New England
Eastern Canada
2001

Ex **onMobil** Travel Publications

ACKNOWLEDGMENTS

We gratefully acknowledge the help of our representatives for their efficient and perceptive inspection of the lodging and dining establishments listed; the establishments' proprietors for their cooperation in showing their facilities and providing information about them; the many users of previous editions of the Mobil Travel Guide who have taken the time to share their experiences; and for their time and information, the thousands of chambers of commerce, convention and visitors bureaus, city, state, and provincial tourism offices, and government agencies who assisted in our research.

PHOTO CREDITS

Barrett & MacKay Photography: 524, 630; **Randa Bishop Photography:** 356, 396; **Eliot Cohen Photography:** 249; **FPG International:** Walter Bibikow: 113, 155; Hanson Carroll: 506; David Doody: 654; Peter Gridley: 534; Kent Knudson: 672; Richard Laird: 407; Maria Pape: 280; Clyde H. Smith: 15, 380; **Robert Holmes Photography:** 26, 38, 175, 326, 609, 669; **International Stock:** Kindra Clineff: 201; Anne Gardon/Reflexion: 590; Andre Jenny: 479, 486; Perry Mastrovito/Reflexion: 584; Buddy Mays: 519; **Susan Cole Kelly Photography:** 17, 228; **McKain/Camden, Rockport, Lincolnville Chamber of Commerce:** 166; **Joanne Pearson/Fair Haven Photographs:** 124, 138, 210, 262, 297, 414, 423, 440, 497; **Paul Rezendes Photography:** 62, 82, 455, 462; **SuperStock:** 31, 43, 102, 192, 236, 310, 323, 346, 365, 428, 527, 531, 543, 546, 558, 575, 616, 624, 635, 640.

Maps © MapQuest 2000, www.mapquest.com

Published by Publications International, Ltd.
7373 North Cicero Avenue
Lincolnwood, IL 60712

info@exxonmobiltravel.com

COVER PHOTO
SuperStock

ISBN 0-7853-4631-7

Manufactured in China.
10 9 8 7 6 5 4 3 2

CONTENTS

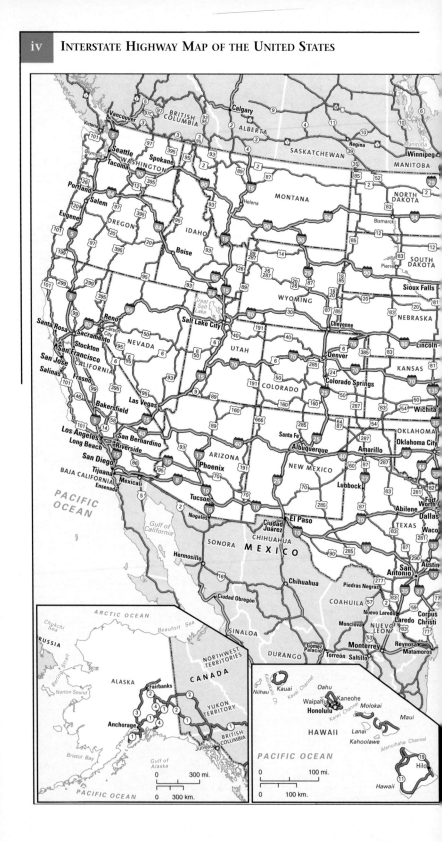

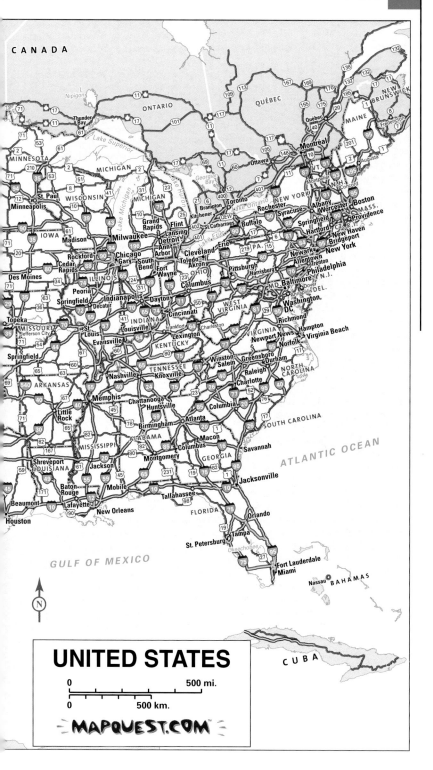

UNITED STATES

0   500 mi.

0   500 km.

MAPQUEST.COM™

Mileage Chart

Distances in chart are in miles. To convert miles to kilometers, multiply the distance in miles by 1.609

Example:
New York, NY to Boston, MA = 215 miles or 346 kilometers (215 x 1.609)

	ALBUQUERQUE, NM	ATLANTA, GA	BALTIMORE, MD	BILLINGS, MT	BIRMINGHAM, AL	BISMARCK, ND	BOISE, ID	BOSTON, MA	BUFFALO, NY	BURLINGTON, VT	CHARLESTON, SC	CHARLESTON, WV	CHARLOTTE, NC	CHEYENNE, WY	CHICAGO, IL	CINCINNATI, OH	CLEVELAND, OH	DALLAS, TX	DENVER, CO	DES MOINES, IA	DETROIT, MI	EL PASO, TX	HOUSTON, TX	INDIANAPOLIS, IN	JACKSON, MS	KANSAS CITY, MO	LAS VEGAS, NV
ALBUQUERQUE, NM		1490	1902	991	1274	1333	966	2240	1808	2178	1793	1568	1649	538	1352	1409	1619	754	438	1091	1608	263	994	1298	1157	894	578
ATLANTA, GA	1490		679	1889	150	1559	2218	1100	910	1158	317	503	238	1482	717	476	726	792	1403	967	735	1437	800	531	386	801	2067
BALTIMORE, MD	1902	679		1959	795	1551	2401	422	370	481	583	352	441	1665	708	521	377	1399	1690	1031	532	2045	1470	600	1032	1087	2445
BILLINGS, MT	991	1889	1959		1839	413	626	2254	1796	2181	2157	1755	2012	455	1246	1552	1597	1433	554	1007	1534	1255	1673	1432	1836	1088	965
BIRMINGHAM, AL	1274	150	795	1839		1509	2170	1215	909	1241	466	578	389	1434	667	475	725	647	1356	919	734	1292	678	481	241	753	1852
BISMARCK, ND	1333	1559	1551	413	1509		1039	1846	1388	1773	1749	1347	1604	594	838	1144	1189	1342	693	675	1126	1597	1582	1024	1548	801	1378
BOISE, ID	966	2218	2401	626	2170	1039		2697	2239	2624	2520	2182	2375	737	1708	1969	2040	1711	833	1369	1977	1206	1952	1852	2115	1376	760
BOSTON, MA	2240	1100	422	2254	1215	1846	2697		462	214	1003	741	861	1961	1003	862	654	1819	2004	1326	741	2465	1890	940	1453	1427	2757
BUFFALO, NY	1808	910	370	1796	909	1388	2239	462		375	899	431	695	1502	545	442	197	1393	1546	868	277	2039	1513	508	1134	995	2299
BURLINGTON, VT	2178	1158	481	2181	1241	1773	2624	214	375		1061	782	919	1887	930	817	567	1763	1931	1253	652	2409	1916	878	1479	1366	2684
CHARLESTON, SC	1793	317	583	2157	466	1749	2520	1003	899	1061		468	204	1783	907	622	724	1109	1705	1204	879	1754	1110	721	703	1102	2371
CHARLESTON, WV	1568	503	352	1755	578	1347	2182	741	431	782	468		265	1445	506	209	255	1072	1367	802	410	1718	1192	320	816	764	2122
CHARLOTTE, NC	1649	238	441	2012	389	1604	2375	861	695	919	204	265		1637	761	476	520	1031	1559	1057	675	1677	1041	575	625	956	2225
CHEYENNE, WY	538	1482	1665	455	1434	594	737	1961	1502	1887	1783	1445	1637		972	1233	1304	979	100	633	1241	801	1220	1115	1382	640	843
CHICAGO, IL	1352	717	708	1246	667	838	1708	1003	545	930	907	506	761	972		302	346	936	1015	337	283	1543	1108	184	750	532	1768
CINCINNATI, OH	1409	476	521	1552	475	1144	1969	862	442	817	622	209	476	1233	302		253	958	1200	599	261	1605	1079	116	700	597	1955
CLEVELAND, OH	1619	726	377	1597	725	1189	2040	654	197	567	724	255	520	1304	346	253		1208	1347	669	171	1854	1328	319	950	806	2100
DALLAS, TX	754	792	1399	1433	647	1342	1711	1819	1393	1763	1109	1072	1031	979	936	958	1208		887	752	1218	647	241	913	406	554	1331
DENVER, CO	438	1403	1690	554	1356	693	833	2004	1546	1931	1705	1367	1559	100	1015	1200	1347	887		676	1284	701	1127	1088	1290	603	756
DES MOINES, IA	1091	967	1031	1007	919	675	1369	1326	868	1253	1204	802	1057	633	337	599	669	752	676		606	1283	992	481	931	194	1429
DETROIT, MI	1608	735	532	1534	734	1126	1977	741	277	652	879	410	675	1241	283	261	171	1218	1284	606		1799	1338	318	960	795	2037
EL PASO, TX	263	1437	2045	1255	1292	1597	1206	2465	2039	2409	1754	1718	1677	801	1543	1605	1854	647	701	1283	1799		758	1489	1051	1085	717
HOUSTON, TX	994	800	1470	1673	678	1582	1952	1890	1513	1916	1110	1192	1041	1220	1108	1079	1328	241	1127	992	1338	758		1033	445	795	1474
INDIANAPOLIS, IN	1298	531	600	1432	481	1024	1852	940	508	878	721	320	575	1115	184	116	319	913	1088	481	318	1489	1033		675	485	1843
JACKSON, MS	1157	386	1032	1836	241	1548	2115	1453	1134	1479	703	816	625	1382	750	700	950	406	1290	931	960	1051	445	675		747	1735
KANSAS CITY, MO	894	801	1087	1088	753	801	1376	1427	995	1366	1102	764	956	640	532	597	806	554	603	194	795	1085	795	485	747		1358
LAS VEGAS, NV	578	2067	2445	965	1852	1378	760	2757	2299	2684	2371	2122	2225	843	1768	1955	2100	1331	756	1429	2037	717	1474	1843	1735	1358	
LITTLE ROCK, AR	900	528	1072	1530	381	1183	1808	1493	1066	1437	900	745	754	1076	662	632	882	327	984	567	891	974	447	587	269	382	1478
LOS ANGELES, CA	806	2237	2705	1239	2092	1702	1033	3046	2572	2957	2554	2374	2453	1116	2042	2215	2374	1446	1029	1703	2310	801	1558	2104	1851	1632	274
LOUISVILLE, KY	1320	419	602	1547	369	1139	1933	964	545	915	610	251	464	1197	299	106	356	852	1118	595	366	1499	972	112	594	516	1874
MEMPHIS, TN	1033	389	933	1625	241	1337	1954	1353	927	1297	760	606	614	1217	539	493	742	466	1116	720	752	1112	586	464	211	536	1611
MIAMI, FL	2155	661	1109	2554	812	2224	2883	1529	1425	1587	583	994	730	2147	1382	1141	1250	1367	2069	1632	1401	1959	1201	1196	915	1466	2733
MILWAUKEE, WI	1426	813	805	1175	763	767	1748	1100	642	1027	1003	601	857	1012	89	398	443	1010	1055	378	380	1617	1193	279	835	573	1808
MINNEAPOLIS, MN	1339	1129	1121	839	1079	431	1465	1417	958	1343	1319	918	1173	881	409	714	760	999	924	246	697	1530	1240	596	1151	441	1677
MONTRÉAL, QC	2172	1241	564	2093	1289	1685	2535	313	397	92	1145	822	1003	1799	841	815	588	1772	1843	1165	564	2363	1892	872	1514	1359	2596
NASHVILLE, TN	1248	242	716	1648	194	1315	1976	1136	716	1086	543	395	397	1240	474	281	531	681	1162	725	541	1328	801	287	423	559	1826
NEW ORLEANS, LA	1276	473	1142	1955	351	1734	2234	1563	1254	1588	783	926	713	1502	935	820	1070	525	1409	1117	1079	1118	360	826	185	932	1854
NEW YORK, NY	2015	869	192	2049	985	1641	2491	215	400	299	773	515	631	1755	797	636	466	1589	1799	1121	622	2235	1660	715	1223	1202	2552
OKLAHOMA CITY, OK	546	944	1354	1227	729	1136	1506	1694	1262	1632	1248	1022	1102	773	807	863	1073	209	681	546	1062	737	449	752	612	348	1124
OMAHA, NE	973	989	1168	904	941	616	1234	1463	1005	1390	1290	952	1144	497	474	736	806	669	541	136	743	1236	910	618	935	188	1294
ORLANDO, FL	1934	440	904	2333	591	2003	2662	1324	1221	1383	379	790	525	1926	1161	920	1045	1146	1847	1411	1180	1738	980	975	694	1245	2512
PHILADELPHIA, PA	1954	782	104	2019	897	1611	2462	321	414	371	685	454	543	1725	768	576	437	1501	1744	1091	592	2147	1572	655	1135	1141	2500
PHOENIX, AZ	466	1868	2366	1199	1723	1662	993	2706	2274	2644	2184	2035	2107	1004	1819	1876	2085	1077	904	1558	2074	432	1188	1764	1482	1360	285
PITTSBURGH, PA	1670	676	246	1719	763	1311	2161	592	217	587	642	217	438	1425	467	292	136	1246	1460	791	292	1893	1366	370	988	857	2215
PORTLAND, ME	2338	1197	520	2352	1313	1944	2795	107	560	233	1101	839	959	2059	1101	960	751	1917	2102	1424	838	2563	1988	1038	1550	1525	2855
PORTLAND, OR	1395	2647	2830	889	2599	1301	432	3126	2667	3052	2948	2610	2802	1166	2137	2398	2469	2140	1261	1798	2405	1767	2381	2280	2544	1805	1188
RAPID CITY, SD	841	1511	1626	379	1463	320	930	1921	1463	1848	1824	1422	1678	305	913	1219	1264	1077	404	629	1201	1105	1318	1101	1458	710	1035
RENO, NV	1020	2440	2623	960	2392	1372	430	2919	2460	2845	2741	2403	2595	959	1930	2191	2262	1933	1054	1591	2198	1315	2072	2073	2337	1598	442
RICHMOND, VA	1876	527	152	2053	678	1645	2496	572	485	630	428	322	289	1760	802	530	471	1309	1688	1126	627	1955	1330	641	914	1085	2444
ST. LOUIS, MO	1051	549	841	1341	501	1053	1628	1181	749	1119	850	512	704	892	294	350	560	635	855	436	549	1242	863	239	505	252	1610
SALT LAKE CITY, UT	624	1916	2100	548	1868	960	342	2395	1936	2322	2218	1880	2072	436	1406	1667	1738	1410	531	1067	1675	864	1650	1549	1813	1074	417
SAN ANTONIO, TX	818	1000	1671	1500	878	1599	1761	2092	1665	2036	1310	1344	1241	1046	1270	1231	1481	271	946	1009	1490	556	200	1186	644	812	1272
SAN DIEGO, CA	825	2166	2724	1302	2021	1765	1096	3065	2632	3020	2483	2393	2405	1179	2105	2234	2437	1375	1092	1766	2373	730	1487	2122	1780	1695	337
SAN FRANCISCO, CA	1111	2618	2840	1176	2472	1749	646	3135	2677	3062	2934	2620	2759	1176	2146	2407	2478	1827	1271	1807	2415	1181	1938	2290	2232	1814	575
SEATTLE, WA	1463	2705	2775	816	2657	1229	500	3070	2612	2997	2973	2571	2827	1234	2062	2368	2413	2208	1329	1822	2350	1944	2449	2249	2612	1872	1256
TAMPA, FL	1949	455	960	2348	606	2018	2677	1380	1276	1438	434	845	581	1941	1176	935	1101	1161	1862	1426	1194	1753	995	990	709	1259	2526
TORONTO, ON	1841	958	565	1762	958	1354	2204	570	106	419	1006	537	802	1468	510	484	303	1441	1512	834	233	2032	1561	541	1183	1028	2265
VANCOUVER, BC	1597	2838	2908	949	2791	1362	633	3204	2745	3130	3106	2705	2960	1368	2196	2501	2547	2342	1463	1956	2483	2087	2583	2383	2746	2007	1390
WASHINGTON, DC	1896	636	38	1953	758	1545	2395	458	384	517	539	346	397	1659	701	517	370	1362	1686	1025	526	2008	1433	596	996	1083	2441
WICHITA, KS	707	989	1276	1067	838	934	1346	1616	1184	1554	1291	953	1145	613	728	785	995	367	521	390	984	898	608	674	771	192	1276

LITTLE ROCK, AR	LOS ANGELES, CA	LOUISVILLE, KY	MEMPHIS, TN	MIAMI, FL	MILWAUKEE, WI	MINNEAPOLIS, MN	MONTRÉAL, QC	NASHVILLE, TN	NEW ORLEANS, LA	NEW YORK, NY	OKLAHOMA CITY, OK	OMAHA, NE	ORLANDO, FL	PHILADELPHIA, PA	PHOENIX, AZ	PITTSBURGH, PA	PORTLAND, ME	PORTLAND, OR	RAPID CITY, SD	RENO, NV	RICHMOND, VA	SALT LAKE CITY, UT	SAN ANTONIO, TX	SAN DIEGO, CA	SAN FRANCISCO, CA	SEATTLE, WA	ST. LOUIS, MO	TAMPA, FL	TORONTO, ON	VANCOUVER, BC	WASHINGTON,DC	WICHITA, KS
00	806	1320	1033	2155	1426	1339	2172	1248	1276	2015	546	973	1934	1954	466	1670	2338	1395	841	1020	1876	1051	624	818	825	1111	1463	1949	1841	1597	1896	707
28	2237	419	389	661	813	1129	1241	242	473	869	944	989	440	782	1868	676	1197	2647	1511	2440	527	549	1916	1000	2166	2618	2705	455	958	2838	636	989
072	2705	602	933	1109	805	1121	564	716	1142	192	1354	1168	904	104	2366	246	520	2830	1626	2623	152	841	2100	1671	2724	2840	2775	960	565	2908	38	1276
530	1239	1547	1625	2554	1175	839	2093	1648	1955	2049	1227	904	2333	2019	1199	1719	2352	889	379	960	2053	1341	548	1500	1302	1176	816	2348	1762	949	1953	1067
81	2092	369	241	812	763	1079	1289	194	351	985	729	941	591	897	1723	763	1313	2599	1463	2392	678	501	1868	878	2021	2472	2657	606	958	2791	758	838
183	1702	1139	1337	2224	767	431	1685	1315	1734	1641	1136	616	2003	1611	1662	1311	1944	1301	320	1372	1645	1053	960	1599	1765	1749	1229	2018	1354	1362	1545	934
308	1033	1933	1954	2883	1748	1465	2535	1976	2234	2491	1506	1234	2662	2462	993	2161	2795	432	930	430	2496	1628	342	1761	1096	646	500	2677	2204	633	2395	1346
493	3046	964	1353	1529	1100	1417	313	1136	1563	215	1694	1463	1324	321	2706	592	107	3126	1921	2919	572	1181	2395	2092	3065	3135	3070	1380	570	3204	458	1616
066	2572	545	927	1425	642	958	397	716	1254	400	1262	1005	1221	414	2274	217	560	2667	1463	2460	485	749	1936	1665	2632	2677	2612	1276	106	2745	384	1184
437	2957	915	1297	1587	1027	1343	92	1086	1588	299	1632	1390	1383	371	2644	587	233	3052	1848	2845	630	1119	2322	2036	3020	3062	2997	1438	419	3130	517	1554
900	2554	610	760	583	1003	1319	1145	543	783	773	1248	1290	379	685	2184	642	1101	2948	1824	2741	428	850	2218	1310	2483	2934	2973	434	1006	3106	539	1291
745	2374	251	606	994	601	918	822	395	926	515	1022	952	790	454	2035	217	839	2610	1422	2403	322	512	1880	1344	2393	2620	2571	845	537	2705	346	953
754	2453	464	614	730	857	1173	1003	397	713	631	1102	1144	525	543	2107	438	959	2802	1678	2595	289	704	2072	1241	2405	2759	2827	581	802	2960	397	1145
076	1116	1197	1217	2147	1012	881	1799	1240	1502	1755	773	497	1926	1725	1004	1425	2059	1166	305	959	1760	892	436	1046	1179	1176	1234	1941	1468	1368	1659	613
62	2042	299	539	1382	89	409	841	474	935	797	807	474	1161	768	1819	467	1101	2137	913	1930	802	294	1406	1270	2105	2146	2062	1176	510	2196	701	728
32	2215	106	493	1141	398	714	815	281	820	636	863	736	920	576	1876	292	960	2398	1219	2191	530	350	1667	1231	2234	2407	2368	935	484	2501	517	785
82	2374	356	742	1250	443	760	588	531	1070	466	1073	806	1045	437	2085	136	751	2469	1264	2262	471	560	1738	1481	2437	2478	2413	1101	303	2547	370	995
27	1446	852	466	1367	1010	999	1772	681	525	1589	209	669	1146	1501	1077	1246	1917	2140	1077	1933	1309	635	1410	271	1375	1827	2208	1161	1441	2342	1362	367
84	1029	1118	1116	2069	1055	924	1843	1162	1409	1799	681	541	1847	1744	904	1460	2102	1261	404	1054	1688	855	531	946	1092	1271	1329	1862	1512	1463	1686	521
67	1703	595	720	1632	378	246	1165	725	1117	1121	546	136	1411	1091	1558	791	1424	1798	629	1591	1126	436	1067	1009	1766	1807	1822	1426	834	1956	1025	390
91	2310	366	752	1401	380	697	564	541	1079	622	1062	743	1180	592	2074	292	838	2405	1201	2198	627	549	1675	1490	2373	2415	2350	1194	233	2483	526	984
74	801	1499	1112	1959	1617	1530	2363	1328	1118	2235	737	1236	1738	2147	432	1893	2563	1767	1105	1315	1955	1242	864	556	730	1181	1944	1753	2032	2087	2008	898
47	1558	972	586	1201	1193	1240	1892	801	360	1660	449	910	980	1572	1188	1366	1988	2381	1318	2072	1330	863	1650	200	1487	1938	2449	995	1561	2583	1433	608
87	2104	112	464	1196	279	596	872	287	826	715	752	618	975	655	1764	370	1038	2280	1101	2073	641	239	1549	1186	2122	2290	2249	990	541	2383	596	674
69	1851	594	211	915	835	1151	1514	423	185	1223	612	935	694	1135	1482	988	1550	2544	1458	2337	914	505	1813	644	1780	2232	2612	709	1183	2746	996	771
82	1632	516	536	1466	573	441	1359	559	932	1202	348	188	1245	1141	1360	857	1525	1805	710	1598	1085	252	1074	812	1695	1814	1872	1259	1028	2007	1083	192
478	274	1874	1611	2733	1808	1677	2596	1826	1854	2552	1124	1294	2512	2500	285	2215	2855	1188	1035	442	2444	1610	417	1272	337	575	1256	2526	2265	1390	2441	1276
	1706	526	140	1190	747	814	1446	355	455	1262	355	570	969	1175	1367	920	1590	2237	1093	2030	983	416	1507	600	1703	2012	2305	984	1115	2439	1036	464
706		2126	1839	2759	2082	1951	2869	2054	1917	2820	1352	1567	2538	2760	369	2476	3144	971	1309	519	2682	1856	691	1356	124	385	1148	2553	2538	1291	2702	1513
26	2126		386	1084	394	711	920	175	714	739	774	704	863	678	1786	394	1062	2362	1215	2155	572	264	1631	1125	2144	2372	2364	878	589	2497	596	705
40	1839	386		1051	624	940	1306	215	396	1123	487	724	830	1035	1500	780	1451	2382	1247	2175	843	294	1652	739	1841	2144	2440	845	975	2574	896	597
90	2759	1084	1051		1478	1794	1671	907	874	1299	1609	1654	232	1211	2390	1167	1627	3312	2176	3105	954	1214	2581	1401	2688	3140	3370	274	1532	3504	1065	1655
47	2082	394	624	1478		337	939	569	1020	894	880	514	1257	865	1892	564	1198	2063	842	1970	899	367	1446	1343	2145	2186	1991	1272	607	2124	799	769
14	1951	711	940	1794	337		1255	886	1337	1211	793	383	1573	1181	1805	881	1515	1727	606	1839	1216	621	1315	1257	2014	2055	1654	1588	924	1788	1115	637
46	2869	920	1306	1671	939	1255		1094	1632	383	1625	1300	1466	454	2637	607	282	2963	1758	2756	714	1112	2232	2043	2931	2972	2907	1522	330	3041	600	1547
55	2054	175	215	907	569	886	1094		539	906	703	747	686	818	1715	569	1234	2405	1269	2198	626	307	1675	954	2056	2360	2463	701	764	2597	679	748
55	1917	714	396	874	1020	1337	1632	539		1332	731	1121	653	1245	1548	1108	1660	2663	1643	2431	1002	690	1932	560	1846	2298	2731	668	1302	2865	1106	890
262	2820	739	1123	1299	894	1211	383	906	1332		1469	1258	1094	91	2481	367	313	2920	1716	2713	342	956	2189	1861	2839	2929	2864	1150	507	2998	228	1391
55	1352	774	487	1609	880	793	1625	703	731	1469		463	1388	1408	1012	1124	1792	1934	871	1727	1331	505	1204	466	1370	1657	2002	1403	1295	2136	1350	161
70	1567	704	724	1654	514	383	1300	747	1121	1258	463		1433	1228	1440	928	1561	1662	525	1455	1263	440	932	927	1630	1672	1719	1448	971	1853	1162	307
69	2538	863	830	232	1257	1573	1466	686	653	1094	1388	1433		1006	2169	963	1422	3091	1955	2884	750	993	2360	1180	2467	2918	3149	82	1327	3283	860	1434
75	2760	678	1035	1211	865	1181	454	818	1245	91	1408	1228	1006		2420	306	419	2890	1686	2683	254	895	2160	1774	2779	2900	2835	1062	522	2968	140	1330
67	369	1786	1500	2390	1892	1805	2637	1715	1548	2481	1012	1440	2169	2420		2136	2804	1335	1308	883	2343	1517	651	987	358	750	1513	2184	2307	1655	2362	1173
20	2476	394	780	1167	564	881	607	569	1108	367	1124	928	963	306	2136		690	2590	1386	2383	341	611	1859	1519	2494	2599	2534	1019	321	2668	240	1046
90	3144	1062	1451	1627	1198	1515	282	1234	1660	313	1792	1561	1422	419	2804	690		3223	2019	3016	670	1279	2493	2189	3162	3233	3168	1478	668	3301	556	1714
37	971	2362	2382	3312	2063	1727	2963	2405	2663	2920	1934	1662	3091	2890	1335	2590	3223		1268	578	2925	2057	771	2322	1093	638	170	3106	2633	313	2824	1775
93	1309	1215	1247	2176	842	606	1758	1269	1643	1716	871	525	1955	1686	1308	1386	2019	1268		1151	1720	963	628	1335	1372	1368	1195	1970	1429	1328	1620	712
30	519	2155	2175	3105	1970	1839	2756	2198	2431	2713	1727	1455	2884	2683	883	2383	3016	578	1151		2718	1850	524	1870	642	217	755	2899	2426	898	2617	1568
83	2682	572	843	954	899	1216	714	626	1002	342	1331	1263	750	254	2343	341	670	2925	1720	2718		834	2194	1530	2684	2934	2869	805	660	3003	108	1274
16	1856	264	294	1214	367	621	1112	307	690	956	505	440	993	895	1517	611	1279	2057	963	1850	834		1326	968	1875	2066	2125	1008	782	2259	837	441
07	691	1631	1652	2581	1446	1315	2232	1675	1932	2189	1204	932	2360	2160	651	1859	2493	771	628	524	2194	1326		1419	754	740	839	2375	1902	973	2094	1044
00	1356	1125	739	1401	1343	1257	2043	954	560	1861	466	927	1180	1774	987	1519	2189	2322	1335	1870	1530	968	1419		1285	1737	2275	1195	1714	2410	1635	624
03	124	2144	1841	2688	2145	2014	2931	2056	1846	2839	1370	1630	2467	2779	358	2494	3162	1093	1372	642	2684	1875	754	1285		508	1271	2481	2601	1414	2720	1531
012	385	2372	2144	3140	2186	2055	2972	2360	2298	2929	1657	1672	2918	2900	750	2599	3233	638	1368	217	2934	2066	740	1737	508		816	2933	2643	958	2834	1784
305	1148	2364	2440	3370	1991	1654	2907	2463	2731	2864	2002	1719	3149	2835	1513	2534	3168	170	1195	755	2869	2125	839	2275	1271	816		3164	2577	140	2769	1843
84	2553	878	845	274	1272	1588	1522	701	668	1150	1403	1448	82	1062	2184	1019	1478	3106	1970	2899	805	1008	2375	1195	2481	2933	3164		1383	3297	916	1448
15	2538	589	975	1532	607	924	330	764	1302	507	1295	971	1327	522	2307	321	668	2633	1429	2426	660	782	1902	1714	2601	2643	2577	1383		2711	563	1217
39	1291	2497	2574	3504	2124	1788	3041	2597	2865	2998	2136	1853	3283	2968	1655	2668	3301	313	1328	898	3003	2259	973	2410	1414	958	140	3297	2711		2902	1977
36	2702	596	896	1065	799	1115	600	679	1106	228	1350	1162	860	140	2362	240	556	2824	1620	2617	108	837	2094	1635	2720	2834	2769	916	563	2902		1272
64	1513	705	597	1655	769	637	1547	748	890	1391	161	307	1434	1330	1173	1046	1714	1775	712	1568	1274	441	1044	624	1531	1784	1843	1448	1217	1977	1272	

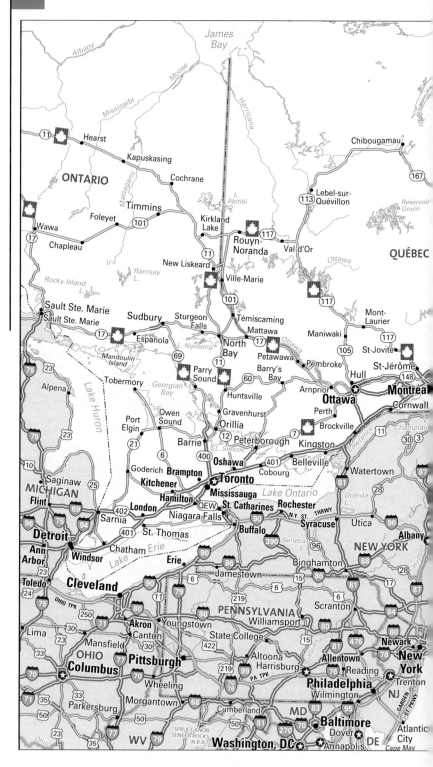

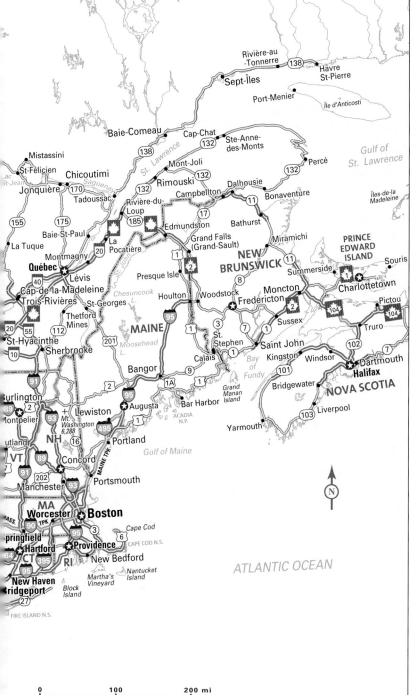

Gagnon

Rivière-au-Tonnerre
138
Havre St-Pierre
Sept-Îles
Port-Menier
Île d'Anticosti
Gulf of St. Lawrence

Baie-Comeau
Cap-Chat
132
Ste-Anne-des-Monts
132
Percé

Mistassini
St-Félicien
Chicoutimi
St. Lawrence
Mont-Joli
132
Rimouski
Jonquière
170
Saguenay
132
Dalhousie
Campbellton
11
Bonaventure
Îles-de-la-Madeleine

Tadoussac
155
175
Rivière-du-Loup
17
Edmundston
Bathurst
PRINCE EDWARD ISLAND
Souris

Baie-St-Paul
185
Grand Falls (Grand-Sault)
Miramichi
1

La Tuque
La Pocatière
20
1
NEW BRUNSWICK
Summerside
Charlottetown

Montmagny
Presque Isle
2
8
Moncton
104
Pictou

Québec
Lévis
Chesuncook L.
Houlton
Woodstock
Fredericton
2
104
Truro

Cap-de-la-Madeleine
40
St-Georges
MAINE
7
1
Sussex
102
7

Trois-Rivières
Thetford Mines
201
Moosehead L.
95
1
St. Stephen
Saint John
Kingston
Windsor
Dartmouth

20
55
112
3
Calais
1
Bay of Fundy
101
Halifax

St-Hyacinthe
Sherbrooke
Bangor
9
Grand Manan Island
Bridgewater
NOVA SCOTIA

10
2
1A
1
103
Liverpool

Burlington
89
2
95
Bar Harbor
ACADIA N.P.
Yarmouth

Montpelier
93
Lewiston
Augusta
1

Mt. Washington 6,288
495
Portland

Rutland
16
Gulf of Maine

VT
89
Concord

91
202
Portsmouth
N

Manchester
93

MA
Worcester
TPK
Boston
Cape Cod

MASS.
90
3
6
CAPE COD N.S.

Springfield
95
Providence

Hartford
95
New Bedford

CT
RI
Nantucket Island

New Haven
Martha's Vineyard

Bridgeport
Block Island

27

FIRE ISLAND N.S.

ATLANTIC OCEAN

0   100   200 mi
0   100   200 km

© MAPQUEST.COM

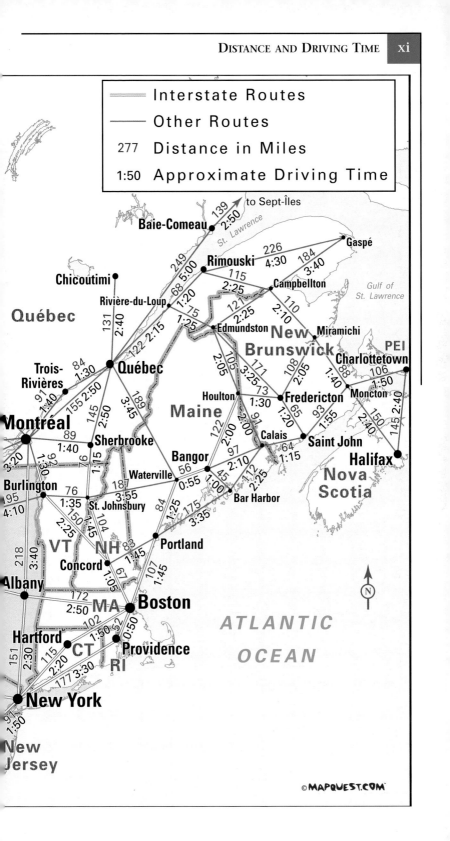

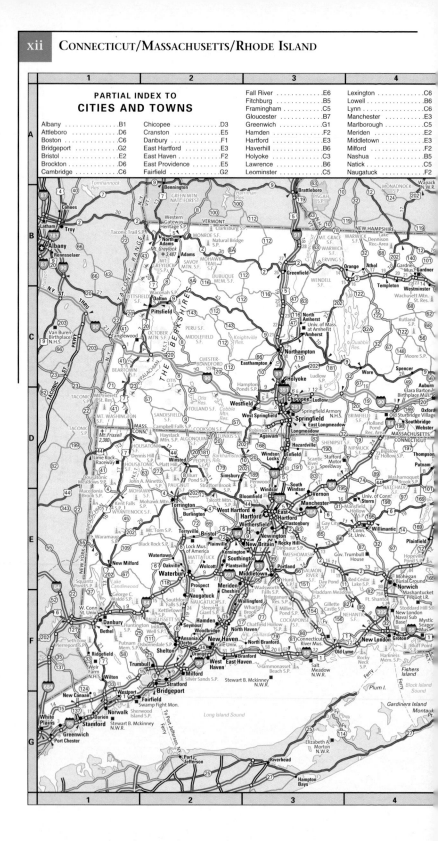

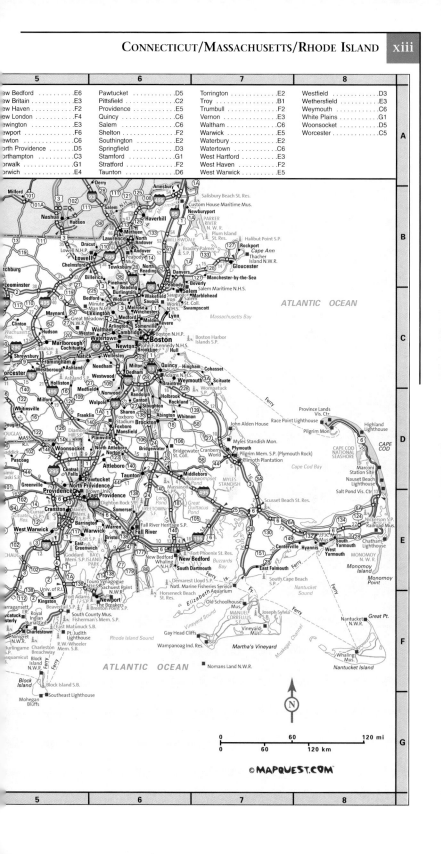

© MAPQUEST.COM

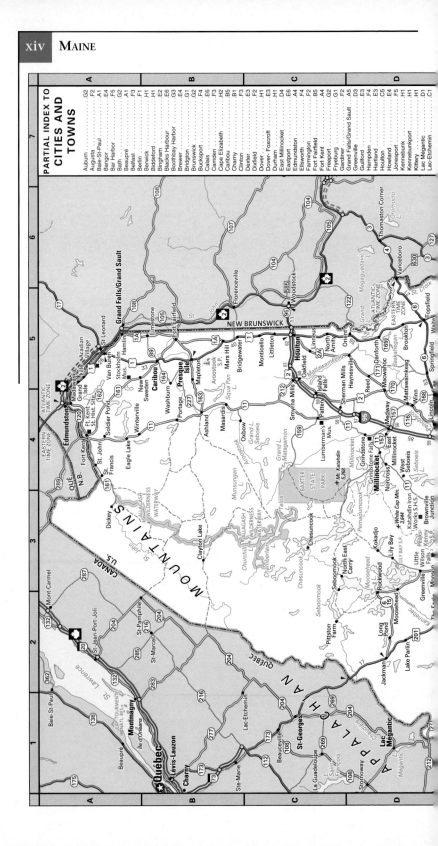

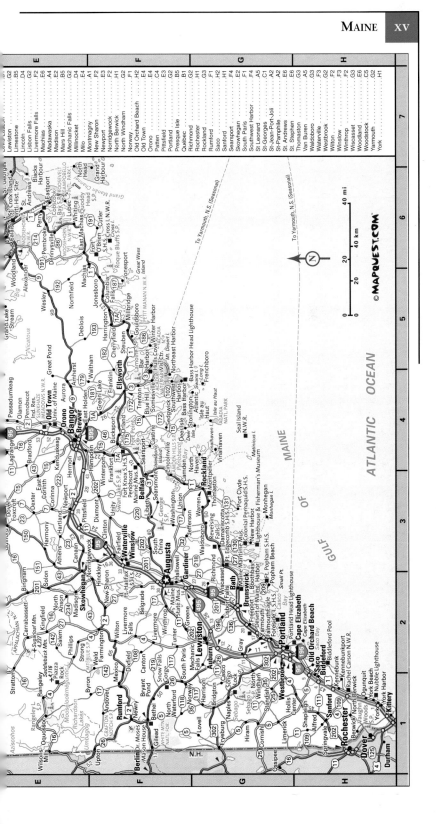

ATLANTIC   OCEAN

MAINE

GULF   OF

© MAPQUEST.COM

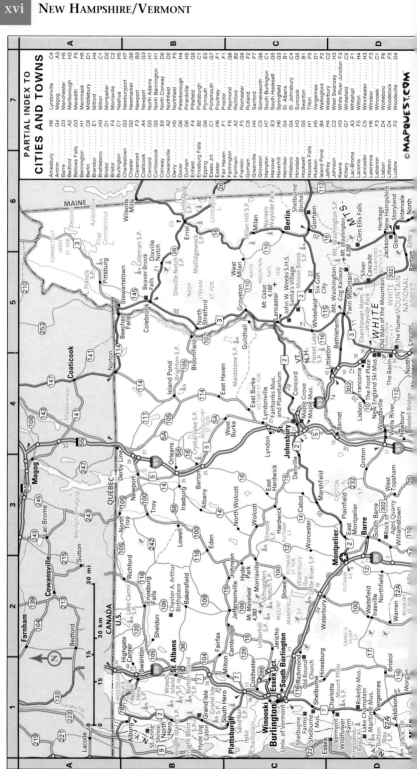

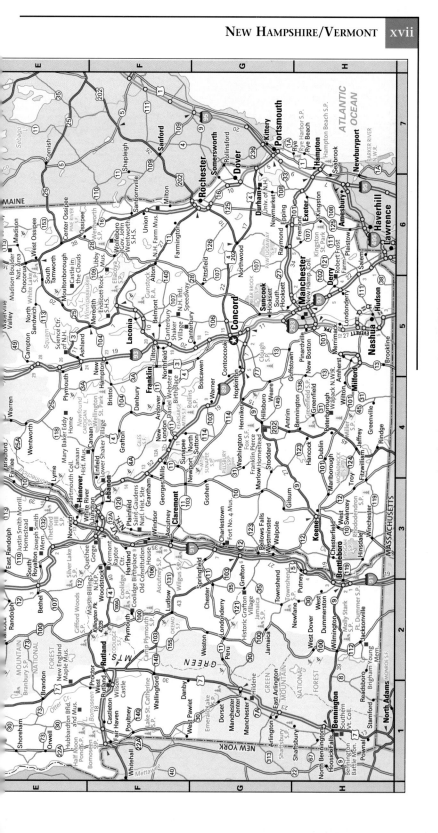

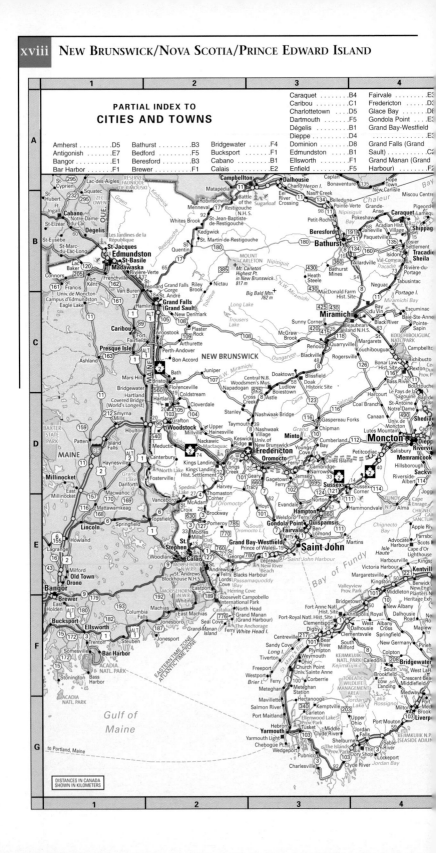

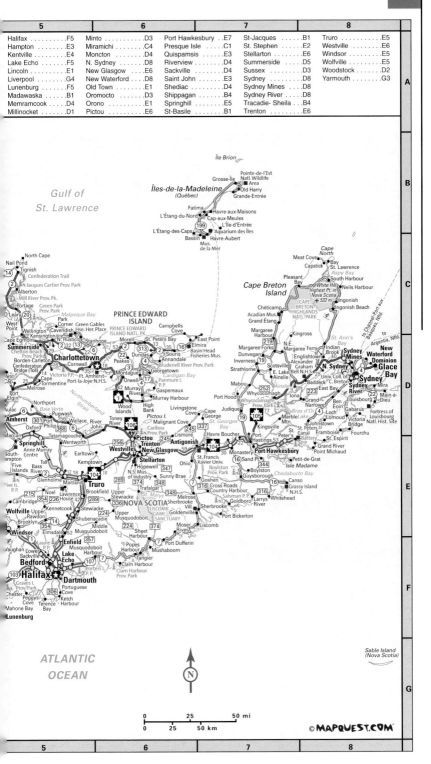

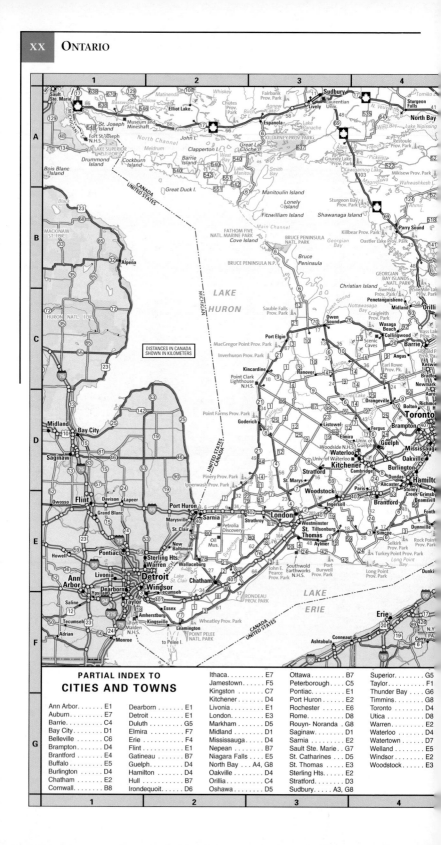

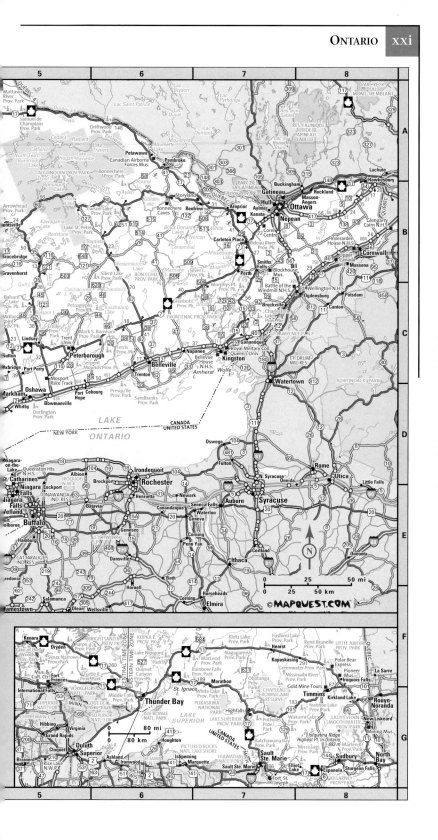

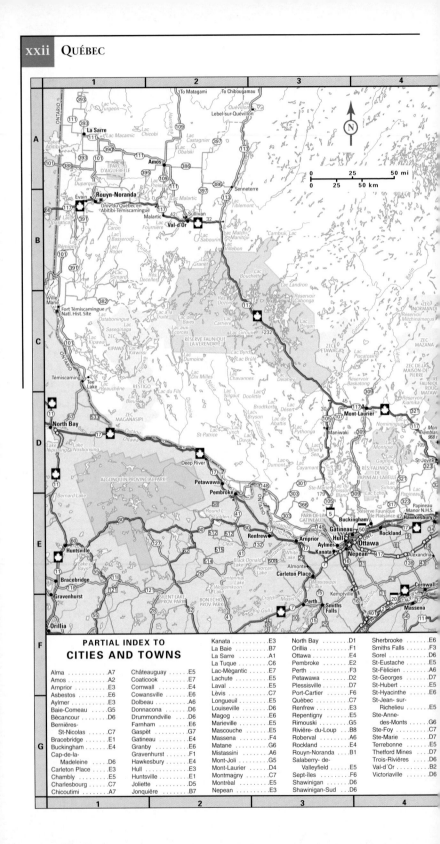

PARTIAL INDEX TO CITIES AND TOWNS

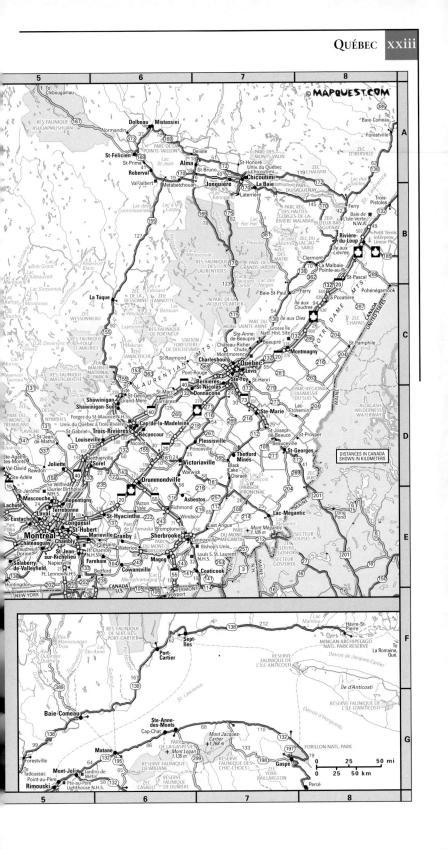

MAP LEGEND

TRANSPORTATION

CONTROLLED ACCESS HIGHWAYS

Free

Toll; Toll Booth

Under Construction

Interchange and Exit Number

Ramp
Downtown maps only

OTHER HIGHWAYS

Primary Highway

Secondary Highway

Multilane Divided Highway
Primary and secondary highways only

Other Paved Road

Unpaved Road
Check conditions locally

HIGHWAY MARKERS

Interstate Route

U.S. Route

State or Provincial Route

County or Other Route

Business Route

Trans-Canada Highway

Canadian Provincial Autoroute

Mexican Federal Route

OTHER SYMBOLS

Distances along Major Highways
Miles in U.S.; kilometers in Canada and Mexico

Tunnel; Pass

One-way Street

Airport

Railroad
Downtown maps only

Auto Ferry; Passenger Ferry

RECREATION AND FEATURES OF INTEREST

National Park

National Forest; National Grassland

Other Large Park or Recreation Area

Military Lands

Indian Reservation

Small State Park with and without Camping

Public Campsite

Trail

Point of Interest

Golf Course
Professional tournament location

Hospital
City maps only

Ski Area

CITIES AND TOWNS

National Capital; State or Provincial Capital

County Seat
State maps only

Cities, Towns, and Populated Places
Type size indicates relative importance

Urban Area
State and province maps only

Large Incorporated Cities

OTHER MAP FEATURES

County Boundary and Name

Time Zone Boundary

+ Mt. Olympus 7,965 Mountain Peak; Elevation
Feet in U.S.; meters in Canada and Mexico

Perennial; Intermittent River

Perennial; Intermittent or Dry Water Body

Dam

Swamp

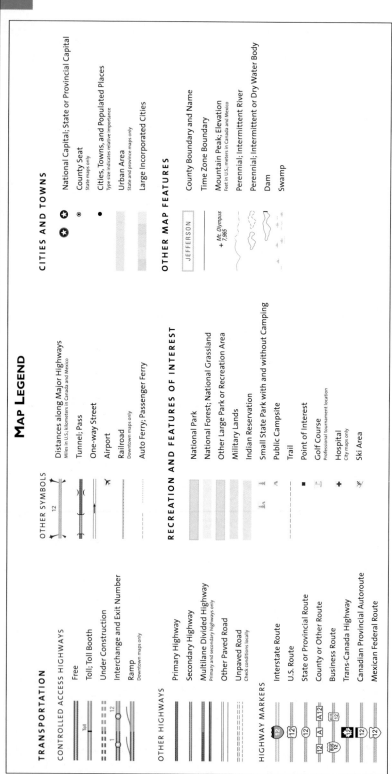

Whoever said the world's getting smaller never had to fuel it.

Each year millions of people become drivers. Meeting this growing demand for energy is complicated, but as ExxonMobil we try to make it look simple. So not only are the familiar faces of Exxon and Mobil still there to help you, they now accept each other's credit cards. We figure you have enough stuff in your wallet already, so now one card works like two.

ExxonMobil

WHETHER YOU'RE IN A...

...TRACK RACE

...TRUCK RACE

...DRAG RACE

...OR THE RAT RACE,

...SUPERFLO® GIVES PROTECTION
THAT'S FAST, PROTECTION THAT LASTS.

High-speed straightaways of the Busch Series. Treacherous mud pits of CORR (Championship Off Road Racing). Earth-shaking quarter miles of NHRA. They're all brutal on a car and its engine. Yet the drivers of these Exxon Superflo® racing vehicles can tell you firsthand, Exxon Superflo motor oil goes the distance. And if it can protect their engines, imagine what it can do for yours.

Superflo races its protection to your engine's vital parts at the start and keeps protecting mile after mile after mile. So protect your car's engine with Exxon Superflo motor oil. Protection That's Fast, Protection That Lasts!™

Would you like to spend less time buying gas?

With *Speedpass,* getting gas just got a little more exciting. All you have to do is wave it at the pump, gas up and go. Fast and easy. You can link it to a major credit card or check card that you *already* have. So call our toll-free number, **1-877-MY MOBIL**, or visit www.speedpass.com to enroll. Join the millions of people who already use *Speedpass.* It's safe, secure and best of all...it's *free*.

Speedpass
Today's way to pay Mobil

Only your garage
could protect it better.

But if you actually use your car, then protect it with Mobil 1® oil and a
Mobil 1 filter. They're like a tag team in your engine. Each one is
engineered for a specific job, but together they're unbeatable. It's the
perfect give-and-take relationship. So, on your next oil change play
matchmaker and be sure to ask for Mobil 1 oil as well as the Mobil 1 filter.

www.mobil1.com/estore
1-800-ASK-MOBIL

Nothing outperforms

WELCOME

For over 40 years, the *Mobil Travel Guide* has provided North American travelers with trusted advice on finding good value, quality service, and the distinctive attractions that give a destination its unique character. Today, the *Travel Guide* is presented by ExxonMobil and is a valued member of the ExxonMobil family of travel publications.

Although you'll notice changes in the *2001 Travel Guide* format—including introduction of the ExxonMobil name—what hasn't changed is our commitment to bring reliable lodging, dining, and sightseeing information to a broad range of travelers. Our nationwide network of professional evaluators offer you their expertise on over 22,000 properties using our 5-Star rating system that has become an industry standard. Whether you're seeking a convenient business meeting locale, an elegant 5-Star celebration, or a leisurely driving trip, it is our hope that you'll rely on the *Travel Guide* as your companion.

As we continue to enhance our products to better meet the needs of the modern traveler, we hope to hear from our most important audience—you, the traveler. Please take the time to complete the customer feedback form at the back of this book or contact us on the Internet at www.exxonmobiltravel.com. We appreciate your input and wish you safe and memorable travels.

Lee R Raymond

Lee R. Raymond
Chairman
Exxon Mobil Corporation

A WORD TO OUR READERS

The exciting and complex development of the US interstate high-way system was formally—and finally—established in 1956, allowing Americans to take to the roads in enormous numbers. They are going on day trips, long weekends, extended family vacations, and business. Traveling across the country, stopping at National Parks, major cities, small towns, monuments, and landmarks remains a fantasy trip for many.

Airline travel, too, is on the increase. Whether for business or pleasure, we can take flights between relatively close cities and from coast to coast.

You, the traveler, deserve the best food and accommodations available in every city, town, or village you visit. But finding suitable accommodations can be problematic. You could try to meet and ask local residents about appropriate places to stay and eat, but that time-consuming option comes with no guarantee of getting the best advice.

That's where the *Mobil Travel Guide* comes in. This trusted, well-established tool can direct you to satisfying places to eat and stay, and to interesting events and attractions in thousands of locations across North America. Prior to the merger with Exxon Corporation, Mobil Corporation had sponsored the Mobil Travel Guide since 1958. Now ExxonMobil presents the latest edition of our annual Travel Guide series in partnership with Consumer Guide publications.

This edition has several new features. We've added driving tours, suggesting "off the beaten path" day trips (or overnight if you choose) to points of interest near a well-established destination. MapQuest has provided our maps this year, including the more-details maps for driving tours. We've also added walking tours. These allow you to stretch your legs and see the sites in and about your destination. Again, you will find maps to help you find your way to monuments, points of historic interest, and maybe even a snack.

Our three-star entries now contain more details. Clearly travelers are looking for good value, and the more information we can offer about restaurants and lodgings, the easier it will be to evaluate your many choices.

Perhaps the biggest difference this year is the addition of color to the travel guides. Pictures of places to stay, things to do, and colorful surroundings along the way might encourage you to make a stop to take your own pictures. Once a seven-volume series, The *Mobil Travel Guides* are now published as a ten book set. This allows us to add more hotel, restaurant, and attraction information, as well as several more maps in each book.

Finally, we've changed the size of the books. With more travelers carrying travel guides in their glove compartment, purse, breast pocket, or briefcase, the new size was chosen to accommodate a better fit.

The hi-tech information database that is the foundation of every title in the *Mobil Travel Guide* series is an astonishing resource: It is enormous, detailed, and continually updated, making it as accurate and useful as it can be. Highly trained field representatives, spread out across the country, generate exhaustive, computerized inspection reports. Senior staff members then evaluate these reports, along with the comments of more than 100,000 readers. All of this information is used to arrive at fair, accurate, and useful assessments of hotels, motels, and restaurants. Mobil's respected and world-famous one- to five-star rating system highlights valuable capsulized descriptions of each site. All of this dependable information, plus details about thousands of attractions and things to do, is in the dynamic Mobil database!

Space limitations make it impossible for us to include every hotel, motel, and restaurant in America. Instead, our database consists of a generous, representative sampling, with information about places that are above-average in their type. In essence, you can confidently patronize any of the restaurants, places of lodging, and attractions contained in the *Mobil Travel Guide* series.

What do we mean by "representative sampling"? You'll find that the *Mobil Travel Guide* books include information about a great variety of establishments. Perhaps you favor rustic lodgings and restaurants, or perhaps you're most comfortable with elegance and high style. Money may be no object or, like most of us, you may be on a budget. Some travelers place a high premium on 24-hour room service or special menu items. Others look for quiet seclusion. Whatever your travel needs and desires, they will be reflected in the *Mobil Travel Guide* listings.

Allow us to emphasize that we have charged no establishment for inclusion in our guides. We have no relationship with any of the businesses and attractions we list, and act only as a consumer advocate. In essence, we do the investigative legwork so you won't have to.

Look over the "How to Use This Book" section that follows. You'll discover just how simple it is to quickly and easily gather all the information you need—before your trip or while on the road. For terrific tips on saving money, travel safety, and other ways to enjoy your travels to the maximum, be sure to read our special section, "Making the Most of Your Trip."

Keep in mind that the hospitality business is ever-changing. Restaurants and places of lodging—particularly small chains or stand-alone establishments—can change management or even go out of business with surprising quickness. Although we have made every effort to double-check information during our annual updates, we nevertheless recommend that you call ahead to be sure a place you have selected is open and still offers all the features you want. Phone numbers are provided, and, when available, we also list fax and Web site information.

We hope that all your travel experiences are easy and relaxing. If any aspects of your accommodations or dining motivate you to comment, please drop us a line. We depend a great deal on our readers' remarks, so you can be assured that we will read and assimilate your comments into our research. General comments about our books are also welcome. You can write us at Mobil Travel Guide, 7373 N Cicero Ave, Lincolnwood, IL 60712, or send e-mail to info@exxonmobiltravel.com.

Take your *Mobil Travel Guide* books along on every trip. You'll be pleased by their convenience, ease of use, and breadth of dependable coverage.

Happy travels in the new millennium!

EDITORIAL CONTRIBUTORS AND CONSULTANTS FOR DRIVING TOURS, WALKING TOURS, ATTRACTIONS, EVENTS AND PHOTOGRAPHY:

Christina Tree has been writing about New England since the late 1960s. She is the author of *How New England Happened: A Guide to New England Through Its History* and is coauthor of several state guides, including the New England *An Explorer's Guide* series and *Best Places to Stay in New England* series. She is also a weekly contributor to *The Boston Globe's* Sunday travel section each year from May through September.

Nancy Lyon is a freelance travel writer and author of *Scatter the Mud: A Traveller's Medley.* Her travel articles appear in several Canadian and US publications including *Travel & Leisure,* Air Canada's *enRoute, The Gazette* (Montréal), and *The New York Times.* She is a contributor to city guides on Montréal and Québec City and to the *Explore America* series.

Mike Michaelson is a writer and editor whose weekly travel page, "Around the Midwest" appears in the Sunday travel section of the *Daily Herald.* He is the author of several travel titles including the *Weekend Getaway Guide* series and *Toronto's Best-Kept Secrets: And New Views of Old Favorites.* His travel articles appear regularly in national magazines, including *National Geographic Traveler* and *Midwest Living.*

How to Use This Book

The *Mobil Travel Guide* is designed for ease of use. Each state has its own chapter. The chapter begins with a general introduction, which provides both a general geographical and historical orientation to the state; it also covers basic statewide tourist information, from state recreation areas to seatbelt laws. The remainder of each chapter is devoted to the travel destinations within the state—cities and towns, state and national parks, and tourist areas—which, like the states, are arranged alphabetically.

The following is an explanation of the wealth of information you'll find regarding those travel destinations—information on the area, on things to see and do there, and on where to stay and eat.

Maps and Map Coordinates

Next to each destination is a set of map coordinates. These are referenced to the appropriate state map in the front of this book. In addition, we have provided maps of selected larger cities and of key neighborhoods within the city sections.

Destination Information

Because many travel destinations are close to other cities and towns where visitors might find additional attractions, accommodations, and restaurants, cross-references to those places are included whenever possible. Also listed are addresses and phone numbers for travel-information resources—usually the local chamber of commerce or office of tourism—as well as pertinent vital statistics and a brief introduction to the area.

What to See and Do

Almost 20,000 museums, art galleries, amusement parks, universities, historic sites and houses, plantations, churches, state parks, ski areas, and other attractions are described in the *Mobil Travel Guides*. A white star on a black background ★ signals that the attraction is one of the best in the state. Since municipal parks, public tennis courts, swimming pools, and small educational institutions are common to most towns, they are generally not represented with the white star on the black background.

Following the attraction's description, you'll find the months and days it's open, address/location and phone number, and admission costs (see the inside front cover for an explanation of the cost symbols). Note that directions are given from the center of the town under which the attraction is listed, which may not necessarily be the town in which the attraction is located. Zip codes are listed only if they differ from those given for the town.

Driving and Walking Tours

New to the *Mobil Travel Guides* are the driving and walking tours. The driving tours are usually day trips—though they can be longer— that make for interesting side trips. This is a way to get off the beaten track and visit an area often overlooked. These trips frequently cover areas of natural beauty or historical significance, and a map of the tour is included with the description. The walking tours focus on a particularly interesting area of a city or town. Again, these can be a break from more everyday tourist attractions. The tours often include places to stop for a meal or snack.

Events

Events—categorized as annual, seasonal, or special—are highlighted. An annual event is one that's held every year for a period of usually no longer than a week to ten days; festivals and fairs are typical entries. A seasonal event is one that may or may not be annual and that is held for a number of weeks or months in the year, such as horse racing, summer theater, concert or opera festivals, and professional sports. Special event listings occur infrequently and mark a certain date or event, such as a centennial or other commemorative celebration.

Major Cities

Additional information on airports and ground transportation, suburbs, and neighborhoods may be included for large cities.

Lodging and Restaurant Listings

ORGANIZATION

For both lodgings and restaurants, when a property is in a town that does not have its own heading, the listing appears under the town nearest its location with the address and town in parentheses immediately after the establishment name. In large cities, lodgings located within 5 miles of major commercial airports are listed under a separate "Airport" heading, following the city listings.

LODGING CLASSIFICATIONS

Each property is classified by type according to the characteristics below. Because the following features and services are found at most motels, lodges, motor hotels, and hotels, they are not shown in those listings:

- Year-round operation with a single rate structure unless otherwise quoted
- European plan (meals not included in room rate)
- Bathroom with tub and/or shower in each room
- Air-conditioned/heated, often with individual room control
- Cots
- Daily maid service
- In-room phones
- Elevators

Motels/Motor Lodges. Accommodations are in low-rise structures with rooms easily accessible to parking (which is usually free). Properties have outdoor room entry and small, functional lobbies. Service is often limited, and dining may not be offered in lower-rated motels and lodges. Shops and businesses are found only in higher-rated properties, as are bellhops, room service, and restaurants serving three meals daily.

Lodges. These differ from motels primarily in their emphasis on outdoor recreational activities and in location. They are often found in resort and rural areas rather than in major cities or along highways.

Hotels. To be categorized as a hotel, an establishment must have most of the following facilities and services: multiple floors, a restaurant and/or coffee shop, elevators, room service, bellhops, a spacious lobby, and recreational facilities. In addition, the following features and services not shown in listings are also found:

- Valet service (one-day laundry/cleaning service)
- Room service during hours restaurant is open
- Bellhops
- Some oversize beds

Resorts. These specialize in stays of three days or more and usually offer American plan and/or housekeeping accommodations. Their emphasis is on recreational facilities, and a social director is often available. Food services are of primary importance, and guests must be able to eat three meals a day on the premises, either in restaurants or by having access to an on-site grocery store and preparing their own meals.

All Suites. All Suites' guestrooms consist of two rooms, one bedroom and one living room. Higher rated properties offer facilities and services comparable to regular hotels.

B&Bs/Small Inns. Frequently thought of as a small hotel, a Bed and Breakfast or an inn is a place of homelike comfort and warm hospitality. It is often a structure of historic significance, with an equally interesting setting. Meals are a special occasion, and refreshments are frequently served in late afternoon. Rooms are usually individually decorated, often with antiques or furnishings representative of the locale. Phones, bathrooms, or TVs may not be available in every room.

Guest Ranches. Like resorts, guest ranches specialize in stays of three days or more. Guest ranches also offer meal plans and extensive outdoor activities. Horseback riding is usually a feature; there are stables and trails on the ranch property, and trail rides and daily instruction are part of the program. Many guest ranches are working ranches, ranging from casual to rustic, and guests are encouraged to participate in ranch life. Eating is often family style and may also include cookouts. Western saddles are assumed; phone ahead to inquire about English saddle availability.

Extended Stay. These hotels specialize in stays of three days or more and usually offer weekly room rates. Service is often limited and dining might not be offered at lower-rated extended-stay hotels.

Villas/Condos. Similar to Cottage Colonies, these establishments are usually found in recreational areas. They are often separate houses, often luxuriously furnished, and rarely offer restaurants and only a small variety of services on the premises.

Conference Centers. Conference Center Hotels are hotels with extended meeting space facilities designed to house multi-day conferences and seminars. Amenities are often geared toward groups staying for longer than one night and often include restaurants and fitness facilities. Larger Conference Center Hotels are often referred to as Convention Center Hotels.

Casinos. Casino Hotels incorporate areas that offer games of chance like Blackjack, Poker, Slot machines, etc. and are only found in states that legalize gambling. Casino Hotels offer a wide range of services and amenities, comparable to regular hotels.

Cottage Colonies. These are housekeeping cottages and cabins that are usually found in recreational areas. Any dining or recreational facilities are noted in our listing.

DINING CLASSIFICATIONS

Restaurants. Most dining establishments fall into this category. All have a full kitchen and offer table service and a complete menu. Parking on or near the premises, in a lot or garage, is assumed. When a property offers valet or other special parking features, or when only street parking is available, it is noted in the listing.

Unrated Dining Spots. These places, listed after Restaurants in many cities, are chosen for their unique atmosphere, specialized menu, or local flavor. They include delis, ice-cream parlors, cafeterias, tearooms, and pizzerias. Because they may not have a full kitchen or table service, they are not given an Mobil Travel Guide rating. Often they offer extraordinary value and quick service.

QUALITY RATINGS

The *Mobil Travel Guide* has been rating lodgings and restaurants on a national basis since the first edition was published in 1958. For years the guide was the only source of such ratings, and it remains among the few guidebooks to rate restaurants across the country.

All listed establishments were inspected by experienced field representatives or evaluated by a senior staff member. Ratings are based upon their detailed inspection reports of the individual properties, on written evaluations of staff members who stay and dine anonymously, and on an extensive review of comments from our readers.

You'll find a key to the rating categories, ★ through ★★★★★, on the inside front cover, All establishments in the book are recommended. Even a ★ place is above average, usually providing a basic, informal experience. Rating categories reflect both the features the property offers and its quality in relation to similar establishments.

For example, lodging ratings take into account the number and quality of facilities and services, the luxury of appointments, and the attitude and professionalism of staff and management. A ★ establishment provides a comfortable night's lodging. A ★★ property offers more than a facility that rates one star, and the decor is well planned and integrated. Establishments that rate ★★★ are professionally managed and staffed and often beautifully appointed; the lodging experience is truly excellent and the range of facilities is extensive. Properties that have been given ★★★★ not only offer many services but also have their own style and personality; they are luxurious, creatively decorated, and superbly maintained. The ★★★★★ properties are among the best in North America, superb in every respect and entirely memorable, year in and year out.

Restaurant evaluations reflect the quality of the food and the ingredients, preparation, presentation, service levels, as well as the property's decor and ambience. A restaurant that has fairly simple goals for menu and decor but that achieves those goals superbly might receive the same number of stars as a restaurant with somewhat loftier ambitions, but the execution of which falls short of the mark. In general, ★ indicates a restaurant that's a good choice in its area, usually fairly simple and perhaps catering to a clientele of locals and families; ★★ denotes restaurants that are more highly recommended in their area; ★★★ restaurants are of national caliber, with professional and attentive service and a skilled chef in the kitchen; ★★★★ reflect superb dining choices, where remarkable food is served in equally remarkable surroundings; and ★★★★★ represent that rare group of the best restaurants in the country, where in addition to near perfection in every detail, there's that special something extra that makes for an unforgettable dining experience.

A list of the four-star and five-star establishments in each region is located just before the state listings.

Each rating is reviewed annually and each establishment must work to maintain its rating (or improve it). Every effort is made to assure that ratings are fair and accurate; the designated ratings are published purely as an aid to travelers. In general, properties that are very new or have recently undergone major management changes are considered difficult to assess fairly and are often listed without ratings.

LODGINGS

Each listing gives the name, address, directions (when there is no street address), neighborhood and/or directions from downtown (in major cities), phone number (local and 800), fax number, number and type of rooms available, room rates, and seasons open (if not year-round). Also included are details on recreational and dining facilities on the property or nearby, the presence of a luxury level, and credit card information. A key to the symbols at the end of each listing is on the inside front cover. (Note that Exxon or Mobil Corporation credit cards cannot be used for payment of meals and room charges.)

All prices quoted in the Mobil Travel Guide publications are expected to be in effect at the time of publication and during the entire year; however, prices cannot be guaranteed. In some localities there may be short-term price variations because of special events or holidays. Whenever possible, these price charges are noted. Certain resorts have complicated rate structures that vary with the time of year; always confirm listed rates when you make your plans.

RESTAURANTS

Each listing gives the name, address, directions (when there is no street address), neighborhood and/or directions from downtown (in major cities), phone number, hours and days of operation (if not open daily year-round), reservation policy, cuisine (if other than American), price range for each meal served, children's meals (if offered), specialties, and credit card information. Additionally, special features such as chef ownership, ambience, and entertainment are noted. By carefully reading the detailed restaurant information and comparing prices, you can easily determine whether the restaurant is formal and elegant or informal and comfortable for families.

TERMS AND ABBREVIATIONS IN LISTINGS

The following terms and abbreviations are used throughout the listings:

A la carte entrees With a price, refers to the cost of entrees/main dishes that are not accompanied by side dishes.

AP American plan (lodging plus all meals).

Bar Liquor, wine, and beer are served in a bar or cocktail lounge and usually with meals unless otherwise indicated (e.g., "wine, beer").

Business center The property has a designated accessible to all guests with business services.

Business serve avail The property can perform/arrange at least two of the following services for a guest: audiovisual equipment rental, binding, computer rental, faxing, messenger services, modem availability, notary service, obtaining office supplies, photocopying, shipping, and typing.

Cable Standard cable service; "premium" indicates that HBO, Disney, Showtime, or similar cable services are available.

Ck-in, ck-out Check-in time, check-out time.

Coin lndry Self-service laundry.

Complete meal Soup and/or salad, entree, and dessert, plus nonalcoholic beverage.

Continental bkfst Usually coffee and a roll or doughnut.

Cr cds: A, American Express; C, Carte Blanche; D, Diners Club; DS, Discover; ER, enRoute; JCB, Japanese Credit Bureau; MC, MasterCard; V, Visa.

D Followed by a price, indicates room rate for a "double"—two people in one room in one or two beds (the charge may be higher for two double beds).

Downhill/X-country ski Downhill and/or cross-country skiing within 20 miles of property.

Each addl Extra charge for each additional person beyond the stated number of persons at a reduced price.

Early-bird dinner A meal served at specified hours, typically around 4:30-6:30 pm.

Exc Except.

Exercise equipt Two or more pieces of exercise equipment on the premises.

Exercise rm Both exercise equipment and room, with an instructor on the premises.

Fax Facsimile machines available to all guests.

Golf privileges Privileges at a course within 10 miles.

Hols Holidays.

In-rm modem link Every guest room has a connection for a modem that's separate from the phone line.

Kit. or Kits. A kitchen or kitchenette that contains stove or microwave, sink, and refrigerator and that is either part of the room or a separate room. If the kitchen is not fully equipped, the listing will indicate "no equipt" or "some equipt."

Luxury level A special section of a lodging, covering at least an entire floor, that offers increased luxury accommodations. Management must provide no less than three of these four services: separate check-in and check-out, concierge, private lounge, and private elevator service (key access). Complimentary breakfast and snacks are commonly offered.

MAP Modified American plan (lodging plus two meals).

Movies Prerecorded videos are available for rental.

No cr cds accepted No credit cards are accepted.

No elvtr In hotels with more than two stories, it's assumed there are elevators; only their absence is noted.

No phones Phones, too, are assumed; only their absence is noted.

Parking There is a parking lot on the premises.

Private club A cocktail lounge or bar available to members and their guests. In motels and hotels where these clubs exist, registered guests can usually use the club as guests of the management; the same is frequently true of restaurants.

Prix fixe A full meal for a stated price; usually one price is quoted.

Res Reservations.

S Followed by a price, indicates room rate for a "single," i.e., one person.

Serv bar A service bar, where drinks are prepared for dining patrons only.

Serv charge Service charge is the amount added to the restaurant check in lieu of a tip.

Table d'hôte A full meal for a stated price, dependent upon entree selection; no a la carte options are available.

Tennis privileges Privileges at tennis courts within 5 miles.

TV Indicates color television.

Under certain age free Children under that age are not charged if staying in room with a parent.

Valet parking An attendant is available to park and retrieve a car.

VCR VCRs in all guest rooms.

VCR avail VCRs are available for hookup in guest rooms.

Special Information for Travelers with Disabilities

The *Mobil Travel Guide* D symbol shown in accommodation and restaurant listings indicates establishments that are at least partially accessible to people with mobility problems.

The *Mobil Travel Guide* criteria for accessibility are unique to our publication. Please do not confuse them with the universal symbol for wheelchair accessibility. When the D symbol appears following a listing, the establishment is equipped with facilities to accommodate people using wheelchairs or crutches or otherwise needing easy access to doorways and rest rooms. Travelers with severe mobility problems or with hearing or visual impairments may or may not find facilities they need. Always phone ahead to make sure that an establishment can meet your needs.

All lodgings bearing our D symbol have the following facilities:

- ISA-designated parking near access ramps
- Level or ramped entryways to building
- Swinging building entryway doors minimum 3900
- Public rest rooms on main level with space to operate a wheelchair; handrails at commode areas
- Elevators equipped with grab bars and lowered control buttons

- Restaurants with accessible doorways; rest rooms with space to operate wheelchair; handrails at commode areas
- Minimum 3900 width entryway to guest rooms
- Low-pile carpet in rooms
- Telephone at bedside and in bathroom
- Bed placed at wheelchair height
- Minimum 3900 width doorway to bathroom
- Bath with open sink—no cabinet; room to operate wheelchair
- Handrails at commode areas; tub handrails
- Wheelchair accessible peephole in room entry door
- Wheelchair accessible closet rods and shelves

All restaurants bearing our D symbol offer the following facilities:

- ISA-designated parking beside access ramps
- Level or ramped front entryways to building
- Tables to accommodate wheelchairs
- Main-floor rest rooms; minimum 3900 width entryway
- Rest rooms with space to operate wheelchair; handrails at commode areas

In general, the newest properties are apt to impose the fewest barriers.

To get the kind of service you need and have a right to expect, do not hesitate when making a reservation to question the management in detail about the availability of accessible rooms, parking, entrances, restaurants, lounges, or any other facilities that are important to you, and confirm what is meant by "accessible." Some guests with mobility impairments report that lodging establishments' housekeeping and maintenance departments are most helpful in describing barriers. Also inquire about any special equipment, transportation, or services you may need.

MAKING THE MOST OF YOUR TRIP

A few hardy souls might look with fondness upon the trip where the car broke down and they were stranded for a week. Or maybe even the vacation that cost twice what it was supposed to. For most travelers, though, the best trips are those that are safe, smooth, and within their budget. To help you make your trip the best it can be, we've assembled a few tips and resources.

Saving Money

ON LODGING

After you've seen the published rates, it's time to look for discounts. Many hotels and motels offer them—for senior citizens, business travelers, families, you name it. It never hurts to ask—politely, that is. Sometimes, especially in late afternoon, desk clerks are instructed to fill beds, and you might be offered a lower rate, or a nicer room, to entice you to stay. Look for bargains on stays over multiple nights, in the off-season, and on weekdays or weekends (depending on location). Many hotels in major metropolitan areas, for example, have special weekend package plans that offer considerable savings on rooms; they may include breakfast, cocktails, and meal discounts. Prices can change frequently throughout the year, so phone ahead.

Another way to save money is to choose accommodations that give you more than just a standard room. Rooms with kitchen facilities enable you to cook some meals for yourself, reducing restaurant costs. A suite might save money for two couples traveling together. Even hotel luxury levels can provide good value, as many include breakfast or cocktails in the price of the room.

State and city sales taxes, as well as special room taxes, can increase your room rates as much as 25 percent per day. We are unable to include this specific information in the listings, but we strongly urge that you ask about these taxes when placing reservations in order to understand the total cost of your lodgings.

Watch out for telephone-usage charges that hotels frequently impose on long-distance calls, credit-card calls, and other phone calls—even those that go unanswered. Before phoning from your room, read the information given to you at check-in, and then be sure to read your bill carefully before checking out. You won't be expected to pay for charges that they did not spell out. (On the other hand, it's not unusual for a hotel to bill you for your calls after you return home.) Consider using your cell phone; or, if public telephones are available in the hotel lobby, your cost savings may outweigh the inconvenience.

ON DINING

There are several ways to get a less-expensive meal at a more-expensive restaurant. Early-bird dinners are popular in many parts of the country and offer considerable savings. If you're interested in sampling a 4- or 5-star establishment, consider going at lunchtime. While the prices then are probably relatively high, they may be half of those at dinner and come with the same ambience, service, and cuisine.

ON PARK PASSES

While many national parks, monuments, seashores, historic sites, and recreation areas may be used free of charge, others charge an entrance fee (ranging from $1 to $6 per person to $5 to $15 per carload) and/or a "use fee" for special services and facilities. If you plan to make several visits to federal recreation areas, consider one of the following National Park Service money-saving programs:

Park Pass. This is an annual entrance permit to a specific unit in the National Park Service system that normally charges an entrance fee. The pass admits the permit holder and any accompanying passengers in a private noncommercial vehicle or, in the case of walk-in facilities, the holder's spouse, children, and parents. It is valid for entrance fees only. A Park Pass may be purchased in person or by mail from the National Park Service unit at which the pass will be honored. The cost is $15 to $20, depending upon the area.

Golden Eagle Passport. This pass, available to people who are between 17 and 61, entitles the purchaser and accompanying passengers in a private noncommercial vehicle to enter any outdoor National Park Service unit that charges an entrance fee and admits the purchaser and family to most walk-in fee-charging areas. Like the Park Pass, it is good for one year and does not cover use fees. It may be purchased from the National Park Service, Office of Public Inquiries, Room 1013, US Department of the Interior, 18th and C Sts NW, Washington, DC 20240, phone 202/208-4747; at any of the 10 regional offices throughout the country; and at any National Park Service area that charges a fee. The cost is $50.

Golden Age Passport. Available to citizens and permanent residents of the United States 62 years or older, this is a lifetime entrance permit to fee-charging recreation areas. The fee exemption extends to those accompanying the permit holder in a private noncommercial vehicle or, in the case of walk-in facilities, to the holder's spouse and children. The passport also entitles the holder to a 50 percent discount on use fees charged in park areas but not to fees charged by concessionaires. Golden Age Passports must be obtained in person. The applicant must show proof of age, i.e., a driver's license, birth certificate, or signed affidavit attesting to age (Medicare cards are not acceptable proof). These passports are available at most park service units where they're used, at National Park Service headquarters (see above), at park system regional offices, at National Forest Supervisors' offices, and at most Ranger Station offices. The cost is $10.

Golden Access Passport. Issued to citizens and permanent residents of the United States who are physically disabled or visually impaired, this passport is a free lifetime entrance permit to fee-charging recreation areas. The fee exemption extends to those accompanying the permit holder in a private noncommercial vehicle or, in the case of walk-in facilities, to the holder's spouse and children. The passport also entitles the holder to a 50 percent discount on use fees charged in park areas but not to fees charged by concessionaires. Golden Access Passports must be obtained in person. Proof of eligibility to receive federal benefits is required (under programs such as Disability Retirement, Compensation for Military Service-Connected Disability, Coal Mine

Safety and Health Act, etc.), or an affidavit must be signed attesting to eligibility. These passports are available at the same outlets as Golden Age Passports.

FOR SENIOR CITIZENS

Look for the senior-citizen discount symbol in the lodging and restaurant listings. Always call ahead to confirm that the discount is being offered, and be sure to carry proof of age. At places not listed in the book, it never hurts to ask if a senior-citizen discount is offered. Additional information for mature travelers is available from the American Association of Retired Persons (AARP), 601 E St NW, Washington, DC 20049, phone 202/434-2277.

Tipping

Tipping is an expression of appreciation for good service, and often service workers rely on tips as a significant part of their income. However, you never need to tip if service is poor.

IN HOTELS

Door attendants in major city hotels are usually given $1 for getting you a cab. Bellhops expect $1 per bag, usually $2 if you have only one bag. Concierges are tipped according to the service they perform. It's not mandatory to tip when you've asked for suggestions on sightseeing or restaurants or help in making reservations for dining. However, when a concierge books you a table at a restaurant known to be difficult to get into, a gratuity of $5 is appropriate. For obtaining theater or sporting event tickets, $5-$10 is expected. Maids, often overlooked by guests, may be tipped $1-$2 per days of stay.

AT RESTAURANTS

Coffee shop and counter service wait staff are usually given 8 percent–10 percent of the bill. In full-service restaurants, tip 15 percent of the bill, before sales tax. In fine restaurants, where the staff is large and shares the gratuity, 18 percent–20 percent for the waiter is appropriate. In most cases, tip the maitre d' only if service has been extraordinary and only on the way out; $20 is the minimum in upscale properties in major metropolitan areas. If there is a wine steward, tip him or her at least $6 a bottle, more if the wine was decanted or if the bottle was very expensive. If your bus person has been unusually attentive, $2 pressed into his hand on departure is a nice gesture. An increasing number of restaurants automatically add a service charge to the bill instead of a gratuity. Before tipping, carefully review your check. If you are in doubt, ask your server.

AT AIRPORTS

Curbside luggage handlers expect $1 per bag. Car-rental shuttle drivers who help with your luggage appreciate a $1 or $2 tip.

Staying Safe

The best way to deal with emergencies is to be prepared enough to avoid them. However, unforeseen situations do happen, and you can prepare for them.

IN YOUR CAR

Before your trip, make sure your car has been serviced and is in good working order. Change the oil, check the battery and belts, and make sure tires are inflated properly (this can also improve gas mileage). Other inspections recommended by the car's manufacturer should be made, too.

Next, be sure you have the tools and equipment to deal with a routine breakdown: jack, spare tire, lug wrench, repair kit, emergency tools, jumper cables, spare fan belt, auto fuses, flares and/or reflectors, flashlights, first-aid kit, and, in winter, windshield wiper fluid, a windshield scraper, and snow shovel.

Bring all appropriate and up-to-date documentation—licenses, registration, and insurance cards—and know what's covered by your insurance. Also bring an extra set of keys, just in case.

En route, always buckle up! In most states it is required by law.

If your car does break down, get out of traffic as soon as possible—pull well off the road. Raise the hood and turn on your emergency flashers or tie a white cloth to the roadside door handle or antenna. Stay near your car. Use flares or reflectors to keep your car from being hit.

IN YOUR LODGING

Chances are slim that you will encounter a hotel or motel fire. The ⛑ in a listing indicates that there were smoke detectors and/or sprinkler systems in the rooms we inspected. Once you've checked in, make sure that any smoke detector in your room is working properly. Ascertain the locations of fire extinguishers and at least two fire exits. Never use an elevator in a fire.

For personal security, use the peephole in your room's door.

PROTECTING AGAINST THEFT

To guard against theft wherever you go, don't bring anything of more value than you need. If you do bring valuables, leave them at your hotel rather than in your car, and if you have something very expensive, lock it in a safe. Many hotels have one in each room; others will store your valuables in the hotel's safe. And of course, don't carry more money than you need; use traveler's checks and credit cards, or visit cash machines.

For Travelers with Disabilities

A number of publications can provide assistance. The most complete listing of published material for travelers with disabilities is available from The Disability Bookshop, Twin Peaks Press, Box 129, Vancouver, WA 98666, phone 360/694-2462. A comprehensive guidebook to the national parks is *Easy Access to National Parks: The Sierra Club Guide for People with Disabilities* ($16), distributed by Random House.

The Reference Section of the National Library Service for the Blind and Physically Handicapped (Library of Congress, Washington, DC 20542, phone 202/707-9276 or 202/707-5100) provides information and resources for persons with mobility problems and hearing and vision impairments, as well as information about the NILS talking program (or visit your local library).

Traveling to Canada

Citizens of the United States do not need visas to enter Canada, but proof of citizenship—passport, birth certificate, or voter registration card—is required. A driver's license is not acceptable. Naturalized citizens will need their naturalization certificates or their US passport to reenter the United States. Children under 18 who are traveling on their own should carry a letter from a parent or guardian giving them permission to travel in Canada.

Travelers entering Canada in automobiles licensed in the United States may tour the provinces for up to three months without fee. Drivers are advised to carry their motor vehicle registration card and, if the car is not registered in the driver's name, a letter from the registered owner authorizing use of the vehicle. If the car is rented, carry a copy of the rental contract stipulating use in Canada. For your protection, ask your car insurer for a Canadian Non-resident Interprovince Motor Vehicle Liability Insurance Card. This card ensures that your insurance company will meet minimum insurance requirements in Canada.

The use of seat belts by drivers and passengers is compulsory in all provinces. A permit is required for the use of citizens band radios. Rabies vaccination certificates are required for dogs or cats.

No handguns may be brought into Canada. If you plan to hunt, sporting rifles and shotguns plus 200 rounds of ammunition per person will be admitted duty-free. Hunting and fishing licenses must be obtained from the appropriate province. Each province has its own regulations concerning the transportation of firearms.

The Canadian dollar's rate of exchange with the US dollar varies; contact your local bank for the latest figures. Since customs regulations can change, it's recommended that you contact the Canadian consulate or embassy in your area. Offices are located in Atlanta, Boston, Buffalo, Chicago, Dallas, Detroit, Los Angeles, Miami, Minneapolis, New York City, Seattle, and Washington, DC. For the most current and detailed listing of regulations and sources, ask for the annually revised brochure "Canada: Travel Information," which is available upon request.

Important Toll-Free Numbers and On-Line Information

Hotels and Motels

Adam's Mark   800/444–2326
www.adamsmark.com

Baymont Inns and Suites
800/428–3438
www.budgetel.com

Best Western   800/780–7234,
TDD 800/528–2222
www.bestwestern.com

Budget Host   800/283–4678
www.budgethost.com

Clarion   800/252–7466

Comfort Inn   800/228–5150
www.choicehotels.com

Courtyard by Marriott   800/321–2211
www.courtyard.com

Days Inn   800/325–2525
www.daysinn.com

Doubletree   800/222–8733
www.doubletreehotels.com

Drury Inns   800/325–8300
www.drury-inn.com

Econo Lodge   800/446–6900
www.econolodge.com

Embassy Suites   800/362–2779
www.embassy-suites.com

Exel Inns of America   800/356–8013
www.exelinns.com

Fairfield Inn
by Marriott   800/228–2800
www.fairfieldinn.com

Fairmont Hotels   800/527–4727
www.fairmont.com

Forte   800/225–5843
www.forte-hotels.com

Four Seasons   800/819–5053
www.fourseasons.com

Friendship Inns   800/453–4511
www.hotelchoice.com

Hampton Inn   800/426–7866
www.hampton-inn.com

Hilton   800/445–8667,
TDD 800/368–1133
www.hilton.com

Holiday Inn   800/465–4329,
TDD 800/238–5544
www.holiday-inn.com

Howard Johnson   800/446–4656,
TDD 800/654–8442
www.hojo.com

Hyatt & Resorts   800/233–1234
www.hyatt.com

Inns of America   800/826–0778
www.innsamerica.com

Inter-Continental   800/327–0200
www.interconti.com

La Quinta   800/531–5900,
TDD 800/426–3101
www.laquinta.com

Loews   800/235–6397
www.loewshotels.com

Marriott   800/228–9290
www.marriott.com

Master Hosts Inns   800/251–1962
www.reservahost.com

Meridien   800/225–5843
www.forte-hotels.com

Motel 6   800/466–8356
www.motel6.com

Nikko Hotels
International   800/645–5687
www.nikkohotels.com

Omni   800/843–6664
www.omnihotels.com

Quality Inn   800/228–5151
www.qualityinn.com

Radisson   800/333–3333
www.radisson.com

Ramada   800/228–2828,
TDD 800/228–3232
www.ramada.com

Red Carpet Inns   800/251–1962
www.reservahost.com

Red Lion   800/733–5466
www.redlion.com

Red Roof Inn   800/843–7663
www.redroof.com

Renaissance   800/468–3571
www.renaissancehotels.com

Residence Inn
by Marriott   *800/331–3131*
    www.marriott.com

Ritz-Carlton   *800/241–3333*
    www.ritzcarlton.com

Rodeway   *800/228–2000*
    www.rodeway.com

Sheraton   *800/325–3535*
    www.sheraton.com

Shilo Inn   *800/222–2244*
    www.shiloinns.com

Signature Inns   *800/822–5252*
    www.signature-inns.com

Sleep Inn   *800/753–3746*
    www.sleepinn.com

Super 8   *800/800–8000*
    www.super8motels.com

Susse Chalet   *800/524–2538*
    www.sussechalet.com

Travelodge   *800/578–7878*
    www.travelodge.com

Vagabond Inns   *800/522–1555*
    www.vagabondinns.com

Westin Hotels
& Resorts   *800/937–8461*
    www.westin.com

Wyndham Hotels
& Resorts   *800/996–3426*
    www.travelweb.com

Airlines

Air Canada   *800/776–3000*
    www.aircanada.ca

Alaska   *800/252–7522*
    www.alaska-air.com

American   *800/433–7300*
    www.aa.com

America West   *800/235–9292*
    www.americawest.com

British Airways   *800/247–9297*
    www.british-airways.com

Canadian   *800/426–7000*
    www.cdnair.ca

Continental   *800/523–3273*
    www.flycontinental.com

Delta   *800/221–1212*
    www.delta-air.com

IslandAir   *800/323–3345*

Mesa   *800/637–2247*
    www.mesa-air.com

Northwest   *800/225–2525*
    www.nwa.com

SkyWest   *800/453–9417*
    www.skywest.com

Southwest   *800/435–9792*
    www.iflyswa.com

TWA   *800/221–2000*
    www.twa.com

United   *800/241–6522*
    www.ual.com

USAir   *800/428–4322*
    www.usair.com

Trains

Amtrak   *800/872–7245*
    www.amtrak.com

Buses

Greyhound   *800/231–2222*
    www.greyhound.com

Car Rentals

Advantage   *800/777–5500*
    www.arac.com

Alamo   *800/327–9633*
    www.goalamo.com

Allstate   *800/634–6186*
    www.bnm.com/as.htm

Avis   *800/831–2847*
    www.avis.com

Budget   *800/527–0700*
    www.budgetrentacar.com

Dollar   *800/800–3665*
    www.dollarcar.com

Enterprise   *800/325–8007*
    www.pickenterprise.com

Hertz   *800/654–3131*
    www.hertz.com

National   *800/227–7368*
    www.nationalcar.com

Payless   *800/729–5377*
    www.800-payless.com

Rent-A-Wreck   *800/944–7501*
    www.rent-a-wreck.com

Sears   *800/527–0770*
    www.budget.com

Thrifty   *800/847–4369*
    www.thrifty.com

FOUR-STAR AND FIVE-STAR ESTABLISHMENTS IN NEW ENGLAND AND EASTERN CANADA

Connecticut

★★★★★ Lodging
The Mayflower Inn, *Washington*

★★★★ Lodging
The Inn At National Hall, *Westport*

★★★★ Restaurants
Miramar, *Westport*
Thomas Henkelmann, *Greenwich*

Maine

★★★★ Lodgings
Bar Harbor Hotel - Bluenose Inn, *Bar Harbor*
The Captain Lord Mansion, *Kennebunkport*
The Inn At Harbor Head, *Kennebunkport*
The Lodge At Moosehead Lake, *Greenville*
The White Barn Inn, *Kennebunkport*

★★★★ Restaurant
The White Barn Restaurant, *Kennebunkport*

Massachusetts

★★★★★ Lodging
Four Seasons Hotel Boston, *Boston*

★★★★ Lodgings
Blantyre, *Lenox*
Boston Harbor Hotel, *Boston*
The Charlotte Inn, *Martha's Vineyard*
The Eliot Hotel, *Boston*
Le Meridien Boston, *Boston*
The Ritz-Carlton, Boston, *Boston*
The Wauwinet, *Nantucket Island*

★★★★ Restaurants
Aujourd'hui, *Boston*
Clio, *Boston*
Grill 23 & Bar, *Boston*
Hamersley's Bistro, *Boston*
L'Espalier, *Boston*
No. 9 Park, *Boston*
Radius, *Boston*
Rowes Wharf Restaurant, *Boston*
Silks, *Lowell*
Wheatleigh, *Lenox*

New Hampshire

★★★★ Lodging
The Balsams, *Dixville Notch*

Vermont

★★★★★ Lodging
Twin Farms, *Woodstock*

★★★★ Lodgings
The Governor's Inn, *Ludlow*
The Inn At Saw Mill Farm, *West Dover*
Rabbit Hill Inn, *St. Johnsbury*
Topnotch At Stowe, *Stowe*

★★★★ Restaurants
Hemingway's, *Killington*
The Inn at Sawmill Farm, *West Dover*

CANADA

New Brunswick

★★★★ Lodging
Kingsbrae Arms, *St. Andrews*

Ontario

★★★★ Lodgings

Chateau Laurier, *Ottawa*

Four Seasons Hotel Toronto, *Toronto*

Hotel Inter-Continental Toronto, *Toronto*

Le Royal Meridien King Edward, *Toronto*

Metropolitan Hotel, The, *Toronto*

Park Hyatt Toronto, *Toronto*

Windsor Arms Hotel, *Toronto*

★★★★ Restaurants

Centro Grill & Wine Bar, *Toronto*

Chiado, *Toronto*

The Fifth, *Toronto*

Hemispheres, *Toronto*

Lai Wah Heen, *Toronto*

North 44 Degrees, *Toronto*

Pangaea, *Toronto*

Scaramouche, *Toronto*

Truffles, *Toronto*

Quebec

★★★★ Lodgings

Hilton Montreal Bonaventure, *Montreal*

Hotel Le Germain, *Montreal*

Loews Hotel Vogue, *Montreal*

Loews Le Concorde, *Quebec City*

★★★★ Restaurants

Cafe Henry Burger, *Mont Tremblant Provincial Park*

Chez la Mere Michel, *Montreal*

L'eau a la Bouche, *Montreal*

La Maree, *Montreal*

Laurie Raphael, *Quebec City*

Le Piment Rouge, *Montreal*

Les Caprices de Nicolas, *Montreal*

Mediterraneo Grill & Wine Bar, *Montreal*

Nuances, *Montreal*

Toque!, *Montreal*

CONNECTICUT

Connecticut is a state of beautiful hills and lakes and lovely old towns with white church steeples rising above green commons. It is also a state with a tradition of high technical achievement and fine machining. Old houses and buildings enchant the visitor; a re-creation of the life of the old sailing ship days at Mystic Seaport leads the traveler back to times long gone.

Adriaen Block sailed into the Connecticut River in 1614. This great river splits Massachusetts and Connecticut and separates Vermont from New Hampshire. It was the river by which Connecticut's first settlers, coming from Massachusetts in 1633, settled in Hartford, Windsor, and Wethersfield. These three towns created a practical constitution called the Fundamental Orders, through which a powerful "General Court" exercised both judicial and legislative duties. The Royal Charter of 1662 was so liberal that Sir Edmund Andros, governor of New England, tried to seize it (1687). To save it, citizens hid the charter in the Charter Oak, which once stood in Hartford.

Population: 3,282,031
Area: 4,872 square miles
Elevation: 0-2,380 feet
Peak: Mount Frissel (Litchfield County)
Entered Union: Fifth of original 13 states (January 9, 1788)
Capital: Hartford
Motto: He who transplanted, still sustains
Nickname: Constitution State
Flower: Mountain Laurel
Bird: American Robin
Tree: White Oak
Time Zone: Eastern
Website: www.tourism.state.ct.us

Poultry, dairy products, and tobacco are the state's most important agricultural products; forest products, nursery stock, and fruit and vegetable produce follow in importance. Aircraft engines, helicopters, hardware, tools, nuclear submarines, and machinery are the principal manufactured products. The home offices of more than 40 insurance companies are located in the state.

When to Go/Climate

Connecticut's climate is the mildest of all the New England states. Coastal breezes help keep the humidity manageable, and mud season (between winter and spring, when topsoil thaws and lower earth remains frozen) is shorter here than in other New England states.

AVERAGE HIGH/LOW TEMPERATURES (°F)

BRIDGEPORT

Jan 29/22	**May** 59/50	**Sep** 66/58
Feb 31/23	**June** 68/59	**Oct** 56/47
Mar 39/31	**July** 74/66	**Nov** 46/38
Apr 49/40	**Aug** 73/65	**Dec** 35/28

HARTFORD

Jan 25/16	**May** 60/48	**Sep** 64/52
Feb 28/19	**June** 69/57	**Oct** 53/41
Mar 38/28	**July** 74/62	**Nov** 42/33
Apr 49/38	**Aug** 72/60	**Dec** 30/21

CALENDAR HIGHLIGHTS

APRIL

Connecticut Storytelling Festival (New London). Connecticut College. Nationally acclaimed artists; workshops, concerts. Phone 860/439-2764.

MAY

Garlicfest (Fairfield). Notre Dame Catholic High School. Vendors prepare international array of garlic-seasoned cuisine. Sales, entertainment. Phone 203/372-6521.

Lobsterfest (Mystic). Seaport. Outdoor food festival. Phone 860/57-0711.

JUNE

Taste of Hartford (Hartford). Main St. Four-day event features specialties of more than 50 area restaurants; continuous entertainment. Phone 860/728-3089.

International Festival of Arts and Ideas (New Haven). Celebration of the arts and humanities. Phone 888/ART-IDEA.

JULY

Riverfest (Hartford). Celebration of America's independence and the Connecticut River. Family entertainment, concerts, food, fireworks display over river.

Mark Twain Days (Hartford). Celebration of Twain's legacy and Hartford's cultural heritage with more than 100 events. Concerts, riverboat rides, medieval jousting, tours of Twain House, entertainment. Phone 860/247-0998.

Barnum Festival (Bridgeport). Commemorates the life of P. T. Barnum.

AUGUST

Pilot Pen International Tennis Tournament (New Haven). Connecticut Tennis Center, near Yale Bowl. Championship Series on the ATP Tour. Phone 888-99-PILOT.

SEPTEMBER

Durham Fair (Middletown). Fairgrounds, in Durham on CT 17. State's largest agricultural fair. Phone 860/349-9495.

OCTOBER

Apple Harvest Festival (Meriden). 3 mi S on CT 120, in Southington, on Town Green. Street festival celebrating local apple harvest. Carnival, arts and crafts, parade, road race, food booths, entertainment. Phone 860/628-8036.

DECEMBER

Christmas Torchlight Parade (Old Saybrook). Over 40 fife and drum corps march down Main St.

Parks and Recreation Finder

Directions to and information about the parks and recreation areas below are given under their respective town/city sections. Please refer to those sections for details.

STATE PARK AND RECREATION AREAS

Key to abbreviations. I.P. = Interstate Park; S.A.P. = State Archaeological Park; S.B. = State Beach; S.C.A. = State Conservation Area; S.C.P. = State Conservation Park; S.Cp. = State Campground; S.F. = State Forest; S.G. = State Garden;

S.H.A. = State Historic Area; S.H.P. = State Historic Park; S.H.S. = State Historic Site; S.M.P. = State Marine Park; S.N.A. = State Natural Area; S.P. = State Park; S.P.C. = State Public Campground; S.R. = State Reserve; S.R.A. = State Recreation Area; S.Res. = State Reservoir; S.Res.P. = State Resort Park; S.R.P. = State Rustic Park.

Place Name	Listed Under
Campbell Falls S.P.	NORFOLK
Chatfield Hollow S.P.	CLINTON
Dennis Hill S.P.	NORFOLK
Dinosaur S.P.	WETHERSFIELD
Fort Griswold Battlefield S.P.	GROTON
Gillette Castle S.P.	EAST HADDAM
Hammonasset Beach S.P.	MADISON
Hatstack Mountain S.P.	NORFOLK
Housatonic Meadows S.P.	CORNWALL BRIDGE
Kent Falls S.P.	KENT
Kettletown S.P.	SOUTHBURY
Lake Waramaug S.P.	NEW PRESTON
Macedonia Brook S.P.	KENT
Rocky Neck S.P.	OLD LYME
Southford Falls S.P.	SOUTHBURY
Squantz Pond S.P.	DANBURY
Talcott Mountain S.P.	HARTFORD
Topsmead S.F.	LITCHFIELD
Wadsworth Falls S.P.	MIDDLETOWN

Water-related activities, hiking, riding, various other sports, picnicking and visitor centers, as well as camping, are available in some of these areas. There are 32 state forests and 92 state parks inland and on the shore. A parking fee ($4-$12) is charged at many of these. Camping, mid-April-September; shore parks $12/site/night; inland parks with swimming $10/site/night; inland parks without swimming $9/site/night; additional charge per person for groups larger than 4 persons. Two- to three-week limit, mid-April-September; three-day limit, October-December. No camping January-mid-April; selected parks allow camping October-December. Forms for reservations for stays of more than two days may be obtained after January 15 by writing to the address in Hartford; these reservations should then be mailed to the park itself; no reservations by phone. Parks and forests are open all year, 8 am-sunset. Most shore parks allow all-night fishing (with permit). Inland swimming areas are open 8 am-sunset. No pets allowed in state park campgrounds. For further information, reservations, and regulations contact Dept of Environmental Protection, Bureau of Outdoor Recreation, 79 Elm St, Hartford 06106; 860/424-3200.

SKI AREAS

Place Name	Listed Under
Mohawk Mountain Ski Area	CORNWALL BRIDGE
Mount Southington Ski Area	MERIDEN
Powder Ridge Ski Area	MIDDLETOWN
Ski Sundown	AVON

FISHING AND HUNTING

Hunting license: nonresident, $42 (firearms). Archery permit (incl big and small game): nonresident, $44. Deer permit: nonresident, $30 (firearms). Fishing license: nonresident, season, $25; 3-day, $8. Combination firearm hunting, fishing license: nonresident, $55. Further information, including the latest regulations, can be obtained from Dept of Environmental Protection, Licensing and Revenue, 79 Elm St, Hartford 06106; 860/424-3105.

Driving Information

Safety belts are mandatory for all persons in front seat of vehicle. Children under 4 years must be in an approved passenger restraint anywhere in vehicle: ages 1-3 may use a regulation safety belt; under age 1 must use an approved safety seat.

INTERSTATE HIGHWAY SYSTEM

The following alphabetical listing of Connecticut towns in *Mobil Travel Guide* shows that these cities are within 10 miles of the indicated interstate highways. A highway map, however, should be checked for the nearest exit.

Highway Number	Cities/Towns within 10 miles
Interstate 84	Danbury, Farmington, Hartford, Manchester, Southbury, Stafford Springs, Vernon, Waterbury.
Interstate 91	Enfield, Hartford, Meriden, Middletown, New Haven, Wethersfield, Windsor, Windsor Locks.
Interstate 95	Branford, Bridgeport, Clinton, Fairfield, Greenwich, Groton, Guilford, Madison, Milford, Mystic, New Haven, New London, Norwalk, Old Saybrook, Stamford, Stonington, Stratford, Westport.
Interstate 395	Groton, New London, Norwich, Plainfield, Putnam.

Additional Visitor Information

Pamphlets, maps, and booklets, including the Connecticut Vacation Guide, are available to tourists by contacting the State of Connecticut, Department of Economic and Community Development, 505 Hudson St, Hartford 06106; 800/282-6863. In addition, *Connecticut*—a monthly magazine published by Communications Intl, 789 Reservoir Ave, Bridgeport 06606—gives a listing of activities around the state; available by subscription or at newsstands.

Connecticut tourism information centers also provide useful information: on I-95 southbound at North Stonington, northbound at Darien, northbound at Westbrook (seasonal); on I-84 eastbound at Danbury, eastbound at Southington (seasonal), westbound at Willington; on I-91 northbound at Middletown, southbound at Wallingford; on Merritt Parkway (CT 15) northbound at Greenwich (seasonal). Also, several privately operated tourism centers are located throughout the state.

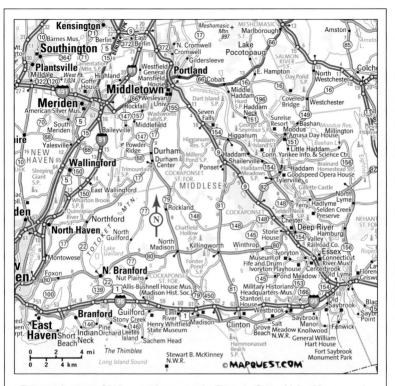

This tour begins in Old Lyme with stops at the Florence Griswold Art Museum and Rocky Neck State Park beach. Continue across the bridge into Old Saybrook, and follow Route 9 to Essex, a picturesque village with shops and restaurants. The Connecticut River Museum is located here, as is the departure point for the Valley Railroad, which runs along the river. (Railroad passengers can connect with a riverboat for a one-hour Connecticut River cruise.) Follow scenic Route 154 to Chester, where you can take the country's oldest continuous ferry (it also carries cars) across to Gillette Castle in East Haddam, or continue over the bridge to East Haddam for a great view of the Victorian Goodspeed Opera House, which stages American musicals and is a destination in its own right. You can return via Route 9 (limited-access highway), or take the scenic way (country roads), Route 82 to Route 156 to I-95, back along the eastern side of the river. Continue west on I-95 to Hammonasset Beach State Park in Madison (the big beach in this area) and then down Route 1, past the town's classic historic homes, to Guilford, site of the Henry Whitfield State Museum, an unusual 1630s stone house. Get back on I-95 and follow it into New Haven. Another trip option (not pictured on the map) is to head east on I-95 to the town of Mystic, the state's top coastal lodgings/attractions hub. Mystic Seaport Museum, Mystic Aquarium, and a shopping mall in the shape of a New England village are popular attractions. Foxwoods Resort Casino, in nearby Ledyard, is the world's largest gambling casino; its complex includes lodging and a museum devoted to the Mashantucket Pequot, the tribe that owns the casino. From Mystic, take I-95 to Stonington (a picturesque fishing village) and then to Watch Hill (a resort town with good beaches). From Stonington, it's a scenic 40-mile coastal drive along Route 1, which passes the Rhode Island fishing resort towns of Charlestown and Narragansett (departure point for ferries to Block Island) and crosses to Jamestown Island in Newport (RI). **(Approx 112 mi; approx 124 mi from Mystic to Jamestown Island)**

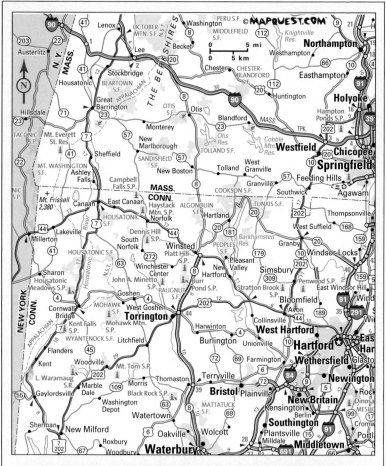

Hartford is the state capital and offers two major tourist sights: the downtown Wadsworth Atheneum and the Mark Twain House. Both are major draws for travelers passing through on the highways that intersect here, making Hartford the logical starting point for a tour west into scenic Litchfield Hills, a town studded with country inns and bed-and-breakfasts. Begin with the Atheneum (a major art museum), then stop at the neighboring Mark Twain and Harriet Beecher Stowe houses (east of downtown). Follow Route 44 west to 202 to continue on to Litchfield, a beautiful New England village with small museums, inns, and restaurants. Take Route 202 west, passing Mount Tom State Park, to New Preston, where you will find antique shops and Lake Waramaug State Park, which offers swimming and fishing. Continue south on Route 202 to New Milford with its big green, colonial homes, antique shops, and restaurants. Turn north on Route 7 to Kent, a major art center with museums and galleries. Kent Falls State Park is also here with its dramatic 200-foot waterfalls. Proceed north to the scenic town of Cornwall Bridge. From here you can return to Litchfield via Goshen, but the most popular return trip follows Route 7 (along the Housatonic River) up through Canaan to Sheffield (MA) and on to Stockbrige, Lee, and Lenox. **(Approx 103 mi; add 44 mi if continuing on to Lenox, MA)**

Avon

See also Bristol, Farmington, Hartford, Wethersfield

Pop 13,937 **Elev** 202 ft **Area code** 860 **Zip** 06001
Web www.travelfile.com/get/ghtd
Information Greater Hartford Tourism District, 234 Murphy Rd, Hartford 06114; 860/244-8181 or 800/793-4480

What to See and Do

Farmington Valley Arts Center. Twenty studios, located in historic stone explosives plant, occupied by artists and artisans and open to public at artist's discretion. Fisher Gallery and Shop featuring guest-curated exhibitions and a juried collection of handmade crafts, gifts, and artwork. (Jan-Oct, Wed-Sat, Sun afternoons; Nov-Dec, daily; closed hols) 25 Arts Center Lane, Avon Park North, off US 44. Phone 860/678-1867. **FREE**

Roaring Brook Nature Center. This 112-acre wildlife refuge has interpretive building with seasonal natural history exhibits, wildlife observation area, 6 mi of marked trails. Gift shop. (Sep-June, Tues-Sun; rest of yr, daily; closed hols) 1½ mi N of US 44, at 70 Gracey Rd in Canton. Phone 860/693-0263. ¢¢

Ski Sundown. Three triple chairlifts, Pomalift; snowmaking, school, patrol, rentals, half-day rate; bar, snack bar. 15 trails. Longest run 1 mi; vertical drop 625 ft. (Dec-Mar, daily) 6 mi W via CT 44, then 1½ mi NE on CT 219, in New Hartford. Phone 860/379-9851 or 860/379-SNOW (snow conditions). ¢¢¢¢

Hotel

★★★ **AVON OLD FARMS HOTEL.** *279 Avon Mountain (06001), E at jct US 44 and CT 10. 860/677-1651; fax 860/677-0364; toll-free 800/836-4000. Email reservations@avonoldfarmshotel. com; www.avonoldfarmshotel.com.* 157 rms, 3 story, 2 suites. Apr-Jun, Sep-Nov: S, D $179; suites $250; under 18 free; lower rates rest of yr. Crib avail, fee. Parking lot. Pool. TV; cable (premium). Complimentary continental bkfst, newspaper. Restaurant. Bar. Meeting rms. Business servs avail. Concierge serv. Dry cleaning. Exercise equipt, sauna. Golf. Tennis, 5 courts. Downhill skiing. Hiking trail. Picnic facilities. Cr cds: A, C, D, DS, MC, V.

Restaurants

★★★ **AVON OLD FARMS INN.** *1 Nod Rd (06001), E at jct US 44 and CT 10, 5 mi off I-84. 860/677-2818. www .avonoldfarmsinn.com.* Own baking. Hrs: 11:30 am-9:30 pm; Sun 10 am-8:30 pm; Sun brunch to 2:30 pm. Res required. Bar. Lunch $6.95-$13.95; dinner $18.95-$26.95. Sun brunch $15.95. Child's menu. 1757 stagecoach stop. Cr cds: A, DS, MC, V.

★★ **DAKOTA.** *225 W Main St (06001). 860/677-4311. www.dakota. com.* Specializes in steak, seafood. Salad bar. Hrs: 5-10 pm; Sat 4-11 pm; Sun 10 am-10 pm. Res accepted. Bar. Lunch, dinner a la carte entrees: $9.95-$23.95. Brunch a la carte entrees: $9.95-$23.95. Child's menu. Casual, rustic atmosphere with a touch of Southwestern decor. Cr cds: A, D, DS, MC, V.

Branford

(F-2) *See also Meriden, Milford, New Haven*

Settled 1644 **Pop** 27,603 **Elev** 49 ft
Area code 203 **Zip** 06405
Web www.cttourism.org
Information CT River Valley & Shoreline Visitors Council, 393 Main St, Middletown 06457; 860/347-0028 or 800/486-3346

Once a busy shipping center, Branford has become a residential and industrial suburb of New Haven. The community's bays and beaches attract many summertime vacationers. Branford's large green, dating from colonial days, is surrounded by public buildings.

What to See and Do

Harrison House. (ca 1725) Classic colonial saltbox restored by J. Frederick Kelly, an early 20th-century architect; stone chimney, herb garden, period furnishings, and farm implements. (June-Sep, Thurs-Sat afternoons; also by appt) 124 Main St. Phone 203/488-4828 or 203/488-2126. **FREE**

Thimble Islands Cruise. Legends of treasures hidden by Captain Kidd, along with picturesque shores and vegetation, have lured people to these 20 to 30 rocky islets in Long Island Sound for more than 250 yrs. Narrated tours (30-45 min) leave hrly aboard the *Volsunga III.* (May-Oct, Tues-Sun) Res required. Departs from Stony Creek Dock. Phone 203/481-3345 or 203/488-9978. ¢¢¢

Motel/Motor Lodge

★★ **DAYS INN.** *375 E Main St (06405). 203/488-8314; fax 203/483-6885; toll-free 800/329-7466.* 74 rms, 2 story. S $75-$80; D $90-$99; each addl $10; suites $245; under 16 free. Crib free. Pet accepted; $10. TV; cable (premium), VCR avail. Pool. Complimentary continental bkfst. Coffee in rms. Restaurant 7 am-2 pm; Sat, Sun to noon. Ck-out 11 am. Valet serv. Meeting rms. Business center. Gift shop. Barber, beauty shop. Refrigerators avail. Cr cds: A, C, D, DS, ER, JCB, MC, V.

Bridgeport

(G-2) *See also Fairfield, Milford, Norwalk, Stratford, Westport*

Settled 1639 **Pop** 141,686 **Elev** 20 ft
Area code 203
Information Chamber of Commerce, 10 Middle St, 14th flr, 06604; 203/335-3800

An important manufacturing city, Bridgeport is home to dozens of well-known companies that produce a highly diversified array of manufactured products. The University of Bridgeport (1927) is also located in the city.

Bridgeport's most famous resident was probably P. T. Barnum. The city's most famous son was 28-inch Charles S. Stratton, who was promoted by Barnum as General Tom Thumb. There was a time when train passengers in and out of Bridgeport occasionally saw elephants hitched to plows; the elephants, of course, were from Barnum's winter quarters. As well as running the "Greatest Show on Earth," Barnum was for a time the mayor of Bridgeport.

What to See and Do

✪ **The Barnum Museum.** Houses memorabilia from P. T. Barnum's life and circus career, including artifacts relating to Barnum's legendary discoveries, General Tom Thumb and Jenny Lind; scale model of 3-ring circus; displays of Victorian Bridgeport; changing exhibits; art gallery. (Tues-Sun; closed hols) 820 Main St. Phone 203/331-9881. ¢¢

Beardsley Zoological Gardens. This 30-acre zoo, the state's only, houses more than 200 animals; Siberian tiger exhibit, farmyard; concession, gift shop. (Daily; closed Jan 1, Thanksgiving, Dec 25) Noble Ave, Beardsley Park, off I-95 exit 27A. Phone 203/394-6565. Zoo ¢¢; Park entrance fee per vehicle ¢

Captain's Cove Seaport. Replica of the HMS *Rose,* the British warship that triggered the founding of the American Navy during the American Revolution. Marina, shops, restaurant, fish market. (Schedule varies) 1 Bostwick Ave, I-95 Exit 26. Phone 203/335-1433. HMS *Rose* ¢¢

Discovery Museum. Planetarium; films; approx 120 hands-on science and art exhibits; children's museum; Challenger Learning Center; changing art exhibits; lectures, demonstrations, and workshops. (Tues-Sun; closed Labor Day, Thanksgiving, Dec 25) 4450 Park Ave, off Merritt Pkwy, Exit 47. Phone 203/372-3521. ¢¢¢

Ferry to Port Jefferson, Long Island. Car and passenger service across Long Island Sound (1 hr, 20 min). (Daily) Union Square Dock, at foot of

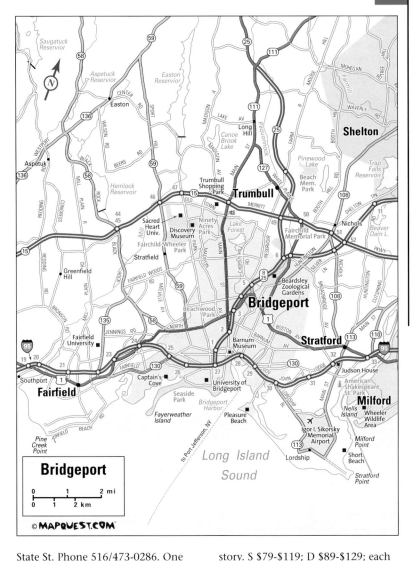

State St. Phone 516/473-0286. One way, individual ¢¢¢

Statue of Tom Thumb. Life-size statue on 10-ft base. Mountain Grove Cemetery, North Ave & Dewey St.

Seasonal Event

Barnum Festival. Commemorates the life of P. T. Barnum. Early July.

Hotels

★★ **HOLIDAY INN.** *1070 Main St (06604). 203/334-1234; fax 203/367-1985; res 800/holiday.* 234 rms, 9

story. S $79-$119; D $89-$129; each addl $10; suites $179-$450; under 16 free; family, wkend rates. Crib free. Pet accepted, some restrictions. TV; cable. Indoor/outdoor pool. Restaurant 6 am-10 pm. Bar 4 pm-midnight. Ck-out noon. Meeting rms. Business center. In-rm modem link. Free covered parking. Free airport, railroad station, bus depot transportation. Exercise equipt. Refrigerator in some suites. Atrium; waterfall. Beach 4 blks. Cr cds: A, D, DS, MC, V.

★★★ **MARRIOTT TRUMBULL HOTEL.** *180 Hawley Ln (06611), N via CT 8/25 to CT 15 (Merritt Pkwy) Exit 51S, 3 blks S to Hawley Ln. 203/ 378-1400; fax 203/378-0632; toll-free 800/682-4095.* 320 rms, 5 story. S $144-$189; D $164-$209; each addl $20; suites $300-$400; under 18 free; wkend rates. Crib free. TV; cable (premium), VCR avail. 2 pools, 1 indoor; whirlpool, poolside serv. Coffee in rms. Restaurants 6:30 am-11 pm. Bars 11-1 am; entertainment. Ck-out noon. Convention facilities. Business center. In-rm modem link. Gift shop. Exercise equipt; sauna. Some refrigerators. Cr cds: A, C, D, DS, ER, JCB, MC, V.

[D] ⚓ 🏋 ⛷ 🏊 [SC] 🚶

Restaurant

★ **BLACK ROCK CASTLE.** *2895 Fairfield Ave (06605). 203/336-3990.* Specializes in flaming Irish whiskey steak, beef. Hrs: 11:30 am-9 pm; Fri, Sat to 11 pm. Closed Jan 1, Dec 25. Res accepted. Lunch a la carte entrees: $4.95-$6.95; dinner a la carte entrees: $9.95-$16.95. Child's menu. Entertainment: Wed-Sun. Valet parking. Castle motif; dining beneath tower. Cr cds: A, D, DS, MC, V.

[D] [SC] ⊷

Bristol

(E-2) *See also Meriden, New Britain, Waterbury*

Settled 1727 **Pop** 60,640 **Elev** 289 ft
Area code 860 **Zip** 06010
Web www.chamber.bristol.ct.us
Information Greater Bristol Chamber of Commerce, 10 Main St; 860/584-4718. Litchfield Hills Travel Council, PO Box 1776, Marbledale 06777; 860/868-2214

Gideon Roberts began making and selling clocks here in 1790. Bristol has since been famous for clocks—particularly for Sessions and Ingraham. Today Bristol is also the home of Associated Spring Corporation; Dana Corp/Warner Electric; Theis Precision Steel; and ESPN, the nation's first all-sports cable television network.

What to See and Do

American Clock and Watch Museum. More than 3,000 timepieces; exhibits and video show on history of clock and watch manufacturing located in historic house built 1801. Also award-winning sundial garden, bookshop. (Apr-Nov, daily; closed Thanksgiving) 100 Maple St. Phone 860/583-6070. ¢¢

Burlington Trout Hatchery. Hatchery building houses incubators and tanks; development of trout from egg to fish. (Daily) 10 mi N via CT 69, then approx 1 mi E on CT 4 to Belden Rd, in Burlington. Phone 860/673-2340. **FREE**

H.C. Barnes Memorial Nature Center. Self-guided trails through 70-acre preserve. Interpretive building features ecological and animal displays. (Sat, also Wed-Fri and Sun afternoons) Trails (daily; closed hols). 175 Shrub Rd, 3 mi N on CT 69. Phone 860/589-6082. ¢

Lake Compounce Theme Park. One of the oldest continuously operating amusement parks in the nation. Over 25 wet and dry attractions including roller coasters, white-water raft ride, vintage trolley, bumper cars, and 1911 carousel. Special events. (June-Aug, Wed-Mon; Sep, wkends) 822 Lake Ave. Phone 860/583-3631. All-day ride pass ¢¢¢¢

Lock Museum of America. Antique locks, displays on lock history and design. (May-Oct, Tues-Sun, limited hrs) 3½ mi NW on CT 72, then W ¾ mi on US 6 to 130 Main St in Terryville. Phone 860/589-6359. ¢¢ 2 blks W is

  Eli Terry, Jr. Waterwheel. Built in the early 1840s, this 20-ft diameter, rack and pinion, breast-type wheel is an excellent example of the type of waterwheel used to supply power to industrial buildings during this period. 160 Main St.

New England Carousel Museum. Displays more than 300 carved, wooden antique carousel figures, including two chariots. Restoration workshop on view. (Apr-Oct, Mon-Sat, also Sun afternoons; rest of yr, Wed-Sat, also Sun afternoons; closed hols) 95 Riverside Ave. Phone 860/585-5411. ¢¢

Annual Events

Balloons Over Bristol. Bristol Eastern High School. More than 60 hot-air balloons from around the country gather to participate in 3-day event; carnival, crafts fair, food booths. Phone 860/584-4718. Memorial Day wkend.

Chrysanthemum Festival. Music, art, theater, hayrides, picking pumpkins, parades and dances, Historical Society tours. Phone 860/584-4718. Late Sep.

B&B/Small Inn

★★★ **CHIMNEY CREST MANOR.** *5 Founders Dr (06010). 860/582-4219; fax 860/584-5903.* 6 units, 3 story, 4 suites. S, D $85-$150; each addl $15. Closed Dec 24-25. Crib free. TV; cable (premium), VCR avail. Complimentary full bkfst. Ck-out 11 am, ck-in 3 pm. Framed artwork, beamed ceilings in 32-rm Tudor-style mansion (1930). Library; sun rm. Totally nonsmoking. Cr cds: A, MC, V.
⊠ 🐾 SC

Clinton

(C-5) *See also Essex, Guilford, Madison, New Haven, Old Saybrook*

Settled 1663 **Pop** 12,767 **Elev** 25 ft
Area code 860 **Zip** 06413
Web www.ClintonCT.com

Information Chamber of Commerce, 50 E Main St, PO Box 334; 860/669-3889; or the Connecticut Valley Tourism Commission, 393 Main St, Middletown 06457; 860/669-3889

What to See and Do

Chamard Vinyards. A 15-acre vineyard and winery offering Chardonnay, Pinot Noir, Merlot, and other varieties. Tours and tastings (Wed-Sat). 115 Cow Hill Rd. Phone 860/664-0299 or 800/371-1609. **FREE**

Chatfield Hollow State Park. Approx 550 acres situated in a heavily wooded hollow with fine fall scenery and natural caves that once provided shelter for Native Americans. Pond swimming, fishing; hiking, ice-skating, picnicking, concessions. Stan-

dard hrs, fees. 7 mi NW via CT 80 & 81, on N Branford Rd in Killingworth. Phone 860/663-2030. ¢¢¢

Stanton House. (1789) 13-rm house connected to general store; original site of first classroom of Yale Univ. Period furnishings, antique American and Staffordshire dinnerware, weapon collection, bed used by Marquis de Lafayette during 1824 visit. (June-Sep, Tues-Sun) 63 E Main St. Phone 860/669-2132. **FREE**

Motel/Motor Lodge

★ **CLINTON MOTEL.** *163 E Main St (06413). 860/669-8850; fax 860/669-3849.* 15 rms, 1 story. Jun-Sep: S $72; D $89; lower rates rest of yr. Crib avail. Parking lot. Pool. TV; cable. Complimentary toll-free calls. Restaurant. Ck-out 11 am, ck-in 1 pm. Fax servs avail. Exercise privileges. Golf. Cr cds: A, DS, MC, V.
🍴 ➳ 🏃 ⊠ 🐾

Restaurant

★ **LOG CABIN RESTAURANT AND LOUNGE.** *232 Boston Post Rd (06413). 860/669-6253.* Specializes in seafood, steak, pasta. Hrs: 11:30 am-9 pm; Fri, Sat to 10 pm; Sun from noon. Closed Dec 25. Res accepted. Bar. Lunch $4.95-$7.95; dinner $10.95-$18.95. Child's menu. Log cabin decor; fireplace. Cr cds: A, D, MC, V.
D ⊠

Cornwall Bridge

See also Kent

Pop 450 (est) **Elev** 445 ft
Area code 860 **Zip** 06754
Information Litchfield Hills Travel Council, PO Box 968, Litchfield 06759; 860/567-4506

The small central valley containing the villages of Cornwall, West Cornwall, and Cornwall Bridge was avoided by early settlers because its heavy stand of pine made the clearing of land difficult.

What to See and Do

Covered bridge. Designed by Ithiel Town, the bridge has been in continuous service since 1837. 4 mi N via US 7 to CT 128 near West Cornwall, at Housatonic River. **FREE**

Housatonic Meadows State Park. A 452-acre park bordering the Housatonic River. Fishing, boating, canoeing; picnicking, camping (dump station). No pets. Standard hrs, fees. 1 mi N on US 7. Phone 860/672-6772 (May-Sep) or 860/927-3238. **FREE**

Mohawk Mountain Ski Area. More than 20 trails and slopes, most with snowmaking; triple, 4 double chair-lifts; patrol, school, rentals; cafeteria. Longest run 1¼ mi; vertical drop 640 ft. (Late Nov-early Apr, daily; closed Dec 25) More than 40 mi of cross-country trails. Night skiing Mon-Sat. 4 mi NE on CT 4, S on CT 128, on Great Hollow Rd in Mohawk Mt State Park. Phone 860/672-6100 (snow conditions), 860/672-6464 or 800/895-5222. ¢¢¢¢

Sharon Audubon Center. National Audubon Society wildlife sanctuary (684 acres) includes nature center, 11 mi of walking trails, self-guided tours, herb and wildflower garden, gift/bookstore. Grounds (daily). Nature center, store (daily; closed hols). Approx 8 mi NW on CT 4 near Sharon. Phone 860/364-0520. ¢¢

B&B/Small Inn

★ CORNWALL INN AND RESTAURANT. *270 Kent Rd; Rte 7 (06754). 860/672-6884; toll-free 800/786-6884.* 13 rms, 2 story, 1 suite. No rm phones. S, D $50-$110; each addl $10; suite $150; under 5 free. Crib free. Pet accepted, some restrictions. TV in some rms, also in sitting rm. Pool. Complimentary continental bkfst. Dining rm 6-9 pm Thurs-Mon; res required. Bar 5-10 pm. Ck-out 11 am, ck-in 2 pm. Bellhop. Bus depot transportation. Downhill ski 5 mi; x-country ski ¼ mi. Picnic tables. Restored 19th-century country inn; antiques. Cr cds: A, DS, MC, V.

Danbury

(F-1) See also Southbury, Woodbury

Settled 1685 **Pop** 65,585 **Elev** 378 ft
Area code 203
Web www.housatonic.org
Information Housatonic Valley Tourism Commission, 30 Main St, PO Box 406, 06813; 203/743-0546 or 800/841-4488

Danbury, originally settled by eight Norwalk families seeking fertile land, played an important role during the American Revolution as a supply depot and site of a military hospital for the Continental Army. After the war and until the 1950s, the community was the center of the hat industry. Zadoc Benedict is credited with the first factory in 1790, which made three hats a day.

What to See and Do

Candlewood Lake. Connecticut's largest lake, more than 14 mi long with approx 60 mi of shoreline, extends one finger into Danbury. Swimming, fishing, boating; picnicking, concession. Fees for some activities. 2 mi NW on CT 37, then E on Hayestown Ave to E Hayestown Rd. Phone 203/354-6928. On the W shore are Pootatuck State Forest and

Squantz Pond State Park. More than 170 acres. Freshwater swimming, scuba diving, fishing, boating (7½ hp limit), canoeing (rentals); hiking, biking, picnicking, concessions. No pets. Standard hrs, fees. 10 mi N on CT 37 & 39 in New Fairfield. Phone 203/797-4165. ¢¢

Scott-Fanton Museum. Includes Rider House (1785), period furnishings, New England memorabilia; Dodd Shop (ca 1790), historical display of hat industry; Huntington Hall, changing exhibits and research library. (Wed-Sun afternoons; closed hols) 43 Main St. Phone 203/743-5200. **Donation**

Annual Event

Taste O' Danbury. Phone 203/790-6970. Sep.

Seasonal Event

Charles Ives Center for the Arts. At Westside campus, Western Connecticut State University, on Mill Plain Rd. Outdoor classical, country, folk, jazz, and pop concerts. Fri-Sun. Phone 203/837-9226. July-Sep.

Motel/Motor Lodge

★★ **RAMADA INN.** *Danbury Newtown Rd (06801), 1½ mi NE at Exit 8. 203/792-3800; fax 203/730-1899; toll-free 800/228-2828.* 181 rms, 2-5 story. S $79-$145; D $79-$155; each addl $15; under 16 free; wkend rates. Pet accepted, some restrictions. TV; cable (premium). Indoor/outdoor pool. Coffee in rms. Restaurant 6:30 am-10:30 pm; Fri to 11 pm; hrs vary wkends. Rm serv. Bar 11-1 am. Ck-out 11 am. Coin lndry. Meeting rms. Business servs avail. In-rm modem link. Valet serv. Health club privileges. Refrigerators, microwaves avail. Cr cds: A, C, D, DS, ER, JCB, MC, V.

Hotels

★★ **BEST WESTERN BERKSHIRE INN.** *11 Stony Hill Rd, US Rte 6 (06801), I-84 Exit 8. 203/744-3200; fax 203/744-3979; res 800/528-1234. Email bw.berkshire@snet.net; www.best western.com/berkshiremotorinn.* 69 rms, 3 story. May-Oct: S, D $110; each addl $8; under 11 free; lower rates rest of yr. Crib avail, fee. Parking lot. TV; cable (premium). Complimentary continental bkfst, newspaper, toll-free calls. Restaurant. Business center. Dry cleaning. Exercise privileges. Golf. Cr cds: A, C, D, DS, MC, V.

★★★ **HILTON DANBURY AND TOWERS.** *18 Old Ridgebury Rd (06810), I-84 E, Exit 2A. 203/794-0600; fax 203/798-2709; res 800/445-8667. www.danbury.hilton.com.* 242 rms, 10 story. S, D $125-$195; each addl $15; family, wkend rates. Crib free. Pet accepted, some restrictions. TV; cable (premium), VCR (movies). Indoor pool; whirlpool, poolside serv. Restaurant 6:30 am-10 pm. Bar 11-2 am; entertainment. Ck-out noon. Meeting rms. Business center. In-rm modem link. Coin lndry. Lighted tennis. Exercise equipt;

sauna. Health club privileges. Microwaves avail. Cr cds: A, DS, MC, V.

★★ **HOLIDAY INN.** *80 Newtown Rd (06810), I-84 Exit 8. 203/792-4000; fax 203/797-0810; toll-free 800/465-4329. Email william@holiday.meyer jabara.com; www.danburyholidayinn. com.* 114 rms, 4 story. S, D $124; suites $139; each addl $10; under 17 free. Crib avail. Pet accepted. Parking lot. Pool. TV; cable (premium), VCR avail. Complimentary coffee in rms, newspaper, toll-free calls. Restaurant. Bar. Ck-out noon, ck-in noon. Meeting rms. Business servs avail. Bellhops. Dry cleaning. Exercise privileges. Golf, 18 holes. Tennis, 8 courts. Video games. Cr cds: A, D, DS, MC, V.

★★ **THE INN AT ETHAN ALLEN.** *21 Lake Ave (06811), I-84 Exit 4, 1 blk W. 203/744-1776; fax 203/791-9673; toll-free 800/742-1776.* 195 rms, 6 story. S $108-$115; D $123-$130; each addl $15; suites $113-$130; under 17 free; wkend rates. TV; cable (premium). Pool. Restaurant 6:30-10 am, noon-2 pm, 5-10 pm; Sat, Sun 7:30 am-2 pm. Bar 4 pm-1 am, wkends from 11:30 am. Ck-out noon. Coin lndry. Meeting rms. Business center. In-rm modem link. Free railroad station, bus depot transportation. Airport transportation. Exercise equipt; sauna. Microwaves avail. Owned by Ethan Allen furniture co. Cr cds: A, DS, MC, V.

Resort

★★ **BEST WESTERN STONY HILL INN.** *46 Stoney Hill Rd US Rte 6 (06801), 1¼ mi E on US 6 Exit 8, between I-84 Exits 8 and 9. 203/743-5533; fax 203/743-4958; res 800/528-1234. Email bw.stonyhillinn@snet.net; www.bestwestern.com/stonyhil.* 36 rms, 1 story. May-Oct: S, D $120; each addl $10; children $10; under 12 free; lower rates rest of yr. Crib avail, fee. Parking lot. Pool. TV; cable (premium). Complimentary continental bkfst, newspaper, toll-free calls. Restaurant 11:30 am-8 pm, closed Mon. Bar. Ck-out 11 am, ck-in 1 pm. Meeting rms. Business center. Coin

lndry. Exercise privileges, sauna.
Golf. Cr cds: A, C, D, DS, MC, V.

D 🐾 ⚖ 🏄 ➷ 🔥 SC 🏄

B&B/Small Inn

★ ★ **THE HOMESTEAD INN.** *5 Elm St (06776), 13 mi N on US 7. 860/354-4080; fax 860/354-7046. www.home steadct.com.* 14 rms, 2 story, 1 suite. May-Oct: S $86; D $96; each addl $10; children $6; under 12 free; lower rates rest of yr. Crib avail. Parking lot. TV; cable. Complimentary continental bkfst, toll-free calls. Restaurant. Ck-out 11 am, ck-in 2 pm. Business servs avail. Gift shop. Golf. Downhill skiing. Cr cds: A, C, D, DS, MC, V.

➷ 🏄 ➷ 🔥

Restaurants

★ ★ **CIAO CAFE AND WINE BAR.** *2B Ives St (06810). 203/791-0404.* Specializes in veal Christine, rigatoni with tortanella cheese. Hrs: 11:30 am-10 pm; Fri, Sat to 11 pm; Sun brunch to 2 pm. Closed Labor Day, Dec 25. Res accepted; required Fri, Sat. Bar. Wine list. Lunch a la carte entrees: $5.95-$8.95; dinner a la carte entrees: $8.75-$16.95. Sun brunch $7.95. Contemporary decor. Cr cds: A, MC, V.

D

★ **THE HEARTH.** *US 7 (06804), NE via I-84 to Exit 7, 5 mi N on US 7. 203/775-3360.* Specializes in open-hearth steak, seafood. Hrs: noon-9 pm; Fri, Sat to 9:30 pm; Sun 1-8 pm. Closed Mon; Thanksgiving, Dec 24, 25; Feb. Lunch $4.75-$7; dinner $8.95-$22.95. Complete meals: $11.50-$23. Child's menu. Open-hearth cooking in center of restaurant. Cr cds: A, MC, V.

➷

★ ★ **TWO STEPS DOWNTOWN GRILLE.** *5 Ives St (06810), I-84 Exit 5. 203/794-0032.* Specializes in fajitas, baby back ribs. Hrs: 11-12:30 am; Fri, Sat to 1:30 am; Sun brunch 10 am-2 pm. Closed Labor Day, Dec 25. Res accepted. Bar. Lunch $5.95-$7.95; dinner $7.95-$15.95. Sun brunch $7.95. Child's menu. Former firehouse; lower level has Western decor. Cr cds: A, D, MC, V.

D ➷

East Haddam

See also Essex, Middletown

Pop 6,676 **Elev** 35 ft **Area code** 860
Zip 06423 **Web** www.cttourism.org
Information CT River Valley & Shoreline Visitors Council, 393 Main St, Middletown 06457; 860/347-0028 or 800/486-3346

The longest remaining swinging bridge in New England crosses the Connecticut River to Haddam.

What to See and Do

Amasa Day House. (1816) Period furnishings include some pieces owned by 3 generations of the Day family; stenciled floors and stairs. (June-Labor Day, Fri-Sun) Under reconstruction, phone ahead. 4 mi N on CT 149 at jct CT 151 in Moodus. Phone 860/873-8144 or 860/247-8996. ¢¢

Gillette Castle State Park. The 184-acre park surrounds a 24-rm castle built by turn-of-the-century actor/playwright William Gillette; medieval German design with dramatically decorated rms. (Late May-mid-Oct, daily; mid-Oct-mid-Dec, Sat and Sun) Picnicking and hiking trails in the surrounding park. Standard hrs. Under reconstruction, call ahead. 4 mi SE via local roads to 67 River Rd. Phone 860/526-2336. Castle ¢¢

Goodspeed Opera House. Home of the American Musical Theatre (1876). Performances of American musicals (Apr-Dec, Wed-Sun eves, matinees Wed, Sat, and Sun) Guided tours (June-Sep, Mon and Sat; fee). On CT 82 at East Haddam Bridge. Phone 860/873-8668. Tours ¢

Nathan Hale Schoolhouse. One-rm school where the American Revolutionary patriot taught during winter of 1773; period furnishings, memorabilia. Church has bell said to have been cast in Spain in A.D. 815 (Memorial Day-Labor Day, Sat, Sun, and hols, limited hrs) Main St (CT 149), at rear of St. Stephen's Church. Phone 860/873-9547 (church). **FREE**

Sightseeing.

   Camelot Cruises, Inc. Offers Connecticut River cruises, Long Island cruises, Murder Mystery cruises, and evening music excursions. Long Island cruises (mid-June-Labor Day, Tues-Thurs and Sat-Sun; after Labor Day-mid-Oct, Sun). Murder Mystery cruises (April-Dec, Fri and Sat eves). W on CT 82, across river at Marine Park in Haddam. Phone 860/345-8591. ¢¢¢¢¢

Eagle Aviation. Scenic airplane rides over the Connecticut River Valley. (Daily; closed Dec 25-Jan 8) Goodspeed Airport & Seaplane Base, Goodspeed Landing, Lumberyard Rd. Phone 860/873-8568 or 860/873-8658. ¢¢¢¢¢

Goodspeed Opera House, East Haddam

B&B/Small Inn

★ ★ **BISHOPSGATE INN.** *7 Norwich Rd (06423). 860/873-1677; fax 860/873-3898. Email ctkegel&assoc@ bishopsgate.com; www.bishopsgate.com.* 6 rms, 2 story, 1 suite. Apr-Dec: D $150; suites $150; each addl $25; lower rates rest of yr. Crib avail. Pet accepted, some restrictions. Parking lot. TV; cable. Complimentary full bkfst, coffee in rms, newspaper, toll-free calls. Ck-out 11 am, ck-in 1 pm. Fax servs avail. Concierge serv. Sauna. Golf, 18 holes. Picnic facilities. Cr cds: DS, MC, V.

Enfield

(D-3) *See also Windsor Locks; also see Holyoke and Springfield, MA*

Settled 1680 **Pop** 45,532 **Elev** 150 ft
Area code 860 **Zip** 06082
Web www.cnctb.org

Information Connecticut North Central Tourism Bureau, 111 Hazard Ave; 860/763-2578 or 800/248-8283

Located on the Connecticut River, Enfield was an important embarking point for flat-bottom boats transporting wares to Springfield, Massachusetts, in the 18th century. The Enfield Society for the Detection of Horse Thieves and Robbers was founded here over a century ago. Jonathan Edwards, a famous theologian, delivered his fire and brimstone sermon "Sinners in the Hands of an Angry God" here in 1741.

What to See and Do

Martha A. Parsons House. (1782) Constructed on land put aside for use by parsons or ministers, this house holds 180 yrs worth of antiques collected by the Parsons family; tables brought from West Indies, George Washington memorial wallpaper. (May-Oct, Sun afternoons or by appt) 1387 Enfield St. Phone 860/745-6064. **FREE**

Old Town Hall (Purple Heart Museum). Includes inventions of the Shakers, a religious sect that observed a doctrine of celibacy, common property, and community living; medals and service memorabilia, 46-star flag; local historical displays and artifacts. (May-Oct, Sun afternoons or by appt) 1294 Enfield St. Phone 860/745-1729. **FREE**

Motel/Motor Lodge

★★ **RED ROOF INN.** *5 Hazard Ave (06082). 860/741-2571; fax 860/741-2576; toll-free 800/843-7663.* 109 rms, 2 story. S $34.99-$42.99; D $39.99-$46.99; under 18 free. Crib free. Pet accepted. TV; cable (premium). Restaurant adj 6:30-12:30 am. Ck-out noon. Business servs avail. In-rm modem link. X-country ski 15 mi. Cr cds: A, C, D, DS, MC, V.

Hotel

★★★ **RADISSON HOTEL SPRING-FIELD.** *1 Bright Meadow Blvd (06082). 860/741-2211; fax 860/741-6917; res 800/333-3333.* 181 rms, 6 story. S $104-$114; D $114-$124; each addl $10; under 18 free; wkend rates. Crib free. TV; cable (premium), VCR avail. 2 pools, 1 indoor; whirlpool, life-guard (summer wkends). Restaurant 6:30 am-2 pm, 5:30-10 pm; Sat, Sun from 7 am. Bar 11 am-midnight; Sun to 11 pm; entertainment. Ck-out 11 am. Meeting rms. Business servs avail. In-rm modem link. Concierge serv. Free airport, railroad station, bus depot transportation. Lighted tennis. Exercise equipt; sauna. Health club privileges. Game rm. Lawn games. Some in-rm steam baths. Pic-nic area. Cr cds: A, C, D, DS, ER, JCB, MC, V.

B&B/Small Inn

★★ **THE SHAKER INN AT THE GREAT STONE DWELLING.** *447 Rte 4A (03748). 603/632-7810; toll-free 888/707-4257. www.theshakerinn. com.* 24 rms, 4 story. S $105; D $155; each addl $15; under 18 free. Crib avail. Parking lot. TV; cable. Compli-mentary full bkfst, toll-free calls. Restaurant 8 am-8:30 pm, closed Mon. Bar. Ck-out 11 am, ck-in 3 pm. Meeting rms. Business servs avail. Gift shop. Golf, 18 holes. Downhill skiing. Beach access. Supervised chil-dren's activities. Hiking trail. Cr cds: A, D, DS, MC, V.

Essex

See also Clinton, East Haddam, Middle-town, Old Lyme, Old Saybrook

Pop 5,904 **Elev** 100 ft **Area code** 860 **Zip** 06426 **Web** www.cttourism.org

Information CT River Valley & Shore-line Visitors Council, 393 Main St, Middletown 06457; 860/347-0028 or 800/486-3346

What to See and Do

Connecticut River Museum. Displays include full-rigged ship models, navi-gation instruments, full-size repro-duction of world's first submarine. Waterfront park adj. (Tues-Sun; closed hols) At foot of Main St at river. Phone 860/767-8269. ¢¢

Valley Railroad. Scenic 12-mi steam train excursion along Connecticut River to Chester; can opt to connect with a riverboat for 1-hr Connecticut River cruise (addl fare). Cruise pas-sengers are returned to Essex via later connecting trains. Turn-of-the-cen-tury equipment. Various attractions. (Early May-late Oct, days vary; also Christmas trips) 1 Railroad Ave. Phone 860/767-0103. Train ¢¢¢; Train and cruise ¢¢¢¢

Annual Event

Deep River Ancient Muster. 2½ mi N via CT 9, at Devitt's Field, Main St, in Deep River. Approx 60 fife and drum corps recall Revolutionary War period; displays. Two days mid-July.

B&B/Small Inn

★★★ **THE COPPER BEECH INN.** *46 Main St (06442), W off CT 9 Exit 3. 860/767-0330; toll-free 888/809-2056. www.copperbeechinn.com.* 13 rms, 2 story. D $180; children $30. Parking lot. TV; cable. Complimen-tary continental bkfst, toll-free calls. Restaurant 5:30-10 pm, closed Mon. Bar. Ck-out 11 am, ck-in 2 pm. Meet-ing rm. Concierge serv. Golf. Tennis. Cr cds: A, C, D, MC, V.

★★ **GRISWOLD INN.** *36 Main St (06426). 860/767-1776; fax 860/767-*

0481. Email griswoldinn@snet.net; www.griswoldinn.com. 30 rms, 3 story. S, D $90-$185; each addl $10. Crib $10. TV in sitting rm. Complimentary continental bkfst. Restaurant (see also GRISWOLD INN). Ck-out 11 am, ck-in 2 pm. Business servs avail. Inn since 1776. Fireplace in spacious library. Many antiques. Near Connecticut River. Cr cds: A, MC, V.

Restaurants

★★★ **COPPER BEECH INN.** 46 Main St. 860/767-0330. www.copper beechinn.com. Specializes in bouillabaisse, breast of duck, veal. Own baking. Hrs: 5:30-8 pm; Sat to 9 pm; Sun 1-6:30 pm. Closed Mon, Tues (Jan-Mar); Jan 1, Dec 24, 25. Res accepted; required Sat. Dinner a la carte entrees: $20.75-$26.25. Jacket. In restored Victorian building (1889); once residence of prominent ivory importer. Cr cds: A, D, MC, V.

★★★ **GRISWOLD INN.** 36 Main St. 860/767-1776. www.griswoldinn.com. Specializes in prime rib, local seafood, game (winter). Own sausage. Hrs: 11:45 am-9 pm; Fri, Sat to 10 pm; Sun from 11 am; Sun brunch to 2:30 pm. Closed Dec 24, 25. Res accepted. Bar. Lunch $6.95-$12.95; dinner $12.95-$22.95. Sun brunch $12.95. Child's menu. Entertainment: banjo concerts Fri, Sun; jazz pianist Sat. 1776 inn. Family-owned. Cr cds: A, MC, V.

★★ **SAGE AMERICAN BAR & GRILL.** 129 W Main St (06412), 5 mi NW on CT 9 Exit 6, E on Main St, near Goodspeed Theater. 860/526-9898. Specializes in seafood, prime rib, steak. Hrs: 5-11 pm; Sun from 4 pm. Res accepted. Dinner $13.95-$23.95. Child's menu. In converted 19th-century mill with wheels and belts overhead. Overlooks waterfall, brook, covered walking bridge. Cr cds: A, D, DS, MC, V.

★★ **STEVE CENTERBROOK CAFE.** 78 Main St (06409), E of CT 9 Exit 3. 860/767-1277. Specializes in grill items, pasta. Hrs: 5:30-9 pm. Closed Mon. Res accepted. Bar. Dinner a la carte entrees: $15.95-$19.50. Victorian house; country decor. Cr cds: A, MC, V.

Valley Railroad, Essex

Fairfield

(G-2) *See also Bridgeport, Milford, Norwalk, Stamford, Stratford*

Settled 1639 **Pop** 53,418 **Elev** 15 ft
Area code 203

Information Chamber of Commerce, 1597 Post Rd, 06430; 203/255-1011

A small band of colonists led by Roger Ludlowe settled Fairfield two years after the Pequot were subdued in the Great Swamp Fight. In 1779, British troops under General Tyron marched into the area and requested that the people submit to royal authority. When this was refused, the village was put to the torch.

What to See and Do

Connecticut Audubon Society Birdcraft Museum and Sanctuary. Established in 1914, this vest-pocket, 6-acre sanctuary houses natural history museum with wildlife displays, dinosaur footprints, and observational beehive; trails, ponds. (Sat-Sun, limited hrs) 314 Unquowa Rd. Phone 203/259-0416. **FREE**

Connecticut Audubon Society Fairfield Nature Center and Larsen Sanctuary. Center features Connecticut wildlife and flora, solar greenhouse, natural history library, nature store. (Tues-Sat; also Sun in spring, fall; closed hols) **Donation.** Adj is 160-acre sanctuary with 6 mi of trails through woodlands, meadows, ponds, streams. (Daily) Trail for the disabled. 2325 Burr St. Phone 203/259-6305. Sanctuary ¢

Fairfield Historical Society. Museum with permanent displays of furniture, paintings, maritime memorabilia, dolls, toys, farm implements, clocks; changing exhibits of history, costumes, decorative arts; genealogical and research library. (Daily; closed hols) 636 Old Post Rd. Phone 203/259-1598. ¢¢

Ogden House. (ca 1750) Maintained by the Fairfield Historical Society, this 18th-century saltbox farmhouse, with authentic furnishings, has been restored to the time of its building by David and Jane Ogden; mid-18th-century kitchen garden. (Mid-May-mid-Oct, Thurs and Sun; other times by appt) 1520 Bronson Rd. Phone 203/259-1598. ¢¢

Annual Events

Garlicfest. Notre Dame Catholic High School, 220 Jefferson St. Vendors prepare international array of garlic-seasoned cuisine. Sales, entertainment. Phone 203/372-6521. Three days early May.

Dogwood Festival. At Greenfield Hill Congregational Church, 1045 Old Academy Rd. Herbs, plants, arts and crafts, walking tours, music programs, food. Phone 203/259-5596. Early or mid-May.

Chamber Arts and Crafts Festival. On Sherman Green. Phone 203/255-1011. Mid-June.

Motel/Motor Lodge

★★ **FAIRFIELD INN AND RESTAURANT.** *417 Post Rd (06430). 203/255-0491; fax 203/255-2073; toll-free 800/347-0414.* 80 rms, 2 story. S $68.50; D $75.50; each addl $10; under 15 free. Crib $10. TV; cable (premium). Pool. Restaurant noon-9 pm. Bar to 1 am; entertainment. Ckout 11 am. Meeting rms. In-rm modem link. Cr cds: A, C, D, MC, V.
🏊 ⛵ 🐾 SC

Farmington

See also Bristol, Hartford, New Britain, Wethersfield

Settled 1640 **Pop** 20,608 **Elev** 245 ft
Area code 860 **Zip** 06032
Web www.travelfile.com/get/ghtd
Information Greater Hartford Tourism District, 234 Murphy Rd, Hartford 06114; 860/244-8181 or 800/793-4480

In 1802 and 1803, 15,000 yards of linen cloth were loomed in Farmington, and 2,500 hats were made in a shop on Hatter's Lane. There were silversmiths, tinsmiths, cabinetmakers, clockmakers, and carriage builders. Today, Farmington is a beautiful community—one of New England's museum pieces. It is also the home of Miss Porter's School (1844), a well-known private preparatory school for girls.

What to See and Do

Hill-Stead Museum. (1901) Colonial revival-style country house designed by Theodate Pope in collaboration with McKim, Mead, and White for industrialist A. A. Pope; contains Pope's collection of French impressionist paintings and decorative arts. Set on 152 acres, which includes a sunken garden. One-hr tours. (Tues-Sun) 35 Mountain Rd. Phone 860/677-9064. ¢¢¢

Stanley-Whitman House. (ca 1720) This is one of the finest early 18th-century houses in the United States; period furniture, local artifacts, changing displays, 18th-century herb and flower gardens. (May-Oct, Wed-Sun afternoons; Nov-Apr, Sun afternoons, also by appt) 37 High St. Phone 860/677-9222. ¢¢

Annual Event

Farmington Antiques Weekend. Polo Grounds. One of the largest antique events in Connecticut; approx 600 dealers. Phone 860/871-7914. Mid-June.

Hotel

★★★ **HARTFORD FARMINGTON MARRIOTT.** *15 Farm Springs Rd (06032), in Farm Springs Office Complex. 860/678-1000; fax 860/677-8849; res 800/627-7468; toll-free 800/228-9190. Email hartfarm@marriott.com; www.marriot.com.* 381 rms, 4 story. S, D $79-$145; suites $250-$500; studio rms $145; under 18 free; wkend rates. TV; cable (premium), VCR avail. 2 pools, 1 indoor; whirlpool, poolside serv. Restaurant 6:30 am-midnight. Bar 11:30-1 am; Fri, Sat to 2 am; Sun to midnight; entertainment. Ck-out noon. Coin lndry. Convention facilities. Business center. In-rm modem link. Gift shop. 2 tennis courts. Downhill ski 15 mi. Exercise equipt. Game rm. Lawn games. Some bathrm phones. Refrigerator in some suites. Private patios, balconies. Luxury level. Cr cds: A, DS, MC, V.

⊠ 🖍 ⌖ 🕅

All Suite

★★ **CENTENNIAL INN.** *5 Spring Ln (06032). 860/677-4647; fax 860/676-0685; toll-free 800/852-2052. Email sales@centennialinn.com; www.centennialinn.com.* 112 kit. suites, 2 story. S, D $119-$209; family, wkend rates. Crib free. Pet accepted. TV; cable (premium), VCR (movies $4). Pool; whirlpool. Complimentary continental bkfst, coffee in rms. Ck-out noon. Coin lndry. Meeting rms. Business center. In-rm modem link. Downhill ski 15 mi. Exercise equipt. Fireplaces. Balconies. Grills. On 12 wooded acres. Cr cds: A, DS, MC, V.

D 🖎 ⌖ ⊠ 🕅 🖍 ⌖ 🕅

Extended Stay

★★ **FARMINGTON INN OF GREATER HARTFORD.** *827 Farmington Ave, Rtes. 4 & 10-Farmington Center (06032), I-84 Exit 39 to CT 4. 860/677-2821; fax 860/677-8332; toll-free 800/648-9804. Email corner.house@snet.net; www.farmingtoninn.com.* 59 rms, 2 story, 13 suites. Apr-Jun, Sep-Oct: S $139; D $149; suites $169; each addl $20; under 18 free; lower rates rest of yr. Crib avail. Pet accepted, some restrictions. Parking garage. TV; cable (premium), VCR avail, CD avail. Complimentary continental bkfst, coffee in rms, newspaper. Restaurant 11 am-10 pm, closed Sun. Bar. Ck-out 11 am, ck-in 2 pm. Meeting rms. Business center. Bellhops. Concierge serv. Dry cleaning. Gift shop. Salon/barber avail. Exercise privileges. Golf. Tennis, 8 courts. Downhill skiing. Beach access. Bike rentals. Supervised children's activities. Hiking trail. Picnic facilities. Cr cds: A, C, D, DS, MC, V.

D 🖎 ⌖ 🕅 ⊠ 🖍 ⌖ 🕅 ⊠ 🔥 **SC** 🕅 🖈

Restaurants

★★ **APRICOT'S.** *1593 Farmington Ave (06032). 860/673-5405.* Specializes in fresh seafood. Hrs: 11:30 am-10 pm; Fri, Sat to 10:30 pm; Sun to 9 pm; Sun brunch 11:30 am-2:30 pm. Res required. Bar. Lunch a la carte entrees: $7-$12; dinner a la carte entrees: $15-$28. Sun brunch $7-$14.95. Child's menu. Entertainment: pianist Wed-Sat. Converted trolley house. Cr cds: A, D, DS, MC, V.

D ⊟

★ **STONEWELL.** *354 Colt Hwy (06032), CT 6. 860/677-8855.* Specializes in seafood, steak. Hrs: 11:30 am-10 pm; Sun brunch to 3 pm. Closed July 4, Dec 25. Res accepted. Bar. Lunch $4.95-$11.95; dinner $6.25-$17.95. Sun brunch $12.95. Child's menu. Entertainment: Fri, Sat sing-along. Informal atmosphere. Large stone fireplace. Cr cds: A, D, MC, V.

D **SC** ⊟

Glastonbury

(see Hartford)

Greenwich

(G-1) *See also Norwalk, Stamford.*

Settled 1640 **Pop** 58,441 **Elev** 71 ft
Area code 203
Information Chamber of Commerce, 21 W Putnam Ave, 06830; 203/869-3500

Greenwich (GREN-itch) is on the New York state line just 28 miles from Times Square. Behind the city's old New England facade, community leaders continue searching for ways to preserve 18th-century charm in the face of present-day economic, political, and social problems.

What to See and Do

Audubon Center in Greenwich. This 485-acre sanctuary includes self-guided nature trail and 8-mi hiking trail; interpretive building with exhibits. Resident workshop for adults. (Tues-Sun; closed hols, hol wkends) 613 Riversville Rd, 8 mi NW. Phone 203/869-5272. ¢¢

Bruce Museum. Arts and sciences museum features exhibits, lectures, concerts, and educational programs. (Tues-Sat) 1 Museum Dr. Phone 203/869-0376. ¢¢

Bush-Holley House. (1732) Headquarters of the Historical Society of the Town of Greenwich. Residence of a successful 18th-century farmer, it became the site of the Cos Cob art colony at the turn of the century. Exhibits include late 18th-century Connecticut furniture; paintings by Childe Hassam, Elmer Livingston MacRae, John Henry Twachtman; sculptures by John Rogers; pottery by Leon Volkmar. (Tues-Fri and Sun, afternoons; closed hols) S off US 1, at 39 Strickland Rd in Cos Cob. Phone 203/869-6899. ¢¢

Putnam Cottage/Knapp Tavern. (ca 1690) Near this tavern, Revolutionary General Israel Putnam made a daring escape from the Redcoats in 1779; museum exhibits, rare scalloped shingles, herb garden, restored barn on grounds. (Sun, Wed, and Fri; also by appt) 243 E Putnam Ave. Phone 203/869-9697. ¢

Hotels

★★★ HOMESTEAD INN. *420 Field Point Rd (06830). 203/869-7500; fax 203/869-7502. www.homesteadinn.com.* 17 rms, 2 story, 5 suites. D $300; suites $395; under 14 free. Valet parking avail. TV; cable (premium), VCR avail. Complimentary newspaper, toll-free calls. Restaurant 8 am-9 pm. Bar. Ck-out noon, ck-in 3 pm. Meeting rm. Business servs avail. Bellhops. Concierge serv. Dry cleaning. Golf. Beach access. Cr cds: A, C, D, JCB, MC, V.

★★★ HYATT REGENCY GREENWICH. *1800 E Putnam Ave (06870), NE via I-95 Exit 5, then E on US 1. 203/637-1234; fax 203/637-2940; res 800/233-1234. www.hyatt.com.* 374 rms, 4 story. S $219-$275; D $254-$280; each addl $25; suites $325-$850; under 18 free; wkend rates. TV; cable (premium), VCR avail. Indoor pool; whirlpool. Restaurant 6:30 am-11 pm. Rm serv 6-1 am. Bar 11:30 am-midnight; Fri, Sat to 1 am. Ck-out noon. Convention facilities. Business center. In-rm modem link. Gift shop. Exercise equipt; sauna, steam rm. Health club privileges. 4-story atrium; skylights; garden paths and waterways. Luxury level. Cr cds: A, DS, MC, V.

B&Bs/Small Inns

★★ HARBOR HOUSE INN. *165 Shore Rd (06870), I-95 Exit 5, E on US 1, S on Sound Beach Ave, W on Shore Rd. 203/637-0145; fax 203/698-0943. Email hhinn@aol.com; www.hhinn@aol.com.* 23 rms, 3 story. Apr-Dec: S, D $209; lower rates rest of yr. Parking lot. TV; cable (DSS), VCR avail, CD avail. Complimentary continental bkfst, newspaper. Restaurant nearby. Ck-in 3 pm. Business servs avail. Concierge serv. Coin lndry. Exercise privileges. Golf. Beach access. Bike rentals. Picnic facilities. Cr cds: A, D, MC, V.

★★ **STANTON HOUSE INN.** *76 Maple Ave (06830). 203/869-2110; fax 203/629-2116. Email shiinn@aol.com; www.inns.com.* 20 rms, 3 story, 2 suites. S, D $105; suites $149; each addl $20; under 10 free. Parking lot. Pool. TV; cable, VCR avail. Complimentary continental bkfst. Restaurant nearby. Ck-out 11 am, ck-in 3 pm. Business center. Dry cleaning. Exercise privileges. Golf. Tennis, 2 courts. Beach access. Bike rentals. Hiking trail. Picnic facilities. Cr cds: A, C, D, DS, MC, V.

Restaurants

★★★ **JEAN-LOUIS.** *61 Lewis St (06830), corner of Greenwich Ave and Lewis St, downtown. 203/622-8450. www.restaurantjeanlouis.com.* Specializes in seafood, poultry. Own baking. Hrs: noon-9 pm; Sat 6-10 pm. Closed Sun. Res accepted. Wine cellar. Lunch a la carte entrees: $21-$29; dinner a la carte entrees: $30-$35. Street parking. Jacket. Cr cds: A, D, MC, V.

★★ **TERRA RISTORANTE ITALIANO.** *156 Greenwich Ave (06830). 203/629-5222.* Specializes in wood-fired pizza. Hrs: noon-10 pm; Fri, Sat to 11 pm; Sun 5:30-9:30 pm. Closed some major hols. Res accepted. Wine, beer. Lunch a la carte entrees: $4-$25; dinner a la carte entrees: $13-$29. Italian villa decor; arched ceiling with original frescoes. Cr cds: A, D, MC, V.

★★★★ **THOMAS HENKELMANN.** *420 Field Point Rd, I-95 Exit 3 (Arch St). 203/869-7500. www.thomashenkelmann.com.* Chef Thomas Henkelmann creates dishes that combine touches of his native Germany with French techniques at this early American dining room. The inn and restaurant, which Henkelmann owns with his wife Theresa Carroll, reside in a charmingly renovated 1799 farmhouse with a relaxing French and English antique-filled decor. Try the baked peaches with marzipan he recalls from a favorite childhood combination. Specializes in veal, game, seafood. Own baking. Hrs: 7 am-9:30 pm; Sat, Sun from 8 am. Closed Jan 1, Labor Day. Res accepted. Bar. Wine cellar. Bkfst $10.50-$16; lunch $15-$23; dinner $26-$34. Valet parking. Jacket (dinner). Cr cds: A, D, MC, V.

★ **TUCSON CAFE.** *130 E Putnam Ave (06830), I-95 Exit 4 to US 1 S. 203/661-2483.* Specializes in chicken fajitas, quesadillas, innovative Southwestern dishes. Hrs: 11:30-1 am; Sun from 4 pm. Closed Easter, Thanksgiving, Dec 25. Res accepted. Bar. Lunch $7.50-$13.50; dinner $8.50-$22. Entertainment: jazz Wed. Parking. Skylight. Native Amer artwork. Cr cds: A, D, MC, V.

Groton

(F-4) *See also Mystic, New London, Norwich*

Settled 1705 **Pop** 9,837 **Elev** 90 ft
Area code 860 **Zip** 06340
Web www.mysticmore.com

Information Connecticut's Mystic & More, 470 Bank St, PO Box 89, New London 06320; 860/444-2206 or 800/TO-ENJOY (outside CT)

Groton is the home of a huge US naval submarine base. It is also the place where the Electric Boat Division of the General Dynamics Corp, world's largest private builder of submarines, built the first diesel-powered submarine (1912) and the first nuclear-powered submarine, *Nautilus* (1955). Pfizer Inc. operates one of the largest antibiotic plants in the world and maintains a research laboratory here.

What to See and Do

Charter fishing trips. Several companies offer full- and ½-day saltwater fishing trips for both small and large groups. Phone 800/TO-ENJOY for details.

Fort Griswold Battlefield State Park. Includes 135-ft monument to 88

Revolutionary soldiers slain here in 1781 by British troops under the command of Benedict Arnold. Park (daily). Monument and museum (Memorial Day-Labor Day, daily; Labor Day-Columbus Day, Sat and Sun). 1½ mi S of US 1 on Monument St & Park Ave. Phone 860/449-6877 or 860/445-1729. **FREE**

Historic Ship *Nautilus* **& Submarine Force Museum.** Permanent home for *Nautilus*, world's first nuclear-powered submarine. Self-guided, audio tour; museum exhibits depicting history of the US Submarine Force; working periscopes; authentic submarine control rm; 4 mini-subs; mini-theaters. Picnicking. (Spring-fall, daily; winter, Wed-Mon; closed Jan 1, Thanksgiving, Dec 25, also 1 wk early May and early Dec) 2 mi N on CT 12 at Crystal Lake Rd. Phone 860/694-3174 or 800/343-0079. **FREE**

Oceanographic cruise. A 2½-hr educational cruise on Long Island Sound aboard marine research vessels *Enviro-lab II* and *Enviro-lab III*. Opportunity to use nets and scientific instruments to explore marine environment first hand. (June-Aug) Avery Point. Phone 800/364-8472. ¢¢¢

Motels/Motor Lodges

★ ★ **CLARION INN.** *156 Kings Hwy (06340).* 860/446-0660; fax 860/445-4082; toll-free 800/252-7466. 69 rms, 2 story, 34 kits. July-Oct: S, D, kit. units $76-$139; each addl $10; suites $89-$179; under 18 free; lower rates rest of yr. Crib free. TV; cable (premium). Indoor pool; whirlpool. Restaurant 6 am-10 pm; wkends from 7 am. Rm serv. Bar 11-1 am. Ck-out 11 am. Coin lndry. Meeting rms. Business servs avail. Valet serv. Barber, beauty shop. Exercise equipt; sauna. Game rm. Many refrigerators; some wet bars. Balconies. Picnic tables, grills. Cr cds: A, C, D, DS, MC, V.
≈ ⨯ ≋ 🐾 SC

★ ★ **QUALITY INN.** *404 Bridge Street (06340).* 860/445-8141; fax 860/445-8141. 110 rms, 3 story.; each addl $10; under 18 free. Crib avail. Parking lot. Pool, childrens pool. TV; cable (premium). Complimentary continental bkfst, coffee in rms, newspaper. Restaurant 2-8 pm, closed Sun. Bar. Ck-out 11 am, ck-in 4 pm. Meeting rm. B/W printing avail.

Coin lndry. Exercise equipt. Golf, 18 holes. Tennis, 4 courts. Supervised children's activities. Picnic facilities. Cr cds: A, D, DS, MC, V.
D ⨯ ⨲ ≋ ⨯ ≋ 🔥

🔲

Guilford

See also Branford, Clinton, Madison, New Haven

Founded 1639 **Pop** 19,848 **Elev** 20 ft **Area code** 203 **Zip** 06437

Information Destination Guilford, 115 State Square, Dept MOB; 203/453-9677

Guilford was settled by a group of Puritans who followed Rev. Henry Whitfield here from England. One of the residents, Samuel Hill, gave rise to the expression "run like Sam Hill" when he repeatedly ran for political office.

What to See and Do

Henry Whitfield State Museum. (1639) One of the oldest houses in the state and among the oldest of stone houses in New England. Restored with 17th- and 18th-century furnishings; exhibits; herb garden. Gift shop. (Wed-Sun; closed hols) ½ mi S on Whitfield St. Phone 203/453-2457. ¢¢

Hyland House. (1660) Restored and furnished in 17th-century period, herb garden; guided tours. (Early June-Oct, Tues-Sun) A map of historic homes in Guilford avail. 84 Boston St. Phone 203/453-9477. ¢

Thomas Griswold House Museum. (ca 1775) Fine example of a saltbox house; costumes of 1800s, changing historical exhibits, period gardens, restored working blacksmith shop. (Early June-Oct, Tues-Sun; winter by appt) 171 Boston St. Phone 203/453-3176 or 203/453-5517. ¢

All Suite

★ **TOWER SUITES MOTEL.** *320 Boston Post Rd (06437).* 203/453-9069; fax 203/458-2727. 1 story, 15 suites. May-Dec: suites $89; each addl $10; under 12 free; lower rates rest of yr. Crib avail. Parking lot. TV; cable (premium). Complimentary coffee in rms, toll-free calls. Restaurant nearby. 24-hr rm serv. Ck-out 11 am, ck-in 1 pm. Business servs avail. Golf. Tennis. Beach access. Supervised children's activities. Picnic facilities. Cr cds: A, DS, MC, V.

Restaurant

★★ SACHEM COUNTRY HOUSE.
111 Goose Ln (06437), At I-95 Exit 59. 203/453-5261. Specializes in seafood, prime rib. Hrs: 4-10 pm; Sun from 10:30 am; Sun brunch to 2:30 pm. Res required Fri, Sat. Dinner $10.95-$14.95. Sun brunch $12.95. Child's menu. In 18th-century house; fireplace. Family-owned. Cr cds: A, MC, V.
D

Hartford

(E-3) *See also Avon, Farmington, Wethersfield*

Settled 1633 **Pop** 139,739 **Elev** 50 ft
Area code 860
Web www.grhartfordcvb.com
Information Greater Hartford Convention & Visitors Bureau, One Civic Center Plaza, Suite 300, 06103; 860/728-6789 or 800/446-7811 (outside CT)

The capital of Connecticut and a major industrial and cultural center on the Connecticut River, Hartford is headquarters for many of the nation's insurance companies.

Roots of American democracy are deep in Hartford's history. The city was made virtually independent in 1662 by Charles II, but an attempt was made by Sir Edmund Andros, governor of New England, to seize its charter. The document was hidden by Joseph Wadsworth in a hollow tree since known as the Charter Oak. The tree was blown down in 1856; a plaque on Charter Oak Avenue marks the spot.

Hartford has what is said to be the oldest continuously published newspaper in the United States, the *Courant*. Founded in 1764, it became a daily in 1837. Trinity College (1823), the American School for the Deaf, Connecticut Institute for the Blind, and the Institute of Living (for mental illness) are located in the city.

Transportation

Hartford Bradley Intl Airport. Information 860/627-3000; lost and found 860/627-3340; cash machines, Terminal B, Concourse A.
Car Rental Agencies. See IMPORTANT TOLL-FREE NUMBERS.
Public Transportation. Buses (Connecticut Transit), phone 860/525-9181.
Rail Passenger Service. Amtrak 800/872-7245.

What to See and Do

Bushnell Park. The 41-acre park contains 150 varieties of trees and a restored 1914 carousel (schedule varies; fee); concerts and special events (spring-fall). Downtown, between Jewell, Elm, and Trinity Sts. Phone 860/246-7739. **FREE**
Butler-McCook Homestead. (1782) Preserved house, occupied by 4 generations of one family (1782-1971), has possesions dating back 200 yrs; collection of Victorian toys; Japanese armor; Victorian garden. (Mid-May-mid-Oct, Tues, Thurs, and Sun afternoons; closed hols) 396 Main St. Phone 860/522-1806 or 860/247-8996. ¢¢
Center Church and Ancient Burying Ground. Church (1807) is patterned after London's St. Martin-in-the-Fields, with Tiffany stained-glass windows. Cemetery contains markers dating back to 1640. Main & Gold Sts.
Connecticut Audubon Society Holland Brook Nature Center. On 38 acres adj to Connecticut River, the center features a variety of natural history exhibits including discovery rm. Nature store; many activities. (Tues-Sun; closed hols, Dec 25-Jan 1) 5 mi SE via CT 2 at 1361 Main St, in Glastonbury. Phone 860/633-8402. Discovery rm ¢
Connecticut Historical Society. Library contains more than 2 million

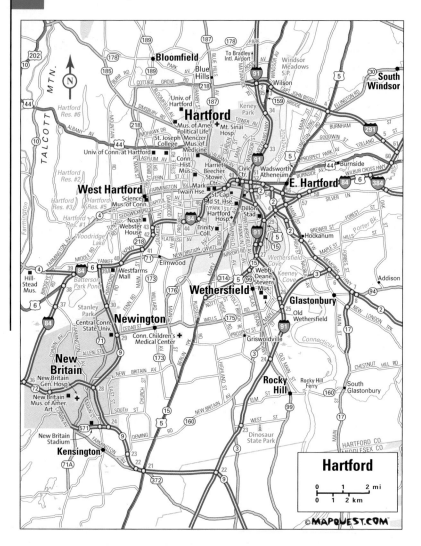

Hartford

books and manuscripts (Memorial Day-Labor Day, Tues-Fri; rest of yr, Tues-Sat; closed hols). Museum has 9 galleries featuring permanent and changing exhibits on state history (Memorial Day-Labor Day, Tues-Fri, Sun afternoons; rest of yr, Tues-Sun afternoons; closed hols). 1 Elizabeth St. Phone 860/236-5621. ¢¢

Elizabeth Park. Public gardens feature 900 varieties of roses and more than 14,000 other plants; first municipal rose garden in country; greenhouses (all yr). Outdoor concerts in summer; ice-skating in winter. (Daily) Prospect & Asylum Aves. Phone 860/242-0017. **FREE**

Harriet Beecher Stowe House. (1871) The restored Victorian cottage of the author of *Uncle Tom's Cabin* contains original furniture, memorabilia. Tours. (Tues-Sat, also Sun afternoons; also Mon June-Columbus Day and Dec) 73 Forest St. Phone 860/525-9317. ¢¢¢

Mark Twain House. (1874) *Tom Sawyer, Huckleberry Finn* and other books were published while Samuel Clemens (Mark Twain) lived in this 3-story Victorian mansion featuring the decorative work of Charles Comfort Tiffany and the Associated Artists; Tiffany-glass light fixtures, windows, and Tiffany-designed stencilwork in gold and silver leaf. Tours. (Tues-Sat, also Sun afternoons; also Mon June-Columbus Day and Dec) 351 Farmington Ave. Phone 860/493-6411. ¢¢¢

Noah Webster Foundation and Historical Society. This 18th-century homestead was birthplace of America's first lexicographer, writer of the *Blue-Backed Speller* (1783) and the *American Dictionary* (1828). Period furnishings, memorabilia; costumed guides; period gardens. (Open Thurs-Mon; closed hols) 227 S Main St in West Hartford. Phone 860/521-5362. ¢¢

Old State House. (1796) Oldest state house in nation, designed by Charles Bulfinch; restored Senate chamber with Gilbert Stuart portrait of Washington; displays and rotating exhibitions. Tourist information center; museum shop. Guided tours by appt. (Daily; closed hols) 800 Main St. Phone 860/522-6766. **FREE**

Raymond E. Baldwin Museum of Connecticut History. Exhibits include Colt Collection of Firearms; Connecticut artifacts, including original 1662 Royal Charter; portraits of Connecticut's governors. Library features law, social sciences, history, genealogy collections, and official state archives. (Mon-Fri; closed hols) Connecticut State Library, 231 Capitol Ave, opp Capitol. Phone 860/566-4777 or 860/566-3056. **FREE**

Science Center of Connecticut. Computer lab; mini-zoo; physical sciences discovery rm; walk-in replica of sperm whale; hands-on aquarium; "KaleidoSight," a giant walk-in kaleidoscope; planetarium shows; changing exhibits. (Tues-Sat, also Sun afternoons, also Mon during summer; closed hols) 950 Trout Brook Dr in West Hartford. Phone 860/231-2824. ¢¢

Sightseeing tours.

Heritage Trails Sightseeing. Guided and narrated tours of Hartford. (Daily) Phone 860/677-8867. ¢¢¢¢

Hartford on Tour. One- and two-hr walking tours of various historic neighborhoods. (May-July and Sep-Oct, Sat and Sun) ¢¢

Connecticut River Cruise. The *Lady Fenwick*, a reproduction of an 1850s steam yacht, makes 1 to 2½ hr trips on the Connecticut River. (Memorial Day-Labor Day, daily; after Labor Day-Oct, Fri-Sun)

Departs from Charter Oak Landing. Phone 860/526-4954. ¢¢

State Capitol. (1879) Guided tours (1 hr) of the restored, gold-domed capitol building and the contemporary legislative office building (Apr-Oct, Mon-Sat; rest of yr, Mon-Fri; closed hols, also Dec 25-Jan 1); includes historical displays. 210 Capitol Ave, at Trinity St. Phone 860/240-0222. **FREE**

Talcott Mountain State Park. The 557-acre park features the 165-ft Heublein Tower, on mountaintop 1,000 ft above Farmington River; considered best view in state. (3rd Sat Apr-Labor Day, Thurs-Sun; after Labor Day-1st wkend Nov, daily) Picnicking, shelters. 8 mi NW via US 44, off CT 185, near Simsbury. Phone 860/677-0662.

University of Hartford. (1877) 7,600 students. Independent institution on 300-acre campus. Many free concerts, operas, lectures, and art exhibits. 4 mi W, at 200 Bloomfield Ave in West Hartford. Phone 860/768-4100. Located here is

Museum of American Political Life. Exhibits include life-size mannequins re-creating political marches from 1830s-1960s; 70-ft wall of historical pictures and images; political television commercials since 1952. (Tues-Sun afternoons; closed hols) In the Harry Jack Gray Center. Phone 860/768-4090. **FREE**

☒ **Wadsworth Atheneum.** One of nation's oldest continuously operating public art museums with more than 40,000 works of art, spanning 5,000 yrs; 15th to 20th-century paintings, American furniture, sculpture, porcelains, English and American silver, the Amistad Collection of African American art; changing contemporary exhibits. (Tues-Sun; closed hols) Free admission Thurs and Sat morning. 600 Main St. Phone 860/278-2670 or 860/278-2670 (recording). ¢¢

Annual Events

Taste of Hartford. Main St, downtown. Four-day event features specialties of more than 50 area restaurants; continuous entertainment. Phone 860/728-3089. Mid-June.

Riverfest. Celebration of America's independence and the Connecticut River. Family entertainment, concerts, food, fireworks display over river. Early July.

Mark Twain Days. Celebration of Twain's legacy and Hartford's cultural heritage with more than 100 events. Concerts, riverboat rides, medieval jousting, tours of Twain House, entertainment. Phone 860/247-0998. Wkend mid-July.

Mark Twain House, Hartford

Christmas Crafts Expo I & II. Hartford Civic Center. Exhibits and demonstrations of traditional and contemporary craft media. First 2 wkends Dec.

City Neighborhoods

Many of the restaurants, unrated dining establishments, and some lodgings listed under Hartford include neighborhoods as well as exact street addresses. Geographic descriptions of these areas are given.

Civic Center District. South of Church St, west of Main St, north of Elm St, and east of Union Place.

Franklin Ave Area. South of Southern Downtown; along Franklin Ave between Maple Ave on the north and Victoria Rd on the south.

Southern Downtown. Area east and south of Civic Center District; south of State St, west of Prospect St and Charter Oak Place, and north of Wyllys St.

Hotels

★★★ **CROWNE PLAZA.** *50 Morgan St (06120), jct I-84 Exit 52 and I-91 Exit 32, in Civic Center District.* 860/549-2400; fax 860/527-2746; toll-free 800/227-6963. 342 rms, 18 story. S $79.95-$119.95; D $89.95-$129.95; each addl $10; suites $225; under 18 free; wkend rates. Crib free. Pet accepted. TV; cable (premium), VCR avail. Pool; poolside serv. Restaurant 6:30 am-10 pm. Bar 4 pm-2 am. Ck-out noon. Convention facilities. Business center. In-rm modem link. Free airport transportation. Exercise equipt. Cr cds: A, C, D, DS, JCB, MC, V.

D ▦ ≃ 才 ⊠ ▨ SC 才

★★★ **GOODWIN HOTEL.** *1 Haynes St (06013), opp Hartford Civic Center at Goodwin Square.* 860/246-7500; fax 860/247-4576; toll-free 800/922-5006. www.goodwinhotel.com. 113 rms, 6 story, 11 suites. S, D $119; suites $175. Crib avail, fee. Pet accepted, some restrictions, fee. Valet parking avail. TV; cable (DSS), VCR avail. Complimentary newspaper. Restaurant 6:30 am-10 pm. Bar. Ck-out noon, ck-in 3 pm. Meeting rms. Business servs avail. Bellhops. Dry cleaning. Exercise privileges. Golf. Tennis. Downhill skiing. Video games. Cr cds: A, C, D, DS, MC, V.

D ▦ ≊ 朿 ⫴ 才 ⫴ ⊠ ▨

★★★ **HILTON.** *315 Trumbull St (06103), at Civic Center Plaza.* 860/728-5151; fax 860/240-7247; res 800/445-8667. www.hartford.hilton. com. 384 rms, 22 story, 6 suites. S, D $199; suites $600; each addl $20; under 18 free. Crib avail. Parking garage. Pool, whirlpool. TV; cable (premium). Complimentary coffee in rms, newspaper, toll-free calls. Restaurant 6:30 am-8 pm. Bar. Ck-out noon, ck-in 3 pm. Conference center, meeting rms. Business center. Bellhops. Concierge serv. Dry cleaning, coin lndry. Exercise equipt, sauna. Golf, 18 holes. Video games. Cr cds: A, C, D, DS, MC, V.

D ⫴ ≃ 才 ⫴ ⊠ ▨ 才

★★ **HOLIDAY INN.** *363 Roberts St (06108), I-84, Exit 58, E of Downtown.* 860/528-9611; fax 860/289-0270; toll-

*free 800/465-4329. Email gmehc@
lodgian.com.* 130 rms, 5 story. S, D
$65-$85; under 18 free; wkend rates.
Crib free. Pet accepted. TV; cable
(premium). Indoor pool. Complimentary coffee in rms. Restaurant 6
am-10 pm. Rm serv. Bar 4 pm-midnight. Ck-out noon. Coin lndry.
Meeting rms. Business servs avail. In-
rm modem link. Valet serv. Exercise
equipt. Some refrigerators. Cr cds: A,
DS, MC, V.

★★ **RAMADA INN CAPITOL HILL.**
*440 Asylum St (06103), opp State Capi-
tol Building, in Civic Center District.
860/246-6591; fax 860/728-1382.* 96
rms, 9 story. S $49-$65; D $55-$65;
each addl $10. Crib free. Pet
accepted, some restrictions. TV; cable
(premium). Ck-out noon. Business
servs avail. Free valet parking. Cr cds:
A, D, DS, MC, V.

★★★ **SHERATON HARTFORD
HOTEL.** *100 E River Dr (06108), S via
I-91 Exit 3 to Pitkin, I-84 Exit 53.
860/528-9703; fax 860/289-4728; res
800/325-3535; toll-free 888/530-9703.
Email sheratonhtfd@yahoo.com.* 212
rms, 8 story, 3 suites. Mar-Jun, Sep-
Oct: S $199; D $219; suites $350;
each addl $10; under 16 free; lower
rates rest of yr. Crib avail. Parking
lot. Indoor pool. TV; cable (premium), VCR avail. Complimentary
coffee in rms, newspaper, toll-free
calls. Restaurant 6:30 am-11 pm. Bar.
Ck-out noon, ck-in 3 pm. Meeting
rms. Business center. Bellhops.
Concierge serv. Dry cleaning. Gift
shop. Exercise privileges. Golf, 18
holes. Tennis, 5 courts. Hiking trail.
Picnic facilities. Video games. Cr cds:
A, C, D, DS, ER, JCB, MC, V.

Restaurants

★★ **BUTTERFLY.** *831 Farmington
Ave (06119), W on Farmington Ave.
860/236-2816.* Specializes in Szechwan cuisine. Hrs: 11 am-11 pm; Sun
brunch to 4 pm. Closed Thanksgiving. Res accepted. Bar. Lunch a la
carte entrees: $5.50-$6.95; dinner a
la carte entrees: $5.95-$14.95. Sun

brunch $12.95. Parking. Contempo-
rary decor. Cr cds: A, DS, MC, V.

★★★ **CARBONE'S.** *588 Franklin
Ave (06114). 860/296-9646.* Specializes in fettucine carbonara, vitello
cuscinetto. Own baking, desserts.
Hrs: 11:30 am-9:30 pm; Fri to 10 pm;
Sat 5-10 pm. Closed Sun; hols. Res
accepted. Bar. Lunch $8-$11; dinner
$12-$20. Parking. Tableside preparation. Family-owned. Cr cds: A, D,
MC, V.

★ **HOT TOMATOES.** *1 Union Pl
(06103), in Civic Center District.
860/249-5100.* Specializes in pasta,
veal. Hrs: 11:30 am-11 pm; Fri to
midnight; Sat 5 pm-midnight; Sun
from 4 pm. Res accepted. Bar. Lunch
a la carte entrees: $6.95-$8.95; dinner a la carte entrees: $8.95-$18.95.
Cr cds: A, D, MC, V.

★★ **MAX DOWNTOWN.** *185 Asylum St (06103), Southern Downtown.
860/522-2530.* Specializes in black
Angus beef, stone pies. Hrs: 11:30
am-10 pm; Sat from 5 pm; Sun from
4:30 pm. Closed hols. Res accepted.
Bar. Lunch a la carte entrees: $6.95-
$9.95; dinner a la carte entrees:
$9.95-$23. Child's menu. Intimate
bistro atmosphere. Cr cds: A, D, DS,
MC, V.

★★★ **PASTIS.** *201 Ann St. (06103).
860/278-8852.* Specializes in steak
frettes, co qau vin, cassoulet. Hrs:
11:30 am-10 pm; Fri 11 pm; Sat 5-11
pm. Closed Sun. Res accepted. Wine
list. Lunch $6.95-$16.95; dinner
$15.95-$24.95. Cr cds: A, D, MC, V.

★★ **PEPPERCORN'S GRILL.** *357
Main St (06106), Southern Downtown.
860/547-1714.* Specializes in orange
ravioli, veal chops, osso buco. Hrs:
11:30 am-10 pm; Thurs to 11 pm; Fri
to midnight; Sat 5 pm-midnight.
Closed Sun; hols. Res accepted. Bar.
Lunch a la carte entrees: $6.95-
$16.95; dinner a la carte entrees:
$16.95-$45. Child's menu. Parking.
Contemporary bistro atmosphere. Cr
cds: A, D, MC, V.

Unrated Dining Spot

RESTAURANT BRICCO. *78 LaSalle Rd (06903). 860/233-0220.* Specializes in Australian lamb, stone pies. Own baking, desserts. Hrs: 11 am-3 pm, 5-10 pm; Fri, Sat to 11 pm; Sun 4-9 pm. Lunch $11-$14; dinner $15-$25. Child's menu. Family-owned. Cr cds: MC, V.
D

Kent

See also Cornwall Bridge, New Preston

Pop 2,918 **Elev** 395 ft **Area code** 860 **Zip** 06757
Information Litchfield Hills Travel Council, PO Box 968, Litchfield 06759; 860/567-4506

Kent, a small community near the western border of Connecticut, has become an art and antique center. Home to a large art colony, the surrounding area is characterized by massive hills that overlook the plain of the Housatonic River. The village of Kent was incorporated in 1738, after the tract of land was sold in a public auction. Although early development was based on agriculture, by the middle of the 19th century Kent was a booming industrial village with three iron furnaces operating in the area.

What to See and Do

Kent Falls State Park. This 295-acre park is beautiful in spring when the stream is high and in fall when leaves are changing; 200-ft cascading waterfall. Stream fishing, hiking, picnicking. Standard fees. (Daily) 5 mi N on US 7. Phone 860/927-4100 or 860/927-3238.

Macedonia Brook State Park. These 2,300 acres provide one of the state's finest nature study areas, as well as views of the Catskills and Taconic mountains. Trout-stocked stream fishing, hiking, picnicking. Camping (late Apr-Sep) on 84 sites in open and wooded settings. Standard fees. (Daily) 2 mi E on CT 341, N on Macedonia Brook Rd. Phone 860/927-4100 or 860/927-3238.
FREE

Sloane-Stanley Museum and Kent Furnace. New England barn houses Eric Sloane's collection of early American tools, re-creation of his studio, artifacts, works; on site of old Kent furnace (1826); video presentation. (Mid-May-Oct, Wed-Sun) 1 mi N on US 7. Phone 860/927-3849 or 860/566-3005. ¢¢

Annual Event

Fall Festival. 1 mi N on US 7, on grounds of the Connecticut Antique Machinery Museum. Exhibits include steam and traction engines, road roller (ca 1910), windmill, threshers, broom making, shingle sawing, antique cars, steamboats, tractors, and trucks. Phone 860/927-0050. Late Sep.

B&B/Small Inn

★★ **FIFE'N DRUM RESTAURANT & INN.** *53 N Main St (06757-0188), on Main St (CT 7). 860/927-3509; fax 860/927-3509.* 8 rms. Apr-Oct: D $95-$110; each addl $12.50; lower rates rest of yr. TV. Complimentary coffee. Restaurant (see also FIFE 'N DRUM). Bar 11:30 am-11 pm; wkends to midnight; entertainment. Ck-out 11 am, ck-in 2 pm. Gift shop. Downhill/x-country ski 11 mi. Balconies. Cr cds: A, DS, MC, V.

Restaurant

★★★ **FIFE 'N DRUM.** *59 N Main St, on Main St (CT 7). 860/927-3509. www.fifendrum.com.* Specializes in roast duckling, filet mignon au poivre, sweetbreads. Own baking. Hrs: 11:30 am-9 pm; Sat to 10:30 pm; Sun brunch to 3 pm. Closed Tues; Dec 25. Res accepted. Bar. Wine cellar. Lunch $4.50-$7.95; dinner $8.95-$24.50. Sun brunch $15.95. Child's menu. Cr cds: A, D, DS, MC, V.
D

Lakeville

See also Cornwall Bridge, Norfolk

Settled 1740 **Pop** 1,800 (est)
Elev 764 ft **Area code** 860 **Zip** 06039

Information Litchfield Hills Travel Council, PO Box 968, Litchfield 06759; 860/567-4506

Lakeville, located on Lake Wononscopomuc in the Litchfield Hills area, developed around a major blast furnace once owned by Ethan Allen. The furnace and nearby metals foundry cast many of the weapons used in the American Revolution as well as the guns for the USS *Constellation*. When the furnace was torn down in 1843, the first knife manufacturing factory was erected there. Nearby is the famous Hotchkiss School, a coed prep school.

What to See and Do

Holley House. Museums of 18th- and 19th-century history include 1768 iron-master's home with 1808 Classical-revival wing, Holley Mfg Co pocketknife exhibit from 1876, hands-on 1870s kitchen exhibit illustrating the debate over women's roles. 1876 Living History Tours (4 tours daily). (Mid-June-mid-Oct, Sat, Sun, and hol afternoons; also by appt) Main St at Millerton Rd. Phone 860/435-2878. Tours ¢¢ Also here is

Salisbury Cannon Museum. Hands-on exhibits illustrate contributions of local iron industry to American Revolution. Includes ice house, cutting tools, outhouse, 19th-century heritage gardens, and Nature's Medicine Cabinet exhibit. Same hrs as Holley House. **FREE**

Annual Event

Grand Prix at Lime Rock. Phone 800/RACE-LRP. Memorial Day wkend.

Seasonal Events

Sports car racing. Lime Rock Park, 2 mi S on CT 41, then 4 mi E on CT 112, at jct US 7. Sat and Mon hols. Phone 800/RACE-LRP.

Music Mountain Summer Music Festival. On Music Mt, 5 mi NE via US 44, 3 mi S on CT 126 to Falls Village, then 2½ mi E on CT 126 to top of Music Mt Rd. Performances by known ensembles and guest artists; also jazz series. Sat, Sun. Phone 860/824-7126 (box office). Mid-June-early Sep.

Motels/Motor Lodges

★★ **INN AT IRON MASTERS.** *229 N Main St PO Box 690 (06039), on US 44, ½ mi W of CT 41. 860/435-9844; fax 860/435-2254. Email ironmstr@ discovernet.net; www.innatironmstrs. com.* 27 rms, 1 story, 1 suite. Apr-Oct: S $135; D $145; suites $185; each addl $15; under 12 free; lower rates rest of yr. Crib avail. Pet accepted, some restrictions. Parking lot. Pool. TV; cable. Complimentary continental bkfst, coffee in rms. Restaurant. Ck-out 11 am, ck-in 2 pm. Fax servs avail. Gift shop. Golf. Tennis. Downhill skiing. Hiking trail. Picnic facilities. Cr cds: A, MC, V.

★ **SHARON MOTOR LODGE.** *1 Calkinstown Rd (06069), 7 mi S on CT 41. 860/364-0036; fax 860/364-0462.* 22 rms. May-Oct: S, D $69-$125; lower rates rest of yr. Crib $10. TV; cable. Pool. Restaurant opp 7:30 am-10:30 pm. Ck-out 11 am. Business servs avail. Downhill/x-country ski 10 mi. Cr cds: A, DS, MC, V.

Resort

★★★ **INTERLAKEN INN.** *74 Interlaken Rd (06039), 2½ mi SW on CT 112. 860/435-9878; fax 860/435-2980; toll-free 800/222-2909. Email info@interlakeninn.com; www.interlakeninn.com.* 75 rms, 2 story, 8 suites. May-Oct: S, D $199; suites $289; lower rates rest of yr. Crib avail, fee. Pet accepted, some restrictions, fee. Parking lot. Pool. TV; cable. Complimentary coffee in rms, toll-free calls. Restaurant 6:30 am-10 pm. Bar. Meeting rms. Business center. Bellhops. Concierge serv. Dry cleaning. Gift shop. Exercise privileges, sauna. Golf. Tennis, 2 courts. Downhill skiing. Beach access. Bike rentals. Supervised children's activities. Hiking trail. Picnic facilities. Cr cds: A, DS, MC, V.

B&Bs/Small Inns

★★ **RAGAMONT INN.** *8 Main St (06068), 1 mi N on US 44, at jct CT 41. 860/435-2372.* 10 rms, 2 story. 7 rms with A/C. No rm phones. S $60-

$95; D $70-$105; each addl $10; under 5 free. Closed Nov-May. TV in some rms; cable. Restaurant (see also RAGAMONT INN). Ck-out 11 am, ck-in 2 pm. Built in 1830; country inn atmosphere with antiques. Cr cds: A, DS, MC, V.

★★ **WAKE ROBIN INN.** *Rte 41 (06039), ¼ mi S on CT 41. 860/435-2515; fax 860/435-2000. www.wake robininn.com.* 39 rms, 2 story. Apr-Nov: S, D $95-$250; each addl $10; lower rates rest of yr. Crib free. Pet accepted. TV; cable (premium). Ck-out noon, ck-in 2 pm. Former girls school (1896); antiques. Library, sitting rm. On hill. Cr cds: A, MC, V.

Litchfield

See also Bristol, Cornwall Bridge

Settled 1720 **Pop** 8,365 **Elev** 1,085 ft
Area code 860 **Zip** 06759
Web www.litchfieldhills.com
Information Litchfield Travel Council, PO Box 968; 860/567-4506

Litchfield, on a plateau above the Naugatuck Valley, has preserved a semblance of the 18th century through both its many early homes and its air of peace and quiet. Because the railroads laid their main lines below in the valley, industry largely bypassed Litchfield. The Rev. Henry Ward Beecher and his sister, Harriet Beecher Stowe, author of *Uncle Tom's Cabin,* grew up in Litchfield. Tapping Reeve established the first law school in the country here in the late 18th century.

What to See and Do

Haight Vineyard and Winery. First Connecticut winery; one of the few to grow vinifera grapes in New England. Tours, tastings, vineyard walk, picnic tables, gift shop. (Daily; closed hols) Chestnut Hill Rd. Phone 860/567-4045. **FREE**

Litchfield Historical Society Museum. Exhibits include American fine and decorative arts and county historical displays, research library, changing exhibits, video presentation. (Mid-Apr-mid-Nov, Tues-Sun; closed hols) On the Green, at jct East & South Sts. Phone 860/567-4501. ¢¢ Adj is

Tapping Reeve House. (1773) **and Law School** (1784) Period furnishings in house used as America's first law school; graduates included Aaron Burr and John C. Calhoun; garden. (June-mid-Oct, Tues-Sun; closed July 4, Labor Day) South St. Phone 860/567-4501. ¢

Topsmead State Forest. This 511-acre forest includes an English Tudor mansion overlooking a 40-acre wildlife preserve. Tours of mansion (2nd and 4th wkends, June-Oct). Phone 860/567-5694 or 860/485-0226. **FREE**

White Memorial Foundation, Inc. The 4,000-acre conservation area is contiguous with part of Bantam Lake shoreline (largest natural lake in the state), the Bantam River, and several small streams and ponds. Rolling woodland has wide variety of trees, flowers, ferns, mosses; 35 mi of trails; woodland birds, both nesting and in migration; and other woodland animals. The Conservation Center has displays and exhibits, extensive nature library with children's rm (daily; fee). Swimming, fishing, boating; hiking trails, including "trail of the senses." Cross-country skiing. Camping. 2½ mi W on US 202. Phone 860/567-0857.

Annual Event

Open House Tour. Tour of Litchfield's historic homes, special exhibits, tea, and luncheon. Phone 860/567-9423. Early July. 4¢¢¢-in advance, 5¢¢¢-same day

B &Bs/Small Inns

★★ **LITCHFIELD INN.** *432 Bantam Rd Rte 202 (06759). 860/567-4503; fax 860/567-5358; toll-free 800/499-3444. Email litchfieldinn@ compuserve; www.litchfieldinnct.com.* Apr-Dec: S $115; D $125; suites $200; each addl $10; under 16 free; lower rates rest of yr. Crib avail, fee. Parking lot. TV; cable (premium), VCR avail. Complimentary continental bkfst, toll-free calls. Restaurant 11:30 am-10 pm. Bar. Ck-out 11 am, ck-in 3 pm. Business center. Dry cleaning. Gift shop. Exercise privileges. Golf, 18 holes. Tennis, 2 courts. Downhill skiing. Bike rentals. Hiking trail. Picnic facilities. Cr cds: A, D, MC, V.

★★ **TOLLGATE HILL INN & REST.** *Rte 202 & Tollgate Rd (06759), 2½ mi NE of the Green on US 202.* 860/567-4545; fax 860/567-8397; toll-free 800/445-3903. 15 rms, 2 story, 5 suites. May-Dec: S $110; D $140; suites $175; each addl $15; lower rates rest of yr. Crib avail. Pet accepted, some restrictions, fee. Parking lot. TV; cable, VCR avail. Complimentary continental bkfst. Restaurant noon-7 pm, closed Tue. Bar. Ck-out 11 am, ck-in 1 pm. Meeting rms. Business servs avail. Concierge serv. Golf, 18 holes. Tennis, 16 courts. Downhill skiing. Cr cds: A, D, DS, MC, V.

Restaurants

★★★ **TOLLGATE HILL.** *Rte 202 and Tollgate Rd.* 860/567-4545. *www.litchfieldct.com/dng/tollgate.html.* Specializes in fresh fish, shellfish pie, seasonal foods. Hrs: noon-9 pm; Sun 11 am-8 pm. Closed Mon, Tues. Res accepted. Bar. Wine cellar. Lunch $7-$11; dinner $18-$23. Entertainment: Sat. A historic waystation (1745). Early Amer decor; fireplaces. Cr cds: A, D, DS, MC, V.

★★ **VILLAGE RESTAURANT.** *25 West St (06759), on the Green.* 860/567-8307. Specializes in fresh seafood, steak. Hrs: 11:30 am-10 pm; Sun brunch 11 am-3:30 pm. Closed Dec 25. Res accepted. Bar. Lunch a la carte entrees: $6-$10; dinner a la carte entrees: $12-$20. Sun brunch $8-$12. Child's menu. Overlooks village green. Cr cds: A, C, MC, V.

★★★ **WEST STREET GRILL.** *43 West St (06759).* 860/567-3885. Hrs: 11:30 am-9 pm; Fri, Sat to 10 pm. Closed Dec 25; also Mon in Nov-May. Res accepted; required Fri, Sat. Bar. Wine cellar. Lunch a la carte entrees: $4.95-$14.95; dinner a la carte entrees: $6.95-$25.95. Child's-menu. Contemporary black-white decor. Cr cds: A, MC, V.

Litchfield Church

Madison

See also Branford, Clinton, Guilford, New Haven

Settled 1649 **Pop** 15,485 **Elev** 22 ft
Area code 203 **Zip** 06443
Web www.MadisonCT.com

Information Chamber of Commerce, 22 Scotland Ave, PO Box 706; 203/245-7394; Tourism Office, 22 School St; 203/245-5659

What to See and Do

Allis-Bushnell House and Museum. (ca 1785) Period rms with four-corner fireplaces; doctor's office and equipment; exhibits of costumes, dolls, household implements; original paneling; herb garden. (Early June-Labor Day, Wed, Fri, and Sat, limited hrs; other times by appt) 853 Boston Post Rd. Phone 203/245-4567. **Donation**

Deacon John Grave House. Frame garrison colonial house (1685). (Memorial Day-Labor Day, Tues-Sun; spring and fall, wkends only) Academy & School Sts. Phone 203/245-4798. **Donation.**

Hammonasset Beach State Park. More than 900 acres with 2-mi beach on Long Island Sound. Saltwater swimming, scuba diving, fishing, boating; hiking, picnicking (shelters), camping, Nature Center. Standard

fees. 1 mi S of I-95 Exit 62. Phone
203/245-1817.

B&B/Small Inn

★★ **MADISON BEACH HOTEL.** *94
W Wharf Rd (06443). 203/245-1404;
fax 203/245-0410. www.madisonbeach
hotel.com.* 29 rms, 4 story, 6 suites.
May-Oct: D $115; suites $150; each
addl $15; under 12 free; lower rates
rest of yr. Crib avail. Pet accepted,
some restrictions, fee. Parking lot. TV;
cable (premium). Complimentary
continental bkfst, toll-free calls.
Restaurant 11:30 am-1 pm. Bar. Ck-
out 11 am, ck-in 2 pm. Meeting rms.
Business servs avail. Dry cleaning.
Beach access. Cr cds: A, D, DS, MC, V.

Restaurants

★★★ **CAFE ALLEGRA.** *725 Boston
Post Rd (06443). 203/245-7773. www.
allegracafe.com.* Specializes in regional
and international dishes. Hrs: 11:30
am-10 pm; Sat 5:30-10:30 pm; Sun 1-
8:30 pm. Closed Jan 1, Dec 25. Res
accepted. Bar. Wine cellar. Lunch a la
carte entrees: $5.95-$9.95; dinner a
la carte entrees: $13.95-$21.95.
Child's menu. Entertainment:
pianist, harpist Sun. Garden atmosphere; 3 dining rms. Cr cds: A, D,
MC, V.

★★ **FRIENDS AND COMPANY.** *11
Boston Post Rd (06443). 203/245-
0462.* Specializes in fresh seafood,
steak, seasonal dishes. Own baking,
desserts. Hrs: noon-10 pm; Mon,
Tues from 5 pm; Sun from 4:30 pm.
Closed Thanksgiving, Dec 25; also
last Mon in June. Bar. Lunch $5.75-
$8.95; dinner $5.75-$15.50. Child's
menu. Cr cds: A, D, DS, MC, V.

Manchester

(E-3) See also Hartford, Storrs, Windsor

Settled 1672 **Pop** 51,618 **Elev** 272 ft
Area code 860 **Zip** 06040
Web www.travelfile.com/get/ghtd

Information Greater Hartford
Tourism District, 234 Murphy Rd,
Hartford 06114; 860/244-8181 or
800/793-4480

The "city of village charm" has the
peaceful air of another era, with
great trees and 18th-century houses.
Manchester, once the silk capital of
the western world, is still a major
manufacturing center with more
than 100 industries—many more
than a century old.

What to See and Do

Cheney Homestead. (ca 1780) Birthplace of the brothers that launched
the state's once-promising silk industry; built by Timothy Cheney, clock-
maker. Paintings and etchings, early
19th-century furniture, replica of
schoolhouse. (Limited hrs) 106 Hartford Rd. Phone 860/643-5588. ¢

**Connecticut Firemen's Historical
Society Fire Museum.** Located in
1901 firehouse, this museum exhibits
antique fire-fighting equipment and
memorabilia, including leather fire
buckets, hoses, and helmets; hand-
pulled engines; horse-drawn hose
wagon; old prints and lithographs.
(Mid-Apr-mid-Nov, Fri-Sun) 230 Pine
St. Phone 860/649-9436. **Donation**

Lutz Children's Museum. Houses participatory exhibits on natural and
physical science, art, ethnology, and
history; live animal exhibit; outdoor
"playscape" area. (Tues-Sun; closed
hols) 247 S Main St. Phone 860/643-
0949. ¢¢

Oak Grove Nature Center. More
than 50 acres of woods, fields,
streams, pond, and trails. (Daily) Oak
Grove St. Phone 860/647-3321. **FREE**

Wickham Park. More than 200 acres
with gardens, including Oriental,
woods, ponds; log cabin (refreshments wkends); playgrounds, picnic
areas; aviary and small zoo; tennis
courts, softball fields (Apr-Oct, daily).
1329 W Middle Tpke, entrance on
US 44, off I-84 Exit 60. Phone
860/528-0856. Parking fee ¢

Motels/Motor Lodges

★ **CONNECTICUT MOTOR
LODGE.** *400 Tolland Tpke (06040), at
I-84 Exit 63. 860/643-1555; fax
860/643-1881.* 31 rms. S $40-$45; D
$55-$65; each addl $5. Crib $5. TV;

cable. Restaurant adj 7 am-11 pm.
Ck-out 11 am. Cr cds: A, C, D, DS,
JCB, MC, V.

★ **MANCHESTER VILLAGE MOTOR INN.** *100 E Center St (06040). 860/
646-2300; fax 860/649-6499; toll-free
800/487-6499.* 44 rms, 2 story. S
$39.95-$49.50; D $49.50-$57.50;
each addl $5; under 18 free. Crib
free. Pet accepted. TV; cable (premium), VCR (movies). Complimentary coffee in lobby. Restaurant opp
6:30 am-9 pm. Ck-out 11 am. Business servs avail. Sundries. Balconies.
Picnic tables. Cr cds: A, C, D, DS,
MC, V.

All Suite

★★ **CLARION SUITES INN.** *191
Spencer St (06040). 860/643-5811; fax
860/643-5811; res 800/CLARION; toll-
free 800/992-4004. Email clarion
manch@aol.com.* 104 kit. suites, 2
story. S, D $99-$139; under 16 free;
wkend rates. Crib free. Pet accepted;
$250 refundable and $10/day. TV;
cable, VCR. Heated pool; whirlpool.
Complimentary full bkfst. Complimentary coffee in rms. Restaurant
adj 6:30 am-midnight. Ck-out noon.
Coin lndry. Meeting rms. Business
servs avail. Sundries. Gift shop. Grocery store. Drug store. Valet serv. Free
airport, railroad station transportation. Downhill/x-country ski 20 mi.
Exercise equipt. Lawn games. Balconies. Cr cds: A, DS, MC, V.

Restaurants

★★★ **CAVEY'S FRENCH RESTAU-
RANT.** *45 E Center St (06040).
860/643-2751.* Own baking. Hrs: 6-9
pm. Closed Sun, Mon; hols. Res
accepted; required Sat. Bar. Wine cellar. Dinner a la carte entrees: $19-
$27. Prix fixe: $55. Parts of building
from old mansions. Cr cds: A, MC, V.

★★★ **CAVEY'S ITALIAN RESTAU-
RANT.** *45 E Center St (06040).
860/643-2751.* Hrs: 11:30 am-2:30
pm, 5:30-9:30 pm. Closed Sun, Mon;
hols. Res accepted; required Sat. Bar.
Lunch a la carte entrees: $8-$12; dinner a la carte entrees: $13-$19. Enter-

tainment: Fri, Sat. Country Mediterranean decor. Family-owned since
1933. Cr cds: A, MC, V.

Meriden

(E-2) *See also Hartford, Middletown,
New Haven*

Settled 1661 **Pop** 59,479 **Elev** 144 ft
Area code 203 **Zip** 06450
Web www.mayormeriden.com
Information City Hall, Mayor's
Office, 142 E Main St; 203/630-4000

Located in the heart of the central
Connecticut Valley, Meriden was
named after Meriden Farm in War-
wickshire, England. Once called the
"silver city of the world" because its
principal business was the manufacture of silver products, Meriden now
has a broad industrial base.

What to See and Do

Castle Craig Tower. Road leads to
tower atop East Peak, site of Easter
sunrise services. (May-Oct) In Hubbard Park, 2 mi W on I-691/CT 66.

Mount Southington Ski Area. Triple,
double chairlifts, 3 T-bars, J-bar;
snowmaking, patrol, school, rentals;
cafeteria, lounge. 12 trails; longest
run approx 1 mi; vertical drop 425 ft.
Night skiing. (Dec-Mar, daily) Approx
10 mi W; ½ mi W of I-84 Exit 30, at
Mt. Vernon Rd in Southington.
Phone 203/628-0954 or 800/982-
6828 (CT; snow conditions). ¢¢¢¢

Solomon Goffe House. (1711) Gam-
brel-roofed house features period fur-
nishings, artifacts. Costumed guides.
(July-Aug, Sat and Sun; rest of yr, 1st
Sun of month) 677 N Colony St.
Phone 203/634-9088. ¢

Annual Events

Daffodil Festival. Hubbard Park, W
Main St. Approx 500,000 daffodils in
bloom; various events. Mid-Apr.

Apple Harvest Festival. 3 mi S on CT
120, in Southington, on Town
Green. Street festival celebrating

local apple harvest. Carnival, arts and crafts, parade, road race, food booths, entertainment. Phone 860/628-8036. Seven days early Oct.

Motels/Motor Lodges

★★ **HAMPTON INN.** *10 Bee St (06450), I-91 N Exit 16, I-91 S Exit 17. 203/235-5154; fax 203/235-7139; toll-free 800/426-4329.* 125 rms, 4 story. S, D $75-$85; under 18 free; wkend rates. Crib free. TV; cable (premium). Complimentary continental bkfst. Coffee in rms. Restaurant nearby. Ck-out noon. Meeting rms. Business servs avail. In-rm modem link. Cr cds: A, C, D, DS, MC, V.
☐ ☒ ☒ SC

★★ **HOLIDAY INN EXPRESS.** *120 Laning St (06489), 6 mi N on CT 10 to Laning St, 2 blks N of I-84 Exit 32. 860/ 276-0736; fax 860/276-9405; toll-free 800/465-4329.* 122 rms, 3 story. May-Oct: S $59-$69; D $64-$74; each addl $6; under 18 free; lower rates rest of yr. Crib free. TV; cable, VCR avail. Pool. Complimentary continental bkfst. Restaurant adj 11:30 am-10 pm. Ck-out 11 am. Meeting rms. Business servs avail. In-rm modem link. Valet serv. Downhill ski 5 mi. Exercise equipt. Some refrigerators. Cr cds: A, C, D, DS, ER, JCB, MC, V.
☐ ☒ ☒ ☒ ☒ ☒ SC

Hotel

★★ **RAMADA PLAZA INN.** *275 Research Pkwy (06450). 203/238-2380; fax 203/238-3172; res 800/228-2828; toll-free 800/272-6232. Email locmd@ primehospitality.com; www.ramada. com.* 140 rms, 6 story. 10 suites. Apr-Oct: S $139; D $149; suites $175; each addl $10; under 18 free; lower rates rest of yr. Crib avail. Pet accepted. Parking lot. Indoor pool. TV; cable (premium). Complimentary coffee in rms, newspaper. Restaurant 6:30 am-10 pm. Bar. Ck-out noon, ck-in 2 pm. Meeting rms. Business center. Bellhops. Dry cleaning, coin lndry. Gift shop. Free airport transportation. Exercise equipt, sauna. Golf. Tennis, 6 courts. Video games. Cr cds: A, C, D, DS, ER, JCB, MC, V.
☐ ☒ ☒ ☒ ☒ ☒ ☒ ☒ SC ☒

Restaurant

★★ **BRANNIGAN'S.** *176 Laning St (06489), S on CT 10. 860/621-9311.* Specializes in barbecue ribs, seafood. Hrs: 11 am-10 pm; Sun brunch 11 am-2:30 pm. Closed Memorial Day, Dec 25. Res accepted. Bar. Lunch $4.95-$8.95; dinner $4.95-$15.95. Sun brunch $10.95. Child's menu. Cr cds: A, MC, V.
☐ ☒

⛽

Middletown

(E-3) *See also Hartford, Meriden*

Settled 1650 **Pop** 42,762 **Elev** 51 ft
Area code 860 **Zip** 06457
Web www.cttourism.org
Information CT Valley Tourism Commission, 393 Main St; 860/347-0028 or 800/486-3346

On the Connecticut River between Hartford and New Haven, Middletown was once an important shipping point for trade with the West Indies. The first official pistol-maker to the US Government, Simeon North, had his factory here in 1799. Today Middletown boasts diversified industry and one of the longest and widest main streets in New England.

What to See and Do

Powder Ridge Ski Area. Quad, 3 chairlifts, handletow; patrol, school, rentals, snowmaking; bar, restaurant, cafeteria, nursery. 14 trails; vertical drop 500 ft. (Nov-Apr, daily) 5 mi SW off CT 147, on Powder Hill Rd in Middlefield. Phone 860/349-3454. ¢¢¢¢

Wadsworth Falls State Park. These 285 acres surround Wadsworth Falls and lookout. Pond swimming, stream fishing; hiking along wooded area with mountain laurel display, picnicking. Beautiful waterfall with overlook. Standard hrs, fees. 3 mi SW off CT 66, on CT 157. Phone 860/566-2304.

Annual Event

Durham Fair. Fairgrounds, in Durham on CT 17. State's largest agricultural fair. Phone 860/349-9495. Last wkend Sep.

Motels/Motor Lodges

★★ **COMFORT INN.** *111 Berlin Rd (06416), 4 mi N on CT 372, E of I-91 Exit 21.* 860/635-4100; fax 860/632-9546; toll-free 800/228-5150. 77 rms, 4 story. S $54; D $61; each addl $6; under 18 free. Crib free. Pet accepted; $75 refundable. TV; VCR avail. Swimming privileges. Complimentary continental bkfst. Restaurant opp 5:30 am-10 pm. Ck-out 11 am. Health club privileges. Cr cds: A, C, D, DS, ER, JCB, MC, V.
[D] [symbols]

★★ **HOLIDAY INN.** *4 Sebethe Dr (06416), W of I-91 Exit 21.* 860/635-1001; fax 860/635-0684; res 800/465-4329. 145 rms, 3 story. S $79-$139; D $89-$149; each addl $10; suites $149; under 18 free; wknd rates. Crib free. TV; cable (premium). Indoor pool. Restaurant 6 am-10 pm. Bar. Ck-out 11 am. Coin lndry. Meeting rms. Business servs avail. In-rm modem link. Valet serv. Sundries. Airport transportation. Exercise equipt; sauna. Health club privileges. Lawn games. Picnic tables. Cr cds: A, DS, MC, V.
[symbols]

Hotel

★★★ **RADISSON HOTEL AND CONFERENCE CENTER.** *100 Berlin Rd (06416), 4 mi N on CT 72, E of I-91 Exit 21.* 860/635-2000; fax 860/635-6970; res 800/333-3333. Email rhi_crom@radisson.com. 211 rms, 4 story. S $69-$99; D $79-$109; suites $195-$350; under 18 free; wknd rates. Crib free. TV; cable, VCR avail. Indoor pool; whirlpool, poolside serv. Coffee in rms. Restaurants 6:30 am-10:30 pm. Bar noon-1 am; entertainment Sat. Ck-out noon. Meeting rms. Business servs avail. In-rm modem link. Gift shop. Exercise equipt; sauna. Some bathrm phones. Cr cds: A, DS, MC, V.
[symbols]

[gas pump symbol]

Milford

(F-2) *See also Bridgeport, Fairfield, New Haven, Stratford*

Settled 1639 **Pop** 49,938 **Elev** 89 ft
Area code 203 **Zip** 06460
Web www.newhavencvb.org or www.milfordct.com

Information Greater New Haven Convention and Visitors Bureau, 59 Elm St, 1st flr, New Haven 06510; 203/777-8550 or 800/332-STAY

What to See and Do

Milford Historical Society Wharf Lane Complex. Three historical houses incl Eells-Stow House (ca 1700), believed to be oldest house in Milford and featuring unusual "dog sled" stairway; Stockade House (ca 1780), first house built outside the city's early stockade; and Bryan-Downs House (ca 1785), 2-story early American structure housing more than 400 Native American artifacts spanning more than 10,000 yrs. (Memorial Day-Columbus Day, Sun; also by appt) 34 High St. Phone 203/874-2664. ¢

Milford Jai-Alai. Pari-mutuel wagering. Restaurant. (Tues-Sat eves; matinees Tues, Wed, Sat, and Sun) 311 Old Gate Lane, off I-95 Exit 40. Phone 203/877-4242.

Annual Event

Oyster Festival. Milford Center, town green. Arts and crafts exhibits, races, boat tours, games, food, entertainment. Phone 203/878-4225. Mid-Aug.

Motel/Motor Lodge

★★ **HAMPTON INN.** *129 Plains Rd (06460).* 203/874-4400; fax 203/874-5348; res 800/426-7866. Email mifpl01@hi-hotel.com. 147 rms, 3 story, 1 suite. Feb-Oct: S, D $95; suites $125; lower rates rest of yr. Crib avail. Parking lot. TV; cable (premium). Complimentary continental bkfst, coffee in rms, newspaper, toll-free calls. Restaurant nearby. Meeting rm. Business servs avail. Dry cleaning, coin lndry. Exercise equipt. Golf,

18 holes. Video games. Cr cds: A, C, D, DS, MC, V.

⊡ 🎿 🏃 ⇙ 🐾 SC

Restaurants

★ **ALDARIO'S.** *240 Naugatuck Ave (06460). 203/874-6096. Email sante123@aol.com; www.aldarios.com.* Specializes in seafood, veal. Salad bar. Hrs: 11:30 am-10 pm; Tues to 9 pm; Sat from 4:30 pm; Sun 12:30-8 pm. Closed Mon; some major hols. Res accepted. Bar. Lunch $4.50-$9.95; dinner $8.95-$16.95. Child's menu. Family-owned. Cr cds: A, D, DS, MC, V.

⊡ ⇙

★★ **THE GATHERING.** *989 Boston Post Rd (06460), US 1. 203/878-6537.* Specializes in fresh fish, steak, prime rib. Salad bar. Hrs: 11:30 am-midnight; Sun noon-8 pm. Closed Dec 25. Res accepted. Bar. Lunch $9.95-$16.95; dinner $9.95-$16.95. Child's menu. Colonial decor. Family-owned. Cr cds: A, MC, V.

⊡ ⇙

★★ **SCRIBNER'S.** *31 Village Rd (06460). 203/878-7019. www.scribnersrestaurant.com.* Specializes in exotic fish, fresh seafood, Angus beef. Hrs: 11:30 am-closing; Sat from 5 pm. Closed most major hols. Res accepted. Bar. Lunch $4.95-$8.95; dinner $17.95-$26.95. Child's menu. Casual dining. Nautical decor. Cr cds: A, MC, V.

⊡ ⇙

Mystic

See also Groton, New London, Norwich, Stonington

Settled 1654 **Pop** 2,618 **Elev** 16 ft
Area code 860 **Zip** 06355
Web www.mysticmore.com

Information Tourist Information Center, Building 1D, Olde Mistick Village; 860/536-1641; or Connecticut's Mystic & More, 470 Bank St, PO Box 89, New London 06320; 860/444-2206 or 800/222-6783 (outside CT)

The community of Mystic, divided by the Mystic River, was a shipbuilding and whaling center from the 17th to the 19th centuries. It derives its name from the Pequot, "Mistuket."

What to See and Do

Denison Homestead. (1717) Restored in the style of 5 eras (18th to mid-20th centuries); furnished with heirlooms of 11 generations of a single family. Guided tour (mid-May-mid-Oct, Wed-Mon afternoons; rest of yr, by appt). 2 mi E of I-95 Exit 90, on Pequotsepos Rd. Phone 860/536-9248. ¢¢

Denison Pequotsepos Nature Center. An environmental education center and natural history museum active in wildlife rehabilitation. The 125-acre sanctuary has more than 7 mi of trails; family nature walks, films, lectures. (Daily; closed hols) 2 mi NE of I-95 Exit 90, on Pequotsepos Rd. Phone 860/536-1216. ¢¢

Mystic Marinelife Aquarium. Exhibits feature more than 6,000 live specimens from all waters of the world; demonstrations with dolphins, sea lions, and the only whales in New England; Seal Island, outdoor exhibit of seals and sea lions in natural settings; penguin pavilion. (Daily; closed Jan 1, Thanksgiving, Dec, also last full wk Jan) 55 Coogan Blvd. Phone 860/536-3323. ¢¢¢

❇ **Mystic Seaport.** This 17-acre complex is the nation's largest maritime museum, dedicated to preservation of 19th-century maritime history. Visitors may board the 1841 wooden whaleship *Charles W. Morgan,* square-rigged ship *Joseph Conrad,* or fishing schooner *L. A. Dunton.* Collection also includes some 400 smaller vessels; representative seaport community with historic homes and waterfront industries, some staff in 19th-century costume; exhibits, demonstrations, working shipyard; children's museum, planetarium (fee), 1908 steamboat cruises (May-Oct, daily; fee); restaurants; shopping; special events throughout the yr. (Daily; closed Dec 25) 75 Greenmanville Ave (CT 27), 1 mi S of I-95 Exit 90. Phone 860/572-5315. ¢¢¢¢

Olde Mistick Village. More than 60 shops and restaurants in 1720s-style New England village on 22 acres; duck pond, millwheel, waterfalls, entertainment, carillon (May-Oct, Sat and Sun). Village (daily). Coogan Blvd & CT 27. Phone 860/536-4941. **FREE**

Annual Event

Lobsterfest. Mystic Seaport. Outdoor food festival. Phone 860/572-5315. Late May.

Motels/Motor Lodges

★ ★ **BEST WESTERN SOVEREIGN HOTEL.** *Rte 27 & I-95 (06355). 860/536-4281; toll-free 800/528-1234.* 150 rms, 2 story, 4 suites. June-Oct: S $109; D $139; suites $279; each addl $5; under 18 free; lower rates rest of yr. Crib avail, fee. Parking lot. Indoor pool. TV; cable. Complimentary full bkfst, coffee in rms, newspaper. Restaurant 6:30 am-9 pm. Bar. Ck-out 11 am, ck-in 3 pm. Meeting rms. Fax servs avail. Bellhops. Dry cleaning. Exercise equipt, sauna, steam rm. Golf. Beach access. Supervised children's activities. Hiking trail. Picnic facilities. Video games. Cr cds: A, D, DS, MC, V.

★ ★ ★ **INN AT MYSTIC.** *Rte 1 & Rte 27 (06355), 2 mi S of I-95 Exit 90. 860/536-9604; fax 860/572-1635; toll-free 800/237-2415. Email idyer@innat mystic.com; www.innatmystic.com.* 67 rms, 2 story. May-Oct: S, D $100-$235; each addl $10; under 18 free; lower rates rest of yr. Crib $10. TV; cable (premium), VCR avail. Heated pool; whirlpool. Complimentary afternoon tea. Restaurant (see also FLOOD TIDE). Bar. Ck-out 11 am. Meeting rm. Business servs avail. Tennis. Some in-rm whirlpools, fireplaces. Some private patios, balconies. Formal gardens. Long Island Sound ¼ mi. Cr cds: A, DS, MC, V.

★ ★ ★ **TWO TREES INN.** *240 Lantern Hill Dr (06339), E on I-95 to Exit 92, NW on CT 2. 860/312-3000; fax 860/885-4050; toll-free 800/369-9663.* 280 rms, 3 story, 60 suites. Late June-early Sept: S, D $150; each addl $20; suites $175; under 18 free; package plans; lower rates rest of yr. Crib $10. TV; cable (premium), VCR avail. Indoor pool; whirlpool. Complimentary continental bkfst. Restaurant 11:30 am-10 pm. Ck-out noon. Business servs avail. Bellhops. Health club privileges. Refrigerators. Foxwoods Casino adj. Cr cds: A, DS, MC, V.

Hotels

★ ★ **COMFORT INN.** *48 Whitehall Ave (06355), I-95, Exit 90. 860/572-8531; fax 860/572-9358; toll-free 800/572-9339. Email cimystic@ connix.com; www.whghotels.com/ cimystic.* 120 rms, 2 story. Jun-Sep: S, D $169; each addl $10; children $10; under 16 free; lower rates rest of yr. Crib avail. Parking lot. TV; cable (premium). Complimentary continental bkfst, newspaper. Restaurant nearby. Ck-out 11 am, ck-in 3 pm. Meeting rms. Dry cleaning. Exercise equipt. Golf. Tennis, 6 courts. Picnic facilities. Cr cds: A, C, D, DS, ER, JCB, MC, V.

★ ★ **DAYS INN.** *55 Whitehall Ave (06355). 860/572-0574; fax 860/572-1164; res 800/329-7466; toll-free 800/572-3993. Email mbiggins@connix. com; www.whghotels.com/dimystic.* 123 rms, 2 story, 2 suites. May-Oct: S, D $199; suites $249; each addl $10; under 18 free; lower rates rest of yr. Crib avail. Parking lot. Pool. TV; cable (premium). Complimentary coffee in rms, newspaper, toll-free calls. Restaurant 6 am-midnight. Ck-out 11 am, ck-in 3 pm. Business center. Dry cleaning. Exercise privileges. Golf. Tennis, 15 courts. Picnic facilities. Cr cds: A, C, D, DS, ER, JCB, MC, V.

★ ★ ★ **FOXWOODS RESORT AND CASINO LEDYARD.** *Rte 2 PO Box 3777 (06339), E on I-95, Exit 92, approx 8 mi W on CT 2. 860/312-3000; res 860/312-3000; toll-free 800/369-9663.* 312 rms, 6 story, 40 suites. July-early Sept: S, D $200; each addl $20; suites $275; under 18 free; lower rates rest of yr. Crib $10. TV; cable (premium), VCR avail. Indoor pool; whirlpool, lifeguard. Restaurants open 24 hrs. Bar 11-1:30 am; entertainment. Ck-out noon. Meeting rms. Business servs avail. In-rm modem link. Concierge serv. Shopping arcade. Barber, beauty shop. Free garage, valet parking. Exercise rm. Some refrigerators. Connected to casino. Cr cds: A, C, D, DS, ER, JCB, MC, V.

Mystic Seaport

★★★ **HILTON.** *20 Coogan Blvd (06355). 860/572-0731; fax 860/572-0328; toll-free 800/445-8667. Email dreed@mptn.org; www.visitmystic.com/hilton.* 171 rms, 4 story, 12 suites. Jun-Aug: S, D $225; suites $375; each addl $20; lower rates rest of yr. Crib avail. Valet parking avail. Indoor pool. TV; cable (premium). Complimentary coffee in rms, newspaper. Restaurant 5:30 am-9:30 pm, closed Sun. Bar. Ck-out 11 am, ck-in 3 pm. Meeting rms. Business center. Bellhops. Concierge serv. Dry cleaning. Gift shop. Exercise privileges. Golf. Tennis. Bike rentals. Supervised children's activities. Cr cds: A, C, D, DS, MC, V.

B&Bs/Small Inns

★ **APPLEWOOD FARMS INN.** *528 Colonel Ledyard Hwy (06339), I-95, Exit 89, N to CT 184, W to Col Ledyard Hwy. 860/536-2022; fax 860/536-6015; toll-free 800/717-4262. Email applewoodfarms@worldnet.att.net; www.visitmystic.com/applewoodfarmsinn.* 5 rms, 2 story, 1 suite. S $109; D $125; suites $150; each addl $25. Pet accepted, some restrictions. Parking lot. TV; cable (premium), VCR avail. Complimentary full bkfst. Restaurant 7 am-10 pm, closed Mon. Ck-out 11 am, ck-in 3 pm. Meeting rm. Business center. Whirlpool. Golf. Tennis. Hiking trail. Picnic facilities. Cr cds: A, DS, MC, V.

★★ **THE OLD MYSTIC INN.** *52 Main St (06372), 1½ mi N on CT 27, then right at stop sign. 860/572-9422;*

fax 860/572-9954. Email omysticinn@ aol.com; www.visit mystic.com/oldmystic inn. 8 rms, 2 story, 1 suite. Jun-Aug: D $135; lower rates rest of yr. Parking lot. TV; cable, VCR avail. Complimentary full bkfst, newspaper. Restaurant nearby. Ck-out 11 am. Business servs avail. Whirlpool. Golf. Tennis. Cr cds: A, MC, V.

★★★ **PALMER INN.** *25 Church St (06340), 3 mi S via CT 215. 860/572-9000.* 6 rms, 5 A/C, 3 story. No rm phones. S, D $115-$225. Children over 16 yrs only. Complimentary continental bkfst; afternoon refreshments. Ck-out 11 am, ck-in 2-6 pm. Near ocean. Mansion built 1907; antiques, stained-glass. Totally non-smoking. Cr cds: A, DS, MC, V.

★★ **RED BROOK INN.** *Rte 184 & Welles Rd (06372), 3 mi N on CT 27 to CT 184, W ½ mi. 860/572-0349; fax 860/572-0349; toll-free 800/290-5619. Email rkeyes1667@aol.com.* 11 rms, 8 A/C, 2 story. No rm phones. S, D $105-$169. Advance payment required. Crib free. TV; cable. Complimentary full bkfst. Restaurants nearby. Ck-out 11 am, ck-in noon. Concierge serv. Fireplaces in 7 rms. Two Colonial buildings (ca 1740 and ca 1770) furnished with period antiques. Totally nonsmoking. Cr cds: A, DS, MC, V.

★★ **WHALER'S INN.** *20 E Main St (06355). 860/536-1506; fax 860/572-1250; toll-free 800/243-2588. Email whalers.inn@riconnect.com.* 41 rms, 18 with shower only, 2 story. May-late Oct: S $99-$105; D $119-$139; suite $175-$210; each addl $10; under 18 free; lower rates rest of yr. Crib $5. TV; cable. Dining rm 11:30 am-9 pm. Ck-out 11 am, ck-in 2 pm. Business servs avail. In-rm modem link. Balconies. Built 1865; Colonial décor. Cr cds: A, DS, MC, V.

Restaurants

★ ★ ★ **BRAVO BRAVO.** *20 E Main St (06355). 860/536-3228.* Specializes in Maryland crab cakes with lobster sauce, pasta with seafood. Hrs: 11:30 am-9 pm; Fri, Sat to 10 pm. Closed Mon. Res accepted. Extensive wine list. Lunch $6.95-$12.95; dinner $13.95-$24.95. Entertainment. Cr cds: A, D, DS, MC, V.
D 🔥

★ ★ ★ **FLOOD TIDE.** *jct US 1 and CT 27. 860/536-8140. www.innat mystic.com.* Specializes in beef Wellington, chateaubriand, Caesar salad. Hrs: 7 am-10 pm; Sun brunch 11 am-2 pm. Res required. Bar. Wine list. Bkfst a la carte entrees: $2-$10. Buffet: $8.95; lunch a la carte entrees: $5.95-$19.95; dinner a la carte entrees: $13.95-$25.95. Sun brunch $15.95. Child's menu. Entertainment: pianist. Parking. Nautical decor; elegant dining with view of sea. Cr cds: A, D, DS, MC, V.
D

★ ★ **GO FISH.** *Olde Mistick Village (06355). 860/536-2662.* Specializes in seafood pasta, go fish crabcakes. Raw bar. Sushi bar. Hrs: 11:30 am-9:30 pm; Fri, Sat to 10:30 pm; Sun to 9:30 pm. Res accepted. Wine, beer. Lunch $5.95-$13.50; dinner $10.95-$19.95. Child's menu. Entertainment. In Olde Mistick Village. Cr cds: A, D, DS, ER, MC, V.
D 🔥 ⌐

★ ★ **J. P. DANIELS.** *CT 27 and CT 184 (06355), ½ mi N on CT 184. 860/ 572-9564. www.synderblox.com/j.p. daniels.* Specializes in veal, seafood. Hrs: 5-9 pm; Sun brunch 11 am-2 pm. Closed Dec 24, 25. Res accepted. Bar. Wine list. Dinner $8.95-$17.95. Sun brunch $13.95. Child's menu. Parking. Elegant dining in relaxed country setting. Cr cds: A, DS, MC, V.
D

★ **MYSTIC PIZZA.** *56 W Main St (06355). 860/536-3700. www.mystic-pizza.com.* Specializes in pizza, pasta. Hrs: 10:30 am-10 pm; Fri, Sat to 11:30 pm. Closed Easter, Thanksgiving, Dec 25. Wine, beer. Lunch a la carte entrees: $2-$8.75; dinner a la carte entrees: $2-$9.25. Child's menu. Parking. Popular pizza parlor

immortalized in the Julia Roberts film by the same name. Family-owned. Cr cds: C, DS, MC, V.
D ⌐

★ ★ **SEAMEN'S INNE.** *105 Greenmanville Ave (06355). 860/536-9649. www.seamensinne.com.* Specializes in prime rib, fresh Atlantic seafood. Hrs: 11:30 am-10 pm; Sun from 10:30 am; Sun brunch to 2 pm; hrs vary off-season. Closed Dec 25. Res accepted. Bar. Lunch $4.95-$9.95; dinner $10.95-$18.95. Sun brunch $9.95. Child's menu. 19th-century sea captain's house decor; overlooks river. Cr cds: A, D, DS, MC, V.
D

★ **STEAK LOFT.** *Olde Mistick Village (06355), 2 mi N on CT 27. 860/536-2661. Email steakloft@aol.com; www. visitmystic.com/steakloft.* Specializes in steak, seafood. Salad bar. Hrs: 11:30 am-9:30 pm. Closed Thanksgiving, Dec 25. Bar. Lunch $3-$12; dinner $11-20. Child's menu. Entertainment: Wed-Sun. Parking. Casual New England atmosphere. Cr cds: A, D, DS, MC, V.
D SC ⌐

New Britain

(E-3) See also Hartford, Meriden, Wethersfield

Settled 1686 **Pop** 75,491 **Elev** 179 ft
Area code 860
Web www.newbritainchamber.org

Information Chamber of Commerce, 1 Court St, 06051; 860/229-1665; or the Central Connecticut Tourism District, 1 Enterprise Grove Plaza, 06051, 860/225-3901

This is the "hardware city." Production of sleigh bells and farm tools began about 1800, followed by locks and saddlery hardware. Many tool, hardware, and machinery manufacturers, including The Stanley Works, organized in 1843, are headquartered in New Britain.

What to See and Do

Central Connecticut State University. (1849) 14,000 students. On campus is Copernican Planetarium and Observatory, featuring one of the largest public telescopes in the United States; planetarium shows (Fri, Sat; children's shows Sat) Phone 860/827-7000. Planetarium shows ¢¢

Hungerford Outdoor Education Center. Outdoor animal areas; trails; gardens; pond; exhibits of natural history, nutrition, and energy; picnicking. (Apr-Oct, Tues-Sun; rest of yr, Tues-Sat) Approx 3 mi S via CT 372, at 191 Farmington Ave in Kensington. Phone 860/827-9064. ¢

New Britain Museum of American Art. Works by outstanding American artists from 1740 to the present; works by Whistler, Church, Sargent, Wyeth; Thomas Hart Benton murals; Sanford Low Collection of American illustrations; Charles and Elizabeth Buchanan Collection of American impressionists. (Tues-Sun afternoons; closed hols) 56 Lexington St. Phone 860/229-0257. **FREE**

New Britain Youth Museum. Exhibits of Americana, cultures of other nations, circus miniatures, dolls, hands-on displays. (Tues-Fri) 30 High St. Phone 860/225-3020. **FREE**

Annual Events

Main Street, USA. Street festival featuring wide variety of ethnic foods, entertainment, rides, arts and crafts. Phone 860/225-3901. Second Sat June.

Dozynki Polish Harvest Festival. Broad St. Street dancing, polka bands, cultural displays, beer, singing, ethnic food, pony and hayrides, Polish arts and crafts. Phone 860/225-3901. Third wkend Sep.

Seasonal Event

Baseball. New Britain Rock Cats (AA team). New Britain Stadium, Willowbrook Park. Phone 860/224-8383. Mid-Apr-Sep.

Motel/Motor Lodge

★★ **CENTRAL INN AND CONFERENCE CENTER.** *65 Columbus Blvd (06051). 860/224-9161; fax 860/224-1796; toll-free 800/272-6232.* 119 rms, 6 story. S, D $45-$95; each addl $10; suites $125; under 19 free; wkend plans. Crib free. Pet accepted, some restrictions; $10. TV; cable (premium), VCR avail. Ck-out noon.

Coin lndry. Meeting rms. Business servs avail. Airport transportation. Garage parking. Downhill ski 5 mi. Cr cds: A, C, D, DS, JCB, MC, V.

🄳 ⬀ 🖂 ⬛ 🐾 🆂🅲

Restaurant

★ **EAST SIDE.** *131 Dwight St (06051). 860/223-1188.* Specializes in German dishes, baked shrimp, steak. Hrs: 2-8 pm. Closed Mon; July 4, Dec 25. Res accepted. Bar. Lunch $4.95-$9.95; dinner $10.95-$16.95. Child's menu. European atmosphere. Family-owned. Cr cds: MC, V.

🄳 ⤴

New Canaan

(G-1) *See also Norwalk, Stamford*

Founded 1801 **Pop** 17,864 **Elev** 300 ft
Area code 203 **Zip** 06840
Information Chamber of Commerce, 111 Elm St; 203/966-2004

New Canaan was settled in 1731 as Canaan Parish, a church society encompassing parts of Norwalk and Stamford. A quiet residential community situated on high ridges, New Canaan has retained its rural character despite its proximity to industrial areas.

What to See and Do

New Canaan Historical Society. The First Town House (original town hall) has costume museum; library; and Cody Drugstore (1845), a restoration of the town's first pharmacy; on grounds of Hanford-Silliman House Museum (ca 1765) are a tool museum, hand press, 1-room schoolhouse, and sculptor John Roger's studio and museum. (Town House, Tues-Sat; other buildings Wed, Thurs, and Sun, limited afternoon hrs; closed hols) 13 Oenoke Ridge Rd. Phone 203/966-1776. ¢¢

New Canaan Nature Center. More than 40 acres of woodland, ponds, and meadows; discovery center with hands-on exhibits; suburban ecology exhibits; solar greenhouse; cider house and maple sugar shed; herb and wildflower gardens; trails, marsh boardwalk; animals. Grounds (daily). Buildings (Tues-Sun; closed hols). 144 Oenoke Ridge Rd. Phone 203/966-9577. **FREE**

Silvermine Guild Arts Center. Art center in rustic 6-acre setting has a school of the arts and three galleries with changing exhibits by member artists and artisans; invitational and juried exhibitions; many educational events and programs. (Tues-Sun; closed Jan 1, Thanksgiving, Dec 25) 1037 Silvermine Rd. Phone 203/966-5617 (galleries) or 203/966-5618 (programs). **FREE**

B&B/Small Inn

★★★ **ROGER SHERMAN INN.** *195 Oenoke Ridge Rd (06840), I-95 Exit 12, N on CT 124. 203/966-4541; fax 203/966-0503. Email info@rogershermaninn.com; www.rogershermaninn. com.* 16 rms, 2 story, 1 suite. S $105; D $160; suites $300. Parking lot. TV; cable, VCR avail. Complimentary continental bkfst, newspaper. Restaurant noon-9 pm. Bar. Ck-out 11 am, ck-in 2 pm. Meeting rms. Business center. Dry cleaning. Golf, 18 holes. Tennis, 6 courts. Hiking trail. Picnic facilities. Cr cds: A, D, MC, V.

ⅅ 🕴 🏂 🛩 🐾 🚶

New Haven

(F-2) *See also Branford, Milford*

Settled 1638 **Pop** 130,474 **Elev** 25 ft
Area code 203
Web www.newhavencvb.org or www.cityofnewhaven.com
Information Greater New Haven Convention & Visitors Bureau, 59 Elm St, 1st flr, 06510; 203/777-8550 or 800/332-STAY

New Haven is only 75 miles from New York City, but it is typically New England. Its colorful history is built into the stones and timbers of the area. Here Eli Whitney worked out the principle of interchangeable parts for mass production. Around the corner, Nathan Hale roomed as a student, not far from where Noah Webster compiled the first dictionary. In addition to all this, Yale University puts New Haven on any list of the world's cultural centers.

Northwest of New Haven is a 400-foot red sandstone cliff called West Rock. In 1661 three Cromwellian judges, who had ordered Charles I beheaded, took refuge here from the soldiers of Charles II.

What to See and Do

Amistad Memorial. This 14-ft bronze relief sculpture is a unique 3-sided form. Each side depicts a significant episode of the life of Joseph Cinque, one of 50 Africans kidnapped from Sierra Leone and slated for sale in Cuba in 1839. After secretly rerouting the slave ship to Long Island Sound, the battle for the would-be slaves' freedom ensued in New Haven. Two years later, their victory was complete. Ed Hamilton sculpted this important piece. In front of City Hall. 165 Church St.

East Rock Park. City's largest park includes Pardee Rose Gardens, bird sanctuary, hiking trails, athletic fields, tennis courts, picnic grounds. Excellent view of harbor and Long Island Sound. (Apr-Oct, daily; rest of yr, Sat, Sun, and hols) 1 mi NE at foot of Orange St, on E Rock Rd. Phone 203/946-6086. **FREE**

Fort Hale Park and Restoration. Here Federal guns kept British warships out of the harbor in 1812. Old Black Rock Fort, from Revolutionary War days, has been restored, and archaeological excavations are in progress. Fort Nathan Hale, from Civil War era, also has been reconstructed. Both offer spectacular views of the harbor. Picnicking. Guided tours. (Memorial Day-Labor Day, daily) 36 Woodward Ave. Phone 203/787-8790. **FREE**

The Green. In 1638, these 16 acres were laid out, making New Haven the first planned city in America. On the town common are 3 churches—United (1813), Trinity Episcopal (1814), and Center Congregational (1813), which is one of the masterpieces of American Georgian architecture. **FREE**

Grove Street Cemetery. First cemetery in the United States divided into family plots. Buried here are Noah Webster, Charles Goodyear, Eli Whitney, and many early settlers of the area. Grove & Prospect Sts. **FREE**

Lighthouse Point. This 82-acre park on Long Island Sound has lighthouse built in 1840, restored antique carousel (fee), bird sanctuary. Beach, bathhouse, playfield, picnic facilities, boat ramp. (Daily) Parking fee (Memorial Day-Labor Day only). End of Lighthouse Rd, 5 mi SE off I-95, Exit 50. Phone 203/946-8005. ¢¢

New Haven Colony Historical Society Museum. Museum of local history; special exhibits, also research library (fee). (Tues-Sun; closed hols) 114 Whitney Ave. Phone 203/562-4183. ¢

Pardee-Morris House. (1750) Built in 18th century, burned by the British in 1779, then rebuilt in 1780 around surviving masonry; American period furnishings; kitchen garden. (June-Aug, Sat and Sun) 325 Lighthouse Rd, S of I-95 Exit 50. Phone 203/562-4183. ¢

Shore Line Trolley Museum. Collection of trolley, interurban, and rapid-transit cars from 15 states and Canada. A National Historic Site. Cars on display include pre-1900 trolleys (1893, 1899), the first commercially produced electric locomotive (1888), and a trolley parlor car. Exhibits on electric railways. Scenic trolley ride in authentic, restored cars; operator narrates on tour of display buildings and restoration shop; trolleys depart every 30 min (inquire for schedule). Picnic grove (May-Oct); gift shop; special events. (Memorial Day-Labor Day, daily; May and after Labor Day-Oct, wkends and some hols; Apr and early- to late-Nov, Sun only; wkend after Thanksgiving-wkend prior to Dec 25, Sat and Sun) 5 mi E via I-95 exit 51 or 52, at 17 River St in east Haven. Phone 203/467-6927. ¢¢¢

Shubert Performing Arts Center. Full-service performing arts venue opened in 1914. Known as the "Birthplace of the Nation's Greatest Hits." Home to dance, musical, comedy, and dramatic performances. (Sep-May) 247 College St. Phone 203/562-5666 or 888/736-2663.

West Rock Nature Center. Nature center features native Connecticut wildlife in outdoor bird and mammal sections; indoor nature house with reptiles and other displays. Hiking trails, picnic areas. (Mon-Fri; closed hols) On Wintergreen Ave, 1 mi N of

Southern Connecticut State Univ. Phone 203/946-8016. **FREE**

⭐ **Yale University.** (1701) 10,000 students. Founded by 10 Connecticut ministers and named for Elihu Yale, an early donor to the school. In September 1969, the undergraduate school became coeducational. 149 Elm St, on N side of New Haven Green. Phone 203/432-2300. Of special interest are

> **The Old Campus.** Nathan Hale (class of 1773) roomed here. One-hr guided walking tours (Mon-Fri, one tour morning, one tour afternoon; Sat, Sun, one tour afternoon). Inquire at Visitor Information Office. 149 Elm St. Phone 203/432-2300. **FREE**

> **Yale Art Gallery.** Collections include Italian Renaissance paintings, American paintings and decorative arts, ancient art, African sculpture, Near and Far Eastern art, and European paintings from the 13th-20th centuries. (Tues-Sat, also Sun afternoons; closed hols) 1111 Chapel St at York St. Phone 203/432-0600. **FREE**

> **Sterling Memorial and Beinecke Rare Book and Manuscript Libraries.** Exhibits of famous collections, Gutenberg Bible. Sterling: (June-Aug, Mon-Sat; rest of yr, daily; closed hols). Beinecke: (Sep-July, Mon-Sat; Aug, Mon-Fri; closed hols). Best approach is from College St via Cross Campus Walk, on High St. Phone 203/432-2798 (Sterling) or 203/432-2977 (Beinecke). **FREE**

> **Collection of Musical Instruments.** Total holdings of 850 musical instruments; permanent displays and changing exhibits; lectures, concerts, special events. (Sep-May, Tues-Thurs afternoons; June, Tues and Thurs afternoons; closed school hols) Under 14 only with adult. 15 Hillhouse Ave. Phone 203/432-0822. ¢

> **Peabody Museum of Natural History.** Exhibits on mammals, invertebrate life, Plains and Connecticut Native Americans, meteorites, minerals and rocks, birds of Connecticut; several life-size dinosaur exhibits including a brontosaurus (60-ft long) reconstructed from original fossil material; dioramas of North American flora and fauna; wkend films (free). (Daily; closed

hols) Free admission Mon-Fri late afternoon. 170 Whitney Ave at Sachem St. Phone 203/432-5050 (recording). ¢¢

Yale Center for British Art. British paintings, prints, drawings, sculpture, and rare books from Elizabethan period to present. Reference library and photo archive. Lectures, tours, films, concerts. (Tues-Sun;

Branford College, Yale University

closed hols) 1080 Chapel St. Phone 203/432-2800. **FREE**

Yale Bowl. An Ivy League football mecca. 2 mi W on Chapel St.

Annual Events

Powder House Day. Marks anniversary of the demand made upon the First Selectman in 1775 by Captain Benedict Arnold for the keys to the Powder House (arsenal). Having obtained the ammunition, Arnold marched his company to Boston to take part in the rebellion. The present governor's footguard appears in authentic Revolutionary War garb to join in ceremonies that are held on the Green. Late Apr or early May.

International Festival of Arts and Ideas. Celebration of the arts and humanities. 195 Church St. Phone 888/ART-IDEA. Late June.

Pilot Pen International Tennis Tournament. Connecticut Tennis Center, near Yale Bowl. Championship Series on the ATP tour. Phone 888-99-PILOT. Mid-Aug.

Downtown Summertime Street Festival. Downtown, along Chapel St. Phone 203/946-7821. Mid-Aug.

Seasonal Events

Long Wharf Theatre. Features new plays as well as classics. Phone 203/787-4282 (box office). Tues-Sun nights, Sep-June. 222 Sargent Dr, at I-95 Exit 46.

New Haven Symphony Orchestra. Woolsey Hall, College & Grove Sts.

Series of concerts by leading artists. Phone 203/776-1444. Oct-mid-Apr.

Yale Repertory Theater. 222 York St. Phone 203/432-1234. Oct-May.

Hotels

★★ **THE COLONY.** *1157 Chapel St (06511). 203/776-1234; fax 203/772-3929; toll-free 800/458-8810. Email info@colonyatyale.com; www.colony atyale.com.* 80 rms, 5 story, 6 suites. Apr-Jun, Sep-Oct: S $89; D $99; suites $175; each addl $10; under 12 free; lower rates rest of yr. Crib avail, fee. Parking garage. TV; cable, VCR avail. Complimentary newspaper, toll-free calls. Restaurant 6:30 am-11 pm. Bar. Ck-out noon, ck-in 3 pm. Meeting rms. Business center. Bellhops. Dry cleaning. Free airport transportation. Exercise privileges. Golf. Cr cds: A, D, MC, V.

🄳 ✗ 🇰 ⟶ 🀄 🇰

★★ **HOLIDAY INN AT YALE UNIVERSITY.** *30 Whalley Ave (06511), adj to Yale Univ. 203/777-6221; fax 203/772-1089; res 800/HOLIDAY.* 160 rms, 8 story. S, D $95; under 12 free. Crib avail, fee. Parking garage. Pool. TV; cable (premium). Complimentary coffee in rms, newspaper, toll-free calls. Restaurant 7 am-10 pm. Bar. Ck-out noon, ck-in 3 pm. Meeting rms. Business center. Bellhops. Dry cleaning. Free airport transportation. Exercise privileges. Golf, 18 holes. Cr cds: A, D, DS, JCB, MC, V.

🄳 ✗ ⟶ 🇰 ⟶ 🀄 🇰

B&B/Small Inn

★★★ **THREE CHIMNEYS.** *1201 Chapel St (06511). 203/789-1201; fax 203/776-7363; toll-free 800/443-1554.* Email chimneysnh@aol.com; www. threechimneysinn.com. 11 rms, 3 story. Jan-Feb, May, Oct-Nov: S, D $180; each addl $25; lower rates rest of yr. Parking lot. TV; cable (premium). Complimentary full bkfst, newspaper. Restaurant nearby. Bar. Ck-out 11 am, ck-in 3 pm. Meeting rms. Business servs avail. Concierge serv. Dry cleaning. Golf. Cr cds: A, DS, MC, V.

D ⅀ ✕

Extended Stay

★★ **RESIDENCE INN.** *3 Long Wharf Dr (06511). 203/777-5337; fax 203/ 777-2808; toll-free 800/331-3131.* Email joannedre@aol.com; www. residenceinn.com. 112 suites. May-Oct: S, D $145; lower rates rest of yr. Crib avail. Pet accepted, fee. Parking lot. Pool, whirlpool. TV; cable (premium). Complimentary continental bkfst, coffee in rms, newspaper, toll-free calls. Restaurant nearby. Ck-out noon, ck-in 3 pm. Meeting rm. Business servs avail. Dry cleaning, coin lndry. Free airport transportation. Exercise privileges. Golf. Downhill skiing. Beach access. Picnic facilities. Cr cds: A, C, D, DS, MC, V.

D ✒ ➤ ⅀ ⅏ ⅃ ⊠ ⅙

Restaurants

★ **INDOCHINE PAVILLION.** *1180 Chapel St (06511). 203/865-5033.* Specializes in spicy chicken, Saigon noodle soup, Saigon sound pancakes. Hrs: 11 am-10 pm. Closed hols. Res accepted. Lunch $4.95-$6.95; dinner $8.75-$17.95. Storefront restaurant; Asian paintings. Cr cds: A, DS, MC, V.

D

★★ **LA MIRAGE.** *111 Scrub Oak Rd (06773), N on I-91 Exit 13, 1½ mi S on Scrub Oak Rd. 203/239-1961.* Specializes in baked stuffed shrimp, prime rib. Hrs: 6-10 pm. Closed Mon; July 4, Dec 25. Res accepted. Bar. Dinner $10.95-$18.95. Entertainment. Family-owned. Cr cds: A, MC, V.

⊒

New London

(F-4) See also Groton, Mystic, Norwich, Stonington

Settled 1646 **Pop** 28,540 **Elev** 33 ft
Area code 860 **Zip** 06320
Web www.mysticmore.com
Information Connecticut's Mystic and More, 470 Bank St, PO Box 89; 860/444-2206 or 800/222-6783

New London is a seagoing community and always has been; it has one of the finest deep-water ports on the Atlantic coast. From the first days of the republic into the 20th century, whalers brought fortunes home to New London. Townspeople still welcome all ships—submarines, cutters, yachts, cruisers. Today the city's manufacturing industries include turbines, steel fabrication, high-tech products, medicines, electronics, and other products.

What to See and Do

Eugene O'Neill Theater Center. Complex includes National Playwrights Conference, National Critics Institute, National Music Theater Conference, National Puppetry Conference, National Theater Institute. Staged readings of new plays and musicals during summer at Barn Theater, Amphitheater and Instant Theater (June-Aug). W via US 1, at 305 Great Neck Rd in Waterford. Phone 860/443-5378.

Ferries. Most operate yr around.

New London-Orient Point, NY. Five auto ferries make 1½-hr trip across Long Island Sound. High-speed passenger ferry makes a 40-min trip daily. (Daily; no trip Dec 25) Departs from 2 Ferry St. Advance res required for vehicles. Phone 860/443-7394. ¢¢¢- ¢¢¢¢

New London-Block Island, RI. Auto ferry makes 2-hr crossing; one round-trip (mid-June-Labor Day). Phone 860/442-9553. (See BLOCK ISLAND, RI) Individuals, vehicles ¢¢¢¢

New London-Fishers Island, NY. Auto ferries *Race Point* and *Munnatawket* make crossing to Fishers Island; several departures daily. Departs from New London Pier, foot of State St. Phone

860/443-6851 or 516/788-7463. One way: pedestrian ¢¢; vehicle and driver ¢¢¢¢

Joshua Hempsted House. (1678) Oldest house in city; restored, 17th- and 18th-century furnishings; Hempsted family diary detailing life in the house during colonial times. (Mid-May-mid-Oct, Tues-Sun afternoons) 11 Hempstead St. Phone 860/443-7949 or 860/247-8996. ¢¢ Admission includes

Nathaniel Hempsted House. (1759) One of two surviving examples of mid-18th-century cut-stone architecture in state. Stone exterior bake oven, 7 rms with period furnishings. (Mid-May-mid-Oct, Tues-Sun afternoons) Phone 860/443-7949 or 860/247-8996.

Lyman Allyn Art Museum. Colonial silver; 18th- and 19th-century furniture; collection of dolls, doll houses; American and European paintings; Oriental and primitive art. (Tues-Sun; closed hols) 625 Williams St. Phone 860/443-2545. ¢¢

Monte Cristo Cottage. Restored boyhood home of playwright and Nobel prize winner Eugene O'Neill; houses research library and memorabilia. Multimedia presentation, literary readings. (Labor Day-Memorial Day, Mon-Fri afternoons) 325 Pequot Ave. Phone 860/443-0051 or 860/443-5378. ¢¢

Ocean Beach Park. Swimming in ocean, olympic-size pool, waterslide; sheltered pavilion, boardwalk, picnic area, concessions, miniature golf; novelty shop, amusement arcade, entertainment. (Sat before Memorial Day-Labor Day, daily; arcade open all yr) 3 mi S on Ocean Ave, on Long Island Sound. Phone 800/510-7263. Per vehicle ¢¢

Science Center of Eastern Connecticut. Regional science museum located on 415-acre Connecticut Arboretum with trees and shrubs native to the area (daily). Major exhibit on eastern Connecticut's natural and cultural history entitled "Time and the River: The Story of Land and People in the Thames River Basin"; workshops and courses; field trips, special programs; nature trail, herb garden; museum shop. (Tues-Sun; closed hols) 33 Gallows Lane, N of I-95 Exit 83. Phone 860/442-0391. ¢¢

Shaw Perkins Mansion. (1756) Naval HQ for state during Revolution; genealogical and historical library. Unique paneled cement fireplace walls. 305 Bank St. Phone 860/443-1209. ¢

Sunbeam Fleet Nature Cruises. Trips to observe humpback, minke, finback, and other whales and schools of dolphins and porpoises from aboard the 100-ft *Sunbeam Express;* naturalist will answer questions. (July-Aug, days vary) Also cruises to view bald eagles and seals (Jan-Feb). Res suggested. Departs from dock near Niantic River bridge in Waterford, W via I-95 exit 74, S on CT 161, left on CT 156 to first dock on left past bridge. Phone 860/443-7259. ¢¢¢¢

US Coast Guard Academy. (1876) 800 cadets. Visitors' Pavilion with multimedia show (May-Oct, daily). US Coast Guard Museum (daily; closed hols). Cadet parade-reviews (fall, spring, usually Fri). Barque *Eagle,* 295 ft, open to visitors (Fri-Sun, when in port; limited hrs); photography permitted. Mohegan Ave, 1 mi N on I-95 Exit 83. Phone 860/444-8270. **FREE**

Ye Antientiest Burial Ground. (1653) Huntington St. **FREE**

Ye Olde Towne Mill. (1650) Built for John Winthrop Jr. founder of New London and Connecticut's sixth governor; restored 1981; overshot waterwheel (closed to public). Mill St & State Pier Rd, under Gold Star Bridge.

Annual Events

Connecticut Storytelling Festival. Connecticut College. Nationally acclaimed artists; workshops, concerts. Phone 860/439-2764. Late Apr.

Sail Festival. City Pier. Phone 860/443-8331. One wknd July.

Motels/Motor Lodges

★ **NIANTIC INN.** *345 Main St (06357), I-95 Exit 72, approx 3 mi W on CT 156.* 860/739-5451; fax 860/691-1488. 24 suites, 3 story. Mid-May-late Oct: suites $145; each addl $30; under 12 free; lower rates rest of yr. Crib free. TV; cable. Complimentary coffee in rms. Restaurant nearby. Ck-out 11 am. Business servs avail. Refrigerators. Picnic tables. Swim-

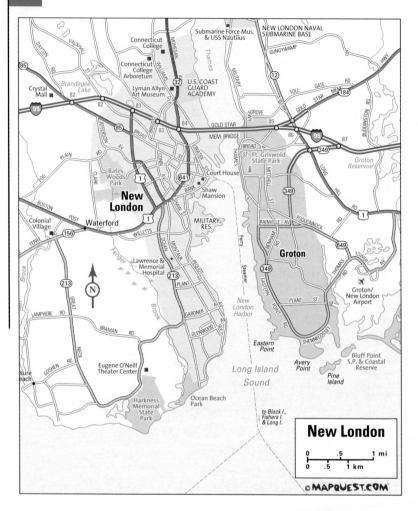

New London

© MAPQUEST.COM

ming beach opp. Cr cds: A, D, DS, MC, V.

★★★ **RADISSON.** *35 Governor Winthrop Blvd (06320), I-95 Exit 83N. 860/443-7000; fax 860/443-1239; res 800/333-3333.* 120 rms, 5 story. S, D $65-$155; each addl $20; suites $75-$165; under 18 free; wkend packages. Crib free. TV; cable (premium). Indoor pool; whirlpool. Restaurant 6:30 am-9 pm. Bar 11-1 am. Ck-out noon. Meeting rms. Business center. In-rm modem link. Bellhops. Valet serv. Sundries. Free airport, railroad station, bus depot transportation. Lighted tennis privileges. Health club privileges. Refrigerator, wet bar in most suites. Cr cds: A, DS, MC, V.

★★ **RED ROOF INN.** *707 Colman St (06320), I-95, Exit 82A. 860/444-0001; fax 860/443-7154; res 800/ THEROOF.* 108 rms, 2 story. May-Oct: S $39.99-$57; D $34.99-$77; each addl $5; under 18 free; higher rates special events; lower rates rest of yr. Crib free. Pet accepted. TV; cable (premium), VCR avail. Complimentary coffee in lobby. Restaurant nearby. Ck-out noon. Meeting rms. Business servs avail. In-rm modem link. Cr cds: A, DS, MC, V.

★ **STARLIGHT MOTOR INN.** *256 Flanders Rd (06357), 6 mi S on I-95 Exit 74, at jct CT 161. 860/739-5462; fax 860/739-0567.* 48 rms, 2 story. May-Sept: S, D $44-$99; lower rates rest of yr. TV; cable (premium), VCR

avail. Pool. Restaurant nearby. Cr
cds: A, C, D, DS, MC, V.

🏊 📶 🔥 SC

Hotel

★★ **RAMADA INN.** *248 Flanders Rd
(06357), 6 mi S on I-95 Exit 74, at jct
CT 161.* 860/739-5483; fax 860/739-
4877; toll-free 800/942-8466. www.
ramada.com. 50 rms, 2 story, 12 suites.
May-Oct: S, D $139; suites $259; each
addl $10; under 15 free; lower rates
rest of yr. Crib avail. Parking lot. Pool.
TV; cable (premium). Complimentary
continental bkfst, coffee in rms, newspaper, toll-free calls. Restaurant. Ck-
out 11 am, ck-in 3 pm. Business
center. Dry cleaning, coin lndry. Golf.
Beach access. Cr cds: A, C, D, DS, JCB,
MC, V.

D 🚶 🏊 📶 🔥 SC 🏃

B&B/Small Inn

★★ **QUEEN ANNE INN.** *265
Williams St (06320).* 860/447-2600;
fax 860/443-0857; toll-free 800/347-
8818. *Email info@queen-anne.com;
www.queen-anne.com.* 10 rms, 3 story.
S $95; D $145. Street parking. TV;
cable. Complimentary full bkfst.
Restaurant. Ck-out 11 am, ck-in 3
pm. Fax servs avail. Whirlpool. Golf.
Cr cds: A, C, D, DS, MC, V.

🚶 📶 🔥

Restaurant

★ **CONSTANTINE'S.** *252 Main St
(06357), 5 mi W on CT 156.* 860/739-
2848. Specializes in fresh seafood.
Hrs: 11 am-9 pm; Fri, Sat to 10 pm;
summer hrs vary. Closed Mon;
Thanksgiving, Dec 25. Bar. Lunch $2-
$8.50; dinner $6.95-$20.95. Child's
menu. View of Long Island Sound.
Family-owned. Cr cds: A, DS, MC, V.

D 🖪

New Preston

See also Cornwall Bridge, Kent

Pop 1,217 **Elev** 700 ft **Area code** 860
Zip 06777

Information Litchfield Hills Travel
Council, PO Box 968, Litchfield
06759; 860/567-4506

What to See and Do

**Historical Museum of Gunn Memor-
ial Library.** House built 1781; contains collections and exhibits on area
history, paintings, furnishings,
gowns, dolls, dollhouses, and tools.
(Thurs-Sun afternoons) 4 mi SW via
CT 47 at jct Wykeham Rd, on the
green in Washington. Phone
860/868-7756. **FREE**

🔳 **The Institute for American Indian
Studies.** A museum of Northeastern
Woodland Indian artifacts with permanent exhibit hall. Exhibits include
changing Native American art displays, also a replicated indoor long-
house, outdoor replicated Algonkian
village, simulated archaeological site,
and nature trail. Special programs.
(Apr-Dec, daily; rest of yr, Wed-Sun;
closed hols) 4 mi SW via CT 47 to CT
199S, then 1½ mi to Curtis Rd in
Washington. Phone 860/868-0518. ¢¢

Lake Waramaug State Park. Swimming, fishing, scuba diving; field
sports, hiking, ice-skating, camping,
picnicking. Standard hrs, fees. 5 mi N
on Lake Waramaug Rd (CT 478).
Phone 860/868-2592 or 860/868-
0220 (camping).

Annual Event

Women's National Rowing Regatta.
Lake Waramaug State Park. Mid-May.

B&Bs/Small Inns

★★★ **BOULDERS INN.** *E Shore Rd
(CT 45) (06777), 1½ mi N.* 860/868-
0541; fax 860/868-1925; toll-free
800/555-2685. *Email boulders@boul-
dersinn.com; www.bouldersinn.com.* 6
rms in inn, 2 story, 8 rms in cottages,
3 rms in carriage house. MAP: S
$200-$300; D $250-$350; each addl
$50. Restaurant (see also BOUDERS).
Bar. Ck-out 11:30 am. Business servs
avail. In-rm modem link. Tennis.
Downhill ski 20 mi; x-country ski 5
mi. Rec rm. Refrigerators, fireplace in
cottages and carriage house. Balconies. Canoes, rowboats, sailboats,
paddleboats. Bicycles. Hiking. Private
beach on lake. Cr cds: A, DS, MC, V.

🐾 📺 🎿 ⛷️ 📶 🔥

★★ **HOPKINS INN.** *22 Hopkins Rd (06777), 2 mi N on CT 45, ½ mi W.* 860/868-7295; fax 860/868-7464. 11 rms, 2 share bath, 3 story. No A/C. No rm phones. Apr-Dec: S, D $67-$150; each addl $7. Closed rest of yr. Restaurant (see also HOPKINS INN). Bar. Ck-out 11 am, ck-in 1 pm. Lake Waramaug opp, private beach. Established 1847. Cr cds: A, MC, V.

Restaurants

★★★ **BOULDERS.** *East Shore Rd, CT 45.* 860/868-0541. www.boulders inn.com. Own baking. Hrs: 6-9 pm; Sun 5-8 pm. Closed Tues; Dec 25; also Mon in winter. Res accepted; required wknds. Dinner a la carte entrees: $17.50-$24. In turn-of-the-century summer home. Cr cds: A, MC, V.

D

★★ **HOPKINS INN.** *22 Hopkins Rd.* 860/868-7295. Email besra@snet.net; www.thehopkinsinn.com. Specializes in roast duck a l'orange, sweetbreads, Wienerschnitzel. Hrs: noon-2 pm, 6-9 pm; Fri, Sat to 10 pm; Sun 12:30-8:30 pm; hrs vary off-season. Closed Mon; also Jan-Mar. Res accepted. Bar. Lunch $10-$14; dinner $18-$21. Child's menu. Terrace dining. In old inn on hill overlooking lake. Cr cds: A, DS, MC, V.

★★★ **LE BON COIN.** *US 202 (06777).* 860/868-7763. Specializes in sweetbreads, Dover sole. Hrs: noon-2 pm, 5-9 pm; Sun from 5 pm. Closed Tues, Wed; Jan 1, Memorial Day, Dec 25. Res accepted. Bar. Wine list. Lunch a la carte entrees: $4.75-$10; dinner a la carte entrees: $12.75-$19. Child's menu. Country French atmosphere. Cr cds: MC, V.

D

Niantic

(see New London)

Norfolk

See also Lakeville, Riverton

Founded 1758 **Pop** 2,060
Elev 1,230 ft **Area code** 860
Zip 06058
Information Litchfield Hills Travel Council, PO Box 968, Litchfield 06759; 860/567-4506

What to See and Do

Historical Museum. Located in former Norfolk Academy (1840). Exhibits on history of Norfolk including displays of a country store and post office as well as a children's rm with an 1879 doll house. (Late May-mid-Oct, Sat and Sun; rest of yr, by appt) On the green. Phone 860/542-5761. **FREE**

State parks.

Campbell Falls. Winding trails through woodland composed of many splashing cascades; focal point is Campbell Falls. Fishing, hiking, picnicking. 6 mi N on CT 272. Phone 860/482-1817. **FREE**

Dennis Hill. A unique summit pavilion (formerly a summer residence) is located at an elevation of 1,627 ft, providing a panoramic view of the Litchfield Hills and beyond. Picnicking, hiking, cross-country skiing. 2 mi S on CT 272. Phone 860/482-1817. **FREE**

Hatstack Mountain. A 34-ft-high stone tower at the summit, 1,716 ft above sea level, provides an excellent view of Long Island Sound, the Berkshires, and peaks in New York. A ½-mi trail leads from parking lot to tower. Picnicking, hiking. 1 mi N on CT 272. Phone 860/482-1817. **FREE**

Seasonal Event

Norfolk Chamber Music Festival. Musical performances Fri, Sat evenings in acoustically superb 1906 Music Shed located on grounds of 19th-century estate; also picnicking, indoor performances, and art gallery before concerts; informal chamber music recitals Thurs and Sat. E. B. Stoeckel Estate at jct US 44, CT 272. Phone 860/542-3000 (June-Oct) or 203/432-1966 (rest of yr). Mid-June-mid-Sep.

B&B/Small Inn

★ **MOUNTAIN VIEW INN.** *67 Litchfield Rd (CT 272) (06058), off US 44. 860/542-6991; fax 860/542-5689. Email mvinn@snet.net; www.mvinn. com.* 8 rms, 2 story, 2 suites. May-Oct: S $95; D $135; each addl $25; children $25; under 12 free; lower rates rest of yr. Crib avail. Parking lot. TV; cable. Complimentary full bkfst. Restaurant nearby. Bar. Ck-out 11 am, ck-in 3 pm. Meeting rms. Business center. Golf, 9 holes. Tennis, 2 courts. Downhill skiing. Cr cds: DS, MC, V.

Norwalk

(G-1) See also Bridgeport, Fairfield, Greenwich, Stamford

Founded 1651 **Pop** 78,331 **Elev** 42 ft
Area code 203
Information Coastal Fairfield County Tourism District, 297 West Ave, 06850; 203/854-7825 or 800/866-7925

Norwalk's growth was heavily influenced by Long Island Sound. The city evolved rapidly from an agriculturally based community to a major seaport, then to a manufacturing center known for high-fashion hats, corsets, and clocks. The Sound still plays an important part in Norwalk's development, providing beauty, recreation and, of course, oysters.

What to See and Do

Charter fishing trips. Several companies offer full- and half-day saltwater fishing excursions. Contact the Coastal Fairfield County Tourism District for details.

Ferry to Sheffield Island Lighthouse. *Island Girl* departs from Hope Dock, jct Washington and N Water St, in South Norwalk. Ferry through Norwalk Harbor to historic lighthouse (1868) on 3-acre island. Tour. Picnicking. (Memorial Day-June, wkends; July-Labor Day, daily) Phone 203/838-9444. Round trip ¢¢¢

Historic South Norwalk (SoNo). Nineteenth-century waterfront neighborhood on National Register featuring historical buildings, unique shops, art galleries, and restaurants. 1 mi SE via I-95 Exit 14N/15S, bounded by Washington, Water, N & S Main Sts, in South Norwalk. Phone 800/866-7925.

Lockwood-Mathews Mansion Museum. (1864-68) Fifty-room Victorian mansion built by financier LeGrand Lockwood; 42-ft skylit rotunda, ornamented doors and carved marble, inlaid woodwork throughout, period furnishings, musical boxes, and mechanical music exhibit; 1-hr guided tour. Victorian Ice-Cream Social (mid-July) and Antiques Show (late Oct). (Tues-Fri and Sun, limited hrs; July and Aug, also Sat; closed hols, also mid-Dec-Feb) 295 West Ave. ¢¢

Maritime Aquarium at Norwalk. Hands-on maritime museum featuring shark touch tank and harbor seal pool; 125 species, touch tanks, films on IMAX screen, boat building exhibit. Guided harbor study tours. (Daily; closed Thanksgiving, Dec 25) 2 mi S via I-95 exit 14N or 15S, at 10 N Water St. Phone 203/852-0700, ext 206. ¢¢

Mill Hill Historic Park. Complex of historic early American buildings include the Town House Museum (ca 1835), Fitch House Law Office (ca 1740), and schoolhouse (1826); also old cemetery. (May-Oct, Sun) Wall St & East Ave. Phone 203/846-0525. **FREE**

St. Paul's-on-the-Green. This 14th-century-style Gothic church contains the Seabury Altar, medieval stained glass, exquisite needlepoint, antique organ. Also here is colonial cemetery. (Daily by appt) 60 East Ave. Phone 203/847-2806. **FREE**

WPA Murals. America's largest collection of Works Progress Administration murals depict life in south eastern Fairfield County in the 1930s. (Mon-Fri; closed hols) City Hall, 125 East Ave (parking entrance, Sunset Hill Ave). Phone 203/854-7702 or 203/866-0202. **FREE**

Annual Events

Round Hill Scottish Games. Cranbury Park. Heritage celebration with Highland dancing, pipe bands, caber tossing, clan tents, Scottish and American food. Phone 203/324-1094. Late June or early July.

SoNo Arts Celebration. Washington St, in Historic South Norwalk. Juried crafts, kinetic sculpture race, entertainment, concessions, block party. First wkend Aug.

Oyster Festival. Veteran's Park, East Norwalk. Three-day event featuring entertainment, boat rides, concessions. Wkend after Labor Day.

International In-water Boat Show. Cove Marina, Calf Pasture Beach Rd. Phone 212/922-1212. Mid-Sep.

Motel/Motor Lodge

★★ **FOUR POINTS HOTEL BY SHERATON.** *426 Main Ave (06851). 203/849-9828; fax 203/846-6925; toll-free 800/329-7466.* 127 rms, 4 story. S, D $169; each addl $10; under 18 free; wkend rates. Crib free. TV; cable (premium). Coffee in rms. Restaurant 7 am-10 pm. Bar. Ck-out noon. Coin lndry. Meeting rms. Business servs avail. Sundries. Exercise equipt. Health club privileges. Cr cds: A, C, D, DS, MC, V.

Hotel

★★★ **DOUBLETREE CLUB HOTEL - NORWALK.** *789 Connecticut Ave (06854). 203/853-3477; fax 203/855-9404; toll-free 800/222-8733.* 267 rms, 8 story. S, D $149. Crib avail. Parking garage. Indoor pool. TV; cable (premium), VCR avail. Complimentary coffee in rms, newspaper, toll-free calls. Restaurant. Bar. Conference center, meeting rms. Business center. Dry cleaning, coin lndry. Exercise equipt. Golf, 18 holes. Downhill skiing. Cr cds: A, C, D, DS, ER, JCB, MC, V.

B&B/Small Inn

★★ **THE SILVERMINE TAVERN.** *194 Perry Ave (06850), jct Silvermine Ave. 203/847-4558; fax 203/847-9171.* 10 rms, 2 story, 1 suite. Sep-Oct: S $80; D $145; suites $185; each addl

$20; lower rates rest of yr. Parking lot. TV; cable (premium), VCR avail. Complimentary continental bkfst, newspaper. Restaurant noon, closed Tue. Bar. Ck-out 11 am, ck-in 4 pm. Meeting rms. Business center. Gift shop. Cr cds: A, C, D, MC, V.

Restaurants

★★ **MESON GALICIA.** *10 Wall St (06850).* 203/866-8800. Specializes in seafood, duckling, lamb. Hrs: noon-10 pm. Closed Mon; hols. Res accepted; required Fri, Sat. Bar. Lunch a la carte entrees: $9-$16; dinner a la carte entrees: $17.50-$25. Bldg once a trolley barn (1800s). Cr cds: A, C, D, DS, ER, MC, V.

★★★ **PASTA NOSTRA.** *116 Washington St (06854).* 203/854-9700. Specializes in Italian cuisine. Hrs: 5-10 pm. Closed Sun-Tues. Res required wkends. Dinner $17-$29. Cr cds: DS, MC, V.

★★ **SILVERMINE TAVERN.** *194 Perry Ave.* 203/847-4558. Specializes in New England fare, fresh seafood. Hrs: noon-3 pm, 6-10 pm; Sun 3-9 pm; Sun brunch 11 am-2:30 pm. Closed Tues; Dec 25. Res accepted. Bar. Lunch $6.50-$11.95; dinner $15.50-$24.95. Buffet: (Thurs) $17.50. Sun brunch $18.50. Child's menu. 18th-century Colonial tavern overlooking mill pond; antiques. Country store opp. Family-owned. Cr cds: A, C, D, ER, MC, V.

Norwich

(E-4) See also Groton, New London

Settled 1659 **Pop** 37,391 **Elev** 52 ft
Area code 860 **Zip** 06360
Web www.mysticmore.com

Information Connecticut's Mystic and More, 470 Bank St, PO Box 89, New London 06320; 860/444-2206 or 800/863-6569 (outside CT)

Norwich was one of the first cities chartered in Connecticut. Since the end of the 18th century it has been a leader in the industrial development of the state. Here the colony's first paper mill was opened in 1766, and the first cut nails in America were made in 1772. Cotton spinning began about 1790.

There are three distinct sections: NorwichTown to the northwest, a living museum of the past; the business section near the Thames docks; and a central residential section with many 19th-century homes.

What to See and Do

Indian Leap. The falls was a favorite resort and outpost of the Mohegan. Legend has it that a band of Narragansetts, during the Battle of Great Plains in 1643, fled from pursuing Mohegans. As they came upon the falls, many were forced to jump off the cliffs and into the chasm below, hence the name. Can be viewed from the Monroe St footbridge. Yantic Falls off Yantic St. **FREE**.

Leffingwell Inn. (1675) Scene of American Revolution councils. Museum, period rms. (Mid-May-Labor Day, Tues-Sun; rest of yr, by appt) 348 Washington St at CT Tpke Exit 81E. Phone 860/889-9440. ¢¢

Mohegan Park and Memorial Rose Garden. Picnic and play area, swimming area (June-Labor Day, daily). Rose garden; best time to visit, June-Sep. (Daily) Entrances on Judd Rd & Rockwell St. Phone 860/823-3759. **FREE**

Native American Burial Grounds. Resting place of Uncas, chief of the Mohegans (more popularly known as Mohicans) who gave the original land for the settlement of Norwich. Sachem St, off CT 32.

The Old Burying Ground. Burial place of many American Revolutionary soldiers, including French soldiers; also Samuel Huntington, signer of the Declaration of Independence. Entrance from E Town St; brochure avail at Cemetery Lane entrance.

Slater Memorial Museum and Converse Art Gallery. Roman and Greek casts, Vanderpoel Collection of Oriental Art, 17th to 20th-century American art and furnishings, chang-

ing exhibits. (Sep-June, daily; rest of yr, Tues-Sun; closed hols) Approx 1 mi N via I-395 Exit 81E, on campus of Norwich Free Academy, 108 Crescent St. Phone 860/887-2506. **Donation**

Tantaquidgeon Indian Museum. Works of Mohegan and other New England tribes, past and present; also displays of Southeast, Southwest, and Northern Plains Native Americans. (May-Oct, Tues-Sun) 5 mi S on CT 32, at 1819 Norwich-New London Tpke, in Uncasville. Phone 860/848-9145. **Donation**

Annual Events

Chelsea Street Festival. Chelsea district. Fine arts, entertainment, hayrides, children's events. Phone 860/887-2789. Third Sat May.

Blue Grass Festival. Strawberry Park. Phone 860/886-1944. Late May.

Rose-Arts Festival. Broadway & Washington Sts. Crowning of Rose Queen, arts and crafts shows, children's activities, entertainment, international food festival, flower competition, golf tournament, bicycle and road races. Ten days late June-early July.

Harbor Day. Brown Memorial Park, at waterfront. Raft race, boat rides, dunking booth, arts and crafts, entertainment. Phone 860/886-1463. Late Aug.

Historic Norwichtown Days. Norwichtown Green. Living history events, crafts, parade. Phone 860/887-2808. Second wkend Sep.

Hotel

★★ **RAMADA INN.** *10 Laura Blvd (06360). 860/889-5201; fax 860/889-1767; toll-free 800/272-6232. Email dl_mcghee@hotmail.com; www.ramada.com.* 127 rms, 6 story, 1 suite. Jun-Oct: S $149; D $159; suites $250; each addl $10; under 18 free; lower rates rest of yr. Crib avail. Parking lot. Indoor pool. TV; cable, VCR avail. Complimentary continental bkfst, coffee in rms, newspaper. Restaurant 6 am-9 pm. Bar. Ck-out 11 am, ck-in 3 pm. Meeting rms. Business servs avail. Bellhops. Dry cleaning. Exercise privileges. Golf, 18

holes. Tennis, 4 courts. Video games.
Cr cds: A, C, D, DS, JCB, MC, V.

🔲 🏃 🖌 🛏 🎿 🖼 🐾 **SC**

Resort

★ ★ ★ **THE SPA AT NORWICH
INN.** *607 W Thames St (06360), CT
32. 860/886-2401; fax 860/886-9483;
toll-free 800/-ASK-4SPA. www.
thespaatnorwichinn.com.* 65 rms in
inn, 3 story, 70 villas. May-Oct: S, D
$130-$150; suites $165-$245; lower
rates rest of yr. TV; cable, VCR avail
(movies). 2 pools; whirlpool. Restaurant. Bar 4 pm-midnight; Fri, Sat to 1
am; entertainment Fri, Sat. Ck-out
noon. Meeting rms. Business center.
Concierge serv. Railroad station
transportation. Lighted tennis, pro.
Exercise rm; sauna. Massage. Lawn
games. Built in 1929 as gathering
place for prominent persons. Cr cds:
A, DS, MC, V.

🔲 🖌 🛏 🎿 🖼 🐾

Restaurant

★ ★ **KENSINGTON ROOM.** *607 W
Thames St, CT 32. 860/886-2401.* Specializes in classic New England cuisine. Own baking, desserts. Hrs: 6
am-11 pm; Sun brunch 11:30 am-
2:30 pm. Res accepted. Bar. Bkfst buffet: $6.95- $12.95; lunch a la carte
entrees: $10.95-$14.95; dinner a la
carte entrees: $19-$29. Sun brunch
$15.95. Georgian Colonial decor;
antiques. Cr cds: A, MC, V.

🔲

Old Lyme

(F-3) *See also Essex, New London, Old
Saybrook*

Settled 1665 **Pop** 6,535 **Elev** 17 ft
Area code 860 **Zip** 06371
Web www.mysticmore.com
Information Connecticut's Mystic
and More, 470 Bank St, PO Box 89,
New London 06320; 860/444-2206 or
800/863-6569

Once, long ago, they say a sea captain lived in every house in Old
Lyme. Fortunately, a good many of
the houses are still standing on the
tree-lined streets of this sleepy old
village. Named for Lyme Regis, England, it is a summer resort and an
artists colony, one of the first on the
coast.

What to See and Do

Florence Griswold Museum. (1817)
Stately late-Georgian mansion that
housed America's most celebrated art
colony at the turn of the century.
Paintings by Willard Metcalf, Childe
Hassam, and other artists of the
colony; exhibits of 18th- and 19th-
century New England furnishings
and decorative arts. (May-Dec, Tues-
Sat, also Sun afternoons; rest of yr,
Wed-Sun afternoons; closed hols) 96
Lyme St, 1 blk W off CT Tpke Exit
70. Phone 860/434-5542. ¢¢¢-¢¢¢¢.

Rocky Neck State Park. Approx 560
acres with ½-mi frontage on Long
Island Sound. Saltwater swimming,
scuba diving, fishing; hiking, picnicking (shelters, concessions),
camping. Standard hrs, fees. 6 mi E
via I-95 Exit 72, on CT 156 in East
Lyme. Phone 860/739-5471.

B&Bs/Small Inns

★ ★ ★ **BEE AND THISTLE INN.** *100
Lyme St (06371). 860/434-1667; fax
860/434-3407; res 860/434-1667; toll-
free 800/622-4046. Email info@beeand
thistleinn.com.* 11 rms, 3 story, 1 cottage. S $75-$150; D $75-$155; each
addl $15; cottage $210. Children
over 12 yrs only. Closed 2 wks Jan.
TV in cottage. Restaurant (see also
BEE AND THISTLE INN). Rm serv
8:30-10 am. Bar noon-11 pm; guitarist Fri; harpist Sat. Ck-out 11 am,
ck-in 2 pm; cottage: ck-out noon, ck-
in 3 pm. Picnic tables. Colonial
house (1756); antique furniture. 5
acres on river. Cr cds: A, DS, MC, V.

★ ★ ★ **OLD LYME INN.** *85 Lyme St
(06371). 860/434-2600; fax 860/434-
5352; toll-free 800/434-5352. Email
olinn@aol.com; www.oldlymeinn.com.*
13 rms, 2 story. Jun-Oct: D $160;
each addl $30; under 12 free; lower
rates rest of yr. Pet accepted, some
restrictions. Parking lot. TV; cable.
Complimentary continental bkfst,
newspaper, toll-free calls. Restaurant
11 am-9 pm. Bar. Ck-out noon, ck-in
3 pm. Meeting rms. Business servs
avail. Cr cds: A, C, D, DS, MC, V.

🔲 🐾 🎿 🖼

Restaurants

★ ★ ★ **BEE AND THISTLE INN.** *100 Lyme St. 860/434-1667. Email info@beeanthistleinn.com; www.beeand thistleinn.com.* Hrs: 8 am-10 pm. Closed Tues; Dec 24, 25; also 2 wks Jan. Res accepted. Bar. Bkfst a la carte entrees: $3.50-$7; lunch a la carte entrees: $8.95-$12; dinner a la carte entrees: $19-$28. Entertainment: guitar duo Fri; harpist Sat. In Colonial house (1756); 4 fireplaces. Cr cds: A, DS, MC, V.

★ ★ ★ **OLD LYME INN.** *85 Lyme St. 860/434-2600. Email olinn@aol.com; www.oldlymeinn.com.* Own baking. Hrs: noon-2 pm, 6-9 pm; Sun brunch 11 am-3 pm. Res accepted. Bar. Wine list. Lunch $6.95-$10.95; dinner $19.95-$27.95. Entertainment: jazz guitarist Fri, Sat. Restored 1850 home; 3 fireplaces, many antiques; murals by local artist. In historic district. Cr cds: A, DS, MC, V.

D ⊣

Old Saybrook

See also Clinton, Essex, New London, Old Lyme

Settled 1635 **Pop** 9,552 **Elev** 31 ft
Area code 860 **Zip** 06475
Web www.oldsaybrook.ct.com
Information Chamber of Commerce, 146 Main St, PO Box 625; 860/388-3266; or the Connecticut Valley Tourism Commission, 393 Main St, Middletown 06457; 860/347-0028

Old Saybrook, at the mouth of the Connecticut River, is popular with summer vacationers. It is the third-oldest named community in Connecticut and is the oldest officially chartered town in the state. It was also the original site of Yale College until 1716.

What to See and Do

Fort Saybrook Monument Park. Nearly 18-acre park with remains of Fort Saybrook, first military fortification in the state; picnicking. (Daily) On College St, at Saybrook Point. **FREE.**

General William Hart House. (1767) Provincial Georgian-style, colonial residence of well-to-do New England merchant and politician; features include 8 corner fireplaces, one of which is decorated with Sadler and Green transfer-print tiles illustrating Aesop's Fables; original wainscoting; Federal-style pieces, several of which are Hart family items; antique furniture, costumes, artifacts; on grounds are re-created colonial gardens, including award-winning herb garden. (Mid-June-mid-Sep, Fri-Sun, limited hrs). 350 Main St. Phone 860/388-2622. **Donation**

Annual Events

Arts and Crafts Show. Town Green, Main St. More than 200 artists and craftspersons exhibiting. Phone 860/388-3266. Last full wkend July.

Christmas Torchlight Parade. More than 40 fife and drum corps march down Main St. Second Sat Dec.

Motels/Motor Lodges

★ ★ **HERITAGE MOTOR INN.** *1500 Boston Post Rd (06475). 860/388-3743. Email heritagemotorinn@aol.com.* 12 rms, 1 story, 1 suite. May-Sep: S $90; D $100; suites $140; each addl $7; under 12 free; lower rates rest of yr. Crib avail. Parking lot. Pool. TV; cable. Restaurant nearby. Ck-out 11 am, ck-in 3 pm. Golf, 9 holes. Tennis, 7 courts. Cr cds: A, D, DS, MC, V.
🎿 🐾 ⊠ 🔫 🦽

★ **SANDPIPER MOTOR INN.** *1750 Boston Post Rd (06475), I-95 Exit 66. 860/399-7973; fax 860/399-7387; toll-free 800/323-7973. Email innkeeper@ sandpiper; www.thesanpiper.com.* 32 rms, 3 story, 12 suites. May-Oct, Dec: S $95; D $110; suites $135; under 4 free; lower rates rest of yr. Crib avail. Parking lot. Pool. TV; cable (DSS), VCR avail. Complimentary continental bkfst, newspaper. Restaurant 12-9:30 pm. 24-hr rm serv. Ck-out 11 am, ck-in 2 pm. Business servs avail. Exercise equipt. Golf. Beach access. Supervised children's activities. Cr cds: A, DS, MC, V.
D 🐾 🎿 ⊠ 🔫 🦽

★ ★ ★ **SAYBROOK POINT INN AND SPA.** *2 Bridge St; CT 154 (06475). 860/395-2000; fax 860/388-*

1504; toll-free 800/243-0212. 62 rms, 3 story, 7 suites. May-Oct: S, D $179-$259; suites $299-$495; under 12 free; lower rates rest of yr. Crib avail. TV; cable, VCR avail (movies). 2 pools, 1 indoor; whirlpool. Restaurant 8 am-9 pm. Bar noon-1 am. Ckout noon. Coin lndry. Meeting rms. Business servs avail. In-rm modem link. Bellhops. Valet serv. Concierge serv. Gift shop. railroad station transportation. Exercise rm: sauna. Touring bicycles. Health club privileges. Refrigerators, wet bars. Balconies. Cr cds: A, C, D, DS, MC, V.

D ⇌ 🕱 ⇥ 🐾 SC

Resort

★★★ WATER'S EDGE RESORT AND CONFERANCE CENTER.
1525 Boston Post Rd (06498), 5 mi W on US 1. 860/399-5901; fax 860/399-6172; toll-free 800/222-5901. www. watersedge-resort.com. 98 rms, 3 story. May-Oct: S, D $295; suites $335; each addl $25; under 16 free; lower rates rest of yr. Crib avail. Valet parking avail. Indoor/outdoor pools, childrens pool, whirlpool. TV; cable, VCR avail. Complimentary coffee in rms, newspaper, toll-free calls. Restaurant 7 am-9 pm. Bar. Ck-out noon, ck-in 3 pm. Meeting rms. Business center. Bellhops. Dry cleaning, coin lndry. Gift shop. Exercise equipt, sauna, steam rm. Golf. Tennis, 2 courts. Downhill skiing. Beach access. Supervised children's activities. Picnic facilities. Cr cds: A, D, DS, MC, V.

D 🐾 ⇗ 🕱 ⟿ ⇌ 🕱 ✈ ⟿ 🔥 🕱

Restaurants

★★ ALEIA'S. *1687 Boston Post Rd (06475), 5 mi W on US 1, Exit 65. 860/399-5050. www.aleias.com.* Specializes in fish, pasta, steak. Hrs: 5-9 pm; Fri, Sat to 10 pm. Closed Sun, Mon. Res accepted. Bar. Dinner $13.50-$19.95. Child's menu. Entertainment: pianist Fri, Sat. Bistro atmosphere. Cr cds: A, MC, V.

D

★★ DOCK AND DINE. *College St (06475), S on Main St to the water. 860/388-4665. Email dockdinect@aol. com.* Seafood menu. Specializes in fresh seafood, steak, ribs. Hrs: 11 am-9 pm. Closed Mon, Tues (mid-Oct-

mid-Apr); Thanksgiving, Dec 24, 25. Res accepted. Bar. Lunch $5.95-$10.95; dinner $11.95-$21.95. Child's menu. Entertainment: Fri-Sun (summer). View of Sound, dock. Cr cds: A, C, D, DS, ER, MC, V.

D ⇥

★ SAYBROOK FISH HOUSE. *99 Essex Rd (06475). 860/388-4836. www.saybrookfishhouse.com.* Specializes in fresh seafood. Hrs: noon-10 pm; early bird dinner Mon-Fri 4:30-6 pm, Sat 4-5:30 pm. Closed Thanksgiving, Dec 25. Bar. Lunch $4.95-$8.95; dinner $11.95-$19.95. Child's menu. Tables covered with brown packing paper. Cr cds: A, C, D, DS, ER, MC, V.

D SC ⇥

Plainfield

(E-4) *See also Norwich, Putnam*

Settled 1689 **Pop** 14,363 **Elev** 203 ft
Area code 860 **Zip** 06374
Web www.webtravels.com/quietcorner

Information Northeast Connecticut Visitors District, PO Box 598, Putnam 06260; 860/928-1228 or 888/628-1228

What to See and Do

Plainfield Greyhound Park. Parimutuel betting. Restaurant, bar. No minors. Races every 15 min. (All yr) Phone 860/564-3391. ¢¢

Prudence Crandall House. Site of New England's first academy for black girls (1833-34). Restored 2-story frame building with changing exhibits, period furnishings, research library. Gift shop. (Wed-Sun; closed Thanksgiving; also mid-Dec-mid-Jan) W on CT 14A at jct CT 169 in Canterbury. Phone 860/546-9916. ¢

Quinebaug Valley Trout Hatchery. A 1,200-acre hatchery for brook, brown, and rainbow trout. Exhibits and displays (daily). Fishing by permit only (Mar-May, wkends and hols). Trout Hatchery Rd, at end of Cady Lane, in Central Village. Phone 860/564-7542. **FREE**

Motels/Motor Lodges

★ **PLAINFIED YANKEE MOTOR INN.** *55 Lathrop Rd (06354), I-395 Exit 87.* 860/564-4021; fax 860/564-4021. 48 rms, 2 story. Late May-mid-Oct: S $69; D $75; each addl $10; under 18 free; wkly rates; lower rates rest of yr. Crib $10. TV; cable (premium). Ck-out 11 am. Meeting rms. Business servs avail. Health club privileges. Refrigerators avail. Picnic tables. Cr cds: A, C, D, DS, MC, V.
🄳 ⛄ 🔥

★ **PLAINFIELD MOTEL.** *66 E Main St (06070), on CT 14 at I-395 Exit 89.* 860/564-2791; fax 860/564-4647. 35 rms. S, D $42-$59; each addl $10. Crib $10. Pet accepted, some restrictions; $7. TV; cable (premium). Pool. Restaurant adj 5:30 am-9 pm; wkends 24 hrs. Ck-out noon. Coin lndry. Business servs avail. Sundries. Picnic tables, grills. Cr cds: A, C, D, DS, MC, V.
🄳 🐾 🛏 ⛄ 🔥

Putnam

(D-4) *See also Plainfield*

Pop 9,031 **Elev** 290 ft **Area code** 860
Zip 06260
Web www.webtravels.com/quietcorner
Information Northeast Connecticut Visitors District, PO Box 598; 860/928-1228 or 888/628-1228

Named for Revolutionary War hero Israel Putnam, this town is situated on four small hills. Because it was located at Cargill Falls on the Quinebaug River and a railroad station served as a connecting point between New York and Boston, Putnam at one time ranked eighth in New England in the volume of freight handled.

What to See and Do

🏛 **Roseland Cottage.** (1846) Influential abolitionist publisher Henry C. Bowen's summer home. One of the most important surviving examples of a Gothic-revival "cottage," complete w/period furnishings. Located on Woodstock Hill. With its bright pink exterior and picturesque profile, it stands in contrast to the otherwise colonial character of this New England village. Surrounded by original outbldgs, incl one of the oldest indoor bowling alleys in the country; aviary. Boasts one of the oldest parterre gardens in New England, edged by 1,800 ft of dwarf boxwood. Presidents Grant, Hayes, Harrison, and McKinley attended Bowen's celebrated 4th of July parties here. (June-mid-Oct, Wed-Sun; closed hols) 7 mi NW via CT 171 & 169 in Woodstock. Phone 860/928-4074. ¢¢

Motel/Motor Lodge

★★ **KINGS INN.** *5 Heritage Rd (06260), I-395 Exit 96.* 860/928-7961; fax 860/963-2463; toll-free 800/541-7304. Email kingputnam@aol.com. 40 rms, 2 story, 1 suite. Mar-Oct: S $72; D $78; suites $120; each addl $8; under 12 free; lower rates rest of yr. Crib avail. Pet accepted. Parking lot. Pool. TV; cable, VCR avail. Complimentary continental bkfst, coffee in rms, newspaper. Restaurant 11am-1am. Bar. Ck-out 11 am, ck-in 2 pm. Meeting rms. Business servs avail. Dry cleaning. Exercise privileges. Golf, 18 holes. Hiking trail. Picnic facilities. Cr cds: A, D, DS, MC, V.
🐾 🏃 🛏 🏌 ⛷ ⛄ 🔥 SC

B&B/Small Inn

★★★ **INN AT WOODSTOCK HILL.** *94 Plaine Hill Rd (06267), W on CT 171 to CT 169, then 1 mi N.* 860/928-0528; fax 860/928-3236. Email innwood@snet.net; www.woodstockhill.com. 22 rms, 3 story, 7 suites. May-Oct: S $82-$145; D $90-$155; each addl $12; suites $100-$155; lower rates rest of yr. TV; cable (premium), VCR avail. Complimentary continental bkfst. Restaurant 11 am-2 pm, 5:30-9 pm; Sun to 7:30 pm; closed Mon. Limited rm serv. Bar. Ck-out 11 am, ck-in 2 pm. Business servs avail. Concierge serv. Lawn games. Fireplaces. Library, sitting rm. Historic building (1815). Cr cds: A, D, MC, V.
🄳 ⛄ 🔥

Ridgefield

(F-1) *See also Danbury, New Canaan, Norwalk, Stamford*

Settled 1709 **Pop** 20,919 **Elev** 749 ft
Area code 203 **Zip** 06877
Web www.ridgefield.net

Information Chamber of Commerce, 9 Bailey Ave, PO Box 191; 203/438-5992 or 800/FUN-1708; or Housatonic Valley Tourism Commission, Box 406, 72 West St, Danbury 06813; 203/743-0546 or 800/841-4488 (outside CT)

Ridgefield is unusual among communities settled in the 19th century because it has a main street of boulevard width—99 feet lined with tree-shaded houses. On this street in 1777, Benedict Arnold (still a revolutionary) set up barricades and fought the Battle of Ridgefield against General Tyron.

What to See and Do

Aldrich Museum of Contemporary Art. Changing exhibits, sculpture garden (daily; free). Museum (Tues-Sun afternoons). 258 Main St. Phone 203/438-4519. ¢¢

Keeler Tavern. Restored 18th-century tavern, stagecoach stop, home. Once Revolutionary patriot HQ; British cannonball still embedded in wall. Summer home of architect Cass Gilbert. Period furnishings, gardens, tours, museum shop. (Wed, Sat, and Sun afternoons; closed Jan) 132 Main St. Phone 203/438-5485. ¢¢

B&Bs/Small Inns

★★★ **THE ELMS INN.** *500 Main St (06877). 203/438-2541; fax 203/438-2541. Email www.innkeeper@elmsinn; www.elmsinn.com.* 15 rms, 3 story, 5 suites. Crib avail. TV; cable. Complimentary continental bkfst, newspaper, toll-free calls. Restaurant nearby, closed Mon. Ck-out noon, ck-in 1 pm. Dry cleaning. Golf. Cr cds: A, C, D, MC, V.
🛉 ▧ 🐾

★★★ **STONEHENGE INN.** *US 7 (06877), 1 mi S of jct CT 35 and US 7.*

203/438-6511; fax 203/438-2478. 12 rms, 2 story, 4 suites. S $90; D $145; suites $165. Valet parking avail. TV; cable (premium), VCR avail. Complimentary continental bkfst, newspaper. Restaurant 6-11 pm, closed Mon. Bar. Ck-out 11 am, ck-in 1 pm. Meeting rms. Business servs avail. Concierge serv. Dry cleaning. Golf. Tennis. Hiking trail. Cr cds: A, D, DS, MC, V.
D 🛉 🐾 ▧ 🐾

★★★ **WEST LANE INN.** *22 West Ln (06877). 203/438-7323; fax 203/438-7325. Email westlanein@aol.com; www.westlaneinn.com.* 17 rms, 3 story. Jun-Jul, Sep-Oct: S $120; D $185; each addl $10; under 1 free; lower rates rest of yr. Crib avail. Parking lot. TV; cable, VCR avail. Complimentary continental bkfst, coffee in rms, newspaper, toll-free calls. Restaurant noon-10 pm, closed Mon. Ck-out 11 am, ck-in 2 pm. Meeting rm. Business center. Concierge serv. Dry cleaning. Exercise privileges. Golf, 18 holes. Tennis, 4 courts. Cr cds: A, D, DS, MC, V.
▧ 🛉 🐾 🛉 🛉 ▧ 🐾 🛉

Restaurants

★★★ **THE ELMS.** *500 Main St, CT 35. 203/438-9206.* Specializes in game, lobster, seafood. Own baking. Hrs: 11 am-9 pm. Closed Mon; Easter, Dec 25. Res required (dinner). Bar. Wine cellar. Lunch $7.95-$14.95; dinner $23-$27. Child's menu. Oldest continuously run inn in Ridgefield; established 1799. Family-owned. Cr cds: A, D, DS, MC, V.

★★★ **STONEHENGE.** *35 Stonehenge Rd. 203/438-6511.* Specializes in fresh brook trout, rack of lamb, game. Own baking. Hrs: 6-11 pm; Sun brunch noon-2:30 pm. Closed Mon. Res accepted; required wkends. Wine cellar. Dinner $14-$28. Complete meals: $46. Sun brunch $26. Valet parking. Restored home (1853) near pond. Cr cds: A, MC, V.
SC

Riverton

See also Hartford, Norfolk

Pop 500 (est) **Elev** 505 ft
Area code 860 **Zip** 06065
Information Litchfield Hills Travel
Council, PO Box 968, Litchfield
06759; 860/567-4506

Lambert Hitchcock, one of America's greatest chairmakers, built his
original chair factory here in 1826.
His famous stenciled chairs and cabinet furniture are now prized pieces.
The old factory is still in operation,
and some antiques are on display.
Today, the grand colonial houses
and tree-lined streets of this New
England village are filled with
emporiums and shops.

What to See and Do

Hitchcock Museum. Collection of
original 18th-century furnishings by
Hitchcock and others, displayed in
historic church (1829). (Apr-Dec,
Thurs-Sun) CT 20, center of village.
Phone 860/738-4950. **Donation**

Solomon Rockwell House. (1813)
Antebellum house built by early
industrialist; Hitchcock chairs,
antique clocks, Revolutionary and
Civil War memorabilia, wedding
gown collection, melodeon. (June-
Oct, Thurs-Sun afternoons) 3 mi SW
on CT 20, 2 mi S on CT 8, at 225
Prospect St in Winsted. Phone
860/379-8433. ¢

Annual Event

Riverton Fair. 1800s country village
fair, held since 1909; chopping, sawing, and pie-eating competitions; displays; art and crafts; entertainment.
Second wkend Oct.

Simsbury

(D-2) *See also Avon, Farmington, Hartford*

Settled 1660 **Pop** 22,023 **Elev** 181 ft
Area code 860 **Zip** 06070
Web www.grhartfordcvb.com
Information Greater Hartford
Tourism District, 1 Civic Center
Plaza, Hartford 06103; 860/728-6789
or 800/446-7811

Hopmeadow Street, in this characteristic New England village, is so
named because hops were grown in
the area to supply early distillers.
Simsbury's handsome Congregational Church was built in 1830.

After it was founded, Simsbury
developed steadily until 1676, when
the settlers fled in terror during King
Philip's War. Scouts returning three
days later found the settlement in
ashes. Soon the village was reconstructed and activity was again stimulated by the discovery of copper at
East Granby (then part of Simsbury).

What to See and Do

Massacoh Plantation-Simsbury Historic Center. Restored Victorian carriage house. Furnished buildings and
exhibits represent 3 centuries of
community life; industrial and agricultural tools, old meetinghouse, icehouse, first copper coins struck in
America (1737). Tours. (Sun-Fri afternoons) 800 Hopmeadow St. Phone
860/658-2500. ¢¢

Simsbury Farms. Recreational facility
covering 300 acres; picnicking, iceskating, tennis, swimming, golf,
cross-country skiing, nature and family fitness trails, volleyball, paddle
tennis. (Daily; some activities seasonal) Fees for most activities. 100
Old Farms Rd. Phone 860/658-3836
or 860/658-3200.

Motel/Motor Lodge

★ **IRON HORSE INN.** *969 Hopmeadow St (06070), CT 10. 860/658-
2216; fax 860/651-0822; toll-free
800/245-9938. Email jgogu745102@*

aol.com; www.ironhorseofsimsbury.com.
26 rms, 3 story, 1 suite. Apr-Dec: S
$79; D $89; suites $160; lower rates
rest of yr. Crib avail. Pet accepted,
some restrictions, fee. Parking lot.
Pool. TV; cable. Complimentary
newspaper. Restaurant. Ck-out 11
am, ck-in 1 pm. Business servs avail.
Coin lndry. Exercise privileges,
sauna. Golf. Tennis. Downhill skiing.
Cr cds: A, MC, V.

⬛⬛⬛⬛⬛⬛⬛⬛⬛⬛ SC

Hotel

★★★ **SIMSBURY INN.** *397 Hopmeadow St (06070). 860/651-5700; fax
860/651-8024; toll-free 800/634-2719.
Email si@simsburyinn.com; www.
simsburyinn.com.* 91 rms, 3 story, 7
suites. Apr-Jun, Sep-Nov: S, D $169;
lower rates rest of yr. Crib avail, fee.
Parking lot. Indoor pool, lap pool,
whirlpool. TV; cable (premium), VCR
avail. Complimentary continental
bkfst, newspaper, toll-free calls.
Restaurant 11:30 am-9:30 pm, closed
Mon. Bar. Ck-out 11 am, ck-in 3 pm.
Meeting rms. Business center. Bellhops. Dry cleaning, coin lndry. Free
airport transportation. Exercise privileges. Golf. Tennis. Downhill skiing.
Bike rentals. Hiking trail. Picnic facilities. Cr cds: A, D, DS, MC, V.

⬛⬛⬛⬛⬛⬛⬛⬛⬛⬛⬛⬛

B&B/Small Inn

★★ **SIMSBURY 1820 HOUSE.** *731
Hopmeadow St (06070). 860/658-
7658; fax 860/651-0724; toll-free 800/
879-1820. www.simsbury1820house.
com.* 32 rms, 3 story. S, D $115-$185;
each addl $10. TV. Complimentary
continental bkfst. Restaurant 5:30-
8:30 pm. Ck-out 11 am, ck-in 3 pm.
Business servs avail. Private patios,
balconies. Built 1820; antiques.
Veranda. Cr cds: A, DS, MC, V.

⬛⬛⬛

Restaurants

★★ **CHART HOUSE.** *4 Hartford Rd
(06070), 2 mi S on CT 10, at jct CT
185. 860/658-1118. www.chart-house.
com.* Specializes in steak, prime rib,
fresh seafood. Own dressings. Hrs: 5-
9 pm; Sun from 4 pm; early-bird dinner 5-6:30 pm. Res accepted. Bar.
Dinner $14-$32. Child's menu. Former tavern (1780); period furnish-

ings, antiques. Cr cds: A, C, D, DS,
ER, MC, V.

⬛

★ **ONE-WAY FARE.** *4 Railroad St
(06070). 860/658-4477.* Specializes in
chili, homemade soups, hamburgers.
Hrs: 11 am-midnight; Sun brunch
10:30 am-3 pm. Closed Labor Day,
Thanksgiving, Dec 25. Bar. Lunch
$4.50-$16.50; dinner $4.50-$16.50.
Sun brunch $3.95-$16.50. Old brick
railroad station (1874); railroad
memorabilia. Cr cds: A, MC, V.

⬛⬛

⬛

Southbury

See also Danbury, Waterbury, Woodbury

Settled 1673 **Pop** 15,818 **Elev** 257 ft
Area code 203 **Zip** 06488
Information Litchfield Hills Travel
Council, PO Box 968, Litchfield
06759; 860/567-4506

What to See and Do

Bullet Hill Schoolhouse. One of the
oldest school buildings in the country, estimated to have been built in
1789, in use until 1942; some experts
believe it antedates the American
Revolution; early schooling exhibits.
(April-May, limited hours; rest of yr,
by appt) ½ mi E of I-84 Exit 15, on
US 6. Phone 203/264-8781. **Donation**

State parks.

Southford Falls. Approx 120 acres.
Former site of Diamond Match Co.
Stream and pond fishing, ice skating; bridle trail nearby, scenic hiking along Eight Mile River,
picnicking. (Daily) 4 mi SE via CT
67 & 188. Phone 203/264-5169. ¢

Kettletown. The name of this park
is derived from the time when settlers first arrived and purchased
this tract of land from the Native
Americans for one brass kettle.
Swimming, fishing; hiking, sports
field, picnicking, camping. Nature
trail for the disabled. Standard hrs,
fees. 5 mi S via I-84, Exit 15. Phone
203/264-5169.

Hotel

★★★ **HILTON SOUTHBURY HOTEL.** *1284 Strongtown Rd (06488). 203/598-7600; fax 203/598-7591; res 800/445-8667. Email stbsh_6m@ hilton.com; www.hilton.com.* 198 rms, 3 story. S $95-$140; suites $125-$315; under 12 free; ski plans; wkend, hol rates. Pet accepted. TV; cable (premium), VCR avail. Indoor pool; whirlpool, poolside serv. Coffee in rms. Restaurant 6:30 am-10:30 pm. Bar. Ck-out noon. Convention facilities. Business servs avail. In-rm modem link. Bellhops. Valet serv. Sundries. Exercise equipt; sauna. Cr cds: A, C, D, DS, MC, V.

Restaurant

★★ **TARTUFO.** *900 Main St S (06488). 203/262-8001. www.tartufos. com.* Specializes in fettuccine with truffles, risotto alla Piemontese. Hrs: noon-2:30 pm, 5-9 pm; Sun brunch noon-2:30 pm. Closed hols. Res accepted. Bar. Lunch a la carte entrees: $6.50-$14; dinner a la carte entrees: $14.95-$23. Sun brunch $18.95. Child's menu. Entertainment: jazz Thurs-Sat. Country setting. Cr cds: A, DS, MC, V.

Southington

(see Meriden)

Stafford Springs

See also Enfield, Storrs, Windsor; also see Springfield, MA

Settled 1719 **Pop** 4,100 **Elev** 591 ft **Area code** 860 **Zip** 06076

Information Connecticut Northcentral Tourism & Visitors Bureau, 111 Hazard Ave, Enfield 06082; 860/763-2578 or 800/248-8283

Stafford Springs is known for its production of woolen fabrics, printed circuits, and industrial filters.

What to See and Do

Civilian Conservation Corps Museum. New Deal program devoted to state and national parks is commemorated. Video and photograph exhibits, equipment and uniforms, camp memorabilia. (Late May-Aug, afternoons) 166 Chestnut Hill Rd (CT 190). Phone 860/684-3430. **Donation**

Mineral Springs. Located here are the springs that gave the town its name. In 1771, John Adams, future president of the United States, came to bathe in the springs after hearing of their healing effects. Spring St, between Grace Episcopal Church and the library. **FREE**

Seasonal Event

Stafford Motor Speedway. CT 140W. A ½-mi paved oval track for stock car racing. Phone 860/684-2783. Apr-Sep.

Stamford

(G-1) See also Greenwich, New Canaan, Norwalk

Settled 1641 **Pop** 108,056 **Elev** 10 ft **Area code** 203

Information Greater Stamford Convention & Visitors Bureau, 733 Summer St, 06901; 203/359-4761

Stamford is a corporate headquarters, manufacturing and research center as well as a residential suburb of New York City. More than 20 *Fortune* 500 corporations are located in this area. An assortment of marinas and beaches provide recreation on Long Island Sound.

What to See and Do

First Presbyterian Church. (1958) Contemporary building shaped like a fish, designed by Wallace Harrison; glass by Gabriel Loire of Chartres, France; 56-bell carillon tower (1968).

Summer concerts (July, Thurs night, Sun morning; June and Aug, Sun morning). 1101 Bedford St. Phone 203/324-9522. **FREE**

University of Connecticut-Bartlett Arboretum. Collections of dwarf conifers, rhododendrons, azaleas, wildflowers, perrenials, and witches brooms; ecology trails and swamp walk are within the natural woodlands surrounding the gardens. Grounds (daily). 151 Brookdale Rd, off High Ridge Rd, 1 mi N of Merritt Pkwy (CT 15) Exit 35. Phone 203/322-6971. **FREE**

Whitney Museum of American Art at Champion. Local branch of Whitney Museum of New York offers changing exhibits, gallery talks (Tues, Thurs, and Sat), concerts, and other related programs and activities. (Tues-Sat) Atlantic St & Tresser Blvd, downtown. Phone 203/358-7630 or 203/358-7652. **FREE**

Annual Event

Festival of Arts. Mill River Park. Various exhibits of performing and visual arts. Late June.

Motel/Motor Lodge

★ **SUPER 8.** *32 Grenhart Rd (06902), I-95 Exit 6. 203/324-8887; fax 203/964-8465; res 800/800-8000. Email stamfordsuper8@usa.com; www.super8.com.* 98 rms, 4 story, 1 suite. May-Aug: S $79; D $89; suites $99; lower rates rest of yr. Crib avail. TV; cable (DSS). Complimentary continental bkfst, newspaper. Restaurant nearby. Ck-out 11 am, ck-in 2 pm. Fax servs avail. Cr cds: A, D, DS, ER, MC, V.

🖼️ 🐾 SC

Hotels

★★ **HOLIDAY INN SELECT.** *700 Main St (06901), I-95 Exit 8. 203/358-8400; fax 203/358-8872; toll-free 800/408-7640. www.holiday-inn.com.* 385 rms, 10 story. S, D $99-$139; suites $400-$500; under 12 free; wkend rates. Crib free. TV; cable (premium), VCR avail. Indoor pool. Coffee in rms. Restaurants 6-11 am, 5-11 pm. Bar noon-midnight; wkends to 1:30 am. Ck-out noon. Coin lndry. Convention facilities. Business center. Gift shop. Garage. Free railroad station transportation. Exercise

equipt. Health club privileges. Some refrigerators. Microwaves avail. Luxury level. Cr cds: A, C, D, DS, JCB, MC, V.

D 🖼️ 🏋️ 🖼️ 🐾 SC 🏃

★★★ **SHERATON STANFORD HOTEL.** *2701 Summer St (06905). 203/359-1300; fax 203/359-6474; res 888/627-8315. www.sheraton.com.* 409 rms, 5 story, 36 suites. Sep-Dec: S, D $260; suites $650; each addl $15; under 17 free; lower rates rest of yr. Crib avail. Parking garage. Indoor pool, lap pool, whirlpool. TV; cable (premium), VCR avail. Complimentary coffee in rms, newspaper. Restaurant 6 am-11 pm. 24-hr rm serv. Bar. Ck-out noon, ck-in 3 pm. Conference center. Business center. Bellhops. Concierge serv. Dry cleaning, coin lndry. Gift shop. Exercise equipt, sauna, steam rm. Golf. Picnic facilities. Video games. Cr cds: A, C, D, DS, MC, V.

D 🐾 🏋️ 🖼️ 🖼️ 🏃 🖼️ 🐾 SC 🏃

★★★ **STAMFORD MARRIOTT HOTEL.** *2 Stamford Forum (06901). 203/357-9555; fax 203/324-6897; res 800/732-9689; toll-free 800/228-9290.* 506 rms, 17 story. S, D $145-$164; each addl $10; suites $250-$440; wkend rates. Crib free. Covered parking $3/day. TV; cable (premium), VCR avail. Indoor/outdoor pool; whirlpool, poolside serv. Restaurant 6:30 am-2 pm, 5-10 pm; Sat, Sun 7 am-10 pm. Bars; entertainment. Ck-out noon. Coin lndry. Convention facilities. Business center. In-rm modem link. Gift shop. Beauty shop. Exercise rm; sauna, steam rm. Game rm. Luxury level. Cr cds: A, C, D, DS, MC, V.

D 🖼️ 🏋️

★★★ **THE WESTIN STAMFORD.** *1 1st Stamford Pl (06901), I-95 Exit 7 N. 203/967-2222; fax 203/351-1836. www.ittsheraton.com.* 480 rms, 10 story. S, D $145; each addl $20; suites $200-$500; wkend rates. Crib free. Garage: self-park free, valet parking $6. TV; cable (premium), VCR avail. Indoor pool; whirlpool, poolside serv. Coffee in rms. Restaurants 6 am-10:30 pm. Bar 11:30-1:00 am. Ck-out noon. Convention facilities. Business center. In-rm modem link. Concierge serv. Gift shop. Tennis. Exercise equipt. Health club privileges. Some bathrm phones;

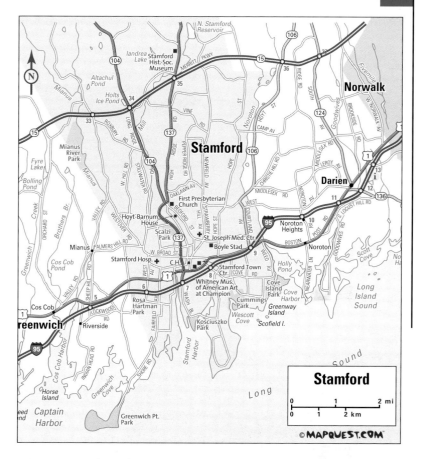

Stamford

microwaves avail. Cr cds: A, C, D, DS, ER, JCB, MC, V.

🄳 🏃 🏊 🏋 🚭 🔥 SC 🏌

Extended Stay

★★ **STAMFORD SUITES.** *720 Bedford St (06901), I-95 Exit 7.* 203/359-7300; fax 203/359-7304. Email *admin@stamford.newcastlehotels.com; www.stamfordsuites.com.* 45 suites. July-Oct: S $229; suites $229; each addl $15; under 12 free; lower rates rest of yr. Crib avail. Parking garage. Pool, lap pool, childrens pool, whirlpool. TV; cable (DSS). Complimentary continental bkfst, coffee in rms, newspaper, toll-free calls. Restaurant nearby. Ck-out noon, ck-in 3 pm. Business center. Bellhops. Concierge serv. Dry cleaning. Exercise privi-

leges. Golf. Tennis, 2 courts. Beach access. Cr cds: A, C, D, DS, MC, V.

🄳 🏃 🏌 🏊 🏋 🚭 🔥 🏌

Restaurants

★ **CRAB SHELL.** *46 Southfield Ave (06902), at Stamford Landing.* 203/967-7229. *www.mv.com/users/lindaknight/crabshell.* Specializes in grilled seafood, Maryland blue crab, ribs. Hrs: 11 am-11 pm. Bar. Lunch $6.95-$12.95; dinner $8.95-$29.95. Child's menu. Parking. Waterfront dining. Cr cds: A, D, MC, V.

🄳 ⬛

★★ **GIOVANNI'S.** *1297 Long Ridge Rd (06903), S on Merritt Pkwy, Exit 34, E at Stoplight.* 203/322-8870. *www.giovannis.com.* Specializes in steak and chops, seafood. Own pasta. Hrs: 11:30 am-3 pm, 4-10 pm; Sat from 4 pm; Sun 1-9 pm. Closed Thanksgiving,

Dec 25. Bar. Lunch $6-$11; dinner $12-$27.95. Child's menu. Three dining rms with semiformal atmosphere; lobster tank in lobby. Family-owned. Cr cds: A, C, D, DS, ER, MC, V.

★★ **IL FALCO.** *59 Broad St (06902), I-95 Exit 7.* 203/327-0002. Specializes in pasta, veal, fresh seafood. Hrs: 11 am-11 pm. Closed Sun; some major hols. Res accepted. Bar. Lunch a la carte entrees: $9.50-$15.50; dinner a la carte entrees: $11.50-$22. Parking. Pleasant atmosphere. Cr cds: A, D, MC, V.

★★ **LA BRETAGNE.** *2010 W Main St (US 1) (06902), I-95 Exit 5.* 203/324-9539. *Email labretagne@snet.net.* Specializes in seafood, veal, duck. Hrs: noon-10 pm. Closed Sun; most major hols. Res accepted; required Sat. Bar. Lunch $9-$18; dinner $21-$28. Child's menu. Parking. Cr cds: A, D, MC, V.

Covered bridge, Southford Falls State Park

★★ **LA HACIENDA.** *222 Summer St (06901), I-95 Exit 8.* 203/324-0577. Specializes in fresh fish, game. Hrs: 11 am-midnight. Closed Thanksgiving, Dec 25. Res accepted. Bar. Lunch $8.95-$14.95; dinner $10.95-$17.95. Parking. Multi-level dining. Southwestern decor. Cr cds: A, D, MC, V.

★ **MEERA INDIAN CUISINE.** *227 Summer St (06901), I-95 N Exit 8.* 203/975-0477. Specializes in tandoori chicken, chicken tikka kebab. Salad bar. Hrs: 11 am-11 pm. Res accepted. Bar. Lunch a la carte entrees: $5-

$12.95. Buffet: $8.95; dinner a la carte entrees: $5-$12.95. Indian decor. Cr cds: A, D, MC, V.

Stonington

See also Groton, Norwich, Mystic, New London, Old Lyme, Old Saybrook; also see Westerly, RI

Settled 1649 **Pop** 16,919 **Elev** 7 ft
Area code 860 **Zip** 06378
Web www.mysticmore.com

Information Connecticut's Mystic and More, 470 Bank St, PO Box 89, New London 06320; 860/444-2206 or 800/863-6569 (outside CT)

Until their defeat at Mystic Fort in 1637, the Pequot dominated the area around Stonington. In 1649, the first European settlers came here from Rehoboth, Massachusetts. Connecticut and Massachusetts both claimed ownership of the territory. In 1662, permanent control was granted to Connecticut by charter from King Charles II. Three years later the area was officially called Mystic, and in 1666 the name was changed to Stonington (which includes Stonington Borough).

The conclusion of the King Philip War in 1676 effectively ended the Native American threat in southern New England. The local economy, based on farming, shipping, and manufacturing, thrived. Prior to the Civil War, whaling and sealing expeditions left Stonington's port at regular intervals. After the war, maritime interests flourished as Stonington served as the connecting point for rail and steamer service to New York City. Today this maritime heritage is represented by a commercial fishing fleet and recreational boating.

What to See and Do

Old Lighthouse Museum. First government-operated lighthouse in Connecticut (1823); exhibits include Stonington-made firearms, stoneware, ship models, whaling gear, China trade objects, folk art, local artifacts. Children's gallery. Visitors can climb the tower for a panoramic view of Long Island Sound. (May-June and Sep-Oct, Tues-Sun; July-Aug, daily; rest of yr, by appt) 7 Water St. Phone 860/535-1440 (summer) or 860/535-1492 (winter). ¢

B&B/Small Inn

★ ★ **RANDALL'S ORDINARY.** *Rte 2 (06359), N of I-95 Exit 92. 860/599-4540; fax 860/599-3308; toll-free 877/599-4540. Email info@randalls ordinary.com; www.randallsordinary. com.* 13 rms, 2 story, 5 suites. Jul-Oct: S, D $165; suites $350; each addl $15; lower rates rest of yr. Crib avail. TV; cable (premium). Complimentary newspaper. Restaurant 7 am-9 pm. Bar. Ck-out 11 am, ck-in 2 pm. Meeting rms. Business center. Concierge serv. Gift shop. Golf. Hiking trail. Picnic facilities. Cr cds: A, MC, V.

Storrs

(E-4) *See also Hartford, Manchester, Stafford Springs*

Pop 12,198 **Elev** 600 ft **Area code** 860 **Zip** 06268
Web www.webtravels.com/quiet corner
Information Northeast Connecticut Visitors District, PO Box 598, Putnam 06260; 860/928-1228 or 888/628-1228

What to See and Do

Ballard Institute and Museum of Puppetry. Features changing exhibits from collection of more than 2,000 puppets. Gives visitors appreciation of puppetry as artform. (Mid-Apr-mid-Nov, Fri and Sat) 6 Boum Pl. Phone 860/468-4605. **FREE**

Caprilands Herb Farm. More than 30 different theme gardens using herbs, spices, and wild grasses; 18th-century farm building; lunchtime lectures (Apr-Dec; fee). Tea program (Sun). Basket and bookshops. (Daily) 8 mi SW via US 44 to 534 Silver St in Coventry. Phone 860/742-7244. **FREE**

Nathan Hale Homestead. (1776) Country-Georgian-style structure built by Nathan's father, Richard. Restored, many original furnishings. (Mid-May-mid-Oct, afternoons) 8 mi SW via US 44 to 2299 South St in Coventry. Phone 860/742-6917 or 860/247-8996. ¢¢

University of Connecticut. (1881) 26,200 students. On campus are state's largest public research library, art galleries, museums, animal barns, biological and floricultural greenhouses (tours; free). (See SEASONAL EVENT) SE on I-84 Exit 68, then S on CT 195. Phone 860/486-3530 or 860/486-2000; for campus tours phone 860/486-4866. Also here are

  William Benton Museum of Art. Permanent collection including American and European paintings, sculpture, prints, and drawings; changing exhibits. (Tues-Sun; closed hols and between exhibitions) 245 Glenbrook Rd. Phone 860/486-4520. **FREE**

  Connecticut State Museum of Natural History. Exhibits on Native Americans, mounted birds of prey, honey bees, sharks, minerals. (Thurs-Mon, afternoons) Wilbur Cross Bldg. Phone 860/486-4460. **FREE**

Seasonal Event

Connecticut Repertory Theatre. Univ of Connecticut, Harriet S. Jorgensen Theatre. Musicals, comedies, and dramas. Nightly. Phone 860/486-4226. July and Sep-May exc Jan.

Stratford

(F-2) *See also Bridgeport, Fairfield, Milford, Norwalk*

Settled 1639 **Pop** 49,389 **Elev** 25 ft
Area code 203 **Zip** 06497

Information Chamber of Commerce, 10 Middle St, PO Box 999, 06601-0999; 203/335-3800

A fine port on the Housatonic River, Stratford has been a hub of shipbuilding and industry for more than three centuries.

What to See and Do

Boothe Memorial Park. Former Boothe homestead (1663-1949) on 30 acres; unusual, historical buildings; Boothe home and carriage house (mid-May-late Oct, Tues-Sun). Americana Museum, blacksmith shop, architecturally eccentric "technocratic cathedral," flower gardens, rose garden, picnicking, playgrounds, park (daily). Other buildings (Memorial Day-late Oct, daily) Main St. Phone 203/381-2068 or 203/385-4085. **FREE**

Captain David Judson House. (ca 1750) Restored and furnished Colonial house, period furnishings and crafts, slave quarters, tool display, local history exhibits. (Late May-Oct, Wed, Sat, Sun; closed Memorial Day, July 4) 967 Academy Hill. Phone 203/378-0630. ¢ Admission includes

> **Catharine B. Mitchell Museum.** Changing and permanent exhibits depict history of the Stratford area 1639-1830; local memorabilia. (Same hrs as Judson House)

Motel/Motor Lodge

★ **HONEYSPOT LODGE.** *360 Honeyspot Rd (06497). 203/375-5666; fax 203/378-1509.* 93 rms, 2 story. S $32.95-$55; D $39.95-$60; each addl $8; under 18 free. Crib avail. TV; cable (premium). Pool. Ck-out noon. Meeting rms. Business servs avail. Cr cds: A, C, D, DS, MC, V.

Hotel

★★ **RAMADA INN STRATFORD.** *I-95 (06615), near Igor I. Sikorsky Memorial Airport. 203/375-8866; fax 203/375-2482; res 800/2RAMADA.* 145 rms, 6 story. S, D $85-$100; each addl $10; under 18 free; wkend rates. Crib free. TV; cable (premium). Indoor pool. Restaurant 6:30 am-2 pm, 5-10 pm; Sun 7 am-9 pm. Bar. Ck-out noon. Meeting rms. Business

servs avail. Free airport, railroad station, bus depot transportation. Health club privileges. Cr cds: A, DS, MC, V.

Terryville

(see Bristol)

Vernon

(E-3) *See also Hartford, Manchester, Windsor*

Pop 29,841 **Elev** 350 ft **Area code** 860 **Zip** 06066
Web www.travelfile.com/get/ghtd
Information Greater Hartford Tourism District, 234 Murphy Rd, Hartford 06114; 860/244-8181 or 800/793-4480

Motel/Motor Lodge

★★ **QUALITY INN AND CONFERENCE CENTER.** *51 Hartford Tpke (06066). 860/646-5700; fax 860/646-0202; res 800/221-2222; toll-free 800/235-4667.* 127 rms, 2 story. S $49.95-$79; D $79-$125; under 18 free. Crib free. TV; cable (premium). Pool. Continental bkfst. Restaurant 11:30 am-10 pm, Sat, Sun, hols 7 am-11 pm. Rm serv 11:30 am-9 pm; Sun from noon. Bar 11:30 am-midnight; Fri, Sat to 1 am. Ck-out 11 am. Coin lndry. Meeting rms. Business servs avail. In-rm modem link. Valet serv. Sundries. Par-3 golf; miniature golf. Health club privileges. Game rm. Refrigerators. Cr cds: A, C, D, DS, MC, V.

B&B/Small Inn

★★ **TOLLAND.** *63 Tolland Green (06084), approx ¾ mi N on I-84, Exit 68, N on CT 195. 860/872-0800; fax 860/870-7958; toll-free 877/465-0800. Email tollinn@ntplx.net; www.tolland inn.com.* 5 rms, 2 story, 2 suites. S $85; D $95; suites $150. Parking lot. TV; cable, VCR avail. Complimentary full bkfst, toll-free calls. Restaurant nearby. Business servs avail. Concierge serv. Gift shop. Golf. Tennis. Cr cds: A, C, D, DS, MC, V.

Restaurant

★ **REIN'S NEW YORK-STYLE DELI.**
435 Hartford Tpke (06066). 860/875-1344. Specializes in corned beef, lox and bagels, pastrami. Hrs: 7 am-midnight. Bar. Bkfst $3.75-$8.95; lunch, dinner $3.75-$8.95. Child's menu. New York-style delicatessen. Cr cds: A, C, MC, V.

🅳

Washington

Area code 860

B&B/Small Inn

★ ★ ★ ★ ★ **THE MAYFLOWER INN.**
118 Woodbury Rd / Rte 47 (06793), 4 mi W. 860/868-9466; fax 860/868-1497. Email inn@mayflowerinn.com; www.mayflowerinn.com. This 1920-inn reflects its name in the 25 bedrooms and suites as well as the public areas. Guests will feel like royalty with the nine acres of flowers, fully equipped fitness center, tennis courts, oil paintings, Oriental rugs, clocks, and antiques. The elegantly decorated guestrooms feature four post beds, marble bathrooms with deep tubs and mahogany wainscoting. 17 rms, 3 story, 8 suites. S, D $450; suites $850. Parking lot. Pool. TV; cable (premium), VCR avail. Complimentary full bkfst, newspaper. Restaurant 7:30 am-9 pm. 24-hr rm serv. Bar. Ck-out 1 pm, ck-in 3 pm. Meeting rm. Business servs avail. Concierge serv. Dry cleaning. Gift shop. Exercise rm, sauna, steam rm. Golf. Tennis. Downhill skiing. Bike rentals. Cr cds: A, MC, V.

Waterbury

(E-2) *See also Bristol, Meriden, New Britain*

Settled 1674 **Pop** 108,961 **Elev** 290 ft
Area code 203
Information Waterbury Region Convention & Visitors Bureau, 21 Church St, 06702-2106; 203/597-9527

Waterbury, fourth-largest city in Connecticut, was once an important manufacturing center for brass-related products. Today, high-technology manufacturing and the banking industry dominate the economy. Waterbury's location near major highways provides quick and direct access to all Eastern cities.

What to See and Do

Brass Mill Center. More than 1 million-sq-ft indoor mall with many shops, food court, and 12-screen movie theater. (Daily) I-84 Exit 22 or 23, at 495 Union St. Phone 203/755-5003.

Mattatuck Museum. Industrial history exhibit, decorative arts, period rms, paintings and prints by Connecticut artists. (July-Aug, Tues-Sat; rest of yr, Tues-Sun; closed hols) 144 W Main St. Phone 203/753-0381.
FREE

Quassy Amusement Park. More than 30 different rides and activities set against Lake Quassapaug; beach, swimming, boating; miniature golf, petting zoo, picnicking, concession. (Late May-Labor Day, daily; Apr-late May and Labor Day-Oct, wkends) 5 mi W on I-84 Exit 17, on CT 64 in Middlebury. Phone 203/758-2913. All-day pass ¢¢¢; Parking fee ¢¢

Motel/Motor Lodge

★ **KNIGHTS INN.** *2636 S Main St (06706), I-84 Exit 19 to CT 8 Exit 29. 203/756-7961; fax 203/754-6642.* 84 rms, 2 story. S $39.95-$45.95; D $45.95-$55.95; each addl $8; under 18 free. Crib free. Pet accepted; $8. TV; cable (premium). Pool. Restaurant open 24 hrs. Bar. Ck-out 11 am.

Meeting rms. Business center. Valet serv. Sundries. Balconies. Cr cds: A, C, D, DS, MC, V.

Hotel

★★ **SHERATON WATERBURY.** *3580 E Main St (06705). 203/573-1000; fax 203/573-1349; toll-free 800/541-0469. Email sales@waterbury.new castlehotels.com; www.sheraton.com.* 279 rms, 4 story, 10 suites. Sep-Oct: S, D $109; each addl $10; under 18 free; lower rates rest of yr. Crib avail. Pet accepted. Parking lot. Indoor pool, whirlpool. TV; cable (premium), VCR avail. Complimentary coffee in rms, newspaper, toll-free calls. Restaurant. Bar. Conference center, meeting rms. Business servs avail. Bellhops. Concierge serv. Dry cleaning, coin lndry. Gift shop. Exercise equipt, sauna, steam rm. Golf. Downhill skiing. Cr cds: A, C, D, DS, MC, V.

B&B/Small Inn

★★ **HOUSE ON THE HILL BED & BREAKFAST.** *92 Woodlawn Terrace (06710). 203/757-9901. Email mv houseonthehill@aol.com.* 3 story, 4 suites. Suites $165; each addl $25. Pet accepted, some restrictions. Parking lot. TV; cable, VCR avail. Complimentary full bkfst, coffee in rms, newspaper. Restaurant nearby. Ck-out 11 am, ck-in 3 pm. Meeting rms. Exercise privileges. Golf, 18 holes. Tennis, 8 courts. Picnic facilities. Cr cds: A, C, D, DS, MC, V.

Westport

(G-1) *See also Bridgeport, Fairfield, Norwalk, Stamford*

Settled 1648 **Pop** 24,410 **Elev** 78 ft
Area code 203 **Zip** 06880
Web www.bcnnews.com/westport/chamber

Information Chamber of Commerce, 180 Post Rd E, PO Box 30; 203/227-9234

Westport is a fashionable community on Long Island Sound 45 miles from New York City. Well-known writers and many successful actors, illustrators, and corporate and advertising executives make their homes here. Westport is surrounded by wooded hills and has three municipal beaches and a state park on the Sound.

Annual Events

Westport Handcrafts Fair. Staples High School Field House. Features 100 crafts artisans. Phone 203/227-9318. Memorial Day wkend.

Antique Dealers Outdoor Show and Sale. Phone 203/227-9234. Early Sep.

Seasonal Events

Westport Country Playhouse. Broadway and pre-Broadway presentations by professional companies. Mon-Sat nights; matinees Wed and Sat; children's shows Fri. Phone 203/227-4177. Mid-June-mid-Sep. 25 Powers Court, on Post Rd E.

Levitt Pavilion for the Performing Arts. Jesup Green, on the Saugatuck River. Nightly free outdoor performances of classical, jazz, pop, rock; dance, children's series. Phone 203/226-7600. Late June-late Aug.

Hotels

★★★★ **THE INN AT NATIONAL HALL.** *2 Post Rd W (06880). 203/221-1351; fax 203/221-0276; toll-free 800/628-4255. Email info@innatnational hall.com; www.innatnationalhall.com.* Fifteen rooms and suites, uniquely decorated with vibrant colors and charming European style, are housed in this 1873 Italianate structure on the Saugatuck River. Several chambers boast soaring, two-story ceilings with loft bedrooms, crystal chandeliers and beautiful river views. Todd English's sleek Miramar restaurant adds a final excellent touch to this National Hall Historic District property with innovative Mediterranean cuisine. 8 rms, 3 story, 7 suites. May-Oct: S, D $350; suites $500; each addl $50; lower rates rest of yr. Crib avail. Valet parking avail. TV; cable (premium), VCR avail, CD avail. Complimentary continental bkfst, coffee in rms, newspaper, toll-free calls. Restaurant 6 pm-10 pm, closed Mon. Ck-out noon, ck-in 3 pm. Meeting rm. Business servs avail. Bellhops. Concierge serv. Dry cleaning. Gift shop. Exercise privileges. Golf. Cr cds: A, C, D, MC, V.

★★ **WESTPORT INN.** *1595 Post Rd E (06880). 203/259-5236; fax 203/254-8439; toll-free 800/446-8997. Email westportinn@snet.net; www. westportinn.com.* 114 rms, 2 story, 2 suites. Mar-Oct: S $154; D $164; suites $389; each addl $10; under 16 free; lower rates rest of yr. Crib avail. Pet accepted, some restrictions, fee. Parking garage. Indoor pool, whirlpool. TV; cable, VCR avail. Complimentary coffee in rms, newspaper, toll-free calls. Restaurant 6 am-9 pm. Bar. Ck-out noon, ck-in 3 pm. Meeting rms. Business servs avail. Dry cleaning. Exercise equipt, sauna. Golf. Cr cds: A, C, D, DS, MC, V.

B&B/Small Inn

★★ **THE INN AT LONGSHORE.** *260 Compo Rd S (06880). 203/226-3316; fax 203/227-5344.* 10 rms, 3 story, 3 suites. Apr-Oct: S $110; D $150; suites $175; lower rates rest of yr. Crib $15. TV; cable. Pool. Playground. Complimentary coffee in rms. Complimentary continental bkfst. Restaurant 11:30 am-2:30 pm, 5:30-11 pm. Ck-out noon, ck-in 3 pm. Business servs avail. Lighted tennis. Golf, 18 holes, greens fee $22, pro, putting green, driving range. Built as a private estate in 1890; overlooks Long Island Sound. Cr cds: A, MC, V.

Restaurants

★★★ **COBB'S MILL INN.** *12 Old Mill Rd (06880), NW on CT 57, 4 mi N of Merritt Pkwy (CT 15). 203/227-7221. www.cobbsmillinn.com.* Specializes in steak, chops, seafood. Hrs: 11 am-11 pm; early-bird dinner Mon-Thurs 5-6:30 pm. Res accepted. Bar. Lunch a la carte entrees: $6-$11; dinner a la carte entrees: $19-$27. Valet parking. In 200-yr-old grist and lumber mill; Colonial decor, pewter dis-

play. Overlooks waterfall, lake. Cr cds: A, C, D, DS, ER, MC, V.

★ **CONNOLLY'S.** *221 Post Rd W (06880), in Westbank Shopping Center. 203/226-5591.* Specializes in seafood, steak. Salad bar. Hrs: 11 am-10 pm. Closed hols. Bar. Lunch $4.50-$10.95; dinner $5.50-$18.95. Child's menu. Cr cds: A, DS, MC, V.

★★★★ **MIRAMAR.** *2 Post Road W. 203/222-2267.* Housed in the Inn at National Hall is another star establishment conceived by celebrity-chef Todd English. The innovative Mediterranean menu is offered in an elegantly understated room of monochromatic tones and sophisticated ambiance. Thankfully, the service is friendly and knowledge and the kitchen delivers fantastic, elaborate compositions that please both the eye and palate. Mediterranean rustic yet refined menu. Specializes in top sirloin. Hrs: 5:30-10 pm, Sun 5-9 pm. Closed Mon. Res required. Wine list. Dinner $19-$32. Cr cds: A, D, MC, V.

★★ **NISTICO'S RED BARN.** *292 Wilton Rd (06880), at Merritt Pkwy (CT 15) Exit 41. 203/222-9549. www. redbarnrestaurant.com.* Specializes in Angus beef, rack of lamb, prime rib. Hrs: 11 am-11 pm; Sun brunch sittings 11:30 am and 1:30 pm. Closed Dec 24, 25. Res accepted. Lunch $5.95-$12.95; dinner $14.95-$29.95. Sun brunch $16.95. Child's menu. Entertainment: pianist Fri, Sat. Valet parking Sat. Cr cds: A, DS, MC, V.

Wethersfield

(E-3) *See also Avon, Hartford, Windsor*

Settled 1634 **Pop** 25,651 **Elev** 45 ft
Area code 860 **Zip** 06109
Web www.wethhist.org

Information Wethersfield Historical Society, 150 Main St; 860/529-7656

Wethersfield, "the most ancient towne in Connecticut," has a rich heritage. Settled by a group of Massachusetts colonists, it became the commercial center of the Connecticut River communities and an important post in the trade between the American colonies and the West Indies. Agriculture, especially corn, rye, and, later, the famous red onion, was the source of Wethersfield's trade. During the years of the American Revolution, notable figures, such as George Washington and Count de Rochambeau, came to Wethersfield and decided upon plans that became part of US history. Many existing buildings date from the American Revolution.

With the birth and development of the railroad and the shift of trade to the coastal villages, Wethersfield's importance as an industrial and commercial center declined.

What to See and Do

Buttolph-Williams House. (ca 1700) Restored building contains fine collection of pewter, delft, fabrics, period furniture. (May-Oct, Wed-Mon, limited hrs) 249 Broad St, at Marsh St. Phone 860/529-0460, 860/529-0612, or 860/247-8996. ¢

◪ **Dinosaur State Park.** While excavating the site of a new building, a stone slab bearing the 3-toed tracks of dinosaurs, which roamed the area 200 million yrs ago, was discovered. Construction was halted, and a 65-acre area was designated a state park. Eventually, more than 2,000 prints were unearthed. A geodesic dome was set up over parts of the trackway to protect the find. Visitors are able to examine the crisscrossing tracks and view a skeletal cast and life-size models of the area's prehistoric inhabitants. Nature trails, picnicking. Exhibit center (Tues-Sun; closed Jan 1, Thanksgiving, Dec 25). Park (daily). 3 mi S via I-91 Exit 23, off West St in Rocky Hill. Phone 860/529-8423. ¢

First Church of Christ, Congregational United Church of Christ. Church established 1635; the Meetinghouse (1761; restored 1973) is the third one to stand on or near this site. (Mon-Fri; also by appt) Main & Marsh Sts. Phone 860/529-1575. **FREE**

Hurlburt-Dunham House. Georgian house updated in Italianate style.

Rich in decoration, including original Rococo Revival wallpapers, painted ceilings, and a varied collection of furniture. (Mid-Mar-mid-May, mid-Oct-Dec 25, Sat and Sun; mid-May-mid-Oct, Thurs-Sun) 212 Main St. Phone 860/529-7656. ¢¢

Webb-Deane-Stevens Museum. Consists of three 18th-century houses that stand at the center of old Wethersfield: the Joseph Webb house (1752), the Silas Deane house (1766), and the Isaac Stevens house (1788). The houses have been restored and are furnished with objects to reflect the different ways of life of their owners—a merchant, a diplomat, and a tradesman; also flower and herb gardens. (May-Oct, Wed-Mon; rest of yr, Fri-Sun) 211 Main St. Phone 860/529-0612. Combination ticket. ¢¢¢

Wethersfield Museum. Changing exhibit galleries; permanent Wethersfield exhibit. (Tues-Sun) Keeney Memorial Cultural Center, 200 Main St. Phone 860/529-7161. ¢

Motel/Motor Lodge

★★ **RAMADA INN.** *1330 Silas Deane Hwy (06109). 860/563-2311; fax 860/529-2974; toll-free 800/228-2828.* 112 rms, 4 story. S, D $42-$59; under 18 free. Crib free. Pet accepted. TV; cable (premium), VCR avail. Complimentary continental bkfst. Restaurant adj 11 am-10 pm. Bar; entertainment Fri, Sat. Ck-out noon. Coin lndry. Meeting rms. Business servs avail. In-rm modem link. Downhill ski 20 mi. Health club privileges. Some in-rm whirlpools. Cr cds: A, C, D, DS, MC, V.

🄳 ➶ 🗺 🖼 🔥 SC

Windsor

(E-3) *See also Enfield, Hartford, Manchester*

Settled 1633 **Pop** 27,817 **Elev** 57 ft
Area code 860 **Zip** 06095

Information Chamber of Commerce, 261 Broad St, PO Box 9, 06095-0009; 860/688-5165; or the Tobacco Valley Convention & Visitors Dis-

trict, 111 Hazard Ave, Enfield
06082; 860/763-2578

Windsor was first settled by members
of an expeditionary group from the
original Plymouth Colony. A farming
center since the 17th century, it is
only nine miles north of Hartford.
The village is divided by the Farmington River; there is a green and
many colonial houses on each side
of the river.

What to See and Do

Connecticut Trolley Museum. Unlimited 3-mi ride on vintage trolleys;
static displays. (Memorial Day-Labor
Day, daily; rest of yr, wkends) 58
North Rd. Phone 860/627-6540. ¢¢¢

Oliver Ellsworth Homestead. (1781)
Home of one of five men who
drafted the Constitution; third Chief
Justice of the United States and one
of the first senators from Connecticut; Washington and Adams visited
the house. Restored to period; many
original Ellsworth furnishings. (May-
Oct, Tues, Wed, Sat) 778 Palisado
Ave. Phone 860/688-8717. ¢¢

The First Church in Windsor. (1630)
United Church of Christ Congregational. Classic Georgian-style architecture (1794); cemetery (1644)
adjacent. Request key at church
office, 107 Palisado Ave. (Daily) 75
Palisado Ave. Phone 860/688-7229.
FREE

Windsor Historical Society. Walking
tours of the Lt. Walter Fyler House
(1640) and the Dr. Hezekiah Chaffee
House (1765); period costumes and
furnishings; Puritan cemetery. (Apr-
Oct, Tues-Sat; Nov-Mar, Mon-Fri) 96
Palisado Ave. Phone 860/688-3813. ¢¢

Motels/Motor Lodges

★★ COURTYARD BY MARRIOTT.
*1 Day Hill Rd (06095). 860/683-0022;
fax 860/683-1072.* 149 rms, 2 story. S,
D $119; suites $139; wkend rates.
Crib free. TV; cable (premium), VCR
avail. Indoor pool; whirlpool. Complimentary coffee in rms. Restaurant
6:30-10:30 am, 5-10 pm; Sat-Sun 7-
11 am, 5-10 pm. Ck-out 1 pm. Coin
lndry. Meeting rms. Business servs
avail. In-rm modem link. Valet serv.
Sundries. Exercise equipt. Game rm.
Refrigerator in suites. Balconies. Mar-

ble courtyard, gazebo. Cr cds: A, C,
D, DS, MC, V.

★★ RESIDENCE INN. *100 Dunfey
Ln (06095). 860/688-7474; fax 860/
683-8457.* 96 kit. suites, 2 story. S, D
$129-$159. Crib avail. Pet accepted;
$100. TV; cable (premium), VCR
avail. Pool; whirlpool. Complimentary continental bkfst. Complimentary coffee in rms. Ck-out noon.
Coin lndry. Meeting rm. Business
servs avail. In-rm modem link. Valet
serv. Free airport transportation.
Lawn games. Some fireplaces. Picnic
tables, grill. Cr cds: A, C, D, DS, JCB,
MC, V.

Windsor Locks

(D-3) *See also Enfield, Hartford, Windsor; also see Springfield, MA*

Pop 12,358 **Elev** 80 ft **Area code** 860
Zip 06096
Information Chamber of Commerce,
PO Box 257; 860/623-9319

What to See and Do

New England Air Museum. One of
the largest and most comprehensive
collections of aircraft and aeronauti-
cal memorabilia in the world. More
than 80 aircraft on display including
bombers, fighters, helicopters, and
gliders dating from 1909-present era;
movies; jet fighter cockpit simulator.
Tour guides. (Daily; closed Thanksgiving, Dec 25) Adj to Bradley International Airport, 3 mi SW via I-91
Exit 40, W on CT 20 to CT 75, follow
signs. Phone 860/623-3305. ¢¢¢

Noden-Reed House and Barn.
Housed in 1840 house and 1825
barn are antique sleigh bed, 1871
taffeta evening dress, 1884 wedding
dress, antique quilts, kitchen utensils, 1880s newspapers and periodicals. (May-Oct, Sun afternoons) 58
West St. Phone 860/627-9212. **FREE**

Old New Gate Prison. Site of a copper mine (1707) converted to Revolutionary prison for Tories (1775-82)
and a state prison (until 1827); self-
guided tour of underground caverns

where prisoners lived. (Mid-May-Oct, Wed-Sun) 8 mi W on US 91 to Exit 40; in East Granby at jct Newgate Rd and CT 120. Phone 860/653-3563 or 860/566-3005. ¢¢

Trolley Museum. Exhibits include more than 50 antique trolley cars from 1894-1949; operating trolleys take visitors on 3-mi ride through countryside; electric passenger trains also operate some wkends. (Memorial Day-Labor Day, daily; rest of yr, Sat, Sun, and hols; closed Thanksgiving, Dec 25) In East Windsor at 58 North Rd (CT 140); from Windsor Locks proceed NE on I-91 to exit 45, then ¾ mi E on CT 140 (for clarification of directions, phone ahead). Phone 860/627-6540. ¢¢¢ On grounds is

Connecticut Fire Museum. Collection of fire engines and antique motorcoaches from 1856-1954. (June-Aug, daily; Apr-May and Sep-Oct, Sat and Sun) Phone 860/623-4732. ¢

Hotels

★★★ DOUBLETREE HOTEL. 16 Ella Grasso Tpke (06096), near Hartford Bradley Intl Airport. 860/627-5171; fax 860/627-8405; toll-free 800/222-8733. 200 rms, 5 story. S, D $69-$119; each addl $10; suites $150-$195; under 18 free; wkend rates; higher rates Dec 31. Crib avail. TV; cable (premium), VCR avail. Indoor pool; whirlpool. Restaurant 6:30 am-10 pm. Bar 4-11 pm. Ck-out noon. Coin lndry. Meeting rms. Business servs avail. Bellhops. Valet serv. Free airport, railroad station transportation. Exercise equipt; sauna. Game rm. Cr cds: A, C, D, DS, ER, JCB, MC, V.

★★ HOMEWOOD SUITES BY HILTON. 65 Ella Grasso trpke (06096), near Hartford Bradley Intl Airport. 860/627-8463; fax 860/627-9313; res 800/225-5466. Email wndlk01@ hws-hotel.com. 132 kit. suites, 2-3 story. S, D $99-$140. Crib free. Pet accepted, some restrictions; $10. TV; cable, VCR (movies). Pool. Complimentary continental bkfst. Complimentary coffee in rms. Restaurant nearby. Ck-out noon. Coin lndry. Business center. In-rm modem link. Valet serv. Sundries. Gift shop. Free airport, railroad station transportation. Exercise equipt. Lawn games.

Picnic tables. Cr cds: A, C, D, DS, MC, V.

★★ SHERATON BRADLEY. 1 Bradley International Airport (06096), at Hartford Bradley Intl Airport. 860/627-5311; fax 860/627-9348; res 800/325-3535; toll-free 877/422-5311. Email jdzen@sheratonbradley.com; www.sheraton.com/bradleyairport. 236 rms, 10 story, 1 suite. Jan-Jun, Sep-Nov: S, D $205; suites $500; lower rates rest of yr. Crib avail, fee. Pet accepted, some restrictions, fee. Valet parking avail. Indoor pool. TV; cable (premium). Complimentary coffee in rms, newspaper. Restaurant 6:30 am-1 pm. Bar. Ck-out noon, ck-in 3 pm. Meeting rms. Business center. Bellhops. Concierge serv. Dry cleaning. Gift shop. Exercise equipt, sauna, steam rm. Golf, 18 holes. Tennis. Downhill skiing. Supervised children's activities. Video games. Cr cds: A, C, D, DS, JCB, MC, V.

Woodbury

See also Bristol, Danbury, Waterbury

Pop 1,290 **Elev** 264 ft **Area code** 203 **Zip** 06798
Web www.litchfieldhills.com
Information Litchfield Hills Travel Council, PO Box 968, Litchfield 06759; 860/567-4506

What to See and Do

Flanders Nature Center. Large conservation area with woodland hiking trails, wildlife marshes, wildflower trails. Self-guided tour; special events including maple syrup demonstration (Mar). (Daily) Church Hill & Flanders Rd. Phone 203/263-3711. FREE

Glebe House and Gertrude Jekyll Garden. (ca 1770) Minister's farmhouse or *glebe*, where Samuel Seabury was elected America's first Episcopal bishop in 1783; restored with 18th-century furnishings, original paneling; garden designed by Gertrude Jekyll. (Apr-Nov, Wed-Sun afternoons; rest of yr, by appt) On Hollow Rd off US 6. Phone 203/263-2855. ¢¢

B&B/Small Inn

★ **CURTIS HOUSE.** *506 Main St S (06798). 203/263-2101; fax 203/263-6265.* 18 rms, 12 with bath, 12 A/C, 3 story. S $33.60-$72; D $61.60-$123.20; each addl $10. TV in most rms; cable (premium). Restaurant (see also CURTIS HOUSE). Bar. Ck-out 11 am, ck-in 1 pm. Downhill/x-country ski 5 mi. Oldest inn in state (1754). Cr cds: DS, MC, V.

🐾 🎿

Restaurants

★★ **CAROLE PECK'S GOOD NEWS CAFE.** *694 Main St S (06798). 203/266-4663.* Specializes in wok-seared shrimp, free-range rotisserie chicken. Hrs: 11 am-10 pm. Closed Tues; hols. Res accepted. Bar. Lunch a la carte entrees: $5.95-$9.95; dinner a la carte entrees: $11.50-$20. Child's menu. Entertainment: jazz Sat. Modern cafe with changing artwork. Cr cds: A, D, MC, V.

[D]

★ **CURTIS HOUSE.** *506 Main St S. 203/263-2101.* Hrs: noon-9 pm. Closed Dec 25. Res accepted hols. Bar. Lunch complete meals: $7.50-$11.50; dinner complete meals: $13.50-$20. Child's menu. 3 dining rms. Family-owned. Cr cds: DS, MC, V.

[D] 🍴

MAINE

Here are the highest tides (28 feet in Passamaquoddy Bay), the tastiest potatoes, and the tartest conversation in the country. Flat Yankee twang and the patois of French Canadians make Maine's speech as salty as its sea. Hunters, anglers, canoeists, and campers appreciate its 6,000 lakes and ponds, and summer vacationers enjoy its 3,500 miles of seacoast even though the water is a bit chilly.

Downeasters brag about the state's temperature range from -46° to 105°F as well as its famous lobsters. Paper and allied products are the chief manufactured products; machine tools, electronic components, and other metal products are important. Food canning and freezing are major industries. Potatoes, blueberries, poultry, eggs, dairy products, and apples are leading farm crops.

Population: 1,253,040
Area: 30,995 square miles
Elevation: 0-5,268 feet
Peak: Mount Katahdin (Piscataquis County)
Entered Union: March 15, 1820 (23rd state)
Capital: Augusta
Motto: I lead
Nickname: Pine Tree State
Flower: Pine Cone and Tassel
Bird: Chickadee
Tree: Eastern White Pine
Fair: August 9-18, 2001, in Skowhegan
Time Zone: Eastern
Website: www.visitmaine.com

Maine's first settlement (1604) was on St. Croix Island; it lasted one winter. Another early settlement was established near Pemaquid Point. The short-lived Popham Colony, at the mouth of the Kennebec River, built America's first transatlantic trader, the *Virginia*, in 1607. Until 1819 Maine was a part of Massachusetts. It was admitted to the Union in 1820.

Most of Maine's 17.6 million acres of forest land is open to public recreational use including more than 580,000 acres owned by the state. For more information about recreational use of public and private forest land, contact the Maine Bureau of Public Lands, 207/287-3061, or the Maine Forest Service at 207/287-2791.

When to Go/Climate

Maine is a large state affected by several different weather patterns. Coastal temperatures are more moderate than inland temperatures, and fog is common in spring and fall. In general, winters are cold and snowy. Summers are filled with warm, sunny days and cool, clear nights. Fall's famous "nor'easters" can bring high tides, gale-force winds, and huge amounts of rain to the coastal areas.

AVERAGE HIGH/LOW TEMPERATURES (°F)

CARIBOU

Jan 19/-2	May 62/40	Sep 64/43
Feb 23/7	June 72/49	Oct 52/34
Mar 34/15	July 77/55	Nov 38/24
Apr 47/29	Aug 74/52	Dec 42/6

PORTLAND

Jan 30/11	May 63/43	Sep 69/49
Feb 33/14	June 73/52	Oct 59/38
Mar 41/25	July 79/58	Nov 47/30
Apr 52/34	Aug 77/57	Dec 35/18

Parks and Recreation Finder

Directions to and information about the parks and recreation areas below are given under their respective town/city sections. Please refer to those sections for details.

NATIONAL PARK AND RECREATION AREAS

Key to abbreviations. I.H.S. = International Historic Site; I.P.M. = International Peace Memorial; N.B. = National Battlefield; N.B.P. = National Battlefield Park; N.B.C. = National Battlefield and Cemetery; N.C.A. = National Conservation Area; N.E.M. = National Expansion Memorial; N.F. = National Forest; N.G. = National Grassland; N.H.P. = National Historical Park; N.H.C. = National Heritage Corridor; N.H.S. = National Historic Site; N.L. = National Lakeshore; N.M. = National Monument; N.M.P. = National Military Park; N.Mem. = National Memorial; N.P. = National Park; N.Pres. = National Preserve; N.R.A. = National Recreational Area; N.R.R. = National Recreational River; N.Riv. = National River; N.S. = National Seashore; N.S.R. = National Scenic Riverway; N.S.T. = National Scenic Trail; N.Sc. = National Scientific Reserve; N.V.M. = National Volcanic Monument.

Place Name	Listed Under
Acadia N.P.	same
St. Croix Island I.H.S.	CALAIS
White Mountain N.F.	BETHEL

STATE PARK AND RECREATION AREAS

Key to abbreviations. I.P. = Interstate Park; S.A.P. = State Archaeological Park; S.B. = State Beach; S.C.A. = State Conservation Area; S.C.P. = State Conservation Park; S.Cp. = State Campground; S.F. = State Forest; S.G. = State Garden; S.H.A. = State Historic Area; S.H.P. = State Historic Park; S.H.S. = State Historic Site; S.M.P. = State Marine Park; S.N.A. = State Natural Area; S.P. = State Park; S.P.C. = State Public Campground; S.R. = State Reserve; S.R.A. = State Recreation Area; S.Res. = State Reservoir; S.Res.P. = State Resort Park; S.R.P. = State Rustic Park.

Place Name	Listed Under
Aroostook S.P.	PRESQUE ISLE
Baxter S.P.	same
Camden Hills S.P.	CAMDEN
Cobscook Bay S.P.	MACHIAS
Crescent Beach S.P.	PORTLAND
Ferry Beach S.P.	SACO
Fort Knox S.P.	BUCKSPORT
Fort O'Brien Memorial S.P.	MACHIAS
Fort Point S.P.	BUCKSPORT
Grafton Notch S.P.	BETHEL
Lake St. George S.P.	BELFAST
Lamoine S.P.	ELLSWORTH
Mount Blue S.P.	RUMFORD
Popham Beach S.P.	BATH
Rangeley Lake S.P.	RANGELEY
Reid S.P.	BATH
Roque Bluffs S.P.	MACHIAS
Sebago Lake S.P.	SEBAGO LAKE
Two Lights S.P.	PORTLAND

Water-related activities, hiking, biking, various other sports, picnicking and visitor centers, as well as camping, are avail in many of these areas. Most state parks and historic sites are open seasonally, 9 am-sunset; Popham Beach, John

CALENDAR HIGHLIGHTS

FEBRUARY

Kennebunk Winter Carnival (Kennebunk). Snow sculpture contests, snow palace moonwalk, magic show, ice-skating party, chili and chowder contests, children's events. Phone 207/985-6890.

MAY

Maine State Parade (Lewiston). Downtown Lewiston and Auburn. Maine's largest parade; over 30,000 people represent 60 communities. Phone Androscoggin County Chamber of Commerce, 207/783-2249.

JUNE

Windjammer Days (Boothbay Harbor). Old schooners that formerly sailed the trade routes and now cruise the Maine coast sail en masse into harbor. Waterfront food court, entertainment, street parade, children's activities. Phone 207/633-2353.

JULY

Great Whatever Family Festival Week (Augusta). More than 60 events incl tournaments, carnival, barbecue, parade, and fireworks. Festivities culminate with the canoe and kayak regatta on the Kennebec River between Augusta and Gardiner. There are also canoe and kayak races. Phone Kennebec Valley Chamber of Commerce, 207/623-4559.

Bangor Fair (Bangor). One of the country's oldest fairs. Horse racing, exhibits, stage shows. Phone 207/942-9000.

Festival de Joie (Lewiston). Central Maine Civic Center. Celebration of Lewiston and Auburn's Franco-American heritage. Features ethnic song, dance, cultural activities, traditional foods. Phone Androscoggin County Chamber of Commerce, 207/783-2249.

Schooner Days and North Atlantic Blues Festival (Rockland). Three-day festival celebrating Maine's maritime heritage; features Parade of Schooners, arts, entertainment, concessions, fireworks; blues bands and club crawl. Phone 207/596-0376.

AUGUST

Maine Lobster Festival (Rockland). A 5-day event centered around Maine's chief marine creature, with a huge tent cafeteria serving lobster and other seafood. Parade, harbor cruises, maritime displays, bands, entertainment. Phone 207/596-0376.

Skowhegan State Fair (Skowhegan). One of the oldest fairs in the country (1818). Mile-long midway, stage shows, harness racing; contests, exhibits. Phone 207/474-2947.

DECEMBER

Christmas by the Sea (Camden). Celebration of holiday season with musical entertainment, horse-drawn wagon rides, Holiday House Tour, Santa's arrival by lobsterboat. Phone 207/236-4404.

Paul Jones Memorial, and Reid are open yr-round. Most areas have day-use and/or parking fees, $1-$2.50/person; annual pass, $40/vehicle, $20/individual. Camping May-Oct (areas vary), nonresidents $11-$17/site, residents $9-$13/site; reservation fee $2/night. Camping reservations may be made by mail to the Bureau of Parks and Lands, Station #22, Augusta 04333, Attn Reservation Clerk; in person at the office of the Bureau of Parks and Lands in Augusta; by phone, 207/287-3824 or 800/332-1501 (ME). Maine historic sites fee $1.50-$2.

Pets on leash only in most parks. No dogs on beaches (or at Sebago Lake campground). For information contact the Bureau of Parks and Lands, Maine Dept of Conservation, State House Station #22, Augusta 04333; 207/287-3821.

SKI AREAS

Place Name	Listed Under
Camden Snow Bowl	CAMDEN
Carter's X-C Ski Center	BETHEL
Lonesome Pine Trails	FORT KENT
Lost Valley Ski Area	AUBURN
Mountain Jefferson Ski Area	LINCOLN
Saddleback Ski & Summer Lake Preserve	RANGELEY
Shawnee Peak at Pleasant Mountain Ski Area	BRIDGTON
Sugarloaf/USA Ski Area	KINGFIELD
Sunday River Ski Resort	BETHEL

FISHING AND HUNTING

Nonresident fishing license: $50; 12-15 years, $7; 15-day license, $38; 7-day license, $34; 3-day license, $21; 1-day license, $9. Nonresident hunting license for birds and animals except deer, bear, turkey, moose, bobcat, and raccoon: $55; incl all legal game species: $85. These fees do not incl agent fees which range from $1-$2. More detailed information on the state's regulations is available in the brochures *Maine Hunting and Trapping Laws* and *Maine Open Water Fishing Laws* from the Maine Fish and Wildlife Dept, Station 41, 284 State St, Augusta 04333; 207/287-8000.

Driving Information

Every person must be in an approved passenger restraint anywhere in vehicle: children under age 4 must use an approved safety seat. For further information phone 207/871-7771.

INTERSTATE HIGHWAY SYSTEM

The following alphabetical listing of Maine towns in *Mobil Travel Guide* shows that these cities are within 10 miles of the indicated interstate highway. A highway map, however, should be checked for the nearest exit.

Highway Number	Cities/Towns within 10 miles
Interstate 95	Augusta, Bangor, Bath, Biddeford, Brunswick, Freeport, Houlton, Kennebunk, Kittery, Lincoln, Millinocket, Newport, Ogunquit, Old Orchard Beach, Orono, Portland, Saco, Scarborough, Waterville, Wells, Yarmouth, York.

Additional Visitor Information

The pulp and paper industry mills throughout Maine offer tours of their woodlands and manufacturing facilities at various times of the year. For further information contact the Maine Pulp & Paper Association Information Office, 104 Sewall St, PO Box 5670, Augusta 04332; 207/622-3166.

There are 8 official information service centers in Maine; visitors who stop by will find information and brochures helpful in planning stops to points of interest. Their locations are as follows: in Bethel, on US 2; at Kittery, between I-95 & US 1; in Fryeburg (summer only), on US 302; in Calais, on Union St, off US 1; in Hampden, on I-95N at mile marker 169, on I-95S between mile markers 171 & 172; in Houlton, on Ludlow Rd; in Yarmouth, between I-95 exit 17 & US 1.

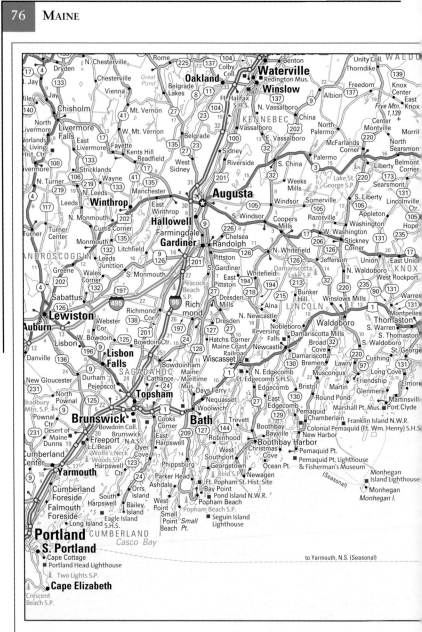

Most tourists stick to coastal Route 1 when it splits from I-95 at Brunswick (Bowdoin College museums and the Joshua Chamberlain Museum, outstanding summer music and theater). Bath is worth a stop to see the Maine Maritime Museum and Shipyard. Traffic streams down a peninsula to Boothbay Harbor, a resort village with a footbridge across its harbor that is a departure point for numerous excursion boats. Rockland is the next must-see stop on Route 1 (the Farnsworth Art Museum and Wyeth Center, Owls Head Transportation Museum, many art galleries, departure point for ferries to Vinalhaven and North Haven and Maine Windjammers). Camden, a town backed by hills (Camden Hills State Park) and filled with inns, restaurants, and shops, is next. Belfast, another interesting old port, is a departure point for excursion boats and for the Belfast & Moosehead Lake Railroad Company excursion train. Continue up coastal Route 1 to Ellsworth, then turn down Route 3 to Mount Desert Island, site of Acadia National Park. The big tourist

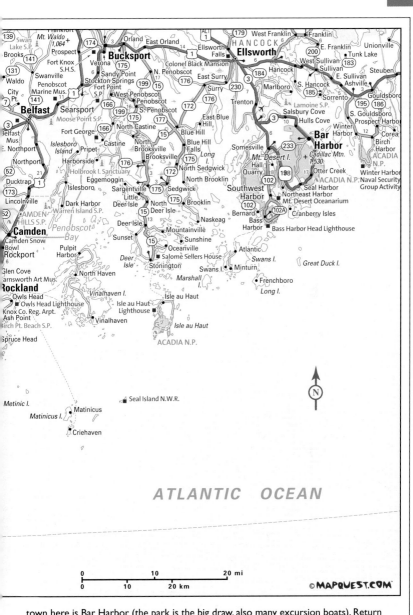

town here is Bar Harbor (the park is the big draw, also many excursion boats). Return the same way, taking the ferry to Yarmouth or Nova Scotia. Another option is to continue north on Route 1 past Ellsworth (the turnoff for Bar Harbor). Here Route 1 changes, becoming far quieter, especially after the turnoff for Schoodic Point, which is part of Acadia National Park. The obvious next stop is in Machias where the Burnham Tavern Museum tells the area's revolutionary history. Most people make a detour at the cliffside walking trails of Quoddy Head State Park (the easternmost point in the United States) before continuing on to Lubec and over the bridge to Campobello to see the Roosevelt Campobello International Park with Franklin D. Roosevelt's summer home as its centerpiece. The park also includes a golf course and extensive hiking trails. Most return the same way to Bar Harbor. **(Approx 306 mi; add 128 mi if continuing on to Lubec)**

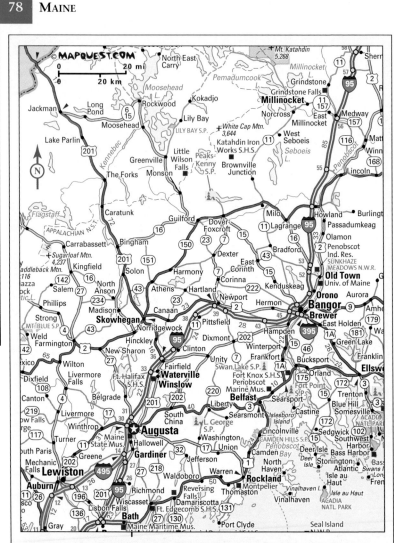

This tour begins on I-95 at Augusta, Maine's state capital (the Maine State Museum, Old Fort Western) and follows Route 27 through the Belgrade Lakes, then up Route 201 along the Kennebec River through Skowhegan (summer theater) and the picturesque villages of Solon and Bingham. Continue on up into The Forks, New England's prime whitewater rafting area, and a popular tourist destination in its own right. Rafting is available daily spring through fall on the Kennebec River through Kennebec Gorge, and the road is lined with dozens of outfitters. Continue on to Jackman (North Woods outpost, eateries, outfitters), and head east on Route 6/15 along the Moose River Valley to Rockwood on Moosehead Lake, New England's largest lake and prime moose-watching base. Mount Kineo, off Rockwood, features hiking and excursions. Fishing is big here, and many old "camps" cater to anglers and families. Route 15 leads south along the lake, past Squaw Mountain (a ski resort) to Greenville, hub of sea plane services to remote North Woods fishing camps. The Moosehead Marine Museum is the departure point for the Katahdin excursion boat, a former lake steamer. From Greenville, continue on to Baxter State Park and Mount Katahdin (Maine's highest mountain and terminus of the Appalachian Trail), via the "Golden Road." Return through Millinocket to I-95. **(Approx 300 mi)**

Acadia National Park

See also Bar Harbor, Northeast Harbor, Southwest Harbor

(On Mount Desert Island, S and W of Bar Harbor; entrance off ME 3)
Waves crashing against a rocky coastline, thick woodlands abundant with wildlife, and mountains scraping the sky—this, Acadia National Park, is the Maine of storybooks. Occupying nearly half of Mount Desert Island, with smaller areas on Isle au Haut, Little Cranberry Island (see CRANBERRY ISLES), Baker Island, Little Moose Island, and part of the mainland at Schoodic Point, Acadia amazes visitors. It is a sea-lashed granite coastal area of forested valleys, lakes, and mountains, all created by the force of the glaciers. At 40,000 acres, Acadia is small compared to other national parks; however, it is one of the most visited national parks in the United States, and the only national park in the northeastern United States. A 27-mile loop road connects the park's eastern sights on Mount Desert Island, and ferry services take travelers to some of the smaller islands. Visitors can explore 1,530-foot Cadillac Mountain, the highest point on the Atlantic Coast of the United States; watch waves crash against Thunder Hole, creating a thunderous boom; or swim in the ocean at various coastal beaches. A road to the summit of Cadillac provides views of Frenchman, Blue Hill, and Penobscot bays.

Mount Desert Island was named by the French explorer Samuel de Champlain in 1604. Shortly thereafter French Jesuit missionaries settled here until driven off by an armed vessel from Virginia. This was the first act of overt warfare between France and England for control of North America. Until 1713, the island was a part of French Acadia. It was not until after the American Revolution that it was extensively settled. In 1916, a portion of the area was proclaimed Sieur de Monts National Monument. It was changed to Lafayette National Park in 1919,

and finally, in 1929, it was enlarged and renamed Acadia National Park.

Like all national parks, Acadia is a wildlife sanctuary. Fir, pine, spruce, many hardwoods, and hundreds of varieties of wildflowers thrive. Nature lovers will be delighted with the more than 120 miles of trails; park rangers take visitors on various walks and cruises, pointing out and explaining the natural, cultural, and historical features of the park. Forty-five miles of carriage roads offer bicyclists scenic rides through Acadia. Copies of ranger-led programs and trail maps are available at the visitor center.

There is saltwater swimming at Sand Beach and freshwater swimming at Echo Lake. Snowmobiles are allowed in some areas and cross-country skiing is available. Most facilities are open Memorial Day-Sep; however, portions of the park are open year round; picnic grounds are open May-Oct. Limited camping is available at two park campgrounds: Blackwoods, open year round, requires reservations from mid-June-mid-Sep; Seawall, open late May-late Sep, is on a first-come, first-served basis. The park headquarters, 2½ mi W of Bar Harbor (see) on ME 233 provides visitor information (Nov-Apr, daily; closed Jan 1, Thanksgiving, Dec 24, 25). For further information contact the Superintendent, PO Box 177, Bar Harbor 04609; 207/288-3338. Golden Eagle, Golden Age, and Golden Access passports accepted (see MAKING THE MOST OF YOUR TRIP). Park entrance fee (subject to change) ¢¢; Per vehicle ¢¢¢ In the park are

Visitor Center. 3 mi NW of Bar Harbor at Hulls Cove. (May-Oct, daily)

The Robert Abbe Museum. Exhibits feature Native American prehistoric and ethnographic artifacts. (Mid-May-Oct, daily) At Sieur de Monts Spring. Phone 207/288-3519. ¢

Islesford Historical Museum. In Islesford, on Little Cranberry Island, 2 mi S of Seal Harbor, a ½-hr boat trip from Northeast Harbor. (See CRANBERRY ISLES) **FREE**

Isle au Haut (EEL-oh-HO). Mountains rise more than 540 feet on this island of forested shores and cobble-

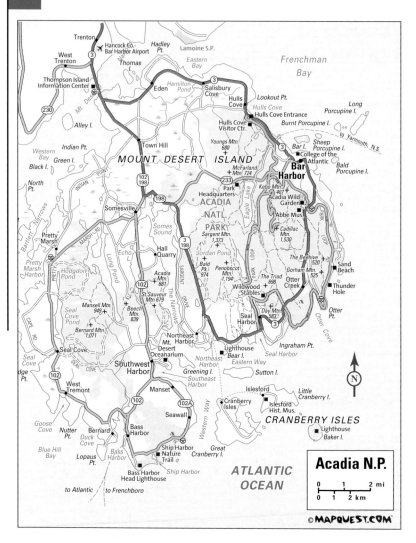

stoned beaches; hiking trails, small primitive campground (advance mail reservations; phone 207/288-3338 for reservation form). A ferry from Stonington (see DEER ISLE) takes visitors on the 45-min trip to island (Mon-Sat; closed hols; fee).

Ferry Service. Connects Islesford, Great Cranberry Island, and Northeast Harbor on a regular schedule all yr. Phone 207/244-3575. ¢¢¢

★ **Park tours.** Narrated sightseeing trips through the park. Buses leave Main St, Bar Harbor. (June-early Oct) For tickets and information on tour schedules and fees contact Testa's Cafe, 53 Main St, Bar Harbor. Phone 207/288-3327. ¢¢¢

Naturalist Sea Cruises. Marine life and history of the area are explained. Cruises visit Frenchman Bay (phone 207/288-3322), Islesford (phone 207/276-5352), and Baker Island (phone 207/276-3717). (Daily during summer season, schedules and fees vary)

Auto Tape Tours. A scenic, 56-mile self-guided tour gives a mile-by-mile description of points of interest, history, and geology of the park. Tape available May-Oct at visitor center. Cassette player and tape rental, deposit required; or tape may be purchased. ¢¢-¢¢¢¢

Allagash Wilderness Waterway

See also Fort Kent

In 1970 the Allagash River was designated a national wild river. Stretching 95 miles through 200,000 acres of lakes, rivers, and timberland in Maine's northern wilderness, this waterway is a favorite of canoeists. A good put-in point is Chamberlain Thoroughfare, at the junction of Chamberlain and Telos lakes. The trip ends at Allagash Village, eight miles north of Allagash Falls, near the Canadian border, where the Allagash flows into the St. John River. Some canoe experience is necessary before attempting the entire trip as high winds can be a problem on the lakes and, depending on the level of the Allagash, the rapids can be dangerous.

Registration is required upon entering and leaving the waterway; rangers are at Allagash Lake, Chamberlain Thoroughfare, Eagle Lake, Churchill Dam, Long Lake Thoroughfare, and the Michaud Farm. Supplies and canoes must be brought in; gasoline is not available. There are restrictions regarding the size of parties using the waterway, as well as watercraft permitted. Numerous primitive campsites accessible only by water are scattered along the waterway (mid-May-mid-Oct). Campsite fee per person, per night ¢¢

For further information and rules contact the Bureau of Parks & Lands, Maine Department of Conservation, Northern Regional Office, BMHI Complex, Bldg H, 106 Hogan Rd, Bangor, 04401; 207/941-4014.

Auburn

(G-2) *See also Lewiston*

Settled 1797 **Pop** 24,309 **Elev** 188 ft
Area code 207 **Zip** 04210
Web www.androscoggincounty.com
Information Androscoggin County Chamber of Commerce, 179 Lisbon, PO Box 59, Lewiston 04243-0059; 207/783-2249

Auburn, together with its sister city Lewiston, make up an important manufacturing center. In 1836, the first organized shoe company was started here. The Minot Shoe Company prospered, selling more than $6 million in shoes by 1900, and becoming the fifth-largest shoe company in the United States by 1920. When the depression hit, the company suffered a severe blow. The city continued to expand, however, and today Auburn is one of the largest cities in the state.

What to See and Do

Androscoggin Historical Society Library and Museum. Exhibits trace local, county, and state history. (Wed-Fri; closed hols) Museum, library. County Bldg, 2 Turner St at Court St. Phone 207/784-0586. **FREE**

Norlands Living History Center. Life as it was lived a century ago; clothing, customs. Yr-round working farm with oxen, horses, cows, crops, and seasonal activities. Features 19th-century Victorian home of Washburn family; school, library, church, farmer's cottage, barn. Tours (Aug, daily). Picnicking. (See ANNUAL EVENTS) 25 mi N just off ME 4, in Livermore. Phone 207/897-4366. Tours ¢¢

Skiing. Lost Valley Ski Area. Two double chairlifts, T-bar; snowmaking, patrol, school, rentals; bar, restaurant. (Dec-mid-Mar, daily) Follow signs off ME 11. Phone 207/784-1561. ¢¢¢¢

Annual Events

Maple Days. Norlands Living History Center. Mid-Mar.

Acadia National Park

Heritage Days. Norlands Living History Center. Thurs-Sun, last wkend June.

Autumn Celebration. Norlands Living History Center. Sep.

Augusta

(F-2) *See also Waterville*

Settled 1628 **Pop** 21,325 **Elev** 153 ft
Area code 207 **Zip** 04330
Web www.augustamaine.com
Information Kennebec Valley Chamber of Commerce, University Dr, PO Box E, 04332-0192; 207/623-4559

Augusta, the capital of Maine, began in 1628 when men from Plymouth established a trading post on the site of Cushnoc, a Native American village. From there, Fort Western was built in 1754 to protect settlers against Native American raids, and the settlement grew. Today, 39 miles from the sea, Augusta is at the head of navigation on the Kennebec River; some of the town's leading industries include steel and food processing and service-related industries.

What to See and Do

Old Fort Western. Fort complex built in 1754 by Boston merchants; main house and reproduction blockhouse, watchboxes, and palisade. Costumed staff interprets 18th-century life on the Kennebec River. (Mid-June-Labor Day, daily; after Labor Day-Columbus Day, Sat and Sun, limited hrs) City Center Plaza, 16 Cony St. Phone 207/626-2385. ¢¢

State House. (1829-32) The original design for this impressive bldg was by Charles Bulfinch (architect of the Massachusetts State House). Remodeled and enlarged (1909-10), it rises majestically above Capitol Park and the Kennebec River. On its 185-ft dome is a statue, designed by W. Clark Noble, of a classically robed woman bearing a pine bough torch. (Daily; closed hols) State & Capitol Sts. Phone 207/287-2301. **FREE** Also here are

Maine State Museum. Exhibits of Maine's natural environment, prehistory, social history, and manufacturing heritage. "This Land Called Maine" features 5 natural history scenes as well as a presentation of 40 spectacular gems and gem minerals found in Maine. "Made in Maine" presents 19th-century products and manufacturing technologies and incl a water-powered woodworking mill, a 2-story textile factory, and more than 1,000 Maine-made objects.

Other exhibits examine the early economic activities of agriculture, fishing, granite quarrying, ice harvesting, lumbering, and shipbuilding. Also featured are a display of military, political, and geographical artifacts relating to the formation of the state of Maine as well as an exhibition of early 19th-century wall decoration. Gift shop. (Daily; closed hols) Phone 207/287-2301. **FREE**

Blaine House. (1833) House of James G. Blaine, Speaker of the US House of Representatives and 1884 presidential candidate. Since 1919, this 28-rm house has been official residence of Maine's governors. Originally built in Federal style, it was remodeled several times and today appears semicolonial. Tours (Tues-Thurs, limited hrs; closed hols). State & Capitol Sts. Phone 207/287-2301. **FREE**

Annual Event

Great Whatever Family Festival Week. Augusta/Gardiner area. More than 60 events incl tournaments, carnival, barbecue, parade, and fireworks. Festivities culminate with the canoe and kayak regatta on the Kennebec River between Augusta and Gardiner. There are also canoe and kayak races. Contact Chamber of Commerce. Ten days late June-early July.

Motels/Motor Lodges

★★ **BEST WESTERN SENATOR INN.** 284 Western Ave; I-95 (04330), at I-95 Exit 30. 207/622-5804; fax 207/622-8803; toll-free 877/772-2224. 103 rms, 1-2 story. July-Aug: S $79-$99; D $89-$109; each addl $9; suites $149-$189; under 18 free; lower rates rest of yr. Crib free. Pet accepted, some restrictions; $50. TV; cable (premium), VCR avail (movies). 2 heated pools, 1 indoor. Playground. Complimentary full bkfst. Complimentary coffee in rms. Restaurant 6:30 am-10 pm. Rm serv. Bar to 1 am. Ck-out noon. Coin lndry. Meeting rms. Business servs avail. In-rm modem link. Sundries. Exercise rm; sauna. Massage. Indoor putting green. Game rm.

Some refrigerators, fireplaces. Picnic tables. Cr cds: A, C, D, DS, MC, V.

★★ **COMFORT INN.** 281 Civic Center Dr (04330). 207/623-1000; fax 207/623-3505; res 800/228-5150; toll-free 800/808-1188. Email lsearcy@fine hotels.com. 99 rms, 3 story. Late June-mid-Oct: S, D $89-$139; each addl $10; under 18 free; higher rates camp wkends; lower rates rest of yr. Crib free. TV; cable (premium). Indoor pool; wading pool, whirlpool. Complimentary continental bkfst. Restaurant 11 am-10 pm. Bar. Ck-out 11 am. Meeting rms. Business servs avail. Valet serv. X-country ski 10 mi. Exercise equipt; sauna. Cr cds: A, D, DS, MC, V.

★ **MOTEL 6.** 18 Edison Dr (04330). 207/622-0000; fax 207/622-1048; toll-free 800/440-6000. 68 rms, 2 story. Late June-Sep: S $32.99; D $38.99; each addl $3; under 18 free. Crib free. Pet accepted, some restrictions. TV; cable (premium). Complimentary coffee in lobby. Restaurant nearby. Ck-out noon. Coin lndry. Cr cds: A, D, DS, MC, V.

★★ **SUSSE CHALET INN.** 65 Whitten Rd (04330), off ME Tpke, Augusta-Winthrop Exit. 207/622-3776; fax 207/622-3778; res 800/524-2538. Email ingleinns@aol.com; www.susse chalet.com. 59 rms, 8 kit, 2 story. S $45.70-$51.70; D $47.70-$67.70; kit $63.70-$80.70. Crib $5. TV; cable (premium). Heated pool. Complimentary continental bkfst. Restaurant nearby. Ck-out 11 am. Coin lndry. Meeting rm. Business servs avail. Cr cds: A, D, DS, MC, V.

Hotel

★ **TRAVELODGE HOTEL.** 390 Western Ave (04330). 207/622-6371; fax 207/621-0349; res 800/578-7878; toll-free 888/636-2463. Email maine hotel@aol.com. 128 rms, 2 story, 3 suites. Jul-Oct: S, D $70; under 17 free; lower rates rest of yr. Pet accepted. Parking lot. Pool, children's pool. TV; cable (premium). Complimentary continental bkfst, coffee in rms, newspaper. Restaurant 4-10 pm. Bar. Ck-out 11 am, ck-in 2 pm. Business center. Coin lndry. Exercise equipt. Golf. Cr cds: A, C, D, DS, MC, V.

[D] 🔊 🏋 ⚓ 🏃 ✈ 🔥 SC 🎿

B&B/Small Inn

★★ **WINGS HILL INN.** *Rte 27 (04918), I-95 Exit 31B, 15 mi N on ME 27. 207/495-2400; fax 207/495-3920; toll-free 800/50-WINGS. Email winghill@aol.com.* 9 rms, 5 with shower only, 2 story. No A/C. No rm phones. June-Sep: S, D $95; each addl $20; ski plans; wkend rates (2-day min); lower rates rest of yr. TV in common rm; cable, VCR avail. Complimentary full bkfst. Restaurant nearby. Ck-out 11 am, ck-in 2-6 pm. Some balconies. Renovated farmhouse built 1800; antique quilts. Totally nonsmoking. Cr cds: DS, MC, V.

🏋 🔊 🎿 🛏 🔥

Bailey Island

See also Brunswick

Elev 20 ft **Area code** 207 **Zip** 04003
Web www.midcoastmaine.com
Information Chamber of Commerce of the Bath-Brunswick Region, 59 Pleasant St, Brunswick 04011; 207/725-8797

At the terminus of ME 24 S, along the northern shore of Casco Bay, lies Bailey Island, the most popular of the 365 Calendar Islands. Together with Orr's Island, to which it is connected by a cribstone bridge, Bailey is a resort and fishing center. Originally called Newwaggin by an early trader from Kittery, Bailey Island was renamed after Deacon Timothy Bailey of Massachusetts, who claimed the land for himself and banished early settlers. Bailey Island and Orr's Island partially enclose an arm of Casco Bay called Harpswell Sound—the locale of John Whittier's poem "The Dead Ship of Harpswell" and of Harriet Beecher Stowe's "Pearl of Orr's Island."

What to See and Do

Bailey Island Cribstone Bridge. Unique construction of uncemented granite blocks laid honeycomb fashion, allowing the tides to flow through. On ME 24 S, over Will Straits. **FREE**

Giant Staircase. Natural rock formation dropping 200 ft in steps to ocean. Scenic overlook area. Washington St. **FREE**

Motel/Motor Lodge

★ **COOK'S ISLAND VIEW MOTEL.** *Rte 24 (04003), on ME 24. 207/833-7780.* 18 rms, 3 kits. No A/C. July-Labor Day, hol wkends: D $80; kit. units $15 addl; under 18 free; lower rates after Memorial Day-June, after Labor Day-Oct. Closed rest of yr. Pet accepted, some restrictions. TV; cable. Pool. Restaurant nearby. Ck-out 11 am. Cr cds: A, MC, V.

🔊 ⚓ 🔥

B&Bs/Small Inns

★ **BAILEY ISLAND MOTEL.** *PO Box 4 Rte 24 (04003), on ME 24. 207/833-2886; fax 207/833-7721. Email rhblack@gwi.net; www.bailey islandmotel.com.* 11 rms, 2 story. 1 kit. No A/C. No rm phones. Mid-June-early Oct: D $95; each addl $10; under 10 free; lower rates May-mid-June, Oct. Closed rest of yr. Crib free. TV; cable. Complimentary continental bkfst. Ck-out 11 am. Picnic tables. Balconies. On ocean. Totally nonsmoking. Cr cds: A, D, DS, MC, V.

🛏 🔥

★★ **LOG CABIN ISLAND INN.** *PO Box 410 (04003). 207/833-5546; fax 207/833-7858. Email info@logcabin maine.com.* 8 rms, 2 with shower only, 1 suite, 4 kit. units. Memorial Day-Labor Day: S, D $109-$199; each addl $19.95; suite $199; kit. units $125-$145; wkly rates; hols 2-day min; lower rates rest of yr. Closed Nov-Mar. TV; cable, VCR (movies). Complimentary full bkfst. Complimentary coffee in rms. Restaurant 5-8 pm. Ck-out 11 am, ck-in 3 pm. Business servs avail. Gift shop. Refrigerators; some in-rm whirlpools, fireplaces. Balconies. Built in 1940s. Log cabin; panoramic view of bay, islands. Totally nonsmoking. Cr cds: A, DS, MC, V.

Restaurant

★ COOK'S LOBSTER HOUSE. *Garrison Cove Rd (04003), off ME 24. 207/833-2818. www.milepost.org/co/ cookslobster.* Specializes in baked stuffed lobster, shore dinners, steak. Raw bar. Hrs: 11 am-10 pm. Bar. Lunch $2.95-$9.95; dinner $9.25-$26.95. Child's menu. Dockage. Family-owned. Cr cds: DS, MC, V.
D

Bangor (E-4)

Settled 1769 **Pop** 33,181 **Elev** 61 ft
Area code 207 **Zip** 04401
Web www.bangorregion.com
Information Bangor Region Chamber of Commerce, 519 Main St, PO Box 1443; 207/947-0307

In 1604, Samuel de Champlain sailed up the Penobscot River to the area that was to become Bangor and reported that the country was "most pleasant and agreeable," the hunting good, and the oak trees impressive. As the area grew, these things remained true. Begun as a harbor town, like many of Maine's coastal areas, Bangor turned to lumber when the railroads picked up much of the shipping business. In 1842, it became the second-largest lumber port in the country.

Bangor received its name by mistake. An early settler, Reverend Seth Noble, was sent to register the new town under its chosen name of Sunbury; however, when officials asked Noble for the name, he thought they were asking him for the name of a tune he was humming, and replied "Bangor" instead. Today, the city is the third-largest in Maine and a trading and distribution center.

What to See and Do

Bangor Historical Museum. (Thomas A. Hill House, 1834) Tour of first floor of Greek Revival house; second-floor gallery features changing exhibits. (June-mid-Sep, Mon-Fri and Sun afternoons; Mar-May and mid-Sep-Dec, Tues-Fri afternoons) 159 Union St, at High St. Phone 207/942-5766. ¢

Cole Land Transportation Museum. Exhibits on more than 200 vehicles incl vintage cars, horse-drawn logging sleds, and fire engines. Historic photographs of Maine also on display. (May-early Nov, daily) 405 Perry Rd. Phone 207/990-3600. ¢¢

Monument to Paul Bunyan. A 31-ft-tall statue commemorating the legendary lumberjack. Main St, in Bass Park. **FREE**

Annual Events

Kenduskeag Stream Canoe Race. Phone 207/947-1018. Mid-Apr.

Bangor Fair. One of country's oldest. Horse racing, exhibits, stage shows. Phone 207/947-5555. Late June-1st wk Aug.

Seasonal Event

Band concerts. Paul Bunyan Park. Phone 207/947-1018. Tues eves, July-Aug.

Motels/Motor Lodges

★ BEST INN BANGOR. *570 Main St (04401). 207/942-1234; fax 207/942-1234; res 800/237-8466. www.bestinn. com.* 50 rms, 2 story, 1 suite. Jul-Aug: S $75; D $80; suites $160; lower rates rest of yr. Pet accepted. TV; cable. Complimentary continental bkfst, coffee in rms, toll-free calls. Restaurant 7 am-9 pm. Bar. Ck-out noon, ck-in 1 pm. Meeting rm. Fax servs avail. Dry cleaning. Exercise privileges. Golf. Cr cds: A, C, D, DS, MC, V.

★★ BEST WESTERN WHITE HOUSE INN. *155 Littlefield Ave (04401), W at I-95 Exit 44. 207/862-3737; fax 207/862-3737; res 800/528-1234. www.bestwestern.com/white houseinnbangor.* 61 rms, 3 story, 5 suites. May-Oct: S, D $100; suites $120; each addl $10; under 12 free; lower rates rest of yr. Crib avail, fee. Pet accepted, some restrictions. Parking lot. Pool. TV; cable (premium), VCR avail. Complimentary continental bkfst, coffee in rms, toll-free calls.

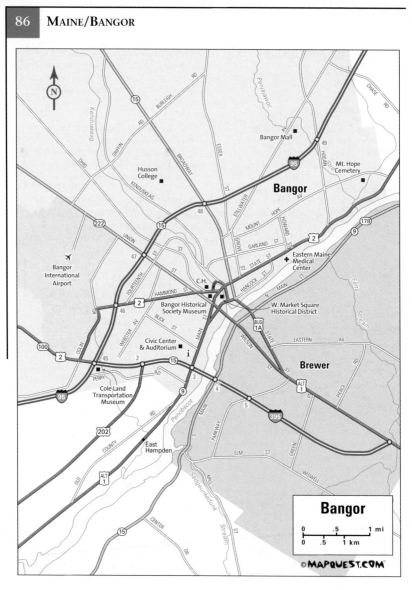

Bangor

0   .5   1 mi
0   .5   1 km

©MAPQUEST.COM

Restaurant. Bar. Ck-out 11 am. Business center. Dry cleaning, coin lndry. Gift shop. Sauna. Golf. Tennis, 5 courts. Downhill skiing. Picnic facilities. Cr cds: A, C, D, DS, ER, MC, V.

★★ **COMFORT INN.** *750 Hogan Rd (04401). 207/942-7899; fax 207/942-6463; res 800/228-5150.* 96 rms, 2 story. Mid-June-Oct: S $49-$89; D $59-$99; each addl $5; under 19 free; lower rates rest of yr. Crib free. Pet accepted; $6. TV; cable (premium). Pool. Complimentary continental bkfst, coffee in rms. Ck-out noon. Meeting rms. Business servs avail.

Sundries. Free airport transportation. Game rm. Exercise equipt. X-country ski 10 mi. Shopping mall adj. Cr cds: A, D, MC, V.

★★ **DAYS INN.** *250 Odlin Rd (04401). 207/942-8272; fax 207/942-1382; toll-free 800/329-7466.* Email *daysinn@midmaine.com.* 101 rms, 2 story. July-Oct: S $50-$65; D $55-$85; each addl $6; under 12 free; lower rates rest of yr. Crib free. Pet accepted; $6. TV; cable (premium), VCR avail. Indoor pool; whirlpool. Complimentary continental bkfst. Restaurant adj 11-

1 am. Ck-out 11 am. Business servs avail. In-rm modem link. Sundries. Free airport transportation. Downhill/x-country ski 12 mi. Game rm. Cr cds: A, C, D, DS, JCB, MC, V.

★ **ECONO LODGE.** *327 Odlin Rd (04401). 207/945-0111; fax 207/942-8856; res 800/553-2666; toll-free 800/393-0111.* 128 rms, 4 story. S $29.95-$65.95; D $39.95-$85.95; under 19 free. Crib free. Pet accepted. TV; cable (premium). Complimentary coffee in lobby. Ck-out 11 am. Coin lndry. Business servs avail. In-rm modem link. Downhill/x-country ski 7 mi. Some refrigerators, microwaves. Cr cds: A, DS, MC, V.

★★ **FAIRFIELD INN.** *300 Odlin Rd (04401), I-95 Exit 45 B. 207/990-0001; fax 207/990-0917; res 800/228-2800.* 153 rms, 3 story. Mid-June-mid-Oct: S, D $49.95-$84.95; each addl $3; under 18 free; lower rates rest of yr. Crib free. TV; cable (premium). Indoor pool; whirlpool. Complimentary continental bkfst. Restaurant adj 6 am-10 pm. Ck-out noon. Coin lndry. Meeting rm. Business servs avail. In-rm modem link. Downhill ski 7 mi; x-country ski 5 mi. Exercise equipt; sauna. Cr cds: A, D, DS, MC, V.

Hotels

★★ **FOUR POINTS BY SHERATON.** *308 Godfrey Blvd (04401), at Intl Airport. 207/947-6721; fax 207/941-9761; res 800/325-3535; toll-free 800/228-4609. Email rooms@bangor.newcastlehotels.* 101 rms, 9 story. S, D $98-$155; each addl $15; under 18 free. Crib free. Pet accepted. TV; cable (premium). Pool. Complimentary coffee in rms. Restaurant 6 am-2:30 pm, 5-11 pm. Bar 2 pm-midnight. Ck-out noon. Meeting rms. Business center. In-rm modem link. Gift shop. Validated parking. Airport transportation. Downhill/x-country ski 7 mi. Exercise equipt. Enclosed walkway to airport. Cr cds: A, DS, MC, V.

★★ **HOLIDAY INN.** *404 Odlin Rd (04401), 3 mi W on I-395, near Intl Airport. 207/947-0101; fax 207/947-7619; toll-free 800/914-0101. Email hibgror@ctel.net; www.holiday-inn.com/bangor-odlin.* 207 rms, 3 story. July-Aug: S $99; D $109; each addl $10; under 18 free; lower rates rest of yr. Crib avail. Pet accepted. Parking lot. Indoor/outdoor pools, whirlpool. TV; cable (premium). Complimentary coffee in rms, newspaper, toll-free calls. Restaurant 6 am-9 pm. Bar. Ck-out noon, ck-in 2 pm. Meeting rms. Business center. Bellhops. Dry cleaning, coin lndry. Free airport transportation. Exercise equipt, sauna. Golf. Tennis, 5 courts. Downhill skiing. Cr cds: A, C, D, DS, JCB, MC, V.

★★ **HOLIDAY INN.** *500 Main St (04401). 207/947-8651; fax 207/942-2848; res 800/465-4329; toll-free 800/799-8651. Email hibgrms@ctel.net; www.holiday-inn.com/bangor-civic.* 113 rms, 4 story, 8 suites. July-Oct: S, D $99; suites $200; each addl $10; under 18 free; lower rates rest of yr. Crib avail. Pet accepted, some restrictions. Parking lot. Pool. TV; cable (premium), VCR avail. Complimentary coffee in rms, newspaper, toll-free calls. Restaurant 7 am-9 pm. Bar. Ck-out noon, ck-in 2 pm. Meeting rms. Business center. Dry cleaning, coin lndry. Free airport transportation. Exercise privileges. Golf, 18 holes. Tennis, 2 courts. Downhill skiing. Supervised children's activities. Video games. Cr cds: A, C, D, DS, JCB, MC, V.

B&Bs/Small Inns

★★ **THE LUCERNE INN.** *1A Bar Harbor Rd (04429), 11 mi E on US 1A. 207/843-5123; fax 207/843-6138; toll-free 800/325-5123. Email info@lucerneinn.com; www.lucerneinn.com.* 22 rms, 3 story, 8 suites. July-Oct: S, D $99-$159; each addl $15; package plans. Lower rates rest of yr. Crib avail, fee. Pet accepted, some restrictions, fee. Parking lot. Pool. TV; cable (DSS), VCR avail. Complimentary continental bkfst, newspaper, toll-free calls. Restaurant. Bar. Ck-out 11 am, ck-in 2 pm. Meeting rms. Business center. Gift shop. Golf, 9 holes. Downhill skiing. Hiking trail. Cr cds: A, MC, V.

★★ **QUALITY INN PHENIX.** *20 Broad St (04401), in West Market Sq.* *207/947-0411; fax 207/947-0255.* 32 rms, 4 story. July-late-Oct: S, D $75-$150; lower rates rest of yr. Crib free. Pet accepted. TV; cable, VCR avail. Complimentary continental bkfst. Restaurant adj 7 am-midnight. Ck-out noon, ck-in 1 pm. Guest lndry. Meeting rm. Business servs avail. Exercise equipt. Refrigerator avail. Restored commercial bldg (1873) located in West Market Square; furnished with antique reproductions. Near river. Cr cds: A, DS, MC, V.

D ⏴ 🐾 ⚡ ⤳ 🕴 🏃 ⛵ 🔥

Restaurants

★ **CAPTAIN NICK'S SEAFOOD HOUSE.** *1165 Union St (04401).* *207/942-6444.* Specializes in lobster, seafood, local dishes. Hrs: 11 am-10 pm. Closed Thanksgiving, Dec 25. Res accepted. Bar. Lunch $3.50-$7.25; dinner $6.95-$17.95. Child's menu. Cr cds: A, C, DS, ER, MC, V.

D SC

★★ **MILLER'S.** *427 Main St (04401).* *207/945-5663.* Specializes in prime rib, fresh seafood, rotisserie chicken. Salad bar. Dessert bar. Own baking. Hrs: 11 am-10 pm; Sun 10 am-9 pm; Sun brunch to noon. Closed Dec 25. Res accepted. Lunch $3.95-$7.50; dinner $8.95-$21.95. Sun brunch $6.95. Child's menu. Two separate dining areas. Family-owned. Cr cds: A, DS, MC, V.

D SC

★★ **PILOTS GRILL.** *1528 Hammond St (04401). 207/942-6325.* Specializes in baked stuffed lobster, baked haddock, prime rib. Own desserts. Hrs: 11 am-2 pm, 5-9 pm; Sun 11 am-8 pm. Closed July 4, Dec 25. Res accepted. Bar. Lunch $5.95-$9.95; dinner $8.95-$19.95. Child's menu. Family-owned since 1940. Cr cds: A, C, D, DS, ER, MC, V.

⊟ D

Bar Harbor

(F-5) *See also Cranberry Isles, Northeast Harbor, Southwest Harbor*

Pop 2,768 **Elev** 20 ft **Area code** 207 **Zip** 04609 **Web** www.acadia.net/bhcc **Information** Chamber of Commerce, 93 Cottage St, PO Box 158; 207/288-5103

Bar Harbor, the largest village on Mount Desert Island, has a summer population of as many as 20,000 and is headquarters for the surrounding summer resort area. The island, which includes most of Acadia National Park, is mainly rugged granite, forested and flowered, with many bays and inlets where sailing is popular. In the mid-1800s, socially prominent figures, including publisher Joseph Pulitzer, had elaborate summer cottages built on the island. The era of elegance ebbed, however, with the Great Depression, World War II, and the "Great Fire of 1947," which destroyed many of the estates and scorched more than 17,000 acres. As a result, the forests in the area now have younger, more varied trees bearing red, yellow, and orange leaves instead of just evergreens.

What to See and Do

The Abbe Museum. Major collection of Native American artifacts, many unearthed in the immediate area. (May-Oct) ME 3 S to Sieur de Monts Exit. Phone 207/288-3519. ¢

🔲 **Acadia National Park.** (see) Borders town on W & S. HQ 2½ mi W on ME 233. Phone 207/288-3338. ¢¢

Bar Harbor Historical Society Museum. Collection of early photographs of hotels, summer cottages, and Green Mt cog railroad; hotel registers from the early to late 1800s; maps, scrapbook of the 1947 fire. (Mid-June-Oct, Mon-Sat; closed hols) 34 Mount Desert St, Jesup Memorial Library. Phone 207/288-4245. **FREE**

Bar Harbor Whale Watch Co. Offers variety of cruises aboard catamarans *Friendship V* or *MV Seal* to view whales, seal, puffin, osprey, lobster, and more. Also nature cruises and fishing trips. Cruises vary in length and destination. (May-Oct, daily)

Depart from Bluenose Ferry Terminal. 1 mi N on ME 3. Phone 207/288-2386 or 800/WHALES-4.

Ferry service to Yarmouth, Nova Scotia. Passenger and car carrier *Bluenose* makes 6-hr trips (cabins avail). Phone 888/249-7245. ¢¢¢¢

Fishing. Fresh water in many lakes and streams (check regulations, obtain license). Salt water off coast; commercial boat operators will arrange trips.

The Jackson Laboratory. An internationally known mammalian genetics laboratory conducting research relevant to cancer, diabetes, AIDS, heart disease, blood disorders, birth defects, aging, and normal growth and development. Audiovisual and lecture programs (early-June-late Aug, Tues and Thurs afternoons; closed 1 wk late July and 1 wk mid-Aug). 2 mi S on ME 3. **FREE**

Natural History Museum. More than 50 exhibits depicting animals in their natural settings; 22-ft Minke whale skeleton. Interpretive programs; evening lectures in summer (Wed). (June-Labor Day, daily; rest of yr, by appt) Eden St. In historic Turrets Bldg on College of the Atlantic waterfront campus. Phone 207/288-5015. ¢¢

Oceanarium-Bar Harbor. An extension of the Mt Desert Oceanarium in Southwest Harbor (see); features incl harbor seals, salt-marsh walks, viewing tower; also lobster museum with hands-on exhibits. (Mid-May-mid-Oct, Mon-Sat) 9 mi N on ME 3. Phone 207/288-5005. ¢¢ Also included is the

> **Lobster Hatchery.** Young lobsters are hatched from eggs to ½ inch in length, then returned to ocean to supplement supply; guides narrate process. (Mid-May-mid-Oct, Mon-Sat)

Annual Event

Art Exhibit. Village Green. Third wkend in July and Aug.

Motels/Motor Lodges

★★ **ATLANTIC EYRIE LODGE.** *6 Norman Rd (04609). 207/288-9786; fax 207/288-8500; toll-free 800/422-2883. Email atlanticeyrie@acadia.net;* www.barharbor.com/eyrie. 58 rms, 4 story. July-Aug: S, D $144; each addl $10; lower rates rest of yr. Crib avail. Parking lot. Pool. TV; cable. Complimentary continental bkfst, newspaper, toll-free calls. Restaurant nearby. Ck-out 11 am, ck-in 3 pm. Meeting rm. Business servs avail. Coin lndry. Golf. Cr cds: A, MC, V.

![symbols]

★★★ **BAR HARBOR HOTEL-BLUENOSE INN.** *90 Eden St (04609). 207/288-3348; fax 207/288-2183; toll-free 800/445-4077. www.acadia.net/bluenose.* From its hilltop location on Mount Desert Island, this inn offers breathtaking views of Frenchman Bay. The property's 97 rooms and suites are spread between the Mizzentop and Stenna Nordica buildings. Guests can explore nearby Acadia National Park or walk down to the dock and catch the Bluenose Ferry for a day trip to Yarmouth, Nova Scotia. 49 rms, 48 suites. 3-4 story. July-Aug: S, D $149-$279; suites $279-$349; each addl $15; lower rates April-June, Sep-Oct. Closed rest of yr. TV; cable (premium), VCR avail. 2 heated pools, 1 indoor; whirlpool. Complimentary coffee in rms. Restaurant 7-10:30 am, 5:30-9:30 pm. Rm serv during dining hrs. Bar 5-11 pm. Ck-out 11 am, ck-in 3 pm. Coin lndry. Meeting rm. Business servs avail. Bellhops. Gift shop. 18-hole golf privileges. Whale watching, sailing, kayaking, hiking, bicycle riding nearby. Exercise equipt. Refrigerators; fireplaces, bathrm phones in suites only. Balconies. Ocean view. Totally non-smoking. Cr cds: MC, V.

![symbols]

★★ **BAR HARBOR MOTEL.** *100 Eden St Rte 3 (04609). 207/288-3453; fax 207/288-3598; toll-free 800/388-3453. Email bhmotel@acadia.net;* www.barharbormotel.com. 54 rms, 1 story, 24 suites. July-Aug: S, D $114; suites $149; each addl $10; lower rates rest of yr. Crib avail. Parking lot. Pool. TV; cable. Complimentary toll-free calls. Restaurant nearby. Ck-out 11 am, ck-in 2:30 pm. Business servs avail. Gift shop. Golf. Hiking trail. Picnic facilities. Cr cds: DS, MC, V.

![symbols]

★★ BAR HARBOR QUALITY INN.
40 Kebo St; Me 3 and Mt Desert St (04609). 207/288-5403; fax 207/288-5473; res 800/228-5151; toll-free 800/282-5403. Email quality@acadia.net; www.acadia.net/quality. 76 rms, 2 story. July-Aug: S, D $169; each addl $10; under 18 free; lower rates rest of yr. Crib avail. Parking lot. Pool, whirlpool. TV; cable. Complimentary coffee in rms, newspaper. Restaurant 6:30 am-5 pm. Bar. Ck-out 2 pm, ck-in 11 pm. Business center. Coin lndry. Gift shop. Golf, 18 holes. Tennis, 2 courts. Picnic facilities. Cr cds: A, C, D, DS, ER, JCB, MC, V.

★★ BEST WESTERN INN.
Rte 3 (04609), 4 mi W on ME 3. 207/288-5823; fax 207/288-9827; res 800/528-1234. www.bestwesterninn.com. 70 rms, 1 story, 2 suites. July-Sep: S, D $105; suites $135; each addl $5; under 13 free; lower rates rest of yr. Crib avail. Pet accepted, some restrictions, fee. Parking lot. Pool. TV; cable (premium). Complimentary continental bkfst, toll-free calls. Ck-out 11 am, ck-in 2 pm. Coin lndry. Gift shop. Golf. Hiking trail. Cr cds: A, C, D, DS, MC, V.

★ CADILLAC MOTOR INN.
336 Main St (04609). 207/288-3831; fax 207/288-9370; toll-free 888/207-2593. Email cadillac@acadia.net; www.cadillacmotorinn.com. 43 rms, 2 story, 4 suites. July-Aug: S, D $99; suites $165; each addl $15; under 12 free; lower rates rest of yr. Crib avail, fee. Parking lot. TV; cable. Complimentary newspaper. Restaurant nearby. Ck-out 11 am, ck-in 3 pm. Fax servs avail. Golf, 18 holes. Picnic facilities. Cr cds: A, DS, MC, V.

★★ CROMWELL HARBOR MOTEL.
359 Main St (04609). 207/288-3201; toll-free 800/544-3201. Email www.cromwellharbor@webtv.net; www.cromwellharbor.com. 25 rms. July-Aug: S $98; D $115; each addl $10; lower rates rest of yr. Parking lot. Pool. TV; cable (premium). Complimentary coffee in rms, toll-free calls. Restaurant. Ck-out 11 am, ck-in 2 pm. Internet dock/port avail. Golf, 18 holes. Tennis, 2 courts. Cr cds: A, MC, V.

★★ DREAMWOOD PINES MOTEL.
RR 2 Box 1100 (04609), 4 mi N on ME 3. 207/288-9717; fax 201/288-4194. www.acapia.net/dreamwood. 20 rms, 1 story, 2 suites. July-Aug: D $98; each addl $8; lower rates rest of yr. Crib avail, fee. Pet accepted, some restrictions, fee. Parking lot. Pool. TV; cable. Complimentary coffee in rms, toll-free calls. Restaurant. Ck-out 11 am, ck-in 3 pm. Fax servs avail. Golf. Picnic facilities. Cr cds: DS, MC, V.

★ EDENBROOK MOTEL.
96 Eden St (04609). 207/288-4975; toll-free 800/323-7819. Email edenbrook@acadia.net; www.acadia.net/edenbrook/office.html. 46 rms, 1 story, 1 suite. July-Aug: S, D $90; suites $110; each addl $5; children $5; lower rates rest of yr. Crib avail, fee. Parking lot. TV; cable. Complimentary coffee in rms, toll-free calls. Restaurant nearby. Ck-out 11 am, ck-in 2 pm. Golf. Cr cds: A, DS, MC, V.

★ EDGEWATER COTTAGES AND MOTEL.
Old Barharbor Rd (04672), Salisbury Cove, 5 mi W on ME 3. 207/288-3491; fax 207/288-3491; res 888/310-9920. www.sourcemaine.com/edgewatr. 23 units, 1-2 story, 8 motel rms, 4 kits. 11 kit. cottages, 4 apts (2-bedrm). July-Labor Day: S, D $97; kits. $107; each addl $10; kit. cottages, apts $78-$130; wkly rates; lower rates mid-Apr-June, early Sep-Oct. Closed rest of yr. TV; cable (premium). Complimentary coffee in lobby. Ck-out 11 am. Coin lndry. Refrigerators; some fireplaces. Patios, balconies. Picnic tables, grills. On Frenchman Bay; swimming beach. Cr cds: MC, V.

★★ GOLDEN ANCHOR INN.
55 West St (04609). 207/288-5033; fax 207/288-4577; toll-free 800/328-5033. www.goldenanchorinn.com. 88 rms, 4 kit. units, 2 story. July-early Sep: S, D $110-$185; each addl $10; under 5 free, 5-12 $2.50; lower rates Apr-June, early Sep-Oct. Closed rest of yr. Crib free. TV; cable. Heated pool; whirlpool. Complimentary bkfst buffet in season. Restaurant 7 am-10 pm. Rm serv 1-9 pm. Bar from noon. Ck-out 11 am. Business servs avail. In-rm modem link. Balconies. On ocean. Private pier, dockage; whale

watching cruises in season. Cr cds: D, DS, MC, V.

⊡ ⚡ ⚑ ⛱ 🎿 🎣 ⛷ 🔥 🚶

★ **HIGGINS HOLIDAY HOTEL.** *43 Holland Ave (04609). 207/288-3829; fax 207/288-4982; toll-free 800/345-0305. Email cooper@midmaine.com; www.higginsholidaymotel.amtg.com.* 18 rms, 2 story, 7 suites. July-Aug: S, D $89; suites $175; each addl $7; lower rates rest of yr. Crib avail, fee. Parking lot. TV; cable. Complimentary coffee in rms, toll-free calls. Restaurant nearby. Ck-out 11 am, ck-in 2 pm. Golf. Cr cds: DS, MC, V.

⊡ 🎣 ⛱ 🔥

★ **HIGH SEAS.** *RR 1 Box 1085 (04609), 4 mi N on ME 3. 207/288-5836; toll-free 800/959-5836.* 34 rms. July-Aug: S, D $68-$98; under 12 free; lower rates May-June, Sep-mid-Oct. Closed rest of yr. Crib $2. TV; cable. Heated pool. Restaurant 6 am-9 pm. Ck-out 11 am. Refrigerators avail. Cr cds: DS, MC, V.

⛱ ⛱ 🔥 SC

★ **MAINE STREET MOTEL.** *315 Main St (04609). 207/288-3188; fax 207/288-2317; toll-free 800/333-3188. Email cwitham@acadia.net; www.mainestreetmotel.com.* 44 rms, 1-2 story. July-Aug: S, D $88-$98; each addl $10; under 16 free; lower rates Apr-June, Sep-Oct. Closed rest of yr. Crib $10. TV; cable (premium). Restaurant adj from 11 am. Ck-out 11 am. Business servs avail. Cr cds: A, DS, MC, V.

⊡ ⛱ 🔥

★★ **PARK ENTRANCE MOTEL.** *RR 2 Box 180 Hamor Ave (04609), Hamor Ave, 2½ mi N off ME 3, adj Acadia Park Entrance. 207/288-9703; fax 207/288-9703; res 800/288-9703.* 58 rms, 24 A/C, 2 story, 6 kits. (5 no ovens). Aug: S, D $134-$179; kit. units $199-$299; under 18 free; lower rates early May-July, Sep-late Oct. Closed rest of yr. Crib $6. TV; cable (premium). Heated pool; whirlpool. Complimentary coffee in rms. Restaurant nearby. Ck-out 11 am. Business servs avail. Lawn games. Refrigerators avail. Private patios, balconies. Picnic tables, grills. Overlooks bay, beach. Mooring, dock; fishing pier. Cr cds: A, DS, MC, V.

⊡ ⛵ ⛱ ⛱ 🔥

★ **VILLAGER MOTEL.** *207 Main St (04609). 207/288-3211; fax 207/288-2270. Email villager@acadia.net; www.acadia.net/villager.* 52 rms, 2 story. July-Aug: S, D $79-$98; each addl $10; under 11 free; lower rates May-June, Sep-late Oct. Closed rest of yr. Crib $5. TV; cable. Heated pool. Complimentary coffee in lobby. Restaurant nearby. Ck-out 11 am. Cr cds: A, MC, V.

⛱ ⛱ 🔥

★★ **WONDER VIEW INN.** *50 Eden St (10801). 207/288-3358; fax 207/288-2005; toll-free 800/341-1553. Email wonderview@acadia.net; www.wonderviewinn.com.* 79 rms. July-Aug: S $115; D $148; each addl $10; children $10; under 12 free; lower rates rest of yr. Crib avail, fee. Parking lot. Pool. TV; cable. Complimentary newspaper. Restaurant. 24-hr rm serv. Bar. Ck-out 11 am, ck-in 3 pm. Business servs avail. Golf, 18 holes. Tennis, 4 courts. Cr cds: A, DS, MC, V.

🎣 ⛷ ⛱ ⛱ 🔥

Hotels

★★ **ACADIA INN.** *98 Eden St (04609). 207/288-3500; fax 207/288-8424; res 800/638-3636. Email acadiainn@acadia.net; www.acadiainn.com.* 95 rms, 3 story. July-Oct: S, D $159; each addl $20; children $10; under 9 free; lower rates rest of yr. Crib avail. Parking lot. Pool, whirlpool. TV; cable (premium). Complimentary continental bkfst. Restaurant nearby. Ck-out 11 am, ck-in 1 pm. Fax servs avail. Coin lndry. Gift shop. Golf. Picnic facilities. Cr cds: A, DS, MC, V.

⊡ 🎣 ⛱ ⛱ 🔥 SC

★★★ **BAR HARBOR INN.** *Newport Dr (04609). 207/288-3351; fax 207/288-5296; res 800/248-3351. Email bhinn@acadia.net; www.barharborinn.com.* 142 rms, 2 story, 11 suites. Jun-Sep: S, D $269; suites $475; each addl $20; children $20; under 14 free; lower rates rest of yr. Crib avail, fee. Pet accepted, some restrictions, fee. Valet parking avail. Pool, whirlpool. TV; cable (premium), VCR avail. Complimentary continental bkfst, coffee in rms, newspaper, toll-free calls. Restaurant 11:30 am-9:30 pm. Bar. Ck-out 11 am, ck-in 2 pm. Meeting rm. Business servs avail. Bellhops.

Gift shop. Exercise privileges. Golf. Tennis. Beach access. Cr cds: A, D, DS, MC, V.

★★★ **THE BAYVIEW.** *111 Eden St (04609).* 207/288-5861; fax 207/288-3173; toll-free 800/356-3585. Email bayview@barharbor.com. 39 rms, 2-3 story, 7 kit. town homes. No elvtr. Late June-Labor Day: S, D $110-$275; each addl $20; ages 12-18 $10; under 12 free; town homes $390-$440; lower rates mid-May-late June, Labor Day-late Oct. Closed rest of yr. TV; cable (premium), VCR avail. Heated pool; poolside serv. Complimentary bkfst buffet; afternoon refreshments. Restaurant 7-10 am; 5-8:30 pm. Bar 11-1 am. Ck-out 11 am. Meeting rms. Business servs avail. Airport transportation. Lighted tennis privileges. Exercise equipt. Massage. Lawn games. Whirlpool in town homes. Private patios, balconies. Situated on 8 wooded acres with water frontage on Frenchmen Bay. Former estate; Georgian country house furnished with antiques. Fireplaces. Library. Gardens. Cr cds: A, DS, MC, V.

Resort

★★★ **BAR HARBOR REGENCY.** *123 Eden St (04609).* 207/288-9723; fax 207/288-3089; res 800/465-4329. Email bhregency@yahoo.com; www. barharborholidayinn.com. 221 rms, 4 story, 2 suites. July-Aug: S $289; under 18 free; lower rates rest of yr. Crib avail. Parking lot. Pool, childrens pool. TV; cable (premium), VCR avail. Complimentary coffee in rms, newspaper. Restaurant 6:30 am-8 pm. Bar. Ck-out noon, ck-in 3 pm. Meeting rms. Business servs avail. Bellhops. Concierge. Coin lndry. Gift shop. Exercise equipt, sauna. Golf. Tennis, 2 courts. Beach access. Supervised children's activities. Hiking trail. Picnic facilities. Cr cds: A, D, DS, MC, V.

B&Bs/Small Inns

★★ **BLACK FRIAR INN.** *10 Summer St (04609), off Cottage St.* 207/288-5091; fax 207/288-4197. Email blackfriar@blackfriar.com; www.blackfriar. com. 6 rms, 3 story, 1 suite. June-Oct:

S $104; D $109; suites $145; each addl $15; lower rates rest of yr. Parking lot. TV; cable (premium), VCR avail. Complimentary full bkfst. Restaurant nearby. Ck-out 11 am, ck-in 4 pm. Internet access avail. Golf. Tennis. Cr cds: DS, MC, V.

★★ **CANTERBURY COTTAGE.** *12 Roberts Ave (04609).* 207/288-2112; fax 207/288-5681. Email canterbury@ acadia.net; www.acadia.net/cantebury. 4 rms, 3 with shower only, 2 story. No A/C. No rm phones. Mid-June-mid-Oct: S, D $85-$100; each addl $15; hols 2-day min (in season); lower rates rest of yr. Children over 8 yrs only. Cable TV in common rm; VCR. Complimentary full bkfst; afternoon refreshments. Restaurant nearby. Ck-out 11 am, ck-in 2 pm. Built in 1900. Totally nonsmoking. Cr cds: MC, V.

★★★ **CASTLEMAINE.** *39 Holland Ave (04609).* 207/288-4563; fax 207/288-4525; toll-free 800/338-4563. www.castlemaineinn.com. 12 rms, 3 story, 5 suites. July-Aug: S, D $125; suites $175; each addl $25; lower rates rest of yr. Parking lot. TV; cable, VCR avail. Complimentary continental bkfst, toll-free calls. Restaurant 8 am-9 pm. Ck-out 11 am, ck-in 2 pm. Fax servs avail. Exercise privileges. Golf, 18 holes. Tennis, 6 courts. Bike rentals. Hiking trail. Cr cds: MC, V.

★★★ **CLEFTSTONE MANOR.** *92 Eden St (04609).* 207/288-4951; fax 207/288-2089; toll-free 888/288-4951. Email innkeeper@cleftstone.com; www. cleftstone.com. 14 rms, 3 story, 2 suites. June-Oct: S, D $130; suites $165; each addl $20; lower rates rest of yr. Parking lot. TV; cable, VCR avail. Complimentary full bkfst, toll-free calls. Restaurant nearby. Ck-out 11 am, ck-in 3 pm. Meeting rm. Fax servs avail. Concierge. Free airport transportation. Golf. Cr cds: MC, V.

★★ **GRAYCOTE INN.** *40 Holland Ave (04609).* 207/288-3044; fax 207/288-2719. Email innkeepers@graycote inn.com; www.graycoteinn.com. 7 rms, 3 story, 5 suites. June-Oct: S $126; D $130; suites $200; each addl $20; lower rates rest of yr. Parking lot. TV;

cable, VCR avail. Complimentary full bkfst, newspaper. Restaurant nearby. Ck-out 10:30 am, ck-in 3 pm. Exercise privileges. Golf, 18 holes. Tennis, 10 courts. Cr cds: A, DS, MC, V.

★★ **HATFIELD BED & BREAKFAST.** *20 Roberts Ave (04609). 207/288-9655. Email hatfield@hatfieldinn.com; www.hatfieldinn.com.* 6 rms, 3 story. June-Oct: D $115; each addl $25; lower rates rest of yr. Parking lot. TV; cable, VCR avail. Complimentary full bkfst, newspaper, toll-free calls. Restaurant nearby. Ck-out 11 am, ck-in 2 pm. Coin lndry. Gift shop. Salon/barber avail. Golf. Tennis, 10 courts. Beach access. Bike rentals. Hiking trail. Picnic facilities. Cr cds: DS, MC, V.

★★ **HEARTHSIDE BED & BREAKFAST.** *7 High St (04609). 207/288-4533; fax 207/288-9818. Email mobil@hearthsideinn.com; www.hearthsideinn.com.* 9 rms, 3 story. June-Oct: D $120; lower rates rest of yr. Parking lot. TV; cable, VCR avail. Complimentary full bkfst, newspaper, toll-free calls. Restaurant nearby. Ck-out 11 am. Golf, 18 holes. Tennis, 2 courts. Beach access. Bike rentals. Hiking trail. Cr cds: DS, MC, V.

★★★ **INN AT BAY LEDGE.** *1385 Sand Point Rd (04609). 207/288-4204; fax 207/288-5573. Email bayledge@downeast.net; www.innatbayledge.com.* 7 rms, 2 story. June-Oct: D $325; lower rates rest of yr. Parking lot. Pool. TV; cable, VCR avail. Complimentary full bkfst, toll-free calls. Restaurant nearby. Bar. Ck-out 11 am, ck-in 3 pm. Meeting rm. Business servs avail. Exercise privileges, sauna, steam rm. Golf. Tennis, 5 courts. Beach access. Hiking trail. Cr cds: MC, V.

★★★ **MANOR HOUSE INN.** *106 West St (04609). 207/288-3759; fax 207/288-2974; toll-free 800/437-0088. Email manor@acadia.net; www.barharbormanorhouse.com.* 9 rms, 8 suites. June-Oct: S, D $155; suites $175; each addl $20; under 12 free; lower rates rest of yr. Parking lot. TV; cable, CD avail. Complimentary full

bkfst, coffee in rms, newspaper, toll-free calls. Restaurant nearby. Ck-out 10:30 am, ck-in 3 pm. Meeting rms. Business center. Concierge. Exercise privileges, whirlpool. Golf, 18 holes. Tennis, 4 courts. Beach access. Bike rentals. Hiking trail. Picnic facilities. Cr cds: A, DS, MC, V.

★★ **MAPLES INN.** *16 Roberts Ave (04609). 207/288-3443; fax 207/288-0356. Email info@maplesinn.com; www.maplesinn.com.* 6 rms, 3 story, 1 suite. 1 A/C. No rm phones. Mid-June-mid-Oct: S, D $90-$120; each addl $15; suite $150; higher rates Memorial Day wkend; lower rates mid-Apr-mid-June, mid-Oct-early Dec. Closed rest of yr. Children over 8 yrs only. Complimentary full bkfst. Restaurant nearby. Ck-out 11 am, ck-in 2 pm. X-country ski 5 mi. Some fireplaces. Balconies. Restored, turn-of-the-century Victorian inn. Totally nonsmoking. Cr cds: DS, MC, V.

★★★ **MIRA MONTE INN & SUITES.** *69 Mt Desert St (04609). 207/288-4263; fax 207/288-3115; toll-free 800/553-5109. Email mburns@miramonte.com; www.miramonte.com.* 13 rms, 2 story, 3 suites. June-Oct: S, D $175; suites $200; each addl $15; children $15; lower rates rest of yr. Parking lot. TV; cable, VCR avail. Complimentary full bkfst, toll-free calls. Restaurant nearby. Ck-out 11 am, ck-in 2 pm. Meeting rm. Business servs avail. Cr cds: A, D, DS, MC, V.

★★ **THE RIDGEWAY INN.** *11 High St (04609). 207/288-9682; toll-free 800/360-5226. Email info@theridgewayinn.com; www.theridgewayinn.com.* 4 rms, 3 story, 1 suite. July-Oct: S, D $150; each addl $15; lower rates rest of yr. Parking lot. TV; cable, VCR avail. Complimentary full bkfst, newspaper, toll-free calls. Restaurant nearby. Ck-out 11 am, ck-in 2 pm. Golf, 18 holes. Cr cds: MC, V.

★★ **STRATFORD HOUSE INN.** *45 Mt Desert St (04609). 207/288-5189; fax 207/288-4184. Email info@stratfordinn.com.* 10 rms, 2 share bath, 3 story. July-mid-Sep: S, D $75-

$150; each addl $15; under 5 free; lower rates mid-May-June, mid-Sep-mid-Oct. Closed rest of yr. TV, 5 B and W. Complimentary continental bkfst 8-10 am. Ck-out 11 am, ck-in 1 pm. Fireplaces. Music rm. Built by publisher of Louisa May Alcott's "Little Women" (1900); English Tudor design modeled after Shakespeare's house in Stratford-on-Avon, original Jacobean furniture. Totally nonsmoking. Cr cds: DS, MC, V.

★★★ **THORNHEDGE INN.** *47 Mt Desert St (04609). 207/288-5398; res 877/288-5395; toll-free 877/288-5398.* 13 rms, 3 story. 1 A/C. Mid-June-mid-Oct: S, D $80-$140; lower rates mid-May-mid-June. Closed rest of yr. TV; cable. Continental bkfst; evening refreshments. Ck-out 11 am, ck-in noon. Some fireplaces. Queen Anne-style structure built by publisher of Louisa May Alcott's "Little Women" as a summer cottage (1900). Totally nonsmoking. Cr cds: MC, V.

Cottage Colony

★ **EMERY'S COTTAGES ON THE SHORE.** *PO Box 172, Sand Point Rd (04609), Sand Point Rd, 4 mi NE off ME 3. 207/288-3432; res 207/288-3432; toll-free 888/240-3432. Email emeryscottages@acadia.net; www. emeryscottages.com.* 21 cottages, 13 kits. (oven in 6). No A/C. No rm phones. Late June-Labor Day: D $70-$84; kit. units $90-$110; wkly rates; lower rates early May-late June, Labor Day-Oct. Closed rest of yr. Crib free. TV; cable (premium). Complimentary coffee. Ck-out 10 am, ck-in 2 pm. Coin lndry. Refrigerators. Picnic tables, grills. On Frenchman Bay. Cr cds: A, DS, MC, V.

Restaurants

★ **FREDDIE'S ROUTE 66.** *21 Cottage St (04609). 207/288-3708.* Specializes in prime rib, lobster, roast pork. Hrs: 11 am-11 pm. Closed mid-Oct-mid-May. Res accepted. Bar. Lunch, dinner $7.95-$15.95. Child's menu. 1950s-theme decor. Family-owned. Cr cds: A, C, D, DS, ER, MC, V.
D

★ **ISLAND CHOWDER HOUSE.** *38 Cottage St (04609). 207/288-4905.* Specializes in lobster, chowder. Own desserts. Hrs: 11 am-9 pm. Closed Nov-Apr. Res accepted. Bar. Lunch $4.29-$9.99; dinner $8.99-$19.99. Child's menu. Pub decor with model train operating in dining rm. Cr cds: A, DS, MC, V.
D

★ **MIGUEL'S MEXICAN.** *51 Rodick St (04609). 207/288-5117.* Specializes in tostadas, enchiladas, fajitas. Hrs: 5-10 pm. Closed mid-Nov-Mar. Bar. Dinner complete meals: $5.95-$13.95. Child's menu. Mexican atmosphere; artifacts, tiled floors. Cr cds: MC, V.
D

★★ **QUARTER DECK.** *1 Main St (04609). 207/288-5292.* Specializes in lobster crepe a la Reine, sole Marguery hollandaise au supreme. Hrs: 11 am-10 pm; early-bird dinner 4-6 pm. Closed Nov-Apr. Lunch $3.95-$10.95; dinner $10.95-$19.95. Cr cds: A, D, DS, MC, V.
D

★★★ **READING ROOM.** *Newport Dr. 207/288-3351. Email bhinn@ acadia.net; www.barharborinn.com.* Specializes in fresh local seafood. Own baking. Hrs: 5-9 pm. Closed mid-Nov-Easter. Res accepted. Bar. Wine list. Bkfst a la carte entrees: $1.50-$9.50. Buffet: $7.50-9.50; dinner a la carte entrees: $15.95-$24.95. Child's menu. Entertainment: pianist or harpist. Valet parking. Panoramic view of harbor and docks. Cr cds: A, C, D, DS, ER, MC, V.
D

★★ **RINEHART DINING PAVIL-LION.** *Highbrook Rd (04609), off Eden St. 207/288-5663.* Specializes in prime rib, seafood. Hrs: 7 am-9 pm. Closed Nov-Apr. Bar. Bkfst buffet: $7; lunch, dinner $10.95-$19.95. Child's menu. Parking. Octagonal bldg on hill; overlooks harbor. Cr cds: DS, V.
D

Unrated Dining Spot

FISHERMAN'S LANDING. *35 West St (04609). 207/288-4632.* Specializes in lobster, seafood. Hrs: 11 am-8 pm. Closed Oct-May. Bar. Lunch, dinner

$1.50-$9. Lobster tanks; select lobster. Built over water. Family-owned. Cr cds: MC, V.

D

Bath

(G-2) *See also Boothbay Harbor, Brunswick, Freeport*

Pop 9,799 **Elev** 13 ft **Area code** 207
Zip 04530
Web www.midcoastmaine.com
Information Chamber of Commerce of the Bath-Brunswick Region, 45 Front St; 207/443-9751 or 207/725-8797

For more than two centuries Bath has been a shipbuilding center on the west bank of the Kennebec River. The Bath Iron Works, which dates back to 1833, began bldg ships in 1889. It has produced destroyers, cruisers, a battleship, pleasure craft, and steamers, and now also produces patrol frigates. Altogether, Bath has launched more than 4,000 ships from its shores, and launching a ship today is still a great event.

Many fine old mansions, built when Bath was a great seaport, still stand. A restored 19th-century business district, waterfront park, and public landing are also part of the city.

What to See and Do

Fort Popham Memorial. Construction of the fort began in 1861. Never finished, it was garrisoned in 1865-66 and remains an impressive masonry structure with gun emplacements. Picnic tables (no garbage receptacles). (May-Sep, daily) 16 mi S on ME 209 in Popham Beach. Phone 207/389-1335 or 207/287-3821.
FREE

Maine Maritime Museum and Shipyard. Maritime History Bldg has exhibits of models, navigational instruments, scrimshaw, macramé, seafaring crafts and memorabilia, paintings. Tours of original shipyard bldgs, demonstrations of seafaring techniques (seasonal); waterfront pic-nic area and playground. Museum shop. (Daily; closed Jan 1, Thanksgiving, Dec 25) 243 Washington St, 2 mi S of US 1, located on Kennebec River. Phone 207/443-1316. ¢¢¢

Popham Colony. A picturesque drive. In 1607 the first American vessel, the *Virginia,* was built here by colonists who shortly thereafter returned to England, many of them in the ship they had built. On the hilltop nearby is Fort Baldwin, built during WWI. A 70-ft tower offers a panoramic view of the coast and the Kennebec River. 16 mi S on ME 209 on Sabino Head.
FREE

State parks.

Popham Beach. Swimming, tidal pools (mid-Apr-Nov), surfing, fishing; picnicking. (Daily) Standard fees. 12 mi S on ME 209. Phone 207/389-1335. ¢

Reid. Swimming, saltwater lagoon, bathhouse, fishing; picnic facilities, concession. (Daily) Standard fees. 1 mi E on US 1 to Woolwich, then 13 mi SE on ME 127 to Georgetown, then SE. Phone 207/371-2303. ¢¢

Motel/Motor Lodge

★★ **HOLIDAY INN BATH.** *139 Richardson St (04530). 207/443-9741; fax 207/442-8281; res 800/HOLIDAY. Email hibath@aol.com.* 141 rms, 3 story. Late June-early Oct: S, D $85-$119; each addl $10; under 19 free; lower rates rest of yr. Crib free. Pet accepted. TV; cable, premium. Heated pool; whirlpool. Complimentary coffee in rms. Restaurant 6 am-2 pm, 5-10 pm. Bar 11-1 am; Sun from noon; entertainment Wed-Sun. Ck-out noon. Meeting rm. Business servs avail. In-rm modem link. Valet serv. Sundries. Coin lndry. Exercise equipt; sauna. Refrigerators. Cr cds: A, DS, MC, V.

D ⊠ ≋ ⊼ ⊠ ⊠ SC

B&Bs/Small Inns

★★ **FAIRHAVEN INN.** *118 N Bath Rd (04530), 1½ mi N on High St to Whiskeag Rd, left onto Whiskeag Rd to North Bath Rd. 207/443-4391; fax 207/443-6412; toll-free 888/443-4391. Email fairhvn@gwi.net; www.maine coast.com/fairhaveninn.* 8 rms, 2 story.

May-Oct: S $75; D $100; each addl $15; lower rates rest of yr. Crib avail, fee. Parking lot. TV; cable, VCR avail. Complimentary full bkfst. Restaurant 8 am-8 pm. Ck-out 11 am, ck-in 4 pm. Meeting rm. Business servs avail. Concierge. Golf, 18 holes. Tennis, 6 courts. Hiking trail. Picnic facilities. Cr cds: DS, MC, V.

★ ★ ★ **GALEN C. MOSES HOUSE.** *1009 Washington St (04530). 207/442-8771; fax 207/443-6861; toll-free 888/442-8771. Email stay@galenmoses.com.* 4 rms, 2 shower only. No A/C. No rm phones. Mid-May-Oct: S, D $69-$99; wkends 2-day min (in season); lower rates rest of yr. Children over 12 yrs only. Cable TV in common rm, VCR avail (movies). Complimentary full bkfst; afternoon refreshments. Ck-out 11 am, ck-in 3-8 pm. Picnic tables, grills. Built in 1874; antiques. Italian bldg with Victorian interior; stained-glass windows. Totally non-smoking. Cr cds: A, DS, MC, V.

Restaurants

★ ★ **KRISTINA'S.** *160 Centre St (04530). 207/442-8577.* Hrs: 8 am-9 pm. Closed Thanksgiving, Dec 25; Jan; also Mon off-season. Res accepted. Bar. Bkfst $3.25-$7.50; lunch $4.95-$8.95; dinner $10.95-$15.95. Sat, Sun brunch, $3.50-$9.25. Child's menu. Bakery on premises. Cr cds: DS, MC, V.

☐

★ **TASTE OF MAINE.** *US 1 (04579), 1 mi N on US 1. 207/443-4554. www.tasteofmaine.com.* Specializes in lobster, seafood, steak. Hrs: 11 am-9 pm. Lunch $2.95-$24.95?; dinner $2.95-$24.95. Child's menu. Gift shop. Overlooks fork of Kennebec River. Cr cds: A, D, DS, MC, V.

☐

Baxter State Park

See also Millinocket

(18 mi NW of Millinocket via park roads)

While serving as a legislator and as governor of Maine, Percival P. Baxter urged creation of a wilderness park around Mount Katahdin—Maine's highest peak (5,267 feet). Rebuffed but not defeated, Baxter bought the land with his own money and deeded to the state of Maine a 201,018-acre park "to be forever left in its natural, wild state." The park can be reached from Greenville via paper company roads, from Millinocket via ME 157, or from Patten via ME 159.

The Park Authority operates the following campgrounds: Katahdin Stream, Abol and Nesowadnehunk, Roaring Brook (Roaring Brook Road), Chimney Pond (by trail 3.3 miles beyond Roaring Brook), Russell Pond (Wassataquoik Valley, seven miles by trail beyond Roaring Brook), South Branch Pond (at outlet of Lower South Branch Pond), Trout Brook Farm (Trout Brook Crossing). There are cabins ($17/person/night) at Daicey Pond off Nesowadnehunk Road and at Kidney Pond. All areas except Chimney, Kidney, and Daicey ponds have tent space, and all areas except Trout Brook Farm, Kidney, and Daicey ponds have lean-tos; ($6/person/night), water (unprotected, should be purified) and primitive facilities (no indoor plumbing, no running water; some springs); bunkhouses ($7/night) at some campgrounds. Under age 7 free throughout the park.

Reservations should be made by mail (and paid in full) in advance. For detailed information contact the Reservation Clerk, Baxter State Park, 64 Balsam Dr, Millinocket 04462. Swimming, fishing, canoes for rent at Russell Pond, South Branch Pond, Daicey Pond, Kidney Pond, and Trout Brook farm.

The park is open for camping mid-May-mid-October. No pets or motorcycles are permitted. Vehicles exceeding seven feet wide, nine feet high, or 22 feet long will not be admitted. For further information contact Park Manager, 64 Balsam Dr, Millinocket 04462; 207/723-5140. Nonresident vehicle fee ¢¢¢

Belfast

(F-3) *See also Bucksport, Camden, Searsport*

Settled 1770 **Pop** 6,355 **Elev** 103 ft
Area code 207 **Zip** 04915
Information Chamber of Commerce, 29 Front St, PO Box 58; 207/338-5900

Belfast, named for the city in Northern Ireland, was settled in 1770 by Irish and Scottish immigrants. An old seaport on the west shore of Penobscot Bay, Belfast is also a hub of small boat traffic to the bay islands. It is the seat of Waldo County, with sardine canneries, potato processing, window making, and printing as its major industries.

What to See and Do

Lake St. George State Park. More than 360 acres. Swimming, bathhouse, lifeguard, fishing, boating (ramp, rentals); snowmobiling permitted, picnicking, camping. (Mid-May-mid-Oct) Standard fees. 19 mi W on ME 3, near Montville. Phone 207/589-4255.

Annual Event

Belfast Bay Festival. City Park. Parade, concerts, carnival. Phone 207/338-5900. July.

Motels/Motor Lodges

★★ **BELFAST HARBOR INN.** *RR 5 Box 5230, Rte 1 (04915), ½ mi N on US 1. 207/338-2740; fax 207/338-5205; toll-free 800/545-8576. Email stay@belfastharborinn.com; www.belfastharborinn.com.* 61 rms, 2 story. July-Aug: S, D $74-$89; each addl $10; under 12 free; wkly rates; lower rates rest of yr. Crib free. Pet accepted; $5. TV; cable (premium). Pool. Complimentary continental bkfst. Restaurant 11 am-9 pm. Ck-out 11 am. Meeting rm. Business servs avail. Downhill/x-country ski 15 mi. Balconies. Picnic tables. Overlooks Penobscot Bay. Cr cds: A, DS, MC, V.

★ **GULL MOTEL.** *RR 5 Box 5377 (04915), 3 mi N on US 1. 207/338-4030.* 14 rms, 1 story. July-Aug: S, D $79; each addl $7; children $5; under 12 free; lower rates rest of yr. Crib avail, fee. Pet accepted, some restrictions, fee. TV; cable. Complimentary toll-free calls. Ck-out 11 am, ck-in 1 pm. Golf. Cr cds: MC, V.

★ **WONDERVIEW COTTAGES.** *RR 5 Box 5339 (04915), Searsport Ave, 3 Mi NE on US 1, ME 3. 207/338-1455; fax 207/338-1455. Email wondercottages@acadia.net; www.maineguide.com/belfast/wonderview.* 20 kit. cottages, 1 condo. No A/C. July-Labor Day, wkly: kit. cottages for 2-6, $475-$850; lower rates Apr-June, Sep-late Oct. Closed rest of yr. Crib free. Pet accepted. TV; cable. Playground. Restaurant nearby. Ck-out 10:30 am. Lawn games. Fireplaces. Screened porches. Picnic tables, grills. Private beach on Penobscot Bay. Cr cds: DS, MC, V.

B&B/Small Inn

★★ **BELFAST BAY MEADOWS INN.** *192 Northport Ave (04915), S on US 1. 207/338-5715; res 800/335-2370. Email bbmc@baymeadowsinn.com; www.baymeadowinn.com.* 20 rms, 1-3 story. July-Aug: S, D $85-$165; each addl $15; lower rates rest of yr. Crib free. Pet accepted. TV in some rms, sitting rm; cable, VCR avail (free movies). Playground. Complimentary full bkfst. Ck-out 11 am, ck-in 3:30-6:30 pm. Meeting rm. Business servs avail. Refrigerators avail. Turn-of-the-century country inn; antiques. Overlooks bay. Totally nonsmoking. Cr cds: A, DS, MC, V.

Restaurant

★★ **DARBY'S.** *155 High St (04915). 207/338-2339.* Specializes in pad thai, mahogany duck. Own desserts. Hrs: 11 am-3 pm, 5-9 pm. Closed Easter, Dec 25. Res accepted. Bar. Lunch $3.95-$10.95; dinner $6.95-$16.95. Child's menu. Street parking. Cr cds: DS, MC, V.

Bethel (F-1)

Settled 1774 **Pop** 2,329 **Elev** 700 ft
Area code 207 **Zip** 04217
Web www.bethelmaine.com

Information Chamber of Commerce,
PO Box 439; 207/824-2282 or
800/442-5826 (res)

Bethel, on both banks of the winding
Androscoggin River, is built on the
rolling Oxford Hills and is backed by
the rough foothills of the White
Mountains. In addition to being a
year-round resort, it's an educational
and wood products center. One of
Maine's leading preparatory schools,
Gould Academy (founded 1836), is
located here.

What to See and Do

Dr. Moses Mason House Museum.
(1813) Restored home of prominent
congressman who served during
administration of Andrew Jackson.
Antique furnishings, early American
murals. (July-Labor Day, Sat and Sun
afternoons; rest of yr, Mon-Fri, also
by appt) Broad St, in National Historic District. Phone 207/824-2908. ¢

Grafton Notch State Park. The
Appalachian Trail passes through the
notch; interpretive displays, scenic
view, picnicking, fishing. (Memorial
Day-mid-Oct) Approx 9 mi NW via
US 2, ME 26. Phone 207/824-2912. ¢

Skiing.

　Carter's X-C Ski Center. One
　thousand acres with 65 km of
　groomed cross-country trails.
　Rentals, lessons; lounge, shop, two
　lodges. (May-Oct, daily) Middle
　Intervale Rd. Phone 207/539-4848.
　¢¢

　Sunday River Ski Resort. Nine
　quad, 4 triple, 2 double chairlifts
　(incl 4 high-speed detachables, one
　surface lift); patrol, school, rentals,
　ski shop, snowmaking; cafeterias,
　restaurants, bars. 126 runs; longest
　run 3 mi; vertical drop 2,340 ft.
　(Early Oct-mid-May, daily) 112
　cross-country trails adj. Mountain
　biking (late June-Labor Day, daily;
　Labor Day-late Oct, wkends). 6 mi
　NE on US 2. Phone 207/824-3000
　or 800/543-2SKI (reservations).
　¢¢¢¢

**Swimming, picnicking, camping, boat-
ing, fishing.** Songo Lake in Bethel;
Christopher Lake in Bryant Pond; N
and S ponds in Locke Mills; Littlefield beaches and Stony Brook campgrounds. E on ME 26.

White Mountain National Forest.
(see under NEW HAMPSHIRE). More
than 49,000 acres of this forest
extend into Maine SW of here.
Birches and sugar maples turn fall
into a season of breathtaking color.
Fishing. Hiking, rockhounding.
Camping (fee). For information contact the Supervisor, 719 Main St, PO
Box 638, Laconia, NH 03247; or the
Evans Notch Ranger District office in
Bethel. Phone 603/528-8721 (Supervisor) or 207/824-2134 (Ranger). **FREE**

Motels/Motor Lodges

★ **INN AT THE ROSTAY.** *186
Mayville Rd; US 2 (04217). 207/824-
3111; fax 207/824-0482; toll-free
888/754-0072. Email info@rostay.com;
www.rostay.com.* 18 rms, 1 story, 1
suite. Dec-Mar, July, Oct: S $98; D
$110; suites $160; each addl $10;
children $5; under 15 free; lower
rates rest of yr. Pet accepted, some
restrictions, fee. Parking lot. TV;
cable, VCR avail. Complimentary
coffee in rms, newspaper. Restaurant
6:30 am-10 pm. Ck-out 10:30 am, ck-
in 3 pm. Meeting rm. Business servs
avail. Concierge. Coin lndry. Gift
shop. Exercise privileges. Golf, 18
holes. Downhill skiing. Bike rentals.
Supervised children's activities. Hiking trail. Picnic facilities. Cr cds: A,
DS, MC, V.

🄳 🔌 🛁 ⛽ 🏂 🎿 🚶 ⛷ 🔥

★★ **NORSEMAN INN.** *134 Mayville
Rd (04217). 207/824-2002; fax 207/
824-0640; res 207/824-2002. Email
norsemaninn@megalink.net; www.bethel
maine.com.* 22 rms, 2 story, 1 suite.
Feb-Mar, July-Aug: S $98; D $118;
suites $198; each addl $10; lower
rates rest of yr. Crib avail, fee. Parking lot. TV; cable. Complimentary
continental bkfst, toll-free calls.
Restaurant nearby. Ck-out 10:30 am,
ck-in 2 pm. Business servs avail. Coin
lndry. Exercise privileges. Golf, 18
holes. Tennis. Downhill skiing. Hiking trail. Picnic facilities. Cr cds: DS,
MC, V.

🄳 🛁 🏂 🎿 ⛽ 🚶 ⛷ 🔥

★★ **RIVER VIEW.** *357 Mayville Rd (04217), 2 mi NE on US 2 (ME 5/26). 207/824-2808; fax 207/824-6808. Email info@riverresort.com.* 32 kit. units (2-bedrm). Mid-Dec-mid-Apr: D $89-$139; each addl $20; suites $150-$250; 2-day min; higher rates hols; lower rates rest of yr. TV; cable (premium). Indoor pool; whirlpool. Playground. Ck-out 10 am. Tennis. Downhill ski 4 mi; x-country ski 3 mi. Sauna. Game rm. Lawn games. Picnic tables, grills. On river. Cr cds: A, DS, MC, V.

⬇ ➤ 🏌 ➤ 👫 ⛷ ☃ 🔥

Resorts

★★ **BETHEL INN AND COUNTRY CLUB.** *On the Common (04217), at jct US 2, ME 5, 26, 35. 207/824-2175; fax 207/824-2233; toll-free 800/654-0125. Email info@bethelinn.com; www. bethelinn.com.* 129 rms, 2 story, 9 suites. Jan-Mar, June-Sep: S $149; D $300; suites $209; each addl $65; under 15 free; lower rates rest of yr. Crib avail. Pet accepted, some restrictions, fee. TV; cable. Restaurant 5:30-10 pm. Bar. Ck-out 11 am, ck-in 2 pm. Downhill skiing. Bike rentals. Supervised children's activities. Hiking trail. Picnic facilities. Cr cds: A, C, D, DS, MC, V.

🅳 ⬇ ➤ ☃ 🔥

★★★ **GRAND SUMMIT.** *Sunday River Access Rd (04217), 4 mi N on US 2, follow Sunday River signs. 207/824-3500; fax 207/824-3993; toll-free 800/543-2754. www.sundayriver.com.* 140 rms, 3 story, 90 suites. Nov-Mar: Crib avail. Valet parking avail. Pool, lap pool, whirlpool. TV; cable, VCR avail, CD avail. Complimentary coffee in rms. Restaurant 6:30 am-10 pm. Bar. Ck-out 11 am, ck-in 4 pm. Meeting rms. Business center. Bellhops. Concierge. Coin lndry. Gift shop. Exercise privileges, sauna, steam rm. Golf, 18 holes. Tennis, 3 courts. Downhill skiing. Bike rentals. Supervised children's activities. Hiking trail. Cr cds: A, C, D, DS, MC, V.

🅳 ⬇ ➤ 👫 🏌 ➤ ⛷ ☃ 🔥 👤

B&B/Small Inn

★★ **BRIAR LEA INN & RESTAURANT.** *150 Mayville Rd (04217), 1 mi N on US 2 at jct ME 26. 207/824-4717;* fax 207/824-7121; toll-free 877/311-1299. Email briarlea@megalink. net; www.briarleainnrestaurant.com. 7 rms, 3 with shower only. No A/C. No rm phones. Jan-Apr, mid-Sep-mid-Oct: S $79; D $89-$99; each addl $15; ski plans; wkends, hols (2-day min); higher rates hols; lower rates rest of yr. Crib $15. Pet accepted, some restrictions. TV in common rm; cable, VCR avail. Complimentary full bkfst. Restaurant 6:30-11 am, 5-9:30 pm; Sun to noon. Ck-out 11 am, ck-in 4 pm. Downhill ski 5 mi; x-country ski on site. Built in 1850s; farmhouse atmosphere; antiques. Cr cds: A, DS, MC, V.

🐟 ⬇ ➤ 🏌 ➤ 👫 ⛷ ✈ 🔥 👤

Restaurant

★ **MOTHER'S.** *Main St (04217). 207/824-2589.* Specializes in seafood, chicken, pasta. Own soups. Hrs: 11 am-9 pm; Sun brunch to 2 pm. Closed Thanksgiving, Dec 24, 25. Lunch $4.50-$14.50; dinner $6.50-$19. Sun brunch $10.95. Child's menu. Parking. Gothic gingerbread-style house (late 1800s); antiques. Cr cds: C, DS, ER, MC, V.

Bingham

(E-2) *See also Skowhegan*

Settled 1785 **Pop** 1,071 **Elev** 371 ft
Area code 207 **Zip** 04920

What to See and Do

Wilderness Expeditions. Guided raft trips on the Kennebec, Penobscot, and Dead rivers; also canoe outfitting, guided kayaking, and ski tours. (May-Sep, daily) Phone 207/534-7305 or 800/825-9453. ¢¢¢¢

Motel/Motor Lodge

★ **BINGHAM MOTOR INN & SPORTS COMPLEX.** *Rte 201 (04920), 1 mi S on US 201. 207/672-4135; fax 207/672-4138. Email bmisc@ctel.net; ctel.net/~bmisc.* 20 rms. May-Nov: S $48.95; D $58.95; suites $88; each addl $8; under 12 free; lower rates rest of yr. Crib avail. Pet accepted, some restrictions. Parking lot. Pool. TV; cable (premium). Restaurant nearby. Ck-out 10 am, ck-in 1 pm. Business center. Free airport transportation. Golf, 18 holes. Downhill skiing. Hiking trail. Picnic facilities. Cr cds: A, DS, MC, V.

[icons]

Blue Hill

(F-4) *See also Bar Harbor, Ellsworth*

Settled 1722 **Pop** 1,941 **Elev** 40 ft
Area code 207 **Zip** 04614
Information Office of the Town Clerk, PO Box 433; 207/374-2281 or 207/374-5741

Named for a nearby hill that gives a beautiful view of Mount Desert Island, Blue Hill changed from a thriving seaport to a summer colony known for its crafts and antiques. Mary Ellen Chase, born here in 1887, wrote about Blue Hill in *A Goodly Heritage* and *Mary Peters*.

What to See and Do

Holt House. One of the oldest houses in Blue Hill; now home of the Blue Hill Historical Society. Memorabilia. (July-Aug, Tues and Fri afternoons; closed hols) For further information contact the town clerk. ¢

Parson Fisher House. (1814) House designed and built by town's first minister, who also made most of his own furniture and household articles; paintings and woodcuts by the minister; memorabilia. (July-mid-Oct, Mon-Sat afternoons) On ME 15. Phone 207/374-2844. ¢¢

Rackliffe Pottery. Family manufactures wheel-thrown dinnerware from native red-firing clay. Open workshop. (July-Aug, daily; rest of yr, Mon-Sat; closed hols) Ellsworth Rd. Phone 207/374-2297. **FREE**

Rowantrees Pottery. Manufactures functional pottery and wheel-thrown handcrafted dinnerware; 10- to 15-min tours. (June-Sep, daily; rest of yr, Mon-Fri; closed hols) Union St. Phone 207/374-5535. **FREE**

Wooden Boat School. (Daily) Naskeag Rd & Brooklyn. Phone 207/359-4651.

Annual Event

Blue Hill Fair. Sheep dog trials, agriculture and livestock exhibits; midway, harness racing, crafts. Five days Labor Day wkend.

Hotel

★★ **HERITAGE INN.** *Ellsworth (04614), ½ mi E on ME 172.* 207/374-5646. 23 rms, 2 story. No A/C. July-Labor Day: S, D $85; each addl $8; kit. unit $115; lower rates rest of yr. Crib $5. TV; cable. Complimentary coffee in rms. Restaurant nearby. Ck-out 11 am. On hillside, overlooking bay. Cr cds: MC, V.

[icons]

B&B/Small Inn

★★★ **BLUE HILL INN.** *Union St (04614), W on ME 177.* 207/374-2844; fax 207/374-2829; toll-free 800/826-7415. Email bluehillinn@hotmail.com; www.bluehillinn.com. 10 rms, 3 story, 1 suite. July-Oct: S $145; D $165; suites $225; lower rates rest of yr. Street parking. TV; cable (premium). Complimentary full bkfst, coffee in rms, newspaper, toll-free calls. Restaurant. Bar. Meeting rm. Business center. Coin lndry. Gift shop. Tennis, 2 courts. Beach access. Bike rentals. Hiking trail. Picnic facilities. Cr cds: A, MC, V.

[icons]

Restaurant

★★ **JONATHAN'S.** *Main St (04614),* 207/374-5226. *Email mbistro@midmaine.com.* Mediterranean menu. Specializes in braised lamb shank, poached Atlantic salmon. Hrs: 5-10 pm. Closed hols; Mon off-season. Res accepted. Wine, beer. Dinner a la carte entrees: $16-$19.50. Street parking. Cr cds: MC, V.

Boothbay Harbor

(G-3) *See also Damariscotta, Wiscasset*

Pop 1,267 **Elev** 16 ft **Area code** 207
Zip 04538
Web www.boothbayharbor.com

Information Boothbay Harbor Region Chamber of Commerce, PO Box 356; 207/633-2353 or 800/266-8422

Native Americans were paid 20 beaver pelts for the area encompassing Boothbay Harbor. Today, its protected harbor, a haven for boatmen, is the scene of well-attended regattas several times a summer. Boothbay Harbor, on the peninsula between the Sheepscot and Damariscotta rivers, shares the peninsula and adjacent islands with a dozen other communities, incl Boothbay (settled 1630), of which it was once a part.

What to See and Do

Boat Trips.

Balmy Days Cruises. Trips to Monhegan Island (see) with 4-hr stopover. (June-Sep, daily) Also 1-hr harbor cruises with stop at Squirrel Island in Boothbay Harbor (Apr-Oct, daily) and Night Lights cruises (July-Aug, Tues-Sat). Pier 8, Commercial St. Phone 207/633-2284. ¢¢¢-¢¢¢¢¢

Cap'n Fish's Boat Trips and Deep Sea Fishing. Boats make varied excursions: 1¼-3-hr trips; fishing cruises; lobster hauling; puffin, seal, and whale watches; scenic, sunset, and cocktail cruises; fall foliage and Kennebec River trips; charters. (Mid-May-Oct; days vary) Pier 1. Phone 207/633-3244 or 207/633-2626. ¢¢¢-¢¢¢¢¢

Boothbay Railway Village. Specifically geared to young children, incl historical Maine exhibits of rural life, railroads, and antique autos and trucks. Rides on a coal-fired, narrow-gauge steam train to an antique vehicle display. Also on exhibit on 8 acres are displays of early fire equipment, a general store, a 1-rm schoolhouse, and 2 restored railroad stations. (Mid-June-mid-Oct, daily) 1 mi N of Boothbay Center on ME 27. Phone 207/633-4727. ¢¢

Boothbay Region Historical Society Museum. Artifacts of Boothbay Region. (July-Labor Day, Wed, Fri, Sat; rest of yr, Sat only) 70 Oak St. **Donation**

Fishing. In inland waters, Golf Course Brook, Adams, W Harbor, and Knickerbocker ponds in Boothbay; Meadow Brook in E Boothbay. Ocean fishing from harbor docks. Boat rentals; deep-sea fishing.

Picnicking. Boothbay Region Lobstermen's Cooperative, Atlantic Ave. Lobsterman's Wharf, E Boothbay. Robinson's Wharf, ME 27 at bridge, Southport. Boiled lobsters and steamed clams, snacks avail.

Annual Events

Windjammer Days. Schooners that formerly sailed the trade routes and now offer cruises along the Maine coast sail en masse into harbor. Waterfront food court, entertainment, street parade, children's activities. Phone 207/633-2353. Late June.

Antique Show. Phone 207/633-4727. Third wkend July.

Fall Foliage Festival. Foliage drives, harvest suppers, boat trips, country fair. Phone 207/633-4743. Columbus Day wkend.

Harbor Lights Festival. Craft fair, lighted boat parade. Phone 207/633-2353. First Sat Dec.

Motels/Motor Lodges

★★ **CAP'N FISH'S MOTE & MARINA.** *65 Atlantic Ave (04538). 207/633-6605; fax 207/633-6239; toll-free 800/633-0860. www.capnfishs motel.com.* 55 rms, 2 story. June-Aug: S, D $120; each addl $8; under 12 free; lower rates rest of yr. Crib avail. Parking lot. TV; cable. Complimentary toll-free calls. Restaurant nearby. Ck-out 11 am, ck-in 3 pm. Golf. Cr cds: A, MC, V.
🄳 🛉 🗟 🔥

★★ **FLAGSHIP MOTOR INN.** *200 Townsend Ave; ME 27 (04538). 207/633-5094; fax 207/633-7055; toll-free 800/660-5094. Email flagship@ boothbaylodging.com; www.boothbay-lodging.com.* 83 rms, 2 story. July-Aug: S, D $75; each addl $10; children $5; under 18 free; lower rates rest of yr. Parking lot. Pool. TV; cable. Complimentary toll-free calls. Restaurant. Bar. Golf, 18 holes. Tennis, 2 courts. Bike rentals. Picnic facilities. Cr cds: A, DS, MC, V.
🄳 🛉 🗟 🔥

★★ **LAWNMEER INN.** *65 Hendrix Hill Rd (04575), 2½ mi S on ME 27. 207/633-2544; fax 207/633-0762; toll-free 800/633-7645. Email cooncat@ lawnmeerinn.com.* 35 rms, 1-2 story. Some A/C. July-Labor Day: D $88-$140; each addl $25; lower rates: mid-May-June, wkdays after Labor Day-mid-Oct. Closed rest of yr. Pet accepted; $10. TV; cable. Restaurant 7:30-10 am, 6-9 pm. Bar 5:30-9 pm. Ck-out 11 am. Lawn games. Balconies. Built 1898. On inlet; dock. Cr cds: MC, V.

Boothbay Harbor

★★★ **OCEAN GATE INN.** *Rte 27 (04576), 2½ mi SW on ME 27. 207 /633-3321; fax 207/633-2900; toll-free 800/221-5924. Email ogate@ocean gateinn.com.* 67 rms, 1-2 story. 15 A/C. July-Aug: S, D, kit. units $110-$145; each addl $15; suites for 2-4 $160-$190; kit. cottages for 2-8, $1,800/wk; under 12 free; lower rates mid-May-June, Sep-mid-Oct. Closed rest of yr. Crib $5. TV; cable. Heated pool; whirlpool. Playground. Complimentary full bkfst. Complimentary coffee in rms. Ck-out 11 am. Coin lndry. Tennis. Exercise equipt. Refrigerators avail. Lawn games. Private porch on most rms. On 85 wooded-acres. On ocean; dock, boats avail. View of harbor. Cr cds: DS, MC, V.

★ **PINES MOTEL.** *Sunset Rd (04538), Sunset Rd, 1¼ mi SE, off Atlantic Ave. 207/633-4555.* 29 rms. No A/C. July-Aug: S $70; D $80; each addl $6; lower rates May-June, after Sep-mid-Oct. Closed rest of yr. Crib free. Pet accepted. TV; cable. Heated pool. Playground. Ck-out 11 am. Tennis. Lawn games. Refrigerators. Balconies, decks. In wooded area; view of harbor. Cr cds: DS, MC, V.

★ **SEAGATE.** *138 Townsend Ave (04538). 207/633-3900; fax 207/633-3998; toll-free 800/633-1707. Email mef@gwi.net; www.seagatemotel.com.*

25 rms, 1 story. July-Aug: S, D $90; each addl $7; under 12 free; lower rates rest of yr. Crib avail, fee. Parking lot. Pool. TV; cable. Complimentary continental bkfst, newspaper, toll-free calls. Fax servs avail. Golf, 18 holes. Tennis, 2 courts. Cr cds: A, DS, MC, V.

★★ **SMUGGLER'S COVE MOTOR INN.** *Rte 96 (04544), 4¼ mi E on ME 96. 207/633-2800; fax 207/633-5926; toll-free 800/633-3008.* 60 units, 2 story, 6 kit. units (most without ovens). No A/C. Late June-Labor Day: S, D $60-$140; each addl $10; kit. units $85-$140; under 12 free; wkly rates; lower rates after Labor Day-mid-Oct. Closed rest of yr. Crib $10. Pet accepted, some restrictions; $50 deposit, refundable. TV; cable. Heated pool. Restaurant 8-10:30 am, 6-9:30 pm. Bar from 5:30 pm. Ck-out 11 am. Business servs avail. Balconies. On ocean; swimming beach. Cr cds: A, DS, MC, V.

★ **TOPSIDE MOTEL.** *49 Mcknown St (04538), atop Mckown Hill, 1 blk off ME 27. 207/633-5404.* 7 rms, 17 motel rms, 2-3 story, 2 kit. suites. No A/C. No elvtr. July-Aug: D $70-$150; each addl $10; under 8 free; lower rates late May-June, after Labor Day-mid-Oct. Closed rest of yr. Crib free. TV in motel rms; cable. Complimentary continental bkfst. Coffee in rms. Restaurant nearby. Ck-out 11 am. Lawn games. Refrigerator in motel rms. View of bay, harbor. Cr cds: DS, MC, V.

★ **THE WATER'S EDGE MOTEL.**
Ocean Point Rd (04544), 3½ mi E on ME 96. 207/633-2505. 26 units, 1-2 story, 20 kit. units, 8 cottages. No A/C. No rm phones. Late June-late Aug: S, D $75; kit. units $80; kit. cottages $70-$100; lower rates mid-May-late June, late Aug-mid-Oct. Closed rest of yr. Crib $5. Pet accepted, some restrictions; $10. TV; cable. Playground. Ck-out 10 am. Coin lndry. Lawn games. Refrigerators. Balconies. Picnic tables, grills. On ocean; dockage; swimming beach. Cr cds: C, MC.

D 🔾 🖾 🐾

Hotels

★★ **FISHERMAN'S WHARF INN.**
22 Commercial St (04538), at Pier 6. 207/633-5090; fax 207/633-5092; toll-free 800/628-6872. Email fishermans wharf@clinic.net; www.fishermanswharf inn.com. 54 rms, 3 story, 6 suites. July-Aug: S $100; D $110; suites $135; each addl $10; children $5; under 16 free; lower rates rest of yr. Crib avail, fee. Valet parking avail. TV; cable (premium). Complimentary continental bkfst, newspaper, toll-free calls. Restaurant 11:30 am-9 pm. Bar. Ck-out 11 am, ck-in 2 pm. Meeting rm. Business center. Bellhops. Coin lndry. Gift shop. Golf. Cr cds: A, C, D, DS, MC, V.

D 🔾 🛏 🖾 🐾 🏃

★★★ **TUGBOAT INN.** *80 Commercial St/PO Box 267 (04538).* 207/633-4434; toll-free 800/248-2628. www. tugboatinn.com. 62 rms, 3 story, 2 suites. June-Sep: S, D $165; suites $195; each addl $15; under 11 free; lower rates rest of yr. Crib avail, fee. Valet parking avail. TV; cable. Complimentary continental bkfst, toll-free calls. Restaurant 11:50 am-9 pm. Bar. Ck-out 11 am, ck-in 3 pm. Meeting rm. Fax servs avail. Coin lndry. Gift shop. Golf, 18 holes. Cr cds: A, DS, MC, V.

D 🔾 🛏 🖾 🐾

Resorts

★★★ **BROWN'S WHARF MOTEL RESTAURANT & MARINA.** *121 Atlantic Ave (04538), 1 mi SE.* 207/633-5440; fax 207/633-5440; toll-free 800/334-8110. Email brownswharf@

clinic.net; www.brownswharfinn.com. 67 rms, 3 story, 2 suites. June-Aug: S, D $149; suites $139; each addl $15; children $15; under 2 free; lower rates rest of yr. Crib avail. Parking lot. TV; cable (premium), VCR avail. Complimentary full bkfst, coffee in rms, newspaper, toll-free calls. Restaurant 5:30-8:30 pm. Bar. Ck-out 11 am, ck-in 3 pm. Business servs avail. Coin lndry. Golf. Beach access. Cr cds: A, MC, V.

D 🔾 🛏 🐾 SC

★★★ **SPRUCE POINT INN.**
Atlantic Ave (04538), 1½ mi SE off ME 27. 207/633-4152; fax 207/633-7138; toll-free 800/553-0289. Email the point@sprucepointinn.com; www. sprucepointinn.com. 20 rms, 40 suites. July-Aug: S, D $155; suites $185; each addl $10; lower rates rest of yr. Crib avail. Pet accepted. Parking lot. Pool, lap pool, childrens pool, whirlpool. TV; cable (premium), VCR avail. Complimentary coffee in rms. Restaurant. Bar. Meeting rms. Business center. Bellhops. Concierge. Coin lndry. Gift shop. Exercise equipt. Golf, 18 holes. Tennis, 2 courts. Bike rentals. Supervised children's activities. Hiking trail. Picnic facilities. Cr cds: A, C, D, DS, MC, V.

D 🔾 🛏 🏊 🖾 🏃 🐾

B&Bs/Small Inns

★★ **1830 ADMIRAL'S QUARTERS INN.** *71 Commercial St (04538).* 207/633-2474; fax 207/633-5904. Email loon@admiralsquartersinn.com. June-Oct: S $135; D $145; suites $155; each addl $20; under 12 free; lower rates rest of yr. Parking lot. Indoor pool, children's pool. TV; cable, VCR avail. Complimentary full bkfst, coffee in rms, newspaper, toll-free calls. Restaurant nearby. Ck-out 11 am, ck-in 2 pm. Internet access avail. Coin lndry. Gift shop. Exercise privileges. Golf, 18 holes. Tennis, 6 courts. Beach access. Bike rentals. Hiking trail. Picnic facilities. Cr cds: DS, MC, V.

🔾 🛏 🏊 🏃 🐾

★★ **ANCHOR WATCH BED & BREAKFAST.** *9 Eames Rd (04538).* 207/633-7565; fax 207/633-5319. Email diane@lincoln.midcoast.com; www.anchorwqatch.com. 5 rms, 3 story. June-Oct: S, D $140; lower rates rest of yr. Parking lot. TV; cable, VCR avail. Complimentary full bkfst. Restaurant 11 am-9 pm. Ck-out 11 am, ck-in 2 pm. Exercise privileges. Golf, 18 holes. Tennis, 6 courts. Bike rentals. Supervised children's activities. Hiking trail. Picnic facilities. Cr cds: DS, MC, V.

★★ **FIVE GABLES INN.** *335 Murray Hill Rd (04544), 3½ mi E on ME 96. 207/633-4551; toll-free 800/451-5048. Email info@fivegablesinn.com; www. fivegablesinn.com.* 16 rms, 3 story. June-Oct: S $175; each addl $25; lower rates rest of yr. Parking lot. TV; cable, VCR avail. Complimentary full bkfst, newspaper. Restaurant 11 am-midnight. Ck-out 11 am, ck-in 2 pm. Concierge. Gift shop. Golf, 18 holes. Tennis, 2 courts. Beach access. Bike rentals. Hiking trail. Cr cds: MC, V.

★★ **HARBOUR TOWNE INN ON WATERFRONT.** *71 Townsend Ave (04538). 207/633-4300; fax 207/633-4300. Email gtme@gwi.net; www. acadianet/harbourtowneinn.* 12 rms, 3 story, 7 kits. No A/C. Memorial Day-Oct: S, D $99-$175; suite $275; each addl $25; kits. $129-$175; lower rates rest of yr. Crib $25. TV; cable. Complimentary continental bkfst; afternoon refreshments. Restaurant nearby. Ck-out 10 am, ck-in 3:30 pm. Balconies. On harbor. Totally nonsmoking. Cr cds: A, MC, V.

★★ **HOWARD HOUSE LODGE.** *347 Townsend Ave (04538), 1 mi N on ME 27. 207/633-3933; fax 207/633-6244; toll-free 800/466-6697. Email maineair@howardhouselodge.com; www.howardhouselodge.com.* 14 rms, 2 story. July-Oct: S, D $87; each addl $15; children $15; under 10 free; lower rates rest of yr. Parking lot. TV; cable. Complimentary full bkfst. Restaurant nearby. Ck-out 11 am. Fax servs avail. Golf, 18 holes. Tennis, 6 courts. Hiking trail. Cr cds: A, MC, V.

★★ **KENNISTON HILL INN.** *Wiscasset Rd; Rte 27 (04537). 207/633-2159; fax 207/633-2159; toll-free 800/992-2915. Email innkeeper@ maine.com; www.maine.com/inn keeper.* 10 rms, 7 with shower only,

1-2 story. No A/C. No rm phones. Mid-June-Oct: D $69-$110; each addl $25; lower rates rest of yr. Children over 10 yrs only. Complimentary full bkfst; afternoon refreshments. Ck-out 11 am, ck-in 3 pm. Some fireplaces. Restored Colonial-style farmhouse (1786); antiques. Totally nonsmoking. Cr cds: DS, MC, V.

★★ **OCEAN POINT INN.** *Shore Rd PO Box 409 (04544), 6½ mi SE on ME 96 at Ocean Pt. 207/633-4200; toll-free 800/552-5554. www.oceanpoint inn.com.* 61 units, 1-2 story, 50 rms in 5 bldgs, 6 cottage units; 5 kit. units. Some A/C. Late June-early Sep: S, D $96-$160; each addl $10; cottage units $91-$136; kit. units. $925-$1,020/wk; under 13, $5 (cottages only); hol wkends (3-day min); lower rates late May-late June, early Sep-mid-Oct. Closed rest of yr. Crib $5. TV; cable. Heated pool. Dining rm (in season) 7:30-10 am, 6-9 pm; closed Sun, early Sep-mid-Oct. Bar 5-10 pm. Ck-out 11 am, ck-in 3 pm. Refrigerators. Some balconies; porch on cottages. On peninsula at entrance to Linekin Bay. Cr cds: A, DS, MC, V.

Cottage Colony

★ **HILLSIDE ACRES CABINS & MOTEL.** *Adams Pond Rd (04537), 1½ mi N on Adams Rd, off ME 27. 207/ 633-3411; fax 207/633-2295. Email hillside@clinic.net; www.gwi.net/~ hillside.* 4 rms, 2 story, 1 suite. July-Aug: S, D $57; suites $75; each addl $5; lower rates rest of yr. Crib avail, fee. Pet accepted, some restrictions. Parking lot. Pool. TV; cable. Complimentary continental bkfst. Restaurant nearby. Ck-out 10:30 am, ck-in 1 pm. Exercise privileges. Picnic facilities. Cr cds: MC, V.

Restaurants

★ **ANDREW'S HARBORSIDE.** *12 Bridge St (04538), at W end of footbridge. 207/633-4074.* Specializes in seafood, cinnamon rolls. Own soups, desserts. Hrs: 7 am-8 pm. Closed mid-Oct-Apr. Bkfst $2.25-$6.25; lunch $3.95-$10.95; dinner $9.95-

$16.95. Child's menu. Overlooks harbor. Cr cds: DS, MC, V.

D

★ **CHINA BY THE SEA.** *96 Townsend Ave (04538). 207/633-4449.* Hrs: 11 am-10 pm. Closed Thanksgiving, Dec 25. Res accepted. Lunch, dinner $4.50-$14.95. Overlooks harbor. Cr cds: A, C, D, DS, ER, MC, V.

D

★ **EBB TIDE.** *43 Commercial St (04538). 207/633-5692.* Specializes in seafood, omelettes. Own desserts. Hrs: 6 am-9 pm. Closed Dec 25. Bkfst $3-$5.50; lunch $3-$12.95; dinner $7-$12.95. Child's menu. Cr cds: A, MC, V.

Bridgton

(G-1) *See also Poland Spring, Sebago Lake*

Pop 2,195 **Elev** 494 ft **Area code** 207 **Zip** 04009
Information Bridgton Lakes Chamber of Commerce, PO Box 236M; 207/647-3472

Primarily a resort, this community between Long and Highland lakes is within easy reach of Pleasant Mountain (2,007 feet), a recreational area that offers skiing as well as a magnificent view of 50 lakes. Bridgton also has many unique craft and antique shops located within a two-mile radius of the town center.

What to See and Do

Gibbs Avenue Museum. Headquarters of Bridgton Historical Society. Permanent exhibits incl narrow-gauge railroad memorabilia; Civil War artifacts; Sears "horseless carriage" (1911). Special summer exhibits. Genealogy research facility incl Bridgton and Saw River railroad documents. (Sep-June, Tues and Thurs; rest of yr, Tues-Fri; closed hols) Gibbs Ave. Phone 207/647-3699. ¢

Shawnee Peak at Pleasant Mountain Ski Area. Triple, 3 double chairlifts; snowmaking, school, rentals, patrol;

nursery, restaurant, cafeteria, bar. Longest run 1½ mi; vertical drop 1,350 ft. Night skiing. (Late Nov-early Apr, daily) 6 mi W, off US 302. Phone 207/647-8444. ¢¢¢¢

Annual Event

Quilt Show. Town hall. New and old quilts; demonstrations. Contact Chamber of Commerce. Mid-July.

B&B/Small Inn

★★★ **THE INN AT LONG LAKE.** *PO Box 806, Lake House Rd (04055), S on US 302, at jct ME 11. 207/693-6226; toll-free 800/437-0328. Email innatll@megalink.net; www.innatlong lake.com.* 14 rms, 4 story, 2 suites. June-Oct: S $112; D $140; suites $180; each addl $40; children $400; under 6 free; lower rates rest of yr. Parking lot. TV; cable. Complimentary full bkfst, newspaper. Restaurant. Ck-out 11 am, ck-in 3 pm. Meeting rm. Concierge. Gift shop. Golf, 18 holes. Downhill skiing. Beach access. Picnic facilities. Cr cds: DS, MC, V.

Restaurant

★ **BLACK HORSE TAVERN.** *8 Portland Rd (04099). 207/647-5300.* Specializes in ribs, steak, fresh seafood. Hrs: 11 am-10 pm; hrs vary off-season. Closed Thanksgiving, Dec 25. Bar. Lunch $3.95-$7.95; dinner $5.95-$19.95. Sun brunch $1.50-$5.95. Child's menu. In restored homestead. Equestrian motif; saddles, bridles, harnesses on display. Cr cds: DS, MC, V.

D

Brunswick

(G-2) *See also Bailey Island*

Settled 1628 **Pop** 20,906 **Elev** 67 ft
Area code 207 **Zip** 04011
Web www.midcoastmaine.com
Information Chamber of Commerce of the Bath-Brunswick Region, 59 Pleasant St; 207/725-8797

Once a lumbering center and later a mill town, Brunswick is now mainly concerned with trade, health care, and education; it is the home of Bowdoin College and Brunswick Naval Air Station. The city lies northeast of a summer resort area on the shores and islands of Casco Bay. Magnificent Federalist mansions along Federal Street and Park Row remind visitors of Brunswick's past.

What to See and Do

Bowdoin College. (1794) 1,500 students. Nathaniel Hawthorne, Henry Wadsworth Longfellow, Robert Peary, Franklin Pierce, and Joan Benoit Samuelson graduated from here. Tours. Maine St. Phone 207/725-3000. On campus are

Museum of Art. Portraits by Stuart, Feke, and Copley; paintings by Homer and Eakins; Greek and Roman vases and sculpture. (Tues-Sun; closed hols) Walker Art Bldg. Phone 207/725-3275. **FREE**

Peary-MacMillan Arctic Museum. Exhibits relating to Arctic exploration, ecology, and Inuit (Eskimo) culture. (Tues-Sun; closed hols) Hubbard Hall. Phone 207/725-3416. **FREE**

Pejepscot Historical Society Museum. Regional historical museum housed in an 1858 sea captain's home; changing exhibits, research facilities. (Memorial Day-Labor Day, Mon-Sat; rest of yr, Mon-Fri; closed hols) 159 Park Row. Phone 207/729-6606. **FREE** The Society also operates

Joshua L. Chamberlain Museum. Former residence of Maine's greatest Civil War hero, 4-term Governor of Maine, and president of Bowdoin College. Guided tours. (Memorial Day-Labor Day, Tues-Sat; closed hols) 226 Maine St. ¢¢ Combination ticket with Skolfield-Whittier House ¢¢¢

Skolfield-Whittier House. An 18-rm Victorian structure last occupied in 1925; furnishings and housewares of 3 generations. Guided tours. (Memorial Day-Labor Day, Tues-Sat; closed hols) 161 Park Row. ¢¢ Combination ticket with Chamberlain Museum ¢¢¢

Thomas Point Beach. Swimming, lifeguard; picnicking, tables, fireplaces, snack bar, gift shop, arcade, playground, camping (fee). (Memorial Day-Labor Day, daily) Off ME 24, at Cook's Corner. Phone 207/725-6009.

Annual Events

Topsham Fair. N via ME 24 in Topsham. Entertainment; arts and crafts. Phone 207/725-2735. Seven days early Aug.

Bluegrass Festival. At Thomas Point Beach. Phone 207/725-6009. Labor Day wkend.

Seasonal Events

Maine State Music Theater. Pickard Theater, Bowdoin College campus. Broadway musicals by professional cast. Tues-Sat eves; Wed, Fri, Sun matinees. Phone 207/725-8769. Mid-June-Aug.

Bowdoin Summer Music Festival and School. Brunswick High School and Bowdoin College campus. Chamber music, concert series. Phone 207/725-3322. Fri eves, late June-Aug.

Music on the Mall. Downtown. Free outdoor family concert series. Phone 207/725-8797. Wed eves, July and Aug.

Motels/Motor Lodges

★ **ATRIUM TRAVELODGE.** *21 Gurnet Rd Cooks Corner (04011). 207/729-5555; fax 207/729-5149. Email deescees@aol.com.* 186 rms, 3 story. July-Aug: S, D $74-$86; each addl $10; suites $125; under 19 free; lower rates rest of yr. Crib free. Pet accepted. TV; cable, VCR (movies $2.95). Indoor pool; wading pool, whirlpool. Complimentary coffee in lobby. Restaurant 6 am-10 pm. Rm serv. Bar to midnight. Ck-out noon. Meeting rms. Business servs avail. Sundries. Coin lndry. Exercise equipt; sauna. Game rm. Lawn games. Refrigerators. Cr cds: A, MC, V.

★★ **COMFORT INN.** *199 Pleasant St (04011). 207/729-1129; fax 207/725-8310.* 80 rms, 2 story. May-Oct: S, D $80-$89; each addl $7; under 18 free; lower rates rest of yr. Crib free. TV; cable (premium). Complimentary continental bkfst. Restaurant nearby. Ck-out 11 am. Business servs avail. Valet serv Mon-Fri. Cr cds: A, D, DS, MC, V.

★ **ECONO LODGE.** *215 Pleasant St; Rte 1 and I-95 (04011), 2 mi S on US 1 at Jct I-95.* 207/729-9991; fax 207/721-0413; res 800/4CHOICE; toll-free 800/654-9991. 29 rms, 1-2 story. July-Labor Day: D $76-$83; each addl $7; lower rates rest of yr. Crib $3. TV; cable. Pool. Complimentary coffee in lobby. Restaurant nearby. Ck-out 11 am. Coin lndry. Business servs avail. Sundries. Cr cds: A, C, D, DS, MC, V.
D ⊠ ⊠ ⊠

★ **SUPER 8 MOTEL.** *224 Bath Rd (04011).* 207/725-8883; fax 207/729-8766; res 800/800-8000. 70 rms, 2 story, 1 suite. June-Oct: S $57; D $85; suites $95; each addl $5; under 12 free; lower rates rest of yr. Crib avail. Parking lot. TV; cable (premium). Complimentary continental bkfst, newspaper, toll-free calls. Restaurant nearby. Ck-out 11 am, ck-in 3 pm. Fax servs avail. Golf. Downhill skiing. Cr cds: A, DS, MC, V.
D ⊠ ⊠ ⊠ ⊠ ⊠ SC

★ **VIKING MOTOR INN.** *287 Bath Rd (04011).* 207/729-6661; fax 207/729-6661; toll-free 800/429-6661. Email info@vikingmotorinn.com; www.vikingmotorinn.com. 28 rms. July-Oct: S $69; D $79; suites $89; each addl $5; under 12 free; lower rates rest of yr. Crib avail, fee. Pet accepted, some restrictions, fee. Parking lot. Pool. TV; cable. Complimentary toll-free calls. Restaurant nearby. Ck-out 10 am, ck-in 2 pm. Business servs avail. Exercise privileges. Golf, 18 holes. Tennis, 2 courts. Hiking trail. Picnic facilities. Cr cds: A, D, DS, MC, V.
⊠ ⊠ ⊠ ⊠ ⊠ ⊠ ⊠ ⊠ ⊠

B&B/Small Inn

★ ★ ★ **CAPTAIN DANIEL STONE INN.** *10 Water St (04011).* 207/725-9898; fax 207/725-9898; res 800/267-0525. Email cdsi@netquarters.net; www.netquarters.net/cdsi. 34 rms, 3 story, 4 suites. Mid-July-mid-Sep: S, D $125-$145; each addl $10; suites $175-$210; lower rates rest of yr. Crib free. TV; cable, VCR (movies). Complimentary continental bkfst. Dining rm 11:30 am-2 pm, 5-9 pm. Bar 4-10 pm. Ck-out 11 am, ck-in 4 pm. Business servs avail. Bathrm phones; some in-rm whirlpools. Balconies. Antiques. Screened veranda. Former

sea captain's house (1819). Cr cds: A, D, MC, V.
D ⊠ ⊠ ⊠ SC

Restaurant

★ ★ **GREAT IMPASTA.** *42 Maine St (04011).* 207/729-5858. Specializes in pasta, veal. Hrs: 11 am-9 pm. Closed Thanksgiving, Dec 25. Lunch $3.95-$6.95; dinner $7.95-$12.95. Cr cds: A, DS, MC, V.
D

Bu` ⊞ Buksport

Buksport

(F-4) *See also Bangor, Belfast, Ellsworth*

Settled 1762 **Pop** 4,825 **Elev** 43 ft
Area code 207 **Zip** 04416
Web www.bangorregion.com
Information Bangor Region Chamber of Commerce, 519 Main St, PO Box 1443, Bangor 04401; 207/947-0307

Although originally settled in 1762, the Penobscot valley town of Bucksport was so thoroughly burned by the British in 1779 that it was not resettled until 1812. On the east bank of the Penobscot River, Bucksport is a shopping center for the area, but is primarily an industrial town with an emphasis on paper manufacturing. The Waldo Hancock Bridge crosses the Penobscot to Verona Island.

What to See and Do

Accursed Tombstone. Granite obelisk over grave of founder Jonathan Buck bears an indelible mark in the shape of a woman's leg—said to have been put there by a witch whom he had hanged. Buck Cemetery, Main & Hinks Sts, near Verona Island Bridge. **FREE**

Fort Knox State Park. Consists of 124 acres around huge granite fort started in 1844 and used as a defense in the Aroostook War. Structure incl spiral staircases. Hiking, picnicking. Interpretive displays. Tours (Aug, Sep). (May-Oct) Standard fees. S on US 1 across Waldo Hancock Bridge. Phone 207/469-7719. ¢¢

Fort Point State Park. Ocean view. Fishing. Picnicking. (Memorial Day-Labor Day) Standard fees. 8 mi S on US 1. Phone 207/469-6818. ¢

Jed Prouty Tavern. A 1798 hostelry once a stopping place on a stage-coach run. Famous guests were Presidents Martin Van Buren, Andrew Jackson, William Henry Harrison, and John Tyler. Admiral Peary also lodged here while a ship for one of his Arctic expeditions was built nearby. (Daily; closed Dec 25) 52-54 Main St. Phone 207/469-3113 or 207/469-7972. **FREE**

Northeast Historic Film. The Alamo Theatre (1916) houses museum, theater, store, and archives of northern New England film and video. Exhibits present 100 yrs of moviegoing, from nickelodeons to mall cinemas. Video and film presentations interpret regional culture. (Oct-May, Mon-Fri; rest of yr, Mon-Sat) 379 Main St. Phone 207/469-0924. **FREE**

Wilson Museum. Prehistoric, historic, geologic, and art exhibits (late May-Sep, Tues-Sun, also hols). On grounds are John Perkins House (1763-83), Hearse House, Blacksmith Shop (July-Aug, Wed and Sun). 18 mi S via ME 175, 166 in Castine. Phone 207/326-8753. Museum **FREE**; Perkins House ¢¢

Motels/Motor Lodges

★★ **BEST WESTERN.** *52 Main St (04416). 207/469-3113; fax 207/469-3113; toll-free 800/528-1234.* 40 rms, 2-4 story. July-Oct: S $89; D $99; each addl $10; suites $125; under 12 free; lower rates rest of yr. Pet accepted, some restrictions. TV; cable. Restaurant opp 5:30-9:30 pm. Ck-out 11 am. Business servs avail. In-rm modem link. On Penobscot River. Cr cds: A, C, D, DS, MC, V.

★ **BUCKSPORT MOTOR INN.** *Rte 1 (04416), ½ mi NE on US 1 (ME 3). 207/469-3111; fax 207/469-3111; res 800/626-9734. Email bucksprt@aol.com.* 24 rms, 1 story. S, D $72; each addl $5; under 12 free. Pet accepted, some restrictions. Parking lot. TV; cable. Complimentary coffee in rms, toll-free calls. Restaurant nearby. Ck-out 11 am, ck-in noon. Fax servs avail. Golf, 9 holes. Tennis. Picnic facilities. Cr cds: A, DS, MC, V.

B&Bs/Small Inns

★★ **CASTINE INN.** *Main St (04421), 2 mi N on US 1, then 16 mi SE on ME 175 and ME 166. 207/326-4365; fax 207/326-4570. Email relax@castineinn.com; www.castineinn.com.* 19 rms, 4 suites, 3 story. No A/C. No rm phones. Memorial Day-Columbus Day: D $85-$130; each addl $20; suites $135-$210; lower rates May-Memorial Day, after Columbus Day-mid-Dec. Closed rest of yr. Children over 8 yrs only. Complimentary full bkfst. Dining rm 8-9:30 am, 5:30-8:30 pm. Bar 5-10 pm. Ck-out 11 am, ck-in 3 pm. Business servs avail. Built 1898; sitting rm with wood-burning fireplace. Many rms with harbor view; perennial and rose gardens. Totally nonsmoking. Cr cds: MC, V.

★★ **PENTAGOET INN.** *PO Box 4 (04421), 2 mi NE on US 1 to ME 175, then 16 mi S on ME 166 to Castine, at jct Main and Perkins Sts. 207/326-8616; fax 207/326-9382; res 207/326-8616; toll-free 800/845-1701. Email pentagoet@hypernet.com; www.pentagoet.com.* 15 rms, 3 story, 1 suite. July-Aug: S $80; D $130; suites $150; each addl $25; under 12 free; lower rates rest of yr. Pet accepted, some restrictions. Street parking. TV; cable. Complimentary full bkfst, newspaper. Restaurant nearby. Bar. Ck-out 10:30 am, ck-in 2 pm. Fax servs avail. Exercise privileges. Golf, 9 holes. Tennis, 4 courts. Bike rentals. Picnic facilities. Cr cds: MC, V.

Calais (E-6)

Settled 1770 **Pop** 3,963 **Elev** 19 ft
Area code 207 **Zip** 04619
Web www.mainerec.com/calais.html

Information Calais Regional Chamber of Commerce, PO Box 368; 207/454-2308 or 800/377-9748

International cooperation is rarely as warm and helpful as it is between Calais (KAL-iss) and St. Stephen, New Brunswick, just across the St. Croix River in Canada. Because of an early closing law in St. Stephen,

Canadians stroll over to the US for a nightcap, and fire engines and ambulances cross the International Bridge in both directions as needed. (For Border Crossing Regulations, see MAKING THE MOST OF YOUR TRIP.) **Note:** New Brunswick is on Atlantic Time, one hour ahead of Eastern Standard Time.

Calais has a unique distinction—it is located exactly halfway between the North Pole and the Equator. The 45th Parallel passes a few miles south of town; a marker on US 1 near Perry indicates the spot. Bass, togue, trout, and salmon fishing is available in many lakes and streams in Calais, and there is swimming at Meddybemps Lake, 13 miles north on ME 191.

What to See and Do

Moosehorn National Wildlife Refuge. Glacial terrain with forests, valleys, lakes, bogs, and marshes. Abundant wildlife. Hiking, fishing, hunting, cross-country skiing, bird-watching. (Daily) 4 mi N via US 1, on Charlotte Rd. Contact Refuge Manager, PO Box 1077. Phone 207/454-7161. **FREE**

St. Croix Island International Historic Site. In 1604 French explorers Sieur de Monts and Samuel de Champlain, leading a group of approx 75 men, selected this as the site of the first attempted European settlement on the Atlantic Coast north of Florida. Information shelter; no facilities. (Daily) 8 mi S via US 1, opp Red Beach in St. Croix River; accessible only by boat. Phone 207/288-3338. **FREE**

Annual Event

International Festival Week. Celebration of friendship between Calais and St. Stephen, New Brunswick; entertainment, concessions, contests, fireworks, parade. Early Aug.

Motels/Motor Lodges

★ **HESLIN'S MOTEL DINING ROOM.** *Rte 1, Box 111 (04619), 5 mi S on US 1. 207/454-3762; fax 207/454-0148. www.mainrec.com/heslins.* 15 rms. July-Aug: S $55; D $70; suites $100; each addl $5; under 12 free; lower rates rest of yr. TV; cable.

Restaurant 5-9 pm. Bar. Ck-out 10 am, ck-in 1 pm. Meeting rm. Golf, 9 holes. Cr cds: DS, MC, V.

★ **INTERNATIONAL MOTEL.** *276 Main St (04619). 207/454-7515; fax 207/454-3217; toll-free 800/336-7515.* 60 rms, 1 suite. June-Oct: S, D $60; suites $120; each addl $5; under 12 free; lower rates rest of yr. Crib avail. Pet accepted, some restrictions. Parking lot. TV; cable, VCR avail. Complimentary coffee in rms, toll-free calls. Restaurant 6 am-9 pm. 24-hr rm serv. Ck-out 11 am. Fax servs avail. Bellhops. Dry cleaning. Exercise privileges. Golf. Hiking trail. Cr cds: A, C, D, DS, MC, V.

★★ **REDCLYFFE SHORE MOTOR INN.** *ME 1 (04671), 12 mi S on US 1. 207/454-3270; fax 207/454-8723. Email redclyffe1@aol.com.* 17 rms. S, D $62-$73; each addl $5. Closed Dec-Apr. TV; cable (premium). Complimentary coffee in rms. Restaurant 5-9 pm. Ck-out 10 am. Victorian Gothic bldg (1863); on bluff overlooking St. Croix River, Passamaquoddy Bay. Cr cds: A, MC, V.

Restaurant

★ **WICKACHEE.** *282 Main St (04619). 207/454-3400.* Specializes in steak, seafood. Salad bar. Hrs: 6 am-10 pm. Closed Dec 25. Res accepted. Wine, beer. Bkfst $1.75-$4; lunch $2.50-$8.95; dinner $6.95-$13.95. Child's menu. Cr cds: MC, V.

Camden

(F-3) *See also Belfast, Rockland*

Pop 5,060 **Elev** 33 ft **Area code** 207
Zip 04843 **Web** www.camdenme.org
Information Camden-Rockport-Lincolnville Chamber of Commerce, Public Landing, PO Box 919; 207/236-4404

Camden's unique setting—where the mountains meet the sea—makes it a popular four-season resort area. Recreational activities incl boat cruises and boat rentals, swimming, fishing, camping, hiking, and picnicking, as well as winter activities. The poet Edna St. Vincent Millay began her career in Camden.

What to See and Do

Camden Hills State Park. Maine's 3rd-largest state park, surrounding 1,380-ft Mt Megunticook. Road leads to Mt Battie (800 ft). Spectacular view of coast. Hiking, picnic facilities, camping (dump station). (Memorial Day-Columbus Day) Standard fees. 2 mi NE on US 1. Phone 207/236-3109.

Conway Homestead-Cramer Museum. Authentically restored 18th-century farmhouse. Collection of carriages, sleighs, and farm implements in old barn; blacksmith shop, privy, and herb garden. Mary Meeker Cramer Museum contains paintings, ship models, quilts; costumes, documents, and other memorabilia; changing exhibits. (July-Aug, Tues-Fri) On US 1, near city limits. Phone 207/236-2257. ¢

Kelmscott Farm. Working farm established to conserve rare and endangered breeds of farm livestock, incl Cotswold sheep, Nigerian dwarf goats, Kerry cattle, and Gloucestershire Old Spots pigs. Educational demonstrations. Farm tours (Labor Day-Memorial Day, by appt). Museum and gift shop. Picnic area. Special events throughout the yr. (Tues-Sun) N on ME 52, in Lincolnville. Phone 207/763-4088. ¢¢

Maine State Ferry Service. A 20-min trip to Islesboro (Dark Harbor) on *Margaret Chase Smith*. (Mid-May-late Oct, wkdays, 9 trips; Sun, 8 trips; rest of yr, 6 trips daily) 6 mi N on US 1 in Lincolnville Beach. Phone 207/789-5611. ¢¢

Sightseeing cruises on Penobscot Bay. Cruises (1-4 hrs) leave from public landing. Contact Chamber of Commerce. Phone 207/236-4404. ¢¢¢¢

Skiing. Camden Snow Bowl. Double chairlift, 2 T-bars; patrol, school, rentals, toboggan chute and rentals, snowboarding, snowmaking; snack bar, lodge. (Mid-Dec-mid-Mar, daily) S on US 1 to John St to Hosmer Pond Rd. Phone 207/236-3438 or 207/236-4418 (snow conditions). ¢¢¢¢

Windjammers. Old-time schooners leave from Camden and Rockport Harbors for ½- to 6-day trips along the coast of Maine. (May-Oct) For further information, rates, schedules or res, contact the individual companies.

Appledore. Lily Pond Dr. Phone 207/236-8353.

Angelique. PO Box 736. Phone 800/282-9989.

Maine Windjammer Cruises. PO Box 617. Phone 207/236-2938.

Olad and Northwind. PO Box 432. Phone 207/236-2323.

Schooner *Lewis R. French*. PO Box 992. Phone 800/469-4635.

Schooner *Mary Day*. PO Box 798M. Phone 800/992-2218.

Schooner *Roseway*. PO Box 696X. Phone 800/255-4449.

Schooner *Surprise*. PO Box 450. Phone 207/236-4687.

Schooner *Timberwind*. PO Box 247, Rockport 04856. Phone 207/236-3639 or 800/759-9250.

Annual Events

Garden Club Open House Day. Tour of homes and gardens (fee). Contact Chamber of Commerce. Third Thurs July.

Windjammer Weekend. Celebration of windjammer industry; fireworks. Phone 207/236-4404. Labor Day wkend.

Christmas by the Sea. Celebration of holiday season with musical entertainment, horse-drawn wagon rides, Holiday House Tour, Santa's arrival by lobsterboat. Phone 207/236-4404. First wkend Dec.

Seasonal Events

Bay Chamber Concerts. Classical music performances by Vermeer Quartet and guest artists (July and Aug, Thurs and Fri eves). Jazz musicians perform Sep-June (one show each month). Rockport Opera House, Central St in Rockport. Phone 207/236-2823.

Camden Opera House. Elm St. Theater with musical and theatrical performances and concerts. Phone 207/236-4404. July-Aug.

Motels/Motor Lodges

★★ BEST WESTERN. *11 Tannery Ln (04843). 207/236-0500; fax 207/236-4711; res 800/755-7483; toll-free 800/757-4837. Email riverhouse@ acadia.net; www.camdenmaine.com.* 35 rms, 3 story. Mid-July-Labor Day: S, D $149-$199; under 17 free; lower rates rest of yr. Crib free. TV; cable (premium), VCR avail. Indoor pool; whirlpool. Complimentary continental bkfst. Restaurant nearby. Ck-out 11 am. Meeting rms. Business servs avail. In-rm modem link. Sundries. Downhill/x-country ski 5 mi. Exercise equipt. Some refrigerators; many microwaves. Cr cds: A, C, D, DS, JCB, MC, V.

[D] [icons]

★★★ BLACK HORSE INN. *PO Box 558 US 1 Atlantic Hwy (04849), 4 mi N on US 1. 207/236-6800; fax 207/ 236-6509; res 800/374-9085. www. midcoast.com/~blkhorse.* 21 rms, 2 story. June-Oct: S $88; D $98; suites $135; each addl $10; under 12 free; lower rates rest of yr. Crib avail, fee. Parking lot. TV; cable (premium). Complimentary continental bkfst, toll-free calls. Restaurant 7 am-9 pm. Ck-out 11 am, ck-in 3 pm. Fax servs avail. Gift shop. Whirlpool. Downhill skiing. Hiking trail. Cr cds: A, DS, MC, V.

[D] [icons]

★★ CEDAR CREST MOTEL. *115 Elm St (04845). 207/236-4859; toll-free 800/422-4964.* 37 rms, 1-2 story. July-Labor Day: D $99-$125; each addl $10; lower rates May-June, Labor Day-Oct. Closed Nov-Apr. Crib free. TV; cable. Heated pool. Playground. Restaurant 6 am-noon; closed Mon. Ck-out 11 am. Coin lndry. Some refrigerators. Balconies. Cr cds: A, MC, V.

[icons]

★★ GLENMOOR BY THE SEA. *RR 1 Box 3291 (04843), 4 mi N on US 1 in Lincolnville. 207/236-3466; fax 207/ 236-7043. www.maineguide.com/ camden/glenmoor.* 22 units, 7 cottages, 1 kit. unit. Early July-Aug: D $109-$169; each addl $10; cottages $129-$225; under 19 free; lower rates mid-May-early July, Sep-early Nov. Closed rest of yr. Crib $5. TV; cable, VCR avail. Heated pool. Complimen-

tary continental bkfst. Ck-out 11 am. Tennis. Refrigerators avail. Balconies. Sun deck. On ocean. Totally nonsmoking. Cr cds: A, MC, V.

[icons]

★★ MOUNT BATTEL HOTEL. *US Rte 1 RR 3 Box 570 (04849), 4 mi N on US 1. 207/236-3870; fax 207/230-0068; res 800/224-3870. Email mt battle@acadie.net.* 21 rms. July-mid-Oct: S, D $65-$115; each addl $15; lower rates May-June and mid-Oct-early Nov. Closed rest of yr. Crib $5. TV; cable. Complimentary continental bkfst, coffee in rms. Ck-out 11 am. Business servs avail. Refrigerators. Picnic tables, sundeck, gazebo, grill. Totally nonsmoking. Cr cds: A, MC, V.

[icons]

★★ SNOW HILL LODGE. *Atlantic Hwy; US 1 (04849), 4½ mi N on US 1. 207/236-3452; fax 207/236-8052; toll-free 800/476-4775. Email theveiw@ midcoast.com; www.midcoast.com/~the view.* 30 rms, 1 story. June-Aug: S $70; D $80; each addl $10; children $6; lower rates rest of yr. Crib avail, fee. Parking lot. TV; cable. Complimentary continental bkfst. Restaurant nearby. Ck-out 10 am, ck-in 1 pm. Fax servs avail. Downhill skiing. Picnic facilities. Cr cds: A, DS, MC, V.

[icons]

Hotel

★★★ INN AT OCEAN'S EDGE. *US 1 (04843). 207/236-0945; fax 207/236-0609. www.innatoceansedge.com.* 15 rms, 3 story, 1 suite. June-Oct: D $220; suites $250; each addl $35; under 14 free; lower rates rest of yr. TV; cable, VCR avail. Complimentary full bkfst, newspaper. Restaurant nearby. Ck-out 11 am, ck-in 3 pm. Meeting rm. Fax servs avail. Bellhops. Exercise equipt. Golf. Tennis, 5 courts. Downhill skiing. Beach access. Bike rentals. Hiking trail. Cr cds: MC, V.

[icons]

B&Bs/Small Inns

★★★ BLUE HARBOR HOUSE, A VILLAGE INN. *67 Elm St (04843). 207/236-3196; fax 207/236-6523; toll-free 800/248-3196. Email balidog@ midcoast.com; www.blueharborhouse.*

com. 7 rms, 2 story, 3 suites. May-Oct: S, D $145; suites $165; lower rates rest of yr. Parking lot. TV; cable, VCR avail. Complimentary full bkfst, newspaper, toll-free calls. Restaurant closed Sun. Bar. Ck-out 11 am, ck-in 3 pm. Business center. Golf, 18 holes. Tennis, 2 courts. Downhill skiing. Cr cds: A, DS, MC, V.

★★★ CAMDEN WINDWARD HOUSE. *6 High St (04843). 207/236-9656; fax 207/230-0433; toll-free 877/492-9656. Email bnb@windwardhouse.com; www.windwardhouse.com.* 6 rms, 3 story, 2 suites. June-Oct: S, D $165; suites $205; each addl $30; children $30; lower rates rest of yr. Parking lot. TV; cable (premium), VCR avail, CD avail. Complimentary full bkfst, coffee in rms, newspaper, toll-free calls. Restaurant nearby. Ck-out 11 am, ck-in 3 pm. Meeting rms. Business center. Concierge. Gift shop. Exercise privileges. Golf. Tennis, 5 courts. Downhill skiing. Hiking trail. Cr cds: A, MC, V.

★★★ DARK HARBOR HOUSE. *117 Getty Rd (04848), 6 mi N on US 1 to Lincolnville, ferry across Penobscot Bay to Islesboro Island, Ferry Rd, right at N Exit 2 intersections, 2 mi S to Dark Harbor. 207/734-6669; fax 207/734-6938. Email dhhouse@acadia.net; www.darkharborhouse.com.* 11 rms, 3 story, 3 suites. July-Aug: D $160; suites $190; each addl $35; lower rates rest of yr. Parking lot. TV; cable (premium), VCR avail, CD avail. Complimentary continental bkfst, coffee in rms, newspaper, toll-free calls. Restaurant 6-8:30 pm, closed Sun. Ck-out 11 am, ck-in 1 pm. Meeting rm. Golf, 18 holes. Tennis, 2 courts. Bike rentals. Cr cds: MC, V.

★★ ELMS BED & BREAKFAST. *84 Elm St (04843). 207/236-6250; fax 207/236-7330; toll-free 800/755-3567. Email theelms@midcoast.com; www.elmsinn.net.* 6 rms, 3 story. May-Oct: S, D $125; each addl $30; lower rates rest of yr. Parking lot. TV; cable (premium), VCR avail, CD avail. Complimentary full bkfst, coffee in rms, newspaper. Restaurant nearby. Ck-out 10:30 am, ck-in 3 pm. Business center. Gift shop. Golf, 18 holes. Tennis, 2

courts. Downhill skiing. Bike rentals. Hiking trail. Cr cds: DS, MC, V.

★★★ HAWTHORN INN. *9 High St (04843). 207/236-8842; fax 207/236-6181. Email hawthorn@midcoast.com; www.camdeninn.com.* 10 rms, 3 story. June-Dec: S, D $155; each addl $35; lower rates rest of yr. Parking lot. TV; cable, VCR avail, CD avail. Complimentary full bkfst, toll-free calls. Restaurant nearby. Meeting rms. Fax servs avail. Gift shop. Exercise privileges, whirlpool. Golf, 18 holes. Downhill skiing. Bike rentals. Hiking trail. Picnic facilities. Cr cds: A, MC, V.

★★★ INN AT SUNRISE POINT. *PO Box 1344 (04849), 4 mi N on US 1. 207/236-7716; fax 207/236-0820; res 800/435-6278. Email info@sunrise point.com; www.sunrisepoint.com.* 3 rms, 2 story. July-Oct: D $375; lower rates rest of yr. TV; cable, VCR avail. Restaurant nearby. Ck-out 11 am, ck-in 3 pm. B/W printing avail. Golf. Beach access. Cr cds: A, MC, V.

★★ THE LODGE AT CAMDEN HILLS. *PO Box 794 (Rte 1 N) (04843), 1 mi N on US 1. 207/236-8478; fax 207/236-7163; toll-free 800/832-7058. Email burgess@thelodgeatcamdenhills.com; www.thelodgeatcamdenhills.com.* 12 rms, 1 story, 4 suites. July-Oct: S $129; D $155; suites $175; each addl $15; under 18 free; lower rates rest of yr. Crib avail. Parking lot. TV; cable, VCR avail. Complimentary coffee in rms, newspaper, toll-free calls. Restaurant nearby. Ck-out 11 am, ck-in 2 pm. Business servs avail. Exercise privileges. Golf. Tennis. Downhill skiing. Beach access. Bike rentals. Hiking trail. Picnic facilities. Cr cds: A, DS, MC, V.

★★ MAINE STAY BED & BREAKFAST. *22 High St (04843), on US 1. 207/236-9636; fax 207/236-0621. Email innkeeper@mainestay.com; www.mainestay.com.* 6 rms, 2 suites. June-Oct: D $100; suites $150; each addl $40; lower rates rest of yr. Parking lot. TV; cable, VCR avail, CD avail. Complimentary full bkfst, coffee in rms, newspaper, toll-free calls. Restaurant. Ck-out 11 am, ck-in 2 pm. Business center. Concierge. Free airport transportation. Exercise privileges. Golf. Tennis, 5 courts. Downhill skiing. Beach access. Bike rentals. Hiking trail. Picnic facilities. Cr cds: A, MC, V.

★★★ **NORUMBEGA INN.** *63 High St (04843). 207/236-4646; fax 207/236-0824. Email stay@norumbegainn.com; www.norumbegainn.com.* 13 rms, 1 A/C, 4 story, 2 suites. No elvtr. July-mid-Oct: D $155-$325; each addl $35; suites $375-$450; lower rates rest of yr. Children over 7 yrs only. TV in some rms; cable, VCR in suites. Complimentary full bkfst; afternoon refreshments. Restaurant nearby. Ck-out 11 am, ck-in 3 pm. Business servs avail. In-rm modem link. Downhill/x-country ski 4 mi. Lawn games. Some fireplaces. Balconies. Stone castle (1886); hand-carved oak woodwork, baby grand piano, antique billiard table, library within turret. Built by inventor of duplex telegraphy. Murder mystery wkends. Totally nonsmoking. Cr cds: A, DS, MC, V.

★★ **THE VICTORIAN BY THE SEA.** *Sea View Dr (04843), 5 mi N on US 1. 207/236-3785; fax 207/236-0017; toll-free 800/382-9817. Email victbb@mid coast.com; www.victorianbythesea.com.* 5 rms, 3 story, 2 suites. July-Oct: S $135; D $150; suites $205; each addl $20; lower rates rest of yr. Parking lot. Pool. TV; cable, VCR avail, CD avail. Complimentary full bkfst. Restaurant nearby. Ck-out 11 am, ck-in 3 pm. Meeting rm. Golf. Downhill skiing. Hiking trail. Cr cds: A, MC, V.

★★ **WHITEHALL INN INC.** *52 High St (04843). 207/236-3391; fax 207/236-4427; toll-free 800/789-6565. Email stay@whitehall-inn.com; www.whitehall-inn.com.* 50 rms in 3 bldgs, most with bath, 2-3 story. No A/C. MAP, July-mid-Oct: S $85-$100; D $140-$180; each addl $45; under 14, $35; EP avail; lower rates Memorial Day-June. Closed rest of yr. Serv charge 15%. Crib $10. TV; cable in lobby. Afternoon refreshments. Restaurant (see WHITEHALL DINING ROOM). Bar. Ck-out 11 am, ck-in after 3 pm. Meeting rm. Business servs avail. Tennis. Health club privi-

leges. Lawn games. Spacious old resort inn (1834); poet Edna St. Vincent Millay gave a reading here in 1912. Garden with patio. Cr cds: A, MC, V.

Restaurants

★★ **CORK.** *51 Bayview St (04843). 207/230-0533.* Specializes in crab cakes. Hrs: 5:30-9:30 pm. Closed Sun, Mon. Res accepted. Extensive wine

Windjammer Weekend, Camden

list. Dinner $16-$40. Entertainment. Cr cds: A, DS, MC, V.

★★ **THE HELM.** *RR 1, Camden Rd (04856), 1½ mi S on US 1. 207/236-4337.* Specializes in French onion soup, steak au poivre, fresh seafood. Salad bar. Own desserts. Hrs: 11:30 am-9 pm. Closed mid-Dec-early Apr. Res accepted. Bar. Lunch; dinner $7-$17. Child's menu. Parking. Cr cds: DS, MC, V.

★★ **LOBSTER POUND.** *US 1 (04849), 6 mi N on US 1. 207/789-5550.* Specializes in seafood, turkey, steak. Own desserts. Hrs: 11:30 am-8 pm. Closed Nov-Apr. Res accepted. Lunch $4.95-$13.95; dinner $4.95-$13.95. Complete meals: $9.95-$34.95. Child's menu. Parking. Lobster tanks. Fireplace. Gift shop. Overlooks

Penobscot Bay. Family-owned. Cr cds:
A, C, D, DS, ER, MC, V.

★★ **PETER OTT'S.** *16 Bayview St
(04843). 207/236-4032.* Specializes in
local seafood, black Angus beef. Salad
bar. Own desserts. Hrs: 5-9 pm.
Closed Jan 1, Dec 25; also Mon mid-
Sep-mid-May. Bar. Dinner $7.95-
$22.95. Child's menu. Harbor view.
Cr cds: MC, V.

★★ **WATERFRONT.** *40 Bayview St
(04843). 207/236-3747.* Specializes in
seafood. Own desserts. Hrs: 11 am-9
pm. Closed Thanksgiving, Dec 25.
Bar. Lunch $5.95-$13.95; dinner
$12.95-$21.95. Child's menu. Parking. On harbor. Cr cds: A, MC, V.

★★★ **WHITEHALL DINING
ROOM.** *52 High St (US 1). 207/236-
3391. Email stay@whitehall-inn.com;
www.whitehall-inn.com.* Specializes in
seafood, beef, vegetarian specials.
Own baking, desserts. Hrs: 8-9 am, 6-
9 pm. Closed mid-Oct-mid-June. Bar.
Wine list. Bkfst $7.95; dinner $15-
$18. Child's menu. Cr cds: A, MC, V.

Caribou

(B-5) *See also Presque Isle*

Pop 9,415 **Elev** 442 ft **Area code** 207
Zip 04736
Web www.mainerec.com/caribou.html
Information Chamber of Commerce,
111 High St; 207/498-6156

Caribou, the nation's northeastern-
most city, is primarily an agricultural
area but has become diversified in
manufacturing. Located here are a
food processing plant, a paper bag
manufacturing plant, and an electronics manufacturing plant. Swimming, fishing, boating, camping, and
hunting are available in the many
lakes located 20 miles northwest on
ME 161.

What to See and Do

Caribou Historical Center. Museum
housing history of northern Maine.
(June-Aug, Tues-Sat; rest of yr, by
appt) 3 mi S on US 1. Phone
207/498-2556. **Donation**

Nylander Museum. Fossils, rocks,
minerals, butterflies, and shells collected by Olof Nylander, Swedish-
born geologist and naturalist; early
man artifacts; changing exhibits. Gift
shop. (Memorial Day-Labor Day,
Wed-Sun; rest of yr, wkends and by
appt) 393 Main St, ¼ mi S on ME
161. Phone 207/493-4209. **FREE**

Rosie O'Grady's Balloon of Peace **Monument.** Honoring Col Joe W. Kit-
tinger Jr, who in 1984 was the first
balloonist to fly solo across the
Atlantic Ocean, breaking distance
record set earlier by the *Double Eagle
II* flight. 2 mi S on S Main St. **FREE**

Annual Event

Winter Carnival. Phone 207/498-
6156. Feb.

Motels/Motor Lodges

★★★ **CARIBOU INN & CONVEN-
TION CENTER.** *19 Main St (04736),
2 mi S at US 1 and ME 164. 207/498-
3733; res 800/235-0466. Email
cicc3733@aol.com.* 73 rms, 3 story. No
elvtr. S, D $56-$80; suites $98-$106;
each addl $8; under 12 free. Crib
free. TV; cable (premium), VCR avail.
Indoor pool, whirlpool. Restaurant 6
am-2 pm, 5-9 pm; Sat 7 am-2 pm, 5-
9 pm; Sun 7 am-2 pm, 4-8 pm. Bar 5
pm-midnight; entertainment Fri, Sat.
Ck-out 11 am. Coin lndry. Meeting
rms. Business servs avail. Free airport
transportation. X-country ski ½ mi.
Exercise rm; sauna. Health club privileges. Game rm. Rec rm. Refrigerators, minibars. Some balconies. Cr
cds: A, C, D, DS, MC, V.

★★ **CROWN PARK INN.** *Access
Hwy (04736), at jct ME 89 and US 1.
207/493-3311; fax 207/498-3990; toll-
free 888/493-3311.* 60 rms, 2 story. S,
D $50-$58; each addl $10; under 18
free. Crib $7. TV; cable, VCR avail
(movies). Complimentary continental bkfst. Restaurant nearby. Bar 4
pm-1 am. Ck-out 11 am. Coin lndry.
Meeting rm. Business servs avail. In-
rm modem link. Exercise equipt.

Some refrigerators. Cr cds: A, D, DS, MC, V.

🔥 ⛷ 🧖 🎿 🏃

Restaurants

★ **JADE PALACE.** *Skyway Plz (04736), on US 1, in Skyway Plz Mall.* *207/498-3648.* Specializes in sizzling imperial steak, flaming Hawaiian duck, seafood. Hrs: 11 am-10 pm. Closed Thanksgiving. Res accepted. Bar. Lunch $1.95-$5.55. Buffet: $5.95; dinner $4.55-$12.95. Cr cds: A, DS, MC, V.

D **SC**

★ **RENO'S.** *117 Sweden St (04736).* *207/496-5331.* Specializes in pizza, sandwiches, fish. Salad bar. Hrs: 5 am-11 pm. Closed Memorial Day, Thanksgiving, Dec 25. Bkfst $1-$5; lunch $2.50-$7.95; dinner $2.50-$9. Child's menu. Cr cds: DS, MC, V.

D **SC**

Center Lovell

Pop 100 (est) **Elev** 532 ft
Area code 207 **Zip** 04016

This community on Kezar Lake is close to the New Hampshire border and the recreational opportunities of the White Mountain National Forest (see BETHEL). The surrounding region is rich in gems and minerals.

Resort

★★ **QUISISANA LODGE.** *Pleasant Point Rd (04016), 1 mi W of ME 5 on Pleasant Point Rd. 207/925-3500; fax 207/925-1004.www.quisisanaresort. com.* 16 rms in 2 lodges, 38 cottages (1-3 bedrm). No A/C. AP, mid-June-Aug: S $165-$265; D $230-$320; each addl $80; July-Aug (1-wk min). Closed rest of yr. Crib free. TV rm. Dining rm. Box lunches. Ck-out 11 am, ck-in 2 pm. Tennis. Private sand beaches. Waterskiing. Boats, motors; rowboats, canoes. Fishing guides. Windsurfing. Lawn games. Musicals, operas, concerts performed by staff (music students). Game rm. Rec rms. Dancing. Units vary. Refrigerators, fireplaces. Porch in cottages. Lake

sightseeing tours. On Lake Kezar in foothills of White Mts. Cr cds: A, MC, V.

🔥 ⛷ 🎣 🧖 ⛵ 🔥

B&Bs/Small Inns

★★★ **ADMIRAL PEARY HOUSE.** *9 Elm St (04037), 15 mi S on ME 5, W on US 302. 207/935-3365; fax 207/935-3365; toll-free 800/237-8080. Email admpeary@nxi.com; www. admiralpearyhouse.com.* 6 rms, 3 story. July-Oct: S, D $148; each addl $20; lower rates rest of yr. Parking lot. TV; cable, CD avail. Complimentary full bkfst, coffee in rms, newspaper, toll-free calls. Restaurant nearby. Ck-out 11 am, ck-in 3 pm. Meeting rms. Business servs avail. Whirlpool. Golf. Tennis. Downhill skiing. Beach access. Bike rentals. Hiking trail. Cr cds: A, MC, V.

🔥 ⛷ 🎣 🧖 ⛵ ⛵ 🔥

★★ **OXFORD HOUSE INN.** *105 Main St (04037), 15 mi S on ME 5, W on US 302. 207/935-3442; fax 207/935-7046; toll-free 800/261-7206. Email innkeeper@oxfordinn.com.* 5 rms, 3 story. No rm phones. D $80-$125; each addl $15. TV in some rms, sitting rm; cable. Complimentary full bkfst. Restaurant. Ck-out 11 am, ck-in 1 pm. Downhill ski 8 mi; x-country ski on site. Historic house (1913); antiques, verandah. Totally nonsmoking. Cr cds: A, D, DS, MC, V.

🔥 ⛷ 🎣 🧖 🎿 ⛵ 🔥

Chebeague Islands

Pop 300 (est) **Elev** 40 ft
Area code 207 **Zip** 04017

Little Chebeague (sha-BEEG) and Great Chebeague islands, off the coast of Portland in Casco Bay, were at one time a favorite camping spot of various tribes. The Native Americans had a penchant for clams; the first European settlers thus found heaps of clamshells scattered across the land. Those shells were later used to pave many of the islands' roads, some of which still exist today.

Great Chebeague, six miles long and approximately three miles wide, is connected to Little Chebeague at low tide by a sandbar. There are various locations for swimming. Additionally, both islands lend themselves well to exploring on foot or bicycle. At one time, Great Chebeague was home to a bustling fishing and shipbuilding community, and it was a quarrying center in the late 1700s. Today, it welcomes hundreds of visitors every summer.

What to See and Do

Ferry service from mainland.

Casco Bay Lines. From Portland, Commercial & Franklin Sts; 1-hr crossing. (Daily) Phone 207/774-7871. Round trip ¢¢¢

Chebeague Transportation. From Cousins Island, near Yarmouth; 15-min crossing. (Daily) Off-site parking with shuttle to ferry. Phone 207/846-3700. Round trip ¢¢¢

Cranberry Isles

See also Bar Harbor, Northeast Harbor, Southwest Harbor

Pop 189 **Elev** 20 ft **Area code** 207 **Zip** 04625

The Cranberry Isles, named because of the rich, red cranberry bogs that once covered Great Cranberry Isle, lie off the southeast coast of Mount Desert Island. There are five islands in the group: Little and Great Cranberry, Sutton, Bear, and Baker. Great Cranberry, the largest, covers about 900 acres. Baker Island is part of Acadia National Park, and Sutton is privately owned. In 1830, the islands petitioned the state to separate from Mount Desert Island. In the late 1800s, the area was a thriving fishing community.

What to See and Do

✪ Acadia National Park. (see) N on Mount Desert Island.

Ferry service. Ferry connects Little Cranberry and Great Cranberry with Northeast Harbor (see) on Mt Desert

Island; 3-mi, 30-min crossing. (Summer, daily; rest of yr, varied schedule) Phone 207/244-3575. ¢¢¢

Islesford Historical Museum. Exhibits on local island history from 1604. (July-Aug, daily; Sep, by appt) Islesford, on Little Cranberry Island. Phone 207/244-9224. **FREE**

Damariscotta

(G-3) *See also Boothbay Harbor, Wiscasset*

Settled 1730 **Pop** 1,811 **Elev** 69 ft
Area code 207 **Zip** 04543
Information Chamber of Commerce, PO Box 13; 207/563-8340

Damariscotta, whose name is an Abenaki word meaning "river of many fishes," has a number of colonial, Greek-revival, and pre-Civil War houses. With the neighboring city of Newcastle across the Damariscotta River, this is a trading center for a seaside resort region extending to Pemaquid Point and Christmas Cove.

What to See and Do

Chapman-Hall House. (1754) Restored house with original whitewash kitchen, period furniture; local shipbuilding exhibition. (July-early Sep, Mon-Sat) Main & Church Sts. ¢

Colonial Pemaquid State Memorial. Excavations have uncovered foundations of jail, tavern, private homes. Fishing, boat ramp; picnicking; free parking. (Memorial Day-Labor Day, daily) Standard fees. 14 mi S via ME 130, in New Harbor. Phone 207/677-2423. Also here is

Fort William Henry State Memorial. Reconstructed 1692 fort tower; museum contains relics, portraits, maps, and copies of Native American deeds (fee).

✪ Pemaquid Point Lighthouse Park. Incl 1827 lighthouse that towers above the pounding surf (not open to public), Fishermen's Museum housed in old lightkeeper's dwelling (donation), art gallery, and some recreational facilities. Fishermen's Museum (Memorial Day-Columbus

Day, daily; rest of yr by appt). 15 mi S at end of ME 130 on Pemaquid Point. Phone 207/677-2494 or 207/677-2726. Park ¢

St. Patrick's Church. (1808) Early Federal architecture; Revere bell in steeple. One of the oldest surviving Catholic churches in New England. W to Newcastle, then 2 mi N off US 1. Phone 207/563-3240.

Swimming. Pemaquid Beach, N of lighthouse.

Motel/Motor Lodge

★★ **OYSTER SHELL MOTEL.** *3063 Bristol Rd (04543), 1½ mi N on US 1 Business. 207/563-3747; fax 207/563-3747; toll-free 800/874-3747. Email oystrshl@lincoln.midcoast.com; www. lincoln.midcoast.com/~oystrshl.* 18 kit. suites, 4 story. No elvtr. July-Labor Day: S, D $95-$119; under 12 free; lower rates rest of yr. Crib free. TV; cable (premium). Heated pool. Complimentary coffee in rms. Restaurant nearby. Ck-out 11 am. X-country ski 2 mi. Microwaves. Balconies. Overlooks saltwater bay. Totally nonsmoking. Cr cds: A, MC, V.

🏊 ⛱ 🛄 🐾

B&Bs/Small Inns

★★★ **THE BRADLEY INN.** *3063 Bristol Rd (04554). 207/677-2105; fax 207/677-3367; res 800/942-5560. Email bradley@lincoln.midcoast.com; www.bradleyinn.com.* 16 rms, 3 story, 1 suite. June-Oct: S, D $135; suites $195; children $35; lower rates rest of yr. Parking lot. TV; cable. Complimentary full bkfst. Restaurant 5-9 pm. Bar. Ck-out 11 am. Meeting rms. Gift shop. Exercise privileges. Golf, 9 holes. Beach access. Bike rentals. Hiking trail. Cr cds: A, MC, V.

D 🛋 🏋 🚶 🎿 🛄 🐾

★★ **BRANNON-BUNKER INN.** *349 Rte 129 (04573), 4½ mi S on ME 129. 207/563-5941; res 207/563-5941; toll-free 800/563-9225. Email brbnlinn@ lincoln.midcoast.com.* 7 rms, 2 story, 1 suite. June-Oct: S $70; D $75; suites $125; each addl $10; children $5; under 18 free; lower rates rest of yr. Crib avail, fee. Parking lot. TV; cable, VCR avail. Complimentary continental bkfst. Ck-out 11 am, ck-in 2 pm.

Meeting rm. Golf, 18 holes. Downhill skiing. Picnic facilities. Cr cds: A, C, D, DS, MC, V.

D ⛷ 🏋 🎿 🛄 🔥

★★ **DOWN EASTER INN.** *222 Bristol Rd (04543). 207/563-5332; fax 207/563-5332.* 22 rms, 2 story. No A/C. No rm phones. Memorial Day-Oct: S $63.50; D $70-$80; each addl $10; under 16 free. Closed rest of yr. TV. Complimentary continental bkfst. Restaurant 6:30-10 am, 11 am-3 pm, 5-9 pm. Ck-out 11 am, ck-in 2 pm. Antiques. Lawn games. Greek Revival farmhouse (1785); built by a ship chandler whose ancestors were among the first settlers of Bristol. Cr cds: MC, V.

D 🛄 🐾 SC

★★★ **NEWCASTLE INN.** *60 River Rd (04553), SW on US 1 Business (Main St) across bridge, follow left to River Rd, ½ mi E of US 1. 207/563-5685; fax 207/563-6877; toll-free 800/ 832-8669. Email innkeep@newcastle inn.com; www.newcastleinn.com.* 13 rms, 3 story, 1 suite. June-Oct: S, D $220; suites $240; each addl $40; lower rates rest of yr. TV; cable (premium). Restaurant, closed Mon. Bar. Ck-out 11 am, ck-in 3 pm. Meeting rms. Cr cds: A, MC, V.

🛄 🐾

Restaurant

★★ **BACKSTREET LANDING.** *Elm St Plz (04543). 207/563-5666.* Specializes in seafood, vegetarian dishes. Own desserts. Hrs: 11 am-8 pm. Closed Jan 1, Thanksgiving, Dec 25; Wed Nov-Apr. Bar. Lunch $3.95-$13.95; dinner $8.95-$20.95. Child's menu. On river; scenic view. Cr cds: C, D, DS, ER, MC, V.

D

Deer Isle (F-4)

Settled 1762 **Pop** Deer Isle 1,829; Stonington 1,252 **Elev** 23 ft
Area code 207 **Zip** 04627
Web www.acadia.net/deerisle

Information Deer Isle/Stonington Chamber of Commerce, PO Box

459, Stonington 04681; 207/348-6124 in season

A bridge over Eggemoggin Reach connects these islands with the mainland. There are two major villages here—Deer Isle (the older) and Stonington. Lobster fishing and tourism are the backbone of the economy, and Stonington also cans sardines. Fishing, sailing, tennis, and golf are available in the area.

What to See and Do

Isle au Haut. (EEL-oh-HO) Reached by ferry from Stonington. Much of this island—with hills more than 500 ft tall, forested shores, and cobblestone beaches—is in Acadia National Park (see).

Isle au Haut Ferry Service. Service to the island and excursion trips avail. Phone 207/367-5193.

Resort

★★ **GOOSE COVE LODGE.** *Goose Cove Rd (04683), 3 mi S on Sunset Rd, then 1½ mi W on Goose Cove Rd. 207/348-2508; fax 207/348-2624; toll-free 800/728-1963. Email goosecove@goosecovelodge.com; www.goosecovelodge.com.* 23 rms, 2 story, 5 suites. July-Aug: S $140; D $180; suites $210; each addl $40; children $20; under 1 free; lower rates rest of yr. Crib avail. Parking lot. TV; cable (premium), VCR avail. Complimentary full bkfst, coffee in rms, toll-free calls. Restaurant. Bar. Ck-out 10 am, ck-in 3 pm. Meeting rm. Business servs avail. Gift shop. Exercise privileges. Golf, 9 holes. Tennis, 2 courts. Beach access. Bike rentals. Supervised children's activities. Hiking trail. Picnic facilities. Cr cds: A, DS, MC, V.

B&B/Small Inn

★★★ **PILGRIMS INN.** *Main St (04627), on ME 15. 207/348-6615; fax 207/348-7769. www.pilgrimsinn.com.* 15 rms, 3 share bath, 4 story. No A/C. MAP, July and Aug: D $160-$180; each addl $65; kit. cottage $215; wkly rates; lower rates mid-May-June and Sep-late Oct. Serv charge 15%. Closed rest of yr. Dining rm 8-9 am, 7 pm (one sitting; by res only). Honor bar. Ck-out 11

am, ck-in 1-5 pm. Gift shop. Fireplaces in library/sitting rm. Antiques. On ocean. Built 1793. Cr cds: A, DS, MC, V.

Eastport

(E-6) *See also Lubec*

Settled 1780 **Pop** 1,965 **Elev** 60 ft
Area code 207 **Zip** 04631
Web www.nemaine.com/eastportcc

Information Chamber of Commerce, PO Box 254; 207/853-4644

At the southern end of Passamaquoddy Bay, Eastport is a community with 150-year-old houses and ancient elms. The average tide at Eastport is approximately 18 feet, but tides up to 25 feet have been recorded here. Eastport was the site of one of the country's first tide-powered electric generating projects, and though never completed, it resulted in the construction of two tidal dams. The city also boasts of being the nation's salmonid aquaculture capital, where millions of salmon and trout are raised in pens in the chilly off-shore waters.

What to See and Do

Barracks Museum. This 1822 bldg once served as the officers' barracks for a nearby fort, which was held by British troops during the War of 1812. Museum. (Memorial Day-Labor Day, Tues-Sat afternoons) 74 Washington St. **FREE**

Ferry to Deer Island, New Brunswick. A 20-min trip; camping, picnicking on Deer Island. (June-Sep, daily) For schedules, fees inquire locally. (For Border Crossing Regulations, see MAKING THE MOST OF YOUR TRIP.) ¢¢

Fishing. Pollock, cod, flounder, and others caught from wharves. Charter boats avail for deep-sea fishing in sheltered waters.

***Old Sow* Whirlpool.** One of largest in Western Hemisphere; most active 3 hrs before high tide. Between Dog & Deer islands. **FREE**

Passamaquoddy Indian Reservation. Champlain, in 1604, was the first European to encounter members of this Algonquin tribe. Festivals and ceremonies throughout the yr (see ANNUAL EVENT). About 5 mi N on ME 190 at Pleasant Point. Phone 207/853-2551. **FREE**

Whale-watching trips. Boat excursions during the summer to view whales in the bay.

Annual Events

Indian Festival. At Passamaquoddy Indian Reservation. Ceremonies, fireworks, traditional celebrations. Second wkend Aug.

Salmon Festival. Tours of aquaculture pens; music, crafts, educational displays; farm-raised Atlantic salmon dinners. Phone 207/853-4644. Sun after Labor Day.

Motel/Motor Lodge

★★ **THE MOTEL EAST.** *23A Water St (04631). 207/853-4747; fax 207/ 853-4747. Email moteleastport@acadia. net; www.userpages.acadia.net/motel eastport.* 9 rms, 2 story, 5 suites. S $80; D $85; suites $95; each addl $10; under 18 free. Crib avail. Pet accepted, some restrictions, fee. Parking lot. TV; cable. Complimentary coffee in rms, newspaper, toll-free calls. Restaurant 11 am-9 pm. Ck-out 11 am, ck-in 3 pm. Fax servs avail. Beach access. Hiking trail. Picnic facilities. Cr cds: A, C, D, DS, ER, MC, V.

B&Bs/Small Inns

★★ **TODD HOUSE.** *1 Capen Ave (04631). 207/853-2328; fax 207/853-2328.* 6 rms, 2 story, 2 suites. July-Sep: S $45; D $80; suites $90; children $5; lower rates rest of yr. Pet accepted. Parking lot. TV; cable (premium), VCR avail. Complimentary continental bkfst. Restaurant. Ck-out 10 am, ck-in 2 pm. Free airport transportation. Cr cds: MC, V.

★★ **WESTON HOUSE BED & BREAKFAST.** *26 Boyton St (04631). 207/853-2907; fax 207/853-0981; toll-free 800/853-2907.* 5 rms, 2 share baths. No A/C. S, D $50-$75; each addl $15. Complimentary full bkfst; afternoon refreshments. Restaurant

nearby. Ck-out 11 am, ck-in 1 pm. Lawn games. Picnic tables. Restored 19th-century residence; sitting rm with tin ceiling. Cr cds: A, MC, V.

Cottage Colony

★ **SEAVIEW CAMPGROUND.** *16 Norwood Rd (04631), E on ME 190. 207/853-4471. Email info@eastport maine.com; www.eastportmaine.com.* 4 rms, 1 story. July-Aug: S, D $75; lower rates rest of yr. Pet accepted, some restrictions, fee. Parking lot. TV; cable (premium). Restaurant. Ck-out 10 am, ck-in noon. Business center. Coin lndry. Gift shop. Exercise privileges. Beach access. Hiking trail. Picnic facilities. Cr cds: DS, MC, V.

Ellsworth

(F-4) *See also Bar Harbor*

Settled 1763 **Pop** 5,975 **Elev** 100 ft
Area code 207 **Zip** 04605
Web www.acadia.net/eacc

Information Chamber of Commerce, 163 High St, PO Box 267; 207/667-5584 or 207/667-2617

This is the shire town and trading center for Hancock County—which includes some of the country's choicest resort territory, incl Bar Harbor. In the beginning of the 19th century, Ellsworth was the second biggest lumber shipping port in the world. Its business district was destroyed by fire in 1933, but was handsomely rebuilt, contrasting with the old residential streets.

What to See and Do

John Black Mansion. (ca 1820) Georgian house built by a local landowner; antiques. Garden; carriage house with old carriages and sleighs. (June-mid-Oct, Mon-Sat) W Main St. Phone 207/667-8671. ¢¢

Lamoine State Park. A 55-acre recreation area around beach on Frenchman Bay. Fishing, boating (ramp);

picnicking, camping. (Memorial Day-mid-Oct, daily) Standard fees. 8 mi SE on ME 184. Phone 207/667-4778. ¢

Stanwood Sanctuary (Birdsacre) and Homestead Museum. Trails, ponds, and picnic areas on 130-acre site. Collections incl mounted birds, nests, and eggs. Wildlife rehabilitation center with shelters for injured birds, incl hawks and owls. Museum was home of pioneer ornithologist, photographer, and writer Cordelia Stanwood (1865-1958). Sanctuary and rehabilitation center (daily; free); museum (mid-June-mid-Oct, daily). Gift shop. On Bar Harbor Rd (ME 3). Phone 207/667-8460. Tours of museum ¢¢

Motels/Motor Lodges

★ **COLONIAL TRAVELODGE.** *321 High St; Rte 3 (04605). 207/667-5548; fax 207/667-5549; res 800/578-7878. Email colonial@acadia.net; www. acadia.net/colonial.* 64 rms, 2 story, 4 suites. July-Aug: S $110; D $120; suites $159; each addl $6; under 17 free; lower rates rest of yr. Crib avail, fee. Pet accepted, some restrictions. Parking lot. Indoor pool, whirlpool. TV; cable (DSS), VCR avail. Complimentary continental bkfst, coffee in rms, newspaper, toll-free calls. Restaurant 11:30 am-9 pm. Ck-out 11 am, ck-in 2 pm. Fax servs avail. Golf. Hiking trail. Cr cds: A, DS, MC, V.

D 🐾 🏋 🛌 🏊 🔥 SC

★ **ELLSWORTH MOTEL.** *24 High St (04605). 207/667-4424; fax 207/667-6942. Email ruthk@acadia.net.* 16 rms, 2 story. July-Aug: S $48; D $64; each addl $6; children $6; lower rates rest of yr. Crib avail, fee. Parking lot. Pool. TV; cable. Restaurant. Golf. Cr cds: MC, V.

🏋 🛌 🏊 🔥

★★ **HOLIDAY INN.** *215 High St (04605), US 1 and ME 3. 207/667-9341; fax 207/667-7294; res 800/401-9341; toll-free 800/465-4329. Email hielwme@acadia.net; www.holidayinn ellsworth.com.* 103 rms, 2 story. July-Aug: S $109-$119; D $119-$129; each addl $10; under 19 free; lower rates rest of yr. Crib free. Pet accepted. TV; cable, premium. Indoor pool; whirlpool, poolside serv. Complimentary coffee in rms. Restaurant 7-11 am, 5-10 pm. Bar 4 pm-1 am. Ck-out noon. Coin lndry. Meeting rms. Business

servs avail. In-rm modem link. Sundries. Indoor tennis. X-country ski 15 mi. Exercise equipt; sauna. Near river. Cr cds: A, C, D, DS, MC, V.

D 🐾 🏋 🏊 🛌 🏊 🏃 🔥 🐾 SC

★ **HOMESTEAD MOTEL.** *RR 3 (04605), 1 mi W on US 1 (ME 3). 207/667-8193; fax 207/667-8193.* 14 rms, some A/C. July-Aug: S $47-$52; D $48-$62; each addl $5; under 12 free; lower rates mid-May-June, Sep-mid-Oct. Closed rest of yr. TV; cable. Complimentary coffee in lobby. Ck-out 11 am. Some refrigerators. Totally nonsmoking. Cr cds: A, DS, MC, V.

🛌 🔥

★★ **TWILITE MOTEL.** *147 Bucksport Rd (04605), 1 mi W on US 1 (ME 3). 207/667-8165; fax 207/667-0289; toll-free 800/395-5097. Email twilie@downeast.net; www.twilitemotel. com.* 22 rms, 1 story. June-Aug: S, D $86; each addl $8; under 12 free; lower rates rest of yr. Crib avail. Pet accepted, some restrictions, fee. Parking lot. TV; cable, VCR avail. Complimentary continental bkfst, coffee in rms, toll-free calls. Ck-out 11 am, ck-in 2 pm. Business center. Coin lndry. Gift shop. Golf, 18 holes. Tennis, 4 courts. Cr cds: A, D, DS, MC, V.

🐾 🏋 🏃 🛌 🔥 SC 🏃

Restaurants

★★ **ARMANDO'S.** *ME 1 (04640), 7 mi NE on US 1. 207/422-3151.* Specializes in pasta, seafood. Hrs: 5-9 pm. Closed Sun, Mon; Jan 1, Easter, Dec 25; Tues-Thurs in winter. Res accepted. Bar. Dinner $8.95-$16.95. Two-sided, stone fireplaces. Cr cds: MC, V.

★ **HILLTOP HOUSE.** *Bar Harbor Rd (04605), 1 mi S on ME 3. 207/667-9368. Email htop@acadia.net.* Specializes in steak, seafood, pizza. Own baking. Hrs: 11 am-9 pm. Closed Jan 1, Thanksgiving, Dec 25. Bar. Lunch $2.25-$9.95; dinner $4.25-$16.95. Child's menu. Cr cds: A, C, D, DS, ER, MC, V.

D

Fort Kent

(A-4) *See also Edmundston, NB, Canada*

Settled 1829 **Pop** 4,268 **Elev** 530 ft
Area code 207 **Zip** 04743
Web www.sjv.net/seefkme
Information Chamber of Commerce,
PO Box 430; 207/834-5354 or
800/733-3563.

Fort Kent, at the northern end of
famous US 1 (the other end is at Key
West, Florida), is the chief community of Maine's "far north." A bridge
across the St. John River leads to
Clair, New Brunswick. (For Border
Crossing Regulations, see MAKING
THE MOST OF YOUR TRIP.) The
town is a lumbering, farming, hunting, and fishing center, and canoeing, downhill and cross-country
skiing, and snowmobiling are popular here. A campus of the University
of Maine is located here.

What to See and Do

Canoeing. Fort Kent is the down-
stream terminus of the St. John-
Allagash canoe trip, which starts at E
Seboomook on Moosehead Lake, 156
mi and 6 portages away. (See ALLA-
GASH WILDERNESS WATERWAY)

Cross-country skiing. Fort Kent has
11½ mi of scenic intermediate and
advanced trails. **FREE**

Fishing. Guides, boats, and gear avail
for short or long expeditions up the
Fish River chain of lakes for salmon
or trout; St. John or Allagash rivers
for trout.

Fort Kent Block House. Built in
1839, during the Aroostook Bloodless
War with Britain, used for training
exercises and as a guard post.
Restored; antique hand tools in
museum; interpretive displays. Picnicking. (Memorial Day-Labor Day,
daily) N edge of town. Phone
207/834-3866 or 207/764-2040. **FREE**

**Fort Kent Historical Society Museum
and Gardens.** Former Bangor and
Aroostook railroad station, built in
early 1900s, now houses historical
museum. (Usually last 2 wks June-1st
wk Aug, Tues-Sat) For further information contact the Chamber of
Commerce. 54 W Main St.

Skiing. Lonesome Pine Trails. Thirteen trails, 2,300-ft slope with 500-ft
drop; beginners slope and tow; rope
tow, T-bar; school, patrol; lodge, concession. (Dec-Apr, Wed and Fri-Sun,
also hols) Forest Ave. Phone 207/834-
5202. ¢¢¢¢

Annual Event

Can Am Crown Sled Dog Races. Late
Feb-early Mar.

Freeport

(G-2) *See also Bath, Brunswick,
Yarmouth*

Pop 6,905 **Elev** 130 ft **Area code** 207
Zip 04032 **Web** www.freeportusa.com
Information Freeport Merchants Association, Hose Tower Information Center, 23 Depot St, PO Box 452MTG;
207/865-1212 or 800/865-1994

It was in Freeport that legislators
signed papers granting Maine independence from Massachusetts and,
eventually, its statehood. The town is
home to the renowned L.L. Bean
clothing and sporting goods store; its
major industries incl retail, tourism,
crabbing, and crabmeat packing.

What to See and Do

Atlantic Seal **Cruises.** Cruises aboard
40-ft, 28-passenger vessel on Casco
Bay to Eagle Island and Robert E.
Peary house museum; also seal- and
bird-watching trips, fall foliage sightseeing cruises. (Schedules vary) Tickets must be purchased at Main St
office, S Freeport. Depart from Town
Wharf, foot of Main St in S Freeport,
2 mi S on S Freeport Rd. Phone
207/865-6112. ¢¢¢¢

🌟 **Factory outlet stores.** Freeport is
home to more than 120 outlet stores
and centers that offer brand-name
merchandise at discounted prices,
incl the famous L.L. Bean clothing
and sporting goods store, which
stays open 24 hrs a day. For a list of
outlet stores contact the Freeport
Merchants Association.

Mast Landing Sanctuary. A 140-acre area maintained by the Maine Audubon Society. Hiking, cross-country skiing. (Daily) Upper Mast Landing Rd, 1½ mi E. Phone 207/781-2330. **FREE**

Winslow Memorial Park. Campground with swimming, boating (fee); cross-country skiing, picnicking. (Schedule varies) Staples Point, 5 mi S off US 1, I-95. Phone 207/865-4198. ¢

Motels/Motor Lodges

★ **CASCO BAY INN.** *107 US 1 (04032). 207/865-4925; fax 207/865-0696; toll-free 800/570-4970. Email cascobayinn@aol.com.* 30 rms, 2 story. July-mid-Oct: S, D $74-$89; each addl $7; lower rates mid-Apr-June, mid-Oct-mid-Dec. Closed rest of yr. TV; cable. Continental bkfst. Restaurant nearby. Ck-out 11 am. Totally nonsmoking. Cr cds: DS, MC, V.

⬛ 🐾 🐾 ⬛ 🔥

★★ **COASTLINE INN.** *537 US 1 (04032). 207/865-3777; fax 207/865-4678; toll-free 800/470-9494. Email jeffyork@gwi.net; www.coastlineinn-maine.com.* 108 rms, 2 story. May-Oct: S $89; D $99; each addl $10; lower rates rest of yr. Pet accepted. Parking lot. TV; cable (DSS), VCR avail. Complimentary continental bkfst, coffee in rms, newspaper, toll-free calls. Restaurant nearby. Business center. Coin lndry. Golf. Downhill skiing. Picnic facilities. Cr cds: A, DS, JCB, MC, V.

⬛ 🐾 🏊 🐾 ⬛ 🔥 🚶

Hotel

★★ **FREEPORT INN.** *31 US Rte 1 (04032), Exit 17 off I-95. 207/865-3106; fax 207/865-6364; toll-free 800/998-2583. Email info@freeportinn.com; www.freeportinn.com.* 78 rms, 3 story, 1 suite. June-Oct: S, D $100; suites $220; each addl $10; under 18 free; lower rates rest of yr. Crib avail, fee. Pet accepted, some restrictions. Parking lot. Pool. TV; cable (premium). Complimentary newspaper, toll-free calls. Restaurant. Bar. Ck-out 11 am, ck-in 3 pm. Business servs avail. Dry cleaning. Exercise privileges. Golf. Cr cds: A, D, DS, MC, V.

⬛ 🐾 🏊 🐾 🏊 🚶 ⬛ 🔥

B&Bs/Small Inns

★★ **181 MAIN STREET BED & BREAKFAST.** *181 Main St (04032). 207/865-1226; toll-free 800/235-9750. Email bb181main@aol.com; www.members.aol.com/bb181main/index.htm.* 7 rms, 2 story. 4 A/C. No rm phones. Memorial Day-Oct: S $85; D $110; lower rates rest of yr. Children over 14 yrs only. TV in sitting rm; cable, VCR. Pool. Complimentary full bkfst. Restaurant nearby. Ck-out 11 am, ck-in 3-7 pm. X-country ski 2 mi. Antiques. Library. Restored Greek Revival Cape (ca 1840); Colonial furnishings. Totally nonsmoking. Cr cds: MC, V.

🏊 🏊 🐾 🐾

★★ **THE BAGLEY HOUSE.** *1290 Royalsborough Rd (04222), I-95 Exit 20, then 6 mi N on ME 136. 207/865-6566; fax 207/353-6372; toll-free 800/765-1772. Email balyhse@aol.com; www.bagleyhouse.com.* 7 rms, 2 story, 1 suite. June-Oct: S $90; D $150; suites $150; each addl $15; under 12 free; lower rates rest of yr. Crib avail. Parking lot. TV; cable (premium). Complimentary full bkfst. Ck-out 11 am, ck-in 3 pm. Meeting rm. Gift shop. Golf. Downhill skiing. Hiking trail. Picnic facilities. Cr cds: A, D, DS, JCB, MC, V.

⬛ 🐾 🚶 🐾 🔥 **SC**

★★ **BREWSTER HOUSE BED & BREAKFAST.** *180 Main St (04032). 207/865-4121; fax 207/865-4221; toll-free 800/865-0822. www.brewsterhouse.com.* 5 rms, 3 story, 2 suites. May-Dec: S $115; D $125; suites $165; each addl $20; lower rates rest of yr. Parking lot. TV; cable (premium). Complimentary full bkfst, toll-free calls. Restaurant nearby. Ck-out 11 am, ck-in 3 pm. Business center. Gift shop. Golf, 9 holes. Tennis, 4 courts. Downhill skiing. Cr cds: A, DS, MC, V.

🏊 🚶 🐾 🐾 🔥 🚶

★★★ **HARRASEEKET INN.** *162 Main St (04032). 207/865-9377; fax 207/865-1684; toll-free 800/342-6423. Email harraseeke @aol.com; www.stayfreeport.com.* 84 rms, 3 story, 4 suites. June-Oct: S, D $205; suites $275; each addl $25; under 12 free; lower rates rest of yr. Crib avail, fee. Valet parking avail. Indoor pool, lap pool, whirlpool. TV; cable, VCR avail. Complimentary full bkfst, coffee in rms. Restaurant. Bar. Ck-out 11 am, ck-in 3 pm. Meeting rms. Business center. Concierge. Dry cleaning. Gift shop. Exercise privileges. Golf. Downhill skiing. Picnic facilities. Cr cds: A, C, D, DS, MC, V.

★★ **KENDALL TAVERN B&B.** *213 Main St (04032). 207/865-1338; fax 207/865-3544; toll-free 800/341-9572. Email hpetergrove@earthlink.net.* 7 rms, 3 story. June-Nov: S $105; D $120; each addl $15; lower rates rest of yr. Crib avail. Parking lot. TV; cable, VCR avail. Complimentary full bkfst, newspaper. Restaurant nearby. Ck-out 11 am, ck-in 3 pm. Business center. Coin lndry. Whirlpool. Golf, 18 holes. Tennis. Downhill skiing. Cr cds: A, C, D, DS, MC, V.

★★ **WHITE CEDAR INN.** *178 Main St (04032). 207/865-9099; toll-free 800/853-1269. www.members.ad.com/bedandbrk/cedar.* 7 rms, 6 with shower only, 2 story. No rm phones. July-Oct, wkends in June, Nov, Dec: S, D $95-$130; each addl $15; lower rates rest of yr. Children over 11 yrs only. TV in sitting rm; cable. Complimentary full bkfst. Restaurant adj 11 am-10 pm. Ck-out 11 am, ck-in 3 pm. Bellhops. Former home of Arctic explorer Donald MacMillan. Totally nonsmoking. Cr cds: A, DS, MC, V.

Restaurants

★ **CORSICAN.** *9 Mechanic St (04032). 207/865-9421. www.dinefreeport.com.* Continental menu. Specializes in pesto and tomato pizza, vegetable lasagne, calzones. Hrs: 11 am-9 pm. Closed Jan 1, Thanksgiving, Dec 25. Wine, beer. Lunch $4-$9.95; dinner $4-$14.95. Cr cds: D, DS, MC, V.

★ **GRITTY MCDUFF'S.** *183 Lower Main St (US 1) (04032). 207/865-4321. Email gritty@grittys.com; www.grittys.com.* Specializes in seafood, pizza. Hrs: 11 am-11 pm. Res accepted. Bar. Lunch $4.25-$12.50; dinner $4.25-$12.50. Child's menu. Casual decor. Cr cds: A, MC, V.

★★ **JAMESON TAVERN.** *115 Main St (US 1) (04032). 207/865-4196.* Specializes in seafood, steak. Hrs: 11 am-10 pm. Closed Dec 25. Res accepted. Bar. Lunch $4.95-$9.50; dinner $10.25-$21.95. Child's menu. Parking. Historic tavern (1779); final papers separating Maine from the Commonwealth of Massachusetts were signed here. Cr cds: A, D, DS, MC, V.

★ **LOBSTER COOKER.** *39 Main St (US 1) (04032). 207/865-4349. www.lobstercooker.com.* Specializes in fresh crab and lobster rolls, chowder. Hrs: 10 am-8 pm. Wine, beer. Lunch a la carte entrees: $2.95-$12.95; dinner a la carte entrees: $2.95-$12.95. Parking. Lobster tank. Historic bldg (1816). Cr cds: A, MC, V.

★★★ **THE MAINE DINING ROOM.** *162 Main St. 207/865-1085. Email harraseeket@aol.com; www.harraseeket.com.* Specializes in organic cuisine. Own baking. Hrs: 6-9 pm; Sun brunch 11 am-2 pm. Res accepted. Bar. Wine cellar. Dinner $18-$32. Complete meals for 2: $60. Sun brunch $25.95. Child's menu. Parking. Colonial decor; some antiques. Cr cds: A, C, D, DS, ER, MC, V.

Greenville (D-3)

Settled 1824 **Pop** 1,884 **Elev** 1,038 ft
Area code 207 **Zip** 04441
Web www.moosehead.net/moose/chamber.html

Information Moosehead Lake Region Chamber of Commerce, PO Box 581; 207/695-2702 or 207/695-2026

Greenville is a starting point for trips into the Moosehead Lake region (see). Until it was incorporated in 1836, it was known as Haskell, in honor of its founder Nathaniel Haskell.

What to See and Do

Baxter State Park. (see) Approx 45 mi NE via private paper company roads.

Beautiful Maine harbor

Lily Bay State Park. A 924-acre park on Moosehead Lake. Swimming, fishing, boating (ramp); picnicking, camping (dump station), snowmobiling permitted (Mid-May-mid-Oct). Standard fees. 8 mi N via local roads, near Beaver Cove. Phone 207/695-2700 (seasonal).

Moosehead Marine Museum. On steamboat *Katahdin,* berthed in East Cove. Exhibits of the steamboat era and the Kineo Hotel; cruises avail. (July-Labor Day, daily; mid-May-June and rest of Sep, Sat and Sun) Phone 207/695-2716. Cruises ¢¢¢¢

Skiing. Moosehead Resort on Big Squaw Mountain. Double, triple chairlifts, T-bar, pony lift; novice-to-expert trails; rentals, school, patrol, snowmaking; cafeteria, restaurant, bar, nursery, lodge. Longest run 2½ mi; vertical drop 1,750 ft. (Late Nov-Apr, daily) Cross-country trails. Chairlift rides (June-mid-Oct; fee). 5 mi NW on ME 6/15, then 2 mi W on access road. For further information contact the Chamber of Commerce.

Annual Event

Moose Mainea. Various locations around Greenville. Celebration honoring the moose. Canoe race, rowing regatta, fly-fishing championship, Tour de Moose bike race. Family Fun Day with parade, crafts, entertainment. Moose-sighting tours. Phone 207/695-2702. Mid-May-mid-June.

Motels/Motor Lodges

★ **CHALET MOOSEHEAD LAKE-FRONT MOTEL.** *Rte 15 (04442), 1 mi W, off ME 6/15. 207/695-2950; fax 207/695-2950; toll-free 800/290-3645.* Email mlodz@ctel.net; www.moosehead lodging.com. 15 rms, 2 story, 15 suites. Jan-Feb, July-Oct: S $68; D $75; suites $105; each addl $10; children $10; lower rates rest of yr. Pet accepted, some restrictions, fee. Parking lot. TV; cable (premium). Complimentary coffee in rms, toll-free calls. Restaurant. Ck-out 10 am, ck-in noon. Fax servs avail. Gift shop. Golf. Downhill skiing. Beach access. Picnic facilities. Cr cds: A, DS, MC, V.

★ **INDIAN HILL.** *S Main St (04441), ½ mi S on ME 6/15. 207/695-2623; fax 207/695-2950; toll-free 800/771-4620.* Email mlodz@ctel.net; www.moosehead lodging.com. 15 rms, 1 story. Jan-Mar, July-Oct: S, D $65; each addl $10; children $10; lower rates rest of yr. Parking lot. TV; cable (premium). Complimentary coffee in rms, toll-free calls. Restaurant. Ck-out 10:30 am, ck-in noon. Gift shop. Golf, holes. Downhill skiing. Picnic facilities. Cr cds: A, DS, MC, V.

★ **KINEO VIEW MOTOR LODGE.** *Rte 15 (04441), 2 mi S on ME 15/6. 207/695-4470; fax 207/695-4656; toll-free 800/659-8439. www.maineguide. com/moosehead/kineo.html.* 12 rms, 2 story. No A/C. Memorial Day-mid-Oct: D $65-$75; each addl $5; under 13 free; wkly rates; lower rates rest of yr. Pet accepted; $5. TV. Whirlpool. Complimentary continental bkfst in season. Ck-out 10:30 am. Downhill ski 9 mi; x-country ski on site. Game rm. Lawn games. Balconies. Picnic tables. Lake views. Cr cds: A, DS, MC, V.

Hotel

★ **GREENWOOD.** *Rte 15; Rockwood Rd (04442), 3 mi NW on ME 6/15. 207/695-3321; fax 207/695-2122; toll-free 800/477-4386.* Email grenwood@ moosehead.net. 15 rms, 2 story. June-

Sep: S $59.95; D $64.95; each addl $5; children $5; lower rates rest of yr. Crib avail, fee. Pet accepted, some restrictions, fee. Parking lot. Pool. TV; cable (premium); VCR avail. Complimentary continental bkfst, coffee in rms, newspaper. Restaurant nearby. Ck-out 10:30 am, ck-in 2 pm. Business servs avail. Golf, 10 holes. Tennis, 2 courts. Downhill skiing. Beach access. Supervised children's activities. Hiking trail. Picnic facilities. Cr cds: A, C, D, DS, MC, V.

D ⭧ 🕭 🏊 🕸 ⛷ 🎿 🛶 🔥

B&Bs/Small Inns

★★ **GREENVILLE INN.** *Norris St (04441). 207/695-2206; fax 207/695-0335; toll-free 888/695-6000. Email gvlinn@moosehead.net; www.greenville inn.com.* 4 rms, 2 story, 2 suites. June-Oct: S, D $165; suites $235; each addl $20; children $20; lower rates rest of yr. Parking lot. TV; cable. Complimentary continental bkfst, toll-free calls. Restaurant 6-8:30 pm, closed Sun. Bar. Ck-out 11 am, ck-in 3 pm. Concierge. Golf, 9 holes. Tennis, 2 courts. Downhill skiing. Cr cds: DS, MC, V.

🏊 🕸 ⛷ ✈ 🛶 🔥

★★★★ **THE LODGE AT MOOSE-HEAD LAKE.** *Lily Bay Rd (04441), 2 mi N. 207/695-4400; fax 207/695-2281. Email innkeeper@lodgeatmoose headlake.com.* This romantic nature retreat offers five lodge rooms and three adjacent carriage house suites all with charming rustic interiors incl hand-carved poster beds, twig tables, and woodsy fabrics. Most guestrooms afford dramatic sunset views over the water and Squaw Mountain. Explore nearby Lily Bay State Park or take part in the year-round recreations of the lake and surrounding wilderness. 5 rms, 3 suites, 2 story. No rm phones. Open New Year's-late March; mid-May-late Oct; S, D $175-$395; 2 night min. Children over 14 yrs welcome. TV; cable, VCR, 250-video library. Complimentary full bkfst, coffee in rms. Ck-out 11 am, ck-in 3 pm. Concierge. Business servs avail. Outdoor activities: fly-fishing, moose safari, hiking, mountain biking, kayaking, horseback riding. Winter activities: downhill ski 10 mi; x-country ski 2 mi; dog sledding. Fire-

places, jacuzzis in all rooms. Pool table. Electric blankets, robes. Totally nonsmoking. Cr cds: A, DS, MC, V.

🕭 🕸 🏊 🛶 🔥

⛽

Houlton (C-5)

Settled 1805 **Pop** 6,613 **Elev** 366 ft
Area code 207 **Zip** 04730
Web www.greaterhoulton.com

Information Greater Houlton Chamber of Commerce, 109 Main St; 207/532-4216

Houlton prospered first from lumber, then from the famous Maine potatoes. It is young by New England standards, but was the first town settled in Aroostook County. Industries incl woodworking and wood chip and waferboard factories. It is two miles from the Canadian border and a major port of entry. Swimming is available at Nickerson Lake. Fishing is available in several nearby lakes. (For Border Crossing Regulations, see MAKING THE MOST OF YOUR TRIP.)

What to See and Do

Aroostook Historical and Art Museum. Pioneer exhibits, local historical items incl model and artifacts from Hancock Barracks, memorabilia from the now closed Ricker College. (By appt) 109 Main St. Phone 207/532-4216. **FREE**

Hancock Barracks. Second northernmost Federal outpost in the country; manned by troops from 1828-46. Garrison Hill, 1 mi E on US 2. **FREE**

Market Square Historic District. These historic 1890s bldgs show a high degree of design artistry. Contact Chamber of Commerce for walking tour maps. Main St between Kendall and Broadway. **FREE**

Museum of Vintage Fashions. Contains 17 rms of men's, women's, and children's vintage fashions. Dress-makers shop, hat boutique, bridal rm, haberdashery. (June-early Oct, Mon-Thurs, also Fri-Sun by appt only) 25 mi SW via US 2 to Island Falls, on Sherman St. Phone 207/463-2404 or 207/862-3797. **Donation**

Annual Events

Meduxnekeag River Canoe Race. Late Apr.

Houlton Fair. Entertainment, concessions, rides. Early July.

Houlton Potato Feast Days. Last full wkend Aug.

Motels/Motor Lodges

★ ★ **IVEYS MOTOR LODGE.** *Hwy 1 & I-95 (04730), I-95 Exit 62. 207/532-4206; fax 207/532-4206; toll-free 800/244-4206. www.mainerec.com/ivey. html.* 24 rms. June-mid-Oct: S $48-$64; D $64-$68; each addl $8; lower rates rest of yr. Crib $8. TV; cable (premium). Complimentary coffee in rms. Restaurant adj open 24 hrs. Bar 4 pm-midnight. Ck-out 11 am. Meeting rms. Business servs avail. Health club privileges. Refrigerators. Cr cds: A, C, D, DS, MC, V.

★ **SCOTTISH INN.** *239 Bangor St (04730), 1 mi S on US 2A. 207/532-2236; fax 207/532-9893.* 43 rms. May-mid-Nov: S, D $44-$48; each addl $6; lower rates rest of yr. Crib $6. Pet accepted; $6. TV; cable (premium). Complimentary coffee in lobby. Restaurant nearby. Ck-out 11 am. Business servs avail. Refrigerators. Cr cds: A, MC, V

★ ★ **SHIRETOWN MOTOR INN.** *282 North St at I-95 (04730), on North Rd, 1 mi N of US 1, N of I-95 Exit 62. 207/532-9421; toll-free 800/441-9421.* 51 rms. June-mid Oct: S, D $60-$62; each addl $10; suites $72; kit. units $72. Crib $7. TV; cable (premium). Indoor pool. Complimentary coffee in lobby. Restaurant 5-10 pm. Bar to 1 am. Ck-out 11 am. Coin lndry. Meeting rms. Business servs avail. Tennis. Exercise equipt. Refrigerators. Cr cds: A, MC, V

★ **STARDUST.** *672 North St (04730), 2 mi N. 207/532-6538; fax 207/532-4143; toll-free 800/437-8406. Email rjlngstf@javanet.com.* 11 rms, 1 story, 1 suite. Jan-Mar, June-Sep: S $35; D

$45; suites $55; lower rates rest of yr. Pet accepted, some restrictions, fee. Parking lot. TV; cable, VCR avail. Restaurant nearby. Ck-out 11 am, ck-in 3 pm. Business servs avail. Exercise privileges. Golf, 9 holes. Tennis, 3 courts. Downhill skiing. Hiking trail. Picnic facilities. Cr cds: A, DS, MC, V.

Kennebunk

(H-1) *See also Kennebunkport, Old Orchard Beach, Portland, Saco*

Settled 1650 **Pop** 8,004 **Elev** 50 ft
Area code 207 **Zip** 04043
Web www.kkcc.maine.org
Information Chamber of Commerce, 17 Western Ave, ME 9-Lower Village, PO Box 740; 207/967-0857

The original settlement that was to become Kennebunk was at one time a part of Wells. When Maine separated from Massachusetts in 1820, Kennebunk separated from Wells. Once a shipbuilding community on the Mousam and Kennebunk rivers, Kennebunk today is the principal business center of a summer resort area that includes Kennebunkport (see) and Kennebunk Beach.

What to See and Do

Brick Store Museum. A blk of restored 19th-century bldgs incl William Lord's Brick Store (1825); exhibits of fine and decorative arts, historical and maritime collections. (Tues-Sat; closed hols) 117 Main St, US 1, opp library. Phone 207/985-4802. ¢¢

Taylor-Barry House. (ca 1803) Sea captain's Federal period house with furniture, stenciled hallway; 20th-century artist's studio. (June-Sep, Tues-Fri afternoons) 24 Summer St. Phone 207/985-4802. ¢¢

Annual Event

Winter Carnival. Snow sculpture contests, snow palace moonwalk, magic show, ice-skating party, chili and chowder contests, children's events. Phone 207/985-6890. Feb.

Motels/Motor Lodges

★ **ECONO LODGE KENNEBUNK.**
55 York St (04043). 207/985-6100; fax 207/985-4031; toll-free 800/336-5634. 46 rms, 2 story. July-mid Oct: S, D $99-$149; each addl $10; under 18 free; lower rates rest of yr. Crib $10. TV; cable. Pool. Complimentary continental bkfst. Complimentary coffee in rms. Ck-out 11 am. Balconies. Some refrigerators; microwaves avail.

D 🛏 🐾 SC

★ **TURNPIKE MOTEL.** *77 Old Alewive Rd (04043), at ME Tpke Exit 3 N. 207/985-4404.* 24 rms, 2 story. July-Aug: S, D $70; lower rates rest of yr. Crib avail, fee. Parking lot. TV; cable. Complimentary coffee in rms, toll-free calls. Restaurant nearby. Ck-out 11 am, ck-in 1 pm. Golf. Tennis. Cr cds: MC, V.

🍴 🍳 🛏 🔥

B&Bs/Small Inns

★★ **ARUNDEL MEADOWS INN.**
1024 Portland Rd (04046), 2 mi N on US 1 in Arundel. 207/985-3770. www.biddeford.com/arundel_meadows-inn. 7 rms, 2 story, 2 suites. No rm phones. June-Oct: S, D $75-$95; each addl $20; suites $100-$125; wkly rates; lower rates rest of yr. Children over 11 yrs only. TV in some rms; cable. Complimentary full bkfst. Ck-out 11 am, ck-in 2 pm. Some fireplaces. Picnic tables, grills. Sitting rm. Restored farmhouse (1827); artwork, antiques, garden. Totally nonsmoking. Cr cds: MC, V.

🛏 🐾

★★★ **THE BEACH HOUSE.** *211 Beach Ave (04043). 207/967-3850; fax 207/967-4719. Email inkeeper@beachhseinn.com; www.beachhseinn.com.* 34 rms, 4 story, 1 suite. June-Oct: D $210; suites $350; each addl $25; lower rates rest of yr. Parking lot. TV; cable, VCR avail, CD avail. Complimentary continental bkfst, newspaper. Restaurant nearby. Ck-out 11 am, ck-in 3 pm. Business servs avail. Concierge. Dry cleaning. Golf, 18 holes. Tennis, 4 courts. Beach access.

Bike rentals. Hiking trail. Cr cds: A, MC, V.

D 🍳 🍴 🛏 🐾 🔥 🏊

★★ **THE KENNEBUNK INN.** *45 Main St (04043). 207/985-3351; fax 207/985-8865. www.thekennebunkinn.com.* 24 rms, 3 story, 4 suites. June-Oct, Dec: S $95; D $55; suites $155; each addl $10; children $10; under 20 free; lower rates rest of yr. Crib avail, fee. Pet accepted, some restrictions. Parking lot. TV; cable (premium), VCR avail. Complimentary continental bkfst, newspaper, toll-free calls. Restaurant 5-9 pm. Bar. Ck-out 11 am, ck-in 3 pm. Meeting rms. Business center. Concierge. Gift shop. Exercise privileges. Golf. Tennis, 7 courts. Beach access. Hiking trail. Picnic facilities. Cr cds: A, DS, MC, V.

D 🍽 🍳 🍴 🛏 🏇 🔥 🏊 🚶

Restaurants

★★★ **GRISSINI.** *27 Western Ave (04043). 207/967-2211.* Specializes in fresh pasta, wood-oven pizza. Hrs: 5-9 pm. Closed Thanksgiving. Res accepted. Bar. Wine list. Dinner $10.95-$17.95. Child's menu. Parking. Cr cds: A, DS, MC, V.

D

★★ **THE KENNEBUNK INN.** *45 Main St. 207/985-3351.* Specializes in grilled loin of lamb, flaming creme brulee. Hrs: 5-9:30 pm. Closed Dec 25. Res accepted. Bar. Dinner $11-$19. Child's menu. Parking. Inn built 1799; stained-glass windows. Cr cds: A, C, DS, MC, V.

★★★ **WINDOWS ON THE WATER.** *12 Chase Hill Rd (04043), E on ME 35 to Chase Hill Rd. 207/967-3313. Email jphughes@biddeford.com; www.windowsonthewater.com.* Specializes in lobster. Hrs: 11 am-10 pm. Closed Dec 25. Res accepted. Wine list. Lunch $6.90-$12.90; dinner $12.90-$25.90. Child's menu. Contemporary decor; views of river, marina. Open kitchen. Cr cds: A, C, D, DS, ER, MC, V.

D

Kennebunkport

(H-1) *See also Kennebunk, Old Orchard Beach, Portland, Saco*

Settled 1629 **Pop** 3,356 **Elev** 20 ft
Area code 207 **Zip** 04046
Web www.kkcc.maine.org

Information Chamber of Commerce, 17 Western Ave, ME 9-Lower Village, PO Box 740, Kennebunk 04043; 207/967-0857

At the mouth of the Kennebunk River, this coastal town is a summer and winter resort, as well as an art and literary colony. It was the home of author Kenneth Roberts and the scene of his novel *Arundel*. During the Bush administration, the town achieved fame as the summer residence of the 41st President.

What to See and Do

Architectural Walking Tour. Tours of historic district (June-Sep, Thurs) Phone 207/985-4802. ¢¢

The Nott House. (1853) Greek Revival house with original wallpaper and furnishings from the Perkins-Nott family. Tours. (June-mid-Oct, Tues-Fri afternoons) 8 Maine St. Phone 207/967-2751. ¢¢

School House. (1899) Headquarters of the Kennebunkport Historical Society. Houses collections of genealogy, photographs, maritime history, and many artifacts and documents on Kennebunkport's history. (Wed-Fri afternoons) 135 North St. Phone 207/967-2751. **FREE**

Seashore Trolley Museum. Approx 200 antique streetcars from US and abroad; special events. (Late May-mid-Oct, daily) 3½ mi N on Log Cabin Rd (North St). Phone 207/967-2800 or 207/967-2712. ¢¢¢

Swimming. Colony Beach and Goose Rocks Beach.

Motels/Motor Lodges

★★ **CAPE ARUNDEL INN.** *208 Ocean Ave (04046), between Spouting Rock and Blowing Cave, 2½ mi S. 207/967-2125; fax 207/967-1199.* 7 inn rms, 6 motel rms. No A/C. Mid-June-late-Oct: inn rms $145-$180; motel rms $175; each addl $20; lower rates late-Apr-mid-June, late-

Oct-mid-Dec. Closed rest of yr. TV in motel rms; cable. Complimentary continental bkfst. Restaurant 6-9 pm. Ck-out 11 am. Balconies on motel rms. Victorian-style inn (1890); turn-of-the-century decor. Overlooks seacoast. Totally nonsmoking. Cr cds: A, DS, MC, V.
D ⭐ ⛵ 🏊 🐾

★★ **RHUMB LINE MOTOR LODGE.** *Ocean Ave (04046), 3 mi SE. 207/967-5457; fax 207/967-4418; toll-free 800/337-4862. Email info@rhumbline maine.com; www.rhumblinemaine.com.* 56 rms, 3 story, 3 suites. July-Sep: S $149; D $159; suites $159; each addl $10; under 12 free; lower rates rest of yr. Crib avail. Parking lot. Indoor/outdoor pools, whirlpool. TV; cable. Complimentary continental bkfst, toll-free calls. Restaurant. Bar. Ck-out 11 am, ck-in 2 pm. Meeting rms. Business servs avail. Exercise equipt, sauna. Golf, 18 holes. Tennis, 5 courts. Downhill skiing. Beach access. Picnic facilities. Cr cds: A, DS, MC, V.
D ⭐ 🏊 🎿 🎾 ⛵ 🐾 🏌 SC

★★ **SHAWMUT INN.** *Turbat's Creek Rd (04046), 3 mi E on Ocean Ave to Turbat's Creek Rd. 207/967-3931; fax 207/967-4158; toll-free 800/876-3931. Email shawmutreservations@juno.com.* 82 rms, some A/C, 2 suites, 1-3 story, 37 kits. No elvtr. July-Aug: S, D $99-$169; MAP avail; wkend packages; lower rates rest of yr. Crib $10. TV; cable. Saltwater pool; poolside serv. Complimentary full bkfst. Restaurant 8-10:30 am, noon-2:30 pm, 6-10 pm. Bar 11:30-1 am; entertainment wkends. Ck-out 11 am. Meeting rms. Business servs avail. Gift shop. Town transportation by trolley. Tennis privileges, pro. 18-hole golf privileges. Lawn games. Private patios, balconies. Picnic tables. Historic inn (1913) located on more than 20 acres along ocean. Cr cds: A, C, D, DS, MC, V.
D ⭐ 🎾 ⛵ 🐾 SC

★★ **VILLAGE COVE INN.** *29 S Maine St (04046), ½ mi SE. 207/967-3993; fax 207/967-3164; toll-free 800/879-5778. Email info@villagecoveinn. com.* 32 rms, 1-2 story. July-Aug: S, D $129-$179; each addl $25; under 12 free; lower rates rest of yr. Crib $20. TV; cable. 2 pools, 1 indoor; poolside serv in season. Complimentary full bkfst. Restaurant 7:30-10 am, 5:30-9:30 pm; varied hrs off-season. Bar 11:30 am-closing, off-season from 4:30 pm; entertainment wkends. Ck-out 11 am. Meeting rms. Business servs avail. Refrigerators. Totally non-smoking. Cr cds: A, DS, MC, V.

★★ **YACHTSMAN LODGE & MARINA.** *Ocean Ave (04046), ¼ mi to Dock Sq. 207/967-2511; fax 207/967-5056. Email innkeeper@yachtman. com.* 29 rms. Some A/C. July-early Sep: D $139-$175; each addl $15; lower rates May-June, early Sep-Oct. Closed rest of yr. TV; cable (premium). Complimentary continental bkfst. Restaurant opp 8 am-8 pm. Ck-out 11 am. Business servs avail. Refrigerators. Patios. Picnic tables, grill. On river; marina, dockage. Cr cds: A, MC, V.

Hotels

★ **AUSTINS INN TOWN HOTEL.** *28 Dock Sq (04046). 207/967-4241; toll-free 888/228-0548. www.austinn townhotel.com.* 12 rms, 3 story, 2 suites. July-Oct: S, D $69; suites $138; each addl $15; lower rates rest of yr. Crib avail. Parking lot. TV; cable (premium). Restaurant nearby. Ck-out 1 pm, ck-in 11 pm. Meeting rm. Concierge. Gift shop. Golf. Tennis, 6 courts. Beach access. Bike rentals. Cr cds: DS, MC, V.

★★★ **KENNEBUNKPORT INN.** *1 Dock Sq (04046). 207/967-2621; fax 207/967-3705; toll-free 800/248-2621. www.kennebunkportinn.com.* 34 rms, 3 story. June-Oct: S $239; D $310; each addl $35; lower rates rest of yr. Parking lot. Pool. TV; cable. Restaurant. Bar. Fax servs avail. Golf. Tennis, 2 courts. Cr cds: A, MC, V.

★★ **SCHOONERS INN.** *127 Ocean Ave (04046). 207/967-5333; fax 207/967-2040. Email info@schoonersinn. com; www.schoonersinn.com.* 17 rms, 2 story. June-Oct: S, D $135-$175; each addl $10; suite $250; under 12 free; wkends (2-day min); higher rates hols; lower rates rest of yr. Crib avail, fee. Parking lot. TV; cable, VCR avail. Complimentary continental bkfst.

Restaurant nearby. Bar. Ck-out 11 am, ck-in 4 pm. Beach access. Cr cds: A, MC, V.

★★ **SEASIDE HOUSE & COT-TAGES.** *Goochs Beach (04046), ¾ mi S on ME 35. 207/967-4461; fax 207/967-1135. www.kennebunkbeach.com.* 22 rms, 2 story. July-Aug: S $189; D $199; lower rates rest of yr. Crib avail. Pet accepted, some restrictions, fee. Parking lot. TV; cable. Complimentary continental bkfst. Restaurant nearby. Ck-out 11 am, ck-in 2 pm. Business servs avail. Coin lndry. Gift shop. Golf. Downhill skiing. Beach access. Cr cds: A, MC, V.

Resorts

★★★ **COLONY HOTEL.** *140 Ocean Ave, (04046). 207/967-3331; fax 207/967-8738; toll-free 800/552-2363. Email reservations@thecolonyhotel.com; www.thecolonyhotel.com/maine.* 125 rms in hotel, annex and motel, 2-4 story. No A/C. July-early Sep (wkends 2-day min in hotel), MAP: D $175-$375; each addl $30; EP avail off-season; lower rates mid-May-June, Sep-late Oct. Closed rest of yr. Crib free. Pet accepted; $22. TV in some rms. Heated saltwater pool. Dining rm 7:30-9:30 am, 6:30-8:30 pm; Sun brunch 11 am-2 pm; poolside lunches in season. Bar. Ck-out 11 am, ck-in 3 pm. Meeting rms. Business servs avail. In-rm modem link. Bellhops. Gift shop. Tennis privileges. Golf privileges. Putting green. Private beach. Bicycles. Lawn games. Soc dir in summer; entertainment; movies. On trolley route. Spacious grounds; on ocean peninsula. Family-operated since 1948. Totally non-smoking. Cr cds: A, MC, V.

★★★ **NONANTUM RESORT.** *95 Ocean Ave (04046), ¾ mi S, ½ mi S of ME 9. 207/967-4050; fax 207/967-8451; toll-free 800/552-5651. Email stay@nonantumresort.com; www. nonantumresort.com.* 116 rms, 26 kit units, 3-4 story. Late May-early Sep: S, D $129-$229; each addl $10; lower rates Apr-late May, early Sep-Nov. Closed rest of yr. TV; cable. Heated pool; poolside serv. Restaurant 7:30-10:30 am, 6-9 pm. Bar; entertainment (in season). Ck-out 11 am. Meeting rm. Business servs avail. Bellhops. Lawn games. Some refrigerators, microwaves. Picnic tables. One of oldest operating inns in state. On Kennebunk River; dockage. Lighthouse. Cr cds: A, MC, V

B&Bs/Small Inns

★★ **BREAKWATER INN AND RESTAURANT.** *133 Ocean Ave (04046), 1 mi S on Ocean Ave. 207/967-3118. www.thebreakwaterinn.com.* 20 rms, 2 suites. June-Aug: S $165; D $175; suites $125; each addl $25; lower rates rest of yr. Crib avail. Parking lot. TV; cable. Complimentary continental bkfst, toll-free calls. Restaurant 5:30-9 pm. Bar. Ck-out 11 am, ck-in 2 pm. Golf. Beach access. Cr cds: A, MC, V.

★★★ **BUFFLEHEAD COVE.** *Bufflehead Cove Rd (04046), S on ME 35. 207/967-3879.* 5 rms, 3 with shower only, 2 story. No rm phones. Late June-late Oct: S, D $135-$250; 2-day min in season; open wknds only Jan-Mar. Children over 11 yrs only. Complimentary full bkfst; afternoon refreshments. Ck-out 11 am, ck-in 3 pm. Concierge serv. Many fireplaces. Balconies. Picnic tables. On river, swimming. Secluded late 19th-century shingle cottage on Kennebunk River. Riverboats avail. Totally nonsmoking. Cr cds: DS, MC, V.

★★★ **CAPTAIN FAIRFIELD INN.** *8 Pleasant St (04046), at Village Green. 207/967-4454; fax 207/967-8537; toll-free 800/322-1928. Email jrw@captain fairfield.com; www.captainfairfield.com.* 9 rms, 2 story. June-Oct: S, D $180; suites $275; each addl $25; under 6 free; lower rates rest of yr. Parking lot. TV; cable (premium), VCR avail. Complimentary full bkfst, newspaper, toll-free calls. Restaurant nearby. Ck-out 11 am, ck-in 2 pm. Business servs avail. Concierge. Golf. Tennis. Beach access. Bike rentals. Hiking trail. Picnic facilities. Cr cds: A, D, DS, MC, V.

★★★ **THE CAPTAIN JEFFERDS INN.** *5 Pearl St (04046), 5 blks S on Ocean Ave, left at River Green, then left at next corner. 207/967-2311; fax 207/964-0721; toll-free 800/839-6844. Email captjeff@captainjeffersinn; www. captainjeffersinn.com.* 15 rms, 3 story, 6 suites. May-Oct: D $90; suites $285; each addl $20; children $20; lower rates rest of yr. Pet accepted, some restrictions, fee. Parking lot. TV; cable, VCR avail. CD avail. Complimentary full bkfst, coffee in rms, newspaper. Restaurant nearby. Ck-out 11 am, ck-in 3 pm. Gift shop. Golf. Tennis. Cr cds: A, MC, V.

★★★★ **THE CAPTAIN LORD MANSION.** *6 Pleasant St (04046), 1 blk E of Ocean Ave, at Pleasant and Green Sts. 207/967-3141; fax 207/967-3172. Email captain@biddeford.com; www. captainlord.com.* This inn's lemon yellow, black-shuttered facade is a prelude to the warm service and charming accommodations that lie within. Originally built in 1812 as a private residence, the mansion is now listed on the National Register of Historic Places and has been operated by the same innkeepers for over 20 years. Rates incl a full breakfast served in the country-style kitchen. 16 rms, 3 story; 4 rms with double jacuzzi in main inn. May-Dec: D $159-$299; each addl $25; suite $399; 2-day min wknds, 3-day min hol wknds; lower rates rest of yr. Children over 12 yrs only. Complimentary full bkfst; afternoon refreshments. Restaurants nearby. Ck-out 11 am, ck-in after 3 pm. Meeting rms. Business servs avail. Gift shop. Cassette player. Fireplaces. Deluxe rm with refrigerators. Some bathrooms with heated tile floors. Totally nonsmoking. Cr cds: A, MC, V.

★★ **ENGLISH MEADOWS INN.** *141 Port Rd (04043), I-95 (ME Tpke) Exit 3, then 5 mi S on ME 35. 207/967-5766; fax 207/967-3868; toll-free 800/272-0698. Email emi@cybertours. com; www.englishmeadowsinn.com.* 10 rms, 30 story, 10 suites. May-Oct: S $120; D $130; suites $160; each addl $20; under 6 free; lower rates rest of yr. Parking lot. TV; cable, VCR avail. Complimentary full bkfst. Restaurant. Concierge. Golf, 18 holes. Downhill skiing. Beach access. Bike rentals. Supervised children's activi-

ties. Hiking trail. Picnic facilities. Cr
cds: A, MC, V.

★★★★ THE INN AT HARBOR
HEAD. *41 Pier Rd (04046), at Cape
Porpoise Harbor. 207/967-5564; fax
207/967-1294. Email harborhead@
cybertours.com; www.harborhead.com.*
This 100-year-old shingled farmhouse
is intimate and informal with five
uniquely decorated romantic guestrooms filled with antiques, books,
chintz, and paddle fans. Stop by the
ocean-view breakfast room for a
morning meal, then head to nearby
Goose Rocks Beach, or just sit on the
dock and watch the day pass. The inn
overlooks picturesque Cape Porpoise
Harbor. 4 rms, 2 story, 2 suites. Rm
phones avail. Open Feb-mid-Dec. Late
May-mid-Oct: S, D $190-$315; suites
$290-$315; lower rates rest of yr. Children over 12 yrs only. Complimentary
full bkfst; afternoon refreshments. Ck-
out 11 am, ck-in 3 pm. Some balconies. Private beach. Totally
nonsmoking. Cr cds: A, MC, V.

★★★ MAINE STAY INN & COT-
TAGES. *34 Maine St (04046). 207/
967-2117; fax 207/967-8757; toll-free
800/950-2117. Email innkeeper@
mainestayinn.com; www.mainestayinn.
com.* 14 rms, 2 story, 3 suites. July-
Aug, Oct: S, D $180; suites $225; each
addl $25; children $10; under 17 free;
lower rates rest of yr. Crib avail, fee.
Parking lot. TV; cable (premium),
VCR avail. Complimentary full bkfst,
coffee in rms, toll-free calls. Restaurant nearby. Ck-out 3 pm, ck-in 11
pm. Meeting rm. Business servs avail.
Concierge. Gift shop. Golf, 18 holes.
Tennis, 2 courts. Picnic facilities. Cr
cds: A, MC, V.

★★★ OLD FORT INN. *8 Old Fort
Ave (04046), S on Ocean Ave to Old
Fort Ave. 207/967-5353; fax 207/967-
4547; toll-free 800/828-3678. Email
ofi@ispchannel.com; www.oldfortinn.com.*
16 rms, 2 story, 2 suites. June-Oct: S
$150; D $195; suites $350; each addl
$25; lower rates rest of yr. Parking
lot. Pool. TV; cable (DSS). Complimentary full bkfst, coffee in rms, toll-
free calls. Restaurant nearby. Ck-out
11 am, ck-in 3 pm. Meeting rm. Business center. Coin lndry. Gift shop.

Free airport transportation. Golf,
holes. Tennis. Hiking trail. Picnic
facilities. Cr cds: A, C, D, DS.

★★ TIDES INN BY THE SEA. *252
Kings Hwy (04046), ME 9 to Dyke Rd,
left at end to inn. 207/967-3757; fax
207/967-5183. Email tidesinn@cyber
tours.com; www.tidesinnbythesea.com.*
25 rms, 4 share bath, 3 with shower
only, 3 story, 3 kits. No A/C. No rm
phones. Mid-June-Labor Day (3-day
min wkends): D $165-$225; kit.
units $1,200-$2,600/wk; lower rates
mid-May-mid-June and Labor Day-
Columbus Day. Closed rest of yr.
Crib $20. TV in lobby, some rms.
Dining rm (see also THE BELVIDERE
ROOM). Ck-out 10:30 am, ck-in 3
pm. Swimming beach. Built as inn
1899; antiques. Original guest book
on display; signatures incl T. Roosevelt and Arthur Conan Doyle. Cr
cds: A, MC, V.

★★★★ THE WHITE BARN INN.
*37 Beach Ave (04046). 207/967-2321;
fax 207/967-1100. Email innkeeper@
whitebarninn.com; www.whitebarninn.
com.* Twenty-five rooms are tucked
away amidst this inn's lush greenery
and gardens and all incl continental
breakfast, afternoon tea, and luxurious touches of fresh flowers and fruit,
CD players, and terry robes. The
unique pool is sunk into a natural
stone patio complete with private
poolside cabanas for massage
appointments. Finish the day at the
inn's nationally recognized New England restaurant. 16 rms, 3 story, 9
suites. June-Oct: D $395; suites $525;
lower rates rest of yr. Valet parking
avail. Pool, whirlpool. TV; cable (premium), VCR avail, CD avail. Complimentary continental bkfst, coffee in
rms, newspaper. Restaurant 5-11 pm.
Bar. Ck-out 11 am, ck-in 3 pm. Meeting rm. Business servs avail.
Concierge. Dry cleaning. Salon/bar-
ber avail. Exercise privileges. Golf, 18
holes. Tennis, 2 courts. Downhill skiing. Beach access. Bike rentals. Hiking
trail. Cr cds: A, MC, V.

Restaurants

★ **ALISSON'S.** *5 Dock Sq (04046). 207/967-4841. Email alissons@ cybertour.net.* Specializes in extra-long lobster roll. Hrs: 11 am-9 pm; Fri, Sat to 10 pm. Closed Thanksgiving, Dec 25. Bar. Lunch $5-$8; dinner $11-$16. Child's menu. Two store-front rms; 2nd floor overlooks Dock Sq. Family-owned. Cr cds: A, DS, MC, V.
Ⓓ

★★ **ARUNDEL WHARF.** *43 Ocean Ave (04046). 207/967-3444. www. arundelwharf.com.* Specializes in seafood. Hrs: 11 am-9 pm. Closed Nov-Mar. Res accepted. Bar. Lunch $4-$15; dinner $13-$25. Fireplace. Cr cds: A, C, D, DS, ER, MC, V.
Ⓓ

★ **BARTLEY'S DOCKSIDE DINING.** *Western Ave (04046), by the bridge. 207/967-5050. Email bart@int-usa.net; www.int-usa.net/bartley/.* Specializes in seafood-stuffed haddock, bouillabaisse, blueberry pie. Hrs: 11 am-10 pm. Closed mid-Dec-Apr. Res accepted. Lunch $2.95-$14.95; dinner $6.50-$23.95. Child's menu. Parking. View of water. Family owned. Cr cds: A, MC, V.
Ⓓ

★★ **THE BELVIDERE ROOM.** *252 Kings Hwy. 207/967-3757.* Specializes in lobster burrito, wild game, shellfish ragout. Own baking, ice cream. Hrs: 5-9 pm. Closed mid-Oct-mid-May. Res accepted (dinner). Bar. Wine list. Bkfst $4.95-$7.95; dinner $16.95-$30.95. Child's menu. In historic inn. View of beach and ocean; antique china; player piano. Family-owned. Cr cds: A, MC, V.

★★ **BREAKWATER INN.** *133 Ocean Ave. 207/967-3118. www.the breakwaterinn.com.* Specializes in lobster, fresh seafood. Own desserts. Hrs: 5-9 pm. Closed late Oct-early May. Res accepted. Bar. Dinner $13.95. Child's menu. Parking. Built 1883 as guest house; view of river, ocean. Cr cds: A, MC, V.

★ **MABEL'S LOBSTER CLAW.** *124 Ocean Ave (04046). 207/967-2562.* Specializes in lobster Savannah, baked stuffed lobster. Own desserts. Hrs: 11 am-3 pm, 5-9 pm. Closed Wed; early Nov-Apr. Res accepted. Lunch $5-$9; dinner $12.95-$24.

Child's menu. Family-owned. Cr cds: A, MC, V.
Ⓓ

★★★ **SEASCAPES.** *77 Pier Rd (04046), 2 mi NE off ME 9, on Pier. 207/967-8500. www.seascapes restaurant.com.* Specializes in medallions of roasted lobster, Christina's shrimp, sugar cane-planked seafood grille. Hrs: 5-10 pm. Closed Mon, Tues; Nov-mid-Apr. Res accepted. Wine list. Dinner $19.95-$26.95. Entertainment: pianist Wed-Sun in season. Parking. Situated over tidal harbor. Cr cds: A, C, D, DS, ER, MC, V.

★★★★ **THE WHITE BARN RESTAURANT.** *37 Beach St. 207/ 967-2321. www.whitebarninn.com.* This restaurant, which dates back to 1820, is housed in two restored barns. The menu changes weekly and offers prix-fixe dinners of contemporary New England cuisine. Wine tastings, cigar dinners, and receptions are held in the "Wine Room," which is located in the wine cellar and can accommodate up to fourteen guests. Specializes in fresh Maine seafood, seasonal game. Menu changes wkly. Hrs: 5-9 pm. Closed 2 weeks in Jan. Res required. Bar. Wine cellar. Dinner prix fixe: 4-course $67. Entertainment: pianist. Cr cds: A, MC, V.
Ⓓ

⛽

Kingfield (E-2)

Pop 1,114 **Elev** 560 ft **Area code** 207 **Zip** 04947

On a narrow intervale in the valley of the Carrabassett River, Kingfield once had several lumber mills. The town was named after William King, Maine's first governor, and was the birthplace of F. E. and F. O. Stanley, the twins who developed the Stanley Steamer. There is good canoeing, hiking, trout fishing, and hunting in nearby areas.

What to See and Do

Carrabassett Valley Ski Touring Center. Approx 50 mi of ski touring trails. Center offers lunch (daily); school, rentals; skating rink (fee), rentals; trail information area; shop. (Early Dec-late Apr, daily) Half-day rates. 15 mi N via ME 16/27. Phone 207/237-2000. ¢¢¢¢

Sugarloaf/USA Ski Area. Two quad, triple, 8 double chairlifts, T-bar; school, patrol, rentals, snowmaking; lodge, restaurants, coffee shop, cafeteria, bars, nursery, health club, shops. Six Olympic runs, 45 mi of trails; longest run 3½ mi; vertical drop 2,820 ft. (Early Nov-May, daily) 65 mi of cross-country trails. 15 mi N on ME 16/27. Phone 207/237-2000 or 800/THE-LOAF (res only). ¢¢¢¢

Hotel

★ ★ **THE HERBERT HOTEL.** *Main St (04947). 207/265-2000; fax 207/265-4597; res 800/THEHERB.* 31 rms, 4 story, 5 suites. July-Mar: S $59; D $79; suites $125; each addl $10; under 12 free; lower rates rest of yr. Crib avail. Pet accepted, some restrictions. Valet parking avail. Indoor pool. TV; cable (DSS), VCR avail. Complimentary continental bkfst, coffee in rms, newspaper, toll-free calls. Restaurant 5:30-9:30 pm. Bar. Ck-out 11 am, ck-in noon. Meeting rms. Business servs avail. Dry cleaning, coin lndry. Gift shop. Exercise equipt, sauna, steam rm. Golf, 18 holes. Downhill skiing. Supervised children's activities. Hiking trail. Picnic facilities. Cr cds: A, C, D, DS, JCB, MC, V.

Resort

★ ★ ★ **GRAND SUMMIT HOTEL.** *Sugarloaf/USA (04947), 16 mi N, 2 mi SW of ME 27 on Sugarloaf Mt. 207/237-2222; fax 207/237-2874; toll-free 800/527-9879. Email smhotel@somtel. com; www.sugarloaf.com.* 100 rms, 6 story, 20 suites. Jan-Mar: S, D $235; suites $350; each addl $10; children $10; under 16 free; lower rates rest of yr. Crib avail, fee. Parking lot. Indoor/outdoor pools, lap pool, whirlpool. TV; cable (premium), VCR avail. Complimentary coffee in rms. Restaurant 6 am-8 pm. Bar. Meeting rms. Bellhops. Concierge. Coin lndry. Gift shop. Exercise rm, sauna, steam rm. Golf, 18 holes. Tennis, 3 courts.

Downhill skiing. Bike rentals. Supervised children's activities. Hiking trail. Picnic facilities. Cr cds: A, C, D, DS, ER, MC.

Restaurant

★ ★ **LONGFELLOW'S.** *Main and Kingfield Sts (04947). 207/265-4394.* Specializes in prime rib, seafood, chicken, beef. Hrs: 11 am-9 pm. Res accepted. Lunch $2.95-$6.75; dinner $5.50-$13.50. Child's menu. One of town's oldest bldgs (1860s). Cr cds: MC, V.

Kittery

(H-1) See also York; also see Portsmouth, NH

Settled 1623 **Pop** 9,372 **Elev** 22 ft
Area code 207 **Zip** 03904
Web www.kittery-eliot-chamber.org
Information Chamber of Commerce, US 1, PO Box 526; 207/439-7545 or 800/639-9645

This old sea community has built ships since its early days. Kittery men built the *Ranger*, which sailed to France under John Paul Jones with the news of Burgoyne's surrender. Across the Piscataqua River from Portsmouth, NH, Kittery is the home of the Portsmouth Naval Shipyard, which sprawls over islands on the Maine side of the river.

What to See and Do

Factory Outlet Stores. Approx 120 outlet stores can be found throughout Kittery. For a complete listing, contact the Chamber of Commerce.

Fort Foster Park. A 92-acre park with beach, fishing pier; picnicking, pavilion, baseball field, cross-country skiing in winter. (June-Aug, daily; May and Sep, Sat and Sun) Entrance fee per individual and per vehicle. NE via ME 103 to Gerrish Island. Phone 207/439-3800.

Fort McClary Memorial. Restored hexagonal blockhouse on site of 1809 fort. Interpretive displays; picnicking. (Memorial Day-Labor Day, daily) For further information contact the Chamber of Commerce. 3½ mi E of US 1 in Kittery Point. **FREE**

Hamilton House. (ca 1785) This Georgian house, situated overlooking the Salmon Falls River, was redecorated at the turn of the century with a mixture of antiques, painted murals, and country furnishings to create an interpretation of America's Colonial past. Perennial garden, flowering trees and shrubs, and garden cottage. Tours. (June-mid-Oct, Tues, Thurs, Sat, and Sun afternoons) N on I-95 to ME 236, then approx 10 mi NW to Vaughan Lane in South Berwick. Phone 207/384-5269. ¢¢

John Paul Jones State Memorial. Memorial to the sailors and soldiers of Maine. Hiking. (Daily) River bank, E side of US 1 at entrance to Kittery. **FREE**

Kittery Historical and Naval Museum. Exhibits portray history of US Navy and Kittery—Maine's oldest incorporated town—as well as southern Maine's maritime heritage. (June-Oct, Mon-Fri; rest of yr, Fri and by appt) Rogers Rd, off US 1 by Rotary at ME 236. Phone 207/439-3080. ¢¢

Sarah Orne Jewett House. (1774) Novelist Sarah Orne Jewett spent most of her life in this fine Georgian residence. Interior restored to recreate the appearance of the house during her time (1849-1909). Contains some original 18th- and 19th-century wallpaper; fine paneling. Her own bedroom-study has been left as she arranged it. (June-mid-Oct, Tues, Thurs, Sat, and Sun) N on I-95 to ME 236, then approx 10 mi NW to 5 Portland St in South Berwick. Phone 207/384-2454. ¢¢

Motel/Motor Lodge

★★ **DAYS INN.** *2 Gorges Rd (03904), US 1 Bypass S. 207/439-5555; fax 207/439-5555; toll-free 800/329-7466.* 108 rms, 1-3 story. Late June-early Sep: S $89.90; D $94.90; each addl $6; under 18 free; package plans off-season; lower rates rest of yr. Crib free. TV; cable (premium); VCR avail (movies). Indoor pool; sauna. Restaurant 7-11 am, 5-9 pm; off-season hrs vary. Bar 5 pm-midnight. Ck-out 11 am. Coin lndry. Meeting rms. Business servs avail. Valet serv. Sundries. Refrigerators, microwaves avail. Cr cds: A, D, DS, MC, V.

D ⌖ ⌖ ⌖ SC

B&B/Small Inn

★★ **COACHMAN INN.** *380 US Rte 1 (03904), adj Kittery Outlet Mall. 207/439-4434; fax 207/439-6757; toll-free 800/824-6183. www.visit-maine. com/coachman.* 43 rms, 2 story, 1 suite. July-Aug: S $110; D $115; suites $132; each addl $10; under 14 free; lower rates rest of yr. Crib avail. Parking lot. Pool. TV; cable (premium). Complimentary continental bkfst, toll-free calls. Restaurant nearby. Ck-out 3 pm, ck-in 11 pm. Business servs avail. Golf. Tennis. Cr cds: A, DS, MC, V.

D ⌖ ⌖ ⌖ ⌖ ⌖ SC

Restaurants

★ **CAPTAIN SIMON'S GALLEY.** *90 Pepperell Rd (ME 103) (03905). 207/439-3655.* Specializes in fresh seafood, steak, chicken. Hrs: 11 am-9 pm; off-season hrs vary. Closed Thanksgiving, Dec 25; also Tues (off season). Res accepted. Bar. Lunch $2.95-$8.95; dinner $6.95-$14.25. Sun brunch $1.99-$5.95. Nautical decor. Original hand-hewn beams from 17th-century boathouse; views of pier, lighthouses. Cr cds: A, DS, MC, V.

D

★★ **WARREN'S LOBSTER HOUSE.** *11 Water St (03904). 207/439-1630. www.lobsterhouse.com.* Specializes in lobster Thermidor, fresh seafood. Salad bar. Own baking. Hrs: 11 am-9 pm; Fri, Sat to 10 pm; hrs vary off-season. Closed Jan 1, Dec 24-25. Bar. Lunch $4.50-$9.95; dinner $9.95-$15.95. Sun brunch $10.95. Child's menu. Nautical decor; view of waterfront. Cr cds: A, C, D, ER, MC, V.

D

Lewiston

(G-2) *See also Auburn*

Settled 1770 **Pop** 39,757 **Elev** 210 ft
Area code 207
Web www.androscoggincounty.com
Information Androscoggin County
Chamber of Commerce, 179 Lisbon
St, PO Box 59, 04243-0059; 207/783-
2249

Maine's second-largest city is 30
miles up the Androscoggin River
from the sea, directly across the river
from its sister city of Auburn (see).
Known as the Twin Cities, both are
strong manufacturing and service-
oriented communities. Lewiston was
the first of the two cities to harness
the water power of the Androscoggin
Falls; however, both cities have bene-
fitted from the river.

What to See and Do

Bates College. (1855) 1,500 students.
New England's oldest and the
nation's second-oldest coeducational
institution of higher learning; originally the Maine State Seminary, it
was renamed after a prominent
Boston investor. Liberal arts and sciences. On its well-landscaped campus are the Edmund S. Muskie
Archives (1936 alumnus and former
Senator and US Secretary of State)
and a beautiful chapel containing a
hand-crafted tracker-action organ.
College St & Campus Ave. Phone
207/786-6255 or 207/786-6330. Also
on campus are

> **Mount David.** A 340-ft rocky hill
> offering a view of Lewiston, the
> Androscoggin Valley, and the Presi-
> dential Range of the White Mts to
> the west.

> **Olin Arts Center.** Multilevel facil-
> ity overlooking campus lake
> houses a concert hall and a
> Museum of Art that contains a
> variety of changing and perma-
> nent exhibits (Tues-Sun; closed
> hols). Phone 207/786-6158
> (museum) or 207/785-6135 (cen-
> ter). **FREE**

Annual Events

Maine State Parade. Downtown
Lewiston and Auburn. Maine's
largest parade; over 30,000 people
representing 60 communities. Tele-
vised statewide. Phone 207/784-
0599. First wkend May.

Lewiston-Auburn Garden Tour. Tour
of 6 gardens in the area. Ticket pur-
chase required. Phone 207/782-1403.
July.

Festival de Joie. Central Maine Civic
Center. Celebration of Lewiston and
Auburn's Franco-American heritage.
Features ethnic song, dance, cultural
activities, traditional foods. July.

Motels/Motor Lodges

★ **CHALET.** *1243 Lisbon St (04240).
207/784-0600; fax 207/786-4214; toll-
free 800/733-7787.* 74 units, 2-3 story,
8 suites, 7 kit. units (some equipt).
No elvtr. Mid-May-mid-Nov: S $36; D
$40-$45; each addl $5; suites $60-
$85; kit. units $5 addl; under 13 free;
lower rates rest of yr. Crib $5. TV;
cable (premium). Indoor pool; whirlpool. Restaurant 6-11 am. Bar 4 pm-
midnight. Ck-out 11 am. Coin lndry.
Downhill/x-country ski 15 mi. Exercise equipt; sauna. Refrigerators avail.
Picnic tables, grills. Cr cds: A, D, DS,
MC, V.

⊡ ⌂ ⇌ ⇥ 🚶 ⇲ �

★★ **RAMADA INN CONFERENCE
CENTER.** *490 Pleasant St (04240).
207/784-2331; fax 207/784-2332; res
800/272-6232. www.ramadamaine.
com.* 117 rms, 2 story. Mid-May-mid-
Oct: S $74.90; D $89-$99; each addl
$10; suites $149; studio rms $79-$99;
under 18 free. Crib free. TV; cable.
Indoor pool; whirlpool. Complimentary bkfst buffet. Coffee in rms.
Restaurant 7 am-1:30 pm, 5-10 pm.
Bar 11-1 am; entertainment. Ck-out
11 am. Coin lndry. Meeting rms.
Business center. In-rm modem link.
Gift shop. Downhill ski 10 mi. Exercise equipt; sauna. Cr cds: A, D, DS,
MC, V.

⊡ ⇥ ⇌ 🚶 ⇲ ⚙

★ **SUPER 8.** *1440 Lisbon St (04240).
207/784-8882; fax 207/784-1778; toll-
free 800/800-8000. www.super8.com.*
49 rms. July-Sep: S $40.88-$43.88; D
$55.88; each addl $6; under 12 free;
lower rates rest of yr. Crib free. TV;

cable, VCR avail (movies). Complimentary continental bkfst. Restaurant nearby. Ck-out 11 am. Downhill/x-country ski 15 mi. Cr cds: A, C, D, DS, MC, V.

D 🔒 ⚡ ➤ ◰ 🔥

Lincoln (D-4)

Pop 5,587 **Elev** 180 ft **Area code** 207 **Zip** 04457
Web www.mainerec.com/linchome. html
Information Chamber of Commerce, 75 Main St, PO Box 164; 207/794-8065 or 800/794-8065

What to See and Do

Mount Jefferson Ski Area. Novice, intermediate, and expert trails; T-bar, rope tow; patrol, school, rentals; lodge, concession. Longest run 0.7 mi, vertical drop 432 ft. (Jan-Mar, Tues, Wed, Sat, and Sun; daily during school vacations) 12 mi NE via ME 6 in Lee. Phone 207/738-2377. ¢¢¢¢

Motel/Motor Lodge

★ **BRIARWOOD MOTOR INN.** *Outer W Broadway, (04457), 1 mi S. 207/794-6731.* 24 rms, 2 story, 1 suite. June-Nov: S $40; D $45; under 10 free; lower rates rest of yr. Crib avail, fee. Pet accepted, some restrictions. TV; cable. Complimentary newspaper, toll-free calls. Restaurant nearby. Bar. Meeting rm. Salon/barber avail. Golf. Downhill skiing. Beach access. Picnic facilities. Cr cds: A, DS, MC, V.

D 🔒 ⚡ ➤ 👤 ◰ 🔥

Lubec

(E-6) *See also Eastport*

Pop 1,853 **Elev** 20 ft **Area code** 207 **Zip** 04652

Quoddy Head State Park, the easternmost point in the United States, is located in Lubec. There is a lighthouse here, as well as the Franklin D. Roosevelt Memorial Bridge, which stretches over Lubec Narrows to Campobello Island. Herring smoking and sardine packing are local industries.

What to See and Do

Roosevelt Campobello International Park. Canadian property jointly maintained by Canada and US. Approx 2,800 acres incl the 11-acre estate where Franklin D. Roosevelt had his summer home and was stricken with poliomyelitis. Self-guided tours of 34-rm house, interpretive guides avail; films shown in visitor center; picnic sites in natural area; observation platforms and interpretive panels at Friar's Head; vistas. No camping. (Sat before Memorial Day-Columbus Day, daily) 1½ mi E off ME 189 on Campobello Island. Phone 506/752-2922. **FREE**

Motel/Motor Lodge

★ **EASTLAND.** *Rte 189 (04652), 4 mi W. 207/733-5501; fax 207/733-2932.* 20 rms. Some A/C. Mid-June-Oct: S $38-$45; D $52-$62; each addl $4; under 17, $2; lower rates rest of yr. Crib free. Pet accepted; $3. TV; cable (premium). Ck-out 10 am. Complimentary coffee in lobby. Airport for small planes adj. Cr cds: A, DS, MC, V.

D 🐾 ⚡ 👣 ◰ 🔥

B&B/Small Inn

★★ **HOME PORT INN.** *45 Main St (04652). 207/733-2077; fax 207/733-2950; toll-free 800/457-2077. www.homeportinn.com.* 7 rms, 2 story. No rm phones. Memorial Day-mid-Oct: S, D $60-$80; each addl $10. Closed rest of yr. TV in sitting rm; VCR avail. Complimentary continental bkfst. Restaurant (see HOME PORT INN). Ck-out 10 am, ck-in 2 pm. Gift shop. Picnic tables. Built 1880; antiques, library. Totally nonsmoking. Cr cds: A, DS, MC, V.

D ⚡ 👣 ◰ 🔥

Restaurant

★★ **HOME PORT INN.** *45 Main St. 207/733-2077. Email carmant@ nemaine.com.* Specializes in seafood, beef, chicken. Hrs: 5-8 pm. Closed mid-Oct-May. Res accepted. Wine, beer. Dinner $9.99-$18.99. Dining rm of inn; antiques displayed. Cr cds: DS, MC, V.

D

Machias

(E-6) *See also Lubec*

Settled 1763 **Pop** 2,569 **Elev** 70 ft
Area code 207 **Zip** 04654
Information Machias Bay Area Chamber of Commerce, PO Box 606; 207/255-4402

For almost a hundred years before 1750, Machias (muh-CHY-as) was the headquarters for a number of pirates incl Samuel Bellamy, called the Robin Hood of Atlantic pirates. After pirating abated, Machias became a hotbed of Revolutionary fervor. Off Machiasport, downriver, the British schooner *Margaretta* was captured (June 1775) in the first naval engagement of the war. Today the area is noted particularly for hunting, fishing, and nature trails. Bear, deer, puffin, salmon, and striped bass abound nearby. The University of Maine has a branch in Machias.

What to See and Do

Burnham Tavern Museum. (1770) Memorabilia from 1770-1830. (June-Sep, Mon-Fri; rest of yr, by appt) Main St, just off US 1 on ME 192. Phone 207/255-4432. ¢

Ruggles House. (1820) This home exhibits Adam-style architecture and unusual "flying" staircase. Intricate wood carving, period furnishings. (June-mid-Oct, daily) 20 mi S on US 1, then ¼ mi off US 1 in Columbia Falls. Phone 207/483-4637 or 207/546-7903. ¢

State parks.

  Cobscook Bay. Fishing, boating (ramp); hiking, picnicking, snowmobiling permitted, camping (dump station). (Mid-May-mid-Oct, daily) Standard fees. 20 mi NE on US 1 near Whiting. Phone 207/726-4412. ¢

  Fort O'Brien Memorial. Remains of a fort commanding the harbor, commissioned by Washington in 1775. Hiking, picnicking. (Memor-ial Day-Labor Day, daily) 5 mi E on ME 92. **FREE**

  Roque Bluffs. Oceanfront pebble beach, freshwater pond, swimming, fishing; picnicking. (Mid-May-mid-Oct, daily) 7 mi S, off US 1. Phone 207/255-3475. ¢

Annual Event

Wild Blueberry Festival. Third wkend Aug.

Motel/Motor Lodge

★ **BLUEBIRD MOTEL.** *Rte 1 (04654), 1 mi W on US 1.* 207/255-3332. 40 rms, 1 story. July-Sep: S $54; D $60; each addl $4; children $2; under 12 free; lower rates rest of yr. TV; cable (premium). Restaurant nearby. Ck-out 11 am. Golf, 9 holes. Tennis. Cr cds: A, MC, V.

★ **MAINELAND MOTEL.** *Rte 1 (04630), 1 mi E on US 1.* 207/255-3334. *Email maineland@nemaine.com; www.freeyellow.com/members8/visit maine.* 30 rms, 1 story. May-Sep: S $40; D $48; each addl $5; under 12 free; lower rates rest of yr. Pet accepted, fee. Parking lot. TV; cable (premium). Complimentary coffee in rms, toll-free calls. Restaurant nearby. Ck-out 11 am, ck-in 1 pm. Exercise privileges. Golf. Tennis, 2 courts. Picnic facilities. Cr cds: A, C, D, DS, MC, V.

Millinocket (D-4)

Pop 6,956 **Elev** 350 ft **Area code** 207
Zip 04462
Web www.mainerec.com/millhome.
html
Information Katahdin Area Chamber of Commerce, 1029 Central St; 207/723-4443

What to See and Do

Baxter State Park. (see) 18 mi NW via state park road. Phone 207/723-5140.

Motels/Motor Lodges

★★ **ATRIUM.** *740 Central St (04462). 207/723-4555; fax 207/723-6480.* 82 rms, 3 story, 10 suites. June-Oct: S $65-$75; D $70-$80; each addl $5; suites $90; under 18 free; ski plans; lower rates rest of yr. Crib free. Pet accepted. TV; cable, VCR avail. Indoor pool; wading pool, whirlpool. Playground. Complimentary bkfst buffet. Restaurant nearby. Bar 4 pm-midnight. Ck-out noon. Coin lndry. Meeting rms. Sundries. X-country ski 10 mi. Exercise equipt. Rec rm. Some refrigerators; microwaves avail; bathrm phone, wet bar in suites. Cr cds: A, MC, V.

Cape Porpoise

★★ **BEST WESTERN HERITAGE MOTOR INN.** *935 Central St (04462). 207/723-9777; fax 207/723-9777; toll-free 800/528-1234.* 49 rms, 2 story. June-Aug: S $69; D $79; each addl $10; under 12 free; lower rates rest of yr. Crib free. Pet accepted, some restrictions. TV; cable. Complimentary continental bkfst. Restaurant 4-10 pm. Bar. Ck-out 11 am. Meeting rm. Business servs avail. Sundries. Exercise equipt. Whirlpools. Refrigerators avail. Cr cds: A, D, DS, MC, V.

★ **PAMOLA MOTOR LODGE.** *973 Central St (04462). 207/723-9746; fax 207/723-9746.* 29 rms, 1-2 story, 3 kits. Mid-May-mid-Oct: S $39; D $54; each addl $6; under 18 free; lower rates rest of yr. Crib free. TV; cable. Pool; whirlpool. Complimentary continental bkfst. Restaurant 11 am-9 pm. Bar 4 pm-1 am; entertainment Fri, Sat. Ck-out 11 am. Business servs avail. Game rm. Some balconies. Cr cds: A, C, D, DS, MC, V.

Monhegan Island

(G-3) *See also Boothbay Harbor, Damariscotta, Rockland*

Settled 1720 **Pop** 88 **Elev** 50 ft
Area code 207 **Zip** 04852

Monhegan Plantation, nine miles out to sea, approximately two miles long and one mile wide, is profitably devoted to lobsters and summer visitors. Rockwell Kent and Milton Burns were among the first of many artists to summer here. Today, the warm-weather population is about 20 times the year-round number. There is more work in winter: by special law, lobsters may be trapped in Monhegan waters only from January to June. This gives them the other six months to fatten. Monhegan lobsters thus command the highest prices.

Leif Ericson may have landed on Monhegan Island in AD 1000. In its early years, Monhegan Island was a landmark for sailors, and by 1611 it was well known as a general head-quarters for European fishermen, traders, and explorers. For a time, the island was a pirate den. Small compared to other Maine islands, Monhegan is a land of contrasts. On one side of the island sheer cliffs drop 150 feet to the ocean below, while on the other side, Cathedral Woods offers visitors a serene haven.

What to See and Do

Boat and ferry service.
    Ferry from Port Clyde. *Laura B* makes 11-mi journey (1 hr, 10

min) from Muscongus Bay. (July-Oct, 2-3 trips daily; May-June, 1 trip daily; rest of year, Mon, Wed, Fri; no trips hols) No cars permitted; res required. Foot of ME 131. Phone 207/372-8848. ¢¢¢¢

Trips from Boothbay Harbor. *Balmy Days* makes trips from mainland (see BOOTHBAY HARBOR). (June-Sep, daily) Phone 207/633-2284. ¢¢¢¢

 **Monhegan Lighthouse.** Historic lighthouse has been in operation since 1824; automated since 1959. Magnificient views. **FREE**

Moosehead Lake

(D-2) *See also Greenville, Rockwood*

(N of Greenville; approx 32 mi E of Jackman)

Web www.moosehead.net/moose/chamber.html

Information Moosehead Lake Region Chamber of Commerce, PO Box 581, Greenville 04441; 207/695-2702 or 207/695-2026.

The largest of Maine's countless lakes, Moosehead is also the center for the state's wilderness sports. The source of the Kennebec River, Moosehead Lake is 40 miles long and 20 miles wide, with many bays, islands, ponds, rivers, and brooks surrounding it. Its waters are good for ice-fishing in the winter, and trout, landlocked salmon, and togue can be caught in the summer. The lake is located in the heart of Maine's North Woods. Here is the largest moose population in the continental United States. Moose can best be seen in the early morning or at dusk. Being placid creatures, the moose allow watchers plenty of time to snap pictures. It is possible to hunt moose in northern Maine in season, but only by permit granted through a lottery.

Greenville (see), at the southern tip of the lake, is headquarters for moose-watching, hunting, fishing, camping, whitewater rafting, canoeing, hiking, snowmobiling, and cross-country and alpine skiing. The town has an airport with two runways, one 3,000 feet long. Other communities around Moosehead Lake incl Rockwood, Kokadjo, and Greenville Junction.

Newport

(E-3) *See also Skowhegan*

Pop 3,036 **Elev** 202 ft **Area code** 207 **Zip** 04953

Motel/Motor Lodge

★★ **LOVLEY'S MOTEL.** *½ mi W at jct US 2, ME 11/100, N of I-95 Newport-Detroit Exit 39.* 207/368-4311; fax 207/368-4311; toll-free 800/666-6760. 63 rms, 1-2 story, 3 kits. (no ovens, equipt). June-Nov: S $29.70-$49.90; D $39.90-$89.90; each addl $5; kit. units $8 addl; lower rates rest of yr. Crib $8. Pet accepted. TV; cable (premium). Heated pool; whirlpool. Complimentary coffee in rms. Restaurant nearby. Ck-out 11 am. Coin lndry. Business servs avail. Lawn games, gliders. Picnic tables. Cr cds: A, DS, MC, V.

B&B/Small Inn

★★ **BREWSTER INN.** *37 Zions Hill Rd (04930), 14 mi N on ME 7 to Main St.* 207/924-3130; fax 207/924-9768. *Email brewster@nconline.net; www.bbonline.com/me/brewsterinn.* 7 rms, 3 with shower only, 2 story, 2 suites. No rm phones. S, D $59-$69; each addl $10; suites $79-$89; wkly rates. Crib free. TV; cable, VCR avail. Complimentary full bkfst; afternoon refreshments. Restaurant nearby. Ck-out 11 am, ck-in 3 pm. Downhill ski 15 mi. Some fireplaces; refrigerators avail. Built in 1935; original fixtures. Totally nonsmoking. Cr cds: A, DS, MC, V.

Restaurant

★ **LOG CABIN DINER.** *ME 2 (04953), 3 mi E on ME 2 and 100.*

207/368-4551. Specializes in steak, seafood. Own desserts. Hrs: 11 am-8 pm; Sat, Sun 7 am-9 pm. Closed Dec-Mar. Bkfst $1.95-$14.95; lunch, dinner $1.95-$14.95. Child's menu. Family-owned. Cr cds: MC, V.

D SC

Northeast Harbor

(F-4) *See also Bar Harbor*

Pop 650 (est) **Elev** 80 ft
Area code 207 **Zip** 04662

This coastal village is located on Mount Desert Island, a land of rocky coastlines, forests, and lakes. The island is reached from the mainland by a short bridge.

What to See and Do

Acadia National Park. (see) N via ME 3.

Ferry Service. Connects Northeast Harbor with the Cranberry Isles (see); 3-mi, 30-min crossing. (Summer, daily; rest of yr, schedule varies) Phone 207/244-3575. ¢¢¢

Motel/Motor Lodge

★★ **KIMBALL TERRACE INN.** *Huntington Rd (04662), 2 lks SE of ME 3. 207/276-3383; fax 207/276-4102; toll-free 800/454-6225. Email www. kimballterrace@acadia.net; kimball terraceinn.com.* 70 rms, 3 story. July-Aug: S, D $145; each addl $10; under 5 free; lower rates rest of yr. Crib avail, fee. Pet accepted, some restrictions. Parking lot. Pool. TV; cable (DSS). Complimentary toll-free calls. Restaurant. Bar. Meeting rms. Fax servs avail. Gift shop. Golf, 18 holes. Tennis, 2 courts. Cr cds: A, DS, MC, V.

D ⬛🔧🏂🏊🏊🏂

B&Bs/Small Inns

★★ **ASTICOU INN.** *Asticou Way (04662), 1 mi NE on ME 3, 198. 207/ 276-3344; fax 207/276-3373; toll-free 800/258-3373. Email asticou@acadia. net; www.asticou.com.* 35 rms, 3 story, 12 suites. July-Aug: S $250; D $300; suites $350; each addl $30; under 13

free; lower rates rest of yr. Crib avail, fee. Parking lot. Pool. TV; cable (DSS), VCR avail, CD avail. Complimentary continental bkfst, newspaper. Restaurant 7 am-10 pm. Bar. Ck-out noon, ck-in 3 pm. Meeting rms. Business servs avail. Concierge. Dry cleaning, coin lndry. Golf. Tennis. Bike rentals. Supervised children's activities. Hiking trail. Picnic facilities. Cr cds: MC, V.

🔧🏂🏊🏊🏂🏂

★★ **MAISON SUISSE INN.** *144 Main St (04662). 207/276-5223; toll-free 800/624-7668. Email maison@ acadia.net; www.maisonsuisse.com.* 6 rms, 2 story, 4 suites. July-Aug, Oct: S, D $135; suites $205; each addl $15; children $10; under 12 free; lower rates rest of yr. Crib avail, fee. TV; cable (premium), VCR avail. Restaurant nearby. Ck-out 11 am, ck-in 3 pm. Golf. Tennis, 2 courts. Cr cds: A, MC, V.

🏂🏂✈🏂🏂

Restaurants

★ **DOCKSIDER.** *14 Sea St (04662). 207/276-3965.* Specializes in seafood. Hrs: 11 am-9 pm; hrs vary spring, fall. Closed mid-Oct-mid-May. Wine, beer. Lunch, dinner $1.95-$16.95. Child's menu. Rustic, nautical decor. Cr cds: MC, V.

D

★★ **JORDAN POND HOUSE.** *Park Loop Rd (04675), on grounds of Acadia National Park. 207/276-3316. Email arcadia@arcadia.net; www.jordanpond. com.* Specializes in homemade ice cream, popovers. Hrs: 11:30 am-8 pm; hrs vary off-season. Closed Nov-late May. Res accepted. Lunch $6.50-$16; dinner $6.50-$16. Child's menu. Cr cds: A, DS, MC, V.

D

Norway

(F-1) *See also Poland Spring*

Pop 4,754 **Elev** 383 ft **Area code** 207
Zip 04268

Information Oxford Hills Chamber of Commerce, PO Box 167, South Paris 04281; 207/743-2281

What to See and Do

Pennesseewasee Lake. This 7-mi-long lake, covering 922 acres, received its name from the Native American words meaning "sweet water." Swimming, beaches, waterskiing, boating (marina, rentals, launch), fishing for brown trout, bass, and perch; ice-skating. Contact Chamber of Commerce. W of town. **FREE**

Motel/Motor Lodge

★ **GOODWIN'S MOTOR INN.** *191 Main St (04281), ½ mi W on ME 26. 207/743-5121; fax 207/743-5121; toll-free 800/424-8803.* 24 rms. S $40; D $48; under 12 free; higher rates special events. Pet accepted. TV; cable. Restaurant nearby. Ck-out 11 am. Downhill/x-country ski 6 mi. Some refrigerators. Two family units. Cr cds: A, C, D, DS, MC, V.

B&B/Small Inn

★★★ **WATERFORD INN.** *258 Chadbourne Rd (04088), 8 mi W via ME 118, then S on ME 37 to Chadbourne Rd. 207/583-4037; fax 207/583-4037; res 207/583-4037. Email inn@qwi.net.* 8 rms, 2 story, 1 suite. S, D $110; suites $110; each addl $30; children $30. Crib avail, fee. Pet accepted, some restrictions, fee. Parking lot. TV; cable (premium), VCR avail, VCR avail, CD avail. Complimentary full bkfst. Restaurant 5-9 pm. Ck-out 11 am, ck-in 2 pm. Meeting rm. Fax servs avail. Golf, 9 holes. Downhill skiing. Beach access. Bike rentals. Hiking trail. Cr cds: A.

Restaurants

★ **BARJO.** *210 Main St (04268). 207/743-5784.* Specializes in marinated sirloin tips, homemade chicken pie. Salad bar. Hrs: 11 am-9 pm. Closed Mon. Lunch $3.50-$8.95; dinner $4.95-$8.95. Cr cds: DS, MC, V.

★★ **MAURICE RESTAURANT FRANCAIS.** *109 Main St (04281), 1 mi N on ME 26. 207/743-2532.* Specializes in escalope de veau flambe, roast duck a l'orange. Own desserts.

Hrs: 11:30 am-2 pm, 4:30-8:30 pm; Fri, Sat 4:30-9 pm; Sun brunch 11 am-2 pm. Closed Thanksgiving, Dec 24, 25. Res accepted. Lunch $3-$9.95; dinner $10.95-$16.95. Sun brunch $3-$9.95. Cr cds: A, C, D, DS, ER, MC, V.

Ogunquit

(H-1) *See also Kennebunk, Kittery, Wells, York*

Pop 974 **Elev** 40 ft **Area code** 207 **Zip** 03907 **Web** www.ogunquit.org

Information Chamber of Commerce, PO Box 2289; 207/646-2939

Here Maine's "stern and rockbound coast" becomes a sunny strand—a great white beach stretching three miles, with gentle (though sometimes chilly) surf. The Ogunquit public beach is one of the finest on the Atlantic. Marine views, with the picturesque little harbor of Perkins Cove, have attracted a substantial art colony.

What to See and Do

Marginal Way. A beautiful and unusual walk along the cliffs overlooking the ocean, with tidepools at the water's edge.

Ogunquit Museum of American Art. Twentieth-century American sculpture and painting. (July-mid-Sep, daily) 183 Shore Rd, at Narrow Cove. Phone 207/646-4909. **FREE**

Seasonal Event

Ogunquit Playhouse. 1 mi S on US 1. Established in the early 1930s. Top plays and musicals with professional actors. Phone 207/646-5511. Late June-Labor Day wkend.

Motels/Motor Lodges

★★ **THE BEACHMERE INN.** *12 Beachmere Pl (03907). 207/646-2021; fax 207/646-2231; toll-free 800/336-3983. Email info@beachmereinn. com.* 54 units in inn, motel, and cottages, 52 with bath, 2-3 story, 51 kits. Mid-June-Labor Day: D $100-$195;

each addl $10; spring, fall plans; lower rates late Mar-mid-June, after Labor Day-mid-Dec. Closed rest of yr. Crib $5. TV; cable, VCR (free movies). Playground. Complimentary continental bkfst. Restaurant nearby. Ck-out 11 am. Business servs avail. 9-hole golf privileges. Many microwaves; some fireplaces. Private patios, balconies. Picnic tables, grills. Victorian-style inn (1889). On ocean, swimming beach. Cr cds: A, MC, V.

★ **BRIARBROOK MOTOR INN.** *US 1 (03907). 207/646-7571. www. briarbrook.com.* 18 rms, 2 kit. units. Late June-Labor Day: D $82-$89; each addl $12; under 13, $10; kit. units $695/wk; lower rates mid-Apr-late June, after Labor Day-Oct. Closed rest of yr. Crib $9. TV; cable. Heated pool. Complimentary coffee in lobby. Restaurant adj 7 am-10 pm. Ck-out 11 am. Refrigerators. Picnic tables. On trolley route. Ogunquit Playhouse adj. Cr cds: A, DS, MC, V.

★★ **JUNIPER HILL INN.** *196 US Rte 1 (03907). 207/646-4501; fax 207/646-4595; toll-free 800/646-4544. Email juniperhill@ogunquit.com; www. ogunquit.com.* 101 rms, 2 story. May-Oct: S $49; D $59; each addl $15; children $15; lower rates rest of yr. Crib avail. Parking lot. Indoor/outdoor pools, whirlpool. TV; cable (premium). Complimentary newspaper, toll-free calls. Restaurant nearby. Ck-out 11 am, ck-in 2:30 pm. Fax servs avail. Coin lndry. Exercise equipt, sauna. Golf, 18 holes. Tennis, 2 courts. Cr cds: A, D, DS, MC, V.

★★ **MEADOWMERE.** *US 1 (03907), at Bourne's Ln. 207/646-3162; fax 207/646-6952; toll-free 800/633-8718. www.meadowmere.com.* 35 rms, 1-2 story. Some rm phones. Late June-Labor Day: S, D $86-$100; each addl $10; under 12, $5; higher rates hols; lower rates late Apr-late June, after Labor Day-mid-Oct. Closed rest of yr. TV; cable. Pool. Complimentary continental bkfst. Restaurant adj 7 am-9 pm. Ck-out 11 am. Refrigerators. Balconies. On trolley route. Cr cds: A, DS, MC, V.

★★ **THE MILESTONE.** *333 US Rte 1 (03907). 207/646-4562; fax 207/646-1739; toll-free 800/646-6453. Email milestone@ogunquit.com; www.ogun quit.com.* 70 rms, 2 story. June-Aug: S, D $149; each addl $15; children $15; lower rates rest of yr. Crib avail. Parking lot. Pool, whirlpool. TV; cable (premium). Complimentary newspaper, toll-free calls. Restaurant nearby. Ck-out 11 am, ck-in 2:30 pm. Fax servs avail. Exercise equipt. Golf, 18 holes. Tennis, 2 courts. Cr cds: A, D, DS, MC, V.

★★ **NORSEMAN MOTOR INN.** *41 Beach St (03907), 2 blks E at beach. 207/646-7024; fax 207/646-0655; toll-free 800/822-7024. Email norseman resorts@cybertours.com; www.ogunquit beach.com.* 94 rms, 1-3 story. No elvtr. Early July-late Aug: S, D $95-$185; each addl $15; lower rates early Apr-early June, late Aug-Oct. Closed rest of yr. Crib free. TV; cable. Restaurant 6:30 am-11 pm; off-season to 9 pm. Ck-out 11 am. Bellhops. Sundries. Many refrigerators. Private patios, balconies, decks. Rms vary. On beach.

★★ **RIVERSIDE.** *159 Shore Rd (03907), 1 mi S on Shore Rd at Perkins Cove. 207/646-2741; fax 207/646-0216. Email riverside@cybertours.com; www.riversidemotel.com.* 42 rms, 2 story. June-Aug: S, D $160; each addl $15; children $15; under 6 free; lower rates rest of yr. Crib avail, fee. Parking lot. TV; cable. Complimentary continental bkfst, toll-free calls. Restaurant nearby. Ck-out 11 am, ck-in 2 pm. Golf. Tennis. Cr cds: MC, V.

★★ **SEA CHAMBERS MOTOR LODGE.** *25 Shore Rd (03907). 207/646-9311; fax 207/646-0938. Email info@seachambers.com; www.sea chambers.com.* 43 rms, 2-3 story. No elvtr. Mid-June-Aug (4-day min July-Aug; 3-day min some hol wkends): S, D $118-174; each addl $15; lower rates Apr-mid-June, Sep-mid-Dec. Closed mid-Dec-Mar. Crib free. TV; cable. Heated pool. Complimentary continental bkfst. Ck-out 11 am. Business servs avail. Bellhops. Tennis. Golf privileges. Health club privileges.

Refrigerators. Most rms with ocean view. Sun decks. Cr cds: A, DS, MC, V.

★★ **SEA VIEW MOTEL.** *225 US Rte 1 (03907), ¼ mi N. 207/646-7064; fax 207/646-7064; res 207/646-7064. Email seavu@loa.com.* 40 rms, 2-3 story. No elvtr. July-Aug: S, D $79-$139; each addl $10; higher rates hols; lower rates rest of yr. Crib free. TV; cable (premium). Heated pool; whirlpool. Complimentary coffee. Restaurant nearby. Ck-out 11 am. Meeting rm. Exercise equipt. Refrigerators. Cr cds: A, MC, V.

★★★ **SPARHAWK RESORT MOTEL.** *41 Shore Rd (03907), ¼ mi SE. 207/646-5562; res 207/646-5562.* 51 rms, 36 suites. June-Aug: Crib avail, fee. Parking lot. Pool. TV; cable (premium). Complimentary continental bkfst, toll-free calls. Restaurant nearby. Ck-out 11 am, ck-in 2 pm. Fax servs avail. Golf, 18 holes. Tennis. Cr cds: MC, V.

★ **STAGE RUN MOTEL.** *238 Rte 1 (03907). 207/646-4823; fax 207/641-2884. Email stagerun@cybertours.com.* 24 rms, 2 story. July-Labor Day: S, D $89-$129; lower rates early Apr-June, early Sep-Oct. Closed rest of yr. Crib $10. TV; cable; VCR avail. Heated pool. Restaurant opp 6 am-9 pm. Ck-out 11 am. Refrigerators. Balconies. Near ocean, swimming beach. Cr cds: A, MC, V.

★★ **TOWNE LYNE MOTEL.** *US Rte (03907), 1½ mi N. 207/646-2955; fax 207/646-1812. Email smiletownelyne@gwi.net.* 20 rms, 1 story. July-Aug: D $115; lower rates rest of yr. TV; cable. Complimentary coffee in rms, newspaper, toll-free calls. Restaurant nearby. Ck-out 11 am, ck-in 2 pm. Cr cds: A, DS, MC, V.

Hotels

★★★ **GORGES GRANT HOTEL.** *239 US Rte 1 (03907), ½ mi N on US 1. 207/646-7003; fax 207/646-0660; toll-free 800/646-5001. Email gorges grant@ogunquit.com; www.ogunquit. com.* 81 rms, 2 story. May-Oct: S, D $164; each addl $15; children $15; lower rates rest of yr. Crib avail. Parking lot. Indoor/outdoor pools, whirlpool. TV; cable (premium). Complimentary newspaper, toll-free calls. Restaurant. Ck-out 11 am. Business servs avail. Coin lndry. Exercise equipt. Golf, 18 holes. Tennis, 2 courts. Cr cds: A, D, DS, MC, V.

★★ **THE GRAND HOTEL.** *108 Shore Rd (03907). 207/646-1231. Email info@thegrandhotel.com; www. thegrandhotel.com.* 28 suites, 3 story. Late June-early Sep (2-day min wkdays, 3-day min wkends): S, D $150-$200; lower rates mid-Apr-late June, early Sep-mid-Nov. Closed rest of yr. Crib $10. TV; cable, VCR (movies $4.50). Indoor pool. Complimentary continental bkfst. No rm serv. Restaurant adj 7 am-10 pm. Ck-out 11 am. Refrigerators. Balconies. Cr cds: A, DS, MC, V.

Resorts

★★★ **ANCHORAGE BY THE SEA.** *55 Shore Rd (03907), on Marginal Way. 207/646-9384; fax 207/646-6256. www.anchoragebythesea.com.* 2 rms, 3 story. July-Aug: S, D $215; each addl $15; children $15; under 2 free; lower rates rest of yr. Crib avail, fee. Parking lot. Indoor/outdoor pools, children's pool, whirlpool. TV; cable, VCR avail. Restaurant 7 am-6 pm. Bar. Ck-out 11 am, ck-in 3 pm. Meeting rm. Business servs avail. Sauna. Golf, 18 holes. Tennis, 2 courts. Cr cds: DS, MC, V.

★★ **COLONIAL VILLAGE RESORT.** *266 US 1 (03907), ½ mi N on US 1. 207/646-2794; fax 207/646-2463; toll-free 800/422-3341.* 67 rms, 1-2 story, 29 suites, 24 kit. units (no ovens), 4 kit. cottages (2-bedrm). July-Aug, motel (3-day min in season): D, kit. units $109-$140; each addl $15; suites $135-$173; kit. cottages for 2-4 (1-wk min July-Labor Day) $950/wk; lower rates early Apr-June, Sep-mid-Dec. Closed rest of yr. Crib $10. No maid serv in cottages. TV; cable, VCR avail (movies). 2 pools, 1 indoor; whirlpools. Complimentary continental bkfst. Restaurant nearby. Ck-out 11 am. Coin lndry. Tennis. Game rm. Private deck on cottages. Rowboats. Picnic tables, grills. On Tidal River. Cr cds: A, MC, V.

⛵ 🏊 🛏 🔥

★★ **PINK BLOSSOMS FAMILY RESORT.** *66 Shore Rd (03907). 207/646-7397; fax 207/646-2549; toll-free 800/228-7465. Email office@pinkb. com; www.pinkb.com.* 16 rms, 2 story, 22 suites. July-Aug: D $145; suites $195; each addl $10; lower rates rest of yr. Crib avail. Parking lot. Pool. TV; cable. Ck-out 11 am, ck-in 3 pm. Fax servs avail. Golf, 18 holes. Tennis. Picnic facilities. Cr cds: MC, V.

🅳 🍴 ⛵ 🏊 🔥

★★ **THE TERRACE BY THE SEA.** *11 Wharf Ln (03907). 207/646-3232; res 207/646-2323. Email innkeeper@ß terracebythesea.com; www.terracebythe sea.com.* 36 rms, 2 story. June-Aug: S, D $190; each addl $15; children $15; under 6 free; lower rates rest of yr. Crib avail. Parking lot. Pool. TV; cable. Complimentary continental bkfst. Ck-out 11 am, ck-in 3 pm. Bellhops. Golf, 18 holes. Tennis, 4 courts. Beach access. Cr cds: A, MC, V.

🐾 🍴 ⛵ 🏊 🛏 🔥

B&Bs/Small Inns

★ **ABOVE TIDE INN.** *26 Beach St (03907). 207/646-7454. www.above tideinn.com.* 9 rms, 7 with shower only, 2 story. No rm phones. Mid-June-mid-Sep (3-day min): S, D $125-$160; each addl $20; lower rates mid-Sep-mid-Oct, mid-May-mid-June. Closed rest of yr. TV; cable. Complimentary continental bkfst. Restaurant nearby. Ck-out 11 am, ck-in 2 pm. Massage. Refrigerators. Balconies. Sun deck. Situated on pilings over river; ocean, dune views. Cr cds: MC, V.

🐾 🔥

★★★ **HARTWELL HOUSE.** *118 Shore Rd (03907). 207/646-7210; fax 207/646-6032; res 207/646-7210; toll-free 800/235-8883. Email hartwell@ cybertours.com; www.hartwellhouse inn.com.* 13 rms, 2 story, 3 suites. June-Aug, Oct: S, D $150; suites $180; lower rates rest of yr. Parking lot. TV; cable. Complimentary full bkfst, coffee in rms, toll-free calls. Restaurant, closed Tues. Ck-out 11 am, ck-in 3 pm. Meeting rms. Business center. Golf, 18 holes. Tennis, 4

courts. Beach access. Bike rentals. Hiking trail. Cr cds: A, DS, MC, V.

🅳 🐾 🎿 🏃 ⛵ 🚣 🛏 🔥 🏃

★★ **THE PINE HILL INN.** *14 Pine Hill Rd S (03907). 207/361-1004; fax 207/361-1815. Email pinehill@cyber tours.com.* 6 units, 4 with shower only, 1-2 story, 2-bdrm kit. cottage. No rm phones. Late June-Labor Day: S, D $90-$115; kit. cottage $100; wkly rates cottage; 3-day min cottage; lower rates rest of yr. Children over 12 yrs only in inn rms. TV in cottage, sitting rm; cable. Complimentary full bkfst (inn rms only). Ck-out 11 am, ck-in 4-6 pm. Turn-of-the-century cottage with sun porch. Short walk to ocean. Totally non-smoking. Cr cds: A, MC, V.

🛏 🔥

Restaurants

★★★ **ARROW'S.** *Berwick Rd (03907). 207/361-1100. www.arrows restaurant.com.* Specializes in house-cured prosciutto. Own baking, pastas. Hrs: 6-9 pm. Closed Mon; also late Nov-late Apr. Expansive windows overlook more than 3 acres of perennial, herb, and vegetable gardens. Bar. Wine cellar. Dinner $29.95-$35.95. Valet parking. Renovated 1765 farmhouse; original plank floors, antiques, fresh flowers. Cr cds: MC, V.

★ **BARNACLE BILLY'S.** *Perkins Cove (03907), 1 mi E of US 1. 207/646-5575. Email info@barnbilly.com; www. barnbilly.com.* Specializes in boiled lobster, steamed clams, barbecued chicken. Hrs: 11 am-9 pm; hrs vary mid-Apr-mid-June, mid-Sep-mid-Oct. Closed mid-Oct-mid-Apr; also Mon-Thurs mid-Apr-early-May. Lunch from $5; dinner $7.50-$20. Valet parking. Lobster tank. Fireplaces; nautical decor. Family-owned. Cr cds: A, MC, V.

🅳

★★ **BILLY'S ETC.** *Oarweed Cove Rd (03907), 1 mi S on Shore Rd, in Perkins Cove area. 207/646-4711. Email info@ barnbilly.com; www.barnbilly.com.* Specializes in fresh seafood, lobster, steak. Hrs: 11 am-9 pm. Closed Nov-early May. Bar. Lunch $4.95-$19.95; dinner $4.95-$19.95. Child's menu. Valet parking. Views of river and gardens. Cr cds: A, MC, V.

🅳

★★ **GYPSY SWEETHEARTS.** *10 Shore Rd (03907). 207/646-7021. Email gypsy@cybertours.com; www. gypsysweethearts.com.* Specializes in shrimp margarita, almond-crusted haddock, East Coast crab cakes. Own desserts. Hrs: 5:30-9 pm. Closed Mon. Res accepted. Bar. Dinner $13.95-$22.95. Child's menu. Converted early-1800s home with original decor, perennial gardens, enclosed sunporch. Family-owned. Cr cds: A, DS, MC, V.
D

★★ **HURRICANE.** *52 Oarweed Cove Rd (03907), ½ mi S on Shore Rd, in Perkins Cove area. 207/646-6348. Email hurricane@perkinscove.com; www.perkinscove.com.* Specializes in rack of lamb, baked stuffed lobster, roasted vegetable lasagna. Own desserts. Hrs: 11:30 am-3:30 pm, 5:30-9:30 pm; Fri, Sat 5:30-10:30 pm; winter hrs vary. Closed Thanksgiving, Dec 25. Res accepted; required dinner (May-Sep). Bar. Lunch $7-$15; dinner $14-$26. Sun brunch $7-$15. Entertainment: jazz Sun Oct-May. Limited parking. Panoramic views of ocean. Cr cds: A, C, D, DS, ER, MC, V.

★★★ **JONATHAN'S.** *2 Bourne Ln (03907). 207/646-4777. www. jonathansrestaurant.com.* Specializes in seafood, beef, chicken. Own baking. Hrs: 5-10 pm; Oct-June 5:30-9 pm. Res accepted. Bar. Wine cellar. Dinner $14.50-$21.95. Child's menu. Entertainment: pianist Wed-Sat. Parking. Aquarium; tropical fish. Doll collection. Herb and country rock gardens. Cr cds: A, D, DS, MC, V.
D

★ **OARWEED COVE.** *Oarweed Rd, at Perkins Cove (03907). 207/646-4022. www.oarweed.com.* Specializes in lobster, lobster rolls, chowder. Hrs: 11 am-9 pm. Closed mid-Oct-Apr. Lunch, dinner $3.95-$19.95. Child's menu. Parking. View of ocean. Cr cds: A, DS, MC, V.
D

★ **OGUNQUIT LOBSTER POUND.** *256 US 1 (03907). 207/646-2516.* Specializes in boiled lobster; select your own. Hrs: 5-9:30 pm. Bar. Dinner $5.95-$25. Parking. New England decor; fireplaces. Family-owned. Cr cds: A, DS, MC, V.
D

★★★ **OLD VILLAGE INN.** *30 Main St (03907). 207/646-7088.* Specializes in local seafood, duckling, beef. Hrs: 5:30-9 pm; Fri, Sat to 9:30 pm. Closed Dec 25. Bar. Wine list. Dinner $12.95-$22.95. Child's menu. Town's oldest commercial bldg (1833). Guest rms avail. Cr cds: A, DS, MC, V.

★★ **POOR RICHARD'S TAVERN.** *125 Shore Rd (03907), 1 mi S on Shore Rd to Pine Hill Rd. 207/646-4722.* Specializes in Yankee pot roast, lobster-stuffed filet of sole. Hrs: 5:30-9:30 pm. Closed Sun; also Dec-Mar. Res accepted. Bar. Dinner $12-$24. Valet parking. 1780 inn with orginal hand-hewn beams, brick fireplace, antiques. Cr cds: A, DS, MC, V.
D

★★★ **PROVENCE.** *104 Shore Rd (03907). 207/646-9898. Email info@ 98provence.com; www.98provence.com.* Specializes in fresh local seafood, venison, lamb. Own desserts, ice cream. Hrs: 5:30-9 pm. Closed Tues; also mid-Dec-mid-Apr. Res accepted. Bar. Wine list. Dinner $20-$40. Intimate dining in country-French atmosphere; antiques and china displayed. Cr cds: A, MC, V.
D

Old Orchard Beach

(H-2) *See also Portland, Saco*

Settled 1630 **Pop** 7,789 **Elev** 40 ft
Area code 207 **Zip** 04064
Web www.oldorchardbeachmaine. com

Information Chamber of Commerce, PO Box 600; 207/934-2500 or 800/365-9386

This popular beach resort, 12 miles south of Portland, is one of the long-time favorites on the Maine Coast. It has a crescent beach seven miles long and about 700 feet wide—which in rocky Maine is a good deal of beach. In summer it is the vacation destination of thousands.

What to See and Do

Palace Playland. Amusement park featuring restored 1906 carousel, arcade, games, rides, water slide; concessions. (Late June-Labor Day, daily; Memorial Day-late June, wkends) Fee for individual attractions or one-price daily pass. Off ME 5, on beachfront. Phone 207/934-2001. One-price pass ¢¢¢¢

The Pier. Extends 475 ft into the harbor; features shops, boutiques, restaurant. (May-Sep, daily)

Motels/Motor Lodges

★ **CAROLINA MOTEL.** *1 Roussin St (04064), ½ lk E of Grand Ave (ME 9). 207/934-4476.* 34 kit. units (no ovens), 2 story. No A/C. Late June-early Sep: S, D $115-$150; each addl $8; lower rates May-late June, early Sep-Oct. Closed rest of yr. Crib free. TV; cable. Heated pool. Restaurant 8 am-8 pm. Ck-out 10 am. Some private balconies. On ocean. Cr cds: A, DS, MC, V.

★★ **THE EDGEWATER.** *57 W Grand Ave (04064). 207/934-2221; fax 207/934-3731; toll-free 800/203-2034. Email edgelamb@janelle.com; www. janelle.com.* 35 rms, 2 story, 5 kits. (no ovens). Late June-mid-Aug, Labor Day wknd: S, D $99-$149; each addl $8; under 12 free; lower rates mid-Mar-late June, after Labor Day-mid-Nov. Closed rest of yr. TV; cable. Heated pool. Complimentary coffee in lobby. Restaurant adj 7:30 am-noon, 5-10 pm. Ck-out 11 am. Meeting rm. In-rm modem link. Refrigerators, microwaves. Sun deck. On ocean. Cr cds: A, DS, MC, V.

★ **FLAGSHIP MOTEL.** *54 W Grand Ave. (04064) 207/934-4866; toll-free 800/486-1681. Email info@flagship motel.com; www.flagshipmotel.com.* 27 rms, 24 A/C, 2 story, 8 suites, 1 cottage. July-Labor Day: D $79-$105, suites $89-$110; each addl $8; under 12 free; lower rates mid-May-June, after Labor Day-mid-Oct. Closed rest of yr. Crib free. Pet accepted, some restrictions. TV; cable. Pool. Complimentary coffee in lobby. Restaurant opp 7-11 am, 5-10 pm. Ck-out 11 am. Refrigerators. Balconies. Picnic tables. Opp ocean; beach. Cr cds: A, MC, V.

★★ **FRIENDSHIP MOTOR INN.** *167 E Grand Ave (04064). 207/934-4644; fax 207/934-7592; toll-free 800/969-7100. Email fmi@lamere.net; www. friendshipmotorinn.com.* 71 rms, 2 story, 71 suites. July-Aug: S, D $129; suites $129; each addl $10; children $10; lower rates rest of yr. Crib avail. Parking lot. Pool. TV; cable, VCR avail. Complimentary coffee in rms, toll-free calls. Fax servs avail. Concierge. Coin lndry. Gift shop. Golf, 18 holes. Beach access. Picnic facilities. Cr cds: A, DS, MC, V.

★ **GRAND BEACH INN.** *198 E Grand Ave (04064). 207/934-4621; fax 207/934-4261; toll-free 800/834-9696. Email gbi@int.usa.net.* 87 units, 2-3 story, 37 kits. No elvtr. July-early Sep: S, D $89-$139; suites, kit. units $149-$179; under 13 free; lower rates rest of yr. Closed rest of yr. Crib $10. Pet accepted, some restrictions. TV; cable. Heated pool. Playground. Restaurant 7-11 am. Ck-out 10 am. Coin lndry. Balconies. Picnic tables, grills. Cr cds: A, DS, MC, V.

★ **THE GULL MOTEL INN & COTTAGES.** *89 W Grand Ave (04064). 207/934-4321; fax 207/934-1742; toll-free 877/662-4855. Email info@gullmotel.com; www.gullmotel. com.* 21 kit. units, 2 story, 4 kit. cottages. Late-June-Labor Day: D $75-$115; each addl $10; kit. cottages (2-bedrm) June-Sep $750/wk; lower rates May-late-June, Labor Day-early Oct. Closed rest of yr. Crib $5. TV; cable. Heated pool. Restaurant nearby. Ck-out 10 am. Private patios, balconies. Picnic tables, grills. Cr cds: A, MC, V.

★ **ISLAND VIEW MOTEL.** *174 E Grand Ave (04064). 207/934-4262. Email islandview@lamere.net.* 15 rms, 3 story. July-Aug: S, D $95; lower rates rest of yr. Pet accepted, some restrictions, fee. Parking lot. Pool. TV; cable. Complimentary coffee in rms. Restaurant nearby. Ck-out 10 am, ck-in 1 pm. Business servs avail. Golf. Beach access. Supervised children's activities. Picnic facilities. Cr cds: A, DS, MC, V.

★ **NEPTUNE MOTEL.** *82 E Grand Ave (04064). 207/934-5753; toll-free 800/624-6786.* 4 rms, 3 story, 12 suites. June-Aug: D $98; suites $98; each addl $10; under 16 free; lower rates rest of yr. Crib avail. Parking lot. TV; cable. Restaurant nearby. Ck-out 10 am, ck-in 1 pm. B/W printing avail. Golf, 18 holes. Tennis, 2 courts. Downhill skiing. Beach access. Supervised children's activities. Hiking trail. Picnic facilities. Cr cds: A, DS, MC, V.

★★ **ROYAL ANCHOR RESORT.** *201 E Grand Ave (04064). 207/934-4521; fax 207/934-4521; toll-free 800/934-4521.* 40 rms, 3 story. No A/C. No elvtr. Late June-late Aug: S, D $105-$145; each addl $10-$15; lower rates May-late June and late Aug-mid-Oct. Closed rest of yr. Crib free. TV; cable, VCR avail. Heated pool. Complimentary continental bkfst. Ck-out 10:30 am. Coin lndry. Tennis. Refrigerators, microwaves. Many private patios, balconies. On ocean. Cr cds: A, DS, MC, V.

★ **SEA CLIFF HOUSE & MOTEL.** *2 Sea Cliff Ave (04064). 207/934-4874; fax 207/934-1445; toll-free 800/326-4589.* 35 rms, 2-3 story, 22 kit. suites (2-rm). July-Aug: D $89-$125; each addl $10; lower rates rest of yr. Crib $5. TV; cable, VCR avail. Heated pool. Complimentary coffee in rms. Restaurant nearby. Ck-out 10 am. Refrigerators. Balconies. On ocean, beach. Cr cds: A, DS, MC, V.

★ **SKYLARK MOTEL.** *2 Brown St (04064). 207/934-4235. Email skylark@customnet.com.* 22 rms, 3 story, 3 kit. suites (2-bedrm), 19 kit. units (no ovens). Mid-July-mid-Aug: S, D, kit. units $104-$120; kit. suites $160-$180; wkly rates late June-late Aug; lower rates Apr-mid-July, mid-Aug-Oct. Closed rest of yr. Crib free. TV; cable (premium). Complimentary coffee in lobby. Restaurant nearby. Ck-out 11 am. Coin lndry. Picnic tables, grill. On ocean. Cr cds: A, DS, MC, V.

Hotel

★ **SAND PIPER BEACHFRONT MOTEL.** *2 Cleaves (04064), at Beachfront, ½ blk from Grand Ave (ME 9). 207/934-2733; fax 207/934-2733; toll-free 800/611-9921. Email sandpiper motel@lamere.net; www.welcome.to/ sandpiper.* 22 rms, 2 story. July-Aug: S $85; D $105; each addl $5; under 12 free; lower rates rest of yr. Crib avail, fee. Pet accepted, some restrictions, fee. Parking lot. TV; cable. Complimentary continental bkfst. Restaurant nearby. Ck-out 10 am, ck-in 10 pm. Golf. Beach access. Picnic facilities. Cr cds: A, DS, MC, V.

B&B/Small Inn

★★ **ATLANTIC BIRCHES INN.** *20 Portland Ave (04064). 207/934-5295; fax 207/934-3781; toll-free 888/934-5295. Email info@atlanticbirches.com; www.atlanticbirches.com.* 10 rms, 3 A/C, 2 kit. units (no oven), 2-3 story. No rm phones. Early July-Labor Day: S, D $75-$95; each addl $10; family rates; lower rates rest of yr. Crib free. TV in sitting rm; cable, VCR avail (movies free). Pool. Playground. Complimentary continental bkfst. Restaurant nearby. Ck-out 11 am, ck-in 2 pm. Picnic tables, grills. Restored Victorian house. Swimming beach nearby. Totally nonsmoking. Cr cds: A, MC, V

All Suite

★★ **HORIZON.** *2 Atlantic Ave (04064). 207/934-2323; fax 207/934-3215; toll-free 888/550-1745. Email horizonmotel@hotmail.com; www.horizonmotel.com.* 14 rms, 3 story, 14 suites. June-Sep: S, D $95; suites $95; each addl $8; children $8; lower rates rest of yr. Crib avail. Parking lot. TV; cable. Complimentary coffee in rms, newspaper, toll-free calls. Restaurant nearby. Ck-out 10 am, ck-in 2 pm. Fax servs avail. Coin lndry. Golf. Tennis, 3 courts. Beach access. Cr cds: A, MC, V.

Orono (E-4)

Settled 1774 **Pop** 10,573 **Elev** 80 ft
Area code 207 **Zip** 04473
Web www.bangorregion.com

Information Bangor Region Chamber of Commerce, 519 Main St, PO Box 1443, Bangor 04401; 207/947-0307

The Penobscot River flows through this valley town, which was named for a Native American chief called Joseph Orono (OR-a-no). The "Maine Stein Song" was popularized here in the 1930s by Rudy Vallee.

What to See and Do

University of Maine-Orono. (1865) 11,500 students. This is the largest of 7 campuses of the University of Maine system. On campus are Jordan Planetarium, Hutchins Concert Hall, ornamental and botanical gardens, and the largest library in the state. Main St & College Ave. Phone 207/581-1110 or 207/581-1341 (planetarium). Also on campus is

> **Hudson Museum.** Exhibits relating to history and anthropology. (Tues-Sun) At Maine Center for the Arts. Phone 207/581-1901. **FREE**

Motels/Motor Lodges

★★ BEST WESTERN BLACK BEAR INN. 4 Godfrey Dr (04473), I-95 Exit 51. 207/866-7120; fax 207/866-7433; res 800/528-1234. 68 rms, 3 story. July-Oct: S $75; D $80; each addl $5; suites $109-$119; under 12 free; lower rates rest of yr. Pet accepted. TV; cable (premium), VCR avail. Complimentary continental bkfst, coffee in rms. Restaurant 5-8 pm; closed Sun. Ck-out 11 am. Meeting rms. Business center. Exercise equipt; sauna. Microwaves avail. Cr cds: A, MC, V.

🄳 🠺 🕅 🖃 � SC 🕅

★ MILFORD MOTEL ON THE RIVER. 154 Main St (04461), US 95 Exit 51, US 2A to US 2. 207/827-3200; toll-free 800/282-3330. Email milford@mint.net; www.mint.net/milford.motel. 10 rms, 2 story, 12 suites. May-Sep: S $54; D $59; suites $84; each addl $5; under 16 free; lower rates rest of yr. Pet accepted. TV; cable (premium). Complimentary coffee in rms. Ck-out 10 am, ck-in noon. Coin lndry. Golf, 9 holes. Cr cds: A, DS, MC, V.

🠺 🕃 🕅 🖃 🌙

★★ UNIVERSITY MOTOR INN. 5 College Ave (04473). 207/866-4921; fax 207/866-4550; toll-free 800/321-4921. www.universitymotorinn.com. 48 rms, 2 story. June-Sep: S $48; D $58; each addl $4-$6; under 13 free; higher rates: Univ ME graduation, homecoming; lower rates rest of yr. Crib free. Pet accepted. TV; cable. Pool. Complimentary continental bkfst. Ck-out 11 am. Private patios, balconies. Cr cds: A, D, DS, MC, V.

🄳 🠺 🕃 🏊 🖃 🕅 🖃 🌙

Restaurant

★★ MARGARITA'S. 15 Mill St (04473). 207/866-4863. Hrs: 4 pm-1 am. Bar. Dinner a la carte entrees: $3.25-$12.95. Child's menu. Cr cds: A, DS, MC, V.

🄳 SC

Poland Spring

See also Auburn, Bridgton, Norway, Sebago Lake

Settled 1768 **Pop** 200 (est) **Elev** 500 ft
Area code 207 **Zip** 04274

The Poland Spring Inn, once New England's largest private resort (5,000 acres), stands on a rise near the mineral spring that has made it famous since 1844. Actually, the hotel had even earlier beginnings with the Mansion House built in 1794 by the Ricker brothers. In 1974 the original inn burned and was replaced by a smaller hotel.

What to See and Do

🟥 **Shaker Museum.** Shaker furniture, folk and decorative arts, textiles, tin, and woodenware; early American tools and farm implements displayed. Guided tours of bldgs in this last active Shaker community incl Meetinghouse (1794), Ministry Shop (1839), Boys' Shop (1850), Sisters' Shop (1821), and Spin House (1816). Workshops, demonstrations, concerts, and other special events. Extensive research library (Tues-

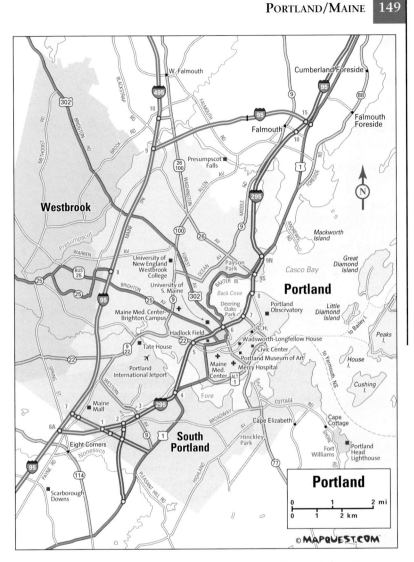

Portland

© MAPQUEST.COM

Thurs, by appt only). (Memorial Day-Columbus Day, Mon-Sat) 1 mi S on ME 26. Phone 207/926-4597. Tour ¢¢

Portland

(G-2) *See also Old Orchard Beach, Scarborough, Yarmouth*

Settled 1632 **Pop** 64,358 **Elev** 50 ft
Area code 207
Web www.visitportland.com

Information Convention & Visitors Bureau of Greater Portland, 305 Commercial St, 04101; 207/772-5800

Maine's largest city is on beautiful Casco Bay, dotted with islands popular with summer visitors. Not far from the North Atlantic fishing waters, it leads Maine in this industry. Shipping is also important. It is a city of fine elms, stately old homes, historic churches, and charming streets.

Portland was raided by Native Americans several times before the Revolution. In 1775 it was bombarded by the British, who afterward burned the town. Another fire, in 1866, wiped out large sections of the city. Longfellow remarked that the ruins reminded him of Pompeii.

What to See and Do

Boat trips. Cruises along Casco Bay, some with stops at individual islands or other locations; special charters also avail. Most cruises (May-Oct). For further information, rates, schedules, or fees contact the individual companies.

Bay View Cruises. Fisherman's Wharf, 184 Commercial St, 04101. Phone 207/761-0496.

Casco Bay Lines. PO Box 4656 DTS, 04112. Phone 207/774-7871.

Eagle Tours Inc. 19 Raybon Rd Extension, York 03909. Phone 207/774-6498.

M/S *Scotia Prince*. A 1,500-passenger cruise ferry leaves nightly for 11-hr crossing to Yarmouth, Nova Scotia. (May-Oct) Staterms avail. Phone 207/775-5616, 800/341-7540, or 800/482-0955 (ME). ¢¢¢¢

Olde Port Mariner Fleet, Inc. PO Box 1084, 04104. Phone 207/775-0727.

The Center for Maine History.

Maine History Gallery. Features Museums Collection with over 2,000 paintings, prints, and other original works of art, and approximately 8,000 artifacts. Collection incl costume and textiles, decorative arts, Native American artifacts and archeological material, political items, and military artifacts. Changing programs and exhibits trace the history of life in Maine. Gallery talks and hands-on workshops also offered. (June-Oct, daily; Dec-May, Tues-Sat) 485 Congress St. Phone 207/774-1822. ¢¢

Research Library. World's most complete collection of Maine history materials. Incl 125,000 books and newspapers, 3,500 maps, 70,000 photos, and 100,000 architectural pieces. Also Fogg collection of autographs and rare original copy of Dunlap version of the Declaration of Independence. (Tues-Sat; closed hols) Phone 207/774-1822. **FREE**-¢¢¢¢

Wadsworth-Longfellow House. (1785) Boyhood home of Henry Wadsworth Longfellow. Built by the poet's grandfather, General Peleg Wadsworth, it is maintained by the Maine Historical Society. Contains furnishings, portraits, and personal possessions of the family. (June-Oct, daily; Dec, limited hrs) 487 Congress St. Phone 207/772-1807 or 207/774-1822. ¢¢

Children's Museum of Maine. Hands-on museum where interactive exhibits allow children to become a Maine lobsterman, storekeeper, computer expert, or astronaut. (Daily) 142 Free St. Phone 207/828-1234. ¢¢

Old Port Exchange. A charming collection of shops, galleries, and restaurants located on the waterfront in late 19th-century brick bldgs. Between Exchange and Pearl Sts, extending 5 blks from waterfront to Congress St.

Portland Museum of Art. Collections of American and European painting, sculpture, prints, and decorative art; State of Maine Collection with works by artists from and associated with Maine; John Whitney Payson Collection (Renoir, Monet, Picasso, and others). Free admission Sat mornings. (Apr-Oct, Tues-Sun; Nov-Mar, Wed-Sun; closed hols) 7 Congress Sq. Phone 207/775-6148 or 207/773-ARTS (recording). ¢¢

Portland Observatory. (1807) This octagonal, shingled landmark is the last surviving 19th-century signal tower on the Atlantic. Newly renovated, with 102 steps to the top. (June-Oct, daily) 138 Congress St. Phone 207/772-5561.

Southworth Planetarium. Astronomy programs, laser light concerts, children's shows. (Fri and Sat; addl shows summer months) 96 Falmouth St. Phone 207/780-4249. ¢¢¢

State parks.

Crescent Beach. Swimming, sand beach, bathhouse, fishing; picnicking, playground, concession. (Memorial Day-Sep) Standard fees. 10 mi SE on ME 77 in Cape Elizabeth. Phone 207/799-5871 (seasonal).

Two Lights. Approx 40 acres along Atlantic Ocean. Fishing; picnicking. (Mid-Apr-Nov) Standard fees.

9 mi SE off ME 77 in Cape Elizabeth. Phone 207/799-5871.

Tate House. (1755) Georgian structure built by George Tate, mast agent for the British Navy. Furnished and decorated in the period of Tate's residence, 1755-1800; 18th-century herb gardens. (July-mid-Sep, Tues-Sun; mid-May-June and mid-Sep-mid-Oct, by appt only; closed July 4, Labor Day) 1270 Westbrook St. Phone 207/774-9781. ¢¢

The Museum at Portland Headlight. (1791) Said to be first lighthouse authorized by the US and oldest lighthouse in continuous use; erected on orders from George Washington. Former lighthouse keeper's quarters now a museum. (June-Oct, daily; Nov-Dec and Apr-May, wkends) 1000 Shore Rd, in Fort Williams Park, Cape Elizabeth. Phone 207/799 2661. ¢

Victoria Mansion. (1858) One of the finest examples of 19th-century architecture surviving in the US. Opulent Victorian interior incl frescoes, carved woodwork, and stained and etched glass. (June-Labor Day wkend, Wed-Sun, also Tues afternoons; wkend after Labor Day-Columbus Day, Fri-Sun; closed July 4, Labor Day) 109 Danforth St at Park St. Phone 207/772-4841. ¢¢

Annual Events

Old Port Festival. Parades, street performances, games, and entertainment to celebrate the revival of the Old Port Exchange. Exchange St. Phone 207/772-6828. Early June.

Sidewalk Art Show. Exhibits extend along Congress St from Congress Sq to Monument Sq. Phone 207/828-6666. Third Sat Aug.

New Year's Eve Portland. Fifteen indoor and many outdoor locations. More than 90 performances, mid-afternoon to midnight; a citywide, nonalcoholic celebration with parade and fireworks. Phone 207/772-9012. Dec 31.

Seasonal Event

Outdoor summer concerts. Deering Oaks Park. Phone 207/874-8793. Tues afternoons-Thurs eves, late June-Aug.

Motels/Motor Lodges

★ ★ **BEST WESTERN MERRY MANOR INN.** *700 Main St (04106), 3½ mi S on US 1, 2 mi off ME Tpke Exit 7. 207/774-6151; fax 207/871-0537. www.seenewengland.com.* 151 rms, 1-3 story. No elvtr. June-late Oct: S $109.95; D $119.95; each addl $10; under 12 free; lower rates rest of yr. Crib $3. Pet accepted. TV; cable (premium), VCR avail (movies). Heated pool. Coffee in rms. Restaurant 6 am-10 pm. Ck-out 11 am. Coin lndry. Meeting rms. Business servs avail. In-rm modem link. Valet serv. Health club privileges. Some refrigerators; microwaves avail. Cr cds: A, D, DS, MC, V.

★ ★ **COMFORT INN.** *90 Maine Mall Rd (04106), 2 mi S at ME Tpke Exit 7, near Intl Jetport. 207/775-0409; fax 207/775-1755; toll-free 800/368-6485. Email 729portland@sunbursthospitality. com.* 128 rms, 3 story. Mid-June-Oct: S, D $119-$149.95; each addl $5; under 19 free; lower rates rest of yr. Crib free. TV; cable (premium). Heated pool. Complimentary continental bkfst. Coffee in rms. Restaurant nearby. Ck-out 11 am. Coin lndry. Business servs avail. In-rm modem link. Valet serv. Free airport transportation. Health club privileges. Cr cds: A, C, D, DS, MC, V.

★ ★ **HOLIDAY INN.** *81 Riverside St (04103), I-95 Exit 8. 207/774-5601; fax 207/774-2103; toll-free 800/465-4329. www.portlandholidayinn.com.* 200 rms, 2 story. July-Oct: S, D $108-$129; under 20 free; lower rates rest of yr. Crib free. TV; cable (premium). Heated pool; whirlpool, poolside serv. Complimentary coffee in rms. Restaurant 6 am-2 pm, 5-10 pm. Bar 11:30-1 am; Sun from noon. Ck-out noon. Coin lndry. Meeting rms. Business servs avail. In-rm modem link. Bellhops. Sundries. Free airport transportation. Exercise equipt; sauna. Refrigerators avail. Picnic tables. Cr cds: A, D, DS, JCB, MC, V.

★ ★ **HOLIDAY INN BY THE BAY.** *88 Spring St (04101). 207/775-2311; fax 207/761-8224; res 800/465-4329;*

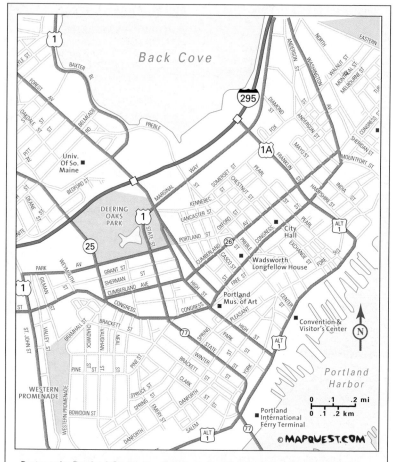

Begin at the Portland Convention & Visitors Bureau Information Center, which is located on Commercial Street down by the water. Portland is compact but has two downtowns: the old waterfront area that is now the Old Port Exchange and Congress Street, which was developed along a ridge several long streets inland. There's a hill involved here, but this walk minimizes it.

From the Visitor Center, follow Center Street (plenty of shops and restaurants) up to the Longfellow House and History Gallery on Congress Street. Detour down Preble to visit the new Portland Public Market, a colorful mix of vendors, cafes, and restaurants, before heading back up to Congress Street. Walk past the galleries of the Maine College of Art to Congress Square, site of the Portland Museum of Art and the Children's Museum. Return along Free Street to Temple turning on Middle to Exchange and down Exchange to Fore Street (maximizing shops/restaurant blocks) back to Center.

toll-free 800/345-5050. www.innbythe
bay.com. 233 rms, 11 story, 2 suites.
June-Oct: S $138; D $148; each addl
$10; under 19 free; lower rates rest of
yr. Crib avail. Valet parking avail.
Indoor pool. TV; cable (premium).
Complimentary coffee in rms, toll-
free calls. Restaurant 6 am-10 pm. Bar.
Ck-out noon, ck-in 3 pm. Business
center. Bellhops. Dry cleaning, coin
lndry. Gift shop. Free airport transportation. Sauna. Golf. Video games.
Cr cds: A, C, D, DS, JCB, MC, V.

★★★ **MARRIOTT.** *200 Sable Oaks
Dr (04106), 4 mi S on I-295 Exit 1, W
to Maine Mall Rd, N to Running Hill
Rd, then W. 207/871-8000; fax 207/
871-7971; res 800/228-9290. www.
marriott.com.* 227 rms, 6 story. Late
May-early Nov: S, D $129-$159;
suites $125-$300; lower rates rest of
yr. Crib free. Pet accepted, some
restrictions. TV; cable (premium),
VCR avail. Indoor pool; whirlpool,
poolside serv. Complimentary coffee
in rms. Restaurant 6:30 am-11 pm.
Bar noon-1 am. Ck-out noon. Meeting rms. Business servs avail. In-rm
modem link. Bellhops. Valet serv.
Gift shop. Exercise equipt; sauna. Cr
cds: A, D, DS, MC, V.

★ **SUSSE CHALET LODGE.** *1200
Brighton Ave (04102). 207/774-6101;
fax 207/772-8697; toll-free 800/258-
1980.* 132 rms, 2 story. July-Oct: S
$59.70; D $69.70-$79.70; under 19
free; lower rates rest of yr. Crib free.
TV; cable (premium). Pool. Complimentary continental bkfst. Restaurant adj open 24 hrs. Ck-out 11 am.
In-rm modem link. Cr cds: A, C, D,
DS, MC, V.

Hotels

★★ **EASTLAND PARK HOTEL.** *157
High St (04101). 207/775-5411; fax
207/775-2872. www.eastlandpark
hotel.com.* 204 rms, 12 story. June-
Oct: S, D $119-$139; each addl $15;
suites $275-$350; under 18 free;
lower rates rest of yr. Crib free.
Garage parking, fee. TV; VCR, cable
(premium). Complimentary coffee in
rms. Restaurant 6:30 am-2 pm, 5:30-
9 pm; Fri, Sat to 10 pm. Bar 5 pm-1

am; entertainment wkends. Ck-out
noon. Meeting rms. Business center.
Concierge. Gift shop. Free airport
transportation. Exercise equipt;
sauna. Refrigerator avail. Cr cds: A,
MC, V.

★★ **HAMPTON INN.** *171 Philbrook
Ave (04106), S on I-295 Exit 1 to
Maine Mall Rd, then right to Philbrook
Ave, near Intl Jetport. 207/773-4400;
fax 207/773-6786; res 800/426-7866.
Email info@portlandhamptoninn.com;
www.portlandhamptoninn.com.* 116
rms, 4 story, 1 suite. May-Oct: S
$119; D $129; suites $139; under 18
free; lower rates rest of yr. Crib avail.
Parking lot. TV; cable (premium).
Complimentary continental bkfst,
coffee in rms, newspaper, toll-free
calls. Restaurant 11 am-1 pm. Ck-out
noon, ck-in 3 pm. Business servs
avail. Dry cleaning. Free airport
transportation. Exercise equipt. Golf.
Tennis, 4 courts. Cr cds: A, C, D, DS,
MC, V.

★ **HOWARD JOHNSON HOTEL.**
*155 Riverside St (04103), ME Tpke Exit
8. 207/774-5861; fax 207/774-5861;
res 800/446-4656. Email info@hojo
portland.com; www.hojoportland.com.*
119 rms, 3 story. June-Oct: S $110; D
$120; each addl $10; under 17 free;
lower rates rest of yr. Crib avail. Pet
accepted. Parking lot. Indoor pool,
whirlpool. TV; cable (DSS), VCR
avail. Complimentary coffee in rms,
newspaper. Restaurant 6 am-11 pm.
Bar. Ck-out noon, ck-in 3 pm. Meeting rms. Business servs avail. Bellhops. Dry cleaning, coin lndry. Gift
shop. Free airport transportation.
Exercise equipt. Golf. Cr cds: A, C, D,
DS, JCB, MC, V.

★★★ **PORTLAND REGENCY
HOTEL.** *20 Milk St (04101), in Old
Port Exchange area. 207/774-4200; fax
207/775-2150; toll-free 800/727-3436.
Email public@theregency.com; www.
theregency.com.* 95 rms, 4 story, 10
suites. Early July-late Oct: S, D $169-
$199; each addl $10; suites $209-
$249; wkend rates off-season; lower
rates rest of yr. Crib free. Valet parking $5. TV; cable (premium), VCR
avail. Complimentary coffee in rms.
Restaurant 6:30 am-9:30 pm; Sat, Sun

from 7 am. Bar 11:30 am-midnight. Ck-out noon. Meeting rms. Business servs avail. In-rm modem link. Concierge. Free airport transportation. Exercise rm; sauna. Massage. Whirlpool. Bathrm phones, minibars. Small, European-style hotel in refurbished, brick armory bldg (1895). Cr cds: A, MC, V.

⬜ 🛏 🔄 🔥

★★★ **SHERATON SOUTH PORTLAND HOTEL.** *363 Maine Mall Rd (04106), 4 mi S at ME Tpke Exit 7, near Intl Jetport. 207/775-6161; fax 207/775-0196; res 800/325-3535. Email nnappi@starlodge.com; www. sheraton.com.* 217 rms, 9 story, 3 suites. June-Oct: S, D $259; suites $400; each addl $10; under 17 free; lower rates rest of yr. Crib avail, fee. Parking lot. Indoor pool, whirlpool. TV; cable (premium). Complimentary coffee in rms, newspaper. Restaurant. Bar. Ck-out 11 am, ck-in 3 pm. Meeting rms. Business servs avail. Bellhops. Concierge. Dry cleaning. Gift shop. Free airport transportation. Exercise equipt, sauna. Golf. Tennis. Cr cds: A, C, D, DS, MC, V.

⬜ 🔄 🔄 🔄 🛏 ✈ 🔄 🔥 SC

Resorts

★★★ **BLACK POINT INN.** *510 Black Point Rd (04074), 4 mi S on US 1, Then 4 Mi SE on ME 207. 207/883-2500; fax 207/883-9976; toll-free 800/258-0003.* 65 rms in inn, 25 units in 4 cottages. MAP, July-Aug: S $220-$260; D $300-$450; each addl $75; suites $400-$450; lower rates May-mid-June, late Oct-Nov. Closed rest of yr. Children over 8 yrs only mid-July-mid-Aug. Serv charge 15%. Crib free. TV; cable (premium), VCR avail (movies). 2 pools, 1 indoor, 1 heated; whirlpools, poolside serv, lifeguard in season. Dining rm (public by res) 8-11 am, noon-5 pm, 6-9 pm. Bar noon-1 am. Ck-out noon, ck-in 3 pm. Meeting rms. Business servs avail. In-rm modem link. Bellhops. Valet serv. Concierge. Gift shop. Barber, beauty shop. Airport transportation. Tennis privileges. 18-hole golf privileges. Bicycles. Exercise rm; sauna. Massage. Lawn games. Many bathrm phones; some balconies. Private beach. 1878 inn;

antiques. Secluded grounds on ocean; rose garden. Cr cds: A, DS, MC, V.

⬜ 🔄 🔄 🔄 🔄 🛏 🔄 🔥

★★★ **INN BY THE SEA.** *40 Bowery Beach Rd (04107), 6 mi SE on ME 77. 207/799-3134; fax 207/799-4779; toll-free 800/888-4287. Email inn maine@aol.com or innbythesea@ aol.com; www.innbythesea.com.* 43 suites. July-Aug: suites $399; each addl $19; lower rates rest of yr. Crib avail, fee. Pet accepted. Valet parking avail. Pool. TV; cable (premium), VCR avail, CD avail. Complimentary coffee in rms, newspaper, toll-free calls. Restaurant 7 am-10 pm. Ck-out noon, ck-in 4 pm. Meeting rms. Business servs avail. Bellhops. Concierge. Dry cleaning. Gift shop. Golf, 18 holes. Tennis. Downhill skiing. Beach access. Hiking trail. Picnic facilities. Cr cds: A, DS, MC, V.

⬜ 🔄 🔄 🔄 🔄 🔄 🛏 🔄 🔥

B&Bs/Small Inns

★★ **INN AT ST. JOHN.** *939 Congress St (04102), near Intl Airport. 207/773-6481; fax 207/756-7629; res 800/636-9127. Email info@innatstjohn.com; www.innatstjohn.com.* 32 rms, 16 share bath, 4 with shower only, 4 story. Some A/C. No elvtr. July-Oct: S, D $49-$134; each addl $6; under 13 free; lower rates rest of yr. Crib free. Pet accepted. TV; cable (premium). Complimentary continental bkfst, coffee in rms. Restaurant nearby. Ck-out 11 am, ck-in varies. Business servs avail. Coin lndry. Free airport, bus depot transportation. Refrigerators, microwaves avail. Built in 1896; European motif, antiques. Cr cds: A, MC, V.

✈ 🔄 🔥

★★ **INN ON CARLETON.** *46 Carleton St (04102). 207/775-1910; toll-free 800/639-1779. Email pcox1@ maine.rr.com.* 7 rms, 3 share bath, 2 with shower only, 3 story, 1 suite. No rm phones. June-Oct: S $65; D $115-$155; each addl $15; suite $225; hols (2-day min); lower rates rest of yr. Children over 8 yrs only. Complimentary full bkfst. Restaurant nearby. Ck-out 11 am, ck-in 4-6:30 pm. Business servs avail. Brick townhouse built 1869; Victorian antiques. Totally nonsmoking. Cr cds: A, MC, V.

★★★ **POMEGRANATE INN.** *49 Neal St (04102). 207/772-1006; fax 207/773-4426; toll-free 800/356-0408. www.innbook.com/pome.html.* 8 rms, 4 with shower only, 3 story. Memorial Day-Oct: S, D $135-$175; wkends and hols (2-day min); lower rates rest of yr. Children over 16 yrs only. TV; cable. Complimentary full bkfst. Ck-out 11 am, ck-in 4-6 pm. Street parking. Some in-rm fireplaces. Colonial Revival house built 1884; antiques, art collection. Totally nonsmoking. Cr cds: A, DS, MC, V.

Old Port Exchange Area, Portland

All Suite

★★★ **EMBASSY SUITES.** *1050 Westbrook St (04102), opp Intl Jetport. 207/775-2200; fax 207/775-4052; toll-free 800/362-2779. Email embassy@ embassysuitesportland.com; www. embassysuitesportland.com.* 119 rms, 6 story, 119 suites. June-Sep: $159-$299, each addl $10, under 18 free, off season packages, lower rates rest of yr. Parking lot. Indoor pool, whirlpool. TV; cable (premium), VCR avail, CD avail. Complimentary full bkfst, coffee in rms, newspaper, toll-free calls. Restaurant 7 am-10 pm.

Bar. Ck-out noon, ck-in 3 pm. Meeting rms. Business center. Dry cleaning. Gift shop. Exercise equipt. Golf, 18 holes. Downhill skiing. Hiking trail. Cr cds: A, D, DS, MC, V.

Restaurants

★★★ **BACK BAY GRILL.** *65 Portland St (04101). 207/772-8833. Email joel@backbaygrill.com; www.backbay grill.com.* Specializes in fresh seafood, grilled dishes, creme brulee. Own baking. Hrs: 5:30-9 pm; Fri, Sat to 10 pm. Closed Sun; hols. Res accepted. Wine cellar. Dinner $14.95-$24.95. In restored pharmacy (1888). Cr cds: A, C, D, DS, MC, V.

★★ **BOONE'S.** *6 Custom House Wharf (04112), off Commercial St. 207/774-5725.* Specializes in shore dinners, seafood, steak. Hrs: 11 am-9 pm. Closed Thanksgiving, Dec 25. Bar. Lunch $4.50-$8.95; dinner $9.95-$19.95. Child's menu. Parking. Fishing port atmosphere; built on wharf. Established in 1898. Cr cds: A, MC, V.

★★ **DI MILLO'S FLOATING RESTAURANT.** *25 Long Wharf (04101). 207/772-2216. www.dimillo. com.* Specializes in seafood, steak, lobster. Hrs: 11 am-11 pm. Closed Thanksgiving, Dec 25. Bar. Lunch $3.75-$11.95; dinner $9.95-$24.95. Child's menu. Parking. Nautical decor; located on waterfront in a converted ferry boat. Family-owned. Cr cds: A, D, DS, MC, V.

★★ **F. PARKER REIDY'S.** *83 Exchange St (04101), In Old Port Exchange Area. 207/773-4731.* Specializes in fresh fish, seafood, steak. Hrs: 11:30 am-10 pm; Fri, Sat to 11 pm; Sun from 4:30 pm. Closed July 4, Thanksgiving, Dec 25. Res accepted. Bar. Lunch $3-$9; dinner $7.95-$16. Child's menu. Originally Portland Savings Bank (1866). Cr cds: A, D, DS, MC, V.

★★★ **FORE STREET.** *288 Fore St (04101). 207/775-2717.* Specializes in spit-roasted pork, applewood-grilled steaks, wood-baked seafood. Own desserts. Hrs: 5-10 pm; Fri, Sat to 10:30 pm. Closed hols. Res accepted. Bar. Wine list. Dinner $10.95-$21.95. Child's menu. Converted 1930s oil tank garage. Unique decor with copper and steel tables, poured-concrete bar. View of harbor and ferry terminal. Cr cds: A, MC, V.

D

★ **NEWICK'S SEAFOOD.** *740 Broadway (04106), S on US 295 to Exit 3, then S to Broadway. 207/799-3090. www.newicks.com.* Specializes in fresh seafood. Hrs: 11:30 am-8 pm; Fri, Sat to 9 pm. Closed Thanksgiving, Dec 25. Bar. Lunch $6.50-$16; dinner $6.50-$16. Child's menu. Parking. Seafood market on premises. Casual dining. Cr cds: A, DS, MC, V.

D

★★ **RIBOLITA.** *41 Middle St (04101). 207/774-2972.* Specializes in risotto. Hrs: 5-9:30 pm. Closed Sun; hols. Res accepted. Dinner $9.50-$16.50. Child's menu. Street parking. Cr cds: MC, V.

★★★ **THE ROMA.** *769 Congress St (04102). 207/773-9873.* Specializes in lobster, fresh seafood, northern Italian dishes. Own desserts. Hrs: 11:30 am-2 pm, 5-9 pm; Sat from 5 pm; Sun 5-8 pm. Closed Memorial Day, Labor Day, Dec 25; also Sun Dec-May. Res accepted. Bar. Lunch $4.95-$9.95; dinner $9.95-$16.95. Child's menu. Parking. Victorian mansion (ca 1885). Fireplaces. Cr cds: A, DS, MC, V.

★★ **STREET & CO.** *33 Wharf St (04101). 207/775-0887.* Specializes in lobster diavolo, scallops in Pernod and cream, shrimp over linguini with tomato caper sauce. Hrs: 5:30-9:30 pm; Fri, Sat to 10 pm. Closed Jan 1, Dec 24, 25. Res accepted. Bar. Dinner $12.95-$19.95. Street parking. 19th century commercial bldg with original floor woodwork. Open kitchen. Cr cds: A, MC, V.

D

★★ **VALLE'S STEAK HOUSE.** *1140 Brighton Ave (04102), at ME Tpke Exit 8. 207/774-4551.* Specializes in seafood, steak. Hrs: 11 am-9 pm; Fri, Sat to 10 pm. Res accepted. Bar. Lunch $3.95-$7.95; dinner $7.95-$14.95. Child's menu. Entertainment: Fri, Sat. Parking. Family-owned. Cr cds: A, DS, MC, V.

D

★★ **VILLAGE CAFE.** *112 Newbury St (04101), near Old Port Exchange area. 207/772-5320. www.villagecafe. daweb.com.* Specializes in fried clams, lobster, veal, steak. Hrs: 11 am-10 pm; Fri, Sat to 11 pm; Sun 11:30 am-8 pm. Closed Thanksgiving, Dec 25. Bar. Lunch $4.25-$8.75; dinner $6.75-$24.95. Child's menu. Parking. Family-owned. Cr cds: A, C, D, DS, ER, MC, V.

D SC

★★ **WALTER'S CAFE.** *15 Exchange St (04101). 207/871-9258. www. walterscafe.com.* Specializes in lobster with angel hair pasta, crazy chicken. Own baking. Hrs: 11 am-3 pm, 5-10 pm; Sun from 5 pm. Closed Jan 1, Dec 25; also 1st Sat in May. Bar. Lunch $6.95-$12.95; dinner $11.95-$17.95. Street parking. Mid-1800s commercial bldg with much original interior; 3 dining areas on 2 levels. Cr cds: A, MC, V.

D

Presque Isle

(B-5) *See also Caribou*

Settled 1820 **Pop** 10,550 **Elev** 446 ft
Area code 207 **Zip** 04769
Web www.mainerec.com/pimaine.html

Information Presque Isle Area Chamber of Commerce, PO Box 672; 207/764-6561 or 800/764-7420

Commercial and industrial center of Aroostook County, this city is famous for its potatoes. A deactivated air base nearby is now a vocational school and industrial park.

What to See and Do

Aroostook Farm—Maine Agricultural Experiment Station. Approx 375 acres operated by Univ of Maine; experiments to improve growing and marketing of potatoes and grain. (Mon-Fri; closed hols) Houlton Rd, 2 mi S on US 1. Phone 207/762-8281. **FREE**

Aroostook State Park. On 577 acres. Swimming, bathhouse, fishing, boating (rentals, ramp on Echo Lake); hiking, cross-country trails, picnicking, camping. (Mid-May-mid-Oct, daily) Snowmobiling permitted. Standard fees. 4 mi S on US 1, then W. Phone 207/768-8341.

Double Eagle II Launch Site Monument. Double Eagle II, the first balloon to travel across the Atlantic Ocean, was launched from this site in 1978. Spragueville Rd, 4 mi S on US 1, then W. **FREE**

University of Maine at Presque Isle. (1903) 1,500 students. During the summer there is the Pioneer Playhouse and an Elderhostel program. In winter, the business bkfst program, theater productions, and a number of other cultural and educational events are open to the public. US 1. Phone 207/768-9400.

Annual Events

Spudland Open Amateur Golf Tournament. Presque Isle Country Club. Mid-July.

Northern Maine Fair. Midway, harness racing, entertainment. First full wk Aug.

Motels/Motor Lodges

★ **BUDGET TRAVELER MOTOR LODGE.** *71 Main St (04769), on Houlton Rd. 207/769-0111; fax 207/764-6836; toll-free 800/958-0111. Email budgeth@prodigy.net.* 53 rms, 6 kit, 2 story. S $29.95; D $35.95-$49.95; each addl $5; under 12 free. Crib $6. TV; cable, VCR avail (movies). Complimentary continental bkfst. Restaurant nearby. Ck-out 11 am. Coin lndry. Business servs avail. Free airport transportation. Refrigerators; microwaves avail. Cr cds: A, MC, V.

[D] [≈] [🐾] [SC]

★ **NORTHERN LIGHTS.** *72 Houlton Rd (04769). 207/764-4441; fax 207/769-6931.* 14 rms. S $26.95; D $39.95; each addl $5; under 12 free. Crib $5. Pet accepted; $10. TV; cable. Morning coffee. Ck-out 11 am. Cr cds: A, DS, MC, V.

[🔾] [🐾] [🎿] [≈] [🐾] [🚶]

Rangeley (E-1)

Settled 1825 **Pop** 1,063 **Elev** 1,545 ft
Area code 207 **Zip** 04970
Web www.rangeleymaine.com
Information Chamber of Commerce, PO Box 317; 207/864-5364 or 800/MT-LAKES (res)

Within ten miles of Rangeley there are 40 lakes and ponds. The six lakes that form the Rangeley chain—Rangeley, Cupsuptic, Mooselookmeguntic, Aziscoos, Upper Richardson, and Lower Richardson—spread over a wide area and give rise to the Androscoggin River. Some of Maine's highest mountains rise beside the lakes. The development of ski and snowmobiling areas has turned this summer vacation spot into a year-round resort.

What to See and Do

Camping. Several designated public camp and picnic sites; wilderness sites on islands.

Fishing. Boats for rent; licensed guides. The lakes are stocked with square-tailed trout and landlocked salmon.

Rangeley Lake State Park. More than 690 acres on Rangeley Lake. Swimming, fishing, boating (ramp, floating docks); snowmobiling permitted, picnicking, camping (dump station). (May-Oct) Standard fees. 4 mi S on ME 4, then 5 mi W via local road. Phone 207/864-3858.

Saddleback Ski and Summer Lake Preserve. Two double chairlifts, 3 T-bars; rentals, school, patrol, snowmaking; cafeteria, bar, nursery, lodge. Longest run 2½ mi; vertical drop 1,830 ft. (Late Nov-mid-Apr, daily) Cross-country trails. 7 mi E off ME 4. Phone 207/864-5671 or 207/864-3380 (snow conditions). ¢¢¢¢

Swimming, boating. Several public beaches and docks on lakefront. Rangeley Lakeside Park on lakeshore has public swimming, picnicking areas.

Wilhelm Reich Museum. Unusual stone bldg housing scientific equipment, paintings, and other memorabilia of this physician-scientist; slide presentation, nature trail, discovery rm. (July-Aug, Tues-Sun; Sep, Sun only) Dodge Pond Rd, 4 mi W off ME 4. Phone 207/864-3443. ¢¢

Annual Events

Sled Dog Race. Teams from eastern US and Canada compete in 20-mi race. Phone 207/864-5364. First wkend Mar.

Logging Museum Field Days. Logging competitions, Miss Woodchip contest, parade, logging demonstrations. Phone 207/864-5595. Last wkend July.

Motel/Motor Lodge

★★ **COUNTRY CLUB INN.** *1 Country Club Dr (04970), 2½ Mi N, Off ME 4/16.* 207/864-3831; fax 207/864-3831. Email ccinn@tdstelme.net; www.rangeleymaine/ccinn. 10 rms in 2 story inn; 9 rms in motel. No A/C. Late May-mid-Oct, late Dec-Mar, MAP: S $114; D $72-$77/person; golf plans; EP avail. Closed Apr, Nov. Serv charge 15%. Crib $5. TV in lobby. Pool. Dining rm 7:30-9 am, 6:30-8 pm. Box lunches. Bar. Ck-out 10:30 am, ck-in 1 pm. Grocery, coin lndry 2½ mi. Free airport transportation. Boat; waterskiing 1½ mi. Downhill/x-country ski 7 mi. Lawn games. Scenic view of mountains, lake. Cr cds: A, DS, MC, V.

⊠ ⊠ ⊠

Resort

★★★ **RANGELEY INN.** *51 Main St (Rte 4) (04970).* 207/864-3341; fax 207/864-3634; toll-free 800/666-3687. Email rangeinn@rangeley.org; www.rangeleyinn.com. 52 rms, 2 story, 1 suite. Jan-Mar, June-Oct: S, D, $69-$119, each addl $6; Kit. units $89-$109; lower rates rest of yr. Crib avail, fee. Parking lot. TV; cable, VCR avail. Restaurant (see RANGELEY INN). Bar. Ck-out 11 am, ck-in 3 pm. Meeting rms. Business center. Coin lndry. Gift shop. Whirlpool. Golf, 18 holes. Tennis, 2 courts. Downhill skiing. Bike rentals. Hiking trail. Picnic facilities. Cr cds: A, DS, MC, V.

⊠ ⊠ ⊠ ⊠ ⊠ ⊠ ⊠ ⊠

Restaurants

★ **PEOPLE'S CHOICE.** *Main St (ME 4) (04970), 1 mi N on ME 4/16.*

207/864-5220. Specializes in fresh seafood. Salad bar. Own baking. Hrs: 6 am-9 pm. Closed Thanksgiving, Dec 25. Res accepted. Bar. Bkfst $2-$7; lunch $3-$9; dinner $7-$15. Child's menu. Entertainment: wkends. Chainsaw-carved lumberjack on display. Cr cds: A, DS, MC, V.

⊡

★★★ **RANGELEY INN.** *51 Main St.* 207/864-3341. Email rangeinn@ rangeley.org; www.rangeleyinn.com. Specializes in fresh seafood, rack of lamb, filet mignon. Own baking. Hrs: 6-9 pm. Closed Dec 25; also Apr-May. Res accepted. Bar. Wine list. Dinner $12.95-$28.95. Child's menu. Elegant decor; oak woodwork, brass chandeliers, tin ceiling. Cr cds: A, DS, MC, V.

⊡

Rockland (G-3)

Settled 1770 **Pop** 7,972 **Elev** 35 ft
Area code 207 **Zip** 04841
Web www.midcoast.com/~rtacc

Information Rockland-Thomaston Area Chamber of Commerce, PO Box 508; 207/596-0376 or 800/562-2529

This town on Penobscot Bay is the banking and commercial center of the region and seat of Knox County. It is also the birthplace of the poet Edna St. Vincent Millay. Its economy is geared to the resort trade, but there is commercial fishing and light industry. It is the railhead for the whole bay. Supplies for boats, public landing, and guest moorings are here.

What to See and Do

Farnsworth Art Museum and Wyeth Center. Cultural and educational center for the region. Collection of over 6,000 works of 18th-20th-century American art. Center houses personal collection of Wyeth family art and archival material. (June-Sep, daily; rest of yr, Tues-Sun) 325 Main St. Phone 207/596-6457. ¢¢ Incl in admission and adj is

Farnsworth Homestead. A 19th-century Victorian mansion with period furniture. (June-Sep, daily)

Maine State Ferry Service. Ferries make 15-mi (1 hr, 15 min) trip to Vinalhaven and 12½-mi (1 hr, 10 min) trip to North Haven. (All-yr, 2-3 trips daily) 517A Main St. Phone 207/596-2202.

Owls Head Transportation Museum. Working display of antique cars, airplanes, and 100-ton steam engine. (Daily) 2 mi S via ME 73, in Owls Head. Phone 207/594-4418. ¢¢

Shore Village Museum. A large collection of lighthouse lenses and artifacts; Civil War collection. Museum shop. (June-mid-Oct, daily; rest of yr, by appt) 104 Limerock St. Phone 207/594-0311. **Donation**

Windjammers. Old-time schooners sail out for 3 to 6 days following the same basic route through Penobscot Bay, into Blue Hill and Frenchman's Bay, stopping at small villages and islands along the way. Each ship carries an average of 30 passengers. (Memorial Day-Columbus Day) For further information, rates, schedules, or res, contact the individual companies.

> **American Eagle.** Phone 800/648-4544.
>
> **The Heritage.** Phone 800/648-4544.
>
> **Issac Evans.** Phone 877/238-1325.
>
> **J. & E. Riggin.** Phone 207/594-1875 or 800/869-0604. ¢¢¢¢
>
> **Nathaniel Bowditch.** Phone 800/288-4098.
>
> **Stephen Taber.** Phone 207/236-3520 or 800/999-7352. ¢¢¢¢
>
> **Victory Chimes.** Phone 800/745-5651.

Annual Events

Schooner Days and North Atlantic Blues Festival. Three-day festival celebrating Maine's maritime heritage, featuring Parade of Schooners, arts, entertainment, concessions, fireworks; blues bands and club crawl. Phone 207/596-0376. Wkend after July 4.

Maine Lobster Festival. A 5-day event centered on Maine's chief marine creature, with a huge tent cafeteria serving lobster and other seafood. Parade, harbor cruises, maritime displays, bands, entertainment. Phone 207/594-5563. First wkend Aug.

Motels/Motor Lodges

★★ **GLEN COVE MOTEL.** *US 1 (04846), 3 mi N. 207/594-4062; toll-free 800/453-6268.* 34 rms, 1-2 story. July-Aug: S, D $79-$119; each addl $10; lower rates rest of yr. Closed Feb. Crib free. TV; cable. Heated pool. Complimentary coffee in lobby. Restaurant nearby. Ck-out 11 am. Refrigerators. Overlooks Penobscot Bay. Cr cds: A, DS, MC, V.

D ⌧ ⌧ ⌧ ⌧

★ **NAVIGATOR MOTOR INN.** *520 Main St (04841), across from State Ferry terminal. 207/594-2131; fax 207/594-7763; toll-free 888/246-4595. Email navigatorinn@hotmail.com.* 81 rms, 4-5 story, 6 kits. Mid-June-Aug: D $70-$99; each addl $10; under 16 free; lower rates rest of yr. Pet accepted, some restrictions. TV; cable. Restaurant 6:30 am-2 pm, 5:30-9:30 pm. Bar 11-1 am. Ck-out 11 am. Coin lndry. Meeting rms. Business servs avail. Downhill ski 10 mi; x-country ski 2 mi. Refrigerators; microwaves avail. Balconies. Near ocean. Cr cds: A, DS, MC, V.

D ⌧ ⌧ ⌧ ⌧

★ **WHITE GATES INN.** *700 Commercial St (04856), 4 mi N on US 1. 207/594-4625; fax 207/594-5993. Email wgates@midcoast.com.* 14 rms, 10 story. July-Aug: S $69; D $79; lower rates rest of yr. Crib avail. Parking lot. TV; cable (premium), VCR avail. Complimentary continental bkfst. Restaurant nearby. Golf. Cr cds: A, DS, MC, V.

⌧ ⌧ ⌧

Resort

★★★ **SAMOSET RESORT.** *220 Warrenton St (04856), ½ mi N on US 1, then E on Waldo Ave. 207/594-2511; fax 207/594-0722; toll-free 800/341-1650. Email info@samoset.com; www.samoset.com.* 150 rms, 4 story. Early July-early Sep: S $195-$230; D $217-$265; each addl $20; suites from $290; under 16 free; ski, golf, tennis plans; lower rates rest of yr. Crib free. TV; cable (premium). 2 pools, 1 indoor; whirlpool, poolside serv. Playground. Supervised children's activities. Coffee in rms. Dining rm 7 am-9 pm. Bar 11:30-1 am; entertainment. Ck-out noon, ck-in after 3 pm. Meeting rms. Business servs avail. In-rm modem link. Valet serv. Concierge. Gift shop. Sports dir. Tennis. Racquetball. 18-hole golf, putting green, driving range, pro, pro shop. Sailing. Dockage in season. Downhill ski 10 mi; x-country ski on site. Fitness trails. Lawn games. Movies. Game rm. Exercise rm; saunas. Massage. Private patios, balconies. Clambakes. On bay. Cr cds: A, MC, V.

[D] [≥] [ĩ] [≁] [≈] [Ӿ] [≥] [≥] [SC]

B&Bs/Small Inns

★★★ **CAPTAIN LINDSEY HOUSE INN.** *5 Lindsey St (04841). 207/596-7950; fax 207/596-2758; toll-free 800/523-2145. Email lindsey@mid coast.com.* 9 rms, 3 story. No elvtr. Mid-June-early Sep: S, D $95-$160; each addl $45; wkends 2-day min (in season); lower rates rest of yr. Children over 10 yrs only. TV; cable. Complimentary continental bkfst; afternoon refreshments. Restaurant 11 am-10 pm. Ck-out 11 am, ck-in 3 pm. In-rm modem link. Street parking. Downhill/x-country ski 10 mi. Built in 1830. Antiques; 1920s walk-in safe. Totally nonsmoking. Cr cds: A, DS, MC, V.

[D] [Ł] [≁] [≥] [Ӿ] [≥] [≥]

★★ **CRAIGNAIR INN.** *533 Clark Island Rd (04859), 5 mi S on US 1, Exit ME 131S. 207/594-7644; fax 207/596-7124; toll-free 800/320-9997. Email innkeeper@craignair.com; www. craignair.com.* 21 rms, 3 story. June-Sep: S $62; D $120; each addl $20; under 5 free; lower rates rest of yr. Crib avail, fee. Pet accepted, some restrictions, fee. Parking lot. TV; cable (premium). Complimentary full bkfst. Restaurant 5:30-9 pm, closed Sun. Bar. Ck-out 11 am, ck-in 3 pm. Meeting rm. Business servs avail. Free airport transportation. Golf. Tennis. Downhill skiing. Beach access. Hiking trail. Picnic facilities. Cr cds: DS, MC, V.

[≥] [Ł] [≥] [ĩ] [≁] [ĩ] [≥] [≥]

★★ **THE LAKESHORE INN BED & BREAKFAST.** *184 Lakeview Dr (04841). 207/594-4209; fax 207/596-6407. Email lakeshore@midcoast.com; www.midcoast.com/~lakshore.* 4 rms, 2 story. S, D $135; each addl $25. Parking lot. TV; cable, VCR avail. Complimentary full bkfst. Restaurant

nearby. Internet dock/port avail. Gift shop. Free airport transportation. Golf. Tennis, 6 courts. Downhill skiing. Beach access. Hiking trail. Cr cds: MC, V.

[Ł] [≥] [ĩ] [≁] [≥]

Restaurants

★ **HARBOR VIEW.** *Thomaston Landing (04861). 207/354-8173.* Specializes in pasta, seafood. Hrs: 11:30 am-9 pm. Closed Thanksgiving, Dec 25; also Sun and Mon Nov-Apr. Bar. Lunch $6.75-$12.95; dinner $9.95-$17.95. Parking. Antiques. View of harbor. Cr cds: A, D, DS, MC, V.

[D] [≁]

★★★ **PRIMO.** *2 S Main St (04841). 207/596-0770. Email info@primo restaurant.com; www.primorestaurant. com.* Italian with seafood menu. Hrs: 5:30-9:30. Closed Tues. Res accepted. Wine list. Dinner $15-$18. Cr cds: A, D, DS, MC, V.

[≥] [SC]

Rockwood (D-3)

Pop 190 (est) **Elev** 1,050 ft
Area code 207 **Zip** 04478

What to See and Do

Moosehead Lake. (see) E & S of town.

Raft trips.

Northern Outdoors, Inc. Specializes in outdoor adventures incl white water rafting on Maine's Kennebec, Penobscot, and Dead rivers (May-Oct). Also snowmobiling (rentals), hunting, and resort facilities. Rock climbing, freshwater kayak touring. Phone 207/663-4466 or 800/765-RAFT. ¢¢¢¢

Wilderness Expeditions, Inc. Whitewater rafting on the Kennebec, Penobscot, and Dead rivers; also canoe trips and ski tours. (May-Sep, daily) Phone 207/534-2242, 207/534-7305, or 800/825-9453. ¢¢¢¢

Motel/Motor Lodge

★ **MOOSEHEAD MOTEL.** *State Rte 15 (04478), on ME 6, 15. 207/534-*

7787. *www.maineguide.com/ moosehead/motel.* 27 rms, 11 A/C, 4 kit. units, 2 story. No rm phones. S, D $47-$56; kit. units $60-$75; each addl $5; family units $60-$75; hunters' plan. TV, some B/W. Restaurant 7-10 am, 5-8 pm; closed Apr, Dec. Ck-out 11 am. Private docks; canoes, boats, motorboats; fishing, hunting guides. Picnic tables, grill. Plane rides avail. Moosehead Lake opp, boat tour. Cr cds: A, DS, MC, V.

Cottage Colony

★ **THE BIRCHES & CATERING.** *Birches Rd (04478), 2 mi NE of ME 6/15. 207/534-7305; fax 207/534-8835; res 800/825-9453. Email wwld@ aol.com; www.birches.com.* 3 rms in main lodge, shared baths; 17 kit. cottages, shower only. No A/C. AP, May-Nov: S $105; D $65/person; wkly rates; housekeeping plan (no maid serv) $550-$750/wk (4 people); lower rates rest of yr. Pet accepted; $5. Dining rm 7-10 am, 6-9 pm; also 11 am-3 pm in season. Box lunches. Bar. Ck-out 10 am, ck-in 3 pm. Business servs avail. Gift shop. Grocery, package store 2 mi. Private beach. Marina, dockage. Boats, motors; canoes, sailboats. Canoe, rafting trips. Moose-watching cruises. Downhill ski 15 mi; x-country ski on site. Ski, kayak, snowmobile rentals. Bicycles. Sauna. Whirlpool. Fishing guides; clean/store area. Rustic log cabins. On Moosehead Lake. Cr cds: A, MC, V.

Rumford

(F-1) *See also Bethel*

Settled 1774 **Pop** 7,078 **Elev** 505 ft
Area code 207 **Zip** 04276
Web www.agate.net/~rvcc
Information River Valley Chamber of Commerce, PO Drawer 598; 207/364-3241

This papermill town is located in the valley of the Oxford Hills, where the Ellis, Swift, and Concord rivers flow into the Androscoggin. The spectacular Penacook Falls of the Androscoggin are right in town. Rumford serves as a year-round resort area.

What to See and Do

Mount Blue State Park. Recreation areas on Lake Webb incl swimming, bathhouse, lifeguard, fishing, boating (ramp, rentals); hiking trail to Mt Blue, cross-country skiing, snowmobiling permitted, picnicking, camping (dump station). (Memorial Day-Labor Day) Standard fees. 4 mi E on US 2 to Dixfield, then 14 mi N on ME 142 in Weld. Phone 207/585-2347.

Motels/Motor Lodges

★★ **BLUE IRIS MOTOR INN.** *US Rte 2 (04278), 5 mi W on US 2. 207/364-4495; toll-free 800/601-1515.* 12 rms, 1 story, 2 suites. S $40; D $48; suites $75; each addl $7; under 12 free. Parking lot. Pool. TV; cable. Complimentary toll-free calls. Restaurant nearby. Ck-out 10 am, ck-in 2 pm. Exercise privileges. Golf, 18 holes. Tennis, 6 courts. Downhill skiing. Cr cds: A, MC, V.

★ **LINNELL MOTEL & REST INN CONFERENCE CENTER.** *986 Prospect Ave (04276), 2 mi W, off US 2. 207/364-4511; fax 207/369-0800; toll-free 800/446-9038. Email innkeeper@ linnellmotel.com; www.linnellmotel. com.* 50 rms, 2 story. S $50; D $60; each addl $5; under 12 free. Crib avail. Pet accepted, fee. Parking lot. TV; cable. Complimentary continental bkfst, newspaper, toll-free calls. Restaurant. 24-hr rm serv. Ck-out 11 am, ck-in 2 pm. Meeting rms. Business center. Coin lndry. Golf, 9 holes. Tennis, 4 courts. Downhill skiing. Hiking trail. Picnic facilities. Cr cds: A, D, DS, MC, V.

★★ **MADISON RESORT INN.** *US Rte 2 PO Box 398 (04276), 4 mi W on US 2. 207/364-7973; fax 207/369-0341; toll-free 800/258-6234. Email madisons@gwi.net.* 60 rms, 38 A/C, 2 story. S $65; D $85-$95; each addl $15; kit. units $95-$125; under 12 free. Crib free. Pet accepted. TV; cable,

VCR avail (movies). Pool; whirlpool. Restaurant 6-10 am, 5-9 pm. Bar 4-10 pm. Ck-out 11 am. Meeting rms. Business servs avail. Downhill/x-country ski 10 mi. Exercise rm; sauna. Lawn games. Refrigerators. Balconies. On river; boats, canoes. Cr cds: A, MC, V.

Saco

(H-2) *See also Old Orchard Beach, Portland*

Settled 1631 **Pop** 15,181 **Elev** 60 ft
Area code 207 **Zip** 04072
Web www.biddefordsacomaine.com
Information Biddeford/Saco Chamber of Commerce, 110 Main St, Suite 1202; 207/282-1567

Saco, on the east bank of the Saco River, facing its twin city Biddeford, was originally called Pepperellboro, until its name was changed in 1805. The city has diversified industry, incl a machine and metalworking plant. Saco is home to the University of Maine system and is only four miles from the ocean.

What to See and Do

Aquaboggan Water Park. More than 40 acres of water and land attractions, incl 5 water slides, wave pool, children's pool, "aquasaucer," games, miniature golf, bumper boats, race cars. Picnicking. (May-Sep, daily) 4 mi N on US 1. Phone 207/282-3112. ¢¢¢¢¢

Dyer Library and York Institute Museum. Public library has arts and cultural programs. Museum features local history, decorative and fine art; American paintings, ceramics, glass, clocks, and furniture; changing exhibits. (Tues-Sat) 371 Main St, on US 1. Phone 207/283-3861 or 207/282-3031. ¢

Ferry Beach State Park. Beach, swimming; picnicking, nature and cross-country trails. (Memorial Day-Labor Day, daily) Standard fees. 3½ mi N via ME 9. Phone 207/283-0067.

Funtown USA. Theme park featuring adult and kiddie rides; log flume ride, Excalibur wooden roller coaster, Grand Prix Racers, games. Picnicking. (Mid-June-Sep, daily; early May-mid-June, wkends) 2 mi NE on US 1. Phone 207/284-5139 or 207/284-7113. ¢¢¢¢

Maine Aquarium. More than 150 forms of marine life, incl seals, penquins, electric eels, sharks, and tropical fish. Touch tanks. Remote-controlled miniature boats. Petting zoo. Snack bar. Picnicking. (Daily) 1½ mi N on US 1. Phone 207/284-4511. ¢¢

Motels/Motor Lodges

★ **CLASSIC.** *21 Ocean Park Rd (04072).* 207/282-5569; *fax 207/282-5569; toll-free 800/290-3909. Email classicmotel@rcn.com; www.classic motel.com.* 18 rms, 2 story, 1 suite. June-Sep: S $80; D $85; suites $150; each addl $10; children $5; under 18 free; lower rates rest of yr. Parking lot. Indoor pool, whirlpool. TV; cable, VCR avail. Complimentary continental bkfst, toll-free calls. Restaurant. Ck-out 11 am. Business servs avail. Exercise privileges. Golf. Tennis, 6 courts. Downhill skiing. Picnic facilities. Cr cds: A, DS, MC, V.

★★ **EASTVIEW.** *924 Portland Rd (04072), 3 mi N.* 207/282-2362; *fax 207/282-2362.* 22 rms. Late June-Labor Day: S $65; D $70; each addl $5; under 12 free; lower rates May-late June, after Labor Day-late Oct. Closed rest of yr. TV; cable. Pool. Restaurant opp 8 am-10 pm. Ck-out 10 am. Lawn games. Some refrigerators. Cr cds: A, MC, V.

★ **SUNRISE MOTEL.** *962 US Rte 1 (04072).* 207/283-3883; *fax 207/284-8888; res 207/283-3883; toll-free 800/467-8674. www.sunrisemotel.com.* 25 rms, 2 story, 8 suites. June-Sep: S, D $85; suites $100; each addl $10; children $10; under 13 free; lower rates rest of yr. Crib avail. Parking lot. Pool, children's pool. TV; cable (premium), VCR avail. Complimentary continental bkfst, toll-free calls. Restaurant. Ck-out 10 am, ck-in 10 pm. Fax servs avail. Coin lndry. Golf. Beach access. Picnic facilities. Cr cds: A, DS, MC, V.

Restaurant

★★ CASCADE INN. *941 Portland Rd (US 1) (04072), at Cascade Rd. 207/283-3271.* Specializes in steak, seafood. Hrs: 11 am-8 pm; Fri, Sat to 9 pm; Sun from 9 am. Bar. Bkfst buffet: $4.95-$5.95; lunch $3.99-$9.95; dinner $5.25-$14.95. Sun brunch $3.95-$5.95. Child's menu. Fireplaces. Cr cds: DS, MC, V.

Scarborough

See also Portland

Pop 12,518 **Elev** 17 ft **Area code** 207
Zip 04074
Web www.visitportland.com

Information Convention & Visitors Bureau of Greater Portland, 305 Commercial St, Portland 04101; 207/772-5800

Scarborough contains some industry, but it is primarily a farming community and has been for more than 300 years. It is also a bustling tourist town during the summer months as vacationers flock to nearby beaches and resorts. The first Anglican church in Maine is here, as is painter Winslow Homer's studio, now a National Landmark.

What to See and Do

Scarborough Marsh Nature Center. Miles of nature and waterway trails through marshland area; canoe tours, special programs (fee). (Mid-June-Labor Day, daily) Phone 207/883-5100 or 207/781-2330. **FREE**

Seasonal Event

Harness racing. On US 1, ME Tpke Exit 6. Scarborough Downs. Eves and matinees. Phone 207/883-4331. Apr-Nov.

Motels/Motor Lodges

★★ HOLIDAY HOUSE INN & MOTEL. *106 E Grand Ave (04074).* 207/883-4417; fax 207/883-6987. 16 rms in motel, 8 rms in inn, 1 A/C. Late June-Labor Day: D $100-$130; each addl $10; lower rates mid-May-mid-June, after Labor Day-Oct. Closed rest of yr. Crib $10. Adults only in inn. TV; cable. Restaurant nearby. Ck-out 10:30 am. Refrigerators. Picnic tables. Ceiling fans. Utility kit. 8 am-4:30 pm. On ocean; sun deck. Cr cds: A, MC, V.

★ LIGHTHOUSE MOTOR INN. *366 Pine Point Rd (04074). 207/883-3213; fax 207/883-3213; toll-free 800/780-3213. Email lighthouseinn@cybertours. com; www.mynextvacation.com.* 22 rms, 2 story. July-Aug: D $150; each addl $15; children $15; lower rates rest of yr. Crib avail, fee. Parking lot. TV; cable. Complimentary continental bkfst. Restaurant nearby. Ck-out 10 am, ck-in 2 pm. Golf, 18 holes. Tennis, 2 courts. Beach access. Cr cds: A, DS, MC, V.

★ MILLBROOK. *321 US 1 (04074). 207/883-6004; res 207/883-6004; toll-free 800/371-6005. Email frontdesk@ millbrookmotel.com; www.millbrook motel.com.* 18 rms, 2 story. July-Aug: S $75; D $80; each addl $5; children $5; under 12 free; lower rates rest of yr. TV; cable (premium). Restaurant. Ck-out 11 am, ck-in 1 pm. Business servs avail. Golf, 18 holes. Tennis, 4 courts. Picnic facilities. Cr cds: DS, MC, V.

Hotel

★★ FAIRFIELD INN. *2 Cummings Rd (04074). 207/883-0300; fax 207/ 883-0300; res 800/228-2800. Email fi380gm@earthlink.net; www.fairfield inn.com/pwmpt.* 120 rms, 3 story. Mid-July-Sep: S $99; D $119; under 18 free; lower rates rest of yr. Crib free. TV; cable (premium). Heated pool. Complimentary continental bkfst. Ck-out noon. Meeting rms. Business servs avail. In-rm modem link. Sundries. Refrigerators. Cr cds: DS, MC, V.

Searsport

(F-4) *See also Belfast, Bucksport*

Settled 1770 **Pop** 2,603 **Elev** 60 ft
Area code 207 **Zip** 04974
Information Chamber of Commerce, Main St, PO Box 139; 207/548-6510

On the quiet upper reaches of Penobscot Bay, this is an old seafaring town. In the 1870s at least ten percent of the captains of the US Merchant Marines lived here. Sea terminal of the Bangor and Aroostook Railway, Searsport ships potatoes and newsprint. This village abounds with antique shops and is sometimes referred to as the "antique capital of Maine."

What to See and Do

Fishing, boating on bay. Town maintains wharf and boat landing, beachside park.

Penobscot Marine Museum. Old Town Hall (1845), Merithew House (ca 1860), Fowler-True-Ross House (1825), Phillips Library, and Carver Memorial Gallery. Ship models, marine paintings, American and Oriental furnishings. (Memorial Day wkend-mid-Oct, daily) Church St, off US 1. Phone 207/548-2529. ¢¢¢

Motel/Motor Lodge

★ **YARDARM MOTEL.** *172 E Main, PO Box 246 (04974), 1 mi NE. 207/548-2404; toll-free 888/676-8006. Email yardarm@searsportmaine.com; www.searsportmaine.com.* 18 rms, 1 story. July-Sep: S $55; D $75; lower rates rest of yr. Crib avail. TV; cable. Complimentary continental bkfst. Restaurant nearby. Ck-out 11 am, ck-in 1 pm. Cr cds: DS, MC, V.
◨ ▥

B&Bs/Small Inns

★★ **BRASS LANTERN INN BED & BREAKFAST.** *81 W Main St (04974). 207/548-0150; fax 207/548-0304; toll-free 800/691-0150. Email stay@brasslanternmaine.com; www.brasslanternmaine.com.* 5 rms, 2 story. June-Oct: S $90; D $95; each addl $20; lower rates rest of yr. Parking lot. TV; cable, VCR avail. Complimentary full bkfst,

coffee in rms, newspaper. Restaurant. Ck-out 11 am, ck-in 4 pm. Meeting rm. Business center. Gift shop. Golf. Tennis. Downhill skiing. Beach access. Hiking trail. Picnic facilities. Cr cds: DS, MC, V.
▨ ◨ ▮ ▮ ▮ ▨ ▨ ▮

★★ **HICHBORN INN.** *Church St (04981), 4 mi N on US 1, Exit Main St. 207/567-4183; res 800/346-1522. www.members.aol.com/hichborn.* 4 rms, 2 share bath. A/C avail. No rm phones. Late May-early Nov: S, D $60-$95; package plans; lower rates rest of yr. Children over 12 yrs only. Complimentary full bkfst; afternoon refreshments. Restaurant nearby. Ck-out noon, ck-in 4 pm. Downhill/x-country ski 20 mi. Built in 1850. Victorian Italianate bldg in original condition; period antiques. Totally nonsmoking. Cr cds: A, MC, V.
◨ ▨ ▮

Sebago Lake

See also Bridgton, Poland Spring

Area code 207

Second-largest of Maine's lakes, this is perhaps the most popular, partly because of its proximity to Portland. About 12 miles long and eight miles wide, it lies among wooded hills. Boats can run a total of more than 40 miles from the south end of Sebago Lake, through the Songo River to the north end of Long Lake. Numerous resort communities are hidden in the trees along the shores. Sebago, home of the landlocked salmon *(Salmo sebago),* is also stocked with lake trout.

What to See and Do

Marrett House and Garden. (1789) Built in Georgian style, but later enlarged and remodeled in the Greek Revival fashion; period furnishings, farm implements. Coin from Portland banks was stored here during the War of 1812, when it was thought that the British would take Portland. Perennial and herb garden. Tours (mid-June-Aug, Tues, Thurs, Sat, and Sun). Approx 2 mi S on ME

25 to center of Standish. Phone 207/642-3032 or 617/227-3956. ¢¢

Sebago Lake State Park. A 1,300-acre area. Extensive sand beaches, bathhouse, lifeguards, fishing, boating (rentals, ramps); picnicking, concession, camping (dump station). No pets. (May-mid-Oct, daily) Standard fees. 2 mi S of Naples off ME 11/114. Phone 207/693-6231 or 207/693-6613 (campground).

The Jones Museum of Glass and Ceramics. A decorative arts museum significant for its collection of both glass and ceramics. More than 7,000 pieces from early times to present. Changing exhibits; gallery tours, library, museum shop. (Mid-May-mid-Nov, daily) 5 mi NW via ME 114 and 107 on Douglas Hill in Sebago. Phone 207/787-3370. ¢¢

Motel/Motor Lodge

★ **SUBURBAN PINES.** *322 Roosevelt Tr (04062), approx 7 mi S on US 302. 207/892-4834; fax 207/892-4841.* 25 rms, 11 kits, 1-3 story. June-Oct: S, D $50-$60; suites $75-$85; under 12 free; lower rates rest of yr. Pet accepted; $50 deposit. TV; cable. Complimentary coffee. Ck-out 11 am. Coin lndry. Picnic table, grill. Maine state picnic area opp. Cr cds: DS, MC, V.
D ⬛ ⬛ ⬛ ⬛

Resort

★★★ **MIGIS LODGE.** *Rte 302 (04077), 8 mi N on US 302. 207/655-4524; fax 207/655-2054. Email migis@ migis.com; www.migis.com.* 6 suites. June-Aug: S $215; D $500; each addl $125; lower rates rest of yr. Crib avail. Parking lot. TV; cable, VCR avail. Complimentary full bkfst, coffee in rms, newspaper. Restaurant. Bar. Meeting rms. Business center. Concierge. Dry cleaning, coin lndry. Gift shop. Exercise rm, sauna. Golf. Tennis. Beach access. Bike rentals. Supervised children's activities. Hiking trail. Picnic facilities. Cr cds: DS, MC, V.
D ⬛ ⬛ ⬛ ⬛ ⬛ ⬛ ⬛ ⬛ ⬛ ⬛

Restaurants

★★ **BARNHOUSE TAVERN RESTAURANT.** *61 ME 35 (04062), at jct US 302. 207/892-2221.* Specializes in seafood casserole, baked stuffed haddock, steak. Hrs: 11 am-10 pm. Closed Dec 25. Res accepted. Bar. Lunch $3.95-$8.95; dinner $7.95-$18.95. Entertainment: Thurs-Sat. Authentically restored post-and-beam barn and farmhouse (1872); country atmosphere, loft dining. Cr cds: A, C, D, DS, ER, MC, V.
D SC

★★★ **OLDE HOUSE.** *Rte 85 (04071), 1 mi N of US 302. 207/655-7841.* Specializes in beef Wellington, lemon chicken, duck. Own baking. Hrs: 5-10 pm. Closed Mon. Res accepted; required hols. Wine list. Dinner $15.95-$22.95. Child's menu. Historic (1790) home. Victorian decor; antiques. Cr cds: DS, MC, V.
D

Skowhegan

(E-2) *See also Newport, Waterville*

Settled 1771 **Pop** 8,725 **Elev** 175 ft
Area code 207 **Zip** 04976
Web www.skowhegan.org

Information Chamber of Commerce, PO Box 326; 207/474-3621 or 800/426-8713

Skowhegan, on the Kennebec River, is surrounded by beautiful lakes. Shoes, paper pulp, and other wood products are made here. In the village's center stands a 12-ton, 62-foot high Native American carved of native pine by Bernard Langlais. Skowhegan is the birthplace of Margaret Chase Smith, who served three terms in the United States House of Representatives and four terms in the Senate.

What to See and Do

History House. (1839) Old household furnishings; museum contains books, china, dolls, and documents. (Mid-June-mid-Sep, Tues-Fri afternoons) Elm St, on the Kennebec River. Phone 207/474-6632. ¢

Annual Events

Skowhegan State Fair. One of oldest in country (1818). mi-long midway, stage shows, harness racing; contests, exhibits. Phone 207/474-2947. Mid-Aug.

Skowhegan Log Days. Parade, fireworks, pig roast, lobster bake, golf tournament, amateur and professional competitions, bean dinner. Com-

Picturesque lighthouse

memorates last log drive on Kennebec River. Phone 207/474-3621. Last full wk Aug.

Motels/Motor Lodges

★★ **BELMONT MOTEL.** *425 Madison Ave (04976). 207/474-8315; fax 207/474-8315; toll-free 800/235-6669.* 36 rms. July-Oct: S $50; D $65; each addl $5; suites $110-$130; higher rates State Fair, special events; lower rates rest of yr. TV; cable (premium). Pool. Restaurants nearby. Ck-out 11 am. Sundries. Downhill ski 5 mi; x-country ski 1 mi. Lawn games. Refrigerators avail. Picnic tables. Cr cds: A, D, DS, MC, V.

★★ **THE TOWNE MOTEL.** *248 Madison Ave (004976). 207/474-5121; fax 207/474-6407; toll-free 800/843-4405.* 33 rms, 1-2 story, 7 kits. July-Oct: S, D $60-$68; each addl $6; kit. units $72-$78; higher rates: state fair, racing; lower rates rest of yr. TV; cable (premium). Pool. Complimentary continental bkfst. Restaurant nearby. Ck-out 11 am. Coin lndry. Downhill/x-country ski 6 mi. Cr cds: A, MC, V.

Restaurants

★★ **CANDLELIGHT.** *1 Madison Ave (04976). 207/474-2978. Email candlelite@wworx.net.* Specializes in beef, seafood. Salad bar. Own baking. Hrs: 11 am-2 pm, 4-9 pm; Sun, Mon to 2 pm; Sat from 4 pm. Closed Dec 25. Res accepted. Bar. Lunch $1.50-

$7.25; dinner $7.95-$14.95. Child's menu. Parking. Cr cds: A, DS, MC, V.

★★ **HERITAGE HOUSE.** *260 Madison Ave (04976). 207/474-5100.* Specializes in fresh seafood, steak, vegetables. Hrs: 11:30 am-2 pm, 5-9 pm; Sat-Mon from 5 pm. Closed July 4, Dec 25. Res accepted. Bar. Lunch $3.95-$6.95; dinner $7.95-$15. Child's menu. Restored home; oak staircase. Cr cds: A, DS, MC, V.

Southwest Harbor

(F-4) *See also Bar Harbor, Cranberry Isles*

Pop 1,952 **Elev** 50 ft **Area code** 207
Zip 04679
Web www.acadia.net/swhtrcoc

Information Chamber of Commerce, PO Box 1143; 207/244-9264 or 800/423-9264

This is a prosperous, working seacoast village on Mount Desert Island. There are lobster wharves, where visitors can watch about 70 fishermen bring their catch, and many shops where boats are constructed. Visitors may rent sail and power boats in Southwest Harbor to explore the coves and islands; hiking trails and quiet harbors offer relaxation.

What to See and Do

Acadia National Park. (see) W, N, and E of village.

Cranberry Cove Boating Co. Cruise to Cranberry Islands. See native wildlife and learn island history. Six departures daily. (Mid-June-mid-Sep, daily) Departs Upper Town Dock. Phone 207/244-5882. ¢¢

Maine State Ferry Service. Ferry makes 6-mi (40 min) trip to Swans Island and 8¼-mi (50 min) trip to Frenchboro (limited schedule). Swans Island (all-yr, 1-6 trips daily). 4 mi S on ME 102 & ME 102A, in Bass Harbor. Phone 207/244-3254 (Bass Harbor) or 207/526-4273.

Mount Desert Oceanarium. More than 20 tanks with Gulf of Maine marine creatures. Touch tank permits animals to be picked up. Exhibits on tides, seawater, plankton, fishing gear, weather. Inquire for information on special events. (Mid-May-mid-Oct, Mon-Sat) Clark Point Rd. Phone 207/244-7330. ¢¢

Wendell Gilley Museum. Art and natural history museum featuring collection of bird carvings by local artist Wendell Gilley; changing exhibits of local and historical art; films. (June-Oct, Tues-Sun; May and Nov-Dec, Fri-Sun) Main St & Herrick Rd. Phone 207/244-7555. ¢¢

B&Bs/Small Inns

★★ **KINGSLEIGH INN 1904.** *373 Main St (04679). 207/244-5302; fax 207/244-7691. Email relax@kingleigh inn.com; www.kingsleighinn.com.* 7 rms, 3 story, 2 suites. June-Oct: D $125; suites $210; each addl $20; under 12 free; lower rates rest of yr. Parking lot. TV; cable. Complimentary full bkfst, newspaper. Restaurant nearby. Ck-out 11 am, ck-in 3 pm. Exercise privileges. Golf. Tennis, 2 courts. Beach access. Bike rentals. Hiking trail. Picnic facilities. Cr cds: MC, V.

★★ **LAMB'S EAR INN BED AND BREAKFAST.** *60 Clark Point Rd (04679). 207/244-9828; fax 207/244-9924. www.acadia.net/lambsear.* 8 rms, 2 with shower only, 2 story. No A/C. No rm phones. Mid-June-mid-Oct: S, D $85-$165; each addl $25;

lower rates May-mid-June. Closed rest of yr. Children over 8 yrs only. TV in some rms; cable. Complimentary bkfst buffet; afternoon refreshments. Restaurant nearby. Ck-out 10:30 am, ck-in 2-6 pm. Captain's house (1857); deck with harbor view. Some in-rm whirlpools, fireplaces. Totally nonsmoking. Cr cds: A, DS, MC, V.

★★ **THE MOORINGS INN.** *Shore Rd Manset, PO Box 744 (04679), 2 mi E, on Shore Rd. 207/244-5523; toll-free 800/596-5523. Email storey@ acadia.net; www.mooringsinn.com.* 6 rms, 2 story, 4 suites. July-Sep: S $65; D $75; suites $100; each addl $10; children $6; lower rates rest of yr. Parking garage. TV; cable. Complimentary continental bkfst, newspaper, toll-free calls. Restaurant. Bar. Meeting rms. Concierge. Golf, 9 holes. Tennis. Beach access. Bike rentals. Hiking trail.

Cottage Colony

★★ **ACADIA CABINS.** *410 Main St. (PO Box 1214) (04679). 207/244-5388. Email info@acadiacabins.com; www.acadiacabins.com.* June-Aug: S, D $79; suites $99; each addl $10; lower rates rest of yr. Parking lot. Pool. TV; cable, VCR avail. Complimentary toll-free calls. Ck-out 10 am, ck-in 2 pm. Coin lndry. Golf. Cr cds: DS, MC, V.

Restaurant

★ **SEAWALL DINING ROOM.** *566 Seawall Rd (04679), 3½ mi E on ME 102A. 207/244-3020. Email seawall motel@acadia.net.* Specializes in seafood, baked stuffed lobster. Own desserts. Hrs: 11:30 am-9 pm; July-Labor Day to 10 pm. Closed Dec-Apr. Res accepted. Lunch, dinner $3.25-$18. Child's menu. Family-owned. Cr cds: A, D, MC, V.

Unrated Dining Spot

BEAL'S LOBSTER PIER. *Clark Point Rd (04679). 207/244-3202.* Specializes in fresh seafood, steamed lobster.

Hrs: 9 am-6 pm; hrs vary off-season. Closed July 4. Wine, beer. Bkfst a la carte entrees: $10-$20; lunch, dinner a la carte entrees: $10-$20. Lobsters boiled to order; self-service. Family-owned since 1930. Cr cds: A, DS, MC, V.

D

Waterville

(F-3) *See also Augusta*

Settled 1754 **Pop** 17,173 **Elev** 113 ft
Area code 207 **Zip** 04901
Web www.mid-mainechamber.com
Information Mid-Maine Chamber of Commerce, One Post Office Square, PO Box 142, 04903; 207/873-3315

A large Native American village once occupied the west bank of the Kennebec River where many of Waterville's factories now stand. An important industrial town, Waterville is the center of the Belgrade and China lakes resort area. Manufactured goods incl men's and women's shirts, paper and molded pulp products, and woolens.

What to See and Do

Colby College. (1813) 1,700 students. This 714-acre campus incl an art museum in the Bixler Art and Music Center (daily; closed hols), a Walcker organ designed by Albert Schweitzer in Lorimer Chapel and books, manuscripts, and letters of Maine authors Edwin Arlington Robinson and Sarah Jewett in the Miller Library (Mon-Fri; closed hols). Mayflower Hill Dr, 2 mi W, ½ mi E of I-95. Phone 207/872-3000.

Old Fort Halifax. (1754) Blockhouse. Bridge over Kennebec gives view of Ticonic Falls. (Memorial Day-Labor Day, daily) 1 mi E on US 201, on Bay St in Winslow, on E bank of Kennebec River. **FREE**

Redington Museum. (1814) Waterville Historical Society collection incl 18th- and 19th-century furnishings, manuscripts, Civil War and Native American relics; historical library; children's rm; apothecary museum.

(Mid-May-Sep, Tues-Sat) 64 Silver St. Phone 207/872-9439. ¢¢

Two-Cent Footbridge. One of the few remaining former toll footbridges in the US. Front St. **FREE**

Seasonal Event

New England Music Camp. 5 mi W on ME 137 to Oakland, then 4 mi S on ME 23; on Pond Rd. Faculty and student concerts, Sun; faculty concerts, Wed; student recitals, Fri. Phone 207/465-3025. Late June-late Aug.

Motels/Motor Lodges

★★ **COMFORT INN & SUITES.** *332 Main St (04901). 207/873-2777; fax 207/872-2838.* 78 rms, 4 story, 25 suites. Apr-Oct: S $89; D $99; suites $129; each addl $4; lower rates rest of yr. Crib avail, fee. Parking lot. Indoor pool. TV; cable (premium). Complimentary full bkfst, coffee in rms, toll-free calls. Restaurant nearby. Ck-out 11 am, ck-in 3 pm. Fax servs avail. Dry cleaning, coin lndry. Exercise equipt. Picnic facilities. Cr cds: A, C, D, DS, MC, V.
D ⊠ ⟁ ⊠ ⊠ SC

★★ **HOLIDAY INN.** *375 Main St (04901). 207/873-0111; fax 207/872-2310; toll-free 800/465-4329. Email hiwvlme@mint.net; www.acadia.net/ hiwat-cm.* 138 rms, 3 story. May-Oct: S $85; D $95; each addl $10; suite $150; under 19 free; lower rates rest of yr. Crib free. Pet accepted. TV; cable (premium), VCR avail. Indoor pool; whirlpool. Complimentary coffee in rms. Restaurant 6 am-2 pm, 5-10 pm. Bar 11-1 am. Ck-out noon. Coin lndry. Meeting rms. Business servs avail. In-rm modem link. Sundries. Exercise equipt; sauna. Refrigerators, microwaves avail. Cr cds: A, C, D, DS, JCB, MC, V.
D ⟲ ⊠ ⟁ ⊠ ⊠ SC

Hotel

★★ **BEST WESTERN WATERVILLE.** *356 Main St (04901), at I-95 Exit 34. 207/873-3335; fax 207/873-3335; res 800/528l234.* 86 rms, 2 story. July-Oct: S $94; D $104; suites $129; each addl $10; under 12 free; lower rates rest of yr. Crib avail, fee. Pet accepted, some restrictions. Parking lot. Pool, whirlpool. TV; cable (premium), VCR avail. Complimentary coffee in rms, newspaper. Restaurant 6 am-10 pm. Ck-out noon, ck-in 2 pm. Meeting rms. Business servs avail. Dry cleaning. Exercise privileges, sauna. Golf. Tennis. Cr cds: A, C, D, DS, MC, V.

Restaurants

★★ **JOHN MARTIN'S MANOR.** *54 College Ave (04901). 207/873-5676.* Specializes in prime rib, popovers, seafood. Salad bar. Hrs: 11 am-9 pm. Closed Dec 25. Res accepted. Bar. Lunch $3.95-$7.45; dinner $6.95-$15.95. Child's menu. Cr cds: A, D, DS, MC, V.

★ **WEATHERVANE.** *470 Kennedy Memorial Dr (04901), at I-95 Exit 33. 207/873-4522.* Specializes in seafood. Raw bar. Hrs: 11 am-9 pm. Closed Thanksgiving, Dec 24, 25. Lunch a la carte entrees: $1.99-$10.95; dinner a la carte entrees: $6-$19.95. Child's menu. Fireplaces. Cr cds: MC, V.

Unrated Dining Spot

BIG G'S DELI. *Outer Benton Dr (04901), 2 mi NE. 207/873-7808.* Specializes in sandwiches, bkfst dishes. Hrs: 6 am-7 pm; Fri, Sat to 9 pm. Bkfst $3-$5; lunch, dinner $5-$9. Child's menu. Deli with self serv. Paintings of entertainers. Cr cds: A, MC, V.

Wells

See also Kennebunk, Ogunquit, York

Settled 1640 **Pop** 7,778 **Elev** 70 ft
Area code 207 **Zip** 04090
Web www.wellschamber.org
Information Chamber of Commerce, PO Box 356; 207/646-2451

One of the oldest English settlements in Maine, Wells includes Moody, Wells Beach, and Drake's Island. It was largely a farming center, with some commercial fishing, until the resort trade began in the 20th century. Charter boats, surf casting, and pier fishing attract fishermen; seven miles of beaches entice swimmers.

What to See and Do

Rachel Carson National Wildlife Refuge. Approx 4,500 acres of salt marsh and coastal edge habitat; more than 230 species of birds may be observed during the yr. Visitor center; 1-mi interpretive nature trail. (All yr, sunrise-sunset) Located along coastline between Kittery Point and Cape Elizabeth; visitor center 3 mi NE on ME 9. Phone 207/646-9226. **FREE**

Wells Auto Museum. Approx 80 antique cars dating from 1900 trace progress of the automotive industry. Also displayed is a collection of nickelodeons, picture machines, and antique arcade games to play. (Memorial Day wkend-Columbus Day wkend, daily) US 1. Phone 207/646-9064. ¢¢

Wells Natural Estuarine Research Reserve. Approx 1,600 acres of fields, forest, wetlands, and beach. Laudholm Farm serves as visitor center. Programs on coastal ecology and stewardship, exhibits and tours. Reserve (daily). Visitor center (May-Oct, daily; rest of yr, Mon-Fri). 1½ mi N of Wells Corner on ME 1. Phone 207/646-1555. **FREE**

Motels/Motor Lodges

★★ **ATLANTIC MOTOR INN.** *37 Atlantic Ave (04090), 2 mi S on US 1, then E on Mile Rd to Atlantic Ave. 207/646-7061; fax 207/641-0607; res 800/727-7061. Email ami@cybertours. com; www.atlanticmotorinn.com.* 27 rms, 3 story, 8 suites. July-Aug: S, D $179; suites $159; each addl $15; children $15; under 1 free; lower rates rest of yr. Crib avail, fee. Parking garage. Pool. TV; cable (premium). Complimentary toll-free calls. Restaurant. Ck-out 11 am, ck-in 2 pm. Golf, 18 holes. Tennis, 2 courts. Beach access. Cr cds: A, DS, MC, V.

★ **LAFAYETTES OCEANFRONT RESORT.** *PO Box 639, 393 Mile Rd (04090), S on US 1, E on Mile Rd. 207/ 646-2831; fax 207/646-6770. Email stay@wellsbeachmaine.com.* 128 rms, 15 with shower only, 2-3 story. Early July-Labor Day: S, D $80-$150; kit. units $115-$150; family rates; in-season and hols (2-5 day min); lower rates rest of yr. Crib $10. TV; cable. Restaurant adj 7 am-10 pm. Ck-out 11 am. Meeting rms. Business servs avail. Sundries. Coin lndry. Indoor pool; whirlpool. Refrigerators. Many balconies. On beach. Cr cds: A, MC, V.

D ⛱ 🖼 🔥

★ **NER BEACH MOTEL.** *395 Post Rd (04054), 2 mi S on US 1. 207/646-2636; fax 207/641-0968.* 43 rms, 2 story. July-Aug: D $109; each addl $8; lower rates rest of yr. Crib avail, fee. Pet accepted, some restrictions, fee. Parking lot. Pool. TV; cable. Restaurant nearby. Ck-out 11 am, ck-in 2 pm. Golf, 18 holes. Beach access. Picnic facilities. Cr cds: DS, MC, V.

🐾 🧗 🖼 🔥

★★ **SEAGULL MOTOR INN.** *1413 Post Rd (US Rte1) (04090), ¼ mi S on US 1, 2¼ mi SE of ME Tpke Exit 2. 207/646-5164; fax 207/641-8301; toll-free 800/573-2485. Email info@ seagullvacations.com; www.seagull vacations.com.* 24 rms, 1 story. July-Aug: S, D $92; each addl $12; lower rates rest of yr. Crib avail, fee. Parking lot. Pool, whirlpool. TV; cable. Restaurant. Ck-out 11 am, ck-in 2 pm. Business servs avail. Golf. Supervised children's activities. Picnic facilities. Cr cds: A, D, DS, ER, MC, V.

D 🧗 🖼 🔥

★ **SEA MIST RESORT MOTEL.** *1524 Post Rd (04090), on US 1, at ME 9B. 207/646-6044; fax 207/641-2199; toll-free 800/448-0925. www.seamist motel.com.* 68 rms, 2 story. July-Labor Day: D $85-$95; wkly rates; lower rates Apr-June, Labor Day-early Dec. Closed rest of yr. Crib $5. TV; cable. Indoor pool; whirlpool. Playground. Restaurant nearby. Ck-out 10 am. Lawn games. Refrigerators, microwaves. Balconies. Picnic tables, grills. Cr cds: DS, MC, V.

D ⛱ 🖼 🧗 🔥

★ **SUPER 8.** *820 Main St (04073), approx 9 mi N on ME 109. 207/324-8823; fax 207/324-8782.* 49 rms, 2 story. Apr-Sep: S $43.88-$46.88; D $55.88-$60.88; each addl $5; under 13 free; lower rates rest of yr. Crib free. TV; cable, VCR avail (movies). Complimentary coffee in lobby. Ck-out 11 am. Business servs avail. Refrigerator, microwave avail. Cr cds: A, D, DS.

D ⛱ 🧗 🔥 ✈ 🖼 🔥

★ **VILLAGE GREEN MOTEL & COTTAGES.** *773 Post Rd (04090), 2 mi S on US 1. 207/646-3285; fax 207/646-4889.* 18 rms, 2 story, 1 suite. July-Aug: S $72; D $95; suites $115; each addl $10; children $10; lower rates rest of yr. Pool. TV; cable. Restaurant nearby. Fax servs avail. Beach access. Cr cds: A, DS, MC, V.

🖼 🔥 🔥

★ **WELLS-MOODY MOTEL.** *119 Post Rd; US 1, PO Box 371 (04054), 2½ mi S on US 1. 207/646-5601. Email wells-moody@cybertours.com; www. wellsmoodymotel.com.* 24 rms, 1 story. July-Aug: S $99; D $109; each addl $10; children $10; lower rates rest of yr. Parking lot. Pool. TV; cable (premium). Complimentary toll-free calls. Restaurant 5 am-10 pm. Ck-out 11 am, ck-in 2 pm. Golf. Tennis. Beach access. Picnic facilities. Cr cds: A, DS, MC, V.

🧗 🔥 🖼 🔥

Resort

★★ **GARRISON SUITES.** *1099 Post Rd; US 1 (04090). 207/646-3497; toll-free 800/646-3497. Email info@ garrisonsuites.com; www.garrisonsuites. com.* 15 rms, 2 story, 20 suites. June-Aug: S, D $95; suites $150; each addl $10; children $10; under 6 free; lower rates rest of yr. Crib avail, fee. Parking lot. Pool. TV; cable. Complimentary coffee in rms, toll-free calls. Restaurant nearby. Ck-out 11 am, ck-in 1 pm. Free airport transportation. Exercise privileges. Golf, 18 holes. Tennis, 2 courts. Beach access. Picnic facilities. Cr cds: MC, V.

🧗 🔥 🖼 🧗 🖼 🔥

Cottage Colony

★ **WATERCREST COTTAGES & MOTEL.** *1277 Post Rd; Rte 1 (04090), ½ mi S on US 1, 1½ mi SE of ME Tpke Exit 2. 207/646-2202; fax 207/646-7067; toll-free 800/847-4693. Email wc@watercrestcottages.com; www.*

watercrestcottages.com. 9 motel rms, 4 kits., 50 kit. cottages. July-late Aug, hol wkends: S, D $64-$74; each addl $10; cottages for 2-8 (late June-Labor Day, 1-wk min) $435-$735/wk; lower rates May-June, late Aug-mid-Oct. Closed rest of yr. Crib free. Pet accepted, some restrictions. TV; cable, VCR avail (free movies). Heated pool; whirlpool. Playground. Restaurant nearby. Ck-out 11 am; cottages 10 am. Coin lndry. Lawn games. Exercise equipt. Microwaves in cottages. Picnic tables, grills. Screened porch on cottages. Cr cds: DS, MC, V.

D 🐾 ➰ 🖈 ⬆ 🔥

All Suite

★★★ **VILLAGE BY THE SEA.** *Rte1 S (04090). 207/646-1100; fax 207/ 646-1401; toll-free 800/444-8862. Email reservations@vbts.com; www.vbts. com.* 3 story, 99 suites. July-Aug: S $164; D $179; suites $179; each addl $10; under 14 free; lower rates rest of yr. Crib avail, fee. Parking lot. Indoor/outdoor pools, children's pool, whirlpool. TV; cable, VCR avail. Ck-out 10 am, ck-in 3 pm. Fax servs avail. Coin lndry. Gift shop. Golf. Tennis, 6 courts. Supervised children's activities. Picnic facilities. Cr cds: A, DS, MC, V.

D 🖈 🖈 ➰ ⬆ 🔥 SC

Restaurants

★★ **GREY GULL.** *475 Webhannet Dr (04090). 207/646-7501. www.thegrey gullinn.com.* Specializes in seafood, beef. Hrs: 5:30-9 pm. Closed Mon-Wed mid-Dec-mid Mar. Res accepted. Bar. Dinner $10.95-$22.95. Child's menu. Classical guitarist Sun; Irish entertainment Tues. Valet parking (in season). 19th-century inn located on ocean. Guest rms avail. Cr cds: A, DS, MC, V.

★ **HAYLOFT.** *US 1 (04054), 2½ mi S on US 1 (Post Rd). 207/646-4400. www.thehayloft.com.* Specializes in broasted chicken, Maine seafood, Angus beef. Hrs: 11 am-9 pm. Closed wk before Dec 25. Lunch $3.95-$7.95; dinner $6.95-$19.95. Child's menu. Country farm decor. Cr cds: A, DS, MC, V.

D

★★ **LITCHFIELD'S.** *2135 Post Rd (04090), 1 mi N on US 1. 207/646-5711.* Specializes in seafood, steak, pasta. Raw bar. Own desserts. Hrs: 11:30 am-9 pm; Fri, Sat to 9:30 pm; Sun to 8 pm; Sun brunch 11 am-3 pm. Closed Dec 25. Res accepted. Bar. Lunch $4.95-$10.95; dinner $8-$35. Sun brunch $15.95. Child's menu. Entertainment: pianist. Parking. Cr cds: A, D, DS, MC, V.

D

★★ **LORD'S HARBORSIDE.** *352 Harbor Rd (04090), at harbor. 207/646-2651.* Specializes in fresh seafood, chowders, lobster. Hrs: noon-8 pm; Fri, Sat to 9 pm; varied hrs off-season. Closed mid-Oct-Apr. Lunch, dinner $4.95-$19.95. Child's menu. Parking. Nautical dining rm overlooking harbor. Family-owned. Cr cds: MC, V.

D

★ **MAINE DINER.** *2265 Post Rd (04090), 1¾ mi N on US 1. 207/646-4441. Email eat@mainediner.com; www.mainediner.com.* Specializes in homemade chowders, lobster pie. Own desserts. Hrs: 7 am-9 pm; Columbus Day-Memorial Day to 8 pm. Closed Thanksgiving, Dec 25. Wine, beer. Bkfst $1.35-$7.95; lunch $2.50-$9.95; dinner $5.95-$13.95. Child's menu. Traditional diner decor. Cr cds: DS, MC, V.

D

★★ **STEAKHOUSE.** *1205 Post Rd (04090), 1 mi S. 207/646-4200.* Specializes in steak, seafood. Hrs: 4:30-9 pm. Closed Mon; also mid-Dec-Mar. Dinner $7.95-$18.95. Child's menu. Parking. Antique farm implements and ship models displayed. Cr cds: D, MC, V.

D

Wiscasset

(G-3) *See also Bath, Boothbay Harbor, Damariscotta*

Settled 1653 **Pop** 3,339 **Elev** 50 ft **Area code** 207 **Zip** 04578

Many artists and writers live here in beautiful old houses put up in the golden days of clipper ship barons and sea captains. Chiefly a summer resort area centered around its harbor, Wiscasset is half as populous as it was in 1850. Its pictorial charm is extraordinary even on the picturesque Maine coast. A noted sight in Wiscasset are the remains of two ancient wooden schooners, which were hauled into the harbor in 1932.

What to See and Do

Lincoln County Museum and Old Jail. First penitentiary built in the District of Maine (1809-11). Jailer's house has changing exhibits, relics of Lincoln County. (July and Aug, Tues-Sun) Federal St, ME 218. Phone 207/882-6817. ¢

Maine Art Gallery. Exhibits by Maine artists. (Mid-May-early-Oct, Tues-Sun; rest of yr Thurs-Sun) Warren St, in Old Academy Bldg (1807). Phone 207/882-7511. **Donation**

Musical Wonder House-Music Museum. (1852) Talking machines, antique musical boxes, player pianos shown and played in historical settings; antique furnishings; gift shop. (Late May-mid-Oct, daily) 18 High St. Phone 207/882-7163 or 800/336-3725. ¢¢- ¢¢¢¢

Nickels-Sortwell House. (1807) Classic Federal-style elegance. Built for a shipmaster in the lumber trade, William Nickels, it was used as a hotel between 1820-1900. The mansion was then bought by Mayor Alvin Sortwell of Cambridge, MA, as a private home. Graceful elliptical stairway; many Sortwell family furnishings; restored garden. (June-mid-Oct, Wed-Sun) 121 Main St at Federal St, US 1. Phone 207/882-6218 or 617/227-3956. ¢¢

Pownalborough Court House. (1761) Oldest pre-Revolutionary court house in Maine. Three-story bldg houses furnished courtrm, judges' chambers, spinning rm, tavern, bedrms, parlor, and kitchen. Nature trails along river; picnic areas; Revolutionary cemetery. (Wed-Sat; July and Aug also Sun afternoon) 8 mi N on ME 27, then 3 mi S on ME 128 in Dresden, bordering Kennebec River. Phone 207/882-6817. ¢¢

Motels/Motor Lodges

★★★ **COD COVE INN.** *22 Crossroads (04556), jct US 1 and ME 27. 207/882-9586; fax 207/882-9294; toll-free 800/882-9586. Email covei@gwi. net.* 30 rms, 2 story, 1 cottages. July-Labor Day: S, D $115-$175; suite $175; each addl $10; higher rates Columbus Day wkend; lower rates mid-Apr-June, Labor Day-late Oct. TV; cable. Heated pool; whirlpool. Complimentary continental bkfst. Restaurant opp 6-9 am. Ck-out 11:30 am. Meeting rms. Business servs avail. In-rm modem link. Refrigerators; some fireplaces. Balconies. Colonial-style bldg. Overlooks bay. Cr cds: A, MC, V.

🄳 ⬥ 🔧 ⤢ ⛱ ✈ ▨ 🔥

★ **WISCASSET MOTOR LODGE.** *596 Bath Rd (04578), 3 mi S on US 1. 207/882-7137; fax 207/882-7137; toll-free 800/732-8168. Email info@ wiscassetmotorlodge.com.* 22 rms, 2 story, 6 cabins. Some A/C. July-Labor Day: S, D $39-$68; each addl $8; lower rates Apr-June and after Labor Day-Oct. Closed rest of yr. Crib $5. TV; cable. Complimentary continental bkfst (July-Labor Day). Ck-out 11 am. Cr cds: DS, MC, V.

🄳 ➦ ⬥ 🧍 🔥

B&B/Small Inn

★★ **SQUIRE TARBOX INN.** *1181 Main Rd (04578), US 1 to ME 144, then 8 mi S. 207/882-7693; fax 207/882-7107. Email squiretarbox@ime.net; www.squiretarboxinn.com.* 11 rms, 2 story. July-Oct: S $97; D $154; each addl $32; lower rates rest of yr. Parking lot. TV; cable, VCR avail. Complimentary full bkfst. Restaurant. Bar. Ck-out 11 am, ck-in 2 pm. Fax servs avail. Golf, 16 holes. Tennis. Bike rentals. Hiking trail. Cr cds: A, DS, MC, V.

🧍 🔧 ✈ ▨ 🔥

Cottage Colony

★ **BAY VIEW INN & COTTAGES.** *179 US 1, (04556), ½ mi N. 207/882-6911; toll-free 800/530-2445. www. mainesunshine.com/bayview.* July-Aug: S $65; D $95; lower rates rest of yr. Crib avail. Pet accepted, fee. Street parking. Pool. TV; cable. Restaurant nearby. Ck-out 11 am, ck-in 3 pm. Golf, 18 holes. Cr cds: A, DS, MC, V.

Restaurant

★★ **LE GARAGE.** *Water St (04578), 1 blk S of US 1.* 207/882-5409. Specializes in char-broiled marinated lamb, broiled seafood platter, chicken pie. Own baking. Hrs: 11:30 am-2:30 pm, 5-8:30 pm; Sun 11 am-8 pm. Closed Mon; hols; Jan. Res accepted. Bar. Lunch $3.95-$18.95; dinner $7.95-$18.25. View of bay. Cr cds: MC, V. D

Yarmouth

(G-2) *See also Brunswick, Freeport, Portland*

Settled 1636 **Pop** 7,862 **Elev** 100 ft
Area code 207 **Zip** 04096
Web www.omnisystem.com/yarmouth/chamber/
Information Chamber of Commerce, 158 Main St; 207/846-3984

Yarmouth is a quaint New England village ten miles north of Portland (see) on US 1. There are many well maintained older homes and specialty shops. It is linked by a bridge to Cousins Island in the bay.

What to See and Do

Yarmouth Historical Society Museum. Two galleries with changing exhibits of local and maritime history, fine and decorative arts. Local history research rm; historical lecture series. (July-Aug, Mon-Fri afternoons; rest of yr, Tues-Sat) 3rd floor, Merrill Memorial Library, Main St. Phone 207/846-6259. **FREE**

  Old Ledge School. (1738) Restored 1-rm schoolhouse. (By appt) W Main St. Phone 207/846-6259. **FREE**

Annual Event

Clam Festival. Celebration of soft-shelled clam. Arts and crafts, entertainment, parade, fireworks. Third wkend July.

Restaurant

★★ **CANNERY.** *106 Lafayette St (04096).* 207/846-1226. Specializes in fresh local seafood. Hrs: 11:30 am-9 pm; Fri, Sat to 9:30 pm. Closed Thanksgiving, Dec 25. Bar. Lunch $6.95-$12.95; dinner $10.95-$17.95. Child's menu. Nautical decor; view of river, marina. Cr cds: A, MC, V. D

York

(H-I) *See also Kittery, Ogunquit, Wells*

Settled 1624 **Pop** 9,818 **Elev** 60 ft
Area code 207 **Zip** 03909
Web www.yorkme.org
Information The Yorks Chamber of Commerce, 599 US 1, PO Box 417; 207/363-4422

Originally named Agamenticus by the Plymouth Company, which settled the area in 1624, the settlement was chartered as a city—the first in America—in 1641 and renamed Gorgeanna. Following a reorganization in 1652, the "city" in the wilderness took the name York. The present-day York area includes York Village, York Harbor, York Beach, and Cape Neddick.

What to See and Do

Old York Historical Society. Tours of 7 bldgs dating from the early 1700s. (Mid-June-Sep, Tues-Sun) Visitor orientation and tickets at Jefferds Tavern. Administration Office houses museum offices (Mon-Fri) and historical and research library. Phone 207/363-4974. Per bldg ¢; Combination ticket ¢¢¢

  Elizabeth Perkins House. Turn-of-the-century summer house on the banks of the York River, at Sewall's Bridge. Former home of a prominent York preservationist. The furnishings reflect the Colonial-revival period.

  Emerson-Wilcox House. Built in 1742, with later additions. Served at various times as a general store, tavern, and post office as well as the home of 2 of the town's prominent early families. Now contains a series of period rms dating from 1750; antique furnishings.

George Marshall Store. Mid-19th-century general store houses local art exhibits. On Lindsay Rd at the York River. **FREE**

Jefferds Tavern and Schoolhouse. Built by Capt Samuel Jefferds in 1750 and furnished as a tavern in coastal Maine in the late 18th century; used as an orientation center and educational facility. Schoolhouse adj is probably the state's oldest surviving 1-rm schoolhouse; contains exhibit on 1-rm schooling in Maine.

John Hancock Warehouse. Owned by John Hancock until 1794, this is one of the earliest surviving customs houses in Maine. Used now to interpret the maritime history of this coastal village. Lindsay Rd at York River.

Old Gaol. Built in 1719 with 18th-century additions. One of the oldest English public bldgs in the US, it was used as a jail until 1860. Has dungeons and cells for felons and debtors, as well as galleries of local historical artifacts, late 1800s photography exhibit. On US 1A.

Sayward-Wheeler House. (1718) Home of the 18th-century merchant and civic leader Tory Jonathan Sayward. Tours. (June-mid-Oct, Sat and Sun) 79 Barrell Lane, 2 mi S in York Harbor. Phone 603/436-3205. ¢¢

Annual Event

Harvest Fest. Juried crafts, ox-roast, colonial theme. Mid-Oct.

Motel/Motor Lodge

★★ **YORK COMMONS INN.** *362 US 1 (03909).* 207/363-8903; fax 207/363-1130; toll-free 800/537-5515. 90 rms. Mid-June-mid-Oct: S, D $89-$99; each addl $5; under 18 free; lower rates rest of yr. Crib free. Pet accepted, some restrictions. TV; cable. Indoor pool. Complimentary bkfst. Complimentary coffee in rms. Restaurant opp 11 am-8 pm. Business servs avail. Sundries. Refrigerators, microwaves avail. Cr cds: A, DS, MC, V.

🄳 🔌 ⚓ ≈ 🔥

Resorts

★★ **ANCHORAGE MOTOR INN.** *265 Long Beach Ave (03910).* 207/363-5112; fax 207/363-6753. Email info@ anchorageinn.com; www.anchorageinn. com. 179 rms, 3 story. Late June-Aug: S, D $119-$154; suites $195-$245; lower rates rest of yr. Crib $10. TV; cable. 3 pools; 2 indoor; whirlpool, poolside serv. Restaurant adj 7 am-9 pm. Bar. Ck-out 11 am. Meeting rms. Business servs avail. Golf privileges. Exercise equipt. Lawn game. Balconies. Refrigerators. Opp ocean. Cr cds: A, MC, V.

🄳 🎿 ⚓ 🏃 🖼 🔥

★★★ **STAGE NECK INN.** *22 Stage Neck Rd (03911), 1 mi E on US 1A.* 207/363-3850; fax 207/363-2221; toll-free 800/222-3238. Email reserve@ stageneck.com; www.stageneck.com. 60 rms, 3 story. Apr-Oct: S $280; D $285; each addl $10; children $5; under 12 free; lower rates rest of yr. Crib avail, fee. Parking lot. Indoor/outdoor pools, lifeguard, whirlpool. TV; cable, VCR avail, CD avail. Complimentary coffee in rms, newspaper. Restaurant 7:30 am-9 pm. Bar. Ck-out 11 am, ck-in 3 pm. Meeting rms. Business servs avail. Bellhops. Dry cleaning, coin lndry. Exercise equipt, sauna. Golf. Tennis, 2 courts. Beach access. Bike rentals. Hiking trail. Cr cds: A, DS, MC, V.

🄳 ⚓ 🌡 🎿 🏃 🖼 ≈ 🔥

B&Bs/Small Inns

★★ **DOCKSIDE GUEST QUARTERS.** *Harris Island Rd (03909), ME 103 to Harris Island Rd.* 207/363-2868; fax 207/363-1977; toll-free 800/ 270-1977. Email info@docksidegq.com; www.docksidegq.com. 16 rms, 2 story, 6 suites. July-Oct: S, D $142; suites $114; each addl $10; children $10; under 12 free; lower rates rest of yr. Crib avail. Parking lot. TV; cable, VCR avail. Complimentary toll-free calls. Restaurant 11 am-9 pm, closed Mon (see DOCKSIDE). Bar. Ck-out 11 am, ck-in 3 pm. Meeting rms. Business servs avail. Concierge. Gift shop. Exercise privileges. Golf. Tennis, 4 courts. Bike rentals. Picnic facilities. Video games. Cr cds: A, DS, MC, V.

🄳 🌡 🏃 🎿 🔥 ≈ 🔥

★★ **EDWARDS HARBORSIDE INN.** *(03911), 1 mi E on US 1A.* 207/363-3037; fax 207/363-1544; res 800/273-

2686. www.yorkharbor.com. 8 rms, 3 story, 2 suites. June-Oct: D $90-$170; each add $20; suites $210-$2140; higher rates wkends; lower rates rest of yr. TV; cable, VCR avail. Ck-out 11 am, ck-in 3 pm. Golf. Tennis, 2 courts. Cr cds: MC, V.

★ **HOMESTEAD INN BED AND BREAKFAST.** *8 S Main St (US 1A) (03910), 4 mi E on US 1A. 207/363-8952; fax 207/363-8952. Email homestedbb@aol.com; www.members. aol.com/homstedbb.* 4 rms, 2 share bath, shower only, 3 story. No A/C. No elvtr. No rm phones. S, D $65; each addl $10; wkly rates. Closed Nov-Mar. Children over 12 yrs only. Complimentary continental bkfst. Restaurant nearby. Ck-out 11 am, ck-in 2 pm. Business servs avail. Opp beach. Built in 1905; former boarding house. Totally nonsmoking. Cr cds: A, MC, V.

★★ **YORK HARBOR INN.** *Rte 1A (03911), 1 mi E. 207/363-5119; fax 207/363-7151; res 800/343-3869. Email info@yorkharborinn.com.* 33 rms, 23 with shower only, 2 story. Apr-Oct: D $109-$209; 2-day min most wkends; higher rates New Year's Eve; lower rates rest of yr. Crib $10. TV; cable, VCR avail. Complimentary continental bkfst. Restaurant (see YORK HARBOR INN). Ck-out 11 am, ck-in 2:30 pm. Business servs avail. Golf privileges. Whirlpool. Balconies. Some fireplaces. bathrm phones. Ocean opp. Original section from 1637 is now sitting rm. Cr cds: A, MC, V.

Restaurants

★★★ **CAPE NEDDICK INN.** *1233 US 1 (03902). 207/363-2899. www. yorkme.org/dining/capeneddickinn.html.* Specializes in seafood, beef. Own baking. Hrs: 5-10 pm. Closed Dec 25. Res accepted. Bar. Wine list. Dinner $16-$27. Upscale country inn atmosphere; original artwork. Cr cds: DS, MC, V.

★★ **DOCKSIDE.** *Harris Island Rd. 207/363-2722. www.docksidegq.com.* Specializes in Maine seafood, roast duckling. Salad bar. Hrs: 7:30 am-2 pm, 5:30-9 pm; hrs vary off-season. Closed Mon; also Nov-Memorial Day. Res accepted. Bar. Bkfst $5.50-$9.50; lunch $5.50-$9.50; dinner $9.95-$19.95. Child's menu. Nautical decor; overlooks harbor and marina. Family-owned. Cr cds: DS, MC, V.

Nubble Lighthouse, York

★★ **FAZIO'S ITALIAN.** *38 Woodbridge Rd (03909). 207/363-7019. Email fazios@fazios.com; www.fazios. com.* Specializes in fresh pasta. Hrs: 11 am-9 pm. Closed hols. Bar. Lunch, dinner $6.50-$14.95. Child's menu. Mural of Italian street market; photos from '30s and '40s. Cr cds: A, C, D, DS, ER, MC, V.

★★★ **YORK HARBOR INN.** *US 1A, 1 mi E. 207/363-5119. Email gary inkeep@aol.com; www.yorkharborinn. com.* Specializes in seafood, lobster. Hrs: 5:30-9 pm. Closed Mon-Thurs in Jan-mid-May. Res accepted Fri, Sat. Bar. Wine cellar. Dinner $16.95-$24.95. Child's menu. Ocean and harbor views. Cr cds: A, D, MC, V.

MASSACHUSETTS

L eif Ericson—or even a French or Spanish angler—may have originally discovered the Cape Cod coast. However, the first recorded visit of a European to Massachusetts was that of John Cabot in 1497. Not until the Pilgrims landed at Provincetown and settled at Plymouth was there a permanent settlement north of Virginia. Ten years later, Boston was founded with the arrival of John Winthrop and his group of Puritans.

Native American wars plagued Massachusetts until the 1680s, after which the people experienced a relatively peaceful period combined with a fast-growing, mostly agricultural economy. In the 1760s, opposition to British taxation without representation exploded into the American Revolution. It began in Massachusetts, and from here, the American tradition of freedom and justice spread around the world. The Constitution of Massachusetts is the oldest written constitution still in effect. The New England town meeting, a basic democratic institution, still governs most of its towns. The state had a child labor law in 1836, a law legalizing trade unions in 1842, and the first minimum wage law for women and children.

Population: 6,175,169
Area: 7,826 square miles
Elevation: 0-3,491 feet
Peak: Mount Greylock (Berkshire County)
Entered Union: Sixth of original 13 states (February 6, 1788)
Capital: Boston
Motto: By the sword we seek peace, but peace only under liberty
Nickname: Bay State
Flower: Mayflower
Bird: Chickadee
Tree: American Elm
Time Zone: Eastern
Website: www.mass-vacation.com

Massachusetts proved to be fertile ground for intellectual ideas and activities. In the early 19th century, Emerson, Thoreau, and their followers expounded the Transcendentalist theory of the innate nobilty of man and the doctrine of individual expression, which exerted a major influence on American thought, then and now. Social improvement was sought through colonies of idealists, many of which hoped to prove that sharing labor and the fruits of labor were the means to a just society. Dorothea Dix crusaded on behalf of the mentally disturbed, and Horace Mann promoted universal education. In 1831, William Lloyd Garrison, an ardent abolitionist, founded his weekly, *The Liberator*. Massachusetts was the heartland of the Abolitionist movement and her soldiers fought in the Civil War because they were convinced it was a war against slavery.

Massachusetts was also an important center during the Industrial Revolution. After the Civil War the earlier success of the textile mills, like those in Lowell, generated scores of drab, hastily built industrial towns. Now these towns are being replaced by modern plants with landscaped grounds. Modern industry is as much a part of Massachusetts as the quiet sandy beaches of Cape Cod, with their bayberry and beach plum bushes.

Massachusetts has also been home to several generations of the politically prominent Kennedy family. John F. Kennedy, 35th president of the United States, was born in the Boston suburb of Brookline, as were his younger brothers, Senators Robert and Edward.

The Bay State offers mountains, ocean swimming, camping, summer resorts, freshwater and saltwater fishing, and a variety of metropolitan cultural advantages. No other state in the Union can claim so much history in so small an area, for in Massachusetts each town or city has a part in the American story.

When to Go/Climate

Massachusetts enjoys a moderate climate with four distinct seasons. Cape Cod and the Islands offer milder temperatures than other parts of the state and rarely have snow, while windchill in Boston (the windiest city in the United States) can make temperatures feel well below zero and snow is not uncommon.

AVERAGE HIGH/LOW TEMPERATURES (°F)

BOSTON

Jan 36/22	**May** 67/50	**Sep** 73/57
Feb 38/23	**June** 76/60	**Oct** 63/47
Mar 46/31	**July** 82/65	**Nov** 52/38
Apr 56/40	**Aug** 80/64	**Dec** 40/27

WORCESTER

Jan 31/15	**May** 66/45	**Sep** 70/51
Feb 33/17	**June** 75/54	**Oct** 60/41
Mar 42/25	**July** 80/60	**Nov** 47/31
Apr 54/35	**Aug** 77/59	**Dec** 35/20

Parks and Recreation Finder

Directions to and information about the parks and recreation areas below are given under their respective town/city sections. Please refer to those sections for details.

NATIONAL PARK AND RECREATION AREAS

Key to abbreviations. I.H.S. = International Historic Site; I.P.M. = International Peace Memorial; N.B. = National Battlefield; N.B.P. = National Battlefield Park; N.B.C. = National Battlefield and Cemetery; N.C.A. = National Conservation Area; N.E.M. = National Expansion Memorial; N.F. = National Forest; N.G. = National Grassland; N.H.P. = National Historical Park; N.H.C. = National Heritage Corridor; N.H.S. = National Historic Site; N.L. = National Lakeshore; N.M. = National Monument; N.M.P. = National Military Park; N.Mem. = National Memorial; N.P. = National Park; N.Pres. = National Preserve; N.R.A. = National Recreational Area; N.R.R. = National Recreational River; N.Riv. = National River; N.S. = National Seashore; N.S.R. = National Scenic Riverway; N.S.T. = National Scenic Trail; N.Sc. = National Scientific Reserve; N.V.M. = National Volcanic Monument.

Place Name	Listed Under
Adams N.H.S.	QUINCY
Blackstone River Valley N.H.C.	WORCESTER
Boston African American N.H.S.	BOSTON
Cape Cod N.S.	same
Frederick Law Olmsted N.H.S.	BOSTON
John F. Kennedy N.H.S.	BOSTON
Longfellow N.H.S.	CAMBRIDGE
Lowell N.H.P.	LOWELL
Minute Man N.H.P.	CONCORD
Salem Maritime N.H.S.	SALEM
Saugus Iron Works N.H.S.	SAUGUS
Springfield Armory N.H.S.	SPRINGFIELD

CALENDAR HIGHLIGHTS

APRIL

Boston Marathon (Boston). Famous 26-mile footrace from Hopkinton to Boston. Phone 617/236-1652.

Reenactment of Battle of Lexington and Concord (Lexington). Massachusetts Ave. Reenactment of opening battle of American Revolution; parade. Phone Lexington Historical Society, 781/862-1703.

Daffodil Festival (Nantucket Island). Festival is marked by over a million blooming daffodils. Parade of antique cars, prize for best tailgate picnic. Phone Chamber of Commerce, 508/228-1700.

JUNE

La Festa (North Adams). Ethnic festival, food, entertainment, events. Phone 413/66-FESTA.

JULY

Harborfest (Boston). Hatch Shell on the Esplanade. Concerts, chowder fest, children's activities, Boston Pops Orchestra, fireworks. Phone 617/227-1528.

Green River Music and Balloon Festival (Greenfield). Hot-air balloon launches, craft show, musical entertainment, food. Phone 413/733-5463.

SEPTEMBER

The "Big E" (Springfield). Largest fair in the Northeast; entertainment, exhibits, historic Avenue of States, Storrowton Village; horse show, agricultural events, "Better Living Center" exhibit. Phone 413/737-2443.

OCTOBER

Haunted Happenings (Salem). Various sites. Psychic festival, historical exhibits, haunted house, costume parade, contests, dances. Phone Salem Halloween Office, 978/744-0013.

NOVEMBER

Thanksgiving Week (Plymouth). Programs for various events may be obtained by contacting Destination Plymouth. Phone 508/747-7525 or 800/USA-1620.

DECEMBER

Stockbridge Main Street at Christmas (Stockbridge and West Stockbridge). Events incl a re-creation of Norman Rockwell's painting. Holiday marketplace, concerts, house tour, silent auction, sleigh/hay rides, caroling. Phone 413/298-5200.

STATE PARK AND RECREATION AREAS

Key to abbreviations. I.P. = Interstate Park; S.A.P. = State Archaeological Park; S.B. = State Beach; S.C.A. = State Conservation Area; S.C.P. = State Conservation Park; S.Cp. = State Campground; S.F. = State Forest; S.G. = State Garden; S.H.A. = State Historic Area; S.H.P. = State Historic Park; S.H.S. = State Historic Site; S.M.P. = State Marine Park; S.N.A. = State Natural Area; S.P. = State Park; S.P.C. = State Public Campground; S.R. = State Reserve; S.R.A. = State Recreation Area; S.Res. = State Reservoir; S.Res.P. = State Resort Park; S.R.P. = State Rustic Park.

Place Name	Listed Under
Beartown S.F.	GREAT BARRINGTON
Brimfield S.F.	SPRINGFIELD
Fall River Heritage S.P.	FALL RIVER
Fort Phoenix Beach S.R.	NEW BEDFORD
Granville S.F.	SPRINGFIELD
Holyoke Heritage S.P.	HOLYOKE
Lawrence Heritage S.P.	LAWRENCE
Lowell Heritage S.P.	LOWELL
Lynn Heritage S.P.	LYNN
Mohawk Trail S.F.	NORTH ADAMS
Mount Greylock S.R.	NORTH ADAMS
Myles Standish S.F.	PLYMOUTH
Natural Bridge S.P.	NORTH ADAMS
Nickerson S.P.	BREWSTER
October Mountain S.F.	LEE
Savoy Mountain S.F.	NORTH ADAMS
Scusset Beach S.P.	SANDWICH
Shawme-Crowell S.F.	SANDWICH
Walden Pond S.R.	CONCORD
Western Gateway Heritage S.P.	NORTH ADAMS

Water-related activities, hiking, riding, various other sports, picnicking, and visitor centers, as well as camping, are available in many of these areas. Day-use areas (approx Memorial Day-Labor Day, some areas all yr): $2/car. Camping (approx mid-Apr-Oct, schedule may vary, phone ahead; 2-wk max, last Sat May-Sat before Labor Day at many parks): campsites $6-$10/day; electricity $2/day. Pets on leash only in S.P.; no pets in bathing areas. Information avail from Dept of Environmental Management, Division of Forests & Parks, 617/727-3180.

SKI AREAS

Place Name	Listed Under
Bousquet Ski Area	PITTSFIELD
Brodie Mountain Ski Area	PITTSFIELD
Butternut Basin Ski Area	GREAT BARRINGTON
Jiminy Peak Ski Area	GREAT BARRINGTON
Mount Tom Ski Area	HOLYOKE
Otis Ridge Ski Area	GREAT BARRINGTON

FISHING AND HUNTING

Deep-sea and surf fishing are good; boats are available in most coastal towns. For information on saltwater fishing, contact Division of Marine Fisheries, phone 617/727-3193. Inland fishing is excellent in more than 500 streams and 3,000 ponds. Nonresident fishing license $37.50; 3-consecutive-day nonresident license $23.50. Nonresident hunting license: small game $65.50; big game $99.50. Inquire for trapping licenses. Fees subject to change. Licenses issued by town clerks, selected sporting good stores, or from Division of Fisheries and Wildlife, phone 617/727-3151 or 800/ASK-FISH. Information on freshwater fishing, regulations, and a guide to stocked trout waters and best bass ponds are also available from Division of Fisheries and Wildlife.

Driving Information

Safety belts are mandatory for all persons. Children under 13 years must be in a federally approved child safety seat or safety belt anywhere in vehicle: it is recommended that children 40 lbs and under use a federally approved child safety seat and be placed in the back seat. For further information, phone 617/624-5070 or 800/CAR-SAFE (MA).

INTERSTATE HIGHWAY SYSTEM

The following alphabetical listing of Massachusetts towns in *Mobil Travel Guide* shows that these cities are within 10 miles of the indicated Interstate highways. A highway map, however, should be checked for the nearest exit.

Highway Number	Cities/Towns within 10 miles
Interstate 90	Boston, Cambridge, Framingham, Great Barrington, Holyoke, Lee, Lenox, Natick, Newton, Pittsfield, Springfield, Stockbridge and West Stockbridge, Sturbridge, Sudbury Center, Waltham, Wellesley, Worcester.
Interstate 91	Amherst, Deerfield, Greenfield, Holyoke, Northampton, Springfield.
Interstate 93	Andover, Boston, Lawrence, Lowell.
Interstate 95	Bedford, Boston, Burlington, Concord, Danvers, Dedham, Foxboro, Framingham, Lexington, Lynn, Lynnfield, Natick, Newton, Saugus, Sudbury Center, Waltham, Wellesley.

Additional Visitor Information

The Massachusetts Office of Travel and Tourism, 617/727-3201, has travel information. For a free *Massachusetts Getaway Guide* phone 800/447-MASS.

Many properties of the Society for the Preservation of New England Antiquities (SPNEA) are located in Massachusetts and neighboring states. For complete information on these properties contact the SPNEA Headquarters, 141 Cambridge St, Boston 02114; 617/227-3956. For information regarding the 71 properties owned and managed by The Trustees of Reservations, contact 527 Essex St, Beverly, MA 01905; 508/921-1944.

Massachusetts has many statewide fairs, though none is considered the official state fair; contact the Massachusetts Dept of Agriculture, Division of Fairs, 617/727-3037.

There are several visitor centers located in Massachusetts; they are located on the MA Turnpike (daily, 9 am-6 pm) at Charlton (eastbound and westbound), Lee (eastbound), and Natick (eastbound); also I-95 at Mansfield, between Exits 5 and 6 (northbound); and on MA 3 at Plymouth (southbound).

Travel south from Boston on Route 3 (a limited-access highway) to Plymouth, site of Plymouth Rock (a replica of the Mayflower), and Plimoth Plantation, (a museum village of the Pilgrim settlement as it was in 1627). This is also a major lodging place with beach and pond swimming and boat excursions. Most tourists continue on Route 3 to Cape Cod, following Route 6 east down the spine of the Cape, and stopping in Sandwich (Sandwich Glass Museum, beaches, lodging) and Hyannis (departure point for ferries to Nantucket, Martha's Vineyard). The scenic alternative to this highway is Route 6A, which parallels Route 6, threading all the old towns on Massachusetts Bay. Routes 6 and 6A meet at the Orleans Rotary, the point where the Cape narrows and changes direction (it's frequently compared to an arm, bent upward at the elbow; this is the elbow). The visitor center for the Cape Cod National Seashore is just beyond in Eastham, and the remaining 12 miles are all about beaches. Route 6 ends in Provincetown, famed for its monument, museum, art galleries, inns, restaurants, and overall "scene." **(Approx 230 mi)**

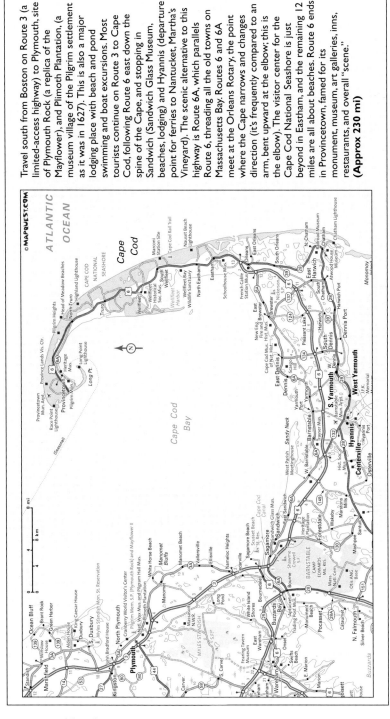

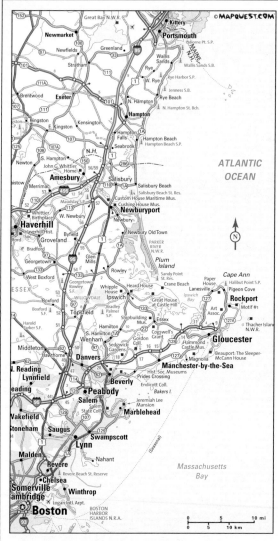

From Boston, take Route 1A to Marblehead, an 18th-century port/yachting center with historic homes, inns, shops, and restaurants. Continue on to Salem to visit the Peabody Museum/Essex Institute, Salem Maritime National Historic site, House of Seven Gables, and Salem Witch Museum, as well as historic homes, inns, shops, and restaurants. From Salem, take Route 128 to Gloucester, site of the Cape Ann Historical Museum, Hammond Castle Museum, historic homes, beaches, restaurants, shops, harbor excursions, and whale watching. Continue around Cape Ann on Route 127A, stopping at Rockport to visit its art museum, shops, and galleries on Bearskin Neck, a prime resort lodging hub for the North Shore. The scenic tour continues on Route 133 through Essex (shipbuilding museum, kayaking, water excursions, restaurants, historic homes) to Ipswich (17th-century historic homes and Crane Beach—best on the North Shore) and on up Route 1A through Rowley and Newbury (historic homes) to Newburyport. A prime departure point for whale watching, this historic old port offers many points of interest, including the famous, Federalist-era architecture of High Street; the Custom House Museum; and the Parker River National Wildlife Refuge with hiking and limited beaching. Newburyport also has ample lodging, restaurants, and outstanding shopping in its rehabbed early 19th-century downtown. If you want, continue north along the coast passing through Portsmouth (NH), a tourist-geared old port and site of Strawbery Banke Museum, and on up to Maine's South Coast towns. **(Approx 76 mi; add 40 mi if continuing on to Portsmouth, NH)**

Amesbury

(B-6) *See also Haverhill, Newburyport*

Settled 1654 **Pop** 14,997 **Elev** 50 ft
Area code 978 **Zip** 01913
Information Alliance for Amesbury, 5
Market Sq, 01913-2440; 978/388-
3178

In 1853, Jacob R. Huntington, "the
Henry Ford of carriage-making,"
began a low-cost, high-quality carriage industry that became the economic backbone of Amesbury.

What to See and Do

Amesbury Sports Park. Winter snow
tubing. Summer go-carts, golf range,
miniature golf, bumper boats, volleyball park. Restaurant, lounge. (Daily;
closed hols) 12 Hunt Rd. ¢¢¢

Bartlett Museum. (1870) Houses
memorabilia of Amesbury's history
dating from prehistoric days to settlement and beyond. The Native
American artifact collection, consisting of relics of local tribes, is considered one of the finest collections in
the state. (Memorial Day-Labor Day,
Wed-Sun afternoons; after Labor
Day-Columbus Day, Sat and Sun) 270
Main St. Phone 978/388-4528. ¢

John Greenleaf Whittier Home. John
Greenleaf Whittier lived here from
1836 until his death in 1892; 6 rms
contain books, manuscripts, pictures,
and furniture; the Garden Room,
where he wrote "Snow-Bound" and
many other works, remains
unchanged. (May-Oct, Tues-Sat) 86
Friend St. Phone 978/388-1337. ¢¢

Amherst (C-3)

Founded 1759 **Pop** 35,228 **Elev** 320 ft
Area code 413 **Zip** 01002
Web www.amherstcommon.com
Information Chamber of Commerce,
11 Spring St; 413/253-0700

Amherst College, founded in 1821 to
educate "promising but needy
youths who wished to enter the Ministry," has educated several of the
nation's leaders, including Calvin
Coolidge and Henry Ward Beecher.
Amherst is also the seat of the University of Massachusetts and of Hampshire College. This attractive,
academic town was the home of three
celebrated American poets: Emily
Dickinson, Eugene Field, and Robert
Frost; Noah Webster also lived here.

What to See and Do

Amherst College. (1821) 1,550 students. On the tree-shaded green in
the middle of town. The Robert Frost
Library owns approx half of Emily
Dickinson's poems in manuscript
and has a Robert Frost collection, as
well as materials of Wordsworth,
Eugene O'Neill, and others. Phone
413/542-2000. Also on campus are

Pratt Museum of Geology. (1884)
Some of the finest collections of
dinosaur tracks, meteorites, minerals, and fossils; also the world's
largest mastodon skeleton. (Academic yr, daily; closed school hols)
FREE

Mead Art Museum. A notable art
collection is housed here. (Sep-July,
daily; Aug, by appt) **FREE**

Amherst History Museum. In 18th-
century Strong House. House reflects
changing tastes in local architecture
and interior decoration; extensive
collection of 18th- and 19th-century
textiles and artifacts; gallery (Mid-
May-mid-Oct, Wed and Sat, afternoons). Eighteenth-century herb and
flower garden open to the public
(spring-summer). 67 Amity St. Phone
413/256-0678. ¢¢

Emily Dickinson Homestead. (1813)
Birthplace and home of Emily Dickinson. Selected rms open for tours by
appt (afternoons: May-Oct, Wed-Sat;
Mar-Apr and Nov-mid-Dec, Wed and
Sat). 280 Main St. Phone 413/542-
8161. ¢¢

Hadley Farm Museum. Restored 1782
barn houses agricultural implements,
tools, and domestic items dating
from 1700s; broom-making
machines. (May-mid-Oct, Tues-Sun)
5 mi SW at jct MA 9, 47, at 147 Russell St in Hadley. **FREE**

Jones Library. Building houses collections of the Amherst authors; incl an
Emily Dickinson rm with some of

Dickinson's personal articles, manuscripts, and a model of her bedrm. Historical collection (Mon-Sat); library (Sep-May, daily; rest of yr, Mon-Sat; closed hols). 43 Amity St. Phone 413/256-4090. **FREE**

National Yiddish Book Center. This 37,000-sq-ft, non profit facility was developed by Aaron Lansky to preserve Yiddish literature and its history and ensure its lasting legacy. Book Repository houses a core collection of 120,000 Yiddish books—the largest in the world—and 150,000 folios of rare Yiddish and Hebrew sheet music. Book Processing Center, shipping and receiving area, and Bibliography Center are all open for viewing as rare books are catalogued and shipped to libraries across the country. Vistor Center incl 3 exhibit halls, a kosher dairy kitchen, and educational story rails that introduce visitors to the books and the Center's important work. Reading Room, Yiddish Resource Center, Yiddish Writers Garden. Also galleries for print, spoken, and performing arts. Bookstore; museum store. (Sun-Fri) MA 116, on campus of Hampshire College. Phone 800/535-3595. **FREE**

University of Massachusetts. (1863) 25,000 students. State's major facility of public higher education. More than 150 bldgs on 1,200-acre campus. Tours (daily). N edge of town on MA 116. Phone 413/545-4237 or 413/545-0306 (visitor center). Also here is

Fine Arts Center and Gallery. A variety of nationally and internationally known performances in theater, music, and dance. Art gallery (daily). Performances (Sep-May). Phone 413/545-2511.

Seasonal Event

Maple sugaring. NW via MA 116 to Sunderland, then 2 mi N on MA 47. Visitors are welcome at maple camps, daily. Mount Toby Sugar House, phone 413/665-3127. Late Feb-Mar.

Motel/Motor Lodge

★ **HOWARD JOHNSON INN.** *401 Russell St (01035), MA 9 at jct MA 116. 413/586-0114; fax 413/584-7163; res 800/446-4656. Email hojo-hadley@aol.com.* 100 rms, 3 story. S $59-$109; D $69-$109; each addl $10; suites $79-$152; under 18 free; higher rates special events. Crib free. Pet accepted. TV; cable (premium). Pool. Complimentary bkfst. Ck-out noon. Meeting rm. Business servs avail. In-rm modem link. Downhill ski 16 mi; x-country ski 12 mi. Exercise equipt. Health club privileges. Private patios, balconies. Cr cds: A, DS, MC, V.

D 🐾 🛂 🕊 🏃 🖼 🔥 **SC**

B&Bs/Small Inns

★★ **ALLEN HOUSE VICTORIAN INN.** *599 Main St (01002). 413/253-5000. Email allenhouse@webtv.net; www.allenhouse.com.* 7 rms, 5 with shower only, 2 story. Rm phones avail. Apr-Nov: S $55-$105; D $65-$135; each addl $10-$20; higher rates college events; lower rates rest of yr. Children over 8 yrs only. TV in sitting rm. Complimentary full bkfst; afternoon refreshments. Restaurant nearby. Ck-out 11 am, ck-in mid-afternoon. Queen Anne-style house built 1886; many antiques. Totally nonsmoking. Cr cds: DS, MC, V.

🖼 🔥

★★ **LORD JEFFREY INN.** *30 Boltwood Ave (01002). 413/253-2576; fax 413/256-6152; toll-free 800/742-0358. Email lordjefferyinn@pinnacle-inns.com; www.pinnacle-inns.com/lordjefferyinn/.* 40 rms, 3 story, 8 suites. Apr-Oct: S $109; D $119; suites $189; each addl $10; under 12 free; lower rates rest of yr. Crib avail, fee. Pet accepted, some restrictions, fee. Street parking. TV; cable, VCR avail. Restaurant 7 am-10 pm. Bar. Ck-out 11 am, ck-in 3 pm. Meeting rms. Business center. Gift shop. Exercise privileges. Golf Tennis, 4 courts. Downhill skiing. Bike rentals. Hiking trail. Video games. Cr cds: A, D, DS, MC, V.

D 🐾 🛂 🏌 🕊 🏃 🎿 🖼 🔥 🏃

Andover and North Andover

(B-6)

Settled ca 1643 **Pop** Andover: 29,151; North Andover: 22,792 **Elev** 164 ft

Area code 978 **Zip** Andover: 01810; North Andover: 01845

Information Merrimack Valley Chamber of Commerce, 264 Essex St, Lawrence 01840-1496; 978/686-0900

An attempt was made in Andover in the 19th century to surpass Japan's silk industry by growing mulberry trees on which silkworms feed. But Andover has had to be content with making electronic parts and woolen and rubber goods instead. Its true fame rests on Phillips Academy, the oldest incorporated school in the United States, founded in 1778 by Samuel Phillips.

What to See and Do

Amos Blanchard House (1819) also **Barn Museum**(1818) and **Research Library** (1978). House features period rms, special local history exhibits, 17th-to-20th-century themes. Barn Museum features early farm equipment, household items, hand-pumped fire wagon. Library houses local history, genealogy, and special collections. Guided tours (by appt). (Mon-Fri, also by appt; closed hols) 97 Main St. Phone 978/475-2236. ¢

Phillips Academy. (1778) 1,200 students. A coed residential school for grades 9-12. On 450 acres with 170 bldgs, many of historical interest. The Cochran Sanctuary, a 65-acre landscaped area, has walking trails, a brook, and two ponds. (Daily) Main St, MA 28. Phone 978/749-4000. Also on grounds are

Addison Gallery of American Art. More than 7,000 works, incl paintings, sculpture, and photographs. Changing exhibits. Ship model collection tracing era of sail through steam engine. (Sep-July, Tues-Sun; closed hols) Phone 978/749-4016. **FREE**

Robert S. Peabody Foundation for Archaeology. Exhibits on physical, cultural evolution of man; prehistoric archaeology of New England, New Mexico, Mexico, Canada. (Tues-Sat; closed hols) Phillips & Main Sts. Phone 978/749-4490. **FREE**

Stevens-Coolidge Place. House, interior, and extensive gardens are maintained as they were in the early 20th century by diplomat John Gardener Coolidge and his wife, Helen Stevens Coolidge. Collection of Chinese porcelain, Irish and English cut glass, linens, and clothing. Early American furnishings. House (late Apr-Oct, Sun afternoons). Gardens (daily; free). 137 Andover St, in North Andover. Phone 978/682-3580. House ¢¢

Motels/Motor Lodges

★★ **HOLIDAY INN.** *4 Highwood Dr (01876), I-495 Exit 39. 978/640-9000; fax 978/640-0623; res 800/HOLIDAY. Email hitadosm@aol.com.* 237 rms, 5 story. S, D $119; under 18 free; wkend rates. TV; cable (premium). Complimentary coffee in rms. Restaurant 6:30 am-2 pm, 5-10 pm. . Bar; entertainment Wed. Ck-out noon. Meeting rms. Business servs avail. In-rm modem link. Sundries. Exercise equipt; sauna. Indoor pool; whirlpool. Some refrigerators. Cr cds: A, C, D, DS, MC, V.

★★ **RAMADA HOTEL.** *311 Lowell St (01810), 2½ mi W on MA 133, 1 blk E of I-93 Exit 43A. 978/475-5400; fax 508/470-1108; toll-free 800/323-1351.* 179 rms, 2 story. S $99-$129; D $109-$139; each addl $12; suites $125-$250; under 18 free; group, wkend rates. Crib free. Pet accepted. TV; cable. 2 pools, 1 indoor; whirlpool. Restaurant 6:30 am-2 pm, 5-10 pm. . Bar 11:30-1 am. Ck-out noon. Meeting rms. Business servs avail. Valet serv. Airport transportation. Indoor tennis, pro. 9-hole par 3 golf, greens fee $12-$14. Exercise equipt; sauna. Microwaves avail. Cr cds: A, C, D, DS, ER, JCB, MC, V.

★ **SUSSE CHALET INN.** *1695 Andover St (01876), I-495 Exit 39. 978/640-0700; fax 978/640-1175; res 800/524-2538.* 133 rms, 5 story. S, D $54.70-$68.70; each addl $7; under 18 free. TV; cable (premium). Complimentary continental bkfst. Restaurant adj 10 am-10 pm. Ck-out 11 am. In-rm modem link. Sundries. Coin lndry. Pool. Cr cds: A, D, DS, ER, JCB, MC, V.

★★★ **WYNDHAM.** *123 Old River Rd (01810). 978/975-3600; fax*

978/975-2664. 293 rms, 5 story. S, D $175; under 18 free; family rates; package plans. Crib free. Pet accepted, some restrictions. TV; cable (premium), VCR avail (movies). Complimentary coffee in lobby. Restaurant 6:30 am-10 pm. to 11 pm. Bar 5 pm-12:30 am; entertainment wkends. Ck-out noon. Convention facilities. Business servs avail. In-rm modem link. Bellhops. Valet serv. Sundries. Gift shop. Airport, Railroad station transportation. Exercise equipt; sauna. Indoor pool; whirlpool. Lawn games. Some refrigerators. Many balconies. Cr cds: A, C, D, DS, JCB, MC, V.

Hotel

★★ **TAGE INN-ANDOVER.** *131 River Rd (01810), 1 blk SW of I-93 Exit 45. 978/685-6200; fax 978/689-0128; res 800/322-8243. Email info@ andovertage.com; www.tageinn.com.* 177 rms, 3 suites, 4 story. May-Oct: S, D $79; suites $110; each addl $8; under 17 free; lower rates rest of yr. Crib avail. Parking lot. Indoor pool, whirlpool. TV; cable (premium). Complimentary continental bkfst, coffee in rms, newspaper, toll-free calls. Restaurant 5-10 pm. Bar. Ck-out noon, ck-in 3 pm. Meeting rms. Business servs avail. Dry cleaning, coin lndry. Exercise equipt. Golf. Tennis, 2 courts. Video games. Cr cds: A, D, DS, MC, V.

B&B/Small Inn

★★★ **ANDOVER INN.** *10 Chapel Ave (01810), ¾ mi S on MA 28. 978/475-5903; fax 978/475-1053; toll-free 800/242-5903. www.andoverinn. com.* 23 rms, 3 story. S $95; D $110; each addl $10; suites $140; under 12 free. Pet accepted, some restrictions. TV; VCR avail. Dining rm 7:30 am-9:45 pm. Bar 11:30 am-midnight. Ck-out noon. Meeting rms. Business center. In-rm modem link. Valet serv. Beauty shop. On campus of Phillips Academy. Cr cds: A, C, D, DS, MC, V.

Restaurants

★★ **CASSIS.** *16 Post Office Ave (01810). 978/474-8788.* French

menu. Specializes in duck nagret with green peppercorn sauce, potato dauthinoix and fresh peaches, scallops with tadouli, lobster vinigarette and mache. Hrs: 5:30-9 pm. Closed Sun, Mon. Res accepted. Wine, beer. Dinner $18-$23. Entertainment. Chef-owned. Cr cds: MC, V.

★ **CHINA BLOSSOM.** *946 Osgood (01845), at MA 125 and Sutton St. 978/682-2242.* Hrs: 11 am-9 pm. Closed Thanksgiving. Bar. Lunch, dinner a la carte entrees: $6.95-$26. Family-owned. Cr cds: A, C, D, DS, MC, V.

Barnstable (Cape Cod)

See also Hyannis, South Yarmouth

Settled 1637 **Pop** 40,949 **Elev** 37 ft
Area code 508 **Zip** 02630
Web www.capecodchamber.org

Information Cape Cod Chamber of Commerce, US 6 & MA 132, PO Box 790, Hyannis 02601-0790; 508/362-3225 or 888/33-CAPECOD

Farmers first settled Barnstable because the marshes provided salt hay for cattle. Later the town prospered as a whaling and trading center, and when these industries declined, land development made it the political hub of the Cape. It is the seat of Barnstable County, which incl the entire Cape; like other Cape communities, it does a thriving resort business.

What to See and Do

Cape Cod Art Association Gallery. Changing exhibits, exhibitions by New England artists; demonstrations, lectures, classes. (Apr-Nov, daily, limited hrs; rest of yr, inquire for schedule) On MA 6A. Phone 508/362-2909. **FREE**

Donald G. Trayser Memorial Museum. Marine exhibits, scrimshaw, Barnstable silver, historic documents. (July-mid-Oct, Tues-Sat afternoons) In Old Custom House and Post Office, Main St on Cobb's

Hill, MA 6A. Phone 508/362-2092. **Donation**

Hyannis Whale Watcher Cruises. View whales aboard the *Whale Watcher,* a 297-passenger supercruiser, custom designed and built specifically for whale watching. Naturalist on board will narrate. Cafe on board. (Apr-Oct, daily) Res necessary. Barnstable Harbor. Contact PO Box 254. Phone 508/362-6088. ¢¢¢¢

Sturgis Library. Oldest library bldg (1644) in US has material on the Cape, incl maritime history; genealogical records of Cape Cod families. Research fee for nonresidents. (Mon-Sat; closed hols; limited hrs) On Main St, MA 6A. Phone 508/362-6636. ¢¢

West Parish Meetinghouse. (1717) Said to be the oldest Congregational church in country; restored. Congregation established in London, 1616. Regular Sun services are held here all yr. Jct US 6, MA 149 in West Barnstable. **FREE**

B&Bs/Small Inns

★★★ **ACWORTH INN.** *4352 Old Kings Hwy, Rte 64 (02637), 2 mi E on MA 6A. 508/362-3330; fax 508/375-0304; toll-free 800/362-6363. www. acworthinn.com.* 4 rms, 2 with shower only, 2 story, 1 suite. Some A/C. No rm phones. Late May-Oct: S, D $100-$125; each addl $20; suite $185; wkends, hols (2-day min); lower rates rest of yr. Children over 12 yrs only. TV in common rm; cable. Complimentary full bkfst. Restaurant nearby. Ck-out 11, ck-in 3-10 pm. Concierge serv. Farmhouse built in 1860. Totally nonsmoking. Cr cds: A, DS, MC, V.

★★★ **ASHLEY MANOR.** *3660 Main St (02630). 508/362-8044; fax 508/362-9927; toll-free 888/535-2246. Email ashleymn@capecod.net; www. ashleymanor.net.* 6 rms, 2 story, 4 suites. July-Oct: S, D $135; lower rates rest of yr. Parking lot. TV; cable, VCR avail. Complimentary full bkfst, coffee in rms, newspaper, toll-free calls. Restaurant nearby. Ck-out 11 am, ck-in 2 pm. Meeting rms. Business servs avail. Concierge serv. Free airport transportation. Exercise equipt, whirl-

pool. Golf. Tennis. Picnic facilities. Cr cds: A, DS, JCB, MC, V.

★★★ **BEECHWOOD INN.** *2839 Main St (02630), MA 6A. 508/362-6618; fax 508/362-0298; toll-free 800/609-6618. Email info@beechwoodinn. com; www.beechwoodinn.com.* 6 rms, 3 story. May-Oct: S, D $180; each addl $25; lower rates rest of yr. Crib avail. Parking lot. TV; cable, VCR avail. Complimentary full bkfst, newspaper. Restaurant nearby. Ck-out 11 am, ck-in 2 pm. Business servs avail. Exercise privileges. Golf. Tennis, 8 courts. Beach access. Bike rentals. Hiking trail. Cr cds: A, DS, MC, V.

★★ **HONEYSUCKLE HILL B&B.** *591 Old Kings Hwy, (02668), 3 mi W on MA 6A. 508/362-8418; fax 508/362-8386; res 508/362-8418; toll-free 800/441-8418. Email stay@honeysuckle hill.com; www.honeysucklehill.com.* 4 rms, 2 story, 1 suite. May-Oct: S $120; D $140; suites $200; lower rates rest of yr. Parking lot. TV; cable, VCR avail. Complimentary full bkfst, newspaper, toll-free calls. Restaurant nearby. Ck-out 11 am, ck-in 3 pm. Business center. Concierge serv. Gift shop. Exercise privileges. Golf. Tennis. Picnic facilities. Cr cds: A, DS, MC, V.

Restaurants

★★ **BARNSTABLE TAVERN AND GRILLE.** *3176 Main St (02630). 508/362-2355.* Specializes in black Angus beef, fresh native seafood, desserts. Hrs: 11:30 am-10 pm; Fri, Sat to 11 pm. Closed Dec 24, 25. Bar. Lunch $3.95-$10.95; dinner $10.95-$21.95. Child's menu. Inn and tavern since 1799. Cr cds: A, MC, V.

★★ **HARBOR POINT.** *Harbor Point Rd (02630), 1¼ mi E. 508/362-2231.* Specializes in fresh seafood, steak. Hrs: 11:30 am-10:30 pm; wkends to midnight; Sun brunch 11 am-3 pm. Closed Feb-Mar. Res accepted. Bar. Lunch $2.95-$10.95; dinner $15.95-$22.95. Sun brunch $10.95. Child's menu. Overlooking bay, marsh abundant with wildlife. Fountain. Cr cds: A, C, DS, MC, V.

★★ **MATTAKEESE WHARF.** *271 Mill Way (02630), on Barnstable Harbor. 508/362-4511.* Specializes in bouillabaisse, baked stuffed shrimp, lobster. Own pasta. Hrs: 11:30 am-10 pm; Sun to 9 pm; early-bird dinner Sun-Fri 4:30-6 pm; Sun brunch to 2:30 pm. Closed late Oct-Apr. Res accepted. Bar. Lunch $5.25-$12; dinner $10.95-$19.95. Sun brunch $8.95. Child's menu. Entertainment: wkends. Valet parking. View of boats in harbor; nautical motif. Family-owned. Cr cds: A, DS, MC, V.

Bedford (C-6)

Pop 12,996 **Elev** 135 ft **Area code** 781 **Zip** 01730

Motels/Motor Lodges

★★ **RAMADA INN.** *340 Great Rd (01730). 781/275-6700; fax 617/275-3011; toll-free 800/272-6232.* 99 rms, 3 story. Apr-Oct: S, D $69-$119; each addl $10; under 18 free; wkend, hol rates. Crib free. TV; cable (premium). Heated pool. Complimentary full bkfst, coffee in rms. Restaurant 6:30-10:30 am, 5-9 pm; Sat 7-11 am, 5-9 pm; Sun 7 am-noon. Bar. Ck-out noon. Meeting rms. Business servs avail. Valet serv. Exercise equipt. Cr cds: A, C, D, DS, JCB, MC, V.

★ **TRAVELODGE.** *285 Great Rd (01730), Exit 31B, 1 mi N of I-95 on MA 4/225. 617/275-6120; fax 617/275-0407; toll-free 800/578-7878.* 42 rms, 2 story. S $59-$79; D $69-$89; each addl $6; under 14 free. Crib $6. TV; cable. Pool. Complimentary coffee. Restaurant nearby. Ck-out 11 am. In-rm modem link. Balconies. Cr cds: A, D, DS, MC, V.

Hotel

★★★ **RENAISSANCE.** *44 Middlesex Tpke (01730), MA 3 Exit 26 to MA 62. 781/275-5500; fax 781/275-8956.* 285

rms, 2-3 story. S, D $170-$210; suites $200-$225; wkend rates; under 18 free. Crib free. Pet accepted, some restrictions. TV; cable (premium), VCR avail. Indoor pool; whirlpool, poolside serv. Restaurant (see also HAVILLAND'S GRILLE). Rm serv 24 hrs. Complimentary coffee delivered to rms. Bar 11:30-1 am; entertainment. Ck-out 1 pm. Convention facilities. Business center. In-rm modem link. Concierge serv. Indoor and outdoor tennis, pro. Exercise rm; sauna. Health club privileges. Refrigerators, minibars. On 24 wooded acres. Cr cds: A, D, DS, JCB, MC, V.

Unrated Dining Spot

HAVILLAND'S GRILLE. *44 Middlesex Tpke. 781/275-5500.* Specializes in Mediterranean cuisine featuring grilled seafood. Own baking. Hrs: 6:30 am-10 pm; Sat, Sun from 7:30 am. Closed Dec 25. Res accepted. Bar. Bkfst $4.95-$11.95; lunch $7-$14; dinner $10-$26. Child's menu. Cr cds: A, D, DS, MC, V.

Berkshire Hills

Web www.berkshires.org

Information Berkshire Visitors Bureau, Berkshire Common, Pittsfield 01201; 413/443-9186 or 800/237-5747

This western Massachusetts resort area is just south of Vermont's Green Mountains, but has neither the ruggedness nor the lonesomeness of the range to its north. The highest peak, Mount Greylock (elevation: 3,491 feet), is cragless and serene. Farms and villages dot the landscape. The area is famous for its variety of accommodations, culture, and recreation. There are also countless summer homes and camps for children by the lakes, ponds, and brooks.

Berkshire County is about 45 miles long from north to south, and half that from east to west. It has 90 lakes and ponds, 90,000 acres of state forest, golf courses, ski areas, ski touring centers, numerous tennis facilities, and campsites. The area first became famous when Nathaniel Hawthorne wrote *Tanglewood Tales,* and it has since become distinguished for its many summer cultural activities, incl the Tanglewood Music Festival at Tanglewood (see LENOX) and the Berkshire Theatre Festival (see STOCKBRIDGE AND WEST STOCKBRIDGE).

Beverly

(B-6) *See also Danvers*

Settled 1626 **Pop** 38,195 **Elev** 26 ft
Area code 978 **Zip** 01915
Information North Shore Chamber of Commerce, 5 Cherry Hill Dr, Danvers 01923; 978/774-8565

When George Washington commissioned the first US naval vessel, the schooner *Hannah,* on September 5, 1775, at Glover's Wharf in Beverly, the town was already well established. In 1693, the local Puritan minister's wife, Mistress Hale, was accused of witchcraft. She was so far above reproach that the charge—and the hysteria—collapsed. Today, Beverly is a popular summer resort area. Saltwater fishing, boating, and scuba diving are available near Glover's Wharf.

What to See and Do

Balch House. (1636) One of the two oldest wood-frame houses in America. Born in 1579, John Balch came to America in 1623 as one of the first permanent settlers of Massachusetts Bay. (Mid-May-mid-Oct, Wed-Sun; closed hols) Inquire about combination ticket (incl Hale and Cabot houses). 448 Cabot St. Phone 978/922-1186. ¢¢

Cabot House. (1781) HQ of Beverly Historical Society. Brick mansion of Revolutionary War privateer John Cabot, built a yr after it was written that "the Cabots of Beverly are now said to be by far the most wealthy in New England." Continental navy exhibit; period rms; portrait and primitive art collection; dolls; military and changing exhibits. (Wed-Sat) Inquire about combination ticket

(incl Hale and Balch Houses). 117 Cabot St. Phone 978/922-1186. ¢¢

Hale House. (1694) Built by the Rev John Hale, who was active in the witchcraft trials and whose own wife was accused of witchcraft. Rare wallpaper and furnishings show changes through the 18th and 19th centuries. (Mid-June-Labor Day, Fri-Sun afternoons; also by appt; closed hols) Inquire about combination ticket (incl Cabot and Balch Houses). 39 Hale St. Phone 978/922-1186. ¢¢

"Le Grand David and his own Spectacular Magic Company." Resident stage magic company, New England's longest running theatrical attraction. This 2¼-hr stage magic production features magic, music, comedy, and dance; 500 costumes, two dozen sets and backdrops; 50 magic illusions. (Sun) Additional performances at Larcom Theatre (1912), 13 Wallis St. Advance tickets recommended. Cabot Street Cinema Theatre (1920), 286 Cabot St. Phone 978/927-3677. ¢¢¢¢

Wenham Museum. Doll collection representing cultures from 1500 B.C. to present; toy room, dollhouses; changing arts, crafts, and antique exhibits. Claflin-Richards House (ca 1660) containing collections of quilts, costumes, fans, period furniture. Winslow Shoe Shop displays history of shoemaking; early ice-cutting tools; research library. (Daily; closed hols) 2½ mi N on MA 1A, at 132 Main St in Wenham. Phone 978/468-2377. ¢¢

Seasonal Events

North Shore Music Theatre. 62 Dunham Rd, at MA 128N Exit 19. Broadway musicals and plays; children's musicals; celebrity concerts. Phone 978/922-8500. Late Apr-late Dec.

Band concerts. Lynch Park Bandshell Sun eve; downtown Ellis Square, Thurs eve. Late June-mid-Aug.

Restaurant

★ ★ **BEVERLY DEPOT.** *10 Park St (01915), MA 62 Bridge St to end. 978/927-5402.* Continental menu. Specializes in fresh seafood, steak, prime rib. Salad bar. Hrs: 5-11 pm; Sun from 4 pm. Bar. Dinner $9-$22.

Child's menu. In 1800s train depot. Cr cds: A, D, DS, MC, V.

Boston (C-6)

Founded 1630 **Pop** 574,283 **Elev** 0-330 ft **Area code** 617
Web www.bostonusa.com

Information Greater Boston Convention & Visitors Bureau, 2 Copley Pl, Suite 105, 02116; 617/536-4100 or 888/733-2678

Suburbs Braintree, Burlington, Cambridge, Dedham, Framingham, Lexington, Lynn, Newton, Quincy, Saugus, Waltham, Wellesley. (See individual alphabetical listings.)

Greater Boston is a fascinating combination of the old and the new. It consists of 83 cities and towns in an area of 1,057 square miles with a total population of more than three million people. Boston proper is the hub of this busy complex, which many proper Bostonians still believe is the hub of the universe.

Boston is a haven for walkers; in fact, strolling along its streets is advised to get a true sense of this most European of all American cities. If you drive, a map is invaluable. Traffic is heavy. The streets (many of them narrow and one-way) run at odd angles and expressway traffic speeds.

Boston's wealth of historic sights makes it a must for all who are interested in America's past. John Winthrop and 800 colonists first settled in Charlestown, just N of the Charles River, and moved to Boston in 1630. Arriving too late to plant, 200 colonists died during the first winter, mostly of starvation. In the spring, a ship arrived with provisions, and the new Puritan commonwealth began to thrive and grow. Fisheries, fur trapping, lumbering, and trading with Native Americans were the foundation of Boston's commerce. The port is still viable, with 250 wharves along 30 miles of berthing space.

The American Revolution began here in 1770. British troops fired on an angry mob, killing six in what has since been called the "Boston Massacre." In 1773, the Boston Tea Party dumped East Indian tea into the bay in a dramatic protest against restriction of colonial trade by British governors. Great Britain closed the port in retaliation. The course of history was set.

In April, 1775, British General Thomas Gage decided to march on Concord to capture military supplies and overwhelm the countryside. During the night of April 18-19, Paul Revere, William Dawes, and Samuel Prescott spread the news to Lexington and Concord in a ride immortalized, somewhat inaccurately, by Henry Wadsworth Longfellow. The American Revolution had begun in earnest; the Battle of Bunker Hill followed the battles of Lexington and Concord. On March 17, 1776, General William Howe, commander of the British forces, evacuated the city.

Boston's list of distinguished native sons incl John Hancock, Samuel Adams, Paul Revere, Henry Ward Beecher, Edward Everett Hale, Ralph Waldo Emerson, William Lloyd Garrison, Oliver Wendell Holmes (father and son), and hundreds of others.

Mention Boston and many people will automatically think of the gentry of Beacon Hill, with their elegant homes and rigid social code. However, the Irish have long had a powerful influence in Boston's politics and personality, while a stroll down an Italian neighborhood on the North End will be like stepping back to the old country.

Boston today has managed to retain its heritage and charm while thriving in the modern age. Urban renewal and increased construction have reversed an almost 40-year slump that plagued Boston earlier inthe 20th century. With more than 100 universities, colleges, and trade and vocational schools in the area, Boston is a city as full of vigor and promise for the future as it is rich with the past.

Transportation

Car Rental Agencies. See IMPORTANT TOLL-FREE NUMBERS.

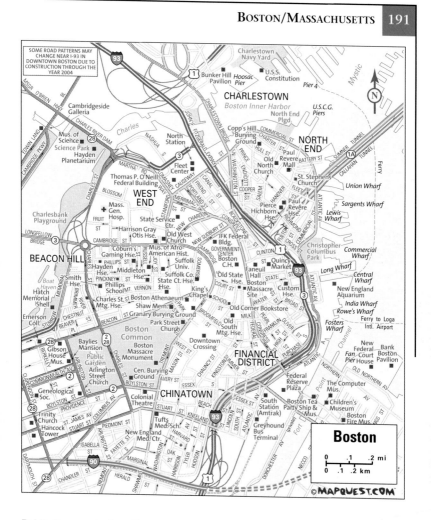

Boston

0 .1 .2 mi

0 .1 .2 km

© MAPQUEST.COM

Public Transportation.
Buses, subway, and elevated trains (Massachusetts Bay Transportation Authority), visitor pass available, phone 617/722-3200.

Rail Passenger Service.
Amtrak 800/872-7245.

Logan International Airport.
Information 617/561-1800 or 800/235-6426; lost and found 617/561-1714; weather 617/936-1234; cash machines, Terminals A, B, C.

What to See and Do

Bell's Laboratory. Restored lab where telephone was born when Alexander Graham Bell first sent speech sounds electrically over a wire. Charts and instruments Bell used; first telephone switchboard; first commercial telephone. (Daily) New England Telephone Bldg, 185 Franklin St, in lobby. Phone 617/743-9800. **FREE**

Blue Hills Trailside Museum. Visitor center for the 5,700-acre Blue Hills Reservation. Deer, turkey, otter, snakes, owls, and honeybees. Exhibit hall with natural science/history displays, incl Native American wigwam; viewing tower. Activities incl hikes, films, animal programs. Special events incl maple sugaring (Mar), Hawks Wkend (Sep), and Honey Harvest (Oct). Visitor center and bldgs (Tues-Sun; schedule may vary) Phone 617/333-0690. ¢¢

Boston African American National Historic Site. Incl **African Meeting House.** Part of the Museum of Afro-American History. Built by free black

Bostonians in 1806, bldg was an educational and religious center and site of founding of New England Anti-Slavery Society in 1832. (Memorial Day-Labor Day, Mon-Fri; rest of yr, by appt) 30-min tour (hrly on the hr) of Meeting House by museum staff. Smith Ct, off Joy St on Beacon Hill. Phone 617/742-5415. **FREE** Meeting House is starting point for the

Black Heritage Trail. Marked walking tour conducted by National Park Service, past sites in the Beacon Hill section that relate the history of 19th-century black Boston.

Old State House, Boston

Brochure and maps are at National Park Visitor Center, 46 Joy St, 2nd floor. Two-hr guided tours by National Park Service (by appt). Phone 617/742-5415. **FREE**

Boston Common. A 48-acre tract set aside in 1634 for a cow pasture and training field, and, by law, still available for these purposes. Free speech is honored here, and you may find groups discussing anything from atheism to zoology. At the far side of the Common is the

Central Burying Ground. The grave of Gilbert Stuart, the painter, is here; technically not a part of the Common, although in it. Proceed W, crossing Charles St, and enter the

Public Garden. Formal gardens, rare trees carefully labeled. Pond with the famous swan boats in summer and skating in winter (fee).

Boston Harbor Islands National Park Area. Incl 30 islands in Boston Harbor; visitors have access to only 10. Of these, George's Island is the hub, providing water shuttles to other undeveloped islands. George's Island is also popular due to Civil War-era Fort Warren, a National Historic Landmark (guided tours avail). Boston Light, the country's oldest continually used lighthouse, is on Little Brewster Island, which is reachable by excursion boat. George's Island is open daily; Little Brewster is open to the public on Saturdays by reservation only. Camping permitted on selected islands. Phone 617/223-8666.

Boston Public Library. (1895) Italian Renaissance bldg by Charles McKim incl central courtyard and fountain. Mural decorations, bronze doors, sculpture. Contemporary addition (1972), by Philip Johnson, houses large circulating library, recordings, and films. Film and author programs; exhibits. Central Library. (Mon-Sat; schedule may vary) Phone 617/536-5400. **FREE**

Boston Tea Party Ship and Museum. Atmosphere of the Boston Tea Party (1773) is re-created. Visitors may board the full-size working replica of the Tea Party Ship and throw tea chests overboard. Exhibits, artifacts, audiovisual presentations place the event in historical perspective; costumed tour guides. Complimentary tea served. (Daily; closed Dec, Jan, and Feb) Congress St Bridge, on Harborwalk. Phone 617/338-1773. ¢¢

Boston University. (1839) 28,000 students. Information center located at 771 Commonwealth Ave in George Sherman Union (Phone 617/353-2169); also located here is the George Sherman Union Gallery. Mugar Memorial Library houses papers of Dr. Martin Luther King, Jr, as well as those of Robert Frost, Isaac Asimov, and other writers and artists. Boston University Art Gallery exhibits at the School for the Arts, 855 Commonwealth Ave. Commonwealth Ave near Kenmore Sq. Campus tours from the Admissions Office, 121 Bay State Rd. Phone 617/353-2318.

Children's Museum of Boston. Participatory exhibits on science, disabilities, cultural diversity, computers, and games; play activities. (July-Labor Day, daily; rest of yr, Tues-Sun; closed Jan 1, Thanksgiving, Dec 25) 300 Congress St, near South Station. Phone 617/426-8855. ¢¢¢

Franklin Park Zoo. "Bird's World" indoor/outdoor aviary complex with natural habitats; African tropical forest; hilltop range with camels, antelopes, zebras, mouflon; children's zoo. (Daily; closed Thanksgiving, Dec 25) 1 Franklin Park Rd. Near the intersection of Columbia Rd & Blue Hill Ave. Phone 617/442-2002. ¢¢-¢¢¢

Frederick Law Olmsted National Historic Site. Former home and office of the founder of landscape architecture in America. Site archives contain documentation of firm's work. Site also incl landscaped grounds designed by Olmsted. Guided tours. (Fri-Sun) 99 Warren St, in Brookline. Phone 617/566-1689. **FREE**

★ **The Freedom Trail.** A walking tour through downtown Boston that passes 16 points of interest, plus other exhibits, monuments, and shrines just off the trail, some of which are part of Boston National Historical Park. The trail is marked by signs and a red sidewalk line. Brochures are available at the Greater Boston Convention & Visitors Bureau information centers at the Prudential Plaza (phone 617/536-4100) and on the Boston Common. The Boston National Park Visitor Center (daily) dispenses an excellent free map and offers seasonal guided tours. Phone 617/242-5689.

State House. (1795) Designed by Charles Bulfinch, the nation's first professional architect, it has since had wings added to both sides. Inside are statues, paintings, and other interesting materials. Hall of Flags on 2nd floor; House and Senate Chambers, State Library on 3rd floor. Tours (Mon-Sat; closed hols). Beacon St at head of Park St. Phone 617/727-3676. **FREE**

Park Street Church. (1809) Often called "Brimstone Corner" because brimstone for gunpowder was stored here during the War of 1812. William Lloyd Garrison delivered his first antislavery

address here in 1829. Tours. (July-Aug, Tues-Sat; Sun services all yr) 1 Park St. Phone 617/523-3383. **FREE**

Granary Burying Ground. Once the site of the town granary. The graves of John Hancock, Samuel Adams, Paul Revere, Benjamin Franklin's parents, many governors, another signer of the Declaration of Independence, and the martyrs of the Boston Massacre are here. (Daily) Tremont St opp end of Bromfield St.

King's Chapel. (1754) The first Anglican church in Boston (1686) became in 1786 the first Unitarian church in America. adj is the King's Chapel Burying Ground. Tremont St at School St. **FREE**

Site of the first US free public school. (1635) It was the Boston Public Latin School. School St opp Old City Hall. Across the street is

Statue of Benjamin Franklin. (1856) by Richard S. Greenough. Continue W on School St to Parker House, a hotel where Ho Chi Minh and Malcolm X once worked as waiters.

Old South Meeting House. (1729) This was the site of many important town meetings about the British, incl those that sparked the Boston Tea Party. Multimedia exhibition depicts its 300-yr history. (Daily; closed hols) 310 Washington St. Phone 617/482-6439. ¢

Old State House. (1713) Boston's oldest public bldg, the Old State House served as the seat of the Royal Governor and Colonial Legislature until the Revolution. The Boston Massacre took place outside the bldg on Mar 5, 1770. From the balcony, the Declaration of Independence was first proclaimed to the citizens of Boston. Houses permanent and changing exhibits related to Boston history (daily). Reference and photograph library at 15 State St (Mon-Fri; fee). 206 Washington St, at State St. Phone 617/720-3290. ¢¢

Site of the Boston Massacre. Marked by a circle of cobblestones in the pavement. 30 State St.

Faneuil Hall Marketplace. Bostonian Peter Faneuil bequeathed this 2-

story, bronze-domed bldg to the city in 1742 as a public meeting hall and marketplace. Called the "Cradle of Liberty" because it was the scene of mass meetings during the pre-Revolutionary period, the bldg and two other restored structures today house a bustling marketplace of more than 100 specialty shops, 20 restaurants and pubs, and a variety of pushcarts and food stalls. Marketplace (daily). adj is a military museum—the Ancient and Honorable Artillery Company Museum—chartered in 1638 as a school for officers. (Mon-Fri; closed hols) Merchants Row. Phone 617/523-1300 or 617/227-1638 (museum). **FREE**

Paul Revere House. (ca 1680) This is the only 17th-century structure left in downtown Boston. It was from this house that the silversmith left for his historic ride on Apr 18, 1775. The interior features 17th- and 18th-century decorative arts and contains Revere artifacts and memorabilia. (Apr-Dec, daily; rest of yr, Tues-Sun) 19 North Sq. Phone 617/523-2338. **¢¢**

Old North Church. (1723) The oldest church bldg in Boston. From the steeple's highest window were hung 2 lanterns, sending Paul Revere on his historic ride to warn the militia in Lexington. (Daily) Also Sun services. 193 Salem St, at foot of Hull St. Phone 617/523-6676. **Donation**

Copp's Hill Burying Ground. First burials date from 1660. During the Revolution, British cannon here were trained on Charlestown and Bunker Hill, across the Charles River. Rev Cotton Mather and Edmund Hart, builder of the US frigate *Constitution,* are buried here. (Daily) Hull & Snow Hill Sts.

Bunker Hill Monument. A 221-ft granite obelisk commemorates the Battle of Bunker Hill, which took place on June 17, 1775. Ranger-conducted battle talks (June-Oct, on the hr); musket firing demonstrations (mid-June-Labor Day, Wed-Sun). Spiral staircase (294 steps) to top of monument, no elevator. Four sides viewing Boston area. (Daily; closed Jan 1, Thanksgiving, Dec 25) Monument Sq, Charlestown, a few blks from the *Constitution.* Phone 617/242-5641. **FREE**

USS *Constitution.* "Old Ironsides," launched in 1797, was engaged in more than 40 battles without defeat. Oldest commissioned Navy ship afloat in world. 20-min tours. Museum with ship artifacts is adj. (Daily) Located in Charlestown Navy Yard, Boston National Historical Park. I-93: northbound, Exit 25 and follow signs across Charlestown bridge; southbound, Exit 28 to Sullivan Sq and follow signs. Phone 617/426-1812. **FREE**

Gibson House Museum. Victorian townhouse with period furnishings. Tours (May-Oct, Wed-Sun afternoons; Nov-Apr, Sat and Sun; closed hols). 137 Beacon St. Phone 617/267-6338. **¢¢**

Guided walking tours. Boston by Foot. 1½-hr architectural walking tours incl the heart of Freedom Trail (Tues-Sat); Beacon Hill (daily, departures vary); Victorian Back Bay Tour (Fri and Sat); North End (Sat); children's tour (Sat-Mon, one departure daily); downtown Boston (Sun). All tours (May-Oct). Tour of the month each 4th Sun; custom tours. Contact 77 N Washington St, 02114. Phone 617/367-2345 or 617/367-3766 (recording). **¢¢¢**

Guild of Boston Artists. Changing exhibits of paintings, graphics, and sculpture by New England artists. (Sep-June, Tues-Sat; closed Jan 1, Thanksgiving, Dec 25) 162 Newbury St. Phone 617/536-7660. **FREE**

Harrison Gray Otis House. (1796) Otis, a lawyer and statesman, built this first of 3 houses designed for him by Charles Bulfinch. A later move to Beacon Hill left this house as a rooming house for 100 yrs. Restored to reflect Boston taste and decoration of 1796-1820. Some family furnishings. Reflects the proportion and delicate detail Bulfinch introduced to Boston, strongly influencing the Federal style in New England. Museum. HQ for the Society for the Preservation of New England Antiquities; send stamped, self-addressed legal-size envelope to Society for guide to 22 historic homes (02114). Tours (Wed-Sun). 141 Cambridge St, enter from Lynde St. Phone 617/227-3956. **¢¢**

Institute of Contemporary Art.
Occupies a 19th-century Richardsonian-style bldg once used as a police station. Exhibits of contemporary art: painting, sculpture, video, and photography. Docent-guided tours (Sat and Sun afternoons). Also film, video, music, dance, poetry, lectures, and performance art in the ICA Theater. Gallery (Wed-Sun). Bookstore (daily). Free admission Thurs eve. 955 Boylston St, opp Prudential Center. Phone 617/266-5152. ¢¢

Isaac Royall House. (1637) Originally built as a 4-rm farmhouse by John Winthrop, first governor of Bay State Colony; enlarged in 1732 by Isaac Royall. Example of early Georgian architecture; examples of Queen Anne, Chippendale, and Hepplewhite furnishings. (May-Sep, Wed-Sun) ¾ mi S off I-93, at 15 George St in Medford. Phone 781/396-9032. ¢¢

Isabella Stewart Gardner Museum. This was the home of this patron of the arts from 1902 until her death in 1924. Paintings, sculpture, and a flower display are in the enormous Venetian-style central courtyard, surrounded by 3 floors of galleries (Tues-Sun; closed hols). Concerts (late Sep-May, Sat and Sun afternoons; fees). 280 The Fenway. Phone 617/734-1359 (concert information) or 617/566-1401 (museum). ¢¢¢

John F. Kennedy National Historic Site. The birthplace and early childhood home of the nation's 35th president is restored in appearance to 1917, the year of his birth. Ranger-guided tours. (Wed-Sun; closed Jan 1, Thanksgiving, Dec 25) Golden Eagle Passport accepted (see MAKING THE MOST OF YOUR TRIP.). 83 Beals St, in Brookline. Phone 617/566-7937. ¢

John Hancock Observatory. The observatory, considered the best place to see Boston, is located on the 60th floor of the John Hancock Tower. It offers a panoramic view of Boston and eastern Massachusetts and exciting multimedia exhibits of Boston, past and present. They incl "Boston 1775," a sound and light show about Boston since revolutionary days; a taped narration by the late Walter Muir Whitehill, architectural historian; and a lighted display of New England scenes. In addition, "Aviation Radio" allows visitors to tune in on the cross-talk between planes at Logan International's tower while viewing the action at the airport. (Daily; closed Thanksgiving, Dec 25) At Copley Square. Phone 617/247-1977. ¢¢

Louisburg Square. This lovely little residential square with its central park is the ultimate in traditional Boston charm. Louisa May Alcott, William Dean Howells, and other famous Bostonians have lived here. It is one of the most treasured spots in Boston. Christmas caroling is traditional here.

The Mother Church, the First Church of Christ, Scientist. Tours. (Tues-Sat; also Sun after services; closed hols) Christian Science Center, Huntington & Massachusetts Aves. Phone 617/450-3790. **FREE** adj is

> **Christian Science Publishing Society.** (*The Christian Science Monitor.*) Inquire about tours. Mapparium, a walk-through stained-glass globe, is here. (Tues-Sat; closed hols) Bible exhibit (Wed-Sun; closed Jan, hols). Massachusetts Ave at Clearway St. Phone 617/450-3790 or 617/450-3793. **FREE**

■ **Museum at the John Fitzgerald Kennedy Library.** Designed by I. M. Pei, the library is considered one of the most beautiful contemporary works of architecture in the country. The library tower houses a collection of documents from the Kennedy administration as well as audiovisual programs designed to re-create the era. (Daily; closed Jan 1, Thanksgiving, Dec 25) Picnic facilities on oceanfront. 5 mi SE on I-93, off Exit 15, at University of Massachusetts Columbia Point campus, Dorchester. Phone 617/929-4523. ¢¢

Museum of Fine Arts. Chinese, Japanese, Indian, Egyptian, Greek, Roman, European, and American collections; also silver, period rms, and musical instruments. Gallery lectures, films; library; children's programs; changing exhibits; restaurants; auditorium. (Daily; closed Thanksgiving, Dec 25) Free admission Wed, late afternoon-evening. 465 Huntington Ave. Phone 617/267-9300. ¢¢¢

Museum of Science. One of the finest and most modern science museums in the world, with many hands-on exhibits. "Seeing the Unseen," giant dinosaur model; "Human Body Discovery Space," health and environment displays; live animal, physical science, and special effects demonstrations. Children's Discovery Room. Omnimax Theatre (fee). (Daily; closed Thanksgiving, Dec 25) Science Park, on Charles River Dam Bridge between Storrow Dr and Memorial Dr. Advance tickets recommended. Phone 617/523-6664 or 617/723-2500. ¢¢¢-¢¢¢¢ Also here are

Charles Hayden Planetarium. Shows approx 50 min. (Same hrs as museum) Children under 4 yrs not admitted. Phone 617/523-6664. Additional fee ¢¢

Computer Museum. Films, computer animations, robot demonstrations, tours. Exhibits incl a Virtual Fish Tank, the Best Software for Kids Gallery, history of computers from 1940 to present; the latest in personal computers, artificial intelligence, computer graphics, and image processing. Phone 617/523-6664.

New England Aquarium. One of the largest cylindrical saltwater tanks in world, stocked with hundreds of specimens of marine life. Permanent exhibits incl marine mammals, birds, and reptiles. Freshwater gallery, marine life in American rivers, incl exotic animals from the Amazon Basin area. Electric eel, turtles, and a 4,000-gallon replica of an Amazon rain forest. Adj is *The Discovery*, a barge where sea lion demonstrations are presented. (Daily; closed morning of Jan 1, Thanksgiving, Dec 25) Whale watches (mid-Apr-mid-Oct; phone for res). Central Wharf. Phone 617/973-5200 or 617/973-5281 (res). ¢¢¢¢

Nichols House Museum. (1804) Typical domestic architecture of Beacon Hill from its era; only home on Beacon Hill open to the public. Attributed to Charles Bulfinch; antique furnishings and art from America, Europe, and the Orient from the 17th to early 19th centuries. Collection of Rose Standish Nichols, landscape designer and writer. (Tues-Sat) 55 Mt Vernon St. Phone 617/227-6993. ¢¢

Professional sports.

American League Baseball (Boston Red Sox). Fenway Park. 4 Yawkey Way. Phone 617/267-9440.

NBA (Boston Celtics). Fleet Center. 1 Fleet Center Pl. Phone 617/523-6050.

NHL (Boston Bruins). Fleet Center. 1 Fleet Center Pl. Phone 617/624-1050.

Shopping. Downtown Crossing, Boston's traditional shopping area, is anchored by Filene's Basement and Macy's. Filene's Basement, billed as the country's first discount store, remains a major attraction with bargain hunters. **The Back Bay Area** offers upscale shopping in Copley Place with more than 100 stores among its retail, office, hotel, and residential complex. Numerous boutiques, art galleries, and antique shops line Newbury St. On the waterfront, **Faneuil Hall Marketplace** offers dozens of shops and restaurants in early 19th-century market bldgs. Neighboring **Haymarket Sq** hosts the "Haymarket," an open-air farmers market with a colorful array of reasonably priced produce, meat, fish, and cheese (Fri and Sat, afternoons).

Sightseeing tours.

Bay State Cruise Company. All-day sail to Provincetown and Cape Cod from Commonwealth Pier. 2½- and 3½-hr harbor and island cruises aboard *Spirit of Boston* highlighting adventure and history. (Mid-June-Labor Day, daily; May-mid-June and after Labor Day-Columbus Day, Sat and Sun only) Commonwealth Pier, World Trade Center. Contact Bay State Cruise Company. Phone 617/748-1428. ¢¢¢¢

Boston Tours From Suburban Hotels. Escorted bus tours departing from suburban hotels and motels along I-95/MA 128. Also departures from metrowest suburban hotels in Natick/Framingham area. Tours follow Freedom Trail and incl stops at Old North Church, "Old Ironsides," Faneuil Hall Marketplace, and Cambridge. Six-hr tour (daily). 56 Williams St, in Waltham. Phone 781/899-1454. ¢¢¢¢

Brush Hill Tours. Fully lectured 3-hr bus tours of Boston/Cambridge (late Mar-mid-Nov); ½-day tours of Lexington/Concord, Salem/Marblehead (mid-June-Oct), and Plymouth (May-Oct); full-day tours of Cape Cod (incl Provincetown) and Newport, RI (June-Sep). Also 1½-hr tours along Freedom Trail aboard the Beantown Trolleys. Departures from major downtown hotels, Copley Square, and Boston Common (daily). Phone 617/236-2148 or 781/986-6100. ¢¢¢¢

Symphony Hall. Home of Boston Symphony (late Sep-early May) and Boston Pops (May-mid-July, Tues-Sun). Huntington & Massachusetts Aves. Phone 617/266-1492.

Trinity Church. (1877) Episcopal. This Henry Hobson Richardson bldg, the inspiration of Phillips Brooks, was the noblest work of the architect. The interior was decorated by John LaFarge and has five of his windows as well as two by William Morris of England. Phillips Brooks, the ninth rector of Trinity Church, is known for his beautiful Christmas carol, "O Little Town of Bethlehem." His statue, by Augustus Saint Gaudens, stands outside the North Transept of the Church. Daniel Chester French created Brooks' bust in the Baptistry. Phillips Brooks preached at Trinity Church for 22 yrs. Theodore Parker Ferris, one of the outstanding preachers of the 20th century, was the 15th rector of Trinity Church and preached here for 30 yrs. Phone 617/536-0944.

⭐ **Walking tour.** Through the Common, Public Garden, and Beacon Hill. Start at Park & Tremont Sts, walk NW up the hill on Park St to the

> **State House.** Walk W 2 blks to Walnut St, turn right 1 blk to Mt Vernon St.
>
> **Nichols House Museum.** Continue W on Mt Vernon St to
>
> **Louisburg Square.** Walk S on Willow St, turn left to Spruce St, and follow it 1 blk to the
>
> **Boston Common.** At the far side of the Common is the
>
> **Boston Massacre Monument.** Commemorates this 1770 event, which has been called the origin of the Revolution. At the SW corner of the Common is the

> **Central Burying Ground.** Proceed W, crossing Charles St, and enter the
>
> **Public Garden.** Just W of the Public Garden is the
>
> **Back Bay area.** Walk along Boylston St, S side of Public Garden, 2 blks to
>
> **Copley Square.** Here is
>
> **Trinity Church.** Opp church is the
>
> **John Hancock Observatory.** Nearby is the
>
> **Boston Public Library.**

"Whites of Their Eyes." Specially designed pavilion houses multimedia reenactment of the Battle of Bunker Hill using life-size figures and eyewitness narratives. Audience "viewpoint" from atop Breed's Hill. Continuous 30-min shows. (Apr-Nov, daily; closed Thanksgiving) Bunker Hill Pavilion, 55 Constitution Rd, just W of the USS *Constitution* in Charlestown. Phone 617/241-7575. ¢¢

Annual Events

Patriots Day Celebration. Third Mon Apr.

Boston Marathon. Famous 26-mi footrace from Hopkinton to Boston. Apr 17.

Bunker Hill Day. Mid-June.

Harborfest. Hatch Shell on the Esplanade. Boston Pops Orchestra, fireworks. Late June-early July.

Esplanade Concerts. Musical programs by the Boston Pops in the Hatch Shell on the Esplanade. Two wks July.

Charles River Regatta. Third Sun Oct.

First Night Celebration. Boston Common. Dec 31.

Additional Visitor Information

Literature and information is available at the Greater Boston Convention & Visitors Bureau, Prudential Tower, PO Box 990468, 02199; 617/536-4100; the Prudential Visitor Center; and at the visitor information center on Tremont St, Boston Common (daily; closed Jan 1, Thanksgiving, Dec 25). The National Park Visitor Center (daily) at 15 State St also has helpful information. All have informative brochures with maps of the Freedom Trail and Black History Trail.

Bostix, located in Faneuil Hall Marketplace, offers half-price tickets for music, theater, and dance performances on the day of performance; also provides cultural information and calendar of events. (Tues-Sun; closed Thanksgiving, Dec 25) Phone 617/723-5181 (recording).

City Neighborhoods

Many of the restaurants, unrated dining establishments, and some lodgings listed under Boston incl neighborhoods as well as exact street addresses. Geographic descriptions of these areas are given.

Back Bay. S of Memorial Dr along the Charles River Basin, W of Arlington St, N of Stuart St and Huntington Ave, and E of Boston University campus and Brookline.

Beacon Hill. S of Cambridge St, W of Somerset St, N of Beacon St, and E of Charles St.

Copley Square. S of Boylston St, W of Trinity Church (Trinity St), N of St. James Ave, and E of the Public Library (Dartmouth St).

Downtown Crossing Area. At intersection of Washington St and Winter and Summer Sts; area S of State St, N of Essex St, E of Tremont St, and W of Congress St. **East of Downtown Crossing Area:** E of Congress St. **South of Downtown Crossing Area:** S of Essex St.

Faneuil Hall/Quincy Market Area. S and W of the John F. Fitzgerald Expy (I-93), N of State St, and E of Congress St.

Financial District. S of State St, W and N of the John F. Fitzgerald Expy (I-93), and E of Congress St.

North End. Bounded by Boston Harbor and the John F. Fitzgerald Expy (I-93).

South End. S of I-90, W of John F. Fitzgerald Expy (I-93), N of Massachusetts Ave, and E of Columbus Ave.

Theatre District. S of Boylston St, W of Tremont St, N of I-90, and E of Arlington St.

Motel/Motor Lodge

★★ **RAMADA AIRPORT HOTEL.** *225 McClellan Hwy (02128), 1 mi N of Logan Intl Airport on MA 1A.* 617/569-5250; fax 617/569-5159; toll-free 800/RAMADA. 356 rms, 12 story. S $119-$209; D $129-$219; each addl $10; under 18 free; lower rates off season. Crib free. TV; cable (premium). Pool. Coffee in rms. Restaurant 6-11:30 am, 5-10 pm. Bar 11-2 am. Ck-out noon. Meeting rms. Business servs avail. In-rm modem link. Gift shop. Free airport transportation. Exercise equipt. Microwaves avail. Cr cds: A, C, D, DS, JCB, MC, V.
D ⊷ 🏋 ✈ ⊷ 🔥 SC

Hotels

★★ **BEST WESTERN.** *342 Longwood Ave (02115), in Back Bay.* 617/731-4700; fax 617/731-6273; res 800/528-1234; toll-free 800/462-6786. Email innlwm@erols.com; www.best western.com. 140 rms, 8 story, 20 suites. Apr-Oct: S $209; D $219; suites $249; each addl $15; under 17 free; lower rates rest of yr. Crib avail. Valet parking avail. TV; cable (premium), VCR avail. Complimentary newspaper. Restaurant 6:30 am-1 pm. Bar. Ck-out noon, ck-in 3 pm. Meeting rms. Business servs avail. Bellhops. Concierge serv. Dry cleaning. Gift shop. Salon/barber avail. Exercise rm. Golf. Tennis. Video games. Cr cds: A, C, D, DS, ER, JCB, MC, V.
D 🏌 🏊 🏋 🎿 ⊷ 🔥

★★★★ **BOSTON HARBOR HOTEL.** *Rowes Wharf (02110), on the Waterfront, in Financial District.* 617/439-7000; fax 617/330-9450; toll-free 800/752-7077. Email reservations@bhh.com; www.bhh.com. This hotel affords lovely views of the harbor. All 230 rooms, housed behind the well-recognized "grand arch" facade, are elegantly furnished to reflect historic Boston with interesting artwork and marble bathrooms. An exceptional antique chart collection is displayed off the lobby, which also hosts the fine Rowes Wharf restaurant. 204 rms, 16 story, 26 suites. D $295; suites $385. Crib avail. Pet accepted. Valet parking avail. Indoor pool, whirlpool. TV; cable (DSS), VCR avail. Complimentary newspaper. Restaurant. 24-hr rm serv. Bar. Ck-out 1 pm, ck-in 3 pm. Meeting rms.

Business center. Bellhops. Concierge serv. Dry cleaning. Gift shop. Free airport transportation. Exercise rm, sauna, steam rm. Golf. Tennis, 20 courts. Downhill skiing. Supervised children's activities. Picnic facilities. Video games. Cr cds: A, C, D, DS, MC, V.

★★★ BOSTON MARRIOTT LONG WHARF. *296 State St (02109), on Waterfront, in Faneuil Hall/Quincy Market Area.* 617/227-0800; *fax 617/227-2867; toll-free 800/228-9290. www.marriott.com/boslw.* 400 rms, 7 story, 10 suites. Apr-Nov: S, D $365; suites $450; each addl $30; under 18 free; lower rates rest of yr. Crib avail. Valet parking avail. Indoor pool, whirlpool. TV; cable (DSS), VCR avail. Complimentary coffee in rms, newspaper, toll-free calls. Restaurant 7 am-10 pm. Bar. Conference center, meeting rms. Business center. Bellhops. Concierge serv. Dry cleaning, coin lndry. Gift shop. Exercise equipt, sauna. Tennis. Cr cds: A, D, DS, MC, V.

★★ THE BOSTON PARK PLAZA HOTEL. *64 Arlington St (02116), in Back Bay, opp Boston Public Garden.* 617/426-2000; *fax 617/426-5545; toll-free 800/225-2008.* 960 rms, 15 story. S $189-$269; D $209-$289; each addl $20; suites $375-$1,500. Crib $10. Garage $23; valet. TV; cable (premium). Pool privileges. Restaurant 6:30 am-midnight. Bar 11-1:30 am. Ck-out noon. Convention facilities. Business center. In-rm modem link. Concierge serv. Shopping arcade. Barber, beauty shop. Exercise equipt. Health club privileges. Refrigerators. Cr cds: A, D, DS< MC, V.

★★★ CHARLES STREET INN. *94 Charles St (02114).* 617/371-0008; *fax 617/371-0009; toll-free 877/772-8900. Email info@charlesstreetinn.com; www. charlesstreetinn.com.* 8 rms, 5 story. May-Oct: suites $280; each addl $50; lower rates rest of yr. Parking garage. TV; cable, VCR avail, CD avail. Complimentary continental bkfst, coffee in rms, newspaper, toll-free calls. Restaurant nearby. Ck-out 11 am, ck-in 3 pm. Business servs avail. Concierge serv. Dry cleaning. Exer-

cise privileges. Golf, 18 holes. Tennis, 2 courts. Cr cds: A, D, DS, MC, V.

★★★ THE COLONNADE HOTEL. *120 Huntington Ave (02116), in Back Bay, opp Hynes Convention Center, adj Copley Plaza Shopping Center.* 617/424-7000; *fax 617/424-1717; toll-free 800/962-3030. www.colonnadehotel. com.* 273 rms, 11 story, 12 suites. Mar-Nov: S, D $425; suites $1050; each addl $25; under 18 free; lower rates rest of yr. Crib avail. Pet accepted. Valet parking avail. Pool, lifeguard. TV; cable (DSS), VCR avail, CD avail. Complimentary newspaper, toll-free calls. Restaurant 6:30 am-1 pm. 24-hr rm serv. Bar. Ck-out noon, ck-in 3 pm. Conference center, meeting rms. Business center. Bellhops. Concierge serv. Dry cleaning. Exercise equipt. Golf. Tennis. Supervised children's activities. Cr cds: C, D, DS, MC, V.

★★ COPLEY INN. *19 Garrison St (02116), in Back Bay.* 617/236-0300; *fax 617/536-0816; toll-free 800/232-0306. Email info@copleyinn.com; www. copleyinn.com.* 20 rms, 5 story. Apr-Nov: S, D $135; lower rates rest of yr. Crib avail. TV; cable. Restaurant nearby. Cr cds: A, MC, V.

★★ COPLEY SQUARE. *47 Huntington Ave (02116), in Copley Square, Exit 22 off MA Tpke.* 617/536-9000; *fax 617/267-3547; toll-free 800/225-7062. www.copleysquarehotel.com.* 143 rms, 7 story, 5 suites. Apr-Oct: S, D $285; suites $385; each addl $20; under 16 free; lower rates rest of yr. Crib avail. Parking garage. TV; cable (premium). Complimentary coffee in rms. Restaurant 11:30 am-10:30 pm. Bar. Ck-out noon, ck-in 3 pm. Business servs avail. Bellhops. Concierge serv. Dry cleaning. Golf. Bike rentals. Cr cds: A, C, D, DS, ER, MC, V.

★★★ DOUBLETREE SUITES. *400 Soldiers Field Rd (02134), W of Back Bay, N of Brookline, I-90 Exit Storrow Dr.* 617/783-0090; *fax 617/783-0897; res 800/222-8733.* 310 suites, 16 story. S, D $149-$289; each addl $20; under 18 free; wkend packages. Crib free. TV; cable (premium). Indoor

pool; whirlpool. Complimentary coffee in rms. Restaurant 6:30 am-10 pm. Bar 11:30-12:45 am; entertainment Wed-Sat. Ck-out noon. Coin lndry. Convention facilities. Business center. In-rm modem link. Concierge serv. Exercise equipt; sauna. Game rm. Bathrm phones, refrigerators, minibars; some microwaves. Some private patios, balconies. On river. Cr cds: A, C, D, DS, ER, JCB, MC, V.

★★★ **THE FAIRMONT COPLEY PLAZA.** *138 St. James Ave (02116), in Copley Square.* 617/267-5300; fax 617/437-0794; toll-free 800/527-4727. *www.fairmont.com.* 379 rms, 6 story, 61 suites. June, Sep-Oct: S $289; D $319; each addl $30; under 17 free; lower rates rest of yr. Crib avail. Valet parking avail. TV; cable (DSS). Complimentary newspaper. Restaurant 5:30-11 pm. 24-hr rm serv. Ck-out 1 pm, ck-in 3 pm. Conference center, meeting rms. Business center. Bellhops. Concierge serv. Dry cleaning. Gift shop. Salon/barber avail. Exercise privileges. Golf. Tennis. Video games. Cr cds: A, C, D, DS, MC.

★★★★★ **FOUR SEASONS HOTEL BOSTON.** *200 Boylston St (02116), in Boston Common, in Downtown Crossing Area.* 617/338-4400; fax 617/423-0154; res 800/332-3442. There are 216 guestrms and 72 suites in this luxurious hotel overlooking the Public Garden and Beacon Hill; even the 45-ft indoor pool has a spectacular view. Dine on renowned cuisine at Aujourd'hui or listen to evening jazz in The Bristol Lounge. For special events, guests can book one of 8 function rooms, incl a magnificent ballroom perched above the garden. 216 rms, 15 story. S, D $465-$605; each addl $40; suites $605-$3,500; under 18 free; wkend rates. Crib free. Pet accepted, some restrictions. Valet, garage parking $27. TV; cable (premium), VCR avail (movies). Indoor pool; whirlpool, poolside serv. Restaurants 6:30-11:30 pm; Sat to 12:30 am (see also AUJOURD'HUI and BRISTOL LOUNGE). Rm serv 24 hrs. Bar 11-2 am; entertainment. Ck-out 1 pm. Ck-in 3 pm. Convention facilities. Business center. In-rm modem link; 2-line phones. Concierge serv. Gift shop. Exercise rm; sauna. Massage. Overnight valet lndry, 1-hr pressing. Bathrm phones. Minibars. Cr cds: A, D, DS, MC, V.

★★★ **HARBORSIDE HYATT CONFERENCE CENTER AND HOTEL.** *101 Harborside Dr (02128), at Logan Intl Airport, on Boston Harbor.* 617/568-1234; fax 617/567-8856; toll-free 800/233-1234. Email hrbrside@cs.com; *www.bostonhy.com.* 270 rms, 14 story. S $230-$410; D $255-$435; suites $895. Crib free. TV; cable, VCR avail. Indoor pool; whirlpool. Coffee in rms. Restaurant 6 am-11 pm. Bar. Ck-out noon. Conference facilities. Business center. In-rm modem link. Free airport transportation. Exercise equipt; sauna. Refrigerator in suites. Adj to water shuttle. Cr cds: A, C, D, DS, ER, JCB, MC, V.

★★ **HARBORSIDE INN.** *185 State St (02109).* 617/723-7500; fax 617/670-2010. *www.hagopianhotels.com.* 54 rms, 8 story, 2 suites. Mar-Oct: S, D $200; suites $330; each addl $15; under 18 free; lower rates rest of yr. Parking garage. TV; cable (premium). Complimentary continental bkfst. Restaurant 6 am-1 pm. Bar. Ck-out noon, ck-in 3 pm. Fax servs avail. Concierge serv. Dry cleaning. Exercise equipt. Golf, 18 holes. Cr cds: A, D, DS, MC, V.

★★★ **HILTON BACK BAY.** *40 Dalton St (02115), in Back Bay adj to Hynes Convention Center.* 617/236-1100; fax 617/867-6104; toll-free 800/874-0663. *www.hilton.com/hotels/bosbhhf.* 385 rms, 26 story. S $215-$280; D $235-$300; each addl $20; suites $450-$1,000; family rates; package plans. Pet accepted, some restrictions. Garage $17. TV; cable (premium). Indoor pool. Restaurant 7 am-midnight. Bar 5:30 pm-12:30 am. Ck-out noon. Convention facilities. Business center. In-rm modem link. Concierge serv. Gift shop. Exercise equipt. Some balconies. Cr cds: A, C, D, DS, ER, JCB, MC, V.

★★★ **HILTON LOGAN AIRPORT.** *85 Terminal Rd (02128), on grounds of Logan Intl Airport.* 617/569-9300; fax 617/568-6800. 516 rms, 14 story. S $129-$195; D $149-$245; each addl $20; suites $400; family, wkend rates.

Crib free. Pet accepted, some restrictions. TV; cable (premium). Pool; poolside serv, lifeguard. Coffee in rms. Restaurant 5:30 am-10:30 pm. Bar 11-2 am. Ck-out 11 am. Convention facilities. Business center. In-rm modem link. Concierge serv. Free airport transportation. Exercise equipt. Many mini-bars. Cr cds: A, C, D, DS, ER, MC, V.

Swan Boats in Boston's Public Garden

★★ HOLIDAY INN SELECT
BOSTON. *5 Blossom St (02114), at Cambridge St at Government Center. 617/742-7630; fax 617/742-4192; res 800/HOLIDAY.* 303 rms, 14 story. Apr-Nov: S, D $199-$259; each addl $20; under 19 free; wkend rates; higher rates graduation wkends; lower rates rest of yr. Crib free. Garage $20. TV; cable (premium). Pool. Restaurant 6 am-11 pm. Bar. Ck-out noon. Coin lndry. Meeting rms. Business servs avail. In-rm modem link. Valet serv. Exercise equipt. Health club privileges. Overlooks Charles River. Luxury level. Cr cds: A, D, DS, MC, V.

★★★★ LE MERIDIEN BOSTON.
250 Franklin St (02110), in Financial District. 617/451-1900; fax 617/423-2844; toll-free 800/543-4300. Email meridien@lemeridienboston.com; www.lemeridienboston.com. 309 rms, 9 story, 17 suites. May-June, Sep-Oct: S $405; D $435; suites $1400; each addl $30; under 12 free; lower rates rest of yr. Pet accepted, some restrictions. Valet parking avail. Indoor pool, lap pool, whirlpool. TV; cable (premium), VCR avail. Complimentary coffee in rms, newspaper, toll-free calls. Restaurant 7 am-10 pm. 24-hr rm serv. Bar. Ck-out 1 pm, ck-in 3 pm. Conference center, meeting rms. Business center. Bellhops. Concierge serv. Dry cleaning. Gift shop. Exercise rm, sauna. Golf, 18 holes. Tennis, 4 courts. Supervised

children's activities. Cr cds: A, C, D, DS, MC, V.

★★★ LENOX.
710 Boylston St (02116), Copley Square. 617/536-5300; fax 617/266-7905; toll-free 800/225-7676. Email info@lenoxhotel.com; www.lenoxhotel.com. 209 rms, 11 story, 3 suites. Apr-May, Sep-Oct: S, D $308; suites $498; each addl $40; under 17 free; lower rates rest of yr. Crib avail. Valet parking avail. TV; cable, VCR avail. Complimentary newspaper, toll-free calls. Restaurant 5:30-11 pm. Bar. Ck-out noon, ck-in 3 pm. Meeting rms. Business center. Bellhops. Concierge serv. Dry cleaning. Free airport transportation. Exercise equipt. Golf. Tennis. Cr cds: A, C, D, DS, ER, JCB, MC, V.

★★★ OMNI PARKER HOUSE.
60 School St (02108), 1 blk N of Boston Common, Downtown Crossing Area. 617/227-8600; fax 617/742-5729; toll-free 800/843-6664. Email makram@omnihotels.com; www.omnihotels.com. 552 rms, 14 story. June, early Sep-mid-Nov: S, D $109-$205; suites $199-$225; under 18 free; wkend rates; lower rates rest of yr. Crib free. Garage $24. TV; cable (premium), VCR avail. Restaurant (see also PARKER'S) Bar 6:30 am-midnight; entertainment exc Sun. Ck-out noon. Convention facilities. Business servs avail. In-rm modem link. Concierge serv. Gift shop. Health club privileges. Oldest continuously-operating

hotel in the US. Cr cds: A, D, DS, MC, V.

★★★ **RADISSON.** *200 Stuart St (02116), in Theatre District.* 617/482-1800; fax 617/451-2750; res 800/333-3333. www.radisson.com/bostonma. 356 rms, 24 story. Valet parking avail. Indoor pool. TV; cable (premium). Complimentary coffee in rms, newspaper, toll-free calls. Ck-out noon, ck-in 3 pm. Conference center, meeting rms. Business center. Bellhops. Concierge serv. Dry cleaning. Gift shop. Exercise equipt. Golf. Cr cds: A, C, D, DS, ER, JCB, MC, V.

★★★ **REGAL BOSTONIAN.** *Faneuil Hall Marketplace (02109), near Logan Intl Airport, in Faneuil Hall/Quincy Market Area.* 617/523-3600; fax 617/523-2454; res 800/222-8888; toll-free 800/343-0922. Email bostonianhotel@earthlink.net; www.millennium-hotels.com/boston. 201 rms, 7 story. S, D $245-$345; each addl $20; suites $450-$625; under 18 free; wkend rates. Valet parking $24. TV; cable (premium), VCR avail. Complimentary coffee in lobby. Restaurant (see also SEASONS). Rm serv 24 hrs. Bar 2 pm-1 am; entertainment Tues-Sat. Ck-out 3 pm. Meeting rms. Business center. In-rm modem link. Concierge serv. Tennis privileges. Exercise equipt. Health club privileges. Bathrm phones, minibars; some in-rm whirlpools, fireplaces. Many balconies. 1 blk to harbor. Cr cds: A, DS, MC, V.

★★★★ **THE RITZ-CARLTON, BOSTON.** *15 Arlington St (02117), at Newbury St, in Back Bay.* 617/536-5700; fax 617/536-9340; res 800/241-3333. Boasting a great location in the heart of old Boston, this hotel's rooms have pristine views of the public garden, Beacon Hill, or the Charles River and are within walking distance of historic sites, shopping, and the financial district. French provincial furnishings and evening piano music are good examples of the property's old-style grandeur. Service is genuine and continually attentive. 275 rms, 17 story. S, D, suites $435-$725; presidential suite $2,500; each addl $20; under 12 free. Crib free. Pet accepted, some restric-

tions, $30. TV; cable. Restaurants 6:30 am-midnight. Rm serv 24 hrs. Concierge serv. Barber. Airport transportation avail. Exercise equipment; sauna. Bathrm phones. Cr cds: A, DS, MC, V.

★★★ **SEAPORT.** *1 Seaport Ln (02210), E of Downtown Crossing Area.* 617/385-4500; fax 617/385-4001; toll-free 877/seaport. Email info@seaport hotel.com. 427 rms, 18 story. S $240-$315; D $265-$340; each addl $25; suites $500-$1500; under 12 free; package plans. Pet accepted, some restrictions. Valet parking $22; garage parking $18. TV; cable (premium), VCR avail. Complimentary coffee in rms. Restaurant 6:30-11 am, 11:30 am-2 pm, 5:30-11 pm. Bar 11-1 am. Ck-out 1 pm. Convention facilities. Business center. In-rm modem link. Concierge serv. Gift shop. Exercise rm; sauna. Massage. Indoor pool. Bathrm phones, minibars; refrigerators, microwaves, wet bars avail. On harbor. Luxury level. Totally non-smoking. Cr cds: A, C, D, DS, MC, V.

★★ **SUSSE CHALET HOTEL.** *800 Morrissey Blvd (02122), I-93 Exit 12, 3 mi S of Downtown Crossing Area.* 617/287-9100; fax 617/265-9287; toll-free 800/886-0056. Email ctesta@boston hotel.com; www.bostonhotel.com. 174 rms, 3 story, 1 suite. Aug-Oct: S, D $159; suites $215; under 18 free; lower rates rest of yr. Crib avail. Pet accepted. Parking lot. Pool, lifeguard. TV; cable (premium). Complimentary continental bkfst, toll-free calls. Restaurant 6:30 am-10 pm. Bar. Ck-out 11 am, ck-in 2 pm. Meeting rm. Business servs avail. Dry cleaning, coin lndry. Gift shop. Free airport transportation. Exercise privileges. Golf. Picnic facilities. Cr cds: A, C, D, DS, MC, V.

★★★ **SWISSOTEL BOSTON.** *1 Ave de Lafayette (02111), in Financial District.* 617/451-2600; fax 617/451-0054; res 888/-73-swiss; toll-free 800/621-9200. www.swissotel.com. 459 rms, 22 story, 42 suites. Apr-Oct: S, D $379; suites $409; each addl $25; under 16 free; lower rates rest of yr. Crib avail. Pet accepted, some restrictions. Valet parking avail. Indoor pool, lap pool, lifeguard, whirlpool.

TV; cable (premium), VCR avail, CD avail. Complimentary coffee in rms, newspaper. Restaurant 7 am-11 pm. 24-hr rm serv. Bar. Ck-out noon, ck-in 3 pm. Conference center, meeting rms. Business center. Bellhops. Concierge serv. Dry cleaning. Gift shop. Exercise rm, sauna, steam rm. Golf. Cr cds: A, C, D, DS, MC, V.

⬛⬛⬛⬛⬛⬛⬛

★★★ THE TREMONT BOSTON.

275 Tremont St (02116), in Theatre District, 2 blks from Boston Common. 617/426-1400; fax 617/338-7881; res 800/WYNDHAM. 322 rms, 15 story. S, D $144-$250; each addl $10; under 18 free; wkend rates. Crib free. Valet parking $24. TV; cable (premium), VCR. Coffee in rms. Restaurant 6:30 am-11:30 pm. Bar noon-midnight; entertainment Thurs-Sun. Ck-out noon. Convention facilities. Business center. In-rm modem link. Concierge serv. Gift shop. Exercise equipt. Luxury level. Cr cds: A, MC, V.

⬛⬛⬛⬛⬛⬛

★★★ WESTIN COPLEY PLACE HOTEL.

10 Huntington Ave (02116), in Copley Sq, I-90 Copley Sq Exit. 617/262-9600; fax 617/424-7483; toll-free 800/937-8461. www.westin.com. 800 rms, 36 story. S $189-$280; D $219-$310; each addl $25; suites $400-$1,500; under 18 free. Crib free. Pet accepted, some restrictions. TV; cable (premium). Indoor pool; whirlpool. Coffee in rms. Restaurants (see also PALM and TURNER FISHERIES). Rm serv 24 hrs. Entertainment. Ck-out noon. Convention facilities. Business center. In-rm modem link. Concierge serv. Barber. Valet parking $24. Airport transportation. Exercise equipt; sauna. Health club privileges. Minibars. Copley Place shopping gallery across skybridge. Luxury level. Cr cds: A, D, DS, MC, V.

⬛⬛⬛⬛⬛⬛⬛

★★★ XV BEACON.

15 Beacon St (02108). 617/670-1500; fax 617/670-2525. www.xvbeacon.com. 61 rms, 10 story, 2 suites. Apr-Dec: S $395; lower rates rest of yr. Crib avail. Valet parking avail. TV; cable (premium), VCR avail, CD avail. Complimentary full bkfst, newspaper. Restaurant. 24-hr rm serv. Bar. Ck-out noon, ck-in 3 pm. Meeting rm. Business servs avail. Bellhops. Concierge serv. Dry clean-

ing. Exercise privileges. Golf, 18 holes. Tennis, 4 courts. Cr cds: A, C, D, DS, MC, V.

⬛⬛⬛⬛⬛⬛⬛

B&B/Small Inn

★★ NEWBURY GUEST HOUSE.

261 Newbury St (02116), in Back Bay, between Gloucester and Fairfield. 617/437-7666; fax 617/262-4243. www.hagopianhotels.com. 32 rms, 4 story. Mar-Dec: S $85-$130; D $95-$140; each addl $10; under 3 free; higher rates: marathon, graduations. Parking $15. TV; cable. Complimentary continental bkfst. Ck-out noon, ck-in 3 pm. Sitting rm. Built 1882. Cr cds: A, DS, MC, V.

⬛⬛

All Suite

★★★★ THE ELIOT HOTEL.

370 Commonwealth Ave (02215), at Massachusetts Ave, in Back Bay. 617/267-1607; fax 617/536-9114; toll-free - 800/-44ELIOT. Email hoteleliot@aol.com; www.eliothotel.com. This 95-suite property is located in the prestigious Back Bay area of Boston and is convenient to the Hynes Convention Center and various shopping, entertainment, and cultural sites. All suites feature French doors to the bedrooms, Italian marble baths, and down comforters. The hotel, surrounded by lush greenery, is also home to the critically acclaimed Clio restaurant serving contemporary French-American cuisine. 16 rms, 9 story, 79 suites. Apr-June, Sep-Nov: S $395; D $415; suites $415; each addl $20; under 12 free; lower rates rest of yr. Crib avail. Pet accepted. Valet parking avail. TV; cable (DSS), VCR avail, CD avail. Complimentary newspaper, toll-free calls. Restaurant 5:30-10:30 pm. 24-hr rm serv. Bar. Meeting rms. Business center. Bellhops. Concierge serv. Dry cleaning. Exercise privileges. Golf. Bike rentals. Supervised children's activities. Video games. Cr cds: A, D, MC, V.

⬛⬛⬛⬛⬛⬛⬛

Conference Center

★★★ SHERATON BOSTON HOTEL.

39 Dalton St (02199), at Prudential Center, in Back Bay. 617/236-

2000; fax 617/236-1702; res 800/325-3535. Email boston_sales@sheraton. com; www.sheraton.com. 1,181 rms, 29 story. D $189-$269; each addl $20; suites from $260; under 18 free; wkend rates. Crib free. Pet accepted. Garage $23; valet $24. TV; cable (premium). Indoor/outdoor pool; whirlpool. Coffee in rms. Restaurant 6:30-1:30 am. Bars 11:30-2 am; entertainment. Rm serv 24 hrs. Ck-out noon. Convention facilities. Business center. In-rm modem link. Gift shop. Exercise equipt. Luxury level. Cr cds: A, DS, JCB, MC, V.

🅳 🦮 🏊 🛋 🏋 🛏 🔥 🚶

Restaurants

★★★ **AMBROSIA ON HUNTINGTON.** *116 Huntington Ave (02116), in Copley Square. 617/247-2400. www. ambrosiaonhuntington.com.* Specializes in St. Pierre fish imported from France, grilled meats, sushi. Hrs: 11:30 am-2 pm, 5:30-10 pm; Fri to 11 pm; Sat 5-11 pm; Sun 5-9 pm. Closed hols. Lunch $8-$17; dinner $16-$37. Valet parking $7 (dinner). Spacious and elegant atmosphere. Cr cds: A, D, DS, MC, V.

🅳 🛋

★★★ **ANAGO.** *65 Exeter St, in Back Bay. 617/266-6222. www.anagoboston. com.* Specializes in chilled shellfish platter, baked vegetable casserole, fire-roasted chicken. Hrs: 5:30-9:30 pm. Res accepted. Bar. Wine cellar. Dinner $18-$33. Child's menu. Entertainment: jazz Sun. Valet parking. Elegant dining. Cr cds: A, D, MC, V.

🅳

★★ **ANTHONY'S PIER 4.** *140 Northern Ave (02210), E of Downtown Crossing Area, adj to World Trade Center. 617/423-6363. www.pier4.com.* Specializes in smoked salmon, lobster, bouillabaisse. Hrs: 11:30 am-11:30 pm; Sat, Sun from noon. Closed Dec 25. Res accepted. Bar. Lunch $9.95-$26.95; dinner $13.95-$26.95. Parking. Jacket in main dining rm. Nautical decor; view of city and Boston Harbor. Family-owned. Cr cds: A, D, DS, MC, V.

🅳

★★★ **AQUITAINE.** *569 Tremont St (02118). 617/424-8577.* Specializes in steak frittes, duck ravioli. Hrs: 5:30-

10 pm; Thur, Fri to 11 pm, Sat, Sun 10 am-11 pm, Res accepted. Wine, beer. Dinner $18-$24. Brunch $8.95-$12.95. Cr cds: A, D, MC, V.

🅳 🦞

★★★★ **AUJOURD'HUI.** *200 Boylston St. 617/338-4400. www.fshr.com.* Although nominally a French restaurant, this landmark in the Four Seasons Hotel really serves New American cuisine with French and Asian highlights. Appetizers incl Beluga caviar, veal sweetbreads, and duck prosciutto. For the main course, diners can either order a la carte (lobster, grouper, lamb, beef tenderloin, etc.) or opt for one of several awe-inspiring tasting menus. Own baking. Menu changes seasonally. Hrs: 6:30 am-2:30 pm, 5:30-10:30 pm; Sat 7 am-noon, 5:30-10:30 pm; Sun 7-11 am, 6-10:30 pm; Sun brunch 11:30 am-2:00 pm. Res accepted. Bar. Wine cellar. Bkfst a la carte entrees: $15-$20; lunch a la carte entrees: $27-$32; dinner a la carte entrees: $60-$100. Cr cds: A, C, D, DS, ER, MC, V.

🅳 🛋

★★★ **BAY TOWER.** *60 State St (02109), 33rd floor, in Faneuil Hall/Quincy Market Area. 617/723-1666. www.baytower.com.* Specializes in rack of lamb, sauteed Maine lobster, creative French cuisine with a touch of global fusion. Hrs: 5:30-9:30 pm; Fri to 10:30 pm; Sat to 10:15 pm. Closed Sun; Dec 25. Res accepted. Bar. Dinner $22-$36. Parking. Harbor view. Cr cds: A, D, DS, MC, V.

🅳 🛋

★★★ **BIBA.** *272 Boylston St (02116), in Back Bay. 617/426-7878.* Hrs: 11:30 am-2:30 pm, 5:30-9:30 pm; Fri to 10:30 pm; Sat 5:30-10:30 pm; Sun 11:30 am-3 pm, 5:30-9:30 pm. Closed hols. Res accepted. Bar. Lunch a la carte entrees: $8-$16; dinner a la carte entrees: $28-$40. Valet parking. Cr cds: A, D, DS, MC, V.

🅳

★★ **BOB THE CHEF'S.** *604 Columbus Ave (02118), in S End. 617/536-6204. www.bobthechefs.com.* Specializes in chicken and ribs combo, Creole jambalaya, mustard-fried catfish. Hrs: 11:30 am-10 pm; Thurs-Sat to 11 pm; Sun 11 am-9 pm; Sun brunch to 3:30 pm. Closed Mon; hols. Bar. Lunch, dinner $8.95-$13.95. Sun brunch $12.95. Entertainment: jazz Thurs, Fri. Bistro decor; intimate dining. Cr cds: A, DS, MC, V.

★ ★ ★ **BRASSERIE JO.** *120 Huntington Ave. 617-425-3240. www.colonade hotel.com.* Specializes in parisian steak, frites, lobster bouillabisse. Hrs: 6:30 am-11 pm, Sat 7 am-11 pm. Res accepted.Wine list. Lunch $8-$15; dinner $16-$25. Child's menu. Casual, lively atmosphere. Cr cds: A, C, D, DS, MC, V.
D 🍴 ⊒

★ ★ **BRISTOL LOUNGE.** *200 Boylston St. 617/338-4400.* Specializes in tapas, seasonal dishes. Own baking. Hrs: 11 am-10:30 pm. Closed Sat. Res accepted. Bar. Lunch $16-$26; dinner $26-$39. Sun brunch $35. Entertainment: pianist, jazz duo. Valet parking. Art Deco decor with large windows overlooking Boston Gardens and flowered terrace. Cr cds: A, D, DS, MC, V.
⊒

★ ★ **BROWN SUGAR CAFE.** *129 Jersey St (02215), 2 blks S of Fenway Park, near Back Bay. 617/266-2928. www.boston.sidewalk.com.* Specializes in fisherman madness, mango curry, pad Thai country-style. Hrs: 11 am-10 pm; Fri to 11 pm; Sat noon-11 pm; Sun noon-10 pm. Closed Jan 1, July 4, Thanksgiving. Res accepted. Bar. Lunch $5.50-$7; dinner $8-$13. Parking. Thai decor. Cr cds: D, DS, MC, V.
D

★ ★ **CAFE BUDAPEST.** *90 Exeter St. 617/266-1979.* Specializes in veal goulash, cherry soup, chicken paprikash. Own baking. Hrs: noon-3 pm, 5-10:30 pm; Sun 1-9 pm. Closed Jan 1, Dec 25; also wk of July 4. Res accepted. Bar. Lunch $14.50-$16.50; dinner $19.50-$33. Complete meals: $42. Entertainment: violinist, pianist Tues-Sat. Jacket. Original paintings. Old World atmosphere. Family-owned. Cr cds: A, D, DS, MC, V.
D ⊒

★ ★ **CAFE FLEURI.** *250 Franklin St, in Financial District. 617/451-1900. www.lemeridienboston.com.* Specializes in roasted Cornish hen, swordfish

stir-fry, Boston clam chowder. Hrs: 7 am-10 pm; Sat, Sun from 7:30 am; Sun brunch 11 am-4 pm. Res accepted. Bar. Bkfst $10.25-$17.95; lunch $15-$22; dinner $20-$25. Sun brunch $42. Child's menu. Entertainment: jazz Sun. Valet parking. Cr cds: A, D, MC, V.
D

★ ★ ★ **CAFE LOUIS.** *234 Berkley St (02116), in Back Bay. 617/266-4680. www.louis.com.* Specializes in local seafood. Hrs: 11:30 am-10 pm; Mon to 3 pm. Closed Sun; hols. Wine cellar. Lunch a la carte entrees: $9-$17; dinner a la carte entrees: $16-$32. Complete meals: $59. Entertainment: jazz in summer. Free valet parking. Contemporary cafe. Cr cds: A, MC, V.
D

★ **CAFE MARLIAVE.** *10 Bosworth St (02108), in Beacon Hill. 617/423-6340.* Specializes in fresh seafood, beef. Hrs: 11 am-10 pm. Closed Sun; hols. Res accepted. Bar. Lunch $5-$10.50; dinner $9-$22. Parking. Original artwork. Cr cds: A, D, DS, MC, V.
⊒

★ ★ **THE CAPITAL GRILLE.** *359 Newbury St (02115), in Back Bay. 617/262-8900.* Specializes in dry-aged 24-oz Porterhouse steak, broiled lobster, shrimp scampi. Hrs: 5-10 pm; Thurs-Sat to 11 pm. Closed July 4. Res accepted. Bar. Wine cellar. Dinner a la carte entrees: $16.95-$28.95. Valet parking. Cr cds: A, D, DS, MC, V.
D ⊒

★ ★ **CASA ROMERO.** *30 Gloucester St (02117), in Back Bay, enter on alley off Gloucester St. 617/536-4341. www. casaromero.com.* Specializes in marinated pork tenderloin, giant shrimp in cilantro and tomatillos. Hrs: 5-10 pm; Fri, Sat to 11 pm. Closed Jan 1, July 4, Dec 25. Res accepted. Dinner $12-$19.50. Authentic Mexican decor. Family-owned. Cr cds: DS, MC, V.
D

★ ★ **CHARLEY'S.** *284 Newbury St (02115), at Gloucester, in Back Bay. 617/266-3000. www.great-food.com.* Specializes in fresh seafood, baby-back ribs, steaks. Hrs: 11:30 am-11 pm; Fri, Sat 11 am-midnight. Res accepted. Bar. Lunch $5.99-$10.99;

dinner $8.99-$22.95. Child's menu. Renovated Victorian school. Cr cds: A, D, DS, MC, V.

★★ **CIAO BELLA.** *240A Newbury St (02116), at Fairfield, in Back Bay. 617/536-2626. Email dine@ciaobella.com; www.ciaobella.com.* Specializes in veal chops, swordfish chops, seafood. Hrs: 11:30 am-11 pm; Thurs-Sat to 11:45 pm; Sun brunch to 3:30 pm. Closed Thanksgiving, Dec 25. Res accepted. Bar. Lunch a la carte entrees: $6.50-$14.95; dinner a la carte entrees: $8.95-$33.95. Sun brunch $4.95-$11.50. Valet parking (Tues-Sat evening). European decor. Cr cds: A, D, DS, MC, V.

★ **CLAREMONT CAFE.** *535 Columbus Ave (02118), in the S End. 617/247-9001. www.claremontcafe.com.* Specializes in herb-roasted chicken, seafood, tapas. Hrs: 7:30 am-10 pm; Fri to 10:30 pm; Sat 8 am-10:30 pm; Sun brunch 9 am-3 pm. Closed Mon; hols. Bkfst $3.50-$9.95; lunch $4.95-$9.95; dinner $12.95-$21.95. Sun brunch $6.50-$10.95. Valet parking. Corner cafe with artwork by local artists. Cr cds: A, MC, V.

★★★★ **CLIO.** *370 A Commonwealth Ave. 617/536-7200. www.bestbest.com.* Housed in Back Bay's Eliot Hotel, this clubby, intimate dining room offers dramatically prepared, French-American cuisine in an atmosphere of leopard carpets, chocolate walls, and plush sofaseating. Although portions are tiny, flavors are ultracreative and the tasting menu provides a convenient way to sample chef Ken Oringer's over-the-top dishes. Morning hours are making the restaurant a popular power-breakfast hangout. Specializes in seared dayboat scallops, carmelized swordfish au poivre, aromatic glazed short ribs. Hrs: 5:30-10:30 pm. Closed Mon. Res accepted. Bar. Wine list. Bkfst a la carte entrees: $3-$16; dinner a la carte entrees: $22-$34. Valet parking. Cr cds: A, C, D, DS, MC, V.

★★★ **DAVIDE.** *326 Commercial St (02109), in the N End. 617/227-5745. www.davideristorante.com.* Specializes in potato gnocchi, veal chop with fontina and prosciutto. Own pasta, ice cream. Hrs: 11:30 am-11 pm; Sat, Sun 5-11 pm. Bar. Dinner a la carte entrees: $14-$28. Valet parking. Cr cds: A, DS, MC, V.

★★ **DAVIO'S.** *269 Newbury St (02116), in Back Bay. 617/262-4810.* Specializes in veal chops, homemade pasta, pizza. Hrs: 11:30 am-11 pm. Closed Thanksgiving, Dec 25. Res accepted. Bar. Lunch $3.95-$12.95; dinner $3.95-$26.95. Child's menu. Valet parking. Cr cds: A, D, DS, MC, V.

★★★ **THE DINING ROOM.** *15 Arlington St. 617/536-5700. www.ritzcarlton.com.* French menu. Hrs: 5:30-11:30 pm. Closed Mon. Res accepted; required wkends. Wine cellar. Dinner complete meals: 3-course $61, 4-course $69, 5-course $75. Child's menu. Entertainment: pianist. Valet parking. Jacket. Cr cds: A, C, D, DS, MC, V.

★ **DURGIN PARK.** *30 N Market St (02109), in Faneuil Hall/Quincy Market Place. 617/227-2038.* Specializes in prime rib, Indian pudding, strawberry shortcake. Own soups. Hrs: 11:30 am-10 pm; Sun to 9 pm. Closed Dec 25. Bar. Lunch a la carte entrees: $4.95-$16.95; dinner a la carte entrees: $5.95-$16.95. Near Faneuil Hall. Established 1826. Cr cds: A, D, DS, MC, V.

★★ **THE EXCHANGE.** *148 State St (02109), in Faneuil Hall/Quincy Market Area. 617/723-7755. www.exchangebistro.com.* Specializes in tournedos a la Neptune, slow-braised chicken, rack of lamb. Hrs: 11:30 am-2:30 pm; 5:30-10 pm; Sat from 5:30 pm. Closed Sun; also. Res accepted. Bar. Lunch $6-$12; dinner $18-$25. Entertainment: jazz Fri, Sat. Valet parking. Cr cds: A, C, D, DS, MC, V.

★★★ **THE FEDERALIST.** *15 Beacon St. 617/670-2515. www.xvbeacon.com.* Seafood menu. Specializes in red abolone, sirloin steak. Hrs: 7 am-10 pm; Fri, Sat to 10:30 pm. Res accepted. Wine list. Lunch $9-$13; dinner $34-$44. Jackets. 18th century decor. Cr cds: A, C, D, DS, ER, JCB, MC, V.

★ ★ **FILIPPO.** *283 Causeway St (02114), in N End.* 617/742-4143. Specializes in cappello del Contadino. Hrs: 11:30 am-10 pm; Sun from noon. Closed Thanksgiving, Dec 25. Res accepted. Bar. Wine list. Lunch $5.50-$8.50; dinner $12.95-$28.50. Child's menu. Valet parking. Italian decor with large murals. Cr cds: A, MC, V.

D ⊒

★ ★ **GALLERIA ITALIANO.** *177 Tremont St (02111), in Theatre District.* 617/423-2092. Menu changes bi-monthly. Hrs: 11 am-10 pm; Mon to 2:30; Fri to 11 pm; Sat 5:30-11 pm. Closed Sun; hols. Res accepted. Wine, beer. Lunch, dinner $19-$28. Entertainment: italian music Sun. Street parking. Classic trattoria decor. Cr cds: A, D, DS, MC, V.

D

★ ★ ★ **GINZA.** *16 Hudson St (02111), Downtown Crossing Area.* 617/338-2261. www.bostondine.com. Specializes in maki special, sushi. Hrs: 11:30-4 am. Res accepted. Wine, beer. Lunch $7.50-$11.75; dinner $12.50-$38.50. Upscale Japanese dining with sushi bar. Cr cds: A, D, MC, V.

D

★ **GRAND CHAU-CHOWS.** *45 Beach St (02111).* 617/292-5166. Specializes in seafood. Hrs: 10-3 am; Fri, Sat to 4 am. Res accepted. Wine, beer. Lunch $4.25-$4.95; dinner $4.95-$19.95. Entertainment. Cr cds: A, DS, MC, V.

D

★ ★ ★ ★ **GRILL 23.** *161 Berkeley St (02116), at Stuart, in Back Bay.* 617/542-2255. www.grill23.com. The grand space of this 5,000 sq-ft restaurant alone will thrill visitors with its Corinthian columns, sensual lighting, rich mahogany, and vaulted ceilings. The food is also engaging, focusing on prime, dry-aged beef and creatively prepared seafood incorporating market-fresh fruits and vegetables. The restaurant is housed in the historic, 75-year old Salada Tea Building. Menu changes wkly. Hrs: 5:30-10:30 pm; Fri, Sat to 11 pm. Closed . Res accepted. Bar. Dinner a la carte entrees: $18.75-$29.75. Valet parking. Cr cds: A, D, DS, MC, V.

D ⊒

★ ★ ★ ★ **HAMERSLEY'S BISTRO.** *553 Tremont St (02116), in S End.* 617/423-2700. Email bistroham@aol.com; www.hamersleysbistro.com. Nationally recognized chef Gordon Hamersley creates a seasonally changing menu and a pleasant blending of France and New England at his namesake bistro. The dining room is at once classy and comfortable with cozy banquettes, soft yellow walls, and an open kitchen. The menu manages this same great balance with the deliciously simple, specialty roast chicken with garlic, lemon, and parsley. Specializes in crispy duck confit, imported Dover sole, pan-roasted lobster. Hrs: 6-10 pm; Sat, Sun from 5:30 pm. Closed . Bar. Dinner a la carte entrees: $23-$36. Valet parking. Cr cds: A, D, DS, MC, V.

D

★ ★ ★ **HUNGRY I.** *71½ Charles St (02114), Beacon Hill.* 617/227-3524. Specializes in pate maison, venison au poivre. Hrs: 11 am-2 pm, 6-9 pm; Sat from 6 pm; Sun brunch 11 am-2 pm. Closed July 4, Thanksgiving, Dec 25. Res accepted. Lunch, dinner a la carte entrees: $20-$30. Sun brunch $30. 1840s house in historic district. Fireplaces. Cr cds: A, C, D, MC, V.

★ ★ ★ **ICARUS.** *3 Appleton St (02116), in the S End.* 617/426-1790. www.icarusrestaurant.com. Specializes in grilled shrimp with mango and jalapeño sorbet, seared duck breast, game. Hrs: 6-10 pm; Sat to 10:30 pm; Sun 5-9:30 pm. Closed hols. Res accepted; required wkends. Bar. Dinner $19-$29. Prix fixe: $39. Entertainment: jazz Fri. Valet parking. Converted 1860s bldg. Cr cds: A, D, DS, MC, V.

★ ★ **JAE'S CAFE AND GRILL.** *212 Stuart St (02116), in Theatre District.* 617/451-7722. Email jaescafe@aol.com. Specializes in sushi, pad Thai, okdol bibim bab. Hrs: 11 am-10:30 pm; Fri, Sat to 11 pm; Sun noon-10 pm. Bar. Lunch $8.95-$9.95; dinner $7.95-$15.95. Street parking. Cr cds: A, D, DS, MC, V.

D

★ ★ **JIMMY'S HARBORSIDE.** *242 Northern Ave (02210), E of World Trade Center, Financial District.* 617/423-1000. www.jimmyharborside.com. Specializes in shrimp, lobster, broiled

Closed ... ... 1.
Lunch a la carte entrees. $9-$22; dinner a la carte entrees: $10-$32. Child's menu. Valet parking. Nautical decor. Family-owned. Cr cds: A, D, DS, MC, V.

D

★★★ **JULIEN.** *250 Franklin St. 617/451-1900. www.lemeridienboston. com.* Specializes in seafood, lamb, breast of duck. Own baking. Hrs: noon-10 pm; Mon, Sat 6-10 pm. Closed Sun; wk of July 4. Res accepted. Bar. Wine list. Lunch a la carte entrees: $14.50-$18.50. Complete meals: $25; dinner a la carte entrees: $25-$34. Prix fixe: $62. Entertainment: pianist. Valet parking. Jacket. Elegant surroundings; high carved-wood ceilings, crystal chandeliers. Former Federal Reserve Bank Bldg. Cr cds: A, D, DS, MC, V.

★★ **KASHMIR.** *279 Newbury St (02116), in Back Bay. 617/536-1695. www.kashmirfoods.com.* Specializes in tandoori tikki dal, tandoori duck kadahi, tandoori seafood masala. Hrs: 11 am-11 pm. Res accepted. Wine, beer. Lunch buffet: $8.95; dinner a la carte entrees: $12.95-$19.95. Complete meals: $14.95-$39.95. Child's menu. Valet parking. Jacket evenings. Indian artifacts and decor. Cr cds: A, D, MC, V.

★★★★ **L'ESPALIER.** *30 Gloucester St (02115), in Back Bay. 617/262-3023. www.lespalier.com.* Ingredients from local farms and the sea are expertly prepared at this New England-French restaurant housed in an 1886 Back Bay townhouse. The restaurant opened in 1978 and current chef/owner Frank McClelland and his wife, Catherine, took over ten years later. An excellent prix fixe, or more extensive degustation menu, is offered in the main room, salon, or wood-wrapped library. Specializes in grilled beef short ribs with black bean mango salsa, ragout of dayboat wolf fish, pan-roasted free-range chicken in tamarind orange glaze with radishes. Own baking. Hrs: 6-10 pm. Closed Sun; hols. Res accepted. Dinner prix fixe: $68. Cr cds: A, C, D, DS, MC, V.

D

★★ **LALA ROKH.** *97 Mt Vernon St (02108), Beacon Hill. 617/720-5511.* Specializes in authentic Persian dishes. Own baking. Hrs: 5:30-10 pm. Closed hols. Res accepted. Wine. Dinner $14-$17. Several dining areas with authentic decor; Iranian art. Cr cds: A, D, DS, MC, V.

D

★★ **LES ZYGOMATES.** *129 S St (02111). 617/542-5108. www.winebar. com.* French menu. Specializes in steak au poive, scallops. Hrs: 11:30 am-10:30 pm; Fri, Sat to 11 pm. Closed Sun. Res accepted. Wine, beer. Lunch $9-$14; dinner $14-$22. Entertainment: jazz. In Old Leather District. Cr cds: A, D, DS, MC, V.

★★ **LOCKE OBER.** *3 Winter Pl (02108), Downtown Crossing Area. 617/542-1340. www.lockeober.com.* Specializes in Wienerschnitzel, baked lobster Savannah. Hrs: 11:30 am-2 pm, 5:30-10 pm; Sat from 5:30 pm. Closed Sun; . Bar. Lunch $11.50-$20; dinner $22.75-$55. Jacket. Built in 1875. Old World atmosphere. Cr cds: A, D, DS, MC, V.

★★★ **LUCIA.** *415 Hanover St (02113), in N End. 617/523-9148. www.luciarestaurante.com.* Specializes in linguini with seafood, homemade pasta, grilled veal chops. Hrs: 4-11 pm; Fri-Sun from noon. Closed Thanksgiving, Dec 25. Res accepted. Bar. Wine list. Lunch $4-$10; dinner $8.95-$17. Child's menu. Valet parking. Painted frescoes on walls and ceilings. Cr cds: A, MC, V.

★★★ **MAISON ROBERT.** *45 School St (02108), Downtown Crossing Area. 617/227-3370. www.maisonrobert.com.* Specializes in rack of lamb, fresh seafood. Hrs: 11:30 am-9:30 pm; Sat from 5:30 pm. Closed Sun; hols. Res accepted. Bar. Lunch $9-$22; dinner $17-$32. Valet parking. Jacket. Cr cds: A, D, MC, V.

D

★★★ **MAMMA MARIA.** *3 N Sq (02113), in N End. 617/523-0077. www.mammamaria.com.* Menu changes seasonally. Hrs: 5-10 pm; Fri, Sat to 11 pm. Closed hols. Res accepted. Bar. Dinner a la carte entrees: $18-$28. Valet parking. Private dining rms. Overlooks historic area; Paul Revere house across square. Cr cds: A, D, DS, MC, V.

★ ★ ★ **MARCUCCIO'S.** *125 Salem St (02113), in N End.* 617/723-1807. Specializes in sea bass with parsley sauce, calamari with black olive-balsamic sauce, seared scallops with marjoram-walnut pesto. Hrs: 5-10 pm; Fri, Sat to 11 pm. Closed hols. Res accepted. Wine list. Dinner $16-$22. Complete meals: $55-$65. Child's menu. Street parking. Cr cds: MC, V.

★ ★ ★ **METROPOLIS CAFE.** *584 Tremont St (02118), in S End.* 617/247-2931. Specializes in corn soup, sage and lavender roasted lamb, warm chocolate pudding cake with vanilla ice cream. Own pasta. Hrs: 5:30-10 pm; Fri, Sat to 11 pm; Sat, Sun brunch 9 am-3 pm. Closed Jan 1, Thanksgiving, Dec 25. Res accepted. Bar. Wine list. Dinner $12.95-$18.95. Sun brunch, $3.95-$6.95. Valet parking. Bistro decor with high ceilings, brass tables. Cr cds: A, MC, V.

★ ★ ★ **MISTRAL.** *223 Columbus Ave (02116), in S End.* 617/867-9300. www.mistralbistro.com. Specializes in grilled portobello mushrooms, steamed black mussels, confit of duck, and foie gras in brioche. Hrs: 5:30-11 pm. Closed Thanksgiving, Dec 25. Res accepted. Bar. Dinner $16-$35. Valet parking. Mediterranean garden atmosphere. Cr cds: A, D, DS, MC, V.

★ ★ ★ **MORTON'S OF CHICAGO.** *1 Exeter Plz (02116), at Boylston, in Back Bay.* 617/266-5858. www.mortons.com. Specializes in prime dry-aged beef, fresh seafood. Hrs: 5:30-11 pm; Sun 5-10 pm. Closed . Res accepted. Bar. Dinner a la carte entrees: $18.95-$29.95. Valet parking. Menu recited. Cr cds: A, D, MC, V.

★ ★ ★ ★ **NO. 9 PARK.** *9 Park St (02108).* 617/742-9991. Chef Barbara Lynch creates French and Italian-influenced, American-fusion cuisine at this "in-crowd" hot spot on the Boston Common. Flavors are intense

and assertive, and the cafe and two dining rooms have a noise level to match, heightened by the hard-surfaced terrazzo flooring and dark wood. Beaded lamps and black and white historical photos of the area decorate the otherwise minimalist space. Indian menu. Hrs: 11:30 am-2:30 pm; 5:30-10 pm; Sat from 5:30 pm. Closed Sun; hols. Lunch, dinner $19 -$33. Entertainment. Cr cds: D, DS, MC, V.

★ ★ ★ **THE OAK ROOM.** *138 St. James Ave.* 617/267-5300. www.fairmont.com. Specializes in steak, seafood. Own baking. Hrs: 5:30-10 pm; Fri, Sat to 11 pm. Res accepted. Bar. Dinner a la carte entrees: $18.95-$39.95. Complete meals: $38-$68. Valet parking. Turn-of-the-century decor with carved moldings, crystal chandeliers. Cr cds: A, D, DS, MC, V.

★ ★ **PALM.** *200 Dartmouth St.* 617/867-9292. Specializes in steak, lobster, Italian dishes. Own baking. Hrs: 11:30 am-10:30 pm; Sat 5-11 pm; Sun 5-9:30 pm. Closed hols. Bar. Lunch a la carte entrees: $8-$16. Complete meals: $10-$30; dinner $14-$50. Valet parking. Caricatures of regular clientele on walls. Family-owned since 1926. Cr cds: A, D, DS, MC, V.

★ ★ ★ **PARKER'S.** *60 School St.* 617/227-8600. Specializes in Boston scrod, Boston cream pie. Salad bar. Hrs: 6:30 am-10 pm; Sat, Sun from 7 am. Res accepted. Bar. Bkfst $8-$10; lunch $10-$15; dinner $20-$30. Child's menu. Entertainment: pianist. Valet parking. Cr cds: A, D, DS, MC, V.

★ ★ ★ **PIGNOLI.** *79 Park Plaza (02116), in Back Bay.* 617/338-7500. Hrs: 11:30 am-10 pm; Fri, Sat to 11 pm; Sun from 5:30 pm. Bar. Lunch $8-$16; dinner $11-$32. Patio dining. Cr cds: A, D, DS, MC, V.

★ ★ **PLAZA III KANSAS CITY STEAK.** *101 S Market St (02109), in Faneuil Hall/Quincy Market Area.* 617/720-5570. Specializes in steaks, prime rib, fresh seafood. Hrs: 11 am-10 pm; Fri, Sat to 11 pm; Sun to 9 pm. Res accepted. Lunch, dinner a la carte entrees: $7.50-$28.50. Cr cds: A, D, DS, MC, V.

★★★★ **RADIUS.** *8 High St (02108), Downtown, Dewey Sq.* *617/426-1234.* Specializes in seared Maine scallops, Australian farm-raised loin of lamb, saffron-scented New Zealand langoustines. Hrs: 11 am-2:30 pm, 5:30-10 pm, Fri to 11 pm; Sat 5:30-11 pm. Res recommended. Bar. Lunch $8-$19; dinner $21-$37. Valet parking. Modern French cuisine in a playfully sophisticated setting. Private dining room; semiprivate dining, tasting table. Cr cds: C, D, MC, V.

Sailboats on the Charles River, Boston

★★ **RISTORANTE TOSCANO.** *47 Charles St (02114), Beacon Hill.* *617/723-4090.* Specializes in veal, fish, pasta. Hrs: 5:30-9:30 pm; Sun to 9 pm. Closed hols. Res accepted. Bar. Dinner $18-$30. Valet parking. Authentic Italian decor. Cr cds: A, MC, V.

★★★★ **ROWES WHARF.** *70 Rowes Wharf.* *617/439-3995.* *www.bhh.com.* Located in the Boston Harbor Hotel, this dining room has a splendid, har-

bor view and a daily changing, New England-style menu. Chef David Bruce's creative, seasonal dishes might incl fricassee of lobster and chorizo with sweet corn pudding. The dining room has a nautical touch but is anything but rustic with rich wood paneling, royal blue upholstered chairs, and fresh flowers. Specializes in roast rack of Vermont lamb, Maine lobster sausage over lemon pasta, seared yellowfin tuna. Own baking. Hrs: 6:30 am-10 pm; Sat 5:30-10 pm; Sun brunch 10:30 am-2 pm, 5:30-9 pm. Res accepted. Wine cellar. Bkfst a la carte entrees: $6-$11; lunch a la carte entrees: $11-$19; dinner a la carte entrees: $28-$38. Sun brunch $21-$47. Child's menu. Valet parking. Cr cds: A, D, DS, MC, V.

★★★ **SAGE.** *69 Prince St (02113).* *617/248-8814.* *www.restaurantsage. com.* Hrs: 5:30-10:30 pm. Closed Sun.. Res accepted. Dinner $16-$25. Garage. Menu changes monthly. Cr cds: A, D, DS, MC, V.

★★★ **SALTS.** *798 Main St (02139).* *617/876-8444.* *www.salts.netrelief.com.* Specializes in roast rabbit, duck with lavender, halibut. Hrs: 5:30-10 pm. Closed Sun, Mon. Dinner $15-$25. Cr cds: D, MC, V.

★★★ **SEASONS.** *Faneuil Hall Market Place.* *617/523-3600.* Specializes in roast duckling, seasonal dishes. Own baking, pasta. Hrs: 6:30 am-10 pm; Sat, Sun 7 am-11 pm. Res accepted. Bar. Extensive wine list. Bkfst $8-$16; lunch $10-$24; dinner $26-$37. Child's menu. Valet parking. Rooftop restaurant overlooks Faneuil Hall and city. Cr cds: A, D, DS, MC, V.

★★★ **SEL DE LA TERRE.** *255 State St (02109).* *617/720-1300.* *www. eseated.com.* Specializes in grilled pepped sirloin, bouillabaisse of day-boat monkfish. Hrs: 11:30 am-10:30 pm. Res accepted. Wine list. Lunch $7-$14; dinner $8-$21. Child's menu. Garage. Cr cds: A, D, MC, V.

★★ **TAPEO.** *266 Newbury St (02116), in Back Bay.* *617/267-4799.* *www.tapeo.com.* Specializes in tapas, paellas. Hrs: 5:30-10:30 pm; Thurs,

Fri to 11:30 pm; Sat noon-11:30 pm; Sun noon-10:30 pm. Closed Thanksgiving, Dec 24, 25. Res accepted. Bar. Lunch a la carte entrees: $2.50-$7.50; dinner a la carte entrees: $17-$22. Valet parking. Spanish decor; hand-painted tile tapas bar, fireplaces. Cr cds: A, D, MC, V.

D

★★ **TATSUKICHI.** *189 State St (02109), in Faneuil Hall/Quincy Market Area.* 617/720-2468. Specializes in kushiage, shabu shabu, sukiyaki. Hrs: 11:45 am-2:30 pm, 5-10 pm. Closed Sun; also July 4, Thanksgiving, Dec 25. Res accepted. Bar. Lunch $7-$10; dinner $14-$22. Street parking. Cr cds: A, D, DS, MC, V.

D

★ **TERRAMIA.** *98 Salem St (02113), in the N End.* 617/523-3112. Specializes in Maine lobster fritter, open-face seafood ravioli, roasted pork tenderloin in spicy prune sauce. Hrs: 5-10 pm; Fri to 10:30 pm; Sat 4-10:30 pm; Sun 1-10 pm. Closed hols. Res accepted. Wine, beer. Dinner $10.50-$27. Child's menu. Street parking. Cr cds: A, D, DS, MC, V.

D

★★★ **TOP OF THE HUB.** *800 Boylston St (02199), at top of Prudential Bldg, in Back Bay.* 617/536-1775. *www.topofthehub.com.* Hrs: 11:30-2 am, Sun-Wed to 1 am. Closed Dec 25. Res accepted. Bar. Wine list. Lunch a la carte entrees: $6-$15; dinner a la carte entrees: $18-$30. Entertainment: jazz. Panoramic view of Charles River and downtown Boston. Cr cds: A, C, D, DS, MC, V.

D

★★★ **TORCH.** *26 Charles St. (02114).* 617/723-5939. *www.boston torch.com.* Specializes in hanger seared steak, seared foie gras with green apple and juniper. Hrs: Tue-Sun 5-10 pm. Closed Mon. Res recommended. Beer, wine. Dinner $17-$26. Casual. Chef-owned. Cr cds: A, D, DS, ER, JCB, MC, V.

D

★ **TRATTORIA IL PANINO.** *120 S Market (02109), in Faneuil Hall/Quincy Market Area.* 617/573-9700. *www.go boston/ilpanino.* Specializes in zuppe

de pesce, il panino sandwich, lobster ravioli. Hrs: 11:30 am-10 pm; Fri, Sat to 11 pm. Closed Dec 25. Res accepted. Bar. Lunch $7.95-$13.95; dinner $10.95-$23.95. Entertainment: jazz, blues Thurs-Sat. Street parking. Entertainment. Cr cds: A, D, DS, MC, V.

D

★★ **TRUC.** *560 Tremont (02118), in the S End.* 617/338-8070. Email truc-boston@aol.com. Specializes in country French cuisine. Hrs: 6-10 pm. Closed Sun, Mon; also hols. Res accepted. Wine, beer. Dinner $19-$23. Valet parking. Cr cds: C, MC, V.

★★ **TURNER FISHERIES.** *10 Huntington Ave.* 617/424-7425. *www.westin.com.* Specializes in clam chowder, crab cakes, Oriental bamboo steamer basket. Hrs: 11 am-10:30 pm; Sun brunch to 2:30 pm. Res accepted. Bar. Lunch $9-$15; dinner $17-$27. Sun brunch $28.50. Child's menu. Entertainment: jazz Tues-Sat. Valet parking. Cr cds: A, D, DS, MC, V.

D

★★ **VAULT.** *105 Water St (02109), in Faneuil Hall/Quincy Market Area.* 617/292-9966. *www.gotoboston.com.* Specializes in pulled pork with jalapeño corn bread, steamed Maine lobster, steak and potatoes. Hrs: 11:30 am-10:30 pm; Thurs, Fri to 11 pm; Sat from 5:30 pm. Closed Sun; also July 4, Thanksgiving, Dec 25. Res accepted. Bar. Lunch, dinner a la carte entrees: $15-$29. Street parking. Cr cds: A, D, DS, MC, V.

★★ **WHITE STAR TAVERN.** *565 Boylston St (02116), in Back Bay, opp Hancock Bldg.* 617/536-4477. Hrs: 10:30 am-midnight; Sun from 10 am; Sun brunch 11 am-3 pm. Closed Thanksgiving, Dec 25. Bar. Lunch a la carte entrees: $4.95-$9.95; dinner a la carte entrees: $8.95-$15.95. Sun brunch $9.95. Colorful interior. Cr cds: A, C, D, DS, MC, V.

D

★★ **YE OLDE UNION OYSTER HOUSE.** *41 Union St (02108), in Faneuil Hall/Quincy Market Area.* 617/227-2750. Email uoh@unionshore.net; www.unionoysterhouse.com. Specializes in shore dinners, seafood platters. Hrs: 11 am-10 pm; Sun brunch 11 am-3 pm. Closed Thanksgiving, Dec 25. Res accepted. Bar. Lunch $7-$16; dinner $14.95-$25. Sun brunch $9.95. Child's menu. Valet parking. Historic oyster bar established 1826; originally a silk and dry goods shop (1742). Family-owned. Cr cds: A, D, DS, MC, V.

★ **ZUMA'S TEX-MEX CAFE.** *7 N Market St (02109), in Faneuil Hall/ Quincy Market Area. 617/367-9114.* Specializes in fajitas, enchiladas, neon margaritas. Hrs: 11:30 am-1 am; Sat to 2 am; Sun noon-10 pm. Closed Dec 25. Bar. Lunch $5-$12; dinner $5-$12. Cr cds: A, D, DS, MC, V.

Unrated Dining Spots

CAFFE VITTORIA. *294 Hanover St (02113). 617/227-7606.* Specializes in coffee, pastries. Hrs: 8 am-midnight. Res accepted. Wine, beer. Entertainment. Cr cds: A, MC, V.

RUBIN'S KOSHER DELICATESSEN. *500 Harvard St (02446), W on Beacon St. 617/731-8787.* Hrs: 9 am-8:30 pm; Fri 7 am-3 pm; Sun 8 am-8 pm. Closed Sat; Jewish hols. Lunch $3.50-$12; dinner $6.50-$15. Entertainment. Parking. Family-owned. Cr cds: C, DS, MC, V.

Bourne (Cape Cod)

See also Buzzards Bay, Sandwich

Settled 1627 **Pop** 16,064 **Elev** 19 ft
Area code 508 **Zip** 02532
Web www.capecodchamber.org
Information Cape Cod Chamber of Commerce, US 6 & MA 132, PO Box 790, Hyannis 02601-0790; 508/362-3225 or 888/33-CAPECOD

Named for Jonathan Bourne, a successful whaling merchant, this town has had a variety of industries since its founding. Originally a center for herring fishing, the town turned to manufacturing stoves, kettles, and later, freight cars. Bourne's current prosperity is derived from cranberries and tourism.

What to See and Do

Aptucxet Trading Post. A replica of a 1627 trading post, which may have been the first of its kind in America. Native American artifacts; rune stone believed to be proof of visits to the area by the Phoenicians in 400 B.C.; artifacts in 2 rms. On grounds are herb garden, site of original spring, saltworks; Railroad station built for President Grover Cleveland for use at his Gray Gables home, his summer White House; Dutch-style windmill; picnic area adj to Cape Cod Canal. (July-Aug, daily; last 2 wkends May and June and Sep-mid-Oct, Tues-Sun) 24 Aptucxet Rd, off Shore Rd, ½ mi W of Bourne Bridge. Phone 508/759-9487. ¢

Bourne Scenic Park. Swimming pool, bathhouse; playground, picnicking, bike trails, recreation bldg, camping (fee), store. (Apr-Oct, daily) North bank of Cape Cod Canal. Phone 508/759-7873.

Industrial tour. Pairpoint Crystal Co. (est 1837) Handmade lead crystal ware, glassblowing demonstrations. Viewing (Mon-Fri). Store (daily). 851 Sandwich Rd (MA 6A), in Sagamore. Phone 508/888-2344. **FREE**

Braintree (C-6)

Settled 1634 **Pop** 33,836 **Elev** 90 ft
Area code 781 **Zip** 02184
Web www.southshorechamber.org
Information S Shore Chamber of Commerce, 36 Miller Stile Rd, Quincy 02169; 781/479-1111

What to See and Do

Abigail Adams House. Birthplace of Abigail Smith Adams (1744), daughter of a local clergyman, wife of President John Adams, mother of President John Quincy Adams. Period furnishings. (July-Labor Day, Tues-Sun) North & Norton Sts, 2 mi E in Weymouth. Phone 781/335-1849. ¢¢

General Sylvanus Thayer Birthplace.
(1720) Thayer, a soldier and educator, served as fifth Superintendent of
West Point, 1817-33. House contains
17th- and 18th-century furnishings,
military exhibits, and local historical
displays. (Mid-Apr-mid-Oct, Sat and
Sun afternoons, also by appt) 786
Washington St. Phone 781/848-1640.
¢¢ Adj is a

Reconstructed 18th-Century Barn.
Houses farm equipment, ice cutting and wood tools; costumes;
research library and genealogical
records. (Mon-Fri; also by appt)
FREE

Motels/Motor Lodges

★★ **DAYS INN BRAINTREE-
BOSTON.** *190 Wood Rd (02184), MA
128 Exit 6. 781/848-1260; fax 781/
848-9799; res 800/329-7466; toll-free
800/348-4667. Email daysbrtree@aol.
com.* 103 rms, 3 story. S $65-$80; D
$75-$90; each addl $5; suites $150-
$200; under 18 free. Crib free. Pet
accepted, some restrictions. TV; cable
(premium). Complimentary continental bkfst. Restaurant nearby. Ck-
out 11 am. Meeting rm. Business
servs avail. Valet serv. Microwaves
avail. Boston tours. Cr cds: A, DS,
MC, V.
D 🔧 ☒ 🖐 SC

★★ **HOLIDAY INN RANDOLPH.**
*1374 N Main St (02368), ¼ mi from
MA 128, Exit 5A. 781/961-1000; fax
781/963-0089; res 800/HOLIDAY.
Email hirandolph@aol.com.* 158 rms, 4
story, 1 suite. July-Oct: S $149; lower
rates rest of yr. Crib avail, fee. Parking lot. Pool. TV; cable (premium).
Restaurant 7 am-8 pm. Bar. Ck-out
noon. Meeting rms. Business servs
avail. Bellhops. Coin lndry. Golf. Cr
cds: A, D, DS, MC, V.
D 🛠 ☒ 🖐 ☒ 🔧

★★★ **SHERATON BRAINTREE
HOTEL.** *37 Forbes Rd (02184), at MA
128 Exit 6. 781/848-0600; fax 781/
843-9492; res 800/325-3535. www.
sheraton.com/braintree.* 376 rms, 2-6
story. S, D $149-$209; each addl $15;
suites $189-$395; under 18 free;
wkend rates. Crib free. TV; cable (premium). 2 pools, 1 indoor. Restaurant
6:30 am-11 pm. Bar; entertainment
Tues-Sat. Ck-out noon. Meeting rms.

In-rm modem link. Bellhops.
Concierge serv. Sundries. Gift shop.
Exercise rm; steam rm, sauna. Some
bathrm phones. Cr cds: A, D, DS,
MC, V.
D 🔧 🖐 ☒ 🖐 SC

Hotel

★★ **HOLIDAY INN EXPRESS.** *909
Hingham St (02370), approx 10 mi S of
MA 93 on MA 3, Exit 14. 781/871-
5660; fax 781/871-7255; res 800/HOL-
IDAY. www.hiexpress.com/rocklandma.*
68 rms, 2 story, 8 suites. May-Nov: S,
D $114; suites $135; each addl $12;
children $12; lower rates rest of yr.
Crib avail. Pet accepted, fee. Parking
lot. TV; cable (DSS). Complimentary
continental bkfst, newspaper, toll-
free calls. Restaurant nearby. Ck-out
11 am, ck-in 3 pm. Meeting rm. Business center. Dry cleaning, coin lndry.
Exercise privileges. Golf. Video
games. Cr cds: A, C, D, DS, MC, V.
D 🔧 🖐 🖐 🔧 ☒ 🖐 SC 🔧

Restaurant

★★ **CAFFE BELLA.** *19 Warren St
(MA 139) (02368), 3 mi S on MA 28.
781/961-7729.* Specializes in grilled
meats and seafood. Own baking,
pasta. Menu changes seasonally. Hrs:
5-10 pm. Closed Sun; July 4, Thanksgiving, Dec 25. Bar. Dinner $12.50-
$27.50. Mediterranean decor. Cr cds:
A, C, D, ER, MC, V.
D

Brewster (Cape Cod)

Settled 1656 **Pop** 8,440 **Elev** 39 ft
Area code 508 **Zip** 02631
Web www.capecodchamber.org

Information Cape Cod Chamber of
Commerce, US 6 & MA 132, PO Box
790, Hyannis 02601-0790; 508/362-
3225 or 888/33-CAPECOD

What to See and Do

**Cape Cod Museum of Natural His-
tory.** Exhibits on wildlife and ecology
of the area; art exhibits; library; lectures; films; nature trails; field walks;

trips to Monomoy Island. Gift shop. (Daily; closed hols) MA 6A, West Brewster. Phone 508/896-3867 or 800/479-3867. ¢¢

✪ **New England Fire and History Museum.** This 6-bldg complex houses an extensive collection of fire-fighting equipment and incl the Arthur Fiedler Memorial Fire Collection; diorama of Chicago fire of 1871; engines dating from the Revolution to the 1930s; world's only 1929 Mercedes Benz fire engine; life-size reproduction of Ben Franklin's firehouse; 19th-century blacksmith shop; largest apothecary shop in the country, containing 664 gold-leaf bottles of medicine; medicinal herb gardens; library; films; theater performances. Guided tours. Picnic area. (Memorial Day wkend-mid-Sep, daily; mid-Sep-Columbus Day, wkends) ½ mi W of MA 137 on MA 6A. Phone 508/896-5711. ¢¢

Nickerson State Park. Swimming, fishing, boating (ramp); bicycling (Cape Cod Rail Trail), picnicking, camping (dump station). Standard fees. 3 mi E, off MA 6A. Phone 508/896-3491. **FREE**

Stoney Brook Mill. Museum upstairs incl historical exhibits, weaving. Corn grinding (July and Aug, Thurs-Sat afternoons). Old Grist Mill in West Brewster, on site of one of first gristmills in America. Phone 508/896-6745. **FREE**

Resort

★★★ **OCEAN EDGE RESORT AND GOLF CLUB.** *2907 Main St (02631), 2½ mi E on MA 6A.* 508/896-9000; *fax 508/896-9123; toll-free 800/343-6074. Email oceanedge@oceanedge.com; www. oceanedge.com.* 2 story. May-Oct: S, D $315; suites $500; lower rates rest of yr. Crib avail, fee. Parking lot. Indoor/outdoor pools, lap pool, children's pool, lifeguard, whirlpool. TV; cable (premium), VCR avail. Complimentary coffee in rms, newspaper. Restaurant 7 am-midnight. Bar. Ck-out 10 am, ck-in 4 pm. Meeting rms. Business center. Bellhops. Concierge serv. Dry cleaning. Gift shop. Exercise privileges, sauna. Golf, 18 holes. Tennis, 11 courts. Beach access. Bike rentals. Supervised children's activities. Hiking trail. Picnic facilities.

Video games. Cr cds: A, C, D, DS, MC, V.

🄳 ⛷ 🏕 🎣 🏊 🚣 🏃 🏌 🔥 🚶

B&Bs/Small Inns

★★★ **BRAMBLE INN.** *2019 Main St (02631), MA 6A.* 508/896-7644; *fax 508/896-9332.* 8 rms, 2 story. No rm phones. Late May-mid-Oct: D $95-$125. Closed Jan-Apr. Children over 8 yrs only. TV in some rms; cable (premium). Complimentary full bkfst. Restaurant (see also BRAMBLE INN). Ck-out 11 am, ck-in 2 pm. Two bldgs (1849-61); many antiques. Intimate, country atmosphere. Cr cds: A, MC, V.

🏖 🔥

★★★ **BREWSTER FARMHOUSE INN.** *716 Main St (02631).* 508/896-3910; *fax 508/896-4232; toll-free 800/892-3910. Email bnbinn@capecod.net.* 5 rms, some rms with shower only, some share bath, 2 story, 1 suite. No rm phones. Late May-Oct: D $110-$175; suite $220; lower rates rest of yr. Children over 16 only. TV; cable (premium). Heated pool; whirlpool. Complimentary full bkfst; afternoon refreshments. Ck-out 11 am, ck-in 3 pm. Business servs avail. Lawn games. Refrigerators. Balconies. Picnic tables. Built 1850; antiques and reproductions. Totally nonsmoking. Cr cds: A, C, D, DS, MC, V.

🏊 🏖 🔥

★★ **CAPTAIN FREEMAN INN.** *15 Breakwater Rd (02631).* 508/896-7481; *fax 508/896-5618; toll-free 800/843-4664. Email visitus@capecod.net; www. captainfreemaninn.com.* 12 rms, 3 story. May-Oct: S $145; D $165; suites $220; each addl $30; lower rates rest of yr. Parking lot. Pool, whirlpool. TV; cable, VCR avail. Complimentary full bkfst, newspaper, toll-free calls. Restaurant nearby. Ck-out 11 am. Meeting rm. Business center. Concierge serv. Gift shop. Free airport transportation. Golf. Tennis. Beach access. Bike rentals. Hiking trail. Cr cds: A, MC, V.

⛷ 🏕 🎣 🏊 🚣 🔥 🚶

★★ **GREYLIN HOUSE.** *2311 Main St (02631).* 508/896-0004; *fax 508/896-0005; toll-free 800/233-6662. Email greylinhouse@earthlink.net; www. capecodtravel.com/greylin.* 5 rms, 2 story. May-Sep: S $85; D $125; lower rates rest of yr. Pet accepted, some restrictions, fee. Parking lot. TV; cable, VCR avail. Complimentary continental bkfst, newspaper, toll-free calls. Restaurant nearby. Ck-out 11 am, ck-in 2 pm. Fax servs avail. Concierge serv. Golf. Cr cds: DS, MC, V.

★★★ **HIGH BREWSTER.** *964 Satucket Rd (02631), W on Main St, L on Stony Brook Rd, L on Satucket Rd. 508/896-3636; fax 508/896-3734; toll-free 800/203-2634.* 3 rms in main house, 2 story, 4 air-cooled kit. cottages. No rm phones in main house. Memorial Day-Labor Day: D $90-$110; kit. cottages $150-$210; under 16 free; wkly rates. Closed Jan-Mar. Crib free. Pet accepted, some restrictions; $25-$50. Complimentary continental bkfst. Restaurant (see also HIGH BREWSTER INN). Ck-out 11 am, ck-in 3 pm. Lawn games. Antiques; library. Situated on 3 acres, house (1738) overlooks Lower Mill Pond. Adj is historic gristmill and herring run. Cr cds: A MC, V.

★★ **INN AT THE EGG.** *1944 Old Kings Hwy (Rte 6A) (02631). 508/896-3123; fax 508/896-6821; toll-free 800/259-8235. innattheegg.com.* 3 rms, 2 story. May-Oct: D $170; lower rates rest of yr. Parking lot. TV; cable (premium). Complimentary full bkfst. Restaurant nearby. Ck-out noon, ck-in 3 pm. Gift shop. Golf. Beach access. Bike rentals. Hiking trail. Cr cds: MC, V.

★★ **ISAIAH CLARK HOUSE.** *1187 Main St (02631), MA 6A. 508/896-2223; fax 508/896-2138; res 800/822-4001. Email innkeeper@isaiahclark. com; www.isaiahclark.com.* 7 rms, 2 story. May-Oct: S $135; D $150; lower rates rest of yr. Parking lot. TV; cable, VCR avail, CD avail. Complimentary full bkfst, coffee in rms, newspaper. Restaurant nearby. Golf. Tennis. Picnic facilities. Cr cds: A, DS, MC, V.

★★ **OLD SEA PINES INN.** *2553 Main St (02631). 508/896-6114; fax 508/896-7387. Email seapines@c4.net; www.oldseapinesinn.com.* 23 rms, 18 with bath, 18 A/C, 3 story. No rm phones. June-Oct: S, D $55-$115;

suite $155; each addl $20; lower rates rest of yr. Children over 8 yrs only exc in family suites. Complimentary full bkfst. . Bkfst in bed avail. Serv bar 2-10 pm. Ck-out 11 am, ck-in 2 pm. Business servs avail. Some fireplaces. Antiques. Founded 1907 as School of Charm and Personality for Young Women. On 3½ acres. Totally nonsmoking. Cr cds: A D, MC, V.

★★ **RUDDY TURNSTONE.** *463 Main St (02631). 508/385-9871; fax 508/385-5696; toll-free 800/654-1995.* 5 rms, 1 with shower only, 2 story, 1 suite. No rm phones. Mid-June-mid-Oct: S, D $95-$120; suite $150; wkends, hols (2-3-day min); lower rates rest of yr. Children over 10 yrs only. Complimentary full bkfst. Ck-out 11 am, ck-in 1 pm. Bellhops. Concierge serv. Lawn games. Picnic tables. Early 19th-century Cape Cod house; antique furnishings. Totally nonsmoking. Cr cds: DS, MC, V.

Restaurants

★★★ **BRAMBLE INN.** *2019 Main St. 508/896-7644.* Specializes in tenderloin of beef, rack of lamb, assorted seafood curry. Own baking. Hrs: 6-9 pm. Res accepted. Dinner complete meals: $42-$52. Parking. Built in 1861; 4 dining areas, incl enclosed porch. Cr cds: A, DS, MC, V.

★★★ **CHILLINGSWORTH.** *2449 Main St (02631), 1 mi E of jct MA 6A and MA 124. 508/896-3640. Email webchill@chillingsworth.com; www. chillingsworth.com.* Specializes in seafood, veal, pheasant. Menu changes daily. Hrs: 2 sittings: 6-7:30 pm and 8-9:30 pm. Closed Dec-Apr. Dinner prix fixe: $65. Cr cds: A, D, DS, MC, V.

★★★ **HIGH BREWSTER INN.** *964 Satucket Rd. 508/896-3636.* Specializes in fresh local seafood, beef, lamb. Hrs: 5:30-10 pm. Closed Mon, Tues; Dec-Mar. Res required. Dinner complete meals: $30-$50. Parking. Intimate atmosphere; 3 dining areas in 1738 structure; low ceilings, open beams, and wide plank floors;

antiques. Colonial bldg and decor. Cr cds: A, MC, V.

★★★ **OLD MANSE INN AND RESTAURANT**. *1861 Main St (02631), MA 6A. 508/896-3149. www.oldmanseinn.com.* Specializes in steamed lobster, braised lamb shank, lemon buttermilk pudding cake. Hrs: 5:30-9:30 pm. Closed Mon; Jan-Apr. Wine list. Dinner $14-$19. Parking. Two dining rms in early 19th-century inn; antiques. Romantic setting. Guest rms avail. Cr cds: A, DS, MC, V.

Brockton (D-6)

Settled 1700 **Pop** 92,788 **Elev** 112 ft
Area code 508
Web www.metrosouthchamber.com
Information Metro *S* Chamber of Commerce, 60 School St, 02301; 508/586-0500

Half of the Union Army in the Civil War marched in Brockton-made shoes. Known as the nation's "shoe capital" until the 20th century, diverse manufacturing and service industries contribute to the city's economic base today. Brockton was home of boxing champions Rocky Marciano and "Marvelous Marvin" Hagler.

What to See and Do

Brockton Historical Society Museums. The Heritage Center, main bldg of the complex, consists of Shoe Museum, Fire Museum, and "The Homestead," an early Brockton shoemaker's home. "The Homestead" features exhibits on Thomas Edison, who electrified the first shoe factory in the world in Brockton in 1883, and former local shoemaker and undefeated world champion boxer, Rocky Marciano. (Sun afternoons or by appt) 216 N Pearl St. Phone 508/583-1039. ¢

Fuller Museum of Art. Permanent exhibits of 19th- and 20th-century American art; children's gallery; changing exhibits; lectures, gallery talks, and tours. Museum (Tues-Sun afternoons; closed hols). 455 Oak St,

on Porter's Pond. Phone 508/588-6000. ¢¢

Annual Event

Brockton Fair. Fairgrounds. Midway, agricultural exhibits, entertainment. Phone 508/586-8000. Early July.

Motel/Motor Lodge

★★ **BEST WESTERN.** *1005 Belmont St (02301), on MA 123 at jct MA 24, opp VA Hospital. 508/588-3333; fax 508/588-3333; res 800/528-1234.* 64 rms, 2 story. S, D $49-$69; each addl $5; under 12 free. Crib free. TV; cable (premium). Pool. Restaurant 7 am-10 pm; Mon-Wed to 9 pm; Sun to noon. Bar 11-1 am; entertainment Thur-Sat. Ck-out noon. Meeting rms. Business servs avail. In-rm modem link. Sundries. Downhill ski 11 mi. Health club privileges. Cr cds: A, D, DS, MC, V.

Hotel

★★ **HOLIDAY INN BOSTON METRO SOUTH.** *195 Westgate Dr (02301), in Westgate Mall at jct MA 24, 27. 508/588-6300; fax 508/580-4384; res 800/361-2116.* 187 rms, 3 story. 3 suites. May-Oct: S, D $109; suites $189; each addl $10; under 17 free; lower rates rest of yr. Crib avail. Parking lot. Indoor pool, whirlpool. TV; cable (premium), VCR avail. Complimentary coffee in rms, newspaper, toll-free calls. Restaurant 6:30 am-8 pm. Bar. Ck-out noon, ck-in 3 pm. Meeting rms. Business servs avail. Bellhops. Dry cleaning, coin lndry. Exercise equipt, sauna. Golf, 18 holes. Tennis, 12 courts. Picnic facilities. Video games. Cr cds: A, D, DS, JCB, MC, V.

Restaurant

★ **CHRISTOS.** *782 Crescent St (02402), adj Eastside Shopping Plaza. 508/588-4200.* Specializes in steak, Greek salads. Hrs: 11 am-11 pm; Thurs-Sat to midnight; Sun from noon. Closed Thanksgiving, Dec 25. Bar. Lunch $2.75-$6.95; dinner $5.95-$10.50. Family-owned. Cr cds: D, DS, MC, V.

Burlington (C-6)

Settled 1641 **Pop** 23,302 **Elev** 218 ft
Area code 781 **Zip** 01803

Motel/Motor Lodge

★★ **COURTYARD BY MARRIOTT.**
240 Mishawum Rd (01801), 5 mi E on
I-95, Exit 36. 781/932-3200; fax
781/935-6163; toll-free 800/321-2211.
121 rms, 3 story. S, D $139-$169;
each addl $5; suites $159-$189; family rates; package plans. Crib avail.
TV; cable (premium). Complimentary
coffee in rms. Restaurant adj 11:30
am-11:30 pm. Bar 5-11 pm. Ck-out 1
pm. Meeting rms. Business servs
avail. In-rm modem link. Valet serv.
Sundries. Coin lndry. Airport, Railroad station transportation. Exercise
equipt. Health club privileges. Pool.
Cr cds: A, C, D, DS, MC, V.

Hotels

★★★ **BOSTON MARRIOTT.** 1 Mall
Rd (01803), MA 128/I-95 Exit 33B.
781/229-6565; fax 781/229-7973; toll-free 800/371-3625. www.marriott.com.
419 rms, 9 story. S, D $159-$189;
suites $250-$400; family rates wkends.
TV; cable (premium). 2 pools, 1
indoor; whirlpool, poolside serv, lifeguard. Restaurant 6 am-10 pm;
wkends from 7 am. Rm serv to midnight. Bar 4 pm-1 am; entertainment. Ck-out noon. Coin lndry.
Convention facilities. Business servs
avail. In-rm modem link. Concierge
serv. Gift shop. Beauty shop. Exercise
equipt; sauna. Massage. Game rm.
Refrigerators avail. Luxury level. Cr
cds: A, C, D, DS, ER, JCB, MC, V.

★★ **HAMPTON INN.** 315
Mishawum Rd (01801), 5 mi E on I-95,
Exit 36. 781/935-7666; fax 781/933-6899. 99 rms, 5 story. May-Oct: S
$189; lower rates rest of yr. Crib
avail, fee. Valet parking avail. TV;
cable (premium). Complimentary
continental bkfst, coffee in rms,
newspaper, toll-free calls. Restaurant.
Ck-out noon, ck-in 3 pm. Business

servs avail. Dry cleaning. Exercise
privileges. Golf. Cr cds: A, C, D, DS,
MC, V.

Conference Center

★★★ **MARRIOTT COPLEY PLACE.**
110 Huntington Ave (02116), in Copley
Sq. 617/236-5800; fax 617/236-5885;
toll-free 800/228-9290. www.marriott.
com/marriott/bosco. 1,100 rms, 38
story, 47 suites. May-Nov: S, D $369;
suites $850; each addl $20; under 17
free; lower rates rest of yr. Crib avail.
Valet parking avail. Indoor pool, lap
pool, whirlpool. TV; cable (premium),
VCR avail. Complimentary coffee in
rms, newspaper. Restaurant 6:30 am-10 pm. 24-hr rm serv. Bar. Ck-out
noon, ck-in 4 pm. Conference center,
meeting rms. Business center. Bellhops. Concierge serv. Dry cleaning.
Gift shop. Exercise rm, sauna, steam
rm. Golf. Tennis. Cr cds: A, C, D, DS,
ER, JCB, MC, V.

Restaurant

★★ **DANDELION INN.** 90 Burlington Mall Rd (01803), I-95 Exit 32B.
781/273-1616. Specializes in fresh
seafood, steak. Salad bar. Hrs: 11:30
am-2:30 pm, 5-10 pm; Sat from 5
pm; Sun 4-9 pm. Closed hols. Res
accepted. Bar. Lunch $5.95-$12.95;
dinner $7.95-$29.95. Child's menu.
Greenhouse decor. Cr cds: A, C, D,
DS, MC, V.

Buzzards Bay (Cape Cod)

Pop 3,250 **Elev** 10 ft **Area code** 508
Zip 02532
Web www.capecodchamber.org

Information Cape Cod Chamber of
Commerce, US 6 & MA 132, PO Box
790, Hyannis 02601-0790; 508/362-3225 or 888/33-CAPECOD

Cape Cod is said to face "four seas":
Buzzards Bay, Nantucket Sound, the
Atlantic Ocean, and Cape Cod Bay.

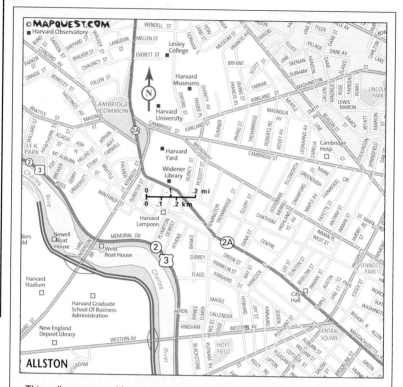

This walk covers roughly a square mile and includes Harvard University's historic yard and art museum, the heart of the lively Harvard Square area, and some major historic sites.

Begin at the Harvard Square T (subway stop), a quick link with downtown Boston. Walk down Brattle Street, past dozens of shops and restaurants and historic sites such as the Blacksmith House (immortalized in Longfellow's poem: "Under a spreading chestnut tree/The village smithy stand's). Spaced out among shops and university buildings are impressive pre-Revolutionary era homes, including the 1759 mansion that served as Washington's headquarters during the siege of Boston (now the Longfellow Historic Site). From the Longfellow Historic Site, the walk cuts through the Harvard Episcopal Campus to Berkley Street and the Cambridge Common with its many monuments, including one to the elm under which Washington took command of his forces. Cross the Common to Massachusetts Avenue and walk through Harvard Yard to the Fogg Art Museum, returning back along Massachusetts Avenue (you've come almost full circle) to the T.

There is a jagged, irregular shoreline here, dotted with hundreds of summer resorts, public and private beaches, yacht clubs, and fishing piers.

The area of Buzzards Bay is at the western entrance to the Cape Cod Canal. Among the better-known towns on the mainland shore are Nonquit and south Yarmouth (see), west of New Bedford; and Fairhaven, Crescent Beach, Mattapoisett, Wareham, and Onset, to the east. On the Cape side are Monument Beach, Pocasset, Silver Beach, West Falmouth, Woods Hole (see), and the string of Elizabeth Islands, which ends with Cuttyhunk.

What to See and Do

Cape Cod Canal Cruises. Cruises with historical narration. Also evening cocktail and entertainment cruises. (June-Oct, daily; May, Sat and Sun) 3 mi W via MA 6, 28, Onset Town Pier. Phone 508/295-3883. ¢¢

Porter Thermometer Museum. The world's only thermometer museum houses an enormous collection of more than 2,700 of these instruments. (Daily) 49 Zarahemla Rd, just E of jct I-495 & I-195, in Onset. Phone 508/295-5504. **FREE**

Motel/Motor Lodge

★ **BAY MOTOR INN.** *223 Main St (02532). 508/759-3989; fax 508/759-3199. Email bmotorinn@capecod.net; www.capecodtravel.com/baymotorinn.* 6 rms, 1 story, 2 suites. June-Sep: S $89; D $99; suites $125; each addl $10; children $10; lower rates rest of yr. Crib avail. Pet accepted, some restrictions, fee. Parking lot. Pool. TV; cable. Complimentary coffee in rms, toll-free calls. Restaurant nearby. Ck-out 11 am, ck-in 3 pm. Fax servs avail. Bellhops. Golf, 18 holes. Tennis, 2 courts. Bike rentals. Cr cds: A, DS, MC, V.

Cambridge

(C-6) *See also Boston*

Settled 1630 **Pop** 95,802 **Elev** 40 ft
Area code 617
Web www.cambcc.org/cambchmbr
Information Chamber of Commerce, 859 Massachusetts Ave, 02139; 617/876-4100

Across the Charles River from Boston, Cambridge is world-famous for its educational institutions, but for the most part it is an industrial city. It is also known as a research center. It was named for Cambridge, England's famous university town.

What to See and Do

The Blacksmith House. (1808) Home of Dexter Pratt, the village blacksmith made famous by Longfellow; now a bakery and coffee shop. (Daily, limited hrs; closed hols) 56 Brattle St. Phone 617/354-3036.

Christ Church. (Episcopal, 1759) The oldest church bldg in Cambridge. It is a fine Georgian Colonial bldg designed by Peter Harrison. It was used as a colonial barracks during the Revolution. (Daily) Zero Garden St at the Common. Phone 617/876-0200. **FREE**

Harvard University. 18,179 students. This magnificent university, America's oldest, was founded in 1636. Two yrs later, when a minister named John Harvard died and left half his estate and his considerable personal library, it was named for him. Incl Harvard and Radcliffe colleges as well as 10 graduate and professional schools. Harvard Yard, as the original campus is called, is tree-shaded and occupied by stately red-brick bldgs. Harvard Square. In and around the yard are

Massachusetts Hall. Oldest bldg (1720) and architectural inspiration for the campus. **FREE**

Widener Library. (1915) Has an enormous Corinthian portico; more than 3,000,000 books. Near it are Houghton, with a fine collection of rare books, and Lamont, the first undergraduate library in America. S side of Harvard Yard. **FREE**

University Hall. (1813-15) Designed by Charles Bulfinch, made of Chelmsford granite in contrast to the surrounding brick, and one of the Yard's most handsome bldgs. **FREE**

Fogg Art Museum. European and American paintings, sculpture, decorative arts, drawings, prints, photographs; changing exhibits. (Daily; closed hols) Free admission Sat mornings. 32 Quincy St. Phone 617/495-9400. ¢¢

Harvard Museum of Natural History. Contains four museums in one bldg, incl Peabody Museum of Archaeology & Ethnology, Museum of Comparative Zoology, Botanical Museum, and Mineralogical & Geological Museum. Exhibits range from pre-Columbian art to dinosaurs, rare gems, and the famous Blaschka glass flowers. Extensive research collections. (Daily; closed hols) 26 Oxford St. Phone 617/495-3045. ¢¢

The Houses of Harvard-Radcliffe. Between Harvard Square and the Charles River and NE of Harvard Yard between Shepard and Linnaean Sts.

John F. Kennedy School of Government. (1978) Contains library, classrooms, public affairs forum for lectures. 79 JFK St, on the banks of the Charles River.

Information Center. Provides maps, brochures. (June-Aug, daily; rest of yr, Mon-Sat) Student-guided tours begin here. 1350 Massachusetts Ave. Phone 617/495-1573.

Longfellow National Historic Site. Georgian-style house built in 1759 was Washington's headquarters during the 1775-76 siege of Boston, and Henry Wadsworth Longfellow's home from 1837 until his death in 1882. Longfellow taught at Harvard and his books are located here. (Daily; closed Jan 1, Thanksgiving, Dec 25) Golden Eagle Passport (see MAKING THE MOST OF YOUR TRIP). 105 Brattle St, ½ mi from Harvard. Phone 617/876-4491. ¢

Massachusetts Institute of Technology. (1861) 9,500 students. One of the greatest science and engineering schools in the world. On the Charles River, the campus incl 135 acres of impressive neoclassic and modern bldgs. Information center in the lobby of the main bldg; guided tours, two departures (Mon-Fri). 77 Massachusetts Ave. Phone 617/253-4795. On campus are

MIT Museum. Collections and exhibits that interpret the Institute's social and educational history, developments in science and technology, and the interplay of technology and art. (Tues-Sun; closed hols) 265 Massachusetts Ave. Phone 617/253-4444. ¢¢ Part of the museum, but in a separate bldg is

Hart Nautical Galleries. Shows ship and marine engineering development through displays of rigged merchant and naval ship models; changing exhibits. (Daily) 77 Massachusetts Ave. **FREE**

List Visual Arts Center at MIT. Changing exhibits of contemporary art. (Sep-June, daily; closed hols) The MIT campus also has an outstanding permanent collection of outdoor sculpture, incl works by Calder, Moore, and Picasso, and significant architecture, incl bldgs by Aalto, Pei, and Saarinen. Walking tour map at information center. Wiesner Bldg, 20 Ames St.

Radcliffe College. (1879) 2,700 women. Coordinate institution with Harvard. Unique women's educational and scholarly resources incl the Arthur and Elizabeth Schlesinger Library on the History of Women in America (at 3 James St). More than 850 major collections of history of women from 1800 to present. Admissions office at 8 Garden St. Phone 617/495-8601.

Motels/Motor Lodges

★★ **BEST WESTERN.** 220 Alewife Brook Pkwy (02138). 617/491-8000; fax 617/491-4932; res 800/491-4914. www.bwhomestead.com/22025.html. 69 rms, 4 story. S $99-$199; D $109-$209; under 19 free. Crib $15. TV; cable (premium). Indoor pool; whirlpool. Complimentary continental bkfst. Restaurant adj 11:30 am-11:30 pm; Sun, Mon to 10:30 pm. Bar to 12:30 am. Ck-out noon. Meeting rm. Business servs avail. In-rm modem link. Health club privileges. Refrigerators avail. Cr cds: A, C, D, DS, ER, JCB, MC, V.

⬚ ⬚ ⬚ SC

★ **HARVARD SQUARE HOTEL.** *110 Mount Auburn St (02138). 617/864-5200; fax 617/864-2409; res 800/458-5886.* 73 rms, 4 story. S, D $99-$199; under 17 free. Crib free. Garage parking $16. TV; cable (premium). Restaurant 7 am-9 pm. Ck-out 11 am. Business servs avail. In-rm modem link. Cr cds: A, C, D, DS, MC, V.

⬚ ⬚ ⬚ SC

★ ★ ★ **THE INN AT HARVARD.** *1201 Massachusetts Ave (02138), 1 blk E of Harvard Sq. 617/491-2222; fax 617/520-3711; res 800/222-8733; toll-free 800/458-5886.* 113 rms, 4 story. S, D $169-$299; suites $250-$550; under 17 free; higher rates commencement. Crib free. Valet parking $20. TV; cable (premium). Complimentary coffee in lobby. Restaurant 6:30-11 pm; Sat, Sun from 7 am. Bar. Ck-out noon. Meeting rms. Business servs avail. In-rm modem link. Bellhops. Concierge serv. Valet serv. Health club privileges. Cr cds: A, DS, MC, V.

⬚ ⬚ ⬚ SC

Hotels

★ ★ ★ **CAMBRIDGE CENTER MARRIOTT.** *2 Cambridge Center (02142). 617/494-6600; fax 617/494-0036; res 800/228-9290.* 431 rms, 26 story. Mar-Aug: S, D $229-$259; suites $400; under 18 free. Crib free. Covered valet parking $18. TV; cable (premium), VCR avail. Pool; whirlpool, poolside serv. Coffee in rms. Restaurant 6:30 am-11 pm. Bar noon-1 am; entertainment. Ck-out noon. Convention facilities. Business center. In-rm modem link. Coin lndry. Shopping arcade. Exercise equipt; sauna. Massage. Health club privileges. Some refrigerators; microwaves avail. Luxury level. Cr cds: A, D, DS, JCB, MC, V.

⬚ ⬚ ⬚ ⬚ ⬚ ⬚

★ ★ ★ **THE CHARLES.** *1 Bennett St (02138), 1 blk S of Harvard Sq. 617/864-1200; fax 617/661-5053; toll-free 800/882-1818. Email reservations@ charleshotel.com; www.charleshotel. com.* 249 rms, 10 story, 44 suites.

Apr-June, Sep-Nov: S, D $500; suites $700; lower rates rest of yr. Crib avail. Pet accepted. Valet parking avail. Indoor pool, lap pool, whirlpool. TV; cable (premium), VCR avail, CD avail. Complimentary newspaper, toll-free calls. Restaurant. 24-hr rm serv. Bar. Ck-out 1 pm, ck-in 3 pm. Meeting rms. Business center. Bellhops. Concierge serv. Dry cleaning. Gift shop. Salon/barber avail. Exercise rm, sauna, steam rm. Golf. Bike rentals. Supervised children's activities. Hiking trail. Picnic facilities. Video games. Cr cds: A, C, D, JCB, MC, V.

⬚ ⬚ ⬚ ⬚ ⬚ ⬚ ⬚ ⬚ SC ⬚

★ ★ **HOLIDAY INN.** *30 Washington St (02143), I-93N Exit Cambridge-Somerville, NE on MA 28. 617/628-1000; fax 617/628-0143; toll-free 800/ 465-4329. Email hisomervil@aol.com.* 184 rms, 9 story. S $145-$185; D $155-$205; each addl $10; under 19 free; wkend rates. Crib free. TV; cable (premium). Indoor pool; whirlpool, lifeguard. Restaurant 6:30 am-noon, 5-10 pm. Bar 11:30-1 am; Fri, Sat to 2 am. Ck-out noon. Coin lndry. Meeting rms. Business servs avail. In-rm modem link. Sundries. Free parking. Exercise rm; sauna. Refrigerators avail. Cr cds: A, C, D, DS, ER, JCB, MC, V.

⬚ ⬚ ⬚ ⬚ ⬚ SC

★ **HOWARD JOHNSON HOTEL.** *777 Memorial Dr (02139). 617/492-7777; fax 617/492-6038; toll-free 800/654-2000.* 201 rms, 16 story. S $90-$185; D $110-$225; each addl $10; under 18 free. Crib free. Pet accepted. TV; cable (premium). 5th-floor indoor pool. Restaurant 7-11 am, 5-10 pm. Bar 4 pm-2 am. Ck-out noon. Meeting rms. Business servs avail. In-rm modem link. Some refrigerators; microwaves avail. Some balconies. On river. Cr cds: A, C, D, DS, ER, JCB, MC, V.

⬚ ⬚ ⬚ ⬚ ⬚ SC

★ ★ ★ **HYATT REGENCY.** *575 Memorial Dr (02139). 617/492-1234; fax 617/491-6906; toll-free 800/233-1234.* 469 rms, 16 story. S, D $159-$270; each addl $25; suites from $450; under 18 free; seasonal, wkend rates. Crib free. Garage $16. TV; cable (premium), VCR avail. Indoor pool; whirlpool. Restaurant 6:30 am-11 pm. Bar 11-1:30 am. Ck-out noon. Convention facilities. Business center. In-rm modem link. Concierge serv. Shopping arcade. Exercise equipt; sauna, steam rm. Refrigerators avail. Private patios, balconies. On river. Luxury level. Cr cds: A, D, DS, JCB, MC, V.

★★★ **ROYAL SONESTA.** *5 Cambridge Pkwy (02142). 617/491-3600; fax 617/806-4232; toll-free 800/766-3782. www.sonesta.com/boston.* 377 rms, 10 story, 23 suites. May-June, Sep-Oct: S, D $279; suites $600; each addl $25; under 17 free; lower rates rest of yr. Crib avail. Valet parking avail. Indoor/outdoor pools, whirlpool. TV; cable (premium), VCR avail. Complimentary newspaper. Restaurant 6:30 am-1 pm. Bar. Ck-out noon, ck-in 3 pm. Conference center, meeting rms. Business center. Bellhops. Concierge serv. Dry cleaning. Gift shop. Exercise equipt, sauna. Golf. Tennis. Video games. Cr cds: A, C, D, DS, ER, JCB, MC, V.

★★★ **SHERATON COMMANDER HOTEL.** *16 Garden St (02138), on Cambridge Common. 617/547-4800; fax 617/868-8322; toll-free 800/325-3535.* 175 rms, 7 story. S $165-$279; D $185-$299; each addl $20; kit. suites $249-$770; under 17 free. Crib free. TV; cable (premium). Coffee in rms. Restaurant 6:30 am-10:30 pm. Bar noon-1 am. Ck-out noon. Meeting rms. Business servs avail. In-rm modem link. Concierge serv. Free parking. Exercise equipt. Some in-rm whirlpools, refrigerators. Cr cds: A, C, D, DS, JCB, MC, V.

B&B/Small Inn

★★★ **A CAMBRIDGE HOUSE BED AND BREAKFAST INN.** *2218 Massachusetts Ave (02140). 617/491-6300; fax 617/868-2848; res 800/232-9989. Email innach@aol.com; www. acambridgehouse.com.* 15 rms, 4 story. Apr-July, Sep-Nov: S $189; D $275; each addl $45; under 6 free; lower rates rest of yr. Parking lot. TV; cable (premium), VCR avail. Complimentary full bkfst, coffee in rms, newspa-

per. Restaurant. Business center. Cr cds: A, D, DS, MC, V.

Restaurants

★★ **BLUE ROOM.** *1 Kendall Sq (02139). 617/494-9034. Email theblue room@aics.net; www.theblueroom.com.* Specializes in multiethnic dishes. Hrs: 5:30-10 pm; Fri, Sat to 11 pm; Sun brunch 11 am-2:30 pm. Closed hols. Res accepted. Bar. Dinner $16-$22. Sun brunch $16.95. Entertainment: pianist. Original artwork from local artists. Cr cds: A, C, D, DS, MC, V.

★★ **BOMBAY CLUB.** *57 JFK St (02138), at Harvard Sq. 617/661-8100. Email sorabh@1x.netcom.com.* Specializes in kebabs, breads. Hrs: 11:30 am-11 pm. Closed Thanksgiving, Dec 25. Res accepted. Bar. Lunch $6.95-$13.95. Buffet: $7.95-$11.95; dinner $6.95-$13.95. Sun brunch, $11.95. Indian art. Cr cds: A, C, D, MC, V.

★★ **CHEZ HENRI.** *1 Shepard St (02138). 617/354-8980.* Specializes in chicken with tarragon vinegar. Hrs: 6-10 pm; Fri, Sat 5:30-11 pm; Sun 5:30-9 pm. Closed Memorial Day, July 4. Bar. Dinner a la carte entrees: $14.95-$21.95. Complete meals: $30. Sun brunch $5-$12. Cr cds: A, D, DS, MC, V.

★★ **COTTONWOOD CAFE.** *1815 Massachusetts Ave (02140), in Porter Exchange Bldg. 617/661-7440.* Specializes in fresh pasta, fresh seafood, seasonal additions. Hrs: 11:45 am-3 pm, 5:30-9:30 pm; Fri, Sat 5:30-10:30 pm; Sun 10:30 am-2:45 pm, 5-9 pm. Closed July 4, Dec 25. Res accepted. Bar. Lunch $4-$9; dinner $11-$20. Parking. Casual atmosphere. Southwestern decor. Cr cds: A, DS, MC, V.

★★ **DALI.** *415 Washington St (02143). 617/661-3254. www.dali restaurant.com.* Specializes in tapas, piedra. Hrs: 5-11 pm. Closed hols Bar. Dinner $14-$22. Street parking. Spanish decor. Cr cds: A, D, MC, V.

★ **GRENDEL'S DEN.** *89 Winthrop St (02138), on Harvard Sq. 617/491-1160.* Specializes in fresh fish, vegetarian dishes, cheese fondue. Salad bar. Hrs: 4 pm-1 am. Closed Thanksgiving, Dec 24, 25. Bar. Dinner a la carte entrees: $5-$12. Casual dining; busy atmosphere. Family-owned since 1971. Cr cds: A, C, D, DS, MC, V.

D ⬥

★ ★ ★ **HARVEST.** *44 Brattle St (02138). 617/868-2255. www.the harvest.com.* Specializes in mustard seed crusted monk fish with crab cakes, grilled porterhouse lamb chops with eggplant and feta cheese custard. Hrs: noon-10:30 pm, Fri, Sat to 11 pm; Sun 11:30 am-10 pm. Res accpeted. Wine list. Lunch $10-$15; dinner $19-$29. Child's menu. Outdoor garden terrace. Cr cds: A, D, DS, MC, V.

D ⬥ ⬥

★ ★ **HELMAND.** *143 1st St (02142). 617/492-4646. www.helmand restaurant.sbweb.switchboard.com.* Specializes in authentic Afghani dishes. Own baking. Hrs: 5-10 pm; Fri, Sat to 11 pm. Closed Jan 1, Thanksgiving, Dec 25. Res accepted. Dinner $9.95-$16.95. Afghani decor with high ceilings. Cr cds: A, MC, V.

D

★ ★ **HENRIETTA'S TABLE.** *1 Bennett St, Harvard Sq. 617/661-5005.* Specializes in New England pot roast, chicken pot pie, fresh fish. Own baking, pasta. Hrs: 6:30-11 am, noon-3 pm, 5:30-10 pm; Fri to 11 pm; Sat 7 am-3 pm, 5:30-11 pm; Sun 7-10:30 am, 5:30-10 pm; Sun brunch noon-3 pm. Res accepted (exc Sat, Sun bkfst). Bar. Bkfst $6.50-$12; lunch $6.50-$12.50; dinner $10.50-$18.50. Sun brunch $32. Child's menu. Windows face courtyard; open kitchen; market on site. Cr cds: A, D, MC, V.

D

★ ★ **LA GROCERIA.** *853 Main St (02139), off Central Sq. 617/876-4162.* Specializes in antipasto. Own pasta. Hrs: 11:30 am-10 pm; Sat 2-10:30 pm; Sun 1-10 pm; early-bird dinner 4-6:30 pm. Closed Jan 1, Thanksgiving, Dec 25. Res accepted. Bar. Lunch $4.95-$8.95; dinner $9.95-$16.95. Child's menu. Valet parking wkends. Family-owned. Cr cds: A, DS, MC, V.

D ⬥

★ **REDBONES.** *55 Chester St (02144), 1 mi N off Massachusetts Ave at Davis Sq. 617/628-2200. www.*

redbonesbbq.com. Specializes in ribs. Hrs: 11 am-10 pm. Closed Thanksgiving, Dec 25. Bar. Lunch $3.95-$7.95; dinner $5.95-$14.95. Street parking. Southwestern decor Cr cds: A, DS, MC, V..

D

★ ★ ★ **RIALTO.** *1 Bennett St, Harvard Sq. 617/661-5050. www.rialto-restaurant.com.* Specializes in grilled sirloin, seasonal game, fresh seafood. Own baking, pasta. Hrs: 5:30-10 pm; Fri, Sat to 11 pm. Closed hols. Res accepted. Bar. Wine list. Dinner $19-$29. Validated parking. 1940s supper club atmosphere; original artwork. Cr cds: A, D, MC, V.

D ⬥

★ ★ ★ **SANDRINE'S.** *8 Holyoke St (02138). 617/497-5300. www.boston sidewalk.com.* Specializes in choucroute, frog legs, tarte flambe. Hrs: 11:30 am-2:30 pm, 5:30-10 pm; Sun, Mon from 5:30 pm; Fri, Sat to 10:30 pm. Res accepted. Bar. Wine list. Lunch $6-$16; dinner $15-$30. Child's menu. Street parking. Classic bistro decor; casual dining. Cr cds: A, MC, V.

D

★ ★ ★ **UPSTAIRS AT THE PUDDING.** *10 Holyoke St (02138), in Harvard Sq, in Hasty Pudding Club. 617/864-1933. www.upstairsatthepudding.com.* Specializes in rack of lamb, hand-rolled pasta. Own desserts. Hrs: 11:30 am-2:30 pm, 6-10 pm; Sun brunch 11 am-2 pm. Closed Dec 25. Bar. Lunch a la carte entrees: $8-$12; dinner a la carte entrees: $16-$30. Sun brunch $8-$14. Terrace dining. Located on 3rd floor of bldg (1885) housing famous Harvard College club, of which 5 Presidents were members; collection of century-old theater posters. Cr cds: A, D, MC, V.

D

Unrated Dining Spots

CREMALDI'S. *31 Putnam Ave (02139). 617/354-7969.* Specializes in pesto, manicotti, veal Marsala. Own pasta, soups. Hrs: 10 am-7 pm. Closed Sun; July 4, Thanksgiving, Dec 25. Lunch $5-$10; dinner $6-$15. Entertainment. Cr cds: A, C, D, DS, MC, V.

D

EAST COAST GRILL. *1271 Cambridge St (02139). 617/491-6568.* Specializes in grilled fish, barbecued beef and pork. Hrs: 5:30-10 pm; Fri, Sat to 10:30 pm. Closed Dec 25. Dinner a la carte entrees: $12-$16. Entertainment. Cr cds: A, DS, MC, V.
[D]

Cape Cod

Web www.capecodchamber.org
Information Cape Cod Chamber of Commerce, US 6 & MA 132, PO Box 790, Hyannis 02601-0790; 508/362-3225 or 888/33-CAPECOD

The popularity of the automobile changed Cape Cod from a group of isolated fishing villages, big estates, and cranberry bogs into one of the world's prime resort areas. The Cape's permanent population of about 201,000 witnesses this change each year with the arrival of nearly a 500,000 summer people.

A great many motels have sprung up since World War II, and cottages line the beaches in some areas. Yet the villages have remained virtually unchanged. The long main streets of villages like Yarmouthport and Brewster are still lined with old houses, some dating from the 17th century. The sea wind still blows across the moors below Truro and the woods of the Sandwich Hills.

The Cape is about 70 miles long and bent like an arm with its fist upraised. Buzzards Bay and the Cape Cod Canal are at the shoulder; Chatham and Nauset beach are at the elbow; and Provincetown is the fist. Since the Cape extends so far out toward the warm Gulf Stream (about 30 miles), its climate is notably gentler than that of the mainland; summers are cooler and winters milder. It has almost 560 miles of coastline, most of which is gleaming beach—the Cape being composed of sand rather than bedrock. As if to please every taste, many towns on the Cape have two coasts—the Nantucket Sound beaches with warm, calm waters; the Atlantic Ocean beaches with colder water and high breakers; or Cape Cod Bay with

cool, calm waters. Inland woods are dotted with 365 clear freshwater ponds, known as kettle ponds.

Surf casting (day and night) and small-boat and deep-sea fishing are major sports along the entire Cape coastline. At least a dozen varieties of game fish are found, incl giant tuna.

The current summer gaiety belies the Cape's hardy pioneer history. It was in Provincetown harbor that the *Mayflower* first set anchor for the winter and the first party of Pilgrims went ashore. Eighteen years earlier, in 1602, Cape Cod was named by the English explorer Bartholomew Gosnold after the great schools of fish he saw in the bay.

The following towns, villages, and special areas on Cape Cod are included in the *Mobil Travel Guide*. For full information on any one of them, see the individual alphabetical listing: Barnstable, Bourne, Brewster, Buzzards Bay, Cape Cod National Seashore, Centerville, Chatham, Dennis, Eastham, Falmouth, Harwich, Hyannis, Orleans, Provincetown, Sandwich, south Yarmouth, Truro and North Truro, Wellfleet, Woods Hole.

Cape Cod National Seashore

This recreation area consists of 44,600 acres, incl submerged lands located offshore along the eastern part of Barnstable County. Headquarters are at south Wellfleet. Exhibits, interpretive programs at the Salt Pond Visitor Center in Eastham (Mid-Feb-Dec, daily; Jan-mid-Feb wkends only), phone 508/255-3421; Province Lands Visitor Center on Race Point Rd in Provincetown (mid-Apr-Nov, daily), phone 508/487-1256. Numerous private homes are within park boundaries. Swimming, lifeguards at designated areas (late June-Labor Day), fishing; hunting, bicycle trails, self-guided nature trails, guided walks, and evening programs in summer. Parking at beaches (fee); free after Labor Day. Buttonbush Trail has Braille trail markers. For further

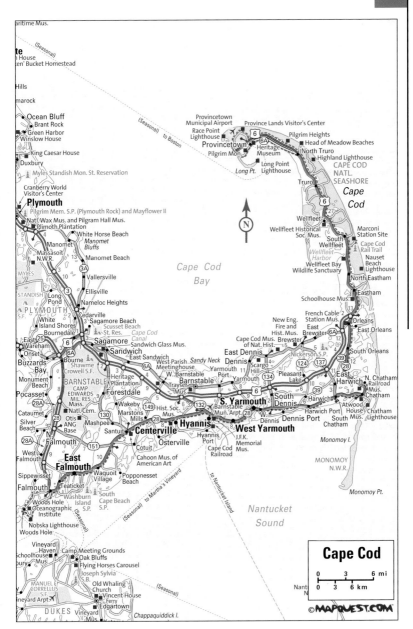

information contact the Superintendent, 99 Marconi Site, Wellfleet 02667; 508/349-3785.

Centerville (Cape Cod)

(E-8) *See also Hyannis*

Pop 9,190 **Elev** 40 ft **Area code** 508 **Zip** 02632
Web www.capecodchamber.org
Information Cape Cod Chamber of Commerce, US 6 & MA 132, PO Box 790, Hyannis 02601-0790; 508/362-3225 or 888/33-CAPECOD

What to See and Do

Centerville Historical Society Museum. Houses 14 exhibition rms interpreting Cape Cod's history, art, industry, and domestic life. Displays incl early American furniture, housewares, quilts, dolls, costumes, Crowell carved birds, Sandwich glass collection, marine rm, tool rm, research library. (June-mid-Sep, Wed-Sun; winter by appt) 513 Main St. Phone 508/775-0331. ¢¢

Osterville Historical Society Museum. Sea captain's house with 18th- and 19th-century furnishings; Sandwich glass, Chinese porcelain, majolica and Staffordshire pottery; doll collection. Special events throughout the summer. Boat-bldg museum, ship models; catboat *Cayugha* is on display. Restored Cammett House (ca 1730) is on grounds. (Mid-June-Sep, Thurs-Sun afternoons; other times by appt) 3 mi SW, at jct West Bay & Parker Rds in Osterville. Phone 508/428-5861. **FREE**

Motels/Motor Lodges

★ **CENTERVILLE CORNERS MOTOR LODGE.** *1338 Craigville Beach Rd (02632). 508/775-7223; fax 508/775-4147; toll-free 800/242-1137. Email ccorners@cape.com; www.center villecorners.com.* 46 rms, 2 story, 2 suites. July-Aug: S, D $130; suites $150; each addl $10; under 15 free; lower rates rest of yr. Crib avail, fee. Pet accepted, some restrictions, fee. Parking lot. Indoor pool, lifeguard. TV; cable. Complimentary continen-

tal bkfst. Restaurant nearby. Ck-out 11 am, ck-in 2 pm. Business center. Sauna. Golf. Tennis. Beach access. Picnic facilities. Cr cds: A, DS, MC, V.

★★ **TRADE WINDS INN.** *780 Craigville Beach Rd (02632), 1 mi E. 508/775-0365; toll-free 877/444-7966. www.twiceapecod.com.* 31 rms, 2 story, 4 suites. July-Aug: S, D $179; suites $215; each addl $10; children $10; under 2 free; lower rates rest of yr. Crib avail, fee. Parking lot. TV; cable. Complimentary continental bkfst. Restaurant nearby. Bar. Ck-out 11 am, ck-in 2 pm. Meeting rm. Fax servs avail. Golf. Tennis. Beach access. Cr cds: A, MC, V.

B&B/Small Inn

★★ **ADAM'S TERRACE GARDENS INN.** *539 Main St. (02632). 508/775-4707; fax 508/775-4707. Email adams terra@capecod.net; www.bedand breakfast.com.* 8 rms, 2 story. June: S $55; D $90; each addl $20; children $20; lower rates rest of yr. TV; cable. Ck-out 11 am, ck-in 3 pm. Meeting rm. Golf. Cr cds: MC, V.

Restaurant

★★★ **REGATTA OF COTUIT.** *4631 Falmouth Rd (02635), 3 mi W on MA 28, E of jct MA 130. 508/428-5715. www.theregattas.com.* Specializes in swordfish with scallion and lemon, lacquered duck, chocolate seduction cake. Own herb garden. Menu changes frequently. Hrs: 5-10 pm. Res accepted. Dinner a la carte entrees: $18-$26. 1790 Federal-style mansion with 8 dining rms; early American decor; fireplaces; many antiques. Cr cds: A, MC, V.
D

Unrated Dining Spot

WIMPY'S SEAFOOD CAFE AND MARKET. *752 Main St (02655), W on MA 28. 508/428-6300.* Specializes in local seafood, clambakes, lamb. Hrs: 11 am-9 pm; Sun brunch 11 am-2 pm; early-bird dinner 4-6 pm; hrs vary off-season. Closed Thanksgiving, Dec 24 (eve), 25. Res accepted. Bar. Lunch $6-$9; dinner $7-$19.95.

Sun brunch $6.95-$10.95. Child's menu. Parking. Indoor atrium; garden and fountain. Fireplaces. Cr cds: D, DS, MC, V.

Chatham (Cape Cod)

Settled 1656 **Pop** 6,579 **Elev** 46 ft
Area code 508 **Zip** 02633
Web www.capecodchamber.org
Information Chamber of Commerce, PO Box 793; 800/715-5567; or the Cape Cod Chamber of Commerce, US 6 & MA 132, PO Box 790, Hyannis 02601-0790; 508/362-3225 or 888/33-CAPECOD

Chatham is among the Cape's fashionable shopping centers. Comfortable estates in the hilly country nearby look out on Pleasant Bay and Nantucket Sound. Monomoy Island, an unattached sand bar, stretches ten miles S into the sea. It was once a haunt of "moon-cussers"—beach pirates who lured vessels aground with false lights and then looted the wrecks.

What to See and Do

Gristmill. 1797. (Daily) Shattuck Place, off Cross St, W shore of Mill Pond in Chase Park. Phone 508/945-5158. **FREE**

Monomoy National Wildlife Refuge. Wilderness area reached from Chatham (access by boat only, special regulations apply). Main St past Chatham Lighthouse, turn left onto Morris Island Rd, follow signs to HQ on Morris Island. Vista of Pleasant Bay, Monomoy Island, and Atlantic Ocean. Surf fishing; more than 250 species of birds. No camping. (Daily) For further information contact Refuge Manager, Great Meadows NWR, Weir Hill Rd, Sudbury 01776. Phone 508/945-0594 or 508/443-4661. **FREE**

Old Atwood House. (1752) Chatham Historical Society. Memorabilia of Joseph C. Lincoln, Cape Cod novelist. Shell collection, murals by Alice Stallknecht, "Portrait of a New England Town." (Mid-June-Sep, Wed-Sat

afternoons; schedule may vary) Stage Harbor Rd, ½ mi off MA 28. Phone 508/945-2493. ¢¢

Railroad Museum. Restored "country Railroaddepot" houses scale models, photographs, Railroadmemorabilia, and relics; restored 1910 New York Central caboose. (Mid-June-mid-Sep, Tues-Sat) Depot Rd, off Main St, MA 28. **Donation**

Seasonal Events

Monomoy Theatre. 776 Main St. Ohio Univ Players in comedies, musicals, dramas, classics. Phone 508/945-1589. Tues-Sat. Late June-late Aug.

Band Concerts. Kate Gould Park. Fri eve. Late June-early Sep.

Motels/Motor Lodges

★ **CHATHAM HIGHLANDER.** *946 Main St (02633). 508/945-9038; fax 508/745-5731. Email highlandl@ capecod.net; www.realmass.com/ highlander.* 28 rms. Late-June-early Sep: S, D $96; wkends (2-day min); hols (3-day min); lower rates rest of yr. Closed Dec-Apr. TV; cable. Complimentary coffee in rms. Restaurant nearby. Ck-out 10:30 am. 2 pools. Refrigerators. Picnic tables. Cr cds: DS, MC, V.
D ⬛ 🔥

★ **THE CHATHAM MOTEL.** *1487 Main St (02633). 508/945-2630; toll-free 800/770-5545. www.chatham motel.com.* 32 rms, 1 story. July-Aug: D $135; suites $165; lower rates rest of yr. Crib avail. Street parking. Pool. TV; cable. Golf. Tennis. Picnic facilities. Cr cds: MC, V.
D 🛆 🔥 🔥 ⬛ 🔥 🔥

★ ★ **CHATHAM TIDES WATERFRONT MOTEL.** *394 Pleasant St (02559), ½ mi S of MA 28 at foot of Pleasant St. 508/432-0374; fax 508/ 432-4289; res 508/432-0379. Email ctides@capecod.net; www.allcapecod. com/chathamtides.* 24 kit. units in motel and townhouses, suites avail. Some A/C. July-Aug: S, D $135-$155; each addl $20; kit. suites, townhouses $1,200-$1,650/wk; lower rates Sep-May. TV; cable. Ck-out 11 am. Some microwaves. Sun decks. On private beach. Cr cds: A, DS, MC, V.
D 🛆 🔥

★★★ DOLPHIN OF CHATHAM INN AND MOTEL. *352 Main St (02633). 508/945-0070; fax 508/945-5945; toll-free 800/688-5900. www.dolphininn.com.* 38 rms, 3 kits. Late June-early Sep: S, D $144-$219; each addl $15; suites $199-$229; kit. units $154; 2-bedrm kit. cottages $1,500/wk; lower rates rest of yr. TV; cable. Heated pool; whirlpool. Coffee in rms. Restaurant 8-11 am. Ck-out 10 am. Business servs avail. Some refrigerators, in-rm whirlpools; microwaves avail. Some private patios. Picnic tables, grills. Cr cds: A, D, DS, MC, V.

Head of the Meadow Beach, Cape Cod National Seashore

★★ THE HAWTHORNE. *196 Shore Rd (02633), off MA 28. 508/945-0372. www.thehawthorne.com.* 26 rms, 1 story. July-Aug: S, D $165; each addl $20; lower rates rest of yr. Parking lot. TV; cable (premium). Restaurant nearby. Ck-out 11 am, ck-in 2 pm. Fax servs avail. Golf. Tennis. Beach access. Picnic facilities. Cr cds: A, MC, V.

★ SEAFARER OF CHATHAM. *2079 Main St (02633), MA 28 and Ridgevale Rd. 508/432-1739; fax 508/432-1739; toll-free 800/786-2772. Email seafarer@capecod.net; www.seafarerofchatham.com.* 20 rms, 1 story. July-Aug: S, D $125; each addl $10; children $10; lower rates rest of yr. Crib avail, fee. Parking lot. TV; cable. Complimentary coffee in rms. Restaurant nearby. Ck-out 11 am, ck-in 2 pm. Fax servs avail. Golf. Tennis, 12 courts. Cr cds: A, MC, V.

Resorts

★★★ CHATHAM BARS INN. *297 Shore Rd (02633), at Seaview St. 508/945-0096; fax 508/945-5491; toll-free 800/527-4884. Email welcome@chathambarsinn.com; www.chathambarsinn.com.* 41 rms in inn, 1-3 story, no elvtr, 28 cottages, 1-12 bedrm. Some A/C. Mid-June-mid-Sep: S, D $190-$410; suites $375-$1,000; lower rates rest of yr. Crib avail. TV; cable, VCR avail (free movies). Heated pool. Free supervised children's activities (Mid-June-Labor Day); ages 4-12. Dining rm 8 am-9 pm. Box lunches, clambakes in season. Bar noon-1 am, entertainment (in season). Ck-out 11 am, ck-in 3 pm. Meeting rms. Business servs avail. In-rm modem link. Bellhops. Valet serv. Concierge serv. Tennis, pro. Putting green. Exercise equipt. Complimentary boat shuttle. Lawn games. Rec rm. Many balconies. Spacious cottages. On 22 acres; private beach. Cr cds: A, DS, MC, V.

★★★ PLEASANT BAY VILLAGE RESORT. *PO Box 772 (02633), 3 mi N on MA 28 in Chathamport. 508/945-1133; fax 508/945-9701; toll-free 800/547-1011. www.pleasantbayvillage.com.* 58 rms, 20 kits., 10 suites (1-2 bedrm). Early June-Aug: S, D, kit. units $215-$245; each addl $15-$20; 1-bedrm suites $355; 2-bedrm suites (2-day min) $395-$415; lower rates mid-May-early June, Sep-mid-Oct. Closed rest of yr. Crib avail. TV; cable. Heated pool; poolside serv. Playground. Restaurant 8-11 am. Ck-out 11 am. Business servs avail. In-rm modem link. Sundries. Lawn games. Refrigerators, microwaves avail. On 6 landscaped acres. Extensive Chinese gardens; waterfall; ornamental pond. Cr cds: A, MC, V.

★★★ WEQUASSETT INN. *on Pleasant Bay (02633), 5 mi NE on MA 28. 508/432-5400; fax 508/432-5032; toll-free 800/225-7125. www.wequassett.*

com. 98 rms, 6 suites, 1 and 2 story. Mid-Apr-mid-Nov: S, D $210-$450; suites $450-$800. Closed rest of yr. Crib free. TV; cable (premium), VCR avail. Heated pool; poolside serv. Supervised children's activities (in season); ages 3-12 yrs. Complimentary coffee in rms. Dining rm 7 am-10 pm. 7 am-11 pm. Ck-out 11 am, ck-in 3 pm. Business center. Valet serv. Gift shop. Airport, bus depot transportation avail. Tennis, pro. Golf privileges. Exercise rm. Massage. Minibars. Some fireplaces. Many private patios, balconies. Private beach. Lawn games; bocce, croquet, shuffleboard. Basketball court, volleyball. Sailboats, windsurfing, deep-sea fishing charters, whale-watching cruises. Cr cds: A, DS, MC, V.

B&Bs/Small Inns

★★★ CAPTAIN'S HOUSE INN. *369 Old Harbor Rd (02633). 508/945-0127; fax 508/945-0866; toll-free 800/315-0728. Email info@captainshouseinn.com; www.captainshouseinn.com.* 17 rms, 2 story, 2 suites. May-Oct: D $200; lower rates rest of yr. Parking lot. TV; cable (premium), VCR avail. Complimentary full bkfst, coffee in rms, newspaper. Restaurant nearby. Ck-out 11 am, ck-in 2 pm. Business center. Concierge serv. Gift shop. Exercise privileges, whirlpool. Golf. Tennis, 2 courts. Beach access. Bike rentals. Hiking trail. Cr cds: A, DS, MC, V.

★★★ CHATHAM TOWN HOUSE INN. *11 Library Ln (02633), in Chatham Center. 508/945-2180; fax 508/945-3990; toll-free 800/242-2180. Email reservations@chathamtownhouse.com; www.chathamtownhouse.com.* 25 rms, 2 story, 2 suites. June-Oct: S, D $350; suites $425; each addl $25; lower rates rest of yr. Crib avail. Parking lot. Pool, whirlpool. TV; cable, VCR avail. Complimentary full bkfst, coffee in rms, newspaper, toll-free calls. Restaurant 5:30-9:30 pm, closed Mon. Bar. Ck-out noon, ck-in 3 pm. Meeting rms. Business center. Concierge serv. Dry cleaning. Salon/barber avail. Exercise privileges. Golf, 9 holes. Tennis, 12 courts. Supervised children's activi-

ties. Picnic facilities. Cr cds: A, C, D, DS, JCB, MC, V.

★★★ CRANBERRY INN. *359 Main St (02633). 508/945-9232; fax 508/945-3769; toll-free 800/332-4667. Email info@cranberryinn.com; www.cranberryinn.com.* 16 rms, 2 story, 2 suites. June-Sep: S, D $230; suites $230; lower rates rest of yr. Parking lot. TV; cable. Complimentary full bkfst, newspaper. Restaurant nearby. Bar. Fax servs avail. Concierge serv. Exercise privileges. Beach access. Bike rentals. Hiking trail. Picnic facilities. Cr cds: A, MC, V.

★★★ MOSES NICKERSON HOUSE INN. *364 Old Harbor Rd (02633). 508/945-5859; fax 508/945-7087; toll-free 800/628-6972. Email tmnhi@mediaone.net; www.capecodtravel.com/mosesnickersonhouse.* 7 rms, 2 story. Late May-mid-Oct: S, D $129-$179; lower rates rest of yr. Children over 14 yrs only. TV avail. Complimentary full bkfst. Restaurant nearby. Ck-out 10:30 am, ck-in 2:30 pm. Lawn games. Antiques. Library/sitting rm. Built 1839. Totally nonsmoking. Cr cds: A, MC, V.

★★ OLD HARBOR INN. *22 Old Harbor Rd (02633). 508/945-4434; fax 508/945-7665; toll-free 800/942-4434. Email brazohi@capecod.net; www.capecod.com/oldharborinn.* 7 rms, 2 story, 1 suite. June-Oct: S, D $259; suites $259; each addl $25; under 12 free; lower rates rest of yr. Parking lot. TV; cable, VCR avail. Complimentary full bkfst, newspaper, toll-free calls. Ck-out 11 am, ck-in 3 pm. Meeting rm. Business center. Concierge serv. Gift shop. Golf, 9 holes. Tennis, 2 courts. Cr cds: MC, V.

★★ PORT FORTUNE INN. *201 Main St (02633). 508/945-0792; res 800/750-0792. Email portfor@capecod.net; www.capecod.net/portfortune.* 13 rms, 2 story. June-Sep: S, D $160; each addl $25; lower rates rest of yr. Parking lot. TV; cable. Complimentary continental bkfst, toll-free calls. Ck-out 11 am, ck-in 2 pm. Fax servs avail. Golf. Tennis. Beach access. Bike rentals. Hiking trail. Cr cds: A, MC, V.

★★★ **QUEEN ANNE INN.** *70 Queen Anne Rd (02633). 508/945-0394; fax 508/945-4884; toll-free 800/545-4667. Email info@queenanneinn.com; www.queenanneinn.com.* 34 rms, 3 story, 4 suites. July-Aug: S, D $189; suites $260; each addl $25; children $25; lower rates rest of yr. Crib avail. Parking lot. Pool, whirlpool. TV; cable, VCR avail, CD avail. Complimentary full bkfst, newspaper, toll-free calls. Restaurant 8 am-11 pm, closed Tue. Bar. Ck-out 11 am, ck-in 2 pm. Concierge serv. Dry cleaning, coin lndry. Exercise privileges. Golf. Tennis, 3 courts. Beach access. Bike rentals. Hiking trail. Cr cds: A, DS, MC, V.

Restaurants

★★ **THE BISTRO.** *595 Main St (02633). 508/945-5033.* Specializes in grilled marinated stuffed chicken breast, pan-roasted cape sea scallops. Hrs: 5:30-10 pm. Wine, beer. Dinner $16.50-$25. Entertainment. Cr cds: A, C, D, MC, V.

★★ **CHATHAM SQUIRE.** *487 Main St (02633). 508/945-0945. Email squire@capecod.net.* Specializes in local seafood. Raw bar. Hrs: 11:30 am-10:30 pm. Bar. Lunch $4.95-$11.95; dinner $9.95-$21.95. Child's menu. Nautical decor. Cr cds: A, DS, MC, V.

★★ **CHRISTIAN'S.** *443 Main St (02633). 508/945-3362. www.christianrestaurant.com.* Specializes in fresh local seafood, homemade meatloaf, oysters. Hrs: 5-10 pm. Bar. Dinner $8-$20. Entertainment: pianist. Two-level dining. Built 1819. Cr cds: A, C, DS, MC, V.

★★ **IMPUDENT OYSTER.** *15 Chatham Bars Ave (02633). 508/945-3545.* Specializes in seafood. Hrs: 11:30 am-3 pm, 5-10 pm. Res required. Bar. Lunch $6.95-$12.95; dinner $14-$23. Child's menu. Cathedral ceilings, stained-glass windows. Cr cds: A, MC, V.

Chicopee

(see Springfield)

Concord

See Lexington, Sudbury Center

Settled 1635 **Pop** 17,076 **Elev** 141 ft
Area code 978 **Zip** 01742
Web www.ultranet.com/~conchamb/

Information Chamber of Commerce, 2 Lexington Rd, in Wright Tavern; 978/369-3042; or visit the Heywood St Information Booth (Apr-Oct)

This town shares with Lexington the title of Birthplace of the Republic. But it was Ralph Waldo Emerson who saw to it that the shot fired "by the rude bridge" was indeed heard 'round the world.

The town's name arose because of the "peace and concord" between the settlers and the Native Americans in the 17th century. The famous Concord grape was developed here in 1849 by Ephraim Bull.

The town of Lincoln, adjoining Concord on the E, was the scene of a running battle with the Redcoats on their withdrawal toward Boston. Here the harassing fire of the Minutemen was perhaps most effective.

What to See and Do

Codman House. (ca 1740) Originally a 2-story, L-shaped Georgian mansion. In 1797-98 it was more than doubled in size by Federal merchant John Codman to imitate an English country residence. Family furnishings. Grounds have many unusual trees and plants; formal Italian garden. (June-mid-Oct, Wed-Sun afternoons) Codman Rd, 5 mi S of MA 2 via Bedford Rd in Lincoln. Phone 781/259-8843. ¢¢

Concord Free Public Library. Modern public library, historical collections of famous Concord authors. On display is a mantelpiece from the US

Capitol (ca 1815). Also statues of Emerson and others by Daniel Chester French. (Nov-May, daily, limited hrs Sun; rest of yr, Mon-Sat) 129 Main St at Sudbury Rd. Phone 978/318-3300. **FREE**

Concord Museum. Where Concord's history begins–*Exploring Concord* film and self-guided *Why Concord?* history galleries; Revolutionary War artifacts, incl Paul Revere's lantern; Ralph Waldo Emerson's study; a gallery dedicated to Henry D. Thoreau incl the desk where he penned *Walden*; Concord-made clocks, silver, and furniture in period room settings. (Daily; closed Easter, Thanksgiving, Dec 25) 200 Lexington Rd. Phone 978/369-9609. ¢¢¢

DeCordova Museum & Sculpture Park. Contemporary art museum on 35 acres of parkland overlooking Flint's Pond; changing exhibits, lectures, films, special events. (Tues-Sun) Concerts in summer (Sun). SE on Sandy Pond Rd in Lincoln. Phone 781/259-8355. ¢¢

Drumlin Farm Education Center. Demonstration farm with domestic and native wild animals and birds; gardens; hayrides; special events. (Tues-Sun and Mon hols; closed Jan 1, Thanksgiving, Dec 25) 2½ mi S on MA 126, then E on MA 117 (S Great Rd) in Lincoln. Phone 781/259-9807. ¢¢

Fruitlands Museums. Four museums, incl the Fruitlands Farmhouse, the scene of Bronson Alcott's experiment in community life, which contains furniture, books, and memorabilia of the Alcott family and the Transcendentalists; Shaker Museum, formerly in the Harvard Shaker Village, with furniture and handicrafts; Picture Gallery, with American primitive portraits and paintings by Hudson River School artists; American Indian Museum, with prehistoric artifacts and Native American art. Hiking trails with views W to Mt Wachusett and N to Mt Monadnock. Tearoom; gift shop. (Mid-May-mid-Oct, Tues-Sun and Mon hols) 102 Prospect Hill Rd. 15 mi W via MA 2, Exit 38A, in Harvard. Phone 978/456-9028. ¢¢¢

Great Meadows National Wildlife Refuge. Nature trails through wetland and upland woodland (daily). More than 200 bird species frequent this diverse habitat area. Nature trails, hiking, cross-country skiing, snowshoeing; canoeing and boating on Sudbury and Concord rivers (no rentals). Concord Unit, Dike Trail; Monsen Rd off MA 62, 1 mi E from Concord Center. Contact Refuge Manager, Weir Hill Rd, Sudbury 01776. Phone 978/443-4661. **FREE**

Gropius House. (1937-38). Family home of architect Walter Gropius. First bldg he designed upon arrival in the US in 1937; blends New England traditions and Bauhaus principles of function and simplicity with New England's bldg materials and environment. Original furniture, artwork. (June-mid-Oct, Fri-Sun afternoons; rest of yr, Sat and Sun 1st full wkend of each month) 68 Baker Bridge Rd, SE in Lincoln. Phone 781/259-8843 or 978/227-3956. ¢¢

Minute Man National Historical Park. North Bridge Unit, Monument St, contains famous Minuteman statue by Daniel Chester French and reconstructed North Bridge over Concord River. Interpretive talks are given. North Bridge Visitor Center at 174 Liberty St has exhibits, rest rms. (Daily; closed Jan 1, Thanksgiving, Dec 25) Battle Road Visitor Center, off MA 2A in Lexington, has exhibit rm, movie, and orientation program. (Mid-May-Oct, daily) Contact Superintendent, 174 Liberty St. Phone 978/369-6993. **FREE**

The Old Manse. (1770) Parsonage of Concord's early ministers, incl Rev William Emerson, Ralph Waldo Emerson's grandfather. Nathaniel Hawthorne lived here for a time and made it the setting for *Mosses from an Old Manse*. Original furnishings. (Mid-Apr-Oct, Mon-Sat, also Sun afternoons) Monument St at the North Bridge. Phone 978/369-3909. ¢¢¢

Orchard House and School of Philosophy. Here Louisa May Alcott wrote *Little Women*. Alcott memorabilia. Guided tours. (Apr-Dec, daily; closed hols, also early-mid-Jan) 399 Lexington Rd. Phone 978/369-4118. ¢¢

Ralph Waldo Emerson House. Ralph Waldo Emerson's home from 1835-82. Original furnishings and family memorabilia; 30-min guided tours. (Mid-Apr-late Oct, Thurs-Sun, limited hrs Sun) 28 Cambridge Tpke, at Lexington Rd (MA 2A). Phone 978/369-2236. ¢¢

Sleepy Hollow Cemetery. The Alcotts, Ralph Waldo Emerson, Nathaniel Hawthorne, Margaret Sidney, Daniel Chester French, and Henry David Thoreau are buried here. Bedford St, NE of square.

⊞ Walden Pond State Reservation. Located in this 304-acre park is a replica of Thoreau's cabin; also trail to cairn that marks site of original cabin. Swimming, fishing; hiking trails, interpretive programs. (All yr, daylight hrs) Standard fees. ½ mi S of MA2 on MA 126. Phone 978/369-3254. Per vehicle ¢

The Wayside. 19th-century authors Nathaniel Hawthorne, the Alcotts, and Margaret Sidney, author of the *Five Little Peppers* books, lived here. Orientation program; 45-min tours (May-Oct) 455 Lexington Rd (MA 2A). Phone 978/369-6975.

Annual Event

Patriots' Day Parade. Events, reenactments. Mon nearest Apr 19 (or Sat if the 19th).

Motel/Motor Lodge

★★ **HOLIDAY INN BOXBOR-OUGH WOODS.** 242 Adams Pl (01719), MA 111 at I-495 Exit 28. 978/263-8701; fax 978/266-9429; res 800/HOLIDAY. Email box_sales@fine-hotels.com. 143 rms, 2-3 story. S, D $119-$139; each addl $10; suites $199; under 18 free. Crib free. TV; cable (premium), VCR avail. Indoor pool. Coffee in rms. Restaurant 6:30 am-11 pm; Sat, Sun from 7 am. Bar 11 am-midnight. Ck-out noon. Meeting rms. Business servs avail. In-rm modem link. Valet serv. Sundries. Downhill/x-country ski 10 mi. Exercise equipt; sauna. Coin lndry. Lawn games. Refrigerators, microwaves avail. Private patios, balconies. Picnic tables. Cr cds: A, D, DS, MC, V.

🄳 🗗 🖛 🏂 🖼 🖄 SC

Hotel

★★ **BEST WESTERN.** 740 Elm St (01742), I-495 Exit 29, 7 mi E on MA 2. 978/369-6100; fax 978/371-1656; res 800/528-1234. Email concordbw1@aol.com; www.bestwestern.com. 106 rms, 2 story. Apr-July, Sep-Oct: S $129; D $139; each addl $10; under 12 free; lower rates rest of yr. Crib

avail. Pet accepted, some restrictions, fee. Parking lot. Pool. TV; cable (premium). Complimentary continental bkfst, newspaper. Restaurant. Ck-out noon, ck-in 2 pm. Business servs avail. Exercise equipt. Golf. Downhill skiing. Cr cds: A, C, D, DS, ER, JCB, MC, V.

🄳 🗗 🖂 🏂 🖛 🏂 🖼 🖄

B&Bs/Small Inns

★★ **COLONIAL INN.** 48 Monument Sq (01742). 978/369-9200; fax 978/371-1533; toll-free 800/370-9200. Email colonial@concordscolonialinn.com; www.concordscolonialinn.com. 45 rms, 3 story, 11 suites. June-Oct: S $179; suites $350; each addl $10; lower rates rest of yr. Crib avail, fee. Parking lot. TV; cable (premium). Complimentary newspaper, toll-free calls. Restaurant 7 am-10:30 pm. Bar. Ck-out 11 am, ck-in 2:30 pm. Meeting rms. Business servs avail. Concierge serv. Dry cleaning. Gift shop. Golf, 18 holes. Tennis. Downhill skiing. Bike rentals. Hiking trail. Picnic facilities. Cr cds: A, D, DS, MC, V.

🄳 🖈 🏂 🖛 🏂 🖼 🖄

★★ **HAWTHORNE INN.** 462 Lexington Rd (01742). 978/369-5610; fax 978/287-4949. Email inn@concordmass.com. 7 rms, 2 story. No rm phones. S $110-$150; D $125-$210. Complimentary continental bkfst; afternoon refreshments. Ck-out 11 am, ck-in 3 pm. Railroad station transportation. X-country ski 2 mi. Microwaves avail. Antiques; original artwork. Library/sitting rm with fireplace. Totally nonsmoking. Cr cds: A, DS, MC, V.

🏂 🖼 🖄

Restaurant

★★ **COLONIAL INN.** 48 Monument Sq. 978/369-2373. www.concords colonialinn.com. Specializes in fresh seafood, roast prime rib, regional specialties. Hrs: 7 am-11 pm; Sun brunch 10:30 am-2:30 pm. Bar. Bkfst $1.85-$9; lunch $3.75-$12; dinner $14.95-$25.95. Sun brunch $20.95. Built in 1716; Henry David Thoreau's house. Cr cds: A, C, D, DS, MC, V.

🄳

Danvers

(B-6) *See also Beverly*

Settled 1636 **Pop** 24,174 **Elev** 48 ft
Area code 978 **Zip** 01923
Web www.northshorechamber.org
Information North Shore Chamber of Commerce, #5 Cherry Hill Dr; 978/774-8565

This small industrial town was once Salem Village—a community started by settlers from Salem looking for more farmland. In 1692, Danvers was the scene of some of the most severe witchcraft hysteria; twenty persons were put to death.

What to See and Do

Glen Magna Farms. A 20-rm mansion; 1790-1890 furnishings; Chamberlain gardens. Derby summer house was built by Samuel McIntire (1794); on the roof are two life-size carvings (reaper and milkmaid) by the Skillin brothers; reproduction of 1844 gazebo. Various special events and programs. (June-Sep, Tues and Thurs exc hols; also by appt) 2 mi N on US 1, then ¼ mi E via Centre St to Ingersoll St. Phone 978/774-9165. ¢¢

Rebecca Nurse Homestead. The house (ca 1680), an excellent example of the New England saltbox, was the homestead of Rebecca Nurse, a saintly woman accused of and executed for witchcraft during the hysteria of 1692. House incl restored rms with furnishings from 17th and 18th centuries; outbuildings, a reproduction of the 1672 Salem Village Meetinghouse and exhibit areas. (Mid-June-mid-Sep, Tues-Sun; mid-Sep-Oct, wkends; rest of yr, by appt; closed hols) 149 Pine St. Phone 978/774-8799. ¢¢

Witchcraft Victims' Memorial. Memorial incl names of those who died, as well as quotes from 8 victims. 176 Hobart St.

Annual Event

Danvers Family Festival. Exhibits, fireworks, races, music. Late June-early July.

Motels/Motor Lodges

★ ★ COURTYARD BY MARRIOTT. *275 Independence Way (01923). 978/777-8630; fax 978/777-7341; toll-free 800/321-2211. www.courtyard. com.* 122 rms, 3 story. Mid-Apr-mid-Nov: S, D $109-$129; suites $129-$149. Crib free. TV; cable (premium). Heated pool. Complimentary coffee in rms. Restaurant 6:30-10 pm; wkends from 7 am. Bar 5-10 pm. Ck-out 1 pm. Coin lndry. Meeting rms. Business servs avail. In-rm modem link. Valet serv. Sundries. Exercise equipt. Refrigerator in suites; microwaves avail. Cr cds: A, C, D, DS, MC, V.

★ ★ DAYS INN BOSTON / SALEM. *152 Endicott St (01923). 978/777-1030; fax 978/777-0264; res 800/329-7466. Email 6260@hotelcendant.com.* 129 rms, 2 story. May-Oct: S, D $69.95-$99.95; each addl $8; under 18 free; wkly, hol rates; lower rates rest of yr. Crib free. TV; cable (premium). Pool. Complimentary continental bkfst. Restaurant adj open 24 hrs. Ck-out 11 am. Coin lndry. Business servs avail. In-rm modem link. Sundries. Picnic tables.Cr cds: A, DS, MC, V.

★ ★ QUALITY INN. *Trask Ln (01923), N on MA 128 at Exit 21. 978/774-6800; fax 978/774-6502; toll-free 800/782-7841.* 125 rms, 2 story. S, D $99-$130; each addl $10; suite $250; under 18 free. Crib free. TV; cable (premium), VCR avail (movies). Indoor pool; whirlpool, poolside serv. Restaurant 7 am-10 pm. Bar; pianist Tues-Thurs, combo Fri-Sat. Ck-out 11 am. Meeting rms. Business servs avail. In-rm modem link. Sundries. Airport transportation. Health club privileges. Microwaves avail. Private patios, balconies. Indoor tropical garden. Cr cds: A, C, D, DS, ER, JCB, MC, V.

★ ★ RESIDENCE INN BY MARRIOTT. *51 Newbury St (01923). 978/*

777-7171; fax 978/774-7195; toll-free 800/331-3131. www.residenceinn.com. 96 suites, 2 story. Suites $89-$189; wkly, wkend rates. Crib avail. Pet accepted, some restrictions. TV; cable. Pool. Complimentary continental bkst. Restaurant nearby. Ck-out noon. Coin lndry. Business servs avail. In-rm modem link. Valet serv. Lighted tennis. Exercise equipt. Sport court. Refrigerators, microwaves. Balconies. Picnic tables. Cr cds: A, C, D, DS, JCB, MC, V.

★ **SUPER 8.** 225 Newbury St (01923), US 1N. 978/774-6500; fax 978/762-6491. 78 rms, 2 story, 11 kit. units. Mid-June-mid-Oct: S, D $56-$66; each addl $5; kit. units $79; under 16 free; lower rates rest of yr. Crib free. Pet accepted. TV. Pool. Complimentary continental bkfst. Restaurant 11:30 am-10 pm. Bar to 12:30 am; entertainment Thurs-Sat. Ck-out 11 am. Meeting rms. Business servs avail. Microwaves avail. Cr cds: A, D, DS, MC, V.

Hotel

★★★ **SHERATON FERNCROFT RESORT.** 50 Ferncroft Rd (01923), US 1 and I-95. 978/777-2500; fax 978/750-7959; res 800/325-2525. 367 rms, 8 story. S, D $169-$260; each addl $15; suites $250-$800; under 18 free. Crib free. TV; cable (premium), VCR avail. 2 pools, 1 indoor; whirlpool, poolside serv, lifeguard. Coffee in rms. Restaurant 6:30 am-11 pm. Bar 11-1 am. Ck-out 11 am. Meeting rms. Business center. In-rm modem link. Airport transportation. Gift shop. Lighted tennis, pro. Golf, pro, putting green, driving range. X-country ski on site. Exercise equipt. Lawn games. Refrigerators, microwaves avail. Private patios. Cr cds: A, DS, MC, V.

Restaurants

★★ **THE HARDCOVER.** 15-A Newbury St (01923), at jct MA 114, enter from US 1N. 978/774-1223. Specializes in seafood, steak, prime rib. Salad bar. Hrs: 5-10 pm; Fri, Sat to 11 pm; Sun 4-9 pm. Bar. Dinner $13.95-$29.95. Child's menu. Walls lined with books, rare prints, paintings. Fireplaces. Cr cds: A, C, D, DS, ER, MC, V.

★★ **LEGAL SEAFOODS.** 210 Andover St (01960), S on MA 128, in Northshore Mall. 978/532-4500. www.legalseafoods.com. Specializes in seafood. Hrs: 11 am-10 pm; Fri, Sat to 11 pm; Sun to 9 pm. Closed Thanksgiving, Dec 25. Res accepted. Bar. Wine list. Lunch a la carte entrees: $5.25-$11.95; dinner a la carte entrees: $10.95-$19.95. Child's menu. Cr cds: A, DS, MC, V.

Dedham (C-6)

Settled 1635 **Pop** 23,782 **Elev** 120 ft
Area code 781 **Zip** 02026
Web www.nvcc.com

Information Neponset Valley Chamber of Commerce, 190 Vanderbilt Ave, Suite 1, Norwood 02062-5047; 781/769-1126

What to See and Do

Dedham Historical Society. Small but important collection of 16th-19th-century furniture; collection of work by silversmith Katharine Pratt; world's largest public collection of Dedham and Chelsea pottery; changing exhibits. Also 10,000-volume historical and genealogical library. (Tues-Fri, also some Sat; closed hols) 612 High St. Phone 781/326-1385. Museum ¢; Library ¢¢

Fairbanks House. (1636) One of the oldest frame houses still standing in the US. Fine example of 17th-century architecture, furnished with Fairbanks family heirlooms; guided tours. (May-Oct, Tues-Sat, also Sun afternoons) 511 East St, at Eastern Ave, off US 1. Phone 781/326-1170. ¢¢

Hotel

★★★ **HILTON AT DEDHAM PLACE.** 25 Allied Dr (02026), off I-95 Exit 14. 781/329-7900; fax 781/329-5552; toll-free 800/345-6565. Email hilton@gis.net; www.dedhamplace.

hilton.com. 249 rms, 4 story. S $119-$245; D $134-$260; each addl $15; suites $400-$600; under 18 free; wkend rates. Crib free. Pet accepted. TV; cable (premium). Indoor pool; whirlpool, poolside serv (in season). Coffee in rms. Restaurant 6:30 am-10 pm. Bar 11-1 am; pianist. Ck-out noon. Meeting rms. Business center. In-rm modem link. Garage, valet parking. Lighted tennis. Exercise rm; sauna. Bathrm phones; refrigerators avail. Cr cds: A, C, D, DS, ER, JCB, MC, V.

Conference Center

★★ **HOLIDAY INN BOSTON-DED-HAM.** 55 Ariadne Rd (02026), jct US 1 and I-95 (Ma 128), Exit 15A. 781/329-1000; fax 781/329-0903; res 800/HOLIDAY; toll-free 800/465-4329. Email hidedham@gis.net; www.holiday-inn. com/bos-dedham. 195 rms, 8 story. Apr-Oct: S, D $139; each addl $10; under 18 free; lower rates rest of yr. Crib avail. Parking lot. Indoor pool, lifeguard. TV; cable (premium), VCR avail. Complimentary coffee in rms, toll-free calls. Restaurant 6:30 am-10 pm. Bar. Ck-out noon, ck-in 3 pm. Meeting rms. Business center. Bellhops. Concierge serv. Dry cleaning, coin lndry. Exercise equipt. Downhill skiing. Picnic facilities. Video games. Cr cds: A, D, DS, JCB, MC, V.

Deerfield

Settled 1669 **Pop** 5,018 (town); 600 (village) **Elev** 150 ft **Area code** 413 **Zip** 01342 **Web** www.historic-deerfield.org

Information Historic Deerfield, Inc, PO Box 321; 413/774-5581

Twice destroyed by French and Native American attacks when it was the northwest frontier of New England, and almost forgotten by industry, Deerfield is noted for its unspoiled meadowland, beautiful houses, and nationally famous boarding schools (Deerfield Academy, 1797, a coeducational preparatory school; the Bement School, a coeducational school; and Eaglebrook School for boys).

In 1675, the Bloody Brook Massacre (King Philip's War) crippled the settlement, which was then a struggling frontier outpost. In 1704 (Queen Anne's War), half of the resettled town was burned. Forty-nine inhabitants were killed, and more than 100 were captured and taken to Canada.

The village boasts that it has one of the most beautiful streets in America, known just as The Street, a mile-long stretch of 80 houses, many dating from the 18th and early 19th centuries.

What to See and Do

Historic Deerfield, Inc. Maintains 14 historic house museums (fee) furnished with collections of antique furniture, silver, ceramics, textiles. A 28,000-sq-ft Collections Study Center features changing exhibits and study-storage displays of portions of the museum's collections. Daily walking tours, meadow walk, antique forums and workshops, special events wkends. Information Center is located at Hall Tavern, The Street. (Daily; closed Thanksgiving, Dec 24, 25) Phone 413/774-5581. Guided tours ¢¢¢

Memorial Hall Museum. (1798) The first bldg of Deerfield Academy; contains colonial furnishings, Native American relics. (May-Oct, daily) Memorial St. Phone 413/774-7476. ¢¢

B&B/Small Inn

★★★ **DEERFIELD INN.** 81 Old Main St (01342), 413/774-5587; fax 413/775-7221; toll-free 800/926-3865. Email information@deerfieldinn.com; www.deerfieldinn.com. 23 rms, 2 story. May-Oct: S $216; D $255; lower rates rest of yr. Crib avail, fee. Street parking. TV; cable. Complimentary full bkfst, coffee in rms, newspaper, toll-free calls. Restaurant 6-9 pm. Bar. Ck-out noon, ck-in 2 pm. Meeting rms. Business servs avail. Gift shop. Golf, 9 holes. Downhill skiing. Supervised children's activities. Hiking trail. Picnic facilities. Cr cds: A, D, MC, V.

Dwight Bardard House Museum, Deerfield

Restaurants

★ ★ ★ **DEERFIELD INN.** *81 Old Main St. 413/774-5587. www.deerfield inn.com.* Specializes in fresh seafood, rack of lamb, veal dishes. Hrs: noon-2 pm, 6-9 pm. Closed Dec 25. Res accepted. Bar. Lunch $6-$12; dinner $20-$23. Child's menu. Afternoon tea 4-5 pm. Colonial decor. Built 1884. 14 museum houses nearby. Cr cds: A, D, MC, V.

D

★ ★ ★ **SIENNA.** *6B Elm St. (01373). 413/665-0215. www.siennarest.com.* Specializes in soft shell crabs, roasted duck breast. Hrs: 5:30-9:30 pm. Closed Mon, Tue. Res accepted. Wine list. Dinner $20-$23. lot, street. Chef owned. Cr cds: MC, V.

Dennis (Cape Cod)

Settled 1639 **Pop** 13,864 **Elev** 24 ft
Area code 508 **Zip** 02638
Web www.dennischamber.com

Information Chamber of Commerce, PO Box 275, S Dennis 02660; 508/398-3568 or 800/243-9920; or the information booth at jct MA 28 & 134

Dennis heads a group, often called "The Dennises," that incl Dennisport, East Dennis, South Dennis, West Dennis, and Dennis. It was here, in 1816, that Henry Hall developed the commercial cultivation of cranberries. Swimming beaches are located throughout the area.

What to See and Do

Jericho House and Historical Center. (1801) Period furniture. Barn museum contains old tools, household articles, model of salt works, photographs. (July-Aug, Wed and Fri) At jct Old Main St & Trotting Park Rds in West Dennis. **Donation**

Josiah Dennis Manse. (1736) and **Old West School House** (1770) Restored home of minister for whom town was named; antiques, Pilgrim chest, children's rm, spinning and weaving exhibit, maritime wing. (July-Aug, Tues and Thurs) 77 Nobscusset Rd. **Donation**

Annual Event

Festival Week. Canoe and road races, antique car parade, craft fair, antique show. Late Aug.

Seasonal Event

Cape Playhouse. On MA 6A. Summer theater, Mon-Sat. Children's Theater (Fri mornings). Phone 508/385-3911 (box office) or 508/385-3838. Late June-Labor Day.

Motels/Motor Lodges

★ ★ **BREAKERS MOTEL.** *61 Chase Ave (02639), 1 mi S of MA 28. 508/398-6905; fax 508/398-7360; toll-free 800/540-6905. Email breakocea@aol. com; www.capecodtravel.com/breake.* 37 rms, 2 story, 3 suites. July-Aug: ; each addl $15; children $15; under 12 free; lower rates rest of yr. Crib avail. Parking lot. Pool. TV; cable. Complimentary continental bkfst. Restaurant nearby. Ck-out 3 pm, ck-in 11 pm. Golf. Beach access. Cr cds: A, MC, V.

★★ **COLONIAL VILLAGE RESORT.**
426 Lower County Rd (02639), ½mi S of MA 28. 508/398-2071; fax 508/398-2071; toll-free 800/287-2071. www. sunsol.com/colonialvillage. 49 rms, 1-2 story, 29 kits., 10 kit. cottages (4-rm, no A/C). July-Labor Day: S, D $94-$120; each addl $10; kit. units $105; kit. cottages $750/wk; each addl $60; lower rates mid-May-June, after Labor Day-mid-Oct. Closed rest of yr. TV; cable. 2 pools, 1 indoor; whirlpool, sauna. Restaurant nearby. Ck-out 11 am. Meeting rms. Fireplace, oven in cottages. Private beach. Cr cds: DS, MC, V.

★★ **CORSAIR OCEANFRONT MOTEL.** *41 Chase Ave (02639), 1 mi S of MA 28. 508/398-2279; fax 508/760-6681; toll-free 800/345-5140. Email corsair@capecod.net; www. virtualcapecod.com/market/corsair.* 25 kit. units, 2 story. July-Aug: S, D $145-$225; each addl $10; suite $275; packages avail; higher rates hols; lower rates Apr-June, Sep-Nov. Closed rest of yr. TV; cable (premium), VCR avail. 2 pools, 1 indoor; whirlpool. Supervised children's activities (in season); ages 5-14. Complimentary continental bkfst (off season). Restaurant adj 8 am-9 pm (in season). Ck-out 11 am. Coin lndry. Lawn games. Microwaves avail. Enclosed sun deck. On private beach. Cr cds: A, MC, V.

★ **THE GARLANDS.** *117 Old Wharf Rd (02639), 1 mi S of MA 28. 508/ 398-6987.* 2 story, 20 suites. July-Aug: S, D $120; each addl $11; lower rates rest of yr. Parking lot. TV; cable. Restaurant nearby. Ck-out 10 am, ck-in 2 pm. Golf. Tennis.

★ **HUNTSMAN MOTOR LODGE.**
829 Main St, Rte 28 (02670), ¼ mi W of MA 134 on MA 28. 508/394-5415; toll-free 800/628-0498. Email info@the huntsman.com; www.thehuntsman.com. 27 rms, 2 story, 9 kits. Mid-June-early Sep: S $52-$59; D $61-$79; each addl $6-$10; kit. units $79; wkly rates; lower rates mid-Apr-mid-June, early Sep-Oct. Closed rest of yr. Crib $4. TV; cable. Pool. Complimentary coffee in lobby. Restaurant adj 7 am-2 pm. Ck-out 11 am. Lawn games.

Refrigerators avail. Picnic tables, grills. Cr cds: A, MC, V.

★ **SEA LORD RESORT MOTEL.** *56 Chase Ave (02639), 1 mi S of MA 28. 508/398-6900. www.sunsol.com/ sealord.* 27 rms, 3 story. July-Aug: S $95; D $119; each addl $10; lower rates rest of yr. Crib avail. Parking lot. Pool. TV; cable, VCR avail. Ck-out 11 am, ck-in 2 pm. Golf. Tennis, 20 courts. Beach access. Bike rentals. Hiking trail. Picnic facilities. Cr cds: DS, MC, V.

★ **SEA SHELL.** *45 Chase Ave (02639), 1 mi S of MA 28. 508/398-8965; fax 508/394-1237; toll-free 800/ 698-8965. Email ssmotel@flash.net; www.virtualcapecod.com/market/sea shellmotel.* 16 rms, 2 story, 1 suite. July-Sep: D $120; suites $220; each addl $15; children $15; lower rates rest of yr. Crib avail. Parking lot. TV; cable. Complimentary continental bkfst. Restaurant. Business servs avail. Exercise privileges. Golf. Tennis. Beach access. Picnic facilities. Cr cds: A, DS, MC, V.

★★ **SESUIT HARBOR.** *1421 Main St (02641), 2 mi E on MA 6A. 508/ 385-3326; fax 508/385-3326; toll-free 800/359-0097. www.capecod.net/sesuit.* 19 rms, 2 story. June-Aug: D $98; each addl $12; children $6; under 12 free; lower rates rest of yr. Crib avail. Parking lot. Pool. TV; cable. Restaurant nearby. Ck-out 10:30 am, ck-in 1 pm. Business servs avail. Golf. Tennis. Picnic facilities. Cr cds: MC, V.

★★ **SOUNDINGS SEASIDE RESORT.** *79 Chase Ave (02639), 1 mi S of MA 28. 505/394-6561; fax 508/374-7537. www.thesoundings.com.* 102 rms, 1-2 story, 15 kits. Late June-Labor Day: S, D $110-$230; each addl $16; package plans; lower rates late Apr-late June, after Labor Day-mid-Oct. Closed rest of yr. TV; cable (premium). 2 pools, 1 indoor; poolside serv, sauna. Restaurant 7-11 am. Ck-out 11 am. Meeting rms. Business servs avail. In-rm modem link. Gift shop. Putting green. Refrigerators.

Balconies. Sun decks. On 350-ft private beach. Cr cds: A, MC, V.
⌖ ⌖

★★ **SPOUTER WHALE MOTOR INN.** *405 Old Wharf Rd PO Box 127 (02639), 1 mi S of MA 28. 508/398-8010; fax 508/760-3214. Email spouter@capercod.net; www.capecod.net/spouter.* 38 rms, 2 story. July-Aug: S $140; D $48; each addl $10; lower rates rest of yr. TV; cable. Restaurant nearby. Ck-out 11 am, ck-in 1:30 pm. Golf. Tennis, 3 courts.
⌖ ⌖ ⌖ ⌖

★★ **THREE SEASONS MOTOR LODGE.** *421 Old Wharf Rd (02639), 1 mi S of MA 28. 508/398-6091; fax 508/998-3762.* 63 rms, 2 story. Late June-Labor Day: D $115-$160; each addl $15; lower rates late May-late June, after Labor Day-Oct. Closed rest of yr. TV; cable. Restaurant 8 am-3 pm; 5-10 pm. Ck-out 11 am. Balconies. On private beach. Cr cds:A, MC, V.
⌖ ⌖

★ **WEST DENNIS MOTOR LODGE.** *691 Main St Rte 28 (02670), ¼ mi W of MA 134 on MA 28. 508/394-7434; fax 508/394-1672. Email capecodbay reosrt@aol.com; www.sunsol.com/west dennis.* 22 rms, 2 story. July-Labor Day: S $49-$56; D $55-$69; each addl $6-$10; lower rates rest of yr. Crib $7. TV; cable, VCR avail. Pool. Restaurant adj 7 am-2 pm. Ck-out 11 am. Refrigerators; microwaves avail. Cr cds: A, MC, V.
⌖ ⌖ ⌖

Resorts

★★ **EDGEWATER BEACH RESORT.** *95 Chase Ave (02639), 1 mi S of MA 28. 508/398-6922; fax 508/760-3447. www.edgewatercapecod.com.* 61 rms, 2 story, 28 suites. June-Sep: D $205; suites $210; each addl $15; children $10; lower rates rest of yr. Parking lot. Indoor/outdoor pools, whirlpool. TV; cable, VCR avail. Restaurant. Ck-out 11 am, ck-in 3 pm. Exercise equipt, sauna. Golf. Tennis. Beach access. Cr cds: A, DS, MC, V.
⌖ ⌖ ⌖ ⌖ ⌖ ⌖

★★ **LIGHTHOUSE INN.** *1 Lighthouse Rd (02670), 1 mi S of MA 28. 508/398-2244; fax 508/398-5658. Email inquire@lighthouse inn.com; www.lighthouseinn.com.* 53

rms, 15 suites. July-Aug: S $110; D $206; suites $244; each addl $25; children $5; under 9 free; lower rates rest of yr. Crib avail. Parking lot. Pool, children's pool. TV; cable. Complimentary full bkfst. Restaurant 8 am-9 pm. Bar. Ck-out 11 am, ck-in 3 pm. Meeting rms. Business servs avail. Bellhops. Coin lndry. Gift shop. Golf. Tennis. Beach access. Supervised children's activities. Cr cds: MC, V.
⌖ ⌖ ⌖ ⌖ ⌖ ⌖ ⌖

B&Bs/Small Inns

★★ **BY THE SEA GUESTS.** *57 Chase Ave (02639), 1 mi S of MA 28. 508/398-8685; fax 508/398-0334; toll-free 800/447-9202. Email bythesea@capecod.net; www.bytheseaguests.com.* 12 rms, 3 story, 5 suites. June-Sep: S, D $140; suites $1,350; each addl $20; children $15; lower rates rest of yr. Crib avail, fee. Parking lot. TV; cable, VCR avail, CD avail. Complimentary continental bkfst, newspaper, toll-free calls. Restaurant nearby. Ck-out 11 am, ck-in 2 pm. Business servs avail. Concierge serv. Coin lndry. Free airport transportation. Golf, 18 holes. Tennis, 4 courts. Beach access. Picnic facilities. Cr cds: A, C, D, MC, V.
⌖ ⌖ ⌖ ⌖ ⌖ ⌖

★★ **CAPTAIN NICKERSON INN.** *333 Main St (02660), approx 4 mi S on MA 134, W on Duck Pond Rd to Main St. 508/398-5966; fax 508/398-5966; toll-free 800/282-1619. Email capt nick@capecod.net; www.bbonline.com/ma/captnick/.* 4 rms, 2 story, 1 suite. May-Oct: S $112; D $117; suites $130; each addl $15; lower rates rest of yr. Crib avail, fee. Parking lot. TV; cable, VCR avail. Complimentary full bkfst, newspaper, toll-free calls. Restaurant. Ck-out 11 am, ck-in 3 pm. Fax servs avail. Concierge serv. Golf. Tennis, 12 courts. Bike rentals. Hiking trail. Cr cds: DS, MC, V.
⌖ ⌖ ⌖ ⌖ ⌖ SC

★★ **FOUR CHIMNEYS INN.** *946 Main St (02638). 508/385-6317; fax 508/385-6285; toll-free 800/874-5502. Email chimneys4@aol.com; www.four chimneysinn.com.* 8 air-cooled rms, 3 story. No rm phones. June-Sep: D $95-$140; wkly rates; lower rates Oct-May. Closed late Dec-mid-Feb. TV in sitting rm; cable (premium). Complimentary continental bkfst. Restaurant nearby. Ck-out 11 am, ck-in 3 pm. Lawn games. Balconies. Picnic tables. Opp lake. Former summer residence (1875); antiques. Cr cds: A, MC, V.

☒ ☒

★★ **ISAIAH HALL BED AND BREAKFAST INN.** *152 Whig St (02638). 508/385-9928; fax 508/385-5879; toll-free 800/736-0160. Email info@isaiahhallinn.com; www.isaiah hallinn.com.* 9 rms, 2 story, 1 suite. June-Aug: S $124; D $134; suites $163; each addl $20; lower rates rest of yr. Parking lot. TV; cable, VCR avail. Complimentary continental bkfst, toll-free calls. Restaurant nearby. Ck-out 11 am, ck-in 2 pm. Internet dock/port avail. Gift shop. Golf. Tennis. Cr cds: A, DS, MC, V.

☒ ☒ ☒ ☒

Restaurants

★★ **CAPTAIN WILLIAM'S HOUSE.** *106 Depot St (02639), ½ mi S of MA 28. 508/398-3910.* Specializes in lobster, prime rib, fresh seafood, homemade pasta. Hrs: 4:30-8:30 pm. Closed Jan-Mar. Res accepted. Bar. Dinner $12.95-$19.95. Child's menu. Sea captain's house (1820). Colonial decor. Cr cds: A, D, DS, MC, V.

D

★★ **CHRISTINE'S.** *581 Main St (02638), 2 mi S on MA 134, 3 mi W on MA 28. 508/394-7333.* Specializes in chicken Christine, local seafood, Lebanese dishes. Hrs: 4-10 pm; earlybird dinner 4-6 pm. Res accepted. Bar. Lunch $4.95-$6.95; dinner $8.95-$17.95. Child's menu. Entertainment: nightly in season; off season, wkends. Parking. Contemporary decor. Cr cds: A, DS, MC, V.

D

★ **MARSHSIDE.** *28 Bridge St (02641), 3 mi E on MA 6A to jct MA 134, L at Light. 508/385-4010.* Specializes in fresh seafood, lobster salad, homemade pies. Hrs: 7 am-9 pm; Sun brunch 8 am-3 pm. Closed Thanksgiving, Dec 25. Bkfst $2.95-$5.95; lunch $4.95-$7.95; dinner $6.95-$13.95. Sun brunch $2.95-$5.95. Child's menu. Cozy atmos-

phere; knick-knacks, artificial flowers. Cr cds: A, C, D, DS, MC, V.

D

★★★ **RED PHEASANT INN.** *905 Main St (02638), MA 6A. 508/385-2133. www.redpheasantinn.com.* Specializes in salmon, rack of lamb, roast lobster. Hrs: 5-11 pm. Res accepted. Bar. Dinner a la carte entrees: $15-$25. Valet parking. Once a barn (ca 1795); many antiques. Family-owned. Cr cds: DS, MC, V.

D

★ **ROYAL PALACE.** *369 Main St (02638), 2 mi S on MA 134, 3 mi W on MA 28. 508/398-6145.* Specializes in Cantonese and Mandarin dishes. Hrs: 4 pm-midnight. Res accepted. Bar. Dinner $6.50-$14.95. Parking. Cr cds: A, DS, MC.

★★ **SCARGO CAFE.** *799 MA 6A (02638). 508/385-8200. Email scargo@ capecod.net; www.scargocafe.com.* Specializes in chicken wildcat, mussels Ferdinand, grapenut custard. Hrs: 11 am-10 pm. Closed Thanksgiving, Dec 25. Bar. Lunch $3.95-$10.95; dinner $9.95-$17.95. Child's menu. Parking. Former residence (1865); opp nation's oldest stock company theater. Cr cds: A, C, DS, MC, V.

D

★ **SWAN RIVER.** *5 Lower County Rd (02639), 2 mi S on MA 134. 508/394-4466. www.swanriverseafoods.com.* Specializes in blackened fish-of-the-day, fried clams, fresh lobster. Hrs: noon-9 pm. Closed mid-Sep-late May. Res accepted. Bar. Lunch $5-$10; dinner $12-$16. Child's menu. Parking. Nautical decor; overlooks Swan River. Family-owned. Cr cds: A, DS, MC, V.

D

Eastham (Cape Cod)

See also Orleans

Settled 1644 **Pop** 4,462 **Elev** 48 ft
Area code 508 **Zip** 02642
Web www.capecod.net/eastham/
chamber

Information Chamber of Commerce, PO Box 1329; 508/240-7211 or 508/255-3444 (Summer only); or visit the Information Booth at MA 6 & Fort Hill

On the bay side of the Cape, in what is now Eastham town, the *Mayflower* shore party met their first Native Americans. Also in the town is a magnificent stretch of Nauset Beach, which was once a graveyard of ships. Nauset Light is an old friend of mariners.

What to See and Do

Eastham Historical Society. 1869 schoolhouse museum; Native American artifacts; farming and nautical implements. (July-Aug, Mon-Fri afternoons) Just off US 6. Phone 508/255-0788. **Donation** The society also maintains the

Swift-Daley House. (1741) Cape Cod house contains period furniture, clothing, original hardware. (July-Aug, Mon-Fri afternoons or by appt) On US 6. Phone 508/255-1766. **FREE**

Eastham Windmill. Oldest windmill on the Cape (1680); restored in 1936. (Late June-Labor Day, daily) Windmill Green, in town center. **Donation**

Motels/Motor Lodges

★ **BLUE DOLPHIN INN.** *5950 Rte 6 (02651), 3 mi N of National Seashore Entrance. 508/255-1159; fax 508/240-3676; toll-free 800/654-0504. Email bludolphin@capecod.net; www.capecod. net/bluedolphin.* 48 rms, 1 story, 1 suite. June-Sep: S, D $109; suites $155; each addl $10; under 15 free; lower rates rest of yr. Crib avail, fee. Parking lot. Pool. TV; cable (premium). Restaurant. Bar. Fax servs avail. Coin lndry. Exercise privileges. Golf. Tennis. Picnic facilities. Cr cds: A, MC, V.

🄳 🛍 🏃 🛏 🟙 🖎 🏊

★★ **CAPTAIN'S QUARTERS MOTEL AND CONFERENCE CENTER.** *Rte 6 (02651), approx 2 mi N on US 6. 508/775-1566; fax 508/240-0280. Email cqmcc@aol.com; www. captains_quarters.com.* 75 rms. Late-June-Labor Day: S, D $84-$105; each addl $8; lower rates mid-Apr-late-June, after Labor Day-mid-Nov. Closed rest of yr. Crib free. TV; cable. Heated pool. Complimentary conti-

nental bkfst. Restaurant nearby. Ck-out 11 am. Meeting rms. Tennis. Lawn games. Bicycles. Health club privileges. Refrigerators. Picnic tables, grill. Near beach. Cr cds: A, C, D, DS, MC, V.

🄳 🏃 🛏 🖎 🏊

★ **EAGLE WING GUEST MOTEL.** *960 Rte 6 (02642), 1½ mi S on US 6. 508/240-5656; fax 508/240-5657; toll-free 800/278-5656. Email eaglewing@ capecod.net; www.eaglewingmotel.com.* 19 rms, 1 story, 3 suites. July-Aug: S, D $109; suites $218; each addl $25; under 21 free; lower rates rest of yr. Parking lot. Pool. TV; cable. Complimentary coffee in rms. Restaurant nearby. Ck-out 11 am, ck-in 3 pm. Business center. Concierge serv. Exercise privileges. Golf. Hiking trail. Cr cds: DS, MC, V.

🛍 🛏 🟙 🖎 🏊 SC 🏃

★★ **EASTHAM OCEAN VIEW MOTEL.** *Rte 6 (02642), 2½ mi N of Orleans Rotary. 508/255-1600; fax 508/240-7104; toll-free 800/742-4133.* 31 rms, 2 story. June-Aug: S $85; D $89; suites $129; each addl $10; under 12 free; lower rates rest of yr. Crib avail, fee. Pool. TV; cable. Complimentary coffee in rms. Restaurant nearby. Ck-out 11 am, ck-in noon. Golf. Picnic facilities. Cr cds: A, C, D, DS, MC, V.

🛍 🛏 🖎 🏊

★★ **MIDWAY MOTEL & COTTAGES.** *5460 US 6 (02651), 2½ mi N of Eastham Visitor Center. 508/255-3117; fax 508/255-4235; toll-free 800/755-3117. Email inquire@midway motel.com; www.midwaymotel.com.* 9 rms, 1 story. June-Aug: S $90; D $96; lower rates rest of yr. Crib avail. Parking lot. TV; cable (premium), VCR avail. Complimentary coffee in rms, newspaper. Restaurant nearby. Business servs avail. Exercise privileges. Golf. Tennis. Bike rentals. Hiking trail. Picnic facilities. Cr cds: A, DS, MC, V.

🛍 🏃 🟙 🖎 🏊

★★ **SHERATON FOUR POINTS HOTEL.** *3800 Rte 6 (02642), ½ mi N of Eastham Visitor Center. 508/255-5000; fax 508/240-1870; toll-free 800/533-3986. Email sheraton@cape.com; www.virtual-valley.com/fourpoints/.* 107 rms, 2 story. July-Aug: S, D $147.90-$174; each addl $10; suites $225;

under 18 free; MAP avail; lower rates rest of yr. Crib $5-$10. TV; cable (premium). 2 pools, 1 indoor; whirlpool, poolside serv. Restaurant 7-11 am, 6-9 pm. Bar to 11 pm. Ck-out 11 am. Meeting rms. Business servs avail. In-rm modem link. Tennis. Exercise equipt; sauna. Health club privileges. Game rm. Some refrigerators. Cr cds: A, C, D, DS, MC, V.

`D` `F` `≈` `T` `≈` `M` `SC`

★ ★ **VIKING SHORES RESORT.** *Rte 6 (02651), 3 mi N on US 6, at jct Nauset Rd. 508/255-3200; fax 508/240-0205; toll-free 800/242-2131. Email viking@cape.com; www.vsp.cape.com/~viking.* 40 rms. Mid-June-Labor Day: S, D $89-$98; each addl $8; under 12 free; wkly rates; lower rates mid-Apr-mid-June, after Labor Day-early Nov. Closed rest of yr. Crib free. TV; cable (premium). Heated pool. Complimentary continental bkfst. Restaurant adj. Ck-out 11 am. Meeting rm. Tennis. Lawn games. Refrigerators. Picnic tables, grills. Cr cds: A, DS, MC, V.

`D` `F` `≈` `≈` `M`

Resort

★ **TOWN CRIER MOTEL.** *3620 US 6 (02642), ½ mi N of Eastham Visitor Center. 508/255-4000; fax 508/255-7491; toll-free 800/932-1434. Email joe111@msn.com; www.towncriermotel. com.* 35 rms, 1 story. July-Aug: S, D $109; each addl $10; under 12 free; lower rates rest of yr. Parking lot. Indoor pool. TV; cable. Restaurant. Ck-out 11 am, ck-in 2 pm. Golf. Tennis. Picnic facilities. Cr cds: A, D, DS, MC, V.

`T` `F` `≈` `T` `≈` `M` `SC`

B&Bs/Small Inns

★ ★ **OVERLOOK INN OF CAPE COD.** *3085 County Rd; Rte 6 (02642). 508/255-1886; fax 508/240-0545; res 508/255-1886. Email stay@ overlookinn.com.* 10 rms, 4 A/C, 3 story. Late June-mid-Sep: D $95-$165; lower rates rest of yr. Complimentary full bkfst; afternoon refreshments. Restaurant nearby. Ck-out 11 am, ck-in 2 pm. Rec rm. Lawn games. Picnic tables. Health club

privileges. 1869 sea captain's house; many antiques. Cr cds: A, MC, V.

`≈` `M` `SC`

★ ★ **PENNY HOUSE INN.** *4885 Rte 6 (02651), on MA 6, ½ mi N of Eastham Center. 508/255-6632; fax 508/255-4893; toll-free 800/554-1751. Email pennyhouse@aol.com; www. pennyhouseinn.com.* 12 rms, 2 story, 1 suite. May-Oct: S, D $145; suites $265; each addl $30; children $15; under 8 free; lower rates rest of yr. Crib avail, fee. Parking lot. TV; cable, VCR avail. Complimentary full bkfst, coffee in rms, newspaper, toll-free calls. Restaurant nearby. Ck-out 11 am, ck-in 2 pm. Meeting rms. Business center. Concierge serv. Gift shop. Exercise privileges. Golf, 18 holes. Tennis, 9 courts. Beach access. Bike rentals. Hiking trail. Picnic facilities. Cr cds: A, DS, MC, V.

`F` `T` `F` `T` `F` `≈` `M` `T`

Cottage Colony

★ **CRANBERRY COTTAGES.** *RR 1; 785 MA 6 (02642), ¾ mi N of Orleans Rotary. 508/255-0602; toll-free 800/ 292-6631. www.sunsol.com/cranberry cottages.* 14 cottages, 7 kits. Some A/C. Late June-Labor Day: S, D $82-$87; each addl $10; 2-bedrm kit. cottages for 1-6, $650-$750/wk; lower rates rest of yr. Crib free. TV; cable (premium). Ck-out 10 am, ck-in 3 pm. Refrigerators; microwaves avail. Grill. Cape Cod cottages in shady grove. Cr cds: DS, MC, V.

`≈` `M`

Fall River

(E-6) *See also New Bedford; also see Providence, RI*

Settled 1656 **Pop** 92,703 **Elev** 200 ft
Area code 508
Web www.frchamber.com

Information Fall River Area Chamber of Commerce, 200 Pocasset St, 02721; 508/676-8226

The city's name, adopted in 1834, was translated from the Native American "quequechan." In 1892, Fall River was the scene of one of the most famous murder trials in American history—that of Lizzie Borden, who was acquitted of the ax murders of her father and stepmother. Water power and cotton textiles built Fall River into one of the largest cotton manufacturers in the world, but its industry is now greatly diversified.

What to See and Do

◪ **Battleship Cove.** Five historic naval ships of the WWII period. The submarine *Lionfish*, a WWII attack sub with all her equipment intact, and the battleship USS *Massachusetts* are open to visitors. The *Massachusetts*, commissioned in 1942, was active in the European and Pacific theaters of operation in WWII and now houses the state's official WWII and Gulf War Memorial; on board is a full-scale model of a Patriot missile. Also here are *PT Boat 796, PT Boat 617*, and the destroyer USS *Joseph P. Kennedy, Jr,* which saw action in both the Korean and Vietnam conflicts and the Cuban missile blockade. The PT boats may be viewed from walkways. A landing craft (LCM) exhibit is located on the grounds. Gift shop; snack bar. (Daily; closed Jan 1, Thanksgiving, Dec 25) At jct MA 138, I-195. Phone 508/678-1100. ¢¢¢

Factory Outlet District. Fall River is an extensive factory outlet area. 638 Quequechan St. Phone 508/675-5519 or 800/424-5519.

Fall River Heritage State Park. Nine acres on the riverfront; sailing. Visitor center (daily) has multimedia presentation on how Fall River developed into the greatest textile producer in the country; tourist information. (Daily; closed Jan 1, Dec 25) Davol St. Phone 508/675-5759. **FREE**

Fall River Historical Society. Historical displays in 16-rm Victorian mansion. Exhibits of toys, dolls, china and glassware, costumes; artifacts relating to the Lizzie Borden trial. Gift shop. (Apr-May, Sep-Dec, Tues-Fri; June-Aug, Tues-Fri, also Sat and Sun afternoons; closed hols) 451 Rock St. Phone 508/679-1071. ¢¢

Marine Museum. 103 ship models on display, incl a 28-ft, 1-ton model of the *Titanic*, trace the growth of maritime steam power from the early 1800s to 1937; paintings, photographs, artifacts. (Summer, Mon-Fri, also wkend afternoons; winter, Wed-Fri, also wkend afternoons; closed Jan 1, Thanksgiving, Dec 25) 70 Water St. Phone 508/674-3533. ¢¢

St. Anne's Church and Shrine. (1906) Designed by Canadian architect Napoleon Bourassa, the upper church is constructed of Vermont blue marble; the lower church is of solid granite. In the upper church are stained-glass windows produced by E. Rault in Rennes, France, a "Casavant Freres" organ and exceptional oak wood ornamentation in the vault of the ceiling. The shrine is in the lower church. S Main St, facing Kennedy Park. Phone 508/674-5651. **FREE**

Motel/Motor Lodge

★★ **HAMPTON INN WESTPORT.** *53 Old Bedford Rd (02790), 6 mi E on I-195, Exit 10. 508/675-8500; fax 508/675-0075; res 800/426-7866. Email flrwp01@hi-hotel.com.* 133 rms, 4 story. Apr-Aug: S, D $69-$99; under 18 free; lower rates rest of yr. Crib free. TV; cable (premium), VCR avail (movies). Complimentary continental bkfst, coffee in rms. Restaurant adj 11 am-10 pm. Ck-out noon. Meeting rms. Business servs avail. In-rm modem link. Sundries. Valet serv. Airport, Railroad station transportation. Lighted tennis. Exercise equipt; sauna. Whirlpool. Some refrigerators. Cr cds: A, MC, V

D ⛵ 🏋 ⤋ 🐾 SC

Hotel

★★ **QUALITY INN FALL.** *1878 Wilbur Ave (02725), I-195 Exit 4 508 /678-4545; fax 508/678-9352; toll-free 800/228-5151. Email qualityinn@ meganet.net.* 104 rms, 2 story, 2 suites. May-Oct: S, D $179; suites $250; each addl $10; under 18 free; lower rates rest of yr. Crib avail. Pet accepted, some restrictions. Parking lot. Indoor pool. TV; cable (DSS), VCR avail. Complimentary continental bkfst, coffee in rms, newspaper. Restaurant 11:50 am-10 pm. Bar. Ck-out noon, ck-in 3 pm. Meeting rm. Business servs avail. Dry cleaning, coin lndry. Exercise equipt. Golf, 18 holes. Picnic facilities. Cr cds: A, C, D, DS, JCB, MC, V.

D 🐟 🏋 🏊 ⤋ 🏋 ⤋ 🐾

Restaurants

★ **MCGOVERN'S.** *310 Shove St (02724). 508/679-5010. Email rest 310@aol.com.* Specializes in seafood, steak. Hrs: 11 am-7 pm; Fri to 8 pm; Sat 7 am-9 pm; Sun 7 am-8 pm. Closed Mon; Dec 25. Res accepted. Bkfst $2-$3; lunch $4-$6; dinner $5-$12. Child's menu. Memorabilia from New England Steamship Line on walls. Family-owned. Cr cds: A, D, DS, MC, V.

[D] [→]

★ ★ **WHITE'S OF WESTPORT.** *66 MA 6 (02790), 6 mi E on I-195 Exit 9. 508/675-7185.* Specializes in steak, ribs, seafood. Hrs: 11 am-10 pm. Closed Dec 25. Res accepted. Bar. Lunch $4.95-$8.50; dinner $8.25-$14.95. Child's menu. Nautical decor; artifacts. Family-owned. Cr cds: A, DS, MC, V.

[D] [→]

Falmouth (Cape Cod)

Settled ca 1660 **Pop** 27,960 **Elev** 10 ft
Area code 508 **Zip** 02540
Web www.capecodchamber.org
Information Cape Cod Chamber of Commerce, US 6 & MA 132, PO Box 790, Hyannis 02601-0790; 508/362-3225 or 888/33-CAPECOD

What to See and Do

Ashumet Holly & Wildlife Sanctuary. Massachusetts Audubon Society. A 45-acre wildlife preserve with holly trail, herb garden, observation beehive. Trails open dawn to dusk. (Tues-Sun) Ashumet Rd, off Currier Rd; just N of MA 151. ¢¢

Falmouth Historical Society Museums. Julia Wood House (1790) and **Conant House** (ca 1740) Whaling collection; period furniture, 19th-century paintings, glassware, silver, tools, costumes; widow's walk; memorial park; Colonial garden. (Mid-June-mid-Sep, Mon-Fri; rest of yr, by appt) Katharine Lee Bates exhibit in Conant House honors author of "America the Beautiful."

(Mid-June-mid-Sep, Mon-Fri) On village green. Phone 508/548-4857. ¢¢

Island Queen. Passenger boat trips to Martha's Vineyard; 600-passenger vessel. (Late May-mid-Oct) Phone 508/548-4800. ¢¢¢

Annual Event

Barnstable County Fair. 8 mi N on MA 151. Horse and dog shows, horse-pulling contest; exhibits. Phone 508/563-3200. Last wk July.

Seasonal Event

College Light Opera Co at Highfield Theatre. Off Depot Ave, MA 28. Nine-wk season of musicals and operettas with full orchestra. Phone 508/548-0668 (after June 15). Mon-Sat. Late June-Labor Day.

Motels/Motor Lodges

★ ★ **ADMIRALTY INN.** *51 Teaticket Hwy (02541). 508/548-4240; fax 508/457-0535; res 800/341-5700. Email motels@capecod.net; www.vacationinn properties.com.* 70 rms, 2 story, 28 suites. July-Aug: S, D $170; suites $180; each addl $10; lower rates rest of yr. Parking lot. Indoor/outdoor pools, whirlpool. TV; cable (premium), VCR avail. Restaurant 7:30 am-9 pm. Bar. Ck-out 11 am, ck-in 2 pm. Meeting rms. Fax servs avail. Golf, 18 holes. Tennis, 6 courts. Supervised children's activities. Picnic facilities. Cr cds: A, C, D, DS, MC, V.

[D] [🏃] [🏌] [➳] [🔥] [🐾]

★ ★ **BEST WESTERN FALMOUTH MARINA TRADEWINDS.** *26 Robbins Rd (02541), 1 blk S of MA 28. 508/548-4300; fax 508/548-6787; toll-free 800/341-5700. www.vacationinn properties.com.* 46 rms, 2 story, 17 suites. June-Sep: S, D $165; suites $225; each addl $10; under 12 free; lower rates rest of yr. Parking lot. Pool. TV; cable (premium). Complimentary continental bkfst, coffee in rms, toll-free calls. Restaurant nearby. Ck-out 11 am, ck-in 3 pm. Golf. Cr cds: A, C, D, DS, MC, V.

[🏃] [➳] [🔥] [🐾]

★ **MARINER MOTEL.** *555 Main St (02540). 508/548-1331; res 800/233-2939.* June-Sep: S, D $99; each addl $10; under 17 free; lower rates rest of yr. Crib avail, fee. Parking lot. Pool. TV; cable, VCR avail. Restaurant nearby. Ck-out 11 am, ck-in 2 pm. Golf. Picnic facilities. Cr cds: A, C, D, DS, MC, V.

★★ **RED HORSE INN.** *28 Falmouth Hts Rd (02540), 1 blk off MA 28. 508/548-0053; fax 508/540-6563; toll-free 800/628-3811. www.redhorseinn.com.* 22 rms, 2 story, 2 suites. June-Sep: S $148; D $170; suites $178; each addl $25; lower rates rest of yr. Crib avail. Parking lot. Pool, lap pool. TV; cable (DSS). Complimentary continental bkfst, newspaper. Restaurant nearby. Ck-out 11 am, ck-in 11 pm. Business servs avail. Concierge serv. Exercise privileges. Golf. Tennis, 4 courts. Cr cds: A, MC, V.

Hotel

★★ **THE FALMOUTH RAMADA ON THE SQUARE.** *40 N Main St (02540). 508/457-0606; fax 508/457-9694; toll-free 800/272-6232. www.ramada.com.* 72 rms, 2 story. July-Aug: S, D $139-$199; each addl $10; suites $179-$249; under 18 free; hol rates; higher rates some special events; lower rates rest of yr. Crib free. TV; cable, VCR (movies). Indoor pool. Restaurant 7 am-10 pm. Bar 11 am-10 pm. Ck-out 11 am. Meeting rms. Business center. In-rm modem link. Cr cds: A, MC, V.

Resort

★★ **SEA CREST RESORT AND CONFERENCE CENTER.** *350 Quaker Rd (02556), 5 mi N on MA 28 Exit 151. 508/540-9400; fax 508/548-0556; toll-free 800/225-3110. Email 74161.672@compuserve.com; www. sumware.com/seacrest.* 266 rms, 1-3 story. Mid-June-mid-Sep: S, D $160-$240; under 17 free; MAP avail; higher rates hols; lower rates rest of yr. Crib $12.50. TV; cable. 2 pools, 1 indoor; whirlpool; poolside serv, lifeguard. Playground. Free supervised children's activities (in season); ages over 3. Restaurant 7-10:30 am, 5:30-11 pm. Snack bar, deli. Bar 11:30-1 am; entertainment. Ck-out 11 am, ck-in 3 pm. Grocery, coin lndry, pkg store 1 mi. Convention facilities. Business center. In-rm modem link. Bellhops. Valet serv. Concierge serv. Gift shop. Sports dir. Tennis. Putting green. Swimming beach. Windsurfing. Lawn games. Soc dir. Game rm. Exercise equipt; sauna. Refrigerators. Balconies. Picnic tables. On ocean. Cr cds: A, D, DS, MC, V.

B&Bs/Small Inns

★★ **BEACH HOUSE AT FALMOUTH HEIGHTS.** *10 Worcester Ct (02540), E on MA 28. 508/457-0310; fax 508/548-7895; toll-free 800/351-3426. www.capecodbeachhouse.com.* 7 rms, 2 story, 1 suite. July-Aug: D $169; suites $189; lower rates rest of yr. Parking lot. Pool. TV; cable. Complimentary continental bkfst. Restaurant. Golf. Tennis. Beach access. Bike rentals. Picnic facilities. Cr cds: MC, V.

★★★ **CAPT. TOM LAWRENCE HOUSE.** *75 Locust St (02540). 508/540-1445; fax 508/457-1790; toll-free 800/266-8139. Email capttom house@aol.com; www.sunsol.com/ captaintom.* 6 rms, 2 story, 1 suite. May, Oct: D $165; suites $200; lower rates rest of yr. Crib avail. Parking lot. TV; cable. Complimentary full bkfst, newspaper. Restaurant nearby. Golf. Bike rentals. Hiking trail. Cr cds: A, MC, V.

★★ **ELM ARCH INN.** *26 Elm Arch Way (02540), ¼ blk S of MA 28. 508/548-0133.* 24 rms, 8 A/C, 12 baths, 2 story. No rm phones. Mid-June-mid-Oct: D $70-$90; each addl $8-$10; lower rates rest of yr. TV in some rms; cable (premium). Pool. Complimentary morning coffee in season. Restaurant nearby. Ck-out 11 am, ck-in after noon. Screened terrace. Built 1810; private residence of whaling captain. Bombarded by British in 1814; dining rm wall features cannonball hole. Cr cds: A, MC, V.

★★★ **GRAFTON INN.** *261 Grand Ave S (02540). 508/540-8688; fax 508/540-1861; toll-free 800/642-4069. Email alamkid@aol.com; www.grafton inn.com.* 10 rms, 3 story. June-Oct: D $210; under 16 free; lower rates rest of yr. Parking lot. TV; cable. Complimentary full bkfst, newspaper, toll-free calls. Restaurant nearby. Ck-out 11 am, ck-in 9 pm. Exercise privileges. Golf, 18 holes. Tennis, 8 courts. Beach access. Bike rentals. Hiking trail. Cr cds: A, MC, V.

★★ **INN ON THE SOUND.** *313 Grand Ave (02540). 508/457-9666; fax 508/457-9631; toll-free 800/564-9668. Email innontheso@aol.com; www.innon thesound.com.* 10 rms, 2 story. May-Oct: S, D $225; each addl $30; under 16 free; lower rates rest of yr. Parking lot. TV; cable. Complimentary full bkfst, coffee in rms, newspaper. Restaurant nearby. Ck-out 11 am, ck-in 3 pm. Business center. Golf. Tennis. Beach access. Cr cds: A, DS, MC, V.

★★★ **LA MAISON CAPPELLARI AT MOSTLY HALL.** *27 Main St (02540). 508/548-3786; fax 508/548-5778. Email mostlyhall@aol.com.* 6 rms, shower only, 3 story. No rm phones. May-Oct: S, D $125-$135; wkends, hols (2-, 3-day min); lower rates rest of yr. Closed Jan. Children over 16 yrs only. TV in sitting rm. Complimentary full bkfst; afternoon refreshments. Restaurant nearby. Ck-out 11 am, ck-in 3 pm. Concierge serv. Bicycles. Greek-revival house built 1849; wrap-around porch, garden gazebo. Totally nonsmoking. Cr cds: A, D, DS, MC, V.

★★★ **THE PALMER HOUSE INN.** *81 Palmer Ave (02540). 508/548-1230; fax 508/540-1878; toll-free 800/472-2632. Email innkeepers@palmerhouse inn.com; www.palmerhouseinn.com.* 16 rms, 3 story, 1 suite. June-Oct: S $140; D $150; suites $260; each addl $30; lower rates rest of yr. Parking lot. TV; cable. Complimentary full bkfst, newspaper, toll-free calls. Restaurant nearby. Meeting rm. Business center. Concierge serv. Gift shop. Golf. Tennis. Bike rentals. Cr cds: A, C, D, DS, MC, V.

★★★ **WILDFLOWER INN.** *167 Palmer Ave (02540). 508/548-9524; fax 508/548-9524; toll-free 800/294-5459. Email wldflr167@aol.com; www. wildflower-inn.com.* 5 rms, 3 story, 1 suite. May-Oct: D $195; suites $225;

each addl $25; under 12 free; lower rates rest of yr. Parking lot. TV; cable (premium), VCR avail. Complimentary full bkfst, coffee in rms, newspaper. Restaurant nearby. Business center. Concierge serv. Gift shop. Whirlpool. Golf. Tennis. Bike rentals. Picnic facilities. Cr cds: A, MC, V.

Conference Center

★★★ **NEW SEABURY RESORT AND CONFERENCE CENTER.** *Rock Landing Rd (02649), 3 mi S of jct MA 28, 151, off Mashpee Rotary. 508/477-9111; fax 508/477-9790; res 508/477-9400; toll-free 800/999-9033. Email info@newseabury.com; www.new seabury.com.* 160 rms, some A/C, kits. Mid-June-Aug: S, D $210-$380; patio and pool villas $275-$380; lower rates rest of yr. Crib $10. TV; cable (premium), VCR (movies). Seaside freshwater pool; wading pool. Supervised children's activities (July-Aug). Dining rm 7 am-10 pm. Bar noon-1 am; entertainment in season. Ck-out 10 am, ck-in 4 pm. Grocery. Coin lndry. Convention facilities. Business center. In-rm modem link. Airport transportation. Sports dir. 16 all-weather tennis courts, pro. Two 18-hole golf courses, pro, putting green, driving range. Miniature golf. Sailboats, wind surfing. Bike trails. Exercise rm. Trips to islands, whale watching, deep-sea fishing avail. Private patios, balconies. On 2,300 acres. Cr cds: A, C, D, MC, V.

Restaurants

★★ **COONAMESSETT INN.** *311 Gifford St (02540). 508/548-2300. Email cmicathi@aol.com; www.capecod restaurants.org.* Specializes in New England seafood. Hrs: 11:30 am-9 pm; Sun brunch 11 am-2 pm. Res accepted. Bar. Lunch $6-$16; dinner $16-$27. Sun brunch $9-$18. Entertainment: in season. Valet parking. Built 1796. Cathedral ceiling. Large windows with view of pond. Tranquil setting. Family-owned. Cr cds: A, MC, V.

★ **FLYING BRIDGE.** *220 Scranton Ave (02540). 508/548-2700. Email*

micathi@aol.com; www.capecod
restaurants.org. Specializes in seafood.
Hrs: 11:30 am-10 pm; Fri, Sat to 11
pm. Bar. Lunch $5.95-$15.95; dinner
$5.95-$15.95. Child's menu. Entertainment: Fri. Valet parking. Cr cds:
A, MC, V.

★ **GOLDEN SAILS CHINESE.** *143
Main St (02536). 508/548-3526.* Specializes in Szechwan, Cantonese,
Mandarin dishes. Hrs: 11:30-1 am;
Fri, Sat to 2 am; Sun noon-1 am.
Closed Thanksgiving. Bar. Lunch a la
carte entrees: $4.25-$5.25; dinner a
la carte entrees: $3.25-$13.50. Parking. Cr cds: A, C, D, DS, ER, MC, V.

★★★ **REGATTA OF FALMOUTH
BY THE SEA.** *217 Clinton Ave
(02540), at Falmouth Harbor entrance,
end of Scranton Ave. 508/548-5400.
www.theregattas.com.* Specializes in
soft shell crab, roasted red pepper
vinaigrette. Own desserts. Hrs: 4:30-
10 pm. Closed Oct-Memorial Day.
Res accepted. Wine list. Dinner a la
carte entrees: $17.50-$26. Parking.
French decor; antiques. View of harbor and sound. Family-owned. Cr
cds: A, MC, V.

Foxboro (D-6)

Settled 1704 **Pop** 14,637 **Elev** 280 ft
Area code 508 **Zip** 02035
Web www.nvcc.com

Information Neponset Valley Chamber of Commerce, 190 Vanderbilt
Ave, Suite 1, Norwood 02062;
781/769-1126

What to See and Do

Professional sports.

NFL (New England Patriots).
Foxboro Stadium, S on US 1.
Phone 508/543-8200.

Hotel

★★ **COURTYARD BY MARRIOTT-
FOXBOROUGH.** *35 Foxborough Blvd
(02035). 508/543-5222; fax 508/543-
0445; toll-free 800/321-2211. Email*
cy.bosfb.gm@marriott.com; www.
courtyard.com/bosfb. 149 rms, 3 story,
12 suites. Apr-Oct: S, D $139; suites
$169; lower rates rest of yr. Crib
avail. Parking lot. Indoor pool, whirlpool. TV; cable. Complimentary coffee in rms, newspaper, toll-free calls.
Restaurant 7 am-10 pm. Ck-out
noon, ck-in 3 pm. Meeting rms. Business servs avail. Dry cleaning, coin
lndry. Exercise privileges. Golf, 18
holes. Cr cds: A, D, DS, MC, V.

Conference Center

★★ **HOLIDAY INN.** *31 Hampshire St
(02048), 3 mi S on MA 140, off I-95
Exit 7A, in Cabot Industrial Park.
508/339-2200; fax 508/339-1040; res
800/465-4329. www.holiday-inn.com/
bos-mansfield.* 202 rms, 2-3 story. S
$99-$159; D $109-$169; each addl
$10; suites $300; under 18 free;
wkend rates. Crib free. TV; cable (premium), VCR avail. Indoor pool.
Complimentary coffee in rms.
Restaurant 6:30 am-10 pm. Bars
11:30-1 am; entertainment. Ck-out
noon. Coin lndry. Meeting rms. Business servs avail. In-rm modem link.
Bellhops. Lighted tennis. Exercise rm.
Some in-rm whirlpools. Private
patios, balconies. Cr cds: A, MC, V.

Restaurant

★★ **LAFAYETTE HOUSE.** *109
Washington St (US 1) (02035), 3 mi N
of I-495 Exit 14A, US 1. 508/543-
5344. www.lafayettehouse.com.* Specializes in roast beef, seafood. Hrs:
noon-10 pm. Bar. Lunch $5.95-$8.95;
dinner $12.95-$19.95. Child's menu.
Historic Colonial tavern built in
1784. Cr cds: A, C, D, DS, MC, V.

Framingham (C-5)

Settled 1650 **Pop** 64,989 **Elev** 165 ft
Area code 508 **Zip** 01701

Framingham is an industrial, commercial, and residential community.
Framingham Centre, the original

town, was bypassed by the railroad in the 19th century and is two miles N of downtown.

What to See and Do

Danforth Museum of Art. Six galleries, incl a children's gallery; changing exhibits, special events; art reference library. (Wed-Sun afternoons; closed Aug and hols) 123 Union Ave. Phone 508/620-0050. ¢¢

Garden in the Woods. A 45-acre botanical garden and sanctuary. Exceptional collection of wildflowers and other native plants; variety of gardens and habitats. HQ of Northeast Wildflower Society. (Mid-June-Oct, Tues-Sun; mid-Apr-mid-June, daily) Guided walks (inquire for schedule). Visitor center; museum shop. 180 Hemenway Rd. Phone 508/877-6574 (recording). ¢¢¢

Hotel

★★★ SHERATON FRAMINGHAM HOTEL. *1657 Worcester Rd (01701), I-90 Exit 12.* 508/879-7200; *fax 508/875-7593; res 800/325-3535; toll-free 800/277-1150. www.sheraton framingham.com.* 365 rms, 6 story, 5 suites. Mar-May, Sep-Nov: S, D $239; suites $378; each addl $15; under 16 free; lower rates rest of yr. Crib avail. Pet accepted, some restrictions, fee. Parking garage. Indoor/outdoor pools, lap pool, lifeguard, whirlpool. TV; cable (premium). Complimentary coffee in rms, newspaper, toll-free calls. Restaurant 6:30 am-10 pm. Bar. Ck-out noon, ck-in 3 pm. Conference center, meeting rms. Business center. Bellhops. Concierge serv. Dry cleaning. Gift shop. Exercise rm, sauna, steam rm. Golf. Tennis. Supervised children's activities. Cr cds: A, C, D, DS, ER, JCB, MC, V.

Gloucester (B-7)

Settled 1623 **Pop** 28,716 **Elev** 50 ft
Area code 978 **Zip** 01930
Web www.cape-ann.com/cacc

Information Cape Ann Chamber of Commerce, 33 Commercial St; 978/283-1601 or 800/321-0133

It is said that more than 10,000 Gloucester men have been lost at sea in the last three centuries—which emphasizes how closely the community has been linked with seafaring. Today it is still a leading fishing port—although the fast schooners made famous in *Captains Courageous* and countless romances have been replaced by diesel trawlers. Gloucester is also the center of an extensive summer resort area that incl the famous artists' colony of Rocky Neck.

What to See and Do

"Beauport," the Sleeper-McCann House. (1907-34) Henry Davis Sleeper, early 20th-century interior designer, began by bldg a 26-rm house, continually adding rms with the help of Halfdan Hanson, a Gloucester architect, until there were 40 rms; 25 are now on view, containing extraordinary collection of antique furniture, rugs, wallpapers, ceramics, glass; American and European decorative arts. Many artists, statesmen, and businessmen were entertained here. (Mid-May-mid-Sep, Mon-Fri; mid-Sep-mid-Oct, daily) 75 Eastern Point Blvd. Phone 978/283-0800. ¢

Cape Ann Historical Museum. Paintings by Fitz Hugh Lane; decorative arts and furnishings; Federal-style house (ca 1805). Emphasis on Gloucester's fishing industry; fisheries/maritime galleries and changing exhibitions depict various aspects of Cape Ann's history. (Tues-Sat; closed hols, also Feb) 27 Pleasant St. Phone 978/283-0455. ¢

Gloucester Fisherman. Bronze statue by Leonard Craske, a memorial to anglers lost at sea. On Stacy Blvd on the harbor.

Hammond Castle Museum. (1926-29). Built like a medieval castle by inventor Dr. John Hays Hammond, Jr; contains a rare collection of art objects. Great Hall contains pipe organ with 8,200 pipes; concerts (selected days throughout the yr). (Memorial Day-Labor Day, daily; after Labor Day-Columbus Day, Thurs-Sun; rest of yr, Sat and Sun; closed Jan 1, Thanksgiving, Dec 25). 80 Hesperus Ave, off MA 127. Phone 978/283-2081. ¢¢

Sargent House Museum. Late 18th-century Georgian residence, built for Judith Sargent, an early feminist writer and sister of Governor Winthrop Sargent; also home of her second husband, John Murray, leader of Universalism. Period furniture, china, glass, silver, needlework, early American portraits, paintings by John Singer Sargent. (Memorial Day-Columbus Day, Fri-Mon; closed hols) 49 Middle St. Phone 978/281-2432. ¢

Annual Events

St. Peter's Fiesta. A 4-day celebration with sports events, fireworks, procession, Blessing of the Fleet. Phone 978/283-1601. Last wkend June.

Waterfront Festival. Arts and crafts show, entertainment, food. Phone 978/283-1601. Third wkend Aug.

Schooner Festival. Races, parade of sail, maritime activities. Phone 978/283-1601. Labor Day wkend.

Seasonal Event

Whale Watching. Half-day trips, mornings and afternoons. Phone 978/283-1601. May-Oct.

Motels/Motor Lodges

★ **ATLANTIS MOTOR INN.** *125 Atlantic Rd (01930). 978/283-0014; fax 978/281-8994; toll-free 800/732-6313.* July-Sep: D $150; each addl $8; under 12 free; lower rates rest of yr. Crib avail. Parking lot. Pool. TV; cable (premium). Restaurant 7:30 am-11 pm. Ck-out noon, ck-in 3 pm. Fax servs avail. Golf. Beach access. Cr cds: A, MC, V.

[icons]

★★ **BEST WESTERN BASS ROCKS OCEAN INN.** *107 Atlantic Rd (01930), in Bass Rocks. 978/283-7600; fax 978/281-6489; res 800/528-1234.* Email bassrocks@prodigy.net; www.best western.com/bassrocksoceaninn. 48 rms, 2 story. June-Oct: S, D $200; each addl $8; under 12 free; lower rates rest of yr. Crib avail, fee. Parking lot. Pool. TV; cable, VCR avail. Complimentary continental bkfst. Restaurant nearby. Ck-out noon, ck-in 2 pm. Fax servs avail. Golf, 18 holes. Tennis, 2 courts. Beach access.

Bike rentals. Hiking trail. Picnic facilities. Cr cds: A, C, D, DS, MC, V.

[icons]

★★ **CAPTAINS LODGE MOTEL.** *237 Eastern Ave (01930), on Rte 127. 978/281-2420; fax 978/283-0322.* 47 rms, 7 kits. July-Sep: S, D $95; each addl $7; kit. units $102; lower rates rest of yr. Crib $7. TV; cable (premium). Heated pool. Restaurant 6 am-2 pm; Sat, Sun 7 am-noon. Ck-out 11 am. Tennis. Cr cds: A, C, D, DS, MC, V.

[icons]

★ **THE MANOR INN.** *141 Essex Ave (01930). 978/283-0614; fax 978/283-3154.* 12 rms, 2 story, 3 suites. June, Oct: D $79; suites $139; each addl $15; under 12 free; lower rates rest of yr. Crib avail. Pet accepted, fee. Parking lot. TV; cable. Complimentary full bkfst, newspaper, toll-free calls. Restaurant. Ck-out 11 am, ck-in 2 pm. Meeting rms. Business center. Bellhops. Coin lndry. Tennis, 2 courts. Beach access. Supervised children's activities. Hiking trail. Picnic facilities. Cr cds: A, DS, MC, V.

[icons]

★ **VISTA MOTEL.** *22 Thatcher Rd (01930), MA 128N to Exit 9, left on MA 127A. 978/281-3410; fax 978/283-7335.* Email vistamotel@juno.com; www.vistamotel.com. 40 rms, 2 story. May-Aug: S, D $110; lower rates rest of yr. Pet accepted, some restrictions, fee. Parking lot. Pool. TV; cable (premium). Complimentary continental bkfst, coffee in rms. Restaurant nearby. Ck-out 10 am, ck-in 8 pm. Exercise privileges. Golf. Tennis. Cr cds: A, DS, MC, V.

[icons]

Resort

★★ **OCEAN VIEW INN AND RESORT.** *171 Atlantic Rd (01930). 978/283-6200; fax 978/282-9548; res 978/283-6200; toll-free 800/315-7557.* Email oviar@snore.net; www.ocean viewinnandresort.co. 63 rms, 3 story. May-Oct: S, D $69-$190; lower rates rest of yr. Crib $10. Pet accepted. TV; cable, VCR avail. 2 heated pools. Restaurants 7 am-9:30 pm. Ck-out 11 am, ck-in 2 pm. Meeting rms. Business servs avail. In-rm modem link. Luggage handling. Rec rm. Lawn games. Some balconies. On ocean.

Several bldgs have accommodations, incl turn-of-the-century English manor house. Cr cds: A, MC, V.

B&B/Small Inn

★★ GEORGE FULLER HOUSE.

148 Main St (01929), W on MA 128, Exit 15 to Main St (MA 133). 978/768-7766; fax 978/768-6178; toll-free 800/477-0148. 7 rms, 6 with shower only, 3 story, 3 suites. June-Oct: S, D $100-$155; each addl $15; under 6 free; lower rates rest of yr. TV; cable. Complimentary full bkfst. Restaurant nearby. Ck-out 11 am, ck-in 3-6 pm. In-rm modem link. Some balconies. Picnic table. An 1830 Federal-style house near the Essex River; antique furnishings. Totally nonsmoking. Cr cds: A, C, D, DS, MC, V.

Restaurants

★ CAMERON'S.

206 Main St (01930). 978/281-1331. Specializes in native seafood, prime rib, Italian sauteed specialties. Hrs: 11 am-9:30 pm; Sun 8 am-10 pm. Closed Dec 25. Res accepted. Bar. Lunch $3.95-$7.95; dinner $6.95-$12.95. Child's menu. Entertainment: Wed-Sun. Family-owned since 1936. Cr cds: A, MC, V.

★★ GLOUCESTER HOUSE RESTAURANT.

7 Seas Wharf (01930). 978/283-1812. Specializes in seafood. Hrs: 11:30 am-9 pm; winter hrs vary. Closed Thanksgiving, Dec 25. Res accepted. Bar. Lunch a la carte entrees: $5.95-$11.95; dinner a la carte entrees: $9.95-$21.95. Child's menu. Entertainment: Thurs-Sun. Gift shop. Nautical decor; view of fishing harbor. Family-owned since 1958. Cr cds: A, D, DS, MC, V.

Humpback Whale

★★ WHITE RAINBOW.

65 Main St (01930). 978/281-0017. Specializes in Maui onion soup, sauteed lobster, seafood skewer. Hrs: 5:30-9:30 pm; Sat 6-10 pm. Closed Dec 24, 25; also Mon mid-Sep-June. Res accepted. Bar. Wine list. Dinner $17.95-$22.95. A la carte entrees: $8.50-$11.95. An 1830 landmark bldg. Cr cds: A, C, D, DS, MC, V.

Great Barrington

Settled 1726 **Pop** 7,725 **Elev** 721 ft
Area code 413 **Zip** 01230
Web www.greatbarrington.org
Information Southern Berkshire Chamber of Commerce, 362 Main St; 413/528-1510 or 413/528-4006

As early as 1774, the people of Great Barrington rose up against the King, seizing the courthouse. Today Great Barrington is the shopping center of the southern Berkshire resort country. Writer, professor, and lawyer James Weldon Johnson, cofounder of the NAACP, and W. E. B. du Bois, black author and editor, lived here. Another resident, the poet William Cullen Bryant, was the town clerk for 13 years.

What to See and Do

Beartown State Forest. Swimming, fishing, boating; hunting, bridle and hiking trails, snowmobiling, picnicking, camping. Standard fees. Approx 5 mi E on MA 23. Phone 413/528-0904.

Colonel Ashley House. (1735) Elegance of home reflects Col Ashley's prominent place in his society. One political meeting he held here produced the Sheffield Declaration, forerunner to Declaration of Independence. Period furnishings. Adj to Bartholowmew's Cobble. (July-Aug, Wed-Sun; Memorial Day-June and Sep-Columbus Day, wkends; also open Mon hols) 9 mi S via MA 7 & 7A to Ashley Falls, then ½ mi on Rannapo Rd to Cooper Hill Rd. Phone 413/229-8600. ¢¢

Skiing.

Butternut Basin. Triple, 5 double chairlifts, Pomalift, rope tow; patrol, school, rentals, snowmaking; nursery (wkends and hols after Dec 26), Cafeterias, wine rm; electronically-timed slalom race course. Longest run 1.8 mi; vertical drop 1,000 ft. (Dec-Mar, daily) Also 7 mi of cross-country trails; rentals. 2 mi E on MA 23. Phone 413/528-2000 or 800/438-SNOW. ¢¢¢¢

Otis Ridge. Double chairlift, T-bar, J-bar, 3 rope tows; patrol, school, rentals, snowmaking; cafeteria. Night skiing (Tues-Sat). Longest run 1 mi; vertical drop 400 ft. (Dec-Mar, daily) 16 mi E on MA 23. Phone 413/269-4444. ¢¢¢¢

Catamount. 7 mi W on NY 23 (see HILLSDALE, NY).

Annual Event

Berkshire Craft Fair. Monument Mt Regional High School. Juried fair with more than 100 artisans. Phone 413/528-3346, ext 28. Early Aug.

Motels/Motor Lodges

★ **BARRINGTON COURT.** *400 Stockbridge Rd (01230), 1 mi N on US 7.* 413/528-2340. 23 rms, 2 story, 2 kit. suites. Late June-Labor Day: S, D $75-$115; each addl $5; kit. suites $175-$200; higher rates wkends in June-Aug (2-day min); lower rates rest of yr. Crib $10. TV; cable. Pool. Playground. Complimentary coffee in rms. Restaurant nearby. Ck-out 11 am. Downhill/x-country ski 2 mi. Lawn games. Refrigerators. Balconies. Cr cds: A, MC, V.
🏊 🖼 🔀 🐾

★ **LANTERN HOUSE MOTEL.** *254 Stockbridge Rd; Rte 7 (01230).* 413/528-2350; fax 413/528-0435; toll-free 800/959-2350. 14 rms, 1 story. Dec-Feb, July-Oct: S $120; D $150; each addl $5; children $5; lower rates rest of yr. Parking lot. Pool. TV; cable. Complimentary coffee in rms. Restaurant nearby. Bar. Ck-out 11 am, ck-in 1 pm. Business center. Golf. Downhill skiing. Cr cds: MC, V.
🏊 🛏 🖼 🔀 🐾 🎿

★ **MONUMENT MOUNTAIN MOTEL.** *249 Stockbridge Rd (01230), 1 mi N on US 7.* 413/528-3272; fax 413/528-3132. 18 rms. July-Oct: S, D $55-$115; each addl $5-$10; wkend rates; ski plans; lower rates rest of yr. TV; cable. Pool. Playground. Complimentary coffee in rms. Restaurant nearby. Ck-out 11 am. Business servs avail. Lighted tennis. Downhill/x-country ski 3 mi. Lawn games. Picnic tables, grills. 20 acres on river. Cr cds: A, MC, V.
D 🏊 🎿 🖼 🔀 🐾 ✈

B&Bs/Small Inns

★★ **THE EGREMONT INN.** *10 Sheffield Rd (01258), 3 mi SW off MA 23.* 413/528-2111; fax 413/528-3284; res 413/528-2111; toll-free 800/859-1780. Email egremontinn@taconic.net; www.egremontinn.com. 19 rms, 3 story. Jan-Feb, July-Oct: D $150; each addl $20; lower rates rest of yr. Crib avail. Parking lot. Pool. TV; cable (DSS), VCR avail. Complimentary continental bkfst, newspaper. Restaurant 5-10 pm. Bar. Ck-out 11 am, ck-in 2 pm. Meeting rms. Fax servs avail. Golf. Tennis, 2 courts. Downhill skiing. Hiking trail. Picnic facilities. Cr cds: A, DS, MC, V.
🦽 🎿 🏊 🛏 🏌 🖼 🔀 🐾

★★ **RACE BROOK LODGE.** *864 S Undermountain Rd (01257), approx 9 mi S on MA 41.* 413/229-2916; fax 413/229-6629; res 888/725-6343. Email rblodge@bcn.net; www.rblodge.com. 21 rms, some with shower only, 3 story. No rm phones. June-Aug: S, D $105-$145; each addl $15; under 5 free; min stay wkends (summer); lower rates rest of yr. Pet accepted, some restrictions. TV; cable in common rm. Complimentary full bkfst. Restaurant adj 5:30-9:30 pm. Bar. Ck-out 11 am, ck-in 2-3 pm. Meeting rm. Downhill/x-country ski 7 mi. Lawn games. Barn built in 1790s. Rustic decor. Totally nonsmoking. Cr cds: A, MC, V.

★★ **THORNEWOOD INN & RESTAURANT.** *453 Stockbridge Rd (01230), jct MA 7 and MA 183. 413/528-3828; fax 413/528-3307; res 413/528-3828; toll-free 800/458-1008. Email inn@thornewood.com; www. thornewoodinn.com.* 13 rms, 2 story. June-Oct: S $115; D $195; each addl $30; children $30; under 8 free; lower rates rest of yr. Crib avail, fee. Parking lot. Pool. TV; cable, VCR avail. Complimentary full bkfst, newspaper. Restaurant 5 am-10 pm. Bar. Ck-out 11:30 am, ck-in 3 pm. Meeting rm. Business servs avail. Gift shop. Exercise privileges, sauna. Golf, 18 holes. Tennis, 8 courts. Downhill skiing. Hiking trail. Video games. Cr cds: A, DS, MC, V.

★★★ **WINDFLOWER INN.** *684 S Egremont Rd (01258), 3 mi W of US 7 on MA 23. 413/528-2720; fax 413/528-5147; toll-free 800/992-1993. Email wndflowr@windflowerinn.com; www.windflowerinn.com.* 13 rms, 2 story. June-Oct: S $125; D $160; each addl $25; children $25; lower rates rest of yr. Crib avail, fee. Parking lot. Pool. TV; cable (DSS). Complimentary full bkfst. Restaurant. Meeting rm. Internet dock/port avail. Golf, 18 holes. Tennis. Downhill skiing. Hiking trail. Picnic facilities. Cr cds: A.

Restaurants

★★★ **CASTLE STREET CAFE.** *10 Castle St (01230). 413/528-5244. www.castlestreetcafe.com.* Specializes in grilled fresh fish, grilled steak, pasta. Hrs: 5-11 pm. Closed Tues; Thanksgiving, Dec 25. Bar. Wine cellar. Dinner a la carte entrees: $9-$22. Intimate, sophisticated bistro atmosphere. Cr cds: A, MC, V.

★★ **JODI'S COUNTRY CAFE.** *327 Stockbridge Rd (01230). 413/528-6064.* Specializes in fresh fish, fresh pasta, steaks. Hrs: 11 am-4 pm; Fri-Sun 9 am-9 pm. Res accepted. Bar. Bkfst $1.95-$6.95; lunch $3.95-$8.95; dinner $12.95-$20.95. Child's menu. Entertainment: wkends June-Oct. Porch dining. Antique decor, original 250-yr-old bldg, hardwood floors. Cr cds: A, C, D, DS, ER, MC, V.

★★ **JOHN ANDREW'S RESTAURANT.** *MA 23 (01258), 6 mi S. 413/528-3469.* Specializes in Napoleon of grilled shrimp, crisp duck confit. Hrs: 5-10 pm; Sun 4-9 pm. Closed Wed Sep-June. Bar. Wine list. Dinner $13-$22. Child's menu. View of gardens. Cr cds: MC, V.

★★ **THE OLD MILL.** *53 Main St (Rte 23) (01258), 4 mi W on MA 23. 413/528-1421.* Specializes in fresh filet of salmon, baby rack of lamb, sauteed calf liver with smoked bacon. Hrs: 5-10 pm. Closed Thanksgiving, Dec 25. Bar. Dinner $16-$24. Child's menu. Parking. In grist mill. Built in 1978. Cr cds: A, D, MC, V.

★★ **PAINTED LADY.** *785 S Main St (01230). 413/528-1662.* Specializes in fresh seafood, pasta, veal. Hrs: 5-10 pm; Sun from 4 pm. Closed Wed; Dec 24, 25. Res accepted. Bar. Dinner $12.95-$22.95. Child's menu. Formal, intimate dining in Victorian house. Cr cds: DS, MC, V.

★★★ **SPENCER'S.** *453 Stockbridge Rd. 413/528-3828. www.thornewood. com.* Specializes in fresh seafood, salads. Own desserts. Hrs: 5-9:30 pm. Closed Mon, Tues; Jan 1; also Mon, Wed (Sep-mid-June). Res accepted. Bar. Wine cellar. Dinner a la carte entrees: $15-$20. Entertainment: jazz Sat. Parking. Family-owned since 1977. Cr cds: A, DS, MC, V.

Unrated Dining Spot

MARTIN'S. *49 Railroad St (01230). 413/528-5455.* Specializes in omelets, soups. Hrs: 6 am-3 pm. Closed Jan 1, Dec 25. Bkfst $2.85-$5.50; lunch $2.50-$5.50. Child's menu. Informal atmosphere. Cr cds: A, MC, V.

Greenfield (B-3)

Settled 1686 **Pop** 18,666 **Elev** 250 ft
Area code 413 **Zip** 01301
Web www.co.franklin.ma.us
Information Franklin County Chamber of Commerce, 395 Main St, Box 898; 413/773-5463

The center of a prosperous agricultural area, Greenfield is also the home of many factories and a center for winter and summer sports, hunting, and fishing. The first cutlery factory in America was established in Greenfield in the early 19th century.

What to See and Do

Northfield Mountain Recreation and Environmental Center. On site of Northeast Utilities Hydro Electric Pumped storage plant. Bus tours to the upper reservoir and underground powerhouse (May-Oct). Hiking, camping, riverboat ride, and picnicking. (Dec-Mar, Mon-Fri; May-Oct, Wed-Sun) Fee for some activities. MA 63 in Northfield. Phone 413/659-3714.

Annual Events

Green River Music and Balloon Festival. Hot-air balloon launches, craft show, musical entertainment, food. Phone 413/773-5463. July.

Franklin County Fair. Four days starting Thurs after Labor Day.

Motel/Motor Lodge

★ **HOWARD JOHNSON LODGE.** *125 Mohawk Tr (01301), 1 blk E of I-91 Exit 26. 413/774-2211; fax 413/772-2637; toll-free 888/244-2211.* 100 rms, 2 story. S $54-$84; D $58-$94; each addl $10; under 18 free; higher rates: special events, some wkends; lower rates rest of yr. Crib free. TV. Pool. Coffee in rms. Restaurant 6 am-10 pm; Fri, Sat to 2 am. Bar 11-1 am. Ck-out noon. Meeting rms. Valet serv. Sundries. Putting green, miniature golf. Downhill ski 20 mi; x-country ski 12 mi. Private patios, balconies. Cr cds: A, C, D, DS, ER, JCB, MC, V.

[D] [≥] [⊠] [⌂] [SC]

Hotel

★★★ **BRANDT HOUSE.** *29 Highland Ave (01301). 413/774-3329; fax 413/772-2908; toll-free 800/235-3329. Email info@brandthouse.com; www.brandthouse.com.* 9 rms, 3 story, 2 suites. June, Oct: suites $205; lower rates rest of yr. Crib avail, fee. Pet accepted, some restrictions, fee. Parking lot. TV; cable, VCR avail. Complimentary full bkfst, coffee in rms, newspaper, toll-free calls. Restaurant nearby. Ck-out 11 am, ck-in 2 pm. Meeting rms. Business servs avail. Exercise privileges. Golf, 18 holes. Tennis. Downhill skiing. Bike rentals. Hiking trail. Picnic facilities. Cr cds: A, DS, MC, V.

[⌂] [⌂] [⌂] [⌂] [⌂] [⌂] [⌂] [⌂] [⌂]

Restaurants

★★ **ANDIAMO.** *Huckle Hill Rd (01337), 8 mi N on I-91, Exit 28A. Follow signs to top of mountain. 413/648-9107. www.sandri.com.* Specializes in veal, pasta, steaks. Hrs: 5-9 pm; Fri, Sat to 10 pm; Sun 4-9 pm. Closed Dec 24, 25. Res accepted. Bar. Dinner $12.95-$22.95. Entertainment: Fri, Sat. Dining in greenhouse-style rm. Cr cds: A, D, DS, MC, V.

[D] [⊠]

★★ **FAMOUS BILL'S.** *30 Federal St (01301). 413/773-9230.* Specializes in lobster, prime rib, seafood. Own desserts. Hrs: 4-10 pm; Fri, Sat to 11 pm; Sun 11 am-8 pm. Res accepted. Bar. Lunch $3.75-$11.95; dinner $6.95-$17.95. Child's menu. Family-owned. Cr cds: MC, V.

[D] [SC] [⊠]

★★ **HERM'S.** *91 Main St (01301). 413/772-6300.* Specializes in seafood, chicken, steak. Hrs: 11:30 am-9 pm; Fri, Sat to 10 pm. Closed Sun; Thanksgiving, Dec 25. Res accepted. Bar. Lunch $6.95-$15.95; dinner $6.95-$15.95. Child's menu. Cr cds: A, DS, MC, V.

[D] [SC] [⊠]

Harwich (Cape Cod)

Settled ca 1670 **Pop** 10,275 **Elev** 55 ft
Area code 508 **Zip** 02646
Web www.capecodchamber.org

Information Harwich Chamber of Commerce, PO Box 34; 508/432-1600; or the Cape Cod Chamber of Commerce, US 6 & MA 132, PO Box 790, Hyannis 02601-0790; 508/362-3225 or 888/33-CAPECOD

Harwich, whose namesake in England was dubbed "Happy-Go-Lucky Harwich" by Queen Elizabeth, is one of those towns made famous in New England literature. It is "Harniss" in the Joseph C. Lincoln novels of Cape Cod. A local citizen, Jonathan Walker was immortalized as "the man with the branded hand" in Whittier's poem about helping escaped slaves; Enoch Crosby of Harwich was the Harvey Birch of James Fenimore Cooper's novel *The Spy*. Today, summer people own ¾ of the land.

What to See and Do

Brooks Free Library. Houses 24 John Rogers's figurines. (Mon-Sat; closed hols) 739 Main St, Harwich Center. Phone 508/430-7562. **FREE**

Harwich Historical Society. Incl Brooks Academy Bldg and Revolutionary War Powder House. Native American artifacts, marine exhibit, cranberry industry articles, early newspapers and photographs. Site of one of the first schools of navigation in US. (Usually mid-June-mid-Sep, Thurs-Sun; schedule may vary) 80 Parallel St, at Sisson Rd, in Harwich Center. Phone 508/362-3225. **FREE**

Red River Beach. A fine Nantucket Sound swimming beach (water 68°-72°F in summer). Off MA 28, S on Uncle Venies Rd in S Harwich. Sticker fee per wkday ¢¢; Wkends and hols ¢¢¢

Saquatucket Municipal Marina. Boat ramp for launching small craft. (May-mid-Nov) Off MA 28 at 715 Main St. Phone 508/432-2562. Daily ¢¢¢

Annual Event

Cranberry Harvest Festival. Family Day, antique car show, music, arts and crafts, fireworks, carnival, parade. Phone 508/432-1600 or 800/441-3199. One wk mid-Sep.

Seasonal Event

Harwich Junior Theatre. Plays for the family and children through high-school age. Res required. Willow & Division Sts, West Harwich. Phone 508/432-2002. July-Aug, daily; Sep-June, monthly.

Motels/Motor Lodges

★ **HANDKERCHIEF SHOALS MOTEL.** *888 Main St; Rte 28 (02661), on MA 28 at Deep Hole Rd.* 508/432-2200. 26 rms. No A/C. Late June-Labor Day: S, D $70-$78; each addl $8; lower rates mid-Apr-late June, after Labor Day-Oct. Closed rest of yr. Crib free. TV; cable. Pool. Restaurant nearby. Ck-out 11 am. Lawn games. Refrigerators, microwaves. Cr cds: DS, MC, V.

★★ **WYCHMERE VILLAGE.** *767 Main St-Rte 28 (02646), ¾ mi E of Harwich Port on MA 28.* 508/432-1434; fax 508/432-8904; toll-free 800/432-1434. Email info@wychmere.com; www.wychmere.com. 25 units, 2 A/C, 11 kits. Mid-June-mid-Sep: D $75-$85; each addl $10; kit. units $90-$130; cottage with kit. for 4, $850/wk; lower rates rest of yr. Crib $10. TV; cable. Heated pool. Playground. Coffee in lobby. Restaurant opp 7 am-noon. Ck-out 11 am. Lawn games. Refrigerators. Picnic tables, grill. Cr cds: A, MC, V.

Resort

★ **COACHMAN MOTOR LODGE.** *774 Main St (02646), 1 mi E of Harwich Port on MA 28.* 508/432-0707; fax 508/432-7951; toll-free 800/524-4265. Email coachmanmotorinn@prodigy.net; www.coachmanmotorinn.com. 28 rms. July-Aug: D $98-$110 (2-day min); each addl $10; apt for 4-5, $735; package plans off-season; lower rates Sep-mid-Nov, May-July. Closed rest of yr. Crib free. TV; cable (premium). Pool. Restaurant 7 am-midnight. Ck-out 11 am. Refrigerators avail. Cr cds: A, MC, V.

B&Bs/Small Inns

★★ **AUGUSTUS SNOW HOUSE.**
528 Main St (02646). 508/430-0528; fax 508/432-6638; toll-free 800/320-0528. Email info@augustussnow.com. 5 rms, some A/C, 2 story. Late May-mid-Oct: S, D $145-$160; wkends (2-day min); lower rates rest of yr. Children over 12 yrs only. TV; cable. Complimentary full bkfst; afternoon refreshments. Restaurant nearby. Ck-out 11 am, ck-in 2 pm. Concierge serv. Free airport transportation. Some in-rm whirlpools. Built in 1901; Victorian decor. Totally nonsmoking. Cr cds: A, DS, MC, V.

★★ **CAPE COD CLADDAGH INN.**
77 Main St (02671), 2½ mi W on MA 28. 508/432-9628; fax 508/432-6039; toll-free 800/356-9628. Email claddagh@capecod.net; www.capecodcladdaghinn.com. 11 rms, 2 story. May-Oct: S $150; D $85; each addl $25; lower rates rest of yr. Crib avail. Pet accepted, some restrictions. Parking lot. Pool. TV; cable. Complimentary full bkfst. Restaurant. Bar. Business servs avail. Gift shop. Golf. Bike rentals. Hiking trail. Cr cds: A, MC, V.

★★ **COUNTRY INN.** *86 Sisson Rd (02646), 1 mi S on MA 124. 508/432-2769; fax 508/430-1455; toll-free 800/231-1722. www.countryinncapecod.com.* 6 rms, 1 story. June-Oct: D $90; each addl $15; lower rates rest of yr. TV; cable. Complimentary continental bkfst. Restaurant. Bar. Ck-out 11 am, ck-in 2 pm. Cr cds: A, MC, V.

★★★ **DUNSCROFT BY THE SEA.**
24 Pilgrim Rd (02646), MA 39 S to MA 28, then E, right turn before Congregational Church. 508/432-0810; fax 508/432-5134; toll-free 800/432-4345. Email dunscroft@capecod.net; www.dunscroftbythesea.com. 9 rms, 2 story, 1 suite. D $175. Street parking. TV; cable, VCR avail. Complimentary full bkfst. Ck-out 11 am, ck-in 2 pm. Meeting rms. Golf. Tennis, 5 courts. Beach access.

Bike rentals. Hiking trail. Picnic facilities. Cr cds: A, MC, V.

★ **SEA HEATHER INN.** *28 Sea St (02646), 1 blk S of MA 28. 508/432-1275; fax 508/432-1275; toll-free 800/789-7809. Email goldencape@aol.com; www.seaheather.com.* 20 rms, 1-2 story. Mid-June-mid-Sep: S, D $95-$175; each addl $15; lower rates rest of yr. Children over 10 yrs only. TV; cable. Complimentary continental bkfst. Restaurant nearby. Ck-out 11 am. Lawn games. Some refrigerators, microwaves. Early American decor; porches, ocean view. Near beach. Totally nonsmoking. Cr cds: A, MC, V.

Conference Center

★★ **SEADAR INN.** *Bank St Beach (02646), 2 blks S of MA 28. 508/432-0264; fax 508/430-1916; res 800/888-5250. www.seadarinn.com.* 23 rms, 2 story, 3 suites. July-Aug: Crib avail. Valet parking avail. TV; cable (premium). Complimentary continental bkfst, newspaper. Restaurant nearby. Ck-out 11 am. Business servs avail. Bellhops. Concierge serv. Free airport transportation. Golf. Tennis, 6 courts. Beach access. Bike rentals. Picnic facilities. Cr cds: A, C, D, DS, MC, V.

Restaurant

★★ **L'ALOUETTE.** *787 Main St (02646), 2 mi E on MA 28. 508/430-0405.* Own baking. Menu changes frequently. Hrs: 5-10 pm. Closed Mon; Dec 25; also Feb. Res required. Dinner a la carte entrees: $15-$22. Intimate French atmosphere. Cr cds: A, DS, MC, V.

Haverhill (B-6)

Settled 1640 **Pop** 51,418 **Elev** 27 ft
Area code 978
Web www.chamber.mva.net
Information Chamber of Commerce, 87 Winter St, 01830; 978/373-5663

Haverhill is a thriving manufacturing and commercial center located along the Merrimack River. Long known for its role in the manufacture of women's shoes, Haverhill now boasts a highly diversified high-tech industrial base. The city features fine neighborhoods of early 19th-century homes. The Quaker poet John Greenleaf Whittier was born here.

A statue at Winter and Main streets commemorates the remarkable Hannah Dustin, who, according to legend, was kidnapped by Native Americans in March, 1697, and escaped with the scalps of ten of her captors.

What to See and Do

Haverhill Historical Society. Located in The Buttonwoods, an early 19th-century house. Period furnishings, china, glass, Hannah Dustin relics, memorabilia from turn-of-the-century theaters, Civil War artifacts, and archaeological collection. Also on grounds is the John Ward House (1641), furnished with colonial items; and an 1850s shoe factory with displays. Guided tours. (Wed, Thurs, also Sat and Sun afternoons) 240 Water St, MA 97. Phone 978/374-4626. ¢¢

John Greenleaf Whittier Birthplace. Whittier family homestead since the 17th century, this is the setting of his best-known poems, incl "Snow-Bound," and "Barefoot Boy." His writing desk and mother's bedrm, built over a rock too large to move, are here. The house is furnished with original pieces and arranged as it would have appeared in his childhood. Grounds (69 acres) still actively farmed. (Tues-Sun; closed Jan 1, Thanksgiving, Dec 25) 305 Whittier Rd, I-495 to Exit 52, 1 mi E on MA 110. Phone 978/373-3979. ¢

Hotel

★★ **BEST WESTERN.** *401 Lowell Ave (01832), at jct MA 110, 113, off I-495 Exit 49. 978/373-1511; fax 978/373-1517; res 800/528-1234; toll-free 888/645-2025.* 126 rms, 3 story. July-Oct: S, D $159; under 17 free; lower rates rest of yr. Crib avail. Parking lot. Indoor pool, whirlpool. TV; cable (DSS). Complimentary continental bkfst, coffee in rms, newspaper, toll-free calls. Restaurant. Ck-out noon, ck-in 3 pm. Business servs avail. Dry cleaning, coin lndry. Cr cds: A, C, D, DS, MC, V.

All Suite

★★ **COMFORT SUITES.** *106 Bank Rd (01832), I-495 Exit 49. 978/374-7755; fax 978/521-1894; res 800/517-4000. www.hotelchoice.com/hotel/ma063/.* 131 rms, 4 story, 131 suites. Apr-Oct: S $125; D $139; suites $139; each addl $10; under 18 free; lower rates rest of yr. Crib avail. Parking lot. TV; cable (DSS). Complimentary continental bkfst, coffee in rms, newspaper. Restaurant. Meeting rms. Business center. Concierge serv. Dry cleaning, coin lndry. Exercise privileges, whirlpool. Golf. Tennis, 6 courts. Downhill skiing. Beach access. Hiking trail. Picnic facilities. Video games. Cr cds: A, C, D, DS, ER, JCB, MC, V.

Holyoke

(C-3) *See also South Hadley, Springfield*

Settled 1745 **Pop** 43,704 **Elev** 270 ft
Area code 413 **Zip** 01040
Information Greater Holyoke Chamber of Commerce, 177 High St; 413/534-3376

Captain Elizur Holyoke explored the Connecticut Valley as early as 1633. His name is preserved in a rich and bustling industrial city made possible with the development of the great river by an unusual set of power canals.

What to See and Do

Holyoke Heritage State Park. Canalside park; visitor center features cultural, environmental, and recreational programs, slide show, and exhibits on the region and on Holyoke's history as a planned city, its canals, industries, and people. Mt Park Merry-Go-Round also here (Sat and Sun afternoons; expanded summer hrs). Restored train cars run periodically (fee); inquire for schedule. (Wed-Sun afternoons) Phone 413/534-1723. **FREE** Also on the site and adj is

Children's Museum. Participatory museum. Exhibits incl paper-making, sand pendulum, bubble making, TV studio, tot lot, "Cityscape," and other changing exhibits. (Tues-Sun) 444 Dwight St. Phone 413/536-KIDS. ¢¢

Mount Tom Ski Area and Summer-Side. Thirteen slopes and trails; 3 double chairlifts, 2 T-bars, J-bar, half-pipe; snowmaking, school, patrol, ski shop, rentals; cafeteria, snack bar, restaurant. Longest run 3,600 ft; vertical drop 680 ft. (Mid-Dec-mid-Mar, daily) SummerSide incl wave pool, 4,000-ft alpine slide, 400-ft water slide, chairlift to five-state view. (Mid-June-Labor Day, daily; Memorial Day-mid-June and early Sep-fall, wkends) 2 mi N on US 5 off I-91. Phone 413/536-0416. ¢¢¢¢- ¢¢¢¢¢

Wistariahurst Museum. Victorian mansion, family home of noted silk manufacturer William Skinner. House highlights incl interior architectural detail unique to late 19th and early 20th centuries, incl a leather-paneled room, conservatory, and music hall; period furniture, decorative arts. Textile and archival collections available for research scholars. Changing exhibits. Carriage house has collection of Native American materials and natural history. (Wed, Sat, Sun afternoons; schedule may vary) 238 Cabot St. Phone 413/534-2216. ¢

Motel/Motor Lodge

★★ **HOLIDAY INN.** *245 Whiting Farms Rd (01040), off I-91 Exit 15. 413/534-3311; fax 413/533-8443; res 800/HOLIDAY.* 219 rms, 4 story. S $76-$80; D $86-$90; each addl $10; family rates; higher rates some college events. Crib free. Pet accepted; $25. TV; cable. Indoor pool; whirlpool, poolside serv. Restaurant 6:30 am-10 pm. Bar 11:30-2 am; entertainment Tues-Sat. Ck-out 11 am. Meeting rms. Bellhops. Concierge serv. Downhill ski 3 mi. Exercise equipt; sauna. Game rm. Luxury level. Cr cds: A, D, DS, MC, V.

D ⬛ ⬛ ⬛ ⬛ ⬛ ⬛ ⬛

B&B/Small Inn

★ **YANKEE PEDLAR INN.** *1866 Northampton St (01040), at jct US 202. 413/532-9494; fax 413/536-8877. www.infoyankeepedlar.com.* May-Aug: S $79; D $89; suites $99; lower rates rest of yr. Crib avail. Parking lot. TV; cable (premium), VCR avail. Complimentary continental bkfst, coffee in rms. Restaurant, closed Mon. Bar. Ck-out 11 am, ck-in 2 pm. Business servs avail. Gift shop. Golf. Cr cds: A, MC, V.

D ⬛ ⬛ ⬛ ⬛

Restaurants

★★★ **DELANY HOUSE.** *Rte 5 at Smith's Ferry (01040). 413/532-1800. Email info@delaneyhouse.com.* Specializes in fresh seafood, game. Own pastries, ice cream. Hrs: 5-9 pm; Fri, Sat to 9:30 pm; Sun 1-7 pm. Closed Jan 1, Dec 25. Res accepted. Bar. Wine cellar. Dinner $12-$23. Child's menu. Entertainment: dancing Fri, Sat. Valet parking. Patio dining. Late 18th-century furnishings. Cr cds: A, C, D, DS, ER, MC, V.

D ⬛

★★ **YANKEE PEDLAR.** *1866 Northamptons (US 5). 413/532-9494. Email info@yankeepedlar.com; www.yankee pedlar.com.* Specializes in fresh fish, veal, beef. Own baking. Hrs: 11:30 am-10 pm; Sun 3-8 pm. Closed Mon; Dec 25. Bar. Lunch $3.75-$12.50; dinner $8.95-$19.95. Sun brunch $13.95. Entertainment: Thurs-Sat. Cr cds: A, MC, V.

D

Hyannis (Cape Cod)

(E-8) *See also Martha's Vineyard, South Yarmouth*

Settled 1639 **Pop** 14,120 **Elev** 19 ft
Area code 508 **Zip** 02601
Web www.hyannis.com

Information Chamber of Commerce, 1481 Rte 132; 508/362-5230 or 877/HYANNIS.

Hyannis is the main vacation and transportation center of Cape Cod. Recreational facilities and specialty areas abound, incl tennis courts, golf courses, arts and crafts galleries, theaters, and antique shops. There are libraries, museums, and the Kennedy Memorial and Compound. Candle-making tours are available. Scheduled airliners and Amtrak stop here, and it is also a port for boat trips to Nantucket Island and Martha's Vineyard. More than six million people visit the village every year, and it is within an hour's drive of the many attractions on the Cape.

What to See and Do

Hyannis-Nantucket or Martha's Vineyard Day Round Trip. (May-Oct) Also hrly sightseeing trips to Hyannis Port (late Apr-Oct, daily); all-day or ½-day deep-sea fishing excursions (late Apr-mid-Oct, daily). Hy-Line, Pier #1, Ocean St Dock. Phone 508/778-2600. Harbor/sightseeing trips ¢¢¢; Fishing/ferry ¢¢¢¢

John F. Kennedy Hyannis Museum. Photographic exhibits focusing on President Kennedy's relationship with Cape Cod; 7-min video presentation. Gift shop. (Mon-Sat, also Sun afternoons) 397 Main St, in Old Town Hall. Phone 508/790-3077. ¢

John F. Kennedy Memorial. Circular fieldstone wall memorial 12 ft high with presidential seal, fountain, and small pool honors late president who grew up nearby. Ocean St.

Swimming. Craigville Beach. SW of town center. **Sea St Beach.** Overlooking Hyannis Port harbor, bathhouse. **Kalmus Park.** Ocean St, bathhouse. **Veteran's Park.** Ocean St. Picnicking at Kalmus and Veteran's Parks. Parking fee at all beaches.

Seasonal Event

Cape Cod Melody Tent. Summer musical theater in-the-round, daily; children's theater. 21 W Main St. Phone 508/775-9100. Wed morning, July-early Sep.

Motels/Motor Lodges

★ **BUDGET HOST MOTEL.** *614 Rte 132 (02601), 1 blk W of jct MA 28, 132.* 508/775-8910; fax 508/775-6476; toll-free 800/322-3354. Email hymotel@capecod.net. 40 rms, 2 story, 8 kits. Late June-Labor Day: D $55-$85; each addl $10; under 17 free; lower rates rest of yr. Crib free. TV; cable (premium). Pool. Complimentary coffee in rms. Restaurant adj open 11:30 am-midnight. Ck-out 11 am. Refrigerators. Cr cds: A, D, DS, MC, V.

[D] [icons]

★★ **CAPTAIN GOSNOLD VILLAGE.** *230 Gosnold St (02601).* 508/775-9111. 36 units, 16 kits., 18 kit. cottages. Some A/C. Many rm phones. Late June-Labor Day: D $75; each addl $10; kit. units $95; cottages (1-3 bedrm) $150-$260; under 5 free; lower rates mid-Apr-mid-June, Labor Day-Nov. Closed rest of yr. Crib free. TV; cable, VCR avail (free movies). Pool; lifeguard. Playground. Restaurant nearby. Ck-out 10:30 am. Lawn games. Refrigerators, microwaves. Picnic tables, grills. Cr cds: MC, V.

[icons] SC

★ **COUNTRY LAKE LODGE.** *1545 Rte 132 (02601), Iyanough Rd, 2½ mi NW on MA 132, ¾ mi S of Exit 6.* 508/362-6455; fax 508/362-8050. Email cllholtco@aol.com; www.countrylakelodge.com. 20 rms, 1 story. June-Aug: S $74; D $84; each addl $10; lower rates rest of yr. Crib avail. Parking lot. Pool. TV; cable. Complimentary toll-free calls. Restaurant nearby. Ck-out 11 am, ck-in 2 pm. Golf. Tennis. Bike rentals. Picnic facilities. Cr cds: A, DS, MC, V.

[icons]

★★ **HERITAGE HOUSE HOTEL.** *259 Main St (02601).* 508/775-7000; fax 508/778-5687; toll-free 800/352-7189. www.capeheritagehotel.com. 143 rms, 3 story. July 4-Labor Day: D $75-$125; each addl $12; under 16 free; package plans; lower rates rest of yr. Crib free. TV; cable (premium). 2 pools, 1 indoor; whirlpool, lifeguard. Sauna. Restaurant 7-10 am. Ck-out 11 am. Meeting rms. Balconies. Cr cds: A, C, D, DS, MC, V.

[icons] SC

★ **HOWARD JOHNSON.** *447 Main St (02601), near Barnstable County Airport.* 508/775-3000; fax 508/771-1457; toll-free 800/446-4656. 39 rms, 2 story. July-Labor Day: S, D $95-$120; under 18 free; higher rates hol wkends; lower rates rest of yr. Crib $10. TV; cable. Indoor pool; whirlpool. Restaurant 1-4 pm. Bar 10-1 am. Ck-out 11 am. Business servs avail. Refrigerators avail. Cr cds: A, MC, V.

⌨ ✕ ◪ ◈ **SC**

★★ **HYANNIS DAYS INN.** *867 Rte 132 (02601).* 508/771-6100; fax 508/775-3011; res 800/329-7466; toll-free 800/368-4667. *www.sunsol.com/days inn.* 97 rms, 2 story, 2 suites. June-Oct: S, D $190; suites $250; each addl $8; children $8; under 16 free; lower rates rest of yr. Crib avail. TV; cable. Restaurant nearby. Ck-out 11 am, ck-in 2 pm. Golf. Tennis, 4 courts. Cr cds: A, C, D, DS, JCB, MC, V.

🛐 📱 ◪ ◈

★★ **RAMADA INN REGENCY.** *1127 Rte 132 (01601), MA 132.* 508/775-1153; fax 508/790-4318; res 800/676-0000. 196 rms, 2 story. July-Sep: S, D $99-$159; each addl $10; suites $119-$199; higher rates hols; lower rates rest of yr. Crib free. TV; cable. Indoor pool; lifeguard. Restaurant 7 am-10 pm. Bar noon-1 am. Ck-out 11 am. Meeting rms. Business servs avail. Concierge serv. Game rm. Balconies. Cr cds: A, C, D, DS, ER, MC, V.

D 📱 📱 ◪ 🛐 ✕ 📱 ◈

Hotels

★★ **COMFORT INN-CAPE COD/HYANNIS.** *1470 Rte 132 (02601).* 508/771-4804; fax 508/790-2336; res 800/228-5150. Email comfort inn@capecod.net; www.comfortinn-hyannis.com. 103 rms, 3 story, 1 suite. May-Oct: S, D $175; suites $195; each addl $10; under 16 free; lower rates rest of yr. Crib avail. Pet accepted, some restrictions. Parking lot. Indoor pool, lifeguard, whirlpool. TV; cable (premium). Complimentary continental bkfst, coffee in rms, newspaper, toll-free calls. Ck-out noon, ck-in 4 pm. Meeting rm. Business servs avail. Dry cleaning. Exercise privi-

leges. Golf. Tennis. Video games. Cr cds: A, C, D, DS, ER, JCB, MC, V.

D 📱 🛐 📱 ⌨ 🛐 ✕ ◪ ◈ **SC**

★★★ **INTERNATIONAL INN.** *662 Main St (02601).* 508/775-5600; fax 508/775-3933; toll-free 877/5CUDDLES. Email intinn@capecod.net; www.cuddles.com. 37 rms, 2 story, 104 suites. Feb, June-Oct: S, D $90; suites $150; lower rates rest of yr. Crib avail. Parking lot. Indoor/outdoor pools, lifeguard. TV; cable (premium), VCR avail. Complimentary coffee in rms. Restaurant 7-10. Bar. Ck-out 11 am, ck-in 3 pm. Gift shop. Exercise privileges, sauna. Golf. Tennis. Cr cds: C, D, DS, ER, MC, V.

D 📱 🛐 📱 ⌨ 🛐 ✕ ◪

★★ **SHERATON FOUR POINTS HOTEL.** *MA 132 (02601), at Bearse's Way.* 508/771-3000; fax 508/778-6039; res 800/598-4559; toll-free 800/325-3535. www.sheraton.com. 256 rms, 2 story, 6 suites. June-Oct: S, D $189; each addl $15; lower rates rest of yr. Crib avail. Indoor/outdoor pools, lifeguard, whirlpool. TV; cable (premium). Complimentary coffee in rms, newspaper. Restaurant 7 am-11 pm. Bar. Ck-out 11 am, ck-in 4 pm. Conference center, meeting rms. Business servs avail. Bellhops. Dry cleaning. Gift shop. Exercise equipt. Golf. Tennis. Cr cds: A, D, DS, MC, V.

D 🛐 📱 ⌨ 🛐 ◪ ◈

Resort

★★★ **SHERATON HYANNIS RESORT.** *W End Circle (02601),* 508/775-7775; fax 508/778-6039; res 800/598-4559. www.sheraton.com. 226 rms, 2 story, 8 suites. May-Oct: S, D $209; each addl $15; lower rates rest of yr. Crib avail. Parking lot. Indoor/outdoor pools, lifeguard, whirlpool. TV; cable (premium). Complimentary coffee in rms, newspaper. Restaurant 7 am-11 pm. Bar. Ck-out 11 am, ck-in 4 pm. Business center. Bellhops. Concierge serv. Dry cleaning. Gift shop. Salon/barber avail. Exercise rm, sauna, steam rm. Golf, 18 holes. Tennis, 2 courts. Cr cds: A, C, D, DS, ER, JCB, MC, V.

D 🛐 📱 ⌨ 🛐 ◪ ◈ 🛐

B&Bs/Small Inns

★★ **SEA BREEZE INN.** *270 Ocean Ave (02601). 508/771-7213; fax 508/862-0663. Email seabreeze@capecod.net; www.seabreezeinn.com.* 14 rms, 2 story. June-Sep: S $80; D $90; each addl $15; lower rates rest of yr. Street parking. TV; cable. Complimentary continental bkfst. Restaurant nearby. Golf. Beach access. Bike rentals. Cr cds: A, DS, MC, V.

★★ **SIMMONS HOMESTEAD INN.** *288 Scudder Ave (02647), ½ mi W on Main St to Scudder Ave. 508/778-4999; fax 508/790-1342; toll-free 800/637-1649. Email simmonsinn@aol.com; www.capecodtravel.com/simmonsinn.* 12 rms, 2 story, 1 suite. May-Oct: S $160; D $180; suites $300; each addl $20; children $10; under 12 free; lower rates rest of yr. Crib avail. Pet accepted, fee. Parking lot. TV; cable, VCR avail, CD avail. Complimentary full bkfst, newspaper. Restaurant nearby. Ck-out 11 am, ck-in 2 pm. Meeting rm. Business servs avail. Concierge serv. Free airport transportation. Exercise privileges, whirlpool. Golf. Tennis, 11 courts. Beach access. Bike rentals. Hiking trail. Picnic facilities. Cr cds: A, DS, MC, V.

Restaurants

★ **DRAGON LITE.** *620 Main St (02601). 508/775-9494.* Specializes in beef and chicken Szechuan, coconut shrimp, Mongolian beef. Hrs: 11:30 am-10 pm. Closed Thanksgiving. Res accepted. Bar. Lunch $4-$6; dinner $5-$15. Street parking. Chinese decor. Cr cds: A, D, DS, MC, V.

D

★ **EGG & I.** *521 Main St (02601). 508/771-1596. Email gigis@gis.net.* Specializes in crow's nest eggs, original bkfsts. Hrs: 6 am-1 pm. Closed Dec-Feb; wkends only Mar, Nov. Res accepted. Bkfst $2-$10; lunch $2-$10. Child's menu. Street parking. Family dining. Cr cds: A, C, D, DS, ER, MC, V.

D SC

★ **ORIGINAL GOURMET BRUNCH.** *517 Main St (02601). 508/771-2558. www.capecod.com.* Hrs: 7 am-3 pm.

Closed Thanksgiving, Dec 25. Wine, beer. Bkfst $2.95-$8; lunch $2.95-$8. Street parking. Casual dining spot. Cr cds: A, MC, V.

★★ **PADDOCK.** *W Main St (02601). 508/775-7677. www.capecodtravel.com/thepaddock.* Specializes in fresh local seafood, roast L.I. duckling. Hrs: 11:30 am-2:30 pm, 5-10 pm. Closed mid-Nov-Mar. Res accepted. Bar. Wine list. Lunch $4.95-$9.50; dinner $13.95-$24.95. Child's menu. Entertainment: pianist. Valet parking. Victorian decor. Family-owned. Cr cds: A, D, DS, MC, V.

D

★★ **PENGUINS SEA GRILL.** *331 Main St (02601). 508/775-2023. Email penguins@capecod.net.* Specializes in seafood, wood-grilled meat, pasta. Hrs: 5-10 pm. Closed Thanksgiving, Dec 25. Res accepted. Bar. Dinner $14-$19. Child's menu. Cr cds: A, C, D, DS, ER, MC, V.

D

★★ **RISTORANTE BAROLO.** *297 N St (02601). 508/778-2878.* Specializes in antipasti, chicken saltimbocca. Hrs: 4 pm-midnight. Closed Jan 1, Easter, Dec 25. Res required. Bar. Dinner $7.95-$21.95. Italian decor. Cr cds: A, D, MC, V.

D

★★ **ROADHOUSE CAFE.** *488 S St (02601), 2 mi W on S St. 508/775-2386. www.roadhousecafe.com.* Specializes in grilled veal chop, cioppino, thin-crust pizza. Hrs: 4-11 pm. Closed Dec 24, 25. Res accepted. Bar. Dinner $5.95-$22.95. Valet parking. In 1903 house. Cr cds: A, D, DS, MC, V.

D

★ **SAM DIEGO'S.** *950 Lyanough Rd (MA 132) (02601), 1½ mi W on MA 132. 508/771-8816.* Specializes in fajitas, enchiladas, baby-back ribs. Own baking. Hrs: 11:30 am-midnight. Closed Easter, Thanksgiving, Dec 25. Bar. Lunch $2.95-$5.95; dinner $6.95-$12.95. Child's menu. Mexican decor. Cr cds: A, DS, MC, V.

D

★ **STARBUCKS.** *668 Rte 132 (02601). 508/778-6767. Email starbucks@capecod.net.* Specializes in hamburgers, fish, Mexican dishes. Hrs: 11:30 am-midnight. Closed Dec

25. Res accepted. Bar. Lunch $5.95-$12.95; dinner $5.95-$12.95. Child's menu. Parking. Coney Island beach house decor. Cr cds: A, D, DS, MC, V.

D

Unrated Dining Spot

BARBYANN'S. *120 Airport Rd (02601). 508/775-9795.* Specializes in hamburgers, prime rib, seafood. Hrs: 11:30 am-11 pm; Sun 11 am-10 pm; Sun brunch 11 am-3 pm. Closed Thanksgiving, Dec 25. Bar. Lunch $3.95-$6.95; dinner $6.95-$12.95. Sun brunch $3.95-$6.95. Child's menu. Parking. Antique toys. Cr cds: A, D, DS, MC, V.

D

Ipswich

See also Boston, Gloucester

Settled 1633 **Pop** 11,873 **Elev** 50 ft
Area code 978 **Zip** 01938

Information Ipswich Visitors Center-Hall Haskell House, S Main St, next to Town Hall; 508/356-8540

Ipswich is a summer resort town and home of the Ipswich clam; it has beaches nearby and a countryside of rolling woodland. Historically, Ipswich claims to have been the nation's first lacemaking town, the birthplace of the US hosiery industry, and of the American independence movement. In 1687 the Reverend John Wise rose in a meeting and denounced taxation without representation. His target was the hated Sir Edmund Andros, the British Colonial governor.

Andros and the lace are gone, but Ipswich retains the aura of its past. Besides a fine green, it has nearly 50 houses built before 1725, many from the 17th century.

What to See and Do

Crane Beach. Among the best on the Atlantic coast; 5 mi of beach; lifeguards, bathhouses, refreshment stand, trail. (Daily) End of Argilla Rd, on Ipswich Bay. Phone 978/356-4354. Per vehicle ¢¢¢; Summer wkends ¢¢¢¢

John Heard House. (1795) Bought as memorial to Thomas F. Waters, house has Chinese furnishings from the China sea trade. (Schedule same as Whipple House) 40 S Main St. Combination fee for both houses ¢¢

The John Whipple House. (1640) Contains 17th- and 18th-century furniture; garden. (May-mid-Oct, Wed-Sat, also Sun afternoons; closed hols) 53 S Main St, on MA 1A. Phone 978/356-2811. ¢¢ Opp is

Annual Event

Old Ipswich Days. Arts and crafts exhibits, games, clambakes, entertainment. Late July.

Motel/Motor Lodge

★★ **COUNTRY GARDEN INN & MOTEL.** *101 Main St (01969), 3 mi N on MA 1A. 978/948-7773; fax 978/948-7947; toll-free 800/287-7773. Email reserve@countrygardenmotel.com.* 19 rms, 12 with shower only, 1-3 story, 4 suites. No elvtr. May-Oct: S $65; D $75; each addl $15; suites $135; under 12 free; hols 2-day min; lower rates rest of yr. Children over 12 yrs only. Crib avail. TV; cable (premium), VCR avail (movies). Complimentary coffee in rms. Ck-out 10 am, ck-in after 1 pm. Business servs avail. X-country ski 2 mi. Lawn games. Some in-rm whirlpools, refrigerators, fireplaces. Picnic tables. Built in 1901. Cr cds: A, C, D, DS, MC, V.

B&B/Small Inn

★★★ **MILES RIVER COUNTRY INN B&B.** *823 Bay Rd (01936), 3 mi S on MA 1A. 978/468-7206; fax 978/468-3999. Email milesriver@mediaone.net; www.milesriver.com.* 8 rms, 2 share bath, 2 with shower only, 3 story. No A/C. No elvtr. No rm phones. June-Oct: S, D $90-$165; each addl $15; suite $210; lower rates rest of yr. Crib $15. Complimentary full bkfst. Restaurant nearby. Ck-out 11 am, ck-in 3 pm. Many fireplaces. Built in 1790s; Colonial American decor, antiques. Totally nonsmoking. Cr cds: A, MC, V.

Restaurants

★★★ **1640 HART HOUSE.** *51 Linebrook Rd (01938). 978/356-9411. www.1640harthouse.com.* Specializes in deep-dish escargot, grilled boneless duck breast. Hrs: 11:30 am-9 pm; Sat 4-10 pm; Sun noon-9 pm; earlybird dinner 4-6 pm. Closed Dec 25. Res accepted. Bar. Lunch $5-$11; dinner $10-$17. Child's menu. Entertainment: Fri, Sat. Parking. Serving food since 1700s. Cr cds: A, C, D, DS, MC, V.

D -◄

★★ **STEEP HILL GRILL.** *40 Essex Rd (01938). 978/356-1121. www. jackrabbitsflats.com.* Specializes in seasonal cuisine. Hrs: 5-10 pm. Closed Mon; hols. Res accepted. Bar. Dinner $13.95-$17.95. Child's menu. Parking. Colonial tavern decor. Cr cds: A, D, DS, MC, V.

D

Hotel

★★ **HAMPTON INN.** *224 Winthrop Ave (01843), I-495 Exit 42A. 978/975-4050; fax 508/687-7122; res 800/426-7866.* 126 rms, 5 story. Aug-Oct: S, D $99; under 18 free; lower rates rest of yr. Crib free. TV; cable. Complimentary continental bkfst. Restaurant nearby. Ck-out noon. Meeting rm. Business servs avail. In-rm modem link. Exercise equipt. Refrigerators, microwaves avail. Cr cds: A, MC, V.

D 示 ➡ ▨ SC

Restaurant

★★ **BISHOP'S.** *99 Hampshire (01840). 978/683-7143. Email bishop rest@worldnet.att.net.* Specializes in lobster, roast beef, Arabic dishes. Hrs: 11:30 am-9 pm; Sat 4-10 pm; Sun 2-9 pm. Closed Thanksgiving, Dec 25. Bar. Lunch $4.50-$9; dinner $11-$25. Entertainment: Fri, Sat. Moorish, Mediterranean decor. Family-owned. Cr cds: A, C, D, DS, MC, V.

D -◄

Lawrence (B-6)

Founded 1847 **Pop** 70,207 **Elev** 50 ft **Area code** 978
Information Chamber of Commerce, 264 Essex St, 01840; 508/686-0900

Lawrence was founded by a group of Boston financiers to tap the water power of the Merrimack River for the textile industry. As textiles moved out, diversified industries have been attracted to the community.

What to See and Do

Lawrence Heritage State Park. Twenty-three acres in city center incl restored Campagnone Common; canal and riverside esplanades. Visitor center in a restored workers' boardinghouse has participatory exhibits on the worker's experiences with industry in Lawrence and their contribution to the city's vitality. (Daily; closed Jan 1, Thanksgiving, Dec 25) Canal St. Phone 978/794-1655 or 978/685-2591. **FREE**

Lee

Founded 1777 **Pop** 5,849
Elev 1,000 ft **Area code** 413
Zip 01238

Lee's major industry has been papermaking since the first years of the 19th century. Today, it is also a summer and ski resort area.

What to See and Do

October Mountain State Forest. Fine mountain scenery overlooking 16,000 acres. Hiking, hunting, snowmobiling, camping on W side of forest. Standard fees. I-90 Exit 2, US 20 westbound. Phone 413/243-1778.

Santarella "Tyringham's Gingerbread House." Former studio of sculptor Sir Henry Kitson, creator of the "Minuteman" statue in Lexington. Built in the early 1930s, the house's major element is the roof, which was designed to look like thatching and to represent the rolling hills of the Berkshires in autumn; the fronting rock pillars and the grottoes between them are fashioned after similar edifices in Europe; Santarella Sculpture garden. Exhibits incl ceramics, glass, paintings, graphics, antiques, objets d'art; also changing exhibits. Sculpture garden with lily pond. (Late May-Oct, daily) 4 mi SE in Tyringham. Phone 413/243-0654. ¢¢

Lighthouse on Cape Cod

Seasonal Event

Jacob's Pillow Dance Festival. Ted Shawn Theatre and Doris Duke Theatre, 8 mi E via US 20, on George Carter Rd in Becket. America's oldest and most prestigious dance festival incl performances by international dance companies. Performances Tues-Sat, some Sun. Phone 413/243-0745 (box office) or 413/637-1322 (info). Late June-Aug.

Motels/Motor Lodges

★★ BEST WESTERN BLACK SWAN INN. *435 Laurel St; Rte 20 W (01238), 2 mi N on MA 20 at Laurel Lake.* 413/243-2700; fax 413/243-2700; toll-free 800/876-7926. Email blkswanma@aol.com; www.travelweb.com/thisco/bw/22036/22036_b.html. 52 rms, 2 story. July-Aug: D $95-$180; suites $120-$215; higher rates wkends (2-day min); lower rates rest of yr. TV; cable, VCR (movies $6). Pool; sauna. Restaurant 5-9 pm. Bar. Ck-out 11 am. Meeting rm. Business center. In-rm modem link. Lawn games. Some refrigerators. Some balconies. Picnic tables. On lake. Cr cds: A, D, DS, MC, V.

D 🐾 ⊷

★★ PILGRAM INN. *165 Housatonic St (01238), ¼ mi N of MA Tpke Exit 2.* 413/243-1328; fax 413/243-2339; toll-free 888/537-5476. Email pilgriminn@aol.com; www.pilgriminn-berkshires.com. 36 rms, 2 story. July-Aug, Oct: S $175; D $195; each addl $10; under 12 free; lower rates rest of yr. Crib avail, fee. Parking lot. Pool. TV; cable. Complimentary continental bkfst, toll-free calls. Restaurant nearby. Ck-out 11 am, ck-in 3 pm. Business center. Coin lndry. Golf. Tennis. Downhill skiing. Cr cds: A, D, DS, MC, V.

D ⊷ 🎿 📠 ⊷
🚫 🔥 🚶

B&Bs/Small Inns

★★★ APPLEGATE. *279 W Park St (01238).* 413/243-4451; fax 413/243-9832; toll-free 800/691-9012. Email lenandgloria@applegateinn.com. 6 rms, 6 with shower only, 2 story. No rm phones. June-Oct: S, D $115-$230; each addl $30; wkends, hols (3-day min); lower rates rest of yr. Children over 12 yrs only. TV in sitting rm. Pool. Complimentary continental bkfst. Restaurant nearby. Ck-out 11 am, ck-in 2 pm. Lawn games. Georgian Colonial built in 1920. Totally nonsmoking. Cr cds: A, MC, V.

🐾 ⊷ 🎿 ⊷ 🚫 🔥 🚶 🚶

★★★ CHAMBERY INN. *199 Main St (US 20W) (01238), at Elm.* 413/243-2221; fax 413/243-3600; toll-free 800/537-4321. 9 rms, 3 story, 9 suites. July-Aug, Oct: S, D, suites $99-$265; each addl $25; 2- or 3-day min wkends; lower rates rest of yr. Over 18 yrs only. TV; cable. Restaurant adj 11:30 am-9 pm. Ck-out 11 am, ck-in 2 pm. Business servs avail. Downhill ski 8 mi. In-rm whirlpools. Berkshires' oldest parochial school (built 1885); recently restored with custom Amish-crafted furnishings. Totally nonsmoking. Cr cds: A, DS, MC, V.

D 🚫 🔥

★★★ DEVONFIELD INN. *85 Stockbridge Rd (01238), at Park St.* 413/

243-3298; fax 413/243-1360; toll-free
800/664-0880. Email ms66jl@aol.com.
10 rms, 3 story. June-Oct: D $110-
$195; each addl $20; suites $155-
$260; lower rates rest of yr; 3-day
min wkends (July-Aug). Children
over 10 yrs only. TV in some rms;
cable. Heated pool. Complimentary
full bkfst. Ck-out 11:30 am, ck-in 2
pm. Business servs avail. Tennis.
Lawn games. Some fireplaces. Picnic
tables. Built by Revolutionary War
soldier; Federal-style rms with
antique furnishings. Cr cds: A, D, DS,
MC, V.

★★★ **FEDERAL HOUSE INN.** *1560
Pleasant St, Rte 102 (01260), 3½ mi S
on MA 102. 413/243-1824; fax 413/
243-1828; res 800/237-5747; toll-free
800/243-1824. www.federalhouseinn.
com.* 9 rms, 2 story. July-Oct: S, D
$180; each addl $25; under 12 free;
lower rates rest of yr. Parking lot. TV;
cable, CD avail. Complimentary full
bkfst, coffee in rms, newspaper.
Restaurant nearby. Ck-out 11 am, ck-
in 3 pm. Fax servs avail. Golf. Tennis.
Downhill skiing. Picnic facilities. Cr
cds: A, DS, MC, V.

★★★ **HISTORIC MERRELL INN.**
*1565 Pleasant St (Rte 102) (01260), 3
mi S on MA 102. 413/243-1794; fax
413/243-2669; toll-free 800/243-1794.
Email info@merrell-inn.com; www.
merrell-inn.com.* 10 rms, 3 story. July-
Oct: S $75-$155; D $85-$165; each
addl $15; suite $135-$215; lower
rates rest of yr. TV in some rms.
Complimentary full bkfst. Ck-out 11
am, ck-in 2 pm. Downhill ski 10 mi;
x-country ski 5 mi. Fireplaces. View
of river. Historic New England inn
(1794); English gardens. Cr cds: A,
MC, V.

★★ **MORGAN HOUSE.** *33 Main St
(01238). 413/243-3661; fax 413/243-
3103; toll-free 877/571-0837.* 11 rms,
6 share bath, 3 story. No rm phones.
July-Oct: S, D $85-$160; each addl
$15; lower rates rest of yr. Crib free.
Complimentary full bkfst. Restaurant
Bar 11-1 am. Ck-out 11 am, ck-in 1
pm. Built 1817. Stagecoach inn

(1853); antiques; country-style decor.
Cr cds: A, D, MC, V.

Restaurants

★★ **CORK N' HEARTH.** *MA 20W
(01238). 413/243-0535.* Specializes in
fresh seafood, veal, beef. Hrs: 5-9 pm.
Closed Mon; Thanksgiving, Dec 24,
25. Res accepted. Bar. Dinner $13.95-
$18.95. Child's menu. 3 dining rms.
Scenic view of lake. Cr cds: A, MC, V.

★★ **SULLIVAN STATION RESTAU-
RANT.** *109 Railroad St (01238).
413/243-2082. www.berkshireweb.com/
dining/menus/sullivanstation.* Specializes in Boston baked scrod, steak,
vegetarian dishes. Hrs: 11:30 am-9
pm. Closed Thanksgiving, Dec 25;
also 2 wks late Feb-early Mar. Res
accepted. Bar. Lunch $4.95-$8.95;
dinner $11.95-$18.95. Railroad memorabilia. Cr cds: A, DS, MC, V.

Lenox

Settled ca 1750 **Pop** 5,069
Elev 1,200 ft **Area code** 413
Zip 01240 **Web** www.lenox.org
Information Chamber of Commerce,
65 Main St, PO Box 646; 413/637-
3646

This summer resort became world-
famous for music when the Boston
Symphony began its Berkshire Festival here in 1939. Nearby is Stockbridge Bowl, one of the prettiest
lakes in the Berkshires.

What to See and Do

**Edith Wharton Restoration (The
Mount).** Edith Wharton's summer
estate; was planned from a book she
coauthored in 1897, *The Decoration of
Houses,* and built in 1902. This Classical Revival house is architecturally
significant; ongoing restoration. On
49 acres, with gardens. Tour of house
and gardens (late May-Labor Day,
daily; after Labor Day-late Oct, Sat
and Sun). (See SEASONAL EVENTS)

Plunkett St at S jct of US 7 & MA 7A. Phone 413/637-1899. ¢¢

Pleasant Valley Wildlife Sanctuary. Sanctuary of the Massachusetts Audubon Society. 1,200 acres with 7 mi of trails; beaver colony; office. (Tues-Sun) Trailside Museum (May-Oct, Tues-Sun). No dogs. On West Mountain Rd, 1½ mi W of US 7/20. Phone 413/637-0320. ¢¢

✪ **Tanglewood.** Where Nathaniel Hawthorne planned *Tanglewood Tales.* Many of the 210 acres, developed into a gentleman's estate by William Aspinwall Tappan, are in formal gardens. Well-known today as the summer home of the Boston Symphony Orchestra and the Tanglewood Music Center, the symphony's training academy for young musicians. (See SEASONAL EVENTS) Grounds (daily; free exc during concerts). On West St, 1½ mi SW on MA 183. Phone 413/637-1600 (summer) or 617/266-1492 (rest of yr).

Main Gate Area. Friends of Tanglewood, box office, music and bookstore, cafeteria, gift shop.

Main House. Original mansion, now administrative bldg for Tanglewood Music Center. Excellent view of Lake Mahkeenac, Monument Mt.

Formal Gardens. Manicured hemlock hedges and lawn, tall pine. Picnicking.

Koussevitzky Music Shed. (1938) The so-called "Shed," where Boston Symphony Orchestra concerts take place; holds 5,000.

Hawthorne Cottage. Replica of "Little Red House" where Hawthorne lived 1850-51, now contains music studios, Hawthorne memorabilia. (Open before each festival concert.)

Chamber Music Hall. Small chamber music ensembles, lectures, seminars, and large classes held here. Designed by Eliel Saarinen, who also designed

Seiji Ozawa Concert Hall. (1941) Festival chamber music programs, Tanglewood Music Center activities; seats 1,200.

Annual Events

Apple Squeeze Festival. Celebration of apple harvest; entertainment,

food, music. Phone 413/637-3646. Usually 3rd wkend Sep.

House Tours of Historic Lenox. Phone 413/637-3646. Fall.

Seasonal Events

Shakespeare & Co. The Mount. Professional theater company performs plays by Shakespeare and Edith Wharton, as well as other events. Four stages, one outdoor. Tues-Sun. Phone 413/637-3353. Late May-early Nov.

Tanglewood Music Festival. Tanglewood Boston Symphony Orchestra. Concerts, Fri and Sat eve and Sun afternoons. Inquire for other musical events. Phone 413/637-1940. July-Aug.

Motels/Motor Lodges

★ **HOWARD JOHNSON EXPRESS INN.** *462 Pittsfield Rd (01240). 413/442-4000; fax 413/440-2630; res 800/446-4656; toll-free 413/442-4000. www.hojo.com.* 44 rms, 2 story, 6 suites. July-Aug: S, D $85-$185; suites $95-$215; under 18 free; wkends (2-3-day min); higher rates fall foliage; lower rates rest of yr. TV; cable. Pool. Complimentary continental bkfst. Restaurant adj 6 am-10 pm. Ck-out 11 am. Business center. Sundries. Many microwaves; some refrigerators. Cr cds: A, MC, V.

D ⤒ ≋ ⊠ 🔥 SC 🏃

★ **LENOX MOTEL.** *525 Pittsfield-Lenox Rd (01240), US 7/20, 4 mi NE. 413/499-0324; fax 413/499-5618. Email lenoxmotel@aol.com; www.lenox motel.com.* 17 rms, 1 story. July-Aug: S, D $145; each addl $10; children $7; under 5 free; lower rates rest of yr. Crib avail, fee. Pet accepted, some restrictions, fee. Parking lot. Pool. TV; cable. Complimentary toll-free calls. Restaurant 6-11. Ck-out 11 am, ck-in 2 pm. Business servs avail. Golf. Tennis. Downhill skiing. Cr cds: A, DS, MC, V.

🏃 ⤒ 🎿 ⛷ ≋ ⊠ 🔥 SC

★★ **THE YANKEE HOME COMFORT.** *461 Pittsfield Rd (01240), 3 mi N on US 7/20. 413/499-3700; fax 413/499-3634; toll-free 800/835-2364. Email yankeehe@javanet.com; www. berkshireinns.com.* 90 rms, 3 story, 6 suites. July-Aug, Oct: S, D $169; suites $259; lower rates rest of yr. Crib avail, fee. Parking lot. Indoor/outdoor pools, whirlpool. TV; cable, CD avail. Complimentary continental bkfst, coffee in rms. Restaurant. Bar. Ck-out 12 pm, ck-in 12 pm. Meeting rms. Business center. Concierge serv. Dry cleaning. Exercise privileges. Golf. Tennis. Downhill skiing. Picnic facilities. Cr cds: A, C, D, DS, MC, V.

Hotels

★ ★ ★ ★ **BLANTYRE.** *16 Blantyre Rd (01240), 1 mi E on MA 20; 3 mi W of I-90 (MA Tpke Exit 2). 413/637-3556; fax 413/637-4282. Email hide@ blantyre.com; www.blantyre.com.* This estate's castlelike, brick facade alone will make visitors feel privileged. The wooded Berkshires are a perfect setting for the property's 100-acres of manicured lawns and gardens, main house, carriage house, and cottages. Rates incl continental breakfast and on-site recreations incl tennis, croquet, and swimming. Rich, carved mahogany furniture and detailing fill the accommodations and there's a wonderful oak library to browse. 12 rms, 2 story, 8 suites. May-Oct: S, D $350; suites $400; each addl $50; lower rates rest of yr. Parking lot. Pool. TV; cable, VCR avail. Complimentary continental bkfst, newspaper. Restaurant 6-9 pm, closed Mon. Bar. Ck-out noon, ck-in 3 pm. Meeting rms. Business center. Bellhops. Concierge serv. Exercise privileges, sauna. Golf. Tennis, 4 courts. Bike rentals. Hiking trail. Cr cds: A, C, D, MC, V.

★ ★ ★ **CRANWELL RESORT AND GOLF CLUB.** *55 Lee Rd (01240), 1/10 mi E of US 7/20. 413/637-1364; fax 413/637-0571; toll-free 800/272-6935. www.cranwell.com.* 93 rms in 7 bldgs, 2-3 story. Mid-June-Oct: S, D $199-$289; under 12 free; suites $289-$439; wkend rates; package plans; lower rates rest of yr. Crib free. TV; cable, VCR avail. Heated pool; poolside serv, lifeguard. Complimentary continental bkfst. Coffee in rms. Restaurant (see WYNDHURST). Bar; entertainment Fri, Sat. Ck-out 11 am. Meeting rms. Business servs avail. In-rm modem link. Tennis. 18-hole golf, greens fee $25-$85, pros, putting green, driving range, golf school. Downhill ski 7 mi; x-country ski on

site. Exercise equipt. Some bathrm phones, fireplaces; microwaves avail. Balconies. Picnic tables. Heliport. Country Tudor mansion on 380 acres. Cr cds: A, D, DS, MC, V.

★ ★ ★ **WHEATLEIGH HOTEL.** *Hawthorne Rd (01240). 413/637-0610; fax 413/637-4507. Email wheatleigh@ taconic.net; www.wheatleigh.com.* 21 rms, 2 story, 2 suites. July-Aug, Oct: D $365; suites $1075; lower rates rest of yr. Valet parking avail. Pool. TV; cable (premium), VCR avail, CD avail. Complimentary newspaper. Restaurant noon-11 pm. 24-hr rm serv. Bar. Ck-out 11 am, ck-in 3 pm. Meeting rms. Business servs avail. Bellhops. Concierge serv. Dry cleaning. Exercise rm. Downhill skiing. Beach access. Bike rentals. Hiking trail. Picnic facilities. Cr cds: A, C, D, MC.

B&Bs/Small Inns

★ ★ **APPLE TREE INN.** *10 Richmond Mountain Rd (10048). 413/637-1477; fax 413/637-2528. Email japple@ berkshire.net; www.appletree-inn.com.* 35 rms, 2 share bath, 3 story, 2 suites. No rm phones. July-Aug: S, D $130-$210; suites $300; 3-day min wkends; some rms 5-day min; lower rates rest of yr. Crib free. TV in some rms; cable. Heated pool. Complimentary continental bkfst. Restaurant (see APPLE TREE). Ck-out 11:30 am, ck-in 2 pm. Tennis. X-country ski 1 mi. Picnic tables. Built in 1885; situated on 22 hilltop acres. Cr cds: A, C, D, DS, MC, V.

★ ★ **BIRCHWOOD INN.** *7 Hubbard St (01240). 413/637-2600; fax 413/637-4604; toll-free 800/524-1646. Email innkeeper@birchwood-inn.com.* 12 rms, 8 with shower only, 2 share bath, 3 story, 8 kit. suites. July-Aug: S, D, kit. suites $90-$210; wkday rates; lower rates rest of yr. Children over 12 yrs only. TV in some rms; cable. Complimentary full bkfst. Restaurant adj 6-10 pm. Ck-out 11:30 am, ck-in 2 pm. Business servs avail. Downhill ski 5 mi; x-country ski adj. Built in 1767; many antiques, gardens. Totally nonsmoking. Cr cds: A, MC, V.

★★★ **BROOK FARM INN.** *15 Hawthorne St (01240). 413/637-3013; fax 413/637-4751; toll-free 800/285-7638. Email innkeeper@brookfarm.com; www.brookfarm.com.* 12 rms, 3 story. June-Oct: S, D $205; each addl $20; lower rates rest of yr. Crib avail. Parking lot. Pool. TV; cable (premium), VCR avail, CD avail. Complimentary full bkfst, newspaper. Restaurant nearby. Business servs avail. Concierge serv. Gift shop. Exercise privileges. Golf. Tennis. Downhill skiing. Cr cds: MC, V.

★★ **CANDLELIGHT INN AND RESTAURANT.** *35 Walker St (01240). 413/637-1555. Email innkeeper@ candlelightinn-lenox.com; www. candlelightinn-lenox.com.* 8 rms, 3 story. No rm phones. July-Oct: D $145-$175; each addl $30; wkly rates; lower rates rest of yr. Children over 10 yrs only. TV in sitting rm. Complimentary continental bkfst. Dining rm noon-9:30 pm. Bar in season. Ck-out 11 am, ck-in 2 pm. Downhill ski 5 mi; x-country ski ½ mi. Built 1885. Cr cds: A, DS, MC, V.

★★★ **THE GABLES INN.** *81 Walker St (01240). 413/637-3416; fax 413/637-3416; toll-free 800/382-9401. www.gableslenox.com.* 18 rms, 3 story, 4 suites. No rm phones. Mid-June-Oct: S, D $90-$210; lower rates rest of yr. Children over 12 yrs only. TV; cable, VCR (free movies). Pool. Complimentary bkfst; afternoon refreshments. Restaurant nearby. Ck-out noon, ck-in 2 pm. Tennis. Downhill ski 5 mi; x-country ski ¼ mi. Some fireplaces. Balconies. Picnic tables. Antiques. Library/sitting rm. Queen Anne-style house (1885), once the home of Edith Wharton. Cr cds: DS, MC, V.

★★★ **GARDEN GABLES INN.** *135 Main St (01240), Downtown in Historic District. 413/637-0193; fax 413/637-4554. Email gardeninn@aol.com; www. lenoxinn.com.* 18 rms, 1 story, 2 suites. June-Oct: D $200; suites $275; each addl $30; under 12 free; lower rates rest of yr. Crib avail. Valet parking avail. Pool, lap pool. TV; cable (premium), VCR avail. Complimentary full bkfst, newspaper, toll-free calls. Restaurant. Ck-out 11 am, ck-in 2 pm. Meeting rms. Business servs avail. Concierge serv. Exercise privileges. Golf, 18 holes. Tennis, 4 courts. Downhill skiing. Beach access. Bike rentals. Hiking trail. Picnic facilities. Cr cds: A, DS, MC, V.

★★ **GATEWAYS INN.** *51 Walker St (01240). 413/637-2532; fax 413/637-1432; toll-free 888/492-9466. Email gateways@berkshire.net; www.gateways inn.com.* 11 rms, 2 story, 1 suite. June-Oct: S $110; D $200; suite $350; each addl $40; lower rates rest of yr. Parking lot. TV; cable. Complimentary full bkfst, coffee in rms, newspaper, toll-free calls. Restaurant, closed Mon. Bar. Ck-out 11 am, ck-in 2 pm. Meeting rms. Business center. Concierge serv. Gift shop. Golf, 18 holes. Tennis, 3 courts. Downhill skiing. Bike rentals. Hiking trail. Cr cds: A, C, D, DS, MC, V.

★★★ **HARRISON HOUSE.** *174 Main St (02114). 413/637-1746; fax 413/637-9957. www.harrison-house. com.* 6 rms, 3 story, 2 suites. June-Oct: S, D $175; suites $240; each addl $50; under 12 free; lower rates rest of yr. Parking lot. TV; cable. Complimentary full bkfst, newspaper. Ck-out 11 am, ck-in 2 pm. Meeting rm. Exercise privileges. Downhill skiing. Beach access. Bike rentals. Supervised children's activities. Hiking trail. Picnic facilities. Cr cds: A, MC, V.

★★★ **KEMBLE INN.** *2 Kemble St (01240). 413/637-4113; toll-free 800/353-4113. www.kembleinn.com.* 14 rms, 3 story. July-Oct: S $145; D $295; each addl $25; lower rates rest of yr. Parking lot. TV; cable. Complimentary continental bkfst. Restaurant nearby. Ck-out 11 am, ck-in 2 pm. Golf, 18 holes. Tennis, 3 courts. Downhill skiing. Cr cds: DS, MC, V.

★★ **ROOKWOOD INN.** *11 Old Stockbridge Rd (01240). 413/637-9750; fax 413/637-1532; toll-free 800/223-9750. Email stay@rookwoodinn.com.* 21 rms, 3 story, 2 suites. Phones in suites. Late June-Aug: D $110-$235;

each addl $15; suite $250-$285; under 12 free; lower rates rest of yr. Crib free. TV in sitting rm and suites. Complimentary full bkfst; afternoon refreshments. Restaurant nearby. Ck-out 11 am, ck-in 3 pm. Bus depot transportation. Downhill ski 5 mi; x-country ski 1 mi. Fireplaces. Balconies. Victorian inn (1885) furnished with English antiques. Totally nonsmoking. Cr cds: A, D, DS, MC, V.

★★★ **THE SUMMER WHITE HOUSE.** *17 Main St (01240). 413/637-4489; fax 413/637-4489; res 413/637-4489; toll-free 800/382-9401. www.thesummerwhitehouse.com.* 6 rms, 3 story. June-Aug: D $195; lower rates rest of yr. Parking lot. Indoor pool. TV; cable (premium). Complimentary continental bkfst, newspaper, toll-free calls. Restaurant nearby. Ck-out 11 am, ck-in 2 pm. Coin lndry. Salon/barber avail. Exercise privileges. Golf. Tennis. Downhill skiing. Beach access. Bike rentals. Hiking trail. Picnic facilities. Cr cds: MC, V.

★★ **THE VILLAGE INN.** *16 Church St (01240), center of town. 413/637-0020; fax 413/637-9756; toll-free 800/253-0917. Email villinn@vgernet.net; www.villageinn-lenox.com.* 32 rms, 3 story, 1 suite. July-Oct: S, D $225; suites $520; each addl $30; lower rates rest of yr. Parking lot. TV; cable (DSS), VCR avail. Complimentary full bkfst, coffee in rms, newspaper. Restaurant 5-9 pm, closed Mon. Bar. Ck-out 11 am, ck-in 2 pm. Meeting rms. Business center. Concierge serv. Gift shop. Exercise privileges, whirlpool. Golf. Tennis, 4 courts. Downhill skiing. Bike rentals. Hiking trail. Cr cds: A, C, D, DS, MC, V.

★ **WALKER HOUSE.** *64 Walker St (01240). 413/637-1271; fax 413/637-2387; toll-free 800/235-3098. Email phoudek@vgernet.net; www.walkerhouse.com.* 8 rms, 2 story. July-Aug, Oct: S $125; D $190; each addl $10; lower rates rest of yr. Pet accepted, some restrictions. Parking lot. TV; cable (premium), VCR avail, CD avail. Complimentary continental bkfst, coffee in rms, newspaper, toll-free calls. Restaurant. Ck-out noon, ck-in 2 pm. Meeting rms. Business servs avail. Exercise privileges. Golf. Tennis, 3 courts. Downhill skiing. Hiking trail. Picnic facilities. Cr cds: A, MC, V.

★★ **WHISTLER INN.** *5 Greenwood St (01240). 413/637-0975; fax 419/637-2190. Email rmears3246@aol.com.* 14 rms, 2 story, 3 suites. July-Aug, Oct: D $90-$225; each addl $25; suites $160-$225; 3-day min summer; lower rates rest of yr. TV; cable; VCR avail. Complimentary full bkfst; afternoon refreshments. Restaurant nearby. Ck-out noon, ck-in 3 pm. Business servs avail. Free bus depot transportation. Downhill ski 5 mi; x-country ski ½ blk. Lawn games. Fireplaces. Picnic tables. Tudor-style mansion built 1820. Library. Music rm with Steinway grand piano, Louis XVI furniture. Cr cds: A, DS, MC, V.

Restaurants

★★ **APPLE TREE.** *10 Richmond Mt Rd. 413/637-1477. www.appletree-inn.com.* Specializes in fresh fish of the day, black Angus steak. Own baking. Hrs: 5:30-9 pm. Closed Mon-Wed off-season. Res accepted. Bar. Dinner $12-$23. Parking. Round dining rm with hillside view. Cr cds: A, D, DS, MC, V.

★★★ **BLANTYRE.** *16 Blantyre Rd. 413/637-3556. www.blantyre.com.* Specializes in fresh game and seafood. Own baking, ice cream. Hrs: 6-8:45 pm; July-Aug also 12:30-1:45 pm. Closed Mon; also Nov-Apr. Res required. Wine cellar. Lunch prix fixe: (July-Aug) 2-course $32, 3-course $40; dinner prix fixe: $75. 18% serv chg. Entertainment: harpist. Valet parking. Jacket. Cr cds: A, C, D, ER, MC, V.

★★ **CAFE LUCIA.** *80 Church St (01240). 413/637-2640.* Specializes in veal, seafood, pasta. Hrs: 5:30-10 pm; hrs vary mid-Sep-May. Closed Mon; Easter, Thanksgiving, Dec 25; also Sun Nov-June. Res accepted. Dinner $13-$28. Cr cds: A, C, D, DS, ER, MC, V.

★ **CAROL'S.** *8 Franklin St (01240). 413/637-8948.* Specializes in bkfst dishes. Hrs: 8 am-2 pm. Closed Wed (Sep-June); Thanksgiving, Dec 25. Bkfst $1.95-$6.50; lunch $1.95-$6.50. Child's menu. Cr cds: A, DS, MC, V.
D SC

★★ **CHURCH STREET CAFE.** *65 Church St (01240). 413/637-2745. Email chustcafe@aol.com.* Specializes in seafood, crab cakes, grilled meat and fish. Hrs: 11:30 am-2 pm, 5:30-9 pm; Fri, Sat to 9:15 pm. Closed Jan 1, Thanksgiving, Dec 25; also Sun, Mon Nov-May. Res accepted. Bar. Lunch $7.95-$13.95; dinner $16.95-$25.50. Bistro-style cafe; New England decor. Cr cds: MC, V.
D

★★★ **GATEWAYS INN.** *51 Walker St. 413/637-2532. Email gateways@ berkshire.net; www.gatewaysinn.com.* Indian menu. Specializes in escargot with gnocchi, rack of lamb Provencal, seasonal dishes. Hrs: 5:30-9 pm. Closed Mon. Res accepted. Wine list. Dinner $18-$26. Parking. Cr cds: A, C, D, DS, ER, MC, V.

★★★ **LENOX 218 RESTAURANT.** *218 Main St (01240). 413/637-4218. www.lenox218.com.* Specializes in Tuscan clam soup; New England seafood cakes; boneless breast of chicken with almonds, sesame, and sunflower seeds. Hrs: 11:30 am-2:30 pm, 5-10 pm. Res accepted. Bar. Lunch $5.95-$8.95; dinner $12.95-$20.95. Child's menu. Parking. Casual elegance; vaulted ceilings and skylights. Cr cds: A, D, DS, MC, V.
D

★★ **LENOX HOUSE.** *55 Pittsfield-Lenox Rd (01240), 5 mi N of MA Tpke Exit 2. 413/637-1341. www.regionnet. com/colberk/lenoxhouse.html.* Specializes in fresh fish, poultry, prime rib. Own baking. Hrs: 11:30 am-9 pm; Fri, Sat to 10 pm. Res accepted. Bar. Lunch $4.75-$9.95; dinner $10.95-$21.95. Parking. Cr cds: A, D, DS, MC, V.
D

★ **PANDA HOUSE CHINESE RESTAURANT.** *506 Pittsfield Rd (01240), 4 mi N on MA 7. 413/499-0660.* Specializes in General Tso's chicken, vegetarian paradise. Hrs: 11:30 am-10 pm; Sun brunch to 3 pm. Closed Thanksgiving, Dec 25.

Res accepted. Bar. Lunch $4.75-$6.25; dinner $7.95-$15.95. Sun brunch $7.95. Parking. Oriental decor. Cr cds: A, D, DS, MC, V.
D

★★★★ **WHEATLEIGH.** *Hawthorne Rd. 413/637-0610.* Polished, mahogany doors lead to this historic hotel's elegant restaurant. The dining room's design is just as regal as the bldg itself, which was modeled in 1893 after a 16th-century Florentine palazzo. Guests dine on contemporary French cuisine (tasting and degustation menus are available) in a beautiful, sun-drenched room filled with oil paintings, hand-carved Chippendale chairs, and sparkling crystal chandeliers. Own baking. Hrs: 6-9 pm. Closed Sun-Thurs. Res required. Dinner 7-course degustation menu (changes every 2-3 days) $95. Valet parking. Cr cds: A, D, DS, MC, V.
D

★★★ **THE WYNDHURST RESTAURANT.** *55 Lee Rd. 413/637-1364. www.cranwell.com.* Specializes in lamb, fresh fish, daily specialties. Own desserts. Hrs: 5-9 pm. Res accepted. Bar. Wine list. Dinner $16.50-$28. Child's menu. Entertainment: Fri, Sat. Formal decor in Tudor mansion; ornately carved fireplace, original artwork. Cr cds: A, DS, MC, V.
D

Leominster (C-5)

Settled 1653 **Pop** 38,145 **Elev** 400 ft
Area code 978 **Zip** 01453
Web www.nc.massweb.org

Information Johnny Appleseed Visitor Center, 110 Erdman Way; 978/840-4300

Leominster (LEMMINst'r) has retained the pronunciation of the English town for which it was named. Known at one time as "Comb City," in 1845 Leominster housed 24 factories manufacturing horn combs. It is the birthplace of "Johnny Appleseed"—John Chapman (1774-1845)—a devout Swedenborgian missionary who traveled throughout America on foot, planting apple orchards and the seeds of his faith. The National Plastics Center and Museum is located here.

Hotel

★★ FOUR POINTS HOTEL LEOMINSTER. *99 Erdman Way (01453), ¼ mi N, at jct MA 2 and 12. 978/534-9000; fax 978/534-0891; res 800/325-3535.* 187 rms, 7 story. S $119-$130; D $134-$145; each addl $15; suites $130-$145; under 18 free. Crib free. TV; cable. Indoor pool. Complimentary continental bkfst Mon-Fri. Restaurant 6:30 am-10 pm. Bar 11:30-1 am. Ck-out noon. Meeting rms. Business center. In-rm modem link. Downhill ski 5 mi. Whirlpool. Cr cds: A, MC, V.

Conference Center

★★★ WACHUSETT VILLAGE INN. *9 Village Inn Rd (01473), 6 mi W on MA 2, Exit 27. 978/874-2000; fax 978/874-1753; res 800/342-1905. www.wachussetvillageinn.com.* 68 rms, 6 story, 6 suites. Jan-Mar, June-Oct: S, D $119; suites $179; each addl $10; children $10; under 12 free; lower rates rest of yr. Crib avail, fee. Pet accepted, some restrictions, fee. Parking lot. Indoor/outdoor pools, lifeguard, whirlpool. TV; cable (premium), VCR avail. Complimentary coffee in rms. Restaurant 7 am-11 pm. Bar. Ck-out 11 am, ck-in 3 pm. Meeting rms. Business servs avail. Dry cleaning, coin lndry. Gift shop. Exercise rm, sauna, steam rm. Golf. Tennis, 2 courts. Downhill skiing. Bike rentals. Supervised children's activities. Hiking trail. Picnic facilities. Cr cds: A, C, D, DS, MC, V.

Lexington

(C-6) *See also Concord*

Settled ca 1640 **Pop** 28,974
Elev 210 ft **Area code** 781 **Zip** 02173
Information Chamber of Commerce Visitors Center, 1875 Massachusetts Ave; 781/862-1450. The center, open daily, offers a diorama depicting the Battle of Lexington and has a walking tour map.

Lexington is called the birthplace of American liberty. On its Green, April 19, 1775, eight Minutemen were killed in what is traditionally considered the first organized fight of the American Revolution. However, in 1908, the US Senate recognized the counterclaim of Point Pleasant, West Virginia as the first battle site. It is still possible to visualize the Battle of Lexington. Down the street came the British, 700 strong. To the right of the Green is the tavern the militia used as headquarters. It was here that 77 Minutemen lined up near the west end of the Green, facing down the Charlestown road. Nearby is a boulder with a plaque bearing the words of Captain John Parker, spoken just before the Redcoats opened fire: "Stand your ground. Don't fire unless fired upon. But if they mean to have a war, let it begin here!" It did—the fight then moved on to Concord.

What to See and Do

Battle Green. The Old Monument, the Minuteman Statue, and the Boulder mark the line of the Minutemen, 7 of whom are buried under the monument. At the center of town.

Lexington Historical Society. Revolutionary period houses. Guided tours. Phone 781/862-1703. 3-house combination ticket ¢¢¢

    Hancock-Clarke House. (1698) Here John Hancock and Samuel Adams were awakened by Paul Revere's alarm on Apr 18, 1775. Furniture, portraits, utensils; small museum. Fire engine exhibit in barn (by appt). (Mid-Apr-Oct, daily) 36 Hancock St. Phone 781/862-1703.

    Buckman Tavern. (1709) Minutemen assembled here before the battle. Period furnishings, portraits. (Mid-Apr-Oct, daily; Nov, wkends only) 1 Bedford St, facing the Battle Green. Phone 781/862-1703.

    Munroe Tavern. (1695) British hospital after the battle. George Washington dined here in 1789. Period furnishings, artifacts. (Mid-Apr-Oct, daily) 1332 Massachusetts Ave. Phone 781/862-1703.

Museum of Our National Heritage. Museum features exhibits on American history and culture, from its founding to the present; also history of Lexington and the American Revolution. (Daily) 33 Marrett Rd (MA 2A), at jct Massachusetts Ave. Phone 781/861-6559. **FREE**

Annual Event

Reenactment of the Battle of Lexington and Concord. Massachusetts Ave. Reenactment of opening battle of American Revolution; parade. Patriots Day. Mon nearest Apr 19.

Motel/Motor Lodge

★★ **HOLIDAY INN EXPRESS.** *440 Bedford St (02420), I-95 Exit 31B. 781/861-0850; fax 781/861-0821.* 204 rms, 2 story. S, D $69-$169; each addl $10; under 12 free. Crib free. TV; cable (premium). Heated pool; whirlpool. Complimentary continental bkfst. Ck-out noon. Coin lndry. Business servs avail. In-rm modem link. Valet serv. Health club privileges. Microwaves avail. Cr cds: A, C, D, DS, JCB, MC, V.

Hotel

★★★ **SHERATON LEXINGTON INN.** *727 Marrett Rd (02421), Exit 30B off I 128/95. 781/862-8700; fax 781/863-0404.* 119 rms, 2 story. S, D $149-$199; each addl $10; under 18 free; wkend rates. Crib free. TV; cable (premium). Pool; poolside serv, lifeguard. Coffee in rms. Restaurant 6:30 am-2:30 pm, 5-10 pm; Sat, Sun 8 am-noon. Bar 11:30 am-11:30 pm. Ck-out noon. Meeting rms. Business servs avail. In-rm modem link. Exercise equipt. Health club privileges. Some private patios, balconies. Picnic tables. Cr cds: A, D, DS, MC, V.

Lowell (B-6)

Settled 1655 **Pop** 103,439 **Elev** 102 ft
Area code 978
Web www.greaterlowellchamber.org
Information Greater Lowell Chamber of Commerce, 77 Merrimack St, 01852; 978/459-8154

In the 19th century, the powerful Merrimack River and its canals transformed Lowell from a handicraft center to a textile industrial center. The Francis Floodgate, near Broadway and Clare streets, was called "Francis' Folly" when it was built in 1848, but it saved the city from flood in 1936. Restoration of the historic canal system is currently in progress.

What to See and Do

American Textile History Museum. Permanent exhibit, "Textiles in America," features 18th to 20th-century textiles, artifacts, and machinery in operation, showing the impact of the Industrial Revolution on labor. Collections of cloth samples, books, prints, photographs, and preindustrial tools may be seen by appt. Tours; activities. Library; education center. Restaurant; museum store. (Tues-Sun; closed Jan 1, Thanksgiving, Dec 25) 491 Dutton St. Phone 978/441-0400. ¢¢

Lowell Heritage State Park. Six mi of canals and associated linear parks and 2 mi of park on the bank of Merrimack River offers boating, boathouse; concert pavilion; interpretive programs. Phone 978/453-0592. **FREE**

Lowell National Historical Park. Established to commemorate Lowell's unique legacy as the most important planned industrial city in America. The nation's first large-scale center for the mechanized production of cotton cloth, Lowell became a model for 19th-century industrial development. Park incl mill bldgs, 5.6-mi canal system. Visitor center at Market Mills, 246 Market St, incl audiovisual show and exhibits (daily; closed Jan 1, Thanksgiving, Dec 25). Free walking and trolley tours (winter and spring). Tours by barge and trolley (May-Columbus Day wkend;

fee), reservations suggested. Downtown. For reservations and information contact Visitor Center, 246 Market St, 01852. Phone 978/970-5000. Located here are

Patrick J. Mogan Cultural Center. Restored 1836 boarding house of the Boott Cotton Mills incl a re-created kitchen, keeper's rm, parlor, and mill girls' bedrm; exhibits on working people, immigrants, and labor history; also local history. (Winter, wkends; rest of yr, daily) 40 French St. **FREE**

Boott Cotton Mills Museum. Industrial history museum with operating looms (ear plugs supplied). Interactive exhibits, video presentations. (Daily; closed Jan 1, Thanksgiving, Dec 25) At foot of John St. ¢¢

New England Quilt Museum. Changing exhibits feature antique, traditional, and contemporary quilts. Museum shop. (May-Nov, Tues-Sun; rest of yr, Tues-Sat; closed hols) 18 Shattuck St. Phone 978/452-4207. ¢¢

University of MA-Lowell. 15,500 students. State-operated university formed by 1975 merger of Lowell Technological Institute (1895) and Lowell State College (1894). Music ensembles at Durgin Hall Performing Arts Center. 1 University Ave. Phone 978/934-4000 or 978/934-4444 (Durgin Hall).

Whistler House Museum of Art. Birthplace of the painter James Abbott McNeill Whistler. Exhibits incl several of his etchings. Collection of 19th- and early 20th-century American art. (May-Oct, Wed-Sun; Mar-Apr and Nov-Dec, Wed-Sat; closed hols) 243 Worthen St. Phone 978/452-7641. ¢

Annual Event

Lowell Folk Festival. Concerts, crafts, and demonstrations, ethnic food, street parade. Last wkend July.

Motels/Motor Lodges

★★ **MARRIOTT COURTYARD.** *30 Industrial Ave E (01852), I-495 Exit 35C to Lowell Connector. 978/458-7575; fax 978/458-1302; res 800/321-2211.* 120 rms, 3 story, 12 suites. S, D $99-$109; suites $129-$139; under 12 free; wkend rates. TV; cable (pre-

mium). Complimentary coffee in rms. Restaurant 6:30-10 am; Sat, Sun 7:30-11:30 am. 5-10 pm. Bar Sun-Thurs 5-10 pm. Ck-out 1 pm. Meeting rms. Business servs avail. In-rm modem link. Valet serv. Sundries. Coin lndry. Airport transportation. Exercise equipt. Pool. Refrigerators avail. Cr cds: A, D, DS, MC, V.

⊡ ⇔ 👖 ⚄ 🛥

★★★ **RADISSON HOTEL.** *10 Independence Dr (01824), ¼ mi S off I-495 Exit 34. 978/256-0800; fax 508/256-0750; toll-free 800/333-3333.* 214 rms, 5 story, 82 suites. S, D $129; each addl $10; suites $149; under 16 free; wkend rates. Crib free. TV; cable (premium), VCR in suites. Indoor pool. Restaurant 6:30 am-2 pm, 5-10 pm. Bar 11 am-midnight. Ck-out noon. Meeting rms. Business servs avail. In-rm modem link. Sundries. Exercise equipt; sauna. Rec rm. Bathrm phone, refrigerator in suites. Cr cds: A, C, D, DS, ER, JCB, MC, V.

⊡ ⇔ 👖 ⚄ 🛥 SC

Hotels

★★ **BEST WESTERN CHELMSFORD INN.** *187 Chelmsford St (01824), I-495 Exit 34. 978/256-7511; fax 978/250-1401; res 800/528-1234; toll-free 888/770-9992. www.bestwestern.com/chelmsfo.* 115 rms, 5 story. June-Oct: S, D $109; each addl $10; under 19 free; lower rates rest of yr. Crib avail. Parking lot. Pool, whirlpool. TV; cable (DSS). Complimentary full bkfst, coffee in rms, newspaper. Restaurant 6 am-midnight. Ck-out noon, ck-in 3 pm. Meeting rms. Business center. Bellhops. Dry cleaning. Exercise privileges, sauna, steam rm. Golf. Downhill skiing. Cr cds: A, C, D, DS, MC, V.

⊡ ⋈ 👖 ⇔ 👖 ⚄ 🔥 SC 👖

★★★ **DOUBLETREE.** *50 Warren St (01852). 978/452-1200; fax 978/453-4674; toll-free 800/876-4586.* 251 rms, 9 story. S, D $89-$129; suites $139-$250; under 18 free. Crib free. TV; cable (premium), VCR avail. Indoor pool; whirlpool, wading pool, poolside serv. Restaurant 6:30 am-10 pm. Bar. Ck-out 11 am. Coin lndry. Convention facilities. Business servs avail. In-rm modem link. Free garage parking. Exercise equipt; sauna. Cr cds: A, C, D, DS, MC, V.

⬚ ⬚ ⬚ ⬚ ⬚ SC

★★★ **WESTFORD REGENCY INN.**
219 Littleton Rd (01886), 10 mi S on MA 110; ¼ mi E of I-495 Exit 32. 978/692-8200; fax 508/692-7403; toll-free 800/543-7801. 193 units, 4 story, 15 suites. S $114; D $140; each addl $8; suites $125-$235; under 18 free; wkend rates. Crib free. Pet accepted, some restrictions. TV; cable (premium). Indoor pool; whirlpool. Restaurant 7 am-10 pm. Bar 11-11 pm; entertainment. Ck-out noon. Convention facilities. Business servs avail. In-rm modem link. Exercise rm; sauna. Bathrm phones; some refrigerators. Atrium in lobby. Cr cds: A, C, D, DS, MC, V.

⬚ ⬚ ⬚ ⬚ ⬚ ⬚ ⬚ ⬚ ⬚

Resort

★★★ **STONEHEDGE INN.** *160 Pawtucket Blvd. (01879).* 978/649-4400; fax 978/649-9256; toll-free 800/648-7070. Email stonehedgeinn@worldnet.att.net; www.stonehedgeinn.com. 30 rms, 2 story. May-June, Sep-Oct: S, D $195; suites $255; lower rates rest of yr. Crib avail. Valet parking avail. Indoor/outdoor pools, whirlpool. TV; cable, VCR avail. Complimentary newspaper. Restaurant 6 am-9 pm. 24-hr rm serv. Bar. Ck-out noon, ck-in 3 pm. Meeting rms. Business servs avail. Bellhops. Concierge serv. Dry cleaning. Exercise rm. Golf. Tennis. Downhill skiing. Bike rentals. Hiking trail. Cr cds: A, C, D, DS, ER, JCB, MC, V.

⬚ ⬚ ⬚ ⬚ ⬚ ⬚ ⬚ ⬚ ⬚

Restaurants

★★★ **COBBLESTONES.** *91 Dutton St (01852).* 978/970-2282. Specializes in chicken marsala, porterhouse steak, game specials. Hrs: 11 am-11 pm. Closed Sun; Labor Day, Thanksgiving, Dec 25. Res accepted. Bar. Lunch $5.95-$7.95; dinner $10.95-$17.95. In restored 1859 bldg. Cr cds: A, DS, MC, V.

★★★ **LA BONICHE.** *143 Merrimack St (01852).* 978/458-9473. Specializes in homemade soups and pates, duck. Hrs: 11 am-2 pm, 5-9 pm; Fri to 9:30 pm; Sat 5-9:30 pm. Closed Sun, Mon. Res accepted. Bar. Lunch $6-$12; dinner $14-$21. Child's menu. Entertainment: musicians Sat. French Provincial decor with natural woodwork. Cr cds: A, MC, V.

⬚

★★★★ **SILKS.** *160 Pawtucket Blvd.* 978/649-4400. www.stonehedgeinn.com. Hrs: 7 am-10 pm, Sun 7 am-9:30 pm. Closed Mon. Res accepted. Wine list. Lunch $10-$14; dinner $22-$34. Brunch $28.50. Entertainment: pianist on Sat night.. Cr cds: A, D, DS, ER, JCB, MC, V.

⬚ ⬚ ⬚

⛽

Lynn

(C-6) See also Boston, Salem

Settled 1629 **Pop** 81,245 **Elev** 30 ft
Area code 781
Web www.lynnchamber.com
Information Chamber of Commerce, 23 Central Ave, Suite 416, 01901; 781/592-2900

Shoe manufacturing began as a home craft in Lynn as early as 1635. Today Lynn's industry is widely diversified. Founded here in 1883, General Electric is the biggest single enterprise. Lynn also has more than three miles of sandy beaches.

What to See and Do

Grand Army of the Republic Museum. Features American Revolution, Civil War, Spanish-American War, and WWI weapons, artifacts, and exhibits. (Mon-Fri by appt; closed hols) 58 Andrew St. Phone 781/477-7085. **Donation**

Lynn Heritage State Park. Five-acre waterfront park; pedalboats, marina. (Daily; closed Jan 1, Dec 25) Visitor center (590 Washington St) with museum-quality exhibits from past to present, from hand-crafted shoes to high-tech items; inquire for hrs. Lynnway. Phone 781/598-1974. **FREE**

Lynn Historical Society Museum/Library. 1836 house with period furnishings; museum wing with changing exhibits. Decorative arts, toys, tools, bicycles, and photographs of Lynn. Library incl manuscripts and diaries from 1600s to present. Library (Mon-Fri; closed hols); museum tours (Mon-Sat, afternoons; closed hols). 125 Green St. Phone 781/592-2465. ¢¢

Lynn Woods Reservation. Wooded area consisting of 2,200 acres. Features walking trails, 18-hole golf course, historic dungeon rock (pirates cave), stone tower; picnic areas, playgrounds. (Daily)

Mary Baker Eddy Historical Home. Restored house where the founder of Christian Science lived from 1875-82. (Mid-May-mid-Oct, Wed and Thurs) 12 Broad St. Phone 781/593-5634. **FREE**

B&B/Small Inn

★ ★ ★ **DIAMOND DISTRICT BREAKFAST INN.** *142 Ocean St (01902), off Lynn Shore Dr at Wolcott.* 781/599-5122; fax 781/595-2200; toll-free 800/666-3076. Email diamond district@msn.com; www.bbhost.com/ diamonddistrict. 11 rms, 1 with shower only, 3 story. June-Oct: S, D $90-$235; each addl $20; under 3 free; lower rates rest of yr. Crib free. Pet accepted, some restrictions; $10. TV. Complimentary full bkfst. Restaurant nearby. Business servs avail. In-rm modem link. Gift shop. Health club privileges. Microwaves avail. Georgian residence built in 1911. Totally non-smoking. Cr cds: A, C, D, DS, MC, V.

![icons]

Lynnfield

Settled 1639 **Pop** 11,274 **Elev** 98 ft
Area code 781 **Zip** 01940

Hotel

★ ★ ★ **SHERATON COLONIAL HOTEL AND GOLF CLUB.** *1 Audubon Rd (01880), N of I-95, MA 128 Exits 42, 43.* 781/245-9300; fax 781/245-0842. 280 rms, 11 story. S $89-$169; D $89-$189; each addl $15; suites $275-$495; wkend rates. Crib free. TV; cable (premium), VCR avail. Indoor pool; whirlpool. Coffee in rms. Restaurant 6:30 am-10:30 pm. Ck-out 11 am. Convention facilities. In-rm modem link. Barber shop. Lighted tennis. 18-hole golf, pro, putting green, driving range. Exercise rm; sauna, steam rm. Some refrigerators; microwaves avail. Cr cds: A, MC, V.

![icons]

Restaurant

★ ★ **KERNWOOD.** *55 Salem St (01940).* 781/245-4011. Specializes in seafood, prime beef. Hrs: 11 am-10 pm. Closed July 4, Dec 25. Bar. Wine list. Lunch $4.95-$10.95; dinner $12-$19. Child's menu. Entertainment: pianist exc Sun. Colonial atmosphere; open-hearth cooking. Family-owned. Cr cds: A, C, D, DS, ER, MC, V.

Marblehead

(C-7) *See also Boston, Salem*

Settled 1629 **Pop** 19,971 **Elev** 65 ft
Area code 781 **Zip** 01945
Web www.marbleheadchamber.org

Information Chamber of Commerce, 62 Pleasant St, PO Box 76; 781/631-2868

A unique blend of old and new, Marblehead is situated on a peninsula 17 miles north of Boston. Originally named Marble Harbor by hardy anglers from Cornwall and the Channel Islands in the 1600s, the town boasts a beautiful harbor and a number of busy boatyards. Pleasure craft anchor in this picturesque port each summer, and a record number of modern racing yachts participate in the annual Race Week. Beaches, boating, fishing, art exhibits, antique and curio shops—all combine to offer a choice of quiet relaxation or active recreation.

What to See and Do

Abbot Hall. Displays the original *Spirit of '76* painting and deed to town (1684) from the Nanepashemet. Museum, Marine Room. Gift shop. (Last wkend May-last wkend Oct, daily; rest of yr, Mon-Fri; closed winter hols) Town Hall, Washington Sq. Phone 781/631-0000. **Donation**

Jeremiah Lee Mansion. (1768) Marblehead Historical Society. Where Genls Glover, Lafayette, and Washington were entertained. Georgian architecture; Marblehead history; antiques of the period, original wallpaper. (Mid-May-mid-Oct, daily; closed hols) 161 Washington St. Phone 781/631-1069. *¢¢*

King Hooper Mansion. (1728) Restored house with garden. Art exhibits. (Mon-Fri, also Sat and Sun afternoons; closed Jan 1, Dec 25) 8 Hooper St. Phone 781/631-2608. **FREE**

Seasonal Event

Sailing races. Phone 781/631-3100. Summer, Wed eve and wkends. Race week 3rd wk July.

B&Bs/Small Inns

★★★ **HARBOR LIGHT INN.** *58 Washington St (01945). 781/631-2186; fax 781/631-2216. Email hli@shore. net; www.harborlightinn.com.* 21 rms, 3 story, 3 suites. May, Nov: S $115; D $125; suites $275; each addl $25; under 14 free; lower rates rest of yr. Parking lot. Pool. TV; cable, VCR avail, CD avail. Complimentary continental bkfst, newspaper, toll-free calls. Restaurant. Ck-out 11 am, ck-in 1 pm. Meeting rm. Business center. Concierge serv. Gift shop. Exercise privileges. Golf. Tennis, 4 courts. Cr cds: A, MC, V.

★★ **MARBLEHEAD INN.** *264 Pleasant St (01945). 781/639-9999; fax 781/639-9996; toll-free 800/399-5843. www.marbleheadinn.com.* 10 units, 3 story. S, D $119-$169; each addl $5. TV; cable (premium), VCR. Complimentary continental bkfst. Restaurants nearby. Ck-out 11 am, ck-in 3 pm. Guest lndry. Picnic tables. Refrigerators, microwaves. Antiques. Victorian inn (1872) near beach. Totally nonsmoking. Cr cds: A, MC, V.

★★ **SEAGULL INN.** *106 Harbor Ave (01945). 781/631-1893; fax 781/631-3535. Email host@seagullinn.com; www.seagullinn.com.* 6 rms, 3 story, 5 suites. May-Oct: S, D $150; suites $150; each addl $25; children $25;

lower rates rest of yr. Crib avail. Pet accepted. Parking lot. TV; cable (premium), VCR avail, CD avail. Complimentary continental bkfst, coffee in rms, newspaper. Restaurant. Bar. Ck-out 11 am, ck-in 2 pm. Meeting rm. Business center. Coin lndry. Gift shop. Exercise privileges. Golf, 18 holes. Tennis, 10 courts. Beach access. Bike rentals. Hiking trail. Picnic facilities. Cr cds: MC, V.

★★ **SPRAY CLIFF ON THE OCEAN.** *25 Spray Ave (01945). 781/631-6789; fax 781/639-4563; toll-free 800/626-1530. Email spraycliff@aol. com; spraycliff.com.* 7 rms, 3 story. May-Oct: S, D $200; each addl $25; lower rates rest of yr. Parking lot. TV; cable (premium), VCR avail, CD avail. Complimentary continental bkfst, newspaper. Restaurant nearby. Ck-out 11 am, ck-in 3 pm. Business servs avail. Golf. Tennis. Beach access. Bike rentals. Hiking trail. Cr cds: A, MC, V.

Restaurants

★ **KING'S ROOK.** *12 State St (01945). 781/631-9838.* Specializes in gourmet pizzas, sandwiches, salads. Hrs: noon-11 pm. Closed Mon; Thanksgiving; Dec 25, 31. Lunch, dinner $4.50-$7.50. Child's menu. Street parking. Family-owned since 1966. Cr cds: DS, MC, V.

★★ **MARBLEHEAD LANDING.** *81 Front St (01945), 1 blk from Washington St. 781/631-1878.* Specializes in seafood. Hrs: 11 am-9 pm. Closed Thanksgiving, Dec 25. Bar. Lunch a la carte entrees: $2.50-$19.95; dinner a la carte entrees: $9.95-$21.95. Sun brunch $2.95-$14.95. Child's menu. Entertainment: Fri, Sun. Windows overlook beach and boating area. Family-owned. Cr cds: A, C, D, DS, ER, MC, V.

★★ **PELLINO'S.** *261 Washington St (01945). 781/631-3344.* Specializes in pasta, seafood, chicken. Hrs: 5-11 pm. Closed Jan 1, Easter, Dec 25. Res required. Bar. Dinner $10.95-$17.95. Parking. Italian decor. Cr cds: A, DS, MC, V.

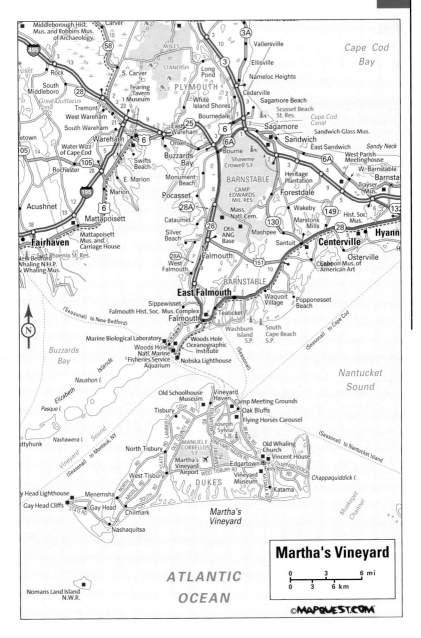

Martha's Vineyard

0   3   6 mi
0   3   6 km

©MAPQUEST.COM

Martha's Vineyard

See also Falmouth, Hyannis, Nantucket Island, Woods Hole

Settled 1642 **Pop** 12,690 **Elev** 0-311 ft
Area code 508 **Web** www.mvy.com
Information Chamber of Commerce, Beach Rd, PO Box 1698, Vineyard Haven 02568; 508/693-0085

This triangular island below the arm of Cape Cod combines moors, dunes, multicolored cliffs, flower-filled ravines, farmland, and forest. It is less than 20 miles from West to East and 10 miles from North to South.

There was once a whaling fleet at the island, but Martha's Vineyard now devotes itself almost entirely to being a vacation playground, with summer houses that range from small cottages to elaborate mansions. The colonial atmosphere still survives in Vineyard Haven, the chief port; Oak Bluffs; Edgartown; West Tisbury; Gay Head, and Chilmark.

Gay Head is one of the few Massachusetts towns in which many inhabitants are of Native American descent.

What to See and Do

Car/passenger boat trips.

Woods Hole, Martha's Vineyard, and Nantucket Steamship Authority. Conducts round-trip service to Woods Hole (all yr, weather permitting). Phone 508/477-8600. ¢¢¢¢

Cape Island Express Lines. New Bedford-Martha's Vineyard Ferry. Daily passenger service (mid-May–mid-Oct) to New Bedford. One-way and same-day round-trips avail. Also bus tours of the island. Schedule may vary; contact Cape Island Express Lines, PO Box 4095, New Bedford, 02741. Phone 508/997-1688. Round-trip ¢¢¢¢

Island Queen. Daily round trips, Falmouth-Martha's Vineyard. (May-Oct) Phone 508/548-4800. Round-trip ¢¢¢

Hyannis-Martha's Vineyard Day Round Trip. Passenger service from Hyannis (May-Oct). Phone 508/778-2600. ¢¢¢¢

Felix Neck Sanctuary. Approx 350 acres with woods, far-reaching salt marshes, pond with large variety of waterfowl, reptile pond, 6 mi of trails; barn, exhibit centers, library. (Daily) 3 mi out of Edgartown on the Vineyard Haven-Edgartown Rd. Phone 508/627-4850. ¢

Historic areas.

Oak Bluffs. In 1835 this Methodist community served as the site of annual summer camp meetings for church groups. As thousands attended these meetings, the communal tents gave way to family tents, which in turn became wooden cottages designed to look like tents. Today, visitors to the community may see these "Gingerbread Cottages of the Campground."

Edgartown. The island's first colonial settlement and county seat since 1642 is the location of stately white Greek Revival houses built by whaling captains. These have been carefully preserved and North Water St has a row of captains' houses unequaled anywhere.

Recreation. Swimming. Many sheltered beaches, among them public beaches at Menemsha, Oak Bluffs, Edgartown, and Vineyard Haven. Surf swimming on S shore. **Tennis.** Public courts in Edgartown, Oak Bluffs, West Tisbury, and Vineyard Haven. **Boat rentals** at Vineyard Haven, Oak Bluffs, and Gay Head. **Fishing.** Good for striped bass, bonito, bluefish, weakfish. **Golf** at Farm Neck Club (phone 508/693-3057) and Mink Meadows (phone 508/693-0600). Bike, moped rentals avail.

✪ **Vincent House.** Oldest known house on the island, built 1672. Carefully restored to allow visitors to see how bldgs were constructed 300 yrs ago. Original brickwork, hardware, and woodwork. (June-early Oct, daily; rest of yr, by appt) Main St in Edgartown. Phone 508/627-4440. **FREE** Also on Main St is

Old Whaling Church. Built in 1843, this is a fine example of Greek Revival architecture. Now a performing arts center with seating for 500. Phone 508/627-4442.

Seasonal Event

Striped Bass and Bluefish Derby.
2,000 entrants compete for cash and prizes. Incl boat, shore, and flyrod divisions. Mid-Sep-mid-Oct.

Hotels

★★★ **HARBOR VIEW HOTEL OF MARTHA'S VINEYARD.** *131 N Water St (02539). 508/627-7000; fax 508/627-8417; toll-free 800/225-6005. www.harbor-view.com.* 113 rms, 4 story, 11 suites. June-Sep: S, D $300; suites $725; each addl $20; under 15 free; lower rates rest of yr. Crib avail. Parking lot. Pool. TV; cable (premium), VCR avail. Complimentary newspaper. Restaurant 8 am-10 pm. Bar. Ck-out 11 am, ck-in 3 pm. Meeting rms. Business center. Bellhops. Concierge serv. Gift shop. Golf. Tennis, 2 courts. Beach access. Bike rentals. Supervised children's activities. Hiking trail. Cr cds: A, C, D, MC, V.

★★★ **KELLEY HOUSE.** *23 Kelly St (02539). 508/627-7900; fax 508/627-8142; res 800/225-6005.* 42 rms, 3 story, 11 suites. June-Sep: S, D $275; suites $525; each addl $20; under 15 free; lower rates rest of yr. Crib avail. Parking lot. Pool, children's pool. TV; cable. Complimentary continental bkfst, coffee in rms, toll-free calls. Restaurant 11:30 am-11 pm. Bar. Ck-out 11 am, ck-in 3 pm. Business servs avail. Bellhops. Concierge serv. Golf. Tennis, 2 courts. Beach access. Bike rentals. Hiking trail. Cr cds: A, MC, V.

Resort

★★ **ISLAND INN.** *Beach Rd (02557). 508/693-2002; fax 508/693-7911; toll-free 800/462-0269. Email innkeeper@islandinn.com; www.islandinn.com.* 51 rms, 2 story, 23 suites. June-Sep: S, D $165; suites $200; each addl $20; under 12 free; lower rates rest of yr. Crib avail. Pet accepted, some restrictions. Street parking. Pool. TV; cable. Complimentary coffee in rms. Restaurant 5-midnight. Ck-out 11 am, ck-in 3 pm. Meeting rms. Coin lndry. Gift shop. Golf. Tennis, 3 courts. Beach access. Bike rentals.

Hiking trail. Picnic facilities. Cr cds: A, C, D, DS, MC, V.

B&Bs/Small Inns

★★ **THE ARBOR INN.** *222 Upper Main St. (02539). 508/627-8137. www.mvy.com/arborinn.* 10 rms, 2 story. June-Sep: S $135; D $185; lower rates rest of yr. TV; cable. Restaurant nearby. Ck-out 11 am, ck-in 2 pm. Cr cds: MC, V.

★★ **ASHLEY INN.** *129 Main St (02539). 508/627-9655; fax 508/627-6629; toll-free 800/477-9655. Email mail@ashleyinnmv.com.* 10 rms, 3 story, 2 suites. Late June-late Sep: S, D $135-$265; suites $265; each addl $15; honeymoon packages; lower rates rest of yr. Children over 12 yrs only. TV; cable. Complimentary continental bkfst. Restaurant adj. Ck-out 11 am, ck-in 2 pm. Some refrigerators, fireplaces. Picnic tables. 1860 sea captain's house; antiques. Totally nonsmoking. Cr cds: A, DS, MC, V.

★ **THE BEACH HOUSE.** *Pennacook and Seaview Aves (02557). 508/693-3955. www.beachhousemv.com.* 9 rms, 3 story. No rm phones. July-Aug: S, D $135-$155; wkends, hols (3-day min); lower rates rest of yr. Children over 10 yrs only. TV. Complimentary continental bkfst. Ck-out 11 am, ck-in 1 pm. Built in 1899; front porch. Opp ocean. Cr cds: A, MC, V.

★★★ **BEACH PLUM INN.** *50 Beach Plum Ln (81432). 508/645-9454; fax 508/645-2801. www.beachpluminn.com.* 11 rms, 2 story, 1 suite. Mid-June-mid-Sep: D $225-$300; suite $325; under 12 free; higher rates hols; lower rates rest of yr. Crib avail. TV; cable (premium), VCR (movies). Playground. Supervised children's activities; ages 3-12. Complimentary full bkfst. Restaurant. Ck-out 11 am, ck-in 2 pm. Business servs avail. In-rm modem link. Concierge serv. Tennis. Lawn games. Balconies. Picnic tables. Built 1890 from salvage of shipwreck. Most rms with ocean view. Gardens. Cr cds: A, D, DS, MC, V.

★★ **CAPTAIN DEXTER HOUSE.**
*35 Pease's Point Way (02539). 508/
627-7289; fax 508/627-3328.* 11 rms,
10 A/C, 1 air-cooled, 2 story. No rm
phones. June-Sep: S, D $135-$195;
each addl $20; lower rates mid-Apr-
May, Oct. Closed rest of yr. Complimentary continental bkfst; afternoon
refreshments. Restaurant nearby. Ck-
out 11 am, ck-in 2 pm. Traditional
white clapboard house built in 1840
by a prominent merchant family;
antiques; flower gardens. Totally
nonsmoking. Cr cds: A, MC, V.
🐕 🔧 🐾

★★ **THE CAPTAIN DEXTER
HOUSE OF VINEYARD HAVEN.** *92
Main St (02568). 508/693-6564; fax
508/693-8448.* 8 rms, 3 story. 6 A/C.
No rm phones. Memorial Day-Oct 1:
D $115-$175; each addl $20; suite
$175; lower rates rest of yr. Children
over 12 yrs only. Complimentary continental bkfst; afternoon refreshments.
Ck-out 11 am, ck-in 2 pm. Sitting garden. Some fireplaces. Old sea captain's
home (1843); antiques. Totally nonsmoking. Cr cds: A, MC, V.
🔧 🐾 SC

★★★★ **THE CHARLOTTE INN.**
*27 S Summer St (02539). 508/627-
4751; fax 508/627-6452.* A romantic
escape whatever the season, this Victorian inn on Martha's Vineyard is
true New England style with wide,
wicker-filled porches, antiques, and
lovely manicured grounds. The property has expanded from the original
1860 Captain's House and is tucked
away off of the Main Street shopping
area. 25 rms located in 5 historic
bldgs. S $295-$850; D $225-$550; 2
suites $750-$850; lower rates off-season. Children over 14 only. Parking
avail. TV; cable (premium); VCR
avail. Concierge serv. Restaurant 6:30-
9:30 pm; closed Mon, Tues off season. Afternoon tea. Cr cds: A, MC, V.
🐕 🔧 🐾

★★ **COLONIAL INN OF
MARTHA'S VINEYARD.** *38 N Water
St (02539). 508/627-4711; fax
508/627-5904; toll-free 800/627-4701.
Email info@colonialinnmvy.com; www.
colonialinnmvy.com.* 50 rms, 4 story, 4
suites. June-Sep: S, D $375; suites
$400; under 16 free; lower rates rest
of yr. Crib avail. Parking lot. TV;
cable (premium), VCR avail. Complimentary continental bkfst, newspa-

per. Restaurant 5:30-11 pm. Bar. Ck-
out 11 am, ck-in 3 pm. Meeting rms.
Business servs avail. Concierge serv.
Gift shop. Salon/barber avail. Exer-
cise privileges. Golf, 18 holes. Tennis,
6 courts. Beach access. Bike rentals.
Hiking trail. Picnic facilities. Cr cds:
A, MC, V.
🅓 🐕 🔧 🐕 🔧 🐾 🐕 🐾

★★ **DAGGETT HOUSE.** *59 N Water
St (02539). 508/627-4600; fax
508/627-4611; toll-free 800/946-3400.
www.mvweb.com/daggett.* 31 rms in 4
bldgs, 2 story, 10 kits. May-Oct: S, D
$150-$225; each addl $20; suites
$155-$550; lower rates rest of yr. Crib
free. TV; cable. Resturant 8-11 am,
5:30-9 pm; Sun brunch to 1 pm. Ck-
out 11 am, ck-in 3 pm. Private pier.
Gardens. Open hearth, antiques in
dining rm, part of historic (1660)
tavern. New England atmosphere.
Totally nonsmoking. Cr cds: A, DS,
MC, V.
🐾 🐾

★★★ **DOCKSIDE INN.** *Circuit Ave
Exit (02557). 508/693-2966; fax
508/696-7293; toll-free 800/245-5979.
Email inns@vineyard.net; vineyard.net/
inns.* 22 rms, 3 story, 5 suites. June-
Sep: S, D $200; suites $350; each addl
$20; lower rates rest of yr. Crib avail.
Parking lot. TV; cable. Complimen-
tary continental bkfst. Restaurant
nearby. Ck-out 11 am, ck-in 3 pm.
Golf, 18 holes. Cr cds: A, DS, MC, V.
🅓 🔧 🐾 🐾

★★ **THE EDGARTOWN INN.** *56 N
Water St (02539). 508/627-4794; fax
508/627-9420. www.edgartowninn.
com.* 20 rms, 3 story. June-Sep: D
$210; lower rates rest of yr. Parking
lot. TV; cable. Complimentary newspaper. Restaurant 8 am-11 pm. Ck-
out 11 am, ck-in 2 pm. Business servs
avail. Golf. Beach access. Picnic facilities. Cr cds: A, MC, V.
🐕 🔧 🐾 🐾

★★ **GREENWOOD HOUSE.** *40
Greenwood Ave (02568). 508/693-
6150; fax 508/696-8113; toll-free 800/
25-9466. Email innkeeper@greenwood
house.com; www.greenwoodhouse.com.*
5 rms, 3 story. Mid-May-mid-Sep: S,
D $169-$249; lower rates rest of yr.
TV; cable. Complimentary full bkfst,
coffee in rms. Restaurant nearby. Ck-
out 10 am, ck-in 2 pm. Business servs
avail. In-rm modem link. Concierge

serv. Lawn games. Refrigerators. Built 1906. Totally nonsmoking. Cr cds: A, C, D, MC, V.

★★★ **THE HANOVER HOUSE.** *28 Edgartown Rd (02568). 508/693-1066; fax 508/696-6099; toll-free 800/339-1066. Email tommrichardson@aol.com; www.hanoverhouseinn.com.* 11 rms, 2 story, 3 suites. May-Oct: D $200; suites $275; each addl $30; under 8 free; lower rates rest of yr. Crib avail, fee. Parking lot. TV; cable. Complimentary continental bkfst, newspaper. Restaurant nearby. Business servs avail. Concierge serv. Golf. Tennis, 5 courts. Beach access. Bike rentals. Picnic facilities. Cr cds: A, DS, MC, V.

★★★ **HOB KNOB INN.** *128 Main St (02539). 508/627-9510; fax 508/627-4560; toll-free 800/696-2723. Email hobknob@vineyard.net.* 16 rms, 3 story. Memorial Day-mid-Oct: S, D $185-$375; lower rates rest of yr. TV; cable. Complimentary full bkfst. Restaurant nearby. Ck-out 11 am, ck-in 2 pm. Meeting rm. Business servs avail. In-rm modem link. Concierge serv. Exercise equipt; sauna. Massage. Bicycle rental. Sun porch; garden. Inn built 1860; many antiques. Totally nonsmoking. Cr cds: A, MC, V.

★★ **LAMBERT'S COVE COUNTRY INN.** *Lambert's Cove Rd (02568), 5 mi W. 508/693-2298; fax 508/693-7890.* 15 rms, 2 story. No rm phones. Late May-early Oct: D $145-$195; lower rates rest of yr. TV in sitting rm. Complimentary full bkfst. Dining rm (public by res) 6-9 pm. Ck-out 11 am, ck-in 2 pm. Tennis. Balconies. Picnic tables. Secluded farmhouse (1790); many antiques. Gardens, apple orchard. Cr cds: A, MC, V.

★★★ **MARTHA'S PLACE B&B.** *114 Main St (02568). 508/693-0253. Email info@marthasplace.com; www.marthasplace.com.* 6 rms, 2 story. June-Sep: D $450; lower rates rest of yr. Parking lot. TV; cable, CD avail. Complimentary continental bkfst, newspaper, toll-free calls. Restaurant nearby. Ck-out 10 am, ck-in 3 pm. Business cen-

ter. Golf. Tennis. Beach access. Cr cds: DS, MC, V.

★★★ **THE OAK HOUSE.** *Seaview & Pequot Aves (02557). 508/693-4187; fax 508/696-7385; res 800/245-5979. www.vineyard.net/inns.* 10 rms, 9 with shower only, 3 story, 2 suites. No elvtr. Mid-June-mid-Sep: S, D $150-$190; suites $250-$260; lower rates rest of yr. Closed Mid-Oct-mid-May. Children over 10 yrs only. TV; cable, VCR avail. Complimentary continental bkfst; afternoon refreshments. Ck-out 11 am, ck-in 4 pm. Street parking. Some balconies. Picnic tables, grills. Opp beach. 1872 summer home for MA governor. Totally nonsmoking. Cr cds: A, DS, MC, V.

★★ **OUTERMOST INN.** *171 Lighthouse Rd (02535). 508/645-3511; fax 508/645-3514. www.outermostinn.com.* 7 rms, 2 story. No A/C. Mid-June-mid-Sep: S, D $240-$320; wkends (2-day min); lower rates mid-Apr-mid-June, mid-Sep-Oct. Children over 12 yrs only. TV. Complimentary full bkfst; afternoon refreshments. Dining rm 6-8 pm. Ck-out 11 am, ck-in 2 pm. Concierge serv. Business servs avail. Balconies. Picnic tables. Picture windows provide excellent views of Vineyard Sound and Elizabeth Islands. Totally nonsmoking. Cr cds: A, DS, MC, V.

★★ **PEQUOT HOTEL.** *19 Pequot Ave (02557). 508/693-5087; fax 508/696-9413; toll-free 800/947-8704. www.pequothotel.com.* 29 rms, 25 with shower only, 3 story. No elvtr. No rm phones. July-Aug: S, D $105-$195; kit. units $245-$385; wkday rates; higher rates July 4; lower rates rest of yr. Closed Nov-Apr. Crib $25. TV in some rms. Complimentary continental bkfst. Restaurant nearby. Ck-out 11 am, ck-in 3 pm. Street parking. Picnic tables. Built in 1920s. Cr cds: A, DS, MC, V.

★★ **POINT WAY INN.** *104 Main St (02539). 508/627-8633; fax 508/627-3838; res 508/627-8633; toll-free 888/711-6633. Email pointwayinn@vineyard.net.* 14 rms, 1-3 story. Late May-Oct: S, D $175-$325; each addl $25;

suites $325; lower rates rest of yr. Pet accepted, some restrictions; $25. TV. Complimentary continental bkfst; afternoon refreshments. Ck-out 11 am, ck-in 2 pm. Lndry serv. Some balconies. Gardens. Totally non-smoking. Cr cds: A, MC, V.

Oak Bluffs Campground, Martha's Vineyard

★★ **SHIRETOWN INN.** *44 N Water (02539). 508/627-3353; fax 508/627-8478; res 800/541-0090. Email paradise@shiretowninn.com; www.shiretowninn.com.* 30 rms, 3 story, 4 suites. July-Sep: S, D $149; suites $279; each addl $20; lower rates rest of yr. Crib avail. Parking lot. TV; cable (premium), VCR avail, CD avail. Complimentary continental bkfst, coffee in rms, toll-free calls. Restaurant. Bar. Ck-out 11 am, ck-in 2 pm. Meeting rms. Business center. Salon/barber avail. Exercise privileges. Golf. Tennis. Beach access. Bike rentals. Hiking trail. Picnic facilities. Video games. Cr cds: A, DS, MC, V.

★★★ **THORNCROFT INN.** *460 Main St (02568). 508/693-3333; fax 508/693-5419; toll-free 800/332-1236. Email innkeeper@thorncroft.com; www.thorncroft.com.* 12 rms, 2 story, 1 suite. June-Sep: D $325; suites $450; lower rates rest of yr. Parking lot. TV; cable, VCR avail. Complimentary full bkfst, coffee in rms, newspaper, toll-free calls. Restaurant nearby. Ck-out 11 am, ck-in 3 pm. Business servs avail. Concierge serv. Gift shop. Free airport transportation. Exercise privileges. Golf. Beach access. Bike rentals. Cr cds: A, C, D, DS, ER, MC, V.

Restaurants

★★★ **COACH HOUSE.** *131 N Water St. 508/627-7000.* Specializes in striped bass with artichokes, sea scallops, duck with sweet potatoes. Hrs: 7-11 am, noon-2 pm, 6-9 pm; Sun brunch 8 am-1:30 pm. Res accepted. Bar. Wine cellar. Bkfst a la carte entrees: $5.95-$12; lunch a la carte entrees: $7.95-$15; dinner a la carte entrees: $24-$34. Sun brunch $16.95. Child's menu. View of harbor. Cigar bar. Cr cds: A, D, MC, V.

★★ **HOME PORT.** *N Rd (02552). 508/645-2679.* Specializes in seafood, lobster. Hrs: 5-10 pm. Closed mid-Oct-mid Apr. Res required. Dinner complete meals: $16-$32. Child's menu. Parking. On harbor; scenic view; nautical atmosphere. Cr cds: MC, V.

★★ **LE GRENIER FRENCH RESTAURANT.** *82 Main St (02568). 508/693-4906.* Specializes in lobster normande, steak au poivre, shrimp pernod. Hrs: 5-10 pm. Res accepted. Dinner a la carte entrees: $18.95-$29.95. Street parking. Elegant bistro. Family-owned since 1979. Cr cds: A, D, DS, MC, V.

★ **LOUIS' TISBURY CAFE.** *350 State Rd (02568). 508/693-3255. Email louis@vineyard.net.* Specializes in eggplant parmesan, rack of lamb, pasta tomato cream shrimp. Hrs: 11 am-10 pm. Closed hols. Lunch, dinner $12.75-$24.95. Child's menu. Parking. Italian cafe style. Cr cds: A, MC, V.

★★ **NAVIGATOR.** *2 Lower Main St (02539). 508/627-4320.* Specializes in seafood. Hrs: 11:30 am-midnight. Closed mid-Oct-mid-May. Bar. Lunch a la carte entrees: $5.95-$11.95; dinner a la carte entrees: $19.95-$29.95. Child's menu. Overlooks harbor.

Family-owned. Cr cds: A, C, D, DS, MC, V.

D

★ ★ ★ **SAVOIR FAIRE.** *14 Church St (02539). 508/627-9864.* Specializes in grilled tuna, soft shell crabs, lobster en brodo. Raw bar in summer. Hrs: 6-10 pm. Closed Nov-Mar. Res accepted. Bar. Wine cellar. Dinner $26-$32. Parking. Cr cds: MC, V.

D

★ ★ **SQUARE RIGGER.** *225 State Rd (02539). 508/627-9968.* Specializes in seafood, grilled entrees, lobster. Hrs: 5-10 pm. Res accepted. Bar. Dinner a la carte entrees: $14-$26. Child's menu. Parking. Open-hearth kitchen in dining rm. Cr cds: A, MC, V.

D SC

★ ★ **WHARF & WHARF PUB.** *Lower Main St (02539), 1 mi E on Main St. 508/627-9966.* Specializes in fresh seafood, seafood Wellington pie, desserts. Hrs: 11:30 am-9:30 pm; Fri, Sat to 10:30 pm. Closed Thanksgiving, Dec 24, 25. Res accepted. Bar. Lunch $5.95-$9.95; dinner $8.95-$17.95. Child's menu. Entertainment: Wed-Sun. Cr cds: A, DS, MC, V.

D ⅃

Nantucket Island

See also Hyannis, Martha's Vineyard

Settled 1659 **Pop** 6,012 **Elev** 0-108 ft
Area code 508 **Zip** 02554
Web www.nantucketchamber.org
Information Chamber of Commerce, 48 Main St; 508/228-1700; Information Bureau, 25 Federal St; 508/228-1700

This is not just an island; it is an experience. Nantucket Island is at once a popular resort and a living museum. Siasconset (SCON-set) and Nantucket Town remain quiet and charming despite heavy tourism. Nantucket, with 49 square miles of lovely beaches and green moors inland, is south of Cape Cod, 30 miles at sea. The island was the world's greatest whaling port from

the late 17th century until New Bedford became dominant in the early 1800s. Whaling prosperity built the towns; tourism maintains them.

There is regular car ferry and passenger service from Hyannis. If you plan to take your car, make advance reservation by mail with the Woods Hole, Martha's Vineyard & Nantucket Steamship Authority, PO Box 284, Woods Hole 02543; 508/477-8600. A great variety of beaches, among them the Jetties, north of Nantucket Town (harbor); and Surfside, on the south shore of the island (surf), offer swimming. Tennis, golf, fishing, sailing, cycling can be arranged.

What to See and Do

Boat trips. Hyannis-Nantucket Day Round Trip. Summer passenger service from Hyannis. Phone 508/778-2600. ¢¢¢¢

⭐ **Main Street.** Paved with cobblestones, lined with elegant houses built by the whaling merchants, and shaded by great elms, this is one of New England's most beautiful streets. The Nantucket Historical Association maintains the following attractions (June-Oct, daily; spring and fall, limited hrs). Phone 508/228-1894. **Note:** Some properties may be closed for renovation.

> **Folger-Franklin Seat & Memorial Boulder.** Birthplace site of Abiah Folger, mother of Benjamin Franklin. Madaket Rd, 1 mi from W end of Main St.

> **Hadwen House.** (1845) Greek Revival mansion; furnishings of whaling period; gardens. Main and Pleasant Sts. ¢¢

> **Jethro Coffin House.** (1686) Nantucket's oldest house. N on North Water to West Chester, left to Sunset Hill. ¢¢

> **Museum of Nantucket History (Macy Warehouse).** Exhibits related to Nantucket history; diorama; craft demonstrations. Straight Wharf. ¢¢

> **Old Fire Hose Cart House.** (1886) Old-time firefighting equipment. Gardner St off Main St. **FREE**

> **Old Gaol.** (1805) Unusual 2-story construction; used until 1933. Vestal St. **FREE**

Old Windmill. (1746) Built of wood from wrecked vessels with original machinery and grinding stones. Corn ground daily during summer. On Mill Hill, off Prospect St. ¢

Whaling Museum. Outstanding collection of relics from whaling days; whale skeleton, tryworks, scrimshaw, candle press. Broad St, near Steamboat Wharf. ¢¢

1800 House. Home of sheriff, early 19th century. Period home and furnishings; large, round cellar; kitchen garden. Mill St, off Pleasant St. ¢¢ General pass for all the above ¢¢¢

Nantucket Maria Mitchell Association. Birthplace of first American woman astronomer; memorial observatory (1908). Scientific library has Nantucket historical documents, science journals, and Mitchell family memorabilia. Natural science museum with local wildlife. Aquarium at 28 Washington St. (Mid-June-Aug, Tues-Sat; library also open rest of yr, Wed-Sat; closed July 4, Labor Day) Combination ticket avail for museum, birthplace, and aquarium. 1 Vestal St. Phone 508/228-9198 or 508/228-0898 (summer). ¢¢

Sightseeing tours.

Barrett's Tours. Offers 1½-hr bus and van tours (Apr-Nov). Phone 508/228-0174. ¢¢¢

Gail's Tours. Narrated van tours (approx 1¾ hrs) of area. Three tours daily. Res recommended. Depart from Information Center at Federal and Broad Sts. Phone 508/257-6557. ¢¢¢¢

Annual Events

Daffodil Festival. Parade of antique cars, prize for best tailgate picnic. Late Apr.

Harborfest. Second wkend June.

Sand Castle Contest. Third Sun Aug.

Christmas Stroll. First Sat Dec.

Motels/Motor Lodges

★★ **HARBOR HOUSE HOTEL.** *S Beach St (02554). 508/228-1500; fax 508/228-7639; res 800/islands. www. nantucketislandresorts.com.* 113 rms, 2-3 story. No elvtr. Late June-mid-Sep: D $245-$285; each addl $20; package plans; lower rates rest of yr. TV; cable (premium). Heated pool; poolside

serv. Restaurant 7:30-10 am, 11:30 am-10 pm. Rm serv in season. Bar noon-1 am; entertainment. Ck-out 11 am. Meeting rms. Business servs avail. In-rm modem link. Bellhops. Concierge serv. Private patios, balconies. Authentic reproductions of Colonial-period furnishings; some antiques. Extensive grounds, elaborate landscaping. Most rms with garden view. Public beach opp. Cr cds: A, C, D, DS, MC, V.

★★ **WHARF COTTAGES.** *New Whale St (02554), on Wharf, foot of Main St. 508/228-4620; fax 508/325-1378.* 25 kit. cottages, 1-2 story. No A/C. Late May-Oct: kit. cottages $295-$575; wkly rates. Closed rest of yr. Crib free. TV; cable (premium). Restaurant nearby. Ck-out 11 am. Coin lndry. Bellhops. Tennis privileges. Balconies. Picnic tables, grills. Dockage. Cr cds: A, MC, V.

Hotel

★★★ **WHITE ELEPHANT RESORT.** *50 Easton St (02554), 4 blks NE. 508/228-2500; fax 508/325-1195; toll-free 800/475-2637.* 80 rms, most A/C, 1-3 story (no elvtr); suites in 15 cottages. Mid-June-mid-Sep: D $340-$590; each addl $20; cottages with kit. $425-$700; lower rates late-May-late-June, mid-Sep-mid-Oct. Closed rest of yr. Crib free. TV; cable (premium). Heated pool; whirlpool, poolside serv, lifeguard. Restaurant 7:30-10:30 am, noon-10 pm in season. Bar noon-1 am; entertainment. Ck-out 11 am. Meeting rm. Business servs avail. In-rm modem link. Concierge serv. Some private patios. Playground. Beach nearby; boat slips for guests only. On harbor; waterfront view from most inn rms. Cr cds: A, C, D, DS, MC, V.

Resort

★★ **NANTUCKET INN.** *27 Macy's Ln (02554), near Memorial Airport. 508/228-6900; fax 508/228-9861; toll-free 800/321-8484. Email ackinn@ nantucket.net; www.nantucket.net/ lodging/nantucketinn.* 100 rms, 1-2 story. June-Sep: S, D $130-$190; each addl $12; under 18 free; lower rates rest of yr. Pet accepted; $25. TV; cable. 2 pools, 1 indoor; whirlpool, lifeguard. Restaurant 7:30-10:30 am, noon-2 pm, 5:30-9 pm. Bars. Ck-out 11 am. Coin lndry. Meeting rms. Business servs avail. Bellhops. Sundries. Free airport transportation. Lighted tennis. Exercise equipt. Refrigerators. Cr cds: A, MC, V.

B&Bs/Small Inns

★★ **CARLISLE HOUSE INN.** *26 N Water St (02554), in Historic District. 508/228-0720. www.nantucket.net/ lodging/carlisle.* 14 rms, 5 share bath, 3 story. No rm phones. Mid-June-mid-Sep: S $75; D $95-$185; each addl $15; suites $250-$275; lower rates rest of yr. Children over 10 yrs only. Complimentary continental bkfst. Restaurant nearby. Ck-out 11 am, ck-in 2 pm. Street parking. Some fireplaces. Antiques. Library/sitting rm. Restored whaling captain's house (1765). Totally nonsmoking. Cr cds: A, MC, V.

★ **THE CARRIAGE HOUSE.** *5 Ray's Ct (02554). 508/228-0326.* 7 rms, 2 story. Mid-June-mid-Oct: S, D $100-$180; lower rates rest of yr. TV in sitting rm; cable. Complimentary continental bkfst. Restaurant nearby. Ck-out 11 am, ck-in 1 pm. Converted 1865 carriage house. Victorian decor. Garden terrace. Totally nonsmoking. Cr cds: A, MC, V.

★★★ **CENTERBOARD GUEST HOUSE.** *8 Chester St (02554). 508/ 228-9696. Email centerbo@nantucket. net; www.nantucket.net/lodging/centerboard.* 6 rms, 3 story, 1 suite. July-Aug: S $225; D $235; suites $375; lower rates rest of yr. Street parking. TV; cable. Cr cds: A, MC, V.

★★ **CENTRE STREET INN.** *78 Centre St (02554). 508/228-0199; fax 508/228-8676; toll-free 800/298-0199. Email inn@nantucket.net; www.centre-streetinn.com.* 13 rms, 6 share bath, 3 story. No rm phones. Late June-late Sep: S $75; D $95-$195; each addl $30; wkends, hols (3-day min); higher rates special hol events; lower rates May-late June, late Sep-mid-Dec. Closed rest of yr. Children over 8 yrs only. Complimentary continental bkfst. Ck-out 11 am, ck-in 3 pm. Concierge serv. Refrigerator avail. Picnic tables. Colonial house built in 1742; some antiques. Totally nonsmoking. Cr cds: A, DS, MC, V.

★★ **COBBLESTONE INN.** *5 Ash St (02554). 508/228-1987; fax 508/228-6698. Email cobble@nantucket.net.* 4 rms, 3 story, 1 suite. June-Sep: S, D $175; suites $265; each addl $20; lower rates rest of yr. Crib avail. Street parking. TV; cable. Complimentary full bkfst. Restaurant nearby. Ck-out 11 am, ck-in 2 pm. Concierge serv. Golf. Cr cds: MC, V.

★ **CORNER HOUSE INN.** *49 Centre St (02554). 508/228-1530. Email cornerhs@nantucket.net; www.corner housenantucket.com.* 15 rms, 3 story, 2 suites. June-Sep: S, D $235; suites $265; each addl $25; lower rates rest of yr. Street parking. TV; cable, VCR avail. Complimentary continental bkfst, toll-free calls. Restaurant nearby. Ck-out 10:30 am, ck-in 1 pm. Business servs avail. Concierge serv. Coin lndry. Exercise privileges. Golf, 18 holes. Tennis, 8 courts. Bike rentals. Picnic facilities. Cr cds: A, MC, V.

★★ **FOUR CHIMNEYS INN.** *38 Orange St (02554). 508/228-1912; fax 508/325-4864.* 10 rms, 8 with shower only, 3 story. No rm phones. Late May-mid-Oct: D $165-$275. Closed rest of yr. TV in sitting rm; cable. Complimentary continental bkfst; afternoon refreshments. Restaurant nearby. Ck-out 11 am, ck-in 1 pm. Concierge serv. Built 1870 for sea captain; many antiques. Garden. Totally nonsmoking. Cr cds: A, MC, V.

★★ **JARED COFFIN HOUSE.** *29 Broad St (02554), in Historic District. 508/228-2400; fax 508/228-8549; res 800/248-2405. Email jchouse@ nantucket.net; www.jaredcoffinhouse. com.* 60 rms, 3 story. May-Oct: D $325; each addl $15; lower rates rest of yr. Crib avail, fee. Parking lot. TV; cable. Complimentary coffee in rms. Restaurant 7:30 am-9 pm. Bar. Ck-out 11 am, ck-in 3 pm. Meeting rms.

Business center. Concierge serv. Gift shop. Golf. Cr cds: A, C, D, DS, ER, JCB, MC, V.

★ **MARTIN HOUSE INN.** *61 Centre St (02554). 508/228-0678. Email martinn@nantucket.net; www. nantucket.net/lodging/martinn.* 13 rms, 4 share bath, 3 story. No A/C. No elvtr. No rm phones. Mid-June-mid-Oct: S $50-$65; D $65-$120; each addl $25; suites $170; under 7 free; lower rates rest of yr. Children over 7 yrs only. TV in common rm; cable (premium). Complimentary continental bkfst. Restaurant opp 6-10 pm. Ck-out 11 am, ck-in 2 pm. In-rm modem link. Street parking. Built in 1803; antiques. Totally nonsmoking. Cr cds: MC, V.

★★ **ROBERTS HOUSE INN.** *11 India St (02554), in Historic District. 508/228-9009; fax 508/325-4046; toll-free 800/588-0087. Email rhinn@aol. com; www.robertshouseinn.com.* 37 rms, 3 story, 2 suites. May-Oct: S $65; D $325; suites $350; each addl $40; lower rates rest of yr. Crib avail. Parking lot. TV; cable. Complimentary continental bkfst, coffee in rms, toll-free calls. Restaurant. Ck-out 11 am, ck-in 2 pm. Business servs avail. Concierge serv. Golf, 9 holes. Cr cds: A, DS, MC, V.

★★ **SEVEN SEA STREET INN.** *7 Sea St (02554), in Historic District. 508/228-3577; fax 508/228-3578. Email seast7@nantucket.net; www. sevenseastreetinn.com.* 11 rms, 2 story, 2 suites. July-Aug: S, D $155-$195; suites $235-$265; off-season package plans; higher rates Christmas stroll wkend; lower rates rest of yr. Children over 5 yrs only. TV; cable, VCR. Complimentary continental bkfst; afternoon refreshments. Restaurant nearby. Ck-out 11 am, ck-in 2 pm. Business servs avail. Whirlpool. Refrigerators. Picnic tables. Library/sitting rm. View of Nantucket Harbor. Totally nonsmoking. Cr cds: A, MC, V.

★★★ **SHERBURNE INN.** *10 Gay St (02554). 508/228-4425; fax 508/228-8114; toll-free 888/577-4425. www. nantucket.net/lodging/sherburne.* 8 rms,

2 story. Mid-June-mid-Oct (3-day min): S, D $125-$235; each addl $25; higher rates: hols, special events; lower rates rest of yr. Children over 6 yrs only. Complimentary continental bkfst. Restaurant nearby. Ck-out 11 am, ck-in 2 pm. Concierge serv. Street parking. Built in 1835 as a silk factory; period antiques, fireplaced parlors. Totally nonsmoking. Cr cds: A, DS, MC, V.

★★ **SHIPS INN.** *13 Fair St (02554). 508/228-0040; fax 508/228-6254. Email shipsinn@nantucket.net.* 12 rms, 10 with bath. No A/C. Mid-May-mid-Oct: S $65-$90; D $145-$175; each addl $25. Closed rest of yr. Crib $10. TV. Complimentary continental bkfst; afternoon refreshments. Dining rm 5:30-9:30 pm. Bar 4:30-10 pm. Ck-out 10:30 am, ck-in 2 pm. Refrigerators. Built in 1831 by sea captain; many original furnishings. Totally nonsmoking. Cr cds: A, MC, V.

★★ **TUCKERNUCK INN.** *60 Union St (02554). 508/228-4886; fax 508/228-4890; toll-free 800/228-4886. www.tuckernuckinn.com.* 18 rms, 2 story, 1 suite. May-Oct: S, D $180; suites $250; each addl $20; lower rates rest of yr. Crib avail, fee. Parking lot. TV; cable, VCR avail. Complimentary toll-free calls. Restaurant. Ck-out 11 am, ck-in 3 pm. Business servs avail. Coin lndry. Golf, 18 holes. Beach access. Cr cds: A, MC, V.

★★★★ **THE WAUWINET.** *120 Wauwinet Rd (02584), 8 mi NE. 508/ 228-0145; fax 508/228-6712; toll-free 800/426-8718. www.wauwinet.com.* This secluded inn, nine miles from the island's center, occupies a thin strip of land bordered by Nantucket Bay and the Atlantic Ocean and affords guests two private beaches. Twenty-six rooms and several individual cottages border a wildlife preserve and are uniquely decorated in classy, New England country decor. The 1988 $8-million renovation brought luxurious detail back to this mid-19th century landmark. 26 rms, 3 story. June-Sep: S, D $590; suites $950; each addl $55; under 12 free; lower rates rest of yr. Parking lot. TV; cable (DSS), VCR avail, CD avail. Complimentary full bkfst, newspaper. Restaurant 8 am-10 pm. Bar. Ck-out 11 am, ck-in 4 pm. Meeting rm. Business servs avail. Concierge serv. Dry cleaning. Golf. Tennis, 2 courts. Beach access. Bike rentals. Hiking trail. Picnic facilities. Cr cds: A, D, MC, V.

Restaurants

★★ **21 FEDERAL.** *21 Federal St. (02554). 508/228-2121.* Specializes in seafood. Own baking, pasta. Menu changes daily. Hrs: 5 pm-1 am. Closed Sun; Jan-Mar. Res accepted. Bar. Dinner $19-$29. Display of old prints, drawings. Cr cds: A, MC, V.

★★ **AMERICAN SEASONS.** *80 Center St. (02554). 508/228-7111.* Specializes in braised rabbit tostada, potato and thyme-crusted sturgeon, homemade desserts. Hrs: 6-10 pm. Closed Jan-Apr. Bar. Dinner $16.50-$23.50. Popular spot features regional cuisine; decorated with country artifacts, hand-painted murals and gameboard tables. Cr cds: A, MC, V.

★ **ATLANTIC CAFE.** *15 S Water St (02554), in Historic District, near Wharf. 508/228-0570. www.atlantic cafe.com.* Specializes in seafood, hamburgers, Mexican dishes. Hrs: 11:30 am-midnight. Closed late Dec-early Jan. Bar. Lunch $5-$12; dinner $8-$21. Child's menu. Nautical decor; ship models. Cr cds: A, C, D, DS, ER, MC, V.

★★ **BOARDING HOUSE.** *12 Federal St (02554). 508/228-9622. www. nantucketrestaurants.com.* Specializes in twin lobster tails, seared yellowfin tuna, pistachio-crusted chocolate finale. Hrs: 5-10 pm. Closed Sun, Mon. Res accepted. Bar. Dinner $20-$32. Original art. Cr cds: A, DS, MC, V.

★★ **CAP'N TOBEY'S CHOWDER HOUSE.** *Straight Wharf (02554), off Main St. 508/228-0836.* Specializes in Cap'n Tobey's clam chowder, Nantucket Bay scallops, Indian pudding. Salad bar. Hrs: 11 am-10 pm. Closed mid-Oct-mid-May. Res accepted. Bar. Lunch $6.95-$9.95; dinner $12.95-$19.95. Child's menu. Nautical decor. Wharf view. Family-owned. Cr cds: A, C, D, DS, ER, MC, V.

★★★ **CHANTICLEER.** *9 New St (02564). 508/257-6231.* Specializes in fresh local seafood, lobster bisque, foie gras. Hrs: noon-2 pm, 6-9 pm. Closed Mon; also late Oct-mid-May. Res required. Bar. Wine cellar. Lunch a la carte entrees: $15-$30; dinner a la carte entrees: $25-$60. Prixe fixe: $65. Parking. Garden dining. Elegant, romantic dining in four dining rms. View of flower and herb gardens, carousel. Cr cds: A, D, MC, V.

★★★ **CIOPPINO'S.** *20 Broad St (02554). 508/228-4622.* Specializes in cioppino, tournedos of beef with lobster topping, grilled salmon fillet. Hrs: 11:30 am-2:30 pm, 5:30-10 pm. Closed Nov-May. Res accepted. Bar. Wine cellar. Lunch a la carte entrees: $8.50-$13.50; dinner a la carte entrees: $19.50-$36. Patio dining. 3 dining rms in turn-of-the-century house. Cr cds: A, D, DS, ER, MC, V.

★★★ **LE LANGUEDOC.** *24 Broad St (02554), in Historic District. 508/228-2552.* Specializes in veal, lamb, fresh fish. Hrs: 5-10 pm. Closed Sun; Jan-Mar. Res accepted. Bar. Lunch $8-$18; dinner $25-$35. Early 1800s bldg in heart of historic district. Cr cds: A, MC, V.

★★ **ROPE WALK.** *1 Straight Wharf (02554). 508/228-8886. www.therope walk.com.* Specializes in fresh local seafood, homemade desserts. Hrs: 11 am-3 pm; 5-10 pm. Closed mid-Oct-mid-May. Bar. Lunch $7.50-$12; dinner $16.50-$26. Child's menu. Nautical artifacts. At end of wharf; view of harbor. Cr cds: MC, V.

★ **TAVERN AT HARBOR SQUARE.** *Straight Wharf (02554), off Main St. 508/228-1266.* Specializes in New England clam chowder, lobster, fresh seafood. Hrs: 11-1 am. Closed Sat, Sun; mid-Oct-late May. Bar. Lunch $6.95-$15.95; dinner $7.95-$20.95. Child's menu. Patio dining. Nautical decor. Wharf view. Cr cds: A, MC, V.

★★★ **TOPPER'S.** *120 Wauwinet Rd. 508/228-0145. www.wauwinet.com.* Specializes in lobster and crab cakes with smoked corn, jalapeno olives and mustard sauce; Nantucket lobster with asparagus, mushrooms, and fettuccine. Hrs: noon-2 pm, 6-10 pm; Sun brunch 11 am-2 pm. Closed Nov-mid-May. Res accepted. Bar. Wine list. Lunch a la carte entrees: $21-$25; dinner a la carte entrees: $34-$52. Sun brunch $36. Within country inn; pickled oak floors; folk art collection. View of Nantucket Bay. Cr cds: A, C, D, MC, V.

[D]

★★ **WEST CREEK CAFE.** *11 W Creek Rd (02554). 508/228-4943.* Specializes in sauteed crab fritter with Georgia peanut vinaigrette; roasted tenderloin with polenta fries and red wine sauce; seared salmon over oven-roasted vegetable risotto and chive oil. Hrs: 6-9 pm; Fri, Sat to 9:30 pm. Closed Tues; also Jan 1, July 4, Dec 25. Res accepted. Bar. Dinner a la carte entrees: $18-$26. Parking. Contemporary, elegant cafe. Cr cds: MC, V.

Natick (C-5)

Pop 30,510 **Elev** 180 ft **Area code** 508 **Zip** 01760 **Web** www.metrowest.org

Information MetroWest Chamber of Commerce, 1671 Worcester Rd, Suite 201, Framingham 01701; 508/879-5600

This town was set aside as a plantation for the "Praying Indians" in 1650 at the request of Revrend John Eliot. A missionary, he believed that he could promote brotherhood between Native Americans and settlers by converting them. After half a century, the Native Americans were crowded out by settlers.

Motels/Motor Lodges

★★ **HAMPTON INN.** *319 Speen St (01760), at MA 9; I-90 Exit 13. 508/653-5000; fax 508/651-9733; res 800/HAMPTON.* 190 rms, 7 story. S, D $90-$99. Crib free. TV; cable (premium). Complimentary continental bkfst. Ck-out noon. Meeting rms. Business servs avail. Exercise equipt. Some refrigerators. Cr cds: A, D, DS, MC, V.

[D] [icons]

★ **TRAVELODGE.** *1350 Worcester Rd (01760). 508/655-2222; fax 508/655-7953; toll-free 800/578-7878. Email sleepbr@banet.net; www.travelodge.com.* 68 rms, 2 story. Apr-Oct: S $109; D $119; each addl $5; under 18 free; lower rates rest of yr. Crib avail. Parking lot. TV; cable (premium). Complimentary continental bkfst, coffee in rms, newspaper, toll-free calls. Restaurant nearby. Ck-out noon, ck-in 1 pm. Fax servs avail. Exercise privileges. Golf. Cr cds: A, DS, ER, JCB, MC, V.

[D] [icons]

Hotels

★★★ **CROWNE PLAZA HOTEL BOSTON - NATICK.** *1360 Worcester St (01760). 508/653-8800; fax 508/653-1708; res 800/2CROWNE. Email crownenati@aol.com; www.crowneplaza.com.* 249 rms, 7 story, 2 suites. May-June, Sep-Oct: S $220; D $240; suites $600; each addl $20; under 13 free; lower rates rest of yr. Crib avail. Valet parking avail. TV; cable (premium), VCR avail. Complimentary coffee in rms, newspaper, toll-free calls. Restaurant 6 am-10 pm. Bar. Ck-out noon, ck-in 3 pm. Meeting rms. Business center. Bellhops. Concierge serv. Dry cleaning. Gift shop. Exercise privileges. Golf. Cr cds: A, C, D, DS, ER, JCB, MC, V.

[D] [icons] [SC]

★★ **SHERBORN INN.** *33 N Main St (01770), 3 mi S on MA 27. 508/655-9521; fax 508/655-5325; res 508/655-9521. Email info@sherborninn.com; www.sherborninn.com.* 4 rms, 2 story. D $120. Crib avail, fee. Parking lot. TV; cable (premium). Complimentary continental bkfst. Restaurant 11:30 am-11 pm. Bar. Ck-out 11 am, ck-in 3 pm. Meeting rms. Business servs avail. Golf. Tennis, 4 courts. Hiking trail. Picnic facilities. Cr cds: A, MC, V.

[D] [icons]

Restaurant

★★ **SHERBORN INN.** *33 N Main St. 508/655-9521. www.sherborninn.com.* Specializes in tenderloin of beef.

Own baking. Hrs: 11:30 am-3 pm, 5-10 pm; Mon-Fri from 5 pm. Res accepted. Bar. Lunch $4.95-$9.50; dinner $13-$24. Entertainment: jazz Tues. Restored tavern decor. Cr cds: A, MC, V.

D

New Bedford (E-6)

Settled 1640 **Pop** 99,922 **Elev** 50 ft **Area code** 508 **Web** www.bristol-county.org

Information Bristol County Convention & Visitors Bureau, 70 N Second St, PO Box 976, 02741; 508/997-1250 or 800/288-6263

Herman Melville, author of *Moby Dick,* said that the brave houses and flowery gardens of New Bedford were one and all harpooned and dragged up from the bottom of the sea. Whaling did in fact build this city. When oil was discovered in Pennsylvania in 1857, the world's greatest whaling port nearly became a ghost town. New Bedford scrapped the great fleet and became a major cotton textile center. More recently, it has thrived on widely diversified industries. New Bedford remains a major Atlantic deep-sea fishing port. The whaling atmosphere is preserved in local museums and monuments, while the Whaling National Historical Park celebrates the town's whaling legacy. In the County Street historic district many of the mansions built for sea captains and merchants still stand.

What to See and Do

Boat trips.

Cape Island Express Lines. New Bedford-Martha's Vineyard Ferry. Bus tours, car rentals on Martha's Vineyard. (Mid-May-mid-Oct, daily) Same-day round-trip and one-way trips avail. Schedule may vary. Phone 508/997-1688. Round-trip ¢¢¢¢

New Bedford-Cuttyhunk Ferry. (Mid-June-mid-Sep, daily; rest of yr, varied schedule) Res suggested. Departs from Fisherman's Wharf, pier 3. Phone 508/992-1432. Round trip ¢¢¢¢

Buttonwood Park and Zoo. Greenhouse; ball fields, tennis courts, playground, picnic area, fitness circuit. Zoo exhibits incl elephants, lions, deer, bears, buffalo; seal pool. (Daily except Thanksgiving, Dec 25, Jan 1) Rockdale Ave. Phone 508/991-6178 (zoo) or 508/991-6175. ¢

Children's Museum. Two floors of hands-on exhibits; 60 acres with nature trails, picnic areas. Special summer and wkend programs. (Tues-Sun; closed hols) From I-195 Exit 12, left on US 6, first right (Tucker Rd), continue 4 mi to 4-way stop, left onto Gulf Rd in *S* Dartmouth. Phone 508/993-3361. ¢¢

Fort Phoenix Beach State Reservation. Swimming; fine view of harbor. Nearby is Fort Phoenix, a pre-Revolutionary fortification (open to the public). Off US 6 & I-95, E via US 6 to Fairhaven, then 1 mi S; follow signs. Phone 508/992-4524. Per vehicle ¢

New Bedford Whaling Museum. Features an 89-ft half-scale model of whaleship *Lagoda.* Galleries devoted to scrimshaw, local artists; murals of whales and whale skeleton; period rms and collections of antique toys, dolls, prints, and ship models. Silent movie presentation (July and Aug). (Daily; closed Jan 1, Thanksgiving, Dec 25) 18 Johnny Cake Hill. Phone 508/997-0046. ¢¢

Rotch-Jones-Duff House and Garden Museum. Whaling era Greek-revival mansion (1834) and garden, has been maintained to reflect the lives of 3 families that lived in the house. (Oct-May, Tues-Sun; rest of yr, Mon-Sat, also Sun afternoons) Museum sponsors concerts and programs throughout the yr. Tours avail, inquire for schedule. Museum shop. 396 County St. Phone 508/997-1401. ¢¢

Seamen's Bethel. (1832) "Whaleman's Chapel" referred to by Melville in *Moby Dick.* Prow-shaped pulpit later built to represent Melville's description. Also many cenotaphs dedicated to men lost at sea. Vespers 3rd Sun each month. (May-Columbus Day, Mon-Sat, also Sun afternoons; rest of yr, by appt) 15 Johnny Cake Hill. Phone 508/992-3295. **Donation**

Annual Events

Feast of the Blessed Sacrament. Madeira Field, N end of town. Portuguese festival. Three days usually beginning 1st wkend Aug.

Blessing of the Fleet. Waterfront. Third Sun Aug.

First Night New Bedford. Historic waterfront and downtown. Celebration of arts and culture; fireworks. Dec 31.

Motel/Motor Lodge

★★ **QUALITY INN.** *500 Hathaway Rd (02740), off I-195 at Exit 13B, near Municipal Airport. 508/997-1231; fax 508/984-7977.* 153 rms, 3 story. S $64-$75; D $69-$82; each addl $5; under 12 free. Crib free. Pet accepted, some restrictions. TV; cable (premium). Indoor pool. Coffee in rms. Restaurant 7 am-11 pm. Bar 4 pm-midnight. Ck-out 11 am. Meeting rm. Business servs avail. In-rm modem link. Coin lndry. Free airport transportation. Golf course opp. Cr cds: A, DS, MC, V.

D ▷ ✈ ▷ 🔥

Hotel

★★ **THE COMFORT INN.** *171 Faunce Corner Rd (02747), W via I-195, Exit 12. 508/996-0800; fax 508/996-0800. www.comfortinndartmouth. com.* 84 rms, 2 story. Apr-Aug: S $90; D $119; each addl $10; lower rates rest of yr. Crib avail. Parking lot. Pool. TV; cable (DSS). Complimentary full bkfst, coffee in rms, newspaper, toll-free calls. Restaurant 11 am-11 pm. Ck-out noon. Business servs avail. Concierge serv. Dry cleaning. Exercise privileges. Golf, 18 holes. Tennis. Beach access. Supervised children's activities. Picnic facilities. Cr cds: A, D, DS, MC, V.

D 🏂 ⛷ ▷ 🕴 ▷ 🐾 SC

Restaurant

★★ **FREESTONE'S CITY GRILL.** *41 William St (02740). 508/993-7477. www.freestones.com.* Specializes in fish chowder, seafood, specialty salads. Hrs: 11 am-10 pm; Fri, Sat to 11 pm. Closed Sun; Labor Day, Thanksgiving, Dec 25. Res accepted. Bar. Lunch $4-$7; dinner $4-$18. Child's menu. Street parking. Renovated bank bldg

(1877); interesting art objects. Cr cds: A, D, DS, MC, V.

D

🅖

Newburyport

Settled 1635 **Pop** 16,317 **Elev** 37 ft
Area code 978 **Zip** 01950
Web www.newburyport.chamber.net

Information Greater Newburyport Chamber of Commerce & Industry, 29 State St; 978/462-6680

Novelist John P. Marquand, who lived in Newburyport, said it "is not a museum piece although it sometimes looks it." High Street is surely a museum of American Federalist architecture. Ship owners and captains built these great houses. The birthplace of the US Coast Guard, Newburyport lies at the mouth of the Merrimack River. The city's early prosperity came from shipping and shipbuilding. It is now a thriving year-round tourist destination.

What to See and Do

Coffin House. (ca 1654) Developed in a series of enlargements, features 17th- and 18th-century kitchens, buttery, and parlor with early 19th-century wallpaper; furnishings of 8 generations. Tours on the hr. (June-mid-Oct, Wed-Sun) 16 High Rd (US 1A). Phone 978/463-2057. ¢¢

Cushing House Museum. (Historical Society of Old Newbury; ca 1810) A Federalist-style mansion, once the home of Caleb Cushing, first envoy to China from US. Museum houses collections of needlework, paperweights, toys, paintings, furniture, silver, clocks, china; library. Also shed, carriage house, and 19th-century garden. (May-Oct, Tues-Sat; closed hols) 98 High St. Phone 978/462-2681. ¢

Custom House Maritime Museum. Collections of artifacts depicting maritime heritage of area; incl ship models, navigational instruments; decorative arts, library. (Apr-late Dec, Mon-Sat, also Sun afternoons) 25 Water St. Phone 978/462-8681. ¢¢

Parker River National Wildlife Refuge. Natural barrier beach formed by 6½ mi of beach and sand dunes is the home of many species of birds, mammals, reptiles, amphibians, and plants; saltwater and freshwater marshes provide resting and feeding place for migratory birds on the Atlantic Flyway. Hiking, bicycling, waterfowl hunting; nature trail. (Daily) Closed to public when parking lots are full. 3 mi E on Plum Island. Contact Refuge Manager, Northern Blvd, Plum Island 01950. Phone 978/465-5753. Pedestrians ¢; Per vehicle ¢¢

Annual Events

Spring Arts & Flower Festival. Downtown. Demonstrations, flower and garden show, crafts, exhibits. Sun, Mon of Memorial Day wkend.

Yankee Homecoming. Celebration incl parades, fireworks, exhibits; river cruises; sailboat and canoe races; craft show; lobster feeds. Last Sat July-1st Sun Aug.

Fall Harvest Festival. Downtown. Juried crafts, music, entertainment, food, baking contest. Sun, Mon of Columbus Day wkend.

Motel/Motor Lodge

★ **SUSSE CHALET INN.** *35 Clarks Rd (01913), Rte 110; 3 mi N on 95 Exit 58B.* 978/388-3400; fax 978/388-9850. 105 rms, 4 story. S, D $69-$89; each addl $6; under 18 free; wkend rates. TV; cable (premium). Complimentary continental bkfst. Restaurant adj 6:30 am-11:30 pm. Ck-out 11 am. Meeting rms. Business servs avail. Health club privileges. Pool. Cr cds: A, C, D, DS, MC, V.
🅳 🛬 🖂 🕇 ⚲ 🔌 🔥

Hotel

★ **GARRISON INN.** *11 Brown Sq (01950), off Pleasant St.* 978/499-8500; fax 978/499-8555. Email services@garrison-inn.com; www.garrison-inn.com. 24 rms, 4 story. June-Oct: S, D $97.50-$107.50 each addl $10; town house $135-$175; lower rates rest of yr. Crib avail. TV; cable (premium), VCR avail. Restaurant (see also DAVID'S). Supervised children's activities; ages 2-12. Bar;

entertainment. Ck-out 11 am, ck-in 3 pm. Meeting rm. Business servs avail. In-rm modem link. Restored historic inn (1809). Cr cds: A, MC, V.
🅳 🔌 🔥

B&Bs/Small Inns

★★ **CLARK CURRIER INN.** *45 Green St (01950).* 978/465-8363. 8 rms, 3 story. May-mid-Jan: S, D $95-$155; lower rates rest of yr. TV in sitting rm. Complimentary bkfst buffet. Restaurant nearby. Ck-out 11 am, ck-in 3 pm. Bus depot transportation. Built 1803 by a shipbuilder. Rms furnished with antiques. Garden with gazebo. Totally nonsmoking. Cr cds: A, DS, MC, V.
🔌 🔥 **SC**

★★ **ESSEX STREET INN.** *7 Essex St (01950).* 978/465-3148; fax 978/462-1907. 19 rms, 3 story. June-Oct: S, D $85-$125; each addl $10; suites $155; kit. unit $175; townhouse $155; lower rates rest of yr. TV. Complimentary continental bkfst. Restaurant nearby. Ck-out 11 am, ck-in 2 pm. Some in-rm whirlpools. Built 1801; fireplace. Cr cds: A, MC, V.
🔌 🔥

★★ **MORRILL PLACE.** *209 High St (01950).* 978/462-2808; fax 978/462-9966; res 888/594-4667. Email morrill@aol.com. 9 rms, 4 share bath, 3 story. No A/C. S, D $72-$95; each addl $10; EP avail; wkly rates. Pet accepted. TV rm; cable, VCR avail. Complimentary continental bkfst. Restaurant nearby. Ck-out noon, ck-in 4 pm. Tennis privileges. 18-hole golf privileges, pro. Built in 1806. Once owned by law partner of Daniel Webster; Webster was frequent visitor. Formal front parlor and library. Cr cds: A, MC, V.
🅳 🐾 🕇 🖇 🔥

★★ **WINDSOR HOUSE.** *38 Federal St (01950).* 978/462-3778; fax 978/465-3443; toll-free 888/873-5296. Email windsorinn@earthlink.net; www.bbhost.com/windsorhouse. 4 rms, 3 story. May-Dec: S, D $145; each addl $35; lower rates rest of yr. Pet accepted, some restrictions. Street parking. TV; cable, VCR avail. Complimentary full bkfst, coffee in rms. Restaurant nearby. Ck-out 11 am, ck-in 4 pm. Meeting rm. Business servs avail.

Exercise privileges. Golf. Tennis. Cr cds: A, DS, MC, V.

Restaurants

★★ **CHEF'S HARVEST.** *38A Washington St (01950). 978/463-1775.* Specializes in veal, fish, pasta. Hrs: 5-10 pm. Closed Tues; Easter, Dec 25. Res accepted. Dinner $5.75-$14.95. Child's menu. Street parking. Casual decor. Cr cds: A, DS, MC, V.

★★★ **DAVID'S.** *11 Brown Sq. 978/462-8077.* Mediterranean menu. Specializes in lobster, scallops, sweet potatoes. Own baking. Hrs: 5-10 pm. Closed Jan 1, Dec 24, 25. Res accepted. Bar. Wine list. Dinner $6.95-$24.50. Prix fixe: $40-$54.50. Child's menu. Entertainment: guitarist Thurs-Sat. Two distinct dining areas: formal dining rm with high ceiling and informal basement pub; separate menus. Cr cds: A, DS, MC, V.

★★★ **GLENN'S GALLEY.** *44 Merrimas St (01950). 978/465-3811.* Hrs: 5:30-10 pm. Closed Mon; Res accepted. Bar. Wine list. Dinner $18-$22. Child's menu. Wed, Thurs, Sun entertainment. Street parking. Bistro decor. Cr cds: A, D, DS, MC, V.

★ **THE GROG.** *13 Middle St (01950). 978/465-8008. www.thegrog.com.* Specializes in seafood. Hrs: noon-1 am. Closed Dec 25. Bar. Lunch $5.95-$14.95; dinner $5.95-$14.95. Entertainment: musicians Thurs-Sun. Tavern atmosphere. Family-owned. Cr cds: A, C, D, DS, ER, MC, V.

★ **JACOB MARLEY'S.** *23 Pleasant St (01950). 978/465-5598.* Specializes in salads. Hrs: 11 am-10 pm; Sun brunch 11 am-2 pm. Closed Dec 25. Bar. Lunch, dinner $8.95-$13.95. Sun brunch $7.95-$10.95. Child's menu. Entertainment: Tues, Sat, Sun. Restored mill; nautical objects. Cr cds: A, MC, V.

★★ **MICHAEL'S HARBORSIDE.** *1 Tournament Wharf (01950), MA 1. 978/462-7785.* Specializes in fresh seafood. Hrs: 11:30 am-3 pm, 5-10 pm; Sun noon-9 pm; winter hrs vary. Closed Thanksgiving, Dec 25. Bar. Lunch $5.95-$11.95; dinner $6.95-$15.95. Entertainment: Sun (summer). Parking. Cr cds: A, DS, MC, V.

★★★ **SCANDIA.** *25 State St (01950). 978/462-6271.* Specializes in seafood, game, vegetarian dishes. Hrs: 10 am-10 pm. Closed Thanksgiving, Dec 25. Res accepted. Bar. Lunch $3.25-$12; dinner $12-$17.95. Child's menu. Traditional, formal decor; original oil paintings. Family-owned. Cr cds: A, DS, MC, V.

★★ **TEN CENTER STREET.** *10 Center St (01950), 1 blk off Market Sq. 978/462-6652.* Specializes in fresh seafood, veal, beef. Own baking. Hrs: 11-1 am. Res accepted. Bar. Lunch a la carte entrees: $5.95-$14.95; dinner a la carte entrees: $6.95-$22.95. Parking. In restored 1800s Federal-style house. Cr cds: A, D, DS, MC, V.

Newton

(C-6) *See also Boston*

Settled 1630 **Pop** 82,585 **Elev** 100 ft
Area code 617
Web www.nnchamber.com

Information Chamber of Commerce, 199 Wells Ave, Suite 208, PO Box 268 Newton Centre 02459; 617/244-5300

Newton, the "Garden City," is actually a city of 13 suburban neighborhoods that have maintained their individual identities. Of the 13, eight have "Newton" in their names: Newton, Newtonville, Newton Centre, Newton Corner, Newton Highlands, West Newton, Newton Upper Falls, and Newton Lower Falls. Five colleges are located here: Boston College, Lasell College, Mount Ida College, Andover-Newton Theological School, and Aquinas Junior College.

What to See and Do

Jackson Homestead. (1809) Once a station on the Underground Railroad. Changing exhibits on Newton history; children's gallery; toys; textiles; and tools. (July-Aug, Mon-Thurs; rest of yr, Mon-Thurs and Sun afternoons; closed hols) 527 Washington St. Phone 617/552-7238. ¢

Motel/Motor Lodge

★ **SUSSE CHALET INN.** *160 Boylston St (02467). 617/527-9000; fax 617/527-4994; toll-free 800/524-2538.* 144 rms in 5 bldgs, 3-6 story. S, D $59.70-$116.70; under 18 free. Crib free. TV; cable (premium). Pool; lifeguard. Complimentary continental bkfst. Restaurant 11:30 am-11:30 pm. Bar to 12:30 am. Ck-out 11 am. In-rm modem link. Coin lndry. Shopping arcade. Barber, beauty shop. Cr cds: A, C, D, DS, MC, V.

Hotels

★★ **HOLIDAY INN NEWTON-BOSTON.** *399 Grove St (02462), I-95 (MA 128) Exit 22. 617/969-5300; fax 617/630-8364; res 800/465-4329.* Aug-Nov: S, D $190; lower rates rest of yr. Crib avail. Parking garage. Pool, lifeguard. TV; cable (premium). Complimentary coffee in rms. Restaurant 6:30 am-midnight. Bar. Ck-out noon, ck-in 3 pm. Business servs avail. Dry cleaning. Exercise equipt. Golf. Downhill skiing. Cr cds: A, C, D, DS, MC, V.

★★★ **MARRIOTT.** *2345 Commonwealth Ave (02466), I-95 Exit 24. 617/969-1000; fax 617/527-6914; toll-free 800/228-9290.* 430 rms, 7 story. Sep-Nov: S, D $169; suites $300-$500; under 18 free; wkend rates; lower rates rest of yr. Crib free. Pet accepted, some restrictions. TV; cable (premium). 2 pools, 1 indoor; whirlpool; poolside serv, lifeguard. Playground. Restaurant 6:30 am-midnight. Bar; entertainment. Ck-out 1 pm. Coin lndry. Convention facilities. Business servs avail. In-rm modem link. Bellhops. Sundries. Barber. X-country ski 1 mi. Exercise equipt; sauna. Canoes. Game rm. Lawn games. Some private patios, balconies. Picnic tables. On Charles River. Luxury level. Cr cds: A, MC, V.

★★★ **SHERATON HOTEL.** *100 Cabot St (02494), Ma 128 Exit 19A. 781/444-1110; fax 617/455-8617; toll-free 800/274-3728. www.sheraton.com.* 247 rms, 5 story, 48 suites. Mid-Apr-mid-Nov: S, D, suites $149-$229; each addl $15; under 18 free; wkend rates. TV; cable (premium). Indoor pool; poolside serv. Restaurant 6:30 am-10 pm. Bar 11:30-1 am, entertainment Thurs-Sat. Ck-out noon. Meeting rms. Business servs avail. Concierge serv. Garage parking. Gift shop. Exercise equipt; sauna. Health club privileges. Cr cds: A, C, D, DS, ER, MC, V.

★★★ **SHERATON NEWTON HOTEL.** *320 Washington St (02158), I-90 Exit 17, in Gateway Center at Newton Corner. 617/969-3010; fax 617/244-5894; toll-free 800/325-3535.* 272 rms, 12 story. S, D $109-$199; each addl $15; wkend rates. Crib free. TV; cable (premium), VCR avail. Indoor pool. Coffee in rms. Restaurant 7 am-10 pm. Bar. Ck-out 11 am. Meeting rms. Business servs avail. In-rm modem link. Bellhops. Exercise rm; sauna. Refrigerators, microwaves avail. Cr cds: A, C, D, DS, ER, MC, V.

Restaurants

★★ **LEGAL SEAFOODS.** *43 Boylston St (02467), 5 mi W on MA 9, in Chestnut Hill Shopping Mall. 617/277-7300.* Specializes in bluefish pate, clam chowder, mussels au gratin. Hrs: 11 am-10 pm; Sun from noon. Closed Thanksgiving, Dec 25. Bar. Lunch $6.95-$13.95; dinner $9.95-$30.95. Child's menu. Fishmarket on premises. Family-owned. Cr cds: A, C, D, DS, ER, MC, V.

★★★ **LUMIERE.** *1293 Washington St (02465). 617/244-9199.* Specializes in sea scallops over potato mousseline, torchon foie gras. Hrs: 5:30-9:30 pm; Fri 5:30-10 pm; Sat 5-10 pm; Sun 5-9 pm. Closed Mon. Res accepted. beer, wine. Dinner $12-$30. Chef-owned. Cr cds: D, MC, V.

★★★ **PILLAR HOUSE.** *26 Quinobeguin Rd (02462), MA 16 and 128 (I-*

95) Exit 21A. 617/969-6500. www
.pillarhouse.com. Specializes in lobster
struedel, spit-roast beef rib, crab
cakes. Hrs: 5-10 pm. Closed Sat, Sun.
Bar. Dinner a la carte entrees: $17-
$30. Parking. In restored 1848 resi-
dence. Family-owned since 1952. Cr
cds: A, DS, MC, V.

D

North Adams

(B-2) See also Williamstown

Settled 1745 **Pop** 16,797 **Elev** 707 ft
Area code 413 **Zip** 01247
Information Northern Berkshire
Chamber of Commerce, 40 Main St;
413/663-3735

North Adams is an industrial community set in the beautiful four-season resort country of the northern
Berkshires. Its factories make electronic components, textile machinery, wire, machine tools, paper
boxes, and other products. Susan B.
Anthony was born in nearby Adams
in 1820.

What to See and Do

MASS MoCA. Center for visual, performing, and media arts. Features
unconventional exhibits and performances by renowned artists and cultural institutions. Rehearsals, art
fabrication shops, and production
studios are open to the public. Tours
avail. (Daily) 87 Marshall St. Phone
413/664-4481. ¢¢¢ Also here is

   Kidspace. Children's gallery presents contemporary art in manner
   that is interesting and accessible.
   Incl hands-on activity stations
   where children can create their
   own works of art. (June-Aug,
   Thurs-Mon; rest of yr, limited hrs)
   Phone 413/664-4481. **FREE**

Mohawk Trail State Forest. Spectacular scenery. Swimming, fishing; hiking and riding trails, winter sports,
picnicking, camping; log cabins.
Standard fees. E on MA 2, near
Charlemont. Phone 413/339-5504.
FREE

Mount Greylock State Reservation.
Mt Greylock, highest point in state
(3,491 ft), is here. War memorial

tower at summit. Fishing; hunting,
cross-country skiing, snowmobiles
allowed, picnicking. Lodge, snacks;
campsites (mid-May-mid-Oct). Visitor center on Rockwell Rd in Lanes-
borough, off MA 7. Standard fees. 1
mi W on MA 2, then N on Notch Rd.
Phone 413/499-4262. **FREE**

Natural Bridge State Park. A water-
eroded marble bridge and rock formations, about 550 million yrs old,
popularized by Nathaniel
Hawthorne. Picnicking. (Mid-May-
mid-Oct) 1¼ mi NE on MA 8. Phone
413/663-6392. Per vehicle ¢¢

Savoy Mountain State Forest. Brilliant fall foliage. Swimming, fishing,
boating (ramp); hiking and riding
trails, hunting, winter sports, picnicking, camping, log cabins. Waterfall. Standard fees. E on MA 2, near
Florida, MA. Phone 413/664-9567 or
413/663-8469. **FREE**

**Western Gateway Heritage State
Park.** Restored freightyard with 6
bldgs around a cobbled courtyard.
Detailed historic exhibits on the con-
struction of Hoosac Railroad Tunnel.
(Daily; closed hols) Behind City Hall
on MA 8. Phone 413/663-8059.
Donation

Annual Events

La Festa. Ethnic festival, ethnic food,
entertainment, events. Phone
413/66-FESTA. Sixteen days beginning mid-June.

Fall Foliage Festival. Parade, entertainment, dancing, children's activities. Phone 413/663-3735. Late
Sep-early Oct.

Northampton

(C-3)

Settled 1673 **Pop** 29,289 **Elev** 140 ft
Area code 413 **Zip** 01060
Web www.northamptonuncommon.
com

Information Chamber of Commerce,
99 Pleasant St; 413/584-1900; or the
Tourist Information Center, 33 King
St; 413/665-0532 (June-Oct)

When the famed concert singer
Jenny Lind honeymooned in this

town on the Connecticut River in 1852, she exclaimed, "Why, this is the paradise of America." But it was not always a peaceful town. Northampton was the scene of a frenzied religious revival movement in the first half of the 18th century. It stemmed from Jonathan Edwards, a Puritan divine who came to be regarded as the greatest preacher in New England. Later, the town was the home of President Calvin Coolidge. A granite memorial on the court house lawn honors Coolidge, who was once mayor. Clarke School for the Deaf is located here.

What to See and Do

Arcadia Nature Center and Wildlife Sanctuary, Massachusetts Audubon Society. Approx 550 acres on migratory flyway; an ancient oxbow of the Connecticut River; self-guiding nature trails; observation tower; courses and programs. Grounds (Tues-Sun). 127 Comba Rd; 4 mi SW on MA 10, follow signs, in Northampton and Easthampton. Phone 413/584-3009. ¢¢

Calvin Coolidge Memorial Room. Displays of the late president's papers and correspondence; also books and articles on Coolidge. Memorabilia incl Native American headdress and beadwork given to him, Mrs Coolidge's needlework, photographs. (Mon-Wed; closed hols; schedule may vary) Phone 413/587-1014. **FREE**

Historic Northampton Museum houses. All houses (Tues-Sun). 46-66 Bridge St. Phone 413/584-6011. ¢¢

> **Damon House.** (1813) Permanent formal parlor exhibit (ca 1820).

> **Shepherd House.** (1798) Incl the lifetime collection of one Northampton family and focuses on family lifestyle at the turn of the 19th century.

> **Parsons House.** (ca 1730) Contains exhibits on local architecture.

Look Park. Miniature train and Christenson Zoo; boating; tennis, picnicking, playgrounds, ball fields; also here is Pines Theater (musical entertainment, children's theater, and puppet programs, summer). Park (all yr). Fees for most facilities. 300 N Main St, NW off MA 9. Phone 413/584-5457. Per vehicle ¢

Smith College. (1871) 2,700 women. The largest private liberal arts college for women in the US. On campus are Paradise Pond, named by Jenny Lind; Helen Hills Hills Chapel; William Allan Neilson Library with more than 1 million volumes; Center for the Performing Arts; Plant House and Botanical Gardens; Japanese Garden. On Elm St (MA 9). Phone 413/584-2700.

Annual Events

Springtime in Paradise. Major arts festival. Memorial Day wkend.

Eastern National Morgan Horse Show. Three-County Fairgrounds. Late July.

Three-County Fair. Agricultural exhibits, horse racing, pari-mutuel betting. Labor Day wk. Phone 413/584-2237.

Seasonal Event

Maple sugaring. Visitors are welcome at many maple camps. Phone 413/584-1900. Mid-Mar-early Apr.

Motels/Motor Lodges

★★ **AUTUMN INN.** *259 Elm St (01060). 413/584-7660; fax 413/586-4808.* 30 rms, 2 story. Apr-Nov: S $68-$80; D $86-$106; each addl $6-$12; suites $110-$135; lower rates rest of yr. Crib free. TV; cable (premium). Pool. Restaurant 7-10 am, 11:30 am-2 pm; wkends 8-11 am. Bar. Ck-out 11 am. In-rm modem link. Downhill ski 5 mi; x-country ski 18 mi. Lawn games. Refrigerator in suites. Picnic table. Smith College opp. Cr cds: A, C, D, MC, V.
🐾 🛏 🏋

★★ **BEST WESTERN NORTHAMPTON.** *117 Conz St (01060), I-91 Exit 18. 413/586-1500; fax 413/586-6549; res 800/528-1234; toll-free 800/941-3066. www.bestwestern.com.* 62 rms, 2 story, 4 suites. July-Oct: S $69; D $79; suites $99; each addl $7; under 12 free; lower rates rest of yr. Crib avail. Parking lot. Pool. TV; cable (premium), VCR avail. Complimentary continental bkfst, coffee in rms, newspaper, toll-free calls. Restaurant nearby. Ck-out 11 am, ck-in 2 pm. Business center. Exercise privileges. Golf, 18 holes. Tennis, 4 courts. Downhill skiing. Supervised children's activities. Hiking trail. Picnic facilities. Cr cds: A, D, DS, MC, V.

D ⚡ ➤ 🎿 ⛷ 🏊 🏋 🎿 ⛷ 🔥 SC 🎿

Hotels

★★ **HOTEL NORTHAMPTON.** *36 King St (01060). 413/584-3100; fax 413/584-9455; toll-free 800/547-3529. www.hotelnorthhampton.com.* 90 rms, 5 story. Sep-Oct: S, D $109-$160; each addl $12; suites $138-$290; under 12 free; higher rates special events; lower rates rest of yr. Crib free. TV; cable (premium). Restaurants 7-1 am. Bar. Ck-out noon. Meeting rms. Business center. Private patios, balconies. Cr cds: A, D, DS, MC, V.

D 🎿 🏊 🔥

★★ **THE INN AT NORTHAMPTON.** *1 Atwood Dr (01060), jct US 5 and I-91 Exit 18. 413/586-1211; fax 413/586-1723; res 413/586-1211; toll-free 800/582-2927. Email innnoho@javanet.com.* June-Oct: S, D $139; suites $159; lower rates rest of yr. Crib avail. Parking lot. Indoor/outdoor pools, children's pool, whirlpool. TV; cable. Complimentary continental bkfst, coffee in rms. Restaurant 4 am-11 pm. Bar. Ck-out 11 am, ck-in 3 pm. Business servs avail. Bellhops. Dry cleaning. Exercise privileges. Golf. Tennis, 2 courts. Downhill skiing. Cr cds: A, D, DS, MC, V.

D 🏊 🎿 ⛷ 🏊 🎿 🏊 🔥

Restaurant

★★ **EASTSIDE GRILL.** *19 Strong Ave (01060). 413/586-3347. Email esgrill@javanet.com.* Specializes in seafood, steak. Hrs: 5-10 pm. Closed Thanksgiving, Dec 25. Bar. Dinner $8.95-$14.95. New Orleans-theme prints. Cr cds: A, C, D, DS, ER, MC, V.

D

North Truro

(see Truro and North Truro)

Orleans (Cape Cod)

See also Eastham

Settled 1693 **Pop** 5,838 **Elev** 60 ft
Area code 508 **Zip** 02653
Web www.capecodchamber.org
Information Cape Cod Chamber of Commerce, US 6 & MA 132, PO Box 790, Hyannis 02601-0790; 508/362-3225 or 888/33-CAPECOD

Orleans supposedly was named in honor of the Duke of Orleans after the French Revolution. The settlers worked at shipping, fishing, and salt production. Its history incl the dubious distinction of being the only town in America to have been fired upon by the Germans during World War I. The town is now a commercial hub for the summer resort colonies along the great stretch of Nauset Beach and the coves behind it. A cable station, which provided direct communication between Orleans and Brest, France, from 1897 to 1959, is restored to its original appearance and open to the public.

What to See and Do

Academy of Performing Arts. Theater presents comedies, drama, musicals, dance. Workshops for all ages. 120 Main St. Phone 508/255-1963.

French Cable Station Museum. Built in 1890 as American end of transatlantic cable from Brest, France. Original equipment for submarine cable communication on display. (July-Labor Day, Tues-Sat afternoons) MA 28 & Cove Rd. Phone 508/240-1735. ¢¢

Nauset Beach. One of the most spectacular ocean beaches on the Atlantic Coast is now within the boundaries of Cape Cod National Seashore (see). Swimming, surfing, fishing, lifeguards. Parking fee. About 3 mi E of US 6 on marked roads.

Motels/Motor Lodges

★★ **THE COVE.** *13 Rte 28 (02653), near jct MA 6A. 508/255-1203; fax 781/255-7736; toll-free 800/343-2233. Email thecove@c4.net; www.thecoveorleans.com.* 47 rms, 1-2 story. July-

Aug: S, D $99-$179 (2-day min); each addl $10; kit. units $159-$179; lower rates rest of yr. Crib $10. TV; cable (premium), VCR. Heated pool. Coffee in rms. Restaurant nearby. Ck-out 11 am. Meeting rm. Business center. Lawn games. Refrigerators, microwaves. Picnic tables, grill. Sun deck. On town cove. Float boat rides avail. Cr cds: A, MC, V.

★ NAUSET KNOLL MOTOR LODGE.
PO 642, 237 Beach Rd (02643), at Nauset Beach, 3 mi E of MA 28 at end of Beach Rd. 508/255-2364; fax 508/255-6901. Email benzsr@cape.com; www.capecodtravel.com. 12 rms, 1 story. June-Aug: S, D $140; each addl $10; children $10; under 6 free; lower rates rest of yr. Crib avail. TV; cable. Restaurant nearby. Ck-out 11 am, ck-in 2 pm. Golf. Tennis. Beach access. Hiking trail. Picnic facilities. Cr cds: MC, V.

★★ OLDE TAVERN MOTEL AND INN.
151 MA 6A, PO 943 (02653). 508/255-1565; toll-free 800/544-7705. www.capecodtravel.com/oldetavern. 30 rms, 1 story. June-Aug: D $110; lower rates rest of yr. Crib avail. Parking lot. Pool. TV; cable (premium). Complimentary continental bkfst. Restaurant nearby. Ck-out 11 am, ck-in 2 pm. Exercise equipt. Golf. Cr cds: A, DS, MC, V.

★ RIDGEWOOD MOTEL AND COTTAGES.
10 Quanset Rd (02662), 2 mi S, jct MA 28 and 39. 508/255-0473. www.indigitweb.com/ridgewood. 18 units, some A/C, 6 cottages. No rm phones. Late June-Labor Day: S, D $69-$80; cottages $500-$610/wk; lower rates rest of yr. Crib $10. TV. Pool. Playground. Complimentary continental bkfst. Ck-out 10 am. Lawn games. Many refrigerators. Picnic tables, grills. Totally nonsmoking. Cr cds: MC, V.

★★ SEASHORE PARK MOTOR INN.
24 Canal Rd (02653), at US 6. 508/255-2500; fax 508/240-2728; toll-free 800/772-6453. 62 rms, 2 story, 24 kits. Late-June-early Sep: S, D $99-$119; each addl $10; under 13 free; kit. units $109-$129; lower rates mid-Apr-late-June, early Sep-Oct. Closed rest of yr. TV; cable. 2 pools, 1 indoor; whirlpool, sauna. Complimentary continental bkfst. Restaurant adj 7 am-midnight. Ck-out 11 am. Business servs avail. Microwaves avail. Private patios, balconies. Sun deck. Totally nonsmoking. Cr cds: A, DS, MC, V.

★★ SKAKET BEACH MOTEL.
203 Cranberry Hwy (02653). 508/255-1020; fax 508/255-6487; toll-free 800/835-0298. Email skaketb@c4.net; www.skaketbeachmotel.com. 45 rms, 2 story, 1 suite. June-Aug: S $91; D $99; suites $164; each addl $11; children $11; lower rates rest of yr. Crib avail. Pet accepted, some restrictions, fee. Parking lot. Pool. TV; cable (premium). Complimentary continental bkfst, coffee in rms, toll-free calls. Restaurant nearby. Ck-out 11 am, ck-in 2 pm. Coin lndry. Golf, 18 holes. Picnic facilities. Cr cds: A, D, DS, MC, V.

B&Bs/Small Inns

★★ KADEE'S GRAY ELEPHANT.
216 Main St. (06243). 508/255-7608. Email kadees@capecod.net. 2 story, 8 suites. June-Aug: suites $140; each addl $25; children $25; lower rates rest of yr. Parking lot. TV; cable. Complimentary coffee in rms. Restaurant noon-9 pm. Bar. Ck-out 10:30 am, ck-in 3 pm. Gift shop. Salon/barber avail. Free airport transportation. Golf. Tennis, 6 courts. Picnic facilities. Cr cds: MC, V.

★★ THE PARSONAGE INN.
202 Main St, PO Box 1501 (02643). 508/255-8217; fax 508/255-8216; toll-free 888/422-8217. Email innkeeper@parsonageinn.com; www.parsonageinn.com. 8 rms, 2 story. June-Sep: D $135; each addl $20; lower rates rest of yr. Street parking. TV; cable. Complimentary full bkfst, coffee in rms. Restaurant nearby. Ck-out 11 am, ck-in 2 pm. Golf. Tennis. Beach access. Bike rentals. Cr cds: A, MC, V.

★★ SHIPS KNEES INN.
186 Beach Rd (02643), 3 mi E; MA 6 Exit 12. 508/255-1312; fax 508/240-1351. 19

air-cooled rms, 8 with bath, 2 story, 2 suites. Some A/C. No rm phones. July-Aug: D $65-$120; each addl $20; suites $110; lower rates rest of yr. Children over 12 yrs only. TV in some rms and in sitting rm; cable. Pool. Complimentary continental bkfst. Ck-out 10:30 am, ck-in 1 pm. Tennis. Picnic tables, grills. Restored sea captain's house (ca 1820); near ocean, beach. Rms individually decorated in nautical style; many antiques, some 4-poster beds. Some rms with ocean view. Totally non-smoking. Cr cds: MC, V.

🖈 🕭 🔊 🐾

Restaurants

★★ **BARLEY NECK INN.** *5 Beach Rd (02653), 1½ mi E on Main St. 508/ 255-0212. Email info@barleyneck.com; www.barleyneck.com.* Specializes in trio salmon medallions, local swordfish steak, braised lamb shank. Hrs: 4-9:30 pm. Res accepted. Dinner $12-$20. Entertainment: pianist. Four separate dining rms, both formal and informal; fireplaces, artwork. Cr cds: A, MC, V.

D

★★★ **CAPTAIN LINNELL HOUSE.** *137 Skaket Beach Rd (02653), Exit 12 off US 6 to W Rd (Left). 508/255-3400. Email info@linnell.com; www.linnell. com.* Specializes in local seafood, rack of lamb. Own baking. Hrs: 5-10 pm. Res accepted. Dinner $16.50-$26. Child's menu. Parking. Sea captain's 1840s mansion; oil paintings; gardens. Cr cds: A, MC, V.

D

★ **DOUBLE DRAGON INN.** *MA 6A & MA 28 (02653). 508/255-4100.* Specializes in Hunan and Cantonese cooking. Hrs: 11:30-1 am. Closed Thanksgiving. Lunch a la carte entrees: $3.50-$5.95; dinner a la carte entrees: $4.25-$12.95. Parking. Chinese decor. Cr cds: A, D, DS, MC, V.

D

★ **LOBSTER CLAW.** *MA 6A (02653). 508/255-1800. www.capecod. com/lobclaw.* Specializes in seafood, lobster, steak. Hrs: 11 am-9 pm. Closed mid-Nov-Mar. Bar. Lunch $4.95-$22.95; dinner $4.95-$22.95. Child's menu. Parking. Nautical decor. Former cranberry packing fac-

tory. Family-owned. Cr cds: A, C, D, DS, ER, MC, V.

D SC

★★ **NAUSET BEACH CLUB.** *222 E Main St (02643), ½ mi E. 508/255-8547. Email nbc@gls.net.* Specializes in soups, salads. Own pasta. Hrs: 5:30-9:30 pm. Closed Sun, Mon off-season. Bar. Dinner $12-$19. Cr cds: A, MC, V.

★★ **OLD JAILHOUSE TAVERN.** *28 W Rd (02653), off MA 6A at Skaket Corners. 508/255-5245. Email jail house@capecod.net.* Specializes in prime rib, veal Orleans, seafood. Hrs: 11-1 am. Closed Thanksgiving, Dec 25. Bar. Lunch $5.25-$10.95; dinner $12.95-$19.75. Parking. Part of old jailhouse. Cr cds: A, DS, ER, MC, V.

D

⛽

Pittsfield

(C-2) *See also Berkshire Hills, Lenox, Stockbridge, and W Stockbridge*

Settled 1743 **Pop** 48,622 **Elev** 1,039 ft **Area code** 413 **Zip** 01201 **Web** www.berkshires.org

Information Berkshire Visitors Bureau, Berkshire Common; 413/443-9186 or 800/237-5747

Beautifully situated in the Berkshire Hills vacation area, this is also an old and important manufacturing center. It is the home of the Berkshire Life Insurance Co (chartered 1851) and of industries that make machinery, plastics, gauges, and paper products.

What to See and Do

Arrowhead. (1780) Herman Melville wrote *Moby Dick* while living here from 1850-63; historical exhibits, furniture, costumes; gardens. Video presentation. Gift shop. HQ of Berkshire County Historical Society. (June-Labor Day, daily; after Labor Day-Oct, Thurs-Mon; rest of yr, by appt) 780 Holmes Rd. Phone 413/442-1793. ¢¢

Berkshire Museum. Museum of art, natural science, and history, featuring American 19th- and 20th-century paintings, works by British and European masters, artifacts from ancient civilizations, exhibits on Berkshire County history; aquarium; changing exhibits; films, lectures, children's programs. (July-Aug, daily; rest of yr, Tues-Sun; closed hols) 39 S St (US 7). Phone 413/443-7171. ¢¢

Canoe Meadows Wildlife Sanctuary. Two hundred sixty-two acres with 3 mi of trails, woods, open fields, ponds; bordering the Housatonic River. (Tues-Sun) Holmes Rd. Phone 413/637-0320. ¢¢

Crane Museum. Exhibit of fine papermaking since 1801, emphasizing distinctive all-rag papers. (June-mid-Oct, Mon-Fri; closed hols) 5 mi E, on MA 9 in Dalton. Phone 413/684-2600. **FREE**

Hancock Shaker Village. An original Shaker site (1790-1960); now a living history museum of Shaker life, crafts, and farming. Large collection of Shaker furniture and artifacts in 20 restored bldgs, incl the Round Stone Barn, set on 1,200 scenic acres in the Berkshires. Exhibits; seasonal craft demonstrations, Discovery Room activities, cafe; farm animals, heirloom herb and vegetable gardens; museum shop; picnicking. (Apr-Nov, daily; Dec-Mar, by appt only) 5 mi W on US 20, at jct MA 41. Phone 413/443-0188. ¢¢¢-¢¢¢¢

Skiing.

Bousquet. Two double chairlifts, 2 rope tows; snowmaking, patrol, school, rentals; cafeteria, bar. Longest run 1½ mi; vertical drop 750 ft. Night skiing. (Dec-Mar, daily) 2 mi S on US 7, then 1 mi W, on Dan Fox Dr. Phone 413/442-8316 or 413/442-2436 (snow conditions). ¢¢¢¢

Jiminy Peak. Triple, 3 double chairlifts, J-bar; patrol, school, rentals; restaurant, 2 cafeterias, bar, lodge. Longest run 2 mi; vertical drop 1,140 ft. (Thanksgiving-Apr 1, daily) Night skiing. Half-day rates.

Also trout fishing; 18-hole miniature golf, Alpine slide, and tennis center (Memorial Day-Labor Day); fee for activities. 9 mi N, then W, between US 7 & MA 43 on Corey Rd in Hancock. Phone 413/738-5500. ¢¢¢¢

Brodie Mountain. Four double chairlifts, 2 rope tows; patrol, school, rentals, snowmaking; bar, cafeteria, restaurant, nursery. (Nov-Mar, daily) Cross-country trails with rentals and instruction. Half-day rates. Tennis, racquetball, winter camping. 10 mi N on US 7 in New Ashford. Phone 413/443-4752. ¢¢¢¢

Cape Cod seafood restaurant

Seasonal Event

South Mountain Concerts. South St. 2 mi S on US 7, 20. Chamber music concerts. Phone 413/442-2106. Sun, Aug-Oct.

Motels/Motor Lodges

★ **ECONO LODGE SPRINGS INN.** *US 7 (01237), 12 mi N. 413/458-5945; fax 413/458-4351; res 800/55econo; toll-free 800/277-0001. www.travel hill.com.* 40 rms, 1-2 story. July-Oct: S $51-$100; D $61-$113; each addl $10; under 12 free; lower rates rest of yr. Crib $10. TV; cable, VCR avail (movies). Heated pool. Complimentary coffee in rms. Restaurant 7 am-10 pm. Bar from 11:30 am; entertainment Sat. Ck-out 11:30 am. Meeting rms. Sundries. Tennis. Downhill/x-country ski opp. Game rm. Refrigerators avail. Some patios, balconies. Cr cds: A, DS, MC, V.

⬛ ▶️ 🔥 🛏️ 🎿 🏊 🖐️

★ **TRAVELODGE.** *16 Cheshire Rd; Rte 8 (01201).* 413/443-5661; fax 413/443-5866; toll-free 800/578-7878. 48 rms, 2 story. July-mid-Oct: S $65-$105; D $81-$120; each addl $6; under 17 free; lower rates rest of yr. Crib free. TV; cable. Complimentary coffee in rms. Restaurant opp 6 am-10 pm. Ck-out 11 am. Coin lndry. Meeting rm. Business servs avail. Downhill ski 5 mi; x-country ski 12 mi. Refrigerators. Picnic table. Cr cds: A, C, D, DS, MC, V.

▶️ 🎿 🏊 SC

Hotel

★★★ **CROWNE PLAZA.** *1 W St (01201).* 413/499-2000; fax 413/442-0449; toll-free 800/227-6963. 179 rms, 12 story. July-mid-Oct: S, D $120-$210; each addl $15; suites $295-$449; under 18 free; wknd rates; package plans; lower rates rest of yr. Crib free. TV; cable (premium). Indoor pool; whirlpool. Coffee in rms. Restaurant 6 am-11 pm. Bar 11:30-1 am. Ck-out noon. Meeting rms. Business servs avail. Beauty shop. Free covered parking. Shopping arcade. Exercise equipt; sauna. Health club privileges. Some refrigerators. Cr cds: A, C, D, DS, MC, V.

🛏️ 🏋️ 🎿 🏊 SC

Resort

★★ **JIMINY PEAK MOUNTAIN RESORT.** *Corey Rd (01237), 13 mi N on US 7, then 2 mi W on Brodie Mountain Rd.* 413/738-5500; fax 413/738-5513; toll-free 888/4JIMINY. Email info@jiminy.com; www.jiminypeak.com. 105 rms, 3 story. Dec-Mar, July-Aug: S, D $239; each addl $15; under 12 free; lower rates rest of yr. Crib avail, fee. Parking lot. Pool, whirlpool. TV; cable (premium), VCR avail. Restaurant 7 am-11 pm. Bar. Ck-out 10:30 am, ck-in 4 pm. Meeting rms. Dry cleaning, coin lndry. Gift shop. Exercise equipt, sauna. Golf. Tennis, 4 courts. Downhill skiing. Supervised children's activities. Hiking trail. Picnic facilities. Cr cds: A, C, D, DS, MC, V.

⛷️ ▶️ 🏋️ 🔥 🛏️ 🏋️ 🏊

Restaurant

★★ **DAKOTA.** *1035 S St (01201), 5 mi S on US 7/20.* 413/499-7900. www.dakotarestaurant.com. Specializes in seafood, hand-cut aged prime beef. Salad bar. Hrs: 5-11 pm; Sun 4-10 pm; early-bird dinner Mon-Fri 5-6 pm, Sat and Sun 4-5 pm; Sun brunch 10 am-2 pm. Closed Thanksgiving, Dec 25. Res accepted. Bar. Dinner $8.95-$19.95. Sun brunch $14.95. Child's menu. Rustic decor. Native Amer artifacts, mounted animals. Cr cds: A, DS, MC, V.

⬛

⛽

Plymouth (D-7)

Settled 1620 **Pop** 45,608 **Elev** 50 ft
Area code 508 **Zip** 02360
Web www.visit-plymouth.com

Information Destination Plymouth, 170 Water St, Suite 10C; 508/747-7525 or 800/872-1620.

On December 21, 1620, 102 men, women, and children arrived on the *Mayflower* to found the first permanent European settlement north of Virginia. Although plagued by exposure, cold, hunger, and disease during the terrible first winter, the colony was firmly established by the next year. Plymouth Rock lies under an imposing granite colonnade, marking the traditional place of landing.

Plymouth now combines a summer resort, beaches, a harbor full of pleasure craft, an active fishing town, and a remarkable series of restorations of the original town.

What to See and Do

Burial Hill. Governor Bradford is buried here. Just W of Town Square.

Cole's Hill. Here Pilgrims who died during the first winter were secretly buried. Across the street from Plymouth Rock.

Cranberry World. Visitor Center with exhibits of the history and cultivation of the cranberry. ½-hr self-guided tours; guided tours by appt. (May-Nov, daily) 225 Water St. Phone 508/747-2350. **FREE**

Harlow Old Fort House. (1677) Pilgrim household crafts; spinning, weaving, and candle-dipping demonstrations; herb garden. (July-Oct, Wed-Sat) 119 Sandwich St. Phone 508/746-0012. ¢¢

Hedge House. (1809) Period furnishings, special exhibits. (June-Oct, Wed-Sat) 126 Water St, opp Town Wharf. Phone 508/746-0012. ¢¢

Howland House. (1666) Restored Pilgrim house has 17th- and 18th-century furnishings. (Memorial Day-mid-Oct, Mon-Sat, also Sun afternoons and Thanksgiving) 33 Sandwich St. Phone 508/746-9590. ¢¢

Mayflower Society House Museum. National HQ of the General Society of Mayflower Descendants. House built in 1754; 9 rms with 17th- and 18th-century furnishings. Formal garden. (July-Labor Day, daily; Memorial Day wkend-June and Sep-Oct, Fri-Sun) 4 Winslow St, off North St. Phone 508/746-2590. ¢¢

Myles Standish State Forest. Approx 15,000 acres. Swimming, bathhouse, fishing, boating; hiking and bicycle trails, riding, hunting, winter sports, picnicking (fee), camping (fee; dump station). S on MA 3, Exit 5, Long Pond. Phone 508/866-2526.

National Monument to the Forefathers. Built between 1859-89 (at a cost of $155,000) to depict the virtues of the Pilgrims. At 81 ft, it is the tallest solid granite monument in the US. (May-Oct, daily) Allerton St. Phone 508/746-1790. **FREE**

Pilgrim Hall Museum. (1824) Decorative arts and possessions of first Pilgrims and their descendants; incl furniture, household items, ceramics; only known portrait of a Mayflower passenger. (Daily; closed Jan 1, Dec 25) 75 Court St, on MA 3A. Phone 508/746-1620. ¢¢

⭐ **Plimoth Plantation.** Living history museum re-creates day-to-day life in 17th-century Plymouth. All exhibits (Apr-Nov, daily). 3 mi S on MA 3A. Phone 508/746-1622. General admission ticket (incl *Mayflower II*) ¢¢¢¢ On the plantation are

Visitor Center. Provides visitors with introduction to this unique museum. Orientation program incl 12-min multi-image screen presentation. Exhibits, educational services; museum shop, restaurants, picnic area.

1627 Pilgrim Village. Fort-Meetinghouse and 14 houses. Costumed people portray actual residents of Plymouth and re-create life in an early farming community.

Hobbamock's (Wampanoag) Homesite. A large bark-covered house representing Hobbamock's dwelling, as well as specially crafted tools and artifacts, depict the domestic environment of the Wampanoag culture. Staff members explain this rich heritage from a modern day perspective.

Mayflower II. This 90-ft bark, a full-size reproduction of the type of ship that carried the Pilgrims, was built in England and sailed to America in 1957. Costumed men and women portray crew and passengers who made the 1620 voyage. At State Pier, on Water St. ¢¢¢

Plymouth Colony Winery. Grape growing area, working cranberry bogs, picnic areas. Tour, wine tasting. Watch cranberry harvest activities in fall (usually last wkend Sep). Winery (Apr-late Dec, daily; Mar, Fri-Sun; also hols). US 44W, left on Pinewood Rd. Phone 508/747-3334. **FREE**

Plymouth Harbor Cruises. One-hr cruises of historic harbor aboard *Pilgrim Belle,* a Mississippi-style paddlewheeler. (Mid-May-Mid-Oct, daily) Departs from State Pier. Phone 508/747-2400. ¢¢

Plymouth National Wax Museum. Pilgrim story told through narrations and animation; incl 26 life-size scenes and more than 180 figures. (Mar-Nov, daily) 16 Carver St. Phone 508/746-6468. ¢¢

Plymouth Rock. Water St, on the harbor.

Provincetown Ferry. Round-trip passenger ferry departs State Pier in the morning, returns in evening. (Mid-June-Labor Day, daily; May-Mid-June and after Labor Day-Oct, wkends) Phone 508/747-2400. ¢¢¢¢

Richard Sparrow House. (1640) Plymouth's oldest restored home; craft gallery, pottery made on premises. (Memorial Day wkend-Thanksgiving, Thurs-Tues; gallery open through late Dec) 42 Summer St. Phone 508/747-1240. ¢

Splashdown Amphibious Tours. One-hr tours of historic Plymouth-half on land, half on water. Hrly departures from Harbor Place and Village Landing. (Mid-Apr-late Oct, daily) Phone 508/747-7658. ¢¢¢¢

Spooner House. (1747) Occupied by Spooner family for 5 generations and furnished with their heirlooms. Collections of Oriental export wares, period furniture. (June-Oct, Wed-Sat) 27 North St. Phone 508/746-0012. ¢¢

Supersports Family Fun Park. Rides, games, sports, mini-golf, bumper boats. (Daily, call for off-season hours; closed Dec 25) W of Plymouth historical area, 108 N Main St, jct MA 58 & 44, in Carver. Phone 508/866-9655. ¢¢- ¢¢¢¢

Swimming. Six public bathing beaches.

Whale watching. Four-hr trip to Stellwagen Bank to view world's largest mammals. (Early May-mid-Oct, daily; early Apr-early May and mid-Oct-early Nov, wkends) Phone 508/746-2643. ¢¢¢¢

Annual Events

Destination Plymouth Sprint Triathlon. Myles Standish State Forest (see). National Championship qualifier incl ½-mi swim, 12-mi bike ride, and 4-mi run. 800/USA-1620. July.

Pilgrim's Progress. A reenactment of Pilgrims going to church, from Cole's Hill to Burial Hill. Each Fri in Aug; also Thanksgiving.

Autumnal Feasting. Plimoth Plantation's 1627 Pilgrim Village. A harvest celebration with Dutch colonists from Fort Amsterdam re-creating a 17th-century event. Activities, feasting, games. Phone 508/742-1622. Columbus Day wkend.

Thanksgiving Week. Programs for various events may be obtained by contacting Destination Plymouth. Phone 508/747-7525 or 800/USA-1620. Nov (starts Thanksgiving wkend).

Motels/Motor Lodges

★ **BLUE SPRUCE MOTEL & TOWN-HOUSES.** *710 State Rd, Rte 3A (02360), 6½ mi S on MA 3A. 508/224-3990; fax 508/224-2279; toll-free 800/370-7080. Email bluesprucemotel@ prodigy.net.* 28 rms, 4 townhouses. June-Aug: S, D $58-$76; each addl $6; townhouses $165-$189; lower rates rest of yr. Crib free. TV. Pool. Restaurant nearby. Ck-out 11 am. Business servs avail. In-rm modem link. Lawn games. Refrigerators. Cr cds: A, MC, V.

D ⌔ ⊠ ⊠ 🔥 SC

★ **COLD SPRING MOTEL & GUEST SUITES.** *188 Court St (02360). 508/ 746-2222; fax 508/746-2744; toll-free 800/678-8667. www.coldspringmotel. com.* 31 rms. Late Mar-late Nov: S, D $59-$89; each addl $5. Closed rest of yr. Crib $5. TV; cable (premium). Complimentary continental bkfst (in season). Restaurant nearby. Ck-out 11 am. Business servs avail. Cr cds: A, MC, V.

★ **GOVERNOR BRADFORD ON THE HARBOR.** *98 Water St (02360). 508/746-6200; fax 508/747-3032; toll-free 800/332-1620. Email onthewater@ governorbradford.com; www.governor bradford.com.* 94 rms, 3 story. June-Oct: S, D $103; each addl $10; under 17 free; lower rates rest of yr. Crib avail. Parking lot. Pool. TV; cable (premium), VCR avail. Complimentary toll-free calls. Restaurant 11 am-11 pm. Ck-out 11 am, ck-in 3 pm. Fax servs avail. Coin lndry. Golf. Cr cds: A, D, DS, MC, V.

⍻ ⌔ ⊠ ⊠ 🔥

★★ **PILGRIM SANDS.** *150 Warren Ave, Rte 3A (02360), 2½ mi SE on MA 3a. 508/747-0900; fax 508/746-8066; toll-free 800/729SAND. Email the-beach@pilgrimsands.com; www. pilgrimsands.com.* 62 rms, 2 story, 2 suites. June-Oct: S $120; D $120; suites $250; each addl $8; lower rates rest of yr. Crib avail. Parking lot. Indoor/outdoor pools, whirlpool. TV; cable (premium). Complimentary toll-free calls. Restaurant. Ck-out 11 am, ck-in 3 pm. Business center. Golf. Beach access. Picnic facilities. Cr cds: A, C, D, DS, ER, JCB, MC, V.

D 🛁 ⍻ ⌔ ⊠ ⊠ 🔥 ⍻

★ **SLEEPY PILGRIM MOTEL.** *182 Court St (02360). 508/746-1962; fax 508/746-0203; res 877/776-6835. Email frontdesk@sleepypilgrim.com; www.sleepypilgrim.com.* 16 rms. Mid-June-late Oct: S $64; D $79; each addl $10; lower rates Apr-mid-June, late Oct-Thanksgiving. Closed rest of yr. Crib $5. TV; cable. Complimentary continental bkfst in season. Restaurant nearby. Ck-out 10 am.

Picnic tables, grills. Cr cds: A, DS, MC, V.

🄳 🖾 🔥

Hotel

★★★ **SHERATON INN.** *180 Water St (02360). 508/747-4900; fax 508/746-2609; res 800/325-3535. Email sheratonplymouth@tiac.net; www. sheratonplymouth.com.* 172 rms, 4 story, 3 suites. May-Oct: S, D $195; suites $295; each addl $15; under 18 free; lower rates rest of yr. Crib avail. Parking lot. Indoor pool, whirlpool. TV; cable (premium). Complimentary newspaper, toll-free calls. Restaurant. Bar. Meeting rms. Business center. Bellhops. Dry cleaning, coin lndry. Exercise equipt, sauna. Video games. Cr cds: A, C, D, DS, MC, V.

🄳 ⏳ 🖾 🏋 🖾 🔥 SC 🏃

B&Bs/Small Inns

★★ **JOHN CARVER INN.** *25 Summer St (02360), at Market St. 508/746-7100; fax 508/746-8299; toll-free 800/274-1620. Email jcireserv@aol.com; www.johncarverinn.com.* 85 rms, 3 story, 6 suites. Apr-Nov: S, D $160; suites $249; lower rates rest of yr. Parking lot. Indoor pool, children's pool, lifeguard, whirlpool. TV; cable (premium). Restaurant 7 am-10 pm. Bar. Ck-out 11 am, ck-in 3 pm. Meeting rms. Business center. Gift shop. Exercise privileges, sauna. Supervised children's activities. Cr cds: A, D, DS, MC, V.

🄳 🖾 🏋 🖾 🔥 🏃

★★ **THE MABBETT HOUSE.** *7 Cushman St (02360). 508/830-1911; fax 508/830-9775; toll-free 800/572-7829. Email bnb@mabbetthouse.com; www.mabbetthouse.com.* 3 rms, 2 story, 1 suite. May-Nov: D $139; suites $210; lower rates rest of yr. Street parking. TV; cable (premium). Complimentary full bkfst. Restaurant nearby. Ck-out 11 am, ck-in 3 pm. Business servs avail. Golf. Tennis, 2 courts. Beach access. Cr cds: A, MC, V.

🏋 🎿 🖾 🔥

Restaurant

★ **HEARTH AND KETTLE.** *25 Summer St. 508/746-7100.* Specializes in fresh seafood. Hrs: 7 am-10 pm; win-

ter hrs vary; early-bird dinner noon-6 pm. Closed Dec 25. Res accepted. Bar. Bkfst $3.99-$7.99; lunch $3.99-$10.99; dinner $9.99-$17.99. Child's menu. Servers dressed in Colonial attire. Cr cds: A, C, D, DS, ER, MC, V.

🄳 ⏺

Provincetown (Cape Cod)

See also Cape Cod National Seashore

Settled ca 1700 **Pop** 3,561 **Elev** 40 ft
Area code 508 **Zip** 02657
Web www.capecodaccess.com/provincetownchamber

Information Chamber of Commerce, 307 Commercial St, PO Box 1017; 508/487-3424

Provincetown is a startling mixture of heroic past and easygoing present. The Provincetown area may have been explored by Leif Ericson in AD 1004. It is certain that the *Mayflower* anchored first in Provincetown Harbor while the Mayflower Compact, setting up the colony's government, was signed aboard the ship. Provincetown was where the first party of Pilgrims came ashore. A bronze tablet at Commercial Street and Beach Highway marks the site of the Pilgrims' first landing. The city attracts many tourists who come each summer to explore the narrow streets and rows of picturesque old houses.

What to See and Do

Expedition Whydah's Sea Lab and Learning Center. Archaeological site of sunken pirate ship *Whydah,* struck by storms in 1717. Learn about recovery of the ship's pirate treasure, the lives and deaths of pirates, and the history of the ship and its passengers. (Apr-mid-Oct, daily; mid-Oct-Dec, wkends and school hols) 16 MacMillan Wharf. Phone 508/487-7955. ¢¢

🌟 **Pilgrim Monument and Museum.** A 252-ft granite tower commemorating the Pilgrims' 1620 landing in the New World; provides an excellent view. (Summer, daily) Phone 508/487-1310. ¢¢ Admission incl

Provincetown Museum. Exhibits incl whaling equipment, scrimshaw, ship models, artifacts from shipwrecks; Pilgrim Room with scale model diorama of the merchant ship *Mayflower;* Donald MacMillan's Arctic exhibit; antique fire engine and firefighting equipment; theater history display. (Summer, daily) Phone 508/487-1310.

Provincetown Art Association & Museum. Changing exhibits; museum store. (Late May-Oct, daily; rest of yr, wkends) 460 Commercial St. Phone 508/487-1750. ¢

Recreation. Swimming at surrounding beaches, incl town beach, W of the village; Herring Cove and Race Point, on the ocean side. Tennis, cruises, beach buggy tours, and fishing avail.

Town Wharf (MacMillan Wharf). Off Commercial St at Standish St. Center of maritime activity. Also here is

Portuguese Princess. 100-ft boats offer 3½-hr narrated whale watching excursions. Naturalist aboard. (Apr-Oct, daily) Phone 508/487-2651 or 800/442-3188 (New England). ¢¢¢¢

Whale Watching. Offers 3½-4-hr trips (mid-Apr-Oct, daily). Research scientists from the Provincetown Center for Coastal Studies are aboard each trip to lecture on the history of the whales being viewed. Dolphin Fleet of Provincetown. Phone 508/349-1900 or 800/826-9300. ¢¢¢¢

Annual Event

Portuguese Festival. Parades, concerts; dance, ethnic food court, children's games; fireworks. Culminates with blessing of the fleet (Sun). Last wk June.

Motels/Motor Lodges

★★ **BLUE SEA MOTOR INN.** 696 *Shore Rd (02657), 1¾ mi E on MA 6A. 508/487-1041; toll-free 888/RNT-ROOM. www.virtualcapecod.com/blue sea.* 43 rms, 1-2 story. July-Aug: S, D $97-$127; each addl $10; kit. units $650-$920/wk; lower rates Sep-Oct, May-June. Closed rest of yr. Crib $10.

TV. Indoor pool; whirlpool. Coffee in lobby. Ck-out 10 am. Coin lndry. In-rm modem link. Refrigerators. Balconies. Picnic tables, grills. On ocean; swimming beach. Cr cds: MC, V.

★★ **BRADFORD HOUSE MOTEL.** 41 *Bradford St (02657). 508/487-0173; fax 508/481-0173. Email bradmotel@ aol.com; www.bradfordhousemotel.com.* 6 rms, 3 story. May-Aug: S, D $175; each addl $25; lower rates rest of yr. Parking lot. TV; cable. Complimentary continental bkfst. Restaurant nearby. Ck-out 11 am, ck-in 2 pm. Exercise privileges. Golf. Tennis, 2 courts. Cr cds: A, MC, V.

★ **SHIP'S BELL INN & MOTEL.** 586 *Commercial St (02657). 508/487-1674; fax 508/487-1675. Email nancy@ships-bell.com; www.shipsbell.com.* 8 rms, 2 story, 11 suites. July-Aug: D $95; suites $225; each addl $15; children $15; lower rates rest of yr. Crib avail, fee. Parking lot. TV; cable, VCR avail. Complimentary newspaper. Restaurant nearby. Ck-out 10 am, ck-in 3 pm. Golf, 8 holes. Tennis, 10 courts. Beach access. Picnic facilities. Cr cds: A, DS, MC, V.

Resorts

★★ **BEST WESTERN CHATEAU MOTOR INN.** 105 *Bradford St W End (02657). 508/487-1286; fax 508/487-3557; res 800/528-1234. Email chateau@bwprovincetown.com; www. bwprovincetown.com.* 54 rms, 2 story. June-Aug: S, D $169; each addl $20; under 17 free; lower rates rest of yr. Crib avail. Parking lot. Pool. TV; cable (premium). Complimentary continental bkfst, coffee in rms, newspaper, toll-free calls. Restaurant nearby. Ck-out 11 am, ck-in 2 pm. Fax servs avail. Concierge serv. Exercise privileges. Golf. Tennis. Bike rentals. Cr cds: A, C, D, DS, MC, V.

★★ **BEST WESTERN TIDES BEACHFRONT.** 837 *Commercial St (02657). 508/487-1045; fax 508/487-1621; res 800/528-1234. Email tides@ bwprovincetown.com; www.bwprovince town.com.* 64 rms, 2 story, 2 suites. July-Aug: S, D $199; suites $249; each addl $20; under 17 free; lower rates rest of yr. Crib avail. Parking lot. Pool. TV; cable (premium). Complimentary coffee in rms, newspaper, toll-free calls. Restaurant 7 am-2 pm. Ck-out 11 am, ck-in 2 pm. Fax servs avail. Concierge serv. Coin lndry. Exercise privileges. Golf. Tennis, 8 courts. Beach access. Cr cds: A, C, D, DS, MC, V.

★★ THE MASTHEAD RESORT.

31-41 Commercial St (02657). 508/487-0523; fax 508/481-9251; res 508/487-0523; toll-free 800/395-5095. www.capecodtravel.com/masthead. 11 rms, 4 suites. June-Sep: S $86; D $165; suites $200; each addl $20; lower rates rest of yr. Crib avail. Valet parking avail. TV; cable, VCR avail. Complimentary coffee in rms, newspaper. Restaurant nearby. Ck-out 11 am, ck-in 4 pm. Fax servs avail. Exercise privileges. Tennis. Beach access. Bike rentals. Hiking trail. Picnic facilities. Cr cds: A, C, D, DS, ER, JCB, MC, V.

★★ PROVINCETOWN INN.

1 Commericial St (02657). 508/487-9500; fax 508/487-2911; res 508/487-9500; toll-free 800/942-5388. Email info@provincetowninn.com; www. provincetowninn.com. 100 rms, 2 story, 2 suites. June-Sep: S, D $139; suites $329; each addl $15; under 12 free; lower rates rest of yr. Parking lot. Pool. TV; cable (premium). Complimentary continental bkfst. Restaurant 6-10 pm. Bar. Ck-out 11 am, ck-in 3 pm. Meeting rms. Business center. Gift shop. Exercise privileges. Golf. Tennis, 4 courts. Beach access. Bike rentals. Hiking trail. Cr cds: A, MC, V.

B&Bs/Small Inns

★★★ BRADFORD GARDENS INN.

178 Bradford St (02657). 508/487-1616; fax 508/487-5596; res 508/487-1616; toll-free 800/432-2334. Email bradford@capecod.net; www.bradford gardens.com. 8 rms, 2 story. May-Sep: each addl $26; lower rates rest of yr. Pet accepted. Parking lot. TV; cable (premium), VCR avail. Complimentary full bkfst, toll-free calls. Restau-

rant nearby. Ck-out 11 am, ck-in 3 pm. Fax servs avail. Cr cds: A, MC, V.

★★ FAIRBANKS INN.

90 Bradford St (02657). 508/487-0386; fax 508/487-3540; toll-free 800/324-7265. Email info@fairbanksinn.com; www. fairbanksinn.com. 14 rms, 11 with bath, 2 story. No rm phones. July-Aug: S, D $89-$175; higher rates hols; lower rates rest of yr. Children over 15 yrs only. TV; cable (premium). Complimentary continental bkfst. Restaurant nearby. Ck-out 11 am, ck-in 2 pm. Concierge serv. Balconies. Picnic tables, grills. Antiques. Built 1776; courtyard. Totally nonsmoking. Cr cds: A, MC, V.

★★ SOMERSET HOUSE.

378 Commercial St (02657). 508/487-0383; fax 508/487-4746; toll-free 800/575-1850. Email somerset@somersethouseinn.com; www.somersethouseinn.com. 13 rms, 10 with bath, 2-3 story. No A/C. Mid-June-Mid-Sep: S, D $75-$130; each addl $20; wkly rates; lower rates rest of yr. TV; cable. Complimentary continental bkfst. Restaurant nearby. Ck-out 11 am, ck-in 3 pm. Refrigerators. Opp beach. Restored 1850s house. Totally nonsmoking. Cr cds: MC, V.

★★ WATERSHIP INN.

7 Winthrop St (02657). 508/487-0094; res 800/330-9413. Email watership@capecod. net; www.capecod.net/watershipinn. 15 rms, 3 story, 2 suites. July-Aug: S $90; D $120; suites $205; each addl $20; lower rates rest of yr. Parking lot. TV; cable. Complimentary continental bkfst. Restaurant nearby. Ck-out 11:30 am, ck-in 2 pm. Concierge serv. Golf, 9 holes. Tennis, 4 courts. Picnic facilities. Cr cds: A, DS, MC, V.

★★ WHITE WIND INN.

174 Commercial St (02657), near Municipal Airport. 508/487-1526; fax 508/487-3985; toll-free 888/449WIND. Email wwinn@capenet.com. 11 rms, 7 A/C, 4 air-cooled, 8 with shower only, 3 story. No elvtr. No rm phones. Late May-mid-Sep: S, D $115-$190; wkend, wkly rates; wkends, hols (2-day min); higher rates hols; lower rates rest of yr. Pet accepted. TV; cable, VCR avail (movies). Complimentary continental bkfst. Restaurant nearby. Ck-out 11 am, ck-in 2 pm. Concierge serv. Refrigerators; some fireplaces. Some balconies. Picnic tables. Opp harbor. Built in 1845; former shipbuilder's home. Totally nonsmoking. Cr cds: DS, MC, V.

All Suite

★★ **WATERMARK INN.** *603 Commercial St (02657). 508/487-0165; fax 508/487-2383. Email info@watermark-inn.com; www.watermark-inn.com.* 10 suites. May-Sep: S, D $240; suites $240; each addl $50; children $25; under 16 free; lower rates rest of yr. Parking lot. TV; cable. Restaurant nearby. Ck-out 11 am, ck-in 3 pm. Internet access avail. Concierge serv. Beach access. Cr cds: A, MC, V.

Restaurants

★★ **CAFE EDWIGE.** *333 Commercial St (02657). 508/487-2008.* Specializes in stir-fry tofu, crab cakes, native Littleneck clams. Hrs: 6 am-1 pm, 6-11 pm. Closed Oct 31; also late May. Res accepted (dinner). Bkfst $5-$10; dinner $10-$20. Street parking. Cathedral ceilings, skylights. Cr cds: A, MC, V.

★★ **DANCING LOBSTER CAFE.** *373 Commercial St (02657), 12 blks E. 508/487-0900.* Specializes in Venetian fish soup, crab ravioli, Provencal seafood stew. Hrs: 11 am-11 pm. Closed Mon; also Dec-May. Res accepted. Bar. Lunch, dinner a la carte entrees: $9.95-$18.95. On beach; harbor views. Cr cds: MC, V.

★★ **FRONT STREET.** *230 Commercial St (02657). 508/487-9715. Email frontst@capecpd.net; www.capecod.net/frontstreet.* Specializes in rack of lamb, tea-smoked duck, chocolate oblivion purse. Own desserts. Hrs: 5-10 pm. Closed Tues; Jan-Apr. Res accepted. Bar. Dinner $12-$21. Street parking. Local artwork displayed. Cr cds: A, DS, MC, V.

★★ **LOBSTER POT.** *321 Commercial St (02657). 508/487-0842. Email lpot@*

wn.net; www.provincetown.com/lobster pot. Mediterranean menu. Specializes in chowder, bouillabaisse, clambake. Hrs: 11 am-9 pm. Closed Jan. Bar. Lunch $7-$12; dinner $10-$17. Lobster and chowder market on premises. Overlooks Cape Cod Bay. Cr cds: A, DS, MC, V.

★★ **NAPI'S.** *7 Freeman St (02657), 1 blk N of Commercial St. 508/487-1145. Email napis@mediaone.net; www.provincetown.com.* Specializes in bouillabaisse, shrimp Santa Fe, banana decadence. Hrs: 5-11 pm; early-bird dinner 5-6 pm. Res accepted. Bar. Dinner $12.95-$22.95. Child's menu. Parking. Extensive vegetarian selections. Gathering place of artists and craftspeople. Large collection of art in various media, incl paintings, sculpture, stained glass, graphics, ceramics and crafts. Cr cds: A, C, D, DS, MC, V.

★ **PUCCI'S HARBORSIDE.** *539 Commercial St (02657). 508/487-1964.* Specializes in hot, spicy chicken wings, grilled seafood. Hrs: 11 am-3 pm, 5-11 pm. Closed Nov-mid-Apr. Res accepted. Bar. Lunch $4-$10; dinner $8-$16. Cr cds: A, MC, V.

★★★ **RED INN RESTAURANT.** *15 Commercial St (02657). 508/487-0050.* Specializes in fresh local seafood and meats. Own desserts. Hrs: 6-11 pm; Sun brunch 11 am-3 pm; Jan-May: wknds only. Closed Dec 25. Res accepted. Dinner $19-$24.95. Sun brunch $9-$15. Parking. Three dining rms in restored Colonial bldg. Many antiques. View of Cape Cod Bay. Cr cds: A, MC, V.

★★ **SAL'S PLACE.** *99 Commercial St (02657). 508/487-1279.* Specializes in steak pizzaiola, grilled shrimp, mousse pie. Hrs: 6-10 pm. Closed Nov-Apr. Res accepted. Dinner a la carte entrees: $10-$19. Child's menu. Southern Italian decor; ocean view. Cr cds: MC, V.

Quincy

(C-6) *See also Boston*

Settled 1625 **Pop** 84,985 **Elev** 20 ft
Area code 617
Information Tourism and Visitors
Bureau, 1250 Hancock St, Suite 802
N, 02169; 888/232-6737

Boston's neighbor to the south,
Quincy (QUIN-zee) was the home of
the Adamses, a great American family whose fame dates from Colonial
days. Family members incl the second and sixth presidents—John
Adams and his son, John Quincy
Adams. John Hancock, first signer of
the Declaration of Independence,
was born here. George Bush, the
41st president, was born in nearby
Milton.

Thomas Morton, an early settler,
held May Day rites at Merrymount (a
section of Quincy) in 1627 and was
shipped back to England for selling
firearms and "firewater" to the
Native Americans.

What to See and Do

⭐ **Adams National Historic Sites Visitor Center.** Administered by the
National Park Service. Tickets to sites
can be purchased here *only*. (Mid-
Apr-mid-Nov, daily) Golden Eagle
Passport accepted (see MAKING THE
MOST OF YOUR TRIP). 1250 Hancock St. Phone 617/770-1175. Combination ticket ¢ Incl

**The Adams National Historic
Site.** The house (1731), bought in
1787 by John Adams, was given
as a national site by the Adams
family in 1946. Original furnishings. 135 Adams St, off Furnace
Brook Parkway.

**John Adams and John Quincy
Adams Birthplaces.** Two 17th-
century saltbox houses. The elder
Adams was born and raised at 133
Franklin St; his son was born in
the other house. While living
here, Abigail Adams wrote many
of her famous letters to her husband, John Adams, when he was
serving in the Continental Con-
gress in Philadelphia and as an
arbitrator for peace with Great
Britain in Paris. Guided tours. 133
& 141 Franklin St.

Josiah Quincy House. (1770) Built
on 1635 land grant, this fine Georgian house originally had a view
across Quincy Bay to Boston Harbor; was surrounded by outbuildings and much agricultural land.
Long the home of the Quincy family; furnished with family heirlooms
and memorabilia. Period wall paneling, fireplaces surrounded by English tiles. Tours on the hr.
(June-mid-Oct, Tues, Thurs, Sat, and
Sun afternoons) 20 Muirhead St.
Phone 617/227-3956. ¢¢

Quincy Historical Society. Museum
of regional history; library. (Mon-Sat)
Adams Academy Bldg, 8 Adams St.
Phone 617/773-1144. ¢

Quincy Homestead. Four generations of Quincys lived here, incl
Dorothy Quincy, wife of John Hancock. Two rms built in 1686, rest of
house dates from the 18th century;
period furnishings; herb garden.
(May-Oct, Wed-Sun) 1010 Hancock
St, at Butler Rd. Phone 617/472-
5117. ¢¢

United First Parish Church. (1828)
Only church in US where two presidents and their wives are entombed:
John Adams and John Quincy Adams
and their wives. Tours (late Apr-mid-
Nov, Mon-Sat and Sun afternoons).
1306 Hancock St, at Washington St.
Phone 617/773-1290. ¢

Annual Events

Quincy Bay Race Week. Sailing
regatta, marine parades, fireworks.
July.

South Shore Christmas Festival. Incl
parade with floats. Sun after Thanksgiving.

Seasonal Event

Summerfest. Concerts on the Green,
Ruth Gordon Amphitheatre. Wed,
mid-June-Aug.

Rockport (B-7)

Settled 1690 **Pop** 7,482 **Elev** 77 ft
Area code 978 **Zip** 01966
Web www.rockportusa.com

Information Chamber of Commerce, PO Box 67M; 978/546-6575 or 888/726-3922

Rockport is a year-round artists' colony. A weather-beaten shanty on one of the wharves has been the subject of so many paintings that it is called "Motif No. 1."

Studios, galleries, summer places, estates, and cottages dot the shore of Cape Ann from Eastern Point southeast of Gloucester all the way to Annisquam.

What to See and Do

Old Castle. (1715) A fine example of early 18th-century architecture and exhibits. (July-Labor Day, daily; rest of yr, by appt) Granite and Curtis Sts, Pigeon Cove. Phone 978/546-9533 or 978/546-6821. **Donation**

The Paper House. Newspapers were used in the construction of the house and furniture. (July-Aug, daily; rest of yr, by appt) 52 Pigeon Hill St. Phone 978/546-2629. ¢

Rockport Art Association. Changing exhibits of paintings, sculpture, and graphics by 250 artist members. Special events incl concerts (see ANNUAL EVENT), lectures, artist demonstrations. (Daily; closed Thanksgiving, Dec 25-Jan 1) 12 Main St. Phone 978/546-6604. **FREE**

Sandy Bay Historical Society & Museums. Early American and 19th-century rms and objects, exhibits on fishing, granite industry, the Atlantic cable, and a children's rm in 1832 home constructed of granite. (July-Labor Day, daily; rest of yr, by appt) 40 King St, near Railroad station. Phone 978/546-9533 or 978/546-6821. **Donation**

Sightseeing tours and boat cruises. Contact the Chamber of Commerce for a list of companies offering sightseeing, fishing, and boat tours.

Annual Event

Rockport Chamber Music Festival. Phone 978/546-7391. Four wkends June or July.

Motels/Motor Lodges

★ **CAPTAIN BOUNTY MOTOR INN.** *1 Beach St (01966). 978/546-9557. www.cape-ann.com.* 22 rms, 3 story, 2 suites. June-Aug: D $110; suites $140; each addl $10; children $5; lower rates rest of yr. TV; cable. Ck-out 11 am, ck-in 1 pm. Golf. Tennis. Cr cds: DS, MC, V.

★ **EAGLE HOUSE MOTEL.** *8 Cleaves St (01966). 978/546-6292; fax 978/540-1136.* 15 rms, 2 story. July-Aug: S, D $94; each addl $7; children $7; lower rates rest of yr. Crib avail. Parking lot. TV; cable, VCR avail, CD avail. Restaurant. Ck-out 11 am, ck-in 1 pm. Bellhops. Concierge serv. Golf. Beach access. Cr cds: A, DS, MC, V.

★ **MOTEL PEG LEG.** *10 Beach St (01966). 978/546-6945; fax 978/546-5157. Email pegleg@cove.com; www.marina.cove/users.pegleg.* 14 rms, 2 story. July-Aug: D $145; each addl $10; lower rates rest of yr. Crib avail. TV; cable (premium). Fax servs avail. Cr cds: DS, MC, V.

★★★ **SANDY BAY MOTOR INN.** *173 Main St (01966). 978/546-7155; fax 978/546-9131; toll-free 800/437-7155. www.sandybaymotorinn.com.* 80 rms, 2 story, 23 kits. Late June-Labor Day: S, D $98-$142; each addl $8; family rates; lower rates rest of yr. Crib free. Pet accepted, some restrictions; deposit. TV; cable (premium), VCR avail. Indoor pool; whirlpool, sauna. Restaurant 7-11 am; wkends, hols to noon. Ck-out 11 am. Coin lndry. Meeting rms. Business servs avail. In-rm modem link. Free railroad station transportation. Tennis. Putting green. Refrigerators avail. Cr cds: A, MC, V.

★★ **TURK'S HEAD MOTOR INN.** *151 S St (01966), 1½ mi S on MA 127A. 978/546-3436.* 28 rms, 2 story, 1 suite. June-Sep: S $95; D $101; suites $155; each addl $8; under 13 free; lower rates rest of yr. Parking lot. TV; cable. Restaurant nearby. Ck-out 11 am, ck-in 2 pm. Golf, 18 holes. Tennis, 3 courts. Beach access. Cr cds: A, DS, MC, V.

B&Bs/Small Inns

★ ★ ★ **ADDISON CHOATE INN.** *49 Broadway (01966). 978/546-7543; fax 978/546-7638; res 800/245-7543. www.cape-ann.com/addison-choate.* 8 rms, 2 with shower only, 3 story, 3 suites; 1 guest house. Some A/C. No elvtr. No rm phones. Children over 11 yrs only. Late June-late Sep: S, D $95; suites $140. TV in common rm; cable, VCR avail (movies). Complimentary continental bkfst. Restaurant nearby. Ck-out 11 am, ck-in 3 pm. Business servs avail. Free Railroad station transportation. Pool. Built in 1851; antiques. Totally nonsmoking. Cr cds: MC, V.

⌘ ⌘ ⌘

★ ★ ★ **EMERSON INN BY THE SEA.** *1 Cathedral Ave (01966), 1½ mi N on MA 127. 978/546-6321; fax 978/546-7043; toll-free 800/964-5550. Email emerson@cove.com; www.emersoninn bythesea.com.* 36 rms, 4 story. July-Labor Day: S $90-$135; D $100-$145; each addl $7; suites $100-$145; lower rates Apr, Nov. Closed rest of yr. Crib $7. TV in lounge. Sauna. Heated saltwater pool; whirlpool. Dining rm 8-11 am, 6-9 pm. Ck-out noon, ck-in after 1 pm. Coin lndry. Meeting rms. Business servs avail. In-rm modem link. Free Railroad station transportation. Lawn games. Spa, massage. Sun deck. Older inn; Victorian décor. Many rms with ocean view. Cr cds: DS, MC, V.

⌘ ⌘ ⌘

★ ★ **THE INN ON COVE HILL.** *37 Mount Pleasant St (01966). 978/546-2701; toll-free 888/546-2701. www. cape-ann.com/covehill.* 11 rms, 3 story. June-Sep: S, D $123; each addl $25; lower rates rest of yr. Parking lot. TV; cable. Complimentary continental bkfst. Restaurant nearby. Ck-out 11 am, ck-in 2 pm. Golf. Cr cds: DS, MC, V.

⌘ ⌘ ⌘

★ ★ **LINDEN TREE INN.** *26 King St (01966). 978/546-2494; fax 978/546-3297; toll-free 800/865-2122. Email ltree@shore.net.* 18 rms, 2 with shower only, 3 story, 4 kit. units, 10 A/C. No rm phones. Mid-June-early Sep (2-day min): S $70; D $99-$109; each addl $15; kit. units $105; under 4 free; lower rates rest of yr. Closed 2

wks Jan. TV in some rms; cable, VCR avail (movies). Complimentary continental bkfst, coffee in rms. Restaurant nearby. Ck-out 11 am, ck-in 2 pm. Business servs avail. Microwaves avail. Some balconies. Picnic tables. Cr cds: MC, V.

⌘ ⌘ ⌘ ⌘ ⌘ ⌘

★ ★ **PEG LEG RESTAURANT AND INN.** *2 King St (01966), MA 128, Rte 127 to 5 Corners. 978/546-2352; toll-free 800/346-2352. www.cape-ann.com.* 33 rms in 5 houses. Mid-June-Labor Day: S, D $85-$140; each addl $10; hol wkends (3-day min); lower rates Apr-mid-June, wkdays after Labor Day-Oct. Closed rest of yr. TV. Complimentary continental bkfst. Restaurant (see PEG LEG). Ck-out 11 am, ck-in 2 pm. 6 sun decks. Totally nonsmoking. Cr cds: A, MC, V.

⌘ ⌘

★ ★ **ROCKY SHORES INN & COTTAGES.** *65 Eden Rd (01966), 1½ mi S on MA 127A to Eden Rd. 978/546-2823; toll-free 800/348-4003.* 11 rms, 1 A/C, 3 story. Mid-Apr-mid-Oct: D $84-$121; each addl $10. Closed rest of yr. TV; cable. Complimentary full bkfst. Ck-out 11 am, ck-in 3 pm. Antiques. Mansion built 1905. Overlooks ocean. Cr cds: A, MC, V.

⌘ ⌘

★ ★ ★ **SEACREST MANOR.** *99 Marmion Way (01966), off MA 127A. 978/546-2211; res 978/546-2211. www.seacrestmanor.com.* 8 rms, 3 story. May-Oct: S $148; D $158; under 12 free; lower rates rest of yr. Parking lot. TV; cable (premium). Complimentary full bkfst, newspaper. Restaurant 7:30 am-9:30 pm. Ck-out 11 am, ck-in 2 pm. Concierge serv. Gift shop. Golf, 9 holes. Tennis. Beach access. Bike rentals. Hiking trail. Cr cds: A, MC, V.

⌘ ⌘ ⌘ ⌘ ⌘ ⌘

★ **SEAFARER INN.** *50 Marmion Way (01966). 978/546-6248; res 800/394-9394. www.rockportusa.com/seafarer.* 5 rms, 2 suites. No A/C. No rm phones. Mid-June-mid-Oct: D $75-$110; suites $160; kit. units $95; lower rates rest of yr. TV. Complimentary continental bkfst. Ck-out 11 am, ck-in 3 pm. On Gap Cove; all rms overlook ocean. 100-yr-old bldg. Totally nonsmoking. Cr cds: MC, V.

⌘ ⌘

★ ★ ★ **SEAWARD INN & COT-TAGES.** *44 Marmion Way (01966), 1 mi S of Rockport Center on Ocean. 978/ 546-3471; fax 978/546-7661; toll-free 877/473-2927. Email info@seawardinn. com.* 38 rms, 3 story, 9 cottages. No A/C. Mid-May-Oct: D $119-$225; each addl $20; under 3 free. Crib free. TV. Natural spring-fed swimming pond. Complimentary full bkfst. Dining rm 8-10 am, 5-9 pm. Ck-out 11 am, ck-in 2 pm. Business servs avail. Airport transportation. Free Railroad station transportation. Lawn games. Refrigerators, microwaves avail. Bird sanctuary. Vegetable and herb garden. On 5 acres. Ocean opp. Cr cds: A, D, DS, MC, V.
ⅅ 🏊 🐾

★ ★ **THE TUCK INN B&B.** *17 High St (01966). 978/546-7260; toll-free 800/789-7260. Email tuckinn@shore. net; www.rockportusa.com/tuckinn/.* 10 rms, 2 story, 1 suite. June-Oct: S $79; D $99; suites $129; each addl $15; children $15; lower rates rest of yr. Parking lot. Pool. TV; cable, CD avail. Complimentary continental bkfst, newspaper. Restaurant nearby. Ck-out 11 am, ck-in 2 pm. Golf, 9 holes. Tennis, 4 courts. Beach access. Bike rentals. Supervised children's activities. Hiking trail. Picnic facilities. Cr cds: MC, V.
⚓ 🚶 🧍 🎿 🏊 🎣 🛷 🐾

★ ★ ★ **YANKEE CLIPPER INN.** *96 Granite St (01966), 5 mi N on MA 127 at MA 128. 978/546-3407; fax 978/546-9730; toll-free 800/545-3699. Email info@yankeeclipperinn.com.* 26 rms in 3 bldgs, 2-3 story, 3-bedrm villa. Late May-late Oct: S, D $99-$269; each addl $25; MAP avail; lower rates late Oct-Dec, Mar-late May. Closed rest of yr. TV; cable, VCR avail (movies). Saltwater pool. Complimentary bkfst. Dining rm (see VERANDA). Ck-out 11 am. Business servs avail. Airport, Railroad station transportation. Some in-rm whirlpools. Movies, slides. Rms vary; some antiques. Sun porches. Terraced gardens overlook ocean. Totally nonsmoking. Cr cds: A, DS, MC, V.
⚓ 🏊 🐾 🐾

Restaurants

★ **BRACKETT'S OCEANVIEW.** *27 Main St (01966). 978/546-2797. www.*

bracketts.com. Specializes in seafood. Hrs: 11 am-8 pm. Closed Nov-mid-Mar. Lunch $3.75-$11.95; dinner $7.95-$16.95. Informal family dining. Cr cds: A, C, D, DS, MC, V.

★ ★ **PEG LEG RESTAURANT.** *1 King St. 978/546-3038. Email mrw@ cove.com; www.pegleginn.com.* Mediterranean menu. Specializes in baked stuffed shrimp, steak, duck. Hrs: 5-9 pm; Sun noon-8 pm. Closed Nov-mid-Apr. Dinner $9.95-$21.95. Greenhouse dining rm (in season). Ocean view. Cr cds: A, MC, V.
ⅅ 🐾

★ ★ ★ **VERANDA AT THE YANKEE CLIPPER.** *127 Granite St. 978/546-7795. Email info@yankeeclipper.com.* Specializes in grilled salmon, garlic-roasted duck. Own baking, pasta. Hrs: 5-9 pm. Res required. Dinner $12-$22. Enclosed porch overlooks ocean. Cr cds: A, D, DS, MC, V.

Salem (B-6)

See Beverly, Danvers, Lynn, Marblehead

Settled 1626 **Pop** 38,091 **Elev** 9 ft
Area code 978 **Zip** 01970
Information Chamber of Commerce, 32 Derby Square; 978/744-0004

In old Salem the story of early New England life is told with bricks, clapboards, carvings, and gravestones. The town had two native geniuses to immortalize it: Samuel McIntire (1757-1811), master builder, and Nathaniel Hawthorne (1804-64), author. History is charmingly entangled with the people and events of Hawthorne's novels. Reality, however, could be far from charming. In the witchcraft panic of 1692, 19 persons were hanged on Gallows Hill, another "pressed" to death; at least two others died in jail. Gallows Hill is still here; so is the house of one of the trial judges.

Early in the 18th century, Salem shipbuilding and allied industries were thriving. Salem was a major port. The Revolution turned commerce into privateering. Then began the fabulous China trade and Salem's heyday. The captains came home, and Sam McIntire built splendid houses for them that still stand. Shipping declined after 1812. Salem turned to industry, which, together with tourism, is the present-day economic base.

What to See and Do

Chestnut Street. Architecturally, one of the most beautiful streets in America; laid out in 1796.

⊠ House of Seven Gables. (1668) Said to be the setting for Nathaniel Hawthorne's classic novel. Audiovisual introduction and guided tours of the "Gables" and Hawthorne's birthplace (1750). On grounds are the Hathaway House (1682) and the Retire Becket House (1655), now the Museum Shop. Garden cafe (seasonal). (Daily; closed Thanksgiving, Dec 25; also first 2 wks Jan) 54 Turner St, off Derby St on Salem Harbor. Phone 978/744-0991. ¢¢¢

Peabody Museum and Essex Institute. Peabody Museum founded by sea captains in 1799 features 5 world-famous collections in 30 galleries. Large collections of marine art, Asian export art. Essex Institute features historical interpretations of area. Peabody Museum (daily; closed Jan 1, Thanksgiving, Dec 25). Essex Institute (Daily) East India Square. Phone 978/745-9500. ¢¢¢ Admission incl

> **Gardner-Pingree House.** (1804) Designed by McIntire; restored and handsomely furnished. (June-Oct, daily; rest of yr, Sat, Sun, and hols) 128 Essex St.

> **John Ward House.** (1684) 17th-century furnishings. (June-Oct, daily; rest of yr, Sat, Sun, and hols) Behind Essex Institute.

> **Crowninshield-Bentley House.** (1727) Rev William Bentley, minister and diarist, lived here 1791-1819. Period furnishings. (June-Oct, daily; rest of yr, Sat, Sun, and hols) Essex St at Hawthorne Blvd.

Peirce-Nichols House. (1782) One of the finest examples of McIntire's architectural genius; authentically furnished. (By appt only) 80 Federal St. Phone 978/745-9500.

Pickering Wharf. Six-acre commercial and residential village by the sea incl shops, restaurants, marina. Adj to Salem Maritime National Historic Site.

Pioneer Village: Salem In 1630. Reproduction of early Puritan settlement, incl dugouts, wigwams, thatched cottages; animals; costumed interpreters; craft demonstrations. Guided tours. (Last wkend May-Oct, daily) Forest River Park, off West St. Phone 978/744-0991 or 978/745-0525. ¢¢

Ropes Mansion and Garden. (late 1720s) Gambrel-roofed, Georgian and Colonial mansion; restored and furnished with period pieces. The garden (laid out 1912) is nationally known for its beauty and variety. (June-Oct, daily; limited hrs Sun) 318 Essex St. Phone 978/745-9500. ¢¢

⊠ Salem Maritime National Historic Site. Nine acres of historic waterfront. Self-guided and guided tours. For guided tours, res contact the Orientation Center, Central Wharf Warehouse, 174 Derby St. Phone 978/740-1660. **FREE** Site incl

> **Visitor Information.** In Central Wharf Warehouse and downtown visitor center at Museum Place, Essex St.

> **Derby Wharf.** Once a center of Salem shipping (1760-1810). Off Derby St.

> **Custom House.** (1819) Restored offices. (Daily; closed Jan 1, Thanksgiving, Dec 25) Derby St, opp wharf. Adj are

> **Scale House** (1829) and **Bonded Warehouse** (1819). Site of 19th-century customs operations. (Apr-Oct, daily)

> **Derby House.** (1761-62). Home of maritime merchant Elias Hasket Derby, the country's first millionaire. In back are the Derby House Gardens, featuring roses, herbs, and 19th-century flowers. Inquire at Central Wharf Warehouse for tour information.

> **Narbonne House.** 17th-century house with archaeological exhibits. Inquire at Central Wharf Warehouse for tour information.

> **West India Goods Store.** (1800) Coffee, teas, spices, and goods for sale. (Daily; closed Jan 1, Thanksgiving, Dec 25) 164 Derby St.

Salem State College. (1854) 9,300 students. 352 Lafayette St. Phone 978/741-6000. On campus are

Chronicle of Salem. Mural, 60 ft by 30 ft, depicts Salem history from settlement to present in 50 sequences. (Mon-Fri; closed hols) Meier Hall. **FREE**

Main Stage Auditorium. This 750-seat theater presents musical and dramatic productions (Sep-Apr). Phone 978/744-3700.

Winfisky Art Gallery. Photographs, paintings, graphics, and sculpture by national and local artists. (Sep-May, Mon-Fri) **FREE**

Library Gallery. Art exhibits by local and national artists. (Mon-Sat) **FREE**

Salem Witch Museum. Multimedia presentation reenacting the witch hysteria of 1692. (Daily; closed Jan 1, Thanksgiving, Dec 25) Washington Sq. Phone 978/744-1692. ¢¢

Stephen Phillips Memorial Trust House. (1804) Federal-style mansion with McIntire mantels and woodwork. Furnishings, rugs, porcelains reflect the merchant and seafaring past of the Phillips family. Also carriage barn with carriages and antique automobiles. (Late May-mid-Oct, Mon-Sat) 34 Chestnut St. Phone 978/744-0440. ¢

Witch Dungeon Museum. Reenactment of witch trial of Sarah Good by professional actresses; tour through re-created dungeon where accused witches awaited trial; original artifacts. (May-Nov, daily) 16 Lynde St. Phone 978/741-3570. ¢¢

Witch House. (1642) Home of witchcraft trial judge Jonathan Corwin. Some of the accused witches may have been examined here. (Mid-Mar-early Dec, daily) 310½ Essex St. Phone 978/744-0180. ¢¢

Annual Events

Heritage Days Celebration. Band concerts, parade, exhibits, ethnic festivals. Mid-Aug.

Haunted Happenings. Various sites. Psychic festival, historical exhibits, haunted house, costume parade, contests, dances. Starts wkend before and incl Halloween.

Hotel

★★ **HAWTHORNE HOTEL.** *18 Washington Square W (01970), Rte 1A N, on the Common. 978/744-4080; fax 508/745-9842; toll-free 800/729-7829. Email info@hawthornehotel.com; www. hawthornehotel.com.* 89 rms, 6 story. July-Oct: S $125-$154; D $125-$172; each addl $12; suites $285; under 18 free; lower rates rest of yr. Crib free. Pet accepted; $15. TV; cable (premium). Restaurant 6:30-11 pm; Sat, Sun from 7 am. Ck-out 11 am. Meeting rms. Business servs avail. In-rm modem link. Lndry serv. Exercise equipt. Health club privileges. Cr cds: A, C, D, DS, MC, V.

House of Seven Gables, Salem

B&Bs/Small Inns

★ **COACH HOUSE INN.** *284 Lafayette St (MA A1A) (01970), at Rte 114. 978/744-4092; fax 978/745-8031; toll-free 800/688-8689. www. salemweb.com/biz/coachhouse.* 10 rms, 3 story, 1 suite. July-Oct: S, D $135; suites $140; lower rates rest of yr. Parking lot. TV; cable, CD avail. Complimentary continental bkfst, coffee in rms, newspaper, toll-free calls. Restaurant nearby. Ck-out 11 am, ck-in 4 pm. Business center. Golf. Tennis. Cr cds: A, DS, MC, V.

★★★ **SALEM INN.** *7 Summer St; Rte 114 (01970).* 978/741-0680; fax 978/744-8924; toll-free 800/446-2995. Email *saleminn@earthlink.net; www. saleminnma.com.* 28 rms, 4 story, 11 suites. May-Oct: S, D $149; suites $179; each addl $15; lower rates rest of yr. Crib avail, fee. Pet accepted, some restrictions, fee. Parking lot. TV; cable. Complimentary continental bkfst, coffee in rms, toll-free calls. Restaurant nearby. Ck-out 11 am, ck-in 3 pm. Fax servs avail. Golf. Cr cds: A, C, D, DS, MC, V.

Restaurants

★ **CHASE HOUSE.** *Pickering Wharf Building K (01970).* 978/744-0000. Specializes in seafood. Hrs: 11 am-11 pm. Closed Thanksgiving, Dec 25. Bar. Lunch $5.50-$10.95; dinner $8.50-$17.95. Child's menu. Entertainment: wkends. Cr cds: A, DS, MC, V.

★★ **GRAPE VINE.** *26 Congress St (01970).* 978/745-9335. *www.shore. net/~gvineamericangrill/italian.* Specializes in pasta, vegetarian entrees, chicken. Hrs: 5-10 pm. Closed hols; also Super Bowl Sun. Res accepted. Bar. Dinner $13-$22. Parking. Eclectic deco dining rm. Cr cds: A, C, D, DS, ER, MC, V.

★★★ **LYCEUM.** *43 Church St (01970).* 978/745-7665. *www.lyceum salem.com.* Specializes in grilled food. Own baking. Hrs: 11 am-3 pm, 5-10 pm; Sat from 5 pm; Sun brunch 11 am-3 pm. Closed Thanksgiving, Dec 25. Res accepted. Bar. Lunch $5.95-$9.95; dinner $13.95-$18.95. Sun brunch $3.95-$8.95. Built in 1830. Alexander Graham Bell presented the first demonstrations of long distance telephone conversations here in 1877. Cr cds: A, DS, MC, V.

★★★ **RED RAVEN'S LIMP NOODLE.** *75 Congress Ave (01970).* 978/745-8558. Specializes in roasted mussels, smoked salmon. Hrs: 5-10 pm. Closed hols. Res accepted. Bar. Wine list. Dinner $14.95-$22.95.

Street parking. Turn-of-the-century Victorian decor; paintings. Cr cds: A.

★ **VICTORIA STATION.** *86 Wharf St (01970).* 978/745-3400. Specializes in prime rib, seafood. Salad bar. Hrs: 11 am-10 pm. Closed Dec 25. Res accepted. Bar. Lunch $5.25-$9.95; dinner $8.95-$19.95. Child's menu. Overlooks harbor. Cr cds: A, C, D, DS, ER, MC, V.

Sandwich (Cape Cod)

Settled 1637 **Pop** 15,489 **Elev** 20 ft
Area code 508 **Zip** 02563
Information Cape Cod Canal Region Chamber of Commerce, 70 Main St, Buzzards Bay 02532; 508/759-6000

The first town to be settled on Cape Cod, Sandwich made the glass that bears its name. This pressed glass was America's greatest contribution to the glass industry.

What to See and Do

⭐ Heritage Plantation. 1899-mid-1930s autos incl a restored and rebuilt 1931 Duesenberg Model J Tourer built for Gary Cooper, a 1908 white steamer, and the first official presidential car, which was used by President Taft. The Military Museum houses the Lilly collection of miniature soldiers and antique firearms. Art Museum has Early American collections of scrimshaw and weather vanes, trade signs, and primitive paintings, incl large Currier & Ives collection; jitney rides (free); ride on restored 1912 carousel; windmill (1800); entertainment (summer). Extensive rhododendron plantings on this 76-acre site. Changing exhibits. Cafe and garden shop. (Mid-May-late Oct, daily) Picnic area opp main parking lot. Grove & Pine Sts. Phone 508/888-3300. ¢¢¢

Hoxie House and Dexter Gristmill. Restored mid-17th-century bldgs. House, operating mill; stone-ground corn meal sold. (Mid-June-mid-Oct, daily) Water St. Phone 508/888-1173. ¢; Combination ticket ¢¢

Sandwich Glass Museum. Internationally renowned collection of exquisite Sandwich Glass (ca 1825-88). (Apr-Oct, daily) Phone 508/888-0251. ¢¢

State parks.

  Scusset Beach. Swimming beach, fishing pier; camping (fee). Standard fees. 3 mi NW on MA 6A across canal, then 2 mi E at jct MA 3 & US 6. Phone 508/362-3225. Day use parking (per vehicle) ¢¢

  Shawme-Crowell State Forest. Approx 2,700 acres. Primitive camping. Standard fees. 3 mi W on MA 130, off US 6. Phone 508/888-0351.

Yesteryears Doll and Miniature Museum. Old First Parish Meeting House (1638) houses antique costumed dolls. (Mid-May-Oct, Mon-Sat) Main & River Sts. Phone 508/888-1711. ¢¢

Motels/Motor Lodges

★ **COUNTRY ACRES MOTEL.** *187 Rte 6A (02563). 508/888-2878; fax 508/888-8511; toll-free 888/860-8650. www.sunsol.com/countryacres/.* 17 rms, 1 cottage. Late June-Labor Day: S, D $65-$85; each addl $8; lower rates rest of yr. Crib $8. TV; cable (premium). Pool. Ck-out 11 am. Lawn games. Refrigerators. Cr cds: A, MC, V

★★ **EARL OF SANDWICH MOTEL.** *378 Rte 6A (02537), 2½ mi E on MA 6A. 508/888-1415; fax 508/833-1039; toll-free 800/442-3275. www.earlof sandwich.com.* 24 rms. Late June-early Sep: S, D $65-$89; each addl $10; lower rates rest of yr. Crib $5. Pet accepted. TV. Complimentary continental bkfst. Restaurant nearby. Ck-out 11 am. Tudor motif. Cr cds: A, MC, V.

★ **OLD COLONY MOTEL.** *436 Rte 6A (02537). 508/888-9716; toll-free 800/786-9716. Email jirenec@aol.com; www.sunsol.com/oldcolony/.* 10 rms, 1 story. June-Aug: S, D $89; each addl $10; lower rates rest of yr. Crib avail, fee. Pool. TV; cable. Complimentary continental bkfst, toll-free calls. Restaurant nearby. Ck-out 11 am, ck-

in 1:30 pm. Golf. Tennis. Picnic facilities. Cr cds: A, C, D, DS, MC, V.

★ **SANDWICH LODGE & RESORT.** *54 Rte 6A (02563). 508/888-2275; fax 508/888-8102; toll-free 800/282-5353.* 68 rms, 2 story, 33 suites, 4 kit. units. July-Aug: D $109; each addl $10; suites $129; kit. units $450/wk; lower rates rest of yr. Crib $5. Pet accepted; $15. TV; cable (premium), VCR avail. 2 pools, 1 indoor; whirlpool. Complimentary continental bkfst. Restaurant adj 11:30 am-9 pm. Ck-out 11 am. Coin lndry. Meeting rms. Game rm. Refrigerators, wet bars. Cr cds: A, MC, V.

★ **SANDY NECK MOTEL.** *669 Rte 6A (02537), 5½ mi E on MA 6A. 508/ 362-3992; fax 508/362-5170; toll-free 800/564-3992. Email snmotel@ capecod.net; www.sandyneck.com.* 12 rms, 1 story, 1 suite. June-Sep: S $89; D $99; suites $125; each addl $10; under 2 free; lower rates rest of yr. Crib avail. Parking lot. TV; cable (premium), VCR avail. Complimentary coffee in rms, toll-free calls. Restaurant noon-11 pm. Ck-out 11 am, ck-in 1 pm. Business servs avail. Golf. Tennis. Beach access. Bike rentals. Hiking trail. Picnic facilities. Cr cds: A, C, D, DS, ER, JCB, MC, V.

★★ **SHADY NOOK INN & MOTEL.** *14 Old Kings Hwy; SR 6A (02563), 508/888-0409; fax 508/888-4039; toll-free 800/338-5208. Email thenook@ capecod.net; www.shadynookinn.com.* 23 rms, 1 story, 7 suites. June-Aug: D $110; suites $160; each addl $10; lower rates rest of yr. Crib avail, fee. Parking lot. Pool. TV; cable. Complimentary continental bkfst. Restaurant nearby. Business servs avail. Golf. Cr cds: A, C, D, DS, MC, V.

★★ **SPRING HILL MOTOR LODGE.** *351 Rte 6A (02537), 2½ mi E on MA 6A. 508/888-1456; fax 508/833-1556; toll-free 800/646-2514. Email raldhurs@ capecod.net.* 24 rms, 2 kit. units. Late June-Labor Day: S, D $95-$115; each addl $10; kit. units $155; lower rates rest of yr. Crib $10. TV; cable (premium). Heated pool. Coffee in rms. Restaurant nearby. Ck-out 11 am.

Tennis. Picnic tables. Refrigerators. Cr cds: A, D, DS, MC, V.

B&Bs/Small Inns

★★★ **BAY BEACH BED & BREAKFAST.** *1 and 3 Bay Beach Ln (02557). 508/888-8813; fax 508/880-5416; toll-free 800/475-6398. Email info@bay beach/cp; www.baybeach.com.* 3 rms, 2 story, 4 suites. June-Sep: S $225; D $285; suites $325; each addl $50; under 16 free; lower rates rest of yr. TV; cable (premium), CD avail. Restaurant nearby. Ck-out noon, ck-in 2 pm. Golf. Tennis. Cr cds: MC, V.

★★ **THE BELFRY INN & BISTRO.** *8 Jarves St (02563). 508/888-8550; fax 508/888-3922; toll-free 800/844-4542. Email info@belfryinn.com.* 9 air-cooled rms, 3 with shower only, 3 story. No elvtr. Late May-mid-Oct: S, D $85-$165; package plans; wkends, hols (2-day min); lower rates rest of yr. Children over 10 yrs only. TV in common rm; cable (premium), VCR avail (movies). Complimentary full bkfst; afternoon refreshments. Restaurant 5-11 pm. Rm serv 24 hrs. Ck-out 11 am, ck-in 3 pm. Business center. In-rm modem link. Valet serv. Concierge serv. Lawn games. Some in-rm whirlpools, fireplaces. Some balconies. Former rectory built 1882; belfrey access. Totally nonsmoking. Cr cds: A, D, MC, V.

★★ **CAPTAIN EZRA NYE HOUSE BED & BREAKFAST.** *152 Main St (02563). 508/888-6142; fax 508/833-2897; toll-free 800/388-2278. Email captnye@aol.com; www.captainezranye house.com.* 5 rms, 2 story, 1 suite. May-Oct: S $95; D $105; suites $120; lower rates rest of yr. Parking lot. TV; cable. Complimentary full bkfst. Restaurant nearby. Ck-out 11 am, ck-in 3 pm. Business center. Golf. Tennis, 2 courts. Beach access. Bike rentals. Hiking trail. Cr cds: A, DS, JCB, MC, V.

★★★ **DAN'L WEBSTER INN.** *149 Main St (02563). 508/888-3622; fax 508/888-5156; toll-free 800/444-5156. Email dwi@capecod.net; www.danl websterinn.com.* 37 rms, 3 story, 17 suites. June-Oct: S, D $149; suites $259; each addl $20; under 11 free; lower rates rest of yr. Crib avail, fee. Parking lot. Pool. TV; cable. Complimentary newspaper. Restaurant 8 am-9 pm. Bar. Ck-out 11 am, ck-in 3 pm. Meeting rms. Business servs avail. Concierge serv. Gift shop. Golf, 18 holes. Hiking trail. Picnic facilities. Cr cds: A, D, DS, MC, V.

★★★ **ISAIAH JONES HOMESTEAD.** *165 Main St (02563). 508/888-9115; fax 508/888-9648; toll-free 800/526-1625. Email info@isaiah jones.com; www.isaiahjones.com.* 5 rms, 1 story, 3 suites. May-Oct: S, D $125; suites $150; lower rates rest of yr. Parking lot. TV; cable. Complimentary full bkfst. Restaurant nearby. Ck-out 11 am, ck-in 3 pm. Meeting rm. Concierge serv. Golf. Tennis. Cr cds: A, D, DS, MC, V.

★★ **VILLAGE INN.** *4 Jarves St (02563). 508/833-0363; fax 508/833-2063; toll-free 800/922-9989. Email capecodinn@aol.com; www.capecodinn. com.* 8 rms, 2 share bath, 3 story. No A/C. No rm phones. June-Oct: D $85-$115; wkends (2-day min); lower rates Nov-May. Children over 8 yrs only. Complimentary full bkfst; afternoon refreshments. Restaurant nearby. Ck-out 11 am, ck-in 3-6 pm. Federal-style house (1837) with wrap-around porch, gardens. Many antique furnishings. Totally non-smoking. Cr cds: A, DS, MC, V.

Restaurants

★ **BOBBY BYRNE'S PUB.** *65 Rte 6A (02563), in Stop and Shop Plaza shopping center. 508/888-6088. Email himself@bobbybyrnes.com; www.bobby byrnes.com.* Specializes in steak, seafood, pasta. Hrs: 11 am-midnight; early-bird dinner 4-6 pm. Closed Thanksgiving, Dec 25. Bar. Lunch $4.95-$7.95; dinner $6.95-$10.50. Child's menu. Family-owned. Cr cds: A, D, DS, MC, V.

★★ **BRIDGE RESTAURANT.** *21 MA 6A (02561), 2 mi W on MA 6A. 508/888-8144.* Specializes in Yankee pot roast, fresh scrod, grape nut custard

pudding. Hrs: 11 am-9 pm. Closed Thanksgiving, Dec 25. Res accepted. Bar. Lunch $1.95-$7.95; dinner $8.95-$16.95. Child's menu. Family-owned since 1953. Cr cds: DS, MC, V.

★★★ **DAN'L WEBSTER INN.** *149 Main St. 508/888-3623. www.danl websterinn.com.* Specializes in seafood, chicken, veal. Own baking. Hrs: 8 am-10 pm; Sun brunch noon-2:30 pm; early-bird dinner 4:30-5:30 pm. Res accepted. Bar. Wine cellar. Bkfst $3.50-$6.95; lunch $5.25-$11.95; dinner $10.95-$23.95. Sun brunch $7-$12.95. Child's menu. Entertainment: pianist. Valet parking. Conservatory dining overlooks garden. Reproduction of 1700s house. Several dining rms; some with fireplace. Cr cds: A, C, D, DS, MC, V.
D

★ **HORIZON'S.** *98 Town Neck Rd (02563). 508/888-6166.* Specializes in fresh seafood, clam bakes, steaks. Hrs: 11 am-10 pm. Closed Nov-Apr. Bar. Lunch $4.95-$7.95; dinner $6.95-$13.95. Child's menu. Entertainment: Sat. Overlooks Cape Cod Bay. Cr cds: A, DS, MC, V.
D

Saugus

(C-6) *See also Boston*

Settled 1630 **Pop** 25,549 **Elev** 21 ft **Area code** 781 **Zip** 01906

Saugus is the birthplace of the American steel industry. The first iron-works were built here in 1646.

What to See and Do

Saugus Iron Works National Historic Site. Commemorates America's first successful integrated ironworks. Reconstructed furnace, forge, mill on original foundations; furnished 17th-century house; museum; working blacksmith shop; 7 working water-wheels; guided tours and demonstrations (Apr-Oct); film. (Daily; closed Jan 1, Thanksgiving, Dec 25) Contact the National Park Service, Saugus Iron Works National Historic Site,

244 Central St. Phone 781/233-0050. **FREE**

Restaurants

★★★ **DONATELLO.** *44 Broadway (01906). 781/233-9975.* Specializes in regional Italian cuisine. Own pasta. Hrs: 11 am-10 pm; Sat to 11 pm; Sun 4-10 pm. Closed July 4, Thanksgiving, Dec 24. Res accepted. Bar. Lunch $6-$10; dinner $5.50-$19.95. Valet parking. Italian decor. Cr cds: A, D, MC, V.
D

★★ **HILLTOP STEAK HOUSE.** *855 Broadway Rte 1 (01906), S on US 1. 781/233-7700.* Specializes in beef, seafood. Hrs: 11 am-10 pm. Closed Thanksgiving, Dec 25. Bar. Lunch $5.99-$9.95; dinner $7.99-$22.99. Child's menu. Cr cds: A, MC, V.
D

Seekonk

(see Providence, RI)

Sheffield

(see Great Barrington)

South Hadley

See also Amherst, Holyoke

Settled ca 1660 **Pop** 13,600 (est) **Elev** 257 ft **Area code** 413 **Zip** 01075 **Information** Chamber of Commerce, 10 Harwich Place; 413/532-6451

Nestled on the banks of the Connecticut River, South Hadley was incorporated as a town in 1775. Twenty years later the first navigable canal in the United States began operation here. The town remained a busy shipping center until 1847, when the coming of the railroad made shipping by river unprofitable. Still visible in spots, the canal is being restored.

What to See and Do

Mount Holyoke College. (1837) 1,950 women. Campus tours (inquire for schedule). College St. Phone 413/538-2000. On grounds are

> **Mount Holyoke College Art Museum.** Small but choice permanent collection of paintings, drawings, prints, and sculpture; also special exhibitions. (Tues-Fri, also Sat and Sun afternoons; closed school hols) Phone 413/538-2245. **FREE**

Joseph Allen Skinner Museum. Housed in a small Congregational church (1846). Collection of Early American furnishings, decorative arts; one-rm schoolhouse. (May-Oct, Wed and Sun afternoons) MA 116. Phone 413/538-2085. **FREE**

Talcott Arboretum. Campus features variety of trees and plantings; Japanese meditation, wildflower, and formal perennial gardens; greenhouse complex has collections of exotic plants; flower show (Mar); tours by appt. (Mon-Fri, also Sat and Sun afternoons; closed hols) Phone 413/538-2199. **FREE**

Old Firehouse Museum. Served as a firehouse 1888-1974; features firefighting equipment, Native American artifacts, items relating to local history and South Hadley Canal. (June-Sep, Wed and Sun; schedule may vary) Phone 413/536-4970. **FREE**

Annual Event

Women's Regatta. Brunelle's Marina. Oct.

South Yarmouth (Cape Cod)

(E-8) *See also Hyannis*

Pop 10,358 **Elev** 20 ft **Area code** 508
Zip 02664
Web www.capecodchamber.org
Information Yarmouth Area Chamber of Commerce, PO Box 479; 800/732-1008; or the Cape Cod Chamber of Commerce, US 6 & MA 132, PO Box 790, Hyannis 02601-0790; 508/362-3225 or 888/33-CAPECOD

Much of the area of the Yarmouths developed on the strength of seafaring and fishing in the first half of the 19th century. South Yarmouth is actually a village within the town of Yarmouth. Well-preserved old houses line Main Street to the north in Yarmouth Port, architecturally among the choicest communities in Massachusetts. Bass River, to the south, also contains many fine estates.

What to See and Do

Captain Bangs Hallet House. Early 19th-century sea captain's home. (June-Sep, Wed-Fri and Sun afternoons; rest of yr, by appt) Botanic trails (all yr; donation). Gate house (June-mid-Sep, daily). Off MA 6A, near Yarmouth Port Post Office. Phone 508/362-3021. ¢¢

Swimming. Nantucket Sound and bayside beaches. Parking fee.

Winslow Crocker House. (ca 1780) Georgian house adorned with 17th-, 18th-, and 19th-century furnishings collected in early 20th century. Incl furniture made by New England craftsmen in the Colonial and Federal periods; hooked rugs, ceramics, pewter. (June-mid-Oct, Tues, Thurs, Sat, and Sun) On Old King's Hwy, US 6A, in Yarmouth Port. Phone 508/362-4385. ¢¢

Motels/Motor Lodges

★ ★ **ALL SEASON MOTOR INN.** *1199 Rte 28 (02664). 508/394-7600; fax 508/398-7160; toll-free 800/527-0359. Email infoline@allseasons.com; www.allseasons.com.* 114 rms, 2 story. July-early Sep: S, D $85-$105; each addl $5; lower rates rest of yr. Crib $5. TV; cable (premium), VCR (movies). Indoor/outdoor pool; whirlpool. Playground. Restaurant 7:30-11 am, noon-3 pm (in season). Ck-out 11 am. Coin lndry. Business servs avail. Exercise equipt; sauna. Game rm. Refrigerators. Private patios, balconies. Picnic tables. Cr cds: A, MC, V.

★★ **AMERICANA HOLIDAY MOTEL.** *99 Main St (02673), 2 mi W on MA 28. 508/775-5511; fax 508/790-0957; toll-free 800/445-4497. Email info@americanaholdiday.com.* 153 rms, 2 story. Late June-Labor Day: S, D $59-$69; each addl $5; suites $85-$105; lower rates Mar-late June, after Labor Day-Oct. Closed rest of yr. Crib free. TV; cable. 3 pools, 1 indoor; whirlpool. Playground. Complimentary coffee. Restaurant nearby. Ck-out 11 am. Putting green. Sauna. Game rm. Lawn games. Refrigerators. Cr cds: A, D, DS, V.

★ **BASS RIVER MOTEL.** *891 Main St, Rte 28 (02664), ½ mi W on MA 28. 508/398-2488; fax 508/398-2488.* 20 rms, 4 kits. July-Aug: S $56; D $58; each addl $6; kit. units $60-$64; wkly rates; lower rates rest of yr. Crib $4. TV; cable. Pool. Restaurant nearby. Ck-out 11 am. Lawn games. Some refrigerators. Picnic tables, grills. Cr cds: DS, MC, V.

★ **BEACH N TOWNE MOTEL.** *1261 Rte 28 (02664), ¼ mi W of Bass River Bridge. 508/398-2311; toll-free 800/ 987-8556.* 21 rms. Late June-late Aug: S, D $60-$67; each addl $5-$7; lower rates Feb-late June, late Aug-Dec. Closed rest of yr. Crib free. TV; cable. Pool. Playground. Coffee in lobby. Restaurant nearby. Ck-out 11 am. Lawn games. Refrigerators. Picnic tables, grills. Library. Cr cds: A, DS, MC, V.

★★ **BEST WESTERN BLUE ROCK MOTOR INN.** *39 Todd Rd (02664), 1 mi N off MA 28, off High Bank Rd. 508/398-6962; fax 508/398-1830; res 800/227-3263. Email bluerock@red jacketinns.com.* 45 rms, 1-2 story. Late June-Labor Day (2-day min wkends): S, D $105-$150; each addl $10; under 12 free; golf plan; lower rates Apr-late June, after Labor Day-late Oct. Closed rest of yr. Crib free. TV; cable. Heated pool; whirlpool. Restaurant 7 am-2:30 pm. Bar 11 am-7 pm. Ck-out 11 am. Meeting rm. Business servs avail. Tennis. 18-hole, par 3 golf, pro, greens fee $31, putting greens. Refrigerators. Private patios, bal-

conies. Overlooks golf course. Cr cds: A, C, D, DS, MC, V.

★★ **BLUE WATER ON THE OCEAN.** *291 S Shore Dr (02664), 1½ mi SW off MA 28. 508/398-2288; fax 508/398-1010; res 800/367-9393. Email bluewater@redjacketinns.com; www.redjacketinns.com/bluewater.* 113 rms, 1-2 story. Late June-Labor Day: D $168-$265; each addl $10; lower rates rest of yr. Crib $5. TV; cable. 2 pools, 1 indoor; whirlpool, poolside serv. Free supervised children's activities (July-Labor Day); ages 6-15. Restaurant 7:30-11 am, noon-2 pm; off-season wkend dinner only. Bar noon-1 am; entertainment Fri, Sat. Ck-out 11 am. Meeting rms. Business servs avail. Bellhops. Sundries. Tennis. Putting green. Sauna. Lawn games. Sun decks. Microwaves avail. On 600-ft private ocean beach. Cr cds: A, MC, V.

★ **CAPTAIN JONATHAN MOTEL.** *1237 Rte 28 (02664), 1 mi W of Bass River Bridge. 508/398-3480; toll-free 800/342-3480.* 21 rms, 2 story. July-Aug: S, D $63-$68; each addl $5; cottage $700-$750/wk; under 12 free; wkly rates; higher rates hols; lower rates rest of yr. Crib free. TV; cable. Pool. Playground. Complimentary continental bkfst. Restaurant nearby. Ck-out 11 am. Lawn games. Microwaves avail. Picnic tables. Cr cds: A, C, D, DS, MC, V.

★ **CAVALIER MOTOR LODGE.** *Rte 28; 881 Main St (02664), ½ mi W on MA 28. 508/394-6575; fax 508/394-6578; res 800/545-3536.* 66 rms, 46 A/C, 1-2 story. July-Aug: S, D $59-$99; each addl $7; kit. units $600-$975; golf plans off season; lower rates late Mar-mid-June, Sep-Oct. Closed rest of yr. TV; cable, VCR avail (movies). Indoor/outdoor pool; wading pool, whirlpool, sauna. Playground. Putting green. Lawn games. Game rm. Refrigerators, microwaves avail. Grills. Cr cds: A, MC, V.

★★ **FLAGSHIP MOTOR INN.** *343 Rte 28 (02673), 2 mi W on MA 28. 508/775-5155; fax 508/790-8255; res 888/810-0044. www.yarmouthresort. com.* 138 rms, 2 story. July-Aug: D

$65-$99; each addl $10; suites $75-$119; under 18 free; lower rates May-June, Sep-Oct. Crib free. TV; cable. 2 pools, 1 indoor; whirlpool. Playground. Ck-out 11 am. Meeting rms. Business servs avail. In-rm modem link. Sauna. Game rm. Many refrigerators. Balconies. Cr cds: DS, MC, V.

D ⊷ 🛏 ⊠ 🐾 🎿

★★ **GULL WING SUITES.** *822 Main St (Rte 28) (02664). 508/394-9300; fax 508/394-1190.* 136 suites, 2 story. July-Labor Day: suites $105-$130; package plans; lower rates rest of yr. Crib avail. TV; cable (premium). 2 pools, 1 indoor; whirlpool, saunas. Restaurant nearby. Ck-out 11 am. Meeting rms. Business servs avail. Game rm. Refrigerators, wet bars. Balconies. Cr cds: A, MC, V.

D ⊷ ⊠ 🐾 SC

★ **HUNTERS GREEN MOTEL.** *553 Main St MA 28 (02673), 2 mi W MA. 508/771-1169; toll-free 800/775-5400.* 74 rms, 2 story. Late June-Labor Day: S, D $54-$64; each addl $6; lower rates mid-Apr-late June, after Labor Day-Oct. Closed rest of yr. Crib $6. TV; cable (premium). Indoor/outdoor pool; whirlpool. Restaurant nearby. Ck-out 11 am. Lawn games. Picnic tables. Cr cds: A, DS, MC, V.

D ⊷ 🐾

★ **LEWIS BAY LODGE.** *149 MA 28 (02673), 3½ mi W. 508/775-3825; fax 508/778-2870; toll-free 800/882-8995. Email info@lewisbaylodge.com.* 68 rms, 2 story. Late June-Aug: S, D $58-$78; higher rates special events; lower rates late Apr-late June, Sep-Oct. Closed rest of yr. Crib $6. TV; cable (premium). 2 pools, 1 indoor; whirlpool. Complimentary continental bkfst. Restaurant nearby. Ck-out 11 am. Exercise equipt. Rec rm. Microwaves avail. Cr cds: A, DS, MC, V.

D ⊷ 🛏 🖂 ⊠ 🐾

★★ **MARINER MOTOR LODGE.** *573 MA 28 (02673), 2 mi W. 508/771-7887; fax 508/771-2811; toll-free 800/445-4050. Email mariner@mariner-capecod.com; www.mariner-capecod.com.* 100 rms, 2 story. July-Aug: S, D $89; each addl $10; under 17 free; lower rates rest of yr. Crib avail, fee. Parking lot. Indoor/outdoor pools, whirlpool. TV; cable. Complimentary continental bkfst,

toll-free calls. Restaurant nearby. Ck-out 11 am, ck-in 2 pm. Meeting rm. Fax servs avail. Exercise privileges, sauna. Golf. Tennis. Picnic facilities. Cr cds: A, DS, MC, V.

D 🐾 ⊀ 🛏 🖂 🛏 🗙 ⊠ 🐾 SC

★★ **OCEAN MIST MOTOR LODGE.** *97 S Shore Dr (02664), ½ mi S of MA 28. 508/398-2633; fax 508/760-3151; toll-free 800/248-6478. Email mist@capecod.net; www.capecod.com/oceanmist.* 63 units, 2 story, 32 loft suites, 21 kit. units. July-Aug: D $179; suites $229-$269; kit. units $179-$219; under 15 free; lower rates Sep-Dec and Feb-June. Closed Jan. Crib $10. TV; cable; VCR avail (movies). Indoor pool; whirlpool. Bkfst avail. Complimentary coffee. Ck-out 11 am. Coin lndry. Business servs avail. Refrigerators, wet bars. On ocean; swimming beach. Cr cds: A, DS, MC, V.

D ⊷ 🐾

★★★ **RED JACKET BEACH MOTOR INN.** *1 S Shore Dr (02664), approx ½ mi S of MA 28 to Seaview Ave. 508/398-6941; fax 508/398-1214; toll-free 800/672-0500.* 150 rms, 1-2 story, 13 cottages. Late June-Labor Day: S, D $160-$250; each addl $10; 2-4 bedrm cottages $200-$2,800/wk; lower rates Apr-late June, after Labor Day-late Oct. Closed rest of yr. Crib free. TV; cable. 2 pools, 1 indoor; whirlpool, poolside serv. Supervised children's activities (July-Labor Day); ages 4-12. Restaurant 7:30-11 am, noon-3 pm; also 6-9:30 pm in season. Bar noon-midnight. Ck-out 11 am. Coin lndry. Meeting rms. Business servs avail. Bellhops. Sundries. Tennis. Putting green. Exercise equipt; sauna. Sailing. Game rm. Lawn games. Refrigerators, microwaves avail. Private patios, balconies. On ocean, beach. Cr cds: MC, V.

D 🐾 🛏 🖂 🛏 🎿 ⊠ 🐾 🎿

★★ **TIDEWATER MOTOR LODGE.** *135 Main St MA 28 (02673), 3½ mi W. 508/775-6322; fax 508/778-5105; res 800/338-6322. Email tidewater@tidewatermi.com; www.tidewatermi.com.* 97 rms, 2 story, 4 suites. July-Aug: S, D $105; suites $159; each addl $6; under 12 free; lower rates rest of yr. Crib avail, fee. Parking lot. Indoor/outdoor pools, whirlpool. TV; cable; VCR avail. Complimentary toll-free calls. Restaurant 7 am-10 pm. Ck-out 11 am, ck-in 2 pm. Fax servs avail. Sauna. Golf. Picnic facilities. Cr cds: A, DS, MC, V.

[icons]

Resort

★★ **RIVIERA BEACH RESORT.** *327 S Shore Dr (02664), 1½ mi off MA 28. 508/398-2273; fax 508/398-1202; toll-free 800/CAPECOD. www.redjacketinns. com/riviera.* 125 rms, 2 story. July-Aug: D $280; each addl $10; under 12 free; lower rates rest of yr. Crib avail. Parking lot. Indoor/outdoor pools, whirlpool. TV; cable, VCR avail. Complimentary toll-free calls. Restaurant. Bar. Bellhops. Golf. Tennis. Beach access. Supervised children's activities. Cr cds: A, MC, V.

[icons]

B&Bs/Small Inns

★★★ **CAPTAIN FARRIS HOUSE BED & BREAKFAST.** *308 Old Main St (02664). 508/760-2818; fax 508/398-1262; toll-free 800/350-9477. Email farris@cape.com; www.captain farris.com.* 6 rms, 2 story, 4 suites. July-Sep: S, D $160; suites $200; each addl $25; lower rates rest of yr. Parking lot. TV; cable, VCR avail, CD avail. Complimentary full bkfst, coffee in rms, newspaper. Restaurant nearby. Ck-out 11 am, ck-in 3 pm. Meeting rms. Business center. Concierge serv. Golf. Tennis. Beach access. Hiking trail. Picnic facilities. Cr cds: A, DS, MC, V.

[icons]

★★ **COLONIAL HOUSE INN & RESTAURANT.** *277 Main St; Rte 6A (02675). 508/362-4348; fax 508/362-8034; res 800/999-3416. Email info@ colonialhousecapecod.co.* July-Aug: S $95; D $105; suites $125; each addl $25; children $10; under 10 free; lower rates rest of yr. Crib avail, fee. Pet accepted, some restrictions, fee. Parking lot. Indoor pool, lap pool, lifeguard, whirlpool. TV; cable (DSS), VCR avail. Complimentary continental bkfst, coffee in rms, newspaper. Restaurant 8 am-9 pm. Bar. Ck-out 11 am, ck-in 1 pm. Business center. Concierge serv. Gift shop. Free airport transportation. Exercise privileges. Golf, 18 holes. Tennis, 5

courts. Beach access. Hiking trail. Picnic facilities. Cr cds: A, DS, MC, V.

[icons]

★★★ **INN AT LEWIS BAY.** *57 Maine Ave (02673), 2 mi W on MA 28. 508/771-3433; fax 508/394-1400; toll-free 800/962-6679. Email manorhse@ capecod.net; www.innatlewisbay.com.* 7 rms, 2 with shower only, 2 story. No rm phones. Mid-May-Oct: S, D $78-$138; wkly rates; wkends, hols (2-day min); lower rates rest of yr. Children over 12 yrs only. Complimentary full bkfst. Ck-out 11 am, ck-in 3-8 pm. Concierge serv. Lawn games. Picnic tables. Beach house built in 1920s. Totally nonsmoking. Cr cds: A, MC, V.

[icons]

★★★ **LIBERTY HILL INN.** *77 Main St (MA 6A) (02675), at Willow St. 508/362-3976; fax 508/362-6485; toll-free 800/821-3977. Email libertyh@ capecod.net.* 9 rms, 3 story. No rm phones. Memorial Day-Columbus Day: D $100-$170; each addl $20; higher rates Presidents Day; lower rates rest of yr. Crib $8. TV. Complimentary full bkfst. Restaurant nearby. Ck-out 11 am, ck-in 3 pm. Concierge serv. Free airport transportation. Antiques. Greek-Revival mansion built 1825 for ship builder. Sitting rm furnished with early-American pieces. Totally nonsmoking. Cr cds: A, MC, V.

[icons] SC

Restaurants

★★ **ABBICCI.** *43 Main St. (02664), on MA 6A. 508/362-3501.* Specializes in authentic Italian cuisine, local seafood, desserts. Hrs: 5-11 pm. Res accepted. Bar. Dinner $10.95-$23.95. Parking. Country inn atmosphere. Cr cds: A, D, MC, V.

[icon]

★★ **HOWE'S COTTAGE.** *134 MA 6A (02675). 508/362-9866.* Specializes in free-range chicken breast grilled and spice-rubbed, quiche of the day, fresh grilled Maine salmon with spicy Thai noodles. Own baking. Hrs: 8-1 am; Sun brunch 9 am-3 pm. Bar. Bkfst $3-$6; lunch $3-$7.50; dinner $11-$23. Sun brunch $3-$8. Parking. In old sea captain's house (1840) with gables and gingerbread ornamentation. Casual decor. Cr cds: A, C, D, DS, MC, V.

★★ **INAHO-JAPANESE RESTAURANT.** *157 Main St (02675), 1½ mi N on Union St to Main St (MA 6), W ½ mi.* 508/362-5522. Specializes in tempura, teriyaki, sushi. Hrs: 5-10 pm. Closed Sun, Mon; Easter, Thanksgiving, Dec 25. Res accepted. Dinner $12-$22. Japanese decor; sushi bar. Cr cds: MC, V.

★★ **RIVERWAY LOBSTER HOUSE.** *MA 28 (02664), 1 blk W of Bass River Bridge.* 508/398-2172. Specializes in lobster, seafood. Hrs: 4-10 pm; Sun from noon; early-bird dinner Mon-Thurs 4:30-6:30 pm. Closed Dec 25. Res accepted. Bar. Lunch, dinner $8.50-$18. Child's menu. Parking. 2 fireplaces. Family-owned. Cr cds: A, D, DS, MC, V.

★ **SKIPPER RESTAURANT.** *152 S Shore Dr (02664), 1 mi E off MA 28, S on Seaview Ave.* 508/394-7406. Specializes in seafood, steak. Hrs: 7 am-10 pm. Closed Oct-Mar. Bar. Bkfst $1.99-$5.95; lunch $3.95-$9.95; dinner $8.95-$18.95. Child's menu. Parking. Nautical motif. Scenic view of Nantucket Sound. Cr cds: A, DS, MC, V.

★★ **YARMOUTH HOUSE.** *335 Main St (02673), 3 mi W on MA 28.* 508/771-5154. Specializes in seafood, beef, chicken. Hrs: 11 am-11 pm; early-bird dinner 3-6 pm. Closed Dec 25. Res accepted. Bar. Lunch a la carte entrees: $3.95-$11.95; dinner a la carte entrees: $8.95-$18.95. Child's menu. Parking. 3 dining rms; working water wheel. Cr cds: A, C, D, DS, ER, MC, V.

Springfield

(D-3) *See also Holyoke*

Settled 1636 **Pop** 156,983 **Elev** 70 ft
Area code 413

Information Greater Springfield Convention & Visitors Bureau, 1441 Main St, 01103; 413/787-1548 or 800/723-1548

Established under the leadership of William Pynchon of Springfield, England, this is now a major unit in the Connecticut River industrial empire. Springfield is also a cultural center with a fine library, museums, and a symphony orchestra, and is the home of Springfield College.

Transportation

Hartford Bradley International Airport. Information 860/292-2000; weather 860/627-3440; cash machines, Terminals A and B.

Car Rental Agencies. See IMPORTANT TOLL-FREE NUMBERS.

Public Transportation. Pioneer Valley Transit Authority, phone 413/781-PVTA.

Rail Passenger Service. Amtrak 800/872-7245.

What to See and Do

Basketball Hall of Fame. Exhibits on the game and its teams and players; shrine to the sport invented here in 1891 by Dr. James Naismith. Historic items on display; free movies; video highlights of great games; life-size, action blow-ups of Hall of Famers. Major features incl: "Hoopla," a 22-min film; and "The Spalding Shoot-Out," the most popular participatory attraction, which allows visitors to try their skill at scoring a basket of varying heights while on a moving sidewalk. (Daily; closed Jan 1, Thanksgiving, Dec 25) 1150 W Columbus Ave, adj to I-91. Phone 413/781-6500. ¢¢

Forest Park. On 735 acres. Nature trails, tennis, swimming pool. Picnicking, playgrounds, ball fields. Zoo (Apr-Oct, daily; rest of yr, Sat and Sun; fee). Duck ponds. Pony rides, train rides (fee for both). Park (all yr). Route 83 off I-91. Phone 413/787-6461 (park) or 413/733-2251 (zoo). Park ¢¢

Indian Motocycle Museum. Part of the vast complex where Indian motorcycles were made until 1953. On display are historical cycles and other American-made machines;

photographs; extensive collection of toy motorcycles; other Native American products, incl an early snowmobile and a 1928 roadster. (Daily; closed Jan 1, Thanksgiving, Dec 25) 33 Hendee St. Phone 413/737-2624. ¢¢

Laughing Brook Education Center and Wildlife Sanctuary. Woodlands and wetlands, 354 acres. Former house (1782) of children's author and storyteller Thornton W. Burgess. Live animal exhibits of wildlife native to New England. Observation areas of pond, field, and forest habitats. 4½ mi of walking trails; picnic area. (Tues-Sun; also Mon hols; closed Jan 1, Thanksgiving, Dec 25) 793 Main St, 7 mi SE in Hampden. Phone 413/566-8034. ¢¢

Municipal Group. Incl renovated Symphony Hall, which together with the Springfield Civic Center offers a performing arts complex presenting a variety of concerts, theater, children's productions, dance and sporting events, and industrial shows; 300-ft campanile, modeled after the bell tower in the Piazza San Marco of Venice. NW side of Court Sq.

Riverside Park. Amusement park, rides, roller coasters; children's area; games and arcades; shows; restaurants. (June-Labor Day, daily; Apr, May, and Sep, wkends only) 5 mi W via MA 57 & MA 159S in Agawam. Phone 413/786-9300. ¢¢¢¢

Springfield Armory National Historic Site. US armory (1794-1968) contains one of the largest collections of military small arms in the world. Exhibits incl "Organ of Guns," made famous by Longfellow's poem "The Arsenal at Springfield." Film, video presentations. (Memorial Day-Labor Day, daily; rest of yr, Tues-Sun; closed Jan 1, Thanksgiving, Dec 25) Old Armory Square Green, Federal & State Sts. Phone 413/734-8551. **FREE**

Springfield Library and Museums. Incl **George Walter Vincent Smith Art Museum.** Italian Renaissance bldg housing collection of Oriental armor, arms, jade, bronzes, and rugs; 19th-century American paintings, sculpture. (Thurs-Sun) State & Chestnut Sts. Phone 413/263-6800. **Connecticut River Valley Historical Museum** with genealogy and local history library; period rms. (Thurs-Sun) Phone 413/263-6800. **Museum**

of Fine Arts has 20 galleries incl outstanding collection of American and European works. (Thurs-Sun) Phone 413/263-6800. **Science Museum** has an exploration center, early aviation exhibit, aquarium, planetarium (fee), African hall, dinosaur hall. (Thurs-Sun) Phone 413/263-6800. Above bldgs all closed. Planetarium shows (Thurs, Sat, and Sun). Library (fall-spring, Mon-Sat; summer, Mon-Fri; closed hols). Inclusive admission ¢¢

State forests.

Brimfield. Swimming, trout fishing from shore (stocked); hiking, picnicking. Standard fees. 24 mi E on US 20, then SE near Brimfield. Phone 413/245-9966. Per vehicle ¢

Granville. Scenic gorge, laurel display. Swimming, fishing; hiking, picnicking, camping. Standard fees. 22 mi W off MA 57. Phone 413/357-6611.

Storrowton Village. A group of restored Early American bldgs: meetinghouse, schoolhouse, blacksmith shop, and homes. Old-fashioned herb garden. Dining (see RESTAURANTS). Guided tours (June-Labor Day, Mon-Sat; rest of yr, by appt; closed hols). Eastern States Exposition, 1305 Memorial Ave, on MA 147 in West Springfield. Phone 413/787-0136. ¢¢

Annual Events

World's Largest Pancake Breakfast. A battle with Battle Creek, Michigan, to see who can serve the "world's largest breakfast." Features pancake bkfst served at a 4-blk-long table. Phone 413/733-3800.

Taste of Springfield. Phone 413/733-3800. Wed-Sun, mid-June.

Indian Day. Indian Motocycle Museum. Gathering of owners and those interested in Indian motorcycles and memorabilia. Phone 413/737-2624. Third Sun July.

Glendi Greek Celebration. Greek folk dances, observance of doctrine and ritual festivities, Greek foods, art exhibits, street dancing. Early Sep.

Eastern States Exposition (The Big E). 1305 Memorial Ave, on MA 147 in West Springfield. Largest fair in the Northeast; entertainment, exhibits; historic Avenue of States, Storrowton Village; horse show; agricultural events; "Better Living Center" exhibit. Phone 413/737-2443. Seventeen days Sep.

Hall of Fame Tip-off Classic. At Springfield Civic Center, 1277 Main St. Official opening game of the collegiate basketball season with 2 of the nation's top teams. Phone 413/781-6500. Mid-Nov.

Motels/Motor Lodges

★★ **DAYS INN.** *437 Riverdale St (01089), off I-91 Exit 13B. 413/785-5365; fax 413/732-7017; toll-free 800/329-7466.* 84 rms. S $38-$58; D $45-$65; each addl $10; higher rates special events. Crib free. TV. Pool. Complimentary continental bkfst. Restaurant nearby. Ck-out 11 am. Meeting rms. Downhill ski 9 mi. Cr cds: A, D, DS, MC, V.

🄳 🏊 🌊 🔌 🐾 SC

★★ **HAMPTON INN.** *1011 Riverdale St (US 5) (01089), on US 5, ¼ mi S of MA Tpke (I-90) Exit 4 or N of I-91 Exit 13B. 413/732-1300; fax 413/732-9883; res 800/HAMPTON.* 126 rms, 4 story. S, D $70; under 18 free. Crib free. TV; cable (premium), VCR avail. Pool. Complimentary continental bkfst. Ck-out noon. Meeting rms. Business servs avail. In-rm modem link. Sundries. Downhill/x-country ski 6 mi. Health club privileges. Cr cds: A, C, D, DS, MC, V.

🄳 🏊 🌊 🔌 🌊 🐾

Hotels

★★ **COMFORT INN AT THE PAR-WICK CENTRE.** *450 Memorial Dr (01020), off MA Tpke (I-90) Exit 5, on Rte 33. 413/739-7311; fax 413/594-5005; res 800/221-2222.* 100 rms, 3 story. S $54-$73; D $61-$80; each addl $7; under 18 free. Crib free. TV; cable (premium). Restaurant 5-10 pm. Bar; entertainment Thurs-Mon. Ck-out 11 am. Coin lndry. Meeting rms. Business servs avail. Valet serv. Cr cds: A, MC, V.

🄳 🌊 🐾 SC

★★ **HOLIDAY INN.** *711 Dwight St (01104). 413/781-0900; fax 413/785-1410; toll-free 800/465-4329.* 245 rms, 12 story. S $85-$110; D $95-$120; suites $130-$210; under 19 free; wkend, family rates. Pet accepted; $25. TV; cable. Indoor pool; whirl-

pool. Restaurant 6:30 am-2 pm, 5-10 pm. Bar from 4:30 pm; Sat, Sun from noon. Ck-out noon. Meeting rm. Downhill/x-country ski 10 mi. Exercise equipt. Game rm. Some refrigerators. Cr cds: A, C, D, DS, ER, JCB, MC, V.

🄳 🐦 🏊 🌊 🔌 🌊 🐾 SC

★★★ **MARRIOTT.** *1500 Main St (01115), at I-91 Springfield Center Exit. 413/781-7111; fax 413/731-8932; toll-free 800/228-9290.* 265 rms, 16 story. S $99-$115; D $139-$149; each addl $10; suites $275; under 18 free; wkend package plans. Crib free. TV. Indoor pool; whirlpool, poolside serv. Complimentary coffee in lobby. Restaurant 6:30 am-11 pm. Bars 11:30-2 am; entertainment. Ck-out 1 pm. Meeting rms. Shopping arcade. Barber, beauty shop. Airport transportation. Downhill/x-country ski 15 mi. Exercise equipt; sauna. Some refrigerators. Luxury level. Cr cds: A, C, D, DS, ER, JCB, MC, V.

🄳 🏊 🌊 🔌 🐾 SC

★★★ **SHERATON HOTEL.** *1 Springfield Center (01144). 413/781-1010; fax 413/734-2349; toll-free 800/426-9004. Email sheraton@ javanet.com.* 304 rms, 12 story. S, D $89-$139; suites $149-$169; under 18 free; wkend rates. Crib free. Garage $7.95; valet. TV; cable (premium). Indoor pool; whirlpool, poolside serv. Restaurant 6:30 am-11 pm. Bar 11:30-2 am; entertainment Fri, Sat. Ck-out noon. Convention facilities. Business center. Shopping arcade. Airport transportation. Exercise rm; sauna, steam rm. Bathrm phones. Cr cds: A, D, DS, MC, V.

🄳 🛎 🌿 🌊 🔌 🌊 🐾 🚶

Restaurants

★★★ **HOFBRAUHAUS.** *1105 Main St (01089), off MA Tpke (I-90) Exit 4, S on US 5, then W on MA 147. 413/737-4905. www.hofbrauhaushouse. com.* Specializes in lobster, Wienerschnitzel, rack of lamb. Hrs: 4-9 pm. Closed Dec 25. Res accepted. Bar. Lunch $2.75-$13; dinner $10.25-$30. Child's menu. Parking. Tableside cooking. Bavarian atmosphere; antiques. Cr cds: A, C, D, DS, ER, MC, V.

🄳 🌊

★ **IVANHOE.** *1422 Elm St (01089), I-91 Exit 13B, on US 5. 413/736-4881.* Specializes in prime rib, fresh seafood. Salad bar. Hrs: 11 am-9 pm. Closed Dec 25. Bar. Lunch $3.95-$8.95; dinner $9.95-$15.95. Sun brunch $11.95. Child's menu. Entertainment. Parking. Contemporary decor. Casual atmosphere. Cr cds: A, C, D, DS, ER, MC, V.

D

★★ **MONTE CARLO.** *1020 Memorial Ave (01089), 1 mi W of I-91, opp Exposition Grounds. 413/734-6431.* Specializes in beef Marsala, veal Francaise, pasta. Hrs: 11 am-10 pm; Sat 4-10 pm; Sun from 4 pm. Closed Mon; Dec 25. Res accepted. Bar. Lunch $4.95-$8.95; dinner $8.95-$16.95. Child's menu. Family-owned. Cr cds: A, C, D, DS, ER, MC, V.

D ⊡

★★★ **OLD STORROWTON TAVERN.** *1305 Memorial Ave (01103), 2 mi W on MA 147, in Eastern States Exposition. 413/732-4188. www. storrowton.com.* Specializes in seafood, veal and beef dishes. Own baking. Hrs: 11 am-2 pm, 5-8 pm. Closed Sun; Jan 1, Dec 25. Res required. Bar. Lunch $5.75-$12; dinner $12-$22. Part of restored Colonial village. Cr cds: A, DS, MC, V.

★★ **STUDENT PRINCE & FORT.** *8 Fort St (01103). 413/734-7475. Email hubie@peoplepc.com; www.student prince.com.* Specializes in jagerschnitzel, sauerbraten. Hrs: 11 am-11 pm; Sun noon-10 pm. Res accepted. Bar. Lunch $4.50-$10; dinner $8.50-$24. Child's menu. Large collection of German beer steins. Family-owned. Cr cds: A, C, D, DS, ER, MC, V.

D ⊡

Stockbridge and West Stockbridge

See also Lenox, Pittsfield

Settled 1734 **Pop** 2,408 and 1,483 **Elev** 842 and 901 ft **Area code** 413 **Zip** Stockbridge, 01262; West Stockbridge, 01266 **Web** www.stockbridgechamber.org

Information Stockbridge Chamber of Commerce, Box 224; 413/298-5200; or visit the Information Booth, Main St

Established as a mission, Stockbridge was for many years a center for teaching the Mahican. The first preacher was John Sergeant. Jonathan Edwards also taught at Stockbridge. The town is now mainly a summer resort but still has many features and attractions open year round. West Stockbridge is a completely restored market village. Its Main Street is lined with well-kept storefronts, renovated in the style of the 1800s, featuring stained glass, antiques, and hand-crafted articles.

What to See and Do

Berkshire Botanical Garden. 15-acre botanical garden; perennials, shrubs, trees, antique roses, ponds; wildflower exhibit, herb, vegetable gardens; solar, semitropical, and demonstration greenhouses. Garden shop. Herb products. Special events, lectures. Picnicking. (May-Oct, daily) 2 mi NW, at jct MA 102, 183 in Stockbridge. Phone 413/298-3926. ¢¢

Chesterwood. Early 20th-century summer residence and studio of Daniel Chester French, sculptor of the Minute Man statue in Concord and of Lincoln in the Memorial in Washington, DC. Also museum, gardens, woodland walk, guided tours. A property of the National Trust for Historic Preservation. (May-Oct, daily) 2 mi S of jct MA 102 & MA 183, in Stockbridge. Phone 413/298-3579. ¢¢¢

Children's Chimes Bell Tower. (1878) Erected by David Dudley Field, prominent lawyer, as a memorial to his grandchildren. Carillon concerts (June-Aug, daily). Main St in Stockbridge.

Merwin House "Tranquility." (ca 1825) Brick house in late Federal period; enlarged with "shingle"-style wing at end of 19th century. European and American furniture and decorative arts. (June-mid-Oct, Tues, Thurs, Sat, and Sun) 14 Main St, in Stockbridge. Phone 413/298-4703. ¢¢

Mission House. (1739) House built in 1739 for the missionary Rev John Sergeant and his wife, Abigail Williams; now a museum of colonial life. Collection of colonial antiques; Native American museum; gardens and orchard. Guided tours. (Memorial Day wkend-Columbus Day wkend, daily) Main & Sergeant Sts in Stockbridge, on MA 102. Phone 413/298-3239. ¢¢

Naumkeag. Stanford White designed this Norman-style "Berkshire cottage" (1886); interior has antiques, Oriental rugs, collection of Chinese export porcelain. Gardens incl terraces of tree peonies, fountains, Chinese garden, and birch walk. Guided tours. (Memorial Day wkend-Columbus Day wkend, daily) Prospect Hill in Stockbridge. Phone 413/298-3239. Gardens ¢¢; House and gardens ¢¢¢

⭐Norman Rockwell Museum. Maintains and exhibits the nation's largest collection of original art by Norman Rockwell. (Daily; closed Jan 1, Thanksgiving, Dec 25) MA 183, in Stockbridge. Phone 413/298-4100. ¢¢¢

Colonial home, Stockbridge

Annual Events

Harvest Festival.
Berkshire Botanical Garden. Celebrates beginning of harvest and foliage season in the Berkshire Hills. Phone 413/298-3926. First wkend Oct.

Stockbridge Main Street at Christmas. Events incl a re-creation of Norman Rockwell's painting. Holiday marketplace, concerts, house tour, silent auction, sleigh/hay rides, caroling. Phone 413/298-5200. First wkend Dec.

Seasonal Event

Berkshire Theatre Festival. Berkshire Playhouse. E Main St, in Stockbridge, entrance from US 7, MA 102. Summer theater (Mon-Sat); Unicorn Theater presents new and experimental plays (Mon-Sat in season); children's theater (July-Aug, Thurs-Sat). Phone 413/298-5576. Late June-late Aug.

B&Bs/Small Inns

★★★ THE INN AT STOCKBRIDGE. Rte 7N (01262), approx 1 mi N 413/298-3337; fax 413/298-3406; toll-free 888/466-7865. Email innkeeper@stockbridgeinn.com; www.stockbridgeinn.com. 8 rms, 2 story, 4 suites. June-Oct: D $255; suites $275; each addl $25; lower rates rest of yr. Parking lot. Pool. TV; cable, VCR avail, CD avail. Complimentary full bkfst, newspaper. Restaurant. Ck-out 11 am, ck-in 2 pm. Meeting rm. Business servs avail. Concierge serv. Golf, 18 holes. Tennis, 4 courts. Downhill skiing. Picnic facilities. Cr cds: A, DS, MC, V.
⬛ 🔖 🛠 🏂 🏊 🛶 🔥

★★★ RED LION INN. 30 Main St (01262). 413/298-5545; fax 413/298-5130. Email marketing@redlioninn.com; www.redlioninn.com. 84 rms, 4 story, 26 suites. July-Aug, Oct, Dec: S, D $195; suites $375; each addl $20; lower rates rest of yr. Crib avail. Street parking. Pool. TV; cable (premium), VCR avail. Complimentary toll-free calls. Restaurant. Bar. Meeting rms. Business servs avail. Concierge serv. Dry cleaning. Gift shop. Exercise equipt. Golf, 18 holes. Tennis, 2 courts. Downhill skiing. Cr cds: A, D, DS.
⬛ 🔖 🛠 🏂 🏊 🛶 🔥

★★★ THE TAGGART HOUSE. 18 W Main St (01262). 413/298-4303. Email info@taggarthouse.com; www.taggarthouse.com. 4 rms. No rm phones. July-Aug: S $235-$295; D $275-$355; wkends 2-3 day min; lower rates rest of yr. Closed Jan-Apr. Children over 18 yrs only. Complimentary full bkfst. Restaurant adj 8 am-10 pm. Ck-out 11:30 am, ck-in 3 pm. In-rm modem link. Tennis privileges. Game rm. Built in late 1800s; country manor house. Totally non-smoking. Cr cds: A, C, D, DS, MC, V.

★★★ **WILLIAMSVILLE INN.** *Rte 41 (01266), 5 mi S on MA 41, 5 mi S of MA Tpke Exit 1. 413/274-6118; fax 413/274-3539. Email williamsville@ taconic.net; www.williamsville.com.* 15 rms, 3 story, 1 suite. July-Oct: S $140; D $150; suites $185; each addl $20; lower rates rest of yr. Crib avail, fee. Pet accepted, some restrictions. Parking lot. Pool. TV; cable (premium), VCR avail. Complimentary full bkfst, toll-free calls. Restaurant nearby. Bar. Ck-out 11 am, ck-in 2 pm. Meeting rms. Business center. Concierge serv. Exercise privileges. Golf. Tennis. Downhill skiing. Beach access. Bike rentals. Hiking trail. Picnic facilities. Cr cds: A, MC, V.

Restaurants

★★ **MICHAEL'S.** *5 Elm St (01262). 413/298-3530.* Specializes in hamburgers, New England clam chowder, fettuccini Alfredo. Hrs: 11 am-9 pm. Closed Dec 25. Res accepted. Bar. Lunch $4.95-$7.95; dinner $8.95-$16.95. Child's menu. Cr cds: A, MC, V.

★★★ **THE RED LION.** *30 Main St. 413/298-5545. www.redlioninn.com.* Specializes in fresh seafood, New England clam chowder, roast prime rib of beef. Hrs: 7 am-9 pm. Res accepted. Bar. Bkfst $5-$12; lunch $8-$15; dinner $17.50-$24. Child's menu. Entertainment: pianist wkends. Parking. Jacket. Cr cds: A, D, DS, MC, V.

★★ **TRUC ORIENT EXPRESS.** *1 Harris St (01266), 5 mi NW on MA 102. 413/232-4204.* Specializes in Banh Xeo (pancake stuffed with shrimp and pork). Hrs: 5-10 pm. Closed Thanksgiving, Dec 25; also Tues Nov-Apr. Res accepted. Bar. Dinner $11.50-$17. Parking. Cr cds: A, MC, V.

★★★ **WILLIAMSVILLE INN.** *MA 41. 413/274-6118. www.williamsville*

inn.com. Specializes in beef, fresh fish, duck. Own baking. Hrs: 6-9 pm. Closed Mon-Wed (Nov-mid-June). Res accepted. Bar. Dinner $16-$25. Parking. Intimate atmosphere in 1797 farmhouse. Cr cds: A, MC, V.

Sturbridge

Settled ca 1730 **Pop** 7,775 **Elev** 619 ft **Area code** 508 **Zip** 01566-1057

Information Tourist Information Center, 380 Main St; 508/347-2761 or 888/788-7274

What to See and Do

🟦 **Old Sturbridge Village.** A living history museum that re-creates a rural New England town of the 1830s. The museum covers more than 200 acres with more than 40 restored bldgs; costumed interpreters demonstrate the life, work, and community celebrations of early 19th-century New Englanders. Working historical farm; many special events; picnic area. (Apr-Oct, daily; closed Dec 25) On US 20W, 2 mi W of jct I-84 Exit 2 & MA Tpke (I-90) Exit 9. Phone 508/347-3362, 508/347-5383 (TTY) or 800/SEE-1830. ¢¢¢¢

Annual Event

New England Thanksgiving. Old Sturbridge Village. Re-creation of early 19th-century Thanksgiving celebration. Incl turkey shoot, hearth cooking, and meetinghouse service. Phone 508/347-3362 or 508/347-5383 (TTY). Late Nov.

Motels/Motor Lodges

★ **ECONO LODGE.** *682 Main St (01518), I-90 Exit 9, I-84 Exit 20W. 508/347-2324; fax 508/347-7320; res 800/555-2666.* 52 rms, 7 suites. June-Oct: S, D $60-$90; each addl $5; lower rates rest of yr. Crib avail. TV; cable. Pool. Ck-out 11 am. Coin lndry. Some refrigerators. Cr cds: A, MC, V.

★★ **OLD STURBRIDGE VILLAGE LODGES.** *Main St Rte 20 (01566), 2* mi W of jct I-84 Exit 3B and MA Tpke (I-90) Exit 9. 508/347-3327; fax 508/347-3018; toll-free 800/733-1830. Email osvlodge@osv.org; www.osv.org. 57 rms, 2 story, 2 suites. July-Oct: S, D $110; suites $130; each addl $5; under 15 free; lower rates rest of yr. Crib avail. Parking lot. Pool. TV; cable. Complimentary coffee in rms, newspaper. Restaurant nearby. Ck-out 11 am, ck-in 3 pm. Fax servs avail. Exercise privileges. Golf. Downhill skiing. Picnic facilities. Cr cds: A, DS, MC, V.

★ ★ ★ PUBLICK HOUSE HISTORIC INN. *295 Main St (01566), on MA 131, 1½ mi S of jct US 20, I-84 Exit 2, off MA Tpke (I-90) Exit 9. 508/347-3313; fax 508/347-1246; toll-free 800/ PUBLICK. Email lodging@publickhouse. com; www.publickhouse.com.* 113 rms, 2 story, 13 suites. June-Oct: S, D $100; suites $165; each addl $5; under 17 free; lower rates rest of yr. Crib avail, fee. Pet accepted, some restrictions, fee. Parking lot. Pool, children's pool. TV; cable. Complimentary continental bkfst, newspaper, toll-free calls. Restaurant. Bar. Ck-out 11 am, ck-in 3 pm. Meeting rms. Business servs avail. Bellhops. Dry cleaning. Gift shop. Golf. Tennis. Downhill skiing. Hiking trail. Picnic facilities. Cr cds: A, D, DS, MC, V.

★ STURBRIDGE COACH MOTOR LODGE. *408 Main St Rte 20 (01566), 2 mi W of jct I-84 Exit 2 and MA Tpke (I-90) Exit 9. 508/347-7327; fax 508/ 347-2954.* 54 rms, 2 story, 2 suites. May-Oct: S $89; D $100; suites $125; each addl $5; under 18 free; lower rates rest of yr. Crib avail, fee. Parking lot. Pool. TV; cable, VCR avail. Complimentary continental bkfst, coffee in rms, toll-free calls. Restaurant, closed Sun. Business servs avail. Golf, 18 holes. Tennis, 2 courts. Hiking trail. Cr cds: A, MC, V.

Hotel

★ ★ COMFORT INN & SUITES. *Hwy 20, 215 Charlton Rd (01566), 1½ mi E at MA Tpke (I-90) Exit 9. 508/ 347-3306; fax 508/347-3514; toll-free 800/228-5151. Email comfort innsturb@cs.com; www.sturbridge comfortinn.com.* 33 rms, 3 story, 44 suites. Apr-Oct: S, D $110; suites $150; each addl $15; under 18 free; lower rates rest of yr. Crib avail. Parking lot. Indoor pool, whirlpool. TV; cable (premium). Complimentary continental bkfst, coffee in rms, newspaper, toll-free calls. Restaurant 6 am-11 pm. Bar. Ck-out 11 am, ck-in 2 pm. Meeting rm. Business servs avail. Dry cleaning, coin lndry. Exercise privileges. Golf, 18 holes. Tennis, 2 courts. Downhill skiing. Supervised children's activities. Cr cds: A, C, D, DS, MC, V.

B&B/Small Inn

★ ★ COLONEL EBENEZER CRAFTS INN. *Fiske Hill Rd (01566), check in at Publick House Inn. 508/ 347-3141; fax 508/347-5073; toll-free 800/782-5425.* 8 rms, 3 story. June-Oct: S, D $90-$155; each addl $5; under 16 free; lower rates rest of yr. Crib $5. TV in sun rm; cable, VCR avail (movies). Pool. Restaurant adj 7 am-10 pm. Ck-out 11 am, ck-in 3 pm. Meeting rm. Business servs avail. Tennis. X-country ski 2 mi. Lawn games. Built 1786; overlooks woods. Cr cds: A, C, D, MC, V.

Conference Center

★ ★ ★ STURBRIDGE HOST HOTEL & CONFERENCE CENTER. *366 Main St (01566). 508/347-7393; fax 508/347-3944; toll-free 800/582-3232. Email str_sales@fine-hotels.com; fine-hotels.com.* 215 rms, 3 story, 5 suites. May-Aug, Oct: Crib avail. Pet accepted, some restrictions, fee. Parking lot. Indoor pool, children's pool, lifeguard, whirlpool. TV; cable, VCR avail, CD avail. Complimentary coffee in rms, newspaper. Restaurant-10 pm. Bar. Ck-out 11 am, ck-in 3 pm. Meeting rms. Business servs avail. Concierge serv. Dry cleaning, coin lndry. Gift shop. Exercise rm, sauna, steam rm. Golf. Tennis, 2 courts. Downhill skiing. Beach access. Supervised children's activities. Hiking trail. Picnic facilities. Cr cds: A, C, D, DS, MC, V.

Restaurants

★★ **PUBLICK HOUSE.** *295 Main St.* 508/347-3313. *www.publickhouse. com.* Specializes in turkey, prime rib, lobster pie. Hrs: 7 am-9 pm. Res accepted. Bar. Bkfst $3.95-$12.95; lunch $7.95-$11.95; dinner $14.95-$27. Child's menu. Entertainment: Fri, Sat. Open hearth. In original Colonial structure built in 1771. Located on historic Sturbridge Common. Cr cds: A, D, MC, V.
SC ⟶

★★ **ROM'S RESTAURANT.** *MA 131 (01566).* 508/347-3349. *www.stur bridge.com.* Specializes in veal parmigiana, chicken cacciatore. Own pasta. Hrs: 11 am-9 pm. Closed Thanksgiving, Dec 25. Res accepted. Lunch $3.95-$7.95; dinner $4.95-$12.95. Child's menu. Family-owned. Cr cds: A, D, DS, MC, V.
D ⟶

★★★ **WHISTLING SWAN.** *502 Main St (01566).* 508/347-2321. Specializes in seafood, steak. Own baking. Hrs: 11 am-midnight. Closed Mon; hols. Res accepted. Bar. Lunch $4.95-$12.95; dinner $12.95-$23.95. Child's menu. Entertainment: pianist, guitarist. Whistling Swan, on 1st floor, has 3 intimate dining areas; offers fine dining. Ugly Duckling Loft offers casual dining in a large dining area; bar. 1800s Greek-Revival house with barn attached; many antiques. Cr cds: A, C, D, DS, ER, MC, V.
D

Crafter at Old Sturbridge Village

Sudbury Center

See also Boston

Settled 1638 **Pop** 14,358 **Elev** 190 ft
Area code 978 **Zip** 01776
Web www.ibeam-net.com/sudbury
Information Board of Selectmen, Loring Parsonage, 288 Old Sudbury Rd, Sudbury; 978/443-8891

Sudbury, which has a number of 17th-century bldgs, is best known for the Wayside Inn at South Sudbury, which was the scene of Longfellow's *Tales of a Wayside Inn* (1863).

What to See and Do

Great Meadows National Wildlife Refuge. Along with the Concord section (8 mi N), this refuge contains 3,400 acres of freshwater wetlands, open water, and upland. More than 200 bird species have been recorded at this diverse habitat area. Visitor center/wildlife education center and HQ (May and Oct, daily; winter, Mon-Fri; closed hols). Nature trail, hiking (daily). Office and visitor center off Lincoln Rd. Contact Refuge Manager, Weir Hill Rd. Phone 978/443-4661. **FREE**

Longfellow's Wayside Inn. (1702) A historical and literary shrine, this is America's oldest operating inn. Originally restored by Henry Ford, it was badly damaged by fire in Dec 1955, and restored again by the Ford Foundation. Period furniture. (Daily; closed July 4, Dec 25) Wayside Inn Rd, 3 mi SW, just off US 20. Phone 978/443-1776. Also on the property are

Martha Mary Chapel. Built and dedicated by Henry Ford in 1940, a nondenominational, nonsectarian chapel. No services; used primarily for weddings. (By appt)

Gristmill. With waterwheel in operation; stone grinds wheat and corn used by inn's bakery. (Apr-Nov, daily)

Redstone School. (1798) "The Little Red Schoolhouse" immortalized in "Mary Had a Little Lamb." (May-Oct, daily)

Annual Events

Reenactment of March of Sudbury Minutemen to Concord on April 19, 1775. More than 200 costumed men muster on Common before proceeding to Old North Bridge in Concord. Phone 978/443-1776. Apr.

Fife & Drum Muster and Colonial Fair. Muster takes place on field across from Longfellow's Wayside Inn. Fife and drum corps from New England and surrounding areas compete. Colonial crafts demonstrations and sales. Last Sat Sep.

Motels/Motor Lodges

★★ **CLARION CARRIAGE HOUSE INN.** *738 Boston Post Rd (01776). 978/443-2223; fax 978/443-5830; res 800/CLARION; toll-free 800/637-0113.* 39 rms, 3 story, 5 suites. No elvtr. S, D $150-$175; suites $175; under 18 free; wkends (2-day min). Crib free. TV; cable (premium), VCR avail (movies). Complimentary full bkfst, coffee in rms. Ck-out 11 am. Business servs avail. Valet serv. Free guest lndry. Exercise equipt. Microwaves avail. Cr cds: A, C, D, DS, MC, V.

★★★ **RADISSON INN.** *75 Felton St (01752), I-495, Exit 24B (MA 20). 508/480-0015; fax 508/485-2242.* 206 rms, 5 story. S, D $89-$159; each addl $10; suites $195-$295; under 18 free; wkend rates. Crib free. TV; cable (premium), VCR avail (movies). Indoor pool; whirlpool. Restaurant 6:30 am-2 pm, 5:30-10 pm; wkend hrs vary. Bar 11:30-1 am. Ck-out noon. Meeting rms. Business servs avail. In-rm modem link. Sundries. Gift shop. Exercise rm; sauna. Raquetball courts. Some refrigerators; microwaves avail. Bathrm phone, wet bar in suites. Balconies in suites. Cr cds: A, D, DS, ER, JCB, MC, V.

Hotel

★★ **BEST WESTERN ROYAL PLAZA HOTEL & TRADE CENTER.**

181 W Boston Post Rd (01752), ½ mi W via MA 20 from I-495 Exit 24B. 508/460-0700; fax 508/480-8218; toll-free 888/543-9500. 430 rms, 6 story, 10 suites. S, D $149; suites $189; each addl $10. TV; cable (premium). Restaurant 11:30 am. Bar. Meeting rms. Cr cds: A, C, D, DS, JCB, MC, V.

B&Bs/Small Inns

★★ **THE ARABIAN HORSE INN.** *277 Old Sudbury Rd (01776). 978/443-7400; fax 978/443-0234; res 978/443-7400; toll-free 800/ARABIAN. Email joanbeers@aol.com.* 4 rms, 2 with shower only, 3 story, 1 suite. June-Nov: S, D $149-$269; lower rates rest of yr. Pet accepted. TV; cable (premium). Complimentary full bkfst, coffee in rms. Restaurant nearby. Ck-out 11 am, ck-in 3 pm. In-rm modem link. X-country ski on site. Some balconies. Built in 1886. Arabian horses, antique cars on site. Totally non-smoking. Cr cds: A, MC, V.

★★ **LONGFELLOW'S WAYSIDE INN.** *72 Wayside Inn Rd (01776). 978/443-1776; fax 978/443-8041; toll-free 800/339-1776. www.wayside.org.* 10 rms, 2 story. Sep-Dec: S $72-$145; D $98-$145; lower rates rest of yr. Complimentary full bkfst. Restaurant (see LONGFELLOW'S WAYSIDE INN). Bar. Ck-out 11 am, ck-in 3 pm. Gift shop. Period furnishings. Historic inn (1716); self-guided tours through restored public rms. National historic site; on grounds are Wayside Gristmill and Redstone School, built by former owner Henry Ford. Totally nonsmoking. Cr cds: A, D, DS, MC, V.

Restaurant

★★ **LONGFELLOW'S WAYSIDE INN.** *72 Wayside Inn Rd. 978/443-1776. www.wayside.org.* Specializes in fresh seafood, prime rib. Hrs: 11:30 am-3 pm, 5-10 pm; Sun, hols noon-10 pm. Closed Dec 25. Res accepted. Bar. Lunch $7.50-$10.50; dinner complete meals: $16-$22. Child's menu. Cr cds: A, C, D, DS, ER, MC, V.

Truro and North Truro (Cape Cod)

Settled Truro: ca 1700 **Pop** Truro/N Truro: 1,573 **Elev** 20 ft **Area code** 508 **Zip** Truro 02666; North Truro 02652 **Web** www.capecodchamber.org

Information Cape Cod Chamber of Commerce, US 6 & MA 132, PO Box 790, Hyannis 02601-0790; 508/362-3225 or 888/33-CAPECOD

Truro, named for one of the Channel towns of England, is today perhaps the most sparsely settled part of the Cape—with great stretches of rolling moorland dotted only occasionally with cottages. On the hill above the Pamet River marsh are two early 19th-century churches; one is now the town hall. The countryside is a favorite resort of artists and writers.

What to See and Do

Fishing. Surf casting on Atlantic beaches. Boat ramp at Pamet and Depot Rds; fee for use, harbor master on duty.

Pilgrim Heights Area. Interpretive display, self-guided nature trails, picnicking, rest rms. Cape Cod National Seashore (see). Off US 6. **FREE**

Swimming. Head of the Meadow. A fine Atlantic beach (fee). N on US 6 & W of Chamber of Commerce booth. **Corn Hill Beach.** On the bay (fee). S on US 6, then E. A sticker for all beaches must be purchased from Truro Chamber of Commerce. No lifeguards. (Mid-June-Labor Day).

Truro Historical Society Museum. Collection of artifacts from the town's historic past, incl shipwreck mementos, whaling gear, ship models, 17th-century firearms, pirate chest, and period rms. (Mid-June-mid-Sep, daily) Highland Rd in N Truro. Phone 508/487-3397. ¢

Motels/Motor Lodges

★ **CROW'S NEST MOTEL.** *496 Shore Rd Box 117 (02652), on MA 6A.* 508/487-9031; toll-free 800/499-9799. www.capecodtravel.com. 33 rms, 2 story. June-Aug: D $86; suites $580; each addl $10; lower rates rest of yr. Parking lot. TV; cable. Complimentary toll-free calls. Restaurant nearby. Golf. Cr cds: DS, MC, V.
⬛⬛

★ **HARBOR VIEW VILLAGE.** *168 Shore Rd PO Box 147 (02652), on MA 6A.* 508/487-1087; fax 508/487-6269. Email hbrview@capecod.net; www.capecod.net/hbrview. 14 rms. July-Aug: D $75; lower rates rest of yr. Parking lot. TV; cable. Restaurant nearby. Ck-out 10 am, ck-in 3 pm. Golf. Beach access. Cr cds: MC, V.
⬛⬛⬛⬛⬛⬛

★ **SEA GULL MOTEL.** *654 Shore Rd (02652).* 508/487-9070. Email seagullmtl@capecod.net. 26 rms, 5 kit. apts. Late June-Labor Day: S, D $78-$100; each addl $10; cottages $820/wk; each addl $70/wk; lower rates mid-Apr-late June, after Labor Day-Oct. Closed rest of yr. TV. Restaurant nearby. Ck-out 10:30 am. Refrigerators, microwaves avail. Sun deck. Private beach. Picnic tables, grills. Cr cds: A, DS, MC, V.
⬛⬛⬛⬛⬛⬛

Resort

★ **EAST HARBOUR MOTEL & COTTAGES.** *618 Shore Rd PO Box 183 (02652), on MA 6A.* 508/487-0505; fax 508/487-6693. Email sonja@eastharbour.com; www.eastharbour.com. 8 rms, 1 story, 1 suite. June-Aug: D $105; suites $140; each addl $32; children $16; lower rates rest of yr. Crib avail, fee. Parking lot. TV; cable. Complimentary coffee in rms. Restaurant nearby. Fax servs avail. Coin lndry. Golf. Beach access. Picnic facilities. Cr cds: A, DS, MC, V.
⬛⬛⬛⬛

Cottage Colony

★★ **KALMAR VILLAGE.** *694 Shore Rd Rte 6A (02652).* 508/487-0585; fax 508/487-5827. ww.kalmarvillage.com. 6 suites. July-Aug: suites $150; lower rates rest of yr. Crib avail. Street parking. Pool. TV; cable (premium). Restaurant nearby. Ck-out 10 am, ck-in 3 pm. Fax servs avail. Coin lndry.

Exercise privileges. Golf, 9 holes. Tennis. Beach access. Picnic facilities. Cr cds: DS, MC, V.

Restaurants

★ **ADRIAN'S.** *535 MA 6 (02652), 4½ mi N on MA 6. 508/487-4360. www. capecod.com/adrians.* Specializes in shrimp pizza, linguine alle vongole, cayenne-crusted salmon. Hrs: 8 am-10 pm. Closed mid-Oct-mid-May. Bar. Bkfst $3.95-$7.50; lunch, dinner $6.95-$19.95. Child's menu. Overlooks Provincetown and bay. Cr cds: A, MC, V.

D

★★ **BLACKSMITH SHOP RESTAURANT.** *17 Truro Center Rd (02666), ¼ mi N on MA 6A. 508/349-6554.* Specializes in local seafood, free-range chicken, pasta. Hrs: 5-10 pm. Closed Dec 25; also Mon, Tues off-season. Res accepted. Bar. Dinner $10-$21. Child's menu. Antiques; carousel horse. Cr cds: A, MC, V.

D

★ **MONTANO'S.** *481 MA 6 (02652). 508/487-2026. Email montanos@ capecod.com.* Specializes in veal saltimbocca, seafood Fra Diavolo, baked stuffed lobster. Hrs: 4-10 pm; early-bird dinner 4-6 pm. Closed Dec 25. Res accepted. Dinner $8.95-$18.95. Child's menu. Nautical decor. Cr cds: A, DS, MC, V.

★ **PAPARAZZI.** *518 Shore Rd (02652), at Beach Point. 508/487-7272.* Specializes in local seafood, prime rib. Salad bar. Hrs: 5-10 pm. Closed Mon, Tues in winter; Dec. Dinner $10-$30. Child's menu. Nautical decor. Overlooks bay. Cr cds: A, DS, MC, V.

Uxbridge

(see Worcester)

Waltham

(C-6) *See Boston*

Settled 1634 **Pop** 57,878 **Elev** 50 ft
Area code 781 **Zip** 02154
Web www.walthamchamber.com/advantage.html

Information Waltham West Suburban Chamber of Commerce, 1 Moody St, Suite 301; 781/894-4700

The name Waltham, taken from the English town of Waltham Abbey, means "a home in the forest," and is still appropriate today, due to the town's many wooded and forested areas. Originally an agricultural community, Waltham is now an industrial center. It is also the home of Bentley College and Regis College.

What to See and Do

Brandeis University. (1948) 3,700 students. The first Jewish-founded nonsectarian university in the US. Its 250-acre campus incl Three Chapels, Rose Art Museum (Sep-May, Tues-Sun; closed hols; free); Spingold Theater Arts Center (plays presented Oct-May; fee); and Slosberg Music Center, with classical and jazz performances (Sep-May). 415 S St. Phone 781/736-4300.

Cardinal Spellman Philatelic Museum. Exhibition gallery; library. (Tues-Thurs, Sat, Sun; closed hols) 4 mi W on US 20, in Weston, at 235 Wellesley St. Phone 781/894-6735. **FREE**

Gore Place. A living history farm, Gore Place may be New England's finest example of Federal-period residential architecture; changing exhibits; 40 acres of cultivated fields. The mansion, designed in Paris and built in 1805, has 22 rms filled with examples of early American, European, and Oriental antiques. (Mid-Apr-mid-Nov, Tues-Sun) On US 20 at the Waltham-Watertown line. Phone 781/894-2798. ¢¢

Lyman Estate "The Vale." (1793) Designed by Samuel McIntire for Boston merchant Theodore Lyman. Enlarged and remodeled in the

1880s, the ballroom and parlor retain Federal design. Landscaped grounds. Five operating greenhouses contain grape vines, camellias, orchids, and herbs. House open by appt for groups only. Greenhouses (Mon-Sat, also Sun afternoons). 185 Lyman St. Phone 781/893-7232 (house) or 781/891-7095 (greenhouses). ¢¢

Motels/Motor Lodges

★★ **HOME SUITES INN.** *455 Totten Pond Rd (02451), I-95 (MA 128) Exit 27A. 781/890-3000; fax 781/890-0233; toll-free 800/424-4021. www. homesuitesinn.com.* 116 rms, 3 story. Sep-Oct: S $75-$115; D $75-$155; each addl $10; suites $89-$169; kit. unit $169; under 18 free; wkly, wkend, hol rates; higher rates special events; lower rates rest of yr. Crib free. TV; cable (premium), VCR (movies). Pool. Complimentary continental bkfst, coffee in rms. Restaurant 11 am-11 pm. Bar to midnight. Ck-out 11 am. Coin lndry. Business servs avail. In-rm modem link. Valet serv. Sundries. Health club privileges. Many refrigerators, microwaves. Picnic tables. Cr cds: A, D, DS, MC, V.

D ⊠ 🐾 ⩘ 🖂

★ **SUSSE CHALET MOTOR LODGE.** *385 Winter (02451), I-95/128 Exit 27A. 781/890-2800; fax 781/890-1021; toll-free 800/258-1980.* 149 rms, 2 and 5 story. S $63.70-$115.70; D $68.70-$119.70; each addl $10; under 18 free. Crib free. TV; cable (premium), VCR avail. Complimentary continental bkfst. Restaurant 11:30 am-11:30 pm. Bar. Ck-out 11 am. Business servs avail. In-rm modem link. Microwaves avail. Cr cds: A, C, D, DS, MC, V.

D 🐾 ⩘ 🖂

Hotels

★★ **BEST WESTERN TLC HOTEL.** *477 Totten Pond Rd (02451), I-95 Exit 27A. 781/890-7800; fax 781/890-4937; res 800/528-1234; toll-free 877/852-4683. www.bestwestern.com.* 100 rms, 6 story. Apr-Nov: S, D $195; each addl $15; under 18 free; lower rates rest of yr. Crib avail. Parking lot. Indoor pool. TV; cable (premium), VCR avail. Complimentary continental bkfst, coffee in rms, newspaper. Restaurant 6:30 am-11

pm. Bar. Ck-out 11 am, ck-in 2 pm. Meeting rms. Business center. Dry cleaning. Exercise privileges. Golf. Cr cds: A, C, D, DS, MC, V.

D 🐾 🐾 ⩘ 🖂 🖂

★★★ **WESTIN.** *70 3rd Ave (02451), on MA 128, I-95 Exit 27a. 781/290-5600; fax 617/290-5626; res 800/937-8461.* 346 rms, 2-8 story. S, D $89-$275; each addl $15; family, wkly, wkend rates. Crib free. TV; cable, VCR avail. Indoor pool; whirlpool. Restaurant 6:30 am-10 pm. Rm serv 24 hrs. Bar; entertainment. Ck-out 1 pm. Convention facilities. Business center. In-rm modem link. Gift shop. Free garage parking. Airport transportation. Exercise equipt; sauna, steam rm. Cr cds: A, D, DS, MC, V.

D 🐾 🖂 ⩘ 🖂 🖂

★★ **WYNDHAM GARDEN HOTEL.** *420 Totten Pond Rd (02451), I-95 (MA 128) Exit 27A. 617/890-0100; fax 617/890-4777; toll-free 800/996-3426.* 148 rms, 6 story. S, D $139-$149; each addl $10; under 18 free; wkend rates. Crib free. TV; cable (premium). Indoor pool; poolside serv. Complimentary bkfst. Coffee in rms. Restaurant 6:30 am-10 pm. Bar 4 pm-midnight. Ck-out noon. Meeting rms. Business servs avail. In-rm modem link.. Exercise equipt. Some refrigerators; microwaves avail. Cr cds: A, D, DS, ER, JCB, MC, V.

D 🐾 🖂 ⩘ 🖂 SC

All Suite

★★★ **DOUBLETREE GUEST SUITES BOSTON/WALTHAM.** *550 Winter St (02451), I-95 (MA 128) Exit 27B. 781/890-6767; fax 781/890-8917; res 800/222-8733. Email sales@ dtgs.com; www.doubletree.com.* 8 story. 275 suites. Apr-June, Sep-Oct: suites $175; each addl $15; under 18 free; lower rates rest of yr. Crib avail. Parking lot. Indoor pool, whirlpool. TV; cable (premium), VCR avail. Complimentary coffee in rms, newspaper, toll-free calls. Restaurant 6:30 am-10 pm. Bar. Ck-out noon, ck-in 3 pm. Meeting rms. Business center. Bellhops. Dry cleaning, coin lndry. Gift shop. Exercise privileges, sauna. Golf. Tennis. Downhill skiing. Cr cds: A, C, D, DS, ER, JCB, MC, V.

D 🐾 🐾 🖂 🖂 🖂 ⩘ 🖂 🖂

Restaurants

★ ★ ★ GRILL AT HOBBS BROOK.
*550 Winter St. 781/487-4263. www.
dtgs.com.* Specializes in grilled dishes.
Hrs: 6:30 am-9:30 pm; Sat 7 am-10
pm; Sun brunch 7 am-2 pm. Res
accepted. Bar. Wine list. Bkfst $6-
$12.95; lunch $8-$20; dinner $13-
$27. Sun brunch $12.95. Child's
menu. Entertainment: pianist. Spacious, elegant rms offer views of
chef's herb and vegetable gardens. Cr
cds: A, D, DS, MC, V.
[D]

★ ★ ★ IL CAPRICCIO. *888 Main St
(02451), 1 mi E on I-95, Exit 26.
781/894-2234.* Specializes in baccala
gnocchi, roast trout. Own pasta. Hrs:
5-10 pm. Closed Sun; . Bar. Wine list.
Dinner $17-$26. Complete meals: $38.
Fine dining. Cr cds: A, DS, MC, V.
[D]

★ ★ R PLACE. *312 Washington St
(02481). 781/237-4560.* Specializes in
Southwestern Caesar salad, Louisiana
crab cakes. Hrs: 5-10 pm. Closed
Mon; Jan 1, Thanksgiving. Wine,
beer. Dinner $16-$23. Street parking.
Fine dining; original artwork. Cr cds:
A, C, D, DS, ER, MC, V.
[D]

★ ★ TUSCAN GRILL. *361 Moody St
(02453). 781/891-5486.* Specializes in
wood-grilled dishes, seasonal items.
Own baking, pasta. Hrs: 5-10 pm.
Closed July 4, Thanksgiving, Dec 24,
25. Res accepted. Bar. Dinner a la
carte entrees: $13.95-$17.95. Parking.
Modern Italian trattoria with open
kitchen. Cr cds: DS, MC, V.
[D]

Wellesley

(C-6) See also Boston

Settled 1661 **Pop** 26,615 **Elev** 141 ft
Area code 781 **Zip** 02181
Web www.wellesleyweb.com/
chamber.htm

Information Chamber of Commerce,
One Hollis St, Suite 111; 781/235-
2446

This Boston suburb was named after
an 18th-century landowner, Samuel
Welles. It is an educational and cultural center. There are four widely
known institutions here: Dana Hall,
girls' preparatory school; Babson College, a business school; Massachusetts Bay Community College; and
Wellesley College.

What to See and Do

Map and Globe Museum. Coleman
Map Bldg features largest physical
map of America, with natural vegetation coloring. From viewing balcony
one sees the same scene an astronaut
would see from 700 mi above the
Earth's surface. Switches operable by
public pinpoint cities and other
points of interest with special lights.
(Tues-Fri, afternoons; also Sat and by
appt) On Babson College Campus,
Babson Park, Forest St and Wellesley.
Phone 781/239-4232. **FREE**

Wellesley College. (1870) 2,200
women. Founded by Henry F.
Durant. 500 wooded acres bordering
Lake Waban. On campus are Davis
Museum and Cultural Center and
Margaret C. Ferguson Greenhouses
(daily). Central & Washington Sts,
on MA 16/135. Phone 781/283-1000.

Motel/Motor Lodge

**★ ★ WELLESLEY INN ON THE
SQUARE.** *576 Washington St
(02181). 781/235-0180; fax 781/235-
5263; toll-free 800/233-4686.* 70 rms,
3-4 story. S $82-$90; D $92-$110;
each addl $10; suites $150; under 18
free. Crib free. TV; cable (premium).
Restaurant 7 am-2:30 pm; 5:30-9:30
pm; Sun hrs vary. Bar 11:30 am-
11:30 pm. Ck-out 11 am. Meeting
rms. Business servs avail. Valet serv.
Cr cds: A, C, D, DS, MC, V.
[⊠] [🐾] [SC]

Restaurant

★ ★ ★ BLUE GINGER. *583 Washington St (02482). 781/283-5790.
www.blueginger.net.* Specializes in sea
bass, calamari. Hrs: 11:30 am-2 pm,
5:30-9:30 pm; Sat from 5:30 pm; Sun
5-9 pm. Closed Mon. Lunch $8-$11;
dinner $18-$25. Cr cds: MC, V.
[D]

Wellfleet (Cape Cod)

Settled ca 1725 **Pop** 2,493 **Elev** 50 ft
Area code 508 **Zip** 02667
Web www.capecod.net/wellfleetcc
Information Chamber of Commerce, PO Box 571; 508/349-2510

Once a fishing town, Wellfleet dominated the New England oyster business in the latter part of the 19th century. It is now a summer resort and an art gallery town, with many tourist homes and cottages. Southeast of town is the Marconi Station Area of Cape Cod National Seashore (see). Fishermen here can try their luck in the Atlantic surf or off deep-sea charter fishing boats.

What to See and Do

Historical Society Museum. Marine items, whaling tools, Marconi memorabilia, needlecraft, photograph collection, marine and primitive paintings. (Late June-mid-Sep, Tues-Sat; schedule may vary) Phone 508/349-9157. ¢

Sailing. Rentals at Wellfleet Marina; accommodates 150 boats; launching ramp, facilities.

Swimming. At numerous bayside and ocean beaches on marked roads off US 6. Freshwater ponds with swimming are scattered through woods E of US 6. Parking sticker necessary mid-June to Labor Day.

Wellfleet Bay Wildlife Sanctuary. Operated by the Massachusetts Audubon Society. Self-guiding nature trails. Natural history summer day camp for children. Guided nature walks, lectures, classes, Monomoy Island natural history tours. Sanctuary (Memorial Day-Columbus Day, daily; rest of yr, Tues-Sun). In S Wellfleet, on W side of US 6. Contact PO Box 236, S Wellfleet 02663. Phone 508/349-2615. ¢¢

Motels/Motor Lodges

★★ **EVEN'TIDE MOTEL & COTTAGES.** *650 Rte 6 (02663), 4 mi S on US 6. 508/349-3410; fax 508/349-7804; toll-free 800/368-0007. Email eventide@capecod.net; eventidemotel.*

com. 23 rms, 2 story, 8 suites. June-Aug: S, D $89; suites $102; each addl $15; children $8; under 17 free; lower rates rest of yr. Crib avail, fee. Parking lot. Indoor pool, lap pool. TV; cable. Complimentary coffee in rms, toll-free calls. Restaurant nearby. Ck-out 11 am, ck-in 1 pm. Fax servs avail. Coin lndry. Golf. Tennis. Hiking trail. Picnic facilities. Cr cds: A, C, D, DS, MC, V.

★ **SOUTHFLEET MOTOR INN.** *Rte 6 (02663), across from Marconi National Seashore entrance. 508/349-3580; fax 508/349-0250; toll-free 800/334-3715. Email sverid@webtv.net; www.capecod.net/sfleet.* 30 rms, 2 story. Late June-Labor Day (2-day min): S, D $88-$110; each addl $10; lower rates Apr-late June, after Labor Day-Oct. Closed rest of yr. Crib free. TV; cable (premium). 2 pools, 1 indoor; whirlpool. Complimentary morning coffee in office. Restaurant adj 8 am-10 pm in season. Bar noon-1 am. Ck-out 11 am. Meeting rm. In-rm modem link. Game rm. Refrigerators. Cr cds: A, MC, V.

★★ **WELLFLEET MOTEL & LODGE.** *146 Rte 6 (02663), 5 mi SE. 508/349-3535; fax 508/349-1192; toll-free 800/852-2900. www.wellfleet motel.com.* 57 rms, 8 suites. Parking lot. Indoor/outdoor pools, whirlpool. TV; cable. Complimentary coffee in rms. Ck-out 11 am, ck-in 2 pm. Meeting rm. Business servs avail. Gift shop. Golf. Hiking trail. Picnic facilities. Cr cds: A, MC, V.

B&Bs/Small Inns

★ **THE HOLDEN INN.** *140 Commercial St (02667), Wellfleet Bay, on Rd to the pier. 508/349-3450. Email striper@gis.net; innweb.com.* 26 rms, 2 story, 1 suite. Aug: S $55; D $85; suites $150; under 12 free; lower rates rest of yr. Parking lot. TV; cable. Ck-out 10 am, ck-in 2 pm. Cr cds: A, MC, V.

★★ **INN AT DUCK CREEK.** *70 Main St (02667). 508/349-9333; fax 508/349-0234; res 508/349-9333. Email duckinn@capecod.net.* 25 rms, 17 with bath, 4 A/C, 2-3 story. No rm phones. July-Aug: D $65-$95; each addl $15; lower rates mid-May-June, Sep-mid-Oct. Closed rest of yr. Crib $10. Complimentary continental bkfst. Restaurant (see DUCK CREEK TAVERN ROOM). Ck-out 11 am, ck-in 1 pm. Former sea captain's house (1815) furnished with period antiques. Sitting porch overlooks Duck Creek. Cr cds: A, MC, V.

Restaurants

★★★ **AESOP'S TABLES.** *316 Main St (02667). 508/349-6450.* Specializes in fresh pasta Neptune, uptown marinated duck, Aesop's oysters. Own baking. Hrs: 5-10 pm. Closed mid-Oct-mid-May. Res accepted. Bar. Wine cellar. Dinner $13-$24. Cr cds: A, D, MC, V.
D

★ **DUCK CREEK TAVERN ROOM.** *70 Main St. 508/349-7369. Email duckinn@capecod.net; www.capecod. net/duckinn.* Specializes in seafood. Hrs: 5 pm-1 am; early-bird dinner 5:30-7 pm. Closed mid-Oct-mid-May. Res accepted. Bar. Dinner $11-$17. Child's menu. Nautical decor; duck decoys. Colonial tavern atmosphere. Cr cds: A, MC, V.

★★ **VANRENSSELAER'S.** *1019 US 6 (02667), 2 mi S on US 6, opp Marconi Station. 508/349-2127. Email yrhall@capecod.com.* Specializes in creative pasta, fresh seafood, black Angus steaks. Salad bar. Hrs: 8 am-9 pm. Closed Dec-Mar. Res accepted. Bar. Bkfst $2.75-$7.95; dinner $8-$19.95. Child's menu. Family-owned. Cr cds: A, D, DS, MC, V.
D

Williamstown

Settled 1749 **Pop** 8,220 **Elev** 638 ft
Area code 413 **Zip** 01267

A French and Indian War hero, Colonel Ephraim Williams, Jr, left a bequest in 1755 to establish a "free school" in West Hoosuck, provided the town be renamed after him. In 1765 the town name was changed to Williamstown, and in 1793 the school became Williams College. The life of this charming Berkshire Hills town still centers around the college.

What to See and Do

Sterling and Francine Clark Art Institute. More than 30 paintings by Renoir, other French Impressionists; old-master paintings; English silver; American artists Homer, Sargent, Cassatt, Remington. Extensive art library (Mon-Fri). Museum shop. Picnic facilities on grounds. (July-Labor Day, daily; rest of year, Tues-Sun; closed Jan 1, Thanksgiving, Dec 25) 225 S St. Phone 413/458-9545 for fees.

Williams College. (1793) 1,950 students. Private liberal arts college; campus has wide variety of architectural styles, ranging from colonial to Gothic. Chapin Library of rare books is one of nation's finest, housing the four founding documents of the US. Hopkins Observatory, the nation's oldest (1836), has planetarium shows. Adams Memorial Theatre presents plays. The Paul Whiteman Collection houses Whiteman's recordings and memorabilia. 1 blk E of central green, US 7. Phone 413/597-3131. Also here is

Williams College Museum of Art. Considered one of the finest college art museums in the country. Houses approx 11,000 pieces. Exhibits emphasize contemporary, modern, American, and non-Western art. Museum shop. (Tues-Sat, also Sun afternoons and Mon hols; closed Jan 1, Thanksgiving, Dec 25) Main St. Phone 413/597-2429. **FREE**

Motels/Motor Lodges

★★★ **1896 HOUSE.** *910 Cold Spring Rd (01267), 2 mi S on US 7 and MA 2. 413/458-8125; toll-free 888/666-1896. Email celebrate@1896house.com; www. 1896house.com.* 30 rms, 1 story, 2 suites. July-Oct: Crib avail, fee. Parking lot. Pool. TV; cable. Complimentary continental bkfst, coffee in rms. Restaurant 5-9 pm. Bar. Ck-out 11 am, ck-in 2 pm. Meeting rms. Fax servs avail. Golf. Tennis, 20 courts. Downhill skiing. Picnic facilities. Cr cds: A, C, D, DS, MC, V.

★★ **BERKSHIRE HILLS MOTEL.** *1146 Cold Spring Rd (01267), 3 mi S* on US 7. 413/458-3950; fax 413/458-5878; toll-free 800/388-9677. Email bhmotel@bcn.net. 20 rms, 2 story. June-Oct: S, D $59-$129; each addl $10; under 3 free; lower rates rest of yr. Crib free. TV; cable. Heated pool. Complimentary buffet bkfst. Restaurant adj 5-10 pm. Ck-out 11 am. Downhill/x-country ski 5 mi. Gazebo in garden; wooded grounds bordering brook. Cr cds: A, C, D, DS, MC, V.

★★ **FOUR ACRES MOTEL.** 213 Main St; Rte 2 (01267). 413/458-8158; fax 413/458-8158. Email foura@bcn.net; www.fouracresmotel.com. 31 rms, 2 story. July-Aug, Oct: S $65; D $75; each addl $10; under 2 free; lower rates rest of yr. Crib avail, fee. Parking lot. Pool, whirlpool. TV; cable (premium). Complimentary continental bkfst, newspaper. Restaurant 11:30 am-10 pm, closed Sun. Bar. Ck-out 1 pm, ck-in 11 pm. Business servs avail. Exercise privileges. Golf. Tennis, 8 courts. Downhill skiing. Picnic facilities. Cr cds: A, C, D, DS, MC, V.

Hotels

★★★ **THE ORCHARDS HOTEL.** 222 Adams Rd (01267). 413/458-9611; fax 413/458-3273; toll-free 800/225-1517. Email the-orchards@worldnet.net. 49 rms, 3 story. Mid-May-mid-Nov: S, D $165-$230; each addl $30; MAP avail; lower rates rest of yr. Crib $10. TV; cable (premium), VCR (movies). Pool; whirlpool. Dining rm (see THE ORCHARDS). Afternoon tea 3:30-4:30 pm. Bar noon-11:30 pm. Ck-out noon, ck-in 4 pm. Business servs avail. In-rm modem link. Concierge serv. Tennis privileges. 18-hole golf privileges, pro, greens fee $55-$75. Downhill/x-country ski 6 mi. Exercise equipt; sauna, steam rm. Bathrm phones; many refrigerators; some fireplaces. Library. Cr cds: A, D, MC, V.

★★★ **WILLIAMS INN.** On the Green (01267), jct US 7 and MA 2. 413/458-9371; fax 413/458-2767; toll-free 800/828-0133. www.williamsinn.com. 103 rms, 3 story. May-Oct: S $110; D $160; each addl $15; under 14 free; lower rates rest of yr. Crib avail. Pet accepted, some restrictions, fee. Park-

ing lot. Indoor pool, whirlpool. TV; cable, VCR avail. Restaurant 7 am-10 pm. Bar. Ck-out 11 am, ck-in 2 pm. Meeting rms. Business center. Bellhops. Dry cleaning. Gift shop. Sauna. Golf. Tennis, 26 courts. Downhill skiing. Bike rentals. Hiking trail. Picnic facilities. Cr cds: A, C, D, DS, MC, V.

Restaurants

★★★ **LE JARDIN.** 777 Cold Spring Rd (01267). 413/458-8032. Specializes in fresh seafood, lamb chops, steak. Own baking. Hrs: 5-10 pm; winter hrs vary. Res accepted. Bar. Dinner $15-$25. Parking. Converted 19th-century estate overlooking trout ponds, waterfall. Guest rms avail. Cr cds: A, C, D, DS, ER, MC, V.

★★★ **THE ORCHARDS.** 222 Adams Rd. 413/458-9611. www.theorchardshotel.com. Own baking. Menu changes daily. Hrs: 7 am-9 pm. Res accepted. Bar. Wine cellar. Bkfst a la carte entrees: $6-$12; lunch a la carte entrees: $8-$16; dinner a la carte entrees: $17-$30. Sun brunch $7-$20. Child's menu. Parking. Scenic view of fountain pond with exotic fish, mountains. Cr cds: A, D, MC, V.

★★ **WATER STREET GRILL.** 123 Water St (01267). 413/458-2175. Specializes in fajitas, fresh seafood, pasta. Hrs: 11 am-11 pm. Closed Easter, Thanksgiving, Dec 25. Res accepted. Bar. Lunch a la carte entrees: $4-$8. Buffet: Mon-Fri $5.95; dinner $7-$14. Child's menu. Entertainment: Fri, Sat. Parking. Locally popular; semi-formal atmosphere. Cr cds: A, MC, V.

★★ **WILD AMBER GRILL.** 101 N St (01267), on US 7. 413/458-4000. Specializes in sesame-seared tuna, seared scallops with roasted pepper sauce, osso buco a la Milanese. Own desserts. Hrs: 5-10 pm. Closed Tues Sep-mid-June; also Jan 1, Thanksgiving, Dec 25. Res accepted. Bar. Dinner $14-$22. Child's menu. Entertainment: Fri, Sat in summer. Terrace dining. Colonial atmosphere. Cr cds: A, MC, V.

Woods Hole (Cape Cod)

See also Martha's Vineyard, Nantucket Island

Pop 1,100 (est) **Elev** 15 ft
Area code 508
Web www.capecodchamber.org

Information Cape Cod Chamber of Commerce, US 6 & MA 132, PO Box 790, Hyannis 02601-0790; 508/362-3225 or 888/33-CAPECOD

A principal port of Cape Cod in the town of Falmouth (see). Ferries leave here for Martha's Vineyard. The Oceanographic Institution and Marine Biological Laboratories study tides, currents, and marine life (closed to the public).

What to See and Do

Bradley House Museum. Model of Woods Hole Village (ca 1895); audio-visual show of local history; restored spritsail sailboat; model ships. Walking tour of village. (July-Aug, Tues-Sat; June and Sep, Wed, Sat; schedule may vary). Phone 508/548-7270. **FREE**

Car/passenger boat trips. Woods Hole, Martha's Vineyard Steamship Authority conducts trips to Martha's Vineyard (all yr). Schedule may vary. Phone 508/477-8600. ¢¢¢

Motel/Motor Lodge

★ **SLEEPY HOLLOW MOTOR INN.** *527 Woods Hole Rd (02543). 508/548-1986; fax 508/548-5932; res 508/548-1980. Email shmotel@capecodnethttp.* 24 rms, 1-2 story. Late June-Labor Day: D $85-$125; lower rates Apr-late June, Labor Day-mid-Nov. Closed rest of yr. Crib $6. TV. Pool. Complimentary coffee in rms. Restaurant nearby. Ck-out 11 am. Refrigerators avail. Cr cds: A, MC, V.
🖼️🖼️

Resort

★★ **NAUTILUS MOTOR INN.** *539 Woods Hole Rd (02543), 3¾ mi S of MA 28. 508/548-1525; fax 508/457-9674; toll-free 800/654-2333. Email jpnautilus@aol.com; www.nautilusinn. com.* 54 rms, 2 story. June-Sep: S, D $158; each addl $6; children $6; lower rates rest of yr. Crib avail, fee. Parking lot. Pool. TV; cable. Restaurant 5-10 pm. Bar. Ck-out 11 am, ck-in 2 pm. Meeting rm. Fax servs avail. Golf. Tennis, 2 courts. Beach access. Bike rentals. Hiking trail. Picnic facilities. Cr cds: A, D, DS, MC, V.
🖼️🖼️🖼️🖼️🖼️🖼️🖼️🖼️🖼️

B&B/Small Inn

★★★ **MARLBOROUGH.** *320 Woods Hole Rd (01240). 508/548-6218; fax 508/457-7519; toll-free 800/320-2322.* 5 rms, 1 cottage, 2 story. Some phones. Late May-mid-Oct: S, D $85-$135; higher rates wkends, hols (2-day min); lower rates rest of yr. TV in sitting rm, cottage. Pool. Complimentary full bkfst; afternoon refreshments. Ck-out 11 am, ck-in 2-6 pm. In-rm modem link. Concierge serv. Free ferry terminal transportation. Cape Cod reproduction built 1942; gardens. Cr cds: MC, V.
🖼️🖼️🖼️

Restaurants

★★ **DOME RESTAURANT.** *533 Woods Hole Rd. 508/548-0800.* Specializes in char-broiled swordfish, duck a la Chambord, prime rib. Hrs: 5-11 pm. Closed mid-Oct-mid-Apr. Res accepted. Bar. Dinner $8.95-$19.95. Child's menu. Entertainment: Fri-Sun. Dining inside oldest geodesic dome in the world (1953), designed by Buckminster Fuller. Harbor view. Cr cds: A, C, D, DS, ER, MC, V.
D SC

★ **LEESIDE.** *Luscombe Ave (01267), adj to steamship docks. 508/548-9744.* Specializes in seafood. Hrs: noon-9 pm. Closed Thanksgiving, Dec 25. Bar. Lunch $4.95-$10.95; dinner $4.95-$10.95. Child's menu. Entertainment: Fri, Sat. Nautical decor. Harbor view. Family-owned. Cr cds: A, MC, V.
D 🖼️

Worcester (C-5)

Settled 1673 **Pop** 169,759 **Elev** 480 ft
Area code 508
Web www.worcester.org
Information Worcester County Convention & Visitors Bureau, 33 Waldo St, 01608; 508/755-7400 or 800/231-7557

The municipal seal of Worcester (WUS-ter) calls it the "Heart of the Commonwealth." One of the largest cities in New England, it is an important industrial center. Also a cultural center, it has some outstanding museums and twelve colleges.

What to See and Do

American Antiquarian Society. Research library is the largest collection of source materials pertaining to the first 250 yrs of American history. Specializing in the period up to 1877, the library has two-thirds of all pieces known to have been printed in this country between 1640 and 1821. (Mon-Fri; closed hols) Guided tours (Wed afternoons, schedule may vary). 185 Salisbury St. Phone 508/755-5221. **FREE**

Blackstone River Valley National Heritage Corridor. This 250,000-acre region extends southward to Providence, RI (see) and incl myriad points of historical and cultural interest. Visitor center at Massachusetts Audubon Society's Broad Meadow Brook Wildlife Sanctuary; tours and interpretive programs. 414 Massasoit Rd. Phone 508/754-7363 or 508/755-8899.

Higgins Armory Museum. Large exhibition of medieval-Renaissance and feudal Japan's arms and armor; paintings, tapestries, stained glass. Armor demonstrations and try-ons. (Tues-Sat, also Sun afternoons; closed hols) 100 Barber Ave. Phone 508/853-6015. ¢¢

New England Science Center. Contains museum with environmental science exhibits; solar/lunar observatory, multimedia planetarium theater, African Hall. Indoor-outdoor wildlife, aquariums; train ride; picnicking. (Daily; closed hols) 222 Harrington Way, 1½ mi E. Phone 508/791-9211. ¢¢¢

Salisbury Mansion. (1772) House of leading businessman and philanthropist Stephen Salisbury. Restored to 1830s appearance. Guided tours. (Thurs-Sun afternoons; closed hols) 40 Highland St. Phone 508/753-8278. ¢

Worcester Art Museum. Fifty centuries of paintings, sculpture, decorative arts, prints, drawings, and photography from America to ancient Egypt; changing exhibits; tours, films, lectures. Cafe, gift shop. (Wed-Sun; closed hols) 55 Salisbury St. Phone 508/799-4406. ¢¢

Worcester Common Outlets. More than 100 outlet stores can be found at this indoor outlet mall. Food court. (Daily) I-290, Exit 16, at 100 Front St. Phone 508/798-2581.

Seasonal Event

Worcester Music Festival of the Worcester County Music Assn. Mechanics Hall. The country's oldest music festival; folkdance companies; choral masterworks; symphony orchestras, guest soloists; young people's program. Seven to 12 concerts. Phone 508/754-3231. Sep-Mar.

Motels/Motor Lodges

★★ **DAYS INN.** *426 Southbridge St (01501), 8 mi S on I-290, Exit 9. 508/832-8300; fax 508/832-4579; toll-free 800/329-7466.* 70 rms, 3 story. June-Oct: S $64-$104; D $71-$114; each addl $10; under 18 free; wkly rates; lower rates rest of yr. Crib free. TV; cable. Complimentary continental bkfst. Ck-out 11 am. Coin lndry. Meeting rms. Valet serv. Some refrigerators. Cr cds: A, C, D, DS, MC, V.
🄳 🕸 🐾 🆂🄲

★★ **HAMPTON INN.** *110 Summer St (01608). 508/757-0400; fax 508/831-9839; toll-free 800/HAMPTON.* 99 rms, 5 story, 10 kits. (no equipt). S, D $55-$85; suites $125. Crib free. Pet accepted. TV; cable (premium); VCR avail. Complimentary bkfst buffet. Restaurant nearby. Ck-out 11 am. Meeting rms. Business servs avail. In-rm modem link. Sundries. Downhill ski 20 mi. Some refrigerators. Lake 3 blks. Cr cds: A, C, D, DS, MC, V.
🄳 🐾 🐀 🕸 🐾 🆂🄲

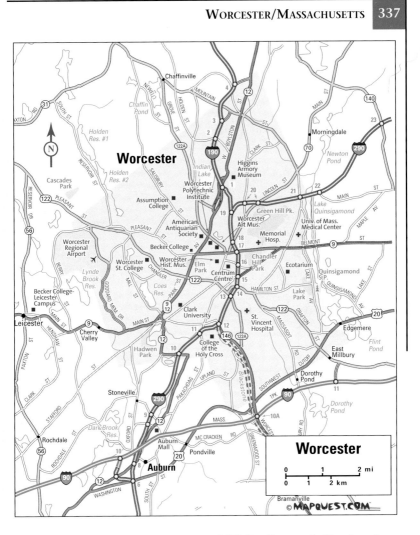

Worcester

© MapQuest.com

★ **WORCHESTER INN AND SUITES.** *50 Oriol Dr (01605), I-290 Exit 20W Or 21E. 508/852-2800; fax 508/852-4605. 114 rms, 3 story. May-Oct: S, D $49-$95; each addl $5; under 18 free; lower rates rest of yr. Crib free. TV; cable. Pool. Playground. Complimentary continental bkfst. Restaurant nearby. Ck-out 11 am. Coin lndry. Meeting rms. Sundries. Lighted tennis. Health club privileges. Some refrigerators. Cr cds: A, D, DS, MC, V.*

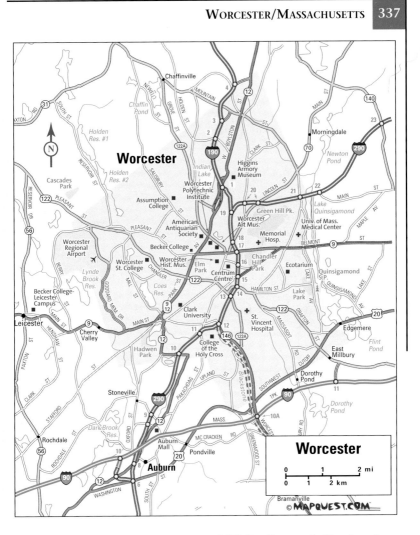

Hotels

★★★ **BEECHWOOD HOTEL.** *363 Plantation St (01605). 508/754-5789; fax 508/752-2060; toll-free 800/344-* *2589. Email www.sales@beechwood hotel.com; www.beechwoodhotel.com. 58 rms, 5 story, 18 suites. S, D $89-$109; each addl $10; suites $119-$139; family rates; higher rates college graduation. Crib free. TV; cable. Restaurant 6:30 am-10 pm. Ck-out 11 am. Business servs avail. Railroad station, bus depot transportation. Downhill/x-country ski 15 mi. Lake 2 blks. Cr cds: A, MC, V.*

★★★ **CROWNE PLAZA WORCESTER.** *10 Lincoln Square (01608), jct I-290 and MA 9. 508/791-1600; fax 508/791-1796; res 800/465-4329. Email gmwor@lodgian.com. 250 rms, 9 story. S $135; D $155; each addl $10; studio rms $135-$155; suites $250-*

$350; under 18 free. Crib free. TV;
cable. 2 pools, 1 indoor; whirlpool,
poolside serv. Restaurant 6:30 am-11
pm. Bar 11-2 am. Ck-out noon. Convention facilities. Bellhops. Valet
serv. Free airport transportation.
Downhill/x-country ski 18 mi. Exercise equipt; sauna. Private patios, balconies. Cr cds: A, MC, V.

D ⚐ ⛵ 🏋 ⚓ SC

Restaurant

★★★ **CASTLE.** *1230 Main St
(01524), 5 mi W on MA 9. 508/892-
9090. www.castlerestaurant.com.* Hrs:
11:30 am-10 pm; Sun from 2 pm.
Closed Mon; Jan 1, Thanksgiving,
Dec 25. Res accepted. Bar. Wine list.
Lunch $8-$25; dinner $20-$45.
Child's menu. Patio dining overlooking lake. Stone replica of 16th-cen-
tury castle complete with medieval
decor. Family-owned. Cr cds: A, C, D,
DS, ER, MC, V.

D

NEW HAMPSHIRE

New Hampshire is a year-round vacation state, offering a variety of landscapes and recreational opportunities within its six unique regions. The lush Lakes Region, dominated by Lake Winnipesaukee, and the Seacoast Region, with its beaches, bays, and historic waterfront towns, are ideal for water sports. The rugged, forested White Mountains offer hiking, camping, dazzling autumn foliage, and excellent skiing. The "little cities" of the Merrimack Valley—Nashua, Manchester, and Concord—are centers of commerce, industry, government, and the arts. Rural 19th-century New England comes alive in the small towns of the Monadnock Region, and many features of these areas come together in the Dartmouth-Lake Sunapee Region, home of Dartmouth College.

Population: 1,109,252
Area: 8,992 square miles
Elevation: 0-6,288 feet
Peak: Mount Washington (Coos County)
Entered Union: Ninth of original 13 states (June 21, 1788)
Capital: Concord
Motto: Live free or die
Nickname: Granite State
Flower: Purple Lilac
Bird: Purple Finch
Tree: White Birch
Time Zone: Eastern
Website: www.visitnh.gov

The mountains in New Hampshire are known for their rugged "notches" (called "gaps" and "passes" elsewhere), and the old valley towns have a serene beauty. Some of the best skiing in the East can be found at several major resorts here. The state's many parks, antique shops, art and theater festivals, and county fairs are also popular attractions, and more than half of New England's covered bridges are in New Hampshire.

David Thomson and a small group of colonists settled on the New Hampshire coast near Portsmouth in 1623. These early settlements were part of Massachusetts. In 1679, they became a separate royal province under Charles the Second. In 1776, the Provincial Congress adopted a constitution making New Hampshire the first independent colony, seven months before the Declaration of Independence was signed.

Although New Hampshire was the only one of the thirteen original states not invaded by the British during the Revolution, its men fought long and hard on land and sea to bring about the victory. This strong, involved attitude continues in New Hampshire to this day. The New Hampshire presidential primary is the first in the nation, and the town meeting is still a working form of government here.

Manufacturing and tourism are the principal businesses here. Electrical and electronic products, machinery, plastics, fabricated metal products, footwear, other leather goods, and instrumentation are manufactured. Farmers sell poultry and eggs, dairy products, apples, potatoes, garden crops, maple syrup, and sugar. Nicknamed the "Granite State," about 200 types of rocks and minerals, including granite, mica, and feldspar, come from New Hampshire's mountains.

When to Go/Climate

New Hampshire experiences typical New England weather—4 distinct seasons with a muddy month or so between winter and spring. Snow in the mountains makes for great skiing in winter; summer temperatures can push up into the 90s.

AVERAGE HIGH/LOW TEMPERATURES (°F)
CONCORD

Jan 30/7	**May** 69/41	**Sep** 72/46
Feb 33/10	**June** 77/51	**Oct** 61/35
Mar 43/22	**July** 80/55	**Nov** 47/27
Apr 56/32	**Aug** 72/46	**Dec** 34/14

MOUNT WASHINGTON

Jan 12/-5	**May** 41/39	**Sep** 46/35
Feb 13/-3	**June** 50/38	**Oct** 36/24
Mar 20/5	**July** 54/43	**Nov** 27/14
Apr 29/16	**Aug** 52/42	**Dec** 17/-6

Parks and Recreation Finder

Directions to and information about the parks and recreation areas below are given under their respective town/city sections. Please refer to those sections for details.

NATIONAL PARK AND RECREATION AREAS

Key to abbreviations. I.H.S. = International Historic Site; I.P.M. = International Peace Memorial; N.B. = National Battlefield; N.B.P. = National Battlefield Park; N.B.C. = National Battlefield and Cemetery; N.C.A. = National Conservation Area; N.E.M. = National Expansion Memorial; N.F. = National Forest; N.G. = National Grassland; N.H.P. = National Historical Park; N.H.C. = National Heritage Corridor; N.H.S. = National Historic Site; N.L. = National Lakeshore; N.M. = National Monument; N.M.P. = National Military Park; N.Mem. = National Memorial; N.P. = National Park; N.Pres. = National Preserve; N.R.A. = National Recreational Area; N.R.R. = National Recreational River; N.Riv. = National River; N.S. = National Seashore; N.S.R. = National Scenic Riverway; N.S.T. = National Scenic Trail; N.Sc. = National Scientific Reserve; N.V.M. = National Volcanic Monument.

Place Name	Listed Under
Saint-Gaudens N.H.S.	HANOVER
White Mountain N.F.	same

STATE PARK AND RECREATION AREAS

Key to abbreviations. I.P. = Interstate Park; S.A.P. = State Archaeological Park; S.B. = State Beach; S.C.A. = State Conservation Area; S.C.P. = State Conservation Park; S.Cp. = State Campground; S.F. = State Forest; S.G. = State Garden; S.H.A. = State Historic Area; S.H.P. = State Historic Park; S.H.S. = State Historic Site; S.M.P. = State Marine Park; S.N.A. = State Natural Area; S.P. = State Park; S.P.C. = State Public Campground; S.R. = State Reserve; S.R.A. = State Recreation Area; S.Res. = State Reservoir; S.Res.P. = State Resort Park; S.R.P. = State Rustic Park.

Place Name	Listed Under
Coleman S.P.	COLEBROOK
Crawford Notch S.P.	BRETTON WOODS
Echo Lake S.P.	NORTH CONWAY
Fort Stark S.H.S.	PORTSMOUTH
Franconia Notch S.P.	same
Greenfield S.P.	PETERBOROUGH
Hampton Beach S.P.	HAMPTON BEACH
Miller S.P.	PETERBOROUGH
Monadnock S.P.	JAFFREY
Moose Brook S.P.	GORHAM

CALENDAR HIGHLIGHTS

MAY

Lilac Time Festival (Franconia). 8 mi W on NH 117, then 4 mi S on US 302, in Lisbon. Celebration of the state flower and observance of Memorial Day. Parade, carnival, vendors, entertainment, special events. Phone 603/436-3988.

JUNE

Portsmouth Jazz Festival (Portsmouth). Two stages with continuous performances on the historical Portsmouth waterfront. Phone 603/436-3988.

Market Square Days (Portsmouth). Summer celebration with 10K road race, street fair, entertainment. Phone 603/436-3988.

JULY

The Old Homestead (Keene). Potash Bowl in Swanzey Center. Drama of life in Swanzey during 1880s based on the Biblical story of the Prodigal Son; first presented in 1886. Phone 603/352-0697.

AUGUST

Mount Washington Valley Equine Classic (North Conway). Horse jumping. Phone Chamber of Commerce, 603/356-3171 or 800/367-3364.

Lakes Region Fine Arts and Crafts Festival (Meredith). Juried show featuring more than 100 New England artists. Music, children's theater, food. Phone Chamber of Commerce 603/279-6121.

League of New Hampshire Craftsmen's Fair (Sunapee). Mt Sunapee State Park. Over 200 craftsmen and artists display and sell goods. Phone 603/224-3375.

SEPTEMBER

New Hampshire Highland Games (Lincoln). Loon Mt. Largest Scottish gathering in Eastern US. Bands, competitions, concerts, workshops. Phone 800/358-SCOT.

Riverfest (Manchester). Outdoor festival with family entertainment, concerts, arts and crafts, food booths, fireworks. Phone 603/623-2623.

Mount Sunapee S.P.	SUNAPEE
Silver Lake S.P.	NASHUA
Wentworth S.P.	WOLFEBORO
White Lake S.P.	CENTER OSSIPEE

Water-related activities, hiking, riding, various other sports, picnicking, and visitor centers, as well as camping, are avail in many of these areas. There is an admission charge at most state parks; children under 12 in family groups are admitted free. Tent camping $12-$20/night; RV camp sites $24-$30/night. For further information contact the New Hampshire Division of Parks & Recreation, PO Box 1856, Concord 03302; 603/271-3556 or 603/271-3628 (camping res).

SKI AREAS

Place Name	Listed Under
Attitash Bear Peak Ski Resort	BARTLETT
Balsams/Wilderness Ski Area	DIXVILLE NOTCH
Black Mountain Ski	JACKSON
Bretton Woods Ski Area	BRETTON WOODS

Cannon Mountain Ski Area	FRANCONIA NOTCH STATE PARK
Dartmouth Skiway Ski Area	HANOVER
Gunstock Recreation Area	LACONIA
Jackson Ski Touring Foundation	JACKSON
King Pine Ski Area	CENTER OSSIPEE
Loon Mountain Recreation Area	LINCOLN/NORTH WOODSTOCK
Mount Cranmore Ski Area	NORTH CONWAY
Mount Sunapee S.P.	SUNAPEE
Pat's Peak Ski Area	CONCORD
Ragged Mountain Ski Area	NEW LONDON
Snowhill at Eastman Ski Area	SUNAPEE
Waterville Valley Ski Area	WATERVILLE VALLEY
Wildcat Ski and Recreation Area	PINKHAM NOTCH

FISHING AND HUNTING

Nonresident season fishing license: $35.50; 15-day, $27.50; 7-day, $23.50; 3-day, $18.50. Nonresident hunting license: $70.50; small game, $36.50; small game 3-day, $17.50; muzzleloader, $28. Combination hunting and fishing license, nonresident: $96. Fees subject to change. For further information and for the *New Hampshire Freshwater and Saltwater Fishing Digests,* pamphlets that summarize regulations, contact the New Hampshire Fish & Game Department, 2 Hazen Dr, Concord 03301; 603/271-3422 or 603/271-3211.

Driving Information

Passengers under 18 years must be in an approved passenger restraint anywhere in vehicle. Children under 4 yrs must be in an approved safety seat anywhere in vehicle. For further information phone 603/271-2131.

INTERSTATE HIGHWAY SYSTEM

The following alphabetical listing of New Hampshire towns in *Mobil Travel Guide* shows that these cities are within 10 miles of the indicated Interstate highways. A highway map should, however, be checked for the nearest exit.

Highway Number	Cities/Towns within 10 miles
Interstate 89	Concord, Hanover, New London, Sunapee.
Interstate 93	Concord, Franconia, Franconia Notch State Park, Franklin, Holderness, Laconia, Lincoln/North Woodstock, Littleton, Manchester, Meredith, Plymouth, Salem.
Interstate 95	Exeter, Hampton Beach, Portsmouth.

Additional Visitor Information

The *New Hampshire Guidebook,* with helpful information on lodging, dining, attractions, and events, is avail from the New Hampshire Office of Travel & Tourism, 172 Pembroke Rd, PO Box 1856, Concord 03302; 603/271-2665 or 800/FUN-IN-NH. For recorded information about events, foliage, and alpine ski conditions phone 800/258-3608.

The League of New Hampshire Craftsmen Foundation offers information on more than 100 galleries, museums, historic sites, craft shops, and craftsmen's studios. Send stamped, self-addressed, business-size envelope to 205 N Main St, Concord 03301.

There are several welcome centers in New Hampshire; visitors who stop by will find information and brochures most helpful in planning stops at points of interest. Open daily: on I-93 at Hooksett, Canterbury, Salem, and Sanborton Boulder; on I-89 at Lebanon, Springfield, and Sutton; on I-95 at Seabrook; and on NH 16 at North Conway. Open Memorial Day-Columbus Day: on NH 9 at Antrim; on US 3 at Colebrook; on US 4 at Epsom; on NH 25 at Rumney; and on US 2 at Shelburne.

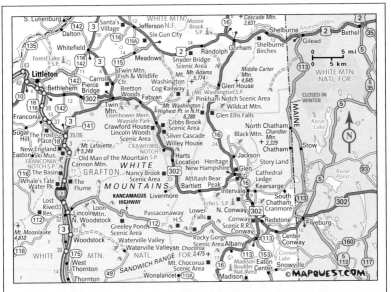

This tour of White Mountains Loop (a national scenic byway) is by
far the most popular in the state. From Boston, take I-93 to
Franconia Notch, where it narrows into Route 3 and offers
turnouts to view landmarks such as the Old Man of the Mountain
(a rocky profile), the tram to the top of Cannon Mountain, The
Flume, and hiking trailheads. Beyond the notch, I-93 and Route 3
divide; follow Route 3 east to Twin Mountain, then go south on
Route 302 to Bretton Woods. This is the departure point for the
Cog Railway to the top of Mount Washington, New England's
highest mountain. The grand Mount Washington Hotel is also here.
The tour continues down through Crawford Notch (features
trailheads and sights like Arethusa Falls) and Bartlett (Attitash Bear
Peak Ski Resort offers a summer Alpine Slide and water slides) to
North Conway. North Conway is the departure point for the
Conway Scenic Railroad and also features a major outlet mall, Echo
Lake State Park, Mount Cranmore ski area, and a summer theater.
From North Conway, backtrack up Route 16, and follow it north
through Pinkham Notch, from which the Mount Washington Auto
Road runs to the top of the mountain. Jackson, a resort village
located just below the notch, offers skiing at Wildcat Mountain and
has a wide selection of lodging. The tourist trail turns east in
Gorham, the town at the top of Pinkham North, and follows the
Androcoggin River into Bethel (ME). An alternative is to stay in
North Conway or Jackson and return to the coast via Route 16,
which joins I-95 at Portsmouth, new Hampshire's old port city.
(Approx 350 mi)

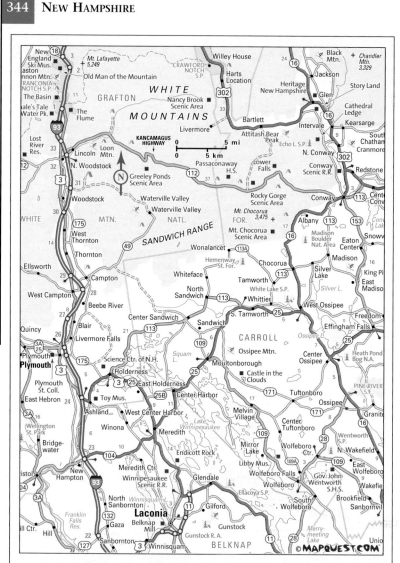

The southwest corner of New Hampshire, known as the Monadnock Region, is popular with travelers from Boston and Rhode Island. Mount Monadnock itself is said to be the second most heavily climbed mountain in the world, and the towns around it are all classic New England villages. From Boston, take Route 2 west to 140 north, then follow Route 12 three miles to Route 202. Arriving in Jaffrey, go west through classic Jaffrey Center to Monadnock State Park and continue on this unnumbered road, passing Dublin Lake and the petting zoo, to Peterborough, where you can take Route 101 to Route 3. The picturesque villages of Hancock, Fitzwilliam, and Greenfield are all within a few miles of this route. **(Approx 150 mi)**

Bartlett

(D-6) See also Bretton Woods, Jackson, North Conway

Pop 2,290 **Elev** 681 ft **Area code** 603
Zip 03812
Information Mount Washington Valley Chamber of Commerce, N Main St, PO Box 2300, North Conway 03860; 603/356-3171

What to See and Do

Attitash Bear Peak Ski Resort. Two high-speed quad, quad, 3 triple, 3 double chairlifts, 2 surface lifts; patrol, school, rentals, snowmaking; nursery, cafeteria, bar. Longest run 1¾ mi; vertical drop 1,750 ft. (Mid-Nov-late Apr, daily) **Summer recreation:** Alpine Slide, water slides, scenic chairlift, horseback riding, mountain biking, hiking, driving range (mid-June-Labor Day, daily; Memorial Day-mid-June and early Sep-mid-Oct, wkends; fees). On US 302. Phone 603/374-2368. ¢¢¢¢

White Mountain National Forest. (see).

Resort

★★ **ATTITASH MOUNTAIN VILLAGE.** *Rte 302 (03812). 603/374-6500; fax 603/374-6509; toll-free 800/862-1600. Email stay@attitashmt village.com; www.attitashmtvillage.com.* 100 rms, 3 story, 100 suites. Jan-Mar, June-Aug: S, D $169; suites $219; lower rates rest of yr. Street parking. Indoor/outdoor pools, lap pool, children's pool, whirlpool. TV; cable, VCR avail. Complimentary coffee in rms. Restaurant 11 am-11 pm. Bar. Ck-out 11 am, ck-in 4 pm. Meeting rms. Business servs avail. Exercise equipt, sauna. Golf. Tennis, 4 courts. Downhill skiing. Supervised children's activities. Hiking trail. Picnic facilities. Cr cds: A, DS, MC, V.
🄳 ⬧ ⬧ ⬧ ⬧ ⬧ ⬧ ⬧ ⬧ ⬧ ⬧

Bretton Woods

See also Franconia, Littleton, Twin Mountain

Settled 1791 **Pop** 10 (est)
Elev 1,600 ft **Area code** 603
Zip 03575

Bretton Woods is located in the heart of the White Mountains, on a long glacial plain in the shadow of Mount Washington (see) and the Presidential Range. Mount Washington was first sighted in 1497; however, settlement around it did not begin until 1771 when the the Crawford Notch, which opened the way through the mountains, was discovered. In the 1770s Governor Wentworth named the area Bretton Woods for his ancestral home in England. This historic name was set aside in 1832 when all the tiny settlements in the area were incorporated under the name of Carroll. For a time, a railroad through the notch brought as many as 57 trains a day and the area grew as a resort spot. A string of hotels sprang up, each more elegant and fashionable than the last. In 1903 the post office, railroad station, and express office reverted to the traditional name—Bretton Woods. Today, Bretton Woods is a resort area at the base of the mountain.

In 1944 the United Nations Monetary and Financial Conference was held here; it established the gold standard at $35 an ounce, organized plans for the International Monetary Fund and World Bank, and chose the American dollar as the unit of international exchange.

What to See and Do

Bretton Woods Ski Area. Quad, triple, 2 double chairlifts, T-bar; patrol, school, rentals, snowmaking; restaurant, cafeteria, bar, child care, lodge. Longest run 2 mi; vertical drop 1,500 ft. (Thanksgiving-Easter, daily) Night skiing (early Dec-Mar, Fri and Sat), 48 mi of cross-country trails. 5 mi E on US 302. Phone 603/278-5000 or 603/278-3333 (snow conditions). ¢¢¢¢

Crawford Notch State Park. One of state's most spectacular passes. Mts

Nancy and Willey rise to the west; Mts Crawford, Webster, and Jackson to the east. Park HQ is at the former site of the Samuel Willey house. He, his family of 6, and 2 hired men died in a landslide in 1826 when they rushed out of their house, which the landslide left untouched. Fishing, trout-feeding pond. Hiking, walking trails on the Appalachian system. Picnicking, concession. Camping (standard fees). Interpretive center. (Late May-mid-Oct) Approx 8 mi SE on US 302. Phone 603/374-2272. In park are

Silver Cascade. A 1,000-ft cataract. N end of Crawford Notch.

Flume Cascade. A 250-ft fall. 3 mi N.

Arethusa Falls. Highest in state; 50 min walk from parking area. 1½ mi SW of US 302, 6 mi N of Bartlett.

Hotel

★★★ MOUNT WASHINGTON HOTEL. *Rte 302 (03575). 603/278-1000; fax 603/278-8838; toll-free 800/258-0330. Email info@mtwashington.com; www.mt washington.com.* 180 rms, 5 story, 20 suites. Feb, Aug-Sep: D $300; suites $500; each addl $70; children $35; under 12 free; lower rates rest of yr. Crib avail. Valet parking avail. Indoor/outdoor pools, whirlpool. TV; cable, VCR avail. Complimentary full bkfst. Restaurant 7 am-9 pm. Bar. Ck-out 11 am, ck-in 3 pm. Meeting rms. Business center. Bellhops. Concierge. Dry cleaning, coin lndry. Gift shop. Exercise privileges, sauna. Golf. Tennis, 12 courts. Downhill skiing. Bike rentals. Supervised children's activities. Hiking trail. Cr cds: A, DS, MC, V.

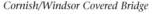

B&Bs/Small Inns

★★★ THE BRETTON ARMS COUNTRY INN. *Rte 302 (03575). 603/278-1000; fax 603/278-8868; toll-free 800/258-0330. Email info@mt washington.com; www.brettonarms.*

com. 31 rms, 3 story, 3 suites. July-Oct: S, D $189; suites $219; lower rates rest of yr. Crib avail. Parking lot. Indoor/outdoor pools, whirlpool. TV; cable (DSS), VCR avail. Restaurant 6-9 pm. Bar. Ck-out 11 am, ck-in 3 pm. Meeting rms. Fax servs avail. Exercise privileges, sauna. Golf. Tennis, 12 courts. Downhill skiing. Bike rentals. Supervised children's activities. Hiking trail. Picnic facilities. Cr cds: A, DS, MC, V.

Cornish/Windsor Covered Bridge

★★ NOTCHLAND INN. *Rte 302 (03812), S on US 302. 603/374-6131; fax 603/374-6168; toll-free 800/866-6131. Email notchland@aol.com; www. notchland.com.* seven rms, 2 story, 6 suites. Sep-Oct, Dec: S $185; D $215; suites $275; lower rates rest of yr. Parking lot. TV; cable (DSS), VCR avail, CD avail. Complimentary full bkfst, coffee in rms, newspaper. Restaurant, closed Mon. Bar. Ck-out 11 am, ck-in 4 pm. Meeting rm. Business center. Concierge. Gift shop. Golf. Downhill skiing. Beach access. Hiking trail. Picnic facilities. Cr cds: A, DS, MC, V.

Restaurant

★ FABYAN'S STATION. *US 302. 603/278-2222.* Specializes in nachos, hamburgers, fresh fish. Hrs: 11:30 am-11:30 pm; hrs vary Apr-mid-June, Oct-late Dec. Bar. Lunch a la carte entrees: $5-$8; dinner a la carte entrees: $7-$14. Child's menu. Converted railway station. Railroad artifacts. Cr cds: A, DS, MC, V.

Center Ossipee

(E-6) *See also Wolfeboro*

Pop 500 (est) **Elev** 529 ft
Area code 603
Web www.ossipeevalley.org
Information Greater Ossipee Area Chamber of Commerce, 127 NH 28, Ossipee, 03864-7300; 603/539-6201 or 800/382-2371

The communities in Ossipee Area are part of a winter and summer sports region centering around Ossipee Lake and the Ossipee Mountains. The mountains also harbor a volcano (dormant for 120 million years) that is considered to be the most perfectly shaped volcanic formation in the world and is rivaled only by a similar formation in Nigeria. A hike up Mount Whittier gives an excellent view of the formation. In the winter, the area comes alive with snowmobiling, dog sledding, cross-country skiing, and other activities.

What to See and Do

King Pine Ski Area. Triple, double chairlifts, 2 J-bars; snowmaking, patrol, school, rentals; night skiing; nursery, snack bar, bar. (Early Dec-late Mar, daily) 11 mi NE via NH 25, 153. Phone 603/367-8896 or 800/367-8897. ¢¢¢¢

Swimming. Ossipee Lake, N and E of village; Duncan Lake, S of village.
Sailing. Silver Lake, N and E of village; also Ossipee Lake. Marinas with small boat rentals.

White Lake State Park. Sandy beach on tree-studded shore. Swimming, trout fishing; hiking, picnicking, concessions, tent camping. (Mid-May-mid-Oct) Snowmobile trails (Dec-Mar). Standard fees. 6 mi N on NH 16. Phone 603/323-7350. June-Aug ¢¢

Colebrook

(B-5) *See also Dixville Notch*

Settled 1770 **Pop** 2,444 **Elev** 1,033 ft
Area code 603 **Zip** 03576
Information North Country Chamber of Commerce, PO Box 1; 603/237-8939

At the west edge of the White Mountains, Colebrook is the gateway to excellent hunting and fishing in the Connecticut Lakes region. The Mohawk and Connecticut rivers join here. Vermont's Mount Monadnock adds scenic beauty.

What to See and Do

Beaver Brook Falls. A scenic glen. 2 mi N on NH 145.

Coleman State Park. On Little Diamond Pond in the heavily timbered Connecticut Lakes region. Lake and stream fishing; picnicking, primitive camping. (Mid-May-mid-Oct) Standard fees. 7 mi E on NH 26, then 5 mi N on Diamond Pond Rd. Phone 603/237-4520.

Columbia Covered Bridge. 75 ft high. 4 mi S on US 3.

Shrine of Our Lady of Grace. Oblates of Mary Immaculate. More than 50 Carrara marble and granite devotional monuments on 25 acres. Special events throughout season. Guided tours (Mother's Day-2nd Sun Oct, daily). 2 mi S on US 3. Phone 603/237-5511. **FREE**

Motel/Motor Lodge

★ **NORTHERN COMFORT MOTEL.** *RR 1, Box 520 (03576), 1 mi S on US 3. 603/237-4440; fax 603/237-4440; res 603/237-4440. Email comfort@ nc1a.net.* 19 rms. S, D $56-$68; each addl $8-$10. Crib free. Pet accepted. TV; cable. Heated pool; whirlpool. Playground. Complimentary continental bkfst June-Sep. Restaurant nearby. Ck-out 11 am. Gift shop. Downhill/x-country ski 12 mi. Exercise equipt. Cr cds: A, DS, MC, V.

D ⊠ ≋ 𝄞 ✈ ⊠ 🔥

Concord

(G-5) *See also Manchester*

Settled 1727 **Pop** 36,006 **Elev** 288 ft
Area code 603 **Zip** 03301
Web www.concordnhchamber.com
Information Chamber of Commerce, 244 N Main St; 603/224-2508

New Hampshire, one of the original 13 colonies, entered the Union in 1788—but its capital was in dispute for another 20 years. Concord finally won the honor in 1808. The state house, begun immediately, was finished in 1819. The legislature is the largest (more than 400 seats) of any state. Concord is the financial center of the state and a center of diversified industry as well.

What to See and Do

Capitol Center for the Arts. Renovated historic theater (1920s) is state's largest. Presents musicals, concerts, dance performances, symphonies, and family entertainment all yr. 44 S Main St. Phone 603/225-1111.

Canterbury Shaker Village. Historic Shaker bldgs; living museum of Shaker crafts, architecture, and inventions. Guided tour of 6 historic bldgs and museum. Restaurant. Gift shop. (May-Oct, daily; Apr and Nov-Dec, Fri-Sun) 15 mi N on I-93 to exit 18, follow signs. 288 Shaker Rd, Canterbury. Phone 603/783-9511. ¢¢¢

Christa McAuliffe Planetarium. Official state memorial to nation's first teacher in space. Changing programs. (Tues-Sun; closed hols, also Apr 12) 3 Institute Dr. I-93 Exit 15E. Phone 603/271-7827. ¢¢

League of New Hampshire Craft-men.
⚑ **Concord Arts & Crafts.** High-quality traditional and contemporary crafts by some of New Hampshire's finest craftsmen; monthly exhibits. (Mon-Sat; closed hols) 36 N Main St. Phone 603/228-8171. **FREE**

Foundation Headquarters. Craft gallery with changing exhibits. Library and resource center for League Foundation members.

(Mon-Fri; closed hols) 205 N Main St. Phone 603/224-1471. **FREE**

Museum of New Hampshire History. Historical museum (founded 1823) with permanent and changing exhibits, incl excellent examples of the famed Concord Coach; museum store. (Tues-Sat, also Sun afternoons). 6 Eagle Sq. Phone 603/226-3189. ¢¢

Pat's Peak Ski Area. Triple, 2 double chairlifts, 2 T-bars, J-bar, pony lift; patrol, school, rentals, ski shop, snowmaking; cafeteria, lounge, nursery. (Dec-late Mar, daily; closed Dec 25) 8 mi N on I-89 to US 202, then 8 mi W to NH 114, then 3 mi S, near Henniker. Phone 603/428-3245. ¢¢¢

Pierce Manse. Home of President Franklin Pierce from 1842-48. Reconstructed and moved to present site; contains many original furnishings and period pieces. (Mid-June-mid-Sep, Mon-Fri; also by appt; closed July 4, Labor Day) 14 Penacook St, 1 mi N of State House. Phone 603/224-0094, 603/224-7668, or 603/225-2068. ¢

State House. Hall of Flags; statues, portraits of state notables. (Mon-Fri; closed hols) Main St; entrance for disabled on Park St. Phone 603/271-2154. **FREE**

Motels/Motor Lodges

★ **BRICK TOWER MOTOR INN.** *414 S Main St (03301). 603/224-9565; fax 603/224-6027.* 51 rms. May-Oct: S $52; D $59-$64; each addl $5; under 12 free; higher rates special events; lower rates rest of yr. Crib free. Pet accepted. TV; cable. Pool. Complimentary continental bkfst. Ck-out 11 am. Some in-rm saunas. Cr cds: A, DS, MC, V.
🐾 ⛱ 🔥 **SC**

★★ **DAYS INN.** *406 S Main St (03301), I-93, Exit 125. 603/224-2511; fax 603/224-6032; toll-free 877/224-2451.* 40 rms, 2 story. July-Sep: S $75; D $85; each addl $10; higher rates: special events, Oct; lower rates rest of yr. Crib free. TV; cable (premium). Pool. Playground. Complimentary continental bkfst. Business servs avail. Ck-out 11 am. Some in-rm whirlpools. Cr cds: A, C, D, DS, MC, V.
⛱ 🏋 ⬆ 🔥

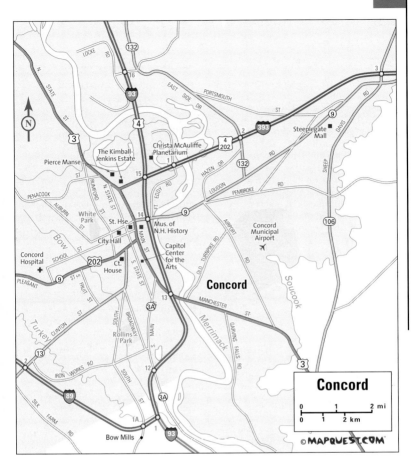

Concord

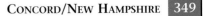

© MAPQUEST.COM

Hotels

★★ **COMFORT INN.** *71 Hall St (03301). 603/226-4100; fax 603/228-2106; res 800/228-5150. Email nhcomfort@aol.com; www.comfortinnconcord.com.* 96 rms, 3 story, 4 suites. May-Oct: S, D $165; suites $250; each addl $10; under 18 free; lower rates rest of yr. Crib avail. Pet accepted, fee. Parking lot. Lap pool, whirlpool. TV; cable (premium). Complimentary continental bkfst, coffee in rms, newspaper, toll-free calls. Restaurant 11 am-10 pm. Ck-out noon, ck-in 3 pm. Meeting rms. Business servs avail. Bellhops. Dry cleaning. Exercise privileges, sauna. Golf, 18 holes. Tennis, 3 courts. Downhill skiing. Video games. Cr cds: A, C, D, DS, ER, JCB, MC, V.

⊡ 🐾 🐕 🕏 🏋 🏊 ⛷ 🎿 ⛷ 🔅 SC

★★ **HAMPTON INN.** *515 South St (03304), on I-89 Exit 1, near jct I-93. 603/224-5322; fax 603/224-4282; res 800/426-7866. Email ccdnh01@hihotel.net.* 145 rms, 4 story. May-Oct: Crib avail. Pet accepted, some restrictions. Parking lot. Indoor pool, whirlpool. TV; cable (premium), VCR avail. Complimentary continental bkfst, coffee in rms, newspaper, toll-free calls. Restaurant nearby. Ck-out noon, ck-in 3 pm. Meeting rms. Dry cleaning, coin lndry. Golf. Tennis. Downhill skiing. Picnic facilities. Cr cds: A, C, D, DS, MC, V.

⊡ 🐾 🕏 🏋 🏊 🎿 ⛷ 🔅

B&B/Small Inn

★★★ **COLBY HILL INN.** *3 The Oaks, Henniker (03242), 17 mi W via US 202 to Henniker, ½ mi W on West-*

ern Ave. 603/428-3281; fax 603/428-9218; toll-free 800/531-0330. Email info@colbyhillinn.com; www.colby hillinn.com. 16 rms, 11 with shower only, 2 story. S $75-$155; D $85-$165; suites $290-$325. Children over 8 yrs only. TV in library; cable. Pool. Complimentary full bkfst. Dining rm (see COLBY HILL INN). Ck-out 11 am, ck-in 2 pm. Downhill/x-country ski 1½ mi. Meeting rm. Business servs avail. In-rm modem link. Lawn games. Some fireplaces. Historic farmhouse (ca 1800) used as tavern, church, meeting house, and private school; sitting rm, antiques. On 5 acres. Totally nonsmoking. Cr cds: A, C, D, DS, MC, V.

⚓ 🛏 🎿 🔥

Restaurants

★★ **COLBY HILL INN.** *3 The Oaks. 603/428-3281. Email info@colbyhill inn.com; www.colbyhillinn.com.* Specializes in tournedos Oscar, chicken Colby Inn, seafood. Hrs: 5:30-8:30 pm; Sun 4:30-7:30 pm. Closed Dec 24, 25. Res accepted. Dinner $18-$34. View of garden. Cr cds: A, D, DS, MC, V.

★ **GRIST MILL.** *520 South St (03304), N on I-89, Exit 1. 603/226-1922.* Specializes in pasta, seafood, bread bowls. Hrs: 11:30 am-10:30 pm. Closed Dec 25. Bar. Bkfst $1.50-$7.95; lunch, dinner $3.99-$12.95. Sun brunch $7.99. Child's menu. On Turkey River. Cr cds: A, DS, MC, V.

[D] 🍽

★ **TIO JUAN'S.** *1 Bicentennial Sq (03301). 603/224-2821.* Specializes in chimichangas, burritos, nachos. Hrs: 4-10 pm; Fri-Sun 3-11 pm. Closed Thanksgiving, Dec 25. Bar. Dinner $4.95-$10.50. Child's menu. Entertainment: guitarist Tues, Thurs. Old Concord police station; cells converted to private rms. Cr cds: A, DS, MC, V.

[D] [SC]

Dixville Notch

(B-5) *See also Colebrook*

Pop 30 (est) **Elev** 1,990 ft
Area code 603 **Zip** 03576

The small village of Dixville Notch shares its name with the most northerly of the White Mountain passes. The Notch cuts through the mountain range between Kidderville and Errol. At its narrowest point, east of Lake Gloriette, is one of the most impressive views in the state. Every four years Dixville Notch is invaded by the national news media, who report the nation's first presidential vote tally shortly after midnight on election day.

What to See and Do

Balsams/Wilderness Ski Area. Chairlift, 2 T-bars; patrol, school, rentals; restaurant, cafeteria, nursery, resort (see). Longest run 2 mi; vertical drop 1,000 ft. (Dec-Mar, daily) Cross-country trails. On NH 26. Phone 603/255-3400, 800/255-0600 (snow conditions exc NH), or 800/255-0800 (snow conditions NH). ¢¢¢¢

Table Rock. Views of New Hampshire, Maine, Vermont, and Québec. ¾ mi S of NH 26, ½ mi E of village of Dixville Notch.

Resort

★★★★ **THE BALSAMS.** *Rte 26 (03576). 603/255-3400; fax 603/255-4221; toll-free 800/255-0600. Email thebalsams@aol.com; www.thebal-sams.com.* 185 rms, 20 suites. July-Aug: S $375; D $470; suites $675; lower rates rest of yr. Crib avail. Valet parking avail. Pool, lifeguard. TV; cable (DSS). Complimentary full bkfst, newspaper. Restaurant. Bar. Ck-out noon, ck-in 4 pm. Meeting rms. Business center. Bellhops. Concierge. Dry cleaning. Gift shop. Salon/barber avail. Exercise equipt, steam rm. Golf. Tennis, 6 courts. Downhill skiing. Bike rentals. Supervised children's activities. Hiking trail. Cr cds: A, DS, MC, V.

[D] 🎱 ⚓ 🎾 ⛳ 🛏 🏃 🎿 🔥 🚶

Dover

(G-6) *See also Portsmouth*

Settled 1623 **Pop** 25,042 **Elev** 57 ft
Area code 603 **Zip** 03820
Web www.dovernh.org
Information Chamber of Commerce, 299 Central Ave; 603/742-2218

With its historic trails and homes, Dover is the oldest permanent settlement in New Hampshire. The town contains the only known existing Colonial garrison.

What to See and Do

Woodman Institute. Garrison House (1675), only garrison in New Hampshire, now visible in nearly its original form. Woodman House (1818), residence of the donor, is now a natural history museum with collections of minerals, Native American artifacts, and displays of mammals, fish, amphibians, reptiles, birds, insects; war memorial rms. Senator John P. Hale House (1813) contains articles of Dover history and antique furniture. (Apr-Jan, Wed-Sun afternoons; closed hols) 182-190 Central Ave, ½ mi S on NH 108. Phone 603/742-1038. ¢¢

Seasonal Event

Cocheco Arts Festival. Mid-July-late Aug.

Motels/Motor Lodges

★★ **DAYS INN.** *481 Central Ave (03820).* 603/742-0400; fax 603/742-7790; res 800/-DAYSINN. Email sleep well@dover-durham-daysinn.com; www. dover-durham-daysinn.com. 50 rms, 3 story, 14 suites. May-Oct: S, D $99; suites $169; each addl $10; under 12 free; lower rates rest of yr. Crib avail. Pet accepted, some restrictions. Parking lot. Indoor pool. TV; cable. Complimentary continental bkfst, newspaper. Restaurant 11 am-midnight. Ck-out 2 pm, ck-in 11 am. Meeting rm. Dry cleaning, coin lndry. Salon/barber avail. Golf, 9 holes. Tennis, 2 courts. Downhill skiing. Hiking trail. Picnic facilities. Cr cds: A, C, D, DS, ER, JCB, MC, V.
D 🔄 🏊 🎿 🚶 🐾 🎣 📶 🐾 🅂🄲

★★★ **NEW ENGLAND CENTER HOTEL.** *15 Strafford Ave (03824),* approx 2 mi S on NH 108, 3 mi W on US 4, 1 mi S on Madbury Rd to Edgewood Rd, on University of NH campus. 603/862-2801; fax 603/862-4897; res 800/590-4334. Email neck.info@unh. edu. 115 rms, 8 story. July-Oct: S $70-$90; D $80-$110; suites $120-$150; lower rates rest of yr. TV; cable (premium), VCR avail. Indoor/outdoor pool privileges. Restaurant 7 am-10 pm. Bar 11 am-11 pm. Ck-out noon. Meeting rms. Business servs avail. Sundries. Tennis privileges. Health club privileges. On 10 wooded acres. Cr cds: A, DS, MC, V.
D 🎣 📶 🐾

B&Bs/Small Inns

★★ **SILVER STREET INN.** *103 Silver St (03820).* 603/743-3000; fax 603/749-5673. 10 rms, 2 share bath, 3 story. May-mid-Oct: S $79; D $89; each addl $10; under 15 free; lower rates rest of yr. Crib free. TV; cable. Complimentary full bkfst. Restaurant nearby. Ck-out 11 am. Business servs avail. Victorian house built ca 1880 for local businessman. Cr cds: A, DS, V.
D 🐾

★★★ **THREE CHIMNEYS INN.** *17 Newmarket Rd (03824).* 603/868-7800; fax 603/868-2964; toll-free 888/399-9777. Email chimney3@3chimneys inn.com; www.threechimneysinn.com. 23 rms, 4 story. Apr-June, Aug-Oct: S, D $209; suites $209; each addl $25; lower rates rest of yr. Parking lot. TV; cable. Complimentary full bkfst, coffee in rms, newspaper. Restaurant 5-9 pm. Bar. Ck-out 11 am, ck-in 4 pm. Meeting rms. Business servs avail. Concierge. Golf, 12 holes. Tennis, 10 courts. Cr cds: A, D, DS, MC, V.
D 🐾 🎿 🚶 🎣 📶 🐾

Restaurants

★★ **FIREHOUSE ONE.** *1 Orchard St (03820).* 603/749-2220. www.firehouse one.com. Specializes in seafood, prime rib, vegetarian dishes. Hrs: 11:30 am-9:30 pm; Mon, Tues 5-9 pm; Sat from 5 pm; Sun 10 am-9 pm. Closed Dec 25. Res accepted; required hols. Bar. Lunch a la carte entrees: $4-$8; dinner a la carte entrees: $8-$18. Sun brunch $8.95. Child's menu. Old restored firehouse (1840); arched doors and windows, tin walls and ceilings, overstuffed chairs. Cr cds: A, D, DS, MC, V.

D ▣

★ ★ ★ **MAPLES.** *17 Newmarket Rd (03824). 603/868-7800. www.three chimneysinn.com.* Specializes in lamb, pastries. Hrs: 6-10 pm. Res accepted. Beer, wine, extensive wine list. Dinner $25-$30. Lot. Smart casual. Cr cds: A, D, DS, MC, V.

D 🔥

★ **NEWICK'S SEAFOOD.** *431 Dover Point Rd (03820). 603/742-3205. www.newicks.com.* Specializes in seafood. Hrs: 11 am-9 pm; hrs vary off-season. Closed Thanksgiving, Dec 25. Lunch, dinner $1.95-$16.95. Serv bar. Seafood market. Gift shop. Nautical accents; overlooks Great Bay. Cr cds: A, D, MC, V.

D ▣

Exeter

(H-6) *See also Hampton Beach, Portsmouth*

Settled 1638 **Pop** 12,481 **Elev** 40 ft **Area code** 603 **Zip** 03833
Web www.exeterarea.org
Information Exeter Area Chamber of Commerce, 120 Water St; 603/772-2411

A venerable preparatory school and Colonial houses belie Exeter's radical history. It had its beginnings in religious nonconformity, led by Reverend John Wheelwright and Anne Hutchinson, both of whom were banished from Massachusetts for heresy. There was an anti-British scuffle in 1734 and by 1774 Exeter was burning Lord North in effigy and talking of liberty. It was made the capital of the state during the Revolution, since there were too many Tories in Portsmouth. Exeter is the birthplace of Daniel Chester French and John Irving.

What to See and Do

American Independence Museum. Site of Revolutionary War-era state treasury bldg; grounds house Folsom Tavern (1775). (May-Oct, Wed-Sun) 1 Governors Ln. Phone 603/772-2622. ¢¢

Gilman Garrison House. (1676-90) Built as a fortified garrison with hewn logs; pulley arrangement to raise and lower door still in place. Substantially remodeled in mid-18th century; wing added with 17th- and 18th-century furnishings. (June-mid-Oct, Tues, Thurs, Sat, and Sun) 12 Water St. Phone 603/436-3205. ¢¢

League of New Hampshire Craftsmen/Exeter. Work in all media by New Hampshire's finest artisans. (Mon-Sat) 61 Water St. Phone 603/778-8282. **FREE**

Phillips Exeter Academy. (1781) 990 students. On 400 acres with more than 100 bldgs. Co-ed school for grades 9-12. Founded by John Phillips, who sought a school for "students from every quarter"; known for its student diversity. On campus are a contemporary library (1971), designed by Louis I. Kahn, the Frederick R. Mayer Art Center, and the Lamont Art Gallery. Phone 603/772-4311.

B&B/Small Inn

★ ★ **INN OF EXETER.** *90 Front St (03833). 603/772-5901; fax 603/778-8757; res 800/267-0525; toll-free 800/782-8444. Emailinfo@innofexeter. com.* 46 rms, 3 story. Mid-June-mid-Nov: S $69-$105; D $79-$125; each addl $15; suites $165; lower rates rest of yr. Crib $7.50. TV; cable. Dining rm 7 am-9 pm; Sat, Sun to 10 pm. Bar 11:45 am-midnight. Ck-out 11 am, ck-in 2 pm. Meeting rm. Business servs avail. Valet serv. On campus of Phillips Exeter Academy. Cr cds: A, DS, MC, V.

D 🔥

Franconia

(D-4) *See also Littleton*

Pop 811 **Elev** 971 ft **Area code** 603 **Zip** 03580

Information Franconia Notch Chamber of Commerce, PO Box 780; 603/823-5661

What to See and Do

Franconia Notch State Park. (see) Approx 7 mi SE via NH 18 & I-93 (Franconia Notch State Pkwy).

Frost Place. Two furnished rms of Robert Frost's home open to public; memorabilia; poetry trail; 25-min video. (July-Columbus Day, Wed-Mon afternoons; Memorial Day-June, Sat and Sun afternoons) 1 mi S on NH 116 to Bickford Hill Rd, right over bridge, left at fork, on to Ridge Rd. Phone 603/823-5510. ¢¢

New England Ski Museum. Details history of skiing in the east; exhibits feature skis and bindings, clothing, art, photographs, and vintage films. Gift shop. (Late May-mid-Oct, daily; Dec-late Mar, Fri-Tues; closed Dec 25) Franconia Notch Pkwy (US 3) exit 2, near Cannon Mt Tramway. Phone 603/823-7177. **FREE**

White Mountain National Forest. (see) SE on NH 18.

Annual Event

Lilac Time Festival. 8 mi W on NH 117, then 4 mi S on US 302, in Lisbon. Celebration of the state flower and observance of Memorial Day. Parade, carnival, vendors, entertainment, special events. Phone 603/431-5388. Late May.

Motels/Motor Lodges

★ **GALE RIVER.** *1 Main St (03580), ½ mi N on NH 18.* 603/823-5655; *fax 603/823-5280; toll-free 800/255-7989. Email galermtl@together.net.* 10 rms, 1 story. Sep-Oct: S, D $82; lower rates rest of yr. Crib avail. Pet accepted, fee. Parking lot. Pool. TV; cable. Complimentary coffee in rms. Restaurant. Ck-out 11 am, ck-in 12 pm. Golf. Downhill skiing. Bike rentals. Hiking trail. Picnic facilities. Cr cds: A, DS, MC, V.

★ ★ ★ **RED COACH INN.** *87 Wallace Hill Rd (03580), I-93 Exit 38.* 603/823-7422; *fax 603/823-5638.* 60 rms, 2 story. S $55-$65; D $70-$110; under 12 free; ski plan; lower rates off season. Crib $5. TV; cable (premium), VCR avail. Indoor pool; whirlpool. Complimentary continental bkfst. Restaurant 6-10:30 am, 5:30-9 pm; hrs vary off season. Meeting rms. Business servs avail. Gift shop. Beauty shop. Downhill ski 4 mi; x-country ski 3 mi. Exercise equipt; sauna. Game rm. Cr cds: A, DS, MC, V.

★ **STONYBROOK MOTEL & LODGE.** *1098 Profile Rd; Rte 18 (03580), 1¼ mi S on NH 18.* 603/823-8192; *fax 603/823-8196.* 23 rms. Some A/C. S, D $59-$75; each addl $7; under 18 free; wkly rates; ski plan; higher rates fall foliage, hol wkends. Crib free. TV; cable. 2 pools, 1 indoor. Playground. Complimentary coffee in rms. Ck-out 11 am. Downhill/x-country ski 2 mi. Game rm. Rec rm. Lawn games. Some refrigerators. Picnic tables, grills. Pond, stream. Cr cds: DS, MC, V.

B&Bs/Small Inns

★ ★ **FOXGLOVE INN.** *Rte 117 (03580), N on NH 18 to NH 117, 3 mi W on NH 117.* 603/823-8840; *fax 603/823-5755; res 888/343-2220. Email foxgloveinn@compuserve.com.* 6 rms, 2 story. No A/C. Rm phone avail. S $75; D $85-$125; ski plans; higher rates foliage season. Children over 12 yrs only. Cable TV avail, VCR avail. Complimentary full bkfst; afternoon refreshments. Ck-out 10 am, ck-in 3 pm. Business servs avail. Downhill ski 5 mi; x-country ski 1 mi. Renovated turn-of-the-century house with cozy rms. Totally nonsmoking. Cr cds: MC, V.

★ ★ ★ **FRANCONIA INN.** *1300 Easton Rd (03580), 2⅛ mi S on NH 116.* 603/823-5542; *fax 603/823-8078; toll-free 800/473-5299. Email info@franconiainn.com; www.franconia inn.com.* 32 rms, 3 story, 6 suites. Feb, July-Oct, Dec: S $86; D $96; suites $146; each addl $10; children $5; under 12 free; lower rates rest of yr. Crib avail. Parking lot. Pool, whirlpool. TV; cable, VCR avail, CD avail. Complimentary coffee in rms, toll-free calls. Restaurant. Bar. Ck-out 11 am, ck-in 3 pm. Meeting rms. PC avail.

Concierge. Golf. Tennis, 4 courts. Downhill skiing. Bike rentals. Supervised children's activities. Hiking trail. Picnic facilities. Cr cds: A, DS, MC, V.

⊡ 🖲 ♿ ⊠ 🛇 🛉 ⊨ 🛏 🐾 **SC**

★★ **HILLTOP INN.** *1348 Main St (03585), 2¼ mi W on NH 117. 603/ 823-5695; fax 603/823-5518; toll-free 800/770-5695.* 6 rms, 2 story, 1 suite. No A/C. No rm phones. S, D $90-$195; each addl $35-$50; suite $90-$130; wkly rates; higher rates fall foliage (2-day min). Pet accepted; $10/day. TV in sitting rm; cable. Complimentary full bkfst; afternoon refreshments. Ck-out 11 am, ck-in 2-6 pm. Downhill ski 8 mi; x-country ski on site. Built 1895; antiques, quilts. Cr cds: A, DS, MC, V.

🐾 🛇 ✈ 🛏 🐾

★ **THE HORSE & HOUND INN.** *205 Wells Rd (03580). 603/823-5501; fax 603/823-5501; toll-free 800/450-5501.* 9 rms, 2 story. Sep-Oct: S $88; D $100; each addl $15; children $15; under 6 free; lower rates rest of yr. Crib avail, fee. Pet accepted, some restrictions, fee. Street parking. TV; cable, VCR avail, CD avail, VCR avail. Complimentary full bkfst, toll-free calls. Restaurant 6-8 pm. Bar. Ck-out 11 am, ck-in 4 pm. Fax servs avail. Golf. Downhill skiing. Hiking trail. Cr cds: A, C, D, DS, MC, V.

🐾 🛇 🛉 🐾

★★ **INN AT FOREST HILLS.** *NH 142 (03580). 603/823-9550; fax 603/823-8701; toll-free 800/280-9550. Email mobil@innfhills.com; www.inn at foresthills.com.* 7 rms, 2 with shower only, 3 story. No A/C. No rm phones. S $85-$105; D $90-$110; each addl $25; ski plans; hols (2-day min); higher rates foliage season. Children over 11 yrs only. TV; cable, VCR avail (movies). Complimentary full bkfst. Ck-out 11 am, ck-in 3-6 pm. Tennis. Downhill ski 5 mi; x-country ski on site. Cottage built in 1890; large front porch, solarium. Totally non-smoking. Cr cds: MC, V.

🖲 🛇 🛉 🛏 🐾

★ **LOVETTS INN.** *1474 Profile Rd (03580), 2 mi S at jct NH 18 and 142. 603/823-7761; fax 603/823-8802; res 603/823-7761; toll-free 800/356-3802. Email lovetts@ncia.net.* 6 rms, 5 with bath, 2 story; 16 guest cottages. Some A/C. S $100-$150; D $140-$190; MAP avail; package plans.

Closed Apr. Crib avail. Pet accepted. TV. Pool. Restaurant (see LOVETT'S INN BY LAFAYETTE BROOK). Bar 6-10 pm. Box lunches. Ck-out 11 am, ck-in after 2 pm. Free bus depot transportation. Downhill ski 3 mi; x-country ski on site. Game rm. Rec rm. Lawn games. Fireplaces in cottages. Historic resort-type inn (1784); on 10 acres with trout pond, streams. Cr cds: A, DS, MC, V.

⊡ 🐾 🖲 🛏 🛏 🐾

★★ **SUGAR HILL INN.** *Rte 117 (03580), ½ mi W on NH 117. 603/ 823-5621; fax 603/823-5639; toll-free 800/548-4748. Email info@sugarhill inn.com; www.sugarhillinn.com.* 10 rms, 2 story, 2 suites. Sep-Oct: D $195; suites $295; each addl $35; under 12 free; lower rates rest of yr. Parking lot. TV; cable. Complimentary full bkfst, coffee in rms, newspaper, toll-free calls. Restaurant. Business servs avail. Gift shop. Whirlpool. Golf, 9 holes. Tennis. Downhill skiing. Bike rentals. Hiking trail. Cr cds: A, MC, V.

🛇 🛉 🛉 🛏 🐾

★★ **SUNSET HILL HOUSE — A GRAND INN.** *231 Sunset Hill Rd (03585), 2 mi W on NH 117. 603/823-5522; fax 603/823-5738; toll-free 800/ 786-4455. Email innkeeper@sunsethill house.com; www.sunsethillhouse.com.* 26 rms, 3 story, 2 suites. Sep-Oct: S $230; D $250; suites $425; each addl $30; children $20; under 11 free; lower rates rest of yr. Crib avail, fee. Parking lot. Pool, whirlpool. TV; cable, VCR avail. Complimentary full bkfst, coffee in rms, newspaper, toll-free calls. Restaurant 5:30-10 pm. Bar. Ck-out 11 am, ck-in 3 pm. Meeting rm. Business center. Concierge. Gift shop. Golf, 9 holes. Tennis, 5 courts. Downhill skiing. Bike rentals. Hiking trail. Picnic facilities. Cr cds: A, D, DS, MC, V.

⊡ 🛇 🛉 🛉 🛏 🛏 🐾 🛉

Restaurants

★★★ **THE FRANCONIA INN.** *1300 Easton Rd. 603/823-5542. Email info@franconiainn.com; www.franconia inn.com.* Specializes in bouillabaisse, rack of lamb, seafood. Own desserts. Hrs: 6-9 pm; hrs vary off-season. Closed Apr-mid-May, Nov. Res accepted. Bar. Dinner $17-$21. Child's menu. Cr cds: A, MC, V.

⊡

★ ★ **HORSE & HOUND.** *205 Wells Rd, off NH 18.* 603/823-5501. Hrs: 6-8 pm. Closed Sun-Tues; Apr-mid-May, mid-Oct-late Nov; also Wed mid-May-July 4. Res accepted. Bar. Dinner $17-$25. Child's menu. Cr cds: A, D, DS, MC, V.

★ ★ **LOVETT'S INN BY LAFAYETTE BROOK.** *1474 Profile Rd.* 603/823-7761. *www.lovettsinn. com.* African menu. Specializes in veal, roast mountain duck. Own baking. Hrs: 6-9 pm. Closed Apr. Res required. Bar. Historic bldg. Cr cds: A, DS, MC, V.

SC

★ ★ **POLLY'S PANCAKE PARLOR.** *672 NH 117 (03585), I-93 Exit 38.* 603/823-5575. Specializes in whole grain pancakes, waffles, sandwiches. Own soups, sausage, desserts. Hrs: 7 am-3 pm; hrs vary Apr, Nov. Closed Thanksgiving-Mar. Res accepted. Bkfst a la carte entrees: $6-$18; lunch, dinner a la carte entrees: $6-$18. Child's menu. In converted carriage shed (1840). Early American decor; antiques. Family-owned. Cr cds: A, DS, MC, V.

Franconia Notch State Park

See also Franconia, Lincoln/North Woodstock Area

(Approx 7 mi SE of Franconia via NH 18 and I-93/Franconia Notch State Pkwy)

This seven-mile pass and state park, a deep valley of 6,440 acres between the Franconia and Kinsman ranges of the White Mountains, has been a top tourist attraction since the mid-19th century. Mounts Liberty (4,460 ft), Lincoln (5,108 ft), and Lafayette (5,249 ft) loom on the east, and Cannon Mountain (4,200 ft) presents a sheer granite face. The Pemigewasset River follows the length of the Notch.

The park offers various recreational activities, including swimming at sandy beach, fishing and boating on Echo Lake (jct NH 18 and I-93 Exit 3); hiking, eight-mile paved bike path through Notch, skiing, picnicking, camping. Fees for some activities. For further information contact Franconia Notch State Park, Franconia 03580; 603/823-5563.

What to See and Do

The Basin. Deep glacial pothole, 20 ft in diameter, at foot of a waterfall, polished smooth by sand, stones, and water. W of I-93 (Franconia Notch State Pkwy), S of Profile Lake.

Cannon Mountain Ski Area. Tramway, quad, triple, 2 double chairlifts, pony lift; patrol, school, rentals, snowmaking; cafeterias, bar (beer and wine), nursery. New England Ski Museum. Longest run 2 mi; vertical drop 2,146 ft. (Late Nov-mid-Apr, daily; closed Dec 25) Tramway rising 2,022 ft vertically over a distance of 1 mi in 6 min, also operates Memorial Day-mid-Oct, daily and on wkends rest of yr (weather permitting). 5 mi S of Franconia via NH 18 and I-93 (Franconia Notch State Pkwy), Exit 2 or 3. Phone 603/823-5563 or 800/552-1234 (snow conditions). Winter ¢¢¢¢; Summer ¢¢

Flume Gorge and Park Information Center. Narrow, natural gorge and waterfall along the flank of Mt Liberty, accessible by stairs and walks; picnicking. Mountain flowers and mosses, Liberty Gorge, the Cascades, covered bridges. Information Center offers 15-min movie introducing park every ½-hr. Interpretive exhibits. Gift shop, cafeteria. (Mid-May-late Oct, daily) 15 mi S of Franconia, I-93 (Franconia Notch State Pkwy), Exit 1. Phone 603/745-8391. ¢¢

Lafayette Campground. Fishing; hiking on Appalachian trail system, picnicking, camping. Fees for some activities. (Mid-May-mid-Oct, daily) 9 mi S of Franconia Village, off I-93 (Franconia Notch State Pkwy). Phone 603/823-9513. ¢¢¢

Old Man of the Mountains. Discovered in 1805, this craggy likeness of a man's face is formed naturally of 5 layers of granite and is 40 ft high; also known as the "Great Stone Face." 1,200 ft above Profile Lake, W of I-93 (Franconia Notch State Pkwy), Exit 2.

Franklin

(F-5) *See also Laconia*

Settled 1764 **Pop** 8,304 **Elev** 335 ft
Area code 603 **Zip** 03235

Franklin was named in 1828 for Benjamin Franklin; until then it was a part of Salisbury. It is the birthplace of Daniel Webster, lawyer, senator, and statesman. The Pemigewasset and Winnipesaukee rivers, joining to form the Merrimack, provide the city with abundant water power.

What to See and Do

Congregational Christian Church. (1820) Church that Daniel Webster attended; tracker action organ. A bust of Webster by Daniel Chester French is outside. (Wed and Thurs mornings, Sun, also by appt) 47 S Main St, on US 3. Phone 603/934-4242. **FREE**

Lakes Region Factory Stores. More than 45 outlet stores. (Daily) Approx 5 mi E on US 3, in Tilton. Phone 603/286-7880.

Motel/Motor Lodge

★ **SUPER 8.** *7 Tilton Rd (03276), 3 mi E on US 3. 603/286-8882; fax 603/286-8788; toll-free 800/800-8000.* 62 rms, 2 story. July-mid-Oct: S $56.88; D $59.88; under 12 free; higher rates special events; lower rates rest of yr. Crib free. TV; cable, VCR avail (movies). Complimentary coffee in lobby. Restaurant adj 6 am-11 pm. Ck-out 11 am. Business servs avail. Sundries. Downhill ski 5 mi. Cr cds: A, DS, MC, V.
🐾 ⊠ 🔥 🏃

B&Bs/Small Inns

★★★ **HIGHLAND LAKE INN.** *32 Maple St (03231), 5 mi W on NH 11. 603/735-6426; fax 603/735-5355. www.highlandlake-inn.com.* 10 rms, shower only, 3 story. No rm phones. S, D $85-$100; each addl $20; 2-day min wkends; higher rates racing wkends, fall foliage, graduation. Children over 8 yrs only. TV in parlor; cable, VCR avail (movies). Complimentary full bkfst. Ck-out 11 am, ck-in 3 pm. Business servs avail. Downhill/x-country ski 5 mi. Lawn games. Picnic tables. On lake. Farm house built in 1767. Totally nonsmoking. Cr cds: A, DS, MC, V.
🐾 ⊠ 🔥

Old Man of the Mountains, Franconia

★★ **MARIA ATWOOD INN.** *71 Hill Rd; Rte 3A (03235), N of jct US 11 and NH 3A. 603/934-3666. Email atwoodinn@cyberportal.net; www.atwoodinn.com.* 7 rms, 3 story. June-Oct: S $65; D $90; lower rates rest of yr. Crib avail. Parking lot. TV; cable, VCR avail, VCR avail. Complimentary full bkfst, coffee in rms, newspaper. Restaurant nearby. Ck-out noon, ck-in 3 pm. Business center. Golf. Cr cds: A, DS, MC, V.
🏃 🔥 🏃

Restaurants

★ **MR D'S.** *428 N Main St (03235), at jct US 11 and NH 3A. 603/934-3142.* Specializes in seafood, steak. Own soups. Hrs: 6 am-8 pm; Fri to 9 pm; Sat to 8:30 pm; Sun from 8 am. Closed hols. Bkfst $1.75-$5.95; lunch $3-$9; dinner $5-$12. Child's menu. Collection of old-fashioned photographs on walls. Cr cds: A, D, DS, MC, V.
D ⊠

★ ★ ★ **OLIVER'S.** *4 Sanborn Rd (03276), approx 3 mi E on NH 11/US 3, at NH 132.* 603/286-7379. *www. oliversrestaurantpub.com.* Specializes in veal, pasta, fresh seafood. Hrs: 11 am-9 pm; Fri, Sat to 10 pm. Res accepted. Bar. Lunch $5.95-$8.95; dinner $9.95-$16.95. Child's menu. Entertainment: Thurs. Country decor; some antiques. Cr cds: A, DS, MC, V.

D

Gorham (C-6)

Settled 1805 **Pop** 3,173 **Elev** 801 ft
Area code 603 **Zip** 03581
Web www.northernwhitemountains. com

Information Northern White Mountains Chamber of Commerce, 164 Main St, PO Box 298, Berlin 03570; 603/752-6060

Commanding the northeast approaches to the Presidential Range of the White Mountains, at the north end of Pinkham Notch (see), Gorham has magnificent views and is the center for summer and winter sports. The Peabody River merges with the Androscoggin in a series of falls. A Ranger District office of the White Mountain National Forest (see) is located here.

What to See and Do

Dolly Copp Campground. Fishing; hiking, picnicking, 176 campsites. 6 mi S on NH 16 in White Mountain National Forest (see). Contact the District Ranger, USDA Forest Service, 80 Glen Rd. Phone 603/466-2713 or 603/466-3984 (camping). ¢¢¢-¢¢¢¢

Libby Memorial Pool and Recreation Area. Natural pool, bathhouses; picnicking. (Summer, daily, weather permitting) ¼ mi S on NH 16. Phone 603/466-9401. ¢

Moose Brook State Park. Views of the Presidential Range of the White Mts; good stream fishing area. Swimming, bathhouse; picnicking, camping, hiking to Randolph Range. (Late May-early Sep) Standard fees. 2 mi W on US 2. Phone 603/466-3860.

Moose Tours. Daily tours leave each evening from the Gorham Informational Booth on a specified route to locate moose for sighting. (Late May-mid-Oct) Main St. Phone 603/752-6060 or 603/466-3103 (departure times). ¢¢¢

Mount Washington. (see) 10 mi S on NH 16.

Motels/Motor Lodges

★ **GORHAM MOTOR INN.** *324 Main St (03581).* 603/466-3381; fax 603/752-2604; toll-free 800/445-0913. 39 rms. S $38-$72; D $42-$84; each addl $6; higher rates fall foliage. Crib free. Pet accepted, some restrictions; $6. TV; cable (premium). Pool. Restaurant nearby. Ck-out 11 am. Downhill/x-country ski 8 mi. Some refrigerators. Cr cds: A, DS, MC, V.

D 🐾 ⚓ 🏊 🖥 🔥

★ ★ **MADISON.** *365 Main St (03581), on US 2.* 603/466-3622; fax 603/466-3664; toll-free 800/851-1136. Email madison@ncia.net. 33 rms, 2 story. May-Oct: S, D $52-$70; each addl $5; higher rates foliage season. Closed rest of yr. Crib $5. TV; cable. Heated pool. Playground. Restaurant opp. Ck-out 11 am. Some refrigerators. Balconies. Cr cds: A, DS, MC, V.

D 🏊 🖥 🔥

★ ★ **ROYALTY INN.** *130 Main St (03581).* 603/466-3312; fax 603/466-5802; toll-free 800/437-3529. Email innkeeper@royaltyinn.com; www.royalty inn.com. 90 rms, 2 story, 2 suites. July-Oct: S $79; D $86; suites $91; each addl $5; children $5; under 3 free; lower rates rest of yr. Crib avail, fee. Pet accepted, fee. Parking lot. Indoor/outdoor pools, lap pool, children's pool, whirlpool. TV; cable (premium), VCR avail. Restaurant. Bar. Ck-out 11 am, ck-in 2 pm. Meeting rms. Business servs avail. Coin lndry. Exercise rm, sauna. Golf, 18 holes. Tennis, 3 courts. Downhill skiing. Bike rentals. Supervised children's activities. Hiking trail. Cr cds: A, C, D, DS, MC, V.

D 🐾 🎿 🚲 ⛳ 🏌 🏊 🎾 ✈ 🖥 🔥

★ ★ ★ **TOWN & COUNTRY MOTOR INN.** *US 2 (03581), ½ mi E.* 603/466-3315; fax 603/466-3318. 160 rms, 2 story. June-Oct: S $48-$64; D $56-$70; each addl $6; suites $70-

$82; golf and ski plans; lower rates rest of yr. Crib $6. Pet accepted. TV; cable, VCR avail. Indoor/outdoor pool; whirlpool. Restaurant 6-10:30 am, 5:30-10 pm. Bar 4:00 pm-12:30 am; entertainment Wed-Sat. Ck-out 11 am. Meeting rms. Business servs avail. Sundries. Golf privileges, putting green. Downhill/x-country ski 6 mi. Snowmobile trails. Exercise equipt; sauna. Game rm. Refrigerators avail. Some in-rm whirlpools. Private patios, balconies. Cr cds: A, C, D, DS, ER, MC, V.

B&B/Small Inn

★★★ PHILBROOK FARM INN. *881 North Rd (03581), 6 mi E on NH 2 to Meadow Rd, left 1 mi to North Rd, then right.* 603/466-3831. *www. journeysnorth.com.* 18 inn rms, 9 share bath, 3 story; two 1-rm cottages, 5 kit. cottages. No A/C. No elvtr. No rm phones. MAP: S $85-$100; D $115-$145; cottages $600/wk; wkly rates. Closed Oct 31-Dec 25; also Apr. Crib $3. Pool. Full bkfst. Dining rm: dinner (1 sitting). Ck-out 11 am (cottages 10 am), ck-in after noon. Downhill ski 15 mi; x-country ski on site. Rec rm. Lawn games. Antiques; sitting rm. Originally a farmhouse (1834), the inn has been in business since 1861. Cr cds: A, DS, MC, V.

Restaurant

★★ YOKOHAMA. *288 Main St (03581).* 603/466-2501. Specializes in sukiyaki, oyako donburi, habachi platter. Hrs: 11 am-9 pm. Closed Mon; Thanksgiving, Dec 25; also 3 wks in Apr. Res accepted. Lunch $4.50-$6.50; dinner $5.75-$13.25. Child's menu. Family-owned. Cr cds: A, D, MC, V.

Hampton Beach

See also Portsmouth

Settled 1638 **Pop** 900 (est) **Elev** 56 ft
Area code 603 **Zip** 03842

Information Chamber of Commerce, 490 Lafayette Rd, Suite 1, PO Box 790; 603/926-8717 or 800/GET-A-TAN

What to See and Do

Fishing. Charter boats at Hampton Beach piers.

Fuller Gardens. Former estate of the late Gov Alvan T. Fuller, featuring extensive rose gardens, annuals, perennials, Japanese garden, and conservatory. (May-Oct, daily) 10 Willow Ave, 4 mi NE via NH 1A, just N of NH 111 in North Hampton. Phone 603/964-5414. ¢¢

Hampton Beach State Park. Sandy beach on Atlantic Ocean. Swimming, bathhouse. Also here is the Sea Shell, a band shell and amphitheater. Camping (hookups). (Late May-Labor Day, daily) Standard fees. 3 mi S on NH 1A. Phone 603/926-3784.

Tuck Memorial Museum. Home of Hampton Historical Society. Antiques, documents, photographs, early postcards, tools, and toys; trolley exhibit; memorabilia of Hampton history. Restored 1-rm schoolhouse; fire station. (Mid-June-mid-Sep; Tues-Fri and Sun, afternoons; rest of yr, by appt) 40 Park Ave, on Meeting House Green, 4 mi N via NH 1A in Hampton. Phone 603/929-0781. **FREE**

Seasonal Events

Hampton Playhouse. 357 Winnacunet Rd, between Hampton and Hampton Beach, Route 101E. Performances in 200-yr-old modernized ox barn. Tues-Sun nights; matinee Wed, Fri; children's shows Sat. Phone 603/926-3073. Mid-June-Labor Day.

Band concerts. On beach. Eves. Late June-Labor Day.

Motel/Motor Lodge

★ HAMPTON BEACH REGAL INN. *162 Ashworth Ave (03842).* 603/926-7758; fax 603/926-7758. 36 rms, 3 story. No elvtr. July-Labor Day: S $85-$95; D $95-$105; kit. suites $129; each addl $8; under 13 free; family rates; lower rates rest yr. Crib $8. TV; cable. Heated pool; whirlpool. Complimentary continental bkfst. Restaurant nearby. Ck-out 11 am. Business servs avail. Game rm. Refrigerators; some in-rm whirlpools. Balconies. Cr cds: A, D, DS, MC, V.

Hotels

★★ **ASHWORTH BY THE SEA.** *295 Ocean Blvd (03842). 603/926-6762; fax 603/926-2002; toll-free 800/345-6736.* 105 rms, 4 story. July-Sep: S, D $95-$189; each addl $20; under 18, $5; lower rates rest of yr. Crib $10. TV; cable (premium); VCR avail. Heated pool; poolside serv. Restaurant 6:30 am-11 pm; dining rm 8-11 am (summer), 11:45 am-2:30 pm, 5-10 pm. Bar; entertainment. Ck-out noon. Meeting rms. Business servs avail. In-rm modem link. Gift shop. Beauty shop. Valet parking. Sun deck. Many balconies. Cr cds: A, D, DS, MC, V.

[icons]

★★ **HAMPTON FALLS INN.** *11 Lafayette Rd (03844), W on NH 101, S on US 1. 603/926-9545; fax 603/926-4155; toll-free 800/356-1729.* 44 rms, 3 story, 4 suites. July-Oct: S, D $169; suites $169; each addl $10; under 12 free; lower rates rest of yr. Crib avail, fee. Pet accepted, some restrictions, fee. Parking lot. Indoor pool, whirlpool. TV; cable, VCR avail. Complimentary continental bkfst, newspaper, toll-free calls. Restaurant 7 am-midnight, closed Mon. Ck-out 11 am, ck-in 2 pm. Meeting rm. Business servs avail. Golf, 18 holes. Tennis, 6 courts. Downhill skiing. Cr cds: A, C, D, DS, MC, V.

[icons]

★★★ **INN OF HAMPTON.** *815 Lafayette Rd (03842), 3 mi N on US 1. 603/926-6771; fax 603/929-2160; toll-free 800/423-4561. www.theinnof hampton.com.* 53 rms, 2 story, 18 suites. May-Oct: S $119; D $139; suites $189; each addl $10; under 11 free; lower rates rest of yr. Crib avail, fee. Parking lot. Indoor pool, whirlpool. TV; cable (premium), VCR avail. Complimentary coffee in rms, newspaper, toll-free calls. Restaurant. Bar. Ck-out 11 am, ck-in 2 pm. Meeting rms. Dry cleaning, coin lndry. Exercise equipt. Golf. Downhill skiing. Cr cds: A, C, D, DS, MC, V.

[icons]

B&Bs/Small Inns

★★★ **D.W.'S OCEANSIDE INN.** *365 Ocean Blvd (03842). 603/926-3542; fax 603/926-3549. Email info@ oceansideinn.com; www.oceansideinn.*

com. 10 rms, 2 story. No rm phones. July-Aug: D $95-$140; each addl $30; wkly rates; lower rates mid-May-June; Sep-mid-Oct. Closed rest of yr. TV; VCR (free movies) in library. Complimentary bkfst. Ck-out 11 am, ck-in 2 pm. Historic bldg (1880). Antiques; opp ocean beach; swimming, sun decks. Totally nonsmoking. Cr cds: A, DS, MC, V.

[icons]

★★ **LAMIE'S INN & TAVERN.** *490 Lafayette Rd (03842), on US 1 at jct NH 27. 603/926-0330; fax 603/929-0017.* 32 rms, 2 story, 1 suite. Late June-Labor Day: S $89-$99; D $109; each addl $10; under 17 free; lower rates rest of yr. Crib free. TV; cable (premium). Restaurant. Bar 4 pm-midnight; entertainment Fri, Sat (in season). Ck-out noon, ck-in 3 pm. Meeting rms. Business servs avail. Valet serv. Airport transportation. Refrigerators avail. Cr cds: A, DS, MC, V.

[icons]

All Suite

★★ **HAMPSHIRE INN.** *20 Spur Rd; Rte 107 (03874), I-95 and NH 107. 603/474-5700; fax 603/474-2886; toll-free 800/932-8520. Email hampshir@ thepipeline.net; www.hampshireinn. com.* 3 story, 35 suites. June-Oct: S, D $119; suites $119; each addl $10; children $10; under 5 free; lower rates rest of yr. Crib avail, fee. Parking lot. Indoor pool, whirlpool. TV; cable (premium), VCR avail. Complimentary continental bkfst, newspaper, toll-free calls. Restaurant nearby. Meeting rms. Business center. Dry cleaning, coin lndry. Gift shop. Exercise equipt. Golf. Tennis. Downhill skiing. Cr cds: A, C, D, DS, MC, V.

[icons]

Restaurant

★ **NEWICK'S FISHERMAN'S LANDING.** *845 Lafayette Rd (03842), 3 mi N on US 1. 603/926-7646. www. newicks.com.* Specializes in fresh seafood. Hrs: 11:30 am-9 pm. Closed Thanksgiving, Dec 25; Mon in winter. Lunch, dinner $2.95-$18.95. Child's menu. Nautical theme; large ship models, artwork. Cr cds: A, DS, MC, V.

[icons]

Hanover (E-3)

Settled 1765 **Pop** 9,212 **Elev** 531 ft
Area code 603 **Zip** 03755
Information Chamber of Commerce, PO Box 5105, 216 Nugget Bldg; 603/643-3115

Established four years after the first settlers came here, Dartmouth College is an integral part of Hanover. Named for the Earl of Dartmouth, one of its original supporters, the school was founded by the Rev Eleazar Wheelock "for the instruction of the youth of Indian tribes and others."

What to See and Do

Dartmouth College. (1769) 5,400 students. Main & Wheelock Sts. Phone 603/646-1110. On campus are

Baker Memorial Library. Bldg features white spire. Two million volumes; notable frescoes by the Mexican artist José Clemente Orozco. (Academic yr, daily) Guide service during vacations (Mon-Fri). Wentworth & College Sts.

Dartmouth Row. Early white brick bldgs incl Wentworth, Dartmouth, Thornton, and Reed halls. Parts of Dartmouth Hall date from 1784. E side of Green.

Hood Museum and Hopkins Center for the Arts. Concert hall, theaters, changing art exhibits. Gallery (daily; free). Performing arts events all yr (fees). Opp S end of Green.

League of New Hampshire Craftsmen. Work by some of New Hampshire's finest craftspeople. (Mon-Sat; closed hols) 13 Lebanon St. Phone 603/643-5050. **FREE**

⊠ **Saint-Gaudens National Historic Site.** Former residence and studio of sculptor Augustus Saint-Gaudens (1848-1907); "Aspet," built ca 1800, was once a tavern. Saint-Gaudens' famous works *The Puritan, Adams Memorial,* and *Shaw Memorial* are among the 100 works on display. Also formal gardens and works by other artists; sculptor-in-residence; interpretive programs. (Memorial Day-Oct, daily) Approx 5 mi S on NH 10, then 12 mi S off NH 12A, in Cornish, across river from Windsor, VT.

Contact Superintendent, RR 3, Box 73, Cornish 03745. Phone 603/675-2175. ¢¢

Skiing.

Dartmouth Skiway. Two double chairlifts; patrol; school; snack bar. Longest run 1 mi; vertical drop 900 ft. (Mid-Dec-Mar, daily) 10 mi N on NH 10 to Lyme, then 3 mi E. Phone 603/795-2143. ¢¢¢¢

Webster Cottage. (1780) Residence of Daniel Webster during his last year as a Dartmouth College student; Colonial and Shaker furniture, Webster memorabilia. (June-mid-Oct, Wed, Sat, and Sun afternoons) 32 N Main St. Phone 603/643-6529. **FREE**

Motels/Motor Lodges

★ **CHIEFTAIN MOTOR INN.** *84 Lyme Rd (03755). 603/643-2550; fax 603/643-5265; toll-free 800/845-3557. Email chieftaininn@quest-net.com; www.chieftaininn.com.* 22 rms, 2 story. May-Oct: S $85; D $95; each addl $10; under 12 free; lower rates rest of yr. Parking lot. Pool. TV; cable. Complimentary continental bkfst. Restaurant nearby. Ck-out 11 am, ck-in 3 pm. Business center. Golf. Tennis. Downhill skiing. Hiking trail. Picnic facilities. Cr cds: A, D, DS, MC, V.

🐾 🏊 🏃 🖼 🏌 ⛱ 🛷 🐾 🏃

★★★ **HANOVER INN.** *Main St & Wheelock St (03755). 603/643-4300; fax 603/646-3744; toll-free 800/443-7024. Email hartson@dartmouth.edu; www.dartmouth.edu/inn.* 92 rms, 5 story, 22 suites. S, D $207-$217; suites $217-$287; ski, golf plans. Crib free. Pet accepted. Covered parking $5; free valet parking. TV; cable, VCR avail. Indoor pool privileges; sauna. Restaurant 7 am-10 pm. Bar 11:30 am-midnight. Ck-out noon. Meeting rms. Business servs avail. Free airport transportation. Bellhops. Valet serv. Gift shop. Lighted tennis privileges, pro. 18-hole golf privileges, greens fee $33, pro, putting green, driving range. Downhill ski 7 mi. Exercise equipt. Health club privileges. Bathrm phones. Georgian-style brick structure owned by college; used as guest house since 1780. Cr cds: A, D, DS, MC, V.

Ⓓ 🐾 🏊 🏃 🖼 🏌 🍴 🛷 🐾 SC

Resort

★ **LOCH LYME LODGE.** *70 Orford Rd, Rte 10 (03768), 11 mi N on NH 10. 603/795-2141; fax 603/795-2141; toll-free 800/423-2141. Email lochlyme lodge@valley.net.* 24 cottages, 12 kits. units, 4 rms in inn, all share bath. No A/C. No rm phones. S, D $42-$90; cottages $420-$725/wk; under 4 free; MAP avail. Cottages closed Sep-May. Crib $6. Pet accepted, some restrictions. Playground. Ck-out 10 am. Tennis privileges. Downhill ski 4 mi; x-country ski 10 mi. Lawn games. Fireplaces, some refrigerators. On Post Pond; swimming beach. Picnic tables, grills. Cr cds: A, D, DS, MC, V.

B&Bs/Small Inns

★★ **ALDEN COUNTRY INN.** *1 Market St (03768), 10 mi N on NH 10 (Lyme Rd), E to the Common. 603/795-2222; fax 603/795-9436; toll-free 800/794-2296. Email info@alden countryinn.com; www.aldencountry inn.com.* 15 rms, 4 story. No elvtr. June-Oct: S $95-$130; D $115-$145; each addl $20; lower rates rest of yr. Complimentary full bkfst. Restaurant 7:30-9:30 am, 5:30-9:30 pm; Sun 5-8 pm. Bar to 9 pm. Ck-out 11 am, ck-in 3 pm. Downhill ski 3 mi; x-country ski 15 mi. Original inn and tavern built 1809; antique furnishings. Cr cds: A, DS, MC, V.

★★★ **DOWD'S COUNTRY INN.** *On the Common (03768), 8 mi N on NH 10. 603/795-4712; fax 603/795-4220.* 22 rms, 2 story. June-Oct: S $70-$125; D $80-$155; lower rates rest of yr. Crib $10. TV in common rm. Complimentary full bkfst. Ck-out 11 am, ck-in 3 pm. Business servs avail. Railroad station, bus depot transportation. Downhill ski 2 mi. Built 1780. Totally nonsmoking. Cr cds: A, D, DS, MC, V.

★ **MOOSE MOUNTAIN LODGE.** *33 Moose Mtn Lodge Rd (03750), E Wheelock St to Etna Center to Etna Rd, follow signs. 603/643-3529; fax 603/643-3529.* 12 rms, 5 share bath, 2 story. No A/C. No rm phones. Jan-mid-Mar, AP: $85-$90/person; Mid-June-late

Oct, Dec 26-late Mar, MAP: $80; family rates. Closed rest of yr. Complimentary coffee in lobby. X-country ski on site. Totally nonsmoking. Cr cds: MC, V.

★★ **WHITE GOOSE INN.** *Rte 10 (03777), 15 mi N on I-91, Exit 15 to Orford. 603/353-4812; fax 603/353-4543. Email whitegoose@valle9.net.* 15 rms, 2 share bath, 8 A/C. No rm phones. May-Oct: S $75; D $85-$105; lower rates rest of yr. Children over 8 yrs only. TV in lobby. Complimentary full bkfst. Ck-out 11 am, ck-in 2 pm. Main bldg (1833) attached to original structure (ca 1770). Circular porch. Totally nonsmoking. Cr cds: A, DS, MC, V.

Restaurants

★★ **JESSE'S.** *RR 120 (03755), 1½ mi S on NH 120. 603/643-4111. www. blueskyrestaurants.com.* Specializes in steak, seafood, Maine lobster. Salad bar. Hrs: 5-9:30 pm; Fri, Sat to 10:30 pm; Sun from 4:30 pm. Bar. Dinner $8.95-$17.95. Child's menu. Open-hearth cooking; mesquite grill. Victorian decor. Cr cds: A, MC, V.

★ **MOLLY'S.** *43 Main St (03755). 603/643-2570. www.mollysrestaurant. com.* Specializes in burgers, creative sandwiches, pasta. Hrs: 11:30 am-10 pm; Fri, Sat to 11 pm. Closed Thanksgiving, Dec 25. Bar. Lunch $5.95-$8.95; dinner $6.95-$14.95. Sun brunch $5.95-$7.50. Greenhouse-type decor; brass railings. Southwestern motif. Cr cds: A, MC, V.

Holderness

See also Meredith, Plymouth

Settled 1770 **Pop** 1,694 **Elev** 584 ft
Area code 603 **Zip** 03245

Holderness is the shopping center and post office for Squam Lake (second-largest lake in the state) and neighboring Little Squam. Fishing, boating, swimming, water sports, and winter sports are popular in this area. The movie *On Golden Pond* was filmed here. A Ranger District office of the White Mountain National Forest (see) is located here.

What to See and Do

League of New Hampshire Craftsmen—Sandwich Home Industries. Work by some of New Hampshire's finest craftspeople. (Mid-May-mid-Oct, daily) 12 mi NE via NH 113, on Main St in Center Sandwich. Phone 603/284-6831. **FREE**

Science Center of New Hampshire. A 200-acre wildlife sanctuary with animals in natural enclosures; features bears, deer, bobcat, otter, and birds of prey; nature trails; animal presentations. Picnicking. (May-Oct, daily) On NH 113. Phone 603/968-7194. *¢¢*

Squam Lake Tours. Two-hr boat tours of area where *On Golden Pond* was filmed. (May-Oct, 3 tours daily) ½ mi S on US 3. Contact PO Box 185. Phone 603/968-7577. *¢¢*

B&Bs/Small Inns

★★★ **GLYNN HOUSE INN.** *43 Highland St (03217), 4 mi S on US 3. 603/968-3775; fax 603/968-3129.* 9 rms, 2 story, 4 suites. No rm phones. S $75-$85; each addl $10; suites $125-$145; wkly rates; hols, wkends (2-day min); higher rates fall foliage. Children over 7 yrs only. TV; VCR (movies). Complimentary full bkfst. Ck-out 11 am, ck-in 3 pm. Tennis privileges. Downhill ski 17 mi; x-country ski 3 mi. Lawn games. Refrigerators. Picnic tables. Built in 1896; gingerbread wraparound porch. Totally nonsmoking. Cr cds: A, DS, MC, V.

★★ **INN ON GOLDEN POND.** *Rte 3 (03245), 4 mi SE of I-93 Exit 24, on US 3. 603/968-7269; fax 603/968-9226. Email innongp@lr.net; www. innongoldenpond.com.* 8 rms, 3 story, 1 suite. No rm phones. Mid-May-Nov: S $80; D $115; each addl $30; suite $140; lower rates rest of yr. Children over 12 yrs only. TV in sitting rm; cable. Complimentary full bkfst. Ck-out 11 am, ck-in 3 pm. Gift shop. Downhill ski 17 mi. Game rm. Lawn games. Built 1879; fireplace; rms individually decorated. On 50

wooded acres; hiking trails, nearby lake. Totally nonsmoking. Cr cds: A, DS, MC, V.

★★★ **MANOR ON GOLDEN POND.** *Manor Dr; Rte 3 and Shepard Hill Rd (03245), Shepard Hill, ½ mi SE on US 3, NH 25. 603/968-3348; fax 603/968-2116; toll-free 800/545-2141. Email manorinn@lr.net; www.manor goldenpond.com.* 25 rms, 2 story. May-Oct: D $210; suites $350; each addl $25; lower rates rest of yr. Parking lot. Pool. TV; cable, VCR avail, CD avail. Complimentary full bkfst, newspaper, toll-free calls. Restaurant. Bar. Ck-out 11 am, ck-in 3 pm. Meeting rm. Fax servs avail. Gift shop. Golf. Tennis. Downhill skiing. Beach access. Picnic facilities. Cr cds: A, MC, V.

Restaurants

★★ **COMMON MAN.** *Main St (03245), 1 mi E of I-93 Exit 24. 603/968-7030.* Specializes in baked stuffed shrimp, lobster bisque, roast prime rib. Hrs: 11:30 am-11 pm. Closed Thanksgiving, Dec 24, 25. Bar. Lunch $3.50-$7.95; dinner $10.95-$16.95. Child's menu. Antiques; rustic decor. Family-owned. Cr cds: A, DS, MC, V. **D**

★★ **CORNER HOUSE INN.** *22 Main St (03227), 12 mi NE on NH 113. 603/284-6219.* Specializes in lobster and mushroom bisque, shellfish saute. Hrs: 11:30 am-9:30 pm; early-bird dinner 5:30-6:30 pm. Closed Thanksgiving, Dec 25; also Mon Nov-May. Lunch $4.50-$11.95; dinner $10.95-$18.95. Victorian-style inn (1849); originally house and attached harness shop. Guest rms avail. Cr cds: A, DS, MC, V. **D**

★★★ **MANOR ON GOLDEN POND.** *US 3. 603/968-3348. www. manorongoldenpond.com.* Menu changes daily. Hrs: 6-8:30 pm. Closed Mon, Tues in Nov-Memorial Day. Res required. Bar. Wine list. Dinner prix fixe: $33, $55. Fireplace. Overlooks Squam Lake, mountains. Cr cds: A, MC, V.

Jackson

(D-6) *See also Bartlett, North Conway*

Settled 1790 **Pop** 678 **Elev** 971 ft
Area code 603 **Zip** 03846
Information Mount Washington Valley Chamber of Commerce, N Main St, PO Box 2300, North Conway 03860; 603/356-3171

At the south end of Pinkham Notch (see), Jackson is a center for skiing and a year-round resort. The Wildcat River rushes over rock formations in the village; Wildcat Mountain is to the north. A covered bridge (ca 1870) spans the Ellis River.

What to See and Do

Heritage-New Hampshire. Path winds among theatrical sets and takes visitors on a walk through 30 events during 300 yrs of New Hampshire history. Each set has animation, sounds, and smells to re-create the past, from a stormy voyage to the New World to a train ride through autumn foliage in Crawford Notch. (Late May-early Oct, daily) 2 mi S on NH 16 in Glen. Phone 603/383-9776. ¢¢

Skiing.

Black Mountain. Triple, double chairlifts, J-bar; patrol, school, rentals; cafeteria, nursery. Longest run 1 mi; vertical drop 1,200 ft. 2½ mi N on NH 16B. Phone 603/383-4490. ¢¢¢¢

Jackson Ski Touring Foundation. Maintains 95 mi of cross-country trails, connecting inns, and ski areas. Instruction, rentals, rescue service. (Dec-mid-Apr, daily; closed Dec 25) Phone 603/383-9355. ¢¢

Story Land. Village of storybook settings; Cinderella's castle, Heidi's grandfather's house; themed rides, incl raft ride, on 35 acres. (Mid-June-Aug, daily; Sep-early Oct, wkends) 2 mi S on NH 16 in Glen. Phone 603/383-4186. ¢¢¢¢

White Mountain National Forest. (see) N & S on NH 16.

Motels/Motor Lodges

★★ **LODGE AT JACKSON VILLAGE.** *Rte 16 (03846). 603/383-0999; fax 603/383-6104; toll-free 800/233-5634. Email mail1@landmarknet.net; www.lodgeatjacksonvillage.com.* 32 rms, 2 story. Sep-Oct: S $255; D $259; each addl $15; under 17 free; lower rates rest of yr. Crib avail, fee. Parking lot. Pool, whirlpool. TV; cable. Complimentary newspaper. Restaurant nearby. Business servs avail. Coin lndry. Golf, 18 holes. Tennis. Downhill skiing. Hiking trail. Picnic facilities. Cr cds: A, DS, MC, V.

⧉ ⧉ ⧉ ⧉ ⧉ ⧉ ⧉ ⧉ ⧉

★★ **RED APPLE INN.** *NH 302 (03838), 3 mi S and W on US 302. 603/383-9680; fax 603/383-9680; toll-free 800/826-3591. www.theredapple inn.com.* 16 rms. S, D $39-$125; each addl $10; under 13 free; ski plans. Closed 2 wks Apr and 3 wks Nov. Crib $10. TV; cable. Pool. Playground. Ck-out 11 am. Downhill ski 2 mi; x-country ski 2 mi. Game rm. Some refrigerators, fireplaces. Picnic tables, grills. In wooded area. Cr cds: A, DS, MC, V.

⧉ ⧉ ⧉ ⧉

Hotel

★★ **ELLIS RIVER HOUSE.** *Rte 16 PO Box 656 (03846). 603/383-9339; fax 603/383-4142; toll-free 800/233-8309. Email innkeeper@erhinn.com; www.erhinn.com.* 20 rms, 3 story, 4 suites. Feb, July-Oct: D $289; each addl $25; lower rates rest of yr. Pet accepted, some restrictions, fee. Parking lot. Pool, whirlpool. TV; cable. Complimentary full bkfst, coffee in rms, newspaper, toll-free calls. Restaurant. Bar. Ck-out 11 am, ck-in 3 pm. Meeting rms. Business servs avail. Concierge. Dry cleaning, coin lndry. Gift shop. Exercise privileges, sauna. Golf, 18 holes. Tennis, 4 courts. Downhill skiing. Hiking trail. Cr cds: A, C, D, DS, ER, MC, V.

⧉ ⧉ ⧉ ⧉ ⧉ ⧉ ⧉ ⧉ ⧉ ⧉ ⧉ ⧉

Resorts

★★ **EAGLE MOUNTAIN HOUSE.** *Carter Notch Rd (03846), 1 mi N. 603/383-9111; fax 603/383-0854; toll-free 800/966-5779. Email reserva-*

tions@eaglemt.com; www.eaglemt.com.
60 rms, 5 story, 30 suites. Feb, July-
Oct: S, D $159; suites $179; each
addl $15; under 17 free; lower rates
rest of yr. Crib avail. Parking lot.
Pool, whirlpool. TV; cable, VCR avail.
Complimentary newspaper, toll-free
calls. Restaurant 8 am-9 pm. Bar. Ck-
out 11 am, ck-in 3 pm. Meeting rms.
Business center. Bellhops. Gift shop.
Exercise equipt, sauna. Golf, 9 holes.
Tennis. Downhill skiing. Hiking trail.
Cr cds: A, C, D, DS, MC, V.

★ ★ ★ **STORYBOOK RESORT INN.**
Jct US 302 and Rte 16 (03838), 2 mi S.
383-6800; fax 603/383-4678. Email
storybk@ncia.net; www.storybookresort.
com. 77 rms, 2 story. Feb-Mar, July-
Oct: S $129; D $159; each addl $10;
children $5; under 16 free; lower
rates rest of yr. Parking lot.
Indoor/outdoor pools, childrens
pool, lifeguard, whirlpool. TV; cable.
Complimentary toll-free calls.
Restaurant 7:45 am-8:30 pm, closed
Mon. Bar. Ck-out 11 am, ck-in 3 pm.
Meeting rms. Business center. Coin
lndry. Exercise equipt, sauna. Golf.
Tennis. Downhill skiing. Hiking trail.
Picnic facilities. Cr cds: A, C, D, DS,
MC, V.

B&Bs/Small Inns

★ ★ ★ **BERNERHOF INN & PRINCE
PLACE RESTAURANT.** Rte 302
(03838), 3 mi S on NH 16, then 1½ mi
W on US 302. 603/383-4414; fax
603/383-0809; res 800/548-8007.
Email stay@bernerhofinn.com; www.
bernerhofinn.com. 9 rms, 2 story, 2
suites. June-Nov: S $95; suites $150;
each addl $25; lower rates rest of yr.
Crib avail. Parking lot. Pool. TV;
cable, VCR avail. Complimentary full
bkfst, newspaper, toll-free calls.
Restaurant. Bar. Meeting rm. Business
servs avail. Gift shop. Exercise privileges, sauna. Golf, 18 holes. Tennis.
Downhill skiing. Cr cds: A, D, DS,
MC, V.

★ ★ ★ **CHRISTMAS FARM INN.** Rte
16B (03846), ¼ mi N. 603/383-4313;
fax 603/383-6495; toll-free 800/443-
5837. 33 rms, 8 A/C, 2 story, 7 cottages. MAP: S $93-$140; D
$156-$250; family rates. Serv charge
15%. TV in some rms. Pool; whirl-

pool, poolside serv. Playground.
Afternoon refreshments. Restaurant
(see CHRISTMAS FARM INN). Bars
from noon. Ck-out 11 am, ck-in after
3 pm. Meeting rm. Business servs
avail. Gift shop. Putting green. Golf
privileges. Downhill ski 1 mi; x-
country on site. Sauna. Rec rm. Lawn
games. Some in-rm whirlpools. Historic bldgs from late 1700s, incl
town's first church and early jail; rms
vary. Cr cds: A, MC, V.

★ ★ **DANA PLACE INN.** NH 16
(03846), 5 mi N in Pinkham Notch.
603/383-6822; fax 603/383-6022; res
800/537-9276. Email contact@dana
place.com; www.danaplace.com. 30
rms, 2 story, 5 suites. Dec-Feb, July-
Oct: D $225; suites $250; each addl
$50; children $20; under 17 free;
lower rates rest of yr. Crib avail. Pet
accepted, some restrictions. Parking
lot. Indoor pool, children's pool,
whirlpool. TV; cable (premium).
Complimentary full bkfst, newspaper, toll-free calls. Restaurant. Bar.
Meeting rm. Business center. Golf.
Tennis, 2 courts. Downhill skiing.
Hiking trail. Picnic facilities. Cr cds:
A, C, D, DS, MC, V.

★ ★ ★ **INN AT THORN HILL.** Thorn
Hill Rd (03846), ¼ mi E of NH 16A.
603/383-4242; fax 603/383-8062; toll-
free 800/289-8990. Email thornhll@
ncia.net; www.innatthornhill.com. 10
rms in 3-story inn, 6 rms in carriage
house, 3 cottages. Some rm phones.
MAP: S $95-$145; D $80-$155/per-
son; package plans. Children over 10
yrs only. TV in parlor of main bldg
and in cottages; cable. Pool; whirlpool. Dining rm 8-9:30 am, 6-9 pm
(public by res). Bar. Ck-out 11 am,
ck-in after 3 pm. Business servs avail.
Downhill ski 2 mi; x-country ski on
site. Lawn games. Some in-rm
whirlpools, wet bars, fireplaces.
Antique furnishings. Totally nonsmoking. Cr cds: A, DS, MC, V.

★ ★ **NESTLENOOK FARM RESORT.**
Dinsmore Rd (03846). 603/383-9443;
fax 603/383-4515; toll-free 800/659-
9443. www.nestlenook.com. 21 rms, 3
story. Dec-Feb, Oct: D $125; under
12 free; lower rates rest of yr. Parking
lot. Indoor/outdoor pools, whirlpool.
TV; cable, VCR avail, CD avail. Com-

plimentary full bkfst, coffee in rms, newspaper. Restaurant nearby. Fax servs avail. Concierge. Gift shop. Sauna, steam rm. Golf, 18 holes. Tennis. Downhill skiing. Bike rentals. Hiking trail. Picnic facilities. Cr cds: DS, MC, V.

★★★ **WENTWORTH RESORT HOTEL.** *Rte 16A and Carter Notch Rd (03846). 603/383-9700; fax 603/383-4265; toll-free 800/637-0013. Email wentwort@nxi.com; www.thewentworth. com.* 43 rms, 3 story, 14 suites. Dec-Feb, June-Oct: S, D $119; suites $219; each addl $10; under 12 free; lower rates rest of yr. Crib avail, fee. Parking lot. Pool, whirlpool. TV; cable, VCR avail, CD avail. Complimentary newspaper, toll-free calls. Restaurant. Bar. Ck-out 11 am, ck-in 2 pm. Meeting rms. Business center. Golf, 18 holes. Tennis. Downhill skiing. Bike rentals. Hiking trail. Picnic facilities. Cr cds: A, C, D, DS, ER, JCB, MC, V.

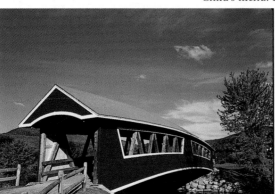

Covered bridge, Jackson

Restaurants

★★ **CHRISTMAS FARM INN.** *Rte 16B. 603/383-4313. www.christmas farminn.com.* Specializes in vegetable-stuffed chicken breast, veal basilico, shrimp scampi. Own baking. Hrs: 8 am-9 pm. Bar. Bkfst $2.45-$4.50; lunch $17.95-$25.95; dinner $17.95-$25.95. In historic bldg (1786). Cr cds: A, DS, MC, V.

★★★ **INN AT THORN HILL.** *Thorn Hill Rd Box A. 603/383-4242. www. innatthornhill.com.* New England

fusion menu. Specializes in pan fried beef tenderloin coated with pastrami spices, roast rack of lamb. Hrs: 6-9 pm. Res reservatons accepted. Extensive wine list. Dinner $21.95-$26.95. Romantic atmosphere. Cr cds: A, DS, MC, V.

★★★ **PRINCE PLACE.** *US 302. 603/383-4414.* Specializes in delices de gruyere, Wienerschnitzel. Own desserts. Hrs: 5-10 pm; hrs vary in fall. Res accepted. Wine list. Lunch $3.50-$9.95; dinner $13-$22. Child's menu. Parking. Host of "A Taste of the Mountains" cooking school. Cr cds: A, DS, MC, V.

★ **RED PARKA PUB.** *US 302 (03838), 3 mi S on US 302. 603/383-4344. www.redparkapub.com.* Specializes in barbecued pork spare ribs, prime rib. Salad bar. Hrs: 4:30-10 pm; Sat, Sun from 4 pm. Closed Thanksgiving, Dec 24, 25. Bar. Dinner $5.95-$18.95. Child's menu. Entertainment: wkends. Parking. One rm in 1914 railroad car. Cr cds: A, D, DS, MC, V.

★★ **WILDCAT TAVERN.** *NH 16A (03846), in Jackson Village. 603/383-4245. www.wildcat innandtavern.com.* Specializes in fresh seafood, veal. Own desserts. Hrs: 11:30 am-9 pm; Fri, Sat to 10 pm. Lunch $4-$10.95; dinner $12-$25. Child's menu. Parking. In historic inn (1896). Cr cds: A, MC, V.

Jaffrey

(H-4) *See also Keene, Peterborough*

Settled 1760 **Pop** 5,361 **Elev** 1,013 ft
Area code 603 **Zip** 03452
Web www.jaffreycoc.org

Information Chamber of Commerce, PO Box 2; 603/532-4549

Jaffrey, on the eastern slopes of Mount Monadnock, has been a summer resort community since the 1840s.

What to See and Do

Barrett House "Forest Hall." (1800) Federal mansion with 3rd-floor ballrm. Twelve museum rms contain some of the most important examples of 18th- and 19th-century furniture and antique musical instruments in New England. Extensive grounds with Gothic Revival summer house on terraced hill behind main house. Guided tours. (June-mid-Oct, Thurs-Sun) 10 mi SE on NH 124, then ¼ mi S on NH 123A (Main St) in New Ipswich. Phone 603/878-2517. ¢¢

✪ **Cathedral of the Pines.** International nondenominational shrine. National memorial for all American war dead; Memorial Bell Tower dedicated to women who died in service. Outdoor altar, gardens, museum. (May-Oct, daily) 3 mi E on NH 124, then 3 mi S, in Rindge. Phone 603/899-3300. **FREE**

Monadnock State Park. Hikers' mecca; 40-mi network of well-maintained trails on Mt Monadnock (3,165 ft). Summit views of all New England states. Picnicking, camping. Ski touring (Dec-Mar). Standard fees. 2 mi W on NH 124, then N. Phone 603/532-8862.

Jefferson

Settled 1772 **Pop** 965 **Elev** 1,384 ft
Area code 603 **Zip** 03583
Web www.northernwhitemountains. com

Information Northern White Mountains Chamber of Commerce, 164 Main St, PO Box 298, Berlin 03570; 603/752-6060

On the slopes of Mount Starr King in the White Mountains, this resort area is referred to locally as Jefferson Hill.

What to See and Do

Santa's Village. Santa and tame deer; unique rides; live shows, computerized animation. Playground; picnic area. (Father's Day-Labor Day, daily; Labor Day-Columbus Day, Sat and Sun) 1 mi NW on US 2, ½ mi W of jct NH 116. Phone 603/586-4445. ¢¢¢

Six Gun City. Western frontier village; cowboy skits, frontier show, fort, Native American camp, homestead, carriage and sleigh museum, general store, snack bar; miniature horse show, pony and burro rides, bumper boats, water slides, and other rides; miniature golf, games, animals, and antiques. (Mid-June-Labor Day, daily; Labor Day-Columbus Day, Sat and Sun) 4 mi E on US 2. Phone 603/586-4592. ¢¢

Annual Event

Lancaster Fair. 6 mi NW in Lancaster. Agricultural exhibits, horse show, entertainment. Labor Day wkend.

Motels/Motor Lodges

★ **EVERGREEN MOTEL.** *US 2 (03583), opp Santa's Village. 603/586-4449.* 18 rms. July-Labor Day: S, D $50-$60; each addl $5; higher rates fall foliage; lower rates May-June and after Labor Day-Oct. Closed rest of yr. Crib free. TV; cable. Heated pool. Restaurant 8 am-8 pm; hrs vary off-season. Ck-out 11 am. Picnic area. Camping, trailer facilities. Cr cds: A, DS, MC, V.
🛤️ 🐾

★ **LANTERN MOTOR INN.** *Rte 2 (03583). 603/586-7151; fax 603/586-7041.* 30 rms. S, D $35-$59; each addl $4. Closed Nov-Apr. Crib $3. TV; cable. Pool; whirlpool. Playground. Coffee in lobby. Ck-out 11 am. Coin lndry. Gift shop. Game rm. Lawn games. On wooded grounds. Cr cds: A, D, DS, MC, V.
🛤️ 📺 🐾

B&B/Small Inn

★ **JEFFERSON INN.** *US 2 (03583). 603/586-7998; fax 603/586-7808; toll-free 800/729-7908. Email jeffinn@ncia. net; www.jeffersoninn.com.* 11 rms, 3 story, 2 suites. No A/C. Some rm phones. S, D $75-$110; each addl $15; suites $120-$165; ski, golf plans; wkends, hols (2-day min). Crib free. TV in common rm. Complimentary full bkfst. Ck-out 11 am, ck-in 3 pm. Concierge serv. Business servs avail.

18-hole golf privileges, greens fee $20. Downhill ski 15 mi; x-country ski opp. Lawn games. Some refrigerators. Renovated Victorian house; wraparound porch. Totally nonsmoking. Cr cds: A, DS, MC, V.

D 🏃 🛏 🖳 🔥

Keene

(H-3) *See also Peterborough*

Settled 1736 **Pop** 22,430 **Elev** 486 ft
Area code 603 **Zip** 03431
Web www.keenechamber.com
Information Chamber of Commerce, 48 Central Sq; 603/352-1303

A modern commercial city, Keene is the chief community of the Monadnock region. Its industries manufacture many products incl furniture, machinery, textiles, and toys.

What to See and Do

Colony Mill Marketplace. Restored 1838 textile mill now transformed into regional marketplace with dozens of specialty shops, an antiques center, numerous dining options, and varied entertainment. (Daily) 222 West St. Phone 603/357-1240.

Horatio Colony House Museum. Stately Federalist home (1806) of son of prominent Keene mill owners. Features treasures collected from Colony's world travels; books, art, antique furniture. (June-mid-Oct, Tues-Sat; rest of year, Sat) 199 Main St. Phone 603/352-0460. **FREE**

Wyman Tavern. (1762) Scene of first meeting of Dartmouth College trustees in 1770; now furnished in 1820s style. (June-Sep, Thurs-Sat) 339 Main St. Phone 603/352-1895. ¢

Annual Events

The Old Homestead. 4 mi S on NH 32, at Potash Bowl in Swanzey Center. Drama of life in Swanzey during 1880s based on the Biblical story of the Prodigal Son; first presented in 1886. Phone 603/352-0697. Mid-July.

Cheshire Fair. Fairgrounds, S on NH 12 in North Swanzey. Exhibits, horse, and ox pulling contests,

entertainment. Phone 603/357-4740. First wk Aug.

Hotel

★★ **BEST WESTERN SOVEREIGN.** *401 Winchester St (03431). 603/357-3038; fax 603/357-4776; res 800/528-1234. www.bwkeene.com.* 131 rms, 2 story. May-Oct: S $175; D $195; under 18 free; lower rates rest of yr. Crib avail. Pet accepted. Parking lot. Indoor pool. TV; cable (premium), VCR avail. Complimentary full bkfst, coffee in rms, newspaper. Restaurant 6:30 am-9:30 pm. Bar. Ck-out noon, ck-in 2 pm. Meeting rms. Business center. Dry cleaning. Exercise privileges. Golf. Downhill skiing. Video games. Cr cds: A, C, D, DS, ER, JCB, MC, V.

D 🏌 🖈 🛏 🖳 🛟 ✈ 🖳 🛶 🏃

B&B/Small Inn

★★★ **CHESTERFIELD INN.** *Rte 9 (03466), 12 mi W on NH 9. 603/256-3211; fax 603/256-6131; toll-free 800/365-5515. Email chstinn@sover. net.* 15 rms, 2 story. S, D $125-$200; each addl $15; higher rates fall foliage. Pet accepted. TV; cable. Complimentary full bkfst. Dining rm 5:30-9 pm. Ck-out 11 am, ck-in 2 pm. Business servs avail. In-rm modem link. Refrigerators; some fireplaces. Some balconies. In renovated farmhouse and barn (1787). Overlooks Green Mts and Connecticut River. Cr cds: A, DS, MC, V.

D 🏌 🖈

Restaurants

★★ **176 MAIN.** *176 Main St. (03431). 603/357-3100. Email ossm@ 176main.com; www.176main.com.* Specializes in Mexican, Italian, and seafood dishes. Hrs: 11:30 am-11 pm; Fri, Sat to midnight; Sun 11 am-10 pm. Closed hols. Bar. Lunch $4.95-$6.95; dinner $9.95-$16.95. Child's menu. Rustic decor; exposed beams. Local artwork. Cr cds: A, D, DS, MC, V.

D 🖳

★ **THE PUB.** *Winchester and Ralston Sts (03431). 603/352-3135.* Greek menu. Specializes in lamb, seafood, prime rib. Hrs: 7 am-10 pm. Res accepted. Bar. Bkfst $1.25-$3.95;

lunch $3.95-$6.95; dinner $5.95-$12.95. Child's menu. Family-owned. Cr cds: A, DS, MC, V.

D ⌐

Laconia

(F-5) *See also Franklin, Meredith, Wolfeboro*

Settled 1777 **Pop** 15,743 **Elev** 570 ft
Area code 603 **Zip** 03246
Information Chamber of Commerce, 11 Veterans Square; 603/524-5531

On four lakes (Winnisquam, Opechee, Pauqus Bay, and Winnipesaukee), Laconia is the commercial center of the area known as the "Lakes Region." Besides the resort trade, it has more than a score of factories whose products include knitting machinery, hosiery, knitted fabrics, ball bearings, and electronic components. The headquarters of the White Mountain National Forest (see) is also located here.

What to See and Do

Cruises on Lake Winnipesaukee.

Queen of Winnipesaukee. This 46-ft sloop sails from M/S *Mount Washington* dock in Weirs Beach. 1½-hr cruises (July-Labor Day, daily; mid-May-June and early Sep-early Oct, wkends); 2-hr evening, moonlight cruises (July-Aug, Tues-Sat). Phone 603/366-5531. ¢¢¢¢

M/S Mount Washington. Leaves Weirs Beach and Wolfeboro on 3¼-hr cruises with stops at Center Harbor or Alton Bay. (Mid-May-late Oct, daily) US Mail boat leaves Weirs Beach on 2-hr cruises (mid-June-mid-Sep). **Moonlight Cruises**, dinner and dancing (July-Labor Day, Tues-Sat eves). Theme cruises (selected dates, June-Oct). Phone 603/366-5531. ¢¢¢¢

Gunstock Recreation Area. A 2,400-acre county-operated park. 7 mi E on NH 11A in Gilford. Phone 603/293-4345 or 800/GUNSTOCK.

Summer. Picnic and camp sites (Memorial Day wkend-Columbus Day wkend; fee; hookups addl; includes swimming privileges); fire-places, stocked pond, blazed trails, playground; special events.

Winter. Skiing; 5 chairlifts, 2 handle tows; patrol, school, rentals, snowmaking; cafeteria, lounge, nursery. Longest run 2 mi; vertical drop 1,400 ft. Cross-country trails. (Nov-Mar, daily; closed Dec 25) ¢¢¢¢

Recreation. The Weirs. Swimming, boating, fishing, sailing, waterskiing. Endicott Memorial Stone with initials of 1652 explorers, S end of beach. (Mid-June-Labor Day, daily) 5 mi N on US 3 at Weirs Beach on Lake Winnipesaukee. Phone 603/524-5046. Parking ¢¢

Surf Coaster. Family water park with wave pool, water slides, "Crazy River" inner tube ride, "Boomerang" rides inside translucent glass tubes; raft rentals, sun decks, showers, children's play areas. Snack bar. (Mid-June-Labor Day, daily; Memorial Day-mid-June, wkends) 6 mi N on US 3, then E on NH 11B, in Weirs Beach. Phone 603/366-4991. ¢¢¢¢

Winnipesaukee Railroad. Scenic train rides along Lake Winnipesaukee; can board in Weirs Beach or Meredith (see).

Seasonal Event

New Hampshire Music Festival. Gilford Middle High School, 5 mi E in Gilford. Symphony/pop concerts. Contact 88 Belknap Mt Rd, Gilford, 03246. Phone 603/524-1000. Fri, July-Aug.

Motels/Motor Lodges

★ **BARTON'S MOTEL.** *1330 Union Ave (03246). 603/524-5674.* 37 rms, 4 kit. cottages. Some rm phones. Mid-June-mid-Sep: S, D $80-$90; each addl $7-$15; kit. units, cottages $145-$150; lower rates rest of yr. Crib free. TV; cable. Heated pool. Restaurant adj 6 am-10 pm. Ck-out 11 am. On lake; row boats; dockage, private beach. Cr cds: A, MC, V.

⊠ 🐾

★★ **BELKNAP MOTEL.** *107 Belknap Point Rd (03246), 5 mi E on NH 11. 603/293-7511; fax 603/528-3552; toll-free 888/454-2537. Email hblinn@cyberportal.net; www.bpmotel.com.* 16 rms, 20 story, 3 suites. June-Aug: S, D $88; suites $108; each addl $15; under 16 free; lower rates rest of yr. Parking lot. TV; cable. Restaurant nearby. Ck-out 10 am, ck-in 3 pm. Internet access avail. Golf. Tennis. Downhill skiing. Beach access. Picnic facilities. Cr cds: A, DS, MC, V.

★ **BIRCH KNOLL.** *867 Weirs Blvd (03246). 603/366-4958; fax 603/366-4081.* 24 rms, 1-2 story. Late June-Labor Day: S, D $65-$89; each addl $8; higher rates special events; lower rates rest of yr. Closed Nov-Mar. Crib $6. TV; cable. Pool. Complimentary coffee. Ck-out 11 am. Business servs avail. Exercise equipt. Rec rm. Some refrigerators avail. Opp beach, boating and canoeing. Picnic tables, grill. Cr cds: A, DS, MC, V.

★★ **B MAE'S RESORT INN & SUITES.** *17 Harris Shore Rd (03246), 6 mi E on NH 11 at jct NH 11B; 14 mi E of I-93 Exit 20. 603/293-7526; fax 603/293-4340; toll-free 800/458-3877. Email bmaes@bmaesresort.com; www.bmaesresort.com.* 59 rms, 2 story, 24 suites. June-Oct: S, D $110; suites $155; each addl $12; children $12; under 12 free; lower rates rest of yr. Crib avail. Parking lot. Indoor/outdoor pools, whirlpool. TV; cable, VCR avail. Complimentary newspaper. Restaurant nearby. Ck-out 11 am, ck-in 3 pm. Meeting rm. Business servs avail. Exercise privileges. Golf. Tennis, 6 courts. Downhill skiing. Picnic facilities. Cr cds: A, C, D, DS, MC, V.

Resorts

★★ **LORD HAMPSHIRE MOTEL & COTTAGES.** *885 Laconia Rd (03289), I-93, Exit 20, 4 mi NE on US 3/NH 11. 603/524-4331; fax 603/524-1897. www.lordhampshire.com.* 8 rms, 1 story, 6 suites. S $85; D $100; suites $125; each addl $25; children $5; under 10 free. Crib avail, fee. Parking lot. TV; cable. Restaurant nearby. Ck-out 11 am, ck-in 1 pm. Fax servs avail. Golf. Tennis. Downhill skiing. Beach access. Picnic facilities. Cr cds: A, MC, V.

★★ **ST. MORITZ TERRACE RESORT.** *937 Weirs Blvd (03246), 5½ mi N on US 3. 603/366-4482; res 603/366-4482.* 1 rms. June-Aug: S, D $75; suites $125; lower rates rest of yr. Crib avail. Parking lot. Pool, children's pool. TV; cable. Ck-out 10:30 am, ck-in 2 pm. Golf, 18 holes. Tennis, 2 courts. Downhill skiing. Beach access. Picnic facilities. Cr cds: MC, V.

B&B/Small Inn

★★ **FERRY POINT HOUSE.** *100 Lower Bay Rd (03269), I-93 Exit 20, 4½ mi E on US 3/NH 11. 603/524-0087; fax 603/524-0959; res 603/524-0087. Email ferrypt@together.net; www.new-hampshire-inn.com.* 7 rms, 2 story. Apr-Oct: D $120; lower rates rest of yr. Parking lot. TV; cable. Complimentary full bkfst. Restaurant nearby. Ck-out 10 am, ck-in 3 pm. Golf, 18 holes. Tennis. Beach access. Hiking trail. Cr cds: A, MC, V.

Restaurant

★★ **HICKORY STICK FARM.** *66 Bean Hill Rd (03220), I-93, Exit 20, 5 mi E on US 3/NH 11, Union Rd 2 mi, follow signs. 603/524-3333. www.hickorystickfarm.com.* Specializes in roast duckling. Own baking. Hrs: 5-9 pm; Sun 10 am-8 pm; hrs vary off-season. Closed Mon. Res accepted. Dinner $12.95-$21.95. Converted Colonial farmhouse, barn. Gift shop. Guest rms avail. Family-owned. Cr cds: A, DS, MC, V.

Lincoln/North Woodstock Area

Pop Lincoln, 1,229; North Woodstock, 600 (est) **Elev** Lincoln, 811 ft; North Woodstock, 738 ft **Area code** 603 **Zip** Lincoln, 03251; North Woodstock, 03262 **Web** www.linwoodcc.org

Information Chamber of Commerce, NH 112, PO Box 358MO, Lincoln; 603/745-6621 or 800/227-4191

In a spectacular mountain setting, the villages of Lincoln and Woodstock lie at the junction of the road through Franconia Notch State Park (see) and the scenic Kancamagus Scenic Byway (NH 112).

What to See and Do

Clark's Trading Post. Entertainment park has trained New Hampshire black bears, haunted house, replica of 1884 firehouse; 30-min ride on White Mt Central Railroad. Museum features early Americana, photo parlor, maple cabin, nickelodeons, ice cream parlor. Bumper boats. (July-Labor Day, daily; Memorial Day-June and Sep-Columbus Day, wkends) 1 mi N of North Woodstock on US 3. Phone 603/745-8913. ¢¢¢

Franconia Notch State Park. (see) 2 mi N on US 3.

Hobo Railroad. Fifteen-mi scenic excursions along the Pemigewasset River. Features restored Pullman Dome dining car. (Daily) Railroad St, off Main. Phone 603/745-2135. ¢¢¢

Lost River Gorge. Natural boulder caves, largest known granite pothole in eastern US; Paradise Falls; boardwalks with 1,900-ft glacial gorge; nature garden with 300 varieties of native shrubs and flowers; geology exhibits; cafeteria, picnicking. (Mid-May-mid-Oct, daily) Appropriate outdoor clothing recommended. 6 mi W of North Woodstock on NH 112, Kinsman Notch. Phone 603/745-8031. ¢¢¢

Skiing. Loon Mountain Recreation Area. A 7,100-ft gondola, 2 triple, 4 double chairlifts, high-speed quad chairlift, pony lift; patrol, school, rentals, shops, snowmaking; restaurant, cafeterias, bar, nursery, lodge (see). Longest run 2½ mi; vertical drop 2,100 ft. (Late Nov-mid-Apr, daily) Cross-country trails (Dec-Mar). **Summer activities** incl: mountain biking (rentals), bike tours, in-line skating, horseback riding, archery, wildlife theater. Gondola also operates Memorial Day-mid-Oct (daily). (See ANNUAL EVENT) 3 mi E of Lincoln off NH 112 (Kancamagus Hwy). Phone 603/745-8111. ¢¢¢¢; Summer ¢¢¢

Whale's Tale Water Park. Wave pool, water slides, "lazy river," children's activity pool; playground, concession, gift shop. (Mid-June-Labor Day, daily; Memorial Day-mid-June, Sat and Sun) N on I-93, Exit 33, then N on US 3. Phone 603/745-8810. ¢¢¢¢

White Mountain National Forest. (see).

Annual Event

New Hampshire Highland Games. Loon Mt. Largest Scottish gathering in Eastern US. Bands, competitions, concerts, workshops. Phone 800/358-SCOT. Three days Sep.

Motels/Motor Lodges

★★ **BEACON RESORT.** *Rte 3 (03262), N on US 3. 603/745-8118; fax 603/745-3783; toll-free 800/258-8934.* 132 rms, 1-2 story, 26 suites, 24 cottages, 47 kits. July-mid-Oct, ski season and hol wkends (3-day min): S, D $65-$150; each addl $10; suites $150; cottages for 2-6, $65-$125; package plans; lower rates rest of yr. Crib $4. TV; cable. 4 pools, 2 indoor; wading pool, whirlpools, saunas. Restaurant 7:30-10:30 am, 5-8:30 pm; summer, wkends, and hols to 9 pm. Bar from 5 pm; entertainment. Ck-out 11 am; cottages 10 am. Coin lndry. Meeting rm. Gift shop. Indoor tennis. Downhill ski 4 mi. Game rm. Lawn games. In-rm whirlpool, fireplace in suites. Screened porch on many cottages. Cr cds: A, DS, MC, V.

D ⚡ ✈ ☰ 🔥

★★ **DRUMMER BOY MOTOR INN.** *Rte 3 (03251), 3 mi N on US 3 at I-93 Exit 33. 603/745-3661; fax 603/745-9829; toll-free 800/762-7275.* 53 rms, 8 kits., 2 kit. cottages. May-Oct: D $70-$160; each addl $5; kit. units $10 addl; suites, kit. cottages for 2-4, $70-$110; 4-bedrm house $250; ski plan; lower rates rest of yr. Crib $5. TV; cable, VCR avail. 2 heated pools, 1 indoor; whirlpool, sauna. Playground. Complimentary continental bkfst (in season). Restaurant nearby. Ck-out 11 am. Coin lndry. Meeting rm. Sundries. Downhill/x-country ski 3 mi. Game rm. Some refrigerators, in-rm whirlpools. Patios, balconies. Picnic tables, grill. Cr cds: A, DS, MC, V.

D ⚡ ☰ ⊠ 🔥 SC

★★ KANCAMABUS MOTOR
LODGE. *Rte 112 PO Box 505 (03251), 1 mi E on NH 112 at I-93 Exit 32. 603/745-3365; fax 603/745-6691; toll-free 800/346-4205. Email info@kanc motorlodge.com; www.kancmotorlodge. com.* 34 rms, 2 story. Jan-Feb, July-Oct: S, D $69; each addl $10; children $5; under 17 free; lower rates rest of yr. Crib avail, fee. Parking lot. Pool. TV; cable. Complimentary toll-free calls. Restaurant 7 am-9 pm. Bar. Ck-out 11 am, ck-in 3 pm. Fax servs avail. Coin lndry. Steam rm. Golf, 10 holes. Downhill skiing. Bike rentals. Hiking trail. Picnic facilities. Cr cds: A, DS, MC, V.

★★ MILL HOUSE INN. *Kancamagus Hwy (03251), 1 mi E of I-93 Exit 32. 603/745-6261; fax 603/745-6896; toll-free 800/654-6183. www.mailatlune. com.* 96 rms, 4 story. Late June-mid-Oct: S, D $89-$99; suites $99-$160; under 17 free; ski, golf plans; lower rates rest of yr. TV; cable, VCR avail. 2 pools, 1 indoor; whirlpools. Restaurant 7 am-10 pm. Ck-out 11 am. Meeting rms. Shopping arcade. Downhill ski 2 mi. Exercise equipt; sauna. Private patios, balconies. Cr cds: A, D, DS, MC, V.

★ MOUNT COOLIDGE MOTEL. *RR 3, Box 337 (03251), 3 mi N on US 3, ½ mi N of I-93 Exit 33. 603/745-8052.* 18 rms. July-Nov: S $36-$62; D $42-$72; each addl $5; lower rates Apr-June. Closed rest of yr. Crib free. TV; cable. Heated pool. Restaurant adj 7:30 am-8:30 pm; closed mid-Oct-mid-May. Ck-out 11 am. On mountain stream. Cr cds: A, DS, MC, V.

★ RED DOORS MOTEL. *RR 1, Box 109A Rte 3 (03251). 603/745-2267; fax 603/745-3646; res 800/527-7596. Email englers@aol.com.* Dec-Feb, July-Oct: S $63; D $73; each addl $5; under 18 free; lower rates rest of yr. Crib avail, fee. Parking lot. Pool. TV; cable (premium). Complimentary coffee in rms, toll-free calls. Restaurant nearby. Ck-out 10 am, ck-in 2 pm. Fax servs avail. Coin lndry. Golf. Downhill skiing. Supervised children's activities. Picnic facilities. Cr cds: A, DS, MC, V.

Resorts

★★ INDIAN HEAD RESORT. *Rte 3 (03251), ½ mi N on US 3 at I-93 Exit 33. 603/745-8000; fax 603/745-8414; toll-free 800/343-8000. Email info@ indianheadresort.com; www.indianhead resort.com.* 98 rms, 2 story. S, D $99-$129; each addl $10; under 12 free; ski plans; higher rates hol wknds. Crib free. TV; cable (premium). 2 pools, 1 indoor; whirlpools, sauna. Restaurant 7 am-9 pm. Bar noon-1 am. Ck-out 11 am. Coin lndry. Meeting rms. Sundries. Gift shop. Lighted tennis. Downhill/x-country ski 5 mi. Game rm. Rec rm. Lawn games. Refrigerators; some in-rm whirlpools. Private patios, balconies. Stocked pond. View of mountains. Cr cds: A, DS, MC, V.

★★ JACK O'LANTERN RESORT. *Rte 3 (03293), 5½ mi S on US 3, W of I-93 Exit 30. 603/745-8121; fax 603/745-4989; toll-free 800/227-4454.* 23 motel rms, 30 cottages (1-3 bedrm), 20 condos. Mid-May-mid-Oct: S, D $66-$110; cottages $64-$108; condos (all-yr) $136-$220; under 12 free; MAP avail in season; golf packages. Closed rest of yr. Crib $12. TV; cable, VCR avail. 2 pools, 1 indoor; wading pool, whirlpool, sauna, poolside serv in summer. Playground. Dining rm 7:30-11 am, 5:30-9 pm. Bar in season. Ck-out 11 am, ck-in 3 pm. Grocery 2 mi. Package store 4 mi. Gift shop. Tennis. 18-hole golf. Swimming beach. Lawn games. Entertainment. Game rm. Rec rm. 300 wooded acres on Pemigewasset River. Cr cds: A, DS, MC, V.

★★★ MOUNTAIN CLUB ON LOON. *Rte 112, Kancamagus Hwy (03251), 3 mi E of I-93 Exit 32, on NH 112. 603/745-2244; fax 603/745-2317; res 800/229-7829. Email rooms@loon.newcastlehotels.com; www. mtnclubonloon.com.* 234 rms, 4-6 story, 117 kit. suites. Dec-mid-Apr: S, D $109-$190; each addl $20; kit. suites $169-$399; under 12 free; ski plans; lower rates rest of yr. Crib free. TV; cable. 2 pools, 1 indoor; whirlpool. Supervised children's activities (July-Aug); ages 5-12. Dining rm 7:30-10:30 am, 11:30 am-2 pm, 5:30-9 pm. Bar; entertainment Tues-Sat (ski season). Ck-out 11 am. Coin lndry. Meeting rms. Bellhops (ski season). Concierge. Tennis. Downhill/x-country ski on site. Exercise equipt; sauna. Game rm. Rec rm. Some in-rm whirlpools. Balconies. Picnic tables. Nature trail. Cr cds: A, DS, MC, V.

★★★ **WOODWARD RESORT.** *Rte 3 (03251), 1 mi N of I-93 Exit 33. 603/745-8141; fax 603/745-3408; res 800/635-8968. Email woodwards@ linwoodnet.com; www.woodwardsresort. com.* 80 rms, 1-2 story. S, D $60-$109; each addl $5; 2-bedrm cottages for 3-6, $100-$140; MAP avail; ski plan. Crib free. TV; cable. 2 pools, 1 indoor; whirlpool. Playground. Restaurant 7:30-10:30 am, 5-8:30 pm. Bar from 4 pm. Ck-out 11 am. Coin lndry. Meeting rm. Tennis. Downhill ski 5 mi. Sauna. Game rm. Lawn games. Refrigerators. Some balconies. Duck pond. On mountain stream. Cr cds: A, DS, MC, V.

B&Bs/Small Inns

★ **WILDERNESS INN BED & BREAKFAST.** *Rtes 3 and 112 (1 blk S on Rte 3) (03262), I-93 Exit 32. 603/745-3890; fax 603/745-6367.* 7 rms in house, 2 share bath, 3 with shower only, 2 story, 1 cottage. No rm phones. S $40-$80; D $45-$105; each addl $10; under 6 free; ski plan; higher rates: hols (2-day min), fall foliage. Crib free. TV in sitting rm; cable. Complimentary full bkfst; afternoon refreshments. Restaurant nearby. Ck-out 11 am, ck-in 3 pm. Downhill/x-country ski 3 mi. Croquet. Built 1912; view of Lost River and mountains. Totally nonsmoking. Cr cds: A, MC, V.

★★ **WOODSTOCK INN.** *135 Main St (03262), N on US 3. 603/745-3951; fax 603/745-3701.* 19 rms, 11 with bath, 8 share bath, 3 story. June-Oct: S $35-$125; D $45-$135; under 12 free (up to 2), each addl child $8; MAP avail; ski packages; higher rates fall foliage, some wkends; lower rates rest of yr. TV; cable, VCR avail. Complimentary full bkfst. Dining rm 7 am-10 pm (see also WOODSTOCK INN). Bar 11:30 am-midnight. Ck-out 11 am, ck-in 2 pm. Gift shop. Downhill/x-country ski 3 mi. Some in-rm

whirlpools, refrigerators, gas fireplaces. Balconies. Victorian house (1890); antique furnishings. Some rms with view of river. Cr cds: A, D, DS, MC, V.

Restaurants

★★ **COMMON MAN.** *Pollard Rd (03217), 1 mi E of I-93 Exit 32. 603/745-3463.* Specializes in prime rib, fresh seafood, pasta. Hrs: 5-9 pm; Fri, Sat to 9:30 pm. Closed Dec 24, 25. Bar. Dinner $9.95-$16.95. Child's menu. Parking. Rustic decor; fireplace, antiques. Converted farmhouse; one of oldest structures in city. Cr cds: A, DS, MC, V.

★★ **GORDI'S FISH & STEAK HOUSE.** *Kancamagus Hwy (03251), at the Depot. 603/745-6635.* Specializes in Maine lobster, prime rib, seafood. Salad bar. Hrs: noon-9 pm; hrs vary off-season. Closed Thanksgiving, Dec 25. Res accepted. Bar. Lunch $4-$8; dinner $6.95-$18.95. Child's menu. Parking. Contemporary bldg with Victorian accents. Olympic ski motif. Cr cds: A, DS, MC, V.

★★ **GOVONI'S ITALIAN.** *Lost River Rd (03262). 603/745-8042.* Specializes in scallop-stuffed scampi, veal parmigiana, homemade desserts. Hrs: 4:30-9 pm. Closed Labor Day-Memorial Day; also Mon-Wed in early June. Bar. Dinner $6.95-$15.95. Child's menu. Parking. White clapboard bldg; formerly a schoolhouse, constructed over mountain stream. Cr cds: MC, V.

★★ **OLD TIMBERMILL PUB & RESTAURANT.** *Main St (03251), at Millfront Marketplace. 603/745-3603.* Specializes in seafood, steak. Hrs: 11:30 am-9 pm. Bar. Lunch, dinner $10-$19. Entertainment: wkends. Converted mill drying shed (1926). Cr cds: A, DS, MC, V.

★ **TRUANTS TAVERNE.** *96 Main St (03262), at jct US 3 and NH 112. 603/745-2239. www.truants.com.* Specializes in seafood, steak. Hrs: 11:30 am-9 pm; Fri, Sat to 10 pm. Closed Thanksgiving, Dec 25. Bar. Lunch $4.95-$10.25; dinner $4.95-$15.50. Child's menu. Parking. Rustic decor

with old schoolhouse motif. Cr cds:
A, DS, MC, V.

D ⊡

★★ **WOODSTOCK INN.** *Main St
(US 3).* 603/745-3951. www.woodstock
innnh.com. Continental menu. Spe-
cializes in seafood, veal. Hrs: 7 am-10
pm. Closed Dec 25. Res accepted.
Bar. Bkfst $2.50-$8.50; lunch $12-
$24; dinner $12-$24. Child's menu.
Entertainment: wkends in season. In
Victorian house (1890). Cr cds: A, D,
MC, V.

D

Littleton

(D-4) *See also Franconia*

Chartered 1784 **Pop** 5,827 **Elev** 822 ft
Area code 603 **Zip** 03561
Web www.littletonareachamber.com
Information Chamber of Commerce,
120 Main St, PO Box 105; 603/444-
6561 or 888/822-2687

Littleton is a resort area a few miles
northwest of the White Mountain
National Forest (see), which maintains a Ranger District office in
nearby Bethlehem. Littleton is also a
regional commercial center; its
industries produce abrasives and
electrical component parts. The
Ammonoosuc River falls 235 feet on
its way through the community.

What to See and Do

Littleton Historical Museum. Photographs, arts and crafts, stereo-
graphs, local memorabilia. (July-Sep,
Wed, Sat afternoons; rest of yr, Wed
afternoons) 2 Union St. Phone
603/444-6586 or 603/444-2637.
FREE

Samuel C. Moore Station. Largest
conventional hydroelectric plant in
New England; 2,920-ft dam across
Connecticut River forms Moore
Reservoir, which extends nearly 11
mi and covers an area of 3,490 acres.
Visitor center has exhibits (daily).
Recreation areas offer hunting, fish-
ing, boat launching, waterskiing; pic-
nicking and nature studies.
(Memorial Day-Columbus Day, daily)

8 mi W on NH 18, 135. Phone
603/638-2327. **FREE**

Motel/Motor Lodge

★★ **EASTGATE MOTOR INN.** *335
Cottage St (03561), I-93 Exit 41.* 603/
444-3971; fax 603/444-3971. 55 rms.
S $44-$64; D $50-$70; each addl $7;
under 6 free. Pet accepted. TV; cable
(premium). Heated pool; wading
pool. Playground. Complimentary
continental bkfst. Restaurant (see
EASTGATE). Bar. Ck-out 11 am.
Meeting rms. Business servs avail.
Downhill ski 7 mi; x-country ski 6
mi. Lawn games. Cr cds: A, C, D, DS,
MC, V.

B&Bs/Small Inns

★★★ **ADAIR COUNTRY INN.** *80
Guider Ln (03574), I-93 Exit 40 at US
302.* 603/444-2600; fax 603/444-
4823; toll-free 888/444-2600. Email
adair@connriver.net; www.adairinn.com.
7 rms, 3 story, 2 suites. Sep-Oct: D
$185; suites $250; each addl $32;
lower rates rest of yr. Parking lot. TV;
cable, VCR avail. Complimentary full
bkfst. Restaurant 5:30-9 pm. Ck-out
11 am, ck-in 3 pm. Meeting rm. Business servs avail. Gift shop. Golf. Tennis. Downhill skiing. Hiking trail. Cr
cds: A, DS, MC, V.

★ **MULBURN.** *2370 Main St (03574),
6 mi E on US 302.* 603/869-3389; fax
603/869-5633. 7 rms, 2 story. No
A/C. No rm phones. S, D $70-$97;
each addl $10; wkly rates; ski, golf
plans; higher rates fall foliage. Closed
Dec 24, 25. Crib $10. TV in lobby.
Playground. Complimentary full
bkfst. Restaurant nearby. Ck-out 10
am, ck-in 3 pm. Downhill/x-country
ski 10 mi. Exercise equipt. Lawn
games. Built 1913 by F.W. Wool-
worth as summer home. Antiques.
Sitting rm. Totally nonsmoking. Cr
cds: A, MC, V.

★★ **THAYER'S INN.** *111 Main St
(03561).* 603/444-6469; fax 603/444-
6469; toll-free 800/634-8179. www.
thayersinn.com. 40 rms, 24 with bath,
4 story, 6 suites (2-bedrm). No elvtr.
Some rm phones. S, D $39-$89;

suites $69-$89; under 6 free; ski, spring break plans. Crib free. TV; cable (premium). Pool privileges. Ck-out 11 am, ck-in 2 pm. Downhill/x-country ski 10 mi. Some refrigerators. Historic inn (1843); antiques, library, sitting rm. Cupola open to public. Cr cds: A, C, D, DS, MC, V.

★★ **WAYSIDE.** *3738 Main St (03574), 6 mi SE on US 302. 603/869-3364; fax 603/869-5765; toll-free 800/448-9557. Email info@thewaysideinn. com.* 14 rms in inn, 2 story; 12 rms in motel, 2 story. Mid-May-late Oct, Dec-late Mar: S $58; D $68-$78; each addl $5; under 12 free; MAP avail; golf, ski plans; lower rates rest of yr. Crib avail. TV in motel rms, living rm of inn; cable. Dining rm 7:30-9:30 am, 6-9 pm. Bar. Ck-out 11 am, ck-in 3 pm. Tennis. 18-hole golf privileges. Downhill ski 8 mi; x-country ski on site. Lawn games. Some in-rm whirlpools, refrigerators. Balconies in motel. Originally 4-rm homestead (1825) for the family of President Franklin Pierce. On Ammonoosuc River; natural sand beach. Cr cds: A, DS, MC, V.

Restaurants

★★ **CLAM SHELL.** *US 302 (03561). 603/444-6445.* Mediterranean menu. Specializes in fresh seafood, prime rib. Salad bar. Own desserts. Hrs: 11:30 am-9 pm; Fri, Sat to 9:30 pm; Sun from noon. Closed Dec 24, 25. Bar. Lunch $4-$8.50; dinner $6.95-$15.95. Child's menu. Cr cds: A, DS, MC, V.

★ **EASTGATE.** *335 Cottage St. 603/444-3971. www.eastgatemotorinn. com.* Specializes in seafood, chicken, prime rib au jus. Hrs: 5-9 pm; Fri, Sat to 9:30 pm. Closed Dec 24. Res accepted. Bar. Dinner $5.95-$15.95. Gazebo with fountain; view of Mt Eustis. Cr cds: A, D, DS, MC, V.

★★ **ITALIAN OASIS.** *106 Main St (03561), in Parker's Marketplace. 603/444-6995.* Specializes in Italian dishes, steak, seafood. Hrs: 11:30 am-10 pm. Closed Easter, Thanksgiving, Dec 25. Res accepted. Bar. Lunch a la carte entrees: $2.95-$6.95; dinner a la carte entrees: $4.95-$14.95. Converted Victorian home (ca 1890). Cr cds: A, DS, MC, V.

★★ **ROSA FLAMINGOS.** *Main St (03574), 6 mi E on US 302. 603/869-3111.* Italian menu. Specializes in tortellini carbonara, fettucine Rosa. Hrs: 5-10 pm; Fri-Sun 11:30 am-4 pm. Closed Easter, Thanksgiving, Dec 25. Res accepted. Bar. Lunch $3.95-$7.50; dinner $5.75-$16.75. Child's menu. Cr cds: A, MC, V.

Lyme

(see Hanover)

Manchester

(H-5) *See also Concord, Nashua*

Settled 1722 **Pop** 99,567 **Elev** 225 ft
Area code 603
Web www.manchester-chamber.org
Information Chamber of Commerce, 889 Elm St, 03101-2000; 603/666-6600

Manchester is a city that has refused to bow to economic adversity. When the Amoskeag Manufacturing Company (cotton textiles), which had dominated Manchester's economy, failed in 1935, it left the city poverty-stricken. With determination worthy of New Englanders, a group of citizens bought the plant for $5,000,000 and revived the city. Now Manchester is northern New England's premier financial center.

What to See and Do

Currier Gallery of Art. One of New England's leading small museums; 13th-20th-century European and American paintings and sculpture, New England decorative art, furniture, glass, silver, and pewter; changing exhibitions, concerts, films, other programs. Tours of Zimmerman House (Frank Lloyd Wright). (Wed-Mon; closed hols) 201 Myrtle Way. Phone 603/669-6144. ¢¢

Manchester Historic Association.
Museum and library with collections
illustrating life in Manchester from
pre-Colonial times to present; fire-
fighting equipment; decorative arts,
costumes, paintings; changing
exhibits. (Tues-Sat; closed hols) 129
Amherst St, 2 blks E of Elm St. Phone
603/622-7531. **FREE**

Palace Theatre. Productions in vintage vaudeville/opera house. 80
Hanover St. Phone 603/668-5588.

**Science Enrichment Encounters
Museum.** More than 60 interactive,
hands-on exhibits demonstrate basic
science principles. (July-Aug, daily;
rest of yr, Thurs eves, Sat and Sun;
closed hols) 200 Bedford St. Phone
603/669-0400. ¢¢

Annual Event

Riverfest. Outdoor festival with family entertainment, concerts, arts and
crafts, food booths, fireworks. Phone
603/623-2623. Labor Day wkend.

Motels/Motor Lodges

★ **ECONO LODGE.** *75 W Hancock St
(03101), I-293 Exit 4. 603/624-0111;
fax 603/623-0268; toll-free 800/553-
2666.* 120 rms, 5 story. S $40; D $45;
each addl $5; under 18 free; wkly,
monthly rates. Crib free. Pet
accepted. TV; cable. Complimentary
coffee in lobby. Restaurant opp 6:30
am-9 pm. Ck-out 11 am. Coin lndry.
Business servs avail. Some refrigerators. Cr cds: A, C, D, DS, MC, V.
D 🐾 ⊠ 🖐 SC

★ **SUPER 8-AIRPORT.** *2301 Brown
Ave (03103), I-293 Exit 2, near Municipal Airport. 603/623-0883; fax 603/
624-9303; toll-free 800/800-8000.* 85 rms,
4 story. June-Labor Day: S $48.88-
$74.88; D $55.88-$79.88; each addl
$5; suites $84.88-$89.88; higher rates
fall foliage; lower rates rest of yr. Crib
free. TV; cable, VCR avail (movies).
Complimentary coffee. Restaurant
nearby. Ck-out 11 am. Meeting rms.
Business servs avail. Valet serv. Free
airport transportation. Refrigerator,
whirlpool in some suites. Cr cds: A,
C, D, DS, MC, V.
D 🖐 ⊠ 🖐 🖐

★ **SUSSE CHALET INN.** *860 S Porter
St (03103), I-293, Exit 1. 603/
625-2020; fax 603/623-7562; toll-free*

800/525-2538. 102 rms, 4 story. S, D
$56.70-$63.70; each addl $7. TV;
cable (premium). Pool. Complimentary continental bkfst. Restaurant
opp 6 am-11 pm. Ck-out 11 am.
Coin lndry. Business servs avail. In-
rm modem link. Sundries. Valet serv.
Refrigerators avail. Cr cds: A, C, D,
DS, MC, V.
D ⊠ ⊠ 🖐 SC

Hotels

★★ **CENTER OF NH HOLIDAY
INN.** *700 Elm St (03101). 603/
625-1000; fax 603/625-4595; res
800/405-4329. Email cnh@grolen.com.*
250 rms, 12 story. S $98-$129; D
$103-$134; suites $195-$495; under
19 free; wknd rates. Crib free. TV;
cable (premium). Indoor pool; whirlpool. Coffee in rms. Restaurant 6:30
am-10 pm. Bar from noon; entertainment Fri, Sat. Ck-out 11 am. Convention facilities. Business servs
avail. In-rm modem link. Gift shop.
Validated indoor parking. Airport
transportation. Exercise equipt;
sauna. Bathrm phone in suites. Cr
cds: A, DS, MC, V.
⊠ 🏋 ⊠ ⊠ 🖐

★★ **COMFORT INN.** *298 Queen City
Ave (03102), I-293 Exit 4. 603/668-
2600; fax 603/668-2600; res 800/228-
5150.* 100 rms, 5 story, 4 suites.
Apr-Oct: S, D $159; suites $200; each
addl $10; under 18 free; lower rates
rest of yr. Crib avail. Pet accepted,
some restrictions. Parking lot. Indoor
pool. TV; cable (premium), VCR avail.
Complimentary continental bkfst,
newspaper, toll-free calls. Restaurant
nearby. Ck-out 11 am, ck-in 3 pm.
Meeting rms. Internet access avail.
Bellhops. Concierge. Dry cleaning,
coin lndry. Free airport transportation. Exercise privileges, sauna. Golf.
Tennis. Hiking trail. Cr cds: A, C, D,
DS, MC, V.
D 🖐 🏋 🍴 ⊠ 🏋 🖐 🖐 SC

★★ **FOUR POINTS HOTEL.** *55 John
E. Devine Dr (03103), I-293 Exit 1.
603/668-6110; fax 603/668-0408; res
800/325-3535. Email www.mht
4ptsso@aol.com; www.fourpoints.
com/manchester.* 119 rms, 4 story, 1
suite. June-Oct: S, D $149; suites
$200; each addl $10; under 17 free;
lower rates rest of yr. Crib avail. Park-

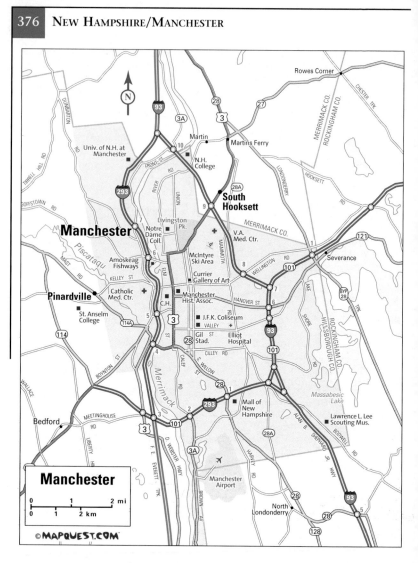

ing lot. Indoor pool, whirlpool. TV; cable (premium). Complimentary coffee in rms, newspaper, toll-free calls. Restaurant 7 am-9 pm. Bar. Ck-out noon, ck-in 2 pm. Meeting rms. Business center. Dry cleaning. Free airport transportation. Exercise privileges. Golf. Downhill skiing. Video games. Cr cds: A, C, D, DS, ER, JCB, MC, V.

D 🐕 🧖 ➳ 👟 ✈ 🛶 🔥 SC 🚶

B&B/Small Inn

★★★ BEDFORD VILLAGE INN.
2 Village Inn Ln (03110), 8 mi SW via NH 101; 5 mi W of I-293, Bedford Exit. 603/472-2001; fax 603/472-2379; toll-free 800/852-1166. Email bvi@tiac.net. 14 suites, 3 story, 2 kits. Suites $155-$195; kits. $250-$375. Crib $15. TV; cable (premium). Afternoon refreshments. Restaurant (see BEDFORD VILLAGE INN). Ck-out 11 am, ck-in 3 pm. Meeting rms. Business servs avail. In-rm modem link. Gift shop. In-rm whirlpools; some wet bars. Some balconies. Converted barn built early 1800s; antique furnishings, rms individually decorated. Cr cds: A, DS, MC, V.

🛶 🔥

Conference Center

★★★ WAYFARER INN AND CONVENTION CENTER. *121 S River Rd (03110), 3 mi S at jct US 3 and NH*

101, 1 blk N of Everett Tpke, Bedford Exit. 603/622-3766; fax 603/623-5796; toll-free 800/544-5064. 194 rms, 2-3 story. No elvtr. S, D $79-$115; each addl $10; suites $175; under 18 free; package plans. Crib free. TV; cable (premium). 2 pools, 1 indoor; whirlpool, poolside serv, lifeguard. Coffee in rms. Restaurant 6:30 am-10 pm; Sat, Sun 7 am-10:30 pm. Bar 11:30-12:30 am; entertainment Thurs-Sat. Ck-out noon. Meeting rms. Business servs avail. In-rm modem link. Valet serv. Sundries. Free airport transportation. Exercise equipt; sauna, steam rm. Some refrigerators. Balconies. Country-inn decor. Cr cds: A, C, D, DS, ER, MC, V.
🄳 🌢 ⚡ ➳ 🏊 🎿 ➳ ◿ SC

Restaurants

★ ★ ★ **BEDFORD VILLAGE INN.** *2 Village Inn Ln. 603/472-2001. www. bedfordvillageinn.com.* Specializes in New England-style dishes. Own baking. Hrs: 7 am-9 pm; Sat, Sun from 8 am. Closed Dec 25. Res accepted. Bar. Wine list. Bkfst $4.50-$10.50; lunch $4.95-$18; dinner $17.50-$31. Sun brunch $6.50-$12.50. Gift shop. Yellow clapboard structure originally part of homestead (1790). Cr cds: A, D, MC, V.
🄳

★ **PURITAN BACKROOM.** *245 Hooksett Rd (03104). 603/669-6890. www.puritanbackroom.com.* Specializes in chicken tenders, barbecued lamb. Own ice cream. Hrs: 11 am-11:30 pm; Wed to midnight; Thurs-Sat to 12:30 am. Closed Thanksgiving, Dec 25. Bar. Lunch, dinner $3.95-$18. Child's menu. Stained-glass windows; many paintings. Cr cds: A, DS, MC, V.
🄳

Meredith

(F-5) *See also Holderness, Laconia, Plymouth*

Founded 1768 **Pop** 4,837 **Elev** 552 ft
Area code 603 **Zip** 03253
Web www.meredithcc.org
Information Chamber of Commerce, PO Box 732; 603/279-6121

Between Lakes Winnipesaukee and Waukewan in the Lakes Region, Meredith is a year-round recreation area.

What to See and Do

League of New Hampshire Craftsmen—Meredith/Laconia Arts and Crafts. Work by some of New Hampshire's finest craftspeople. (Daily) On US 3. Phone 603/279-7920. **FREE**

✪ **Winnipesaukee Scenic Railroad.** Scenic train rides along shore of Lake Winnipesaukee. Board in Meredith or Weirs Beach. (Memorial Day-Columbus Day) Fall foliage trains to Plymouth. Phone 603/279-5253 or 603/745-2135. Excursion ¢¢¢; Dinner train ¢¢¢¢

Annual Events

Great Rotary Fishing Derby. Second wkend Feb.

Lakes Region Fine Arts and Crafts Festival. Juried show featuring more than 100 New England artists. Music, children's theater, food. Last wkend Aug.

Altrusa Annual Antique Show and Sale. Third Sat Sep.

Motels/Motor Lodges

★ **MATTERHORN MOTOR LODGE.** *Rte 25 at Moultonboro Neck Rd (03254), 6 mi NE on NH 25 at Moultonboro Neck Rd. 603/253-4314; fax 603/253-4314.* 28 rms, 2 story. June-Oct: S, D $125; each addl $20; children $10; under 12 free; lower rates rest of yr. Crib avail, fee. Parking lot. Pool. TV; cable (DSS). Complimentary toll-free calls. Restaurant. Ck-out 11 am, ck-in 1 pm. Fax servs avail. Golf, 18 holes. Tennis, 3 courts. Downhill skiing. Picnic facilities. Cr cds: A, C, D, DS, MC, V.
🌢 ⚡ 🏊 🎿 ⛷ ➳ ➳ ◿

★ **MEADOWS LAKESIDE LODGING.** *Rte 25, PO Box 204 (03226), 5 mi NE on NH 25. 603/253-4347; fax 603/253-6171.* 35 rms, 3 story. June-Aug: S $75; D $95; each addl $15; under 4 free; lower rates rest of yr. Crib avail, fee. Pet accepted. Parking lot. TV; cable (DSS). Restaurant nearby. Ck-out 11 am, ck-in 3 pm.

Golf. Beach access. Picnic facilities.
Cr cds: A, DS, MC, V.

B&Bs/Small Inns

★★★ THE INN AT BAY POINT.
312 Daniel Webster Hwy (03253), Rtes 3 and 25. 603/279-7006; fax 603/279-7402; toll-free 800/622-6455. Email info@millfalls.com. 24 rms, 4 story. June-Oct: S, D $139-$249; each addl $15; under 12 free; wkly, wkend rates; ski plans; wkends, hols (2-3-day min); lower rates rest of yr. Crib free. TV; cable, VCR avail (movies). Pool privileges. Whirlpool. Complimentary continental bkfst, coffee in rms. Restaurant 11:30 am-9 pm. Bar. Ck-out 11 am. Meeting rms. Business servs avail. Gift shop. Downhill ski 12 mi; x-country ski on nearby lake. Exercise equipt; sauna. Some refrigerators. Balconies. Picnic tables. On lake; private dock, beach. Cr cds: A, DS, MC, V.

★★★ THE INN AT MILL FALLS.
312 Daniel Webster Hwy #28 (03253), on US 3 at Dover St. 603/279-7000; fax 603/279-6797; toll-free 800/622-6455. Email info@millfalls.com. 54 rms, 5 story. June-Oct: D $89-$195; each addl $15; ski plans; lower rates rest of yr. Crib free. TV; cable, VCR avail (movies). Indoor pool; whirlpool. Complimentary coffee in lobby. Restaurant nearby. Ck-out 11 am, ck-in 3 pm. Meeting rms. Business servs avail. Sauna. Some fireplaces; refrigerators avail. Balconies. On lake. Antique furnishings; some rms with lake view. Adj to historic Mill Falls Marketplace. Cr cds: A, DS, MC, V.

★★★ OLDE ORCHARD INN.
108 Lee Rd, RR Box 256 (03254), approx 7 mi N on NH 25. 603/476-5004; fax 603/476-5419; toll-free 800/598-5845. Email innkeep@oldeorchardinn.com; www.oldeorchardinn.com. 9 rms, 2 story. June-Oct: S, D $100; each addl $25; children $25; lower rates rest of yr. Crib avail, fee. Pet accepted, some restrictions, fee. Parking lot. TV; cable, VCR avail. Complimentary full bkfst, coffee in rms, toll-free calls. Restaurant 5-10 pm. Ck-out 11 am, ck-in 3 pm. Meeting rm. Fax servs avail. Gift shop. Exercise equipt, sauna, whirlpool. Golf, 9 holes. Ten-

nis, 2 courts. Downhill skiing. Beach access. Bike rentals. Supervised children's activities. Hiking trail. Picnic facilities. Cr cds: DS, MC, V.

★★ RED HILL INN.
RR 25B and College Rd (03226), 3 mi N on US 3, E on NH 25B. 603/279-7001; fax 603/279-7003; toll-free 800/573-3445. Email info@redhillinn.com; www.red hillinn.com. 18 rms, 3 story, 8 suites. S $114; D $175; suites $175; each addl $20; children $20. Crib avail, fee. Parking lot. TV; cable, VCR avail, VCR avail. Complimentary full bkfst. Restaurant 8 am-10 pm. Bar. Ck-out 11 am, ck-in 3 pm. Meeting rms. Business center. Gift shop. Golf. Tennis. Downhill skiing. Beach access. Bike rentals. Hiking trail. Cr cds: A, C, D, DS, MC, V.

Restaurants

★★ HART'S TURKEY FARM.
NH 3 and 104 (03253). 603/279-6212. www.hartsturkeyfarm.com. Specializes in turkey, seafood, prime rib. Hrs: 11:15 am-8 pm; Fri, Sat to 8:30 pm. Lunch $3.95-$9.75; dinner $7.95-$15.95. Child's menu. Gift shop. Cr cds: A, D, DS, MC, V.

★★ MAME'S.
8 Plymouth St (03253). 603/279-4631. Email mames@ fcgnetworks.net. Specializes in prime rib, seafood, chicken. Hrs: 11:30 am-9 pm; Fri, Sat 11 am-9:30 pm; Sun from 11 am. Bar. Wine list. Lunch $4-$8.95; dinner $7-$18. Sun brunch $3.95-$6.95. Child's menu. Converted brick house and barn (1825). Cr cds: A, DS, MC, V.

Mount Washington

See also Bretton Woods, Gorham, Jackson

Web www.4seasonresort.com or www.mountwashington.org

Information Mount Washington Valley Chamber of Commerce, N Main

St, PO Box 2300, North Conway 03860; 603/356-5701 or 800/367-3364

(10 mi S of Gorham on NH 16)

Mount Washington is the central peak of the White Mountains and the highest point in the northeastern United States (6,288 feet). At the summit is a 54-acre state park with an information center, first aid station, restaurant, and gift shop. The mountain has the world's first cog railway, completed in 1869; a road to the top dates from 1861. P. T. Barnum called the view from the summit "the second-greatest show on earth."

The weather on Mount Washington is so violent that the timberline is at about 4,000 feet; in the Rockies it is nearer 10,000 feet. In the treeless zone are alpine plants and insects, some unique to the region. The weather station here recorded a wind speed of 231 miles per hour in April, 1934—a world record. The lowest temperature recorded was -49° F; the year-round average is below freezing. The peak gets nearly 15 feet of snow each year.

What to See and Do

Auto road. Trip takes approx 30 min each way. *Note:* Make sure your car is in good condition; check brakes before starting. (Mid-May-mid-Oct, daily, weather permitting) Guided tour service avail (daily). Approaches from the E side, in Pinkham Notch, 8 mi S of Gorham on NH 16. Phone 603/466-3988. ¢¢¢¢ Opp is

> **Great Glen Trails.** All-season, non-motorized recreational trails park featuring biking programs (rentals), fly-fishing instruction and programs, hiking programs (guide or unguided), kayak and canoe tours and workshops in summer; cross-country skiing, snowshoeing, and snow tubing in winter. (Daily; closed Apr) For detailed brochure with schedule and fees, contact NH 16, Pinkham Notch, Gorham 03581. Phone 603/466-2333. ¢¢¢

✪ **Cog railway.** Allow at least 3 hrs for round trip. (May-Memorial Day, wkends; Memorial Day-Nov, daily) Base station road, off US 302, 4 mi E of jct US 3, 302; on W slope of mountain. Phone 603/846-5404 or 800/922-8825. ¢¢¢¢

Hiking trails. Many crisscross the mountain; some reach the top. Hikers should check weather conditions at Pinkham Notch headquarters before climbing. Phone 603/466-2725. **FREE**

Mount Washington Summit Museum. Displays on life in the extreme climate of the summit; rare flora and fauna; geology, history. (Memorial Day-Columbus Day, daily) Top of Mount Washington. Phone 603/466-3388. ¢

Pinkham Notch. (see) SE of Mt Washington on NH 16.

White Mountain National Forest. (see).

Nashua

(H-5) *See also Manchester, Salem*

Settled 1656 **Pop** 79,662 **Elev** 169 ft
Area code 603
Web www.nashuachamber.com
Information Greater Nashua Chamber of Commerce, 146 Main St, 2nd flr, 03060; 603/881-8333

Originally a fur trading post, Nashua's manufacturing began with the development of Merrimack River water power early in the 19th century. The city, second-largest in New Hampshire, has more than 100 diversified industries ranging from computers and tools to beer.

What to See and Do

Anheuser-Busch, Inc. Guided tours of brewery; sampling rm, gift shop. Children only with adult; no pets. 221 Daniel Webster Hwy (US 3) in Merrimack, Everett Tpke Exit 10. Phone 603/595-1202. **FREE** Adj is

> **Clydesdale Hamlet.** Bldgs modeled after a 19th-century European-style farm are the living quarters for the famous Clydesdales (at least 15 are here at all times); carriage house contains vintage wagons. **FREE**

Silver Lake State Park. 1,000-ft sand beach on a 34-acre lake, swimming, bathhouse; picnicking. (Late June-Labor Day) Standard fees. 8 mi W on NH 130 to Hollis, then 1 mi N off NH 122. Phone 603/465-2342.

Mount Washington

Seasonal Event

American Stage Festival. 5 mi NW off NH 101 in Milford. Five plays; music events, children's series. Phone 603/886-7000. June-Sep.

Motels/Motor Lodges

★★ **COMFORT INN.** *10 St. Laurent St (03060), at jct NH 101A, Everett Tpke (US 3) Exit 7E. 603/883-7700; fax 603/595-2107; res 800/228-5150; toll-free 800/762-7482.* 103 rms, 2 story. S $59-$89; D $64-$99; under 18 free. Crib free. TV; cable (premium), VCR avail (movies). Pool. Complimentary continental bkfst. Restaurant adj 11:30 am-10:30 pm; Sun from noon. Bar. Ck-out noon. Meeting rm. Business servs avail. Valet serv. Health club privileges. Refrigerators avail. Cr cds: A, DS, MC, V.

★★ **FAIRFIELD INN.** *4 Amherst Rd (03054), 6 mi N on Everett Tpke (US 3) Exit 11, 1 blk W. 603/424-7500; fax 603/424-7500; toll-free 800/228-2800.* 116 rms, 3 story. June-Labor Day: S $62; D $69; each addl $7; under 18 free; higher rates wkends, fall foliage; lower rates rest of yr. TV; cable (premium). Pool. Complimentary continental bkfst. Restaurant nearby. Ck-out noon. Meeting rm. Business servs avail. In-rm modem link. Valet serv. Sundries. Cr cds: A, C, D, DS, MC, V.

★★ **RED ROOF INN.** *77 Spitbrook Rd (03060), at US 3 Exit 1. 603/888-1893; fax 603/888-5889; res 800/733-* 7663. Email i0122@redroof.com; www.redroof.com. 115 rms, 3 story. May-Oct: S $68; D $77; each addl $7; under 18 free; lower rates rest of yr. Crib avail. Pet accepted. Parking lot. TV; cable (DSS). Complimentary newspaper. Restaurant nearby. Ck-out noon, ck-in 3 pm. Business servs avail. Dry cleaning, coin lndry. Golf. Downhill skiing. Picnic facilities. Video games. Cr cds: A, C, D, DS, MC, V.

★★ **RESIDENCE INN BY MARRIOTT.** *246 Daniel Webster Hwy (03054), 5 mi N on US 3. 603/424-8100; fax 603/424-3128; res 800/331-3131.* 129 kit. suites, 2 story. Kit. suites $102-$160. Crib free. Pet accepted; $50 and $5/day. TV; cable (premium). Pool; whirlpool. Complimentary continental bkfst. Ck-out noon. Coin lndry. Meeting rms. Business servs avail. In-rm modem link. Valet serv. Health club privileges. Sport court. Many fireplaces. Grills. Cr cds: A, DS, MC, V.

Hotels

★★★ **CROWNE PLAZA HOTEL.** *2 Somerset Pkwy (03063), off Everett Tpke (US 3) Exit 8. 603/886-1200; fax 603/595-4199; res 800/962-7482.* 213 rms, 8 story. S, D $89-$129; each addl $10; suites $150-$250; under 18 free; wkend package plans. Crib free. TV; cable. Indoor pool; whirlpool. Complimentary coffee in rms. Restaurant 6 am-10 pm; dining rm from 5:30 pm. Bar 11:30-12:30 am. Ck-out noon. Meeting rms. Business servs avail. In-rm modem link. Gift shop. Beauty shop. Garage parking. Free airport transportation. Tennis. Exercise rm; saunas. Massage. Some in-rm whirlpools; refrigerators avail. 48-seat amphitheater. Luxury level. Cr cds: A, C, D, DS, ER, JCB, MC, V.

★★ **HOLIDAY INN.** *9 Northeastern Blvd (03062), W at US 3 Exit 4.* 603/888-1551; fax 603/888-7193; toll-free 888/801-5661. Email mas1544@aol.com; www.holiday-inn.com. 184 rms, 4 story, 24 suites. May-Oct: S, D $99; suites $139; each addl $10; lower rates rest of yr. Crib avail. Pet accepted. Parking lot. Pool. TV; cable (premium). Complimentary coffee in rms, newspaper, toll-free calls. Restaurant 6:30 am-8 pm. Bar. Ck-out noon, ck-in 3 pm. Meeting rms. Business center. Dry cleaning, coin lndry. Exercise equipt. Golf. Cr cds: A, D, DS, MC, V.

D ◨ ✕ ⊠ ⋀ ⊠ 🐾 ⋀

★★★ **MARRIOTT.** *2200 Southwood Dr (03063), Everett Tpke (US 3) Exit 8.* 603/880-9100; fax 603/886-9489; toll-free 800/362-0962. Oct: S, D $139; suites $275; lower rates rest of yr. Crib avail. TV; cable (DSS). Restaurant 6 am-10 pm. Bar. Ck-out 11 am, ck-in 3 pm. Golf. Tennis. Cr cds: A, C, D, DS, ER, JCB, MC, V.

✕ ⊩ ✈ ⊠

★★★ **SHERATON NASHUA HOTEL.** *11 Tara Blvd (03062), 2 mi S on US 3, at Everett Tpke Exit 1.* 603/888-9970; fax 603/888-4112; res 800/325-3535; toll-free 800/843-8272. www.sheraton.com. 336 rms, 7 story. Sep-Oct: S, D $220; suites $250; each addl $10; lower rates rest of yr. Crib avail. Parking lot. Indoor/outdoor pools, lap pool, lifeguard, whirlpool. TV; cable (premium), VCR avail. Complimentary coffee in rms, newspaper, toll-free calls. Restaurant 7-11. 24-hr rm serv. Bar. Conference center, meeting rms. Bellhops. Concierge. Dry cleaning. Gift shop. Exercise rm, sauna, steam rm. Golf. Tennis. Downhill skiing. Hiking trail. Picnic facilities. Video games. Cr cds: A, C, D, DS, ER, JCB, MC, V.

D ⊠ ✕ ⊩ ⊠ ⋀ ⊠ 🐾 SC

Restaurants

★★ **COUNTRY GOURMET.** *438 Daniel Webster Hwy (03054), 6 mi N on US 3, 1½ mi N of Everett Tpke Exit 11.* 603/424-2755. www.countrygourmet.com. Specializes in seafood, beef, lamb. Hrs: 5-9:30 pm; Fri, Sat to 10 pm; Sun 4-8:30 pm. Closed hols. Res accepted. Bar. Dinner $15-$22.

Child's menu. Entertainment: Thurs-Mon. Originally built 1700s as a tavern. Unique pumpkin-pine wainscoting; original fireplaces and mantels, beamed ceilings. Cr cds: A, D, DS, MC, V.

◨

★ **HANNAH JACK TAVERN.** *Greeley St & Daniel Webster Hwy (03054), E of Everett Tpke Exit 11.* 603/424-4171. Specializes in prime rib, Alaskan king crab legs. Hrs: 11:30 am-8:30 pm; Thurs to 9 pm; Fri to 9:30 pm; Sat 4:30-9:30 pm; Sun from 4 pm. Closed Tues; July 4, Dec 25. Res accepted. Bar. Lunch $5.50-$8.50; dinner $12-$22. Child's menu. Parking. In Colonial bldg over 200 yrs old. Cr cds: A, MC, V.

◨

★ **MODERN.** *116 W Pearl St (03060).* 603/883-8422. Specializes in steak, seafood, chicken. Hrs: 11 am-8 pm. Lunch $2.99-$6.99; dinner $4.99-$17.99. Child's menu. Cr cds: A, C, D, MC, V.

SC ◨

★ **NEWICK'S.** *696 Daniel Webster Hwy (03054), 6 mi N on US 3 Exit 12.* 603/429-0262. Specializes in fresh seafood. Hrs: 11:30 am-8:30 pm; Fri, Sat to 9 pm. Closed Thanksgiving, Dec 25. Bar. Lunch $5.95-$19.95; dinner $5.95-$19.95. Child's menu. Nautical decor. Cr cds: A, DS, MC, V.

D SC ◨

New London

(F-4) *See also Sunapee*

Pop 3,180 **Elev** 825 ft **Area code** 603
Zip 03257

Information Chamber of Commerce, Main St, PO Box 532; 603/526-6575

What to See and Do

Skiing.

Ragged Mountain. Three double chairlifts, T-bar; patrol, school, rentals, snowmaking; cafeteria, bar. Longest run 1½ mi; vertical drop 1,250 ft. (Mid-Nov-Mar, daily) Cross-country skiing. 10 mi E on

NH 11, then 7 mi N on US 4 to Danbury, then 1½ mi E on NH 104 to access road. Phone 603/768-3475. ¢¢¢¢

Seasonal Event

Barn Playhouse. Main St, off NH 11. Live theater presentations nightly; Wed matinees. Also Mon children's attractions. Phone 603/526-4631 or 603/526-6710. Mid-June-Labor Day.

Motels/Motor Lodges

★ **FAIRWAY MOTEL.** *Country Club Ln (03257), at Lake Sunapee Country Club. 603/526-6040; fax 603/526-9622.* 12 rms. S, D $55-$70; each addl $8.50; under 13 free (with 2 adults). Crib free. TV; cable. Pool. Ck-out 11 am. Tennis privileges. Downhill ski 12 mi; x-country ski on site. Cr cds: A, DS, MC, V.

★ **LAMPLIGHTER MOTOR INN.** *6 Newport Rd (03257). 603/526-6484; fax 603/526-9678.* 14 rms, 2 story. S, D $55-$65; kit. units $65-$70; each addl $5. TV; cable, VCR avail. Complimentary continental bkfst. Restaurant nearby. Ck-out 11 am. Business servs avail. Downhill/x-country ski 10 mi. Refrigerators avail. Cr cds: A, DS, MC, V.

B&Bs/Small Inns

★★★ **FOLLANSBEE INN.** *PO Box 92 (03260), 4 mi SE on NH 114. 603/927-4221; fax 603/927-6307; res 603/927-4221; toll-free 800/626-4221. www.follansbeeinn.com.* 23 rms, 3 story. S, D $100; each addl $25; under 12 free. Parking lot. TV; cable (premium), VCR avail. Complimentary full bkfst. Restaurant. Bar. Ck-out 11 am, ck-in 2 pm. Meeting rms. Golf. Tennis, 10 courts. Downhill skiing. Beach access. Bike rentals. Hiking trail. Picnic facilities. Cr cds: MC, V.

★★★ **INN AT PLEASANT LAKE.** *125 N Pleasant St (03257). 603/526-6271; fax 603/526-4111; toll-free 800/626-4907. Email bmackenz@ kear.tds.net; www.innatpleasantlake. com.* 12 rms, some A/C, 3 story. No rm phones. S, D $95-$145; each

addl $25; suite $145; wkly rates. Complimentary full bkfst. Dining rm dinner sitting 6:30 pm. Ck-out 11 am, ck-in 3 pm. Meeting rm. Downhill ski 12 mi; x-country ski 3 mi. Exercise equipt. Some fireplaces. Original Cape farmhouse (1790) converted to summer resort in late 1800s; country antique decor. On Pleasant Lake; private sand beach. Cr cds: A, DS, MC, V.

★★ **NEW LONDON INN.** *140 Main St (03257), I-89 Exit 11, in center of town. 603/526-2791; fax 603/526-2749; toll-free 800/526-2791. Email nlinn@kear.net.* 28 rms, 10 with shower only, 3 story. June-mid-Oct: S $85-$125; D $110-$140; each addl $20; lower rates rest of yr. TV in sitting rm; VCR (free movies). Complimentary continental bkfst. Restaurant (see NEW LONDON INN). Bar from 5 pm. Ck-out 11 am, ck-in 3 pm. Meeting rm. Business servs avail. Downhill/x-country ski 3 mi. Health club privileges. Lawn games. Built 1792. Cr cds: A, MC, V.

Restaurants

★★ **MILLSTONE.** *Newport Rd (NH 11W) (03257). 603/526-4201.* Specializes in veal, seafood, pasta. Own desserts. Hrs: 11:30 am-9 pm. Closed Dec 25. Res accepted. Lunch $5.95-$18.95; dinner $5.95-$18.95. Child's menu. Casual, garden-view dining. Cr cds: A, DS, MC, V.
D

★★ **NEW LONDON INN.** *140 Main St. 603/526-2791. Email nlinn@kear. net; www.newlondoninn.com.* Specializes in garlic-scented New York strip steak, grilled vegetables and shiitake mushroom sampler, herb-crusted Atlantic salmon. Hrs: 5-8:30 pm. Closed Sun. Res accepted; required Fri, Sat. Dinner $13-$22. Child's menu. Colonial decor; overlooks village green, flower gardens. Cr cds: A, MC, V.
D

★★ **POTTER PLACE INN.** *88 Depot St (03216), 8 mi E on NH 11 at jct NH 4. 603/735-5141. Email ppirest@kear. tds.net.* Specializes in veal, roast duckling, fresh seafood and game.

Hrs: 5:30-9 pm. Closed Mon Nov-Apr. Res accepted. Dinner $12-$18. House built 1790s; country atmosphere. Cr cds: A, DS, MC, V.

D

Newport

(G-3) *See also Sunapee*

Settled 1765 **Pop** 6,110 **Elev** 797 ft
Area code 603 **Zip** 03773
Information Chamber of Commerce, 2 N Main St; 603/863-1510

Newport is the commercial headquarters for the Lake Sunapee area. Its industries incl machine tools, woolens, clothing, and firearms. The Town Common Historic District has many churches and Colonial and Victorian houses.

What to See and Do

Fort at No. 4. Reconstructed French and Indian War log fort, complete with stockade, Great Hall, cow barns, and living quarters furnished to reflect 18th-century pioneer living. Exhibits incl Native American artifacts, demonstrations of colonial crafts, and an audiovisual program. (Memorial Day-Labor Day, Wed-Mon; Labor Day-Columbus Day, Sat and Sun) 10 mi W on NH 11/103, then 11 mi S on NH 11/12, near Charlestown. Phone 603/826-5700. ¢¢¢

Motel/Motor Lodge

★ **NEWPORT MOTEL.** *467 Sunapee St (03773), 2 mi E on NH 11/103. 603/863-1440; fax 603/526-9678; toll-free 800/741-2619.* 18 rms. June-Oct: S, D $59.95-$74.95; each addl $7; lower rates rest of yr. TV; cable. Pool. Complimentary coffee. Ck-out 11 am. Downhill ski 5 mi; x-country ski 14 mi. Refrigerators avail. Cr cds: A, C, D, MC, V.

D ⚡ 🏊 ⛷ 🔥

North Conway

(D-6) *See also Bartlett, Jackson*

Settled 1764 **Pop** 2,100 (est)
Elev 531 ft **Area code** 603 **Zip** 03860
Web www.4seasonresort.com
Information Mount Washington Valley Chamber of Commerce, N Main St, PO Box 2300; 603/356-5701 or 800/367-3364

Heart of the famous Mount Washington Valley region of the White Mountains, the area also includes Bartlett, Glen, Jackson, Conway, Redstone, Kearsarge, and Intervale. Mount Washington, seen from the middle of Main Street, is one of the great views in the East.

What to See and Do

Conway Scenic Railroad. Steam and diesel trains depart from restored Victorian station (1874) for 11-mi (55-min) round trip. Valley Train explores the Saco River Valley (mid-May-Oct, daily; mid-Apr-mid-May, Nov and Dec, wkends); Notch Train travels through Crawford Notch (mid-Sep-mid-Oct, daily; late June-mid-Sep, Tues-Sat). Railroad museum. Depot on Main St. Phone 603/356-5251. ¢¢

Covered bridges. In Conway, Jackson, and Bartlett.

Downeast Whitewater Rafting. Specializes in rafting, canoeing, kayak touring, and paddling school. Programs incl guided whitewater rafting trips, whitewater canoe and kayak school, calmwater and whitewater canoe rentals. (May-Oct) US 302, 2 mi E of Center Conway. Phone 603/447-3002. ¢¢¢¢

Echo Lake State Park. Mountain lake in the shadow of White Horse Ledge. Scenic road to 700-ft Cathedral Ledge, dramatic rock formation; panoramic views of the White Mts and the Saco River Valley. Swimming; picnicking. (Late June-Labor Day) Standard fees. 2 mi W, off NH 302. Phone 603/356-2672.

Factory outlet stores. Many outlet malls and stores can be found along NH 16. Contact Chamber of Commerce for more information.

League of New Hampshire Craftsmen. Work by some of New Hampshire's finest craftspeople. (Daily) On NH 16 (Main St). Phone 603/356-2441. **FREE**

Skiing. Mount Cranmore. Express quad, triple, double chairlift to summit, 3 double chairlifts to N, S, and E slopes; patrol, school, rentals, snowmaking; restaurant, bar, cafeterias, day care. Longest run 1¾ mi; vertical drop 1,200 ft. (Dec-Mar, daily) 1 mi E off US 302 (NH 16). Phone 603/356-5543 or 800/786-6754. ¢¢¢¢

White Mountain National Forest. (see) N & S on NH 16; W on US 302.

Annual Events

Mount Washington Valley Equine Classic. Horse jumping. Mid-Aug.

Mud Bowl. (Football) Hog Coliseum. Sep.

Seasonal Event

Eastern Slope Playhouse. Main St, on grounds of Eastern Slope Inn Resort (see MOTELS). Mt Washington Valley Theatre Co presents 4 Broadway musicals. Tues-Sun. Phone 603/356-5776. Late June-early Sep.

Motels/Motor Lodges

★★ **EASTERN SLOPE INN RESORT.** *2760 Main St (03860). 603/356-6847; fax 603/356-8732.* 146 rms, 3 story. S, D $86-$95; each addl $15; townhouse suites $142-$172; under 12 free; ski plans; higher rates fall foliage, hols. TV; cable, VCR avail. Indoor pool; whirlpool. Restaurant noon-midnight; entertainment Fri, Sat. Ck-out 10 am. Coin lndry. Meeting rms. Tennis. Downhill ski 1 mi; x-country ski on site. Sauna. Rec rm. Lawn games. Trout pond. Picnic tables, grills. Golf course adj. Cr cds: A, DS, MC, V.

⊞ ⬟ ⬟ ⬟ ⬟ ⬟ ⬟ ⬟ ⬟ ⬟ ⬟

★ **GOLDEN GABLES INN.** *Rte 16 and US 302 (03860), 1½ mi S on US 302 (NH 16). 603/356-2878; fax 607/356-9094.* 39 rms, 1-2 story. Late June-mid-Oct: S, D $65-$95; each addl $5; lower rates rest of yr. TV; cable (premium). Heated pool. Complimentary coffee. Restaurant nearby. Ck-out 11 am. Downhill/x-country ski 2 mi. Patios, balconies. Cr cds: A, DS, MC, V.

⬟ ⬟ ⬟ ⬟ ⬟ ⬟

★★ **JUNGE'S MOTEL.** *1858 White Mt Hwy Rtes 16 & 302 (03860). 603/356-2886. www.junges motel.com.* 26 rms. Crib avail. Parking lot. Pool. TV; cable, VCR avail. Complimentary toll-free calls. Restaurant nearby. Ck-out 11 am. Golf. Downhill skiing. Hiking trail. Picnic facilities. Cr cds: A, DS, MC, V.

⬟ ⬟ ⬟ ⬟ ⬟ ⬟

★ **SWISS CHALETS VILLAGE INN.** *Rte 16A (03845), 3 mi N. 603/356-2232; fax 603/356-7331; toll-free 800/831-2727. www.swisschalets village.com.* 42 rms, 1-3 story. No elvtr. S $69-$99; D $79-$139; each addl $10; suites $109-$179; under 18 free; ski plans; higher rates fall foliage. Crib free. Pet accepted; $10/day. TV; cable. Heated pool. Complimentary continental bkfst. Ck-out 11 am. Downhill ski 4 mi; x-country ski on site. Game rm. Refrigerators; some in-rm whirlpools; fireplaces. Some balconies. Picnic tables. Rms in Swiss chalet-style bldgs; on 12 acres. Cr cds: A, DS, MC, V.

⬟ ⬟ ⬟ ⬟ ⬟

★ **WHITE TRELLIS MOTEL.** *3245 White Mountain Hwy (03860), Rte 16. 603/356-2492. Email wtm@ncia.net; www.whitetrellismotel.com.* 22 rms, 1 story. July-Oct: S $55; D $145; each addl $8; lower rates rest of yr. Parking lot. TV; cable. Complimentary toll-free calls. Restaurant nearby. Ck-out 10 am, ck-in 1 pm. Exercise privileges. Golf. Tennis, 10 courts. Downhill skiing. Hiking trail. Cr cds: DS, MC, V.

⬟ ⬟ ⬟ ⬟ ⬟ ⬟ ⬟

Hotels

★★★ **NORTH CONWAY GRAND HOTEL.** *Settlers Green and Rte 16 (03860). 603/356-9300; fax 603/356-9300.* 200 rms, 4 story. S, D $79-$165; suites $155-$215; under 18 free; MAP avail; ski plans. Crib $10. TV; cable (premium). Indoor pool; whirlpool. Restaurant 7 am-10:30 pm. Bar 11-1 am; entertainment wkends. Ck-out 11 am. Coin lndry. Meeting rms. Business servs avail. In-rm modem link. Downhill ski 3 mi;

x-country ski 5 mi. Exercise equipt; sauna. Game rm. Bathrm phone, refrigerator, minibar in suites. Cr cds: A, C, D, DS, ER, MC, V.

⊡ 🏃 🍴 🏊 🎿 🏌 🚶 📶 ♨

★★ NORTH CONWAY MOUNTAIN INN.

2114 White Mountain Hwy (03860). 603/356-2803; toll-free 800/319-4405. www.ncmtinn.com. 34 rms, 2 story, 1 suite. July-Oct: S $79; D $99; suites $125; lower rates rest of yr. Crib avail. Pet accepted. Parking lot. TV; cable (premium). Restaurant nearby. Ck-out 11 am, ck-in 1 pm. Exercise privileges. Golf, 18 holes. Tennis, 4 courts. Downhill skiing. Beach access. Bike rentals. Supervised children's activities. Hiking trail. Cr cds: A, DS, MC, V.

⊡ 🐾 🏃 🍴 🏊 🎿 🏌 🚶 🏌 📶 ♨

Resorts

★★ THE FOX RIDGE.

White Mountain Hwy; Rte 16 (03860). 603/356-3151; fax 603/356-0096; toll-free 800/343-1804. Email foxridge@red jacketinns.com; www.foxridgeresort.com. 136 rms, 2 story. July-Aug, Oct: S, D $141; each addl $10; under 16 free; lower rates rest of yr. Crib avail. Parking lot. Indoor/outdoor pools, whirlpool. TV; cable. Complimentary toll-free calls. Restaurant 7:30 am-11 pm. Ck-out 11 am, ck-in 3 pm. Meeting rm. Business servs avail. Bellhops. Coin lndry. Exercise privileges. Golf. Tennis, 3 courts. Downhill skiing. Supervised children's activities. Hiking trail. Picnic facilities. Cr cds: A, MC, V.

⊡ 🎿 🏌 🍴 🏊 🚶 🏌 📶 ♨

★★★ PURITY SPRING RESORT.

HC 63 Box 40 Rte 153 (03849), 9 mi S on NH 153. 603/367-8896; fax 603/367-8664; toll-free 800/373-3754. Email info@purityspring.com; www.purityspring.com. 32 rms, 3 story, 13 suites. Feb, June-Sep: S $129; D $226; suites $226; each addl $52; under 12 free; lower rates rest of yr. Crib avail. Parking lot. Indoor pool, whirlpool. TV; cable, VCR avail. Complimentary coffee in rms. Bar. Ck-out 11 am, ck-in 3 pm. Meeting rms. Business servs avail. Coin lndry. Gift shop. Exercise rm. Golf, 18 holes. Tennis, 5 courts. Downhill skiing. Beach access. Bike rentals. Supervised children's activities. Hiking trail. Picnic facilities. Cr cds: A, D, DS, MC, V.

⊡ 🐾 🎿 🏌 🍴 🏊 🏌 🏌 📶 ♨

★★ RED JACKET MOUNTAIN VIEW.

Rte 16 (03860). 603/356-5411; fax 603/356-3842; res 800/752-2538. www.redjacketmountainview.com. 152 rms, 3 story, 12 suites. Jan-Mar, June-Oct: S, D $229; suites $279; lower rates rest of yr. Crib avail. Parking lot. Indoor/outdoor pools, whirlpool. TV; cable. Complimentary newspaper, toll-free calls. Restaurant 7 am-9 pm. Bar. Ck-out 11 am, ck-in 3 pm. Meeting rms. Fax servs avail. Bellhops. Concierge. Coin lndry. Gift shop. Exercise privileges, sauna. Golf. Tennis, 2 courts. Downhill skiing. Supervised children's activities. Hiking trail. Picnic facilities. Cr cds: A, C, D, DS, MC, V.

⊡ 🎿 🏌 🍴 🏊 🏌 📶 ♨

★★★ WHITE MOUNTAIN HOTEL & RESORT.

W Side Rd (03860). 603/356-7100; fax 603/356-7100; toll-free 800/533-6301. Email dkelly@whitemountainhotel.com; www.white mountainhotel.com. 80 rms, 3 story, 13 suites. July-Oct: S, D $109-$159; suites $149-$199; under 18 free; wkly rates; ski, golf plans; lower rates rest of yr. Crib avail. TV; cable. Heated pool; whirlpool, poolside serv. Dining rm 7-10 am, 11:30 am-9 pm. Rm serv. Bar 11:30-1 am; entertainment, wkends (nightly in season). Ck-out 11 am, ck-in 3 pm. Coin lndry. Meeting rms. Business servs avail. Bellhops. Tennis. 9-hole golf, pro, putting green. Downhill ski 2½ mi. Exercise equipt; sauna. Game rm. Surrounded by White Mt National Forest and Echo Lake State Park. Cr cds: A, DS, MC, V.

⊡ 🎿 🏌 🍴 🏊 🏌 📶 ♨ SC

B&Bs/Small Inns

★★ 1785 INN & RESTAURANT.

3582 N White Mountain Hwy (03860), 2 mi N on NH 16. 603/356-9025; fax 603/356-9862; res 800/421-1785. Email the1785inn@aol.com; www.the1785inn.com. 17 rms, 5 share bath, 12 A/C, 3 story. No rm phones. S $49-$89; D $69-$109; each addl $10-$20; MAP avail; family rates; ski plans; higher rates fall foliage. Crib free. TV in some rms, sitting rm; cable, VCR avail. Pool; poolside serv. Playground. Complimentary full bkfst. Restaurant (see 1785 INN). Bar. Ck-out noon, ck-in 2 pm. Downhill ski 2 mi; x-country ski on site. Lawn games. Picnic tables, grills. Colonial-style bldg (1785); original fireplaces, Victorian antiques. On 6 acres; river, view of Mt Washington. Totally non-smoking. Cr cds: A, DS, MC, V.

★★ **BUTTONWOOD INN.** *Mt Surprise Rd (03860), off Hurricane Mt Rd.* 603/356-2625; fax 603/356-3140; toll-free 800/258-2625. Email innkeeper@buttonwoodinn.com; www.buttonwoodinn.com. 10 rms, 2 story. Sep-Oct: S $125; D $175; each addl $25; children $25; lower rates rest of yr. Parking lot. Pool. TV; cable, VCR avail. Complimentary full bkfst, newspaper, toll-free calls. Restaurant nearby. Meeting rm. Business servs avail. Concierge. Gift shop. Golf. Tennis, 6 courts. Downhill skiing. Hiking trail. Picnic facilities. Cr cds: A, DS, MC, V.

★ **CRANMORE INN.** *80 Kearsarge St (03860), ¼ mi E of US 302 (NH 16).* 603/356-5502; fax 603/356-6052; toll-free 800/526-5502. 18 rms, 3 story. No A/C. Late June-mid-Sep: S $52-$70; D $62-$80; suites $104-$118; wkly, family rates; package plans; higher rates fall foliage; lower rates rest of yr. Crib free. TV rm; cable. Pool. Complimentary bkfst. Dining rm 8-9 am. Ck-out 11 am, ck-in 3 pm. Downhill ski ⅓ mi; x-country ski on site. Health club privileges. Lawn games. In operation since 1863. Cr cds: A, MC, V.

★★ **CRANMORE MOUNTAIN LODGE.** *Kearsarge Rd (03860), off NH 16.* 603/356-2044; fax 603/356-4498; toll-free 800/356-3596. Email c-u@cml1.com; www.cml1.com. 16 rms, 6 A/C, 2-3 story; 40 units in bunkhouse. No rm phones. S, D $69-$125; each addl $10-$15; bunkhouse units $17; suite $150-$225; 2-bedrm townhouse $220; MAP avail winter; wkly rates; ski plans; some lower rates off-season. Crib free. TV in some rms; cable. Pool; whirlpool. Playground. Complimentary full bkfst. Dining rm hrs

vary. Ck-out 11 am, ck-in 3 pm. Coin lndry. Tennis. Downhill ski 1 mi; x-country ski on site. Ice-skating. Game rm. Lawn games. Picnic tables, grills. Historic guest house (1860); once owned by Babe Ruth's daughter. Library, sitting rm, antiques. Located on 12 acres; pond. Farm animals. Cr cds: A, DS, MC, V.

★★ **DARBY FIELD COUNTRY INN & RESTAURANT.** *185 Cahse Hill Rd (03818), 5½ mi S on NH 16, then approx 2 mi W and N on Bald Hill Rd.* 603/447-2181; fax 603/447-5726; toll-free 800/426-4147. Email marc@darbyfield.com; www.darbyfield.com. 14 rms, 3 story, 3 suites. Feb, Sep-Oct, Dec: S $155; D $195; suites $270; each addl $50; children $38; under 2 free; lower rates rest of yr. Parking lot. Pool, whirlpool. TV; cable (premium), VCR avail. Complimentary full bkfst, newspaper. Restaurant 6-9 pm. Bar. Ck-out 11 am, ck-in 2 pm. Meeting rms. Business servs avail. Concierge. Steam rm. Golf. Tennis. Downhill skiing. Hiking trail. Picnic facilities. Cr cds: A, MC, V.

★★ **EASTMAN INN.** *2331 White Mountain Hwy (03860).* 603/356-6707; fax 603/356-7708; toll-free 800/626-5855. Email eastman@eastmaninn.com; www.eastmaninn.com. 14 rms, some A/C, 3 story. S, D $89-$129; higher rates fall foliage; lower rates off season. TV; cable. Complimentary full bkfst. Restaurant nearby. Ck-out 11 am, ck-in 3 pm. Downhill/x-country ski 1 mi. Built 1777. Antiques. Sitting rm with fireplace. Wrap-around porch. Totally nonsmoking. Cr cds: A, DS, MC, V.

★★ **THE FOREST, A COUNTRY INN.** *Rte 16A PO Box 37 (03845), 3¼ mi N on NH 16A.* 603/356-9772; fax 603/356-5652; toll-free 800/448-3534. Email forest@ncia.net; www.forest-inn.com. 11 rms, 3 story. Feb, Sep-Oct: S $125; D $150; lower rates rest of yr. Parking lot. Pool. TV; cable (premium), VCR avail. Complimentary full bkfst, toll-free calls. Ck-out 11 am, ck-in 3 pm. Golf. Tennis, 5 courts. Downhill skiing. Hiking trail. Cr cds: A, DS, MC, V.

★ ★ **MERRILL FARM RESORT.** *428 White Mountain Hwy (03860). 603/447-3866; toll-free 800/445-1017. Email merrill2@ncia.net; www.merrill farm.com.* 45 rms, 3 story, 17 suites. Feb, July-Aug: S, D $99; suites $139; lower rates rest of yr. Crib avail. Street parking. Pool, whirlpool. TV; cable, VCR avail. Complimentary continental bkfst, newspaper. Restaurant nearby. Meeting rms. Exercise equipt, sauna. Golf. Tennis. Downhill skiing. Picnic facilities. Cr cds: A, DS, MC, V.

★ ★ **SNOW VILLAGE INN.** *Stewart Rd (03849), 5 mi S on NH 16, then 6 mi S on NH 153, then 1½ mi E. 603 447-2818; fax 603/447-5268; toll-free 800/447-4345. Email kevin@snow villageinn.com; www.snowvillageinn. com.* 18 rms, 2 story. Feb, Sep-Oct: S $125; D $249; each addl $25; children $25; under 13 free; lower rates rest of yr. Parking lot. TV; cable, VCR avail. Complimentary full bkfst, coffee in rms, newspaper, toll-free calls. Restaurant 8 am-9 pm, closed Wed. Bar. Ck-out 11 am, ck-in 2 pm. Meeting rm. Concierge. Dry cleaning, coin lndry. Sauna. Golf. Downhill skiing. Hiking trail. Picnic facilities. Cr cds: A, D, DS, MC, V.

Conference Center

★ ★ **GREEN GRANITE INN & CON-FERENCE CENTER.** *Rte 16 & 302 (03860). 603/356-6901; fax 603/356-6980; res 800/468-3666. Email granite@nxi.com; www.greengranite. com.* 86 rms, 2 story, 5 suites. June-Oct: S, D $149; suites $229; each addl $10; under 15 free; lower rates rest of yr. Crib avail, fee. Parking lot. Indoor/outdoor pools, whirlpool. TV; cable, VCR avail. Complimentary continental bkfst, coffee in rms, newspaper, toll-free calls. Restaurant nearby. Ck-out 11 am, ck-in 3 pm. Meeting rms. Business servs avail. Bellhops. Coin lndry. Gift shop. Exercise equipt. Golf. Tennis. Downhill skiing. Bike

rentals. Supervised children's activities. Hiking trail. Picnic facilities. Cr cds: A, DS, MC, V.

Restaurants

★ ★ ★ **1785 INN.** *3582 White Mountain Hwy. 603/356-9025. Email the1785inn@aol.com; www.the1785inn. com.* Specializes in rack of lamb, raspberry duckling, veal chop morel. Own baking. Hrs: 5-9 pm; Fri, Sat to 10 pm. Closed Dec 25. Cr cds: D, DS, MC, V.

★ **BELLINI'S.** *33 Seavey St (03860). 603/356-7000. Email angelo@land marknet.net; www.bellinis.com.* Specializes in rigatoni broccoli chicken, veal Marsala, fresh grilled seafood. Hrs: 5-10 pm; Fri, Sat to 11 pm. Closed Mon, Tues. Bar. Dinner $7.95-$17.95. Child's menu. Tuscan country atmosphere. Cr cds: A, D, DS, MC, V.

★ **HORSEFEATHERS.** *Main St (03860). 603/356-2687. www. horsefeathers.com.* Specializes in wood-grilled foods. Hrs: 11:30 am-11:45 pm. Closed Thanksgiving, Dec 25. Bar. Lunch, dinner $6.50-$17.95. Neighborhood nostalgia; landmark restaurant. Cr cds: A, MC, V.

Unrated Dining Spot

PEACH'S. *Main St (03860). 603/356-5860.* Specializes in homemade soups, desserts, salad dressings. Hrs: 7 am-2:30 pm. Closed Thanksgiving, Dec 25. Bkfst $1.25-$5.95; lunch $2-$5.95. Cr cds: A, MC, V.

North Woodstock

(see Lincoln/North Woodstock Area)

Peterborough

(H-4) *See also Jaffrey, Keene, Nashua*

Settled 1749 **Pop** 5,239 **Elev** 723 ft
Area code 603 **Zip** 03458
Information Greater Peterborough
Chamber of Commerce, PO Box 401;
603/924-7234

This was the home of composer
Edward MacDowell (1861-1908).
Edward Arlington Robinson, Stephen
Vincent Benét, Willa Cather, and
Thornton Wilder, among others,
worked at the MacDowell Colony, a
thriving artists' retreat, which made
Peterborough famous.

What to See and Do

Greenfield State Park. A 401-acre
park with swimming, bathhouse,
fishing; picnicking, concessions,
camping (dump station) with separate beach. (Mid-May-mid-Oct) Standard fees. 9 mi N on NH 136, then
W on unnumbered road, near Greenfield. Phone 603/547-3497.

Miller State Park. First of the New
Hampshire parks. Atop 2,288-ft Pack
Monadnock Mt; walking trails on
summit; scenic drive; picnicking.
(June-Labor Day, daily; May and
Labor Day-Nov, Sat, Sun, and hols)
Standard fees. 4 mi E on NH 101.

New England Marionette Opera.
Largest marionette facility in country
devoted to opera. (Mid-May-late Dec,
Sat eves, also Sun matinee; closed
July 4, Thanksgiving) Main St. Phone
603/924-4333.

Peterborough Historical Society.
Exhibits on the history of the area;
historical and genealogical library.
(Mon-Fri; also Sat afternoon July-
Aug) 19 Grove St. Phone 603/924-
3235. July-Aug ¢¢

Sharon Arts Center. Gallery and
crafts center. (Daily) 5 mi SE on NH
123, in Sharon. Phone 603/924-7256.
FREE

Motel/Motor Lodge

★ **JACK DANIELS MOTOR INN.** *Rte
202 (03458), 2 mi N.* 603/924-7548;
fax 603/924-7700; res 603/924-7548.
17 rms, 2 story. Sep-Oct: S $88; D
$98; each addl $10; lower rates rest
of yr. Parking lot. TV; cable. Restaurant. Ck-out 11 am, ck-in 2 pm.
Business servs avail. Golf. Tennis.
Downhill skiing. Cr cds: A, DS,
MC, V.
⊡ ⧖ 🎿 ↗ ⊠ 🔥

B&Bs/Small Inns

★★ **GREENFIELD BED & BREAK-
FAST INN.** *Rtes 31 N & 136 (03047),
3 mi N on US 202, 6 mi NE on NH
136, in center of town.* 603/547-6327;
*fax 603/547-2418; toll-free 800/678-
4144.* 13 rms, 6 with bath, 2 story. D
$49-$89; each addl $20; suite $119-
$149, cottage $159; wkly rates. TV;
cable, VCR (free movies). Complimentary full bkfst. Restaurants nearby. Ck-
out 11 am, ck-in 4 pm. Business servs
avail. Downhill/x-country ski 6 mi.
Cr cds: A, DS, MC, V.
🐾 ⧖ ⊠ 🐾 SC

★★★ **HANCOCK INN.** *33 Main St
(03449), 3 mi N on US 202.* 603/525-
3318; *fax 603/525-9301; toll-free 800/
525-1789. Email innkeeper@hancock
inn.com; www.hancockinn.com.* 15
rms, 30 story. Aug, Oct: S $120; D
$195; suites $235; under 12 free;
lower rates rest of yr. Parking lot. TV;
cable. Complimentary full bkfst, toll-
free calls. Restaurant. Bar. Ck-out 2
pm, ck-in 11 pm. Meeting rms. Business center. Gift shop. Golf, 18 holes.
Tennis, 4 courts. Downhill skiing.
Beach access. Supervised children's
activities. Hiking trail. Picnic facilities. Cr cds: A, D, DS, MC, V.
⊡ 🐾 ⧖ 🎿 ↗ ⊠ 🐾 🏃

Restaurant

★★★ **HANCOCK INN.** *33 Main St.*
603/525-3318. *www.hancockinn.com.*
Specializes in Shaker cranberry pot
roast, roast duckling, apple braised
salmon. Hrs: 6-9 pm. Closed Dec 25.
Res required. Dinner $15-$22.50.
Country decor; antiques. Cr cds: A,
D, DS, MC, V.
⊡

Pinkham Notch

See also Gorham, Jackson, North Conway

Elev 2,000 ft (at highest point)
Web www.4seasonresort.com
Information Mount Washington Valley Chamber of Commerce, N Main St, PO Box 2300, North Conway 03860; 603/356-5701 or 800/367-3364

(Approx 7 mi N on NH 16)

Named for Joseph Pinkham, a 1790 settler, this easternmost White Mountain pass is closest to Mount Washington (see). Headquarters for the Appalachian Mountain Club Hut System is here.

What to See and Do

Glen Ellis Falls Scenic Area. E of NH 16, 12 mi N of Glen in White Mountain National Forest (see).

Skiing.

Wildcat Ski & Recreation Area. Detachable quad, 3 triple, double chairlifts; patrol, school, rentals, snowmaking; cafeteria, nursery. Longest run 2¾ mi; vertical drop 2,100 ft. Gondola. (Mid-Nov-late Apr, daily; closed Thanksgiving, Dec 25) Gondola also operates Memorial Day-late Oct (daily); picnicking. 10 mi N of Jackson on NH 16 in White Mt National Forest (see). Phone 603/466-3326. ¢¢¢¢

Plymouth (E-5)

See also Holderness, Meredith, Waterville Valley

Settled 1764 **Pop** 5,811 **Elev** 660 ft
Area code 603 **Zip** 03264
Web www.plymouthnh.org
Information Chamber of Commerce, PO Box 65; 603/536-1001 or 800/386-3678

Since 1795, Plymouth's varied industries have included lumber, pig iron, mattresses, gloves, and sporting goods. It has been a resort center since the mid-19th century.

What to See and Do

Mary Baker Eddy Historic House. Residence of Mary Baker Eddy from 1860-62, prior to the founding of the Christian Science Church. (May-Oct, Tues-Sun; closed hols) Approx 7 mi W via NH 25 to Stinson Lake Rd, then approx 1 mi N to N side of the Village of Rumney. Phone 603/786-9943. ¢

Plymouth State College. (1871) 3,200 students. A member of the Univ System of New Hampshire. Art exhibits in galleries and Lamson Library. Music, theater, and dance performances in Silver Cultural Arts Center (some fees). Planetarium shows. Tours. 1 blk W of business center. Phone 603/535-5000.

Polar Caves Park. Glacial caves, animal exhibits, local minerals, scenic rock formations; maple sugar museum, gift shops, picnicking. (Early May-late Oct, daily) 5 mi W on Tenney Mt Hwy (NH 25). Phone 603/536-1888. ¢¢¢

Hotel

★ **SUSSE CHALET HOTEL.** *Rte 3 (03264), I-93 Exit 26.* 603/536-2330; *fax 603/536-2686; res 800/524-2538.* 38 rms, 2 story. Sep-Oct: S $76; D $86; each addl $5; under 12 free; lower rates rest of yr. Pet accepted, some restrictions. Parking lot. Pool. TV; cable, VCR avail. Complimentary continental bkfst, toll-free calls. Restaurant nearby. Ck-out 11 am, ck-in 2 pm. Business servs avail. Coin lndry. Exercise privileges. Golf. Cr cds: A, D, DS, MC, V.

Restaurants

★ **JIGGER JOHNSON'S.** *75 Main St (03264).* 603/536-4386. *www.jiggers. com.* Specializes in chicken dijon, steak Diane. Hrs: 11 am-9 pm. Closed Dec 25. Bar. Lunch $2.95-$5.95; dinner $6.95-$11.95. Child's menu. Some street parking. Lively, informal atmosphere. Eclectic decor. Cr cds: A, D, DS, MC, V.

★ **TREE HOUSE.** *3 S Main St (03264). 603/536-4084. Email tree hous@worldpath.net; www.thetreehouse restaurant.com.* Specializes in chicken, steak, seafood. Hrs: 4:30-9 pm; Sun from 11:30 am. Closed Mon; Thanksgiving, Dec 25. Res accepted. Bar. Lunch $3.95-$8.95; dinner $8.95-$14.95. Child's menu. Entertainment: musicians Fri, Sat. Rustic atmosphere; large stone fireplace, vintage items decorate rm. Cr cds: A, D, DS, MC, V.

D

Portsmouth

(G-7) *See also Dover, Exeter, Hampton Beach*

Settled 1630 **Pop** 25,925 **Elev** 21 ft
Area code 603 **Zip** 03801
Web www.portsmouthchamber.org
Information Greater Portsmouth Chamber of Commerce, 500 Market St, PO Box 239, 03802-0239; 603/436-3988 or 603/436-1118

A tour of Portsmouth's famous houses is like a tour through time, with Colonial and Federal architecture from 1684 into the 19th century. Once-time capital of New Hampshire, Portsmouth was also the home port of a dynasty of merchant seamen who grew rich and built accordingly. The old atmosphere still exists in the narrow streets near Market Square.

The United States Navy Yard, located in Kittery, Maine (see), on the Piscataqua River, has long been Portsmouth's major "industry." The peace treaty ending the Russo-Japanese War was signed at the Portsmouth Navy Yard in 1905.

What to See and Do

Children's Museum of Portsmouth. Arts and science museum featuring mock submarine, space shuttle, lobster boat, exhibits, and gallery. (Summer and school vacations, daily; rest of yr, Tues-Sat, also Sun afternoons) 280 Marcy St. Phone 603/436-3853. ¢¢

Fort Constitution. (1808) The first cannon was placed on this site in 1632; in 1694 it was known as Fort William and Mary. Information about a British order to stop gunpowder from coming into the colonies, brought by Paul Revere on Dec 13, 1774, caused the Sons of Liberty from Portsmouth, New Castle, and Rye to attack and capture the next day a fort that held 5 tons of gunpowder. Much of this powder was used at Bunker Hill by the patriots. This uprising against the King's authority was one of the first overt acts of the Revolution. Little remains of the original fort except the base of its walls. Fort Constitution had been built on the same site by 1808; granite walls were added during the Civil War. (Mid-June-early Sep, daily; late May-mid-June and late Sep-mid-Oct, wkends, hols only) 4 mi E on NH 1B in New Castle. **FREE**

★ **Fort Stark State Historic Site.** A former portion of the coastal defense system dating back to 1746, exhibiting many of the changes in military technology from the Revolutionary War through WWII. The fort is situated on Jerry's Point, overlooking the Piscataqua River, Little Harbor, and Atlantic Ocean. (Late May-mid-Oct; Sat and Sun) Wild Rose Lane, approx 5 mi E off NH 1B in New Castle. Phone 603/433-8583. ¢¢

InSight Tours. Specialized tours of Historic Portsmouth and the New Hampshire coastline incl garden, history, nature, and antique tours; 24-hr advance res requested. ¢¢¢¢

Market Square. The old cove of the city follows Market St to Market Sq along the Piscataqua River. Ceres and Bow Sts are especially popular with visitors. Area features craftsmen, unique shops, bookstores, restaurants. NH 95 Exit 7.

Portsmouth Harbor Cruises. Narrated historical tours aboard the 49-passenger M/V *Heritage.* 1½-hr harbor, 2½-hr Isles of Shoals, 1-hr cocktail, 1½-hr sunset cruises, 2½-hr inland river cruise, fall foliage cruise. (Mid-June-Oct) 64 Ceres St, Old Harbor District. Phone 603/436-8084 or 800/776-0915. ¢¢-¢¢¢¢

★ **Portsmouth Historic Homes.** The Historic Associates, part of the Greater Portsmouth Chamber of Commerce, has walking tour maps for 6 historic houses; maps are avail free at the Chamber of Commerce. Phone 603/436-1118. The houses incl

Moffatt-Ladd House. (1763) Built by Capt John Moffatt; later the home of Gen William Whipple, his son-in-law, a signer of the Declaration of Independence. Many original 18th- and 19th-century furnishings. Formal gardens. (Mid-June-mid-Oct, daily) 154 Market St. Phone 603/436-8221. ¢¢

Warner House. (1716) One of New England's finest Georgian houses, with scagliola in the dining rm, restored mural paintings on the staircase walls, beautiful paneling, a lightning rod on the west wall said to have been installed by Benjamin Franklin in 1762, five portraits by Joseph Blackburn, appropriate furnishings. (June-mid-Oct, Tues-Sun) 150 Daniel St, at Chapel St. Phone 603/436-5909. ¢¢

John Paul Jones House. (1758) Where the famous naval commander twice boarded; now a museum containing period furniture, collections of costumes, china, glass, documents, weapons. Guided tours (mid-May-mid-Oct, daily). 43 Middle St, at State St. Phone 603/436-8420. ¢¢

Governor John Langdon House. (1784) John Langdon served 3 terms as governor of New Hampshire and was the first president *pro tempore* of the US Senate. House's exterior proportions are monumental; interior embellished with excellent woodcarving and fine Portsmouth-area furniture. George Washington was entertained here in 1789. Architect Stanford White was commissioned to add the large wing at the rear with dining rm in the Colonial Revival style. Surrounded by landscaped grounds with gazebo, rose and grape arbor, and restored perennial garden beds. Tours (June-mid-Oct, Wed-Sun; closed hols). 143 Pleasant St. Phone 603/436-3205. ¢¢

Rundlet-May House. (1807) Federalist, 3-story mansion. House sits on terraces and retains its original 1812 courtyard and garden layout; landscaped grounds. House contains family furnishings and accessories, incl many fine examples of Federalist craftsmanship and the latest technologies of its time. (June-mid-Oct, Wed-Sun afternoons) 364 Middle St. ¢¢

Wentworth-Gardner House. (1760) Excellent example of Georgian architecture. Elaborate woodwork, scenic wallpaper, magnificent main staircase. (Mid-June-mid-Oct, Tues-Sun afternoons) 50 Mechanic St. Phone 603/436-4406. ¢¢

★ **Star Island and Isles of Shoals.** The M/V *Thomas Laighton* and the M/V *Oceanic* make cruises to historic Isles of Shoals, Star Island walkabouts, whale watch expeditions, lobster clambake river cruises, fall foliage excursion, and others. (Mid-June-Labor Day, daily) Depart from Barker's Wharf, 315 Market St. Phone 603/431-5500. ¢¢¢¢

★ **Strawbery Banke Museum.** Restoration of 10-acre historic waterfront neighborhood; site of original Portsmouth settlement. Forty-two bldgs dating from 1695-1950. Nine houses—Capt Keyran Walsh House (1796), Gov Goodwin Mansion (1811), Chase House (1762), Capt

Take the Market Square exit off I-95, and follow Market Street to signs for Strawbery Banke. Park in the Strawbery Banke lot. Although parking is usually a problem (this compact old downtown was designed for walking), this lot is free and large enough to accommodate many visitors.

From Strawbery Banke (a major attraction), walk back along Marcey Street past Prescott Park with its flower gardens, picnic areas, and amphitheater. If you happen to be visiting in the summer months (early July-late August), you can catch the Prescott Park Arts Festival, which features frequent performances and concerts. Follow Bow Street, perhaps stopping in at some of the specialty shops that line the way, into Market Square. The historic commercial heart of town, Market Square is lined with shops and cafes. Continue up Market Street to the Moffatt-Ladd House, and cut back along the water on Ceres Street. Vary the return by following Pleasant Street, stopping at the Governor Langdon House.

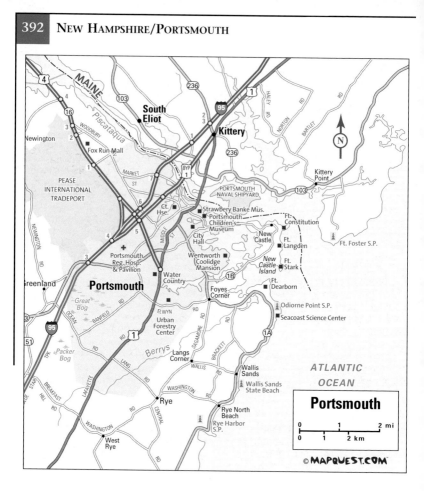

John Wheelwright House (1780), Thomas Bailey Aldrich House (1790), Drisco House (1790s), Rider-Wood House (1840s), Abbott Grocery Store (1943), and the William Pitt Tavern (1766)—are restored with period furnishings. Shops, architectural exhibits, craft shops, and demonstrations; tool, photo, archaeological, and house construction exhibits; family programs and activities, special events, tours; picnicking, coffee shop. (May-Oct, daily) Hancock & Marcy Sts, downtown, follow signs. Phone 603/433-1100. ¢¢¢

Annual Events

Market Square Days. Summer celebration with 10K road race, street fair, entertainment. Phone 603/431-5388. June.

Portsmouth Jazz Festival. Two stages with continuous performances on the historical Portsmouth waterfront. Phone 603/436-7678. Last Sun June.

Motels/Motor Lodges

★★ **HOLIDAY INN.** *300 Woodbury Ave (03801), I-95 Exit at Portsmouth Cir.* 603/431-8000; fax 603/431-2065. 130 rms, 6 story. July-Labor Day: S, D $105.95-$150; suites $190; under 20 free; lower rates rest of yr. Crib free. TV; cable (premium). Indoor pool. Restaurant 6:30 am-9:30 pm. Bar 11:30-1 am; entertainment Tues-Sat. Ck-out 11 am. Meeting rms. Valet serv. Sundries. Exercise equipt. Game rm. Refrigerators avail. Cr cds: A, D, DS, MC, V.

★ **PINE HAVEN MOTEL.** *183 Lafayette Rd (03862), 5 mi S on US 1.* 603/964-8187; fax 603/964-5485; toll-free 877/964-8187. 19 rms, 4 kits. (no oven). Mid-June-Labor Day (2-day min hols and wkends): S $59; D $65-$75; each addl $5; kit. units $78; lower rates rest of yr. Crib $3. TV; cable. Complimentary coffee in rms.

Restaurant nearby. Ck-out 11 am. Refrigerators. Cr cds: A, DS, MC, V.

★★ **PORT MOTOR INN.** *505 Rte 1 Bypass S (03801), at Portsmouth Cir, I-95 Exit 5.* 603/436-4378; fax 603/436-4378; toll-free 800/282-7678. Email *billmacdonald@theportinn.com; www.theportinn.com.* 54 rms, 2 story, 3 suites. July-Oct: S $125; D $139; suites $199; each addl $6; under 12 free; lower rates rest of yr. Crib avail. Parking lot. TV; cable (premium). Complimentary continental bkfst. Restaurant. Ck-out 11 am, ck-in 3 pm. Business servs avail. Golf. Cr cds: A, C, D, DS, MC, V.

★★★ **SHERATON.** *250 Market St (03801).* 603/431-2300; fax 603/431-7805; res 800/325-3505; toll-free 800/325-3535. 181 rms, 5 story, 24 suites. Mid-Apr-late Oct: S, D $135-$185; each addl $10; suites $275-$450; under 18 free; lower rates rest of yr. Crib avail. Garage parking $6. TV; cable (premium). Indoor pool. Complimentary coffee in rms. Restaurant 6:30 am-2:30 pm, 5:30-10 pm. Bar; entertainment. Ck-out 11 am. Meeting rms. Business center. Bellhops. Sundries. Valet serv. Free airport transportation. Exercise equipt; sauna. Minibars; refrigerator in suites. On Piscataqua River. Cr cds: A, C, D, DS, MC, V.

★ **SUSSE CHALET INN.** *650 Borthwick Ave (03801), I-95 Exit 5.* 603/436-6363; fax 603/436-1621; res 800/524-2538. 105 rms, 4 story. June-Labor Day: S, D $69.70-$100.70; under 18 free; lower rates rest of yr. Crib free. TV; cable (premium). Pool. Complimentary continental bkfst, coffee. Restaurant nearby. Ck-out 11 am. Coin lndry. Business servs avail. Refrigerators avail. Cr cds: A, D, DS, MC, V.

Hotels

★★ **COMFORT INN PORTSMOUTH.** *1390 Lafayette Rd (03801), 3 mi S on US 1.* 603/433-3338; fax 603/431-1639; res 800/228-5150; toll-free 800/552-8484. Email *yokens@aol.com; www.yokens.com.* 121 rms, 6 story. July-Aug: S $119; D $129; suites $159; each addl $10; under 11 free; lower rates rest of yr. Crib avail. Parking lot. Indoor pool, lap pool, whirlpool. TV; cable (premium), VCR avail. Complimentary continental bkfst, newspaper, toll-free calls. Restaurant 11 am-8 pm. Bar. Ck-out 11 am, ck-in 2 pm. Meeting rms. Business center. Coin lndry. Gift shop. Exercise equipt. Golf. Tennis, 4 courts. Video games. Cr cds: A, C, D, DS, ER, JCB, MC, V.

★★★ **SISE INN.** *40 Court St (03801).* 603/433-1200; fax 603/433-1200; res 800/267-0525; toll-free 877/747-3466. Email *siseinn@cyberhours.com; www.someplacedifferent.com.* 25 rms, 3 story, 9 suites. May-Oct: S, D $145; suites $220; each addl $15; under 11 free; lower rates rest of yr. Crib avail, fee. Parking lot. TV; cable, VCR avail, CD avail. Complimentary continental bkfst, newspaper, toll-free calls. Restaurant nearby. Ck-out 11 am, ck-in 4 pm. Meeting rms. Business servs avail. Bellhops. Concierge. Dry cleaning. Exercise privileges. Golf. Downhill skiing. Picnic facilities. Cr cds: A, D, MC, V.

B&B/Small Inn

★ **THE INN AT CHRISTIAN SHORE.** *335 Maplewood Ave (03801).* 603/431-6770; fax 603/481-7743. June-Oct: D $100; lower rates rest of yr. Parking lot. TV; cable (premium). Complimentary full bkfst, coffee in rms, toll-free calls. Restaurant nearby. Ck-out 11 am, ck-in 3 pm. Fax servs avail. Exercise privileges. Golf. Cr cds: MC, V.

Restaurants

★★★ **METRO.** *20 High St (03801), off Market Sq.* 603/436-0521. Specializes in clam chowder, fresh seafood, veal Metro. Hrs: 11:30 am-9:30 pm. Closed Sun; Thanksgiving, Dec 25. Bar. Lunch $6-$12; dinner $12-$24. Entertainment: Fri, Sat. Cr cds: A, D, MC, V.

★ **PIER II.** *10 State St (03801), at Memorial Bridge. 603/436-0669.* Specializes in lobster, steak, seafood. Salad bar. Hrs: 11:30 am-10 pm; Fri, Sat to 11 pm. Closed Thanksgiving, Dec 25; Labor Day-May. Res accepted. Bar. Lunch $3-$6.50; dinner $8-$15. Child's menu. Entertainment: Sun-Fri. Valet parking. Overlooks harbor; dockage. Cr cds: A, D, DS, MC, V.

D

★ **YOKEN'S THAR SHE BLOWS.** *1390 Lafayette Rd (03802), 3 mi S of traffic circle on US 1. 603/436-8224. www.yokens.com.* Specializes in steak, native seafood. Hrs: 11 am-8 pm; July-Aug to 9 pm. Closed Thanksgiving, Dec 25. Res accepted. Lunch $3.25-$6.50. Complete meals: $4.95-$6.50; dinner $7.95-$12.95. Child's menu. Nautical decor. Cr cds: A, D, DS, MC, V.

D

Salem (H-6)

Pop 25,746 **Elev** 131 ft **Area code** 603
Zip 03079
Web www.salemnhchamber.org
Information Greater Salem Chamber of Commerce, 220 N Broadway, PO Box 304; 603/893-3177

What to See and Do

America's Stonehenge. A megalithic calendar site dated to 2000 BC, with 22 stone bldgs on more than 30 acres. The main site features a number of stone-constructed chambers and is surrounded by miles of stone walls containing large, shaped monoliths that indicate the rising and setting of the sun at solstice and equinox, as well as other astronomical alignments, incl lunar. (Late Mar-late Dec, daily) 5 mi E of I-93, just off NH 111 in North Salem. Phone 603/893-8300. ¢¢

Canobie Lake Park. Family amusement park; giant roller coaster, log flume, pirate ship, giant Ferris wheel, haunted mine ride; entertainment; lake cruise, fireworks, games, pool; concessions, restaurant. (Memorial Day-Labor Day, daily; Apr-late May, wkends) 1 mi E of I-93, Exit 2. Phone 603/893-3506. ¢¢¢¢

Robert Frost Farm. Home of poet Robert Frost from 1900-11; period furnishings; audiovisual display; poetry-nature trail. (June-Labor Day, daily; after Labor Day-mid-Oct, wkends only) 1 mi SW on NH 38, then NW on NH 28 in Derry. Phone 603/432-3091. ¢¢

Rockingham Park. Thoroughbred horse racing. Live and simulcast racing (daily). Exit 1 off I-93. Phone 603/898-2311.

Motels/Motor Lodges

★ **PARKVIEW INN.** *109 S Broadway; Rte 28 (03079). 603/898-5632; fax 603/894-6579.* Mar-Oct: S $60; D $70; suites $70; each addl $10; lower rates rest of yr. Crib avail. TV; cable. Ck-out 11 am, ck-in 2 pm. Golf. Cr cds: A, C, D, DS, MC, V.

★ **SUSSE CHALET INN.** *8 Keewaydin Dr (03079), I-93 Exit 2. 603/893-4722; fax 603/893-2898; toll-free 800/258-1980.* 104 rms, 4 story. S, D $64.70; under 18 free; seasonal rates. Crib free. TV; cable (premium). Pool. Continental bkfst. Restaurant opp 6 am-11 pm. Ck-out 11 am. Coin lndry. Meeting rm. Business servs avail. In-rm modem link. Cr cds: A, C, D, DS, MC, V.

Hotel

★★ **HOLIDAY INN.** *1 Keewaydin Dr (03079), I-93 Exit 2. 603/893-5511; fax 603/894-6728; res 800/465-4329. Email salemhi@aol.com.* 83 rms, 6 story. May-Oct: S, D $99-$109; lower rates rest of yr. Pet accepted. TV; cable (premium). Pool; poolside serv. Complimentary continental bkfst, coffee in rms. Restaurant 6:30 am-10 pm. Ck-out 11 am. No bellhops. Meeting rms. Business servs avail. In-rm modem link. Exercise equipt. Health club privileges. Refrigerator avail. Cr cds: A, DS, MC, V.

Sunapee

(F-4) *See also New London, Newport*

Pop 2,559 **Elev** 1,008 ft
Area code 603 **Zip** 03782
Web www.sunapeevacations.com
Information Lake Sunapee Business Association, PO Box 400; 603/763-2495 or 800/258-3530

This is a year-round resort community on beautiful Lake Sunapee.

What to See and Do

Lake cruises.

M/V *Mount Sunapee II* Excursion Boat. 1½-hr narrated tours of Lake Sunapee. (Mid-June-Labor Day, daily; mid-May-mid-June and after Labor Day-mid-Oct, Sat and Sun) Lake Ave, Sunapee Harbor, off NH 11. Phone 603/763-4030. ¢¢

M/V *Kearsarge* Restaurant Ship. Buffet dinner while cruising around Lake Sunapee. Phone 603/763-5477. ¢¢¢¢

Mount Sunapee State Park. 2,714 acres. 1 mi S off NH 103. Phone 603/763-2356.

Summer. Swimming beach, bathhouse (fee), trout pool; mountain biking (fee), picnicking, playground, concession, chairlift rides (fee). Displays by artists and craftsmen (see ANNUAL EVENT). (Memorial Day wkend; mid-June-early Sep, daily; early Sep-Columbus Day, wkends)

Winter. Skiing; 3 triple, 3 double chairlifts, pony lift; patrol, school, rentals, snowmaking; cafeteria, nursery; 38 slopes and trails. Snowboarding. (Dec-Mar, daily; closed Dec 25) Phone 800/552-1234 (snow conditions). ¢¢¢¢¢

Snowhill at Eastman Ski Area. Chairlift; patrol, school; concession. Longest run ½ mi; vertical drop 243 ft. (Dec-Mar, Sat, Sun, and hols exc Dec 25) Ski Touring Center has 30 km of cross-country trails; patrol, school, rentals; bar, restaurant (Dec-Mar, Wed-Sun; closed Dec 25). Summer facilities incl Eastman Lake, with swimming, boating, fishing; 18-hole golf, tennis, indoor pool, hiking. 4

mi N on NH 11, then 6 mi N on I-89, Exit 13. Phone 603/863-4500 or 603/863-4240. Cross-country skiing ¢¢¢; Downhill ¢¢¢¢

Annual Event

League of New Hampshire Craftsmen's Fair. Mount Sunapee State Park (see). Over 200 craftsmen and artists display and sell goods. Phone 603/224-3375. Aug.

Motel/Motor Lodge

★ **BURKHAVEN AT SUNAPEE.** *179 Burkehaven Hill Rd (03782), 1½ mi E of NH 11. 603/763-2788; fax 603/763-9065; toll-free 800/567-2788. Email boundbrook@cyberportal.net; www. burkehavenatsunapee.com.* 10 rms, 1 story. Jan-Mar, June-Oct: S, D $84; each addl $8; children $8; lower rates rest of yr. Crib avail. Pet accepted. Parking lot. Pool, whirlpool. TV; cable, VCR avail. Complimentary coffee in rms. Restaurant nearby. Business servs avail. Golf. Tennis, 2 courts. Downhill skiing. Beach access. Bike rentals. Hiking trail. Picnic facilities. Cr cds: A, DS, MC, V.

🐾 🏃 🎿 🍴 🎣 🏊 🚴 🏂 ⛷

B&Bs/Small Inns

★★ **CANDLELITE INN.** *5 Greenhouse Ln (03221), approx 10 mi W on NH 103, N on NH 114. 603/938-5571; fax 603/938-2564; toll-free 888/812-5571. Email candlelite@conknet.com; www.virtualcities.com/nh/candlelite inn.htm.* 6 rms, 2 with shower only, 3 story. No rm phones. S, D $70-$95; wkends (2-day min); higher rates fall foliage, graduation. Complimentary full bkfst. Ck-out 11 am, ck-in 3 pm. Downhill ski 7 mi. Lawn games. Built in 1897; gazebo porch. Totally nonsmoking. Cr cds: A, D, DS, MC, V.

🏃 🎿 🏂 ⛷ 🚴

★★ **DEXTERS INN & TENNIS CLUB.** *258 Stagecoach Rd (03782), I-89 Exit 12, 5 mi W on NH 11, left on Winhill Rd to Stagecoach Rd. 603/763-5571; fax 603/763-5571; toll-free 800/232-5571. Email dexters@tds.net.* 10 rms in lodge, 7 rms in annex, 2 story. No rm phones. MAP, May-Nov (2-day min wkends): S $95-$140; D

$135-$180; each addl $45; kit. cottage (up to 4) $385; EP, golf, tennis plans. Closed rest of yr. Crib $5. Pet accepted; $10. TV in lobby. Pool. Dining rm 8-10 am, 6:30-8:30 pm. Rm serv 24 hrs. Bar 5-10 pm. Ck-out 11 am, ck-in 3 pm. Meeting rms. Business servs avail. Tennis, pro. Lawn games. On 20-acre estate. Cr cds: DS, MC, V.

Twin Mountain

(D-5) *See also Bretton Woods, Franconia, Littleton*

Pop 760 (est) **Elev** 1,442 ft
Area code 603 **Zip** 03595
Web www.twinmountain.org
Information Chamber of Commerce, PO Box 194; 800/245-8946

What to See and Do

Mount Washington. (see) E off US 302.

White Mountain National Forest. (see) E on US 302; SW on US 3.

Motels/Motor Lodges

★★ **FOUR SEASONS MOTOR INN.** *Birch Rd and Rte 3 (03595), Exit 35. 603/846-5708; fax 603/846-5708; res 800/228-5708. www.4seasonsmotorinn. com.* 23 rms, 2 story, 4 suites. Aug-Oct: S $55; D $62; suites $124; each addl $7; under 12 free; lower rates rest of yr. Crib avail. Parking lot. Pool. TV; cable. Complimentary coffee in rms. Ck-out 11 am, ck-in 11

pm. Fax servs avail. Exercise privileges. Golf, 18 holes. Downhill skiing. Supervised children's activities. Hiking trail. Picnic facilities. Video games. Cr cds: DS, MC, V.

★★ **PAQUETTE'S MOTOR INN.** *675 Rte 3 (03595). 603/846-5562; fax 603/846-5562. www.paquettesmotor inn.com.* 33 rms, 2 story. Jan-Mar, July-Aug, Oct: S $48; each addl $6; children $6; under 12 free; lower rates rest of yr. Crib avail, fee. Parking lot. Pool. TV; cable. Complimentary full bkfst. Restaurant, closed Thurs. Ck-out 10:30 am, ck-in 1 pm. Golf, 18 holes. Tennis. Downhill skiing. Bike rentals. Picnic facilities. Cr cds: A, MC, V.

★ **PROFILE DELUXE MOTEL.** *PO Box 99 Rte 3 (03595). 603/846-5522; toll-free 800/682-7222. Email profile deluxe@earthlink.net; www.profiledelux. qpg.com.* 11 rms, 1 story, 2 suites. June-Oct: S, D $55; suites $80; each addl $10; under 12 free; lower rates rest of yr. Crib avail. Parking lot. Pool, lap pool, children's pool. TV; cable (premium). Restaurant nearby. Ck-out 11 am, ck-in 1 pm. Golf. Tennis, 5 courts. Downhill skiing. Hiking trail. Picnic facilities. Cr cds: A, DS, MC, V.

B&B/Small Inn

★★ **NORTHERN ZERMATT INN & MOTEL.** *529 Rte 3 N (03595), 1 mi N of jct US 302. 603/846-5533; fax 603/846-5664; res 800/245TWIN; toll-free 800/535-3214.* 17 rms, 9 A/C, 2-3 story. No rm phones. S $32; D $40-$57; each addl $6; kit. units $57-$79; under 16 free; wkly rates. TV in some rms; cable. Pool. Playground. Complimentary continental bkfst. Restaurant nearby. Ck-out 11 am, ck-in after 3 pm. 18-hole golf privileges. Lawn games. Picnic tables, grills. Former boarding house (ca 1900) for log-

Strawbery Banke Museum, Portsmouth

gers and railroad workers. Cr cds: A, DS, MC, V.

Waterville Valley

(E-5) *See also Lincoln/North Woodstock Area, Plymouth*

Founded 1829 **Pop** 151 **Elev** 1,519 ft
Area code 603 **Zip** 03215
Information Waterville Valley Region Chamber of Commerce, RFD 1, Box 1067, Campton 03223; 603/726-3804

Although the resort village of Waterville Valley was developed in the late 1960s, the surrounding area has been attracting tourists since the mid-19th century, when summer vacationers stayed at the Waterville Inn. Completely encircled by the White Mountain National Forest, the resort, which is approximately 11 miles northeast of Campton, offers a variety of winter and summer activities, as well as spectacular views of the surrounding mountain peaks.

What to See and Do

Waterville Valley Ski Area. Five double, 3 triple chairlifts, quad chairlift, T-bar, J-bar, platter pull; patrol, school; retail, rental, and repair shops; snowmaking; restaurants, cafeterias, lounge, nursery; 48 ski trails; longest run 3 mi; vertical drop 2,020 ft. Limited lift tickets; half-day rates. (Mid-Nov-mid-Apr, daily) Ski Touring Center with 46 mi of cross-country trails; rentals, school, restaurants. Summer facilities incl 9-hole golf, 18 clay tennis courts, hiking, bicycling, rollerblading, horseback riding; small boating, fishing; entertainment. Indoor sports center (daily). 11 mi NE of Campton on NH 49. Contact Waterville Valley Resort, Town Sq. Phone 800/468-2553. ¢¢¢¢

Hotel

★★ BLACK BEAR LODGE. *3 Village Rd (03215). 603/236-4501; fax 603/236-4114; toll-free 800/349-2327. Email blkbear@tog-gether.net;* www.black-bear-lodge.com. 6 story, 107 suites. Dec-Mar, July-Oct: S, D $249; lower rates rest of yr. Crib avail. TV; cable, VCR avail. Restaurant nearby. Ck-out 11 am, ck-in 4 pm. Meeting rms. Golf, 9 holes. Tennis, 18 courts. Cr cds: A, C, D, DS, JCB, MC, V.

Resorts

★★★ SNOWY OWL INN. *4 Village Rd (03215). 603/236-8383; fax 603/236-4890; toll-free 800/766-9969. Email snowy@snowyowlinn.com; www. snowyowlinn.com.* 83 rms, 4 story, 2 suites. Dec-Feb, Sep-Oct: S, D $209; suites $269; each addl $10; under 12 free; lower rates rest of yr. Crib avail. Parking lot. Indoor/outdoor pools, whirlpool. TV; cable. Complimentary continental bkfst, coffee in rms. Restaurant nearby. Ck-out 11 am, ck-in 4 pm. Meeting rms. Business center. Coin lndry. Exercise privileges, sauna. Golf, 9 holes. Tennis, 18 courts. Downhill skiing. Beach access. Bike rentals. Supervised children's activities. Hiking trail. Picnic facilities. Cr cds: A, D, DS, MC, V.

★★ VALLEY INN & TAVERN. *1 Tecumseh Rd (03215). 603/236-8336; fax 603/236-4294; toll-free 800/343-0969. Email info@valleyinn.com; www. valleyinn.com.* 45 rms, 4 story, 4 suites. Jan-Feb, Oct: S, D $169; suites $279; lower rates rest of yr. Crib avail, fee. Parking lot. Indoor/outdoor pools, whirlpool. TV; cable, VCR avail. Complimentary continental bkfst. Restaurant, closed Tue. Bar. Meeting rms. Business servs avail. Coin lndry. Exercise privileges, sauna. Golf. Tennis, 2 courts. Downhill skiing. Bike rentals. Supervised children's activities. Hiking trail. Picnic facilities. Cr cds: A, C, D, DS, MC, V.

Restaurants

★ CHILE PEPPERS. *Town Sq (03215). 603/236-4646.* Specializes in barbecue ribs, chile rellenos, fajitas. Hrs: noon-10 pm. Bar. Lunch $3.95-$7.95; dinner $6.95-$13.95. View of

mountains, Snows Brook waterfall.
Cr cds: A, DS, MC, V.

[D] [⟿]

★★ **WILLIAM TELL.** *Waterville Valley Rd (NH 49) (03223), 3 mi E on NH 49. 603/726-3618.* Specializes in fresh seafood, venison, veal. Hrs: 5-10 pm; Sun from noon. Closed Wed. Res accepted. Bar. Dinner $10.50-$20. Sun brunch $6.25-$9.50. Child's menu. Patio dining overlooking duck pond. Swiss atmosphere. Family-owned. Cr cds: A, DS, MC, V.

[D]

White Mountain National Forest

This national forest and major New Hampshire recreation area includes the Presidential Range and a major part of the White Mountains. There are more than 100 miles of roads and 1,128 miles of foot trails. The Appalachian Trail, with eight hostels, winds over some spectacular peaks. Eight peaks tower more than a mile above sea level; the highest is Mount Washington (6,288 feet); 22 mountains rise more than 4,000 feet. There are several well-defined ranges, divided by deep "notches" and broader valleys. Clear streams rush through the notches; mountain lakes and ponds dot the landscape. Deer, bear, moose, and bobcat roam the wilds; trout fishing is good.

The US Forest Service administers 23 campgrounds with more than 700 sites ($12-$16/site/night), also picnicking sites for public use. There is lodging within the forest; for information, reservations contact the Appalachian Mountain Club, Pinkham Notch, Gorham 03581; 603/466-2727. There are also many resorts, campsites, picnicking, and recreational spots in private and state-owned areas. A visitor center (daily) is at the Saco Ranger Station, 33 Kancamagus Hwy, Conway 03818; 603/447-5448. Information stations are also located at exits 28 and 32 off I-93 and at Franconia Notch State Park Visitor Center. For further information contact the Supervisor, White Mountain National Forest, 719 Main St, Laconia 03246; 603/528-8721.

The following cities and villages in and near the forest are included in the *Guide*: Bartlett, Bretton Woods, Franconia, Franconia Notch State Park, Gorham, Jackson, Lincoln/North Woodstock Area, Mount Washington, North Conway, Pinkham Notch, Twin Mountain, and Waterville Valley. For information on any of them, see the individual alphabetical listing.

Wolfeboro

(F-6) *See also Center Ossipee, Laconia*

Settled 1760 **Pop** 4,807 **Elev** 573 ft
Area code 603 **Zip** 03894
Web www.wolfeboro.com-chamber

Information Chamber of Commerce, PO Box 547; 603/569-2200 or 800/516-5324

Wolfeboro has been a resort area for more than two centuries; it is the oldest summer resort in America. In the winter it is a ski touring center with 40 miles of groomed trails.

What to See and Do

Clark House. Wolfeboro Historical Society is housed in Clark family homestead (1778), a 1-rm schoolhouse (ca 1820), and a firehouse museum. Clark House has period furnishings, memorabilia; firehouse museum contains restored firefighting equipment dating from 1842. (July-Aug, Mon-Sat) S Main St. Phone 603/569-4997. **Donation**

Lake Winnipesaukee cruises. (See LACONIA).

Wentworth State Park. On Lake Wentworth. Swimming, bathhouse; picnicking. (Late June-Labor Day) Standard fees. 6 mi E on NH 109. Phone 603/569-3699.

Wright Museum. Showcases American enterprise during WWII. Collection of tanks, jeeps, and other military vehicles; period memorabilia. (Daily) 77 Center St. Phone 603/569-1212.

Motels/Motor Lodges

★ ★ **LAKE MOTEL.** *280 S Main St (03894), 1 mi S on NH 28, ¾ mi S of jct NH 109. 603/569-1100; fax 603/569-1620.* 30 rms, 5 kit. units. July-Labor Day: S, D $89-$98; each addl $6; kit. units for 2, $630/wk; each addl $8; lower rates mid-May-June and after Labor Day-mid-Oct. Closed rest of yr. Pet accepted, some restrictions. TV; cable. Playground. Coffee in lobby. Restaurant adj 7:30 am-10 pm in summer. Ck-out 11 am. Business servs avail. Sundries. Tennis. Lawn games. On Crescent Lake; private beach, dockage. Cr cds: DS, MC, V.

D 🔄 🛅 🏋 🛏 🔽 🔥

★ ★ **LAKEVIEW INN & MOTOR LODGE.** *200 N Main St (03894). 603/569-1335; fax 603/569-9426.* 14 motel rms, 3 rms in inn, 2 story, 4 kits. July-Oct: S $80; D $90; each addl $5; kit. units $5 addl; lower rates rest of yr. Crib free. TV; cable. Complimentary continental bkfst, coffee in rms. Restaurant 5-9 pm. Bar; entertainment Fri in season. Ck-out 11 am. Business servs avail. Some private patios, balconies. Inn built 1768 on king's land grant. Cr cds: A, MC, V.

D 🛅 🏋 🔽 🔥

★ **PINE VIEW LODGE.** *PO Box 207 (03850), approx 10 mi N on NH 109. 603/544-3800.* 12 rms, 1 story. June-Oct: S, D $85; lower rates rest of yr. Parking lot. TV; cable. Restaurant nearby. Ck-out 11 am, ck-in 3 pm. Coin lndry. Golf. Downhill skiing. Beach access. Hiking trail. Picnic facilities. Cr cds: DS, MC, V.

🛅 🏋 🛅 🏋 🔽 ✖ 🔽 🔥

B&B/Small Inn

★ ★ ★ **THE WOLFEBORO INN.** *90 N Main St (03894). 603/569-3016; fax 603/569-5375; res 800/451-2389. Email postmaster@wolfeboroinn.com.* 44 rms, 3 story, 3 suites, 1 kit. unit. S, D $119-$129; suites $169-$219; kit. $200; under 8 free; wkly rates; higher rates hols. Crib $10. TV; cable, VCR avail. Complimentary continental bkfst. Dining rm 7 am-11:30 pm. Ck-out 11 am, ck-in 3 pm. Business servs avail. Valet serv. Sundries. Downhill ski 20 mi; x-country ski on site. Balconies. On Lake Win-nipesaukee. Original bldg from 1812. Gardens. Cr cds: A, DS, MC, V.

D 🔽 🔽 🏋 SC

Cottage Colony

★ ★ **CLEARWATER LODGES.** *704 N Main St (03894). 603/569-2370; fax 603/569-2370.* 15 kit. cottages (1-2 bedrm), 3-bedrm lodge. No A/C. No rm phones. July-Labor Day: cottages up to 2, $655/wk; cottages up to 4, $850/wk; each addl $80; daily rates; lower rates late May-late June and after Labor Day-late Sept. Closed rest of yr. Crib free. TV in rec rm. Ck-out 10 am, ck-in 3 pm. Coin lndry. Business servs avail. Grocery, package store 3 mi. Private waterfront; boats, motors. Rec rm. Barbecue, picnic areas. Rustic cottages with fireplaces and porches in tall pines on Lake Winnipesaukee. Cr cds: A, DS, MC, V.

🛅 🔥

RHODE ISLAND

Giovanni da Verrazano, a Florentine navigator in the service of France, visited the Narragansett Bay of Rhode Island in 1524; however, it wasn't until 1636 that the first permanent white settlement was founded. Roger Williams, a religious refugee from Massachusetts, bought land at Providence from the Narragansetts. Williams fled what he considered puritanical tyranny and established a policy of religious and political freedom in his new settlement. Soon others began similar communities, and in 1663 King Charles II granted them a royal charter, officially creating the "State of Rhode Island and Providence Plantations."

Although the smallest state in the nation and smaller than many of the counties in the United States, Rhode Island is rich in American tradition. It is a state of firsts. Rhode Islanders were among the first colonists to take action against the British, attacking British vessels in its waters. On May 4, 1776, the state was the first to proclaim independence from Great Britain, two months before the Declaration of Independence was signed. In 1790 Samuel Slater's mill in Pawtucket became America's first successful water-powered cotton mill, and in 1876 polo was played for the first time in the United States in Newport.

Rhode Island has a tradition of manufacturing skill. The state produces machine tools, electronic equipment, plastics, textiles, jewelry, toys, and boats. The famous Rhode Island Red Hen was developed by farmers in Little Compton. Rhode Island is also for those who follow the sea. With more than 400 miles of coastline, visitors can swim, sail, fish, or relax in the many resort areas.

Population: 1,003,464
Area: 1,054 square miles
Elevation: 0-812 feet
Peak: Jerimoth Hill (Providence County)
Entered Union: Thirteenth of original 13 states (May 29, 1790)
Capital: Providence
Motto: Hope
Nickname: Ocean State
Flower: Violet
Bird: Rhode Island Red Hen
Tree: Red Maple
Time Zone: Eastern
Website:
www.visitrhodeisland.com

When to Go/Climate

The weather in Rhode Island is more moderate than in other parts of New England. Breezes off Narraganset Bay make summer humidity bearable and winter temperatures less bitter than elsewhere in the region.

AVERAGE HIGH/LOW TEMPERATURES (°F)

PROVIDENCE

Jan 37/19	May 67/47	Sep 74/54
Feb 38/21	June 77/57	Oct 64/43
Mar 46/29	July 82/63	Nov 53/35
Apr 57/38	Aug 81/62	Dec 41/24

Parks and Recreation Finder

Directions to and information about the parks and recreation areas below are given under their respective town/city sections. Please refer to those sections for details.

CALENDAR HIGHLIGHTS

FEBRUARY

Newport Winter Festival (Newport). Ten days of food, festivities, music. More than 200 cultural and recreational events and activities. Phone 401/849-8048, 800/326-6030, or 401/847-7666.

Mid-winter New England Surfing Championship (Narragansett). Narragansett Town Beach. Phone the Eastern Surfing Association, 401/789-1954.

MAY

Gaspee Days (Warwick). Celebration of the capture and burning of British revenue schooner Gaspee by Rhode Island patriots; arts and crafts, concert, foot races, battle reenactment, muster of fife and drum corps, parade, contests. Phone Gaspee Days Committee, 401/781-1772.

JUNE

Spring Festival of Historic Houses (Providence). Sponsored by the Providence Preservation Society. Tours of selected private houses and gardens. Phone 401/831-7440.

JUNE-JULY

Newport Music Festival (Newport). Chamber and Romantic music, held in Newport's fabled mansions. Phone 401/847-7090.

JULY

Hot-Air Balloon Festival (Kingston). University of Rhode Island. Two-day event features hot-air balloon rides, parachute demonstrations, arts and crafts, music. Phone 401/783-1770.

NATIONAL PARK AND RECREATION AREAS

Key to abbreviations. I.H.S. = International Historic Site; I.P.M. = International Peace Memorial; N.B. = National Battlefield; N.B.P. = National Battlefield Park; N.B.C. = National Battlefield and Cemetery; N.C.A. = National Conservation Area; N.E.M. = National Expansion Memorial; N.F. = National Forest; N.G. = National Grassland; N.H.P. = National Historical Park; N.H.C. = National Heritage Corridor; N.H.S. = National Historic Site; N.L. = National Lakeshore; N.M. = National Monument; N.M.P. = National Military Park; N.Mem. = National Memorial; N.P. = National Park; N.Pres. = National Preserve; N.R.A. = National Recreational Area; N.R.R. = National Recreational River; N.Riv. = National River; N.S. = National Seashore; N.S.R. = National Scenic Riverway; N.S.T. = National Scenic Trail; N.Sc. = National Scientific Reserve; N.V.M. = National Volcanic Monument.

Place Name	Listed Under
Roger Williams N. Mem.	PROVIDENCE

STATE PARK AND RECREATION AREAS

Key to abbreviations. I.P. = Interstate Park; S.A.P. = State Archaeological Park; S.B. = State Beach; S.C.A. = State Conservation Area; S.C.P. = State Conservation Park; S.Cp. = State Campground; S.F. = State Forest; S.G. = State Garden; S.H.A. = State Historic Area; S.H.P. = State Historic Park; S.H.S. = State Historic Site; S.M.P. = State Marine Park; S.N.A. = State Natural Area; S.P. = State Park; S.P.C. = State Public Campground; S.R. = State Reserve; S.R.A. = State Recreation Area; S.Res. = State Reservoir; S.Res.P. = State Resort Park; S.R.P. = State Rustic Park.

Place Name	Listed Under
Burlingame S.P.	CHARLESTOWN
Casimir Pulaski S.P.	GLOCESTER
Colt S.P.	BRISTOL
Fort Adams S.P.	NEWPORT
Goddard Memorial S.P.	EAST GREENWICH
Lincoln Woods S.P.	PROVIDENCE
Misquamicut S.B.	WESTERLY
Salty Brine Beach, Roger Wheeler Beach, and Scarborough Beach S.P.	NARRAGANSETT

Water-related activities, hiking, riding, various other sports, picnicking, and visitor centers, as well as camping, are available in many of these areas. State parks are open sunrise to sunset. Parking fee at beaches: wkdays, $4-$8/car; wkends, hols, $5-$10/car. Camping $8-$12/night; with electric and water $10-$14; sewer additional $5. No pets allowed. A map is available at the Division of Parks & Recreation, Dept of Environmental Management, 2321 Hartford Avenue, Johnston 02919. Phone 401/222-2632.

FISHING AND HUNTING

No license is necessary for recreational saltwater game fishing. Freshwater fishing license: nonresident, $31; 3-day tourists' fee, $16. Both largemouth bass and northern pike can be found in Worden Pond; trout can be found in Wood River.

Hunting license: nonresident, $41. Resident licenses and regulations may be obtained at city and town clerks' offices and at most sporting goods shops. Nonresident licenses may be obtained by contacting DEM-Licensing, 22 Hayes St, Providence 02908; 401/222-3576. For further information write Division of Fish and Wildlife, Dept of Environment Management, Government Center, Wakefield 02879. Phone 401/222-3075.

Driving Information

Children ages 4-12 must be in an approved passenger restraint anywhere in vehicle; age 3 and under must use an approved safety seat. For further information phone Governor's Office of Highway Safety 401/222-3024.

INTERSTATE HIGHWAY SYSTEM

The following alphabetical listing of Rhode Island towns in *Mobil Travel Guide* shows that these cities are within 10 miles of the indicated Interstate highway. A highway map, however, should be checked for the nearest exit.

Highway Number	Cities/Towns within 10 miles
Interstate 95	East Greenwich, Pawtucket, Providence, Warwick, Westerly.

Additional Visitor Information

Contact the Rhode Island Economic Development Corporation Division of Marketing & Communications, 1 W Exchange St, Providence 02903; 401/222-2601 or 800/556-2484. The *Providence Journal-Bulletin Almanac* is an excellent state reference book and may be obtained from the Providence *Journal*, 75 Fountain St, Providence 02902.

There are several information centers in Rhode Island; visitors will find information and brochures most helpful in planning stops at points of interest. Visitor centers are located off I-95 in Richmond (daily) and 7 miles S of Providence in Warwick, at T. F. Green Airport.

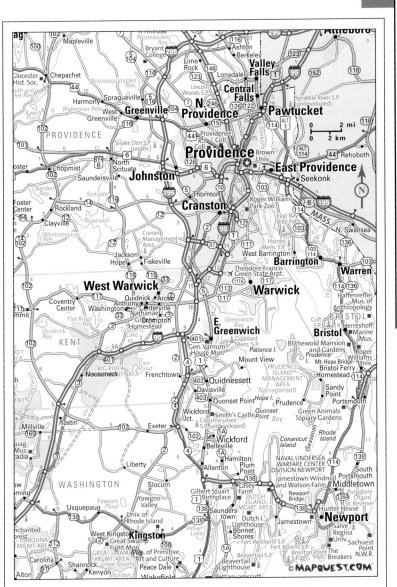

©MAPQUEST.COM

Prime attractions in Providence include Benefit Street and the Rhode Island School of Design Art Museum, John Brown House, Museum of Rhode Island History, and the zoo in Roger Williams Park. The route from Providence to Newport is down 114 with stops at Bristol (Herreshoff Marine Museum, Haffenreffer Museum of Anthropology, Blithewold Mansion and Gardens, colonial homes, inns, restaurants) and Portsmouth (Green Animals topiary gardens, Butterfly Zoo). Newport is the major destination and lodging hub in Rhode Island. Famous for its historic mansions (see detailed listing in Newport under WHAT TO SEE AND DO), Newport also offers visitors such highlights as the International Tennis Hall of Fame, the atmosphere of its colonial neighborhood, the beauty of the waterfront, and summer music festivals. **(Approx 68 mi)**

Block Island

See also Newport, Westerly

(By ferry from Providence, Newport, and Point Judith; by air from Westerly. Also by ferry from New London, CT, and Montauk, Long Island.)

Settled 1661 **Pop** 620 (est) **Elev** 9 ft
Area code 401 **Zip** 02807
Information Chamber of Commerce, Water St, PO Drawer D; 401/466-2982 or 800/383-2474

Block Island, Rhode Island's "air-conditioned" summer resort, covers 21 square miles. Lying 12 miles out to sea from Point Judith, it received its nickname because it is 10-15 degrees cooler than the mainland in summer and consistently milder in winter. Although Verrazano saw the island in 1524, it was named for the Dutch explorer Adriaen Block, who landed here in 1614. Until the resort trade developed, this island community was devoted to fishing and farming. Settler's Rock on Corn Neck Road displays plaques on the boulder listing the first settlers.

In recent years Block Island has become a favorite "nature retreat" for people seeking to escape fast-paced city living. More than 40 rare and endangered species of plants and animals can be found on the island, of which ¼ is in public trust. The Nature Conservancy has designated Block Island as "one of the 12 last great places in the Western Hemisphere."

What to See and Do

Ferry service. Phone 401/783-4613.

Block Island/Montauk, Long Island. (Mid-June-Labor Day, 1 trip daily) Phone 516/668-5009.

Block Island/New London, CT. Two-hr trip. (Mid-June-Labor Day, 1 trip daily, extra trips Fri)

Block Island/Point Judith. Advance reservations for vehicles; all vehicles must be on pier 45 min before sailing. (Mid-June-mid-Sep, 8 round trips daily; early May-mid-June, mid-Sep-Oct, 4 round trips daily; rest of yr, 1 round trip daily)

Block Island/Providence/Newport. Departs from either Providence or Newport. (Late June-Labor Day, 1 trip daily) Nonvehicular ferry.

Fishing. Surf casting from most beaches; freshwater ponds for bass, pickerel, perch; deep-sea boat trips for tuna, swordfish, etc, from Old Harbor.

Fred Benson Town Beach. Swimming, bathhouse, lifeguards; picnicking, concession. Parking. ½ mi N to Crescent Beach.

Natural formations. Mohegan Bluffs. W of Southeast Light lighthouse off Mohegan Trail, are 185-ft clay cliffs that offer a fine sea view. **New Harbor,** 1 mi W on Ocean Ave, is a huge harbor made by cutting through sand bar into Great Salt Pond.

New England Airlines. Twelve-min scheduled flights between Westerly State Airport and Block Island State Airport; also air taxi and charter service to all points. (Daily) Phone 401/466-5881, 401/596-2460, or 800/243-2460.

North Light. Lighthouse built 1867 at tip of island near Settler's Rock, now houses maritime museum. Bordering dunes are seagull rookery and wildlife sanctuary.

Hotels

★★ **SPRING HOUSE.** *52 Spring St (02807). 401/466-5844; fax 401/466-2633; toll-free 800/234-9263. Email springhousehotel@ids.net; www.springhousehotel.com.* 34 rms, 3 story, 15 suites. June-Sep: D $255; suites $300; each addl $20; lower rates rest of yr. Crib avail. Parking lot. TV; cable. Complimentary continental bkfst. Restaurant 6-10 pm. Bar. Ck-out 3 pm, ck-in 11 pm. Meeting rm. Bellhops. Concierge. Coin lndry. Cr cds: A, MC, V.
✈ ➹ 🐾

★★ **SURF MOTEL.** *32 Dodge St (02807). 401/466-2241.* 47 rms, 4 story. July-Aug: S $77; D $99; each addl $11; children $11; lower rates rest of yr. Crib avail. TV; cable. Complimentary continental bkfst, toll-free calls. Restaurant 7 am-10 pm. Ck-out 11 am, ck-in noon. Free airport transportation. Tennis, 3 courts. Beach access. Cr cds: DS, MC, V.
🏌 ✈ ➹ 🐾

B&B/Small Inn

★★★ THE 1661 INN & GUEST HOUSE. *1 Spring St (02807). 401/466-2421; fax 401/466-3162; toll-free 800/626-4773. Email biresorts@aol. com.* 21 units, 6 with shower only, 4 share bath, 2 story, 2 suites, 2 kit. units. No A/C. Many rm phones. July-Sept: S, D $115-$248; suites $229-$325; kit. units $250; wkend rates; 3-day min wkends and hols; lower rates rest of yr. Crib free. Some cable TVs; VCR avail. Playground, petting zoo. Complimentary coffee in rms; full bkfst; afternoon refreshments. Restaurant nearby. Ck-out 11 am, ck-in 1 pm. Bellhops. Free airport transportation. Tennis. Lawn games. Refrigerators. Sun decks. Picnic tables. On ocean. Built 1890; restored Colonial with Early American art and antiques. Cr cds: MC, V.

Restaurants

★★ FINN'S SEAFOOD. *Water St (02807), at Ferry Landing. 401/466-2473. Email dhowarth@netsense.net.* Specializes in seafood, lobster. Hrs: 11:30 am-10 pm. Closed Nov-Apr. Bar. Lunch a la carte entrees: $4.80-$34.50; dinner a la carte entrees: $4.80-$34.50. View of town and harbor. Cr cds: A, MC, V.

★★★ HOTEL MANISSES DINING ROOM. *Spring St (02807). 401/466-2836. www.blockisland.com/eiresorts.* Hrs: 6-9 pm. Bar. Wine cellar. Lunch $9-$21; dinner $15-$25. Prix fixe: $29-$39. Child's menu. Stone-walled dining rm and glass-enclosed garden rm. Cr cds: A, MC, V.

★★ MOHEGAN CAFE. *Water St (02807), opp ferry landing in Historic Downtown District. 401/466-5911.* Specializes in seafood. Hrs: 11:30 am-9 pm. Closed Thanksgiving, Dec 25. Bar. Lunch $3.95-$9.95; dinner $8.95-$18.95. Child's menu. Panoramic view of Old Harbor. Cr cds: A, DS, MC, V.

Bristol

(E-6) *See also Portsmouth, Providence*

Settled 1669 **Pop** 21,625 **Elev** 50 ft
Area code 401 **Zip** 02809
Web www.bristolcountychamber.org
Information Bristol County Chamber of Commerce, 654 Metacom Ave, PO Box 250, Warren 02885-0250; 401/245-0750

King Philip's War (1675-76) began and ended on the Bristol peninsula between Mount Hope and Narragansett bays; King Philip, the Native American rebel leader, headquartered the Wampanoag tribe in the area. After the war ended, Bristol grew into an important port, and by the turn of the 18th century the town was the fourth busiest port in the United States. Bristol was the home of General Ambrose Burnside, Civil War officer and sometime governor and senator. The town was the site of the famous Herreshoff Boatyard, where many America's Cup winners were built. Roger Williams University (1948) is located in Bristol.

What to See and Do

Blithewold Mansion and Gardens. Former turn-of-the-century summer estate; 45-rm mansion surrounded by 33 acres of landscaped grounds; many exotic trees and shrubs incl a giant sequoia. Grounds (open all yr; fee). Mansion and grounds tour (Apr-Oct, Tues-Sun; closed hols). 2 mi S on RI 114 (Ferry Road); on Bristol Harbor overlooking Naragansett Bay. Phone 401/253-2707. Guided tour ¢¢¢

Colt State Park. Three-mi scenic drive around shoreline of former Colt family estate on east side of Narragansett Bay. Fishing, boating; hiking and bridle trails, picnicking. 2½ mi NW off RI 114. Per vehicle ¢ In park is

Coggeshall Farm Museum. Working farm from 18th-19th century; vegetables, herbs, animals; Colonial craft demonstrations. (Tues-Sun; closed Jan) Phone 401/253-9062. ¢¢

Haffenreffer Museum of Anthropology. Brown Univ museum features

Native American objects from North, Central, and South America; Eskimo collections; African and Pacific tribal arts. (June-Aug, Tues-Sun; rest of yr, Sat and Sun) 1 mi E of Metacom Ave, RI 136, follow signs; overlooks Mt Hope Bay. Phone 401/253-8388. ¢

Herreshoff Marine Museum. Herreshoff Mfg Co produced some of America's greatest yachts, incl 8 winners of the America's Cup. Exhibits incl yachts manufactured by Herreshoff, steam engines, fittings; photographs and memorabilia from "golden age of yachting." (May-Oct, Mon-Fri afternoons; also Sat and Sun, limited hours) 7 Burnside St. Phone 401/253-5000. ¢¢

Hope Street. Famous row of Colonial houses. On RI 114.

Prudence Island. Ferry from Church St dock.

Annual Event

Harvest Fair. Coggeshall Farm Museum. Wkend mid-Sep.

Seasonal Events

Blithewold Mansion and Gardens. Concerts. Phone 401/253-2707. June-Aug.

Colt State Park. Concerts in Stone Barn. Sun and Wed, early July-Aug.

Motel/Motor Lodge

★ **KING PHILIP INN.** *400 Metacom Ave (02809). 401/253-7600; fax 401/253-1857; toll-free 800/253-7610.* 45 rms. Mid-May-mid-Oct: S, D $60-$79; each addl $5; under 12 free; higher rates special events; lower rates rest of yr. Crib free. TV; VCR avail. Restaurant 6-11 am, Sat-Sun 7 am-1 pm. Ck-out 11 am. Meeting rms. Business servs avail. Refrigerators. Cr cds: A, DS, MC, V.

⬚⬚⬚⬚

B&Bs/Small Inns

★ ★ ★ **ROCKWELL HOUSE INN.** *610 Hope St (02809), in Historic Downtown Waterfront District. 401/253-0040; fax 401/253-1811; res 401/253-0040; toll-free 800/815-0040.*

Email rockwellinn@ids.net. 4 rms, 1 with shower only, 2 story. No A/C. No rm phones. May-Oct: S, D $125; each addl $25; wkday rates; wkends, hols (2-day min); higher rates July 4th; lower rates rest of yr. Children over 12 yrs only. TV in parlor; VCR. Complimentary full bkfst. Restaurant nearby. Ck-out 11 am, ck-in noon-8 pm. Concierge serv. Business servs avail. Lawn games. Refrigerator avail. Picnic tables. Federal-style house (1809); fireplaces, hand stenciling in many rms. Cr cds: A, DS, MC, V.

⬚⬚⬚⬚⬚⬚⬚

Classic New England light house

★ **WILLIAMS GRANT INN.** *154 High St (02809). 401/253-4222; fax 401/254-0986; toll-free 800/596-4222. Email wmgrantinn@aol.com.* 5 rms, 2 share bath, 2 story. No A/C. No rm phones. May-Oct: S, D $85-$125; wkly rates; wkends, hols (2-day min); lower rates rest of yr. Children over 12 yrs only. Complimentary coffee in rms. Complimentary full bkfst. Restaurant nearby. Ck-out 11 am, ck-in noon-10 pm. House built 1808; original fireplaces, artwork, many antiques. Totally nonsmoking. Cr cds: A, DS, MC, V.

⬚⬚⬚⬚⬚⬚⬚

Restaurants

★ ★ **LOBSTER POT.** *119-121 Hope St (02809). 401/253-9100.* Specializes in lobster, seafood. Hrs: noon-9 pm. Closed Mon. Bar. Lunch $4.75-$12.95; dinner $7.75-$23.95. Child's menu. Entertainment: pianist wkends. On waterfront; view of harbor. Family-owned. Cr cds: A, MC, V.

[D] 🔳

★★ **NATHANIEL PORTER INN.**
*125 Water St (02885), 4 mi N on RI
114. 401/245-6622. www.nathaniel
porterinn.com.* Specializes in filet
with bernaise sauce, seafood. Hrs: 5-
9 pm; Sun brunch 10:30 am-2 pm,
4-8 pm. Closed Mon. Res accepted.
Bar. Dinner $12.95-$21.95. Sun
brunch $19.95. Child's menu.
House built 1795; Colonial decor,
antiques. Guest rms avail. Cr cds: A,
D, DS, MC, V.

🔳

Charlestown

(F-5) *See also Narragansett, Westerly*

Pop 6,478 **Elev** 20 ft **Area code** 401
Zip 02813
Web www.southcountyri.com
Information South County Tourism
Council, Stedman Government Center, 4808 Tower Hill Road, Wakefield
02879; 401/789-4422 or 800/548-4662

Charlestown, named for King Charles
II of England, was originally called
Cross Mills for two gristmills that
once stood here. Charlestown was
first settled along the coast by summer residents and by permanent residents after World War II. The town's
past can be seen in Fort Ninigret, the
historic Native American church, and
the Royal Indian Burial Ground.

What to See and Do

Burlingame State Park. More than
2,000 acres with wooded area. Swimming, lifeguard, fishing, boating; picnicking, concession, tent and trailer
camping (mid-Apr-Oct). Standard
fees. 2 mi SW via US 1, Kings Factory
Rd. Phone 401/322-7337 or 401/322-
7994 (Nov-mid-Apr).

Kimball Wildlife Refuge. Thirty-acre
refuge on S shore of Watchaug Pond
has nature trails and programs. 2½
mi SW on US 1, Windswept Farm
exit, left onto Montauk Rd.

Swimming, fishing. At several Block
Island Sound beaches; S of US 1 on

Charlestown Beach Rd; Green Hill
Rd; Moonstone Rd. **FREE**

Annual Events

Seafood Festival. Ninigret Park.
Seafood vendors, amateur seafood
cook-off, helicopter rides, antique car
show. Phone 401/364-4031. First Sat
and Sun Aug.

**August Meeting of the Narragansett
Indian Tribe.** Narragansett Indian
church grounds. Dancing, music, storytelling. Said to be oldest continuous meeting in the country. Second
week in Aug. Phone 401/364-1101.

Seasonal Event

Theatre-by-the-Sea. Historic barn
theater (1933) presents professionally
staged musicals. Restaurant, bar,
cabaret. Tues-Sun nights; matinees
Thurs; children's shows July-Aug, Fri
only. 7 mi NE via US 1, then S off
Matunuck Beach Rd exit to Cards
Pond Rd in Matunuck. Contact 364
Cards Pond Rd, Matunuck 02879;
401/782-8587. June-Sep.

East Greenwich

(E-5) *See also Warwick*

Pop 11,865 **Elev** 64 ft **Area code** 401
Zip 02818
Web www.eastgreenwichchamber.
com
Information Chamber of Commerce,
5853 Post Rd, Suite 106, PO Box 514;
401/885-0020

Sometimes referred to as "the town on
four hills," East Greenwich, on Narragansett Bay, is a sports and yachting
center. Nathanael Greene and James
M. Varnum organized the Kentish
Guards, who protected the town during the Revolution, here in 1774. The
Guards are still active today.

What to See and Do

Goddard Memorial State Park.
Approx 490 acres with swimming at
Greenwich Bay Beach (bathhouse),
fishing, boating; bridle trails, 9-hole
golf (fee), ice-skating, picnicking, concessions, playing fields, and fireplaces

(fee). E side of Greenwich Cove, E of town via Forge Rd and Ives Rd. Phone 401/884-2010. Per vehicle ¢

Kentish Guards Armory. (1843) HQ of the Kentish Guards, local militia chartered in 1774 and still active; Gen Nathanael Greene was a charter member. (By appt only) 92 Pierce St. Phone 401/821-1628. ¢

Old Kent County Court House. (1750) Remodeled in 1909 and 1995. 125 Main St. Phone 401/886-8606.

Varnum House Museum. (1773) Mansion of Revolutionary War officer and lawyer; period furnishings, Colonial items, gardens. (June-Sep, by appt) 57 Pierce St. Phone 401/884-4110. ¢

Varnum Memorial Armory and Military Museum. (1913) Museum displays uniforms and armaments from the Revolutionary War through the Vietnam War. (By appt) 6 Main St. Phone 401/884-4110. **Donation**

Glocester

Pop 5,011 **Elev** 422 ft **Area code** 401 **Zip** 02859

Information Blackstone Valley Tourism Council, 171 Main St, Pawtucket 02860; 401/724-2200 or 800/454-2882 (Outside RI)

What to See and Do

Brown & Hopkins Country Store. (1799) Nation's oldest continuously operating country store; inside are antiques, gourmet food, penny candy, and a cafe. (Wed-Sun; closed hols) 3 mi SE on RI 100 to US 44 (Main St) in Chepachet. Phone 401/568-4830.

Casimir Pulaski State Park. Park has 100 acres with lake. Swimming beach; cross-country skiing, picnicking. Pavilion (res). (Late May-early Sep) 3 mi SE on RI 100, 6 mi W on US 44. Phone 401/568-2085 or 401/568-2013.

George Washington State Campground. Swimming beach, fishing, boating; hiking trail, picnicking, camping (no fires). Standard fees. (Mid-Apr-mid-Oct) 3 mi SE on RI 100, 4 mi W on US 44. Phone 401/568-2013. ¢

Jamestown

See also Newport

Settled ca 1670 **Pop** 4,999 **Elev** 8 ft **Area code** 401 **Zip** 02835 **Web** www.gonewport.com

Information Newport County Convention & Visitors Bureau, Newport Gateway Center, 23 America's Cup Ave, Newport 02840; 401/849-8048 or 800/976-5122

Jamestown is centered around the Jamestown Ferry landing, but technically the town also includes all of Conanicut—one of three main islands in Narragansett Bay. The island is connected by bridges to Newport on the east (toll) and to the mainland on the west (free). While much of Jamestown was burned by the British in 1775, some old houses do remain.

The restored Conanicut Battery, a Revolutionary redoubt two miles south on Beavertail Road, is open to the public and is the second-highest point on the island.

What to See and Do

Fishing. Striped bass, tuna, flounder, bluefish. For boat charter inquire at East Ferry slip.

Jamestown Museum. Photos and displays pertain to town and old Jamestown ferries. (Late June-Labor Day, Tues-Sat afternoons) 92 Narragansett Ave. Phone 401/423-3771 or 401/423-0784. **Donation** The Jamestown Historical Society also maintains the

  Old Windmill. (1787) Restored to working order. (Mid-June-mid-Sep, Sat and Sun afternoons) 1½ mi N on North Rd. Phone 401/423-1798. **Donation**

Sydney L. Wright Museum. Exhibits of Native American and early Colonial artifacts from Conanicut Island. (Mon-Sat) 26 North Rd, located in the library. Phone 401/423-7280. **FREE**

Watson Farm. (1796) This 280-acre farm on Conanicut Island is being worked as a typical New England farm. Self-guided tour of farm and pastures with focus on land-use history. (June-mid-Oct, Tues, Thurs, and Sun afternoons) North Rd, S of RI 138. Phone 401/423-0005. ¢¢

B&B/Small Inn

★★ **THE BAY VOYAGE.** *150 Conanicus Ave (02835). 401/423-2100; fax 401/423-3209; res 800/225-3522.* 32 kit. suites, 3 story. May-Sept S, D $165-$235; wkly rates; lower rates rest of yr. Crib $15. TV; cable (premium). Pool; whirlpool. Complimentary coffee. Dining rm 6-10 pm; closed Sun, Mon off-season. Ck-out 11 am, ck-in 4 pm. Sauna. Balconies. On Narragansett Bay. Cr cds: A, DS, MC, V.

Kingston

(F-5) *See also Narragansett, Newport, North Kingstown*

Pop 6,504 **Elev** 242 ft **Area code** 401
Zip 02881
Web www.southcountyri.com
Information Chamber of Commerce, 328 Main St, PO Box 289, Wakefield 02880; 401/783-2801; or the South County Tourism Council, Stedman Government Center, 4808 Tower Hill Rd, Wakefield 02879; 401/789-4422 or 800/548-4662

Known as Little Rest until 1825, Kingston was once forest land bought from the Narragansett. Early settlers were farmers who built a water-powered mill in an area still known as Biscuit City. Here, the state constitution was ratified, and a law was passed abolishing slavery in the state. Kingston overlooks a fertile flood plain, which geologists believe was an ancient river. Kingston is also the home of the University of Rhode Island.

What to See and Do

Helme House. (1802) Gallery of the South County Art Association. (Wed-Sun) Kingstown Rd. Phone 401/783-2195. **FREE**

Kingston Library. (1776) Visited by George Washington and Benjamin Franklin, this building housed the Rhode Island General Assembly at the time the British occupied Newport. (Mon-Sat) Kingstown Rd. Phone 401/783-8254.

Museum of Primitive Art and Culture. In 1856 post office building; prehistoric artifacts from New England, North America, South Seas, Africa, Europe, and Asia. (Tues, Wed, and Thurs, limited hrs; also by appt) 2 mi S via RI 108 in Peace Dale at 1058 Kingstown Rd. Phone 401/783-5711. **Donation**

***Night Heron* Nature Cruises.** Offers snorkeling, nature, sunrise, sunset, and undersea nightlife cruises. Each cruise offers 2 or more departures daily. Phone 401/783-9977 or 888/644-8476. ¢¢¢-¢¢¢¢¢

Annual Event

Hot-Air Balloon Festival. Univ of Rhode Island. Two-day event features hot-air balloon rides, parachute demonstrations, arts and crafts, music. Phone 401/783-1770. Late July or early Aug.

Motel/Motor Lodge

★★ **HOLIDAY INN.** *3009 Tower Hill Rd (02874), at jct US 1, RI 138W. 401/789-1051; fax 401/789-0080.* 105 rms, 4 story. May-Oct: S, D $75-$150; each addl $10; under 18 free; lower rates rest of yr. Crib free. TV; cable (premium). Pool; lifeguard. Bar 4 pm-1 am. Ck-out 11 am. Meeting rms. Business servs avail. In-rm modem link. Cr cds: A, C, D, DS, MC, V.

B&B/Small Inn

★★ **LARCHWOOD INN.** *521 Main St (02879). 401/783-5454; fax 401/783-1800; toll-free 800/275-5450. Email larchwoodinn@xpos.com.* 18 rms, 12 with bath, 3 story. Some A/C. Some rm phones. S, D $35-$130; each addl $10. Crib $10. Pet accepted; $5. TV in sitting rm. Restaurant (see LARCHWOOD INN). Bar 11-1 am; entertainment. Ck-out, ck-in noon. Meeting rms. Business servs avail. Private patio. Built 1831. Cr cds: A, C, D, DS, MC, V.

Restaurant

★★ **LARCHWOOD INN.** *521 Main St. 401/783-5454.* Specializes in prime rib, seafood. Hrs: 7:30 am-9 pm; Fri, Sat to 10 pm; early-bird dinner Mon-Fri 5:30-6:30 pm. Res accepted. Bar. Bkfst a la carte entrees: $1.50-$7. Complete meals: $2.95-$6.95; lunch a la carte entrees: $4-$9. Complete meals: $3.95-$6.75; dinner a la carte entrees: $8.95-$13.95. Complete meals: $4.50-$13.95. Country inn. Scottish decor. Family-owned. Cr cds: A, D, DS, MC, V.

D

Little Compton

See also Portsmouth

Pop 3,339 **Area code** 401 **Zip** 02837
Web www.gonewport.com
Information Town Hall, PO Box 523; 401/635-4400; or the Newport County Convention and Visitors Bureau, 23 America's Cup Ave, Newport 02840; 401/849-8048 or 800/976-5122

In Little Compton's old burial ground lie the remains of the first white woman born in New England, Elizabeth Alden Pabodie, the daughter of John and Priscilla Alden.

What to See and Do

Gray's Store (1788). First post office in area (1804) features antique soda fountain, wheeled cheese, candy and tobacco cases. (Daily; closed Sun and hols in winter) 4 Main St in Adamsville, 7 mi NE on local road. Phone 401/635-4566.

Sakonnet Point. Swimming beaches, fishing. Harbor with lighthouse. West Main Rd.

Sakonnet Vineyards. Tour of winery and vineyard. Wine tasting (daily). 162 W Main. Phone 401/635-8486. **FREE**

Wilbor House. (1680) Seventeenth-century house with 18th- and 19th-century additions was restored in 1956 by local historical society; period furnishings, antique farm and household implements. Display of carriages and sleighs in 1860 barn.

Also one-rm schoolhouse, artist's studio. (Mid-June-mid-Sep, Wed-Sun, also by appt) 1 mi S on RI 77 at West Rd. Phone 401/635-4035. ¢¢

Narragansett

See also Block Island, Kingston, Newport

Settled 1675 **Pop** 14,985 **Elev** 20 ft
Area code 401 **Zip** 02882
Web www.southcountyri.com
Information South County Tourism Council, Stedman Government Center, 4808 Tower Hill Rd, Wakefield 02879; 401/789-4422 or 800/548-4662

Part of the township of South Kingstown until 1901, Narragansett was named after the indigenous people who sold their land to the first area settlers. Once a center for shipbuilding, the town's center is still referred to as Narragansett Pier. Between 1878-1920 Narragansett was a well-known, elegant summer resort with many fine "cottages" and hotels. The most prominent landmark of that time was the Narragansett Casino. The casino's main entrance and covered promenade, "the Towers" on Ocean Road, is the only surviving element of that complex; the rest was lost in a devastating fire in 1900. Today Narragansett's most important industries are commercial fishing and tourism. It is also the home of the University of Rhode Island's renowned Graduate School of Oceanography, located at the Bay Campus on South Ferry Road.

What to See and Do

Block Island Ferry. Automobile ferries to Block Island from Point Judith and New London, CT. (Summer, daily) 5 mi S on Ocean Rd, 1 mi W on Sand Hill Cove Rd. Phone 401/783-4613.

Fishing. Wide variety of liveries at Narragansett Pier and the waterfront villages of Jerusalem, opposite side of the Point Judith Pond entrance. Fishing tournaments are held throughout summer.

Point Judith. Fine sea view. 6 mi S of center on Ocean Ave, to Coast Guard Station and Lighthouse.

South County Museum. Antiques representing rural life in 19th-century Rhode Island; costumes, vehicles, and nautical equipment. Farm and blacksmithing displays; toys. Country kitchen, general store, cobbler's shop. Also complete turn-of-the-century letterpress print shop. (May-Oct, Wed-Sun) Located on Canonchet Farm, Boston Neck Rd (RI 1A). Phone 401/783-5400. ¢¢

Swimming. Public beaches at **Narragansett Pier**, pavilion, fees; **Scarborough State Beach**, 1½ mi S on Ocean Ave; **Salty Brine Beach**, Ocean Ave, protected by seawall, fishing; **Roger Wheeler State Beach**, W of Point Judith, playground, picnic tables, concession; parking (fee). Similar facilities at other beaches.

◪ **The Towers.** This Romanesque entrance arch flanked by rounded, conical-topped towers is a grandiose and sad reminder of McKim, Mead, and White's 19th-century casino, destroyed by fire in 1900, and Narragansett's own past as summer mecca for the rich and fashionable. Today the Tourist & Information Center is located here. ¼ mi S on US 1.

Annual Event

Mid-winter New England Surfing Championship. Narragansett Town Beach. For information contact the Eastern Surfing Association, 126 Sayles Ave, Pawtucket, 02860; 401/789-1954. Third Sat Feb.

Motel/Motor Lodge

★★ **VILLAGE INN.** *1 Beach St (02882). 401/783-6767; fax 401/782-2220.* 58 rms, 3 story. Mid-June-Labor Day: S $100-$120; D $115-$168; each addl $10; under 12 free; higher rates some hols; lower rates rest of yr. TV; cable, VCR. Indoor pool; whirlpool, lifeguard. Restaurant 6 am-10 pm; Sat to 11 pm. Bar noon-1 am. Ck-out 11 am. Meeting rms. Business servs avail. Some balconies. Opp ocean; beach. Cr cds: A, DS, MC, V.

D ⇌ ⚒ 🛏 ⊠ 🕭

Restaurant

★★ **COAST GUARD HOUSE.** *40 Ocean Rd (02882). 401/789-0700.* Specializes in seafood, prime rib, swordfish. Hrs: 11:30 am-3 pm, 5-10 pm; Fri, Sat to 11 pm; Sun brunch 10 am-2 pm. Closed Dec 24, 25. Bar. Lunch $6-$10; dinner $13-$20. Sun brunch $13.95. Child's menu. Former Coast Guard station (1888); ocean view. Cr cds: A, D, DS, MC, V.

D ⇌

Newport

(F-6) *See also Jamestown, Portsmouth*

Founded 1639 **Pop** 28,227 **Elev** 96 ft
Area code 401 **Zip** 02840
Web www.gonewport.com

Information Newport County Convention & Visitors Bureau, 23 America's Cup Ave; 401/849-8048 or 800/976-5122

Few cities in the country have a history as rich and colorful as that of Newport, and fewer still retain as much evidence of their great past. The town was founded by a group of men and women who fled the religious intolerance of Massachusetts. They established the first school in Rhode Island the following year. Shipbuilding, for which Newport is still famous, began in 1646. The first Quakers to come to the New World settled in Newport in 1657. They were followed in 1658 by 15 Jewish families who came here from Holland. Newport produced the state's first newspaper, the *Rhode Island Gazette*.

Newport took an active part in the Revolution; local residents set fire to one British ship and continued to fire on others until the British landed 9,000 men and took possession. The city was occupied for two years; it was not until the French fleet entered the harbor that the British withdrew their forces.

Newport's fame as a summer resort began after the Civil War when many wealthy families, including the August Belmonts, Ward McAllister, Harry Lehr, Mrs.

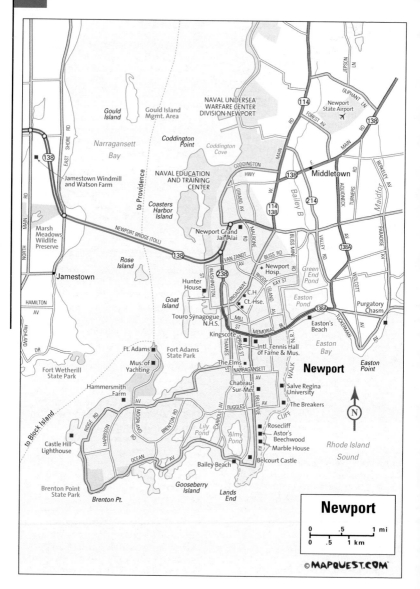

William Astor, and Mrs. Stuyvesant Fish, made the town a center for lavish and sometimes outrageous social events. Parties for dogs and one for a monkey were among the more bizarre occasions. Hostesses spent as much as $300,000 a season entertaining their guests. Although less flamboyant than it was before World War I, the summer colony is still socially prominent.

Today Newport is famous for its boating and yachting, with boats for hire at many wharves. A bridge (toll) connects the city with Jamestown to the west.

What to See and Do

Artillery Company of Newport Military Museum. Military dress of many nations and periods. (June-Sep, Wed-Sat, also Sun afternoons; rest of yr, by appt) 23 Clarke St. Phone 401/846-8488. ¢¢

Brick Market. Home of the Newport Historical Society. Built by Peter Harrison, architect of Touro Synagogue, in 1762 as a market and granary. The

The Breakers, Newport

restored building and surrounding area house boutiques and restaurants. (Daily) Long Wharf & Thames St. Phone 401/846-0813.

CCInc Auto Tape Tours. This 90-min cassette offers a mile-by-mile self-guided tour of Newport. Avail at Paper Lion, Long Wharf Mall, and Gateway Visitor Information Center (next to Marriott Hotel). Incl tape and recorder rental. Tape also may be purchased directly from CCInc, PO Box 227, 2 Elbrook Dr, Allendale, NJ 07401. Phone 201/236-1666. ¢¢¢¢

✪ Cliff Walk. Scenic walk overlooking Atlantic Ocean adjoins many Newport "cottages." Designated a National Recreational Trail in 1975. Begins at Memorial Blvd. **FREE**

Fort Adams State Park. Park surrounds Fort Adams, the second-largest bastioned fort in the US from 1799-1945. The rambling 21-acre fort, constructed of stone over a 33-yr period, is closed due to unsafe conditions; park remains open. Beach swimming, fishing, boating (launch, ramps, hoist); soccer and rugby fields, picnicking. Standard fees. (Memorial Day-Labor Day, daily) Harrison Ave & Ocean Dr. Phone 401/847-2400. Per vehicle ¢¢

Friends Meeting House. (1699) Site of New England Yearly Meeting of the Society of Friends until 1905; meeting house, expanded in 1729-1807, spans 3 centuries of architecture and construction. Guided tours through Newport Historical Society. (By appt) Farewell & Marlborough Sts. Phone 401/846-0813. **FREE**

✪ Historic Mansions and Houses. Combination tickets to the Elms, the Breakers, Rosecliff, Marble House, Hunter House, Chateau-sur-Mer, Kingscote, and Green Animals topiary gardens (see PORTSMOUTH) are avail at any of these houses. (See ADDITIONAL VISITOR INFORMATION)

Astors' Beechwood. Italianate summer residence of Mrs. Caroline Astor, *the* Mrs. Astor. Theatrical tour of house incl actors portraying Mrs. Astor's servants and society guests. (Mid-May-mid-Dec, daily; rest of yr, wkends only) Phone 401/846-3772. ¢¢

Belcourt Castle. (1891) Designed by Richard Morris Hunt in French château style, 62-rm house was residence of Oliver Hazard Perry Belmont and his wife, Alva Vanderbilt Belmont, who built Marble House when married to William K. Vanderbilt. Belcourt is unique for inclusion of stables within main structure; Belmont loved horses. Contains largest collection of antiques and *objets d'art* ¢¢

The Breakers. (1895) Seventy-rm, Northern Italian palazzo designed by Richard Morris Hunt is the largest of all Newport cottages and is impressive by its sheer size; contains original furnishings. Children's playhouse cottage has scale-size kitchen, fireplace, playroom. Built for Mr. and Mrs. Cornelius Vanderbilt. (Apr-Oct, daily) Ochre Point Ave. Phone 401/847-1000. ¢¢ Also here is **The Breakers Stable and Carriage House.** Houses several carriages, incl Vanderbilts' famous coach *Venture.* (July-Labor Day, wkends and hols) ¢¢

Chateau-sur-Mer. (1852) Victorian mansion remodeled in 1872 by Richard Morris Hunt has landscaped grounds with Chinese moon gate. Built for William S. Wetmore, who made his fortune in the China trade. (May-Oct, daily;

rest of yr, wkends) Bellevue Ave. Phone 401/847-1000. ¢¢¢

Edward King House. (1846) Villa by Richard Upjohn is considered one of the finest Italianate houses in the country. Used as senior citizens' center. Tours. (Mon-Fri) 35 King St, Aquidneck Park. Phone 401/846-7426.

The Elms. (1901) Modeled after 18th-century Chateau d'Asnieres near Paris, this restored "cottage" from Newport's gilded age boasts elaborate interiors and formal, sunken gardens that are among the city's most beautiful. Built for Edward J. Berwind, Philadelphia coal magnate. (May-Oct, daily; Nov-Mar, Sat and Sun) Bellevue Ave. Phone 401/847-1000. ¢¢

Hammersmith Farm. The unofficial summer White House during Kennedy Administration, farm dates back to 1640; 28-rm, shingle-style summer house was added in 1887 by John Auchincloss; descendant Hugh D. Auchincloss married Janet Lee Bouvier, mother of Jacqueline Bouvier Kennedy; rambling cottage was site of wedding reception of John and Jacqueline Kennedy. Gardens designed by Frederick Law Olmsted. Gift shop in children's playhouse. Guided tours. (May-Oct, daily) Ocean Dr. Phone 401/846-0420 or 401/846-7346. ¢¢¢

Hunter House. (1748) Outstanding example of Colonial architecture features gambrel roof, 12-on-12 panel windows, broken pediment doorway. Furnished with pieces by Townsend and Goddard, famous 18th-century cabinet makers. (May-Oct, daily; Apr, wkends) 54 Washington St. Phone 401/847-6543. ¢¢¢

Kingscote. (1839) Gothic Revival cottage designed by Richard Upjohn; in 1881 McKim, Mead, and White added the "aesthetic" dining rm, which features Tiffany-glass wall and fixtures. Outstanding Chinese export paintings and porcelains. Built for George Noble Jones of Savannah, GA, Kingscote is considered the nation's first true summer "cottage." (May-Sep, daily; Apr and Oct, wkends) Bellevue Ave. Phone 401/847-1000. ¢¢¢

Marble House. (1892) French-style palace designed by Richard Morris Hunt is the most sumptuous of Newport cottages. Front gates, entrance, central hall are modeled after Versailles. House is named for the many kinds of marble used on interior, which also features lavish use of gold and bronze. Original furnishings incl dining rm chairs made of gilded bronze. Built for Mrs. William K. Vanderbilt. On display are yachting memorabilia and restored Chinese teahouse where Mrs. Vanderbilt held suffragette meetings. (Apr-Oct, daily; rest of yr, wkends) Bellevue Ave. Phone 401/847-1000. ¢¢¢

Rosecliff. (1902) Designed by Stanford White after the Grand Trianon at Versailles, Rosecliff boasts largest private ballrm in Newport and famous heart-shaped staircase. Built for socialite Mrs Hermann Oelrichs. (Apr-Oct, daily) Bellevue Ave. Phone 401/847-6543. ¢¢¢

Samuel Whitehorne House. (1811) Features exquisite furniture, silver, and pewter made by 18th-century artisans; Chinese porcelain, Irish crystal, and Pilgrim-era furniture; garden. (May-Oct, Fri-Mon and hols; or by appt, 24-hr advance notice necessary) 416 Thames St. Phone 401/849-7300. ¢¢

Wanton-Lyman-Hazard House. (ca 1675) Oldest house in Newport, one of the finest Jacobean houses in New England, was site of 1765 Stamp Act riot; restored; 18th-century garden; guided tours. (Mid-June-late Aug, Tues-Sat; closed hols) 17 Broadway. Phone 401/846-0813. ¢

Whitehall Museum House. (1729) Restored, hip-roofed country house built by Bishop George Berkeley, British philosopher and educator; garden. (July-Aug, daily; June, by appt only) 3 mi NE on Berkeley Ave in Middletown. Phone 401/846-3116. ¢¢

✪ **International Tennis Hall of Fame & Museum.** World's largest tennis museum features interactive and dynamic exhibits detailing the history of the sport. Tennis equipt, fashions, trophies, and memorabilia on display in the famous Newport Casino, built in 1880 and designed by McKim, Mead, and White. (Daily; closed Thanksgiving, Dec 25) Grass courts avail (May-Oct). 194 Bellevue Ave. Phone 401/849-3990. ¢¢¢

Newport Art Museum and Art Association. Changing exhibitions of contemporary and historical art are housed in 1864 mansion designed by Richard Morris Hunt in the "stick style" and in 1920 Beaux Arts building. Lectures, performing arts events, evening musical picnics; tours. (Tues-Sat afternoons; closed hols) 76 Bellevue Ave, opp Touro Park. Phone 401/848-8200. ¢¢

Newport Historical Society Museum. Colonial art; Newport silver and pewter, china, early American glass, furniture. (Tues-Sat; closed hols) Walking tours of Colonial Newport (Mid-June-Sep, Fri and Sat; fee). 82 Touro St, adj to Seventh Day Baptist Meeting House. Phone 401/846-0813. **FREE**

Newport Jai Alai. Pari-mutuel betting. (Daily) Fronton & Civic Center, 150 Admiral Kalbfus Rd, at base of Newport Bridge. Phone 401/849-5000.

Old Colony and Newport Railroad. Vintage 1-hr train ride along scenic route to Narragansett Bay. (July-early Sep, Sat and Sun; May-June and mid-Sep-Nov, Sun; also Christmas season) Terminal, America's Cup Ave. Phone 401/624-6951 or 401/683-4549. ¢¢¢

Old Stone Mill. Origin of circular stone tower supported by arches is unknown. Although excavations (1948-49) have disproved it, some people still believe structure was built by Norsemen. Touro Park, Mill St off Bellevue Ave. **FREE**

Redwood Library and Athenaeum. Designed by master Colonial architect Peter Harrison; thought to be oldest library building (1750) in continuous use in US; used by English officers as a club during Revolution. Collections incl part of original selection of books and early portraits. (Mon-Sat; closed hols) 50 Bellevue Ave. Phone 401/847-0292. **FREE**

Seventh Day Baptist Meeting House. (1729) Historical church built by master builder Richard Munday. 82 Touro St, adj to Newport Historical Society. Phone 401/846-0813.

Swimming.

Easton's Beach. Well-developed public beach has bathhouse, snack bar, antique carousel, picnic area, designated surfing area. (Mid-June-Labor Day, daily; early June, wkends). Memorial Blvd, RI 138. Parking ¢¢¢

King Park and Beach. Restrms, picnic area. (Mid-June-Labor Day, daily) Wellington Ave. Phone 401/846-1398.

Touro Synagogue National Historic Site. Oldest synagogue (1763) in US, a Georgian masterpiece by country's first architect, Peter Harrison, contains oldest torah in North America, examples of 18th-century crafts, letter from George Washington; worship services follow Sephardic Orthodox ritual of founders. 72 Touro St. Phone 401/847-4794.

Tours.

Newport Navigation. One-hr narrated cruise of Narragansett Bay and Newport Harbor aboard the *Spirit of Newport*. (May-Oct, daily) Newport Harbor Hotel & Marina. Phone 401/849-3575. ¢¢

Oldport Marine Harbor Tours. One-hr cruise of Newport Harbor aboard the *Amazing Grace*. (May-mid-Oct, daily) America's Cup Ave. Phone 401/847-9109. ¢¢

Viking Boat Tour. One-hr narrated trip incl historic Newport, yachts, waterfront mansions; also avail is extended trip with tour of Hammersmith Farm (see). (May-Oct) *The Viking Queen* leaves Goat Island Marina off Washington St. Phone 401/847-6921. ¢¢- ¢¢¢

Viking Bus Tour. Two-, three-, and four-hr narrated trips cover 150 points of interest, incl mansions and restored areas. (Schedules vary) Three-hr trips incl admission to one mansion; four-hr trip incl admission to two mansions. Leaves from Gateway Tourist Center, America's Cup Ave. Phone 401/847-6921. ¢¢¢

Trinity Church. (1726) First Anglican parish in state (1698), Trinity has been in continuous use since it was built. George Washington and philosopher George Berkeley were communicants. Interior features Tiffany windows and an organ tested by Handel before being shipped from London. Tours. Queen Anne Sq. Phone 401/846-0660. **FREE**

White Horse Tavern. (1673) Oldest operating tavern in the nation. (Daily) 42 Marlborough St. Phone 401/849-3600.

Annual Events

Newport Irish Heritage Month. Throughout the town. A variety of Irish heritage and theme events; films, concerts, plays, arts and crafts, exhibits; food and drink; parade, road race. Phone 401/845-9123. Mar.

Newport Music Festival. Chamber music held in Newport's fabled mansions. Phone 401/847-7090. Three concerts daily, Mid-July.

JVC Jazz Festival. Fort Adams. Phone 401/847-3700. Mid-Aug.

Christmas in Newport. A month-long series of activities incl concerts, tree lighting, and craft fairs. Phone 401/849-6454. Dec.

Additional Visitor Information

The Preservation Society of Newport County publishes material on all Society properties. It sells combination tickets at all buildings under its administration and provides sightseeing information. Phone 401/847-1000.

The Newport County Convention and Visitor's Bureau maintains an information center at 23 America's Cup Ave (daily). Tickets to most tourist attractions are offered for sale. An eight-minute video, maps, general tourist information and group tours and convention information are available. For further information phone 401/849-8048 or 800/976-5122.

Motels/Motor Lodges

★ ★ ★ **HYATT REGENCY NEWPORT.** *1 Goat Island (02840), by causeway from Washington St. 401/849-2600; fax 401/846-7210; toll-free 800/222-8733.* 253 rms, 9 story. Late May-early Sep: S, D $159-$254; each addl $15; suites $275-$550; under 17 free; lower rates rest of yr. Crib free. TV. 2 pools, 1 indoor; poolside serv. Restaurant 6:30 am-10 pm. Bar 10-1 am; entertainment. Ck-out noon. Convention facilities. Business center. In-rm modem link. Airport transportation. Bellhops. Valet serv. Sundries. Gift shop. Beauty shop. Tennis. Exercise equipt; sauna. Some bathrm phones. Some private patios, balconies. Heliport for guests. Marina adj. Cr cds: A, C, D, DS, MC, V.

🅳 � 🛏 🛉 🎿 🔥 🚶

★ ★ **INN ON LONG WHARF.** *142 Long Wharf (02840). 401/847-7800; fax 401/845-0127; toll-free 800/225-3522.* 40 kit. suites, 5 story. May-Sep: S, D $180-$225; higher rates Jazz Festival; lower rates rest of yr. Crib $15. TV; cable (premium). Restaurant 5-11 pm. Bar 4 pm-1 am. Ck-out 11 am. Valet serv. Concierge. Gift shop. Some covered, valet parking. In-rm whirlpools, wet bars. Overlooks harbor. Cr cds: A, DS, MC, V.

🅳 🛏 🛉 🎿 🔥 🚶

★ ★ **INN ON THE HARBOR.** *359 Thames St (02840). 401/849-6789; fax 401/849-2680; res 800/225-3522.* 58 kit. suites, 6 story. May-Sep: S, D $140-$250; wkly rates; higher rates: Jazz Festival, hols; lower rates rest of yr. Crib $15. TV; cable (premium). Restaurant, hrs vary. Bar; entertainment Fri-Sun. Ck-out 11 am. Valet serv. Concierge. Gift shop. Some covered parking; valet. Exercise equipt; sauna. Whirlpool. Overlooks harbor. Cr cds: A, C, D, DS, ER, JCB, MC, V.

🅳 🛉 🎿 🔥 🏀

★ ★ **ROYAL PLAZA HOTEL.** *425 E Main Rd (02842), 2 mi N on RI 138. 401/846-3555; fax 401/846-3666; toll-free 800/825-7072.* 75 rms, 2 story, 13 suites. May-Sep: S, D, suites $119-$189; under 14 free; lower rates rest of yr. Crib avail. TV; cable (premium), VCR avail. Complimentary continental bkfst. Ck-out 11 am. Meeting rm. Airport transportation. Cr cds: A, D, DS, MC, V.

🅳 🎿 🔥 SC

★ ★ **WEST MAIN LODGE.** *1359 W Main Rd (02842), approx 3½ mi N on RI 114. 401/849-2718; fax 401/849-2798; toll-free 877/849-2718.* 55 rms, 2 story. Mar-Dec: S, D $39-$139; each addl $15; under 12 free; higher rates hols; lower rates rest of yr. TV; cable. Restaurant nearby. Ck-out 11 am. Refrigerators avail. Some balconies. Cr cds: A, DS, MC, V.

Hotels

★ ★ **BEST WESTERN MAINSTAY INN.** *151 Admiral Kalbfus Rd (02840). 401/849-9880; fax 401/849-4391; toll-free 877/545-5550. Email* themainstayinn@aol.com. 165 rms, 2 story. July-Aug: S, D $95-$169; each addl $7.50; suites $125-$295; under 12 free; lower rates rest of yr. Crib avail. TV; cable. Pool; poolside serv. Restaurant 6:30 am-10 pm. Bar 11:30-1 am. Ck-out 11 am. Meeting rms. Business servs avail. Some refrigerators. Balconies. Cr cds: A, C, D, DS, MC, V.

★★ COURTYARD BY MARRIOTT.
9 Commerce Dr (02842), 3 mi N on RI 114. 401/849-8000; fax 401/849-8313; toll-free 888/686-5067. 138 rms, 3 story, 10 suites. May-Oct: S, D $219; suites $289; lower rates rest of yr. Crib avail. Parking lot. Indoor/outdoor pools, lap pool, whirlpool. TV; cable; VCR avail. Complimentary full bkfst, coffee in rms, newspaper, toll-free calls. Restaurant 6:30 am-10 pm. Ck-out noon, ck-in 4 pm. Meeting rms. Business servs avail. Dry cleaning, coin lndry. Exercise equipt. Golf. Tennis, 7 courts. Cr cds: A, C, D, DS, MC, V.

★★ THE HOTEL VIKING. One Bellevue Ave (02840). 401/847-3300; fax 401/849-0749; toll-free 800/556-7126. Email www.sales@hotelviking.com; www.hotelviking.com. 224 rms, 5 story, 13 suites. Apr-Sep: S, D $389; suites $1599; each addl $15; under 18 free; lower rates rest of yr. Crib avail. Parking garage. Indoor pool, whirlpool. TV; cable. Complimentary newspaper. Restaurant 7 am-11 pm. Bar. Ck-out 11 am, ck-in 3 pm. Meeting rms. Business servs avail. Bellhops. Concierge. Dry cleaning. Exercise equipt, sauna. Cr cds: A, D, DS, MC, V.

★ HOWARD JOHNSON INN NEWPORT. 351 W Main Rd (02844), on RI 138 at jct RI 114. 401/849-2000; fax 401/849-6047; res 800/446-4656. Email 467@hotel.cendant.com; www.hojo.com. 155 rms, 2 story. Late May-mid-Oct: S $59-$144; D $69-$159; each addl $5; suites $138-$318; studio rms $84-$164; under 18 free; some wknd rates; lower rates rest of yr. Crib free. Pet accepted. TV; cable (premium) VCR avail. Heated pool; whirlpool, lifeguard. Restaurant. Bar 5 pm-1 am. Ck-out 11 am. Meeting

rms. Business servs avail. Valet serv. Sundries. Tennis. Sauna. Some refrigerators. Private patios, balconies. Cr cds: A, DS, MC, V.

★★★ NEWPORT HARBOR HOTEL & MARINA. 49 America's Cup Ave (02840), on RI 138 at the Harbor. 401/847-9000; fax 401/849-6380; toll-free 800/955-2558. Email groupsales@newporthotel.com or individualsales@newporthotel.com; www.newporthotel.com. 133 rms, 4 story. May-Oct: S, D $129-$259; each addl $15; suites $219-$679; under 17 free; lower rates rest of yr. Crib free. TV; cable, VCR avail. Indoor pool. Sauna. Coffee in rms. Ck-out 11 am. Meeting rms. Business servs avail. Cr cds: A, DS, MC, V.

★★★ NEWPORT MARRIOTT HOTEL. 25 America's Cup Ave (02840). 401/849-1000; fax 401/849-3422; res 800/288-2662; toll-free 800/458-3066. www.marriotthotels.com/pvdlw. 310 rms, 7 story, 7 suites. May-Oct: S, D $285; suites $500; under 18 free; lower rates rest of yr. Crib avail. Valet parking avail. Indoor pool, whirlpool. TV; cable (premium), VCR avail. Complimentary coffee in rms, newspaper. Restaurant 6:30 am-11 pm. Bar. Ck-out 11 am, ck-in 4 pm. Conference center, meeting rms. Business center. Bellhops. Concierge. Dry cleaning, coin lndry. Gift shop. Exercise rm, sauna. Golf. Tennis. Cr cds: A, C, D, DS, ER, JCB, MC, V.

★★ NEWPORT RAMADA INN & CONFERENCE CENTER. 936 W Main Rd (02842), 3 mi N on RI 114. 401/846-7600; fax 401/849-6919; toll-free 800/836-8322. Email ramadanpt@aol.com. 133 rms, 2 story, 15 suites. May-Oct: S, D $89; suites $109; each addl $10; under 18 free; lower rates rest of yr. Crib avail. Pet accepted, some restrictions, fee. Parking lot. Indoor pool, lap pool. TV; cable (DSS), VCR avail. Complimentary coffee in rms. Restaurant 6-10 pm. Bar. Ck-out noon, ck-in 2 pm. Meeting rms. Business servs avail. Dry cleaning, coin lndry. Exercise equipt.

Golf. Downhill skiing. Picnic facilities. Cr cds: A, C, D, DS, ER, JCB, MC.

B&Bs/Small Inns

★ **BRINELY VICTORIAN INN.** *23 Brinley St (02840). 401/849-7645; fax 401/845-9634; toll-free 800/999-8523. Email sweetmans@brinleyvitorian.com.* 17 rms, 4 with shower only, 3 story. No rm phones. May-Oct: S, D $115-$199; each addl $15; lower rates rest of yr. Children over 8 yrs only. Complimentary continental bkfst. Restaurant nearby. Ck-out 11 am, ck-in 2 pm. Courtyard with tables. Victorian inn built 1860. Library; antiques; several fireplaces. Rms individually decorated. Cr cds: A, MC, V.

★★★ **FRANCIS MALBONE HOUSE.** *392 Thames St (02840). 401/846-0392; fax 401/848-5956; toll-free 800/846-0392. Email innkeeper@malbone.com; www.malbone.com.* 16 rms, 3 story, 4 suites. Apr-Oct: S, D $295; suites $425; each addl $30; children $30; under 12 free; lower rates rest of yr. Parking lot. TV; cable, VCR avail, CD avail. Complimentary full bkfst, newspaper. Restaurant. Ck-out 11 am, ck-in 2 pm. Meeting rms. Business center. Concierge. Dry cleaning. Gift shop. Exercise privileges. Golf. Tennis. Picnic facilities. Cr cds: A, MC, V.

★★ **THE GREENHOUSE INN.** *30 Wave Ave (02842). 401/846-0310; fax 401/847-2621; toll-free 800/786-0310.* 50 rms, 3 story. S, D $59-$229; each addl $20; suites $99-$250; under 12 free; wknd rates (2-day min June-Oct). TV; cable (premium). Complimentary continental bkfst. Dining rm 11:30 am-9 pm. Ck-out 11 am, ck-in 3 pm. Business servs avail. Refrigerators. On beach. Cr cds: A, C, D, DS, MC, V.

★★ **HAMMETT HOUSE INN.** *505 Thames St (02840). 401/846-0400; fax 401/274-2690; res 800/548-9417.* 5 rms, 3 story. May-Oct: S, D $99-$165; each addl $15; under 5 free; higher rates Jazz, Folk Festivals; lower rates rest of yr. TV; cable (premium). Complimentary continental bkfst. Dining rm 6-10 pm. Ck-out 11 am, ck-in 2

pm. Georgian-style inn (1785) furnished with antique reproductions. Totally nonsmoking. Cr cds: A, DS, MC, V.

★★★ **THE INN AT CASTLE HILL.** *590 Ocean Ave (02840), 4 mi S. 401/849-3800; fax 401/849-3838; toll-free 888/466-1355. Email info@casltehill inn.com.* 21 rms, 10 rms in 3 story inn, 11 rms adj, some share bath. S, D $95-$325; each addl $25. Children over 12 yrs only. Complimentary continental bkfst. Dining rm noon-3 pm, 6-9 pm. Ck-out 11 am, ck-in 3 pm. Victorian house (1874) was summer residence of naturalist Alexander Agassiz; antique furnishings. On ocean; swimming beach. Cr cds: A, DS, MC, V.

★★★ **IVY LODGE.** *12 Clay St (02840). 401/849-6865; fax 401/849-2919; res 401/849-6865; toll-free 800/834-6865. Email innkeepers@ivylodge.com; www.ivylodge.com.* 8 rms, 3 story, 1 suite. May-Oct: S, D $205; suites $325; each addl $60; children $50; under 12 free; lower rates rest of yr. Crib avail. Parking lot. TV; cable (premium). Complimentary full bkfst. Restaurant nearby. Ck-out 11 am, ck-in 3 pm. Golf. Tennis, 6 courts. Cr cds: A, DS, MC, V.

★★★ **MELVILLE HOUSE.** *39 Clarke St (02840). 401/847-0640; fax 401/847-0956. Email innkeeper@ids.net; www.melvillehouse.com.* 7 rms, 2 share bath, 2 story. No rm phones. Early May-early Nov: S, D $115-$145; lower rates rest of yr. Children over 12 yrs only. Complimentary full bkfst; afternoon refreshments. Restaurant nearby. Ck-out 11 am, ck-in after 2 pm. Concierge serv. Sitting rm. Colonial inn (ca 1750); antiques. Cr cds: A, DS, MC, V.

★★ **MILL STREET INN.** *75 Mill St (02840). 401/849-9500; fax 401/848-5131; toll-free 800/392-1316.* 23 suites, 3 story. June-Sep: suites $125-$253; under 16 free; wknd, wkly, hol rates; higher rates: Jazz Festival, Folk Festival; lower rates rest of yr. Crib free. TV; cable (premium). Complimentary continental bkfst; afternoon refreshments. Restaurant nearby. Ck-out 11 am, ck-in 3 pm. Concierge serv. Guest lndry. Business servs avail. Tennis privileges. Health club privileges. Minibars; some refrigerators. Some balconies. Contemporary restoration of historic mill building (1890). Cr cds: A, C, D, MC, V.

⬛ ⬛ ⬛ ⬛ ⬛

★★ **PILGRIM HOUSE.** *123 Spring St (02840). 401/846-0040; fax 401/848-0357; toll-free 800/525-8373. www. pilgrimhouseinn.com.* 11 rms, 2 share bath, 3 story. No rm phones. May-Oct: S, D $65-$155; each addl $25; higher rates Jazz Fest, hols; lower rates rest of yr. Children over 12 yrs only. TV in sitting rm. Complimentary continental bkfst; afternoon refreshments. Restaurant nearby. Ckout 11 am, ck-in after 3 pm. Concierge serv. Victorian inn (ca 1810) near harbor. Rooftop deck. Cr cds: MC, V.

⬛ ⬛

★★ **VICTORIAN LADIES INN.** *63 Memorial Blvd (02840). 401/849-9960; fax 401/849-9960. Email info@ victorianladies.com.* 11 rms, 3 story. Some rm phones. S, D $85-$185. Closed Jan. Children over 10 yrs only. TV. Complimentary full bkfst. Restaurant nearby. Ck-out 11 am, ckin 2 pm. Built 1841; antiques, library, sitting rm. Near ocean. Cr cds: A, DS, MC, V.

⬛ ⬛

★★ **THE WILLOW OF NEW-PORT ROMANTIC INN.** *8 Willow Historic Point (02840). 401/846-5486; fax 401/849-8215. www.newportri. com/users/.* 5 rms, 3 story. May-Oct: S, D $278; lower rates rest of yr. TV; cable (premium). Ck-out 11 am, ckin 3 pm. Cr cds: A, DS, MC, V.

⬛

Extended Stay

★★★ **CLIFFSIDE INN.** *2 Seaview Ave (02840). 401/847-1811; fax 401/848-5850; toll-free 800/845-1811. Email cliff@wsii.com; www.cliffsideinn. com.* 16 rms, 3 story, 7 suites. May-Oct: S, D $225; suites $315; lower rates rest of yr. TV; cable (premium), VCR avail, CD avail. Complimentary full bkfst, coffee in rms, newspaper, toll-free calls. Restaurant nearby. Ck-out 11 am, ck-in 3

pm. Meeting rm. Business servs avail. Concierge. Dry cleaning. Gift shop. Whirlpool. Golf. Beach access. Bike rentals. Hiking trail. Picnic facilities. Cr cds: A, DS, ER, JCB, MC, V.

⬛ ⬛ ⬛ ⬛ ⬛ ⬛

Restaurants

★★★ **CANFIELD HOUSE.** *5 Memorial Blvd (02840). 401/847-0416. www.canfieldhouse.com.* Specializes in chateaubriand. Hrs: 5-11 pm. Res accepted. Dinner $14-$23. Parking. Cr cds: A, C, D, DS, MC, V.

⬛ ⬛

★★ **CHRISTIE'S OF NEWPORT.** *351 Thames St (02840). 401/847-5400.* Mediterranean menu. Specializes in swordfish, fresh lobster, chateaubriand. Hrs: 11:30 am-9:30 pm. Closed Dec 25. Res accepted. Bar. Lunch $5.50-$12; dinner $13-$28. Child's menu. Parking. View of the water. Family-owned. Cr cds: A, DS, MC, V.

⬛ ⬛

★★ **LA FORGE CASINO.** *186 Bellevue Ave (02840). 401/847-0418.* Specializes in fresh native seafood dishes. Hrs: 11:30 am-10 pm; Sun from 9:30 am. Closed Thanksgiving, Dec 25. Res accepted. Bar. Lunch $5.50-$13.50; dinner $14.50-$24. Sun brunch $5.25-$11.95. Child's menu. Entertainment: pianist Fri, Sat. Sidewalk cafe. Built in 1880. Adj to International Tennis Hall of Fame and Tennis Museum. Family-owned. Cr cds: A, MC, V.

⬛ ⬛

★★★ **LA PETITE AUBERGE.** *19 Charles St (02840). 401/849-6669. www.mswebpros.com/auberge.* Specializes in seafood. Hrs: 6-10 pm; Sun 5-9 pm. Closed Jan 1, Thanksgiving, Dec 25. Res accepted. Bar. Wine list. Dinner a la carte entrees: $20-$38. House (1714) of naval hero Stephen Decatur. Colonial decor, fireplaces. Cr cds: A, MC, V.

★★★ **LE BISTRO.** *41 Bowen's Wharf (02840), off America's Cup Ave. 401/849-7778. Email bistroman@aol. com; www.lebistro.com.* Specializes in seafood, black Angus beef. Own baking. Hrs: 11 am-11 pm. Res accepted. Bar. Wine cellar. Lunch $5.50-$12.95;

dinner $9.95-$26.95. Parking. Cr cds: A, DS, MC, V.

★★ **THE MOORING.** *Sayer's Wharf (02840). 401/846-2260. www.mooring restaurant.com.* Specializes in seafood. Hrs: noon-9 pm; Fri, Sat to 10 pm. Closed Mon, Tues Nov-Mar; also Thanksgiving, Dec 25. Bar. Lunch a la carte entrees: $6-$15; dinner a la carte entrees: $8.50-$21. Child's menu. View of harbor, marina. Cr cds: A, D, DS, MC, V.

D ⏎

★★ **PIER.** *W Howard Wharf (02840), off Thames St. 401/847-3645.* Specializes in prime rib, baked stuffed lobster shipyard-style, Pier clambake. Hrs: 11:30-1 am. Closed Dec 25. Res accepted. Bar. Lunch $5.25-$11.95; dinner $9.75-$29.95. Child's menu. Entertainment: Fri, Sat. Patio dining. On Narragansett Bay, overlooking Newport Harbor. Family-owned. Cr cds: A, C, D, DS, MC, V.

D ⏎

★ **RHODE ISLAND QUAHOG COMPANY.** *250 Thames St (02840). 401/848-2330.* Seafood menu. Specializes in barbecue ribs, grilled meats, seafood. Hrs: noon-10 pm. Closed Dec 25. Res accepted. Bar. Lunch a la carte entrees: $4.75-$9.75; dinner a la carte entrees: $10.25-$19.75. Child's menu. Mexican decor in 1894 music hall. Cr cds: A, DS, MC, V.

⏎

★★★ **WHITE HORSE TAVERN.** *26 Marlborough St (02840). 401/849-3600. www.whitehorsetavern.com.* Specializes in rack of lamb, beef Wellington. Own baking. Hrs: 11:30 am-2:30 pm, 6-9:30 pm; Sun 11 am-2 pm. Closed Jan 1, Dec 25. Res accepted. Bar. Wine cellar. Lunch a la carte entrees: $8-$14; dinner a la carte entrees: $18-$32. Sun brunch $14-$19. Parking. Jacket. Oldest operating tavern in America; building (est 1673) originally constructed as a residence. Cr cds: A, C, D, DS, MC, V.

⏎

North Kingstown

See also Providence, Warwick

Settled 1641 **Pop** 23,786 **Elev** 51 ft
Area code 401 **Zip** 02852
Web www.southcountyri.com
Information South County Tourism Council, Stedman Government Center, 4808 Tower Hill Rd, Wakefield 02879; 401/789-4422 or 800/548-4662

North Kingstown was originally part of a much larger area named for King Charles II. The settlement was divided in 1722, creating North Kingstown and South Kingstown, as well as other townships.

What to See and Do

Casey Farm. (ca 1750) Once the site of American Revolution activities, this farm was built and continuously occupied by the Casey family for 200 yrs. Views of Narrangansett Bay and Conanicut Island. Restored and operating farm with animals, organic gardens; 18th-century farmhouse with family paintings, furnishings; outbuildings. (June-Oct, Tues, Thurs, and Sat afternoons) 3½ mi S on RI 1A (past Jamestown Bridge approach), on Boston Neck Rd in Saunderstown. Phone 401/295-1030. ¢¢

Gilbert Stuart Birthplace. Birthplace of portraitist Gilbert Stuart (1755-1828). Antique furnishings; snuffmill powered by wooden waterwheel; partially restored gristmill. Guided tours (½ hr). (Apr-Oct, Sat-Thurs) 5 mi S off RI 1A, 815 Gilbert Stuart Rd, NW of Saunderstown. Phone 401/294-3001. ¢¢

Main Street, Wickford Village. There are 20 houses built before 1804; on side streets are 40 more. E from center.

Old Narragansett Church. (1707) Episcopal. Tours. (Mid-June-Labor Day, Fri-Sun) St. Paul's Church. Church Lane. Phone 401/294-4357.

Smith's Castle. (1678) Blockhouse (ca 1638), destroyed by fire in 1676 and rebuilt in 1678, is one of the oldest plantation houses in the country and the only known existing house where Roger Williams preached; 17th- and 18th-century furnishings;

18th-century garden. (June-Aug, Thurs-Mon, afternoons; May and Sep, Fri-Sun, afternoons; also by appt) 1½ mi N on US 1. Phone 401/294-3521. ¢¢

Annual Events

Wickford Art Festival. In Wickford Village. Approx 250 artists and artisans from around the country. Phone 401/294-6840. Second wkend July

Festival of Lights. House tours, hayrides. First wkend Dec.

Pawtucket

(D-5) *See also Providence*

Settled 1671 **Pop** 72,644 **Elev** 73 ft
Area code 401
Information Blackstone Valley Tourism Council, 171 Main St, 02860; 401/724-2200 or 800/454-2882 (outside RI)

This highly concentrated industrial center, first settled by an ironworker who set up a forge at the falls on the Blackstone River, is recognized by historians as the birthplace of the Industrial Revolution in America. It was here in Pawtucket, named for the Native American phrase "falls of the water," that Samuel Slater founded the nation's first water-powered cotton mill. The town has since become one of the largest cities in the state and a major producer of textiles, machinery, wire, glass, and plastics.

What to See and Do

Slater Memorial Park. Within 200-acre park are sunken gardens; Rhode Island Watercolor Assn Gallery (Tues-Sun); historical Daggett House (fee); carousel (July-Aug, daily; May-June and Sep-Oct, wkends only; fee). Tennis, playing fields, picnicking. Newport Ave off US 1A. Phone 401/728-0500. **FREE**

Slater Mill National Historic Site. Nation's first water-powered cotton mill (1793) was built by Samuel Slater; on site are also Wilkinson Mill (1810) and Sylvanus Brown House (1758). Mill features restored water-power system, incl raceways and 8-

ton wheel; operating machines; spinning and weaving demonstrations; slide show. (June-Labor Day, Tues-Sun; Mar-May and Labor Day-mid-Dec, wkends; closed hols) Roosevelt Ave at Main St. Phone 401/725-8638. ¢¢

Annual Events

St. Patrick's Day Parade. First wkend Mar.

Octoberfest Parade and Craft Fair. First wkend Oct.

Seasonal Events

Pawtucket Red Sox. McCoy Stadium. AAA farm team of the Boston Red Sox. For schedule contact PO Box 2365, 02861; 401/724-7303 or 401/724-7300. Apr-Sep.

Arts in the Park Performance Series. Slater Memorial Park. Tues-Thurs and Sun, July-Aug.

Motel/Motor Lodge

★★ **COMFORT INN.** *2 George St (02860), I-95 Exit 27. 401/723-6700; fax 401/726-6380; toll-free 800/228-5150.* 135 rms, 5 story. S $68-$100; D $72-$100; under 18 free; wkend rates. Crib free. TV; cable (premium). Pool. Restaurant 6:30-12:30 am. Bar. Ck-out noon. Meeting rms. Business servs avail. Health club privileges. Sundries. Balconies. Cr cds: A, C, D, DS, MC, V.

D ⊠ ⤓ 🐾 SC

Portsmouth

See also Bristol, Newport

Founded 1638 **Pop** 16,857 **Elev** 122 ft
Area code 401 **Zip** 02871
Web www.gonewport.com
Information Newport County Convention and Visitor's Bureau, 23 America's Cup Ave, Newport 02840; 401/849-8048 or 800/976-5122

Originally called Pocasset, Portsmouth was settled by a group led by John Clarke and William Coddington, who were sympathizers of Anne Hutchinson of Massachusetts. Soon after the town was first begun

Anne Hutchinson herself, with a number of fellow religious exiles, settled here and forced Clarke and Coddington to relinquish control. Coddington then went south and founded Newport, which temporarily united with Portsmouth in 1640. Fishing, shipbuilding, and coal mining were the earliest sources of revenue. Today, Portsmouth is a summer resort area.

Green Animals Topiary Garden

What to See and Do

The Butterfly Zoo. The only New England operation that breeds, raises, releases, and sells butterflies. View a wide variety of butterflies, incl a preserved specimen of one believed to be the world's largest. (Tues-Sun) 594 Aquidneck Ave, in Middletown. Phone 401/849-9519. ¢¢

⭐ **Green Animals.** Topiary gardens planted in 1880 with California privet, golden boxwood, and American boxwood sculpted into animal forms, geometric figures, and ornamental designs; also rose garden, formal flower beds. Children's toy collection in main house. (May-Oct, daily) Off RI 114. Phone 401/847-6543. ¢¢¢

Prescott Farm and Windmill.
Restored buildings incl an operating windmill (ca 1810), General Prescott's guard house, and a country store stocked with items grown on the farm. (Apr-Nov, daily) Tours (Mon-Fri). 2009 W Main Rd (RI 114), Middletown. Phone 401/847-6230 or 401/849-7300. ¢

Motels/Motor Lodges

★★ **BEST WESTERN INN AND CONFERENCE CENTER.** *144 Anthony Rd (02871). 401/683-3600; fax 401/683-6690; toll-free 800/289-0404.* 85 rms, 2 story. May-Oct: S $85-$89; D $109-$119; each addl $10; suites $150; under 16 free; lower rates rest of yr. Crib free. TV; cable (premium), VCR avail. Indoor pool; lifeguard. Restaurant 6:30 am-9:30 pm; wkends to 10 pm. Bar 4 pm-1 am; entertainment Fri-Sat. Ck-out 11 am. Meeting rms. Business servs avail. In-rm modem link. 18-hole golf privileges. Exercise equipt; sauna. Near beach. Cr cds: A, C, D, DS, ER, JCB, MC, V.
🏊 🏃 🐾 🆂🅲

★ **FOUNDER'S BROOK MOTEL & SUITES.** *314 Boyd's Ln (02871). 401/683-1244; fax 401/683-9129; toll-free 800/334-8765.* Email foundersbrook@juno.com. 8 rms, 1 story, 24 suites. May-Oct: S $129; D $139; suites $159; each addl $10; under 18 free; lower rates rest of yr. Crib avail. Pet accepted, some restrictions, fee. Parking lot. TV; cable. Complimentary toll-free calls. Restaurant nearby. Ck-out 11 am, ck-in 2 pm. Fax servs avail. Coin lndry. Golf. Picnic facilities. Cr cds: A, C, D, DS, MC, V.
🅳 🐾 🏃 ↘ 🐾 🔥

Restaurant

★★★ **SEAFARE INN.** *3352 E Main Rd (02801). 401/683-0577. www.seafareinn.com.* Specializes in seafood, regional American cuisine. Hrs: 5-9 pm. Closed Sun, Mon; Jan 1, Dec 24, 25. Res accepted. Dinner $13.95-$22.95. Jacket. In renovated 1887 Victorian mansion furnished with period pieces. Cr cds: A, D, MC, V.
🅳

Providence

(E-5) *See also Pawtucket, Warwick*

Settled 1636 **Pop** 160,728 **Elev** 24 ft
Area code 401
Web www.providencevb.com
Information Providence Warwick
Convention & Visitors Bureau, One
Sabin St, 02903; 401/751-1177 or
800/233-1636

Grateful that God's providence had
led him to this spot, Roger Williams
founded a town and named it
accordingly. More than three-and-
one-half centuries later, Providence is
the capital and largest city of the
State of Rhode Island and Providence
Plantations, the state's official title.

In its early years Providence was a
farm center. Through the great maritime epoch of the late 18th century
and first half of the 19th century,
clipper ships sailed from Providence
to China and the West Indies. During the 19th century the city
became a great industrial center
which today still produces widely
known Providence jewelry and sil-
verware. Providence is also an
important port of entry.

Providence's long history has created a blend of old and new: modern
hotels and office buildings share the
streets with historic houses. Benefit
Street, overlooking Providence's
modern financial district, has one of
the largest concentrations of Colonial houses in America. The city's
location along the upper Narragansett Bay and numerous cultural
opportunities each provide many
varied attractions for the visitor. In
addition, Providence is the southern
point of the Blackstone River Valley
National Heritage Corridor, a
250,000-acre region that extends to
Worcester, MA (see).

What to See and Do

The Arcade. (1828) First indoor
shopping mall with national landmark status. More than 35 specialty
shops and restaurants. Westminster
St. Phone 401/598-1049.

Brown University. (1764) 7,500 students. Founded as Rhode Island College; school was renamed for
Nicholas Brown, major benefactor
and son of a founder, in 1804. Brown
is the 7th-oldest college in the US.
Pembroke College for Women (1891),
named for the Cambridge, England
alma mater of Roger Williams,
merged with the men's college in
1971. Head of College St on Prospect.
Phone 401/863-1000. Here are

John Carter Brown Library. (1904)
Library houses exhibits, books, and
maps relating to exploration and
settlement of America. (Mon-Sat;
closed school hols) S side of campus green on George St. Phone
401/863-2725. **FREE**

John Hay Library. (1910) Named for
Lincoln's secretary John Hay
(Brown, 1858), library houses
extensive special collections incl
Lincoln manuscripts, Harris collection of American poetry and plays,
university archives. (Mon-Fri) 20
Prospect St, across from Van Wickle
gates. Phone 401/863-3723. **FREE**

Rockefeller Library. (1964) Named
for John D. Rockefeller, Jr (Brown,
1897), library houses collections in
the social sciences, humanities, and
fine arts. (Daily; closed school hols)
College & Prospect. Phone 401/863-
2167 or 401/863-2162. **FREE**

University Hall. (1770) The original
"college edifice" serves as main
administration building.

Wriston Quadrangle. (1952)
Square named for president-emeri-
tus Henry M. Wriston. On Brown
St near John Carter Brown Library.

Cathedral of St. John. (1810) Episcopal. This Georgian structure with
Gothic detail was built on the site of
King's Church (1722). (Sun-Fri;
closed hols) Tour (after Sun services).
271 N Main St, at Church St. Phone
401/331-4622. **FREE**

Culinary Archives & Museum.
Dubbed the "Smithsonian of the
food service industry," this museum
contains over 200,000 items related
to the fields of culinary arts and hospitality collected and donated by
Chicago's Chef Louis Szathmary.
Includes rare US Presidential culinary
autographs; tools of the trade from
the third millennium BC; Egyptian,
Roman, and Asian spoons over 1,000
yrs old; gallery of chefs; original artwork; hotel and restaurant silver; and
periodicals related to the field.

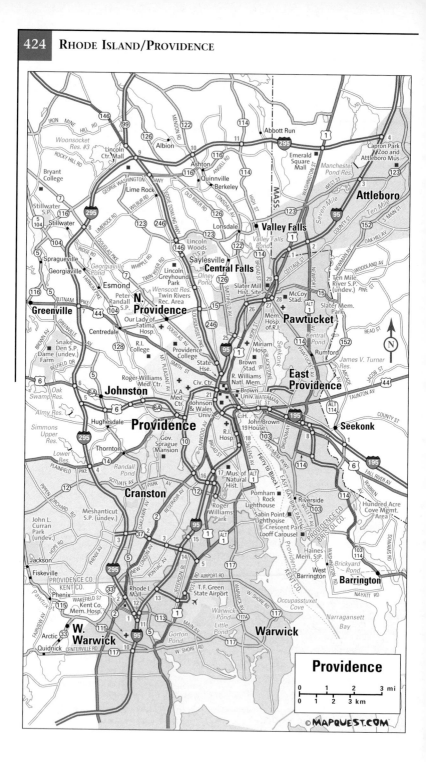

Providence

Guided tours. (Mon-Sat; closed hols) Trade Center at Harborside Campus, 315 Harborside Blvd. ¢¢

First Baptist Meeting House. Oldest Baptist congregation in America, established 1638, erected present building by Joseph Brown in 1775. Sun morning services. (Mon-Fri; closed hols) 75 N Main St, at Waterman St. Phone 401/454-3418. **FREE**

First Unitarian Church. (1816) Organized as First Congregational Church in 1720, the church was designed by John Holden Greene and has the largest bell ever cast by Paul Revere. (Sep-June, Mon-Fri, wkends by appt; rest of yr, Mon-Fri by appt; closed hols) Benefit & Benevolent Sts. Phone 401/421-7970. **FREE**

Governor Stephen Hopkins House. (1707) House of signer of Declaration of Independence and 10-time governor of Rhode Island; 18th-century garden, period furnishings. (Apr-Dec, Wed and Sat afternoons, also by appt) Children only with adult. Benefit & Hopkins Sts, opp courthouse. Phone 401/421-0694. **Donation**

Lincoln Woods State Park. More than 600 acres. Swimming, bathhouse, freshwater ponds, fishing, boating; hiking and bridle trails, ice-skating. Picnicking, concession. Fees for some activities. 5 mi N via RI 146, S of Breakneck Hill Rd. Phone 401/723-7892. Per vehicle ¢

Museum of Rhode Island History at Aldrich House. Exhibits on Rhode Island's history. Headquarters for Rhode Island Historical Society. (Tues-Sun; closed Jan 1, Thanksgiving, Dec 25) 110 Benevolent St. Phone 401/331-8575. ¢¢ Combination ticket for

John Brown House. (1786) Georgian masterpiece by Joseph Brown, brother of John. George Washington was among the guests entertained in house. Museum of 18th-century china, glass, Rhode Island antiques, paintings; John Brown's chariot (1782), perhaps the oldest American-made vehicle extant. Guided tours. (Mar-Dec, Tues-Sun; rest of yr, Sat and Sun; closed hols) 52 Power St, at Benefit St. Phone 401/331-8575. ¢¢ The Historical Society also maintains a

Library. One of the largest genealogical collections in New England; Rhode Island imprints dating from 1727; newspapers, manuscripts, photographs, films. (Sep-May, Wed-Sat; rest of yr, Tues-Fri; closed hols) 121 Hope St, at Power St. **FREE**

North Burial Ground. Graves of Roger Williams and other settlers. 1 mi N of Market Sq on N Main (US 1).

Old State House. Where General Assembly of Rhode Island met between 1762-1900. Independence was proclaimed in Old State House two months before declaration signed in Philadelphia. (Mon-Fri; closed hols) 150 Benefit St. Phone 401/222-2678. **FREE**

Providence Athenaeum Library. (1753) One of the oldest subscription libraries in the US; housed in Greek Revival building designed by William Strickland in 1836. Rare book rm incl original Audubon elephant folios; small art collection. (Mon-Sat; summer, Mon-Fri; closed hols, also 2 wks early Aug) Tours. 251 Benefit St. Phone 401/421-6970. **FREE**

Providence Children's Museum. Many hands-on exhibits, incl a time-travel adventure through Rhode Island's multicultural history, wet-and-wild exploration of water, and hands-on geometry lab. Traveling exhibits. Wkly programs. Gift shop. (Sep-June, Tues-Sun; rest of yr, daily) 100 South St. Phone 401/273-KIDS. ¢¢

Rhode Island School of Design. (1877) 1,960 students. One of the country's leading art and design schools. Tours. 2 College St. Phone 401/454-6100. On campus are

RISD Museum. Collections range from ancient to contemporary. (Tues-Sun; closed hols) 224 Benefit St. Phone 401/454-6345. ¢

Woods-Gerry Gallery. Mansion built 1860-63 has special exhibits by students, faculty, and alumni. (Daily) 62 Prospect St.

Rhode Island State House. Capitol by McKim, Mead, and White was completed in 1901. Building contains a Gilbert Stuart full-length portrait of George Washington and the original parchment charter granted to Rhode Island by Charles II in 1663. *Independent Man* statue on dome. Guided tours. Building (Mon-Fri; closed hols and 2nd Mon Aug). Smith St. Phone 401/222-2357. **FREE**

Roger Williams National Memorial. This 4½-acre park, at site of old town spring, commemorates founding of Providence and contributions made by Roger Williams to civil and religious liberty; slide presentation, exhibit. Visitor information. (Daily; closed Jan 1, Dec 25) 282 N Main St. Phone 401/521-7266. **FREE**

Roger Williams Park. Park has 430 acres of woodlands, waterways, and winding drives. Japanese garden, Betsy Williams' cottage, greenhouses. (Daily; closed Jan 1, Thanksgiving, Dec 25) 3 mi S on Elmwood Ave. Phone 401/785-9450. **FREE** Also in the park are

Museum of Natural History. Anthropology, geology, astronomy, and biology displays; educational and performing arts programs. (Daily; closed Jan 1, Thanksgiving, Dec 25) Elmwood Ave. Phone 401/785-9450. ¢

Zoo. Children's nature center, tropical building, African plains exhibit; Marco Polo exhibits; over 600 animals. Educational programs; tours. (Daily; closed Dec 25) Phone 401/785-3510. ¢¢

Providence Preservation Society. The Providence Preservation Society offers brochures and tour booklets for several historic Providence neighborhoods. (Mon-Fri) 21 Meeting St. Phone 401/831-7440. ¢¢¢

Annual Events

Spring Festival of Historic Houses. Sponsored by the Providence Preservation Society, 21 Meeting St, 02903. Tours of selected private houses and gardens. Phone 401/831-7440. Second wkend June.

WaterFire. Waterplace Park. Floating bonfires in the Providence River accompanied by music. Phone 401/272-31111. Call for schedule.

Motel/Motor Lodge

★ **HIGHWAY MOTOR INN.** *1880 Hartford Ave (02919), jct US 6A and I-295. 401/351-7810.* 35 rms. S $42; D $50; each addl $5; suites $60-$70. TV; cable (premium). Restaurant nearby. Ck-out 11 am. Cr cds: A, MC, V.

🄳 ➴ 🐾

★★ **RAMADA INN.** *940 Fall River Ave (02771), 4 mi E at Exit 1, jct I-195 and MA 114A. 508/336-7300; fax 508/336-2107; toll-free 800/272-6232.* 128 rms, 2 story. S $61-$82; D $66-$85; each addl $10; suites $107-$134; under 18 free; wkend rates. Crib free. TV; cable (premium). Indoor pool; whirlpool. Sauna. Playground. Restaurant 7 am-10 pm. Bar noon-1 am; entertainment. Ck-out noon. Meeting rms. Business center. Tennis. Putting green. Lawn games. Cr cds: A, D, DS, MC, V.

🄳 🏌 ➴ ➴ 🐾 🆂🅲 🏌

Hotels

★★ **DAYS.** *220 India St (02903), 2 mi E on RI 195, Exit 3. 401/272-5577; fax 401/272-0251; toll-free 800/528-9931.* 136 rms, 6 story. Apr-Oct: S $89-$149; D $99-$159; each addl $10; under 12 free; lower rates rest of yr. Crib avail. TV; cable (premium). Restaurant 6:30 am-2 pm, 5-10 pm. Bar 11-1 am. Ck-out 11 am. Meeting rms. Business center. In-rm modem link. Free airport, Rail Road station, bus depot transportation. Exercise equipt. Overlooks harbor. Cr cds: A, C, D, DS, MC, V.

🄳 🏌 🏌 ➴ 🐾

★★ **JOHNSON AND WALES INN.** *MA 114 A and US 44 (02771), I-195E, Exit 1 in MA, Left onto MA 114a to jct US 44, Right on US 44. 508/336-8700; fax 508/336-3414; toll-free 800/232-1772. www.jwinn.com.* 49 rms, 3 story, 37 suites. May-Oct: S, D $120; suites $144; each addl $10; under 18 free; lower rates rest of yr. Crib avail. Parking lot. TV; cable (premium), VCR avail. Complimentary continental bkfst, coffee in rms, newspaper. Restaurant 6:30 am-10 pm. Bar. Ck-out 11 am, ck-in 2 pm. Meeting rms. Business servs avail. Bellhops. Concierge serv. Dry cleaning, coin lndry. Gift shop. Free airport transportation. Exercise privileges. Golf, 18 holes. Tennis, 5 courts. Cr cds: A, C, D, DS, MC, V.

🄳 🏌 🏌 🏌 ➴ 🐾

★★★ **MARRIOTT HOTEL.** *1 Orms St (02904). 401/272-2400; fax 401/273-2686; toll-free 800/937-7768.* 345 rms, 6 story. S, D $99-$179; suites $250; family, wkend rates; higher rates special events. Crib free. Pet accepted. TV; cable (premium), VCR avail. Indoor/outdoor pool; whirlpool, poolside serv, lifeguard. Coffee in rms. Restaurant 6:30 am-11 pm. Bar; entertainment. Ck-out noon. Convention facilities. Business center. In-rm modem link. Bellhops. Sundries. Gift shop. Airport transportation. Exercise equipt; sauna. Game rm. Balconies; some private patios. Cr cds: A, C, D, DS, ER, JCB, MC, V.

★★★ **THE PROVIDENCE BILT-MORE.** *Kennedy Plaza (02903). 401/421-0700; fax 401/455-3050; res 800/448-8355; toll-free 800/294-7709. Email providencebilmore@aol.com.* 244 rms, 18 story. S $120-$190; D $140-$220; each addl $20; suites $199-$750; under 18 free; wkend rates. Crib free. Pet accepted. TV; cable (premium), VCR avail. Restaurant 6:30 am-midnight. Bar noon-1 am; wkends to 2 am. Ck-out noon. Convention facilities. Business center. In-rm modem link. Beauty shop. Garage parking; valet. Exercise equipt. Refrigerators, microwaves avail. Cr cds: A, DS, MC, V.

★★★ **WESTIN.** *1 W Exchange St (02903). 401/598-8000; fax 401/598-8200; res 800/301-1111.* 363 rms, 25 story, 22 suites. S, D $189-$260; each addl $25; suites $260-$1200; under 18 free. TV; cable (premium), VCR avail (movies). Restaurant 6 am-10 pm. Bar to midnight. Ck-out noon. Convention facilities. Business center. In-rm modem link. Concierge. Exercise equipt; sauna. Indoor pool; whirlpool. Minibars; some bathrm phones, refrigerators. Cr cds: A, C, D, DS, ER, JCB, MC, V.

B&Bs/Small Inns

★★ **OLD COURT BED & BREAKFAST.** *144 Benefit St (02903). 401/751-2002; fax 401/272-4830. Email reserve@oldcourt.com; www.oldcourt.com.* 10 rms, 3 story. Mar-Nov: D $165; each addl $20; lower rates rest of yr. Parking lot. TV; cable. Complimentary full bkfst. Ck-out 11:30 am, ck-in 11 pm. Fax servs avail. Cr cds: A, DS, MC, V.

Historic home in Old Providence

★ **STATE HOUSE INN.** *43 Jewett St (02908), near State Capitol Bldg. 401/351-6111; fax 401/351-4261. Email statehouseinn@edgenet.net; www. providence-inn.com.* 10 rms, 3 story. S, D $79-$119; each addl $10; family rates. Crib avail. TV; cable, VCR avail. Complimentary full bkfst. Restaurant nearby. Ck-out 11 am, ck-in 3 pm. Built 1890. Sitting rm. Antiques, fireplaces. Totally non-smoking. Cr cds: A, DS, MC, V.

Restaurants

★★ **ADESSO.** *161 Cushing St (02906). 401/521-0770.* Specializes in pasta dishes, duck, California style wood-oven pizzas. Hrs: 11:30 am-10:30 pm; Fri, Sat to 11:30 pm. Closed July 4, Thanksgiving, Dec 25. Bar. Lunch a la carte entrees: $6.95-$15.95; dinner a la carte entrees: $9.95-$23.95. Parking. Modern decor; open kitchen. Cr cds: A, MC, V.

★★★ **AL FORNO.** *577 S Main St (02903). 401/273-9760. www.alforno. com.* Specializes in pasta, grilled dishes. Hrs: 5-10 pm; Sat from 4 pm. Closed Sun, Mon. Dinner $21-$27.95. Cr cds: A, D, MC, V.

★★ **HEMENWAY'S SEAFOOD GRILL.** *1 Providence-Washington Plz (02903), at S Main St. 401/351-8570. Email mahonaz@aol.com.* Specializes in fresh seafood from around the world. Hrs: 11:30 am-10 pm; Fri, Sat to 11 pm; Sun noon-9 pm. Closed

Thanksgiving, Dec 25. Bar. Lunch $5.45-$11.95; dinner $11.95-$21.95. Child's menu. Valet parking. Cr cds: A, D, DS, MC, V.

[D] [≡]

★★ **OLD GRIST MILL TAVERN.** *390 Fall River Ave (02771), on MA 114A, I-195 Exit 1 in MA. 508/336-8460.* Specializes in prime rib, sirloin, seafood. Salad bar. Hrs: 11:30 am-10 pm; Sun noon-9 pm. Closed Thanksgiving, Dec 25. Bar. Lunch $4.75-$9.95; dinner $7.95-$18.95. Child's menu. Parking. In restored mill (1745); antiques; fireplace. Gardens, pond, wooden bridge over waterfall. Cr cds: A, C, D, DS, MC, V.

[D] [≡]

★★★ **POT AU FEU.** *44 Custom House St (02903). 401/273-8953.* Specializes in classic and regional French dishes. Hrs: noon-1:30 pm, 6-9 pm; Fri, Sat to 9:30 pm. Closed hols; also Sun June-Aug. Res accepted. Bar. Lunch a la carte entrees: $4-$12; dinner a la carte entrees: $12-$29. Prix fixe: $26-$39. Two tiers; bistro atmosphere on lower level, formal dining on upper level. Cr cds: A, C, D, DS, MC, V.

[≡]

Wakefield

(see Kingston)

Warwick

(E-5) *See also East Greenwich, Providence*

Chartered 1647 **Pop** 85,427 **Elev** 64 ft
Area code 401
Web www.warwickri.com

Information Dept of Economic Development, City Hall, 3275 Post Rd, 02886; 401/738-2000, ext 6402 or 800/4-WARWICK

Warwick, the second-largest city in Rhode Island, is the location of T. F. Green Airport, the state's largest commercial airport. With 39 miles of coastline on Narragansett Bay, the city has more than 15 marinas. Warwick is a major retail and indus-

trial center. The geographic diversity of Warwick promoted a decentralized pattern of settlement, which gave rise to a number of small villages including Pawtuxet, Cowesett, and Conimicut.

What to See and Do

Shopping.

Cadillac Shopping Outlet. Discounted brand-name clothing for men, women, and children. (Daily) 1689 Post Rd. Phone 401/738-5145.

Historic Pontiac Mills. Portions of 1863 mill complex have been restored and now house approx 80 small businesses, artisans, and shops. Also open-air market (Sat and Sun). (Daily) 334 Knight St. Phone 401/737-2700.

Warwick Mall. Renovated and expanded; largest mall in the state. Over 80 specialty shops and 4 department stores. Outdoor patio, video wall, topiary gardens. Wkly special events. (Daily) 400 Baldhill Hill Rd. Phone 401/739-7500.

Walking Tour of Historic Apponaug Village. More than 30 structures of historic and/or architectural interest are noted on walking tour brochure available through Dept of Economic Development, Warwick City Hall, 3275 Post Rd, Apponaug 02886. Along Post Rd between Greenwich Ave & W Shore Rd. Phone 1-800/4-WARWICK. **FREE**

Annual Events

Gaspee Days. Celebration of the capture and burning of British revenue schooner *Gaspee* by Rhode Island patriots; arts and crafts, concert, footraces, battle reenactment, fife and drum corps muster, parade, contests. Phone 800/4-WARWICK. May-June.

Warwick Heritage Festival. Revisit history with this wkend reenactment. Nov, Veterans Day wkend. Warwick City Park. Phone 800/4-WARWICK.

Motels/Motor Lodges

★ **FAIRFIELD INN.** *36 Jefferson Blvd (02888), near T.F. Green State Airport. 401/941-6600; fax 401/785-1260.* 115 rms, 5 story. July-Oct: S $74.70; D $84.70; each addl $4-$7; under 18

free; lower rates rest of yr. Crib free.
TV; cable (premium). Pool; lifeguard.
Complimentary continental bkfst.
Restaurant adj open 24 hrs. Ck-out
11 am. Coin lndry. Valet serv. Airport
transportation. Cr cds: A, C, D, DS,
MC, V.

[D] [≈] [✈] [ℵ] [🔥]

★★★ RADISSON AIRPORT HOTEL.
2081 Post Rd (02886), at T.F. Green State Airport. 401/739-3000; fax 401/732-9309; toll-free 800/333-3333. 111 units, 2 story, 39 suites. S, D $89-$150; each addl $15; suites $125-$170; under 18 free; wkend rates. Crib free. TV; cable (premium), VCR avail. Complimentary continental bkfst (Mon-Fri). Restaurant 6:30 am-11 pm. Bar noon-1 am. Ck-out noon. Business servs avail. Bellhops. Valet serv. Concierge. Sundries. Free airport transportation. Wet bar in suites. Cr cds: A, C, D, DS, JCB, MC, V.

[D] [✈] [ℵ] [🔥] [SC]

★★ RESIDENCE INN BY MAR-RIOTT.
500 Kilvert St (02886), near T.F. Green State Airport. 401/737-7100; fax 401/739-2909; res 800/331-3131. 96 kit. suites, 2 story. Kit. suites $140-$190. TV; cable (premium). Indoor pool; whirlpool. Playground. Complimentary continental bkfst. Ck-out noon. Business center. Lawn games. Balconies. Cr cds: A, D, DS, MC, V.

[D] [≈] [ℵ] [✈] [ℵ] [🔥]

Hotels

★★ COMFORT INN.
1940 Post Rd (02886), near T.F. Green State Airport. 401/732-0470; fax 401/732-4247; toll-free 877/805-8997. www. hotelchoice. com. 200 rms, 4 story. Apr-Oct: S, D $159; suites $179; each addl $10; under 17 free; lower rates rest of yr. Crib avail. Parking lot. TV; cable. Complimentary continental bkfst, coffee in rms, newspaper, toll-free calls. Restaurant 5 am-11:30 pm. Bar. Ck-out noon, ck-in 3 pm. Meeting rms. Fax servs avail. Bellhops. Concierge. Dry cleaning. Free airport transportation. Exercise privileges. Golf. Video games. Cr cds: A, D, DS, JCB, MC, V.

[D] [ℵ] [ℵ] [✈] [ℵ] [🔥] [SC]

★★★ CROWNE PLAZA AT THE CROSSING.
801 Greenwich Ave (02886). 401/732-6000; fax 401/732-4839; res 800/227-6963. www.crowne plazari.com. 262 rms, 6 story, 4 suites. Apr-Oct: S $239; D $249; suites $525; each addl $10; lower rates rest of yr. Crib avail. Pet accepted, some restrictions. Parking lot. Indoor pool, whirlpool. TV; cable (premium), VCR avail, CD avail. Complimentary coffee in rms, newspaper. Restaurant 6:30 am-11 pm. Bar. Ck-out 11 am, ck-in 3 pm. Conference center, meeting rms. Business center. Bellhops. Concierge. Dry cleaning, coin lndry. Gift shop. Free airport transportation. Exercise equipt, sauna. Golf. Tennis. Hiking trail. Cr cds: A, C, D, DS, MC, V.

[D] [➹] [ℵ] [ℵ] [≈] [ℵ] [ℵ] [ℵ] [🔥] [SC] [ℵ]

★★★ SHERATON.
1850 Post Rd; US 1 (02886), near T.F. Green State Airport. 401/738-4000; fax 401/738-8206; res 800/325-3535. www. sheraton.com. 206 rms, 5 story, 10 suites. Mar-Nov: S $219; D $229; suites $269; lower rates rest of yr. Crib avail. Pet accepted, some restrictions, fee. Parking lot. Indoor pool. TV; cable (DSS), VCR avail. Complimentary coffee in rms, newspaper. Restaurant 6:30 am-11 pm. Bar. Ck-out noon, ck-in 3 pm. Meeting rms. Business servs avail. Bellhops. Dry cleaning. Free airport transportation. Exercise equipt, sauna. Golf, 18 holes. Tennis, 4 courts. Cr cds: A, C, D, DS, ER, JCB, MC, V.

[D] [➹] [ℵ] [ℵ] [≈] [ℵ] [✈] [ℵ] [🔥]

Restaurant

★★ LEGAL SEAFOODS.
2099 Post Rd (02886). 401/732-3663. www.legalseafoods.com. Specializes in fresh seafood. Hrs: 11:30 am-10 pm; Fri to 10:30 pm; Sat noon-10:30 pm; Sun noon-9 pm. Closed Thanksgiving, Dec 25. Bar. Lunch $5.95-$9.95; dinner $9.95-$16.95. Child's menu. Cr cds: A, C, D, DS, MC, V.

[D]

Westerly

(F-5) *See also Charlestown; also see Mystic and Stonington, CT*

Founded 1669 **Pop** 21,605 **Elev** 50 ft
Area code 401 **Zip** 02891
Web www.southcountyri.com

Information Westerly-Pawcatuck Area Chamber of Commerce, 74 Post Rd, Rte 1; 401/596-7761 or 800/SEA-7636; or the South County Tourism Council, Stedman Government Center, 4808 Tower Hill Rd, Wakefield 02879; 401/789-4422 or 800/548-4662

Westerly, one of the oldest towns in the state, was at one time known for its nearby granite quarries. Today local industries include textiles, the manufacture of fishing line, and tourism.

What to See and Do

Babcock-Smith House. (ca 1732) This 2-story, gambrel-roofed Georgian mansion was residence of Dr. Joshua Babcock, Westerly's first physician and friend of Benjamin Franklin. Later it was home to Orlando Smith, who discovered granite on the grounds. Furniture collection covers 200 yrs; toys date from 1890s; Colonial garden and culinary herb garden. (July-mid-Sep, Wed and Sun; May-June and mid-Sep-mid-Oct, Sun only) 124 Granite St. Phone 401/596-4424 or 401/596-5704. ¢

Misquamicut State Beach. Swimming, bathhouse (fee), fishing nearby; picnicking, concession. (Mid-June-early Sep, daily) Parking fee. 5 mi S off US 1A. ¢¢¢

Watch Hill. Historical community of handsome summer houses, many dating from the 1870s; picturesque sea views. 6 mi S on Beach St, via Avondale. Located here are

  Flying Horse Carousel. Original amusement ride built in 1867. Watch Hill Beach.

  Lighthouse. (1856) Granite lighthouse built to replace wooden one built in 1807; lit by oil lamp until 1933, when replaced by electric. Museum exhibit (Tues and Thurs, afternoons).

Resorts

★★ **BREEZEWAY RESORT L.** *70 Winnapaug Rd (02891), approx 4 mi S on RI 1A, S on Winnapaug Rd. 401/348-8953; fax 401/596-3207; toll-free 800/462-8872. www.info@breezeway resort.com.* 34 rms, 2 story, 18 suites. Jul-Aug: S, D $135; suites $199; each addl $25; children $10; under 11 free; lower rates rest of yr. Crib avail, fee. Parking lot. Pool. TV; cable. Complimentary continental bkfst. Restaurant noon-10 pm. Bar. Ck-out 11 am, ck-in 3 pm. Meeting rm. Bellhops. Concierge. Golf. Tennis. Beach access. Bike rentals. Supervised children's activities. Picnic facilities. Cr cds: A, C, D, DS, MC, V.

🛏️ 🖙 ⤢ ✈ ⊠ 🐾

★★ **WINNAPAUG INN.** *169 Shore Rd (02891). 401/348-8350; fax 401/596-8654; res 800/288-9906. Email winnapauginn@riconnect.com; www.winnapauginn.com.* 47 rms, 3 story, 9 suites. Jul-Aug: S $79; D $179; suites $259; each addl $25; children $15; under 17 free; lower rates rest of yr. Crib avail, fee. Parking lot. Pool. TV; cable (DSS). Complimentary continental bkfst. Restaurant 11:30 am-9 pm. Bar. Ck-out 11 am, ck-in 3 pm. Meeting rms. Golf, 18 holes. Tennis, 3 courts. Beach access. Supervised children's activities. Picnic facilities. Cr cds: A, C, D, DS, MC, V.

D 🐾 🏌 ⤢ ⊠ 🛶 🐾

B&Bs/Small Inns

★★ **SHELTER HARBOR INN.** *10 Wagner Rd (02891). 401/322-8883; fax 401/322-7907; toll-free 800/468-8883. Email shelterharborinn@earth link.net.* 23 rms, 3 with shower only, 2 story. May-Oct: S, D $92-$136; each addl $15-$25; lower rates rest of yr. Crib $15. TV; cable. Playground. Complimentary full bkfst. Restaurant 7:30-10:30 am, 11:30 am-3 pm, 5-10 pm. Bar. Ck-out 11 am, ck-in 2 pm. Meeting rms. Business servs avail. Lawn games. Some balconies. Picnic tables. Originally a farm built early 1800s; guest house and converted barn. Cr cds: A, C, D, DS, MC, V.

D 🐾 🏌 ⊠ 🐾

★★★ **VILLA BED & BREAKFAST.** *190 Shore Rd (02891). 401/596-1054; fax 401/596-6268; toll-free 800/722-9240. Email villa@riconnect.com; www.*

thevillaatwesterly.com. 7 rms, 3 story. Jun-Sep: D $175; each addl $25; lower rates rest of yr. Parking lot. Pool, whirlpool. TV; cable, VCR avail. Complimentary full bkfst, coffee in rms. Restaurant. Ck-out 11 am. Business center. Golf, 18 holes. Tennis, 2 courts. Beach access. Cr cds: A, DS, MC, V.

Cottage Colony

★★ **THE PINE LODGE.** *92 Old Post Rd (02891), 3½ mi N on US 1. 401/ 322-0333; fax 401/322-2010.* 11 rms, 1 story. Jun-Sep: D $100; each addl $15; under 15 free; lower rates rest of yr. Crib avail. Parking lot. TV; cable (DSS). Restaurant nearby. Ck-out 10 am, ck-in 3 pm. Concierge. Golf. Beach access. Picnic facilities. Cr cds: MC, V.

Restaurant

★★ **VILLA TROMBINO.** *112 Ashway Rd (02891). 401/596-3444.* Specializes in pasta, fresh veal, seafood. Hrs: 4-10 pm; early-bird dinner 4-6 pm. Closed Mon; Thanksgiving, Dec 24, 25. Res accepted. Bar. Dinner a la carte entrees: $3.95-$19.95. Child's menu. Cr cds: A, D, DS, MC, V.

VERMONT

Vermont was the last New England state to be settled. The earliest permanent settlement date is believed to be 1724. Ethan Allen and his Green Mountain Boys made Vermont famous when they took Fort Ticonderoga from the British in 1775. Claimed by both New York and New Hampshire, Vermont framed a constitution in 1777. It was the first state to prohibit slavery and the first to provide universal male suffrage, regardless of property or income. For 14 years, Vermont was an independent republic, running its own postal service, coining its own money, naturalizing citizens of other states and countries, and negotiating with other states and nations. Vermont became the 14th state in 1791.

Although Vermont is usually thought of as a farm state, more than 17 percent of the labor force is in manufacturing. Machinery, food, wood, plastic, rubber, paper, and electrical and electronic products are made here. Dairy products lead the farm list, with sheep, maple sugar and syrup, apples, and potatoes following. Vermont leads the nation in its yield of marble and granite; limestone, slate, and talc are also quarried and mined.

Tall steeples dominate the towns, forests, mountains, and countryside where one can walk the 260-mile Long Trail along the Green Mountain crests. Vermont has one of the highest concentrations of alpine ski areas and cross-country ski touring centers in the nation. Fishing and hunting are excellent; resorts range from rustic to elegant.

Population: 562,758
Area: 9,273 square miles
Elevation: 95-4,393 feet
Peak: Mount Mansfield (Lamoille County)
Entered Union: March 4, 1791 (14th state)
Capital: Montpelier
Motto: Freedom and Unity
Nickname: Green Mountain State
Flower: Red Clover
Bird: Hermit Thrush
Tree: Sugar Maple
Fair: September 1-10, 2001, in Rutland
Time Zone: Eastern
Website: www.travel.com

When to Go/Climate

Vermont enjoys four distinct seasons. Comfortable summers are followed by brilliantly colored falls and typically cold New England winters. Heavy snowfall makes for good skiing in winter, while spring thaws bring on the inevitable muddy months. Summer and fall are popular times to visit.

AVERAGE HIGH/LOW TEMPERATURES (°F)
BURLINGTON

Jan 25/8	**May** 67/45	**Sep** 69/49
Feb 28/9	**June** 76/55	**Oct** 57/39
Mar 39/22	**July** 81/60	**Nov** 44/30
Apr 54/34	**Aug** 78/58	**Dec** 30/16

Parks and Recreation Finder

Directions to and information about the parks and recreation areas below are given under their respective town/city sections. Please refer to those sections for details.

CALENDAR HIGHLIGHTS

FEBRUARY

Winter Carnival (Brattleboro). Week-long festival includes ski races, parade, ice show, sleigh rides, road races.

APRIL

Maple Sugar Festival (St. Albans). A number of producers welcome visitors who join sugarhouse parties for sugar-on-snow, sour pickles, and raised doughnuts. Continuing events; arts and crafts; antiques; wood-chopping contests. Website www.stalbanschamber.com. Phone 802/524-5800 or 802/524-2444.

JUNE

Mountain Bike World Cup Race (West Dover). Mount Snow. More than 1,500 cyclists from throughout the world compete in downhill, dual slalom, and circuit racing events. Phone 800/245-7669.

JULY

Festival on the Green (Middlebury). Village green. Classical, modern, and traditional dance; chamber and folk music; theater and comedy presentations. Phone 802/388-0216.

SEPTEMBER

Vermont State Fair (Rutland). Exhibits of arts and crafts, flowers, produce, home arts, pets, animals, maple sugaring. Entertainment, agricultural displays, hot-air ballooning. Daily special events. Phone 802/775-5200.

NATIONAL PARK AND RECREATION AREAS

Key to abbreviations. I.H.S. = International Historic Site; I.P.M. = International Peace Memorial; N.B. = National Battlefield; N.B.P. = National Battlefield Park; N.B.C. = National Battlefield and Cemetery; N.C.A. = National Conservation Area; N.E.M. = National Expansion Memorial; N.F. = National Forest; N.G. = National Grassland; N.H.P. = National Historical Park; N.H.C. = National Heritage Corridor; N.H.S. = National Historic Site; N.L. = National Lakeshore; N.M. = National Monument; N.M.P. = National Military Park; N.Mem. = National Memorial; N.P. = National Park; N.Pres. = National Preserve; N.R.A. = National Recreational Area; N.R.R. = National Recreational River; N.Riv. = National River; N.S. = National Seashore; N.S.R. = National Scenic Riverway; N.S.T. = National Scenic Trail; N.Sc. = National Scientific Reserve; N.V.M. = National Volcanic Monument.

Place Name	Listed Under
Green Mountain N.F.	same

STATE PARK AND RECREATION AREAS

Key to abbreviations. I.P. = Interstate Park; S.A.P. = State Archaeological Park; S.B. = State Beach; S.C.A. = State Conservation Area; S.C.P. = State Conservation Park; S.Cp. = State Campground; S.F. = State Forest; S.G. = State Garden; S.H.A. = State Historic Area; S.H.P. = State Historic Park; S.H.S. = State Historic Site; S.M.P. = State Marine Park; S.N.A. = State Natural Area; S.P. = State Park; S.P.C. = State Public Campground; S.R. = State Reserve; S.R.A. = State Recreation Area; S.Res. = State Reservoir; S.Res.P. = State Resort Park; S.R.P. = State Rustic Park.

Place Name	Listed Under
Branbury S.P.	BRANDON

Burton Island S.P.	ST. ALBANS
Button Bay S.P.	VERGENNES
Calvin Coolidge S.F.	PLYMOUTH
Elmore S.P.	STOWE
Emerald Lake S.P.	MANCHESTER
Gifford Woods S.P.	KILLINGTON
Groton S.F.	BARRE
Jamaica S.P.	NEWFANE
Lake Carmi S.P.	ST. ALBANS
Little River S.P.	WATERBURY
Molly Stark S.P.	WILMINGTON
Mount Ascutney S.P.	WINDSOR
Mount Mansfield S.F.	STOWE
Mount Philo S.P.	SHELBURNE
North Hero S.P.	NORTH HERO
Okemo S.F.	same
Shaftsbury S.P.	BENNINGTON
Silver Lake S.P.	WOODSTOCK
Townshend S.F.	NEWFANE
Wilgus S.P.	WINDSOR
Woodford S.P.	BENNINGTON

Water-related activities, hiking, riding, various other sports, picnicking, camping, and visitor centers are available in many of these areas. Day use areas (Memorial Day wkend-Labor Day, daily): over age 14, $2/person; ages 4-13, $1.50; under 4 free. Boat rentals, $5/hr. Paddleboats, $5/half-hr. Canoe rentals, $5/hr.

Camping: $13/night, lean-to $19 at areas with swimming beaches; $11/night, lean-to $17 at areas without swimming beaches. Reservations of at least 2 days (3 days mid-May-Oct) and maximum of 21 days may be made by contacting park or Department of Forests, Parks, and Recreation, 103 S Main St, Waterbury 05671-0603, with full payment. Pets are allowed on leash only. Phone 802/241-3655.

SKI AREAS

Place Name	Listed Under
Bolton Valley Holiday Resort	BURLINGTON
Bromley Mountain Ski Area	PERU
Burke Mountain Ski Area	LYNDONVILLE
Grafton Ponds Cross-Country Ski Cent	GRAFTON
Haystack Ski Area	WILMINGTON
Killington Resort	KILLINGTON
Mad River Glen Ski Area	WAITSFIELD
Middlebury College Snow Bowl	MIDDLEBURY
Mount Snow Ski Area	WEST DOVER
Mountain Top Cross Country Ski Resort	KILLINGTON
Okemo Mountain Ski Area	OKEMO STATE FOREST
Smugglers' Notch Ski Area	JEFFERSONVILLE
Stowe Mountain Resort	STOWE
Stratton Mountain Ski Area	STRATTON MOUNTAIN
Sugarbush Resort	WARREN
Suicide Six Ski Area	WOODSTOCK

Wild Wings Ski Touring Center   PERU

For brochures on skiing in Vermont contact the Vermont Dept. of Tourism and Marketing, 134 State St, Montpelier 05602; 802/828-3237 or 1-800/VERMONT.

FISHING AND HUNTING

Nonresident fishing license: season $38; 7-day $25; 3-day $18; 1-day $11. Non-resident hunting license: $80; $25 for those under 18 yrs. Nonresident small game license: $35. In order for a nonresident to obtain a hunting license, he/she must prove that he/she holds a license in his/her home state. Bow and arrow license (hunting or combination license also required): nonresident $20. Combination hunting and fishing license: nonresident $100. For *Vermont Guide to Fishing* contact the Fish and Wildlife Dept, 103 S Main St, Waterbury 05671-0501; 802/241-3700.

Driving Information

All vehicle occupants must be secured in federally approved safety belts. Children four years and younger must be secured in an approved child safety device. When the number of occupants exceeds the number of safety belts, children take priority and must be secured. Under one year must use an approved safety seat. For further information phone 802/828-2665.

INTERSTATE HIGHWAY SYSTEM

The following alphabetical listing of Vermont towns in *Mobil Travel Guide* shows that these cities are within 10 miles of the indicated Interstate highways. A highway map should, however, be checked for the nearest exit.

Highway Number	Cities/Towns within 10 miles
Interstate 89	Barre, Burlington, Montpelier, St. Albans, Swanton, Waterbury, White River Junction.
Interstate 91	Bellows Falls, Brattleboro, Fairlee, Grafton, Lyndonville, Newfane, Newport, St. Johnsbury, Springfield, White River Junction, Windsor, Woodstock.

Additional Visitor Information

Vermont is very well documented. The Vermont Official Transportation Map, as well as numerous descriptive folders, are distributed free by the Vermont Dept of Tourism and Marketing, 6 Baldwin St, 05601-1471; 802/828-3237 or 800/VERMONT. Visitor centers are located off I-89 in Guilford (daily); off I-89 in Highgate Springs (daily); off US 4 in Fair Haven (daily); and off I-93 in Waterford (daily).

The Vermont Chamber of Commerce, PO Box 37, Montpelier 05601, distributes *Vermont Traveler's Guidebook* of accommodations, restaurants, and attractions; phone 802/223-3443. *Vermont Life,* one of the nation's best known and respected regional quarterlies, presents photo essays on various aspects of life in the state; available by writing *Vermont Life,* 6 Baldwin St, Montpelier 05602. Another excellent source of information on the state is *Vermont: An Explorer's Guide* (The Countryman Press, Woodstock, VT, 1994) by Christina Tree and Peter Jennison; a comprehensive book covering attractions, events, recreational facilities, accommodations, restaurants, and places to shop. Available in bookstores.

Various books on Vermont are also available from the Vermont Historical Society, Vermont Museum, Pavilion Bldg, 109 State St, Montpelier 05609.

For information regarding Vermont's Long Trail, along with other hiking trails in the state, contact the Green Mountain Club, 4711 Waterbury Stowe Road, Waterbury Center 05677; phone 802/244-7037. The Department of Agriculture, 116 State St, Montpelier 05602, has information on farms offering vacations and maple sugarhouses open to visitors.

Several Vermont-based companies offer inn-to-inn bicycle tours from May through October (months vary). Tours range in length from two days to several

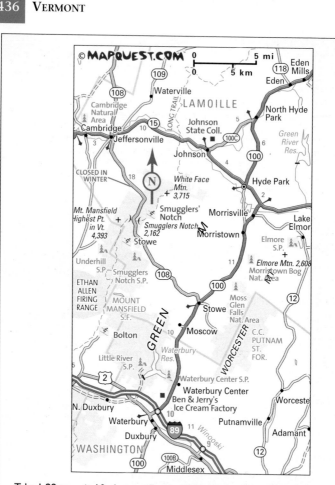

Take I-89 to exit 10, then up Route 100 past the Ben & Jerry's ice cream factory (the state's top tourist attraction) to the village of Stowe. Depending on the season, you can spend your time in Stowe biking, hiking, or cross-country skiing. Take the gondola to the top of Mount Mansfield, Vermont's highest mountain, or visit the many inns, shops, and restaurants found here. From Stowe, continue on to Smugglers' Notch (Route 108), a high, scenic pass that runs from Stowe (open summer only), through the scenic Mount Mansfield State Forest, and on to the village of Jeffersonville. Most tourists return by the same route, but there is an interesting loop return through Johnson and Morristown. Once back at I-89, continue on to Burlington, Vermont's largest city and a departure point for ferries. Visitors will enjoy biking or roller blading along Lake Champlain, shopping, or stopping at the restaurants along the Church Street Marketplace. South of Burlington on Route 7 is the town of Shelburne, which features the Shelburne Museum, Shelburne Farms, and the Vermont Teddy Bear Company. **(Approx 436 mi from Boston)**

Traveling from Woodstock to Rutland, the main access is I-89 to Route 4 via Quechee (Simon Pierce glassworks and restaurant, Quechee Gorge). Woodstock is an old resort town that features a famously beautiful oval green, the Marsh-Billings National Historic Park, Billings Farm Museum, Woodstock Historical Museum, Suicide Six Ski Area, lodging, golf, and restaurants. The tourist route is west from Woodstock on Route 4 with a brief side trip on Route 100A to the Plymouth Notch Historic District, the birthplace of President Coolidge, in Plymouth. Loop back up Route 100 to 4 west by Killington, Vermont's second highest mountain and a major ski area with a lift to the summit, plenty of lodging, and golf. Neighboring Pico Ski Resort has an Alpine Slide. Route 4 is lined with lodging places and joins Route 7 in Rutland (Chaffee Art Museum). This is one of the most popular routes across Vermont.

(**Approx 60 mi**)

Arlington

(G-1) *See also Bennington, Dorset, Manchester and Manchester Center*

Settled 1763 **Pop** 2,299 **Elev** 690 ft
Area code 802 **Zip** 05250

What to See and Do

Candle Mill Village. Three bldgs, incl a gristmill built in 1764 by Remember Baker of the Green Mountain Boys; many music boxes and candles, cookbook and teddy bear displays. (Daily; closed hols) 1½ mi E on Old Mill Rd. Phone 802/375-6068. **FREE**

Fishing. Trout and fly-fishing on the Battenkill River.

Norman Rockwell Exhibition. Hundreds of magazine covers, illustrations, advertisements, calendars, and other printed works displayed in historic 1875 church in the illustrator's home town. Hosts are Rockwell's former models. Twenty-min film. (Daily; closed Easter, Thanksgiving, Dec 25) On VT Historic Rte 7A. Phone 802/375-6423. ¢

Motel/Motor Lodge

★ **CANDLELIGHT MOTEL.** *4893 VT Rte 7A (05250). 802/375-6647; fax 802/375-2566; toll-free 800/34B5294. www.candlelightmotel.com.* 17 rms, 1 story. June-Oct: S $60; D $95; each addl $10; children $10; lower rates rest of yr. Crib avail. Parking lot. Pool. TV; cable. Complimentary continental bkfst, toll-free calls. Restaurant 5-9 pm, closed Tue. Ck-out 11 am, ck-in 1 pm. Fax servs avail. Bellhops. Golf. Tennis, 2 courts. Downhill skiing. Picnic facilities. Cr cds: A, MC, V.

B&Bs/Small Inns

★★★ **ARLINGTON INN.** *3904 Historic Rte 7A (05250). 802/375-6532; fax 802/375-6534; res 802/375-6532; toll-free 800/443-9442. Email arlinn@sover.net; www.arlingtoninn.com.* 19 rms, 2 story. Some rm phones. D $70-$160; each addl $20; wkly rates.

TV in game rm, some rms; cable, VCR avail. Complimentary full bkfst. Restaurant (see ARLINGTON INN). Bar 4-11 pm. Ck-out 11 am, ck-in 2 pm. Meeting rms. Business servs avail. Tennis. Downhill ski 14 mi; x-country ski 1 mi. Game rm. Some private patios. Picnic tables. Greek Revival mansion built in 1848 by railroad magnate, restored to capture charm of the mid-19th century. Cr cds: A, DS, MC, V.

★★★ **ARLINGTONS WEST MOUNTAIN INN.** *River Rd (05250), ½ mi W on VT 313 off VT 7A. 802/375-6516; fax 802/375-6553. Email info@westmountaininn.com; www.westmountain.com.* 14 rms, 3 story, 7 suites. Sep-Oct: S $151; D $285; suites $256; each addl $75; children $45; under 12 free; lower rates rest of yr. Crib avail, fee. Parking lot. TV; cable (DSS), VCR avail. Complimentary full bkfst, newspaper. Restaurant 8 am-8:30 pm. Bar. Ck-out noon, ck-in 2 pm. Meeting rms. Business center. Concierge. Gift shop. Golf. Tennis, 8 courts. Downhill skiing. Supervised children's activities. Hiking trail. Picnic facilities. Cr cds: A, DS, MC, V.

★★ **BATTENKILL INN.** *6342 VT 7A (05250), 3 mi S on VT 7A. 802/362-4213; fax 802/362-0975; toll-free 800/441-1628. Email batnklin@sover.net; www.battenkillinn.com.* 11 rms, 2 story. Sep-Oct: D $150; lower rates rest of yr. Parking lot. TV; cable, VCR avail. Complimentary full bkfst, newspaper. Restaurant nearby. Bar. Ck-out 11 am, ck-in 3 pm. Meeting rms. Business servs avail. Golf. Downhill skiing. Beach access. Hiking trail. Picnic facilities. Cr cds: A, MC, V.

★★ **HILL FARM INN.** *458 Hill Farm Rd (05250), 4 mi N on VT 7A, then ¼ mi E on Hill Farm Rd. 802/375-2269; fax 802/375-9918; toll-free 800/882-2545. Email hillfarm@vermontel.com; www.hillfarminn.com.* 6 rms, 5 suites. Sep-Oct: D $125; suites $110; each addl $20; children $10; lower rates rest of yr. Crib avail, fee. Parking lot. TV; cable, VCR avail. Complimentary full bkfst. Restaurant nearby. Bar. Ck-out 11 am, ck-in 2 pm. Gift shop.

Autumn pumpkins

Golf. Tennis. Downhill skiing. Hiking trail. Cr cds: DS, MC, V.

Restaurant

★★★ **ARLINGTON INN.** *VT 7A. 800/443-9442. Email arlinn@sover.net; www.arlingtoninn.com.* Specializes in pan-fried Maine crab cakes, roast duckling with apple calvados sauce, fresh seafood. Hrs: 5:30-9 pm. Closed Mon; Dec 24, 25. Res accepted. Bar. Wine cellar. Dinner a la carte entrees: $16-$23. Child's menu. View of flower gardens. Cr cds: A, D, DS, MC, V.

Barre

(D-3) *See also Montpelier, Waitsfield, Warren, Waterbury*

Settled 1788 **Pop** 9,482 **Elev** 609 ft **Area code** 802 **Zip** 05641

Information Central Vermont Chamber of Commerce, PO Box 336; 802/229-4619 or 802/229-5711

Barre (BA-rie) has a busy, industrial air. It is home to the world's largest granite quarries and a granite finishing plant. Many highly-skilled European stonecutters have settled here. A popular summer area, Barre serves as an overflow area for nearby ski resorts in winter.

What to See and Do

Goddard College. 400 students. Several bldgs designed by students; formal gardens. Theater, concerts. 5 mi N on VT 14, then 4 mi NE on US 2, in Plainfield. Phone 802/454-8311.

Granite sculptures.

Hope Cemetery. "Museum" of granite sculpture. Headstones rival finest granite carvings anywhere. Carved by craftsmen as final tribute to themselves and their families. On VT 14 at N edge of town.

Robert Burns. Figure of poet stands near city park in downtown. Erected in 1899 by admirers of the poet; regarded as one of the world's finest granite sculptures.

Youth Triumphant. Erected Armistice Day, 1924. Benches around the memorial create a whisper gallery; whispers on one side of oval can be easily heard on other side. City park.

Groton State Forest. This 25,625-acre area includes 3-mi-long Lake Groton (elevation 1,078 ft) and 6 other ponds. Miles of trails have been established to more remote sections of the forest. Nine developed recreation areas. Swimming, bathhouse, fishing, boating (rentals); nature trail, snowmobiling, picnicking, concession, 4 campgrounds (dump station), lean-tos. (Memorial Day-Columbus Day) Standard fees. 19 mi E on US 302, then N on VT 232, near Groton. Phone 802/584-3822.

Rock of Ages Quarry and Manufacturing Division. Skilled artisans creating monuments; picnic area. Visitor center (May-Oct, daily). Manufacturing Divison (all yr, Mon-Fri). 30-min quarry shuttle tour (June-Oct, Mon-Fri; fee). Exit 6 from I-89 or 2 mi S on VT 14, then 3½ mi SE on Main St, in Graniteville. Phone 802/476-3119. **FREE**

Annual Event

Old Time Fiddlers' Contest. Barre Auditorium. Phone 802/476-0256. Usually last wkend Sep.

Motels/Motor Lodges

★★ **DAYS INN OF BARRE.** *173 S Main St (05641). 802/476-6678; fax 802/476-6678; toll-free 800/329-7466.* 42 rms, 1-2 story. S $39-$70; D $49-$85; each addl $6; MAP avail; higher rates special events. Crib free. TV; cable (premium). Indoor pool; whirlpool. Restaurant 7-10 am, 5-9 pm. Bar 4:30 pm-midnight. Ck-out 11 am. Meeting rms. Business servs avail. X-country ski 8 mi. Refrigerators. Cr cds: A, C, D, DS, MC, V.

★★★ **HOLLOW INN AND HOTEL.** *278 S Main St (05641). 802/479-9313; fax 802/476-5242; toll-free 800/998-9444.* 26 motel rms, 15 inn rms, 2 story, 9 kits. Mid-Sep-late Oct: S, D (motel) $80-$85; S, D (inn) $91-$99; each addl $10; kit. units $80-$96; family, wkly rates; lower rates rest of yr. Crib free. Pet accepted. TV; cable (premium), VCR (movies $2.50). Heated pool; whirlpools. Coffee in rms. Complimentary continental bkfst. Ck-out 11 am. Meeting rm. Business servs avail. X-country ski 8 mi. Exercise equipt; sauna. Refrigerators. Some balconies. Picnic tables, grills. Cr cds: A, DS, MC, V.

B&Bs/Small Inns

★★ **GREEN TRAILS INN.** *Stone Rd (05036), 14 mi S on I-89, Exit 5, then E ½ mi to First Rd on R, then 5 mi S. 802/276-3412; toll-free 800/243-3412. www.greentrailsinn.com.* 10 rms, 3 story, 3 suites. D $79; suites $130; each addl $22. Parking lot. TV; cable, VCR avail, VCR avail. Complimentary full bkfst. Restaurant nearby. Bar. Ck-out 11 am, ck-in 3 pm. Meeting rms. Business center. Concierge. Golf. Tennis. Beach access. Hiking trail. Cr cds: DS, MC, V.

★★ **SHIRE INN.** *Main St (05038), approx 15 mi S on VT 110. 802/685-3031; fax 802/685-3871; toll-free 800/441-6908. Email jay@shireinn.com; www.shireinn.com.* 6 rms, 2 story. S

$140; D $145; each addl $25. Street parking. TV; cable, VCR avail, VCR avail. Restaurant 7-9 pm. Ck-out 11 am, ck-in 3 pm. Fax servs avail. Coin lndry. Exercise equipt. Golf. Downhill skiing. Bike rentals. Hiking trail. Picnic facilities. Cr cds: A, DS, MC, V.

Bellows Falls

(G-3) *See also Brattleboro, Springfield*

Settled 1753 **Pop** 3,313 **Elev** 299 ft
Area code 802 **Zip** 05101
Web www.virtualvermont.com/bellowsfalls.html

Information Chamber of Commerce, 34 The Square, PO Box 554; 802/463-4280

The first construction work on a US canal was started here in 1792. Later, nine locks raised barges, rafts, and small steamers over the falls. In 1983, a series of fish ladders extending 1,024 feet was constructed to restore Atlantic salmon and American shad to their migratory route up the Connecticut River. Power from the river helps make this an industrial town; wood products, paper, and wire cord are among the chief products. Ben & Jerry's ice cream has a nationwide distribution center here.

What to See and Do

Adams Gristmill. (1831) Former mill; museum contains early electrical equipment, implements used in paper manufacturing and farming. (By appt) End of Mill St. Phone 802/463-3706.

Green Mountain Railroad. Green Mountain Flyer offers scenic train rides through 3 river valleys. (Late June-Labor Day, Tues-Sun; mid-Sep-Columbus Day, daily) Depot St (at Amtrak station), ¼ mi N. Phone 802/463-3069. ¢¢¢

Native American Petroglyphs. Carvings on rocks, unique among Native American works, by members of an early American people; as early as 1,000 AD. On riverbanks near Vilas Bridge.

Rockingham Meetinghouse. (1787) Restored in 1907; Colonial architecture, antique glass windows; old burying ground with quaint epitaphs. (Mid-June-Labor Day, daily) 5 mi N on VT 103; 1 mi W of I-91 Exit 6 on Old Rockingham Rd in Rockingham. Phone 802/463-3964. ¢

Annual Event

Rockingham Old Home Days. Rockingham Meetinghouse. Celebrates founding of meetinghouse. Dancing, outdoor cafes, sidewalk sales, entertainment, fireworks; pilgrimage to meetinghouse on the last day. First wkend Aug.

Bennington

See also Arlington, Manchester and Manchester Center, Wilmington; also see Williamstown, MA

Settled 1761 **Pop** 16,451 **Elev** 681 ft
Area code 802 **Zip** 05201
Web www.bennington.com
Information Information Booth, Veterans Memorial Dr; 802/447-3311

Bennington was headquarters for Ethan Allen's Green Mountain Boys, known to New Yorkers as the "Bennington Mob," in Vermont's long struggle with New York. On August 16, 1777, this same "mob" won a decisive battle of the American Revolution. Bennington has three separate areas of historic significance: the Victorian and turn-of-the-century bldgs downtown; the Colonial houses, church, and commons in Old Bennington (1 mi W); and the three covered bridges in North Bennington.

What to See and Do

Bennington Battle Monument. A 306-ft monolith commemorates an American Revolution victory. Elevator to observation platform (mid-Apr-Oct, daily). Gift shop. 15 Monument Circle, in Old Bennington. Phone 802/447-0550. ¢

Bennington College. (1932) 450 students. Introduced progressive methods of education; became coeducational in 1969. The Visual and Performing Arts Center has special exhibits. Summer programs and performances. On VT 67A. Phone 802/442-5401.

Bennington Museum. Early Vermont and New England historical artifacts, incl American glass, paintings, sculpture, silver, furniture; Bennington pottery, Grandma Moses paintings, 1925 "Wasp" luxury touring car. Schoolhouse Museum contains Moses family memorabilia; Bennington flag; other American Revolution collections. (Daily; closed Thanksgiving, Dec 25) Genealogical library (by appt). 1 mi W on W Main St. Phone 802/447-1571. ¢¢

Long Trail. A path for hikers leading over the Green Mts to the Canadian border, crosses VT 9 approx 5 mi E of Bennington. A section of the trail is part of the Appalachian Trail.

Old First Church. (1805) Example of early Colonial architecture; original box pews, Asher Benjamin steeple. Guided tours. (Memorial Day-mid-Oct, daily) Monument Ave, in Old Bennington. Phone 802/447-1223. Adj is

Old Burying Ground. Buried here are poet Robert Frost and those who died in the Battle of Bennington.

Park-McCullough House Museum. (1865) A 35-rm Victorian mansion with period furnishings; stable with carriages; costume collection; Victorian gardens; child's playhouse. (Early May-Oct, daily) Special events held throughout the yr. N via VT 67A, in North Bennington. Phone 802/442-5441. ¢¢

Shaftsbury State Park. The 26-acre Lake Shaftsbury, a former millpond, is surrounded by 101 acres of forests and wetlands. Swimming, fishing, boating (rentals); nature and hiking trails, picnicking. (Memorial Day-Labor Day) Standard fees. 10½ mi N on US 7A, in Shaftsbury. Phone 802/375-9978 or 802/483-2001. ¢

Valley View Horses & Tack Shop, Inc. Full-service equestrian facility offers guided trail rides and horse rentals (by the hr). Also "Pony Express" pony rides at the stables for young riders. Western tack shop. (Daily) 9 mi S on US 7 at Northwest Hill Rd in Pownal. Phone 802/823-4649.

Woodford State Park. At 2,400 ft, this 400-acre park has the highest elevation of any park in the state. Swimming, fishing, boating (no motors; rentals); nature and hiking trails, picnicking, tent and trailer sites (dump station), lean-tos. (Memorial Day-Columbus Day) Standard fees. Approx 10 mi E on VT 9. Phone 802/447-7169 or 802/483-2001. ¢

Annual Events

Mayfest. Sat of Memorial Day wkend.
Antique and Classic Car Show. Second wkend after Labor Day.

Motels/Motor Lodges

★ **BENNINGTON MOTOR INN.** *143 W Main St (05201). 802/442-5479; toll-free 800/359-9900. Email zink@together.net; www.thisisvermont. com/pages/bennmotorinn.html.* 16 rms, 1-2 story. May-Oct: S $56-$80; D $58-$80; each addl $7; suites $68-$115; family rates; lower rates rest of yr. Crib $10. TV; cable. Restaurant adj 11 am-10 pm. Ck-out 11 am. Sundries. Downhill/x-country ski 10 mi. Some refrigerators. Balconies. Cr cds: A, DS, MC, V.
⊠ ⊠ 🔥

★★ **BEST WESTERN NEW ENGLANDER MOTOR INN.** *220 Northside Dr (05201). 802/442-6311; fax 802/442-6311; res 800/528-1234.* 52 rms, 2 story, 6 suites. June-Oct: S $110; D $120; suites $145; each addl $7; under 12 free; lower rates rest of yr. Crib avail. Parking lot. Pool. TV; cable. Complimentary continental bkfst, coffee in rms, toll-free calls. Restaurant noon-9 pm. Bar. Ck-out 11 am, ck-in 2 pm. Meeting rm. Business servs avail. Gift shop. Exercise privileges. Golf, 18 holes. Tennis, 2 courts. Picnic facilities. Cr cds: A, C, D, DS, MC, V.
🄳 ⊠ ⊠ ⊠ ⊠ ⊠ ⊠ ⊠ ⊠ ⊠

★ **CATAMOUNT MOTEL.** *500 South St (05201). 802/442-5977; fax 802/447-8765; toll-free 800/213-3608.* 17 rms, 1 story. Aug-Oct: S $79; D $92; each addl $8; lower rates rest of yr. Crib avail. Parking lot. Pool. TV; cable (premium). Complimentary coffee in rms, toll-free calls. Restaurant nearby. Ck-out 11 am, ck-in noon. Fax servs avail. Exercise privi-

leges. Golf. Downhill skiing. Picnic facilities. Cr cds: A, D, DS, MC, V.
⊠ ⊠ ⊠ ⊠ ⊠ 🔥

★★ **FIFE 'N DRUM.** *693 US 7 (05201), 1½ mi S on US 7. 802/442-4074; fax 802/442-8471. Email toberua@sover.net; www.sover.net/~toberua/.* 19 rms, 4 suites. June-Oct: S $92; D $98; suites $105; lower rates rest of yr. Crib avail. Pet accepted, some restrictions, fee. Parking lot. Pool, whirlpool. TV; cable (premium), VCR avail. Complimentary coffee in rms, toll-free calls. Restaurant nearby. Ck-out 11 am, ck-in 1 pm. Fax servs avail. Gift shop. Golf, 18 holes. Tennis, 10 courts. Downhill skiing. Picnic facilities. Cr cds: A, DS, MC, V.
⊠ ⊠ ⊠ ⊠ ⊠ ⊠ 🔥 SC

★ **GOVERNORS ROCK.** *4325 VT 7A (05262), 7 mi N on VT 7A and 6 mi S of Arlington on VT 7A. 802/442-4734; fax 802/719-0703. Email govrock1@sovor.net.* 9 rms, shower only. No rm phones. S $39-$54; D $45-$59; each addl $6; under 12 free. Closed Nov-Apr. TV; cable. Complimentary continental bkfst. Ck-out 10 am. Refrigerators. Picnic tables. Cr cds: MC, V.
⊠ ⊠ ⊠ ⊠ ⊠ 🔥

★ **IRON KETTLE.** *Rte 7A (05262), 6 mi N on VT 7A. 802/442-4316; fax 802/447-1604.* 20 rms. Aug-Oct: S, D $55-$65; each addl $5; lower rates rest of yr. Crib $5. TV. Pool. Complimentary coffee in rms. Ck-out 11 am. Coin lndry. Picnic tables. Cr cds: A, DS, MC, V.
⊠ ⊠ ⊠ ⊠ ⊠ ⊠ 🔥

★ **KNOTTY PINE.** *130 Northside Dr (05201). 802/442-5487; fax 802/442-2231. Email kpine@sover.net; www. bennington.com/knottypine.* 21 rms, 1 story. Sep-Oct: D $76; each addl $8; children $8; lower rates rest of yr. Crib avail. Parking lot. Pool. TV; cable (premium). Complimentary coffee in rms, toll-free calls. Restaurant nearby. Ck-out 11 am, ck-in 1 pm. Fax servs avail. Golf, 18 holes. Tennis, 4 courts. Cr cds: A, DS, MC, V.
⊠ ⊠ ⊠ ⊠ ⊠ 🔥

★★ **VERMONTER MOTOR LODGE.** *2964 West Rd (05201), 3 mi W on VT 9. 802/442-2529; fax 802/442-0879. Email sugarant@vermontel.net; www.*

sugarmapleinne.com. 31 air-cooled units, 18 motel rms, 13 cottages. June-Oct: S $53-$65; D $60-$72; each addl $10; cottages $50-$55; under 12 free; wkly rates; lower rates rest of yr. Crib $5. Pet accepted. TV; cable. Restaurant 7:30-11 am, 5-9 pm. Ck-out 11 am. Business servs avail. X-country ski 20 mi. Lawn games. Refrigerators avail. Picnic tables, grills. Swimming pond. Cr cds: A, DS, MC, V.

B&Bs/Small Inns

★★★ **FOUR CHIMNEYS INN.** *21 West Rd (05201), 1 mi W on VT 9. 802/447-3500; fax 802/447-3692; toll-free 800/649-3503. Email innkeeper@ fourchimneys.com; www.fourchimneys. com.* 9 rms, 3 story. June-Oct: S $115; D $155; each addl $15; children $15; lower rates rest of yr. Parking lot. TV; cable (premium). Complimentary continental bkfst, toll-free calls. Restaurant 6-9 pm, closed Mon. Bar. Ck-out 11 am, ck-in 2 pm. Meeting rms. Business servs avail. Golf, 18 holes. Tennis. Downhill skiing. Hiking trail. Cr cds: A, C, D, DS, MC, V.

★★★ **SOUTH SHIRE INN.** *124 Elm St (05201). 802/447-3839; fax 802/ 442-3547. Email sshire@sover.net; www.southshire.com.* 9 rms, 2 story. July-mid-Oct: S, D $105-$180; each addl $15; lower rates rest of yr. Children over 12 yrs only. TV in carriage house. Complimentary full bkfst. Ck-out 11 am, ck-in 3 pm. Business servs avail. X-country ski 8 mi. Many fireplaces; some in-rm whirlpools. Built 1850; mahogany-paneled library. Totally nonsmoking. Cr cds: A, DS, MC, V.

Cottage Colony

★ **SERENITY MOTEL.** *4379 VT 7A (05262), 7 mi N on VT 7A. 802/442-6490; fax 802/442-5493; toll-free 800/ 644-6490. Email serenity@sover.net; www.thisisvermont.com/pages/serenity. html.* Sep-Oct: S, D $60; each addl $5; under 14 free; lower rates rest of yr. Crib avail. Pet accepted. Parking lot. TV; cable. Complimentary coffee in rms, toll-free calls. Ck-out 10 am,

ck-in 2 pm. Fax servs avail. Picnic facilities. Cr cds: A, DS, MC, V.

Restaurants

★★ **BENNINGTON STATION.** *150 Depot St (05201), corner of River Depot sts. 802/447-1080.* Specializes in seafood, prime rib, turkey. Hrs: 11:30 am-10 pm; Sun 9:30 am-9 pm; early-bird dinner 4:30-6 pm; Sun brunch 11 am-2:30 pm. Res accepted. Bar. Lunch $4.95-$7; dinner $9.95-$16.95. Sun brunch $9.95. Child's menu. Old Railroad station (1898). Cr cds: A, C, D, DS, MC, V.

★★★ **FOUR CHIMNEYS.** *21 West Rd, VT 9. 802/447-3500. Email inn keeper@fourchimneys.com; www.four chimneys.com.* Specializes in salmon with herbs, rack of lamb. Own pastries. Hrs: 6-9 pm; Sun 5-8:30 pm. Closed Mon. Res accepted. Bar. Wine list. Dinner prix fixe: $33.50. Cr cds: A, C, D, DS, MC, V.

★★ **PUBLYK HOUSE.** *782 Harwood Hill (05201), 1½ mi N on VT 7A. 802/442-8301.* Specializes in steak, fresh seafood. Salad bar. Hrs: 11:30 am-10 pm. Closed Thanksgiving, Dec 24, 25. Bar. Lunch $9.95-$18.95; dinner $9.95-$18.95. Child's menu. In converted barn; fireplace. Cr cds: A, D, MC, V.

Brandon

(E-1) *See also Middlebury, Rutland*

Settled 1761 **Pop** 4,223 **Elev** 431 ft
Area code 802 **Zip** 05733
Web www.brandon.org
Information Brandon Area Chamber of Commerce, PO Box 267; 802/247-6401

Brandon is a resort and residential town located at the western edge of the Green Mountains. The first US electric motor was made in nearby Forestdale by Thomas Davenport.

What to See and Do

Branbury State Park. This 96-acre park has swimming, 1,000-ft sand beach, fishing, boating, sailing; nature and hiking trails, picnicking, concession, camping (dump station), lean-tos. (Memorial Day-Columbus Day) Standard fees. 3 mi NE on VT 73, then N on VT 53, E shore of Lake Dunmore. Phone 802/247-5925 or 802/483-2001.

Green Mountain National Forest. (see) E on VT 73.

Mount Independence. Wooded bluff on shore of Lake Champlain, part of American Revolution defense complex. Fort built in 1776 across from Fort Ticonderoga to house 12,000 troops and to protect colonies from northern invasion; evacuated in 1777. Least disturbed major American Revolution site in the country; 4 marked trails show ruins of fort complex. (Late May-early Oct, Wed-Sun) 16 mi W via VT 73 and 73A, in the town of Orwell. Phone 802/759-2412. **Donation**

Stephen A. Douglas Birthplace. Cottage where the "Little Giant" was born in 1813. Douglas attended Brandon Academy before moving to Illinois in 1833. (By appt) 2 Grove St on US 7. Phone 802/247-6401. **FREE**

B&Bs/Small Inns

★★★ **BLUEBERRY HILL INN.** *RR 3 (05733), 6 mi E on VT 73 to Goshen-Ripton Rd, then 4 mi N, follow signs. 802/247-6735; fax 802/247-3983; toll-free 800/448-0707. Email info@ blueberryhillinn.com; www.blueberry hillinn.com.* 12 rms, 1 story. Dec-Mar, June-Oct: S $130; D $200; under 12 free; lower rates rest of yr. Crib avail. Parking lot. TV; cable. Complimentary full bkfst, coffee in rms, toll-free calls. Restaurant. Ck-out noon, ck-in noon. Meeting rms. Business center. Gift shop. Sauna. Golf, 18 holes. Tennis, 2 courts. Downhill skiing. Bike rentals. Supervised children's activities. Hiking trail. Picnic facilities. Cr cds: A, JCB, MC, V.

🄳 🐾 ⊁ 🎿 🏇 🎿 ⛷ ⛷ 🏃

★★ **THE BRANDON INN.** *20 Park St (05733), on Village Green. 802/247-*

5766; fax 802/247-5768; toll-free 800/639-8685. www.brandoninn.com. 35 rms, 25 A/C, 3 story. S $60-$70; D $90-$100; suites $115-$190; mid-wk rates; ski plans; MAP avail; higher rates fall foliage season. Pool. Dining rm 8-9:30 am, 11:30 am-2 pm, 6-9 pm. Bar noon-midnight. Ck-out 11 am. Business servs avail. Downhill ski 20 mi; x-country ski 8 mi. Fireplace in lobby. Built in 1786. Cr cds: A, DS, MC, V.

🄳 🐾 ⊁ 🎿 ⛷ 🐾

★★★ **LILAC INN.** *53 Park St (05733). 802/247-5463; fax 802/247-5499; toll-free 800/221-0720. Email lilacinn@sover.net; www.lilacinn.com.* 9 rms, 2 story. Sep-Oct: S $100; D $200; each addl $30; under 18 free; lower rates rest of yr. Crib avail, fee. Parking lot. TV; cable (premium), VCR avail, CD avail. Complimentary full bkfst, coffee in rms, newspaper, toll-free calls. Restaurant 5:30-9 pm. Bar. Ck-out 11 am, ck-in 3 pm. Meeting rms. Business center. Concierge. Whirlpool. Golf, 18 holes. Tennis, 2 courts. Downhill skiing. Hiking trail. Cr cds: A, D, DS, MC, V.

🄳 🐾 ⊁ 🏇 🎿 🎿 🏃 ⛷ SC 🏃

★★ **MOFFETT HOUSE B & B.** *69 Park St (05733). 802/247-3843; toll-free 800/394-7239.* 5 rms, 3 story, 1 suite. May-Dec: S $70; D $80; suites $200; each addl $15; lower rates rest of yr. Crib avail. Pet accepted, fee. Parking lot. TV; cable, VCR avail, CD avail. Complimentary full bkfst, newspaper. Restaurant 5:30-8:30 pm. Ck-out 11 am, ck-in 2 pm. Meeting rm. Golf. Downhill skiing. Cr cds: MC, V.

🐾 ⊁ 🏇 🎿 ⛷ 🐾

Cottage Colony

★ **THE ADAMS MOTEL.** *1246 Franklin St (05733), 1 mi S. 802/247-6644; fax 802/247-6644; res 802/257-6644.* July-Aug, Oct: S $60; D $65; suites $75; each addl $7; children $7; lower rates rest of yr. Parking lot. Pool. TV; cable. Restaurant 5:30-8:30 pm. Bar. Ck-out 10:30 am, ck-in noon. Meeting rm. Business servs avail. Bellhops. Exercise privileges. Golf. Tennis, 2 courts. Downhill skiing. Supervised children's activities. Hiking trail. Cr cds: A, DS, MC, V.

🄳 🐾 ⊁ 🏇 🎿 🎿 ⛐ 🏃 🎿 🐾 🐾

Restaurant

★★ **LILAC INN.** *53 Park St 802/ 247-5463. Email lilacinn@sover.net; www.lilacinn.com.* Menu changes wkly. Hrs: 8 am-10 pm. Res accepted. Bar. Lunch $10.95-$21; dinner $10.95-$21. Cr cds: A, D, MC, V.

Brattleboro

(H-3) *See also Bellows Falls, Marlboro, Newfane, Wilmington; also see Greenfield, MA and Keene, NH*

Settled 1724 **Pop** 12,241 **Elev** 240 ft
Area code 802 **Zip** 05301
Web www.sover.net/~bratchmb/
Information Brattleboro Area Chamber of Commerce, 180 Main St; 802/254-4565

The first settlement in Vermont was at Fort Dummer (2 miles S) in 1724. Rudyard Kipling married a Brattleboro woman and lived here in the 1890s. Brattleboro is a resort area and an industrial town.

What to See and Do

Brattleboro Museum & Art Center. Exhibits change periodically and feature works by New England artists; history exhibits; permanent display of Estey organ collection; frequent performances and lecture programs. (Mid-May-Nov, Tues-Sun; closed hols) Canal & Bridge Sts. Union Railroad Station. Phone 802/257-0124. ¢

Creamery Bridge. (1879) One of Vermont's best-preserved covered bridges. Approx 2 mi W on VT 9.

Harlow's Sugar House. Observe working sugarhouse (Mar-mid-Apr). Maple exhibit and products. Pick your own fruit in season: strawberries, blueberries, apples; also cider in fall. (Daily; closed Dec 25, also Jan-mid-Feb) 3 mi N via I-91, Exit 4; on US 5 in Putney. Phone 802/387-5852. Sugar house **FREE**

Living Memorial Park. Swimming pool (mid-June-Labor Day); ball fields, lawn games, tennis courts, skiing (T-bar; Dec-early Mar), ice-skating (mid Nov-early-Mar). Picnicking, playground. Special events during summer. Fee for some activities. 2 mi W, just off VT 9. Phone 802/254-5808.

Santa's Land. Christmas theme village; visit with Santa, railroad ride, carousel. Petting zoo; gardens. Concessions. (Memorial Day wkend-Dec 24, daily; closed Thanksgiving) 12 mi N on US 5 or I-91, Exits 4 or 5 in Putney. Phone 802/387-5550. ¢¢

Annual Event

Winter Carnival. Wk-long festival includes ski races, parade, ice show, sleigh rides, road races. Feb.

Seasonal Event

Yellow Barn Music Festival. 10 mi N via I-91 or US 5 in Putney, behind the Public Library. Five-week chamber music festival. Students and well-known guest artists perform concerts. Also Special Performance Series, children's concerts. Phone 802/387-6637 or 800/639-3819. Tues, Fri, Sat eves, some Thurs, Sun, July-Aug.

Motel/Motor Lodge

★ **SUPER 8.** *1043 Putney Rd (05301), I-91, Exit 3 to VT 5, then ¼ mi S. 802/254-8889; fax 802/254-8323; res 800/800-8000.* 64 rms, 2 story. S $43-$47; D $48-$52; each addl $5-$7; under 12 free. Crib free. TV; cable, VCR avail (movies). Complimentary coffee in lobby. Restaurant adj. Ck-out 11 am. Cr cds: A, D, DS, MC, V.

Hotels

★★ **LATCHIS HOTEL.** *50 Main St (05301). 802/254-6300; fax 802/254-6304. www.brattleborough.com/latchis.* 30 rms, 4 story, 3 suites. June-Oct: S $75; D $152; suites $175; each addl $10; under 12 free; lower rates rest of yr. Crib avail. Parking lot. TV; cable. Complimentary continental bkfst, coffee in rms, toll-free calls. Restaurant noon-5:30 pm. Bar. Ck-out 11 am, ck-in 2 pm. Business servs avail. Golf, 18 holes. Tennis, 8 courts. Downhill skiing. Bike rentals. Hiking trail. Cr cds: A, MC, V.

★★ QUALITY INN AND SUITES.
1380 Putney Rd (05301), off I-91 Exit 3. 802/254-8701; fax 802/257-4727; toll-free 800/228-5151. *www.quality innbrattleboro.com.* 92 rms, 2 story. June-Oct: S, D $89-$109; each addl $10; under 18 free; lower rates rest of yr. Crib free. Pet accepted. TV; cable. 2 pools, 1 indoor; whirlpool, sauna. Complimentary full bkfst. Restaurant 6:30-10:30 am, 5-9:30 pm. Bar 4:30-11:30 pm. Ck-out 11 am. Meeting rms. Business servs avail. In-rm modem link. Cr cds: A, DS, MC, V.

D ⊠ ⊠ ⊠ ⊠ SC

Restaurants

★ JOLLY BUTCHER'S. *254 Marlboro Rd (05303), 3 mi W on VT 9, 2½ mi W of I-91 Exit 2.* 802/254-6043. Email jbutcher@together.net. Specializes in steak, fresh seafood. Salad bar. Hrs: 11:30 am-9 pm. Closed Thanksgiving, Dec 25. Bar. Lunch $3.25-$7.95; dinner $7.95-$18.95. Child's menu. Open hearth. Lobster tank. Cr cds: A, DS, MC, V.

D

★ MARINA. *28 Spring Tree Rd (05301), Putney Rd.* 802/257-7563. Specializes in fresh seafood. Hrs: 11 am-10 pm. Bar. Lunch $3.50-$6.75; dinner $6.75-$16.50. Child's menu. Entertainment: Sun. Patio dining. Overlooks West River. Cr cds: A, MC, V.

D ⊟

★★ THE PUTNEY INN. *Depot Rd (05346).* 802/387-5517. *www.putney inn.com.* Specializes in turkey dinner. Hrs: 8 am-8:30 pm. Res accepted. Wine, beer. Lunch $9-$14; dinner $18-$24. Child's menu. Entertainment. Cr cds: A, DS, MC, V.

D ⊠ SC

Burlington

(C-1) *See also Shelburne*

Settled 1773 **Pop** 39,127 **Elev** 113 ft
Area code 802 **Zip** 05401
Web www.vermont.org

Information Lake Champlain Regional Chamber of Commerce, 60 Main St, Suite 100; 802/863-3489

Burlington, on Lake Champlain, is the largest city in Vermont. It is the site of the oldest university and the oldest daily newspaper (1848) in the state, the burial place of Ethan Allen, and the birthplace of philosopher John Dewey. It has a diversity of industries. The lakefront area offers a park, dock, and restaurants.

What to See and Do

Battery Park. View of Lake Champlain and Adirondacks. Guns here drove back British warships in War of 1812. VT 127 & Pearl St.

Bolton Valley Holiday Resort. Resort has quad, 4 double chairlifts, surface lift; school, patrol, rentals, snowmaking; cafeteria, restaurants, bar, nursery; 43 runs, longest run over 3 mi; vertical drop 1,600 ft. (Nov-Apr, daily) Sixty-two mi of cross-country trails. Also summer activities. 20 mi E on Bolton Valley Access Rd, off US 2 in Bolton; I-89 exits 10, 11. Phone 802/434-3444. ¢¢¢¢

Burlington Ferry. Makes 1-hr trips across Lake Champlain to Port Kent, NY (mid-May-mid-Oct, daily). Refreshments. Leaves King St Dock. Phone 802/864-9804. ¢¢¢-¢¢¢¢

Church Street Marketplace. Four traffic-free blocks, from the Unitarian Church designed in 1815 by Peter Banner to City Hall at the corner of Main St. Buildings are a mix of Art Deco and 19th-century architectural styles and house more than 100 shops, restaurants, galleries, and cafes. The bricked promenade is spotted with vendors and street entertainers.

◪ **Ethan Allen Homestead.** Allen's preserved pioneer homestead; re-created hayfield and kitchen gardens, 1787 farmhouse. One-hr guided tours; museum exhibits; audiovisual presentation. (Early May-late Oct, Tues-Sun; also Mon in summer) 2 mi N off VT 127. Phone 802/865-4556. ¢¢

Ethan Allen Park. Part of Ethan Allen's farm. Ethan Allen Tower (Memorial Day-Labor Day, Wed-Sun afternoons and eves) with view of Adirondacks and Lake Champlain to the west, Green Mts to the east. Pic-

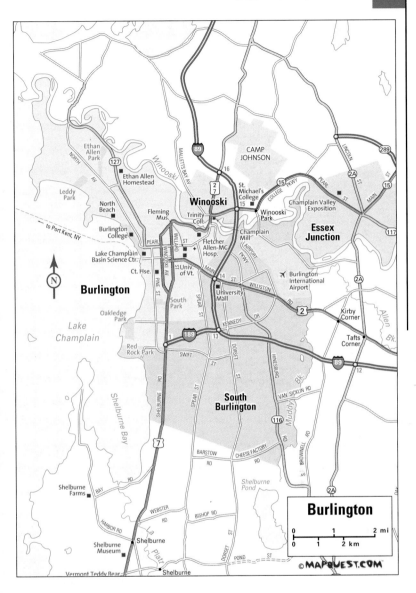

Burlington

nicking. 2½ mi N on North Ave to Ethan Allen Pkwy. **FREE**

Excursion Cruises. *Spirit of Ethan Allen II*, replica of a vintage stern-wheeler and Lake Champlain's largest excursion vessel, offers sight-seeing sunset, moonlight, brunch, and dinner cruises on Lake Champlain; both decks enclosed and heated. Res required for dinner cruises. (June-Oct) Burlington Boathouse, College St. Phone 802/862-8300.

Green Mountain Audubon Nature Center. Center has 230 acres with trails through many Vermont habitats, incl beaver ponds, hemlock swamp, brook, river, marsh, old farm fields, woodland, and sugar orchard. Educational nature center with classes, interpretive programs, and special projects. Open all yr for hiking, snowshoeing, and cross-country skiing. Grounds, office (hrs vary). Fee for some activities. 20 mi SE via I-89, Richmond Exit, in Huntington near the Huntington-Richmond line. Phone 802/434-3068. Adj is

The Birds of Vermont Museum. Displays carvings of 200 species of local birds; also offers nature trails, recorded bird songs. (May-Oct, Mon, Wed-Sun) Phone 802/434-2167. ¢¢

Lake Champlain Basin Science Center. Hands-on activities; live animals native to Lake Champlain incl fish, snakes, turtles, frogs. Connected to University of Vermont Research Lab. (Tours mid-June-Labor Day, daily; Sep-mid-June, wkends) 1 College St. Phone 802/864-1848. ¢¢

Sherman Hollow Cross-Country Skiing Center. Area has 25 mi of groomed, one-way, double-tracked cross-country ski trails; more than 3 mi of lighted trails for night skiing; warming hut; rentals; restaurant. (Dec-Apr) 10 mi SE on I-89 to Exit 11, then E on US 2, then S on Huntington Rd to Sherman Hollow Rd, then W. Phone 802/434-4553. ¢¢¢

St. Michael's College. (1904) 1,700 students. Chapel of St. Michael the Archangel (daily). Also professional summer theater at St. Michael's Playhouse. N via I-89 to Exit 15, then ¼ mi NE on VT 15, in Winooski-Colchester. Phone 802/654-2000 or 802/654-2535.

University of Vermont. (1791) 10,000 students. Fifth-oldest university in New England. Graduate and undergraduate programs. On campus are the **Billings Center**, of architectural significance; **Bailey-Howe Library**, largest in the state; Georgian design **Ira Allen Chapel**, named for the founder; and the **Old Mill**, classroom bldg with cornerstone laid by General Lafayette in 1825. Waterman Building, S Prospect St. Phone 802/656-3480. Also here is

Robert Hull Fleming Museum. American, European, African, pre-Columbian, and Oriental art; changing exhibits. (Limited hrs) Colchester Ave. Phone 802/656-0750. **Donation**

Annual Events

Discover Jazz Festival. A jazz extravaganza with over 150 live performances taking place in city parks, clubs, and restaurants. Phone 802/863-7992. Ten days early June.

Lake Champlain Balloon and Craft Festival. Champlain Valley Exposition. Balloon launches, rides, crafts, food, and entertainment. Three days June.

Seasonal Events

St. Michael's Playhouse. McCarthy Arts Center, St. Michael's College. Summer theater. Professional actors perform 4 plays (2 wks each). Phone 802/654-2535. Tues-Sat, late June-late Aug.

Vermont Mozart Festival. Features 18 chamber concerts in picturesque Vermont settings, incl the Trapp Family Meadow, Lake Champlain ferries, Basin Harbor Club in Vergennes, Waitsfield Round Barn, and Shelburne Farms on Lake Champlain. Phone 802/862-7352. Mid-July-early Aug.

Motels/Motor Lodges

★★ **COMFORT INN.** *1285 Williston Rd (05403), ½ mi E of I-89 on US 2, near Intl Airport.* 802/865-3400; fax 802/865-3400; toll-free 800/228-5150. 105 rms, 3 story. May-Labor Day: S $65-$95; D $74-$109; suites $89-$119; each addl $10; under 18 free; wkend rates; ski plans; higher rates fall foliage season. Crib free. TV; cable (premium). Pool. Complimentary continental bkfst. Restaurant adj 11 am-10 pm. Ck-out noon. Meeting rms. Business servs avail. In-rm modem link. Valet serv. Downhill ski 15 mi; x-country ski 5 mi. Exercise equipt. Some refrigerators. Cr cds: A, DS, MC, V.

★ **HO-HUM MOTEL.** *1660 Williston Rd (05403), 3 mi E on US 2, 1 mi E of I-89 Exit 14E.* 802/863-4551; fax 802/878-8119; toll-free 800/228-7031. 36 rms. Early June-late Oct: S $50-$70; D $65-$80; lower rates rest of yr. Crib free. TV; cable. Pool. Restaurant 7 am-11 pm. Ck-out 11 am. Free airport transportation. Cr cds: A, DS, MC, V.

★★ **HOLIDAY INN.** *1068 Williston Rd (05403), 1½ mi E on US 2, at I-89 Exit 14E.* 802/863-6363; fax 802/863-3061; res 800/holiday; toll-free 800/799-6363. Email holiday@together.net. 174 rms, 4 story. May-Oct: S, D $85-$139; under 19 free; lower rates rest of yr. Crib free. Pet accepted. TV;

cable. 2 pools, 1 indoor; whirlpool. Coffee in rms. Restaurant 6 am-10 pm. Rm serv. Bar noon-2 am, Sat to 1 am, Sun to 10 pm; entertainment Thurs-Sat. Ck-out noon. Meeting rm. Business servs avail. In-rm modem link. Bellhops. Sundries. Free airport transportation. Exercise equipt. Cr cds: A, C, DS, JCB, MC, V.

★ **HOWARD JOHNSON HOTEL.** *1720 Shelburne Rd (05403), 3 mi S on US 7. 802/860-6000; fax 802/864-9919; res 800/874-1554.* 121 rms, 3 story. Mid-June-Labor Day: S, D $80-$120; each addl $10; under 18 free; wkend rates; ski plans; higher rates: college graduation, fall foliage; lower rates rest of yr. Crib free. TV. Indoor pool; whirlpool. Restaurant 6:30-9:30 am, 4:30-9:30 pm. Bar 4 pm-1 am. Ck-out noon. Coin lndry. Meeting rms. Business servs avail. In-rm modem link. Free airport transportation. Downhill ski 20 mi; x-country ski 8 mi. Exercise equipt; sauna. Cr cds: A, C, D, DS, MC, V.

★★ **RESIDENCE INN.** *35 Hurricane Ln (05495), jct I-89 Exit 12 and VT 2A. 802/878-2001; fax 802/878-0025; res 800/331-3131.* 96 kit suites, 2 story. S, D $89-$149; wkly rates; higher rates: graduation, fall foliage. Crib free. Pet accepted. TV; cable (premium). Indoor pool; whirlpool. Playground. Complimentary continental bkfst. Ck-out noon. Coin lndry. Meeting rms. Business servs avail. In-rm modem link. Valet serv. Free airport transportation. Downhill/x-country ski 15 mi. Exercise equipt. Many fireplaces. Balconies. Cr cds: A, D, DS, MC, V.

Hotels

★★ **BEST WESTERN.** *1076 Williston Rd (05403). 802/863-1125; fax 802/658-1296; res 800/528-1234; toll-free 800/371-1125. www.bestwestern. com/windjammerinn.* 177 rms, 2 story. Late-June-mid-Sep: S $70-$110; D $80-$110; each addl $5; suites $80-$109; under 18 free; higher rates fall foliage; lower rates rest of yr. Crib free. Pet accepted; $5. TV; cable (premium). Pool; whirlpool. Complimen-

tary continental bkfst. Restaurant 11:30 am-2:30 pm, 5-10 pm; Sun 10 am-2:30, 4-9 pm. Ck-out 11 am. Coin lndry. Meeting rms. Business servs avail. Free airport transportation. Exercise equipt; sauna. Nature trail. Cr cds: DS, MC, V.

★★ **CLARION HOTEL AND CONFERENCE CENTER.** *1117 Williston Rd (05403), 2 mi E on US 2, I-89 Exit 14E. 802/658-0250; fax 802/660-7516; res 800/CLARION; toll-free 800/272-6232. Email clarion@clarionvermont. com; www.clarionvermont.com.* 130 rms, 2 story. S $60-$110; D $70-$115; each addl $5; under 18 free; higher rates fall foliage season. Crib free. TV; cable, VCR avail (movies). Pool; wading pool. Coffee in rms. Restaurant 6:30 am-10 pm. Rm serv to 9:30 pm. Bar 11-1 am; Sun to 11 pm. Ck-out noon. Meeting rms. Business servs avail. In-rm modem link. Sundries. Free airport transportation. Downhill ski 20 mi; x-country ski 6 mi. Exercise equipt. Cr cds: A, MC, V.

★★ **DAYS INN.** *23 College Pkwy (05446), N on I-89, Exit 15. 802/655-0900; fax 802/655-6851; res 800/329-7466. www.daysinn.com.* 73 rms, 3 story, 12 suites. May-Oct: S $95; D $100; suites $129; each addl $5; under 17 free; lower rates rest of yr. Crib avail. Pet accepted, fee. Parking lot. Indoor pool. TV; cable (premium), VCR avail. Complimentary continental bkfst, newspaper. Restaurant. Ck-out 11 am, ck-in 3 pm. Meeting rm. Business servs avail. Coin lndry. Exercise privileges. Golf. Tennis. Downhill skiing. Hiking trail. Cr cds: A, C, D, DS, ER, JCB, MC, V.

★★ **HAMPTON INN.** *42 Lower Mountain View Dr (05446), N on I-89 Exit 16. 802/655-6177; fax 802/655-4962; toll-free 800/426-7866. Email hamptonll@aol.com; www. hampton-inn.com.* 176 rms, 5 story, 12 suites. Aug-Oct: S $99; D $109; suites $140; lower rates rest of yr. Crib avail. Pet accepted. Parking lot. Indoor pool, whirlpool. TV; cable (DSS), VCR avail. Complimentary continental bkfst, coffee in rms, newspaper, toll-free calls. Restaurant 11:30 am-midnight. Bar. Ck-out 11 am, ck-in 3 pm. Meeting rms. Business center. Dry cleaning, coin lndry. Gift shop. Free airport transportation. Exercise equipt. Golf. Downhill skiing. Video games. Cr cds: A, C, D, DS, ER, JCB, MC, V.

D ⊕ ⚡ 🔧 🏊 🏃 🏃 🏊 SC 🏃

★★★ **INN AT ESSEX.** *70 Essex Way (05452), I-89 Exit 12, then N on VT 2A to VT 15E. 802/878-1100; fax 802/878-0063; toll-free 800/727-4295. Email innfo@innatessex.com; www.inn atessex.com.* 90 rms, 3 story, 30 suites. May-Oct: S, D $175; suites $209; each addl $15; under 12 free; lower rates rest of yr. Crib avail. Parking lot. Pool, lap pool. TV; cable (DSS), VCR avail, CD avail. Complimentary continental bkfst, coffee in rms, newspaper, toll-free calls. Restaurant 6 am-10 pm. 24-hr rm serv. Bar. Ck-out 11 am, ck-in 3 pm. Meeting rms. Business center. Bellhops. Concierge. Dry cleaning. Gift shop. Free airport transportation. Exercise privileges. Golf. Tennis, 10 courts. Downhill skiing. Bike rentals. Hiking trail. Video games. Cr cds: A, C, D, DS, MC, V.

D 🏊 🔧 🏃 🏊 🏃 🏃 🏊 🏃

★★★ **RADISSON.** *60 Battery St (05401). 802/658-6500; fax 802/658-4659; res 800/333-3333. Email Radisson@together.net.* 255 rms. S, D $110-$179; each addl $10; suites $150-$450; under 18 free; higher rates: fall foliage, special events. Crib free. TV; cable (premium). Indoor pool; whirlpool. Coffee in rms. Restaurants 6:30 am-10 pm. Bar; comedy show Fri, Sat. Ck-out noon. Meeting rms. Business servs avail. Concierge. Gift shop. Free garage parking. Free airport transportation. Exercise equipt. View of lake. Luxury level. Cr cds: A, D, DS, MC, V.

D 🏊 🏊 🏃 🏊 🏃 🏃

All Suites

★★ **HOLIDAY INN EXPRESS HOTEL & SUITES.** *1712 Shelburne Rd (05403), 3 mi S on US 7. 802/860-1112; fax 802/860-1112; res 800/465-4329; toll-free 800/874-1554. Email hievermont@aol.com; www.innvermont. com.* 6 rms, 4 story, 78 suites. Aug-Oct: S, D $195; suites $195; each addl $10; under 17 free; lower rates rest of yr. Crib avail. Parking lot. Indoor pool, whirlpool. TV; cable (premium). Complimentary conti-

nental bkfst, coffee in rms, newspaper, toll-free calls. Restaurant 11 am-10 pm, closed Sun. Bar. Ck-out noon, ck-in 2 pm. Meeting rms. Business center. Dry cleaning, coin lndry. Free airport transportation. Exercise privileges, sauna. Golf, 18 holes. Tennis, 4 courts. Downhill skiing. Hiking trail. Picnic facilities. Cr cds: A, C, D, DS, MC, V.

D ⚡ 🔧 🏃 🏊 🏃 🏃 🏊 🏃 SC 🏃

★★ **WILSON INN.** *10 Kellogg Rd (05452), 5 mi N on I-89 Exit 16, N on VT 7 to Severance Rd to Kellogg Rd. 802/879-1515; fax 802/764-5149; toll-free 800/521-2334. Email wilsonin@ together.net; www.wilsoninn.com.* 32 kit. suites, 3 story. No elvtr. S, D $74-$94, higher rates some wkends. Crib free. TV; cable (premium), VCR avail. Heated pool. Playground. Complimentary bkfst buffet. Complimentary coffee in rms. Ck-out 11 am. Coin lndry. Meeting rm. Business servs avail. In-rm modem link. Downhill ski 15 mi; x-country ski 8 mi. Health club privileges. Game rm. Lawn games. Microwaves. Cr cds: A, DS, MC, V.

Conference Center

★★★ **SHERATON HOTEL AND CONFERENCE CENTER.** *870 Williston Rd (05401), 1½ mi E on US 2, at I-89 Exit 14W, near Intl Airport. 802/865-6600; fax 802/865-6670; toll-free 800/677-6576. Email sheraton_ vermont@ittsheraton.com; www.shera-ton.com.* 309 rms, 4 story, 8 suites. July-Oct: S $152; lower rates rest of yr. Crib avail. Pet accepted, some restrictions. Parking lot. Indoor pool, lifeguard, whirlpool. TV; cable (premium). Complimentary coffee in rms, newspaper. Restaurant. Bar. Conference center, meeting rms. Business center. Bellhops. Concierge. Dry cleaning. Gift shop. Free airport transportation. Exercise rm. Golf, 18 holes. Tennis. Video games. Cr cds: A, C, D, DS, ER, JCB, MC, V.

D ⊕ 🔧 🏃 🏊 🏃 ✈ 🏊 🏃 🏃

Restaurants

★ **CARBUR'S.** *115 St. Paul St (05401). 802/862-4106.* Specializes in sandwiches. Hrs: 11 am-10 pm. Closed Thanksgiving, Dec 25. Bar. Lunch $5-$10; dinner $7-$15. Child's menu. Rustic decor, many antiques. Cr cds: A, DS, MC, V.

D SC

★ **DAILY PLANET.** *15 Center St (05401). 802/862-9647.* Specializes in rack of lamb, potato-crusted salmon, Thai pork loin chop. Hrs: 4-11 pm; Fri, Sat to midnight. Closed some major hols. Res accepted. Bar. Dinner $6.75-$14.95. European-style cafe. Frequent art exhibits. Cr cds: A, D, MC, V.

D

★★ **ICE HOUSE.** *171 Battery St (05401). 802/864-1800.* Specializes in fresh seafood, steak. Own desserts. Hrs: 11:30 am-10 pm; Sun from 11 am; early-bird dinner 5-6 pm. Res accepted. Lunch $4.95-$9.95; dinner $12.95-$20.95. Sun brunch $5.75-$8.95. Child's menu. Parking. Converted icehouse. Waterfront view. Cr cds: A, D, DS, MC, V.

★★★ **PAULINE'S.** *1834 Shelburne Rd (05401), US 7. 802/862-1081.* Specializes in fresh seafood, local products. Own baking. Hrs: 11:30 am-2 pm, 5-9:30 pm; early-bird dinner 5-6:30 pm. Closed Dec 24, 25. Res accepted. Bar. Wine list. Lunch $6.95-$8.95; dinner $14.95-$22.95. Sun brunch $5.95-$9.95. Child's menu. Parking. Cherry, oak paneling; lace curtains; some antiques. Cr cds: A, D, DS, MC, V.

D

★★ **PERRY'S FISH HOUSE.** *1080 Shelburne Rd (05403), 2½ mi S on US 7. 802/865-3908. Email fishhouse@ juno.com.* Specializes in fresh seafood, prime rib. Salad bar. Hrs: 5-10 pm; Fri, Sat 4:30-10:30 pm; Sun 10 am-9:30 pm; early-bird dinner 5-6 pm. Closed Thanksgiving, Dec 25. Res accepted. Bar. Dinner $9.95-$19.95. Child's menu. Parking. Nautical decor; lobster tank. Cr cds: A, D, DS, MC, V.

D

★★ **SIRLOIN SALOON.** *1912 Shelburne Rd (05401), 4 mi S on US 7. 802/985-2200.* Specializes in wood-grilled steak, chicken, fresh seafood. Salad bar. Hrs: 4:30-10: pm; Fri to 11 pm; Sat 4-11 pm; Sun 4-10 pm. Closed Thanksgiving, Dec 25. Res

accepted. Bar. Dinner $9.95-$18.95. Child's menu. Parking. Greenhouse dining. Open hearth. Native Amer artwork, artifacts. Cr cds: A, C, D, DS, MC, V.

D

★★ **SWEETWATERS.** *120 Church St (05401). 802/864-9800. Email swi@ middlebury.net; www.sweetwatersbistro. com.* Specializes in salads, bison burgers, char-grilled fish. Own desserts. Hrs: 11:30-1 am. Closed Thanksgiving, Dec 25. Res accepted. Bar. Lunch a la carte entrees: $4.95-$9.95; dinner a la carte entrees: $7.95-$19.95. Sun brunch $7.95-$9.95. Child's menu. Entertainment: Thurs, Fri. Converted bank bldg (1882). Cr cds: A, D, DS, MC, V.

D

Charlotte

(see Shelburne)

Chester

(see Springfield)

Dorset

(G-I) See also Manchester and Manchester Center, Peru

Settled 1768 **Pop** 1,918 **Elev** 962 ft **Area code** 802 **Zip** 05251

This charming village is surrounded by hills 3,000 feet high. In 1776 the Green Mountain Boys voted for Vermont's independence here. The first marble quarry in the country was opened in 1785 on nearby Mount Aeolus.

Seasonal Event

Dorset Theatre Festival. Cheney Rd. Professional theater company presents 5 productions. Phone 802/867-5777. May-Labor Day.

B&Bs/Small Inns

★★ **BARROWS HOUSE INN.** *3156 VT 30 (05251), 1 blk S on VT 30. 802/867-4455; fax 802/867-0132; toll-free 800/639-1620. Email innkeepers@ barrowshouse.com; www.barrowshouse. com.* 28 rms in 9 houses, inn, 3 kits. No rm phones. June-Oct, MAP: S $125-$190; D $185-$235; each addl $30-$50; EP avail; lower rates rest of yr. Crib free. Pet accepted. TV in some rms; VCR avail. Heated pool; sauna, poolside serv. Restaurant (see also BARROWS HOUSE INN). Bar 5-11 pm. Ck-out 11 am, ck-in early afternoon. Bus depot transportation. Meeting rm. Business servs avail. Tennis. Downhill ski 12 mi; x-country ski 6 mi. Bicycles. Lawn games. Game rm. Some refrigerators, fireplaces. Private patios. Picnic tables. Library. Antiques. Gardens. Built in 1804. Cr cds: A, DS, MC, V.

★★★ **DORSET INN.** *Rte 30 (05251), center of town. 802/867-5500; fax 802/867-5542; res 802/867-5500; toll-free 800/835-5284. Email dorset inn@vermontel.net; www.dorsetinn.com.* 31 rms, 29 A/C, 3 story. No rm phones. S, D $75-$100. Adults only. TV in lounge. Restaurant (see also DORSET INN). Bar 4 pm-midnight. Ck-out 11 am, ck-in 2 pm. Antique furnishings. Established in 1796; oldest continuously operating inn in Vermont. Cr cds: A, DS, MC, V.

★★★ **INN AT WEST VIEW FARM.** *Rte 30 (05251), ½ mi S on VT 30. 802/ 867-5715; fax 802/867-0468; toll-free 800/769-4903. Email stay@westview farm.com; www.innatwestviewfarm. com.* 9 rms, 2 story, 1 suite. Sep-Oct: S $150; D $160; suites $180; each addl $20; lower rates rest of yr. Parking lot. TV; cable, VCR avail, CD avail. Complimentary full bkfst, toll-free calls. Restaurant 6-9:30 pm. Bar. Ck-out 11 am, ck-in 3 pm. Golf. Tennis. Downhill skiing. Cr cds: A, MC, V.

Restaurants

★★★ **BARROWS HOUSE INN.** *VT 30. 802/867-4455. Email innkeepers@ barrowhouse.com; www.barrows.com.* Specializes in crab cakes, fresh fish,

fresh vegetables. Own desserts. Hrs: 8-9:30 am, 6-9 pm. Res accepted. Bar. Bkfst a la carte entrees: $8.50; dinner a la carte entrees: $10.95-$25.95. Child's menu. Parking. Greenhouse dining. Cr cds: A, D, DS, MC, V.

★★★ **DORSET INN.** *Church and Main Sts. 802/867-5500. Email dorset@vermontel.net; www.dorsetinn. com.* Specializes in rack of lamb, fresh fish, crispy duck confit. Own baking. Hrs: 7:30-10 am, 5-9 pm. Res recommended. Bar. Wine list. Bkfst $7.50; dinner $12.50-$22. Historic bldg (1796). Colonial decor. Cr cds: A, MC, V.

★★ **INN AT WESTVIEW FARM.** *VT 30. 802/867-5715. Email west view@vermontel.com; www.vtweb. com/innatwestviewfarm.* Specializes in rack of lamb a l'auberge, breast of duck. Own desserts. Hrs: 6-9:30 pm. Closed Tues; also Apr; 1st 2 wks Nov. Bar. Dinner a la carte entrees: $15-$25. In converted 1850 farmhouse. Cr cds: MC, V.

Fairlee

(E-3) *See also White River Junction*

Pop 883 **Elev** 436 ft **Area code** 802 **Zip** 05045
Information Town Offices, Main St, PO Box 95; 802/333-4363

Annual Events

Vermont State Open Golf Tournament. Lake Morey Inn Country Club (see RESORT). Mid-June.

Chicken Barbecue. On the Common, Main St. Phone 802/333-4363. July 4.

Resort

★★ **LAKE MOREY INN.** *Club House Rd (05045), 1 mi W of I-91 on Lake Morey Rd. 802/333-4311; fax 802/333-4553; toll-free 800/423-1211.* 144 rms, 3 story, 22 cottages. MAP, mid-May-Oct: S, D $93-$127/person; each addl $20-$55; cottages (mid-May-mid-Oct only) $80-$99; golf, ski packages; lower rates rest of yr. Crib $10. TV. Indoor/outdoor pool; whirlpool.

Supervised children's activities; ages 3-12. Dining rm (public by res) 7:30-9:30 am, 6:30-9:30 pm. Bar 4-11 pm. Ck-out 11 am, ck-in 2 pm. Business servs avail. In-rm modem link. Bellhops. Two tennis courts. 18-hole golf, greens fee, pro, putting green, driving range. Beach; swimming. Canoes, rowboats. Waterskiing. Windsurfing. Downhill ski 15 mi; x-country ski on site, rentals. Snowmobile trails, sleigh rides, tobogganing. Hiking. Lawn games. Rec rm. Game rm. Exercise equipt; sauna. Refrigerators avail. Balconies. Cr cds: MC, V.

D 🐾 ⛷ 🏊 🎿 ⛷ 🏄 🔥

B&B/Small Inn

★ **SILVER MAPLE LODGE COTTAGES.** *520 US 5 S (05045). 802/333-4326; toll-free 800/666-1946. Email scott@silvermaplelodge.com; www.silvermaplelodge.com.* 15 rms, 2 story. S $69; D $79; each addl $6. Pet accepted, some restrictions. Parking lot. TV; cable, VCR avail, CD avail. Complimentary continental bkfst. Restaurant nearby. Ck-out 11 am, ck-in 2 pm. Concierge. Golf, 18 holes. Tennis. Downhill skiing. Beach access. Bike rentals. Hiking trail. Cr cds: A, DS, MC, V.

🐾 🏊 🎿 ⛷ 🔥

Grafton

See also Bellows Falls, Londonderry, Newfane

Pop 602 **Elev** 841 ft **Area code** 802
Zip 05146
Web www.virtualvermont.com/chamber/greatfallscc/

Information Great Falls Regional Chamber of Commerce, 34 The Square, PO Box 554, Bellows Falls 05101; 802/463-4280

This picturesque New England village is a blend of houses, churches, galleries, antique shops, and other small shops—all circa 1800. Founded in pre-Revolutionary times under the patronage of George III, Grafton became a thriving mill town and modest industrial center after the damming of the nearby Saxton River.

When water power gave way to steam, the town began to decline. Rescued, revived, and restored by the Windham Foundation, it has been returned to its former attractiveness. A creek curling through town and the peaceful air of a gentler era contribute to the charm of this village, considered a paradise for photographers.

What to See and Do

Grafton Ponds Cross-Country Skiing Center. Featuring over 16 mi of groomed trails; school, rentals; concession, warming hut. (Dec-Mar, daily; closed Dec 25) In summer, walking and fitness trails (no fee). Townshend Rd. ¢¢¢

The Old Tavern at Grafton. (1801) Centerpiece of village. Visited by many famous guests over the yrs, incl several presidents and authors; names inscribed over the desk. Furnished with antiques, Colonial decor. Former barn converted to lounge; annex is restored from 2 houses; dining by res. (May-Mar, daily; closed Dec 24, 25) Main St & Townshend Rd. Phone 802/843-2231.

B&Bs/Small Inns

★★ **INN AT WOODCHUCK HILL FARM.** *Woodchuck Hill Rd (05146), 2 mi W of VT 35. 802/843-2398. Email info@woodchuckhill.com; www. woodchuckhill.com.* 5 rms, 3 story, 6 suites. S, D $120; suites $140; each addl $25. Crib avail. Parking lot. Pool. TV; cable, VCR avail, CD avail. Complimentary full bkfst, coffee in rms. Restaurant nearby. Bar. Ck-out 11 am, ck-in 1 pm. Golf, 18 holes. Tennis, 2 courts. Downhill skiing. Hiking trail. Picnic facilities. Cr cds: A, DS, MC, V.

🏊 🎿 ⛷ 🏄 ✈ 🔥

★★★ **OLD TAVERN AT GRAFTON.** *92 Main St (05146), VT 121. 802/843-2231; fax 802/843-2245; toll-free 800/843-1801. Email tavern@sover.net; www.old-tavern.com.* 51 rms, 7 suites. July-Oct, Dec: S, D $195; suites $295; lower rates rest of yr. Crib avail, fee. Parking lot. Pool. TV; cable, VCR avail. Complimentary full bkfst, newspaper, toll-free calls. Restaurant 8 am-9 pm. Bar. Ck-out 11 am, ck-in 4 pm. Meeting rms. Business center. Coin lndry. Gift shop. Golf, 18 holes.

Tennis, 2 courts. Downhill skiing. Bike rentals. Hiking trail. Picnic facilities. Cr cds: A, MC, V.

Green Mountain National Forest

See also Bennington, Manchester and Manchester Center, Rutland, Warren

---

(Extends northward from the Massachusetts border, along the backbone of the Green Mountains)

This 360,000-acre tract lies along the backbone of the Green Mountains, beginning at the Massachusetts line. Its high point is Mount Ellen (4,083 ft). The 260-mile Long Trail, a celebrated hiking route, extends the length of the state; about 80 miles of it are within the forest.

Well-maintained gravel roads wind through the forests of white pine, hemlock, spruce, yellow birch, and sugar maple; there are many recreation areas and privately owned resorts. Hunting and fishing are permitted in the forest under Vermont regulations. There are whitetail deer, black bear, ruffed grouse, and other game, plus brook, rainbow, and brown trout.

Developed and primitive camping, swimming, and picnicking are found throughout the forest, as are privately operated alpine ski areas and ski touring centers. Fees charged at some recreation sites and at developed campsites. Phone 802/747-6700.

What to See and Do

Moosalamoo Recreation Area. 20,000 acres feature trails from which all the forest's diverse natural beauty can be viewed. Winter activities incl cross-country skiing on groomed, specially marked trails; also alpine skiing. The nation's oldest long-distance hiking trail, the Long Trail, runs the Moosalamoo border for nearly 15 mi. Biking allowed on roads and some trails. Camping facilities abound in the area. (Daily) Within Green Mountain

Natl Forest. Phone 802/747-6700 or 802/247-6401.

Highgate Springs

see Swanton

Railroad covered bridge

Jeffersonville

(C-2) *See also Stowe*

Pop 462 **Elev** 459 ft **Area code** 802 **Zip** 05464

What to See and Do

Smugglers' Notch. Resort has 5 double chairlifts, 3 surface lifts; school, rentals, snowmaking; concession area, cafeteria, restaurants, nursery, lodge (see RESORT). 60 runs, longest run over 3 mi; vertical drop 2,610 ft. (Thanksgiving-mid-Apr, daily) More than 25 mi of cross-country trails (Dec-Apr, daily; rentals), ice-skating. Summer activities incl 10 swimming pools, 3 water slides; tennis, miniature golf, driving range. 5 mi S on VT 108. Phone 802/644-8851 or 800/451-8752. ¢¢¢¢

Motel/Motor Lodge

★ **HIGHLANDER MOTEL.** *995 VT Rte 108S (05464), 1½ mi S on VT 108. 802/644-2725; fax 802/644-2725; toll-free 800/367-6471.* 15 rms. No A/C. Late Dec-Apr and late June-Oct: S $58-$64; D $64-$72; each addl $5; dorm rates; higher rates some hols; lower rates rest of yr. Crib free. Pet accepted. TV; cable. Pool; sauna. Playground. Restaurant 7:30-9 am. Ck-out 11 am. Downhill/x-country ski 3 mi. Lawn games. Rec rm. Refrigerators avail. Picnic tables, grill. View of mountains. Cr cds: MC, V.

⬛⬛⬛⬛⬛

Resort

★★★ **SMUGGLER'S NOTCH RESORT.** *4323 VT 108S (05464), 5 mi S on VT 108. 802/644-8851; fax 802/644-1230; res 800/451-8752. www.smuggs.com.* 525 rms, 113 A/C, 1-3 story, 400 kits. Mid-Dec-Mar: S $99-$225; D $109-$249; kit. units $109-$159; 1-5 bedrm apts avail; under 7 free; wkly rates; tennis, ski, golf plans; higher rates hols; lower rates rest of yr. Crib $20. TV; cable (premium), VCR avail (movies). Heated pool; whirlpool, lifeguard. Playgrounds. Supervised children's activities (summer, winter); ages 6 wks-17. Dining rm 7:30 am-10 pm. Bar 11-1 am; entertainment. Ck-out 10 am, 11 am in summer; ck-in 5 pm. Free lndry facilities. Convention facilities. Business servs avail. Grocery, sport shop. Airport, railroad station, bus depot transportation. 12 tennis courts, 2 indoor. Downhill/x-country ski on site. Outdoor ice skating, sleighing. Water slides. Miniature golf; driving range. Lawn games. Bicycles. Hiking. Soc dir; entertainment, movies. Teen rec rm. Exercise equipt; sauna. Massage. Washers in most rms; some fireplaces; microwaves avail. Some balconies. Cr cds: A, D, MC, V.

⬛⬛⬛⬛⬛⬛⬛⬛⬛⬛

B&Bs/Small Inns

★★ **MANNSVIEW INN.** *916 Rte 108 (05464), at Smuggler's Notch. 802/644-8321; fax 802/644-2006; toll-free 888/937-6266. Email rsvp@mannsview.com; www.mannsview.com.* 7 rms, 2 story. Dec-Mar, June-Oct: S $50; D $65; suites $110; lower rates rest of yr. Pet accepted, fee. Parking lot. TV; cable. Complimentary full bkfst, coffee in rms, newspaper. Restaurant. Meeting rm. Whirlpool. Golf. Tennis, 4 courts. Downhill skiing. Bike rentals. Hiking trail. Picnic facilities. Cr cds: A, DS, MC.

⬛⬛⬛⬛⬛⬛⬛⬛

★★ **SINCLAIR INN BED & BREAKFAST.** *389 VT Rte 15 (05465), I-89 N, off Exit 12, N 5 mi to Essex Junction on VT 2A, E on VT 15 10½ mi. 802/899-2234; fax 802/899-2234; toll-free 800/433-4658. Email sinclairinn@worldnet.att.net; www.virtualcities.com/vt.* 6 rms, 2 story, 1 suite. May-Oct: S $140; D $145; each addl $20; under 12 free; lower rates rest of yr. Parking lot. Pool, childrens pool. TV; cable. Complimentary full bkfst, newspaper. Restaurant nearby. Ck-out 11 am, ck-in 3 pm. Meeting rms. Business center. Concierge. Exercise equipt, sauna. Golf. Tennis. Downhill skiing. Beach access. Bike rentals. Hiking trail. Picnic facilities. Cr cds: DS, MC, V.

⬛⬛⬛⬛⬛⬛⬛⬛⬛⬛⬛

★ **SMUGGLER'S NOTCH INN AND RESTAURANT.** *Church St (05464). 802/644-2412; fax 802/644-2881; toll-free 800/845-3101. Email smuginn@pwshift.com.* 11 rms, 2 story. No A/C. S $50; D $60-$125; each addl $10-$15; MAP avail. TV in sitting rm; cable. Pool; whirlpool. Complimentary full bkfst. Dining rm 5-9 pm. Ck-out 11 am, ck-in 2 pm. Downhill ski 4 mi; x-country ski 2 mi. Picnic tables. Old country inn (1789) with large porch. Library; many handmade quilts; antiques. Cr cds: A, DS, MC, V.

⬛⬛⬛⬛⬛⬛⬛⬛

Cottage Colony

★ **STERLING RIDGE INN & CABINS.** *1073 jct Hill Rd (05464). 802/644-8265; fax 802/644-5153; toll-free 800/347-8266. Email vtcabins@sover.net; www.vermont-cabins.* 8 rms, 1 story. Dec-Jan, Sep-Oct: S $55; D $139; suites $175; each addl $12; lower rates rest of yr. Crib avail. Parking lot. Pool, whirlpool. TV; cable (DSS), VCR avail, CD avail. Complimentary full bkfst, newspaper. Ck-out 11 am, ck-in 3 pm. Meeting rms. Business center. Coin lndry. Gift shop. Tennis. Downhill skiing. Bike rentals. Supervised children's activities. Hiking trail. Picnic facilities. Cr cds: MC, V.

Unrated Dining Spot

WINDRIDGE INN. *Main St (05464), Center of Village.* 802/644-5556. *www. virtualvermont.com/windridgeinn.* Eclectic menu. Specializes in rack of lamb, red beans and wild rice, duck with Dijon sauce. Hrs: 7 am-8 pm; Sun-Tues to 3 pm. Closed Dec 25. Res accepted. Bar. Bkfst a la carte entrees: $10.95-$29.95; lunch, dinner a la carte entrees: $10.95-$29.95. Elegant, formal dining in early Amer atmosphere. Cr cds: MC, V.

Killington

See also Plymouth, Rutland, Woodstock

Pop 50 (est) **Elev** 1,229 ft
Area code 802 **Zip** 05751

What to See and Do

Gifford Woods State Park. This 114-acre park has fishing at nearby pond, boat access to Kent Pond. Foot trails (Appalachian Trail passes through park). Virgin forest with picnic facilities. Tent and trailer sites (dump station), lean-tos. (Memorial Day-Columbus Day) Standard fees. On VT 100, 1 mi N of jct US 4. Phone 802/775-5354 or 802/886-2434 (off season).

Skiing.

Killington Resort. Comprises 1,200 acres with 7 mountains (highest elev 4,241 ft); 3 gondolas, 6 high-speed quad, 6 quad, 6 triple, 4 double chairlifts, 8 surface lifts; patrol, school, rentals, snowmaking; mountaintop restaurant (with observation decks), 6 cafeterias, bars, children's center, nursery, lodging. 212 runs; longest run 10 mi, vertical drop 3,150 ft. Snowboarding; snow tubing. (Oct-June, daily) 5 mi SW of jct US 4 & VT 100, N on Killington Rd. Phone 800/621-6867 or 802/422-3261 (ski reports). ¢¢¢¢

Summer activities. Resort activities incl a tennis school (Memorial Day-Sep), 18-hole golf, mountain biking (rentals), in-line skating/skateboarding park, gondola rides to view foliage; 2 water slides (July 4-Sep) Also

Pico Alpine Slide and Scenic Chairlift. Chairlift to top of mountain slope; control speed of own sled on the way down. Sports center and restaurant below. (Late May-mid-Oct) Phone 802/621-6867. ¢¢

Mountain Top Cross-Country Ski Resort. Patrol, school, rentals, snowmaking; concession area, restaurant at inn; 68 mi of cross-country trails. Ice-skating, horse-drawn sleigh rides. (Nov-Apr, daily) N via US 7, then 10 mi NE on unnumbered road, follow signs. Phone 802/483-2311 or 800/445-2100. ¢¢¢¢¢

Motels/Motor Lodges

★★ **GREY BONNET INN.** *831 Rte 100 (05751), ½ mi N of jct US 4.* 802/775-2537; fax 802/775-3371; toll-free 800/342-2086. Email innkeep@ together.net. 40 rms, 3 story. No elvtr. MAP, Dec-Mar: S, D $48-$75; each addl $30; EP avail; family, wkly rates, golf plans; lower rates mid-June-mid-Sep. Closed Apr-May, late-Oct-late Nov. Crib $3. TV. 2 pools, 1 indoor; whirlpool. Playground. Restaurant 7:30-9:30 am, 6-9 pm. Bar. Ck-out 11 am. Meeting rm. Tennis. Downhill ski 2 mi; x-country ski adj. Exercise equipt; sauna. Game rm. Rec rm. Lawn games. Balconies. Cr cds: A, DS, MC, V.

★★ **KILLINGTON PICO MOTOR INN.** *64 US Rte 4 (05751).* 802/773-4088; fax 802/775-9705; toll-free 800/548-4713. Email kpmi@webtv.net; www.killingtonpico.com. 29 rms, 1 story. Dec-Mar: S $49; D $53; lower rates rest of yr. Crib avail. Pool, whirlpool. TV; cable (premium), VCR avail. Complimentary continental bkfst, newspaper, toll-free calls. Restaurant nearby. Bar. Meeting rm. Business servs avail. Concierge. Golf. Downhill skiing. Hiking trail. Picnic facilities. Cr cds: A, C, D, DS, ER, JCB, MC, V.

★★ **SHERBURNE-KILLINGTON MOTEL.** *1946 Rte 4 (05751), 2 blks W of jct VT 100.* 802/773-9535; fax 802/773-0011; toll-free 800/366-0493. Email skmotel@sover.net; www.lodging killington.com. 20 rms. Oct-Apr: S, D $55-$115; each addl $16; under 12 free; ski plan; higher rates winter hol wks; lower rates rest of yr. Crib free. TV; cable, VCR (free movies). Heated pool. Playground. Ck-out 11 am. Downhill/x-country ski ½ mi. Lawn games. Refrigerators. Picnic tables, grills. View of mountains. Cr cds: A, DS, MC, V.

D ⛵ 〰 🔧 🐾 SC

★★ **VAL ROC MOTEL.** *8006 Rte. 4 (05751), ½ mi W of jct VT 100s.* 802/422-3881; fax 802/422-3236; toll-free 800/238-8762. Email valroc@ vermontel.net; www.valroc.com. 24 rms, 1 story. Dec-Mar: S $98; D $100; each addl $14; under 12 free; lower rates rest of yr. Crib avail, fee. Pet accepted, some restrictions, fee. Parking lot. Pool, whirlpool. TV; cable, VCR avail. Complimentary continental bkfst, coffee in rms, toll-free calls. Ck-out 11 am, ck-in 2 pm. Golf. Tennis. Downhill skiing. Bike rentals. Supervised children's activities. Hiking trail. Picnic facilities. Cr cds: A, C, D, DS, MC, V.

🐟 🏃 🎿 ⛵ 🍴 🔧 〰 🔧 🐾

Hotels

★★ **CASCADES LODGE.** *58 Old Mill Rd (05751).* 802/422-3731; fax 802/422-3351; toll-free 800/345-0113. Email info@cascadeslodge.com; www. cascadeslodge.com. 40 rms, 3 story, 6 suites. Dec-Mar, Sep-Oct: S $153; D $189; suites $268; each addl $35; children $25; under 12 free; lower rates rest of yr. Crib avail. Parking lot. Indoor pool, whirlpool. TV; cable (premium), VCR avail. Complimentary full bkfst, coffee in rms, toll-free calls. Restaurant 5-9 pm. Bar. Ck-out 11 am, ck-in 3 pm. Meeting rms. Business center. Concierge. Dry cleaning. Exercise equipt, sauna. Golf. Tennis, 2 courts. Downhill skiing. Bike rentals. Supervised children's activities. Hiking trail. Picnic facilities. Cr cds: A, DS, JCB, MC, V.

D 🏃 🎿 🍴 🔧 〰 🔧 🐾 SC 🏃

★★ **SUMMIT LODGE.** *Killington Mountain Rd (05751), 2 mi S of jct US 4 and VT 100, N on Killington Ski Area Access Rd.* 802/422-3535; fax 802/422-3536; toll-free 800/635-6343. Email summit@vermontel.com; www.summit lodgevermont.com. 45 rms, 2-33 story. No A/C. No elvtr. S $63-$128; D $88-$146; each addl $15; family rates; MAP avail; package plans; higher rates some hols. Serv charge 15% (MAP). Crib free. TV; VCR avail (movies $6). 2 pools, 1 heated; whirlpool, poolside serv. Playground. Dining rm 7:30-9:30 am, 6-9 pm; summer 8-10 am, 6-9 pm. Bar from noon; winter from 4 pm. Ck-out 11 am. Business servs avail. Grocery, package store 2 mi. Tennis, pro. Airport transportation. Downhill ski 1 mi; x-country ski 1 mi. Ice skating. Lawn games. Sauna, steam rm. Massage. Entertainment. Game rm. Rec rm. Racquetball courts. Fireplaces. Balconies. Library. Cr cds: A, DS, MC, V.

♿ ⛵ 🎿 〰 🐾

Resorts

★★★ **CORTINA INN AND RESORT.** *103 US 4 (05751), 4 mi W of jct VT 100.* 802/773-3333; fax 802/775-6948; toll-free 800/451-6108. Email cortina1@aol.com; www.cortina inn.com. 89 rms, 2 story, 7 suites. Dec-Mar, Sep-Oct: S $120; D $189; suites $120; each addl $19; children $5; under 14 free; lower rates rest of yr. Crib avail, fee. Pet accepted, some restrictions, fee. Parking lot. Indoor pool, lap pool, whirlpool. TV; cable, VCR avail, CD avail. Complimentary full bkfst. Restaurant 7 am-9 pm. Bar. Ck-out 11 am, ck-in 3 pm. Meeting rms. Business center. Bellhops. Concierge. Dry cleaning. Gift shop. Free airport transportation. Exercise privileges, sauna. Golf. Tennis, 8 courts. Downhill skiing. Bike rentals. Supervised children's activities. Hiking trail. Picnic facilities. Cr cds: A, C, D, DS, ER, JCB, MC, V.

D 🐟 ♿ ⛵ 🍴 🔧 〰 🎿 🔧 🔧 🏃

★★★ **INN OF THE SIX MOUNTAINS.** *2617 Killington Rd (05751), 4 mi S of jct US 4, VT 100.* 802/422-4302; fax 802/422-4321; res 800/228-4676. Email sixmountains@hotmail. com; www.sixmountains.com. 99 rms, 4 story, 4 suites. Dec-Mar, Sep-Oct: S, D $189; suites $249; each addl $17;

under 12 free; lower rates rest of yr. Crib avail, fee. Parking lot. Indoor/outdoor pools, lap pool, childrens pool, whirlpool. TV; cable. Complimentary coffee in rms. Restaurant 7 am-9:30 pm, closed Mon. Bar. Ck-out noon, ck-in 4 pm. Meeting rms. Business center. Gift shop. Exercise equipt, sauna. Golf. Tennis. Downhill skiing. Bike rentals. Supervised children's activities. Hiking trail. Cr cds: A, C, D, DS, MC, V.

B&Bs/Small Inns

★★★ **RED CLOVER INN.** *7 Woodward Rd (05701), W on US 4 to Woodward Rd. 802/775-2290; fax 802/773-0594; toll-free 800/752-0571. Email redclovr@vermontel.net; www.red cloverinn.com.* 14 rms, 2 story. Jan-Feb, Oct: D $250; suites $450; each addl $60; lower rates rest of yr. Pet accepted, some restrictions, fee. Parking lot. Pool. TV; cable, VCR avail. Complimentary full bkfst. Restaurant 6-9 pm, closed Sun. Bar. Ck-out 11 am, ck-in 2 pm. Meeting rm. Business center. Gift shop. Golf, 18 holes. Tennis, 3 courts. Downhill skiing. Bike rentals. Hiking trail. Cr cds: DS, MC, V.

★★ **VERMONT INN.** *Box 37J Rte 4 (05751), 4 mi W of jct VT 100. 802/775-0708; fax 802/773-2440; toll-free 800/541-7795. Email relax@vermont inn.com; www.vermontinn.com.* 18 rms, 2 story. Dec-Mar, Sep-Oct: D $180; each addl $30; under 12 free; lower rates rest of yr. Parking lot. Pool. TV; cable, VCR avail, CD avail. Complimentary full bkfst, newspaper, toll-free calls. Restaurant (see VERMONT INN). Bar. Ck-out 11 am, ck-in 2 pm. Business servs avail. Concierge. Sauna. Golf. Tennis. Downhill skiing. Hiking trail. Picnic facilities. Cr cds: A, D, MC, V.

Restaurants

★★ **CASCADES LODGE.** *58 Old Mill Rd. 802/422-3731. Email cascades@vermontel.com; www.cascades lodge.com.* Specializes in roast duck with sauce du jour, Caribbean-style crab cakes, paella. Own desserts. Hrs:

7-10 am, 5-9 pm. Closed May. Res accepted. Bar. Bkfst $2.95-$6.95; dinner $10.95-$22.95. Child's menu. Greenhouse-style decor; large picture window offers views of mountains. Cr cds: A, DS, MC, V.

★★★★ **HEMINGWAY'S.** *VT 4 (05751), between jct US 100N and US 100S. 802/422-3886. Email hemwy@sover.net; www.hemingwaysrestaurant.com.* Chef/owner Ted Fondula and his wife Linda have presided over their restaurant since 1982. The prix fixe menu, which can be matched with wines, may incl seared scallops with truffled potatoes and caramelized onion. Honest, humble service stands out in all three unique dining spaces; the intimate stone-wrapped wine cellar, the brick-walled garden rm or the elegant, peach-colored vaulted room. Specializes in Vermont lamb and game birds, lobster ravioli, pan-roasted striped bass. Own pasta, pastries, bread. Hrs: 6-10 pm. Closed Mon, Tues; also mid-Apr-mid-May, first 2 weeks Nov. Res accepted. Dinner prix fixe: $40. Tasting menu: $72. Cr cds: A, C, D, MC, V.

★★ **VERMONT INN.** *VT 4. 802/775-0708. www.vermontinn.com.* Specializes in fresh seafood, veal, lamb. Hrs: 5-9 pm. Closed mid-Apr-Memorial Day. Res accepted. Bar. Dinner $12.95-$20.95. Child's menu. Parking. Fireside dining. View of Green Mts. Cr cds: A, DS, MC, V.

★★ **ZOLA'S GRILLE.** *103 US 4. 802/773-3331. Email cortina1@aol.com.* Specializes in fresh seafood. Hrs: 7-10 am, 5-10 pm. Res accepted; required hols. Bar. Bkfst buffet: $9; dinner $9.95-$21.95. Sun brunch $13.95. Child's menu. Parking. Cr cds: D, DS, MC, V.

Londonderry

See also Grafton, Peru, Stratton Mountain, Weston

Founded 1770 **Pop** 1,506
Elev 1,151 ft **Area code** 802
Zip 05148

Motels/Motor Lodges

★★ **DOSTAL'S RESORT LODGE.**
*441 Magic Mt Access Rd (05148), 3 mi
SE, off VT 11 on Magic Mt Access Rd.
802/824-6700; fax 802/824-6701; toll-
free 800/255-5373. Email dostals@
sover.net; www.dostals.com.* 40 rms, 2
story. Dec-Mar: S, D $139; each addl
$12; under 6 free; lower rates rest of
yr. Crib avail. Parking lot.
Indoor/outdoor pools, lap pool,
whirlpool. TV; cable (premium).
Complimentary newspaper, toll-free
calls. Restaurant. Bar. Ck-out 11 am,
ck-in 3 pm. Meeting rms. Fax servs
avail. Gift shop. Golf, 18 holes. Tennis, 4 courts. Hiking trail. Cr cds: A,
DS, MC, V.

★★ **SNOWDON MOTEL.** *Rte 11
Londonderry Vermont (05148), 1½ mi E
on VT 11. 802/824-6047; fax 802/
824-6047; toll-free 800/419-4600.* 12
rms, 2 story. Jan-Feb, July-Oct: Parking lot. TV; cable (premium). Complimentary full bkfst, toll-free calls.
Restaurant. Ck-out 11 am, ck-in 11
pm. Fax servs avail. Golf, 18 holes.
Tennis, 3 courts. Downhill skiing.
Hiking trail. Picnic facilities. Cr cds:
MC, V.

B&Bs/Small Inns

★ **BLUE GENTIAN LODGE.** *Magic
Mountain Rd (05148). 802/824-5908;
fax 802/824-3531; toll-free 800/456-
2405. Email kenalberti@csi.com; www.
bluegentian.com.* 13 rms, 2 story. Dec-
Feb, Sep-Oct: D $85; each addl $15;
children $10; under 15 free; lower
rates rest of yr. Parking lot. Pool. TV;
cable, VCR avail. Complimentary full
bkfst. Restaurant nearby. Ck-out 10
am, ck-in 2 pm. Gift shop. Golf. Tennis. Downhill skiing. Hiking trail. Cr
cds: MC, V.

★★ **FROG'S LEAP INN.** *RR 1 Box
107 (05148), 1½ mi N on VT 100.
802/824-3019; fax 802/824-3657; toll-
free 877/376-4753. Email frog@frogs
leapinn.com; www.frogsleapinn.com.,* 2
story, 4 suites. Dec-Mar, July-Oct: S
$110; D $135; suites $155; each addl
$20; children $10; under 16 free;
lower rates rest of yr. Crib avail. Pet
accepted, some restrictions, fee. Pool.

TV; cable (DSS), VCR avail. Complimentary full bkfst, coffee in rms,
newspaper, toll-free calls. Restaurant
4-8 pm, closed Mon. Bar. Ck-out 11
am, ck-in 2 pm. Meeting rms. Business center. Gift shop. Golf. Tennis.
Downhill skiing. Hiking trail. Picnic
facilities. Cr cds: A, DS, MC, V.

★★ **LONDONDERRY INN.** *Rte 100
(05155), 3 mi S on VT 100. 802/824-
5226; fax 802/824-3146. Email lond
inn@sover.net; www.bestinns.net/usa/vt/
london.html.* 25 air-cooled rms, 20
baths, some share bath, 3 story. No
rm phones. Mid-Dec-Mar: S $49-$69;
D $59-$79; each addl $13-$19;
higher rates: hols, fall foliage, winter
wkends, Dec 25-31; lower rates rest
of yr. Crib $5. TV in sitting rm; cable.
Pool. Complimentary continental
bkfst. Dining rm 5:30-8:30 pm;
wkends/hols in-season. Ck-out 11
am, ck-in 2 pm. Business servs avail.
Downhill ski 10 mi; x-country ski 4
mi. Lawn games. Former farmhouse
(1826). Cr cds: A, DS, MC, V.

★★ **SWISS INN & RESTAURANT.**
*249 Rte 11 (05148), 1½ mi W on VT
11. 802/824-3442; fax 802/824-6313;
toll-free 800/847-9477. Email swiss
inn@sover.net; www.swissinn.com.* 19
rms, 2 story. Dec-Mar, Jul-Oct: S, D
$99; each addl $15; under 15 free;
lower rates rest of yr. Parking lot.
Pool. TV; cable. Complimentary full
bkfst. Restaurant 5:30-8:30 pm. Bar.
Ck-out 11 am, ck-in 2 pm. Meeting
rms. Fax servs avail. Golf. Tennis.
Downhill skiing. Hiking trail. Cr cds:
MC, V.

Ludlow

(F-2) *See also Plymouth, Springfield,
Weston*

Chartered 1761 **Pop** 2,302
Elev 1,067 ft **Area code** 802
Zip 05149
Web www.virtualvermont.com/cham
ber/ludlow

Information Ludlow Area Chamber
of Commerce, Okemo Market Pl, PO
Box 333; 802/228-5830

What to See and Do

Crowley Cheese Factory. (1882) Oldest cheese factory in US; still makes cheese by hand as in 19th century. Display of tools used in early cheese factories and in home cheesemaking. Watch process and sample product. (Mon-Fri). Phone 802/259-2340. **FREE**

Green Mountain Sugar House. Working maple sugar producer on shore of Lake Pauline. Shop offers syrup, candies, crafts, and gifts. (Daily) 4 mi N on VT 100N. Phone 802/228-7151. **FREE**

Okemo Mountain Ski Area. (See OKEMO STATE FOREST)

B&Bs/Small Inns

★★★ **ANDRIE ROSE INN.** *13 Pleasant St (05149). 802/228-4846; fax 802/228-7910; toll-free 800/223-4846. Email andrie@mail.tds.net; www.andrieroseinn.com.* 23 rms, 6 A/C, 2 story, 9 suites. Some rm phones. Sept-Mar: S, D $110-$160; suites $215-$290; package plans; lower rates rest of yr. TV; cable (premium), VCR avail (free movies). Complimentary full bkfst. Ck-out 11 am, ck-in 3 pm. Business servs avail. Gift shop. Downhill ski ½ mi; x-country ski 1 mi. Some in-rm whirlpools, refrigerators; fireplace in suites. Picnic tables. Grills. Elegant country inn (1829); furnished with antiques. Totally non-smoking. Cr cds: A, MC, V.

★★ **COMBES FAMILY INN.** *953 E Lake Rd (05149), 5 mi N via VT 103, VT 100, follow signs. 802/228-8799; fax 802/228-8704; toll-free 800/822-8799. Email billcfi@tds.net; www.combesfamilyinn.com.* 9 rms, 2 story, 2 suites. Dec-June: S $117; D $124; suites $124; each addl $27; lower rates rest of yr. Crib avail, fee. Pet accepted, some restrictions. Parking lot. TV; cable; VCR avail. Complimentary full bkfst. Restaurant 7-7. Ck-out 11 am, ck-in 2 pm. Business servs avail. Golf, 18 holes. Tennis, 4 courts. Downhill skiing. Picnic facilities. Cr cds: A, DS, MC, V.

★ **ECHO LAKE INN.** *VT 100N (05149), 5 mi N on VT 100. 802/228-8602; fax 802/228-3075; toll-free 800/356-6844. Email echolkinn@aol.com; www.echolakeinn.com.* 29 rms, 3 story, 9 suites. Dec-Mar, Oct: S $229; D $239; suites $309; each addl $20; lower rates rest of yr. Parking lot. Pool, whirlpool. TV; cable. Complimentary full bkfst. Restaurant 6-8:30 pm. Bar. Ck-out 11 am, ck-in 3 pm. Meeting rms. Concierge. Golf. Tennis. Downhill skiing. Beach access. Supervised children's activities. Hiking trail. Picnic facilities. Cr cds: A, MC, V.

★★ **GOLDEN STAGE INN.** *399 Depot St (05153), 3 mi S on VT 103 to VT 131. 802/226-7744; fax 802/226-7882; toll-free 800/253-8226. Email goldenstageinn@tds.net; www.goldenstageinn.com.* 8 rms, 2 story, 1 suite. Dec-Feb, Sep-Oct: S $110; D $125; suites $199; each addl $20; under 10 free; lower rates rest of yr. Parking lot. Pool. TV; cable, VCR avail. Complimentary full bkfst. Restaurant, closed Mon. Bar. Meeting rm. Fax servs avail. Golf, 18 holes. Downhill skiing. Bike rentals. Picnic facilities. Cr cds: MC, V.

★★★★ **THE GOVERNOR'S INN.** *86 Main St (05149). 802/228-8830; fax 802/228-2961; toll-free 800/468-3766. Email kubec@thegovernorsinn.com; www.thegovernorsinn.com.* 8 rms, 3 story, 1 suite. Jan-Feb, Oct: S $180; D $195; suites $275; each addl $40; lower rates rest of yr. Parking lot. TV; cable, VCR avail. Complimentary full bkfst. Restaurant. Bar. Ck-out 11 am, ck-in 2 pm. Concierge. Gift shop. Golf, 9 holes. Downhill skiing. Cr cds: A, MC, V.

Restaurant

★★★ **NIKKI'S.** *44 Pond St (05149), VT 103. 802/228-7797.* Specializes in steak au poivre, fresh seafood, black Angus beef. Hrs: 5-10 pm. Closed Sun, Mon; Thanksgiving. Bar. Wine cellar. Dinner a la carte entrees: $9.95-$21.95. Child's menu. Cathedral ceiling. Cr cds: A, DS, MC, V.

Lyndonville

(C-4) *See also St. Johnsbury*

Settled 1781 **Pop** 1,255 **Elev** 720 ft
Area code 802 **Zip** 05851

Home of small industries and trading center for the surrounding dairy and stock raising farms, Lyndonville lies in the valley of the Passumpsic River. Five covered bridges, the earliest dating from 1795, are located within the town limits.

Covered bridge dating back to the 19th century

What to See and Do

Burke Mountain Ski Area. Area has 2 chairlifts, Pomalift, J-bar; school, rentals, snowmaking; 2 cafeterias, 2 bars, nursery. 30 runs, longest run approx 2½ mi; vertical drop 2,000 ft. Over 57 mi of cross-country trails. (Mid-Nov-mid-Apr, daily) 1 mi N on US 5, then 6 mi NE on VT 114, in Darling State Park. Phone 802/626-3305 or 800/541-5480. ¢¢¢¢

Lake Willoughby. Beaches, water sports, fishing; hiking trails to summit of Mt Pisgah at 2,741 ft. 18 mi N on VT 5A.

Motel/Motor Lodge

★ **COLONADE INN.** *28 Back Center Rd (05851), I-91 Exit 23. 802/626-9316; fax 802/626-1023; toll-free 877/435-3688.* 40 rms, 2 story. Sep-Oct: S $55; D $70; lower rates rest of yr. Parking lot. TV; cable. Complimentary continental bkfst, toll-free calls. Restaurant nearby. Ck-out 11 am, ck-in 3 pm. Fax servs avail. Golf. Downhill skiing. Cr cds: A, D, DS, MC, V.

B&Bs/Small Inns

★ **THE OLD CUTTER INN.** *143 Pinkham Rd (05832), 1 mi N on US 5 to VT 114, then 4 mi N to Burke Mountain Rd. 802/626-5152; fax 802/626-5152. www.pbpub.com/cutter.htm.* 10 rms, 2 story. S $44-$56; D $54-$66; each addl $10-$12; kit. suite $120-$140; under 12 free; MAP avail. Closed Apr, Nov. Crib free. Pet accepted. TV in lobby. Pool. Dining rm (see also OLD CUTTER INN). Ck-out 11 am, ck-in 1 pm. Downhill/x-country ski ½ mi. Lawn games. Picnic tables. Sitting rm. In restored farmhouse (ca 1845) and renovated turn-of-the-century carriage house. Cr cds: MC, V.

★ ★ **THE WILDFLOWER INN.** *Darling Hill Rd. (05851), 1 mi N on US 5 to VT 114, then N to Darling Hill Rd. 802/626-8310; fax 802/626-3039.* 22 rms in 4 bldgs, 2 share bath, 2 story, 9 kit. suites. No A/C. No rm phones. S $74-$84; D $89-$105; suites $120-$200; higher rates fall foliage season. Closed 2 wks Apr and Nov. TV in sitting rm. Heated pool; wading pool, whirlpool, sauna. Free supervised children's activities (Memorial Day-Labor Day); ages 3-12. Complimentary full bkfst. Dining rm (public by res) 5-9 pm. Ck-out 11 am, ck-in 3 pm. Business servs avail. Gift shop. Art gallery. Free bus depot transportation. Tennis on site. Downhill ski 5 mi; x-country ski on site. Hay, sleigh rides. Game rm. Lawn games. Some balconies. Family-oriented inn on 500 acres; barns, farm animals; sledding slopes. Totally nonsmoking. Cr cds: MC, V.

🄳 ⛷ 🏊 🏌 🕊 ⛵ 🔥 🎿

Restaurant

★★ **OLD CUTTER INN.** *143 Pinkham Rd, 1 mi N on US 5 to VT 114, then 4 mi N to Burke Mountain Rd. 802/626-5152. www.pbpub.com/ cutter.html.* Specializes in tournedos of beef, rack of lamb, Rahmschnitzel. Hrs: 5-9 pm. Closed Wed; also Apr, Nov. Res accepted. Bar. Dinner $13-$18.50. Child's menu. Converted 1845 farmhouse. Cr cds: C, D, DS, ER, MC, V.

🄳

Manchester and Manchester Center

(G-1) *See also Arlington, Dorset, Londonderry, Peru, Stratton Mountain*

Settled 1764 **Pop** 3,622 **Elev** 899 and 753 ft **Area code** 802 **Zip** Manchester 05254; Manchester Center 05255 **Web** www.manchesterandmtns.com **Information** Manchester-and-the-Mountains Regional Chamber of Commerce, 3451 Manchester Center; 802/362-2100

These towns have been among Vermont's best-loved year-round resorts for 100 years. The surrounding mountains make them serenely attractive, and the ski business has added to their following. Bromley Mountain, Stratton Mountain, and other areas lure thousands each year. A Ranger District office of the Green Mountain National Forest (see) is located here.

What to See and Do

American Museum of Fly Fishing. Collection of fly fishing memorabilia; tackle of many famous persons, incl Dwight D. Eisenhower, Ernest Hemingway, Andrew Carnegie, Winslow Homer, Bing Crosby, and others.

(Apr-Nov, daily; Dec-Mar, Mon-Fri; closed hols) Corner of VT Historic Rte 7A & Seminary Ave. Phone 802/362-3300. ¢

Emerald Lake State Park. This 430-acre park has rich flora in a limestone-based bedrock. Swimming beach, bathhouse, fishing (also in nearby streams), boating (rentals); nature and hiking trails, picnicking, concession. tent and trailer sites (dump station), lean-tos. (Memorial Day-Columbus Day) Standard fees. 6 mi N on US 7, in North Dorset. Phone 802/362-1655 or 802/483-2001.

✪ **Equinox Sky Line Drive.** A spectacular 5-mi paved road that rises from 600 to 3,835 ft; parking and picnic areas along road; view from top of Mt Equinox. Fog or rain may make mountain road dangerous and travel inadvisable. (May-Oct, daily) No large camper vehicles. 5 mi S on VT Historic Rte 7A. Phone 802/362-1114. Toll ¢¢¢

Factory outlet stores. Many outlet stores can be found in this area, mainly along VT 11/30 and at the intersection of VT 11/30 and VT 7A. Contact the Chamber of Commerce for a complete listing of stores.

Historic Hildene. (1904) The 412-acre estate of Robert Todd Lincoln (Abraham Lincoln's son) incl a 24-rm Georgian manor house, held in the family until 1975; original furnishings; carriage barn, formal gardens, nature trails. (Mid-May-Oct, daily) 2 mi S via VT Historic Rte 7A, in Manchester Village. Phone 802/362-1788. ¢¢¢

Merck Forest and Farmland Center. Includes 2,800 acres of unspoiled upland forest, meadows, mountains, and ponds; 26 mi of roads and trails for hiking and cross-country skiing. Fishing; picnicking, camping (res required). Educational programs. Fees for some activities. 8 mi NW on VT 30 to East Rupert, then 2½ mi W on VT 315. Phone 802/394-7836.

Southern Vermont Art Center. Painting, sculpture, prints; concerts, music festivals; botany trail; cafe. Gift shop. (Late May-mid-Oct, Tues-Sun) 1 mi N off West Rd. Phone 802/362-1405. ¢¢

Vermont Wax Museum. Three Victorian bldgs house 85 life-size wax figures from Mark Twain to JFK. Changing audio and video presentations. On-site wax casting studio.

Fine art gallery features Vermont artists' work in various media. Museum store. (Daily; closed hols) VT 11/30 between VT 7 & 7A. Phone 802/362-0609. ¢¢

Motels/Motor Lodges

★★ **ASPEN MOTEL.** *VT 7A N (05255), 1 mi N on VT 7A. 802/362-2450; fax 802/362-1348. Email aspen@thisisvermont.com; www.thisis vermont.com/aspen.* 24 rms, 1 story, 1 suite. S, D $90; suites $195; each addl $10; children $10. TV; cable. Ck-out 11 am, ck-in 2 pm. Cr cds: A, DS, MC, V.

D 🐾 🔥

★ **THE BRITTANY INN MOTEL.** *Rte 7A S 1056 Main St (05255). 802/362-1033; fax 802/362-0551. www.thisisvt.com/brittany.* 12 rms, 1 story. Aug: D $83; lower rates rest of yr. Crib avail. Parking lot. TV; cable. Complimentary coffee in rms, toll-free calls. Ck-out 11 am, ck-in 2 pm. Fax servs avail. Golf, 18 holes. Downhill skiing. Picnic facilities. Cr cds: A, MC, V.

🐾 🔥 ➤ 🎿 ☇ 🔥

★★ **EYRIE MOTEL.** *158 Bowen Hill Rd (05253), 7 mi N, E of US 7. 802/362-1208; fax 802/362-2948; res 802/362-1208; toll-free 888/EYR1EVT. Email eyrie@together.net; www.thisisver mont.com/eyriemotel.* 12 rms, 1 story. June-Oct: S, D $87; each addl $10; lower rates rest of yr. Parking lot. Pool. TV; cable, VCR avail. Complimentary continental bkfst. Ck-out 11 am, ck-in 3 pm. Golf. Downhill skiing. Hiking trail. Picnic facilities. Cr cds: A, DS, MC, V.

🐾 ➤ 🎿 ☇ 🔥

★★ **FOUR WINDS COUNTRY MOTEL.** *7379 Historic Rte 7A (05255), on VT 7A, 2½ mi N of jct VT 30. 802/362-1105; fax 802/362-0905; toll-free 877/456-7654. Email fwmotel@sover. net; www.fourwindscountrymotel.com.* 18 rms, 1 story. Sep-Oct: D $115; each addl $10; under 18 free; lower rates rest of yr. Crib avail, fee. Parking lot. Pool. TV; cable, VCR avail. Complimentary continental bkfst, coffee in rms, toll-free calls. Restaurant nearby. Ck-out 11 am, ck-in 2 pm. Meeting rm. Business servs avail. Concierge. Dry cleaning. Exercise privileges. Golf.

Tennis, 2 courts. Downhill skiing. Bike rentals. Hiking trail. Picnic facilities. Cr cds: A, MC, V.

D 🐾 🔥 ➤ 🎿 ☇ 🎿 🎿 ☇ 🐾 SC

★★★ **MANCHESTER VIEW.** *VT 7A High Meadow Way (05255), 2 mi N on VT 7A at High Meadow Way. 802/362-2739; fax 802/362-2199; toll-free 800/548-4141. Email manview@vermontel. com; www.manchesterview.com.* 26 rms, 2 story, 10 suites. Dec-Feb, Jul-Oct: S, D $90; suites $220; each addl $12; children $12; lower rates rest of yr. Crib avail, fee. Parking lot. Pool. TV; cable (premium), VCR avail. Restaurant. Ck-out 11 am, ck-in 2 pm. Meeting rm. Business center. Concierge. Golf, 18 holes. Tennis, 2 courts. Downhill skiing. Cr cds: A, C, D, DS, MC, V.

D ➤ 🎿 ☇ 🎿 ☇ 🐾 🔥 🎿

★★ **NORTH SHIRE MOTEL.** *Historic Rte 7A, PO Box 413 (05254), 2½ mi S on VT 7A. 802/362-2336. Email info@northshiremotel.com; www. northshiremotel.com.* 14 rms, 1 story. June-Oct: D $110; each addl $10; lower rates rest of yr. Pool. TV; cable. Complimentary continental bkfst, toll-free calls. Restaurant nearby. Ck-out 11 am, ck-in 1 pm. Concierge. Gift shop. Golf. Downhill skiing. Supervised children's activities. Hiking trail. Picnic facilities. Cr cds: A, DS, MC, V.

🐾 ➤ 🎿 ☇ 🐾 🔥

★ **OLYMPIA MOTOR LODGE.** *7259 Main St (05255), 2½ mi N on VT 7A. 802/362-1700; fax 802/362-1705. Email snt1018@aol.com.* 24 rms, 2 story. Mid-June-Oct: S, D $70-$105; each addl $10; ski plan; lower rates rest of yr. TV; cable (premium). Heated pool. Bar noon-11 pm. Ck-out 11 am. Business servs avail. In-rm modem link. Tennis. Golf privileges, greens fee, pro. Downhill ski 7 mi; x-country ski 3½ mi. Private patios, balconies. Cr cds: A, DS, MC, V.

D 🎿 ☇ 🐾 🔥

★ **STAMFORD MOTEL.** *6458 Main St (05255), US 7. 802/362-2342; fax 802/362-1935. Email stamford@sover. net; www.stamfordmotel.com.* 14 rms, 1-2 story. July-mid-Oct and winter wkends: S, D $56-$65; each addl $6; family, wkly rates; ski plan; lower rates rest of yr. Crib free. TV; cable.

Heated pool. Coffee in rms. Ck-out 11 am. Tennis privileges. Golf privileges, greens fee, pro. Downhill ski 6 mi; x-country ski 2½ mi. Some refrigerators. Balconies. Picnic tables. Cr cds: A, DS, MC, V.

★★ **TOLL ROAD MOTOR INN.** *Box 813 Rte 11-30 (05255), 2¼ mi E on VT 11/30; ¼ mi E of US 7 Exit 4. 802/362-1711; fax 802/362-1715.* 16 rms, 2 story. Dec-Mar, June-Oct: D $109; each addl $10; children $10; lower rates rest of yr. Parking lot. Pool. TV; cable. Complimentary coffee in rms. Restaurant nearby. Ck-out 11 am, ck-in 2 pm. Golf, 18 holes. Tennis, 2 courts. Downhill skiing. Picnic facilities. Cr cds: A, DS, MC, V.

⊠ 🎿 🏌 ⊠ 🔥 ♨

★★★ **WEATHERVANE HOTEL.** *PO Box 378 Historic Rte 7A (05245), 2½ mi S on VT 7A. 802/362-2444; fax 802/362-4616; res 802/362-2444; toll-free 800/262-1317. www.weathervane hotel.com.* 22 rms, 1 story. Sep-Oct: D $145; each addl $10; under 18 free; lower rates rest of yr. Indoor/outdoor pools, whirlpool. TV; cable (premium). Complimentary continental bkfst, coffee in rms. Restaurant nearby. Ck-out 11 am, ck-in 1:30 pm. Fax servs avail. Golf. Downhill skiing. Bike rentals. Hiking trail. Picnic facilities. Cr cds: A, JCB, MC, V.

D 🐾 🎿 ⊠ 🏌 ⊠ 🔥 ♨ 🔥

★ **WEDGEWOOD MOTEL.** *5927 Main St (05255), VT 7A. 802/362-2145; fax 802/362-0190; toll-free 800/254-2145.* Jan-Feb, June-Oct: S $70; D $78; suites $108; under 12 free; lower rates rest of yr. TV; cable (premium). Restaurant nearby. Ck-out 11 am, ck-in 2 pm. Golf. Tennis, 4 courts. Cr cds: A, DS, MC, V.

🏌 🔥 ♨ 🔥 **SC**

Resorts

★★★ **THE EQUINOX.** *3567 Main St (05254), 1 mi S on VT 7A, center of village. 802/362-4700; fax 802/362-4861; toll-free 800/362-4747. Email reservations@equinoxresort.com; www. equinoxresort.com.* 154 rms, 4 story, 29 suites. July-Oct: S $179; D $189; suites $499; each addl $50; under 12 free; lower rates rest of yr. Crib avail, fee. Valet parking avail. Indoor/outdoor pools. TV; cable (premium), VCR avail, CD avail. Restaurant. Bar.

Meeting rms. Business servs avail. Bellhops. Concierge. Dry cleaning. Gift shop. Salon/barber avail. Exercise rm, sauna, steam rm. Golf, 18 holes. Tennis, 3 courts. Downhill skiing. Bike rentals. Hiking trail. Picnic facilities. Cr cds: A, C, D, DS, MC, V.

D 🐾 🎿 ⊠ 🏌 🔥 ⊠ 🔥 ♨ 🔥

★★★ **PALMER HOUSE.** *VT 7A (05255). 802/362-3600; fax 802/362-3600; toll-free 800/917-6245. Email resort@palmerhouse.com; www.palmer house.com.* 34 rms, 16 suites. Jan-Feb, July-Oct: S $120; D $150; suites $250; each addl $20; under 18 free; lower rates rest of yr. Parking lot. Indoor/outdoor pools, lap pool, whirlpool. TV; cable (premium), VCR avail. Complimentary continental bkfst, coffee in rms, newspaper, toll-free calls. Restaurant 11 am-10 pm. Ck-out 11 am, ck-in 2 pm. Fax servs avail. Exercise privileges, sauna. Golf, 9 holes. Tennis, 2 courts. Downhill skiing. Hiking trail. Picnic facilities. Cr cds: A, DS, MC, V.

D 🐾 ⊠ 🏌 🔥 ⊠ 🔥 ♨ 🔥

B&Bs/Small Inns

★★★ **1811 HOUSE.** *Rte 7A (05254), 1 mi S on VT 7A. 802/362-1811; fax 802/362-2443; toll-free 800/432-1811.* 14 rms, 2 story. S $110-$210; D $120-$230; foliage season (2-day min). Children over 16 yrs only. TV avail; cable. Complimentary full bkfst. Bar 5:30-8 pm. Ck-out 11 am, ck-in 2 pm. Tennis privileges. 18-hole golf privileges, pro. Downhill ski 8 mi; x-country ski ½ mi. Game rm. Some fireplaces. Library. Restored 1770 farmhouse; inn since 1811. Canopied beds; antiques; original artwork. Adj to golf course. Cr cds: A, DS, MC, V.

⊠ 🏌 🔥 ♨

★ **BARNSTEAD INN.** *Bonnet St (05255), on VT 30, 2 blks N of jct US 7. 802/362-1619; fax 802/362-0688; toll-free 800/331-1619. www.barnstead inn.com.* 14 rms, 1-3 story. S, D $65-$85; each addl $8; ski plan; higher rates special events. TV; cable. Heated pool. Complimentary coffee in rms. Restaurant nearby. Ck-out 11 am. Tennis privileges. Golf privileges, pro. Downhill ski 10 mi; x-country ski 7 mi. Converted barn (1830s).

Fairgrounds opp. Totally nonsmoking. Cr cds: A, DS, MC, V.

★★★ **INN AT MANCHESTER.** *VT 7A (05254), 1 mi S on VT 7A. 802/362-1793; fax 802/362-3218; toll-free 800/273-1793. Email innkeepers@innatmanchester.com; www.innatmanchester.com.* 18 rms in 2 bldgs, 3 story. Mid-June-Labor Day, mid-Dec-late Mar: D $119-159; each addl $25; wkly rates; package plans; higher rates hols; lower rates rest of yr. Children over 8 yrs only. Serv charge 15%. TV in sitting rm; cable. Pool. Complimentary full bkfst; afternoon refreshments. Dining rm 8-9:30 am. Ck-out 11 am, ck-in 2 pm. Downhill ski 7 mi; x-country ski 2 mi. Private patio. Picnic tables. Antique furnishings. Inn, carriage house (1880). Cr cds: A, DS, MC, V.

★★ **MANCHESTER HIGHLANDS INN.** *216 Highland Ave (05255). 802/362-4565; fax 802/362-4028; toll-free 800/743-4565. Email relax@highlandsinn.com; www.highlandsinn.com.* 15 rms, 3 story. S $105; D $135; each addl $20; under 16 free. Crib avail. Parking lot. Pool. TV; cable (premium), VCR avail, CD avail. Complimentary full bkfst, newspaper, toll-free calls. Restaurant nearby. Bar. Ck-out 11 am, ck-in 2 pm. Meeting rm. Business servs avail. Concierge. Gift shop. Exercise privileges. Golf. Tennis. Downhill skiing. Bike rentals. Cr cds: A, MC, V.

★★★ **RELUCTANT PANTHER INN AND RESTAURANT.** *39 West Rd (05254), off VT 7A. 802/362-2568; fax 802/362-2586; toll-free 800/822-2331. Email panther@sover.net; www.reluctantpanther.com.* 13 rms, 6 suites. MAP, mid-Sept-Oct: S, D $168-$450; wkends (2-day min), hols (3-day min); lower rates rest of yr. Adults only. TV; cable. Complimentary bkfst. Dining rm 6-9 pm; closed Tues, Wed. Ck-out 11 am, ck-in 3 pm. Downhill ski 15 mi; x-country ski 2 mi. Health club privileges. Many fireplaces; whirlpool in suites. Sitting rm. Built 1850. Cr cds: A, MC, V.

★★ **SILAS GRIFFITH INN.** *178 S Main St (05739), 2 mi N on US 7, then W on Main St. 802/293-5567; fax 802/293-5559; res 800/545-1509. Email stay@silasgriffith.com; www.silasgriffith.com.* 13 rms, 3 story, 2 suites. Sep-Oct: S $149; D $159; suites $299; each addl $29; children $19; under 11 free; lower rates rest of yr. Pet accepted, some restrictions. Parking lot. Pool, lap pool, whirlpool. TV; cable, VCR avail. Complimentary full bkfst, toll-free calls. Restaurant 8 am-10 pm. Bar. Ck-out 11 am, ck-in 2 pm. Meeting rms. Business center. Concierge. Gift shop. Golf. Downhill skiing. Beach access. Bike rentals. Hiking trail. Picnic facilities. Cr cds: MC, V.

★★★ **VILLAGE COUNTRY INN.** *Historic Rte 7A (05254), 1 mi S at jct VT 11, 30 and US 7. 802/362-1792; fax 802/362-7238; res 800/370-0800; toll-free 800/370-0300. Email vci@vermontel.com; www.villagecountryinn.com.* 18 rms, 3 story, 14 suites. Oct: S $169; D $179; suites $239; lower rates rest of yr. Parking lot. Pool. TV; cable. Complimentary full bkfst, coffee in rms, toll-free calls. Restaurant 6 am-9 pm. Bar. Ck-out 11 am, ck-in 1 pm. Fax servs avail. Concierge. Gift shop. Exercise privileges. Golf. Tennis, 2 courts. Downhill skiing. Bike rentals. Hiking trail. Cr cds: A, DS, MC, V.

★★★ **WILBURTON INN.** *River Rd (05254), 1½ mi S on VT 7A to River Rd, then ½ mi SE. 802/362-2500; fax 802/362-1107; toll-free 800/648-4944. Email wilbuinn@sover.net; www.wilburton.com.* 35 rms, 1-3 story. Aug-Oct: S, D $120-$215; suites $175; wkly, family rates; higher rates: hols; lower rates rest of yr. TV in most rms. Pool. Complimentary full bkfst. Dining rm (public by res) 8-10 am, 6-9 pm. Rm serv (in season). Bar from 5 pm. Ck-out 11 am, ck-in 1 pm. Business servs avail. Tennis. Golf privileges, greens fee. Downhill ski 6 mi; x-country ski ½ mi. Some refrigerators. Spacious grounds; sculptural displays. Early 1900s Victorian-style inn with mountain view. Cr cds: A, DS, MC, V.

Restaurants

★★★ **CHANTICLEER.** *VT 7A (05255), 3½ mi N on VT 7A. 802/362-1616.* Specializes in rack of lamb, sweetbreads, fresh seafood. Own desserts. Hrs: 2-10 pm. Closed Mon, Tues; Thanksgiving, Dec 25; also Apr, mid-Nov-mid-Dec. Res accepted. Bar. Wine list. Dinner $19.95-$26. Parking. Tableside cooking. Former dairy barn. Fireplace. Cr cds: A, DS, MC, V. **D**

★★ **MARK ANTHONY'S YE OLDE TAVERN.** *N Main St (05255), ½ mi N on US 7. 802/362-0611.* Specializes in poultry and veal dishes, fresh seafood. Hrs: 11 am-9 pm. Res accepted. Bar. Lunch $5.25-$12; dinner $12-$24.95. Parking. Historic 200-yr-old tavern. Cr cds: A, MC, V.

★★ **SIRLOIN SALOON.** *VT 11 (05255), ¼ mi E on VT 11, 30. 802/362-2600. www.sirloinsaloon.com.* Specializes in wood-grilled steak, chicken, seafood. Salad bar. Hrs: 5-10 pm. Closed Thanksgiving. Res accepted. Bar. Dinner $7.95-$19.95. Child's menu. Parking. Open hearth. Converted mill; antiques. Southwestern theme; Native Amer artwork, artifacts. Cr cds: A, D, DS, MC, V. **D**

Marlboro

See also Brattleboro, Wilmington

Settled 1763 **Pop** 924 **Elev** 1,736 ft
Area code 802 **Zip** 05344

What to See and Do

Marlboro College. (1946) 275 students. Arts and sciences, international studies. On campus is Tyler Art Gallery (Mon-Fri; closed hols). 2½ mi S of VT 9. Phone 802/257-4333.

Seasonal Event

Marlboro Music Festival. Marlboro College campus. Chamber music concerts. Phone 215/569-4690. Mid-July-mid-Aug.

B&B/Small Inn

★ **WHETSTONE INN.** *550 South Rd (05344), ½ mi off VT 9 (South Rd), follow Marlboro College signs. 802/254-2500; toll-free 877/254-2500. Email whetston@sover.net.* 11 rms, 3 share bath, 2 story, 3 kits. No A/C. S $35-$60; D $55-$80; each addl $10; kit. units $75-$85; wkly rates. Crib $2. Pet accepted. Restaurant 8-10 am, 7-8 pm (public by res). Ck-out 2 pm, ck-in after 2 pm. Some refrigerators. Picnic tables. 18th-century country inn was originally a stagecoach stop; fireplaces in public rms. Swimming pond. Cr cds: A, D, DS, MC, V.

Restaurant

★ **SKYLINE.** *VT 9 (05344). 802/464-3536.* Specializes in New England dishes. Hrs: 7 am-3 pm; Fri, Sat to 9 pm; Sun to 8 pm. Closed Thanksgiving, Dec 25. Bkfst $2.50-$7.95; lunch, dinner $5.25-$15.95. Child's menu. Early Amer decor; fireplace. On Hogback Mt; 100-mi view from dining rm. Cr cds: A, MC, V. **D** **SC**

Middlebury

(D-1) See also Brandon, Vergennes

Settled 1761 **Pop** 8,034 **Elev** 366 ft
Area code 802 **Zip** 05753
Web www.midvermont.com

Information Addison County Chamber of Commerce Information Center, 2 Court St; 802/388-7951

Benjamin Smalley built the first log house here just before the Revolution. In 1800 the town had a full-fledged college. By 1803 there was a flourishing marble quarry and a women's academy run by Emma Hart Willard, a pioneer in education for women; today, it is known as Middlebury College. A Ranger District office of the Green Mountain National Forest (see) is located here; map and guides for day hikes on Long Trail are available.

What to See and Do

Congregational Church. (1806-09) Built after a plan in the *Country Builder's Assistant* and designed by architect Lavius Fillmore. Architecturally, one of finest in Vermont. (Mid-June-Aug, Fri and Sat) On the Common. Phone 802/388-7634.

Green Mountain National Forest. (see).

Historic Middlebury Village Walking Tour. Contact the Addison County Chamber of Commerce Information Center for map and information. Phone 802/388-7951.

Middlebury College. (1800) 1,950 students. Famous for the teaching of arts and sciences; summer language schools; Bread Loaf School of English and Writers' Conference. W of town on VT 125. Phone 802/443-5000. College includes

Bread Loaf. Site of nationally known Bread Loaf School of English in July and annual Writers' Conference in Aug. Also site of Robert Frost's cabin. In winter, it is the Carroll and Jane Rikert Ski Touring Center. 10 mi E on VT 125.

Emma Willard House. Location of first women's seminary (1814), now admissions and financial aid offices.

Middlebury College Museum of Art. (Tues-Sun; closed Jan 1, Thanksgiving, Dec 25) Phone 802/443-5007. **FREE**

Middlebury College Snow Bowl. Area has triple, 2 double chairlifts; patrol, school, rentals, snowmaking; cafeteria. Fifteen runs. (Early Dec-early Apr, daily; closed Dec 25) 13 mi E on VT 125, just E of Bread Loaf. Phone 802/388-4356. ¢¢¢¢

Old Stone Row. Incl Painter Hall (1815), oldest college bldg in state.

◪ **Starr Library.** Collections of works by Robert Frost and other American writers. (Daily; closed hols)

Sheldon Museum. Comprehensive collection of 19th-century "Vermontiana" in brick house (1829) with black marble fireplaces. Authentic furnishings range from hand-forged kitchen utensils to country and high-style furniture. Museum also features oil portraits, pewter, Staffordshire, clocks, pianos, toys, dolls, and local relics. Guided tours. (June-Oct, Mon-Fri; rest of yr, Wed and Fri; closed hols) 1 Park St. Phone 802/388-2117. ¢¢

UVM Morgan Horse Farm. Breeding and training farm for internationally acclaimed Morgan horses; owned by the Univ of Vermont. Daily workouts and training can be viewed. Guided tours, slide presentations. (May-Oct, daily) 2½ mi NW off VT 23. Phone 802/388-2011. ¢¢

Vermont State Craft Center at Frog Hollow. Restored mill overlooking Otter Creek Falls houses an exhibition and sales gallery with works of more than 300 Vermont craftspeople. Special exhibitions, classes, and workshops. (Spring-fall, daily; rest of yr, Mon-Sat; closed hols) 1 Mill St. Phone 802/388-3177. **FREE**

Annual Events

Winter Carnival. Middlebury College Snow Bowl. Late Feb.

Addison County Home and Garden Show. Exhibits, demonstrations. Usually last wkend Mar.

Festival on the Green. Village green. Classical, modern, and traditional dance; chamber and folk music; theater and comedy presentations. Early July.

Motels/Motor Lodges

★ **BLUE SPRUCE MOTEL.** *2428 Rte 7S (05753), 3 mi S on US 7.* 802/388-4091; fax 802/388-3003; toll-free 800/640-7671. Email stpadd@sover.net. 17 rms, 6 cottages, 3 kits. S, D $58-$75; each addl $10; suites $95-$135; kit. units $10 addl; higher rates in fall. TV; cable. Ck-out 10 am. Downhill ski 8 mi; x-country ski 6 mi. Cr cds: A, C, D, DS, MC, V.
🐾 ⬛ 🔥

★ **GREYSTONE MOTEL.** *US Hwy 7 (05753), 2 mi S on US 7.* 802/388-4935. 10 rms. Mid-May-Oct: S $52-$57; D $60-$70; each addl $8; lower rates rest of yr. TV; cable. Restaurant nearby. Ck-out 10 am. Downhill ski 11 mi; x-country ski 9 mi. Picnic tables. Cr cds: A, DS, MC, V.
🐾 🔥

Hotel

★★ **MIDDLEBURY INN.** *14 Court House Sq (05753), on US 7. 802/388-4961; fax 802/388-4563; toll-free 800/842-4666. Email midinnvt@sover.net; www.middleburyinn.com.* 68 rms, 2 story, 7 suites. S $135; D $150; suites $250; each addl $10; under 18 free. Crib avail. Pet accepted, some restrictions. Parking lot. TV; cable. Complimentary continental bkfst, coffee in rms. Restaurant 7 am-8:30 pm. Bar. Ck-out 11 am, ck-in 3 pm. Meeting rms. Business center. Bellhops. Gift shop. Exercise privileges. Golf, 18 holes. Tennis, 4 courts. Downhill skiing. Cr cds: A, D, DS, MC, V.

B&Bs/Small Inns

★★★ **SWIFT HOUSE INN.** *25 Stewart Ln (05753). 802/388-9925; fax 802/388-9927; res 802/388-9925. Email shi@together.net; www.swifthouseinn.com.* 21 rms, 2 story, 1 suite.D $225; suites $600; each addl $20; under 11 free. Crib avail. Parking lot. TV; cable. Complimentary continental bkfst, coffee in rms, newspaper. Restaurant nearby. Bar. Ck-out 11 am, ck-in 3 pm. Meeting rm. Business center. Gift shop. Salon/barber avail. Exercise privileges, sauna, steam rm. Golf, 18 holes. Downhill skiing. Hiking trail. Picnic facilities. Cr cds: A, C, D, DS, MC, V.

★★ **WAYBURY INN.** *457 E Main Rte 125 (05743), 5 mi SE on VT 125, 1 mi E of US 7. 802/388-4015; fax 802/388-1248; toll-free 800/348-1810. Email thefolks@wayburyinn.com; www.wayburyinn.com.* 11 rms, 3 story, 3 suites. June-Oct: S $95; D $105; suites $140; each addl $10; children $10; lower rates rest of yr. Pet accepted. Parking lot. TV; cable, VCR avail. Complimentary full bkfst, coffee in rms, newspaper, toll-free calls. Restaurant 5-9 pm. Bar. Ck-out 11 am, ck-in 3 pm. Meeting rm. Business servs avail. Concierge. Gift shop. Golf. Tennis. Downhill skiing. Hiking trail. Picnic facilities. Cr cds: C, D, DS, MC, V.

Restaurants

★★ **DOG TEAM TAVERN.** *1338 Dog Team Rd (05753), 4 mi N off US 7. 802/388-7651. www.dogteamtavern. com.* Specializes in sticky buns, baked ham with fritters, fresh seafood. Hrs: 5-9 pm; Sun from noon. Closed Dec 24, 25. Bar. Dinner $9.95-$14.95. Child's menu. Parking. Country atmosphere. Cr cds: C, D, DS, ER, MC, V.

★★ **FIRE AND ICE.** *26 Seymour St (05753). 802/388-7166.* Specializes in steak, seafood. Salad bar. Hrs: 11:30 am-8 pm. Closed Dec 25. Res accepted. Bar. Lunch $8.95-$11.95; dinner $12.95-$20.95. Child's menu. Parking. Eclectic decor, casual. Cr cds: A, C, D, DS, MC, V.

★ **MISTER UP'S.** *Bakery Ln (05753), off Main St, adj to municipal parking lot. 802/388-6724.* Specializes in fresh seafood. Salad bar. Hrs: 11 am-midnight. Closed Thanksgiving, Dec 24, 25. Res accepted. Bar. Lunch a la carte entrees: $5.25-$7.95; dinner a la carte entrees: $9.25-$13.95. Child's menu. Parking. Cr cds: A, D, DS, MC, V.

★★ **WAYBURY INN.** *VT 125. 802/388-4015. Email thefolks@wayburyinn. com; www.wayburyinn.com.* Specializes in fresh fish, steak, rack of lamb. Hrs: 5-9 pm. Res accepted. Bar. Dinner $12.95-$21.95. Child's menu. Parking. Porch dining in summer. Old Colonial stagecoach stop. Cr cds: D, DS, MC, V.

Montpelier

(D-2) See also Barre, Waitsfield, Waterbury

Settled 1787 **Pop** 8,247 **Elev** 525 ft
Area code 802 **Zip** 05602
Web www.central-vt.com

Information Central Vermont Chamber of Commerce, PO Box 336, Barre 05641; 802/229-5711

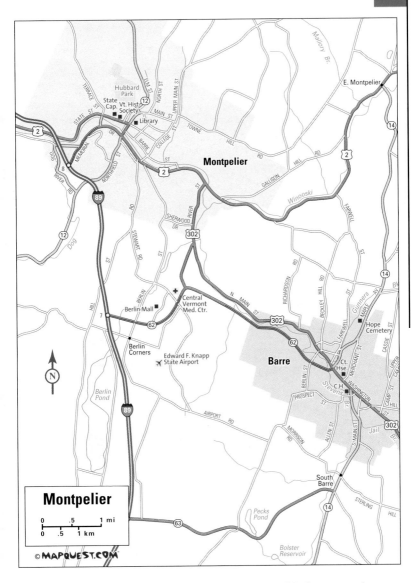

Montpelier

0 .5 1 mi
0 .5 1 km

© MAPQUEST.COM

The state capital, on the banks of the Winooski River, is also a life insurance center. Admiral Dewey, victor at Manila Bay, was born here. A popular summer vacation area, Montpelier absorbs the overflow from the nearby ski areas in winter.

What to See and Do

Hubbard Park. A 110-acre wooded area with picnic area (shelter, fireplaces, water). Stone observation tower (1932). 1 mi NW, on Hubbard Park Dr. Phone 802/223-5141. **FREE**

Morse Farm. Maple sugar and vegetable farm in rustic, wooded setting. Tour of sugar house; view sugarmaking process in season (Mar-Apr); slide show explains process off-season. Gift shop. (Daily; closed Easter, Dec 25) 3 mi N via County Road (follow signs on Main St). Phone 802/223-2740 or 800/242-2740. **FREE**

State House. (1859) Made of Vermont granite; dome covered with gold leaf. (July-mid-Oct, Mon-Fri, also Sat limited hours) State St. Phone 802/828-2228. **FREE**

Thomas Waterman Wood Art Gallery. Oils, watercolors, and etchings by Wood and other 19th-century American artists. Also American artists of the 1920s and '30s; changing monthly exhibits of works of contemporary local and regional artists. (Tues-Sun afternoons; closed hols) In Vermont College Arts Center, at College St. Phone 802/828-8743. ¢

Vermont Department of Libraries. Local and state history collections. (Mon-Fri; closed hols) Pavilion Office Bldg. 109 State St. Phone 802/828-3261. **FREE**

Vermont Historical Society Museum, Library. Historical exhibits. (Tues-Sun; closed hols) Pavilion Office Bldg, adj State House. Phone 802/828-2291. ¢¢

Motels/Motor Lodges

★★ **COMFORT INN.** *213 Paine Turnpike N (05602), on VT 62, ½ mi E of I-89 Exit 7.* 802/229-2222; fax 802/229-2222; toll-free 800/228-5150. Email comfortin@aol.com; www.comfort innsuites. 70 rms, 3 story, 19 suites. Sep-Oct: S $95; D $105; suites $125; each addl $10; under 18 free; lower rates rest of yr. Crib avail. Parking lot. TV; cable (premium), VCR avail. Complimentary continental bkfst, newspaper. Restaurant. Bar. Fax servs avail. Coin lndry. Free airport transportation. Exercise privileges. Golf. Tennis, 2 courts. Downhill skiing. Picnic facilities. Cr cds: A, D, DS, MC, V.

⊡ ⊠ 🏋 ⚟ 🏃 ⚟ 🔀 🔥 SC

★★ **LAGUE INN.** *394 Fisher Rd (05602), 3 mi N on VT 62, opp Central VT Hospital, near E.F. Knapp Airport.* 802/223-2524; fax 802/229-5766. 80 units, 2 story. S $50-$100; D $60-$120; each addl $10; under 6 free; wkly rates; higher rates: hols, fall foliage. Crib free. TV; cable (premium), VCR (movies $5). Indoor pool. Restaurant 6:30 am-9 pm. Bar. Ck-out 11 am. Meeting rms. Business servs avail. Free airport transportation. X-country ski 4 mi. Some refrigerators. Picnic tables. Cr cds: A, DS, MC, V.

⊡ ⊠ ≈ ✕ 🔀 🔥 SC

Hotel

★★★ **CAPITOL PLAZA HOTEL AND CONFERENCE CENTER.** *100 State St (05602). 802/223-5252; fax 802/229-5427; toll-free 800/274-5252. Email capitolplaza@weblizard.net; www.capitolplaza.com.* 56 rms, 4 story. Jul-Oct: S $109; D $119; suites $179; each addl $10; under 15 free; lower rates rest of yr. Crib avail, fee. Parking lot. TV; cable, VCR avail, CD avail. Complimentary coffee in rms, toll-free calls. Restaurant. Bar. Ck-out 11 am, ck-in 3 pm. Meeting rms. Business center. Bellhops. Concierge. Dry cleaning. Gift shop. Salon/barber avail. Exercise privileges. Golf. Tennis, 20 courts. Downhill skiing. Hiking trail. Cr cds: A, DS, MC, V.

⊡ ⊠ 🏋 ⚟ 🏃 ⚟ 🔀 🔥 SC 🏃

B&Bs/Small Inns

★ **BETSY'S BED AND BREAKFAST.** *74 E State St (05602).* 802/229-0466; fax 802/229-5412. Email betsybb@together.net; www.central-vt.com/web/betsybb. 11 rms, 2 story, 1 suite. Sep-Oct: S $80; D $90; suites $130; each addl $5; children $5; lower rates rest of yr. Crib avail. Parking lot. TV; cable, VCR avail, CD avail. Complimentary full bkfst. Restaurant nearby. Ck-out 11 am, ck-in 4 pm. Business servs avail. Coin lndry. Exercise privileges. Golf. Cr cds: A, DS, MC, V.

⊠ 🏋 🏃 🔀 🔥

★★★ **INN AT MONTPELIER.** *147 Main St (05602).* 802/223-2727; fax 802/223-0722. Email mail2inn@aol.com. 19 rms, 2 story, 9 suites. Sep-Oct: S $167; D $177; each addl $15; under 6 free; lower rates rest of yr. Crib avail. Valet parking avail. TV; cable. Complimentary continental bkfst, coffee in rms, newspaper, toll-free calls. Restaurant. 24-hr rm serv. Bar. Meeting rms. Business servs avail. Dry cleaning. Exercise privileges. Golf. Downhill skiing. Supervised children's activities. Hiking trail. Picnic facilities. Cr cds: A, D, DS, MC, V.

⬢ ⚟ ⊠ 🏋 🏃 🔀 SC

★★★ **THE INN ON THE COMMON.** *N Main St (05827), 7 mi E on US 2, 30 mi N on VT 14.* 802/586-9619; fax 802/586-2249; toll-free 800/521-2233. Email info@innonthecommon.com; www.innonthecommon.com. 16 rms in 3 bldgs, 2 story. No A/C. No rm phones. MAP: S $150-$160; D $230-$250; suites $250;

package plans; higher rates fall foliage. Serv charge 15%. Crib free. Pet accepted. TV in sitting rm; VCR. Heated pool. Afternoon refreshments. Dining rm 8-9:30 am, dinner (2 sittings) 6:30, 8 pm. Bar. Ck-out 11 am, ck-in 1 pm. Business servs avail. Tennis. Golf privileges. X-country ski on site. Bicycle rentals. Health club privileges. Lawn games. Antiques. Library. Some fireplaces. Restored Federalperiod houses in scenic Vermont village; landscaped gardens. Extensive film collection. Cr cds: A, DS, MC, V.

★★ **NORTHFIELD INN.** *228 Highland Ave (05663), 10 mi S on VT 12, near Norwich University. 802/485-8558; res 802/485-8558.* 12 rms, 4 story, 2 suites. Jul-Oct: S, D $85-$159; each addl $40; lower rates rest of yr. Parking lot. Pool, lifeguard. TV; cable (premium), VCR avail. Complimentary full bkfst, toll-free calls. Restaurant. Bar. Ck-out 11 am, ck-in 3 pm. Meeting rm. Concierge. Coin lndry. Exercise privileges. Golf, 9 holes. Tennis. Downhill skiing. Beach access. Bike rentals. Hiking trail. Picnic facilities. Cr cds: A, ER, MC, V.

Restaurants

★★ **CHEF'S TABLE.** *118 Main St (05602). 802/229-9202.* Continental menu. Hrs: 11 am-1 pm, 5-9 pm. Closed Sun; most major hols. Res accepted. Bar. Lunch a la carte entrees: $13.50-$18.75; dinner a la carte entrees: $13.50-$18.75. Prix fixe: $30. 15% serv chg. Owned and operated by New England Culinary Institute. Cr cds: A, DS, MC, V.
D SC

★ **LOBSTER POT.** *1028 US 302 (05641). 802/476-9900.* Specializes in seafood, steak. Salad bar. Hrs: 11 am-9 pm; Sun brunch 10 am-2:30 pm. Closed Mon; major hols; also 4th wk Oct. Res accepted. Bar. Lunch $3.95-$7.25; dinner $8.50-$18. Sun brunch $7.47. Child's menu. Family-owned. Cr cds: A, D, MC, V.
D

★★ **MAIN STREET GRILL AND BAR.** *118 Main St (05602). 802/223-3188.* Hrs: 11 am-2 pm, 5-9 pm; Sat, Sun from 5 pm; Sun brunch 10 am-2

pm. Closed hols. Bar. Lunch $4.50-$6.50; dinner $6.95-$11.50. 15% serv chg. Training restaurant for 1st and 2nd year students of New England Culinary Institute. Cr cds: A, C, D, DS, ER, MC, V.
D SC

Mount Mansfield

(see Stowe)

Newfane

(H-2) *See also Brattleboro*

Settled 1774 **Pop** 1,555 **Elev** 536 ft
Area code 802 **Zip** 05345
Information Town Clerk, PO Box 36; 802/365-7772

Originally settled high on Newfane Hill, this is a charming, sleepy town. American poet Eugene Field spent many summer holidays here.

What to See and Do

Jamaica State Park. On 758 acres. Old railroad bed along West River serves as trail to Ball Mt Dam. Fishing; hiking trails, picnicking, tent and trailer sites (dump station), lean-tos. Whitewater canoe races on river. (May-Columbus Day) Standard fees. 13 mi W on VT 30, in Jamaica. Phone 802/874-4600 or 802/886-2434.

Scott Covered Bridge. (1870) Longest single span in state (166 ft), built with lattice-type trusses. Together, the 3 spans total 276 ft. Other 2 spans are of king post-type trusses. Over the West River in Townshend, 5 mi N via VT 30.

Townshend State Forest. A 1,690-acre area with foot trail to Bald Mt (1,580 ft). Hiking trails, picnic sites, tent and trailer sites. Swimming at nearby Townshend Reservoir Recreation Area. (May-Columbus Day) Standard fees. 6 mi N, off VT 30. Phone 802/365-7500 or 802/886-2434.

Windham County Courthouse.
(1825) On the green.

Windham County Historical Society Museum. Contains artifacts from the 21 towns of Windham County; exhibits on the Civil War and the Vermont Regiment. (Memorial Day-Columbus Day, Wed-Sun) Main St. Phone 802/365-4148. **Donation**

B&Bs/Small Inns

★★★ **FOUR COLUMNS INN.** *21 West St (05345), on Village Green. 802/365-7713; fax 802/365-0022; toll-free 800/787-6633.* 15 rms, 4 suites. S, D $110-$125; each addl $25; suites $140-$225. Pet accepted. TV in lounge; cable (premium). Pool. Complimentary full bkfst. Dining rm 6-9 pm, except Tues (guests only) 8-9:30 am (see also FOUR COLUMNS). Bar from 4 pm. Ck-out 11 am, ck-in 2 pm. Business servs avail. Stately 19th-century house; Colonial furnishings. On 150 wooded acres; walking paths, gardens. Totally non-smoking. Cr cds: A, DS, MC, V.

★★ **OLD NEWFANE INN.** *Rte 30 & Village Common (05345), on Village Green. 802/365-4427; toll-free 800/784-4427. www.oldnewfaneinnww.com.* 6 rms, 2 story, 2 suites. Dec-Mar, July-Oct: S $105; D $125; suites $155; under 10 free; lower rates rest of yr. Street parking. TV; cable (premium). Complimentary continental bkfst. Restaurant 6 am-9:30 pm. Bar. Ck-out 1 pm, ck-in 4 pm. Golf, 18 holes. Tennis, 2 courts. Downhill skiing. Cr cds: A, DS, MC, V.

★★★ **WINDHAM HILL INN.** *311 Lawrence Dr (05359), 12 mi N on VT 30, off Windham Hill Rd. 802/874-4080; fax 802/874-4702; toll-free 800/944-4080. Email windham@sover.net; www.windhamhill.com.* 21 rms, 3 story. Oct, Dec: S $240; D $250; each addl $25; lower rates rest of yr. Parking lot. Pool. TV; cable (premium), VCR avail, CD avail. Complimentary full bkfst, toll-free calls. Restaurant. Bar. Meeting rm. Business center. Concierge. Gift shop. Golf. Tennis. Downhill skiing. Hiking trail. Picnic facilities. Cr cds: A, DS, MC, V.

Restaurants

★★★ **FOUR COLUMNS.** *230 West St. 802/365-7713. Email frcolinn@sover.net; www.fourcolumnsinn.com.* Specializes in local lamb, fresh game, fresh fish. Own baking. Hrs: 6-9 pm. Closed Tues; Dec 24-25; also 2 wks Apr. Res accepted. Bar. Wine list. Dinner a la carte entrees: $19-28. Colonial decor. Cr cds: A, C, D, DS, ER, MC, V.

D

★★★ **OLD NEWFANE.** *VT 30. 802/365-4427. www.oldnewfane.com.* Specializes in frogs' legs, wild game. Own baking. Hrs: 6-10 pm. Closed Mon; Apr-late May, Nov-mid-Dec. Res accepted. Bar. Wine list. Dinner $16.95-$28. Historical landmark (1787); Colonial decor. Cr cds: A, DS, MC, V.

Newport

Settled 1793 **Pop** 4,434 **Elev** 723 ft
Area code 802 **Zip** 05855
Information Chamber of Commerce, The Causeway; 802/334-7782

Just a few miles from the Canadian border, Newport lies at the southern end of Lake Memphremagog. Rugged Owl's Head (3,360 ft) guards the western shore of the lake. Recreational activities in the area incl swimming, fishing, boating; camping, skiing, and snowmobiling.

What to See and Do

Goodrich Memorial Library. Artifacts of old Vermont in historic bldg; animal display. (Mon-Sat; closed hols) 70 Main St. Phone 802/334-7902. **FREE**

Haskell Opera House & Library. Historic turn-of-the-century bldg owned jointly by local Canadian and US residents. First floor houses library with reading rm in US, book stacks in Canada. Second floor is replica of the old Boston Opera House (seats 300) with audience in US, stage in Canada. Summer concert series (fee). 8 mi N via US 5, on Caswell Ave in Derby Line, Vermont, and Rock Island, Quebec, Canada. Phone 802/873-3022.

Newport's *Princess.* Cruise Lake Memphremagog in both US and Canadian waters aboard sternwheeler with turn-of-the-century decor. Cruises incl Sightseeing (1½ hrs), Pizza (1½ hrs, res required), Buffet Dinner (2 hrs, res required), Moonlight (1½ hrs), and Weekend Brunch (1½ hrs, res required). (May-Oct, daily; departures vary) City Dock. Phone 802/334-6617. ¢¢¢-¢¢¢¢¢

Northeast Kingdom Tours. Escorted bus tours depart from Newport Municipal Bldg and local motels. Narrated trips (2 and 4 hrs) explore international border region (Vermont/Canada); includes stops at dairy farm and Old Stone House museum. Cruises on Lake Memphremagog and trips to Montréal also avail. 3 Clough St. Phone 802/334-8687.

Old Stone House. (1836) Museum housed in 4-story granite bldg with antique furniture; early farm, household, and military items; 19th-century schoolbooks. (July-Aug, daily; mid-May-June, Sep-mid-Oct, Fri-Tues) 11 mi SE via US 5S or I-91 S to Orleans, then 2 mi NE on unnumbered road to Brownington Village. Phone 802/754-2022. ¢¢

Motels/Motor Lodges

★★ **NEWPORT CITY MOTEL.** *444 E Main St (05855). 802/334-6558; fax 802/334-6557; toll-free 800/338-6558. www.vermonter.com.* 64 rms, 2 story. S, D $58-$75. Crib $6. TV; cable. Indoor pool; whirlpool. Coffee in rms. Restaurant opp 5:30 am-2 pm. Ck-out 11 am. Meeting rm. Business servs avail. In-rm modem link. Sundries. Downhill/x-country ski 15 mi. Exercise equipt. Some refrigerators. Balconies. Cr cds: A, D, DS, MC, V.

★ **SUPER 8.** *444 E Main St (05859), I-91 Exit 25. 802/334-1775; fax 802/334-1994; res 800/800-8000.* 52 rms, 2 story. S $45.88; D $58.88; each addl $6; suites $106; under 12 free. Crib $6. TV; cable. Complimentary continental bkfst. Restaurant nearby. Ck-out 11 am. Business servs avail. Cr cds: A, D, DS, MC, V.

Restaurant

★★ **EAST SIDE RESTAURANT AND PUB.** *25 Lake St (05855). 802/334-2340.* Continental menu. Specializes in fresh seafood, steak, prime rib. Own desserts. Hrs: 11 am-9 pm. Closed Dec 25. Bar. Bkfst $3.25-$5.95; lunch $3.95-$6.95; dinner $7.50-$15. On lake; dockage. Cr cds: DS, MC, V.

North Hero (B-1)

Pop 502 **Elev** 111 ft **Area code** 802
Zip 05474
Web www.champlainislands.com
Information Champlain Islands Chamber of Commerce, PO Box 213; 802/372-5683

What to See and Do

North Hero State Park. A 399-acre park located in the N part of the Champlain Islands; extensive shoreline on Lake Champlain. Swimming, fishing, boating (ramps); hiking trails, playground, tent and trailer sites (dump station), lean-tos. (Memorial Day-Labor Day) Standard fees. 6 mi N, off US 2 near South Alburg. Phone 802/372-8727 or 802/879-5674.

Seasonal Event

Royal Lippizan Stallions of Austria. Summer residence of the stallions. Performances Thurs and Fri eves, Sat and Sun afternoons. For ticket prices, contact Chamber of Commerce. July-Aug.

Motel/Motor Lodge

★★ **SHORE ACRES INN.** *237 Shore Acres Dr (05474). 802/372-8722. Email info@shoreacres.com; www.shore acres.com.* 23 rms, 9 A/C. Mid-June-mid-Oct: S, D $79.50-$129.50; lower rates rest of yr; limited rms avail mid-Oct-May. Pet accepted. TV; cable. Restaurant 7:30-10 am, 5-9 pm. Bar. Ck-out 10:30 am. Driving range. Lawn games. Two tennis courts. Some refrigerators. 50 acres on Lake Champlain; panoramic view. Cr cds: DS, MC, V.

B&Bs/Small Inns

★★★ **NORTH HERO HOUSE INN.** *US 2 (05474), in center of village. 802/ 372-4732; fax 802/372-3218; toll-free 888/525-3644.* 26 rms, 3 story. May-late Oct: S, D $79-$285; each addl $5-$45. Closed rest of yr. TV. Complimentary continental bkfst. Restaurant (see also NORTH HERO HOUSE). Bar 5-11 pm. Ck-out 11 am, ck-in 2 pm. Tennis. Game rm. Lawn games. Some private patios, balconies. Rms vary in size, decor. Built in 1800; fireplace in lobby. On lake; beach, dockage. Cr cds: A, MC, V.

★ **RUTHCLIFFE LODGE & RESORT.** *1002 Quarry Rd (05463), N on US 2, W on VT 129, follow signs. 802/928-3200; fax 802/928-3200; toll-free 800/ 769-8162. Email rcliffe@together.net; www.virtualcities.com/~virtual.* 5 rms, 1 suite. S, D $87; suites $96; each addl $15. Crib avail, fee. Parking lot. TV; cable (premium), VCR avail, CD avail. Complimentary full bkfst, newspaper. Restaurant 8:30 am-9 pm. Bar. Ck-out 11 am, ck-in 2 pm. Golf, 18 holes. Beach access. Bike rentals. Picnic facilities. Cr cds: A, DS, MC, V.

★★ **THOMAS MOTT HOMESTEAD B&B.** *63 Bleu Rock Rd (05440), 14 mi S, off VT 78. 800/348-0843; fax 802/796-3736; toll-free 800/348-0843. Email tmott@together.net; www.thomas-mott-6.6.com.* 5 rms, 2 story. No A/C. S, D $75-$95; each addl $10. Children over 6 yrs only. TV in sitting rm. Complimentary full bkfst; afternoon refreshments. Ck-out 11 am, ck-in 3 pm. X-country ski on site. Rec rm. Complimentary gourmet ice cream. Restored farmhouse (1838); overlooks lake. Totally nonsmoking. Cr cds: A, DS, MC, V.

Restaurant

★★ **NORTH HERO HOUSE.** *VT 2. 802/372-4732. Email nhhlake@aol. com; www.members.aol.com/nhhlake/.*

Hrs: 5-9 pm. Res accepted. Bar. Dinner $11.95-$18.95. Cr cds: A, MC, V.

Okemo State Forest

See also Ludlow, Weston

Information Okemo Mountain Resort, 77 Okemo Ridge Rd, Ludlow 05149; 802/228-4041 or 800/78-OKEMO (lodging res)

Mount Okemo (3,372 ft), almost a lone peak in south central Vermont near Ludlow, commands splendid views of the Adirondacks, the White Mountains, the Connecticut Valley, and Vermont's own Green Mountains. A road goes to within ½ mile of the mountain top (summer, fall; free); from there, it's an easy hike to the fire tower at the top. Surrounding Mount Okemo is the 4,527-acre state forest, which is primarily a skiing area.

Area has 7 quad, 3 triple chairlifts, 2 Pomalifts, J-bar; patrol, school, rentals, snowmaking; cafeteria, restaurants, bar, nursery; 96 runs, longest run 4½ mi; vertical drop 2,150 ft. (Early Nov-mid-Apr, daily) Phone 802/228-4041 or 802/228-5222 (snow conditions). For information about area lodging phone 802/228-5571. ¢¢¢¢

Peru

(G-2) *See also Londonderry, Manchester and Manchester Center*

Settled 1773 **Pop** 324 **Elev** 1,700 ft **Area code** 802 **Zip** 05152

This small mountain village has many fine examples of classic New England architecture, such as the Congregational Church (1846). Spectacular views of the Green Mountains surround this skiing center; also a popular area for fishing, hunting, and hiking.

What to See and Do

Bromley Mountain Ski Area. Area has 2 quad, 5 double chairlifts, 2 mitey-mites, J-bar; patrol, school, rentals, snowmaking; 2 cafeterias, restaurant, 2 lounges, nursery; 41 runs, longest run over 2 mi; vertical drop 1,334 ft. (Mid-Nov-mid-Apr, daily) 2 mi SW on VT 11. Phone 802/824-5522. ¢¢¢

    Summer activities. Include miniature golf, thrill sleds, children's theater. (Mid-June-mid-Oct) Also

    Bromley Alpine Slide. Speed-controlled sled ride and scenic chairlift; cafe, picnic area. Outdoor deck. Multistate view. (Late May-mid-Oct, daily, weather permitting) Phone 802/824-5522. ¢¢

Hapgood Pond Recreation Area. Swimming, fishing, boating; picnicking, camping. Fee for various activities. 2 mi NE on Hapgood Pond Rd, in Green Mt National Forest (see). Phone 802/824-6456. Per vehicle ¢

J. J. Hapgood Store. (1827) General store featuring interesting old items; also penny candy, maple syrup, cheese. (Daily) Main St. Phone 802/824-5911.

Wild Wings Ski Touring Center. School, rentals; warming rm, concession. Twelve mi of groomed trails. 2½ mi N on North Rd. Phone 802/824-6793. ¢¢

Plymouth

(F-2) *See also Killington, Ludlow, Woodstock*

Pop 440 **Elev** 1,406 ft **Area code** 802 **Zip** 05056

Information Town of Plymouth, HC 70, Box 39A; 802/672-3655

Seemingly unaware of the 20th century, this town hasn't changed much since July 4, 1872, when Calvin Coolidge was born in the back of the village store, still in business today. A country road leads to the cemetery where the former president and six generations of his family are buried. Nearby is the Coolidge Visitor's Center and Museum, which displays historical and presidential memorabilia.

What to See and Do

Calvin Coolidge State Forest. A 16,165-acre area. Hiking, snowmobile trails. Picnic facilities. Tent and trailer sites (dump station), primitive camping, lean-tos. (Memorial Day-Columbus Day) Standard fees. 1 mi N off VT 100A, Calvin Coolidge Memorial Hwy. Phone 802/672-3612 or 802/886-2434.

Plymouth Cheese Corp. Cheese, canned products, maple syrup, and honey. Cheese processed Mon-Wed. (Facility open late May-Nov, daily; rest of yr, Mon-Fri; closed Jan 1, Thanksgiving, Dec 25) Phone 802/672-3650. **FREE**

President Calvin Coolidge Homestead. Restored to its early 20th-century appearance. Calvin Coolidge was sworn in by his father in the sitting rm in 1923. The Plymouth Historic District also includes the General Store that was operated by the President's father, the house where the President was born, the village dance hall which served as the 1924 summer White House office, the Union Church with its Carpenter Gothic interior, the Wilder House (birthplace of Coolidge's mother), the Wilder Barn with 19th-century farming equipment, a restaurant, and a visitor center with museum. (Late May-mid-Oct, daily) 1 mi NE on VT 100A, in Plymouth Notch. Phone 802/672-3773. ¢¢

Motel/Motor Lodge

★ **FARMBROOK MOTEL.** *706 Rte 100A (05056), 3 mi NE on VT 100A. 802/672-3621. Email jthistle@webtv. net; www.motel-vt-farmbrook. 12 rms, 2 story. Dec-Mar, Oct: S $55; each addl $7; under 12 free; lower rates rest of yr. Parking lot. TV; cable (premium), CD avail, VCR avail. Complimentary coffee in rms. Restaurant nearby. Ck-out 11 am, ck-in 2 pm. Golf. Downhill skiing. Hiking trail. Picnic facilities. Cr cds: A, D, DS, MC, V.*

Resort

★★★ **HAWK INN AND MOUNTAIN RESORT.** *HCR 70 Box 64 (05056), 8 mi S of US 4 on VT 100. 802/672-3811; fax 802/672-5585; res*

*800/685-4295. Email hawkinn@
vemontel.com; www.hawkresort.com.*
150 houses, townhouses, 50 inn rms.
Late Dec-Feb: 2-4 bedrm houses,
townhouses $250-$700/house; inn
rms (includes bkfst): S, D $169-$279;
wkly, monthly rates; ski plans; MAP
and EP avail; lower rates rest of yr.
Crib free. Maid serv $25/hr (houses,
townhouses). TV; cable (premium),
VCR (movies $3.50). 2 pools; 1
indoor; whirlpool. Playground.
Supervised children's activities (June-
Aug); ages 5-12. Full bkfst. Coffee in
rms. Dining rm 6-10 pm. Rm serv
(inn rms). Box lunches, picnics. Chef
for hire. Bar. Ck-out 11 am, ck-in 4
pm. Grocery 2 mi. Package store 8
mi. Meeting rms. Business servs
avail. In-rm modem link. Valet serv.
Airport, railroad station, bus depot
transportation. Tennis. Swimming in
natural pond. Boats, rowboats,
canoes, sailboats, paddleboats.
Downhill ski 10 mi; x-country ski on
site. Tobogganing, ice skating. Horse-
drawn sleigh rides. Hiking. Bicycles.
Lawn games. Entertainment, movies.
Exercise rm; sauna. Massage. Fishing
guides. Refrigerators, minibars, fieldstone fireplaces. Private patios, balconies. Picnic tables, grills. Nature
trails. Custom-designed vacation
homes. Cr cds: A, DS, MC, V.

Rutland

(F-2) *See also Brandon, Killington*

Settled 1761 **Pop** 18,230 **Elev** 648 ft
Area code 802 **Zip** 05701
Web www.rutlandvermont.com
Information Chamber of Commerce,
256 N Main St; 802/773-2747

This is Vermont's second-largest city.
Its oldest newspaper, the *Rutland Herald,* has been published continuously
since 1794. The world's deepest marble quarry is in West Rutland. The
office of the supervisor of the Green
Mountain National Forest (see) is
located here.

What to See and Do

Chaffee Center for the Visual Arts.
Continuous exhibits of paintings,
graphics, photography, crafts, sculpture. Print rm, gallery shop, annual
art festivals (mid-Aug, Columbus Day
wkend), other special events. (Wed-
Mon; closed hols) 16 S Main St, on
US 7, opp Main St Park. Phone
802/775-0356. **FREE**

Hubbardton Battlefield and Museum.
On July 7, 1777, the Green Mountain
Boys and Colonial troops from Massachusetts and New Hampshire
stopped British forces pursuing the
American Army from Fort Ticonderoga. This was the only battle of
the Revolution fought on Vermont
soil and the first in a series of engage-
ments that led to the capitulation of
Burgoyne at Saratoga. Visitor Center
with exhibits. Battle monument;
trails; picnicking. (Memorial Day-
Columbus Day, Wed-Sun) 7 mi W via
US 4, Exit 5. Phone 802/759-2412. ¢

New England Maple Museum. One of
largest collections of antique maple
sugaring artifacts in the world; 2
large dioramas featuring more than
100 hand-carved figures; narrated
slide show, demonstrations, samples
of Vermont foodstuffs, craft and
maple product gift shop. (Mid-Mar-
Dec 24, daily; closed Thanksgiving) 7
mi N on US 7, in Pittsford. Phone
802/483-9414. ¢¢

Norman Rockwell Museum. More
than 2,000 pictures and Rockwell
memorabilia spanning 60 yrs of
artist's career. Includes the *Four Free-
doms,* Boy Scout series, many magazine covers, incl all 323 from the
Saturday Evening Post, and nearly
every illustration and advertisement.
(Daily; closed hols) Gift shop. E on
US 4. Phone 802/773-6095. ¢¢

⭐ **Vermont Marble Exhibit.** Exhibit
explains how marble is formed and
the process by which it is manufactured. Displays; sculptor at work; balcony view of factory; "Gallery of the
Presidents"; movie on the marble
industry; marble market, gift shop.
(June-Oct, daily; rest of yr, Mon-Sat)
61 Main St, 2 mi W on US 4, then 4
mi N on VT 3 in Proctor, adj to Vermont Marble Co factory. Phone
802/459-3311 or 800/451-4468, ext
436. ¢¢

Wilson Castle. This 32-rm, 19th-cen-
tury mansion on a 115-acre estate

features 19 open proscenium arches, 84 stained-glass windows, 13 imported tile fireplaces, a towering turret and parapet; European and Oriental furnishings, art gallery, sculpture; 15 other bldgs. Picnic area. Guided tours. (Late May-mid-Oct, daily) 2½ mi W on US 4, then 1 mi N on West Proctor Rd. Phone 802/773-3284. ¢¢¢

Annual Events

Green Mountain International Rodeo. PRCA rodeo. Free pony rides, petting zoo. Bands, dancing. Phone 802/773-2747. Mid-June.

Vermont State Fair. Exhibits of arts and crafts, flowers, produce, home arts, pets, animals, maple sugaring. Daily special events. Late-Aug-early-Sep.

Motels/Motor Lodges

★ **HOWARD JOHNSON INN.** *401 S Main St (05701), on US 7. 802/775-4303; fax 802/775-6840.* 96 rms, 2 story. S, D $42-$100; each addl $8; under 18 free. Crib free. TV; cable (premium), VCR avail (movies $2). Indoor pool; sauna. Complimentary continental bkfst. Ck-out noon. Guest lndry. Meeting rms. Business servs avail. Downhill/x-country ski 16 mi. Health club privileges. Game rm. Private patios, balconies. Cr cds: A, DS, MC, V.

★★ **RAMADA LIMITED.** *253 S Main St (05701). 802/773-3361; fax 802/773-4892; toll-free 888/818-3297. Email ramada@vermontel.com.* 76 rms, 2 story, 3 kits. S, D $49-$89; each addl $6-$10; kit. units $89-$129; family rates; higher rates: hol wks. Crib free. TV; cable (premium). Indoor pool; sauna. Bkfst avail. Ck-out noon. Meeting rm. Downhill/x-country ski 16 mi. Health club privileges. Balconies. Cr cds: A, D, DS, MC, V.

Hotels

★★ **COMFORT INN TROLLEY SQUARE.** *19 Allen St (05701). 802/775-2200; fax 802/775-2694; res 800/228-5150; toll-free 800/432-6788.,*

3 story. Feb, Sep-Oct, Dec: S, D $160; lower rates rest of yr. Crib avail. Parking lot. Indoor pool, whirlpool. TV; cable (premium). Complimentary continental bkfst, coffee in rms, newspaper. Restaurant. Ck-out 11 am, ck-in 2 pm. Meeting rms. Fax servs avail. Dry cleaning. Golf. Cr cds: A, C, D, DS, JCB, MC.

★★ **HOLIDAY INN RUTLAND-KILLINGTON.** *476 US Rte 7 S (05701), US 7S. 802/775-1911; fax 802/775-0113; res 800/465-4329; toll-free 800/462-4810. Email info@holiday inn-vermont.com; www.holidayinn-vermont.com.* 150 rms, 2 story. Dec-Mar, July-Oct: S $269; D $269; lower rates rest of yr. Crib avail. Pet accepted, some restrictions. Indoor pool, lap pool, whirlpool. TV; cable (DSS). Complimentary coffee in rms, newspaper. Restaurant 6 am-10:10 pm. Bar. Ck-out noon, ck-in 4:01 pm. Meeting rms. Business center. Bellhops. Dry cleaning, coin lndry. Free airport transportation. Exercise rm, sauna. Golf. Downhill skiing. Supervised children's activities. Cr cds: A, C, D, DS, MC, V.

Resort

★★★ **MOUNTAIN TOP INN.** *195 Mountain Top Rd (05737), 4 mi N on VT 7, then 6 mi NE via Chittenden Rd. 802/483-2311; fax 802/483-6373; toll-free 800/445-2100. Email info@ mountaintopinn.com; www.mountain topinn.com.* 60 units. EP: S, D $90-$115/person; each addl $60; cottages $105/person; MAP avail. Closed Apr and 1st 3 wks Nov. Crib free. TV in lobby; VCR (free movies). Heated pool; sauna, poolside serv. Complimentary coffee in rms. Dining rm (public by res) 8-10 am, noon-2 pm, 6-8:30 pm; Fri, Sat 6-9 pm. Rm serv. Bar noon-11:30 pm. Business servs avail. Gift shop. Bus depot transportation. Tennis. Par-3 golf course, putting green, golf school. Boats, rowboats, canoes. Fly fishing instruction. Downhill ski 8 mi; x-country ski on site; lessons, rental, snow making equipt. Sleigh rides. Hiking trails. Lawn games. Rec rm. Movie rm. Homemade maple syrup. On

mountain top; 1,300 acres; scenic
views. Cr cds: A, DS, MC, V.

B&Bs/Small Inns

**★★★ INN AT RUTLAND BED AND
BREAKFAST.** *70 N Main St (05701).
802/773-0575; fax 802/775-3506; toll-
free 800/808-0575. Email gourmet29@
aol.com; www.innatrutland.com.* 11
rms, 3 story. Feb, Sep-Oct, Dec: S
$175; D $185; each addl $15; lower
rates rest of yr. Parking lot. TV; cable,
CD avail. Compli-
mentary full bkfst,
toll-free calls.
Restaurant nearby.
Ck-out 11 am, ck-in
3 pm. Meeting rm.
Concierge. Free air-
port transportation.
Golf. Tennis, 10
courts. Downhill
skiing. Cr cds: A,
DS, MC, V.

**★★★ MAPLE-
WOOD INN.** *VT
22A S (05743), 18
mi W on US 4 to VT
22A, then S 1 mi
past Fair Haven. 802/
265-8039; fax 802/265-8210; toll-free
800/253-7729. Email maplewd@sover.
net; www.sover.net/~maplewd.* 3 rms, 2
story, 2 suites. Sep-Oct: S, D $105;
suites $150; each addl $20; children
$20; under 12 free; lower rates rest of
yr. Pet accepted, some restrictions,
fee. Parking lot. TV; cable (premium),
VCR avail. Complimentary continental bkfst, toll-free calls. Restaurant
nearby. Bar. Ck-out 11 am, ck-in 3
pm. Meeting rms. Business center.
Exercise privileges. Golf, 18 holes.
Downhill skiing. Hiking trail. Picnic
facilities. Cr cds: A, MC, V.

★★★ TULIP TREE INN. *49 Dam Rd
(05737), 10 mi NE on US 7 to Chittenden Rd, follow signs. 802/483-6213;
fax 802/483-2623; toll-free 800/707-
0017. Email ttinn@sover.net; www.
tuliptreeinn.com.* 9 rms, 2 story. Sep-
Oct, Dec: S, D $199; suites $269;
lower rates rest of yr. Parking lot. TV;
cable (premium), VCR avail. Complimentary full bkfst. Restaurant 7-11
pm. Bar. Ck-out 11 am, ck-in 3 pm.
Golf, 18 holes. Tennis, 4 courts.

Downhill skiing. Beach access. Bike
rentals. Hiking trail. Picnic facilities.
Cr cds: MC, V.

Extended Stay

**★★ BEST WESTERN INN &
SUITES.** *US 4 E (05701), 3 mi E on
US 4. 802/773-3200; fax 802/773-
3200; res 800/528-1234. Email
hoggepenny@aol.com; www.bestwestern
rutland.com.* 56 rms, 2 story, 56
suites. Dec-Mar, Aug-Oct: S, D $134;

Covered bridge over Mad River

suites $99; each addl $10; under 12
free; lower rates rest of yr. Pet
accepted, some restrictions, fee. Parking lot. Pool. TV; cable, VCR avail.
Complimentary continental bkfst,
newspaper, toll-free calls. Restaurant
nearby. Ck-out 11 am, ck-in 4 pm.
Business servs avail. Concierge. Dry
cleaning, coin lndry. Exercise privileges. Golf. Tennis, 2 courts. Downhill skiing. Picnic facilities. Cr cds: A,
C, D, DS, MC, V.

Restaurants

**★★★ COUNTRYMAN'S PLEA-
SURE.** *Townline Rd (05701), 3 mi E
off US 4 near Killington-Pico Ski Area.
802/773-7141. www.countrymans
pleasure.com.* Specializes in roast duck
with raspberry sauce, sauerbraten,
wild game. Own baking. Hrs: 5-10
pm; early-bird dinner to 6 pm. Closed
Sun; Dec 24, 25. Res accepted. Bar.
Dinner $11.95-$22.95. Child's menu.

Restored farmhouse (1824). Sun porch dining. Cr cds: A, C, D, DS, ER, MC, V.
`D` `SC`

★★ **ROYAL'S 121 HEARTHSIDE.** *37 N Main St (05701), US 7, at jct US 4. 802/775-0856.* Specializes in New England dishes, popovers, fresh seafood. Own desserts. Hrs: 11 am-10 pm; Sun noon-9 pm; early-bird dinner Mon-Fri 5-6:30 pm. Res accepted; required hols. Bar. Lunch $5.25-$10.95; dinner $11.95-$19.95. Open-hearth charcoal cooking. Fireplaces. Cr cds: A, MC, V.
`D` `↵`

★★ **SIRLOIN SALOON.** *200 S Main St (05701), US 7. 802/773-7900.* Specializes in wood-grilled steak, chicken, seafood. Salad bar. Hrs: 5-10 pm. Closed Thanksgiving. Res accepted. Bar. Dinner $8.95-$18.95. Child's menu. Native Amer artwork, artifacts. Cr cds: A, D, DS, MC, V.
`D` `↵`

Shelburne

(C-1) *See also Burlington, Vergennes*

Settled 1763 **Pop** 5,871 **Elev** 148 ft
Area code 802 **Zip** 05482
Web www.cvu.cssd.k12.vt.us/shelburn/shelburne.htm
Information Town Hall, 5376 Shelburne Rd, PO Box 88; 802/985-5116

Shelburne is a small, friendly town bordering Lake Champlain. West of town are the Adirondack Mountains; to the east are the Green Mountains. The Shelburne Museum has one of the most comprehensive exhibits of early American life.

What to See and Do

Charlotte-Essex Ferry. Makes 20-min trips across Lake Champlain to Essex, NY (Apr-Jan, daily). 5 mi S on US 7 to Charlotte, then 2 mi W to dock. Phone 802/864-9804. One way, individual ¢; Vehicle ¢¢¢

Mount Philo State Park. A 648-acre mountaintop park offering beautiful views of the Lake Champlain Valley.

Picnicking, camping, lean-tos. Entrance and camp roads are steep; not recommended for trailers. (Memorial Day-Columbus Day) Standard fees. 5 mi S on US 7, then 1 mi E on local road. Phone 802/425-2390 or 802/483-2001.

Shelburne Farms. Former estate of Dr. Seward Webb and his wife, Lila Vanderbilt, built at the turn of the 20th century; beautifully situated on the shores of Lake Champlain. The grounds, landscaped by Frederick Law Olmstead and forested by Gifford Pinchot, once totalled 3,800 acres. Structures incl the Webb mansion, Shelburne House, a 110-rm summer "cottage" built in the late 1800s on a bluff overlooking the lake; a 5-story farm barn with a courtyard of more than 2 acres; and the coach barn, once the home of prize horses. Tours (Memorial Day-mid-Oct, daily; closed hols). Also hay rides; walking trail. Visitor center. Cheese shop (all yr, daily). Overnight stays avail. Harbor & Bay Rds. Phone 802/985-8686 or 802/985-8442 (visitor center). Tours ¢¢¢

★ **Shelburne Museum.** Founded by Electra Webb, daughter of Sugar King H. O. Havemeyer, this stupendous collection of Americana is located on 45 acres of parklike setting with 37 historic bldgs containing items such as historic circus posters, toys, weather vanes, trade signs, and an extensive collection of wildfowl decoys and dolls. American and European paintings and prints (incl works by Monet and Grandma Moses) are on display as well. Also here is the 220-ft sidewheel steamboat *Ticonderoga*, which carried passengers across Lake Champlain in the early part of the century and is now the last vertical beam passenger and freight sidewheel steamer intact in the US; a working carousel and a 5,000-piece hand-carved miniature traveling circus; a fully intact lighthouse; 1-rm schoolhouse; authentic country store; the only 2-lane covered bridge with footpath in Vermont; blacksmith shop; printing and weaving demonstrations; farm equipment and over 200 horse-drawn vehicles on display. Visitor orientation film; free jitney; cafeteria; museum stores; free parking. (Late May-late Oct, daily; rest of yr, limited hrs) On US 7, in center of town. Phone 802/985-3346. ¢¢¢¢

Vermont Teddy Bear Company.
Guided tour of "bear" factory shows
process of handcrafting these famous
stuffed animals. Gift shop. (Mon-Sat,
also Sun afternoons) 6655 Shelburne
Rd (VT 7). Phone 802/985-3001. ¢

Vermont Wildflower Farm. Acres of
wildflower gardens, flower fields, and
woodlands; pond and brook. Changing slide/sound show (every ½-hr).
Gift shop. (May-late Oct, daily) 5 mi
S via US 7. Phone 802/425-3500. ¢¢

Motels/Motor Lodges

★★ **DAYS INN.** *3229 Shelburne Rd
(05482), 1½ mi N on US 7. 802/985-
3334; fax 802/985-3419.* 58 rms, 2
story. July-mid-Sept: S, D $65-$75;
each addl $7; higher rates: fall foliage
season, Labor Day, Columbus Day;
lower rates rest of yr. Crib free. TV;
cable. Pool. Complimentary continental bkfst. Ck-out 11 am. Downhill ski 20 mi. Cr cds: A, D, DS, JCB,
MC, V.

D ⤢ 🏊 ≈ 🔥

★ **ECONO LODGE AND SUITES.**
*3164 Shelburne Rd (05482). 802/985-
3377; fax 802/985-3377; res 800/553-
2666; toll-free 800/825-1882. Email
ghandylodg@aol.com.* 40 rms, 1 story,
20 suites. July-Oct: S $39; D $89;
suites $99; each addl $5; under 16
free; lower rates rest of yr. Crib avail.
Pet accepted, some restrictions, fee.
Parking lot. Pool. TV; cable, VCR
avail. Complimentary continental
bkfst, coffee in rms, newspaper, toll-
free calls. Restaurant 11 am-10 pm.
Bar. Ck-out 11 am, ck-in 2 pm. Business center. Coin lndry. Salon/barber
avail. Golf, 18 holes. Tennis, 2
courts. Downhill skiing. Picnic facilities. Cr cds: A, C, D, DS, MC, V.

D 🐾 🏌 ⤢ 🎾 🏊 ≈ 🔥 SC 🚶

★★ **T-BIRD MOTOR INN.** *4405
Shelburne Rd (05482), ¾ mi N on US 7.
802/985-3663; fax 802/985-9940; toll-
free 800/335-5029.* 24 rms. May-Oct:
D $48-$88; each addl $6-$8; higher
rates: fall foliage season, hol wkends,
graduations. Closed Nov-mid May.
Crib $5. TV; cable. Pool. Complimen-
tary continental bkfst. Restaurant
nearby. Ck-out 11 am. Lawn games.
Some refrigerators. Picnic tables. Cr
cds: A, MC, V.

D ≈ 🔥

B&B/Small Inn

★★★ **SHELBURNE FARMS.** *1611
Harbor Rd (05482). 802/985-8686; fax
802/985-8123.* 26 rms, 7 share bath,
3 story. No A/C. No elvtr. Sept-mid-
Oct: S, D $195-$350; each addl $30;
cottages $240-$300; wkends, hols (2-
day min); lower rates rest of yr. Crib
avail. Cable TV in common rm.
Restaurant 7:30-11:30 am, 5:30-9:30
pm. Ck-out 11 am, ck-in 3 pm. Business servs avail. In-rm modem link.
Luggage handling. Gift shop. Tennis.
Downhill/x-country ski 20 mi. Rec
rm. Lawn games. On lake. Built in
1887; still a working farm. Totally
nonsmoking. Cr cds: A, DS, MC, V.

🎿 ⤢ 🎾 ≈ 🔥

Restaurant

★★★ **CAFE SHELBURNE.** *US 7
(05482). 802/985-3939.* Specializes in
filet of lamb, fresh seafood. Hrs: 5-10
pm. Closed Sun, Mon. Res accepted.
Bar. Wine cellar. Dinner a la carte
entrees: $16-$21. Porch dining.
Provencal bistro atmosphere. Chef-
owned. Cr cds: A, D, MC, V.

Springfield

(G-3) *See also Bellows Falls, Grafton*

Settled 1761 **Pop** 9,579 **Elev** 410 ft
Area code 802 **Zip** 05156
Information Chamber of Commerce,
14 Clinton St; 802/885-2779

The cascades of the Black River once
provided power for the machine tool
plants that stretch along Springfield's
banks. Lord Jeffrey Amherst started
the Crown Point Military Road to
Lake Champlain from here in 1759.
Springfield has been the home of
many New England inventors. It is
also the headquarters of the Amateur
Telescope Makers who meet at Stel-
lafane, an observatory site west of
VT 11.

What to See and Do

Eureka Schoolhouse. Oldest schoolhouse in the state; built in 1790 and
recently restored. Nearby is a 100-yr-
old lattice-truss covered bridge.
(Memorial Day-Columbus Day, daily)

On VT 11 (Charleston Rd). Phone 802/885-2779. ¢¢

Reverend Dan Foster House & Old Forge. Historic parsonage (1785) contains antique furniture, textiles, utensils, farm tools; old forge has working machinery and bellows. Guided tours. (Late June-Sep, Thurs-Mon or by appt) 6 mi N on Valley St to Weathersfield Center Rd in Weathersfield. For further information contact the Chamber of Commerce.

Springfield Art and Historical Society. American art and artifacts. Collections incl Richard Lee pewter, Bennington pottery, 19th-century American paintings, costumes, dolls, toys; Springfield historical items. Changing exhibits. (May-Nov, Tues-Fri; closed hols) 9 Elm Hill. Phone 802/885-2415. **FREE**

Annual Event

Vermont Apple Festival and Craft Show. Family activities, cider pressing, apple pie bake-off, entertainment, crafts. Phone 802/885-2779. Columbus Day wkend.

Motel/Motor Lodge

★★ **HOLIDAY INN EXPRESS.** *818 Charlestown Rd (05156). 802/885-4516; fax 802/885-4595; toll-free 800/465-4329. Email hixpress@aol.com.* 88 rms, 2 story, 2 suites. Jan-Mar, June-Aug, Oct: S, D $125; suites $200; each addl $10; under 14 free; lower rates rest of yr. Crib avail. Pet accepted. Parking lot. Indoor pool. TV; cable. Complimentary continental bkfst, coffee in rms, newspaper. Restaurant 7 am-10 pm. Bar. Ck-out 11 am. Meeting rms. Business center. Dry cleaning, coin lndry. Exercise equipt. Golf, 18 holes. Tennis, 6 courts. Downhill skiing. Bike rentals. Hiking trail. Video games. Cr cds: A, D, DS, MC, V.

Hotel

★★ **HARTNESS HOUSE.** *30 Orchard St (05156). 802/885-2115; fax 802/885-2207; res 800/732-4789. Email innkeeper@hartnesshouse.com; www.hartnesshouse.com.* 41 rms, 2 story, 1 suite. Oct: S $118; D $127;

suites $150; each addl $15; under 14 free; lower rates rest of yr. Crib avail. Parking lot. Pool. TV; cable, VCR avail. Complimentary full bkfst. Restaurant 8 am-9 pm, closed Sun. Bar. Ck-out 11 am, ck-in 3 pm. Meeting rms. Business servs avail. Concierge. Dry cleaning. Gift shop. Exercise privileges. Golf. Tennis, 3 courts. Downhill skiing. Hiking trail. Cr cds: A, C, D, DS, MC, V.

B&Bs/Small Inns

★ **HUGGING BEAR INN.** *244 Main St (05143), 8 mi SW on US 91. 802/875-2412; fax 802/875-3823; toll-free 800/325-0519. Email inn@hugging bear.com; www.huggingbear.com.* 6 rms, 2 story. No A/C. No rm phones. S $55-$65; D $75-$85; each addl $10-$25; higher rates fall foliage. Closed Thanksgiving. Crib free. TV in sitting rm; VCR (free movies). Complimentary full bkfst. Restaurant 7 am-8 pm. Ck-out 11 am, ck-in 3 pm. Gift shop featuring extensive collection of teddy bears. Downhill ski 15 mi; x-country ski 7 mi. Victorian house (ca 1850) furnished with antiques and teddy bears. Totally nonsmoking. Cr cds: A, D, DS, MC, V.

★★★ **THE INN AT WEATHERS-FIELD.** *PO Box 165 106 (05151), N on VT 106, approx ½ mi S of Perkinsville; look for sign. 802/263-9217; fax 802/263-9219; toll-free 800/477-4828. weathersfieldinn.com.* 11 rms, 3 story, 1 suite. Dec-Feb, July-Oct: S $145; D $350; suites $350; each addl $75; lower rates rest of yr. Parking lot. TV; cable. Complimentary full bkfst. Restaurant 6-9 pm, closed Mon. Bar. Ck-out 11 am, ck-in 2 pm. Meeting rms. Concierge. Exercise equipt. Golf. Downhill skiing. Hiking trail. Cr cds: A, C, D, DS, MC, V.

★★ **STONE HEARTH INN.** *698 VT 11 W (05143), I-91 Exit 6, then 12 mi W. 802/875-2525; fax 802/875-4688. Email shinn@vermontel.net; www.virtualvermont.com/shinn.* 10 rms, 3 story. Dec-Feb, Sep-Oct: S $50; D $150; each addl $15; children $10; lower rates rest of yr. Crib avail, fee. TV; cable. Complimentary full bkfst.

Restaurant. Bar. Ck-out 11 am, ck-in 3 pm. Meeting rm. Gift shop. Whirlpool. Golf. Tennis. Downhill skiing. Hiking trail. Picnic facilities. Cr cds: A, DS, MC.

[D] [⚓] [✈] [⛷] [🎿] [🏃]

Restaurant

★★ **HARTNESS HOUSE INN.** *30 Orchard St. 802/885-2115. Email inn keeper@hh.com; www.hh.com.* Specializes in fresh seafood. Hrs: 7 am-9 pm. Res accepted. Bar. Bkfst $5.95; lunch $4.50-$6.95; dinner $11.95-$19.95. Historic bldg (1900). Tours. Cr cds: A, D, DS, MC, V.

[D]

St. Albans

(B-1) *See also Swanton*

Settled 1785 **Pop** 7,339 **Elev** 429 ft
Area code 802 **Zip** 05478
Web www.together.net/~stalbans/chamber.htm

Information Chamber of Commerce, 2 N Main St, PO Box 327; 802/524-2444

This small city is a railroad town (Central Vermont Railway) and center of maple syrup and dairy interests. It was a stop on the Underground Railroad and has had a surprisingly violent history. Smugglers used the city as a base of operations during the War of 1812. On October 19, 1864, the northernmost engagement of the Civil War was fought here when a small group of Confederates raided the three banks in town and fled to Canada with $200,000. In 1866, the Fenians, an Irish organization pledged to capture Canada, had its headquarters here.

What to See and Do

Brainerd Monument. A father's revengeful commemoration of his son's death in Andersonville Prison. Greenwood Cemetery, S Main St.

Burton Island State Park. This 253-acre park offers swimming beach, fishing, canoeing (rentals), boating (rentals, marina with electrical hookups); nature and hiking trails, picnicking, concession, tent sites, lean-tos. (Memorial Day-Labor Day) Standard fees. On island in Lake Champlain; 5 mi W on VT 36, then 3 mi SW on unnumbered road to Kamp Kill Kare State Park access area, where passenger ferry service (fee) is avail to island; visitors may use their own boats to reach the island. Phone 802/879-5674.

Chester A. Arthur Historic Site. Replica of second house of 21st President; nearby is brick church (1830) where Arthur's father was preacher. Exhibit of Chester A. Arthur's life and career. Rural setting; picnic area. (mid-June-mid-Oct, Wed-Sun) 10 mi W via VT 36 to Fairfield, then unpaved road to site. Phone 802/828-3226.

Lake Carmi State Park. This 482-acre park features rolling farmland; 2-mi lakefront, swimming beach, bathhouse, fishing, boating (ramps, rentals); nature trails, picnicking, concession, tent and trailer sites (dump station), lean-tos. (Memorial Day-Labor Day) Standard fees. 15 mi NE on VT 105 to North Sheldon, then 3 mi N on VT 236. Phone 802/879-5674.

St. Albans Historical Museum. Toys, dolls, clothing, railroad memorabilia, farm implements; St. Albans Confederate Raid material, photographs; library and reference rm; re-created doctor's office with medical and X-ray collections; items and documents of local historical interest. (June-Sep, Tues-Sat, also by appt) Church St. Phone 802/527-7933. ¢

Annual Events

Maple Sugar Festival. A number of producers welcome visitors who join sugarhouse parties for sugar-on-snow, sour pickles and raised doughnuts. Continuing events, arts and crafts, antiques, woodchopping contests. Usually last wkend Apr.

Bay Day. Family activity day. Great Race, one-legged running, family games; volleyball, canoeing, and bicycling. Concessions. Fireworks. July 4 wkend.

Civil War Days. Taylor Park. A 3-day event depicting scenes of the Civil War in St. Albans, the northernmost point where the war was fought. Reenactment of major battle, entertainment, antiques. Mid-Oct.

Motel/Motor Lodge

★ **CADILLAC MOTEL.** *213 S Main St (05478). 802/524-2191; fax 802/527-1483. www.motelcadillac.com.* 49 rms, 2 story, 5 suites. Jul-Oct: S $65; D $80; suites $90; each addl $7; children $7; lower rates rest of yr. Crib avail, fee. Pet accepted. Parking lot. Pool. TV; cable. Complimentary toll-free calls. Restaurant nearby. Ck-out 11 am, ck-in 2 pm. Meeting rm. Golf. Tennis. Picnic facilities. Cr cds: A, C, D, DS, MC, V.

Hotel

★★ **COMFORT INN & SUITES.** *813 Fairfax Rd (05478), I-89 Exit 19. 802/524-3300; fax 802/524-3300; res 800/228-5150. Email comfort2@ together.net; www.vtcomfortinn.com.* 46 rms, 3 story, 17 suites. May-Oct: S $89; D $99; suites $139; under 18 free; lower rates rest of yr. Crib avail. Parking lot. Indoor pool. TV; cable (premium). Complimentary continental bkfst, newspaper, toll-free calls. Restaurant nearby. Ck-out 11 am, ck-in 3 pm. Meeting rms. Business servs avail. Coin lndry. Exercise equipt. Golf, 18 holes. Downhill skiing. Cr cds: A, C, D, DS, JCB, MC, V.

St. Johnsbury

(C-4) *See also Lyndonville*

Settled 1787 **Pop** 7,608 **Elev** 588 ft
Area code 802 **Zip** 05819
Web www.vermontnekchamber.org
Information Northeast Kingdom Chamber of Commerce, 30 Western Ave; 802/748-3678 or 800/639-6379

This town was named for Ethan Allen's French friend, St. John de Crève Coeur, author of *Letters from an American Farmer*. The town gained fame and fortune when Thaddeus Fairbanks invented the platform scale in 1830. Fairbanks Scales, maple syrup, and manufacturing are among its major industries.

What to See and Do

Fairbanks Museum and Planetarium. Exhibits and programs on natural science, regional history, archeology, anthropology, astronomy, and the arts. More than 4,500 mounted birds and mammals; antique toys; farm, village, and craft tools; Northern New England Weather Broadcasting Center; planetarium; Hall of Science; special exhibitions in Gallery Wing. (Mon-Sat, also Sun afternoons; closed Jan 1, Dec 25) Planetarium (July-Aug, daily; rest of yr, Sat and Sun only). Museum and planetarium closed hols. Main & Prospect Sts. Phone 802/748-2372. ¢¢

Maple Grove Farm of Vermont. Antique sugarhouse museum. Gift shop. Maple candy factory tours (Mon-Fri; closed hols). Res requested for tours. E edge of town on US 2; I-91, Exit 20 or I-93, Exit 1. Phone 802/748-5141. Tours ¢

St. Johnsbury Athenaeum and Art Gallery. Works by Albert Bierstadt and artists of the Hudson River School. (Mon-Sat; closed hols) 30 Main St (public library and art gallery). Phone 802/748-8291. **Donation**

Seasonal Event

St. Johnsbury Town Band. Courthouse Park. One of the oldest continuously performing bands (since 1830) in the country plays weekly outdoor evening concerts. Contact the Chamber of Commerce for further information. Mon, mid-June-late Aug.

Motels/Motor Lodges

★ **AIME'S MOTEL INC.** *46 VT Rte 18 (05819), 3 mi E at jct US 2, VT 18; I-93 Exit 1. 802/748-3194; toll-free 800/504-6663. Email aimmotel@hcr. net; www.virtualcities.com/vt/aimes motel.htm.* 17 rms, 1 story, 1 suite. Sep-Oct: S $55; D $70; suites $85; each addl $5; under 13 free; lower rates rest of yr. Crib avail. Pet accepted. Parking lot. TV; cable (premium). Restaurant 6 am-9 pm. Ck-out 11 am, ck-in 1 pm. Golf, 18 holes. Downhill skiing. Picnic facilities. Cr cds: A, DS, MC, V.

★★ **FAIRBANKS MOTOR INN.** *32 Western Ave (05819), I-91 Exit 21. 802/748-5666; fax 802/748-1242.* 46 rms, 3 story. S $55-$85; D $65-$95; each addl $10; package plans; higher rates fall foliage. TV; cable (premium). Heated pool. Complimentary continental bkfst. Ck-out 11 am. Business servs avail. In-rm modem link. Putting green. Downhill/x-country ski 15 mi. Health club privileges. Balconies. Picnic tables. On 2 acres along river. Cr cds: A, DS, MC, V.

D 🐾 ⓣ 🏋 ➰ 🏋 ⊠ 🔥

★★ **HOLIDAY MOTEL.** *222 Hastings St (05819), at jct US 2, 5. 802/748-8192; fax 802/748-1244.* 34 rms. *mid*-June-mid-Oct: S $48-$75; D $55-$89; each addl $5; higher rates: fall foliage season, some hols; lower rates rest of yr. TV; cable. Heated pool. Coffee in lobby. Restaurant opp 7 am-9 pm. Ck-out 11 am. Picnic tables. Cr cds: A, DS, MC, V.

➰ ⊠ 🔥

B&B/Small Inn

★★★★ **RABBIT HILL INN.** *Lower Waterford Rd (05848), 10 mi S on VT 18; I-93 Exit NH 44, then 1½ mi N on VT 18. 802/748-5168; fax 802/748-8342; toll-free 800/762-8669. Email info@rabbithillinn.com; www.rabbithill inn.com.* Guests can truly get away from it all at this 15-acre, countryside property. Located in a tiny, rural village and nestled between a river and the mountains, the white-pillared facade and American flag of this inn have charming New England style. Choose from the 21 guest rooms and suites in either the 1825 Main House or the 1795 Tavern Building. 13 rms, 3 story, 8 suites. July-Oct: S $265; D $305; suites $380; each addl $70; lower rates rest of yr. Parking lot. TV; cable (premium), VCR avail, CD avail. Complimentary full bkfst, coffee in rms, toll-free calls. Restaurant 6-8:30 pm (see RABBIT HILL). Bar. Ck-out 11 am, ck-in 2 pm. Concierge. Gift shop. Golf, 18 holes. Downhill skiing. Hiking trail. Picnic facilities. Cr cds: A, MC, V.

D ⓣ 🏋 ➤ 🏌 ⊠ 🖌

Restaurants

★★ **CREAMERY.** *Hill St (05819), 7 mi W on US 2. 802/684-3616.* Specializes in fresh seafood. Own baking, soups. Menu changes daily. Hrs: 11 am-10 pm. Closed Sun, Mon; Jan 1, Dec 24, 25. Res accepted. Bar. Lunch $5-$8; dinner $12-$17. Child's menu. Renovated creamery (1891); antiques, vintage photographs. Cr cds: A, MC, V.

D

★★★ **RABBIT HILL.** *VT 18. 802/748-5168. www.rabbithillinn.com.* Own baking. Menu changes seasonally. Hrs: 6-9 pm. Res required. Bar. Wine cellar. Dinner complete meals: $37. On grounds of historic inn. Cr cds: A, MC, V.

D

Stowe

(C-2) *See also Waterbury*

Settled 1794 **Pop** 3,433 **Elev** 723 ft
Area code 802 **Zip** 05672
Web www.stoweinfo.com

Information Stowe Area Association, PO Box 1320; 802/253-7321 or 800/24-STOWE

Stowe is a year-round resort area, with more than half of its visitors coming during the summer. Mount Mansfield, Vermont's highest peak (4,393 ft), offers skiing, snowboarding, snowshoeing, and skating in the winter. Summer visitors enjoy outdoor concerts, hiking, biking, golf, tennis, and many events and attractions, include a Ben & Jerry's ice cream tour.

What to See and Do

Alpine Slide. Chairlift takes riders to 2,300-ft slide that runs through the woods and open field. Speed controlled by rider. (Memorial Day-mid-June, wkends and hols; mid-June-Labor Day, daily; after Labor Day-mid-Oct, wkends and hols) VT 108, N of Stowe Village. ¢¢¢

Elmore State Park. This 709-acre park offers swimming beach, bathhouse, fishing, boating (rentals); hiking trails (one trail to Elmore Mt fire

Aerial view of Stowe

tower), picnicking, concession, tent and trailer sites (dump station), lean-tos. Excellent views of Green Mt Range; fire tower. (Memorial Day-Columbus Day) Standard fees. N on VT 100, then S on VT 12, at Lake Elmore. Phone 802/888-2982 or 802/479-4280.

Mount Mansfield State Forest. This 38,000-acre forest can be reached from Underhill Flats, off VT 15, or from Stowe, N on VT 108, through Smugglers Notch, a magnificent scenic drive. The Long Trail leads to the summit of Mt Mansfield from the north and south. There are 3 state recreation areas in the forest. **Smugglers Notch** (Phone 802/253-4014 or 802/479-4280) and **Underhill** (phone 802/899-3022 or 802/879-5674) areas offer hiking, skiing, snowmobiling, picnicking, camping (dump station). **Little River Camping Area** (phone 802/244-7103 or 802/479-4280), NW of Waterbury, offers swimming, fishing, boating (rentals for campers only); hiking, camping. (Memorial Day-Columbus Day) Standard fees.

Stowe Mountain Auto Road. A 4½ mi drive to summit. (mid-May-mid-Oct, daily) Approx 6 mi NW of Stowe off VT 108. ¢¢¢

Stowe Mountain Resort. Resort has 8-passenger gondola, quad, triple, 6 double chairlifts, mighty-mite handle tow; patrol, school, rentals, snow-making; cafeterias, restaurants, bar, entertainment, nursery; 45 runs, longest run over 4 mi; vertical drop 2,350 ft. (mid-Nov-mid-Apr, daily) Summer activities incl 3 outdoor swimming pools, alpine slide (mid-June-early Sep, daily); mountain biking (rentals), gondola rides, in-line skate park, fitness center, spa, recreation trail, tennis, golf. NW via VT 108. Phone 802/253-3000 or 800/253-4754. ¢¢¢¢ Nearby is **Mount Mansfield Gondola.** An 8-passenger enclosed gondola ride to the summit of Vermont's highest peak. Spectacular view of the area. Restaurant and gift shop. (Late May-mid-June, wkends; mid-June-mid-Oct, daily) VT 108, N of Stowe Village. ¢¢¢

Stowe Recreation Path. An approx 5-mi riverside path designed for nature walks, bicycling, jogging, and in-line skating. Stowe Village. **FREE**

Annual Event

Stoweflake Balloon Festival. Stoweflake Resort Field, Rte 108. Over 20 balloons launched continuously. Phone 802/253-7321. Second wkend July.

Seasonal Event

Trapp Family Meadow Concerts. Classical concerts in the Trapp Family Lodge Meadow. Phone 802/253-7321. Sun eves, late June-mid-Aug.

Motels/Motor Lodges

★★ **BUCCANEER COUNTRY LODGE.** *3214 Mountain Rd (05672). 802/253-4772; fax 802/253-9486; toll-free 800/543-1293. Email buccaneer@ compuserve.com; www.stoweinfo.com/ buccaneer.* 12 rms, 2 story, 4 kit. suites. mid-Dec-Mar, mid-Sep-mid-Oct: S, D $75-$99; each addl $10-$15; kit. suites $95; under 5 free; wkly rates; ski plans; wkends (2 day min); higher rates: hol wkends, wk of Washington's birthday, Dec 25; lower rates rest of yr. Crib free. TV; cable. Heated pool; whirlpool. Complimentary full bkfst (continental bkfst off-season). Restaurant nearby. Ck-out 11 am. Downhill ski 3 mi; x-country ski 1 mi. Rec rm. Refrigerators. Balconies. Picnic tables, grills. Fireplace. Library. Cr cds: MC, V.

★★ **HOB KNOB INN.** *2364 Mountain Rd (05672), 2½ mi NW on VT 108. 802/253-8549; fax 802/253-7621; toll-free 800/245-8540. Email hobknobinn@aol.com.* 20 rms, 6 kits. Ski season: D $85-$145; each addl $15; kit. units $10 addl; MAP avail; wkly rates; golf, ski plans; higher rates hols, special events; some lower rates off-season. Closed Nov. Crib free. TV. Pool. Complimentary full bkfst (winter), continental bkfst (summer). Restaurant 6-9 pm. Bar. Ck-out 11 am. Downhill ski 5 mi; x-country ski 1½ mi. Some refrigerators, fireplaces. Balconies. Cr cds: A, C, D, DS, MC, V.

★★ **HONEYWOOD COUNTRY LODGE.** *4527 Mountain Rd (05672), 5 mi NW on VT 108. 802/253-4124; fax 802/253-7050; toll-free 800/659-6289. Email honeywd@aol.com; www. honeywoodinn.com.* 12 rms, 1 story, 1 suite. Feb, Sep-Oct, Dec: S, D $125; suites $199; each addl $20; children $10; under 15 free; lower rates rest of yr. Pet accepted, some restrictions, fee. Parking lot. Pool, whirlpool. TV; cable (DSS). Complimentary full bkfst. Restaurant nearby. Ck-out 10 am, ck-in 2 pm. Fax servs avail. Golf. Tennis, 4 courts. Downhill skiing. Bike rentals. Hiking trail. Picnic facilities. Cr cds: A, DS, MC, V.

★★★ **INN AT THE MOUNTAIN.** *5781 Mountain Rd (05672), 6 mi NW on VT 108. 802/253-3656; fax 802/253-3659; toll-free 800/253-4754. www.stowe.com.* 33 rms. MAP: Dec 25-mid-Apr: S, D $145-$180; suites $190-$230; under 12 free; condos $200-$600; learn-to-ski wk rates; golf plans; lower rates rest of yr. Crib $10. TV; cable. Heated pool; whirlpool. Restaurant 7:30-10 am, 5:30-9 pm. Rm serv. Bar 11-2 am. Ck-out 11 am. Meeting rm. Business servs avail. Bellhops. Tennis. Golf privileges. Downhill/x-country ski on site. Snowboarding; lessons, rentals. In-line skate park. Mountain bike center. Exercise equipt; sauna. Rec rm.

Refrigerators, in-rm steam baths. Balconies. Sun deck. Ride attractions. Rms overlook ski slopes. Cr cds: A, D, DS, MC, V.

★★ **INNSBRUCK INN.** *4361 Mountain Rd (05672), 4 mi W on VT 108. 802/253-8582; fax 802/253-2260; toll-free 800/225-8582.* 28 rms, 2 story, 4 kits. mid-Dec-mid-Apr: S $65-$79; D $74-$119; each addl $15; under 12 free; higher rates hol wks; lower rates rest of yr. Crib $10. Pet accepted, some restrictions; $8. TV; cable, VCR avail (movies). Heated pool; whirlpool. Coffee in rms. Restaurant 7:30-9:30 am. Bar (winter only) 3:30 pm-1 am. Ck-out 11 am. Business servs avail. Ski shuttle. Indoor tennis privileges. Downhill ski 2 mi; x-country ski adj. Exercise equipt; sauna. Game rm. Refrigerators. Balconies. Picnic tables. Cr cds: A, DS, MC, V.

★★★ **THE MOUNTAIN RESORT AT STOWE.** *1007 Mountain Rd (05672), 1 mi NW on VT 108. 802/253-4566; fax 802/253-7397; toll-free 800/367-6873. www.stowevt.aol.com.* 30 rms, 7 suites (some with kit.), 7 kit. units. June-Oct, late Dec-Mar: D $89-$175; each addl $8-$20; suites $185-$335; kits. $125-$199; MAP avail; family, wkly rates; golf, ski plans; higher rates: hols, special events; lower rates rest of yr. Crib $5. Pet accepted; $15. TV; cable (premium), VCR avail. 2 pools, 1 indoor; whirlpool. Playground. Coffee in rms. Restaurant 7 am-9 pm. Ck-out 11 am. Business servs avail. Coin lndry. Sundries. Railroad station, bus depot transportation. Tennis. Downhill ski 4 mi; x-country ski 2½ mi. Bicycles. Exercise equipt; saunas. Rec rm. Lawn games. Refrigerators; some in-rm whirlpools; microwaves avail. Some balconies. Picnic tables, grills. Cr cds: A, D, DS, MC, V.

★★ **STOWE MOTEL.** *2043 Mountain Rd (05672), 2 mi NW on VT 108. 802/253-7629; fax 802/253-9971; toll-free 800/829-7629. Email stowemotel@ aol.com; www.stowemotel.com.* 50 rms, 6 suites. Dec-Mar, June-Oct: S, D $92; suites $200; each addl $8; children $4; under 12 free; lower rates rest of yr. Crib avail, fee. Pet accepted, some restrictions, fee. Parking lot. Pool, whirlpool. TV; cable. Complimentary continental bkfst, coffee in rms, toll-free calls. Restaurant nearby. Ck-out 11 am, ck-in 4 pm. Business servs avail. Golf. Tennis. Downhill skiing. Bike rentals. Picnic facilities. Cr cds: A, DS, MC, V.

[icons]

★ ★ SUN AND SKI MOTOR INN.
1613 Mountain Rd (05672), 1½ mi N on VT 108. 802/253-7159; fax 802/253-7150; toll-free 800/448-5223. Email info@stowesunandski.com; www. stowesunandski.com. 22 rms, 2 story, 4 suites. Feb, Sep-Oct, Dec: S $127; D $137; suites $194; each addl $16; children $7; under 12 free; lower rates rest of yr. Crib avail, fee. Parking lot. Pool. TV; cable. Complimentary continental bkfst, coffee in rms. Restaurant nearby. Ck-out 11 am, ck-in 3 pm. Business servs avail. Gift shop. Exercise privileges, sauna. Golf. Tennis. Downhill skiing. Bike rentals. Picnic facilities. Cr cds: A, DS, MC, V.

[icons]

★ ★ SUNSET MOTOR INN.
160 VT Rt 15 W (05661), jct VT 15, 100 10 mi NE. 802/888-4956; fax 802/888-3698; res 800/544-2347. Email sunset@together.net; www.gostowe.com/ member/sunset. 55 rms, 2 story. Sep-Oct, Dec: S $110; D $140; each addl $10; under 12 free; lower rates rest of yr. Crib avail, fee. Parking lot. Pool. TV; cable (premium). Complimentary newspaper. Restaurant 6 am-9 pm. Ck-out 11 am, ck-in 3 pm. Business servs avail. Exercise privileges. Golf, 9 holes. Tennis, 4 courts. Downhill skiing. Picnic facilities. Cr cds: A, D, MC, V.

[icons]

★ ★ TOWN AND COUNTRY RESORT.
876 Mountain Rd (05672), 1 mi N on VT 108. 802/253-7595; fax 802/253-4764; toll-free 800/323-0311. Email tnc@together.net; www.townand countrystowe.com. 45 rms, 2 story. Jan-Mar, June-Oct: S $85; D $95; each addl $15; children $6; under 12 free; lower rates rest of yr. Crib avail, fee. Parking lot. Indoor/outdoor pools, lap pool, children's pool, whirlpool. TV; cable, VCR avail. Complimentary full bkfst, toll-free calls. Restaurant 5:30-9 pm. Bar. Ck-out 11 am, ck-in 2 pm. Meeting rm. Business center. Exercise privileges, sauna. Golf. Tennis. Downhill skiing.

Supervised children's activities. Hiking trail. Picnic facilities. Cr cds: A, C, D, DS, MC, V.

[icons]

Resorts

★ ★ COMMODORES INN.
Rte 100 S (05672), VT 100S. 802/253-7131; fax 802/253-2360; toll-free 800/447-8693. Email commodores@mt-mansfield.com; www.commodoresinn.com. 50 rms, 2 story. mid-Sep-mid-Oct, mid-Dec-mid-Mar: S $78-$98; D $98-$120; each addl $10; under 12 free; wkend rates; higher rates wk of Dec 25; lower rates rest of yr. Crib free. Pet accepted; $10. TV; cable, VCR avail. 2 pools, heated, 1 indoor; wading pool, whirlpools. Complimentary continental bkfst off season. Restaurant 7-10:30 am, 6-9:30 pm. Ck-out 11 am. Meeting rm. Business servs avail. In-rm modem link. Downhill ski 9 mi; x-country ski 6 mi. Exercise equipt; saunas. Game rm. Refrigerators avail. Cr cds: A, DS, MC, V.

[icons]

★ ★ ★ GOLDEN EAGLE RESORT.
511 Mountain Rd (05672), ½ mi NW on VT 108. 802/253-4811; fax 802/253-2561; toll-free 800/626-1010. Email info@stoweagle.com; www.stow eagle.com. 74 rms, 13 suites. Dec-Mar, June-Oct: S $114; D $124; suites $189; each addl $15; under 12 free; lower rates rest of yr. Crib avail, fee. Parking lot. Indoor/outdoor pools, lap pool, whirlpool. TV; cable, VCR avail. Complimentary coffee in rms. Restaurant 7-11. Ck-out 11 am, ck-in 3 pm. Meeting rms. Business center. Coin lndry. Gift shop. Free airport transportation. Exercise equipt, sauna. Golf. Tennis. Downhill skiing. Supervised children's activities. Hiking trail. Picnic facilities. Cr cds: A, C, D, DS, MC, V.

[icons]

★ ★ ★ GREEN MOUNTAIN INN.
18S Main St (05672), on VT 100. 802/253-7301; fax 802/253-5096; toll-free 800/253-7302. Email info@gminn. com; www.greenmountaininn.com. 81 rms, 3 story, 19 suites. Jan-Mar, June-Oct: S $140; D $230; suites $260; each addl $15; under 12 free; lower rates rest of yr. Crib avail. Pet accepted, some restrictions, fee. Park-

ing lot. Pool, whirlpool. TV; cable (premium), VCR avail. Restaurant 11:30 am-9 pm. Bar. Ck-out 11 am, ck-in 2 pm. Meeting rm. Fax servs avail. Bellhops. Dry cleaning. Gift shop. Exercise equipt, sauna, steam rm. Golf. Tennis. Downhill skiing. Cr cds: A, D, DS, MC, V.

★★★ **GREY FOX INN & RESORT.** *990 Mountain Rd (05672), 1 mi W on VT 108. 802/253-8921; fax 802/253-8344; toll-free 800/544-8454. Email info@stowegreyfoxinn.com; www.stowe greyfoxinn.com.* 28 rms, 3 story, 13 suites. Feb-Mar, July-Oct, Dec: S $161; D $171; suites $253; each addl $16; children $7; under 12 free; lower rates rest of yr. Crib avail, fee. Parking lot. Indoor/outdoor pools, lap pool, whirlpool. TV; cable (DSS), VCR avail. Complimentary full bkfst, coffee in rms. Restaurant 8-10:30 pm. Bar. Ck-out 11 am, ck-in 3 pm. Meeting rm. Fax servs avail. Coin lndry. Gift shop. Exercise equipt, sauna. Golf. Tennis. Downhill skiing. Bike rentals. Picnic facilities. Cr cds: A, DS, MC, V.

★★★ **STOWEFLAKE MOUNTAIN RESORT & SPA.** *1746 Mountain Rd (05672), 1½ mi NW on VT 108. 802/ 253-7355; fax 802/253-6858; toll-free 800/253-2232. Email info@stoweflake. com; www.stoweflake.com.* 83 rms, 2 story, 35 suites. Feb, July-Oct: S $80; D $160; suites $170; each addl $10; under 12 free; lower rates rest of yr. Crib avail. Parking lot. Indoor/outdoor pools, children's pool, whirl-pool. TV; cable (DSS), VCR avail. Complimentary coffee in rms. Restaurant 7 am-5:30 pm. Bar. Ck-out 11 am, ck-in 3 pm. Meeting rms. Business center. Bellhops. Concierge. Dry cleaning. Gift shop. Salon/barber avail. Free airport transportation. Exercise rm, sauna, steam rm. Golf, 18 holes. Tennis, 2 courts. Downhill skiing. Bike rentals. Supervised children's activities. Hiking trail. Picnic facilities. Cr cds: A, D, DS, MC, V.

★★★★ **TOPNOTCH AT STOWE.** *4000 Mountain Rd (05672), 4 mi NW on VT 108. 802/253-8585; fax 802/253-9263; toll-free 800/451-8686. Email topnotch@sover.net; www. topnotch-resort.com.* Guests will enjoy the European-country style at this 120-acre resort and spa in Vermont's Green Mountains. There are 90 rooms, suites and townhouses, many with sundecks and views of Mount Mansfield. Dine at Maxwell's for seafood, prime aged meats and game, get pampered at the 23,000 square foot spa or just choose something to read from one of the book-lined rooms. 82 rms, 3 story, 10 suites. Jan-Mar, July-Oct: S, D $310; suites $710; each addl $45; under 12 free; lower rates rest of yr. Crib avail. Pet accepted. Valet parking avail. Indoor/outdoor pools, lap pool, whirlpool. TV; cable (premium), VCR avail. Complimentary coffee in rms, newspaper. Restaurant 7 am-10 pm. Bar. Ck-out 11 am, ck-in 3:30 pm. Meeting rms. Business center. Bell-hops. Concierge. Dry cleaning. Gift shop. Salon/barber avail. Exercise rm, sauna, steam rm. Golf. Tennis. Downhill skiing. Bike rentals. Super-vised children's activities. Hiking trail. Video games. Cr cds: A, C, D, DS, MC, V.

★★★ **TRAPP FAMILY LODGE.** *700 Trapp Hill Rd (05672), 2 mi N on VT 108 then 2 mi W on Trapp Hill Rd. 802/253-8511; fax 802/253-5740; res 800/826-7000. Email info@trapp family.com; www.trappfamily.com.* 73 rms in main lodge, 20 rms in lower lodge, 4 story, 100 guest houses. No A/C. Ski season: S, D $145-$220; each addl $25; guest houses $800-$2,200/wk; under 12 free (off season and summer only); MAP avail; pack-age plans; some higher rates hol wkends; lower rates rest of yr. Crib free. 3 pools, 1 indoor. Dining rm (public by res) 7:30-10:30 am, 5:30-9 pm; Austrian tea rm 10:30 am-5:30 pm. Bar 3:30-10 pm; entertainment, movies. Ck-out 11 am, ck-in 3 pm. Business servs avail. Bellhops. Gift shop. Tennis. Downhill ski 6 mi; x-country ski on site, equipt, instruc-tion. Exercise equipt; sauna. Lawn games. Sleigh rides. Hiking trails; guided nature walks. Many bal-conies. Fireplaces in public rms. Library. Alpine lodge owned by Trapp family, whose lives were por-trayed in *The Sound of Music.* Cr cds: A, DS, MC, V.

B&Bs/Small Inns

★★ **BRASS LANTERN INN.** *717 Maple St (05672). 802/253-2229; fax 802/253-7425; toll-free 800/729-2980. Email brasslntrn@aol.com; www.brass lanterninn.com.* 9 rms, 2 story. S, D $80; each addl $25. Parking lot. TV; cable (premium), VCR avail. Complimentary full bkfst, newspaper, toll-free calls. Restaurant nearby. Bar. Ck-out 10:30 am, ck-in 3 pm. Meeting rm. Business center. Concierge. Gift shop. Exercise privileges, whirlpool. Golf. Tennis, 2 courts. Downhill skiing. Bike rentals. Hiking trail. Picnic facilities. Cr cds: A, MC, V.

★★ **BUTTERNUT INN AND COUNTRY GUEST HOUSE.** *2309 Mountain Rd (05672), 3 mi NW on VT 108. 802/253-4277; fax 802/253-4277; toll-free 800/428-8837.* 18 rms, 3 story. July-Labor Day, mid-Sep-mid-Oct, mid-Dec-Mar: D $45 $75/person; ski plan; lower rates rest of yr. Adults only. TV, some B/W; cable. Heated pool. Complimentary bkfst; afternoon refreshments in sitting rm. Dining rm 8-10 am. Ck-out 11 am, ck-in 3 pm. Downhill ski 4 mi; x-country ski on site. Rec rm. Nature trail. Picnic table, grills. Fireplaces in public areas. Antique furnishings. Library. Totally nonsmoking. Cr cds: MC, V.

★★ **EDSON HILL MANOR.** *1500 Edson Hill Rd (05672), 6 mi NW off VT 108, 1 mi on Edson Hill Rd. 802/253-7371; fax 802/253-4036; toll-free 800/621-0284. Email edsonhill@stowevt.net.* 9 rms in lodge, 16 carriage house units, 25 baths. A/C in lodge rms only. mid-Dec-mid-Apr, MAP: D $95-$125/person; each addl $55; under 4 free; ski, riding and mid-wk plans; lower rates rest of yr. Serv charge 15%. Crib free. Pool. Dining rm 8-10 am, 6-9:30 pm. Bar 4:30 pm-midnight; summer from 5 pm. Ck-out 11 am, ck-in 2 pm. Downhill ski 5 mi; x-country ski on site; marked trails, instruction, rentals. Sleigh rides. Carriage rides. Stocked trout pond. Lawn games. Many fireplaces. Varied accommodations. 225 acres on hillside; view of Green Mts. Cr cds: DS, MC, V.

★★ **SCANDINAVIA INN AND CHALETS.** *3576 Mountain Rd (05672), 3¾ mi NW on VT 108. 802/253-8555; fax 802/253-8555; res 800/544-4229. Email scand@togethor. net; www.scandinaviainn.com.* 18 rms, 3 story, 1 suite. Feb, Oct, Dec: D $129; suites $295; each addl $15; children $15; under 11 free; lower rates rest of yr. Parking lot. Pool, whirlpool. TV; cable, VCR avail. Complimentary full bkfst. Restaurant 7:30 am-11 pm. Ck-out 11 am, ck-in 2 pm. Business servs avail. Coin lndry. Exercise equipt. Golf. Tennis, 20 courts. Downhill skiing. Hiking trail. Cr cds: A, DS, MC, V.

★★★ **STOWEHOF INN.** *434 Edson Hill Rd (05672), 3½ mi N on Edson Hill Rd, off VT 108. 802/253-9722; fax 802/253-7513; toll-free 800/932-7136. www.stowehof.com.* 50 rms, 3 story. Ski season, July-Oct: D $69-$120/person; each addl $35; MAP avail; higher rates: Christmas wk, fall season. Serv charge 15%. Crib free. TV; cable, VCR avail (free movies). Heated pool; whirlpool, poolside serv, sauna. Complimentary full bkfst. Dining rm 8-10 am, 6-9:30 pm; summer also noon-2 pm. Bar 4 pm-1 am. Ck-out noon, ck-in 3 pm. Meeting rm. Business servs avail. Luggage handling. Tennis, pro. Downhill ski 4 mi; x-country ski on site. Rec rm. Lawn games. Sleigh rides. Fireplaces. Private patios, balconies. Library. Trout pond. Cr cds: A, D, DS, MC, V.

★★ **STOWE INN AT LITTLE RIVER.** *123 Mountain Rd (05672), Mt Mansfield Rd at Bridge St, N on VT 108. 802/253-4836; fax 802/253-7308; res 802/253-4836; toll-free 800/227-1108. Email info@stoweinn.com; www.stoweinn.com.* 42 rms, 3 story, 1 suite. Feb, Aug-Oct, Dec: D $210; suites $230; each addl $10; children $10; lower rates rest of yr. Crib avail. Pet accepted. Parking lot. Pool, whirlpool. TV; cable. Complimentary continental bkfst, toll-free calls. Restaurant. Bar. Ck-out 11 am, ck-in 2 pm. Meeting rms. Business center. Exercise privileges. Golf. Tennis.

Downhill skiing. Bike rentals. Hiking trail. Cr cds: A, DS, MC, V.

★★ **THREE BEARS AT THE FOUNTAIN.** *1049 Pucker St Rte 100 (05672). 802/253-7671; fax 802/253-8804; toll-free 800/898-9634. Email threebears@stowevt.net; www.threebearsbandb.com.* 4 rms, 2 story, 2 suites. Feb, Sep-Oct, Dec: D $145; suites $275; each addl $25; under 12 free; lower rates rest of yr. Pet accepted, some restrictions, fee. Parking lot. TV; cable, VCR avail, CD avail. Complimentary full bkfst, newspaper, toll-free calls. Restaurant nearby. Business center. Exercise privileges, whirlpool. Golf. Tennis. Downhill skiing. Picnic facilities. Cr cds: A, MC, V.

★ **WINDING BROOK...A CLASSIC MOUNTAIN LODGE.** *199 Edson Hill Rd (05672). 802/253-7354; fax 802/253-8429; toll-free 800/426-6697. Email windbrklod@aol.com; www.windingbrooklodge.com.* 15 rms, 3 story, 1 suite. Feb, July-Aug, Oct: S $65; D $115; suites $250; each addl $15; under 6 free; lower rates rest of yr. Crib avail. Parking lot. Pool, whirlpool. TV; cable (premium), VCR avail. Complimentary full bkfst, toll-free calls. Restaurant nearby. Ck-out 11 am, ck-in 3 pm. Meeting rm. Business servs avail. Golf, 18 holes. Tennis, 14 courts. Downhill skiing. Bike rentals. Hiking trail. Picnic facilities. Cr cds: A, MC, V.

★★★ **YE OLDE ENGLAND INNE.** *433 Mountain Rd (05672), ¼ mi N on VT 108. 802/253-7558; fax 802/253-8944; toll-free 800/477-3771. Email englandinn@aol.com; www.englandinn.com.* 17 rms, 3 story, 10 suites. Dec-Mar, July-Oct: S, D $349; suites $425; each addl $25; under 12 free; lower rates rest of yr. Crib avail. Pet accepted, some restrictions. Parking lot. Pool, whirlpool. TV; cable, VCR avail. Complimentary full bkfst, coffee in rms, newspaper. Restaurant 11 am-9:30 pm. Bar. Ck-out 11 am, ck-in 3 pm. Meeting rms. Business servs avail. Golf, 18 holes. Downhill ski-ing. Bike rentals. Hiking trail. Picnic facilities. Cr cds: A, DS, MC, V.

Restaurants

★ **CLIFF HOUSE.** *5781 Mountain Rd (05672). 802/253-3000. Email info@stowe.com; www.stowe.com.* Specializes in Rock Cornish game hen, fresh seafood. Hrs: 11 am-3 pm, 5:30-9 pm; Sun, Wed to 2:30 pm. Closed Mon, Tues; Thanksgiving; also mid-Apr-late June, late Oct-mid-Dec. Res required. Lunch buffet: $12.10; dinner complete meals: $42.50. Sun brunch $18.95. View of mountains. Cr cds: A, D, DS, MC, V.

★★★ **ISLE DE FRANCE.** *1899 Mountain Rd (05672). 802/253-7751. Email isledefran@aol.com; www.gostowe.com.* Specializes in lobster Newberg, Dover sole meuniere, chateaubriand. Own bread. Hrs: 6-10 pm. Closed Mon. Res accepted. Bar. Wine list. Dinner a la carte entrees: $14.50-$23. Parking. French provincial decor; formal dining in elegant atmosphere. Cr cds: A, D, MC, V.

★★ **PARTRIDGE INN SEAFOOD RESTAURANT.** *504 Mountain Rd (05672), ½ mi NW on VT 108. 802/253-8000. Email pistowe@together.net.* Mediterranean menu. Specializes in Maine lobster, fresh Cape Cod seafood, pasta. Hrs: 5:30-9:30 pm. Closed first 3 wks Nov. Res accepted. Bar. Dinner $14.50-$19.95. Child's menu. Parking. Fireplace. Cr cds: A, D, DS, MC, V.

★★ **THE SHED.** *1859 Mountain Rd (05672). 802/253-4364.* Specializes in baby back ribs, fresh seafood, calf liver. Hrs: 11 am-midnight. Res accepted. Bar. Lunch $4.95-$9.95; dinner $8.75-$15.95. Sun brunch $12.95. Child's menu. Parking. Brewery on premises. Family-owned. Cr cds: A, D, DS, MC, V.

★ **SWISSPOT.** *128 Main St (05672). 802/253-4622.* Specializes in fondue, pasta, quiche. Hrs: 11:30 am-10 pm. Closed mid-Apr-mid-June. Res accepted. Bar. Lunch $4.95-$8.95; dinner $5.95-$17.95. Child's menu. Patio dining. Built for 1967 Montreal

Expo, then moved here. Cr cds: A, C, D, DS, MC, V.

★★ **WHISKERS.** *1652 Mountain Rd (05672), 1½ mi NW on VT 108. 802/253-8996. Email whiskrest@aol.com.* Specializes in fresh lobster, fresh seafood, prime rib. Own desserts. Hrs: 5-10 pm. Res accepted. Bar. Dinner $8.95-$21.95. Child's menu. Parking. Old farm house, antiques. Lobster tanks. Flower garden. Cr cds: A, C, D, DS, MC, V.

D

Stratton Mountain

See also Londonderry, Manchester and Manchester Center, Peru

Area code 802 **Zip** 05155

What to See and Do

Skiing. Stratton Mountain. A high-speed gondola, high-speed 6-passenger, 4 quad, triple, 3 double chairlifts; patrol, school, rentals, snowmaking; cafeterias, restaurants, bars, nursery, sports center. Ninety runs, longest run 3 mi; vertical drop 2,003 ft. (mid-Nov-mid-Apr, daily) Over 17 mi of cross-country trails (Dec-Mar, daily), rentals; snowboarding. Summer activities incl gondola ride, horseback riding, tennis, golf (school); festivals; concert series. On Stratton Mt access road, off VT 30. Phone 802/297-2200, 802/297-4000, or 800/STRATTON. ¢¢¢¢

Annual Event

Labor Day Street Festival. Stratton Mt. Festival with continuous entertainment, specialty foods, imported beer, activities for children. Phone 802/297-2200. Labor Day wkend.

Seasonal Event

Stratton Arts Festival. Stratton Mt Base Lodge. Paintings, photography, sculpture, and crafts; special performing arts events, craft demonstrations. Phone 802/297-2200. mid-Sep-mid-Oct.

Motel/Motor Lodge

★★ **LIFTLINE LODGE.** *Stratton Mountain Rd (05155). 802/297-2600; fax 802/297-2949; toll-free 900/787-2886.* 91 rms, 2 story, 69 with A/C. mid-Dec-mid-Mar: S, D $125-$135; each addl $15; kit. units $225-$275; under 16 free; wkly rates; ski, golf plans; higher rates fall foliage season; lower rates rest of yr. Crib free. TV; cable. Pool; whirlpools. Restaurant 7-11 am, 5:30-9 pm. Bar 4 pm-1 am; entertainment ski season. Ck-out 11 am. Meeting rms. Business servs avail. In-rm modem link. Lighted tennis. 27-hole golf privileges, greens fee $69, putting green, driving range. Downhill ski adj; x-country ski 1 mi. Exercise equipt; saunas. Rec rm. Cr cds: A, C, D, DS, MC, V.

Resort

★★★ **STRATTON MOUNTAIN INN AND VILLAGE LODGE.** *RR 1 Box 145 (05155), 1½ mi N of jct VT 100N. 802/297-2200; fax 802/297-2939; toll-free 800/787-2886. Email skistratton@intrawest.com; www.stratton.com.* 110 condominiums (1-4 bedrm), 1-4 story. S, D $90-$480; family rates; ski-wk, tennis, golf plans; higher rates hols. TV; cable (premium), VCR (movies $3.50). 4 pools, 1 indoor; whirlpool. Supervised children's activities; ages 1-12. Box lunches. Snack bar. Ck-out 10 am, ck-in 5 pm. Lndry facilities. Package store 5 mi. Meeting rms. Business servs avail. Shopping arcade. Ski shuttle service. Sports dir. 15 tennis courts; indoor lighted tennis, clinic, pro. 27-hole golf, greens fee $49-$82, pro, putting green, driving range. Downhill/x-country ski on site. Racquetball/squash. Bicycles. Game rm. Rec rm. Exercise rm; sauna. Mountain bicycles (rentals). Refrigerators, fireplaces. Private patios, balconies. Picnic tables. Gondola rides (in season). Resort covers 4,000 acres. Cr cds: A, C, D, DS, MC, V.

Swanton

(B-1) *See also North Hero, St. Albans*

Pop 2,360 **Elev** 119 ft **Area code** 802 **Zip** 05488

Information Chamber of Commerce, PO Box 210; 802/868-7200

The location of this town, just two miles east of Lake Champlain, makes it an attractive resort spot.

What to See and Do

missisquoi National Wildlife Refuge. More than 6,400 acres, incl much of the missisquoi River delta on Lake Champlain; primarily a waterfowl refuge (best in Apr, Sep, and Oct), but other wildlife and birds may be seen. Fishing, hunting, hiking and canoe trails. (Daily) 2½ mi W via VT 78. Phone 802/868-4781. **FREE**

Annual Event

Swanton Summer Festival. On Village Green. Band concerts, square dancing, rides, children's events, parades, arts and crafts. Last wkend July.

Resort

★★★ TYLER PLACE FAMILY RESORT. *Old Dock Rd (05460), off I-89. 802/868-3301; fax 802/868-5621; res 802/868-4000. Email tyler@ together.net; www.tylerplace.com.* 12 suites in 1-2-story inn, 27 kit. cottages (3-6 rm). Late May-Labor Day, AP: $77-$198/person; children $35-$81. Closed rest of yr. Crib free. TV rm. 2 pools, 1 indoor pool; wading pool, lifeguard. Supervised children's activities (May-Sep); ages infant-16 yrs. Dining rm 7:30-10:30 am, 12:30-1:30 pm, 6:30-8 pm. Box lunches, buffets. Bar noon-midnight. Ck-out 10 am, ck-in 3 pm. Tennis. Sailing, canoeing, fishing boats, motors (fee). Waterskiing (fee), windsurfing. Nature trails. Soc dir. Rec rm. Exercise rm. Fireplace in cottages. Refrigerator in rms. On 165 acres; private lake shore. Cr cds: A, DS, MC, V.

Vergennes

(D-1) *See also Middlebury, Shelburne*

Settled 1766 **Pop** 2,578 **Elev** 205 ft **Area code** 802 **Zip** 05491

Vergennes is one of the smallest incorporated cities in the nation (1 sq mi). It is also the oldest city in Vermont and the third oldest in New England.

What to See and Do

Button Bay State Park. This 236-acre park on a bluff overlooking Lake Champlain was named for the buttonlike formations in the clay banks; spectacular views of Adirondack Mts. Swimming pool, fishing, boating (rentals); nature and hiking trails, picnicking, tent and trailer sites (dump station). Museum, naturalist. (Memorial Day-Columbus Day) Standard fees. 6 mi W on Button Bay Rd, just S of Basin Harbor. Phone 802/475-2377 or 802/483-2001.

Chimney Point State Historic Site. (1700s) This 18th-century tavern was built on the site of a 17th-century French fort. Exhibits on the Native American and French settlement of Champlain Valley and Vermont. (Memorial Day-Columbus Day, Wed-Sun) 6 mi S via VT 22A, then 8 mi SW via VT 17, at the terminus of the Crown Point Military Rd on shoreline of Lake Champlain. Phone 802/759-2412. ¢

John Strong Mansion. (1795) Federalist house; restored and furnished in the period. (mid-May-mid-Oct, Fri-Sun) 6 mi SW via VT 22A, on VT 17, in West Addison. Phone 802/759-2309. ¢¢

Kennedy Bros Factory Marketplace. Renovated 1920s brick creamery bldg features gifts, crafts, and antique shops. Deli, ice-cream shop, picnic area. (Daily; closed Jan 1, Thanksgiving, Dec 25) 11 Main St. Phone 802/877-2975. **FREE**

Rokeby Museum. (ca 1785) Ancestral home of abolitionist Rowland T. Robinson was a station for the Underground Railroad. Artifacts and archives of 4 generations of the Robinson family. Set on 85 acres, farmstead includes an ice house, a creamery, and a stone smokehouse. Special events yr-round. Tours. (mid-May-mid-Oct, Thurs-Sun) 2 mi N on US 7, 6 mi S of ferry route on US 7, Ferrisburg. Phone 802/877-3406. ¢¢

Motel/Motor Lodge

★ **SKYVIEW MOTEL.** *2956 US Rte 7 (05456), 2 mi N on US 7. 802/877-3410; toll-free 888/799-9090. Email info@skyviewmotel; www.skyviewmotel. com.* 15 rms, 1 story. May-Oct: S $65; D $90; each addl $10; under 12 free; lower rates rest of yr. Crib avail, fee. TV; cable. Complimentary coffee in rms, toll-free calls. Restaurant nearby. Ck-out 11 am, ck-in 1 pm. Golf, 18 holes. Tennis, 2 courts. Downhill skiing. Picnic facilities. Cr cds: A, DS, MC, V.

Resort

★★★ **BASIN HARBOR CLUB.** *Basin Harbor Rd (05491), 6 mi W of US 7, VT 22A. 802/475-2311; fax 802/475-6545; toll-free 800/622-4000. Email info@basinharbor.com; www. basinharbor.com.* 40 rms in lodges, 77 cottages (1-3 bedrm). Mid-May-mid-Oct, AP: S $165; D $220-$405; each addl $5-$70; EP avail mid-May-mid-June, Sep-Oct; wkly rates. Closed rest of yr. Crib avail. Pet accepted, some restrictions. TV avail. Heated pool; poolside serv. Free supervised children's activities (July-Aug); ages 3-15. Dining rm 8 am-10 pm. Box lunches. Bar 11 am-midnight. Ck-out 11 am, ck-in 4 pm. Coin lndry. Business servs avail. Concierge. Gift shop. Airport, Railroad station, bus depot transportation. Rec dirs. Tennis. 18-hole golf, greens fee $42, putting green, driving range. Beach; motorboats, sailboats, canoes, kayaks, cruise boat; windsurfing, waterskiing. Exercise rm. Massage. Fitness, nature trails. Lawn games. Bicycles. Rec rm. Refrigerator in cottages. Family-owned since 1886; Colonial architecture. Located on 700 acres, on Lake Champlain; dockage. 3,200-ft airstrip avail. Cr cds: A, DS, MC, V.

B&Bs/Small Inns

★ **EMERSON GUEST HOUSE.** *82 Main St (05491). 802/877-3293; fax 802/877-3293; toll-free 800/653-3034. Email emersons@sover.net; www. emersonhouse.com.* 6 rms, 3 story, 1 suite. Sep-Oct: D $65; suites $125; each addl $15; under 4 free; lower rates rest of yr. Parking lot. TV; cable. Complimentary full bkfst, newspaper, toll-free calls. Restaurant nearby. Ck-out 11 am, ck-in 4 pm. Business servs avail. Concierge. Golf. Tennis, 2 courts. Downhill skiing. Hiking trail. Picnic facilities. Cr cds: MC, V.

★★★ **STRONG HOUSE INN.** *94 W Main (05491). 802/877-3337; fax 802/877-2599. Email innkeeper@stronghouse inn.com; www.stronghouseinn.com.* 13 rms, 2 story, 1 suite. June-Oct: D $135; under 8 free; lower rates rest of yr. Parking lot. TV; cable (premium), VCR avail, CD avail. Complimentary full bkfst, coffee in rms, newspaper. Restaurant. Bar. Meeting rm. Business servs avail. Gift shop. Golf, 18 holes. Downhill skiing. Hiking trail. Picnic facilities. Cr cds: A, MC, V.

Waitsfield

(D-2) See also Montpelier, Warren, Waterbury

Pop 1,422 **Elev** 698 ft **Area code** 802 **Zip** 05673

Information Central Vermont Chamber of Commerce, PO Box 336, Barre 05641; 802/496-3409 or 800/82-VISIT

This region, known as "the Valley," is a popular area in summer as well as in the winter ski season.

What to See and Do

Mad River Glen Ski Area. Area has 3 double chairlifts, single chairlift; patrol, school, rentals, snowmaking;

cafeterias, restaurant, bar, nursery, telemark program; 33 runs, longest run 3 mi; vertical drop 2,000 ft. (Dec-Apr, daily) On VT 17, 5 mi W of VT 100. Phone 802/496-3551 or 802/496-2001 (snow conditions). ¢¢¢¢

Resort

★★ **TUCKER HILL INN.** *Rte 17 (05673), 1 mi S of VT 100, 1½ mi W on VT 17. 802/496-3983; toll-free 800/ 543-7841. Email tuckerhill@tuckerhill. com; www.tuckerhill.com.* 16 rms, 3 story, 2 suites. Dec-Mar, June-Oct: S $169; D $189; suites $189; each addl $25; lower rates rest of yr. Parking lot. Pool, lap pool. TV; cable (premium), VCR avail. Complimentary continental bkfst, toll-free calls. Restaurant 5-10 pm. Bar. Ck-out 11 am, ck-in 3 pm. Meeting rms. Business center. Bellhops. Concierge. Dry cleaning. Gift shop. Exercise privileges. Golf, 18 holes. Tennis, 2 courts. Cr cds: A, MC, V.

⊡ 🕸 👤 📺 🍽 🏊 🎿 🖼 🐾 SC 🎿

B&Bs/Small Inns

★★ **1824 HOUSE INN BED AND BREAKFAST.** *2150 Main St (05673), 3 mi N on VT 100. 802/496-7555; fax 802/496-7559; toll-free 800/426-3986. Email stay@1824house.com; www. 1824house.com.* 7 rms, 2 story. No rm phones. S, D $75-$135; higher rates: hols, fall foliage. Complimentary full bkfst. Ck-out 11 am, ck-in 4 pm. Downhill ski 6 mi; x-country ski 5 mi. Whirlpool. Lawn games. Restored farmhouse (1824); feather beds, Oriental rugs, down quilts. Totally nonsmoking. Cr cds: A, DS, MC, V.

🕸 📺 🖼 🐾

★★★ **THE INN AT THE ROUND BARN.** *1665 E Warren Rd (05673), 1½ mi S of VT 100 on E Warren Rd. 802/496-2276; fax 802/496-8832. Email roundbarn@madriver.com.* 11 rms, 4 A/C, 2 story. Some rm phones. S $105-$215; D $115-$225; each addl $25. TV in sitting rm. Indoor pool. Complimentary full bkfst. Ck-out 11 am, ck-in 3 pm. Business servs avail. Gift shop. Game rm. X-country ski on site, rentals. In restored farmhouse (ca 1810), named for its historic 12-sided barn (1910). On 235 acres with perennial gardens and 5 ponds. Totally nonsmoking. Cr cds: A, DS, MC, V.

⊡ 🕸 👤 📺 🍽 🎿 🖼 🐾

★★ **LAREAU FARM COUNTRY INN.** *PO Box 563, Rte 100 (05673). 802/496-4949; fax 802/496-7979; toll-free 800/833-0766. Email lareau@ lareaufarminn.com; www.lareaufarm inn.com.* 12 rms, 2 story, 1 suite. Sep-Oct, Dec: S $100; D $125; suites $150; each addl $20; children $15; under 12 free; lower rates rest of yr. Parking lot. TV; cable. Complimentary full bkfst. Restaurant 5:30-9:30 pm. Bar. Ck-out 10:30 am, ck-in 3 pm. Meeting rm. Concierge. Golf. Tennis, 10 courts. Downhill skiing. Beach access. Hiking trail. Cr cds: MC, V.

🕸 👤 📺 🍽 🎿 🖼 🐾

★★ **THE WAITSFIELD INN.** *5267 Main (05673), 1 mi S on VT 100. 802/ 496-3979; fax 802/496-3970; toll-free 800/758-3801. Email waitsfieldinn@ madriver.com; www.waitsfieldinn.com.* 14 rms, 2 story. Dec-Mar, July-Oct: S, D $130; each addl $25; children $25; lower rates rest of yr. Parking lot. TV; cable, CD avail. Complimentary full bkfst. Restaurant nearby. Ck-out 11 am, ck-in 3 pm. Meeting rm. Business servs avail. Gift shop. Golf. Tennis. Downhill skiing. Hiking trail. Cr cds: A, DS, MC, V.

🕸 👤 📺 🍽 🎿 🐾

★ **WHITE HORSE INN.** *999 German Flats Rd (05673). 802/496-3260; fax 802/496-2476; toll-free 800/328-3260. Email whorse@plainfield.bypass.com; www.central-vt.com/web/whorse.* 24 rms, 2 story. Dec-Mar, Sep-Oct: S $65; D $95; each addl $15; children $5; under 12 free; lower rates rest of yr. Pet accepted, some restrictions. Parking lot. TV; cable (premium), VCR avail. Complimentary full bkfst. Restaurant nearby. Ck-out noon, ck-in 3 pm. Meeting rm. Fax servs avail. Golf, 18 holes. Tennis, 4 courts. Downhill skiing. Cr cds: A, DS, MC, V.

🍽 📺 👤 🎿 🖼 🐾

Restaurants

★ **RESTAURANT DEN.** *VT 100 (05673), 1 mi S. 802/496-8880.* Specializes in steak, fresh seafood. Salad bar. Hrs: 11:30 am-11 pm. Closed Thanksgiving, Dec 25. Bar. Lunch

$3.95-$6.95; dinner $8.95-$13.95. Cr cds: A, MC, V.

D

★★ **THE STEAK PLACE AT TUCKER HILL.** *VT 17. 802/496-3983. Email tuckerhill@tuckerhill.com; www.tuckerhill.com.* Hrs: 5-10 pm. Bar. Dinner $8-$14.95. Child's menu. Cr cds: A, MC, V.

Warren

See also Waitsfield, Waterbury

Pop 1,172 **Elev** 893 ft **Area code** 802
Zip 05674
Web www.sugarbushchamber.org
Information Sugarbush Chamber of Commerce, PO Box 173, Waitsfield 05673; 802/496-3409

What to See and Do

Sugarbush Golf Course. An 18-hole championship course designed by Robert Trent Jones, Sr; driving range, 9-hole putting green, championship tees (6,524 yds). Restaurant. (May-Oct, daily) Res recommended. 3 mi NW via VT 100. Phone 802/583-2722. ¢¢¢¢

Sugarbush Resort. Area has 3 quad, 3 triple, 6 double chairlifts, 4 surface lifts; patrol, school, rentals, snowmaking; concession area, cafeteria, restaurant, bar, nursery; 107 runs, longest run over 2 mi; vertical drop 2,600 ft. (Early Nov-early May, daily) 3 mi NW, off VT 100. Phone 802/583-2381, 800/53-SUGAR or 800/583-SNOW (snow conditions). ¢¢¢¢

Sugarbush Soaring Association. Soaring instruction, scenic glider rides. Picnicking, restaurant. (May-Oct, daily) Res preferred. 2 mi NE via VT 100, at Sugarbush Airport. Phone 802/496-2290.

Sugarbush Sports Center. Complete sports and fitness facility with pools and whirlpools, steam rm, saunas, massage. Gym. Indoor/outdoor tennis courts, racquetball/handball, and squash courts. Sports instruction. Fee for activities. (Daily) 3 mi NW via VT 100, in Sugarbush Village. Phone 802/583-2391. ¢¢¢

Motel/Motor Lodge

★ **GOLDEN LION RIVERSIDE INN.** *731 VT 100 (05674), 1 mi N. 802/496-3084; fax 802/496-7438; toll-free 888/867-4491. Email gldnlion@madriver.com; www.madriver.com/lodging/goldlion.* 12 rms, 2 kit. units. No A/C. mid-Sep-mid-Apr: S, D $55-$83; each addl $10; under 6 free; higher rates wkends, hols; lower rates rest of yr. Crib free. Pet accepted. TV; cable. Complimentary full bkfst. Restaurant nearby. Ck-out 11 am. Downhill/x-country ski 3 mi. Picnic table, grill. Cr cds: A, DS, MC, V.

🔌 🛉 🚶 ⛷ 🏊 SC

Resort

★★ **SUGARBUSH VILLAGE CONDOS.** *RR 1 Box 68-12 (05674), 3 mi N on VT 100, then 3 mi W on Sugarbush Access Rd. 802/583-3000; fax 802/583-2373; res 800/451-4326. Email sugares@madriver.com; www.sugarbushvillage.com.* 150 1-5 bedrm kit. condos, 1-5 story. No A/C. Ski season: 1-2 bedrm $90-$330; 3-5 bedrm $335-$440; wkly rates; ski-wk, sports plans; lower rates rest of yr. Crib avail. TV; cable, VCR avail. Pool. Ck-out 10 am. Coin lndry. Downhill ski adj; x-country ski 2 mi. Refrigerators; some microwaves, fireplaces or wood stoves. Private patios, some balconies. Cr cds: A, DS, MC, V.

⛷ 🏊 🏔

B&Bs/Small Inns

★★★ **SUGARBUSH INN.** *2405 Sugarbush Access Rd (05674), then 2 mi W on Sugarbush Access Rd. 802/583-2301; fax 802/583-3209.* 46 rms in inn, 196 kit. condos. No A/C in condos. Dec-Mar: S, D, suites $90-$150; each addl $20-$35; kit. condos $200-$400 (2-day min); ski, golf, tennis plans; higher rates hols; lower rates rest of yr. Crib $10. TV; cable (premium), VCR avail (movies $3.50). 2 pools, 1 indoor; whirlpool. Dining rm 7:30-10 am, 6-10 pm. Bar from 4:30 pm. Ck-out 11 am, ck-in 6 pm. Meeting rms. Business servs avail. Bellhops. Gift shop. Tennis, clinics, pro. 18-hole golf, putting green. Downhill ski ½ mi; x-country ski on site, rentals. Exercise equipt; sauna. Ice skating. Rec rm. Lawn games. Some refrigerators. Some private patios, balconies. Cr cds: A, DS, MC, V.

Sugarbrush Resort, Warren

★★ SUGARTREE COUNTRY INN.
2440 Sugarbush Access Rd (05674), 3 mi N on VT 100 to Sugarbush Access Rd. 802/583-3211; fax 802/583-3203; toll-free 800/666-8907. Email sugar tree@madriver.com; www.sugartree.com. 9 rms, 3 story. Jan-Mar, Sep-Oct: S $115; D $135; each addl $30; lower rates rest of yr. Parking lot. TV; cable (premium), VCR avail. Complimentary full bkfst. Restaurant nearby. Ck-out 11 am, ck-in 3 pm. Fax servs avail. Exercise privileges. Golf, 18 holes. Tennis, 12 courts. Downhill skiing. Hiking trail. Cr cds: A, DS, MC, V.

Villas/Condos

★★ BRIDGES FAMILY RESORT AND TENNIS CLUB. *202 Bridges Circle (05674), 2¼ mi W on Sugarbush Access Rd. 802/583-2922; fax 802/ 583-1018; toll-free 800/453-2922. Email groupsales@bridgesresort.com; www.bridgesresort.com.* 100 rms, 3 story. Dec-Mar, July-Sep: S, D $190; suites $190; lower rates rest of yr. Crib avail, fee. Parking lot. Indoor/outdoor pools, lap pool, children's pool, lifeguard. TV; cable (premium), VCR avail, CD avail. Complimentary coffee in rms, toll-free calls. Restaurant 11 am-3:30 pm. Bar. Ck-out 11 am, ck-in 6 pm. Business servs avail. Concierge. Gift shop. Exercise rm, sauna. Golf, 18 holes. Tennis, 12 courts. Downhill skiing. Supervised children's activities. Hiking trail. Picnic facilities. Cr cds: A, MC, V.

★ POWDER HOUND INN. *203 Powderhound Rd (05674), 1¼ mi N on VT 100, at jct Sugarbush Access Rd. 802/496-5100; fax 802/496-5163; toll-free 800/548-4022. Email phound@ madriver.com; www.powderhoundinn. com.* 2 story, 44 suites. Dec-Mar, July-Aug: S, D $110; suites $110; each addl $10; under 5 free; lower rates rest of yr. Pet accepted, fee. Parking lot. Pool, whirlpool. TV; cable. Complimentary toll-free calls. Restaurant 5-9 pm. Bar. Ck-out 10 am, ck-in 3 pm. Fax servs avail. Golf. Tennis. Downhill skiing. Picnic facilities. Cr cds: A, DS, MC, V.

Restaurants

★★ BASS. *VT 100 (05674), then ¼ mi W on Sugarbush Access Rd. 802/ 583-3100. Email bassrest@accessvt. com.* Specializes in prime rib, lobster, fresh seafood. Hrs: 5-10 pm; from 4 pm during ski season. Closed Wed June-Aug; also late Apr-mid-May. Bar. Dinner a la carte entrees: $9.50-$17.50. Fireplace. Tri-level dining with view of mountains. Cr cds: A, DS, MC, V.

★★★ THE COMMON MAN. *3209 German Flats Rd (05674). 802/583-2800. Email comman@madriver.com.* Specializes in lapin roti, carre d'agneau, escargot maison. Menu changes wkly. Hrs: 6:30-9:30 pm. Closed Mon; Thanksgiving, Dec 25. Res accepted. Dinner a la carte entrees: $10.25-$21. Child's menu. Casual dining in mid-1800s barn. Family-owned. Cr cds: A, D, MC, V.

Unrated Dining Spot

THE WARREN HOUSE RESTAURANT AND RUPERT'S BAR. *2585 Sugarbush Access Rd (05674), 2½ mi W on Sugarbush Access Rd. 802/583-2421. Email warrenhouse@hotmail. com; www.thewarrenhouse.com.* Specializes in International cuisine. Own baking, desserts. Hrs: 5:30-10 pm.

Closed Mon, Tues; also Easter, Dec 25. Res accepted. Bar. Wine list. Dinner $10-$21.95. Child's menu. Entertainment: magician on wkends. Rustic, greenhouse atmosphere. Cr cds: A, MC, V.

Waterbury

(C-2) *See also Barre, Montpelier, Stowe, Waitsfield, Warren*

(see Springfield)
Pop 4,589 **Elev** 428 ft **Area code** 802
Zip 05676
Information Central Vermont Chamber of Commerce, PO Box 336, Barre 05641; 802/229-5711

Centrally located near many outstanding ski resorts, incl Stowe, Mad River Valley, and Bolton Valley, this area is also popular in summer for hiking, backpacking, and bicycling.

What to See and Do

Ben & Jerry's Ice Cream Factory. Half-hr guided tour, offered every 30 min, through ice-cream factory includes slide show, free samples. Gift shop. (Daily; closed Jan 1, Thanksgiving, Dec 25) I-89 Exit 10, then N on VT 100. Phone 802/244-TOUR. ¢

Camel's Hump Mountain. State's 3rd-highest mountain. Trail is challenging. Weather permitting, Canada can be seen from the top. 8 mi SW of town on dirt road, then 3½-mi hike to summit.

Cold Hollow Cider Mill. One of the largest cider mills in New England features 43-inch rack-and-cloth press capable of producing 500 gallons of cider an hr; also jelly-making operations (fall). Samples are served. 3½ mi N on VT 100. Phone 802/244-8771 or 800/327-7537. **FREE**

Little River State Park. This 12,000-acre park offers swimming, fishing; nature and hiking trails, tent and trailer sites (dump station), lean-tos. (Memorial Day-Columbus Day) Standard fees. 2 mi W off, US 2. Phone 802/244-7103 or 802/479-5280.

Long Trail. A 22-mi segment of backpacking trail connects Camel's Hump with Mt Mansfield (see STOWE), the state's highest peak. Primitive camping is allowed on both mountains. Recommended for the experienced hiker.

Winter recreation. Area abounds in downhill, cross-country, and ski touring facilities; also many snowmobile trails.

Hotel

★★ **HOLIDAY INN & SPA WATERBURY.** *45 Blush Hill Rd (05676), at jct I-89 Exit 10 and VT 100 N.* 802/244-7822; fax 802/244-7822; res 800/465-4329; toll-free 800/621-7822. Email holidays@together.net; www.basshotels.com. 79 rms, 2 story. S, D $70-$145; each addl $10; under 12 free; higher rates fall foliage. Crib free. Pet accepted. TV; cable. Pool. Restaurant 7 am-2 pm, 5:30-9 pm; Sat, Sun 7 am-2 pm, 5:30-10 pm. Bar. Ck-out noon. Coin lndry. Meeting rms. Business servs avail. In-rm modem link. Tennis. Downhill/x-country ski 12 mi. Exercise equipt; sauna. Game rm. Picnic tables. Covered bridge. Cr cds: A, DS, MC, V.

B&Bs/Small Inns

★★★ **BLACK LOCUST INN.** *5088 Waterbury-Stowe Rd (05677), 5 mi N on VT 100, I-89 Exit 10.* 802/244-7490; fax 802/244-8473; toll-free 800/366-5592. Email blklocst@sover.net; www.blacklocustinn.com. 6 rms, 2 story. Dec-Mar, May-Oct: S, D $190; lower rates rest of yr. Parking lot. TV; cable, VCR avail, CD avail. Complimentary full bkfst, newspaper. Restaurant nearby. Ck-out 11 am, ck-in 3 pm. Business servs avail. Gift shop. Golf. Tennis, 20 courts. Downhill skiing. Bike rentals. Hiking trail. Picnic facilities. Cr cds: A, D, DS, MC, V.

★ **GRUNBERG HAUS BED AND BREAKFAST.** *94 Pine St (05676), 4 mi S on VT 100.* 802/244-7726; toll-free 800/800-7760. Email grunhaus@aol.com. 11 rms, some share bath, 2 story, 2 cabins. No A/C. No rm phones. S $40-$110; D $59-$130;

each addl $7; wkly rates; ski plan; Complimentary full bkfst; afternoon refreshments. Ck-out 11 am, ck-in 3 pm. Tennis. Downhill ski 12 mi; x-country ski on site. Whirlpool, sauna. Game rm. Balconies. Tyrolean chalet; field stone fireplace, grand piano. On 14 acres; gardens, trails. Cr cds: DS, MC, V.

★ **INN AT BLUSH HILL.** *784 Blush Hill Rd (05676), N of I-89 on VT 100, then left ¾ mi. 802/244-7529; fax 802/244-7314; toll-free 800/736-7522. Email innatbh@aol.com; www.blush hill.com.* 5 rms, 2 story. Sep-Oct: S, D $125; each addl $15; children $15; under 18 free; lower rates rest of yr. Parking lot. TV; cable, VCR avail, CD avail, VCR avail, CD avail. Complimentary full bkfst, coffee in rms, newspaper, toll-free calls. Restaurant nearby. Ck-out 11 am, ck-in 3 pm. Coin lndry. Exercise privileges. Golf, 9 holes. Tennis. Downhill skiing. Bike rentals. Hiking trail. Picnic facilities. Cr cds: A, DS, MC, V.

★★ **THATCHER BROOK INN.** *Rte 100 (05676). 802/244-5911; fax 802/244-1294; toll-free 800/292-5911. Email thatcherinn@aol.com; www. discover-vermont.com/banner/thatcher. htm.* 24 rms, 3 with shower only, 2 story. No A/C. Sep-Mar: S, D $105-$175; each addl $20; under 12 free; ski plans; wkend rates; MAP avail; 2-day min hols; lower rates rest of yr. Crib free. TV; cable, VCR in common rm. Complimentary full bkfst. Restaurant (see THATCHER BROOK). Ck-out 10:30 am, ck-in 3 pm. Business servs avail. Downhill ski 13 mi; x-country ski 10 mi. Rec rm. Built in 1899; twin gazebos with front porch. Cr cds: A, D, DS, MC, V.

Restaurants

★★★ **THATCHER BROOK.** *VT 100N. 802/244-5911. Email info@ thatcherbrook.com; www.thatcherbrook. com.* Specializes in roasted rack of lamb, honey-glazed breast of duck, mushrooms a la Thatcher. Hrs: 5-9:30 pm. Closed Tues. Res accepted. Bar. Dinner a la carte entrees: $12.95-$24.95. Child's menu. Cr cds: A, D, DS, MC, V.

★★★ **VILLA TRAGARA.** *VT 100 (05677). 802/244-5288. www.stowe info.com/villa.* Specializes in pasta, fish. Own baking, pasta. Hrs: 5:30-9:30 pm. Closed Tues in winter. Res accepted. Bar. Wine list. Dinner $12-$17.75. Converted 1820s farmhouse. Cr cds: A, MC, V.

Weathersfield

(see Springfield)

West Dover

(H-2) *See also Wilmington*

Pop 250 (est) **Elev** 1,674 ft
Area code 802 **Zip** 05356
Web www.visitvermont.com/
Information Mount Snow Valley Region Chamber of Commerce, VT 9, W Main St, PO Box 3, Wilmington 05363; 802/464-8092

What to See and Do

Mount Snow Ski Area. Area has 2 quad, 6 triple, 9 double chairlifts; patrol, school, rentals, snowmaking; cafeterias, restaurant, bars, entertainment, nursery. Over 100 trails spread over 5 interconnected mountain areas (also see WILMINGTON); shuttle bus. Longest run 2½ mi; vertical drop 1,700 ft. (Nov-early May, daily) Half-day rates. 9 mi N on VT 100, in Green Mt National Forest. Phone 802/464-8501, 802/464-2151 (snow conditions), or 800/245-SNOW (lodging). ¢¢¢¢

Annual Events

Mountain Bike World Cup Race. Mt Snow. More than 1,500 cyclists from throughout the world compete in downhill, dual slalom, and circuit racing events. Phone 800/245-7669. mid-June.

Mount Snow Foliage Craft Fair. Mt Snow Ski Area (see). New England area artisans exhibit pottery, jewelry, glass, graphics, weaving, and other crafts; entertainment. Columbus Day wkend.

B&Bs/Small Inns

★ **THE INN AT QUAIL RUN.** *106 Smith Rd (05363). 802/464-3362; fax 802/464-7784; toll-free 800/343-7227. Email quailrunvt@aol.com; www. bbonline.com/vt/quailrun.* 14 rms, 2 story. No A/C. No rm phones. S, D $80-$125; each addl $25; ski plans; higher rates fall foliage, hols. Crib free. Pet accepted. TV in some rms; cable. Pool; sauna. Playground. Complimentary full bkfst. Ck-out 11 am, ck-in 3 pm. Business servs avail. Downhill ski 4½ mi; x-country ski on site. Rec rm. Lawn games. Picnic tables. On 12 acres in Green Mountains, view of Deerfield Valley. Totally nonsmoking. Cr cds: A, DS, MC, V.

★★★★ **THE INN AT SAW MILL FARM.** *Rte 100 and Crosstown Rd (05356). 802/464-8131; fax 802/464-1130; res 802/464-8131; toll-free 800/493-1133. Email sawmill@sover.net; www.vermontdirect.com/sawmil.* The architecture and interior design backgrounds of innkeepers Rodney and Ione Williams shine in this meticulously restored 18th-century farm. Weathered siding, exposed beams, stone fireplaces, and antique-American furnishings create a taste of history at the 24-room property. With spectacular food and an unimaginable wine cellar of 36,000 bottles, it's no wonder guests visit just for the dinners. 15 rms, 2 story, 3 suites. Sep-Oct: S $445; D $500; suites $570; each addl $125; children $85; under 12 free; lower rates rest of yr. Parking lot. Pool. TV; cable, VCR avail, CD avail. Complimentary full bkfst, newspaper. Restaurant 6-9:30 pm(see INN AT SAWMILL FARM). Bar. Ck-out noon, ck-in 3 pm. Meeting rm. Business center. Concierge. Gift shop. Exercise privileges. Golf. Tennis. Downhill skiing. Cr cds: A, D, MC, V.

★ **RED CRICKET INN.** *45 Rte 100 N (05356). 802/464-8817; fax 802/464-0508; toll-free 877/473-9274. Email redcrick@sover.net; www.redcricketinn. com.* 22 rms, 1 story, 2 suites. Jan-Mar: S $115; D $125; suites $160; each addl $10; lower rates rest of yr. Parking lot. TV; cable. Complimentary continental bkfst. Restaurant nearby. Meeting rm. Fax servs avail. Sauna. Golf. Downhill skiing. Cr cds: A, DS, MC, V.

★★ **WEST DOVER INN.** *108 Rte 100, Box 1208 (05356). 802/464-5207; fax 802/464-2173. Email wdvr inn@sover.net; www.westdoverinn.com.* 8 rms, 2 story, 4 suites. Jan-Mar, Sep-Oct: S, D $135; suites $200; each addl $30; lower rates rest of yr. Parking lot. TV; cable. Complimentary full bkfst. Restaurant. Bar. Ck-out 11 am, ck-in 2 pm. Meeting rms. Business servs avail. Concierge. Exercise privileges. Golf. Downhill skiing. Hiking trail. Cr cds: A, DS, MC, V.

Restaurant

★★★★ **THE INN AT SAWMILL FARM.** *VT 100 Crosstown Rd. 802/464-8131. Email sawmill@sover.net; www.vermontdirect.com/sawmill.* Housed in an 18th-century barn, visitors travel from miles around just to dine at this historic inn. The menu is dotted with true continental classics and the effect of its combination with faded walls, white exposed beams and a cozy atmosphere is comfortably divine. You might even choose to stay for the night in one of 24 antique-filled rooms. Specializes in seafood, duck, rack of lamb. Own baking. Hrs: 6-9:30 pm. Res accepted. Bar. Wine list. Dinner a la carte entrees: $27-$32. Cr cds: A, DS, MC, V.

D

Weston

(G-2) *See also Londonderry, Peru*

Pop 620 (est) **Elev** 1,295 ft
Area code 802 **Zip** 05161

Once nearly a ghost town, Weston is now a serene village secluded in the beautiful hills of Vermont. Charming old houses are situated around a small common and shops are scattered along Main St. Weston is listed on the National Register of Historic Places.

What to See and Do

Farrar-Mansur House Museum. (1797) Restored house/tavern with 9 rms. Period furnishings, paintings. Guided tours. (July-Aug, Mon-Fri; Memorial Day-Columbus Day, wkends) N side of Common. ¢¢

Greendale Camping Area. Picnicking, camping (fee). 2 mi N on VT 100, 2 mi W on Greendale Rd in Green Mt National Forest (see).

Old mill Museum. Museum of old time tools and industries; tinsmith in residence. Guided tours (July and Aug). (Memorial Day-Columbus Day, daily) On VT 100, in center of village. **Donation**

Vermont Country Store. Just like those Granddad used to patronize—rock candy and other old-fashioned foodstuffs. (Mon-Sat; closed Thanksgiving, Dec 25) On VT 100, S of Village Green. Phone 802/824-3184.

Weston Bowl mill. Wooden bowls, other wooden household products made on premises. Seconds avail. (Daily; closed hols) Just N of Common on VT 100. Phone 802/824-6219. **FREE**

Weston Playhouse. One of the oldest professional theater companies in the state. Restaurant; cabaret. Village Green. Phone 802/824-5288.

B&Bs/Small Inns

★★ **THE COLONIAL HOUSE.** 287 Rte 100 (05161). 802/824-6286; fax 802/824-3934; toll-free 800/639-5033. Email innkeeper@cohoinn.com; www. cohoinn.com. 15 rms, 2 story. Jan-Mar, Oct: S $70; D $100; each addl $15; children $8; under 12 free; lower rates rest of yr. Crib avail. Pet accepted, some restrictions, fee. Parking lot. TV; cable, VCR avail. Complimentary full bkfst. Restaurant 6-7:30 pm. Ck-out 11 am, ck-in 1 pm. Business servs avail. Golf. Tennis, 3 courts. Downhill skiing. Cr cds: C, D, DS, MC, V.

★★ **WILDER HOMESTEAD INN.** 25 Lawrence Hill Rd (05161), near village green. 802/824-8172; fax 802/824-5054; toll-free 877/838-9979. Email

wilder@sover.net. 7 rms, 5 with bath, 3 story. No A/C. No rm phones. S, D $70-$115; each addl $30; higher rates fall foliage, hol wks. Closed 2 wks Apr. Children over 6 yrs only. TV, cable in sitting rm; VCR (free movies). Complimentary full bkfst. Ck-out 11 am, ck-in 2 pm. Gift shop. Downhill ski 10 mi; x-country ski 3 mi. Federal-style country inn; built 1827. Player piano. Overlooks river. Totally nonsmoking. Cr cds: MC, V.

White River Junction

(F-3) *See also Windsor, Woodstock; also see Hanover, NH*

Settled 1764 **Pop** 2,521 **Elev** 368 ft
Area code 802 **Zip** 05001

Appropriately named, this town is the meeting place of the Boston & Maine and Central Vermont railroads, the White and Connecticut rivers, and two interstate highways.

What to See and Do

Quechee Gorge. Often referred to as Vermont's "Little Grand Canyon," the Ottauquechee River has carved out a mile-long chasm that offers dramatic views of the landscape and neighboring towns. About 8 mi W on US 4.

Motel/Motor Lodge

★★ **RAMADA INN-WHITE RIVER JCT.** 259 Holiday Dr (05001), 2 mi SW on US 5; off Sykes ave at jct I-89, I-91. 802/295-3000; fax 802/295-3774; res 800/272-6232; toll-free 800/648-6754. 134 rms, 2 story, 2 suites. Sep-Oct: S, D $145; suites $185; each addl $12; under 12 free; lower rates rest of yr. Crib avail. Pet accepted, some restrictions, fee. Parking lot. Indoor pool. TV; cable (premium). Complimentary continental bkfst, coffee in rms. Restaurant nearby. Ck-out 11 am, ck-in 3 pm. Meeting rms. Business servs avail. Coin lndry. Exercise equipt, sauna. Golf. Cr cds: A, DS, MC, V.

Hotels

★ ★ BEST WESTERN AT THE JUNCTION.
306 N Hartland Rd (05001), 1 blk E of jct I-89, I-91. 802/295-3015; fax 802/296-2581; toll-free 800/528-1234. Email email@ bestwesternjunction.com; www.best westernjunction.com. 2 story. Sep-Oct: S $129; D $139; lower rates rest of yr. Crib avail. Pet accepted, fee. Parking lot. Indoor pool, children's pool, whirlpool. TV; cable (DSS). Complimentary continental bkfst, coffee in rms, newspaper. Restaurant. Ck-out 11 am, ck-in 4 pm. Fax servs avail. Coin lndry. Gift shop. Exercise equipt, sauna. Golf. Tennis. Downhill skiing. Bike rentals. Supervised children's activities. Hiking trail. Picnic facilities. Cr cds: A, MC, V.

★ ★ COMFORT INN.
8 Sykes Ave (05001), I-91 Exit 11. 802/295-3051; fax 802/295-5990; res 800/228-5150; toll-free 800/628-7727. 90 rms, 4 story, 6 suites. June-Oct: S $209; D $219; suites $229; each addl $10; under 18 free; lower rates rest of yr. Crib avail. Parking lot. Pool. TV; cable. Complimentary continental bkfst, newspaper, toll-free calls. Restaurant. Ck-out 11 am, ck-in 2 pm. Meeting rm. Business servs avail. Coin lndry. Exercise privileges. Golf. Tennis, 10 courts. Downhill skiing. Cr cds: A, C, D, DS, MC, V.

B&B/Small Inn

★ ★ STONCREST FARM BED AND BREAKFAST.
1187 Christian St (05088), 3 mi N on VT 5. 802/296-2425; fax 802/295-1135; toll-free 800/ 730-2425. Email gail.sanderson@valley. net; www.stonecrestfarm.com. 6 rms, 4 with shower only, 2 story. No A/C. No rm phones. mid-May-mid-Nov: S $105-$120; D $120-$135; each addl $25; hols (2-day min); lower rates rest of yr. Closed wk of Dec 25. Children over 8 yrs only. Complimentary full bkfst. Ck-out 11 am, ck-in 3-7 pm. Business servs avail. Downhill ski 15 mi; x-country ski 3½ mi. Lawn games. Built in 1810; country Victorian atmosphere. Totally nonsmoking. Cr cds: A, MC, V.

Restaurant

★ ★ A.J.'S.
Sykes Ave (05001), 4 blks E of I-89, I-91. 802/295-3071. Specializes in steak, prime rib, fresh seafood. Salad bar. Hrs: 5-10 pm; Sun 4-9 pm. Res accepted. Dinner $7.95-$16.95. Child's menu. Rustic decor; wood stoves, fireplace. Cr cds: A, D, DS, MC, V.

Wilmington

(H-2) *See also Bennington, Brattleboro, Marlboro, West Dover*

Chartered 1751 & 53 **Pop** 1,968
Elev 1,533 ft **Area code** 802
Zip 05363
Web www.visitvermont.com/
Information Mount Snow Valley Region Chamber of Commerce, VT 9, W Main St, PO Box 3; 802/464-8092

What to See and Do

Haystack Ski Area. Resort has double, 3 triple chairlifts; patrol, school, rentals, snowmaking; concession, cafeteria, bar, nursery, lodges. Over 100 trails spread over 5 interconnecting mountain areas (also see WEST DOVER); shuttle bus. Longest run 1½ mi; vertical drop 1,400 ft. (Dec-Mar, daily) Golf, pro shop; restaurant, bar (early May-mid-Oct). 3 mi NW, off VT 100. Phone 802/464-8501, 802/464-2151 (snow conditions), or 800/245-7669 (lodging). ¢¢¢¢

Molly Stark State Park. A 158-acre park named for wife of General John Stark, hero of Battle of Bennington (1777); on W slope of Mt Olga (2,438 ft). Fishing in nearby lake. Hiking trails, tent and trailer sites (dump station), lean-tos. Fire tower with excellent views. (Memorial Day-Columbus Day) Standard fees. Approx 4 mi E on VT 9. Phone 802/464-5460 or 802/886-2434.

Annual Event

Deerfield Valley Farmers Day Exhibition. Pony pull, midway rides; horse show, livestock judging, entertainment. Late Aug.

Seasonal Event

The Nights Before Christmas.
Throughout Wilmington and West Dover (see). Celebrates holiday season with caroling, torchlight parade, fireworks, tree lighting. Festival of Light, living nativity, and children's hayrides. Phone 802/464-8092. Late Nov-late Dec.

Motel/Motor Lodge

★★ **NORDIC HILLS LODGE.** *34 Look Rd (05363), VT 9 to VT 100n, Left on Coldbrook Rd. 802/464-5130; fax 802/464-8248; toll-free 800/326-5130. Email nordic@together.net.* 27 rms, 3 story. No A/C. No elvtr. S, D $60-$136; each addl $10-$45; higher rates: Presidents wkend, Christmas wk; winter wknds (2-day min). Closed Apr-mid-May. Crib free. TV. Heated pool; whirlpool, sauna. Complimentary full bkfst. Ck-out 11 am. Downhill/x-country ski 1½ mi. Game rm. Lawn games. Family-owned. Cr cds: A, DS, MC, V.

Hotel

★★ **HORIZON INN.** *VT Rte 9 E (05363). 802/464-2131; fax 802/464-8302; toll-free 800/336-5513. Email horizon@sover.net; www.horizoninn. com.* 28 rms, 2 story, 1 suite. Dec-Mar, July-Oct: D $135; suites $300; each addl $10; children $5; under 12 free; lower rates rest of yr. Crib avail. Street parking. Indoor pool, whirlpool. TV; cable, VCR avail, CD avail. Complimentary coffee in rms. Restaurant 7 am-9 pm. Bar. Ck-out 11 am, ck-in 2 pm. Meeting rm. Fax servs avail. Gift shop. Exercise equipt, sauna. Golf. Tennis. Downhill skiing. Beach access. Supervised children's activities. Hiking trail. Picnic facilities. Cr cds: A, DS, MC, V.

B&Bs/Small Inns

★★ **HERMITAGE INN.** *Coldbrook Rd (05363), 2½ mi N on VT 100 to Coldbrook Rd, then 3 mi W. 802/464-3511; fax 802/464-2688. Email hermitag@sover.net; www.hermitageinn.com.* 29

rms. Sep-Apr: S $210; D $250; each addl $70; lower rates rest of yr. Parking lot. Pool. TV; cable, VCR avail. Restaurant 5-11 pm (see HERMITAGE). Bar. Ck-out 11 am, ck-in 2 pm. Internet access avail. Gift shop. Sauna. Golf. Tennis. Downhill skiing. Hiking trail. Cr cds: A, D, MC, V.

★★ **TRAIL'S END - A COUNTRY INN.** *5 Trails End Ln (05363). 802/464-2727; fax 802/464-5532; toll-free 800/859-2585. Email trailsnd@together.net; www.trailsendvt.com.* 13 rms, 2 story, 2 suites. Dec-Mar: S, D $130; suites $190; each addl $30; children $30; lower rates rest of yr. Parking lot. Pool. TV; cable, VCR avail, CD avail. Complimentary full bkfst, newspaper. Restaurant nearby. Ck-out 11 am, ck-in 2 pm. Meeting rm. Business center. Gift shop. Golf. Tennis. Downhill skiing. Hiking trail. Picnic facilities. Cr cds: A, DS, MC, V.

★★ **WHITE HOUSE OF WILMINGTON.** *178 VT 9 E (05363), at jct VT 9, VT 100. 802/464-2135; fax 802/464-5222; toll-free 800/541-2135. Email whitehse@sover.net; www.white houseinn.com.* 23 rms, 2 story, 1 suite. Feb, Oct: S $98; D $168; suites $230; children $30; lower rates rest of yr. Parking lot. Indoor/outdoor pools, lap pool, children's pool. TV; cable, VCR avail, CD avail. Complimentary full bkfst, toll-free calls. Restaurant 5-9 pm, closed Tue pm (see WHITE HOUSE). Ck-out 11 am. Meeting rms. Business servs avail. Concierge. Sauna, steam rm. Golf. Tennis, 4 courts. Downhill skiing. Hiking trail. Picnic facilities. Cr cds: A, D, DS, MC, V.

Restaurants

★★★ **HERMITAGE.** *Coldbrook Rd. 802/464-3511. Email hermitag@sover.net; www.hermitageinn.com.* Specializes in Wienerschnitzel, fresh trout, game. Own baking. Hrs: 5-10 pm. Res accepted. Bar. Wine list. Dinner $14-$25. 15% serv chg. Trout pond. Family-owned. Cr cds: A, D, MC, V.

★★ **WHITE HOUSE.** *178 VT 9E. 802/464-2135. www.whitehouseinn.com.* Specializes in boneless stuffed duck, veal dishes, fresh seafood. Own baking. Hrs: 5-9 pm. Closed Tues. Res accepted. Bar. Wine list. Dinner $16.95-$22.95. Parking. Colonial Revival decor. Cr cds: C, D, DS, ER, MC, V.

[D]

Windsor

(F-3) *See also White River Junction*

Settled 1764 **Pop** 3,714 **Elev** 354 ft **Area code** 802 **Zip** 05089
Information White River Area Chamber of Commerce, PO Box 697, White River Jct 05001; 802/295-6200

Situated on the Connecticut River in the shadow of Mount Ascutney, Windsor once was the political center of the Connecticut Valley towns. The name "Vermont" was adopted, and its constitution was drawn up here. Inventors and inventions flourished here in the 19th century; the hydraulic pump, a sewing machine, coffee percolator, and various refinements in firearms originated in Windsor.

What to See and Do

American Precision Museum. Exhibits incl hand and machine tools; illustrations of their uses and development. Housed in former Robbins and Lawrence Armory (1846). (Late May-Oct, daily; rest of yr, by appt) 196 Main St. Phone 802/674-5781. ¢¢

Constitution House. An 18th-century tavern where constitution of the Republic of Vermont was signed on July 8, 1777. Museum. (mid-May-mid-Oct, Wed-Sun) 16 N Main St, on US 5. Phone 802/672-3773. ¢

Covered bridge. Crossing the Connecticut River; longest in US.

Mount Ascutney State Park. This 1,984-acre park has a paved road to summit of Mt Ascutney (3,144 ft). Hiking trails, picnicking, tent and trailer sites (dump station), lean-tos. (Memorial Day-Columbus Day) Standard fees. 3 mi S off US 5 on VT 44A; I-91 Exit 8. Phone 802/674-2060 or 802/886-2434.

Vermont State Craft Center at Windsor House. Restored bldg features works of more than 250 Vermont craftspeople. (June-Dec, daily; rest of yr, Mon-Sat) Main St. Phone 802/674-6729. **FREE**

Wilgus State Park. This 100-acre park overlooks the Connecticut River. Canoe launching. Hiking trails. Wooded picnic area. Tent and trailer sites (dump station), lean-tos. (Memorial Day-Columbus Day) Standard fees. 6 mi S on US 5. Phone 802/674-5422 or 802/886-2434.

B&B/Small Inn

★ ★ ★ **JUNPIER HILL INN.** *153 Pembroke Rd (05089), ½ mi N of jct US 5. 802/674-5273; fax 802/674-2041; toll-free 800/359-2541. Email inn keeper@juniperhillinn.com; www. juniperhillinn.com.* 160 rms, 30 story. Feb, Sep-Oct, Dec: S, D $150; each addl $25; lower rates rest of yr. Pool. TV; cable, VCR avail, CD avail. Complimentary full bkfst. Restaurant, closed Sun. Bar. Ck-out 11 am, ck-in 3 pm. Meeting rm. Business servs avail. Gift shop. Golf, 9 holes. Tennis, 2 courts. Downhill skiing. Hiking trail. Cr cds: A, D, DS, MC, V.

[D] [icons]

Restaurant

★ ★ **WINDSOR STATION.** *27 Depot Ave (05089). 802/674-2052.* Specializes in seafood, veal, pasta. Own desserts. Hrs: 5:30-9 pm. Closed Mon; Jan 1, Dec 25. Bar. Dinner $10.95-$16.95. Child's menu. Restored Railroad depot (1900). Cr cds: A, D, DS, MC, V.

[D]

Woodstock

(F-3) *See also Killington, Plymouth, White River Junction*

Settled 1768 **Pop** 3,212 **Elev** 705 ft **Area code** 802 **Zip** 05091
Web www.woodstockvt.com

Information Chamber of Commerce, 18 Central St, PO Box 486; 802/457-3555

The antique charm of Woodstock has been preserved, at least in part, by determination. Properties held for generations by descendants of original owners provided built-in zoning long before Historic District status was achieved. When the iron bridge that crosses the Ottauquechee River at Union Street was condemned in 1968, it was replaced by a covered wooden bridge.

What to See and Do

Billings Farm and Museum. Exhibits incl operating dairy farm and an 1890s farmhouse. (May-late Oct, daily) ½ mi N on VT 12. Phone 802/457-2355. ¢¢

Covered bridge. (1968) First one built in Vermont since 1895. Two others cross the Ottauquechee River; one 3 mi W (1877), another 4 mi E, at Taftsville (1836). Center of village.

Kedron Valley Stables. Hayrides, sleigh rides, picnic trail rides; indoor ring; riding lessons by appt. About 5 mi S on VT 106, in S Woodstock. Phone 802/457-1480.

Marsh-Billings-Rockefeller National Historic Park. Incl Marsh-Billings-Rockefeller mansion, which contains extensive collection of American landscape paintings. Mansion is surrounded by 550-acre Mt Tom forest. Interpretive tours of the mansion, its grounds and gardens, and the Mt Tom forest are available. Reservations recommended. Park also offers hiking, nature study, and cross-country skiing. (June-Oct, daily) On Rte 12, ½ mi N of Woodstock Village Green. Phone 802/457-3368. Also here is

Billings Farm & Museum. Museum features a working dairy farm where visitors can learn about modern dairying and 19th-century farm operation. Exhibits depict the activities and culture of rural Vermont life. Incl restored 1890 Farm House with farm office, family living quarters, creamery, and ice house. Gift shop at visitor center. Phone 802/457-2355. ¢¢¢

Silver Lake State Park. This 34-acre park offers swimming beach, bathhouse, fishing, boating (rentals); picnicking, concession, tent and trailer camping (dump station), lean-tos. Within walking distance of Barnard Village. (Memorial Day-Labor Day) Standard fees. 10 mi NW via VT 12

to Barnard, on Silver Lake. Phone 802/234-9451 or 802/886-2434.

Suicide Six Ski Area. Area has 2 double chairlifts, J-Bar; patrol, PSIA school, rentals, snowmaking; cafeteria, wine and beer bar, lodge; 19 runs, longest run 1 mi; vertical drop 650 ft. Site of first ski tow in US (1934). (Early Dec-late Mar, daily) 3 mi N on VT 12 (S Pomfret Rd). Phone 802/457-6661. ¢¢¢¢

Vermont Institute of Natural Science. Property includes a 75-acre preserve with trails (daily). Raptor Center, an outdoor museum, has 26 species of hawks, owls, and eagles (summer, daily; winter, Mon-Sat). Gift shop. 1½ mi SW on Church Hill Rd. Phone 802/457-2779. ¢¢

Walking Tours Around Woodstock. There are 1-2-hr tours of Historic District, covering over 1 mi; depart from Chamber of Commerce information booth on the green. (mid-June-mid-Oct, Mon, Wed, and Sat) Phone 802/457-2450 or 802/457-3458. ¢¢

Woodstock Country Club. An 18-hole championship golf course, 10 tennis courts, paddle tennis, cross-country skiing center with over 35 mi of trails; rentals, instruction, tours. Restaurant, lounge. (Daily; closed Apr and Nov) Fee for activities. S on VT 106. Phone 802/457-2112 or 802/457-2114.

Woodstock Historical Society. Dana House (1807) has 11 rms spanning 1750-1900, incl a children's rm; also silver, glass, paintings, costumes, furniture; research library; Woodstock-related artifacts, photographs. Farm and textile equipment. Gift shop. (mid-May-late Oct, daily) 26 Elm St. Phone 802/457-1822.

Motels/Motor Lodges

★ **BRAESIDE MOTEL.** *Hwy 4 E (05091), 1 mi E on US 4. 802/457-1366; fax 802/457-1366; toll-free 800/303-1366. Email braeside@vermontel. com.* 12 rms. S, D $48-$88. Crib free. TV; cable (premium), VCR avail. Pool. Restaurant nearby. Ck-out 11 am. Downhill ski 6 mi; x-country ski 2 mi. Picnic table. Cr cds: A, MC, V. 🐾 ⛵ 🐾 SC

★ **OTTAUQUECHEE MOTEL.** *US 4 PO Box 418 (05091), 4½ mi W. 802/672-3404; fax 802/672-3215. Email otqlodge@vermontel.com.* 15 rms,

Jenney Farm, Woodstock

14 A/C. S, D $46-$96; each addl $5-$10; higher rates: fall foliage, Christmas wk. TV; cable. Complimentary coffee in rms. Restaurant adj 6 am-9 pm. Ck-out 11 am. Downhill ski 10 mi; x-country ski 5 mi. Refrigerators. Cr cds: D, DS, MC, V.

★ **POND RIDGE MOTEL.** *US 4 (05091), 1½ mi W. 802/457-1667; fax 802/457-1667. Email prm4vt@aol.com; www.vtliving.com/pondridgemotel.* 14 rms, 6 kits. S, D $39-$69; each addl $10; kit. units $69-$150; under 6 free; wkly rates; ski plans; higher rates fall foliage season. Crib $10. TV; cable (premium). Complimentary coffee in rms. Ck-out 10 am. Downhill ski 8 mi; x-country ski 3 mi. Lawn games. Picnic tables, grills. On river; swimming. Cr cds: A, C, D, DS, ER, MC, V.

★★ **THE SHIRE MOTEL.** *46 Pleasant St (05091). 802/457-2211; fax 802/457-5836. Email dotcall@aol.com; www.snirrmotel.com.* 33 rms. May-mid-Sep: S, D $68-$125; under 12 free; higher rates fall foliage. Crib $7. TV; cable. Coffee in lobby. Restaurant nearby. Ck-out 11 am. Business servs avail. Downhill ski 4 mi; x-country ski 1 mi. Refrigerators. Cr cds: A, C, DS, ER, MC, V.

Resort

★ ★ ★ **WOODSTOCK INN & RESORT.** *14 The Green (05091). 802/457-1100; fax 802/457-6699; toll-free 800/448-7900. Email email@ woodstockinn.com; www.woodstockinn. com.* 144 rms, 3 story, 7 suites. July-Oct: S, D $169; suites $545; each addl $25; under 14 free; lower rates rest of yr. Crib avail, fee. Valet parking avail. Indoor/outdoor pools, whirlpool. TV; cable (premium), VCR avail. Complimentary newspaper. Restaurant 7 am-9 pm(see WOODSTOCK INN). Bar. Ck-out 11 am, ck-in 3 pm. Business servs avail. Bellhops. Concierge. Dry cleaning. Gift shop. Exercise rm, sauna, steam rm. Golf, 18 holes. Tennis, 8 courts. Downhill skiing. Bike rentals. Supervised children's activities. Hiking trail. Picnic facilities. Video games. Cr cds: A, JCB, MC, V.

B&Bs/Small Inns

★ ★ **APPLEBUTTER INN.** *Happy Valley Rd (05091), 3 mi E on US 4, then S on Happy Valley Rd. 802/457-4158; toll-free 800/486-1734. Email aplbtrn@aol.com; www.bbonline.com.* 5 rms, 2 story. No rm phones. S, D $70-$135; each addl $15. TV in sitting rm; VCR (free movies). Complimentary full bkfst. Ck-out 10:30 am, ck-in 3 pm. Downhill ski 5 mi; x-country ski 3 mi. Restored Federal-style house (1850); period furnishings. Totally nonsmoking. Cr cds: A, DS, MC, V.

★★ **CANTERBURY HOUSE BED AND BREAKFAST.** *43 Pleasant St (05091), on VT 4. 802/457-3077; fax 802/457-4630; toll-free 800/390-3077. Email innkeeper@thecanterburyhouse. com; www.thecanterburyhouse.com.* 8 rms, 3 story. Sep-Oct: S, D $135; lower rates rest of yr. Parking lot. TV; cable, VCR avail. Complimentary full bkfst. Golf, 18 holes. Tennis, 2 courts. Downhill skiing. Beach access. Bike rentals. Hiking trail. Cr cds: A, MC, V.

★★ **CHARLESTON HOUSE.** *21 Pleasant St (05091). 802/457-3843; fax 802/457-2512; res 888/475-3800. Email nohl@together.net; www.pbpub. com/woodstock/charlestonhouse.htm.* 9 rms, 2 story. No rm phones. S, D $110-$175; hol wkend (2-day min). Complimentary full bkfst. Restaurant nearby. Ck-out 11 am, ck-in 3 pm. Downhill ski 3 mi; x-country ski 1 mi. Greek Revival house built 1835; many antiques. Totally nonsmoking. Cr cds: MC, V.

★★ **FOUR PILLARS.** *Happy Valley Rd (05091), 2½ mi E on VT 4. 802/457-2797; fax 802/457-5138; toll-free 800/ 957-2797. Email fpillars@vermontel. com; www.fourpillarsbb.com.* 4 rms, 1 story, 1 suite. Feb, June-Oct, Dec: D $140; suites $300; each addl $20; lower rates rest of yr. Parking lot. TV; cable, CD avail. Complimentary full bkfst, coffee in rms. Restaurant. Meeting rms. Fax servs avail. Golf, 18 holes. Tennis, 2 courts. Downhill skiing. Bike rentals. Hiking trail. Picnic facilities. Cr cds: MC, V.

★★★ **KEDRON VALLEY INN.** *VT 106 (05071), 5 mi S. 802/457-1473; fax 802/457-4469; toll-free 800/836-1193. Email kedroninn@aol.com; www. innformation.com/vt/kedron.* 26 inn rms, 1-3 story. 10 with A/C. No elvtr. No rm phones. S, D $120-$230; each addl $6.50; MAP avail; mid-wk rates; wkend riding plan; higher rates: fall foliage, Dec 25. Closed Apr. Crib free.

Pet accepted. TV. Restaurant (see KEDRON VALLEY). Bar 5-11 pm. Ck-out 11:30 am, ck-in 3:30 pm. Business servs avail. Downhill ski 7 mi; x-country ski 3 mi. Many fireplaces, wood stoves. Some private patios. Natural pond. Cr cds: A, DS, MC, V.

★★ **THE LINCOLN INN AT THE COVERED BRIDGE.** *530 Woodstock Rd (05091). 802/457-3312; fax 802/457-5808. Email lincon2@aol.com; www.lincolninn.com.* 6 rms, 2 story. Sep-Oct: S $145; D $175; lower rates rest of yr. Crib avail, fee. Parking lot. TV; cable, VCR avail, CD avail. Complimentary full bkfst, newspaper, toll-free calls. Restaurant 6-9 pm, closed Mon. Bar. Ck-out 11 am, ck-in 3 pm. Meeting rms. Business center. Concierge. Golf. Tennis. Downhill skiing. Hiking trail. Picnic facilities. Cr cds: DS, MC, V.

★★★ **MAPLE LEAF INN.** *VT 12 (05031), 9 mi N. 802/234-5342; res 800/51-MAPLE. www.mapleleafinn. com.* 7 rms, 3 story. June-Mar: D $190; lower rates rest of yr. Street parking. TV; cable (DSS), VCR avail. Complimentary full bkfst, newspaper, toll-free calls. Restaurant. Ck-out 11 am, ck-in 3 pm. Business servs avail. Concierge. Gift shop. Golf, 18 holes. Tennis, 3 courts. Downhill skiing. Hiking trail. Cr cds: A, C, D, DS, JCB, MC, V.

★★ **PARKER HOUSE INN.** *1792 Quechee Main St (05059), 5 mi E on US 4. 802/295-6077; fax 802/296-6696. Email parker_house_inn@valley.net; www.theparkerhouseinn.com.* 7 rms, 3 story. Sep-Oct: D $150; each addl $15; children $15; lower rates rest of yr. Parking lot. Indoor/outdoor pools, lap pool, children's pool, lifeguard, whirlpool. TV; cable (DSS), VCR avail. Complimentary full bkfst. Restaurant 5-8 pm. Bar. Ck-out 11 am, ck-in 3 pm. Meeting rm. Exercise privileges. Golf. Tennis, 10 courts. Downhill skiing. Beach access. Bike rentals. Hiking trail. Picnic facilities. Cr cds: A, MC, V.

★★★ **QUECHEE INN AT MARSH-LAND FARM.** *1619 Quechee Main St (05059), I-89 Exit 1, then W on US 4*

½ mi to Clubhouse Rd, then 1 mi N. 802/295-3133; fax 802/295-6587; toll-free 800/235-3133. Email info@quechee inn.com. 24 rms, 2 story. No rm phones. Aug-late Oct, hols, MAP: S $160-$210; D $200-$240; each addl $42; mid-wk rates; package plans; lower rates rest of yr. Crib $10. TV; cable. Swimming, sauna privileges. Complimentary full bkfst; afternoon refreshments. Restaurant 8-10 am, 6-9 pm (see QUECHEE INN AT MARSHLAND FARM). Bar 5-11 pm. Ck-out 11 am, ck-in 2 pm. Meeting rms. Business servs avail. Tennis privileges. Golf privileges. Canoes. Fly fishing clinics. Downhill ski 2 mi; x-country ski on site; instructor, rentals. Bicycles. 1793 farmhouse. Cr cds: A, C, D, DS, MC, V.

★ ★ ★ ★ ★ **TWIN FARMS.** *Stage Rd (05031), 9 mi N on VT 12. 802/234-9999; fax 802/234-9990; toll-free 800/894-6327. www.twinfarms.com.* This 1795 country inn, set on 300 acres of gardens, forests, and meadows, offers guests a restful retreat from their busy lives. Activities incl canoeing, swimming, fishing, tennis, skiing, and biking. Guests will enjoy relaxing in the Furo after a workout at the fitness center. Rates are fully inclusive of all meals, wines, beverage, and recreation equipment. 6 rms. May-Mar: S $800; D $900; suites $1050; lower rates rest of yr. Valet parking avail. TV; cable (DSS), VCR avail, CD avail. Complimentary full bkfst, coffee in rms, newspaper, toll-free calls. Restaurant. Bar. Ck-out noon, ck-in 4 pm. Business center. Concierge. Gift shop. Salon/barber avail. Free airport transportation. Exercise rm, steam rm, whirlpool. Golf. Tennis, 2 courts. Downhill skiing. Bike rentals. Hiking trail. Picnic facilities. Cr cds: A, D, DS, MC, V.

★ ★ **WINSLOW HOUSE.** *492 Woodstock Rd (05031), W on US 4. 802/457-1820; fax 802/457-1820.* 4 rms, 2 story. S $65; D $75-$95; each addl $15; under 6 free; hols (2-day min); higher rates fall foliage. Pet accepted. TV; cable (premium). Complimentary full bkfst. Ck-out 11 am, ck-in 2 pm. Downhill ski 8 mi; x-country ski 3 mi. Lawn games.

Refrigerators. Farmhouse built 1872; period furnishings. Totally nonsmoking. Cr cds: C, D, DS, MC, V.

★ ★ ★ **WOODSTOCKER BED AND BREAKFAST.** *61 River St (Rte 4) (05091), US 4. 802/457-3896; fax 802/ 457-3897. Email woodstocker@valley. net; www.scenesofvermont.com/ woodstocker.* 7 rms, 2 story, 2 suites. Sep-Oct, Dec: S, D $135; suites $155; each addl $20; children $10; under 17 free; lower rates rest of yr. Crib avail. Parking lot. TV; cable, VCR avail, CD avail. Complimentary full bkfst, toll-free calls. Restaurant nearby. Ck-out 11 am. Whirlpool. Golf. Tennis. Downhill skiing. Cr cds: A, MC, V.

Restaurants

★ ★ ★ **BARNARD INN.** *VT 12 (05031), approx 8 mi N. 802/234-9961.* Specializes in noisettes of lamb Green Mountain, roast crisp duck. Hrs: 6-11 pm. Closed Sun, Mon (winter), Mon (summer); Thanksgiving, Dec 25. Res accepted. Bar. Wine list. Dinner a la carte entrees: $19-$25. Child's menu. Parking. Original brick structure of house built ca 1796. Cr cds: A, C, D, MC, V.

★ ★ **BENTLEY'S.** *3 Elm St (05091), center of town. 802/457-3232. Email info@bentleysrestaurant.com; www. bentleysrestaurant.com.* Specializes in gourmet hamburgers, steak, pasta. Hrs: 11:30 am-9:30 pm; Fri, Sat to 10 pm; Sun brunch 11 am-3 pm. Closed Thanksgiving, Dec 25. Res accepted. Bar. Lunch $4.95-$8.95; dinner $9.95-$17.95. Sun brunch $10.95. Child's menu. Cr cds: A, D, DS, MC, V.

★ ★ ★ **KEDRON VALLEY.** *VT 106, 5 mi S. 802/457-1473. www. innformation.com/vt/kedron.* Specializes in salmon in puff pastry, grilled loin of lamb, confit of duck. Own sorbet. Hrs: 6-9 pm. Closed Tues, Wed; also Apr. Res accepted. Bar. Dinner a la carte entrees: $16-$24. Child's menu. Parking. Cr cds: D, MC, V.

★ ★ ★ **PRINCE AND THE PAUPER.** *24 Elm St (05091). 802/457-1818.*

www.princeandpauper.com. Specializes in rack of lamb in puff pastry, crisp roast duck. Own baking. Hrs: 6-9 pm. Closed Thanksgiving, Dec 25. Res accepted. Bar. Wine list. Dinner a la carte entrees: $21-$28. Prix fixe: $35. French country atmosphere. Cr cds: D, MC, V.

★★★ **QUECHEE INN AT MARSH-LAND FARM.** *1119 Quechee Main St, I-89 Exit 1, then W on US 4 ½ mi to Clubhouse Rd, then 1 mi N. 802/295-3133. Email info@quecheeinn.com; www.quecheeinn.com.* Specializes in duck, fresh seafood, lamb. Own baking. Hrs: 6-9 pm. Res accepted. Bar. Wine list. Dinner $17-$24. Child's menu. Entertainment: pianist Fri, Sat. Parking. View of garden and lake. 1793 farmhouse. Cr cds: A, C, D, DS, MC, V.

★★★ **SIMON PEARCE.** *Main St (05059), 5 mi E on US 4. 802/295-1470. www.simonpearce.com.* Specializes in duck, seafood, lamb. Own desserts. Hrs: 11:30 am-2:45 pm, 6-9 pm. Closed Thanksgiving, Dec 25. Wine cellar. Lunch a la carte entrees: $8.75-$12.50; dinner a la carte entrees: $17-$25. Parking. Terrace dining. In renovated mill; overlooks river. Glassblowing, pottery shop. Cr cds: A, D, DS, MC, V.
D

★★★ **WOODSTOCK INN.** *14 The Green. 802/457-1100. Email woodstock.resort@connriver.net; www.woodstockinn.com.* Specializes in jumbo lump crabmeat cake, roast rack of lamb. Hrs: 6-9 pm. Res accepted. Bar. Wine cellar. Dinner a la carte entrees: $19-$26. Child's menu. Parking. Jacket (Memorial Day-Labor Day). Cr cds: A, MC, V.
D

Unrated Dining Spot

PANE E SALUTE. *61 Central St (05091). 802/457-4882.* Specializes in tuscan style pizza, roasted meat, classic pasta dishes, and composed salads. Hrs: noon-2:30 pm, 6-9 pm. Closed Wed. Wine, beer. Lunch, dinner $7.50-$18. Entertainment. Chef owned. Modern cafe decor. Cr cds: DS, MC, V.
D

CANADA

Just north of the United States, with which it shares the world's longest undefended border, lies Canada, the world's largest country in terms of land area. Extending from the North Pole to the northern border of the United States and including all the islands from Greenland to Alaska, Canada's area encompasses nearly four million square miles (10.4 million square kilometers). The northern reaches of the country consist mainly of the Yukon and Northwest territories, which make up the vast, sparsely populated Canadian frontier.

Population: 31,006,347
Area: 6,181,778 square miles (9,970,610 square kilometers)
Peak: Mount Logan, Yukon Territory, 19,850 feet (5,951 meters)
Capital: Ottawa
Speed Limit: 50 or 60 MPH (80 or 100 km/h), unless otherwise indicated

Jacques Cartier erected a cross at Gaspé in 1534 and declared the establishment of New France. Samuel de Champlain founded Port Royal in Nova Scotia in 1604. Until 1759 Canada was under French rule. In that year, British General Wolfe defeated French General Montcalm at Québec and British possession followed. In 1867 the British North America Act established the Confederation of Canada, with four provinces: New Brunswick, Nova Scotia, Ontario, and Québec. The other provinces joined later. Canada was proclaimed a self-governing Dominion within the British Empire in 1931. The passage in 1981 of the Constitution Act severed Canada's final legislative link with Great Britain, which had until that time reserved the right to amend the Canadian Constitution.

Today, Canada is a sovereign nation—neither a colony nor a possession of Great Britain. Since Canada is a member of the Commonwealth of Nations, Queen Elizabeth II, through her representative, the Governor-General, is the nominal head of state. However, the Queen's functions are mostly ceremonial with no political power or authority. Instead, the nation's chief executive is the prime minister; the legislative branch consists of the Senate and the House of Commons.

Visitor Information

Currency. The American dollar is accepted throughout Canada, but it is advisable to exchange your money into Canadian currency upon arrival. Banks and currency exchange firms typically give the best rate of exchange, but hotels and stores will also convert it for you with purchases. The Canadian monetary system is based on dollars and cents, and rates in *Mobil Travel Guide* are given in Canadian currency. Generally, the credit cards you use at home are also honored in Canada.

Goods and Services Tax (GST). Most goods and services in Canada are subject to a 7% tax. Visitors to Canada may claim a rebate of the GST paid on *short-term accommodations* (hotel, motel, or similar lodging) and on *most consumer goods* purchased to take home. Rebates may be claimed for cash at participating Canadian Duty Free shops or by mail. For further information and a brochure detailing rebate procedures and restrictions contact Visitors' Rebate Program, Revenue Canada, Summerside Tax Center, Summerside, PE C1N 6C6; phone 613/991-3346 or 800/66-VISIT (in Canada).

Driving in Canada. Your American driver's license is valid in Canada; no special permit is required. In Canada the liter is the unit of measure for gasoline. One US gallon equals 3.78 liters. Traffic signs are clearly understood and in many cities are bilingual. All road speed limits and mileage signs have been posted in kilometers. A flashing green traffic light gives vehicles turning left the right-of-way, like a green left-turn arrow. The use of safety belts is generally mandatory in all provinces; consult the various provincial tourism bureaus for specific information.

Holidays. Canada observes the following holidays, and these are indicated in text: New Year's Day, Good Friday, Easter Monday, Victoria Day (usually 3rd Mon May), Canada Day (July 1), Labour Day, Thanksgiving (2nd Mon Oct), Remembrance Day (November 11), Christmas, and Boxing Day (December 26). See individual provinces for information on provincial holidays.

Liquor. The sale of liquor, wine, beer, and cider varies from province to province. Restaurants must be licensed to serve liquor, and in some cases liquor may not be sold unless it accompanies a meal. Generally there are no package sales on holidays. Minimum legal drinking age also varies by province. **Note:** It is illegal to take children into bars or cocktail lounges.

Daylight Saving Time. Canada observes Daylight Saving Time beginning the first Sunday in April through the last Sunday in October, except for most of the province of Saskatchewan, where Standard Time is observed year-round.

Tourist information is available from individual provincial and territorial tourism offices (see Border Crossing Regulations in MAKING THE MOST OF YOUR TRIP).

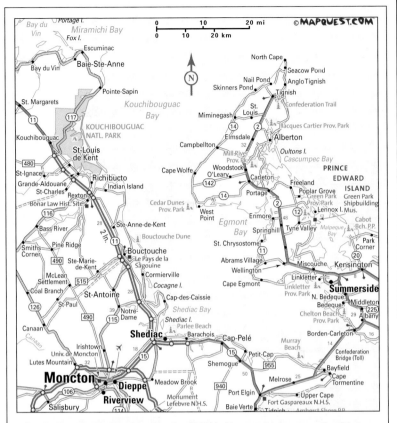

The Northumberland Shore celebrates Old World ways with homespun hand-knit sweaters and rocking chairs on the front porches. Lobster and clam bakes and warm waters and sands especially appeal to visitors. This route goes from Moncton to the world's lobster capital in Shediac and on to the Tantramar Marshes, which are protected from the sea by old Acadian dykes. From Moncton, take 106 south to Sackville. You'll be impressed to see how Sackville's area was reclaimed from the sea by an elaborate system of dikes built by the Acadians. Drop in on Sackville Harness, the only shop in North America still producing handcrafted horse collars and harnesses. Other highlights are the Sackville Waterfowl Park and Owens Art Gallery of Mount Allison University, which has one of Canada's finest collections of Canadian and European art. Five miles east of Sackville on Highway 2, visit Fort Beausejour National Historic Site. Erected in 1751, Fort Beausejour was one of the few forts in Canada to see heavy fighting. Continue on to Aulac, then follow Route 16 to scenic Cape Tormentine. Follow Routes 955, 950, and 133 to Shediac, the world's lobster capital, for great beaches and the warmest water north of Virginia. Enjoy nearby Parlee Beach Provincial Park, then take 134 to Bouchtouche, another Acadian fishing village with wild and beautiful beaches and warm sands. From here, head to Richibucto, where you can learn some local history at the Richibucto River Museum, before continuing on to the grand finale—Kouchibouguac National Park on Kouchibouguac Bay. Some 216 species of birds and 25 species of mammals have been sighted in this national park. Boardwalks lead to a 15-mile sweep of offshore sandbars, tidewater lagoons, grassy salt marshes, peat bogs, and dunes. Inland is a mixed forest of black spruce, white pine, jack pine, yellow birch, and trembling aspen. Enjoy camping, canoeing, hiking, and good swimming in the warm water of the Northumberland Strait. **(Approx 260 mi; 420 km)**

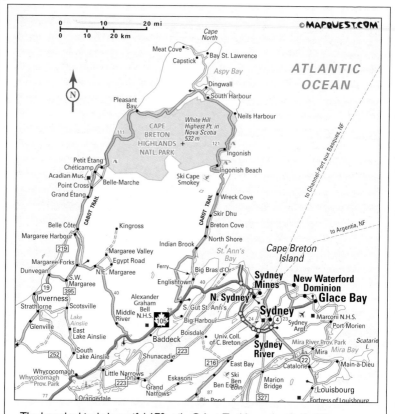

The breathtakingly beautiful 179-mile Cabot Trail hugs the Gulf of St. Lawrence and winds through highlands, over rugged headlands and beside waterfalls, through Acadian villages and the pastoral Margaree Valley. There are many campgrounds, beaches, and lookouts; over 200 species of birds makes this a great place for bird-watching. Cape Breton Island is great music country—whole villages turn out weekly for traditional Cape Breton Island fiddling. From Sydney, take Route 125 to Bras d'Or. Follow the Cabot Trail from South Gut-St. Ann's (home of the Nova Scotia Gaelic College of Arts and Culture) to Igonish to Cape Breton Highlands National Park. Scenic drama is created by the 900-foot-high headlands rising abruptly from the sea, the summit of Cape Smokey, and Beulach Ban Falls. There are spectacular hiking trails throughout. Continue on to Chéticamp, a fishing community with lots of traditional music and festivals, for some of the most spectacular scenery on the trail. Head on to Margaree to fish in the Margaree River, one of the best salmon streams in Canada. At Northeast Margaree, you can visit the Museum of Cape Breton Heritage. Continue on to Baddeck where you can visit the Alexander Graham Bell National Historic Park. The Scottish-born inventor of the telephone did much of his research here on a site overlooking Baddeck Bay. A museum celebrates the genius whose interests extended to aviation, marine engineering, and medical science. Take 105 back to Bras d'Or and Sydney. **(Approx 150 mi; 240 km)**

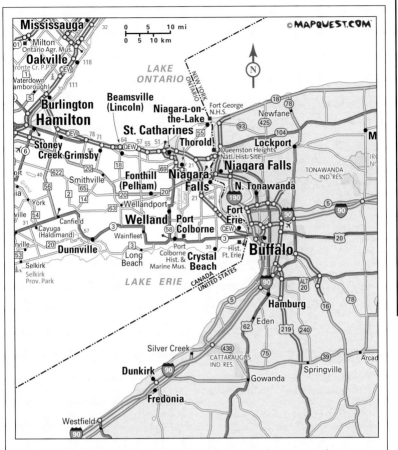

The flashiness of the Canadian side of Niagara Falls is a stark contrast to the more nature-oriented American side; you have to see both. From St. Catherines, located in the heart of the Niagara fruit-growing and wine-making region, take 406 to Welland and the Welland Canal, which links Lake Ontario with Lake Erie 13 miles west of Niagara Falls. The Canal has eight locks, with a total lift of over 300 feet—something to see! The first lock was built here in 1824-29, the present one between 1913-32. Continue on to Port Colborne, the site of Lock 8, said to be the largest single lock in the world. Visit the Historical and Marine Museum before heading over to Crystal Beach for a swim in Lake Erie. Continue on 3 east to Fort Erie, which is linked to the United States by the Peace Bridge. Here you can visit the Fort Erie National Historic Park and the Fort Erie Historical Railroad Museum. Continue on to Niagara Falls, where you surely won't want to miss a Maid of the Mist boat tour through thunder and spray to the base of the falls. Also be sure to visit the top of 500-foot-high Skylon Tower for a panorama of the falls area. Continue on 405 to Niagara-on-the-Lake, which was Upper Canada's first capital between 1791-96. It's a dream of what an early 19th-century town should be. Local attractions include the Niagara Apothecary Museum, Prince of Wales Hotel, preserved 19th-century residences, and the Shaw Festival (early April to mid-October), which features plays by George Bernard Shaw and his contemporaries. **(Approx 55 mi; 87 km)**

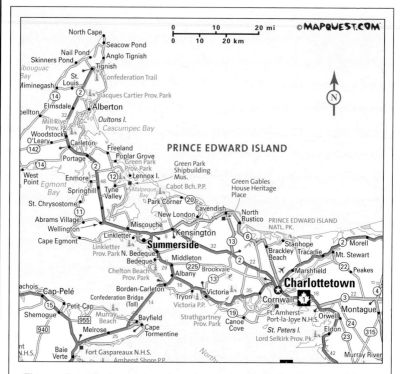

This tour from Charlottetown explores the country of warm beaches, great shifting dune lands, and craggy cliffs immortalized in Lucy Maud Montgomery's best-selling 1908 novel *Anne of Green Gables*. From Charlottetown, take Route 2 to Dunstaffnage, then pick up Route 6 to Dalvay Beach in Prince Edward Island National Park, which preserves some of North America's finest white sand beaches. At Brackley Beach, where the dunes are 60 feet high, you might be lucky enough to spy a red fox, mink, or muskrat. Between Rustico Harbour and Orby Head are six miles of red sandstone cliffs over 90 feet high. Stop at Cavendish to see the Prince Edward Island Marine Aquarium, the Enchanted Lands theme park, and the Royal Atlantic Wax Museum. Here also are the sites of Lucy Maud Montgomery's Cavendish home and her final resting place in the Cavendish Cemetery. In the Cavendish Beach section of the Cavendish Park, you can visit the Green Gables farmhouse (now a museum) featured in the novel. Continue on Route 6 to Stanley Bridge to visit the Prince Edward Island Marine Aquarium and then on to New London to see the green-trimmed white cottage that was Lucy Maud Montgomery's birthplace. It now displays memorabilia of the author. From New London, follow Route 20 for three miles to Route 234 to Burlington to see the remarkable Woodleigh Replicas. These are large-scale stone and concrete models of British castles, churches, and other well-known British landmarks including Shakespeare's Birthplace at Stratford-on-Avon, the Tower of London (containing copies of the British Crown jewels!), and Dunvegan Castle. Some replicas are even large enough to enter. To complete the tour, follow Route 20 to Malpeque, where you can see oyster farming in Malpeque Bay and enjoy a swim at Cabot Provincial Park. **(Approx 63 mi; 102 km)**

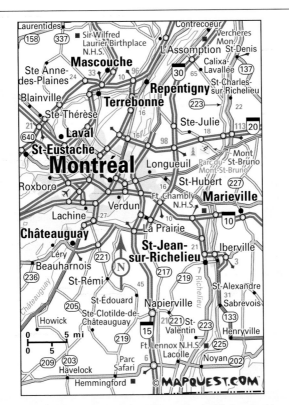

This drive through the fertile Richelieu River valley highlights the historic period when Québec was invaded by Americans—not tourists, but troops—in 1775. From Montréal, take Autoroute 20 east to exit for the pretty village of Beloeil, known for remarkable stone residences and relic-filled churches. Just over the Richelieu River is Mont-St.-Hilaire in the heart of apple orchard country. The highest of the Monteregian hills and a UNESCO Biosphere Reserve, Mont-St.-Hilaire is great for hiking. Continuing south on 223 through the "Valley of the Forts," you'll come to the castlelike Fort Chambly National Historic Park. The original wooden fort was built in 1665 against Iroquois attack. This stone fort replaced it in 1709-11 and was occupied by British troops from 1760-75 and by Americans until 1776. Its 32-foot-high curtain walls jut up from the Richelieu River rapids. Visitors enjoy cycling along the 12-mile long Chambly Canal Bike Path and exploring the old Canal locks. Continue on 223 south to the military town of St.-Jean-Sur-Richelieu, where you can hop a cruise on the Richelieu River and enjoy the hot-air balloon festival that colors the skies for eight days in mid-August. Continue on 223 south to St.-Paul-de-l'île-aux-Noix where you can tour the Fort Lenox National Historic Site on idyllic l'île aux-Noix. This Vaubon style, star-shaped fort is one of the most authentic 19th-century British fortifications in North America. Close by is the Lacolle River Blockhaus, built in 1781. **(Approx 60 mi; 96 km)**

PROVINCE OF NEW BRUNSWICK

New Brunswick, discovered by Jacques Cartier in 1535, was one of the first areas in North America to be settled by Europeans. Established as a province in 1784, it became one of the original provinces of the Canadian Confederation (1867).

New Brunswick's rich historic past is reflected in major restorations such as the Acadian Historical Village near Caraquet, Kings Landing Historical Settlement near Fredericton, and MacDonald Historic Farm near Miramichi. The Acadian influence is found throughout the province, predominantly along the north and east coasts. Caraquet and Moncton are the major centers of Acadian culture.

Pop 714,800 **Land area** 28,354 sq mi (73,437 sq km) **Capital** Fredericton **Web** www.gov.nb.ca/tourism

Information Tourism New Brunswick, PO Box 12345, Woodstock E7M 5C3; 800/561-0123

But there is much more to New Brunswick than history—the Bay of Fundy to the south (featuring some of the highest tides in the world and a great variety of whales), the Reversing Falls in St. John, Magnetic Hill in Moncton, Hopewell Cape Rocks at Hopewell Cape—and always the sea. Some of the finest beaches in Atlantic Canada provide excellent recreational possibilities, exquisite seafood, and the warmest waters north of Virginia. The capital, Fredericton, offers a full range of big-city attractions. The weather is ideal for vacations, June through August being the warmest months. During September and October the fall foliage is a spectacular sight, while the winter months attract many outdoor enthusiasts to ski over 600 miles (1,000 km) of cross-country trails and snowmobile the 5,400 miles (9,000 km) of groomed trails. Angling enthusiasts will be drawn to the world-famous Atlantic salmon river, Miramichi.

Visitor Information Centres are located throughout the province. It is important to note that reservations are not accepted at national parks and only at some provincial parks.

Safety belts are mandatory for all persons anywhere in vehicle. Children under 5 years or under 40 pounds in weight must be in an approved safety seat anywhere in vehicle.

Edmundston (B-1)

*See also Caribou, Fort Kent, and
Presque Isle, ME*

Pop 11,497 **Elev** 462 ft (141 m)
Area code 506
Information Chamber of Commerce,
74 Canada Rd, PO Box 338, E3V 3K9;
506/737-1866

The Madawaska County's origin
revolves around a border dispute
between England and the United
States. From 1785-1845 the areas
around Edmundston, part of the state
of Maine and part of the province of
Quebec, were left without allegiance
to any government. A large portion
was ceded to the United States in
1842 but the Canadian section
remained unattached, prompting residents to issue the "proclamation of
the Republic of Madawaska." Though
eventually becoming a part of New
Brunswick and despite never having
been a reality, the mythical title has
remained, with the coat of arms registered in 1949.

Acadian culture predominates with
almost all of the population speaking
French—but nearly all are bilingual.
The first families to arrive in
Edmundston were Acadian and
French Canadian.

What to See and Do

Edmundston Golf Club. Challenging
18-hole course within the city
attracts people from a large area.
(May-Sep, daily) Victoria St. Phone
506/735-3086. ¢¢¢

Grand Falls. At 75 ft (23 m) high,
one of largest cataracts east of Niagara. Fascinating gorge and scenic
lookouts along trail; museum. Stairs
to bottom of gorge (fee). (Late May-
Oct, daily) 40 mi (64 km) SE, in town
of Grand Falls. Phone 506/473-6013
(May-Oct) or 506/473-3080. ¢

**Les Jardins de la République Provin-
cial Park.** (Gardens of the Republic)
Park of 107 acres (43 hectares) overlooking the Madawaska River.
Amphitheater, scene of music and
film performances; 20-acre (8-
hectare) botanical garden. Heated
swimming pool, boat dock, launch;
tennis, volleyball, softball, horseshoes, bicycling, playground,
indoor game rm, snack bar, 113
campsites (most with electricity;
fee). Park (June-Sep). Various fees. 5
mi (8 km) N via Trans-Canada Hwy
2. Phone 506/735-2525. ¢¢ In the
park is

Antique Auto Museum. Impressive
display of vintage vehicles and
mechanical marvels of the past 70
yrs. (Mid-June-Labour Day, daily)
Phone 506/735-2525. ¢

New Brunswick Botanical Garden.
Conceived and designed by a team
from the prestigious Montreal
Botanical Garden, the garden covers
over 17 acres. More than 30,000
annual flowers and 80,000 plants
are on display. (June-mid-Oct, daily)
Exit 8, 4½ mi (7 km) N on Trans-
Canada Hwy. Phone 506/739-6335.
¢¢

New Denmark Memorial Museum.
Oldest Danish colony in Canada
(1872). Museum bldg is on site of
original immigrant house built in
1872 to house settlers. Household
articles, documents, machinery
belonging to original settlers from
Denmark. (Mid-June-Labour Day,
daily; rest of yr, by appt) 45 mi (72
km) SE in farming community of
New Denmark. Phone 506/553-6724
or 506/553-6764. **FREE**

St. Basile Chapel Museum. Parish
church; replica of first chapel built in
1786. (July-Aug, daily) 321 Main St,
3 mi (5 km) E in St. Basile. Phone
506/263-5971. **FREE**

Annual Events

International Snowmobilers Festival.
Phone 506/737-1866. First wk Feb.

Jazz Festival. Phone 506/739-2104.
Third wkend June.

Foire Brayonne. French heritage festival. Phone 506/739-6608. Late July-
early Aug.

Fredericton (D-3)

Founded 1762 **Pop** 45,000 (est)
Elev 24 ft (7 m) **Area code** 506
Web www.city.fredericton.nb.ca
Information Fredericton Tourism, PO Box 130, E3B 4Y7; 506/460-2041

Over the past 40 years the benefactions of the late Lord Beaverbrook have raised Fredericton from a quiet provincial capital to a major cultural center. Born in Ontario, this British newspaper baron maintained a strong loyalty to New Brunswick, the province of his youth. Wander the elm tree-lined streets through the Green, a lovely park along the St. John River, and admire examples of Beaverbrook's generosity that heighten the city's beauty. Nestled along the tree-shaded Green sits Christ Church Cathedral, an 1853 example of decorated Gothic architecture.

Hopewell Rocks, Fundy Coast

What to See and Do

Beaverbrook Art Gallery. Collection incl 18th-20th-century British paintings, 18th- and early 19th-century English porcelains, historical and contemporary Canadian and New Brunswick paintings, and Salvador Dali's *Santiago el Grande;* Hosmer-Pillow-Vaughan Collection of European fine and decorative arts from the 14th-20th centuries. (Tues-Sun; closed Jan 1, Dec 25) 703 Queen St. Phone 506/458-8545. ¢¢

The Beaverbrook Playhouse. Home of professional company Theatre New Brunswick. Contact PO Box 566, E3B 5A6. 686 Queen St. Phone 506/458-8345.

City Hall. (1876) Seat of municipal government. Guided tours of council chambers; town history depicted in tapestry form. Changing of the Guard (July-Labour Day, Tues-Sat). Tourist Information Centre (May-Sep, daily; rest of yr, Mon-Fri). Queen & York Sts. Phone 506/460-2129. **FREE**

Golf.

Fredericton. Eighteen holes, very picturesque. Golf Club Rd, off Woodstock Rd. Phone 506/458-0003. ¢¢¢¢

Mactaquac. Eighteen-hole championship course. In Mactaquac Provincial Park. Phone 506/363-3011. ¢¢¢¢

Kings Landing Historical Settlement. Settlement of 50 bldg, costumed staff of 100; recalls Loyalist lifestyle of a century ago. Carpenter's shop, general store, school, church, blacksmith shop, working sawmill and gristmill, inn; replica of a 19th-century wood boat (river craft). All restoration and work is done with tools of the period. Settlement (June-early Oct, daily). Tours; children's programs. Restaurants, snack bar. 23 mi (37 km) W on Trans-Canada Hwy at exit 259. Phone 506/363-4999. ¢¢

Mactaquac Fish Hatchery. Has 67 rearing ponds with a potential annual production of 340,000 smolts (young salmon ready to migrate). Visitor center (mid-May-mid-Oct). (Daily) 10 mi (16 km) W on Rte 2/Trans-Canada Hwy. Phone 506/363-3021. **FREE**

Mactaquac Generating Station. Hydroelectric dam has powerhouse with turbines and generators; fish collection facilities at foot of dam. Free guided tours (mid-May-Aug, daily; rest of yr, by appt). 12 mi (19 km) W on Rte 2/Trans-Canada Hwy, exit 274. Phone 506/363-3093.

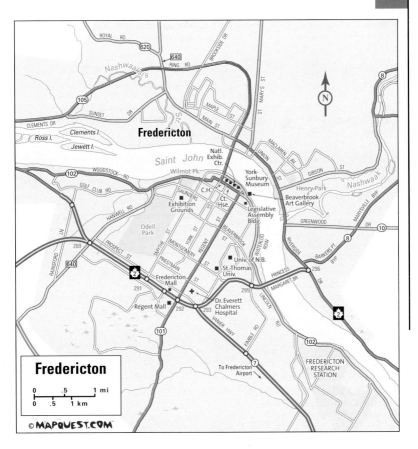

Fredericton

0   .5   1 mi
0   .5   1 km

© MAPQUEST.COM

Mactaquac Provincial Park. Approx 1,400 acres (567 hectares) of farmland and forest overlooking head-pond of Mactaquac Dam. Boating (launch, marinas), swimming beaches, fishing; hiking, camping (hookups, dump station), golf, picnicking, playgrounds, restaurant, store, laundry. Also in the vicinity are an historic village, fish culture station, and a generating plant. Some fees. On Rte 105, 15 mi (24 km) W. Phone 506/460-2041. Per vehicle (summer only) ¢¢

New Brunswick Legislative Assembly. Seat of provincial government; public galleries. Guided tour. Library (Mon-Fri) incl hand-colored engravings of Audubon *Birds of America*. (Mid-June-Labour Day, daily; rest of yr, Mon-Fri) Queen & St. John Sts. Phone 506/453-2527. **FREE**

Odell Park. Unique example of the primeval forest of New Brunswick;

part of original land grant. Approx 400 acres (160 hectares) incl lodge, picnicking, play area, walking paths through woods; deer and other animals; ski trails; arboretum with 1¾ mi (2.8 km) trail. End of Rookwood Ave. Phone 506/460-2230. **FREE**

Officers' Square. Park with Lord Beaverbrook statue; changing of the guard ceremonies (July-Labour Day); band concerts Tues and Thurs eves (late June-Aug), theater in the park (July-Aug). Queen St. On grounds are

Old Officers' Quarters. Typical architecture of Royal Engineers in the Colonial period; stone arches, iron handrails, and stone staircase. Older part (1839-40), near the river, has thicker walls of solid masonry and hand-hewn timbers; later addition (1851) has thinner walls and sawn timbers. ¢ Contains

York-Sunbury Historical Society Museum. Permanent and changing exhibits of military and domestic area history; seasonal exhibitions of history, New Brunswick crafts and fine arts; mounted 42-lb (16-kg) Coleman frog. (July-Aug, daily; May-June and Sep-mid-Oct, Mon-Sat; rest of yr, Mon, Wed, and Fri or by appt) Phone 506/455-6041. ¢¢

University of New Brunswick. (1785) 8,000 students. One of the oldest universities in North America. Tours (by appt). University Ave. Phone 506/453-4793.

Wilmot Park. Wading pool; lighted tennis, ball diamond, picnicking, playground, bowling green. Woodstock Rd. **FREE** Opp is

    Old Government House. (1828) Former residence of Colonial governors; more recently headquarters of Royal Canadian Mounted Police. Not open to public. Woodstock Rd.

Annual Events

Canada Day Celebration. Last wk June-early July. Phone 506/455-3866.

Atlantic Crew Classic Rowing Regatta. Early July. Phone 506/453-9428.

NB Highland Games. Last wkend July. Phone 888/368-8819.

New Brunswick Summer Chamber Music Festival. Phone 506/453-4697. Late Aug.

Fredericton Exhibition. First wk Sep. Phone 506/458-8819.

Writer's Blocks. There is a charge for this fascinating tour, albeit a small one ($5 adults), which is part of the "Learning Quest" program and is given four days a week during the summer. Fredericton has been known as the "Poet's Corner of Canada," and this walk features stops at many of the homes of these literary lions. It includes biographic notes in a performance piece that features work by many famous poets, with recitations and dramatic readings. Walking tour participants try their hand at poems inspired by local masters.

Harvest Jazz and Blues Festival. Mid-Sep. Phone 888/622-5837.

Motels/Motor Lodges

★★ **FREDERICTON INN.** *1315 Regent St (E3C 1A1). 506/455-1430; fax 506/458-5448; toll-free 800/561-8777.* 199 rms, 1-3 story. July-Sep: S $65-$105; D $75-$105; each addl $10; suites $105; kit. unit $115; lower rates rest of yr. Crib $6. Pet accepted. TV; cable, VCR avail. Heated pool; wading pool, whirlpool, poolside serv. Restaurant 6:30 am-11 pm. Bar 4 pm-1 am. Ck-out 11 am. Meeting rms. Business servs avail. In-rm modem link. Bellhops. Sundries. Some in-rm whirlpools. Refrigerators avail. Balconies. Cr cds: A, D, DS, MC, V.

★ **HOWARD JOHNSON.** *480 Riverside Dr (E3B 5E3), N side of Princess Margaret Bridge, ⅛ mi E on Trans-Can 2. 506/472-0480; fax 506/472-0170; toll-free 800/596-4656. www.m2000. mb.ca/howardjohnson/.* 116 rms, 2 story. S $65-$76; D $74-$79; each addl $8; suites $136; under 18 free. Crib free. Pet accepted, some restrictions. TV; cable (premium), VCR avail. Heated pool; whirlpool, poolside serv. Restaurant 7 am-10 pm. Bar 4 pm-1 am. Ck-out noon. Coin lndry. Meeting rms. Business servs avail. In-rm modem link. Valet serv. Airport transportation. Indoor tennis. Downhill ski 10 mi; x-country ski 5 mi. Exercise equipt; sauna. Rec rm. Lawn games. Balconies. Cr cds: A, D, MC, V.

★★ **WANDLYN INN.** *958 Prospect St (E3B 2T8), 1 blk N of Trans-Can 2, Smyth St Exit. 506/462-4444; fax 506/452-7658. Email doreenchase@ wandlyninn.com.* 100 rms, 3 story. S, D $70-$99; studio rms $75-$100; each addl $10; suites $125-$199; under 18 free. Crib free. Pet accepted. TV; cable (premium), VCR avail. 2 pools, 1 indoor; whirlpool, poolside serv. Sauna. Restaurant 7 am-2 pm, 5-9:30 pm. Bar 11-1 am. Ck-out 11 am. Coin lndry. Meeting rms. Business servs avail. Valet serv. Sundries. Refrigerators avail. Cr cds: A, MC, V.

Self-Guided Walking Tour of Downtown Fredericton. Covers 26 attractions within a five-block range. Takes visitors through one of the city's most historic and attractive areas and includes such attractions as City Hall, the Military Compound, the York-Sunbury Historical Museum, the Beaverbrook Art Gallery, Christ Church Cathedral, the provincial Legislative Assembly, Waterloo Row, and the Old Burial Ground.

Hotels

★★★ LORD BEAVERBROOK HOTEL. *659 Queen St (E3B 5E3). 506/455-3371; fax 506/455-1441; res 800/561-7666. Email lhhotel@nbnet. nd.ca; www.lordbeaverbrookhotel.com.* 156 rms, 7 story, 12 suites. May-Oct: S $139; D $149; each addl $10; under 18 free; lower rates rest of yr. Crib avail. Pet accepted, some restrictions. Parking lot. Indoor pool, children's pool, whirlpool. TV; cable, VCR avail. Complimentary coffee in rms, newspaper, toll-free calls. Restaurant 6:30 am-11 pm. Bar. Ck-out 11 am, ck-in 3 pm. Meeting rms. Business center. Dry cleaning. Gift shop. Salon/barber avail. Sauna. Golf. Downhill skiing. Hiking trail. Cr cds: A, D, DS, ER, MC, V.

★★★ SHERATON FREDERICTON. *225 Woodstock Rd (E3B 2H8). 506/457-7000; fax 506/457-4000; toll-free 800/325-3535.* 208 rms, 5 story, 15 suites. May-Oct: S, D $209; suites $239; lower rates rest of yr. Crib avail. Pet accepted. Valet parking avail. Indoor/outdoor pools, children's pool, lifeguard, whirlpool. TV; cable. Complimentary coffee in rms, newspaper, toll-free calls. Restaurant 6 am-11 pm. Bar. Ck-out noon, ck-in 3 pm. Meeting rms. Business center. Bellhops. Dry cleaning. Gift shop. Salon/barber avail. Exercise privileges, sauna. Golf. Downhill skiing. Supervised children's activities. Hiking trail. Video games. Cr cds: A, D, ER, JCB, MC, V.

Fundy National Park

See also Moncton, St. John

Web www.parkscanada.pch.gc.ca/parks/ new-brunswick/fundy/fundye.htm

Information Superintendent, Fundy National Park, PO Box 40, Alma E0A 1B0; 506/887-6000

On the coast between St. John and Moncton (see both), the park's 80 sq mi (207 sq ki) of forested hills and valleys are crisscrossed by mi of hiking trails. Cliffs front much of the rugged coastline. Fish are found in its lakes and streams and the woods are filled with wildlife. The beaches at Herring Cove, Point Wolfe, and Alma are exceptional for viewing the tides. Since the ocean water is frigid, swimming is enjoyed in the heated saltwater pool or one of the lakes; golf, tennis, lawn bowling, picnicking, camping (May-October), cross-country skiing. Programs in amphitheater. Some fees. Guided beach walks (June-August). The park and headquarters are open all yr; visitor area (mid-May-October). Accommodations available in park.

Moncton (D-4)

Pop 55,700 (est) **Elev** 50 ft (15 m)
Area code 506
Web www.greater.moncton.nb.ca

Information Tourism Moncton, 655 Main St, E1C 1E8; 506/853-3590 or 800/363-4558

This commercial and cultural center of the Atlantic provinces is located on the Petitcodiac River, which at low tide becomes a mud flat clus-

Bennet Lake, Fundy National Park

tered with seagulls. As the tide turns, a tidal bore (a small wave) runs upstream to herald the incoming waters. Just off the Trans-Canada Highway another phenomenon awaits the traveler—Magnetic Hill. The experience of sitting in your car, without power, seemingly rolling up the hill, is one remembered by many. There is nothing magnetic about the hill; it is just an optical illusion created by the contours of the countryside. Nearby are the Magnetic Hill Zoo with North American and exotic wildlife and Magic Mountain, a water theme park.

Existing as an Acadian center where English and French cultures have flourished for centuries, Moncton is an excellent beginning for a tour to the northeast along the coast to beautiful Kouchibouquac National Park. Visit the Acadian Museum at the University of Moncton, the Free Meeting House (1821), oldest building in Moncton, which has served nearly every faith, its pioneer cemetery with stones dating to 1816, and the adjacent Moncton Museum.

Nearby Shediac, lobster capital of the world, has a lobster festival in July. From here, northward along the coast of the Northumberland Strait, saltwater fishing and camping provide the visitor with a chance to relax and enjoy the French heritage of the area.

Stretching along the coast are little fishing villages where French-speaking people offer their hospitality. Each year for a few days in early August the village of Cocagne has a bazaar and international regatta—a curious mixture of Acadian and North American cultures. Hydroplane races attract thousands for two days; visitors remain to enjoy the Acadian festival with its special food, handcrafts, dancing, and singing.

What to See and Do

Crystal Palace Amusement Park. Indoor and outdoor attractions incl rides, miniature golf, Science Center, video games, and go-carts. (Daily) 499 Paul St, E in Dieppe. Phone 506/859-4386.

Fort Beausejour National Historic Site. Approx 600 acres (225 hectares). Built by the French between 1751-55 during their long struggle with England for possession of Acadia. Attacked in 1755, the fort was captured by the British under Colonel Monckton, who renamed it Fort Cumberland. Following its capture, the fort was strengthened and its defenses extended. During the American Revolution in 1776 it withstood an attack by revolutionaries under Jonathan Eddy. It was manned by a small garrison during the War of 1812. Three casemates and a massive stone curtain wall have been restored; displays on history and culture of Isthmus of Chignecto; outdoor paintings showing garrison as it existed in 18th century. Picnicking (shelters). Visitor center. Panoramic view of site and surrounding salt marshes. (June-mid-Oct, daily) Contact Chief, Visitor Activities, Aulac E0A 3C0. Approx 37 mi (60 km) E on Hwy 2, Exit 550. Phone 506/536-0720.

Magnetic Hill Zoo. Wild animal park and petting zoo; many species represented, incl wildfowl. (May-Oct, daily) Near Magnetic Hill. Phone 506/384-0303. ¢¢

"The Rocks" Provincial Park. Unique cliffs, caves, and flowerpot-shaped pillars of conglomerate rock interspersed with shale and sandstone layers. Tourist information center has interpretive displays; tour guides avail. Visitors are advised to watch for caution signs, avoid loose cliff sections, not climb any flowerpot or cliff, and return from beach by the time posted at the stairs to avoid problems with rising tide. Picnicking, restaurant. (May-Oct, daily) Contact Parks Branch, Dept of Natural Resources, PO Box 6000, Fredericton E3B 5H. Across Petitcodiac River, then 28 mi (45 km) SE on Hwy 114, "Rocks" Exit, just S of Hopewell Cape. Phone 506/856-2940 or 800/561-0123 (US and CAN). ¢¢

Tidal bore. A small tidal wave running upstream to usher in the Bay of Fundy tides on the normally placid Petitcodiac River. Within one hr water level rises more than 25 ft. The bore arrives twice daily. Main St at Bore View Park.

Motels/Motor Lodges

★★ **COLONIAL INN.** *42 Highfield St (E1C 8T6), ½ blk off Hwy 6. 506/ 382-3395; fax 506/858-8991; toll-free 800/561-4667.* 61 rms, 1-2 story. S $62; D $68; each addl $5; studio rms $75; under 16 free. Crib $5. Pet accepted, some restrictions. TV; cable. Heated pool; whirlpool. Restaurant open 24 hrs. Bar 11 am-midnight. Ck-out noon-2 pm. Meeting rm. Business servs avail. Valet serv. Sundries. Sauna. Some refrigerators. Cr cds: A, D, ER, MC, V.
⬛ ⬛ ⬛ ⬛ SC

★ **ECONO LODGE.** *1905 W Main St (E1E 1H9), Rte 6. 506/382-2587; fax 506/858-5998; res 800/553-2666.*

Email info@econolodgemoncton.com. 67 rms, 5 kit. units, 2 story. S $59; D $79; each addl $5; studio rms $79; kit. units $89; each addl $5; under 12 free; wkly rates. Pet accepted, some restrictions. TV; cable. Heated pool. Restaurant 7 am-9 pm; Sun to 2 pm. Bar. Ck-out 11 am. Business servs avail. Cr cds: A, C, D, DS, ER, MC, V.
⬛ ⬛ ⬛ ⬛ ⬛ ⬛ ⬛ ⬛

★★ **RODD PARK HOUSE INN.** *434 Main St (E1C 1B9), adj Tidal Bore Park. 506/382-1664; fax 506/855-9494; res 800/565-7633. www.rodd-hotels.ca.* 97 rms, 4 story. S $79; D $99; each addl $10; under 19 free. Crib free. Pet accepted, some restrictions. TV; cable (premium). Heated pool. Complimentary coffee in rms. Restaurant 7 am-2 pm, 5-10 pm. Bar. Ck-out noon. Meeting rms. Business servs avail. Valet serv. Cr cds: A, MC, V.
⬛ ⬛ ⬛

Hotel

★★★ **BEAUSEJOUR.** *750 Main St (E1C 1E6). 506/854-4344; fax 506/858-0957; res 800/268-1133. www.delta hotels.com.* 310 rms, 9 story. S, D $109-$151; each addl $15; suites $240-$950; under 18 free; wkend rates. Crib free. Pet accepted. TV; cable (premium). Pool; poolside serv, lifeguard. Coffee in rms. Restaurants 6:30 am-11 pm. Rm serv 24 hrs. Bar 4:30 pm-1 am, wkends from 6 pm, closed Sun. Ck-out noon. Meeting rms. Business servs avail. In-rm modem link. Concierge serv. Gift shop. Barber. Exercise equipt. Minibars; many bathrm phones; some refrigerators. Cr cds: A, D, DS, ER, MC, V.
⬛ ⬛ ⬛ ⬛ ⬛ ⬛ ⬛ ⬛ ⬛ ⬛

B&B/Small Inn

★ **BONACCORD HOUSE B&B.** *250 Bonaccord St (E1C 5M6), at John St. 506/388-1535; fax 506/853-7191.* 3 rms, 3 story, 1 suite. June-Aug: S $45; D $55; suites $55; each addl $10; lower rates rest of yr. Crib avail. Parking lot. TV; cable, VCR avail, CD avail. Complimentary full bkfst, newspaper. Restaurant nearby. Ck-out 10 am, ck-in 2 pm. Dry cleaning. Golf. Downhill skiing. Cr cds: V.
⬛ ⬛ ⬛ ⬛ ⬛ ⬛

St. Andrews (E-2)

See also Calais, ME

Pop 1,760 **Elev** 23 ft (7 m)
Area code 506
Web www.townsearch.com/canada/
nb/standrews
Information Chamber of Commerce
Tourist Information Centre, 46 Reed
Ave, PO Box 89, EOG 2X0; 506/529-
3556

Explored by Champlain and later
settled in 1783 by Loyalists from
New England, this popular seaside
resort is a beautiful village rich in
history. On a peninsula projecting
into Passamaquoddy Bay, fishing,
swimming, sailing, and rockhounding are favorite pastimes. Feast on
fresh lobster, watch the tides swirl
in, visit the specialty shops, or wander down the streets past many
buildings erected before 1800. The
white-framed Greenock Church,
begun in 1822, and the Court
House (1840) and Gaol (1832) are
worth special visits.

From the shore the Fundy Isles dot
the bay, the most famous of which is
Campobello. Here, Franklin Delano
Roosevelt spent his summers from
1905-21 when he was stricken with
infantile paralysis. Tours of Roosevelt's cottage in the International
Park are available.

Northeast toward St. John, the
road to Blacks Harbour affords views
of lighthouses, lovely beaches, and
covered bridges. From this village, a
ferry leaves for Grand Manan Island,
largest of the three islands. This is a
popular vacation destination with
picturesque lighthouses and tiny
fishing villages nestled in the barren
seaside cliffs.

What to See and Do

Algonquin Golf Courses. Opened in
1894, 18-hole championship course
with wooded glades and breathtaking shoreline views (fee). Executive
9-hole woodland course (fee). (Late
Apr-late Oct) Algonquin Hotel, Reed
Ave. Phone 506/529-3062 (summer).

Blockhouse Historic Site. Sole sur-
vivor of coastal defenses built during
War of 1812; restored 1967. (Mid-
May-mid-Oct, daily) In Centennial
Park, Joe's Point Rd. Phone 506/529-
4270. **FREE**

**The Henry Phipps & Sarah Juliette
Ross Memorial Museum.** Private
antique furniture and decorative art
collection of the Rosses. (July-Aug,
daily; May-June and Sep-early Oct,
Tues-Sat) 188 Montague St. Phone
506/529-1824. **FREE**

**Huntsman Marine Science
Center/Aquarium-Museum.** Displays
of coastal and marine environments
with many fish and invertebrates
found in waters of Passamaquoddy
Region; "Touch Tank" allows visitors
to handle marine life found on local
rocky beaches. Displays of live animals include local amphibians, reptiles, and a family of harbor seals.
Exhibits on local geology; seaweed
collection. (May-early Oct, daily)
Brandy Cove Rd. Phone 506/529-
1202. ¢¢

Motels/Motor Lodges

★ **BLUE MOON MOTEL.** *310
Mowat Dr. 506/529-3245; fax
506/529-3245; res 506/529-3245; toll-
free 877/534-5271.* 39 rms, 1 story.
July-Aug: S $55; D $75; each addl
$8; lower rates rest of yr. Crib avail.
Pet accepted, some restrictions. TV;
cable. Restaurant. Ck-out 11 am, ck-
in 1 pm. Business servs avail. Golf,
10 holes. Tennis, 2 courts. Supervised
children's activities. Picnic facilities.
Cr cds: A, D, DS, ER, MC, V.

★ **PICKET FENCE.** *102 Reed Ave
(E0G 2X0). 506/529-8985; fax
506/529-8985.* 17 rms, 1 story. June-
Sep: S, D $55-$75; lower rates rest of
the year. Crib avail. TV; cable (premium). Restaurant nearby. Ck-out
11 am. Golf. Tennis. Beach access. Cr
cds: JCB, MC, V.

★ **SEASIDE BEACH RESORT.** *339
Water St (E5B 2R2). 506/529-3846; fax
506/529-4479; toll-free 800/506-8677.
Email davidsu@mbnet.nb.ca; cside.nb.
ca.* 24 kit. units, 19 with shower
only, 1-2 story, 4 cottages. No A/C.
No rm phones. June-Labour Day: S,
D $65-$75; each addl $5; wkly rates;
lower rates May, early Sep-Oct.
Closed rest of yr. Crib $5. Pet
accepted. TV; cable. Restaurant
nearby. Ck-out 11 am. Coin lndry.

Microwaves avail. Balconies. Picnic tables, grills. Overlooks bay. Cr cds: A, MC, V.

⊡ ❧ ✦ ⊬ 🛪 🛪 ⊠ 🔥

★ **ST. STEPHEN INN.** *99 King St (E3L 2C6), N via Hwy 127, W via Hwy 1 (King St). 800/466-1814; fax 506/466-6148; toll-free 800/565-3088. Email ran99@nb.ca.* 52 rms, 2 story. July-Dec: S $65; D $80; each addl $8; under 17 free; lower rates rest of yr. Crib free. Pet accepted. TV; cable, VCR avail. Restaurant 7 am-10 pm. Meeting rms. Business servs avail. Cr cds: A, MC, V.

❧ 🔥

★★★ **TARA MANOR INN.** *559 Mowat Dr (E5B 2P2), Hwy 127. 506/529-3304; fax 506/529-4755; res 506/529-3304. Email taramanr@nbnet. nb.ca.* 26 rms, 1-3 story, 15 suites. June-late Sep: S, D $98-$148; each addl $10; under 13 free; lower rates May, mid-Sep-mid-Oct. Closed rest of yr. Crib free. TV; cable. Heated pool; whirlpool. Playground. Complimentary coffee in library. Dining rm 7:30-10 am, 6-9 pm. Ck-out 11:30 am. Tennis. Golf privileges. Sauna. Refrigerator in suites. Balconies. Former country estate (1871) of Sir Charles Tupper; antiques. Situated on 16 acres of woods, lawns, and gardens. Cr cds: A, MC, V.

🛪 ⊬ ⊠ 🔥

Hotel

★★★★ **KINGSBRAE ARMS.** *219 King St (E5B 1Y1). 506/529-1897; fax 506/529-1197. Email kingbrae@nbnet. nb.ca; www.kingsbrae.com.* Constructed in 1897, this country-home property is adjacent to the breathtaking Kingsbrae Horticultural Garden and affords views of Passamaquoddy Bay. The inn, located in an oceanside town where Maine and Canada meet, has three suites and five guestrooms with oversized cast iron or whirlpool tubs, feather and down comforters, and period furnishings. Family-style dinners are creative and highlight local produce and seafood. 8 rms, 3 story, 3 suites. Mid-Mar-mid-Oct: S, D $225; suites $250-$350; package plans; wkends 2-day min; lower rates rest of yr. Children over 9 yrs only. Pet accepted, some

restrictions. TV; cable, VCR avail (movies). Heated pool. Complimentary full bkfst; afternoon refreshments. Rm serv 24 hrs. Bar. Ck-out noon, ck-in 3 pm. Business center. In-rm modem link. Bellhops. Valet serv. Concierge serv. Airport transportation. Tennis privileges. Health club privileges. Lawn games. Fireplaces; some in-rm whirlpools. Some balconies. Totally nonsmoking. Cr cds: A, DS, MC, V.

🛪 ⊠ 🔥

Resorts

★★★ **THE ALGONQUIN.** *184 Adolphus St (E5B 1T7). 506/529-8823; fax 506/529-7162; res 800/441-1414. www.salesealg.cphotels.ca.* 250 rms, 54 A/C, 4 story, 42 kit. units. Mid-May-mid-Oct: S, D $119-$219; each addl $20; suites $189-$369; under 18 free. Crib free. Pet accepted. TV; cable, VCR avail. Heated pool; whirlpool, lifeguard. Playground. Supervised children's activities (mid-June-Aug); ages 12 and under. Coffee in rms. Restaurant 7 am-10 pm. Bar; entertainment. Ck-out noon, ck-in 4 pm. Coin lndry. Business servs avail. Bellhops. Valet serv. Concierge serv. Gift shop. Free parking. Tennis. 18-hole golf, greens fee $25-$39, pro, putting green. Bicycle rentals. Exercise rm; sauna. Lawn games. Aerobics. Some in-rm whirlpools, microwaves, fireplaces. On hill; view of water from most rms. Cr cds: A, DS, MC, V.

🛪 ⊠ 🔥

★★★ **PANSY PATCH.** *59 Carleton St (E5B 1M8). 506/529-3834; fax 506/529-9042; toll-free 888/726-7972. Email pansypatch@nb.aibn.com; www.pansypatch.com.* 9 rms, 5 with shower only, 2-3 story, 2 suites. No A/C. May-mid-Oct: S, D $120-$205; each addl $15; suite $170. Closed rest of yr. Cable TV avail and in common rm. Complimentary full bkfst; afternoon refreshments. Restaurant 11 am-3:30 pm, 5-9 pm. Ck-out 11 am, ck-in 3 pm. Business servs avail. In-rm modem link. Bellhops. Gift shop. Tennis privileges. Exercise equipt. Health club privileges. Lawn games. Refrigerator, microwave, fireplace in suite. Some balconies. Built in 1912. Norman cottage architecture; extensive gardens. Totally non-smoking. Cr cds: A, MC, V.

Restaurant

★★ **ST. ANDREWS LIGHTHOUSE.**
1 Patrick St (E0G 2X0), by lighthouse.
506/529-3082. Email jurabob@nbnet.
nb.ca. Specializes in fresh seafood, steak, chicken. Hrs: 11:30 am-2 pm, 5-9 pm. Closed mid-Oct-mid-May. Res accepted. Lunch $3-$19.50; dinner $9.95-$26.50. Child's menu. Lighthouse (1833) on Passamaquoddy Bay. Cr cds: A, D, DS, MC, V.

D

St. John

Founded 1785 **Pop** 78,000 (est)
Elev 100 ft (31 m) **Area code** 506
Web www.city.saint-john.nb.ca
Information Visitor & Convention Bureau, City Hall, 11th floor, PO Box 1971, E2L 4L1; 506/658-2990 or 888/364-4444

The largest city in the province, this deep-sea port was founded by the United Empire Loyalists after the American Revolution. It is Canada's first incorporated city. The heart of the old town is King's Square, where many historic landmarks (including an ancient burial ground) are found.

The Reversing Falls, another of the phenomena caused by the 30-foot (9-meter) tides on the Bay of Fundy, are found near the eastern approach to the city center off Highway 1. Here, the high tidewater is forced back upstream into the St. John River, causing a whirling torrent. A deck, where the tourist bureau is located, overlooks the rapids.

What to See and Do

Barbour's General Store. Restored general store reflecting period 1840-1940; 2,000 artifacts and wide selection of old-fashioned grocery items, china, yard goods, farm implements, cooking tools; re-created post office;

barbershop with wicker barber's chair, collection of shaving mugs; pharmacy with approx 300 samples of "cure-all or kill-alls"; potbellied stove; staff outfitted in period costumes. (Mid-May-mid-Oct, daily) In Market Slip area, downtown. Phone 506/658-2939.

Carlton Martello Tower National Historic Park. Circular coastal forts built for War of 1812; used in WWII as fire command post for harbor defenses (when 2-story superstructure was added); restored powder magazine of 1840s; barrack rm (ca 1865). Panoramic view of city, harbor, and surrounding landscape. Guided tours of tower (June-mid-Oct, daily). Grounds open all yr. Hwy 1, Exit 107. Phone 506/636-4011. ¢¢

Ferry Service to Digby, NS. Car and passenger; 45 mi (72 km). (All yr) Res required. Contact Bay Ferries Ltd, Box 3427, Station B, E2M 4X9. Phone 506/636-4048 or 888/249-7245 (US).

Irving Nature Park. Features winding coastal road and hiking trails. Harbor seals, porpoises, and many species of migrating birds can be viewed offshore. Picnicking. (Daily) Off of Sand Cove Rd on W side of city. Phone 506/653-7367. **FREE**

Loyalist House. (1810-17) Built by David Daniel Merritt, a United Empire Loyalist from New York. Six generations have lived in the house; gracious Georgian mansion remains much as it was when built; excellent craftsmanship. (July-Aug, daily; June and Sep, Mon-Fri; also by appt) 120 Union St. Phone 506/652-3590. ¢¢

New Brunswick Museum. Intl fine art and decorative art objects; human and natural history of New Brunswick. Exhibits incl skeleton of Right Whale and mastodon and geologic "trail through time." Also family discovery center. (Daily; closed Good Fri, Dec 25) The museum's archives and library (Mon-Fri, limited hrs; closed Good Fri, Dec 25) are at 277 Douglas Ave. 1 Market Sq. Phone 506/643-2300 or 506/643-2322 (library). ¢¢¢

Old City Market. Centralized market dating back to 1876 sells fresh meats and vegetables as well as indigenous baskets and handicrafts. Roof is wooden timbers, all wood pegs; fashioned like the hull of an old sailing ship. Magnificent iron gates of market designed in 1880 by local blacksmiths. Bell rung at opening, closing, and noon. (Mon-Sat; closed hols) 47 Charlotte St. Phone 506/658-2820. **FREE**

Rockwood Park. Municipal park with 2,200 acres of woodlands, lakes, and recreational areas, incl golf course, aquatic driving range, and campground. (Daily) Located off Mt Pleasant Ave in city center. Phone 506/658-2883 or 506/652-4050 (campground).

"Trinity Royal" Heritage Preservation Area. A 20-blk heritage area located in the city center; 19th-century residential and commercial architecture; handicrafts and specialty goods.

Annual Events

Loyalist Days' Heritage Celebration. Celebrates the arrival of the United Empire Loyalists in 1783 with reenactment of Loyalist landing; citizens in period costumes; parades, entertainment, sporting events. Phone 506/634-8123. Five days early July.

Festival by the Sea. Ten-day performing arts festival features Canadian entertainers. Phone 506/632-0086. Mid-Aug.

Motels/Motor Lodges

★★ **COLONIAL INN.** *175 City Rd (E2L 3T5). 506/652-3000; fax 506/658-1664; toll-free 800/561-4667. Email colostj@sunday.net.* 94 rms, 82 A/C, 2 story. S $65; D $71; each addl $6; suites $85; under 18 free. Crib free. Pet accepted. TV; cable. Heated pool; whirlpool. Sauna. Restaurant open 24 hrs. Bar 6 pm-2 am. Ck-out noon-2 pm. Meeting rms. Business servs avail. Valet serv. Cr cds: MC, V.

★★ **HOTEL COURTENAY BAY.** *350 Haymarket Sq (E2L 3P1). 506/657-3610; fax 506/633-1773; toll-free 800/563-2489. www.cityhotels.ca.* 125 rms, 5 story. S $59-$69; D $69-$79; each addl $8; under 18 free. Pet accepted. TV; cable (premium). Heated pool. Restaurant 7 am-11 pm. Bar 11 am-11 pm. Ck-out 1 pm. Coin lndry. Meeting rms. Business servs avail. Bellhops. Valet serv. Sundries. Minibars. Some private patios, balconies. Cr cds: A, D, MC, V.

The Legislative Buildings, Fredericton

Hotels

★★ **DELTA BRUNSWICK.** *39 King St (E2L 4W3), above Brunswick Sq shopping mall. 506/648-1981; fax 506/658-0914; res 800/268-1133. Email ksealy@deltahotels.com.* 255 units, 5 story. May-mid-Oct: S, D $125-$135; each addl $10; suites $135-$500; studio rms $135-$145; under 18 free; lower rates rest of yr. Crib free. Pet accepted. Covered parking $8.50; valet $12. TV; cable. Indoor pool; whirlpool. Free supervised children's activities (wkends), over age 2. Restaurant 6:30 am-10 pm (June-Sep). Rm serv 24 hrs. Bar 11-1 am. Ck-out 1 pm. Convention facilities. Business servs avail. Shopping arcade. Exercise equipt; sauna, steam rm. Game rm. Rec rm. Minibars; refrigerators avail. Covered walkway to downtown offices, Market Sq. Cr cds: A, DS, MC, V.

★★★ **HILTON ST. JOHN.** *1 Market Sq (E2L 4Z6). 506/693-8484; fax 506/657-6610; res 800/445-8667; toll-free 800/561-8282.* 197 rms, 12 story. May-Sep: S, D $109-$149; each addl $15; suites $305-$439; lower rates rest of yr. Crib free. Pet accepted, some restrictions. Garage parking $11.44. TV; cable. Indoor pool; whirlpool. Complimentary coffee in rms. Restaurant 6:30 am-11 pm. Bar 11:30-1 am; entertainment. Ck-out noon. Meeting rms. Business center. Concierge serv. Shopping arcade. Barber, beauty shop. X-country ski 2 mi. Exercise equipt; sauna. Health club privileges. Game rm. Rec rm. Refrigerators, minibars. Harbor view. Underground access to Market Sq shopping mall. Cr cds: A, C, D, DS, MC, V.

★ **HOWARD JOHNSON HOTEL.** *400 Main St (E2K 4N5). 506/642-2622; fax 506/658-1529; res 800/446-4656; toll-free 800/475-4656. Email hojos@nb.sympatico.ca; www.hojos.com.* 95 rms, 7 story, 1 suite. June-Oct: S $115; D $125; suites $145; each addl $10; under 18 free; lower rates rest of yr. Pet accepted, some restrictions. Parking garage. Indoor pool, whirlpool. TV; cable (premium), VCR avail. Complimentary coffee in rms, newspaper, toll-free calls. Restaurant 7 am-11 pm. Bar. Ck-out 1 pm, ck-in 1 pm. Business center. Dry cleaning, coin lndry. Exercise equipt. Golf. Tennis, 20 courts. Downhill skiing. Supervised children's activities. Cr cds: A, D, DS, ER, MC, V.

PROVINCE OF NOVA SCOTIA

After a century of struggle between the British and French for control of North America, Nova Scotia became a British possession in 1710, with the seat of government in Halifax. In 1867 it joined with New Brunswick, Ontario, and Québec to form the Confederation of Canada.

Nova Scotia was settled by French, English, Irish, German, Scottish, and African peoples whose languages and traditions add to its flavor. Today a recreational wonderland awaits the tourist with fishing, boating, camping, golf, swimming, and charter cruising—since no part of Nova Scotia is more than 35 miles (56 kilometers) from the sea.

Pop 874,100 **Land area** 20,402 sq mi (52,841 sq km) **Capital** Halifax

Information Tourism Nova Scotia, PO Box 130, Halifax B3J 2M7; 902/424-4248 or 800/565-0000

Major attractions include the Cabot Trail, often described as "the most spectacular drive in North America," the highlands of Cape Breton, the reconstructed Fortress of Louisbourg National Historic Site, and Lunenburg, a World Heritage Site renowned for its Colonial architecture and Fisheries Museum. The Greater Halifax area offers a variety of attractions including parks, noteworthy public gardens, art galleries, universities, theater, outdoor recreation, pubs, fine seafood dining, the world's second-largest harbor, and the Citadel Fortress—Canada's most visited historic site. Nearby is the rugged beauty of Peggy's Cove.

The weather is cool in the spring and late fall; warm in the summer and early fall. East Nova Scotia enjoys relatively mild winters due to the proximity of the Gulf Stream. Nova Scotia observes Atlantic Standard Time.

Safety belts are mandatory for all persons anywhere in vehicle. Children under 40 pounds in weight must be in an approved safety seat anywhere in vehicle. Compliance of passengers under age 16 is the responsibility of the driver. For further information phone 902/424-4256.

Antigonish (E-7)

See also Baddeck

Pop 5,205 **Elev** 15 ft (5 m)
Area code 902
Information Provincial Tourist Bureau, 56 W Street, PO Box 1301, B2G 2L6; 902/863-4921

This harbor town, named for a Micmac word meaning "the place where branches were broken off the trees by bears gathering beechnuts," was settled by Highland Scottish immigrants and American Revolutionary soldiers and their families. West of the Canso Causeway, Antigonish, intersected by rivers, is surrounded by hills from which may be seen the shores of Cape Breton.

What to See and Do

Keppoch Mountain Ski Area. T-bar, Pomalift, triple chairlift; patrol, school, rentals, snowmaking; beginner, intermediate and expert slopes. Ten trails; longest run 5,000 ft (1,524 m), vertical drop 500 ft (152 m). Night skiing. (Dec-Apr, daily; closed Dec 25) Half-day rates. 7 mi (11 km) W. Phone 902/863-3744. ¢¢¢¢

Sherbrooke Village. Restored 1860s village reflects the area's former status as a prosperous river port. Historic bldgs of that era are being restored and refurnished, incl family homes, a general store, drugstore, courthouse, jail, and post office; demonstrations of blacksmith forging, water-powered sawmill operation; horse-drawn wagon rides. Visitors can watch and try spinning, weaving, and quilting. Restaurant. (June-mid-Oct, daily) 40 mi S via Hwy 7, Exit 32. Phone 902/522-2400. ¢¢

St. Ninian's Cathedral. (1874) Built in Roman Basilica style of blue limestone and granite from local quarries. Interior decorated by Ozias LeDuc, Paris-trained Québec artist. Gaelic words *Tigh Dhe* (House of God) appear inside and out, representing the large Scottish population in the diocese who are served by the cathedral. St. Ninian's St. Phone 902/863-2338.

Annual Event

Highland Games. Scottish festival; pipe bands, Highland dancing, traditional athletic events, concert, massed pipe band tattoo. Mid-July.

Motels/Motor Lodges

★★ **GREEN WAY CLAYMORE INN AND CONFERENCE CENTER.** *Church St. (B2G 2M5), S off 104 Exit 33. 902/863-1050; res 888/863-1050. www.grassroots.ns.ca/welcome.html.* 76 rms, 3 story. July-mid-Oct: S $77-$85; D $99-$119; each addl $10; under 18 free; lower rates rest of yr. Crib free. Pet accepted. TV; cable. Indoor pool; whirlpool. Restaurant 7 am-2 pm; also 5:30-8 pm July-mid-Oct. Bar. Ck-out noon. Exercise equipt; sauna. Downhill/x-country ski 7 mi. Some minibars. Cr cds: A, D, ER, MC, V.

⬛⬛⬛⬛⬛⬛ **SC**

★★ **MARITIME INN ANTIGONISH.** *158 Main St (B2G 2B7). 902/863-4001; fax 902/863-2672; toll-free 888/662-7484. Email larry.mclean@ maritimeinns.com.* 34 rms, 2 story. Mid-June-mid-Oct: S, D $75-$85; each addl $10; suites $89-$125; under 18 free; lower rates rest of yr. Crib free. Pet accepted. TV; cable. Restaurant 7 am-9 pm. Bar 4 pm-midnight. Ck-out 11 am. Sundries. Tennis privileges. Downhill ski 7 mi. Cr cds: A, MC, V.

⬛⬛⬛⬛⬛

Hotel

★★ **HEATHER HOTEL AND CONVENTION CENTRE.** *Foord St (B0K 1S0), off Trans-Can Hwy 104 Exit 24. 902/752-8401; fax 902/755-4580; toll-free 800/565-4500. Email heatherh@ns. sympatico.ca.* 77 rms, 2 story. May-Oct: S $80; D $90; each addl $10; lower rates rest of yr. Crib avail. Pet accepted. Parking lot. TV; cable, VCR avail. Complimentary coffee in rms, newspaper, toll-free calls. Restaurant. Bar. Meeting rms. Business servs avail. Dry cleaning. Exercise privileges. Golf. Cr cds: A, D, ER, JCB, MC, V.

D ⬛⬛⬛⬛⬛ **SC**

Restaurant

★★ **LOBSTER TREAT.** *241 Post Rd (B2G 2K6). 902/863-5465.* Specializes in fresh local seafood, steak. Hrs: 11 am-10 pm. Closed Jan-Mar. Res accepted. Bar. Lunch $5.50-$10; dinner $7.95-$25. Child's menu. Former schoolhouse. Cr cds: A, ER, MC, V.

Baddeck (D-8)

Pop 972 **Elev** 100 ft (30 m)
Area code 902
Web www.cbisland.com
Information Tourism Cape Breton, PO Box 1448, Sydney B1P 6R7; 902/563-4636 or 800/565-9464

This tranquil scenic village, situated midway between Canso Causeway and Sydney, is a good headquarters community for viewing the many sights on the Cabot Trail and around the Bras d'Or lakes. Fishing, swimming, hiking, and picnicking are among favorite pastimes along the beautiful shoreline.

What to See and Do

Alexander Graham Bell National Historic Park. Three exhibition halls dealing with Bell's numerous fields of experimentation, including displays on his work with the hearing impaired, the telephone, medicine, marine engineering, and aerodynamics. Expanded hrs, guide service June-Sep. (Daily) Chebucto St, E side of town. Phone 902/295-2069. ¢¢

Cape Breton Highlands National Park. (see) 57 mi N on Cabot Trail.

The Gaelic College. Dedicated to preservation of Gaelic traditions; special summer and winter programs. 13 mi (22 km) E, at exit 11 off Trans-Canada Hwy 105 in St. Ann's. Phone 902/295-3411. On campus are

Craft Centre. Items of Scottish and Nova Scotian origins. Examples of handwoven blankets, ties, shopping bags, kilts, skirts.

The Great Hall of the Clans. Colorful historic display of the Scot—origin, clans, tartans, and migrations. Genealogical and audiovisual section; life and times of Highland pioneers, relics of Cape Breton giant Angus MacAskill. ¢¢

Motels/Motor Lodges

★★★ **AUBERGE GISELE'S INN.** *387 Shore Rd (B0E 1B0), Hwy 305. 902/295-2849; fax 902/245-2033; toll-free 800/304-0466. www.giseles.com.* 70 rms, 3 story, 5 suites. July-Oct: S $125; D $150; suites $200; each addl $15; under 10 free; lower rates rest of yr. Crib avail. Parking lot. TV; cable (premium). Complimentary coffee in rms, newspaper, toll-free calls. Restaurant 7 am-10 pm, closed Sun. Rm serv 24-hr. Bar. Ck-out 10 am, ck-in 4 pm. Meeting rm. Business center. Coin lndry. Gift shop. Sauna, whirlpool. Golf. Tennis, 2 courts. Bike rentals. Cr cds: A, DS, ER, MC, V.

Fortress of Louisbourg, Cape Breton Island

★★ **SILVER DART LODGE.** *Shore Rd (B0E 1B0), ½ mi W on Shore Rd (Rte 205). 902/295-2340; fax 902/295-2484; toll-free 888/662-7484.* 88 rms, 20 A/C, 62 air-cooled, 2 story, 24 kits. Mid-June-mid-Oct: S $55-$85; D $59-$95; each addl $8; under 16 free;

suites $180-$225; cottages, kit. units $85-$95; under 18 free; lower rates May-early June, late Oct. Closed rest or yr. TV. Pool. Dining rm 7-9:30 am, 5:30-9 pm. Bar; entertainment. Ck-out 11 am. Meeting rm. Gift shop. Tennis. Golf privileges. Lawn games. Balconies. Private beach, dock; boat tours. Cr cds: A, ER, MC, V.

★★ TELEGRAPH HOUSE.
Chebucto St (B0E 1B0). 902/295-1100; fax 902/295-1136. 42 rms, 2-3 story. No elvtr. July-Oct: S $57-$80; D $74-$95; each addl $8; under 6 free; lower rates rest of yr. Crib free. TV; cable. Restaurant 7:30 am-8:45 pm. Bar 11-2 am; entertainment. Ck-out 11 am. Meeting rms. Tennis privileges. Golf privileges, greens fee $5. Miniature golf. Some private patios, balconies. Grills. Family-operated since 1860. Cr cds: A, DS, MC, V.

Resort

★★★ INVERARY RESORT. *¼ mi W on Hwy 205. 902/295-3500; fax 902/295-3527; res 800/565-5660. Email inverary@capebretonresorts.com.* 124 rms in motel, inn, 14 cottages, 4 kits. June-mid-Oct: S, D $89-$175; each addl $10; kit. units $175; lower rates rest of yr. Crib $10. TV; cable. Indoor pool; whirlpool. Playground. 2 dining rms 7 am-3 pm, 5:30-8:30 pm; entertainment. Serv bar. Ck-out 10:30 am, ck-in 3 pm. Grocery, coin lndry, package store 2 blks. Convention facilities. Airport transportation. Tennis. Exercise equipt. Private beach. Canoes, paddleboats. Boat tours. Hiking tours. Lawn games. Sauna. Gift shop. Fireplace in some rooms. Balconies. Cr cds: A, DS, MC, V.

Cape Breton Highlands National Park

See also Baddeck

Information Cape Breton Highlands National Park, Ingonish Beach B0C 1L0; 902/224-2306

Cabot Trail, Cape Breton Highlands

In the northern part of Cape Breton Island, this park is bounded on the W by the Gulf of St. Lawrence and on the E by the Atlantic Ocean. The famous Cabot Trail, a modern 184-mi (294-kil) paved highway loop beginning at Baddeck, runs through the park, incl the scenic 66 mi (106 kil) between Ingonish and Cheticamp offering visitors spectacular vistas.

Along the western shore steep hills, to a height of over 1,116 ft (335 meters), rise sharply from the gulf, affording magnificent views of the gulf and the broad plateau covering most of the park interior. The eastern shore is also rocky, indented with numerous coves at the mouths of picturesque valleys. The interior, least seen by visitors, is an area similar to subarctic regions.

Except for the interior, the 370-sq-mi (950-sq-kil) park is covered with a typical Acadian forest of mixed conifers and hardwoods. The interior is covered with heath bogs, and along the seacoast headlands the trees are stunted and twisted into grotesque shapes.

The park is home to many types of wildlife. Moose are numerous and often seen along the hwys. Other animals native to the region range from black bear and whitetail deer to smaller species such as lynx, red fox, and snowshoe hare. Among the approx 200 species of birds to be seen are the red-tailed hawk and bald eagle.

The park is open all yr, but many facilities operate only from mid-May-late October. Information centers are maintained at Ingonish and Cheticamp, the main park entrances along the Cabot Trail. Plan to stop at these facilities, as the staff on duty can provide the latest information on what to see and do within the park. Roadside picnic areas are provided and a variety of self-guiding trails and interpretive events held during summer encourage visitors to learn more about the park's significant areas and features. All visitors must have a park entry permit, which allows access to Cabot Trail, sightseeing facilities, beaches, and trails. Permit ¢¢¢

One of the best ways to see the park is on foot. The hiking trail system is large and diverse, providing access to the area's remote interior as well as allowing you to explore its rugged coastline. After a hike visitors can enjoy a refreshing saltwater swim or just relax on one of the several developed natural sand beaches located within the park.

Golf is another popular sport in the park. The Highlands Golf Links in Ingonish is one of the best 18-hole courses in Canada.

Deep-sea fishing is popular, with local fishermen providing transportation and equipt. For those interested in freshwater fishing, a national park permit can be obtained at park information centers; the season generally runs from mid-April through September. There are fully-equipped campgrounds on the Cabot Trail as well as primitive campsites on the coast.

Resort

★★★ **KELTIC LODGE.** *Middle Head Peninsula (B0C 1L0), on Cabot Tr (Hwy 312).* 902/285-2880; fax 902/285-2859; toll-free 800/565-0444. 100 units, 32 in lodge, 2 story, 2-, 4-bedrm cottages. MAP: S $194-$209; D $263-$278; each addl $75; cottages $418-$556; golf plans. Closed Jan-May, Nov-Dec. TV; cable. Heated pool; lifeguard. Dining rm 7-9:30 am, noon-2 pm, 6-9 pm. Bar. Ck-out 11 am, ck-in 3 pm. Package store 1 mi. Grocery, coin lndry 5 mi. Convention facilities. Business servs avail.

Gift shop. Tennis privileges. Golf privileges, pro, greens fee $55, putting green. Exercise equipt. Lawn games. Some fireplaces. National park adj. Cr cds: A, D, DS, ER, MC, V.

Dartmouth (F-5)

See also Halifax

Founded 1750 **Pop** 62,277 **Elev** 75 ft (23 m) **Area code** 902
Web www.ttg.sba.dal.ca/nstour/halifax
Information Halifax Regional Municipality Tourism Department, PO Box 1749, Halifax B3J 3A5; 902/490-5946

On the eastern side of Halifax Harbour, Dartmouth is Canada's "newest" city (incorporated in 1961) whose history extends back to the 18th century. The opening of the Angus L. MacDonald Bridge in 1955, a direct link to Halifax, and the Murray A. MacKay Bridge helped to make this an industrial city—with the largest naval bases in Canada, oil refineries, and the Bedford Institute of Oceanography. The 22 lakes within its borders make Dartmouth a swimmer's paradise.

What to See and Do

Black Cultural Centre. History and culture of African Americans in Nova Scotia. Library, exhibit rms, auditorium. (Daily) 1149 Main St, Rte 7 at Cherrybrook Rd. Phone 902/434-6223 or 800/465-0767. ¢¢

Quaker Whaler's House. Restored 1785 house. (July-Aug, daily) 59 Ochterloney St. Phone 902/464-2253. **Donation**

Shearwater Aviation Museum. Extensive collection of aircraft and exhibits on the history of Canadian Maritime Military Aviation. Art gallery; photo collection. (Apr-June and Sep-Nov, Tues, Wed, Fri; July-Aug Tues-Fri, Sat, Sun afternoons; rest of yr by appt) 13 Bonaventure Ave, at Shearwater Airport. Phone 902/460-1083. **Donation**

Swimming. Supervised beach, 12 mi (19 km) E on Marine Dr, Rte 207. Many others within city.

Annual Event

Dartmouth Natal Day. Lake Banook. Parade, sports events, rowing and paddling regattas, entertainment, fireworks. First Mon Aug.

Motels/Motor Lodges

★★ **BURNSIDE.** *739 Windmill Rd (Hwy 7) (B3B 1C1), Exit Bedford at Mackay Bridge. 902/468-7117; fax 902/468-1770; res 800/830-4656. Email smt@ns.sympatico.ca.* 92 rms, 3 story. S $59; D, suites $79-$99; each addl $8; under 16 free. TV; cable (premium), VCR avail. Pool. Restaurant 7 am-2:30 pm, 5-8:30 pm. Bar 10-2 am. Ck-out noon. Meeting rms. Business center. Valet serv. Some minibars; microwaves avail. Cr cds: A, D, DS, ER, MC, V.

⌇ ⌇ 🐾 **SC** 🚶

★ **SEASONS MOTOR INN.** *40 Lakecrest Dr (B2X 1V1). 902/435-0060; toll-free 800/792-2497.* 42 rms, 2 story. June-mid-Oct: S, D $51; each addl $3; under 16 free; wkly rates; lower rates rest of yr. Pet accepted. TV; cable, VCR avail (movies). Ck-out 11 am. Business servs avail. X-country ski 5 mi. Refrigerators avail. Cr cds: A, C, D, DS, ER, MC, V.

🔧 ⌇ 🐾 **SC**

Hotels

★★ **HOLIDAY INN HARBOURVIEW.** *99 Wyse Rd (B3A 1L9), on plaza of MacDonald Bridge. 902/463-1100; fax 902/464-1227; res 888/434-0440; toll-free 800/465-4329. Email hi-hbr@istar.ca; www.holidayinn.com/harbourviewns.* 196 rms, 7 story. May-Oct: S $89; D $99; each addl $10; suites $195-$395; under 19 free; wknd rates; lower rates rest of yr. Crib free. Pet accepted, some restrictions. TV; cable. Heated pool. Restaurant 7 am-10:30 pm. Bar 11-1 am. Ck-out noon. Business center. In-rm modem link. Airport transportation. X-country ski 15 mi. Health club privileges. Microwaves avail. Some balconies. Cr cds: A, DS, MC, V.

🔧 ⌇ 🚶 🐾 🚶

★★ **PARK PLACE RAMADA PLAZA.** *240 Brownlow Ave (B3B 1X6). 902/468-8888; fax 902/468-8765; res 800/272-6232; toll-free 800/561-3733. Email ramadart@fox.nstn.ca; www.ramadans.com.* 147 rms, 5 story, 31 suites. May-Oct: S $180; D $190; suites $230; each addl $10; under 18 free; lower rates rest of yr. Crib avail. Pet accepted, some restrictions, fee. Parking lot. Indoor pool, lap pool, children's pool, lifeguard, whirlpool. TV; cable (DSS), VCR avail. Complimentary coffee in rms, newspaper, toll-free calls. Restaurant 6:30 am-10 pm. Bar. Ck-out noon, ck-in 3 pm. Meeting rms. Business center. Bellhops. Dry cleaning. Gift shop. Exercise equipt, sauna. Golf. Supervised children's activities. Hiking trail. Picnic facilities. Cr cds: A, C, D, DS, ER, JCB, MC, V.

D 🔧 🚶 ⌇ 🚶 🔧 ⌇ 🐾 **SC** 🚶

Restaurant

★★ **ROCCO'S.** *300 Prince Albert Rd (B2Y 4J2). 902/461-0211.* Specializes in chicken, seafood, veal. Hrs: 11:30 am-10 pm; Sat from 5 pm; hrs vary Sep-early May. Closed Sun; Jan 1, Dec 24, 25. Res accepted. Bar. Lunch a la carte entrees: $6.50-$8.25; dinner a la carte entrees: $8.95-$17.95. Child's menu. Entertainment. View of lake. Cr cds: A, D, DS, ER, MC, V.

⌇

(⛽)

Digby (F-3)

Pop 2,558 **Elev** 50 ft (15 m)
Area code 902

Information Tourist Information Bureau, 110 Montague Row, PO Box 579, B0V 1A0; 902/245-5714 or 902/245-4769 (winter) or 888/463-4429

Best known for its delicious scallops and harbor sights, this summer resort has many historic landmarks which trace its founding in 1783 by Sir Robert Digby and 1500 Loyalists from New England and New York. This Annapolis Basin town is the ideal headquarters for a day drive southwest down the Digby Neck peninsula, whose shores are washed by the Bay of Fundy with the highest tides in the world. Off Digby Neck are two islands which may be reached by ferry: Long Island and Brier Island, popular sites for rockhounding, whale watching, and birdwatching. Swimming along the sandy beaches and hiking the shores are favorite pastimes in this area of dashing spray, lighthouses, and wildflower-filled forests. A 35-mi (11-kil) drive to the northeast ends in Annapolis Royal and Port Royal, the first permanent European settlements in North America. Marking this is the restored fur trading fort, the Habitation of Port Royal, built by Samuel de Champlain. With high imposing cliffs, gently rolling farmland, and quiet woodland settings, this seacoast drive creates a study in contrasts.

What to See and Do

Ferry Service to St. John, NB. Car and passenger; all yr; summer, up to 3 times daily. Contact BAY Ferries, 94 Water St, PO Box 634, Charlottetown, PEI, C1A 7L3. Phone 888/249-7245.

Fishermen's Wharf. View one of the largest scallop fleets in the world.

Fort Anne National Historic Site. Built between 1702-08 in one of the central areas of conflict between the English and French for control of North America. Of the original site, only the 18th-century earthworks and a gunpowder magazine (1708) remain. Museum in restored officers' quarters. On grounds is Canada's oldest English graveyard, dating from 1720. (Mid-May-mid-Oct, daily; rest of yr, Mon-Fri; closed hols) 28 mi E on Hwy 1, Annapolis Royal Exit. Phone 902/532-2397 or 902/532-2321. **FREE**

Pines Golf Course. An 18-hole championship golf course on provincially owned and operated resort (see RESORTS).

Point Prim Lighthouse. Rocky promontory with view of Bay of Fundy. Lighthouse Rd.

Port Royal National Historic Site. Reconstructed 17th-century fur trading post built by Sieur de Mons; follows plans, bldg techniques of that era. (Mid-May-mid-Oct, daily) 23 mi (38 km) NE via Rte 1, then 6 mi (10 km) W on Port Royal Exit in Annapolis Royal. Phone 902/532-2898. ¢¢

Trinity Church. Only church in Canada built by shipwrights; church cemetery famous for inscriptions of pioneer settlers. (Mon-Fri) Queen St.

Annual Event

Scallop Days. Scallop-shucking contests; grand parade, pet show, entertainment; sporting, fishing, water events. Second wk Aug.

Motels/Motor Lodges

★★ **ADMIRAL DIGBY INN.** *441 Shore Rd. 902/245-2531; fax 902/245-2533; toll-free 800/465-6262. Email admdigby@tarzannet. ns.com; www.digbyns.com.* 46 rms, 2 kit. cottages. Mid-June-mid-Sep: S, D $71-$89; each addl $6-$10; kit. cottages $110; under 12 free; lower rates Apr-mid-June and mid-Sep-Oct. Closed rest of yr. Crib $6. Pet accepted. TV; cable, VCR avail (movies). Heated pool. Restaurant 7:30-10:30 am, 5-9 pm. Bar 5-10 pm. Ck-out 11 am. Coin lndry. Business servs avail. Sundries. Gift shop. Overlooks Annapolis Basin. Cr cds: DS, MC, V.

🅳 🐾 ⓣ ⇔ 🕅 🔥

★★ **COASTAL INN KINGFISHER.** *111 Warwick St (B0V 1A0), off Hwy 101 Exit 26, near St. John Ferry. 902/245-4747; fax 902/245-4866.* 36 rms. S $55; D $65; each addl $7; under 10 free; some lower rates. Crib free. Pet accepted. TV; cable. Playground. Restaurant 7 am-8:30 pm; Sat, Sun 8 am-8:30 pm. Ck-out noon. Coin lndry. Meeting rm. Business servs avail. Microwaves avail. Picnic tables. Beach 4 mi. Cr cds: A, D, ER, MC, V.

🅳 🐾 ⓣ ⇔ 🖉

Resorts

★★ **MOUNTAIN GAP RESORT.** *217 Hwy 1 (B0S 1S0), 4 mi E; Hwy 101 Exits 24, 25. 902/245-5841; fax 902/245-2277; toll-free 800/565-5020. Email mtngap@tartannet.ns.ca; www.*

mountaingap.ns.ca. 102 rms, 1 story, 5 suites. S, D $90; suites $239; each addl $15; under 17 free. Pet accepted. Parking lot. Pool, whirl-pool. TV; cable (premium), VCR avail. Ck-out 11 am, ck-in 2 pm. Meeting rms. Business servs avail. Coin lndry. Gift shop. Golf. Tennis. Beach access. Bike rentals. Super-vised children's activities. Hiking trail. Picnic facilities. Cr cds: A, D, DS, ER, MC, K.

★★★ **THE PINES RESORT.** *103 Shore Rd (B0V 1A0), 1 mi N on Shore Rd. 902/245-2511; fax 902/245-6133.* 84 rms, 3 story, 30 cottages. May-mid-Oct: S $140-$175; D $161-$198; each addl $20; suites $215-$285; MAP: $52/person addl; family rates. Closed rest of yr. Crib free. TV; cable, VCR avail (movies). Heated pool; poolside serv. Playground. Super-vised children's activities (July-Aug); ages 5-12. Dining rm (public by res) 7-10 am, noon-2 pm, 6-9 pm. Lim-ited rm serv. Bar 5-11 pm. Ck-out 11 am, ck-in 3 pm. Grocery store 2 mi. Gift shop. Meeting rms. Business servs avail. Bellhops. Lighted tennis. 18-hole golf, greens fee $35, pro, dri-ving range. Exercise equipt; sauna. Lawn games. Nature trails. Bicycles (rentals). Soc dir. Movies. Fireplace in cottages. Balconies. Veranda. On 300 acres; overlooks Annapolis Basin of Bay of Fundy. Cr cds: A, D, DS, ER, MC, V.

Restaurant

★★ **FUNDY.** *34 Water St, (Rte 101). 902/245-4950. Email fundy@marina. istar.ca.* Specializes in seafood. Hrs: 7 am-10 pm; winter from 11 am. Closed Jan 1, Dec 25. Res accepted. Bar. Bkfst a la carte entrees: $3.50-$8; lunch a la carte entrees: $4.95-$13.90; dinner a la carte entrees: $8.95-$24.95. Child's menu. Enter-tainment. Solarium dining area. On Annapolis basin. Cr cds: A, D, DS, ER, MC, V.

Fortress of Louisbourg National Historic Site

See also Baddeck

(On Cape Breton Island, 22 mi or 35 km south of Sydney via Highway 22)

Web www.fortress.uccb.ns.ca

Information Director, PO Box 160, Louisbourg B0A 1M0; 902/733-2280

This 11,860-acre (4,800-hectare) park incl the massive Fortress erected by the French between 1720-45 to defend their possessions in the New World. Under the terms of the Treaty of Utrecht (1713), France lost New-foundland and Acadia but was per-mitted to keep Cape Breton Island (Isle Royale) and Prince Edward Island (Isle Saint-Jean). English Har-bour, renamed Louisbourg, was then selected by the French as the most suitable point for an Atlantic strong-hold. It served as headquarters for a large fishing fleet and became an important trading center. Later it was used as the base for French privateers preying on New England shipping.

In 1745, after a 47-day siege, Louis-bourg was captured by a volunteer force from New England led by Colonel William Pepperrell and a British fleet under Commodore War-ren. Three yrs later the colony was returned to France by the treaty of Aix-la-Chapelle. In the Seven Yrs' War Louisbourg, after being twice blockaded by British fleets, was finally captured in 1758. In 1760 its fortifications were demolished. Reconstruction of about ¼ of 18th-century Louisbourg is complete.

On the grounds and open are the Governor's apartment, the soldiers' barracks, the chapel, various guard-houses, the Dauphin Demi-Bastion, the King's storehouse, the Engineer's house, the residence of the commissaire-ordonnateur, several private dwellings and storehouses, and the royal bakery. At the Hotel de la Marine, L'Epée Royale, and Grand-champs Inn visitors can sample food in the manner of the 18th-century, while period pastries may be enjoyed at the Destouches house and soldiers' bread purchased at the bakery. Costumed guides interpret the town as it was in 1744 with tours in English and French. Exhibits at various points inside and outside the reconstructed area; walking tours. Park (June-Sep, daily; May and Oct, limited tours). An average visit takes 4-5 hrs; comfortable shoes and warm clothes are advised. ¢¢-¢¢¢

Restaurant

★★ **GRUBSTAKE.** *1274 Main St, adj City Hall.* 902/733-2308. Specializes in seafood, steak. Hrs: noon-10 pm. Closed Sun. Lunch $5.95-$12; dinner $10.95-$35. Entertainment. Early 1800s bldg. At fishing wharf. Cr cds: A, C, MC, V.

Grand Pré

Pop 305 **Elev** 125 ft (38 m)
Area code 902
Information Tourism Nova Scotia, PO Box 130, Halifax B3J 2M7; 902/490-5946 or 800/565-0000

Site of one of the earliest French settlements in North America, this was the setting for Henry Wadsworth Longfellow's poem "Evangeline," which describes the tragic tale of the expulsion of the Acadians by the British in 1755. Its name refers to the extensively diked lands and means "the great meadow." Wolfville, nearby, is the center of the land of Evangeline and the starting point to memorable historic places.

What to See and Do

Grand Pré National Historic Site. Memorial to the Acadian people. Museum (mid-May-mid-Oct). Grounds and gardens (all yr). Phone 902/542-3631. **FREE** On grounds is

Acadian Memorial Church. Display commemorating Acadian settlement and expulsion. Old Acadian Forge; bust of Longfellow; "Evangeline" statue; formal landscaped gardens with original French willows. Guides available. **FREE**

Motels/Motor Lodges

★★ **GREENSBORO INN.** *9016 Commercial St (B4N 3E2), 8 mi W on Hwy 101, Exit 12.* 902/681-3201; fax 902/681-3399; res 800/561-3201. www.valleyweb.com/greensboro. 26 rms. 1 kit. unit. Mid-May-Oct: S $59; D $69-$79, kit. unit $100; under 18 free; each addl $6; lower rates rest of yr. Pet accepted. TV; cable. Indoor pool. Complimentary coffee in lobby. Restaurant adj 11 am-10 pm. Ck-out 11 am. Golf privileges. Downhill/x-country ski 20 mi. Picnic tables. Cr cds: A, D, ER, MC, V.
🦆 ⚓ 🛏 ➶ 🛁 SC

★ **SLUMBER INN-NEW MINAS.** *5534 Prospect rd (D4N 3K8), Hwy 101 W, Exit 12.* 902/681-5000; res 800/914-5005. Email slumberinn@valleyweb.com; www.valleyweb.com/slumberinn. 79 rms, shower only, 2 story. No elvtr. S, D $70-$85; under 12 free. TV; cable (premium); VCR (movies). Restaurant opp. Ck-out 11 am. Business servs avail. Downhill/x-country ski 20 mi. Cr cds: A, D, ER, MC, V.
D ⚓ ➶ 🛁 SC

★★★ **WANDLYN INN.** *7270 Hwy 1 (B4R 1B9).* 902/678-8311; fax 902/679-1253; res 800/561-0000. Email tom.fredericks@wandlyninns.com. 70 units, 3 story. Mid-June-Oct: S $68-$88; D $88-$100; each addl $10; suites $88-$125; under 18 free; lower rates rest of yr. Crib free. Pet accepted. TV; cable, VCR avail. Indoor pool. Restaurant 7 am-9:30 pm. Bar 10-2 am. Ck-out noon. Meeting rms. Business servs avail. Some refrigerators. Picnic tables. Cr cds: A, DS, MC, V.
🦆 🛏 🛁

Resort

★★ **OLD ORCHARD INN.** *Hwy 101, Exit 11 (D0P 1X0).* 902/542-5751; fax 902/542-2276. 105 rms, 3 story, 29 cabins, 10 kits. May-Oct: S, D $79-$88; each addl $8; suites $120; cabins $59-$64 (with kit. $15 addl); family rates; ski plans. Crib free. TV; cable. Indoor pool. Sauna. Playground. Supervised children's activities (winter); ages 5-12. Dining rm 7 am-9 pm. Box lunches. Bar to 2 am. Ck-out 11 am, ck-in 3 pm. Coin lndry 3 mi. Meeting rms. Business center. Grocery, package store 3 mi. Lighted tennis. 18-hole golf privileges. Downhill ski 20 mi; x-country ski on site. Sleigh rides. Lawn games. Some private patios. Picnic tables. Cr cds: A, D, MC, V.

B&Bs/Small Inns

★★★ **BLOMIDON.** *127 Main St (B0P 1X0), off Hwy 101 Exit 10 or 11. 902/542-2291; fax 902/542-7461.* 26 rms, 3 story, 5 suites. May-Oct: S $69-$129; D $79-$139; each addl $10; suites $139; lower rates rest of yr. Crib $12. TV in sitting rm; cable, VCR avail. Complimentary continental bkfst; afternoon refreshments. Dining rm 11:30 am-2 pm, 5-9:30 pm. Ck-out 11 am, ck-in 3 pm. Meeting rms. Business servs avail. Health club privileges. Tennis. Shuffleboard. Library, 2 parlors; antiques. Sea captain's mansion (1879) on 4 acres; period decor. Cr cds: A, D, MC, V.

★★★ **TATTINGSTONE INN.** *434 Main St (B0P 1X0), Hwy 101 Exit 9. 902/542-7696; fax 902/542-7696; res 902/542-7696; toll-free 800/565-7696. Email tattingstone@ns.sympatico.com.* 10 rms, 2 story. Apr-Oct: S, D $85-$158; lower rates rest of yr. TV; cable. Heated pool; steam rm, poolside serv. Dining rm 5-9 pm. Ck-out 11 am, ck-in 3 pm. Business servs avail. Lighted tennis. Some in-rm whirlpools. Former residence (1874), landscaped with many unusual trees. Victorian and Georgian period antiques. Cr cds: A, DS, MC, V.

★★★ **VICTORIA'S HISTORIC INN.** *416 Main St (B0P 1X0), off Hwy 101, Exit 10 or 11. 902/542-5744; fax 902/542-7794; toll-free 800/556-5744. Email victoria.inn@ns.sympatico.ca; www.valleyweb.com/victoriasinn.* 15 rms, 3 story. May-Oct: S, D $89-$175; each addl $15; suite $175; lower rates rest of yr. Complimentary full bkfst. Ck-out 11 am, ck-in 3 pm. Business center. Some balconies. Historic inn built in 1893; period furnishings. Totally nonsmoking. Cr cds: A, MC, V.

Restaurant

★ **PADDY'S PUB AND BREWERY.** *42 Aberdeen St (B4W 2N1), 10 mi W on Hwy 1. 902/678-3199. Email paddys@fox.ns.ca.* Specializes in fish and chips, steak, seafood. Hrs: 11 am-11 pm; Fri, Sat to midnight. Closed Dec 25, 26. Res accepted. Bar. Lunch $3-$7; dinner $5-$15. Sun brunch $3-$6. Child's menu. Entertainment: Fri, Sat. Irish pub atmosphere. Cr cds: A, D, ER, MC, V.

Halifax (F-5)

See also Peggy's Cove

Founded 1749 **Pop** 340,000 **Elev** 25-225 ft (8-69 m) **Area code** 902 **Web** www.explorens.com

Information International Visitors Centre, 1595 Barrington St, B3J 1Z7; 902/490-5946 or 800/565-0000

Capital of Nova Scotia, this largest city in the Atlantic provinces offers a delightful combination of old and new. Founded in 1749 to establish British strength in the North Atlantic, it is growing rapidly as a commercial, scientific, and educational center while continuing to preserve its natural heritage. Centrally situated in the province, it is perfectly suited as the starting point for the Evangeline and Glooscap Trails, the Lighthouse Route, and the Marine Drive with their scenic and historic sights. Located on Bedford Basin, the world's second-largest natural harbor, Halifax recently merged with the town of Dartmouth; this area lies across the harbor and is reached via the MacDonald and MacKay bridges.

What to See and Do

Art Gallery of Nova Scotia. More than 2,000 works on permanent display, incl folk art; changing exhibits. (Tues-Sat, also Sun afternoons; closed hols) Free admission Tues. 1741 Hollis-at-Cheapside. Phone 902/424-7542. ¢¢

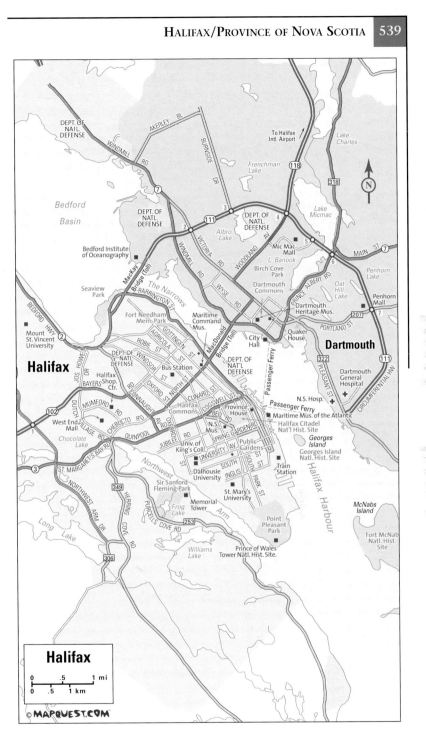

Halifax

```
0        .5        1 mi
0    .5    1 km
```

© MAPQUEST.COM

Bluenose II. Exact replica of famed racing schooner depicted on Canadian dime; public cruises in Nova Scotia waters. At waterfront. Contact Bluenose Preservation Trust. Phone 800/763-1963 or 800/565-0000. ¢¢¢¢

Chapel of Our Lady of Sorrows. Built in one day by 2,000 men; altar carvings date from 1750. South & S Park Sts.

Churches.

St. George's Round Church. (1801) Anglican. Byzantine-style church built at the direction of Edward, Duke of Kent, father of Queen Victoria. Nearby is **St. Patrick's Roman Catholic Church**, a Victorian Gothic building still largely untouched by change. **St. Paul's Church** (1750). Barrington St. First church in Halifax and oldest Protestant church in Canada. "Explosion window" on Argyle St side; during 1917 explosion that destroyed a large portion of the city, the 3rd window of the upper gallery shattered, leaving the silhouette of a human head. Tours (summer; free). (June-Sep, daily) Brunswick & Cornwallis Sts.

Halifax Citadel National Historic Park. Star-shaped hilltop fort built 1828-56 on site of previous fortifications. Excellent view of city and harbor. Audiovisual presentation "Tides of History" (50-min). Restored signal masts, library, barrack rms, powder magazine, expense magazine, defense casemate, and garrison cell. Exhibits on communications, the four Citadels, and engineering and construction. Army Museum; orientation center. Coffee bar serving typical 19th-century soldiers' food; sales outlet; guided tours, military displays by uniformed students, bagpipe music, changing of the guard (summer). (Daily; closed Jan 1, Good Friday, Dec 25) Entrances on Sackville St and Rainnie Dr. Phone 902/426-5080. Fee charged June 15-Labour Day ¢ On grounds are

Maritime Museum of the Atlantic. 1675 exhibits of nautical history incl *Titanic: The Unsinkable Ship* and *Halifax, Halifax Wrecked: The Story of the Halifax Explosion.* (Mid-May-mid-Oct, daily; rest of yr, Tues-Sun; closed hols) 1675 Lower Water St. Phone 902/424-7490. **Donation**

Town Clock. (1803) Halifax's most recognized landmark. Built under supervision of Prince Edward, Duke of Kent, father of Queen Victoria.

Historic Properties (Privateers Wharf). Variety of clothing, specialty shops, restaurants, and pubs housed in several restored 18th-century bldg along the waterfront. (Daily) 1869-70 Upper Water St. Phone 902/429-0530.

Neptune Theatre. Home of internationally recognized theater company; presents 5 main stage plays per season. Small intimate theater with excellent acoustics. Res advised. Corner of Argyle & Sackville Sts. Phone 902/429-7070 or 902/429-7300.

Nova Scotia Museum of Natural History. Permanent exhibits on man and his environment in Nova Scotia; changing exhibits. (June-mid-Oct, daily; rest of yr, Tues-Sun; closed Jan 1, Good Fri, Dec 25) 1747 Summer St. Phone 902/424-7353. ¢

Pier 21. Canada's "Ellis Island"; between 1928, more than a million immigrants and wartime evacuees took their first steps on Canadian soil at Pier 21. Now a National Historic Site, the Pier features traveling exhibits, live performances, Wall of Ships, Immigrant Testimonial Stations, and Wall of Honour. (Tues-Sun) 1055 Marginal Rd. Phone 902/425-7770. ¢¢

Point Pleasant Park. Remains of several forts. Nature trail, monuments, public beach, picnic areas; cross-country skiing. (Daily) Point Pleasant Dr. Phone 902/490-4700. **FREE** On grounds is

Prince of Wales Tower National Historic Park. (1796-97). Built to protect British batteries; said to be first tower of its type in North America. Exhibits portray tower's history, architectural features, and significance as a defensive structure. (July-Labour Day, daily) Phone 902/426-5080. **FREE**

Province House. Oldest provincial Parliament bldg in Canada; office of Premier; legislative library. Guided tours (Mon-Fri; special summer hrs). 1726 Hollis St. Phone 902/424-8967. **FREE**

Public Archives of Nova Scotia. Provincial government records; private manuscripts; maps, photos, genealogies; film and sound archives;

library. (Tues-Sat; closed hols) 6016 University Ave, S end of town. Phone 902/424-6060. **FREE**

Public Gardens. A 16¾ acre (7-hectare) formal Victorian garden with trees, flower beds, fountains; bandstand; duck ponds; concession. (See SEASONAL EVENT) (May-Nov, daily) Spring Garden Rd & South Park St. Phone 880/565-0000. **FREE**

Sightseeing tours.

Double Decker Tours. City tours on double-decker, English-style bus. Tours last approx 1½ hrs. Multiple departure points. (June-Oct, daily) Phone 902/420-1155. ¢¢¢¢

Gray Line bus tours. Phone 800/565-9662; **Cabana Tours,** PO Box 8683, Station A, B3K 5M4, phone 902/423-6066; **Markland Tours,** multilingual minivan tours, phone 902/499-2939

Harbour Hopper Tours. Narrated tours in amphibious vehicles styled after WWII landing craft. (May-Oct, daily) Phone 902/490-8687. ¢¢¢¢¢

Murphy's on the Water. Three boats. Live narration and historical commentary; 2-hr tour. (May-mid-Oct, daily) Murphy's Pier next to Historic Properties. Phone 902/420-1015. ¢¢¢¢-¢¢¢¢¢

York Redoubt National Historic Site. (1793) A 200-yr-old fortification on high bluff overlooking harbor entrance. Features muzzle-loading guns, photo display, picnic facilities, information service. Grounds (daily). (Mid-June-Labour Day, daily) 6 mi (9.7 km) SW via Purcell's Cove Rd. Phone 902/426-5050. **FREE**

Annual Events

Winterfest. Feb.

Multicultural Festival. June.

Atlantic Jazz Festival. July.

Highland Games. July.

International Buskerfest. Aug.

Nova Scotia Air Show. Sep.

Seasonal Event

Public Gardens Band Concerts. Sun afternoons. July-Aug.

Motels/Motor Lodges

★★ **BLUENOSE INN AND SUITES.** *636 Bedford Hwy (B3N 2L8). 902/443-3171; fax 902/443-9368.* 51 units, 1-2 story, 17 kit. suites. June-Oct: S, D $65; each addl $7; kit. suites $89; some wkly rates; lower rates rest of yr. Crib free. Pet accepted. TV; cable, VCR avail. Complimentary continental bkfst. Playground. Restaurant 7-10 pm (off-season). Bar. Ck-out 11 am. Meeting rms. Balconies. Picnic tables. Cr cds: A, C, D, DS, ER, MC, V.

🄳 🌊 ⛷ 🕇 🔧 🛥 🐾

★★ **DELTA BARRINGTON.** *1875 Barrington St (B3J 3L6). 902/429-7410; fax 902/420-6524.* 202 rms, 4 story. S, D $131-$142; each addl $15; suites $289-$475; under 18 free; wkend rates; some lower rates. Crib free. Pet accepted, some restrictions. Parking $15. TV; cable, VCR avail. Indoor pool; whirlpool. Free supervised children's activities (2 days/wk); ages 3-11. Restaurant 6:30 am-2:30 pm, 5-10 pm. Rm serv to 1 am. Bar. Ck-out 1 pm. Meeting rms. Business servs avail. In-rm modem link. Bellhops. Valet serv. Shopping arcade. Barber, beauty shop. Exercise equipt; sauna. Minibars; microwaves avail. Cr cds: A, D, DS, ER, MC, V.

🄳 🌊 ⛷ 🕇 🏊 🕇 🔧 🛥 🐾 🏃

★ **GRAND VIEW.** *Black Point (B0J 1B0), W on Hwy 103, Exit 5, then left ¼ mi on Hwy 213, right at flashing light, 10 Mi on Hwy 3. 902/857-9776; fax 902/857-9776.* 14 rms, 10 kit. units, 2 cottages. No A/C. No rm phones. Mid-June-early Sep: S $47-$55; D $50-$60; each addl $7; cottages $85; under 5 free; wkly rates; lower rates rest of yr. Crib avail. Pet accepted. TV; cable. Playground. Coffee in rms. Ck-out 10:30 am. Near swimming beach; all rms have view of St. Margaret's Bay. Cr cds: MC, V.

🄳 🌊 ⛷ 🕇 🛥 🐾

★★ **HOLIDAY INN SELECT HALIFAX CENTRE.** *1980 Robie St (B3H 3G5), jct Quinpool Rd. 902/423-1161; fax 902/423-9069; res 800/465-4329. Email hiselect@holinnselect.hfx.com.* 232 rms, 14 story. S, D $125-$145; each addl $10; suites $195-$225; under 19 free; wkend rates. Crib free. Pet accepted. TV; cable, VCR avail. Indoor pool; wading pool, whirlpool, poolside serv. Complimentary coffee in rms. Restaurant 6 am-11 pm. Bars noon-1 am. Ck-out 1 pm. Meeting rms. Business center. In-rm modem link. Sundries. Indoor parking. Exercise equipt; sauna. Health club privileges. Microwaves avail. Cr cds: A, C, D, DS, ER, JCB, MC, V.

D ⬛ ⬛ ⬛ ⬛ ⬛ SC ⬛

★★ KEDDY'S HALIFAX. *20 St. Margaret's Bay Rd (B3N 1J4), on Hwy 3, ½ mi W of Armdale Traffic Cir. 902/477-5611; fax 902/479-2150; res 800/561-7666. Email keddyshfx@navnet.net.* 135 rms, 9 story, 14 kits. June-Oct: S $73; D $78; each addl $8; suites $85-$125; kit. units $57-$99; under 19 free; lower rates rest of yr. Crib free. Pet accepted. TV; cable, VCR avail (movies). Indoor pool; whirlpool. Restaurant 7 am-9 pm. Bar 11-1 am. Ck-out 11 am. Meeting rms. Business servs avail. In-rm modem link. Valet serv. Sundries. Sauna. Microwaves avail. Cr cds: A, DS, MC, V.

⬛ ⬛ ⬛

★ SEASONS MOTOR INN. *4 Melrose Ave (B3N 2E2). 902/443-9341; fax 902/443-9344; toll-free 800/792-2498. Email bill.turvey@ns.sympatico.ca.* 36 rms, 4 story, 1 suite. June-Oct: S $66; D $71; suites $76; each addl $50; under 15 free; lower rates rest of yr. Pet accepted. TV; cable. Complimentary continental bkfst. Ck-out 11 am, ck-in noon. Coin lndry. Golf. Cr cds: A, MC, V.

⬛ ⬛ ⬛ ⬛

★★ STARDUST. *1067 Bedford Hwy (B4A 1B5), 9 mi E on Hwy 2. 902/835-3316; fax 902/835-4973.* 50 rms, 25 A/C, 3 story, 32 kits. June-Oct: S $45; D $50; each addl $10; family rms $60; 2-bedrm apts $100; kit. units $35-$45 (equipt $10 addl); under 12 free; lower rates rest of yr. Crib $5. Pet accepted. TV; cable, VCR avail. Restaurant 7 am-10 pm. Serv bar. Ck-out 11 am. Sundries. Some refrigerators. On Bedford Basin. Cr cds: A, ER, MC, V.

⬛ ⬛ ⬛ SC

★★ STARDUST. *1791 St. Margaret's Bay Rd (B3T 1B8). 902/876-2301; fax 902/835-4973.* 12 rms, 2 with shower only, 10 kit. units (no equipt). No A/C. No rm phones. June-Oct: S $40-$50; D $60; each addl $10; kit. units $40-$50; under 12 free; wkly rates;

lower rates rest of yr. TV; cable. Ck-out 11 am. Picnic tables. On lake. Cr cds: A, D, DS, ER, MC, V.

D ⬛ ⬛

★★ WANDLYN INN HALIFAX. *50 Beford Hwy (B3M 2J2). 902/443-0416; fax 902/443-1353; res 800/561-0000. Email bayviewmotorinn@sprint.ca.* 66 rms, 2 story. June-Sep: S $60-$85; D $65-$85; each addl $10; suites $95-$135; under 18 free; lower rates rest of yr. Pet accepted. TV; VCR avail (movies). Restaurant 7-11 am, 5-9 pm. Bar 4-11 pm. Ck-out noon. Meeting rms. Business servs avail. Sundries. Exercise equipt. Microwaves avail. Ocean view from some rms. Cr cds: A, DS, MC, V.

D ⬛ ⬛ ⬛

Hotels

★★★ AIRPORT HOTEL HALIFAX. *60 Bell Blvd (B2T 1K3), off Hwy 102 Exit 6, near Intl Airport. 902/873-3000; fax 902/873-3001; res 800/667-3333.* 147 rms, 3 story, 4 suites. Feb-Apr, July-Sep: S $109; D $119; suites $150; each addl $10; under 19 free; lower rates rest of yr. Crib avail. Pet accepted. Parking lot. Indoor/outdoor pools, whirlpool. TV; cable (DSS). Complimentary coffee in rms, newspaper. Restaurant 6:30 am-8 pm. Bar. Ck-out noon, ck-in 3 pm. Meeting rms. Business center. Bellhops. Coin lndry. Free airport transportation. Exercise equipt. Golf, 18 holes. Video games. Cr cds: A, D, DS, ER, MC, V.

D ⬛ ⬛ ⬛ ⬛ ⬛ ⬛ ⬛ ⬛

★★★ CITADEL. *1960 Brunswick St (B3J 2G7), at foot of Citadel Hill. 902/422-1391; fax 902/429-6672.* 264 rms, 7 and 11 story. S, D $89-$169; each addl $15; suites $250-$305; wkend rates; under 18 free. Crib free. Pet accepted, some restrictions. TV; cable. Indoor pool; whirlpool, poolside serv. Restaurant 7 am-3 pm, 5-11 pm. Bar 11-1 am. Ck-out 1 pm. Meeting rms. Business center. In-rm modem link. Exercise equipt; sauna. Minibars; some refrigerators. Private patios, balconies. Cr cds: A, D, ER, MC, V.

D ⬛ ⬛ ⬛ ⬛ ⬛ ⬛ ⬛ ⬛ ⬛

★★ DELTA HALIFAX. *1990 Barrington St (B3J 1P2), in Scotia Sq. 902/425-6700; fax 902/425-6214; res 800/*

268-1133. *www.deltahotels.com*. 300 rms, 8 story. S, D $129-$159; each addl $20; suites $195-$400; under 18 free. Crib free. Pet accepted, some restrictions. Valet parking $12.95. TV; cable. Heated pool; whirlpool. Restaurant 6:30 am-10 pm. Bars 11-1 am. Ck-out noon. Meeting rms. Business center. Shopping arcade. Beauty shop. Exercise equipt; sauna. Minibars. On Halifax Harbour. Cr cds: A, DS, MC, V.

★★ **INN ON THE LAKE.** *PO Box 29 (B0N 2S0), Exit 5. 902/861-3480; fax 902/861-4883; toll-free 800/463-6465. Email book@innonthelake.com.* 41 rms, 3 story. May-Dec: S, D $90-$104; each addl $10; suites $235-$290; wkly; lower rates rest of yr. Crib free. TV; cable (premium), VCR avail (movies). Pool; poolside serv. Complimentary coffee in rms. Restaurant 7 am-10 pm. Bar 11-1 am. Ck-out 11 am. Meeting rms. Business servs avail. In-rm modem link. No bellhops. Gift shop. Free airport transportation. Tennis. Some refrigerators, microwaves. Some balconies. Picnic tables. On lake. Cr cds: A, MC, V.

★★ **LORD NELSON.** *1515 S Park St (B3J 2L2), across from Public Gardens. 902/423-6331; fax 902/423-7148.* 200 rms, 9 story. S, D $79-$109; each addl $10; suites $99-$150; under 18 free; wkend rates. Crib free. TV; cable. Ck-out 1 pm. Meeting rms. Business servs avail. Shopping arcade. Many microwaves. Cr cds: A, D, DS, ER, MC, V.

★★★ **PRINCE GEORGE.** *1725 Market St. 902/425-1986; fax 902/429-6048.* 206 rms, 6 story. S, D $119-$160; suites $225-$350; under 18 free; wkend rates. Crib free. Pet accepted, some restrictions. Garage $11/night. TV; cable (premium), VCR avail. Indoor pool; poolside serv. Restaurant 6:30 am-11 pm. Rm serv 24 hrs. Bar 11-2 am. Ck-out 1 pm. Convention facilities. Business center. Concierge serv. Gift shop. Exercise equipt. Minibars; microwaves avail. Directly connected to World Trade and Convention Centre and Metro Centre by shuttle elvtr and underground walkway. Cr cds: A, D, DS, JCB, MC, V.

★★★ **SHERATON HALIFAX HOTEL.** *1919 Upper Water St (B3J 3J5), Downtown. 902/422-1700; fax 902/422-5805; res 800/325-3535. www.sheratonhalifax.com.* 349 rms, 6 story. S, D $139-$200; each addl $20; suites $225-$850; under 18 free. Crib free. Pet accepted. Parking $10. TV; cable, VCR avail (movies). Indoor pool; whirlpool, poolside serv. Complimentary coffee in rms. Restaurant 6:30 am-11 pm. Bars 11-2 am; entertainment. Ck-out noon. Convention facilities. Business center. In-rm modem link. Concierge serv. Shopping arcade. Barber, beauty shop. Exercise equipt; sauna. Some bathrm phones; microwaves avail. On ocean, Halifax Harbour. Casino. Cr cds: A, C, D, DS, MC, V.

Resort

★★★ **OAK ISLAND RESORT AND MARINA.** *51 Vaughan Rd, (B0J 3M0), 45 mi W on Hwy 103, Exit 9. 902/627-2600; fax 902/627-2020; toll-free 800/565-5075. Email oakislnd@istar.ca; www.oakislandinn.com.* 66 rms, 3 story, 4 suites. June-Sep: S, D $89; suites $149; each addl $10; lower rates rest of yr. Crib avail. Pet accepted, some restrictions. Parking lot. Indoor pool, whirlpool. TV; cable (DSS). Complimentary coffee in rms. Restaurant. Bar. Ck-out noon, ck-in 3 pm. Meeting rms. Business servs avail. Sauna. Golf. Tennis. Beach access. Supervised children's activities. Hiking trail. Picnic facilities. Cr cds: A, ER, MC, V.

B&Bs/Small Inns

★★ **DAUPHINEE INN.** *167 Shore Club Rd (B0J 1T0), 25 mi W on NS 103. 902/857-1790; fax 902/857-9555; toll-free 800/567-1790. Email stay@dauphineeinn.com; www.dauphineeinn.com.* 6 air-cooled rms, 2 suites. No rm phones. S, D $78-$86; each addl $10; suites $125; under 5 free. Closed Nov-Apr. TV in common rm; cable (premium). Complimentary continental bkfst. Restaurant 5-9 pm. Ck-out 11 am, ck-in 2 pm. Business servs avail. Gift shop. In-rm whirlpool in suites. On swimming beach. Built in 1900; panoramic views of Hubbards Cove. Totally nonsmoking. Cr cds: A, MC, V.

★ **FRESH START.** *2720 Gottingen St (B3K 3C7). 902/453-6616; fax 902/453-6617; toll-free 888/453-6616. Email sisters@ns.sympatico.ca; www.bbcanada.com/2262.html.* 7 rms, 3 story, 1 suite. May-Oct: S $70; D $80; suites $95; lower rates rest of yr. Pet accepted. Parking lot. TV; cable, VCR avail, CD avail. Complimentary full bkfst, toll-free calls. Restaurant. Ck-out 11 am, ck-in 1 pm. Golf, 18 holes. Tennis, 2 courts. Cr cds: A, D, ER, MC, V.

★★★ **HADDON HALL.** *67 Haddon Hill Rd (B0J 1J0), 35 mi W on NS 3. 902/275-3577. Email haddon@tall ships.com; www.haddonhallinn.com.* 9 rms, 2 story, 2 kit. units. June-Oct: S, D, kit. units $150-$400; each addl $15; under 16 free; mid-June-mid-Oct; 2 day min (main house); lower rates rest of yr. TV; cable, VCR avail. Complimentary continental bkfst, coffee in rms. Restaurant 5:30-8:30 pm. Ck-out 10 am, ck-in 11 am. Business servs avail. Bellhops. Valet serv. Tennis. Heated pool. Refrigerator, microwave in kit. units. Built in 1905; panoramic ocean view. Cr cds: A, MC, V

★★ **WAVERLEY INN.** *1266 Barrington St (B3J 1Y5). 902/423-9346; fax 902/425-0167; toll-free 800/565-9346. Email welcome@waverleyinn.com; www.waverleyinn.com.* 32 rms, 3 story. June-Oct: S, D $79-$149; each addl $15; under 12 free; lower rates rest of yr. Crib avail. TV; cable, VCR avail. Complimentary continental bkfst. Restaurant nearby. Ck-out noon, ck-in after noon. Business servs avail. Some in-rm whirlpools; microwaves avail. Historic inn (1876); antiques. Near Halifax Harbour. Cr cds: A, DS, MC, V.

All Suite

★★★ **CAMBRIDGE SUITES HOTEL HALIFAX.** *1583 Brunswick St. 902/420-0555; fax 902/420-9379;* *toll-free 800/565-1263. Email reservations@hfx.cambridgesuites.ns.ca; www.cambridgesuiteshotel.com.* 6 story, 200 suites. May-Oct: S $180; D $195; suites $200; each addl $15; under 17 free; lower rates rest of yr. Crib avail. Valet parking avail. TV; cable, VCR avail, CD avail. Complimentary continental bkfst, coffee in rms, newspaper. Restaurant 9 am-11 pm. Bar. Ck-out 1 pm, ck-in 3 pm. Meeting rms. Business center. Bellhops. Concierge serv. Dry cleaning, coin lndry. Gift shop. Exercise privileges, sauna, steam rm, whirlpool. Golf, 18 holes. Video games. Cr cds: A, D, DS, ER, MC, V.

Restaurants

★ **ALFREDO, WEINSTEIN, AND HO.** *1739 Grafton St (B3J 2W1). 902/421-1977. www.alfredowein-steinho.com.* Specializes in Italian, Chinese, and delicatessen dishes. Sundae bar. Hrs: 11 am-11 pm; Fri, Sat to 4 am. Closed Jan 1, Dec 24-26. Bar. Lunch $5.95-$9.95; dinner $9-$15. Child's menu. Cr cds: A, D, ER, MC, V.

★★ **FIVE FISHERMEN.** *1740 Argyle St (B3J 2W1). 902/422-4421. www.fivefishermen.com.* Specializes in seafood, steak, and steamed mussels. Salad bar. Own desserts. Hrs: 5-11 pm; Sun to 10 pm. Closed Jan 1, Dec 22-25. Res accepted. Bar. Dinner $16.95-$27.95. Former school bldg (1816). Cr cds: A, D, ER, MC, V.

★★★ **SALTY'S ON THE WATERFRONT.** *1869 Upper Water St (B3J 1S9). 902/423-6818. Email saltysns@aol.com.* Specializes in lobster, steak. Hrs: 11:30 am-9:30 pm. Res accepted. Bar. Lunch a la carte entrees: $6.95-$10.95; dinner a la carte entrees: $14-$22. Child's menu. Historic bldg (1800) on waterfront. Nautical decor. Cr cds: A, D, DS, ER, MC, V.

Peggy's Cove (F-5)

See also Halifax

Pop 54 **Elev** 25 ft (8 m)
Area code 902
Information Tourism Nova Scotia, PO Box 130, Halifax B3J 2M7; 902/490-5946 or 800/565-0000

Twenty-seven miles (44 kilometers) southwest of Halifax, this tiny, picturesque village lies nestled in a snug harbor where lobster fishermen live and work. This area is surrounded by bold granite outcroppings where, during a storm, the sea dashes against the shoreline.

Within St. John's Anglican Church, two murals painted by the late William deGarthe, one of Canada's foremost artists, may be viewed. Additional works include carvings of villagers at work scribed into the rock cliff behind deGarthe's home, now a gallery. One of the many lighthouses dotting the Lighthouse Route extending southwest from Halifax to Yarmouth may be seen in this artist's haven.

What to See and Do

Fisheries Museum of the Atlantic. Restored schooner *Theresa E. Connor* and trawler *Cape Sable* serve as floating museum, situated in an old fish plant; *Bluenose* schooner exhibit; aquarium; working dory shop; hall of inshore fisheries, demonstrations rm, theatre, gift shop, gallery; restaurant. (Daily) Bluenose Dr, between Duke & Montague Sts in Lunenburg. Phone 902/634-4794. ¢¢

Town of Lunenburg. (Founded 1753) Walking tour of this historic town provides comprehensive information on its history and unique architectural character. The Tourist Bureau is located on Blockhouse Hill Rd, near Townsend St. Approx 50 mi (80 km) W on Hwy 103.

Motel/Motor Lodge

★ ★ **WINDJAMMER.** *4070 Hwy 3 (B0J 1J0), approx 45 mi W. 902/275-3567; fax 902/275-5867.* 18 rms, 6 A/C. Mid-June-mid-Sep: S $44-$54; D $49-$59; each addl $6; under 12 free; lower rates rest of yr. Crib $5. Pet accepted. TV; cable, VCR avail. Restaurant adj 7:30 am-9 pm. Ck-out

Lighthouse, Peggy's Cove

11 am. Miniature golf. Some refrigerators, microwaves avail. Picnic tables. On lake; swimming beach. Cr cds: A, C, D, DS, ER, MC, V.

Restaurant

★★ **SOU'WESTER.** *NS 333. 902/823-2561. www.peggys-cove.com.* Mediterranean menu. Specializes in seafood chowder, lobster, gingerbread. Own soups, sauces. Hrs: 9 am-8 pm. Closed Dec 24, 25. Bkfst $4.25-$7.25; lunch, dinner $3.25-$17.95. Child's menu. Entertainment. Gift shop. On oceanfront; view of lighthouse and cove. Familyowned. Cr cds: A, D, MC, V.

Truro (E-5)

Settled 1703 **Pop** 12,885 **Elev** 15 ft (5 m) **Area code** 902
Information Chamber of Commerce, 577 Prince St, B2N 1G2; 902/895-6328

After the expulsion of the Acadians following British acquisition of this territory, Truro was resettled in 1760 by 53 Loyalist families from New England. Other settlers followed, mainly from Northern Ireland and those fleeing the American Revolution. After the arrival of the railroad, Truro was incorporated as a town in 1875.

What to See and Do

Acres of the Golden Pheasant. Contains over 50 species of birds, incl pheasants, peacocks, parakeets, finches, and doves. (Daily) Queen St. Phone 902/893-2734. ¢

Colchester County Museum. Exhibits depict human and natural history of the county; changing exhibits. Archives, genealogy library. (June-Sep, Tues-Sun; rest of yr, Tues-Fri; closed hols) 29 Young St. Phone 902/895-6284. ¢

Little White Schoolhouse Museum. One-rm schoolhouse built in 1871,

furnished with desks, artifacts, and textbooks from 1867-1952. (June-Aug, daily; rest of yr, by appt) Arthur St, on grounds of Nova Scotia Teachers College. Phone 902/895-5347, ext 291. **FREE**

Tidal bore. A wave of water rushes *backward* up the Salmon River before high tide. Bores range in height from a ripple up to several ft. A timetable can be obtained from the Chamber of Commerce or by phoning "Dial-a-Tide." Viewing area on Tidal Bore Rd, just off Hwy 102, exit 14. Phone 902/426-5494.

Victoria Park. One thousand-acre national park with hiking trails, outdoor pool, playground, tennis courts, picnic grounds, and baseball field. (Daily) Brunswick St & Park Rd. Phone 902/895-6328. **FREE**

Annual Event

International Tulip Festival. 577 Prince St. Over 250,000 tulips planted. Late May.

Motels/Motor Lodges

★ **PALLISER MOTEL.** *103/104 Tidal Bore Rd (B2N 5B3), Hwy 102 Exit 14. 902/893-8951. Email palliser@ auracom.com.* 42 rms. No A/C. No rm phones. Early May-late-Oct: S $39; D $49; each addl $5; under 10, $5. Closed rest of yr. Crib $5. Pet accepted. TV; cable. Complimentary continental bkfst. Restaurant 7:30 am-8:30 pm. Bar from 11 am. Ck-out 11 am. Meeting rm. Business servs avail. Gift shop. Cr cds: A, DS, MC, V.

★ **STONE HOUSES MOTEL & REST.** *165 Willow St (B2N 4Z9). 902/893-9413; fax 902/897-9937; res 877/600-6638; toll-free 877/660-6638.* 38 rms, 2 story, 2 suites. May-Oct: S $60; D $70; suites $80; each addl $10; under 12 free; lower rates rest of yr. Crib avail. Pet accepted. TV; cable, VCR avail. Complimentary full bkfst, coffee in rms. Restaurant 6 am-10 pm. Bar. Ck-out noon, ck-in 2 pm. Meeting rms. Fax servs avail. Exercise privileges. Golf, 18 holes. Tennis, 6 courts. Downhill skiing. Cr cds: A, MC, V.

★ **WILLOW BEND MOTEL.** *277 Willow St (B2N 5A3). 902/895-5325; fax 902/893-8375; toll-free 800/594-5566.* 27 rms, 9 kits. Mid-June-mid-Sep: S $40-$45; D $42-$55; each addl $5; kits. $39-$49; wkly rates; lower rates rest of yr. Pet accepted. TV; cable (premium), VCR avail. Pool; poolside serv. Bar from 5 pm. Ck-out 11 am. Business servs avail. 18-hole golf privileges. Cr cds: MC, V.

Hotel

★ ★ **BEST WESTERN GLENGARRY.** *150 Willow St (B2N 4Z6). 902/893-4311; fax 902/893-1759; toll-free 800/528-1234. Email bwglen@nsis. com; www.bwglengarry.com.* 90 rms, 3 story. June-Oct: S $86.96-$97.39; D $97.39-$115; each addl $10; suites $180; under 18 free; lower rates rest of yr. Pet accepted. TV; cable, VCR avail (movies). 2 pools, 1 indoor; wading pool, whirlpool, poolside serv. Restaurant 7 am-9 pm; Sun 8 am-8 pm. Bar 5 pm-1 am; entertainment. Ck-out 11 am. Meeting rms. Cr cds: A, C, D, DS, MC, V.

Yarmouth (G-3)

Pop 7,475 **Elev** 140 ft (43 m)
Area code 902
Web www.yarmouth.org
Information Yarmouth County Tourist Assn, PO Box 477, B5A 4B4; 902/742-5355

This historic seaport is the largest town southwest of Halifax and the gateway to Nova Scotia from New England. While the town of Yarmouth was first settled by New Englanders in 1761, the Yarmouth County area was previously inhabited by the MicMac and French Acadians. Today it serves as the hub of the fishing, shipping, and transportation industries of western Nova Scotia.

During the days of sail in the 1800s, this was one of the major shipbuilding and ship owning ports in the world. There is much evidence of this "Golden Age of Sail" to be found in the architecture of many of its fine old homes as well as ship paintings and artifacts exhibited in museums. Travel north on the Evangeline Trail, which passes through French Acadian settlements, fishing centers, and rich orchards and farmlands. South, follow the Lighthouse Route, which parallels the Atlantic coastline and passes near many picturesque lighthouses and fishing ports.

What to See and Do

Cape Forchu Lighthouse. Entrance to Bay of Fundy and Yarmouth Harbour. Route travels along rocky coastline and through colorful fishing villages. County park, picnicking. (Daily) On Cape Forchu Island, 7 mi (11 km) SW, linked by causeway to mainland. **FREE**

Ferry services.

The CAT. Advance res required. Passenger and car ferry service to Bar Harbor, ME. (June-Oct) For, rates, schedule, contact Bay Ferries. Phone 888/249-7245.

MS *Scotia Prince*. Advance res recommended. Passenger and car service between Yarmouth, NS and Portland, ME. (May-Oct, daily) For rates, res, schedule, contact Prince of Fundy Cruises, PO Box 4216, Portland, ME 04101. Phone 207/775-5616, 902/775-5611, 800/341-7540 (Canada and US exc ME), or 800/482-0955 (ME). ¢¢¢-¢¢¢¢

Firefighters' Museum of Nova Scotia. Permanent display of history of firefighting service, incl hand pumps, steamers, horse-drawn apparatus. Gift shop. (July-Aug, daily; rest of yr, Mon-Sat) 451 Main St. Phone 902/742-5525. ¢ In the museum is

National Exhibit Centre. Traveling exhibits change every 6 wks. Contact museum for schedule.

Frost Park. First town cemetery. Gazebo, fountain. Picnicking. Overlooks Yarmouth Harbour, on Water St.

Isaak Walton Killam Library. Unique memorial wall in park behind bldg.

405 Main St, between Parade and Grand Sts. Phone 902/742-5040.

Public wharves. Center of fishing fleet where herring seiners, inshore and offshore scallop draggers, and Cape Island boats can be seen. On Yarmouth Harbour, on each side of BAY Ferry Terminal.

Yarmouth Arts Regional Centre. Center for visual and performing arts for southwestern Nova Scotia (356-seat capacity). Summer theatre, drama, musical comedy, concerts, art shows, courses, workshops, seminars. 76 Parade St. Phone 902/742-8150. ¢¢¢¢

Yarmouth County Museum. Displays history of county with emphasis on Victorian period. Features marine exhibits, period rms, blacksmith shop, stagecoach. Of special interest is a runic stone, found near Yarmouth Harbour in 1812, bearing clear inscription alleged to be left by Leif Ericson on voyage in 1007; Yarmouth Lighthouse lens. (June-Sep, daily; rest of yr, Tues-Sat; closed hols) 22 Collins St. Phone 902/742-5539. ¢

Swordfishing

Annual Events

Festival Acadien de Wedgeport. Parade, costumes. Talent show, concerts, music. During Canada Day wk.

Seafest. Sporting events, entertainment, cultural productions; parade, Queen's Pageant. Fish feast; dory races. Phone 902/742-7585. Mid-July.

Western Nova Scotia Exhibition. Exhibition grounds. Animal judging, equestrian events, agricultural displays, craft demonstrations and exhibits, midway and entertainment; Canada/US ox hauls. Early Aug.

Yarmouth Cup Races. International yacht race; dockside entertainment. Windsurfing races; small craft races. Labour Day wkend.

Motels/Motor Lodges

★★ **BEST WESTERN MERMAID.** *545 Main St (B5A 1J6). 902/742-7821; fax 902/742-2966; res 800/772-2774; toll-free 800/528-1234. Email kelley@ fox.nstn.ca.* 45 rms, 2 story, 5 kits. No A/C. June-Oct: S, D $99-$110; each addl $8; kit. units $110-$135; under 18 free; lower rates rest of yr. Crib $6. Pet accepted, some restrictions. TV; cable. Heated pool. Restaurant nearby. Ck-out 11 am. Coin lndry. Business center. Some refrigerators. Deep sea fishing arranged. Cr cds: A, C, D, DS, ER, JCB, MC, V.

★★ **CAPRI MOTEL.** *8 Herbert St (B5A 1J6), off Main St. 902/742-7168; fax 902/742-2966; toll-free 800/722-2774. Email kelley@fox.nstn.ca.* 35 rms, some A/C, 2 story. S, D $89-$99; each addl $8; suites $95-$135. Crib $6. TV; cable (premium). Pool privileges. Complimentary continental bkfst. Restaurant adj 11:30 am-10 pm. Bar to 2 am. Ck-out 11 am. Business servs avail. Refrigerators avail. Balconies. Cr cds: A, C, D, DS, ER, JCB, MC, V.

★ **LAKELAWN MOTEL.** *641 Main St (B5A 1K2). 902/742-3588; fax 902/742-3588; toll-free 877/664-0664.* 31 rms, 2 story. No rm phones. July-Sep: S $50; D $60; each addl $5; under 12 free; lower rates May-June, Oct. Closed rest of yr. Crib free. Pet accepted, some restrictions. TV; cable. Full bkfst avail. Ck-out 11 am. Business servs avail. Free airport transportation. Cr cds: A, MC, V.

★ **LA REINE MOTEL.** *2 mi N on NS 1. 902/742-9154; fax 902/742-3262; res 902/742-7154.* 23 rms. No A/C. July-Aug: S $54, D $60-$64; each addl $6; under 12 free; lower rates June, Sep-mid-Oct. Closed rest of yr. Crib free. TV; cable (premium). Heated pool. Complimentary coffee in lobby. Restaurant adj 8 am-10 pm. Ck-out 11 am. Business servs avail. Picnic tables. On Doctors Lake. Cr cds: A, DS, MC, V.

★★ **ROAD COLONY HARBOUR INN.** *6 Forest St (B5A 3K8), at ferry terminal. 902/742-9194; fax 902/742-6291; res 800/565-7633.* 65 rms, 4 story, 8 suites. May-Sep: S $80; D $90; under 16 free; suites $101; lower rates rest of yr. Pet accepted. TV; cable, VCR avail (movies). Restaurant 7 am-11 pm. Bar noon-midnight. Meeting rms. Business servs avail. Valet serv. Airport transportation. Health club privileges. Microwaves avail. Cr cds: A, DS, MC, V.

★★ **VOYAGEUR.** *RR 1 (B5A 4A5), 2½ mi NE on Hwy 1. 902/742-7157; fax 902/742-1208.* 33 rms, 4 kits. Mid-June-mid-Sep: S, D $64; each addl $8; kits. $62-$82; family rates; lower rates rest of yr. Crib $6. TV; cable. Restaurant 7 am-10 pm. Ck-out 11 am. Business center. Whirlpool. Microwaves avail. Overlooks Doctors Lake. Cr cds: A, DS, MC, V.

Hotel

★★★ **RODD GRAND YARMOUTH.** *417 Main St (B5A 4B2), near Municipal Airport. 902/742-2446; fax 902/742-4645; res 800/565-7633. www.rodd-hotels.ca.* 138 air-cooled rms, 7 story. June-Oct: S, D $95-$105; each addl $10; suites $120-$130; under 16 free; lower rates rest of yr. Crib free. Pet accepted. TV; cable. Indoor pool. Restaurants 6:30 am-9 pm. Bar 11-1 am. Ck-out 11 am. Meeting rms. Business center. In-rm modem link. Shopping arcade. Free airport, bus depot transportation. Exercise equipt. Microwaves avail. Cr cds: A, DS, MC, V.

B&B/Small Inn

★★★ **THE MANOR INN.** *417 Main St (B0W 1X0), 5 mi N on Hwy 1E. 902/742-2487; fax 902/742-8094; res 888/626-6746; toll-free 800/626-6746. Email manorinn@fox.nstn.ca; www.nsonline.com/manorinn.* 54 rms, 2 story. Mid-June-Sep: S, D $72-$107; under 16 free; lower rates rest of yr. Crib $12. Pet accepted. TV; cable, VCR avail (movies). Heated pool. Dining rm 7-11 am, 5:30-9:30 pm. Sun brunch 11 am-2 pm. Ck-out 11 am, ck-in 2 pm. Business servs avail. Tennis. Lawn games. Microwaves avail. Some balconies. Picnic tables. Rms in Colonial-style inn (ca 1920), coach house, and motel bldg; antiques. Nine landscaped acres on Doctor's Lake; private dock. Cr cds: A, C, D, DS, ER, MC, V.

Restaurants

★★ **AUSTRIAN INN.** *Hwy 1, 3 mi E, Exit 103. 902/742-6202.* Specializes in seafood, veal. Own desserts. Hrs: 11 am-10 pm; Sun-Tues to 9 pm. Closed mid-Dec-Mar. Res accepted. Bar. Lunch $5.35-$19.85; dinner $9.65-$19.85. Sun brunch $11.50. Child's menu. Cr cds: A, MC, V.

★ **CHINA COURT.** *67 Starrs Rd. 902/742-9128.* Hrs: 11 am-8 pm; Fri, Sat to 11 pm; Sun from 11:30 am; Sun brunch to 2:30 pm. Closed hols. Res accepted. Bar. Lunch $3.99-$7.75; dinner $2-$14. Sun brunch $5.95-$10.95. Child's menu. Entertainment. Chinese decor. Cr cds: A, MC, V.

★ **PRINCE ARTHUR STEAK AND SEAFOOD HOUSE.** *73 Starrs Rd (B5A 2T6). 902/742-1129.* Continental menu. Specializes in T-bone steak, shrimp, lobster. Hrs: 11 am-9:30 pm; Sun, Mon 9 am-9 pm; hrs vary off-season. Closed Dec 25. Res accepted. Bar. Bkfst $4.99; lunch $4.99; dinner $9.95-$24.95. Sun brunch $9.95-$11.95. Child's menu. Family-owned. Cr cds: A, D, ER, MC, V.

Province of Ontario

Although first explored by Samuel de Champlain in the 17th century, the Ontario region was not heavily settled until the 18th century by Loyalist refugees from the American Revolution. British settled in what was to become Ontario while French populated Québec. Two territories were formed following the battle of 1759; in 1867 they became provinces in the Dominion of Canada.

This vast province can be divided into northern and southern Ontario; the far northern wilderness dominated by lakes, forests, and logging camps; the southern agricultural and industrial section inhabited by nine-tenths of the population. The province is easily accessible from many points across the United States, with each area offering exciting and beautiful sights for the traveler.

Certainly one of the most spectacular sights is Niagara Falls. Cosmopolitan Toronto, the provincial capital, and Ottawa, the country's capital, offer the tourist a wide spectrum of experiences including theater, fine restaurants, galleries, museums, and recreational facilities. The Stratford Festival in Stratford, the Shaw Festival in Niagara-on-the-Lake, and Upper Canada Village in Morrisburg are not to be missed.

Ontario is also known for its many recreational areas, such as Algonquin and Quetico provincial parks and St. Lawrence Islands National Park. To the north lie Sudbury and Sault Ste. Marie; to the northwest, Thunder Bay, Fort Frances, and Kenora, offering a variety of wilderness activities including canoeing, fishing, and hunting. Perhaps more appealing than any one attraction is the vast, unspoiled nature of the province itself. More than 400,000 lakes and magnificent forests form a huge vacationland just a few miles from the US border, stretching all the way to Hudson Bay.

Ontario lies mostly within the Eastern Time Zone. Travelers should note that fees are charged at international bridges, tunnels, and ferries.

In addition to national holidays, Ontario observes Simcoe Day (first Monday in August).

Safety belts are mandatory for all persons anywhere in vehicle. Children under 40 pounds in weight must be in an approved safety seat anywhere in vehicle.

Pop 9,101,690 **Land area** 412,582 sq mi (1,068,175 sq km)
Capital Toronto
Web www.ontario-canada.com
Information Ministry of Economic Development, Trade, and Tourism, Queen's Park, Toronto M7A 2E1; 800/ONTARIO

Brantford (E-4)

(E-6) See also Hamilton, Stratford

Founded 1784 **Pop** 81,290 **Elev** 815 ft (248 m) **Area code** 519

Information Tourism Brantford, 1 Sherwood Dr, N3T 1N3; 519/751-9900 or 800/265-6299

Brantford is located in the heart of southwestern Ontario along Grand River, a Canadian Heritage River. Captain Joseph Brant, leader of the Iroquois First Nations, crossed the river in 1784. It was through Native and European settlements that Brantford was born. Brantford is equally famous as the place where Alexander Graham Bell lived and invented the telephone.

What to See and Do

Bell Homestead. The house is furnished just as it was when Alexander Graham Bell lived here in the 1870s. Also located here are the first telephone office and artifacts housed in a display center (Tues-Sun; closed Jan 1, Thanksgiving, Dec 25). 57 Charlotte St. Phone 519/756-6220. ¢

Brant County Museum. Collection of Native American artifacts, life histories of Captain Joseph Brant and Pauline Johnson. Also displays of pioneer life in Brant County, incl Brant Square and Brant Corners, where former businesses are depicted. (Wed-Sat; also Sun June-Aug; closed Jan 1, Thanksgiving, Dec 25) 57 Charlotte St. Phone 519/752-2483. ¢

Glenhyrst Art Gallery of Brant. Gallery with changing exhibits of paintings, sculpture, photography, and crafts surrounded by 16-acre (7-hectare) estate overlooking the Grand River. Beautiful grounds and nature trail. (Tues-Sun; closed hols) 20 Ava Rd. Phone 519/756-5932. **FREE**

Her Majesty's Royal Chapel of the Mohawks. (1785) The first Protestant church in Ontario, the "Mohawk Chapel" is the only Royal Native Chapel in the world belonging to six Nations people. (May-June, Wed-Sun afternoons; July-Labour Day, daily; Sep-mid-Oct, Sat and Sun afternoons) 190 Mohawk St. Phone 519/445-4528. ¢¢

Myrtleville House Museum. (1837) Georgian house is one of the oldest in Brant County; original furniture of the Good family, who lived here for more than 150 yrs. On 5½ acres (2 hectares) of parkland. Picnicking. (Mid-Apr-mid-Sep, Tues-Sun; closed hols) 34 Myrtleville Dr. Phone 519/752-3216. ¢

Riverboat Cruises. Big Creek Boat Farm. Dinner cruises on the Grand River. (Mid-May-Sep; res required) ON 54, 4 mi (6.4 km) W of Caledonia. Phone 905/765-4107. ¢¢¢¢

Sanderson Centre for the Performing Arts. This 1919 vaudeville house has been restored and transformed to a theater featuring music, dance, and dramatic performances. 88 Dalhousie St. Phone 519/758-8090 or 800/265-0710.

Woodland Cultural Centre. Preserves and promotes culture and heritage of first Nations of eastern woodland area. Education, research, and museum programs; art shows, festivals. (Daily; closed hols) 184 Mohawk St. Phone 519/759-2650. Museum ¢¢

Annual Events

Riverfest. Three-day festival celebrates the Grand River. Entertainment, fireworks, crafts. Children's activities. Last wkend May. Phone 519/751-9900.

International Villages Festival. Ethnic villages celebrate with ethnic folk dancing, pageantry, and food. Early July.

Six Nations Native Pageant. Forest Theatre, Sour Springs Rd, at Six Nations reserve. Six Nations people reenact their history and culture in natural forest amphitheater. First 3 wkends Fri, Sat Aug. Phone 519/445-4528.

Six Nations Native Fall Fair. Ohsweken Fairgrounds. Native dances, authentic craft and art exhibits. Phone 519/445-4528. Wkend after Labour Day. Phone 519/445-4528.

Motels/Motor Lodges

★★ **BEST WESTERN BRANT PARK INN.** *19 Holiday Dr (N3T 5W5), Park Rd Exit. 519/753-8651; fax 519/753-2619. Email kbrown@bfree.on.ca; www.bestwestern.com/thisco/bw/66036/66036_b.html.* 115 rms, 2 story. June-Sep: S $64.95; D $77.95; each addl $7; under 12 free; lower rates rest of yr. Crib free. TV; cable. Heated pool; wading pool, whirlpool, lifeguard. Playground. Restaurant 6:30 am-9:30 pm. Ck-out 11 am. Meeting rms. Business servs avail. In-rm modem link. Bellhops. Valet serv. Exercise equipt; sauna. Private patios; some balconies. Cr cds: A, D, DS, ER, MC, V.

D ≈ 🐾 ⇄ 🔥 SC

★ **DAYS INN.** *460 Fairview Dr (N3R 7A9). 519/759-2700; fax 519/759-2089. www.daysinn.com/daysinn.html.* 75 rms, 2 story. Apr-Oct: S $56.95; D $66.95; each addl $7; under 12 free; wkly, wkend rates; lower rates rest of yr. Crib free. Pet accepted. TV; cable (premium). Pool privileges. Complimentary coffee in rms. Restaurant 7-1 am. Ck-out 11 am. Meeting rms. Business servs avail. In-rm modem link. Health club privileges. Cr cds: A, D, DS, ER, JCB, MC, V.

D 🐾 ⇄ 🔥 SC

★★ **RAMADA INN.** *664 Colborne St (N3S 3P8). 519/758-9999; fax 519/758-1515; res 800/272-6232. www.ramada.ca.* 98 rms, 2-3 story. No elvtr. May-Sep: S, D $79-$105; each addl $5; under 18 free; family rates; package plans; lower rates rest of yr. Crib free. TV; cable (premium); VCR avail. Complimentary coffee in rms. Restaurant 6:30 am-10 pm. Bar 11-2 am. Ck-out noon. Meeting rms. Business servs avail. In-rm modem link. Bellhops. Valet serv. Sundries. Coin lndry. Tennis privileges. Golf privileges. Downhill ski 6 mi; x-country ski 1 mi. Exercise equipt; sauna. Indoor pool; poolside serv. Game rm. Microwaves avail. Many balconies. Cr cds: A, D, ER, JCB, MC, V.

≈ 🎿 ≈ 🐾 ⇄ 🔥 SC

Restaurant

★★ **OLDE SCHOOL RESTAURANT.** *Hwy 2 W and Powerline Rd W (N3T 5M1). 519/753-3131.* Specializes in steak, seafood. Hrs: 11:30 am-10:30 pm; Sat from 5 pm; Sun brunch 11 am-3 pm. Closed Dec 25. Res accepted; required Sat. Bar. Lunch $6.95-$12.95; dinner $18.95-$26.95. Complete meals: (Mon-Fri) $12.95. Sun brunch $10.95. Entertainment: piano lounge. Restored 1850s schoolhouse; antiques, pioneer and school memorabilia. Cr cds: A, D, DS, ER, MC, V.

D ⇄

⛽

Brockville (C-7)

Settled 1784 **Pop** 21,000 (est)
Elev 300 ft (91 m) **Area code** 613
Web www.brockville.com

Information Tourism Office, 1 King St W, PO Box 5000, K6V 7A5; 613/342-8772, ext 430

Settled by United Empire Loyalists, the town was known as Elizabethtown until 1812 when it was named Brockville after Major General Sir Isaac Brock. It was incorporated as a town in 1832, the first in Ontario. Brockville is the eastern gateway to the Thousand Islands on the St. Lawrence River. It is home to the oldest railway tunnel in Canada, which runs one-quarter of a mile under the city to the riverfront. The city features many Victorian homes along with a historic downtown business section with numerous buildings more than 100 years old.

What to See and Do

Brockville Museum. Devoted to history surrounding the city. Exhibits, workshops, afternoon teas. 5 Henry St. Phone 613/342-4397. ¢¢¢

Thousand Island Cruises. Aboard the *General Brock.* Shallow-draft boat makes trips (1 hr) through heart of the region, incl Millionaires Row and many smaller channels inaccessible to larger boats. (May-late Oct, daily) 14 mi (23 km) W via Hwy 401 to 1000 Islands Pkwy. Phone 613/659-3402 or 800/563-8687. ¢¢¢¢

Annual Events

Great Balloon Rodeo. Mid-June.

Riverfest. Waterfront. Mid-June-early July.

Poker Run. Mid-Aug.

Motels/Motor Lodges

★★ **BEST WESTERN WHITE HOUSE.** *1843 Hwy 2 E (K6V 5T1), 1½ mi E.* 613/345-1622; fax 613/345-4284. 56 rms. S $67; D $72-$77; each addl $5. Crib $5. Pet accepted. TV. Heated pool. Complimentary continental bkfst, coffee in rms. Restaurant 6:30 am-2 pm, 5-9 pm. Ck-out 11 am. Meeting rms. Business servs avail. In-rm modem link. Sundries. Picnic tables. Cr cds: A, C, D, DS, ER, MC, V.

★ **DAYS INN.** *160 Stewart Blvd (K6V 4W6), Hwy 401 Exit 696.* 613/342-6613; fax 613/345-3811. 56 rms, 2 story. Mid-June-mid-Oct: S $57-$64; D $72-$74; each addl $7; under 17 free; lower rates rest of yr. Crib free. TV; cable (premium). Pool. Complimentary coffee in rms. Restaurant 11 am-2 pm, 4:30-9 pm. Bar noon-1 am. Ck-out 11 am. Meeting rms. Business servs avail. Picnic tables. Cr cds: A, C, D, DS, ER, JCB, MC, V.

Hotel

★★★ **ROYAL BROCK.** *100 Stewart Blvd (K6V 4W3), off 401, on 29S Exit 696.* 613/345-1400; fax 613/345-5402. 72 rms, 5 story. S $112-$128; D $124-$140; each addl $12; suites $235-$247; studio rms $121-$133; under 16 free. Crib free. TV; cable (premium). Indoor pool; whirlpool, poolside serv. Supervised children's activities. Restaurant 6:30 am-11 pm. Bar 11:30-2 am; entertainment Mon-Sat. Ck-out noon. Meeting rms. Business servs avail. In-rm modem link. Beauty shop. Tennis. Exercise rm; sauna, steam rm. Massage. Cr cds: A, C, D, DS, ER, JCB, MC, V.

Cornwall

(B-8) *See also Morrisburg*

Pop 46,144 **Elev** 200 ft (62 m)
Area code 613
Web www.visit.cornwall.on.ca

Information Cornwall and Seaway Valley Tourism, Gray's Creek, PO Box 36, K6H 5R9; 800/937-4748

Cornwall is a thriving community located on the banks of the St. Lawrence River. It is connected to Massena, New York by the Seaway International Toll Bridge. The Robert H. Saunders Generating Station, one of the largest international generating stations in the world, is here.

What to See and Do

Inverarden Regency Cottage Museum. (1816) Retirement home of fur trader John McDonald of Garth. Collection of Canadian and English Georgian furniture; houses local picture archives. Tea rm (Sun in summer). (Apr-mid-Nov, daily; rest of yr by appt) Montreal & Boundary Rds. Phone 613/938-9585. **FREE**

Long Sault Parkway. A 6½-mi (10 km) causeway loop connects 11 islands in the St. Lawrence River between Long Sault and Ingleside; 1,300 scenic acres (526 hectares) with beaches and campsites. Toll. 8 mi (13 km) W off ON 2.

United Counties Museum. Old stone house has displays showing early life of the United Empire Loyalists. (Apr-late Nov, daily) 731 Second St W. Phone 613/932-2381. **FREE**

Upper Canada Village. 25 mi (40 km) W on ON 2 in Morrisburg (see).

Annual Events

Raisin River Canoe Races. On Raisin River. Mid-Apr.

Worldfest/Festimonde. Cornwall Civic Complex. Intl folk festival; ethnic music, dancing, displays, costumes. Six days early July.

Williamstown Fair. Mid-Aug.

Awesome August Festival. Balloon lift-off, Cornfest, performances. Mid-Aug.

Motel/Motor Lodge

★★ **BEST WESTERN PARKWAY INN.** *1515 Vincent Massey Dr (K6H 5R6), Hwy 2.* 613/932-0451; fax 613/938-5479. 91 rms, 2 story. S $86; D $110-$145; each addl $6; suites $200; under 18 free. Crib free. Pet accepted. TV; cable (premium). Pool; whirlpool. Coffee in rms. Restaurant 6:30 am-10 pm; Sun to 9 pm. Bar 11-2 am. Ck-out noon. Meeting rms. Business servs avail. In-rm modem link. Valet serv. X-country ski 2 mi. Exercise equipt; sauna. Refrigerators, some fire-places. Cr cds: A, C, D, ER, MC, V.

Fort Frances (F-5)

Pop 8,906 **Elev** 1,100 ft (335 m)
Area code 807
Information Chamber of Commerce, 474 Scott St, P9A 1H2; 807/274-5773 or 800/820-FORT

Across the river from International Falls, Minnesota, Fort Frances is a prosperous paper town and an important border crossing point for visitors from the United States heading for northwestern Canadian destinations. "The Fort" is a popular summer resort town. It is also a major fly-in center for the vast wilderness areas to the north and east, a region of 40,000 lakes.

What to See and Do

Fort Frances Museum. This small museum has changing displays dealing with the indigenous era, the fur trade, and later settlement. (Mid-June-Labour Day, daily; rest of yr, Mon-Sat; closed hols) 259 Scott St. Phone 807/274-7891. Summer admission ¢

Industrial tour. Abitibi Consolidated. The paper manufacturing process is followed from debarking of the logs to the finished paper. (June-Aug, Mon-Fri, by res only) Ages 12 yrs and over only; flat, closed-toe shoes required. 145 3rd St W. Phone 807/274-5311. **FREE**

Noden Causeway. Excellent island views may be seen from this network of bridges. E on ON 11.

Pither's Point Park. This beautiful park has a reconstructed fort, logging tugboat, and a lookout tower with a pioneer logging museum at its base. Tower, fort, and boat (mid-June-Labour Day, daily). Campground (fee) with swimming beach, fishing, boating (rentals adj to park); playground, fitness trail, cafe. (Late June-Labour Day). On Rainy Lake. Phone 807/274-5087 or 807/274-5502. **FREE** Museum ¢

Annual Events

Culturama Festival. Early May.

Fun in the Sun Festival. Late June.

Motel/Motor Lodge

★★ **LA PLACE RENDEZ-VOUS.** *1201 Idylwild Dr (P9A 3M3), 1 mi E on Hwy 11, adj Pither's Point Park.* 807/274-9811; fax 807/274-9553. 54 units, 1-2 story. S $85-$90; D $92-$97; each addl $7; under 12 free. Crib free. TV; cable, VCR avail. Restaurant (see also LA PLACE RENDEZ-VOUS). Bar 11-1 am. Ck-out 11 am. Meeting rms. Business servs avail. In-rm modem link. Whirlpool. Sauna. Some balconies. Picnic tables. On Rainy Lake; swimming beach. Cr cds: A, MC, V.

Restaurant

★★ **LA PLACE RENDEZ-VOUS.** *1201 Idylwild Dr.* 807/274-9811. *www.rendezvoushotel.com.* Specializes in prime rib, walleye. Hrs: 6 am-10 pm. Closed Dec 25. Res accepted. Bar. Bkfst $2.95-$9.95; lunch $4.95-$10.95; dinner $10.50-$19.95. Child's menu. Overlooks Rainy Lake. Family-owned. Cr cds: A, MC, V.

Gananoque

(C-7) *See also Kingston*

Pop 4,863 **Elev** 300 ft (91 m)
Area code 613
Web www.1000islands.on.calgon

Information 1000 Islands Gananoque Chamber of Commerce, 2 King St E, K7G 1E6; 613/382-3250 or 800/561-1595

What to See and Do

1000 Islands Camping Resort. Campground area with pool; tent and trailer sites (hookups, showers, dump station), playground, nature trails, miniature golf (fee). Store, snack bar. Coin lndry. (Mid-May-mid-Oct, daily) 1000 Islands Pkwy, 5 mi (8 km) E. Phone 613/659-3058. Within the park is

Giant Waterslide. A 175-ft (53-m) water slide. (Mid-June-Labour Day, daily) Per hr ¢¢

1000 Islands Skydeck. Atop 400-ft (146-m) tower; elevator to 3 observation decks. (Early May-late Oct, daily) Between spans of the Thousand Islands Intl Bridge, on Hill Island, Lansdowne. Phone 613/659-2335. ¢¢

Baskin Robbins Putt 'n Play. An 18-hole miniature golf course. (May-Oct, daily) 787 King St E. Phone 613/382-7888. ¢¢

Gananoque Boat Line. Three-hr tours through the 1000 Islands with a stop at Boldt Castle; snack bar. (Mid-May-mid-Oct; 1-hr trips July-Aug) Water St. Phone 613/382-2146. ¢¢¢¢

Gananoque Historical Museum. Former Victoria Hotel (1863); parlour, dining rm, bedrm, kitchen furnished in Victorian style. Military and indigenous artifacts; china, glass, 19th- and 20th-century costumes. (June-Oct, daily) 10 King St E. Phone 613/382-4024. ¢

St. Lawrence Islands National Park. (see) 14 mi (30 km) E.

Motels/Motor Lodges

★★ **BEST WESTERN PROVINCIAL.** *846 King St E (K7G 1H3), Hwy 2. 613/382-2038; fax 613/382-8663.* 78 rms. July-Labour Day: S $68-$80; D $78-$98; each addl $6; lower rates Mar-June, after Labour Day-Oct. Closed rest of yr. Crib $6. TV; cable. Heated pool. Restaurant 7:30 am-9:30 pm; off-season to 9 pm. Bar noon-10 pm. Ck-out 11 am. Sundries. Gift shop. Lighted tennis. Some in-rm whirlpools. Cr cds: A, C, D, DS, ER, MC, V.
🅳 🐾 🔽 🖳 🗻 SC

★ **DAYS INN.** *650 King St E (K7G 1H3). 613/382-7292; fax 613/382-4387. Email daysinn@gananoque.com; www.daysinn.com.* 34 rms, 2 story. Late June-Labor Day: S, D $89-$139; suites $149-$189; under 18 free; lower rates rest of yr. Crib free. TV; cable, VCR avail (movies). Heated pool. Complimentary coffee in rms. Restaurant 8 am-10 pm; off-season 11 am-9 pm. Serv bar. Ck-out 11 am. Meeting rms. Business servs avail. Fireplace, in-rm whirlpool in suites. Cr cds: A, C, D, DS, ER, JCB, MC, V.
🅳 🔽 🖳 🗻 SC

★★★ **GANANOQUE INN.** *550 Stone St S (K7G 2A8). 613/382-2165; fax 613/382-7912; res 800/465-3101.* 50 rms, 3 story. No elvtr. Early June-early Sep: S, D $95-$165; suites $120-$250; lower rates rest of yr. Crib free. TV; cable. Restaurant 7 am-11 pm. Bar 11:30-2 am, entertainment Thurs-Sat. Business servs avail. Ck-out 11 am. X-country ski 5 mi. Bicycle, boat rentals. Health club privileges. Some in-rm whirlpools. Balconies. Cr cds: A, ER, JCB, MC, V.
🛗 🔽 🖳 🗻 🧍

B&B/Small Inn

★★★ **TRINITY HOUSE.** *90 Stone St S (K7G 1Z8). 613/382-8383; fax 613/382-1599. Email trinity@kingston.net; www.trinityinn.com.* 8 rms, 3 story, 2 suites. No rm phones. S, D $75-$150; suites $135-$190; MAP avail. TV; cable, VCR avail. Complimentary continental bkfst. Dining rm (public by res) sittings from 5:30 pm; closed Mon. Bar. Ck-out 10 am, ck-in 2 pm. Business servs avail. Victorian mansion (1859) built with bricks imported from Scotland. Victorian gardens. Sun deck overlooking waterfalls. Cr cds: MC, V.
🔽 🗻

Restaurant

★★ **GOLDEN APPLE.** *45 King St W (K7G 2G1), Hwy 2.* 613/382-3300. African menu. Specializes in prime rib, roast lamb, seafood. Hrs: 11 am-9 pm; Sun brunch to 3 pm. Closed Jan-Mar. Res accepted. Lunch a la carte entrees: $5.95-$12.95; dinner complete meals: $14.95-$29.95. Sun brunch $11.95. Child's menu. Converted 1830 mansion; antiques. Exposed stone walls. Cr cds: A, MC, V.

D

Hamilton

(D-4) *See also Brantford, Mississauga, St. Catharines, Toronto*

Pop 306,434 **Elev** 776 ft (237 m)
Area code 905 **Web** www.hamilton-went.on.ca
Information Greater Hamilton Visitor and Convention Services, 1 James St S, 3rd floor, L8P 4R5; 905/546-4222

Thriving both industrially and culturally, Hamilton is Canada's largest steel center. It is located on Hamilton Harbour, spanned by the majestic Skyway Bridge to Toronto, which offers excellent views of the city.

What to See and Do

African Lion Safari. Drive-through wildlife park; exotic animal and bird shows, demonstrations. Admission incl large game reserves, *African Queen* boat, shows, scenic railway; play areas. Camping (June-Sep, fee). Park (Apr-Oct, daily). W on Hwy 8 between Hamilton & Cambridge, on Safari Rd. Phone 519/623-2620. ¢¢¢¢

Andrés Wines. Escorted tours and tastings. (Apr-Dec, daily; rest of yr, by appt) Wine shop. 5 mi (8 km) W at Kelson Rd & S Service Rd, in Grimsby. Phone 905/643-TOUR. ¢

Art Gallery of Hamilton. Collection of more than 8,000 photographs, sculptures, and photographs covering several centuries, by American, Canadian, British, and European artists. Impressive bldg; many intl, national, and regional exhibitions. (Wed-Sun; closed hols) Fee may be higher for some shows. 123 King St W. Phone 905/527-6610. ¢

Battlefield House and Monument. Devoted to the "Battle of Stoney Creek," this 1795 settler's home and monument honors one of the most significant encounters of the War of 1812. Some rms furnished as a farm home of the 1830s. Guides in period costumes. (Open for tours; mid-May-June and early Sep-mid-Oct, Sun-Fri; July-Labour Day, daily; rest of yr, by appt) QEW Exit at Centennial Pkwy, 77 King St in Stoney Creek. Phone 905/662-8458. ¢

Ben Veldhuis Limited. More than 2 acres (1 hectare) of greenhouses; thousands of varieties of cacti, succulents, St. Paulias, and hibiscus; flowering tropical plants. Hibisci bloom all yr. (Daily; closed Jan 1, Dec 25) 154 King St E, off ON 8, W in Dundas. Phone 905/628-6307. **FREE**

Canadian Football Hall of Fame and Museum. Sports museum and national shrine tracing 120 yrs of history of Canadian football. (Daily; closed Sun in winter and spring) 58 Jackson St W. Phone 905/528-7566. ¢¢

Children's Museum. Participatory learning center where children ages 2-13 can expand sensory awareness of the world. "Hands-on" exhibits; changing theme exhibits. (Tues-Sun; closed Dec 25, 26, also Jan and Sep) 1072 Main St E. Phone 905/546-4848. Adults free with child. Per child ¢¢

Dundurn Castle. Home of Sir Allan Napier MacNab, Prime Minister of the United Provinces of Canada (1854-56). The 35-rm mansion is restored to its former splendor. Exhibits, programs, special events featured all yr. Castle (late May-Labour Day and Dec, daily; rest of yr, Tues-Sun; closed Jan 1, Dec 25). 610 York Blvd. Phone 905/546-2872. ¢¢¢

> **Hamilton Military Museum.** Displays Canadian uniforms, equipment, and weapons from ca 1800. (Late May-Labour Day and Dec, daily; rest of yr, Tues-Sun; closed Jan 1, Dec 25) Dundurn Park. Phone 905/546-4974. ¢

Flamboro Downs. Harness racing (all yr). Grandstand seats 3,000; restaurants, lounges. Confederation Cup race for top 3-yr-old pacers in North America held here (Aug). 967 Hwy 5, W in Flamborough. Phone 905/627-3561. ¢¢

Hamilton Place. Live theater and concerts featuring intl artists in a spectacular cultural center. (All yr) 10 MacNab St S. Phone 905/546-3100.

Hamilton's Farmers' Market. Fresh produce, flowers, meat, poultry, fish, cheese, and baked goods are brought from all over the Niagara garden belt. (Tues, Thurs-Sat) 55 York Blvd. Phone 905/546-2096.

Museum of Steam and Technology. An 1859 pumping station contains unique examples of 19th-century steam technology; gallery features permanent and temporary exhibits on modern technology; also special events. Guided tours (daily; closed Jan 1, Dec 25). 900 Woodward Ave. Phone 905/546-4797. ¢¢

Ontario Workers Art & Heritage Centre. Canada's only museum dedicated to preserving the legacy of labor and working people. Incl public resource center, cafe, reading rm, and gift shop. (Wed-Sun) 51 Stuart St. Phone 905/522-3003.
Donation

Royal Botanical Gardens. Colorful gardens, natural areas, and a wildlife sanctuary. Rock Garden with seasonal displays; Laking Garden (herbaceous perennials); Arboretum (world-famous lilacs in late May); Rose Garden; Teaching Garden; woodland, scented, and medicinal gardens. At Cootes Paradise Sanctuary trails wind around more than 1,200 acres (486 hectares) of water, marsh, and wooded ravines. Mediterranean Garden greenhouse wing has particularly interesting displays (fee). Guided tours (fee). Peak period for gardens: May-Sep. (All yr, daily) Information Centre. 680 Plains Rd W at ON 2, 6, and 403. Phone 905/527-1158. ¢¢¢

Whitehern. Former home of the McQuesten family; 19th-century Georgian mansion furnished with original family possessions. Landscaped gardens. (June-Labour Day, daily; rest of yr, Tues-Sun afternoons; closed Jan 1, Dec 25) Jackson St W & McNab Sts. Phone 905/522-2018. ¢¢

Annual Events

Around the Bay Road Race. Canada's oldest footrace (1894). Phone 905/624-0046. Late Mar.

Hamilton International Air Show. Hamilton Civic Airport. Large intl air show. Phone 905/528-4425. Mid-June.

Festival of Friends. Musicians, artists, craftsmen, puppets, dance, mime, theater. Phone 905/525-6644. Second wkend Aug.

Festitalia. Opera, concerts, bicycle race, fashion shows, ethnic foods. Phone 905/529-3498. Mid-Sep.

Hamilton Mum Show. Gage Park, in greenhouses. More than 6,000 blooms. Phone 905/546-2866. First 2 wks Nov.

Motels/Motor Lodges

★★ **ADMIRAL INN.** *3500 Billings Ct (L7N 3N6), N via Hwy 2/6 or QEW. 905/639-4780; fax 905/639-1967.* 67 rms, 2 story. S $54.95; D $62.95; each addl $4; under 12 free. Crib free. TV; cable (premium). Restaurant 7 am-11 pm. Bar 11 am-11 pm. Ck-out 11 am. Meeting rms. Business servs avail. Valet serv. Cr cds: A, D, ER, MC, V.
D ⊠ 🐾 SC

★★ **ADMIRAL INN.** *149 Dundurn St N (L8R 3E7). 905/529-2311; fax 905/529-9100.* 58 rms, 3 story. S $59.95; D $63.95; each addl $4; suites $79.95; under 12 free. Crib free. TV; cable (premium), VCR avail. Restaurant 7 am-11 pm. Ck-out 1 am. Meeting rms. Business servs avail. Valet serv. Downhill/x-country ski 10 mi. Microwaves avail. Cr cds: A, D, MC, V.
🏊 ⊠ 🐾 SC

★ **DAYS INN.** *1187 Upper James St (L9C 3B2). 905/575-9666; fax 905/575-1098. www.daysinn.com/daysinn.html.* 30 rms, 2 story. Late May-late Sep: S $47-$69; D $55-$89; each addl $7; under 13 free; lower rates rest of yr. Crib free. TV; cable (premium), VCR avail. Complimentary coffee in lobby. Restaurant open 24 hrs. Bar. Ck-out 11 am. Meeting rms. Business servs avail. In-rm modem link. Downhill ski 7 mi. Health club privileges. Some refrigerators; microwaves avail. Cr cds: A, D, DS, ER, MC, V.
🏊 ⊠ 🐾 SC

★ **ECONO LODGE.** *175 Main St W (L8P 1J1). 905/528-0611; fax 905/528-1130. www.qualityinn.com.* 57 rms, 2 story. Apr-Sep: S $54.95-$64.95; D $64.95-$74.95; each addl $8; suite $94.29; under 18 free; wkly, hol rates; higher rates wkends (2-day min); lower rates rest of yr. Crib free. TV. Restaurant 7 am-9 pm. Meeting rms. Business servs avail. In-rm modem link. Downhill/x-country ski 15 mi. Microwaves avail. Cr cds: A, C, D, ER, MC, V.

Upper Canada Village, Ontario

★★ **VENTURE INN.** *2020 Lakeshore Rd (L7S 1Y2), N via Hwy 2/6 or QEW. 905/681-0762; fax 905/634-4398. www.ventureinns.com.* 122 rms, 7 story. S $95; D $105; each addl $10; suites $159; under 18 free. Crib free. Pet accepted, some restrictions. TV. Indoor pool; whirlpool. Continental bkfst. Restaurant adj 7-2 am; Sat, Sun 9 am-midnight. Bar; entertainment. Meeting rms. Business servs avail. Valet serv. Sauna. Sun deck. Picnic tables. Opp lake, beach. Cr cds: A, D, DS, ER, MC, V.

Hotels

★ **HOWARD JOHNSON.** *112 King St E (L8N 1A8). 905/546-8111; fax 905/546-8144.* 206 rms, 11 story. S $99; D $109; each addl $10; suites from $139; under 18 free; wkend rates. Crib free. Pet accepted. TV; cable (premium), VCR avail. Indoor pool; whirlpool. Coffee in rms. Restaurant open 24 hrs. Bars 11-2 am. Ck-out noon. Meeting rms. Business servs avail. Barber, beauty shop. Exercise equipt; sauna. Some refrigerators, minibars; microwaves avail. 124-ft (38-m) pool slide. Cr cds: A, C, D, DS, ER, MC, V.

★★ **RAMADA.** *150 King St E (L8N 1B2). 905/528-3451; fax 905/522-2281.* 215 rms, 12 story. S, D $69-$110; each addl $10; suites $187.50-$325; under 19 free. Crib free. Pet accepted. TV; cable, VCR avail. Heated pool; wading pool, whirlpool. Restaurant 7 am-9 pm. Bar Fri-Sat 5:30 pm-2 am. Ck-out 11 am. Meeting rms. Business servs avail. Shopping arcade. Barber, beauty shop. Exercise equipt; sauna. Health club privileges. Refrigerators, microwaves avail. Cr cds: A, C, D, DS, ER, MC, V.

★★★ **SHERATON.** *116 King St W (L8P 4V3), in Lloyd D. Jackson Sq. 905/529-5515; fax 905/529-8266. Email shsales@netaccess.on.ca; www. sheraton.com.* 299 units, 18 story. S, D $185-$200; each addl $15; suites from $225; under 17 free; wkend rates. Crib free. Pet accepted. Parking $7.99. TV; cable (premium). Indoor pool; whirlpool. Complimentary coffee in rms. Restaurant 6:30 am-10:30 pm. Rm serv to 1 am. Bar 11-2 am; entertainment. Ck-out noon. Convention facilities. Business center. In-rm modem link. Shopping arcade. Barber, beauty shop. Downhill/x-country ski 4 mi. Exercise equipt; sauna. Health club privileges. Bathrm phones; microwaves avail. Direct access to Convention Centre and Hamilton Place Concert Hall. Cr cds: A, C, D, DS, ER, JCB, MC, V.

Restaurants

★★★ **ANCASTER OLD MILL INN.** *548 Old Dundas Rd (L9G 3J4), off ON 403 to Mohawk Rd W, then ½ mi to Old Dundas Rd. 905/648-1827.* Specializes in steak, prime rib, fresh

seafood. Own baking. Hrs: 11:30 am-
8:30 pm; Fri, Sat to 9:30 pm; Sun
9:30 am-8:30 pm. Res accepted. Bar.
Wine list. Lunch a la carte entrees:
$9.47-$12.97; dinner a la carte
entrees: $16.95-$24.95. Sun brunch
$22.97. Child's menu. Entertain-
ment: pianist wkends. Originally a
gristmill (1792); tour. Cr cds: A, D,
ER, MC, V.

D

★★★ **SHAKESPEARE'S DINING
LOUNGE.** *181 Main St E (L8N 1H2).
905/528-0689. www.hamilton
shakespeares.com.* Specializes in steak,
seafood, wild game. Hrs: 11:30 am-10
pm; Sat 5-11 pm. Closed Sun; Jan 1,
Dec 25. Res accepted. Bar. Lunch a la
carte entrees: $6.50-$18.95; dinner a
la carte entrees: $13.95-$38.95. Elizabethan decor; antique reproductions.
Family-owned. Cr cds: A, D, ER,
MC, V.

★★ **SIRLOIN CELLAR.** *14½ James
St N (L8R 2J9). 905/525-8620.* Special-
izes in steak, lobster, fresh seafood.
Hrs: 11:30 am-9 pm; Fri to 9:30 pm;
Sat 4:30-9:30 pm; Sun 4:30-8 pm.
Closed hols. Res accepted. Bar. Lunch
$7.95-$15.95; dinner $13.95-$33.95.
Cr cds: A, ER, MC, V.

Kenora (F-5)

Founded 1882 **Pop** 9,817
Elev 1,348 ft (411 m) **Area code** 807
Web www.lakeofthewoods.com
Information Lake of the Woods Visi-
tor Services, 1500 Hwy 17E, P9N
1M3; 807/467-4637 or 800/535-4549

An attractive and prosperous pulp
and paper town, Kenora is also a
popular resort center and gateway
to both the Lake of the Woods area
to the south and the wilderness
country to the north. Fishing, hunting, boating, sailing, and excellent
resort accommodations may be
found here, along with 14,500
islands and 65,000 miles (104,600
km) of shoreline on the lake. Win-

ter activities include ice fishing,
snowmobiling, downhill and cross-
country skiing, curling, and hockey.
The Harbourfront in downtown
Kenora hosts weekend summer festivals. There are many indigenous
pictographs in the area. As fly-in
capital of the country, many visitors
pass through Kenora on the way to
the wilderness of the north.

What to See and Do

Lake cruises. Lake Navigation, Ltd.
The MS *Kenora* makes three 18-mi
(29-km) cruises through the many
islands and channels of Lake of the
Woods (daily). Incl is Devil's Gap,
with its "spirit rock" painting.
Lunch, mid-afternoon, and dinner
cruises. Restaurant, bar. (Mid-May-
early Oct, daily) Harbourfront Wharf.
Phone 807/468-9124. ¢¢¢

Lake of the Woods Museum. Houses
more than 15,000 articles reflecting
local, native, and pioneer history.
(July-Aug, daily; Sep-June, Tues-Sat)
300 Main St. Phone 807/467-2105.
¢¢

Rushing River Provincial Park.
Approx 400 acres (160 hectares).
Beautiful natural setting with a long
and photogenic cascade. Swimming,
fishing, boating; nature and cross-
country skiing trails, picnicking,
playground, camping (fee, res),
museum (summer, daily). Park (all
yr). 12 mi (20 km) E on Hwy 17 & 4
mi (6 km) S on Hwy 71. Phone
807/468-2501 (winter) or 807/548-
4351 (summer). Per vehicle (summer)
¢¢¢

Stone Consolidated. Paper manufacturing process is followed from
debarking of logs to the finished
product. Ages 12 yrs and over only.
Flat, closed-toe shoes required. (June-
Sep, Mon and Wed-Fri, by res only)
504 9th St N. Phone 807/467-3000.
FREE

Annual Events

**ESCAPE (Exciting, Scenic, Cana-
dian/American Powerboat Excursion).** Lake of the Woods. Four-day
event for powerboats to explore the
many channels, islands, and historic
features of the lake. Canadian and
US participants meet in vicinity of
Flag Island, MN. Early July.

Kenora International Bass Fishing Tournament. Three-day competition. Early Aug.

Kenora Agricultural Fair. Kenora Recreation Centre Complex. Three days of competitions and cultural exhibitions incl a midway show. Mid-Aug.

Motels/Motor Lodges

★★ **COMFORT INN.** *1230 Hwy 17 E (P9N 1L9). 807/468-8845; fax 807/468-1588; toll-free 800/228-5150.* 77 rms, 2 story. Mid-June-mid-Sep: S $70-$90; D $75-$100; each addl $4; under 18 free; lower rates rest of yr. Crib free. Pet accepted. TV; cable. Restaurant nearby. Ck-out 11 am. Business servs avail. Cr cds: A, D, DS, ER, MC, V.

D ⬛ ⬛ ⬛ SC

★ **TRAVELODGE.** *800 Hwy 17 E (P9N 1L9). 807/468-3155; fax 807/468-4780.* 42 rms, 1-2 story, 5 kits. Mid-June-mid-Sep: S $75-$80; D $75-$104; lower rates rest of yr. Crib $6. Pet accepted. TV; cable (premium). 2 pools, 1 indoor; whirlpool. Playground. Restaurant 6 am-11 pm. Bar 11-1 am. Ck-out noon. Meeting rms. Business servs avail. Valet serv. Downhill/x-country ski 6 mi. Exercise equipt; sauna. Health club privileges. Picnic tables. Cr cds: A, D, DS, ER, JCB, MC, V.

D ⬛ ⬛ ⬛ ⬛ ⬛ ⬛ SC

Hotel

★★ **BEST WESTERN LAKESIDE INN.** *470 1st Ave S (P9N 1W5), off ON 17 807/468-5521; fax 807/468-4734.* 94 rms, 11 story. S $96; D $106; each addl $10; suites $175-$225; under 12 free. TV; cable (premium). Indoor pool. Complimentary coffee in rms. Restaurant 7 am-10 pm. Bar 11:30-midnight. Ck-out 11 am. Meeting rms. Downhill/x-country ski 4 mi. Sauna. On lakeshore. Cr cds: A, C, D, ER, MC, V.

D ⬛ ⬛ ⬛ ⬛ SC ⬛

Kingston

(C-7) See also Gananoque

Founded 1673 **Pop** 55,051 **Elev** 305 ft (93 m) **Area code** 613
Web www.kingstonarea.on.ca

Information Visitor Welcome Centre, 209 Ontario St, K7L 2Z1; 613/548-4415 or 888/855-4555

Kingston is a city rich in tradition and Kingstonians are justly proud of their city's 300-year history. Since July 1673 when Count Frontenac, Governor of New France, erected a fort on the site of present-day Kingston, the city has played an important part in Canadian history. It was here that the United Empire Loyalists relocated to begin their new life. Kingston also had the honor of being the capital of the United Provinces from 1841-44. However, because Kingston was vulnerable to attack by water from the United States, the capital was moved to Montréal and later to Ottawa. Although Kingston did not retain its position as the capital city, its citizens can boast that it was a Kingstonian, Sir John A. MacDonald, who was the first Prime Minister of Canada and who later became known as the Father of Confederation.

Since Fort Frontenac was built in 1673, Kingston has grown and prospered to become a flourishing city, yet over the years Kingston has not lost its unique charm and grace. In honor of the centennial year, a beautiful waterfront area was created in front of City Hall with a new yacht basin.

Located at the eastern end of Lake Ontario where it empties into the St. Lawrence, Kingston is Canada's freshwater sailing capital.

What to See and Do

Bellevue House National Historic Site. Italianate villa (1840) was home of Sir John A. Macdonald, first Prime Minister of Canada. Restored and furnished with period pieces. Modern display and video presentation at Visitor Centre.

(Apr-Oct, daily; rest of yr, by appt) 35 Centre St. Phone 613/545-8666. ¢¢

Boat trips.

Canadian Empress. This replica of a traditional steamship cruises St. Lawrence and Ottawa rivers on 6 different routes; trips span 4 or 5 nights, some reaching Montréal and Québec City. (Mid-May-Nov) Ages 12 and up. Contact St. Lawrence Cruise Lines, 253 Ontario St, K7L 2Z4. Departs from front of City Hall. Phone 613/549-8091 or 800/267-7868 (res). ¢¢¢¢

Island Queen. Showboat of the 1,000 Islands. Offers 3-hr river cruises through the Islands. (May-Oct, daily) For information and res contact Kingston & The Islands Boatline, 6 Princess St, K7L 1A2. Departs from Kingston Harbour, downtown. Phone 613/549-5544. ¢¢¢

City Hall. Built of limestone in 1843-44 while Kingston was capital of the United Provinces of Canada. (Mon-Fri, daily) 216 Ontario St. Phone 613/546-4291. **FREE**

Confederation Tour Trolley. A 50-min, 10-mi (16-km) narrated tour of Kingston. (Victoria Day-Labour Day, daily on the hr; charters avail) Leaves from Confederation Park, 209 Ontario St. Phone 613/548-4453. ¢¢

Correctional Service of Canada Museum. Displays a variety of artifacts and documents related to the early history of Canadian penitentiaries. Incl displays of contraband weapons and escape devices. 555 King St W. Phone 613/530-3122. **Donation**

Fort Henry. One of Ontario's most spectacular historic sites, the present fortification was built in the 1830s and restored during the 1930s. Guided tour; 19th-century British infantry and artillery drills; military pageantry; exhibits of military arms, uniforms, equipment; garrison life activities. Fort (mid-May-late Sep, daily). E at jct Hwys 2 & 15. Phone 613/542-7388. ¢¢¢

Grand Theatre. Century-old, renovated theater. Live theater, dance, symphonic, and children's performances by professional companies and local groups; summer theater

(see SEASONAL EVENT). (Daily) 218 Princess St. Phone 613/530-2050.

International Ice Hockey Federation Museum. Displays trace history of hockey from its beginning in Kingston in 1885-present. (Mid-June-Labour Day, daily; rest of yr, by appt) 445 Alfred St. Phone 613/544-2355. ¢

MacLachlan Woodworking Museum. (ca 1850) "Wood in the service of humanity" is theme of museum; highlights life of the pioneer farmer in both the field and kitchen, as well as workshops of a cooper, blacksmith, cabinetmaker. (Victoria Day-Labour Day, daily; Mar-mid-May, early Sep-Oct, Wed-Sun) 2993 Hwy 2, 10 mi (16 km) E in Grass Creek Park. Phone 613/542-0543. ¢¢

Marine Museum of the Great Lakes at Kingston. Ships have been built in Kingston since 1678. This museum explores the tales, adventures, and enterprise of "Inland Seas" history. Ship Building Gallery, 1889 Engine Room, with dry dock engines and pumps; artifacts; changing exhibits. Library and archives. The **Museum Ship** *Alexander Henry,* a 3,000-ton icebreaker, is open for tours and b&b accommodations (Victoria Day-Thanksgiving). (May-Dec, daily; rest of yr, Mon-Fri; closed Dec 25) 55 Ontario St, on the waterfront. Phone 613/542-2261. Each museum ¢¢ One blk away is

Pump House Steam Museum. Displays on steam technology, model trains, small engines. (June-Labour Day, daily) 23 Ontario St. Phone 613/542-2261. ¢¢

Military Communications and Electronics Museum. Displays history of Canadian Forces branch and aspects of military communications. Collection ranges from early radios to satellites and modern technology; excellent telephone collection. (Mid-May-Labour Day, daily; rest of yr, Mon-Fri; closed hols in winter) Vimy Barracks, 1 mi (1.6 km) E on ON 2. Phone 613/541-5395. **FREE**

Murney Tower Museum. (1846) Martello tower is now a museum with exhibits of the area's military and social history. Changing exhibits. (Mid-May-Labour Day, daily) King St at Barrie. Phone 613/544-9925. ¢¢

Queen's University. (1841) 13,000 students. Between Barrie, Union, Collingwood, and King Sts. Phone 613/533-2217 (tours). **FREE** On campus are

Agnes Etherington Art Centre. Changing exhibitions of contemporary and historical art. (Tues-Sun; closed hols) University Ave & Queen's Crescent. Phone 613/533-2190. ¢

Miller Museum of Geology and Mineralogy. Collection of rocks, minerals, and fossils from around the world. (Mon-Fri; closed hols) Miller Hall on Union St. Phone 613/533-6767. **FREE**

Royal Military College of Canada. (1876) 800 students. Canada's first military college and first institution of its kind to achieve univ status. E of Kingston Harbour on Hwy 2. On grounds is

Fort Frederick & College Museum. Exhibits depict history of college and the earlier Royal Dockyard (1789-1853); Douglas Collection of small arms and weapons that once belonged to General Porfirio Díaz, president of Mexico from 1886-1912. (Late June-Labour Day, daily) In large Martello Tower. Phone 613/541-6000, ext 6652 (office) or ext 6664 (museum). **FREE**

Annual Event

Pittsburgh Sheepdog Trials. Grass Creek Park. Incl sheep-shearing demonstrations and a variety of related activities. Phone 888/855-4555. Early Aug.

Seasonal Event

It's a Grand Summer. Grand Theatre. Late June-Labor Day. Phone 613/530-2050, ext 6652 (office) or ext 6664 (museum). **FREE**

Motels/Motor Lodges

★★ **BEST WESTERN.** *1217 Princess St (K7M 3E1). 613/549-2211; fax 613/549-4523.* 75 rms, 2 story. S, D $96.50-$139; each addl $10; under 17 free; suites $179-$429. Crib free. TV; cable (premium). Heated pool. Restaurant 7 am-11 pm. Bar 11:30-1 am. Ck-out noon. Meeting rms. Business servs avail. In-rm modem link. Valet serv. Sundries. Fireplaces; some

in-rm whirlpools. Cr cds: A, C, D, DS, ER, MC, V.
🏊 🐕 SC

★ **ECONO LODGE.** *2327 Princess St (Hwy 2) (K7M 3G1), at Sybenham Rd. 613/531-8929; fax 613/531-8929.* 32 rms, 8 kits. May-Labour Day: S $48; D $58-$78; each addl $4; kit. units $4 addl; lower rates rest of yr. Crib $4. Pet accepted; $12/day. TV; cable. Heated pool. Playground. Complimentary coffee in lobby. Restaurant adj 7 am-9 pm. Health club privileges. Ck-out 11 am. Refrigerators. Picnic tables. Grills. Cr cds: A, C, D, ER, MC, V.
D 🐕 🏊 🐕 SC

★★ **FIRST CANADA INN.** *1 First Canada Ct (K7K 6W2), on 401 Exit 617 S. 613/541-1111; fax 613/549-5735.* 74 rms, 2 story. June-Oct 1: S $53.95-$69.95; D $60.95-$76.95; each addl $5; suites $85.95-$125.95; under 12 free; lower rates rest of yr. Crib free. Pet accepted. TV; cable, VCR avail (movies). Complimentary continental bkfst, coffee in rms. Restaurant opp 10-2 am. Bar 4 pm-1 am. Coin lndry. Meeting rms. Business servs avail. Refrigerators. Cr cds: A, D, ER, MC, V.
D 🐕 🐕 SC

★★ **GREEN ACRES.** *2480 Princess St (K7M 3G4). 613/546-1796; fax 613/542-5521; toll-free 800/267-7889.* 32 rms, 3 kits. July-Aug: S $74-$99; D $77-$115; each addl $6; kit. suites $175; lower rates rest of yr. Crib $6. TV; cable (premium), VCR. Heated pool. Playground. Continental bkfst. Coffee in rms. Ck-out 11 am. Coin lndry. Meeting rm. Valet serv. X-country ski 10 mi. Health club privileges. Lawn games. Refrigerators; fireplace, whirlpool in suites; some microwaves. Picnic tables, gas grill. Cr cds: A, MC, V.
🏊 🐕 🐕 SC

★ **HOWARD JOHNSON.** *237 Ontario St (K7L 2Z4). 613/549-6300; fax 613/549-1508.* 94 rms, 6 story. May-late Sep: S, D $99-$160; each addl $10; suites $225-$250; under 18 free; higher rates special events; lower rates rest of yr. Crib free. Pet accepted. TV; cable. Heated pool; whirlpool, poolside serv. Restaurant 7 am-10 pm. Ck-out 11 am. Meeting rms. Business servs avail. Underground free parking. X-country ski 3 mi. Exercise equipt. Health club privileges. On waterfront. Cr cds: A, D, DS, ER, MC, V.

★ **KINGSTON EAST.** *1488 Hwy 15 (K7L 5Y6), ½ mi S of ON 401 Exit 623.* 613/546-6674; fax 613/546-5896. 22 rms. Mid-June-mid-Sep: S, D $60-$75; each addl $5; kit. units $10 addl; lower rates rest of yr. Crib $5. TV. Heated pool. Playground. Restaurant 7 am-7 pm. Ck-out 11 am. Sundries. Some refrigerators. Picnic tables, grills. Cr cds: MC, V.

★ **SEVEN OAKES.** *2331 Princess St (K7M 3G1).* 613/546-3655; fax 613/549-5677. 40 rms. June-Sep 1: S $64; D $68-$74; each addl $5; package plans; lower rates rest of yr. Crib free. Pet accepted. Heated pool; whirlpool. Sauna. Playground. Bar. Ck-out 11 am. Coin lndry. Sundries. Lighted tennis. Refrigerators; some in-rm whirlpools. Picnic tables, grills. Cr cds: A, D, DS, ER, MC, V.

★ **TRAVELODGE HOTEL LA SALLE.** *2360 Princess St (K7M 3G4).* 613/546-4233; fax 613/546-0867. 69 rms, 4 story. May-mid-Sep: S, D $72-$90; under 12 free; lower rates rest of yr. Crib free. TV; cable, VCR avail. Indoor pool; whirlpool. Restaurant 6 am-10 pm. Bar 11 am-11 pm. Ck-out noon. Meeting rms. Business servs avail. Sauna. Sundries. Balconies. Cr cds: A, D, DS, ER, JCB, MC, V.

Resort

★★★ **ISAIAH TUBBS RESORT.** *RR 1, W Lake Rd (K0K 2T0), approx 40 mi W on ON 33 and County Rd 12.* 613/393-2090; fax 613/393-1291. 60 rms in lodge, inn, many A/C, 12 kit. cabins. No phone in cabins. July-Labor Day: S $95-$200; D $150-$220; each addl $10; kit. suites $150-$200; cabins $650-$900/wk; under 5 free; MAP, conference plan avail; lower rates rest of yr. Crib free. TV. 2 pools, 1 indoor; whirlpool. Playground. Free supervised children's activities (July-Aug); ages 4-12. Dining rm 8-1 am. Bar. Ck-out 11 am, ck-in 4 pm. Coin

lndry. Meeting rms. Business servs avail. Tennis. Swimming beach. X-country ski 1 mi. Lawn games. Exercise equipt; sauna. Some refrigerators. Picnic tables, grills. On West Lake, adj Sandbanks Provincial Park. Cr cds: A, D, ER, MC, V.

B&Bs/Small Inns

★★★ **HOCHELAGA.** *24 S Sydenham St (K7L 3G9).* 613/549-5534; fax 613/549-5534. 23 rms, 3 story. S, D $135-$145; each addl $10; under 5 free; lower rates rest of yr. Crib free. TV; cable (premium). Complimentary continental bkfst. Restaurant nearby. Ck-out 11 am, ck-in 3 pm. Business servs avail. Some balconies. Renovated house (1872); period antiques. Cr cds: A, D, ER, MC, V.

★★★ **MERRILL.** *343 Main St E (K0K 2T0), approx 40 mi W ON 33 to ON 49 (Main St).* 613/476-7451; fax 613/476-8283. 14 rms, 3 story, 2 suites. No elvtr. July-Sep: S, D $85-$125; each addl $10; suites $125; under 3 free; lower rates rest of yr. Crib free. TV; cable (premium). Complimentary continental bkfst. Restaurant 11 am-11 pm. Ck-out 11 am, ck-in 3 pm. Meeting rm. Lawn games. Rms individually decorated with period antiques. Brick Victorian house (ca 1878); built for Edwards Merrill, one of Canada's top barristers. Cr cds: A, D, ER, MC, V.

★★★ **ROSEMOUNT INN.** *46 Sydenham St S (K7L 3H1).* 613/531-8844; fax 613/531-9722. Email rosemt@adan.kingston.net. 8 rms, 2 story, 1 cabin. No A/C. No rm phones. S, D $109-$159; each addl $30-$50; cabin $225; wkends, hols (2-day min). Closed mid-Dec-early Jan. Children over 13 yrs only. Complimentary full bkfst, afternoon refreshments. Ck-out 11 am, ck-in 4 pm. Business servs avail. Bellhops. Valet serv. Concierge serv. Gift shop. Some street parking. X-country ski 5 mi. Massage. Fireplace. Built in 1850. Victorian decor; antiques. Totally nonsmoking. Cr cds: A, MC, V.

Restaurant

★★ **AUNT LUCY'S.** *1399 Princess St (K7M 3E9). 613/542-2729.* Specializes in steak, seafood, pasta. Hrs: 10:30 am-10 pm; Fri, Sat to 11 pm; Sun 9:30 am-9 pm. Bar. Lunch, dinner $5.95-$19.95. Sun brunch $10.99. Child's menu. Entertainment. Open-hearth grill. Family-owned. Cr cds: A, DS, MC, V.

D 🖳

Kitchener-Waterloo (D-4)

Pop Kitchener, 139,734; Waterloo, 49,428 **Elev** Kitchener, 1,100 ft (335 m); Waterloo, 1,075 ft (328 m) **Area code** 519 **Web** www.kw-visitor.on.ca

Information Visitor & Convention Bureau, 80 Queen St N, Kitchener N2H 6L4; 519/145-3536 or 800/265-6959

The twin cities of Kitchener-Waterloo were settled in the early 1800s by Mennonites, Amish, and Germans whose cultural heritage is still clearly visible. Not far to the north in Elmira is the heart of Ontario's Pennsylvania German country, with Maple Sugar Festival and tours of Mennonite country. Although Kitchener and Waterloo are separate cities, each takes pride in the achievements of the other. A vigorous spirit of youth and industry pervades both cities, making a visit to the Kitchener-Waterloo area a pleasure for any traveler.

What to See and Do

Bingeman Park. Recreation center on banks of Grand River; swimming (pool, wave pool), watersliding, bumper boats; go-cart track, arcade, roller skating, miniature golf, golf driving range, batting cages, cross-country skiing; picnicking, restaurant; playground, camping. Park (summer, daily; also spring and fall, weather permitting). Campgrounds and restaurant (all yr, daily). Fee for some activities. 1380 Victoria St N, Kitchener. Phone 519/744-1555.

Doon Heritage Crossroads. Re-creation of early 20th-century village (ca 1915) incl museum, grocery store, post office/tailor shop, blacksmith, church, 2 farms, and several houses. (May-late Dec, daily; closed Dec 23) Hwy 401 Exit 275, Homer Watson Blvd. Phone 519/748-1914 or 519/575-4530. ¢¢¢

Farmers Market. More than 100 vendors sell fresh produce, meat, cheese, and handicrafts. Mennonite specialties featured. (All yr, Sat; mid-May-mid-Oct, also Wed). Market Sq, Frederick & Duke Sts, downtown Kitchener. Phone 519/741-2287. **FREE**

Glockenspiel. Canada's first glockenspiel tells fairy tale of Snow White. Twenty-three bells form the carillon. Performance lasts 15 min (4 times daily). King & Benton Sts.

Joseph Schneider Haus. Pennsylvania German Mennonite house (1820), one of area's oldest homesteads, restored and furnished; "living" museum with costumed interpreters; daily demonstrations. Adj Heritage Galleries, incl Germanic folk art; exhibits change every 3 months. (Victoria Day-Labour Day, daily; rest of yr, Tues-Sun; closed Jan 1, Dec 25, 26) 466 Queen St S, Kitchener. Phone 519/742-7752. ¢¢

Kitchener-Waterloo Art Gallery. Six exhibition areas cover all aspects of the visual arts. Gift shop. (Tues-Sun; closed hols) 101 Queen St N, at The Centre in the Square. Phone 519/579-5860. **FREE**

Laurel Creek Conservation Area. Approx 750 acres (305 hectares) of multipurpose area. Dam, swimming beach, boating (no motors); hiking, sports fields, camping (fee), picnicking, reforested areas, bird-watching. (May-mid-Oct) NW corner of Waterloo, bounded by Westmount Rd, Conservation Dr, and Beaver Creek Rd. Phone 519/884-6620. ¢¢

🌟 **Museum & Archive of Games.** Collection incl over 3,500 games. Many "hands-on" exhibits drawn from collection ranging from Inuit bone games to computer games. Exhibits change every 4 months. Archive contains documents pertaining to games and game-playing. (Tues-Thurs and Sun; closed school hols) B.C. Matthews Hall, Univ of Waterloo. Phone 519/888-4424. **FREE**

Waterloo Park. Log schoolhouse built 1820 surrounded by picnic area and lake; playground. Small zoo and band concerts in summer (Sun). Central St, Waterloo. Phone 519/747-8733. **FREE**

Waterloo-St. Jacobs Railway. Streamliner tourist train rolls into the heart of Mennonite farm country. Stops allow exploration of the quaint village of St. Jacobs and the St. Jacobs Farmers Market. Ninety min, round-trip. (May-Oct, daily; Nov-Apr, wkends) Departs Waterloo Station, 10 Father David Bauer Dr. Phone 519/746-1950. ¢¢¢

Woodside National Historic Site. Boyhood home of William Lyon Mackenzie King, Canada's 10th prime minister. 1890s Victorian restoration. Interpretive center has theater and display on King's early life and career. Picnicking. (May-Dec, daily; closed hols) 528 Wellington St N, Kitchener. Phone 519/571-5684. **FREE** Nearby is

> **Pioneer Memorial Tower.** Tribute to industrious spirit of pioneers who first settled Waterloo County. Cemetery on grounds incl graves of several original founders. Excellent view of Grand River. (May-Oct) **FREE**

Annual Events

Waterloo County Quilt Festival. Quilt exhibits, displays, workshops, and demonstrations. Phone 800/265-6959. Nine days mid-May.

Ale Trail. Showcases region's brewing industry and allows visitors to experience the craft of brewing at 6 different area breweries. Phone 800/334-4519. Mid-June.

Kitchener-Waterloo Multicultural Festival. Victoria Park. Phone 519/745-2531. Late June.

Busker Carnival Festival. Intl showcase of street performers. Phone 519/747-8769. Late Aug.

Wellesley Apple Butter & Cheese Festival. Pancake breakfast, farmers market; free tours of farms, cider mill; horseshoe tournament, quilt auction, smorgasbord dinner, model boat regatta, antique cars and tractors. Phone 519/656-3400. Last Sat Sep.

Oktoberfest. Phone 519/748-0800 or 800/265-6959. Early Oct.

Motels/Motor Lodges

★★ **CLARION INN.** *1333 Weber St E. 519/893-1234; fax 519/893-2100.* 102 rms, 2-4 story. S $89-$109; D $99-$129; each addl $10; under 18 free; higher rates Oktoberfest. Crib free. Pet accepted, some restrictions; $50 refundable. TV; cable. Heated pool; whirlpool, poolside serv. Sauna. Complimentary coffee in rms. Restaurant 7 am-9 pm. Bar 11-1 am; entertainment Thurs-Sat. Ck-out 11:30 am. Meeting rms. Business center. Sundries. Some refrigerators; microwaves avail. Balconies. Cr cds: A, C, D, DS, ER, JCB, MC, V.

⌨ 🐾 ➰ 🛏 🔥 SC 🚶

★★ **COMFORT INN.** *220 Holiday Inn Dr (N3C 1Z4), on 401, Exit ON 24 N. 519/658-1100; fax 519/658-6979.* 84 rms, 2 story. S $59-$80; D $67-$95; each addl $4; under 18 free. Crib free. Pet accepted. TV; cable (premium). Complimentary coffee in lobby. Ck-out 11 am. Business servs avail. Sundries. Downhill/x-country ski 4 mi. Cr cds: A, C, D, DS, ER, JCB, MC, V.

🐾 ➣ 🛏 🔥 SC

★ **GATEWAY INN.** *650 Hespeler Rd (N1R 6J8), S ON 24, off ON 401. 519/622-1070; fax 519/622-1512.* 119 rms, 2 story. S $74.95; D $78.95; each addl $7; under 17 free. Crib free. Pet accepted. TV; cable (premium), VCR avail. Heated pool. Playground. Ck-out 11 am. Meeting rms. Business servs avail. Valet serv. Sundries. Game rm. Microwaves avail. Cr cds: A, D, ER, JCB, MC, V.

⌨ 🐾 ➰ 🛏 🔥 SC

★★ **HOLIDAY INN.** *30 Fairway Rd S. 519/893-1211; fax 519/894-8518.* 182 rms, 2-6 story. S $125.95-$145.95; D $136.95-$156.95; each addl $10; suites $205.95-$305.95; under 19 free. Crib free. Pet accepted. TV; cable (premium). Indoor/outdoor pool; poolside serv. Supervised children's activities (July-Aug). Complimentary coffee in rms. Restaurant 6:30 am-10 pm. Bar 11-1 am. Ck-out noon. Meeting rms. In-rm modem link. Valet serv. Downhill/x-country ski 2 mi. Exercise equipt. Microwaves avail. Private patios, balconies. Cr cds: A, C, D, DS, ER, JCB, MC, V.

⌨ 🐾 ➣ ➰ 🏃 🛏 🔥 SC

★ **NEWBURG INN.** *Hwy 7 & 8 W (N0B 2G0), 10 mi W, at ON 8. 519/ 662-3990.* 12 rms. S $50; D $75; each addl $5; suite $75; monthly rates. TV; cable. Complimentary coffee in lobby. Restaurant nearby. Ck-out 11 am. Some refrigerators. Cr cds: A, MC, V.

★★★ **WATERLOO INN.** *475 King St N (N2J 2Z5), 1 mi N on ON 86. 519/884-0220; fax 519/884-0321; toll-free 800/361-4708. www.nrzone. com/waterlooinn/.* 155 rms, 4 story. S $93; D $103; each addl $12; suites from $125; under 16 free. Crib free. Pet accepted. TV; cable. Indoor pool; whirlpool, poolside serv. Complimentary coffee in rms. Restaurant 7 am-10 pm. Rm serv 24 hrs. Bar 11-1 am. Convention facilities. Business servs avail. In-rm modem link. Valet serv. Sundries. Downhill ski 10 mi; x-country ski ½ mi. Exercise equipt; sauna. Game rm. Balconies. Landscaped courtyard. Cr cds: A, D, DS, ER, JCB, MC, V.

Hotels

★★★ **LANGDON HALL.** *RR 33 (N3H 5R8), E on ON 8 to Fountain St. 519/740-2100; fax 519/740-8161. Email langdon@golden.net.* 43 rms, 3 story. 2-day min: S, D $229-$269; suites $369; under 10 free. Crib free. Pet accepted, some restrictions; $25. TV; cable (premium), VCR avail. Heated pool; whirlpool, poolside serv. Complimentary continental bkfst. Restaurant (see also LANGDON HALL). Rm serv 24 hrs. Bar. Ck-out noon. Meeting rms. Business servs avail. In-rm modem link. Gift shop. Tennis. Downhill ski 4 mi; x-country ski on site. Hiking trail. Exercise equipt; sauna, steam rm. Massage. Rec rm. Lawn games. Balconies. Antebellum-style bldg in rural setting. Cr cds: A, D, ER, MC, V.

★★★ **SHERATON.** *105 E King St (N2G 2K8), at Benton. 519/744-4141; fax 519/578-6889.* 201 rms, 9 story. S, D $119-$139; each addl $10; suites $130-$269; studio rms $79; under 18 free; wkend package. Crib free. Pet accepted, some restrictions. TV; cable. Pool; whirlpool, poolside serv. Complimentary coffee in rms.

Restaurant 6:30 am-2 pm, 5:30-10:30 pm. Bar 5 pm-1 am. Ck-out noon. Meeting rms. Business center. In-rm modem link. Free covered parking. Downhill/x-country ski 4 mi. Exercise rm; sauna. Game rm. Miniature golf. Rec rm. Minibars; microwaves avail. Some balconies. Cr cds: A, C, D, ER, MC, V.

★ **SUPER 8.** *730 Hespeler Rd (N3H 5L8), S ON 24, at ON 401. 519/623-4600; fax 519/623-2688.* 106 rms, 7 story, 11 suites. S $99.99; D $109; each addl $10; suites $119; under 12 free; wkly rates; higher rates Octoberfest. Crib free. TV; cable (premium). Indoor pool; whirlpool. Sauna. Complimentary continental bkfst. Coffee in rms. Restaurant nearby. Ck-out 11 am. Coin lndry. Meeting rms. Business servs avail. In-rm modem link. Downhill/x-country ski 5 mi. Game rm. Refrigerators; microwaves avail. Cr cds: A, D, DS, ER, MC, V.

★★ **WALPER TERRACE.** *1 King St W (N2G 1A1), at Queen St. 519/745-4321; fax 519/745-3625; res 800/265-8749. Email service@walper.com; www. walper.com.* 63 rms, 5 story, 22 suites. S, D $99; each addl $10; suites $110-$210; under 16 free; wkend rates. Crib free. TV; cable (premium), VCR avail. Complimentary coffee in rms. Restaurant 7:30-1 am. Bar from 11:30 am. Ck-out noon. Business servs avail. Barber, beauty shop. Free parking. Health club privileges. Restored landmark hotel in the heart of downtown; retains air of old-European elegance. Cr cds: A, D, DS, ER, MC, V.

B&B/Small Inn

★★★ **ELORA MILL.** *77 Mill St W (N0B 1S0), 12 mi N. 519/846-5356; fax 519/846-9180.* 32 rms, 5 story. S, D $150-$170; each addl $50; suites $220; under 13, $25. TV; cable. Complimentary full bkfst. Restaurant (see also ELORA MILL). Bar 4:30 pm-1 am. Ck-out 11:30 am, ck-in 4 pm. Meeting rm. Business servs avail. Valet serv. X-country ski 1 mi. Health club privileges. Some refrigerators, fireplaces. Located in historic pre-Confederation village. Cr cds: A, ER, MC, V.

Restaurants

★ **BARRELS.** *95 Queen St S (N2G 1W1).* 519/745-4451. Specializes in mussels, piglet, pepper steak. Hrs: 11:30 am-9 pm; Fri to 10 pm; Sat 5-10 pm. Closed Sun, Mon; Dec 24, 25. Res accepted. Bar. Lunch a la carte entrees: $6.95-$13.95; dinner a la carte entrees: $10.95-$19.95. Entertainment. Cr cds: A, MC, V.
[D]

★★ **BENJAMIN'S.** *1430 King N (N0B 2N0), N ON 86.* 519/664-3731. Specializes in beef, pasta, seafood. Hrs: 11:30 am-10 pm. Closed Jan 1, Dec 25, 26. Res accepted. Bar. Lunch a la carte entrees: $6.95-$9.25; dinner a la carte entrees: $13.50-$21. Entertainment. Re-creation of 1850s country inn; fireplace, artifacts. Cr cds: A, C, D, DS, ER, MC, V.
[D]

★★★ **CHARCOAL STEAK HOUSE.** *2980 King St E (N2A 1A9).* 519/893-6570. www.cyberdineout.com. Specializes in steak, spareribs, pigtails. Own baking. Hrs: 11:30 am-10 pm; Sat 4:30-11 pm; Sun 10:30 am-9 pm. Res accepted. Bar. Wine list. Lunch a la carte entrees: $7-$16; dinner a la carte entrees: $12-$35. Child's menu. Entertainment. Parking. Cr cds: A, D, ER, MC, V.
[D]

★★★ **ELORA MILL.** *77 Mill St W (N0B 1S0).* 519/846-5356. www.elora mill.com. Own baking. Hrs: 8 am-8 pm; Fri, Sat to 9 pm. Res accepted. Bar. Bkfst a la carte entrees: $7.95; lunch a la carte entrees: $8.95-$13.95; dinner a la carte entrees: $19.95-$29.95. Entertainment. Parking. Restored gristmill (1859). Cr cds: A, D, ER, MC, V.
[D]

★★★ **LANGDON HALL.** *RR 33.* 519/740-2100. Email langdon@golden. net. Specializes in goat cheese quenelle, roasted veal with tarragon, twice-cooked duck. Hrs: noon-9 pm. Res required. Bar. Wine cellar. Lunch $13.75-$19.75; dinner $12.50-$30. Entertainment. Parking. Elegant dining rm overlooking park. Gardens. Cr cds: A, D, ER, MC, V.
[D]

★★ **STONE CROCK.** *59 Church St W (N3B 1M8), 9 mi N ON 86.* 519/669-1521. Specializes in spareribs, turkey, cabbage rolls. Salad bar. Hrs: 7 am-8:30 pm; Sun from 11 am. Closed Dec 25. Bkfst $1.75-$5.75; lunch $5-$9.50; dinner $8.50-$10.95. Child's menu. Entertainment. Parking. Country atmosphere. Gift shop. Cr cds: A, D, ER, MC, V.
[D]

★★★ **SWISS CASTLE INN.** *1508 King St E (N2G 2P1).* 519/744-2391. Chinese menu. Specializes in Wienerschnitzel, lobster tail. Own baking. Hrs: 4:30-9 pm. Closed Mon; hols. Res accepted. Bar. Wine list. Dinner $9.95-$17.95. Child's menu. Entertainment. Parking. Fireplace. Swiss bell collection. Cr cds: A, MC, V.
[D]

★★★ **WATERLOT.** *17 Huron St (N0B 2G0), 11 mi W via ON 8, behind Royal Bank.* 519/662-2020. Email waterlot@sympatico.ca; www3. sympatico.ca/waterlot. Specializes in crab crepes, duckling. Own baking. Hrs: 11:30 am-2 pm, 5-8:30 pm. Closed Mon; Good Friday, Dec 25. Res accepted. Bar. Wine list. Lunch a la carte entrees: $7.95-$13.95; dinner a la carte entrees: $15.50-$28.50. Complete meals: (Sun-Fri) $24. Child's menu. Entertainment. Victorian house (1845); guest rms avail. Cr cds: A, D, MC, V.
[D]

London (E-3)

Pop 300,000 (est) **Elev** 912 ft (278 m)
Area code 519
Web www.city.london.on.ca

Information Tourism London, 300 Dufferin Ave, N6A 4L9; 519/661-4500 or 800/265-2602

Called the "Forest City," London is a busy modern city with charming small-town atmosphere. Located on the Thames River, its street names are similar to those of the other London. A contrast of Victorian architecture and contemporary skyscrapers is prevalent here.

What to See and Do

Double-decker Bus Tour of London. Two-hr guided tour aboard authentic double-decker English bus with stop at Storybook Gardens in Springbank Park and Regional Art Museum. Departs City Hall (Wellington St and Dufferin Ave). (July-Labour Day, daily) Res suggested. Phone 519/661-4500 or 800/265-2602. ¢¢¢

Eldon House. (1834) Oldest house in town; occupied by same family until donated to the city. Furnished much as it was in the 19th century with many antiques from abroad. Spacious grounds, lawns, brick paths, gardens, conservatory-greenhouse. Guided tours (by appt). (Tues-Sun; closed Dec 25) 481 Ridout St N. Phone 519/661-5169. ¢¢

Fanshawe Pioneer Village. Living history museum of 24 bldgs moved to this site to display artifacts and re-create the life of a typical 19th-century crossroads community in southwestern Ontario. Log cabin, barns, and stable; blacksmith, weaver, harness, gun, woodworking, and barber shops; general store, church, fire hall, school, and sawmill; costumed interpreters. (May-Oct, Wed-Sun; Nov-mid-Dec, daily) Also at Fanshawe Conservation Area is Ontario's largest flood control structure; swimming, sailing, fishing (walleye); camping, various sports activities, and nature trails. NE edge of town; E end of Fanshawe Park Rd. Phone 519/457-1296. ¢¢

Grand Theatre. Contemporary facade houses 1901 theater, built by Colonel Whitney of Detroit and Ambrose Small of Toronto. Restored interior, proscenium arch, murals, and cast plasterwork. Professional stock theater (Oct-May). 471 Richmond St. Phone 519/672-8800.

Guy Lombardo Music Centre. Institution housing artifacts belonging to London-born musician. Exhibits on other big band era greats. (Mid-May-Labor Day, Thurs-Mon, daily; other times by appt) 205 Wonderland Rd S, in Springbank Park. Phone 519/473-9003. ¢

London Museum of Archaeology. Traces prehistory of southwestern Ontario; more than 40,000 artifacts show how indigenous people lived thousands of yrs before Columbus was born; archaeological and ethnographic exhibits from southwestern Ontario. Gallery, theater, and native gift shop. (May-Sep, daily; closed Good Fri, Dec 25) 1600 Attawandaron Rd. Phone 519/473-1360. ¢¢ Also here is

Iroquois Village. Ongoing excavation and reconstruction of authentic 500-yr-old Neutral village located on original site. (Admission incl in Museum fee; May-Sep, daily)

London Regional Art and Historical Museums. Changing exhibits on art, history, and culture of the London area; regional, national, and international art. (Tues-Sun; closed Dec 25) 421 Ridout St N. Phone 519/672-4580. **FREE**

London Regional Children's Museum. Hands-on galleries allow children to explore, touch, and discover. Artifacts to touch, costumes to put on, and crafts to make; also special events. (Sep-June, Tues-Sat; July-Aug, daily; closed Jan 1, Dec 25) 21 Wharncliffe Rd S. Phone 519/434-5726. ¢¢

The Royal Canadian Regiment Museum. Displays incl artifacts, battle scenes from 1883-present, weapons, and uniforms. (Tues-Sun; closed hols) Wolseley Hall, Canadian Forces Base. Phone 519/660-5102 or 519/660-5173. **Donation**

Ska Nah Doht Iroquois Village. Re-created Iroquoian village depicting native culture in southwestern Ontario 800-1,000 yrs ago. Guided tours, slide shows, displays; nature trails, picnicking, group camping. Park (daily). Resource Centre & Village (Canada Day-Labor Day, daily; rest of yr, Mon-Fri). 20 mi (32 km) W via ON 2 in the Longwoods Road Conservation Area. Phone 519/264-2420. Per vehicle ¢¢¢

Storybook Gardens. Family-oriented theme park, children's playworld, and zoo, 8 acres (3 hectares) within London's largest park of 281 acres (114 hectares). (Early May-mid-Oct, daily) Springbank Park, Thames River Valley. Phone 519/661-5770. ¢¢¢

Annual Events

The London Air Show & Balloon Festival. Airport. Flying exhibitions (2-hr show); ground displays. Late June.

Royal Canadian Big Band Music Festival. Downtown and Wonderland gardens. Live and recorded big band music; part of Great Canadian Celebration. First wkend July.

Sunfest. Victoria Park. Features 25 music and dance ensembles from around the world, plus 70 food and craft vendors. Phone 519/661-5000 or 800/265-2602. Early July.

Home County Folk Festival. Victoria Park. Three-day outdoor music fest. Mid-July.

Dragon Boat Festival. Fanshawe Conservation area. Mid-Aug.

London Fringe Theatre Festival. City-wide theatrical event. Phone 519/433-3332. Mid-Aug.

Western Fair. Western Fairgrounds. Entertainment and educational extravaganza; horse shows, musicians, exhibits, livestock shows. Ten days early Sep.

Panorama Ethnic Festival. Throughout city. Open house of ethnic clubs; music, dance, food, crafts. Three days late Sep.

Motels/Motor Lodges

★★ **BEST WESTERN.** *591 Wellington Rd (N6C 4R3). 519/681-7151; fax 519/681-3271.* 126 rms, 2 story. S $79; D $109; each addl $8; suites $119-$209; under 12 free. Pet accepted, some restrictions. TV; cable. Pool. Complimentary coffee in rms. Restaurant 6:30 am-9 pm; Sun to 8 pm. Bar 4 pm-midnight. Ck-out 11 am. Meeting rms. Business servs avail. Some in-rm whirlpools. Private patios, balconies. Picnic tables. Cr cds: A, D, DS, ER, MC, V.

D ⭐ ⇔ ⋈ 🔥 SC

★★ **HOLIDAY INN EXPRESS.** *800 Exeter Rd (N6E 1L5), Exit ON 401 at Wellington Rd N. 519/681-1200; fax 519/681-6988.* 125 rms, 2-3 story, 32 suites. S, D $84; each addl $7; under 19 free; suites $92-$96. Crib free. TV; cable (premium), VCR. Complimentary bkfst. Restaurant adj open 24 hrs. Ck-out 11 am. Meeting rms.

Business servs avail. Microwaves avail. Cr cds: A, D, DS, ER, MC, V.

D ⋈ 🔥 SC

★★ **RAMADA INN.** *817 Exeter Rd (N6E 1W1), at ON 401 Interchange 186 N. 519/681-4900; fax 519/681-5065.* 124 rms, 2 story. S, D $99-$109; each addl $10; suites $175-$225; under 18 free. TV; cable. Indoor pool; lifeguard (wkends). Complimentary coffee in rms. Restaurant 6:30 am-10 pm; Sat, Sun from 7 am. Bar 11-1 am. Ck-out 1 pm. Meeting rms. Business servs avail. Valet serv. Sundries. Sauna. Health club privileges. Microwaves avail. Cr cds: A, D, DS, ER, JCB, MC, V.

D ⇔ ⋈ 🔥 SC

Hotels

★★ **DELTA LONDON ARMOURIES.** *325 Dundas St (N6B 1T9). 519/679-6111; fax 519/679-3957. www.deltahotels.com.* 250 rms, 20 story. S $189; D $199; each addl $10; suites $250-$450; under 18 free; wkend rates. Crib free. Pet accepted. TV; cable (premium), VCR avail (movies). Indoor pool; wading pool, whirlpool. Supervised children's activities (July and Aug, daily; rest of yr, Fri-Sun); ages 5-12. Coffee in rms. Restaurant 6:30 am-10 pm. Bar to 2 am. Ck-out noon. Meeting rms. Business center. Concierge serv. Valet parking. Putting green. Exercise equipt; sauna. Health club privileges. Rec rm. Minibars. Some balconies. Luxury level. Cr cds: A, C, D, DS, ER, MC, V.

D 🐾 ⇔ 🧍 ⋈ 🔥 SC 🧍

★★★ **HILTON HOTEL LONDON.** *300 King St (N6R 1S2). 519/439-1661; fax 519/439-9672; toll-free 800/210-9336. www.westin.com.* 331 rms, 22 story. S, D $135-$155; suites $300; under 18 free; wkend rates. Crib free. Pet accepted. TV; cable, VCR avail. Heated pool; wading pool, whirlpool. Restaurant 7 am-11 pm. Bar 11:30-1 am; entertainment. Ck-out 1 pm. Convention facilities. Business servs avail. In-rm modem link. Concierge serv. Gift shop. Exercise equipt; sauna. Health club privileges. Minibars. Luxury level. Cr cds: A, C, D, DS, ER, JCB, MC, V.

D 🐾 ⇔ 🧍 ⋈ 🔥 SC

B&B/Small Inn

★★★ **IDLEWYLD.** *36 Grand Ave (N6C 1K8). 519/433-2891; fax 519/433-2891. www.someplacedifferent. com.* 27 rms, 8 suites. S, D $89-$119; each addl $10; suites $119-$179; under 18 free; wkly rates. Crib free. TV; cable (premium). Complimentary continental bkfst. Ck-out noon, ck-in 3 pm. Business servs avail. In-rm modem link. X-country ski 3 mi. Some balconies. Picnic tables. Victorian mansion (1878); some original decor. Cr cds: A, D, ER, MC, V.

[D] [≽] [⊠] [🐾] [SC]

Restaurants

★ **FELLINI KOOLINI'S.** *153 Albert St (N6A 1L9). 519/642-2300.* Specializes in pizza, pasta. Hrs: 11:30 am-10 pm; Thurs to 11 pm; Fri, Sat to midnight; Sun from 4:30 pm. Closed Jan 1, Dec 25, 26. Bar. Lunch, dinner $7.95-$16.95. Child's menu. Italian country inn decor. Cr cds: A, D, ER, MC, V.

[⊠]

★★ **MARIENBAD.** *122 Carling St (N6A 1H6). 519/679-9940.* Specializes in Wienerschnitzel, beef Tartare. Hrs: 11 am-11 pm. Closed Jan 1, Dec 25. Res accepted. Bar. Lunch a la carte entrees: $5.95-$10.75; dinner a la carte entrees: $8.95-$18.95. Child's menu. Murder mystery dinner 3rd Fri each month. Atrium dining. Original and reproduction 19th-century furnishings. Cr cds: A, D, ER, MC, V.

[D] [⊠]

★★ **MARLA JANE'S.** *460 King St E (N6B 1S9). 519/858-8669. Email marla.jane@gtn.net.* Specializes in Cajun dishes. Hrs: 11:30 am-11 pm; Sun 5-10 pm. Closed Dec 25. Res accepted (dinner). Lunch a la carte entrees: $7.25-$12.95; dinner a la carte entrees: $12.95-$24.95. Herb garden; terrace. Former embassy (ca 1900). Victorian architecture. Stained glass; changing art displays. Cr cds: A, D, DS, ER, MC, V.

[⊠]

★★ **MICHAEL'S-ON-THE-THAMES.** *1 York St (N6A 1A1). 519/672-0111.* Specializes in châteaubriand, fresh seafood. Hrs: 11:30 am-11 pm; Thurs, Fri to midnight; Sat 5 pm-midnight; Sun, hols 5-9 pm. Closed Jan 1, Labour Day, Dec 25. Res accepted. Bar. Lunch a la carte entrees: $5.95-$9.95; dinner a la carte entrees: $9.95-$24.95. Child's menu. Entertainment: pianist Sat, Sun. Tableside cooking. Cr cds: A, D, ER, MC, V.

[⊠]

Mississauga

(D-4) *See also Hamilton, Toronto*

Pop 430,000 **Elev** 569 ft (173 m)
Area code 905
Information City of Mississauga, 300 City Centre Dr, L5B 3C1; 905/896-5058 or 905/896-5000

One of the fastest-growing areas in southern Ontario, Mississauga is a part of the greater Toronto area, bordering Lester B. Pearson International Airport.

Motels/Motor Lodges

★★ **DAYS HOTEL TORONTO AIRPORT.** *6257 Airport Rd (L4V 1E4), near Lester B. Pearson Intl Airport. 905/678-1400; fax 905/678-9130. www.daysinn.com.* 202 rms, 7 story. S $159; D $178; each addl $10; suites $199; under 18 free; wkend rates. Crib free. TV; cable (premium). Indoor pool; whirlpool. Coffee in rms. Restaurant 7 am-midnight. Rm serv. Bar 11 am-1 am. Ck-out noon. Meeting rms. Business servs avail. Bellhops. Gift shop. Barber, beauty shop. Valet serv. Airport transportation. 18-hole golf privileges. Downhill/x-country ski 20 mi. Exercise equipt; sauna. Balconies. Cr cds: A, C, D, DS, ER, JCB, MC, V.

[D] [≽] [⊠] [🏋] [✈] [⊠] [🐾] [SC]

★ **DAYS INN.** *4635 Tomken Rd (L4W 1J9). 905/238-5480; fax 905/238-1031.* 61 rms, 3 story. No elvtr. S, D $60-$100; each addl $5; suites $150; under 18 free. Crib free. Pet accepted. TV; cable, VCR (movies). Complimentary continental bkfst, coffee in rms. Restaurant opp 11:30 am-midnight. Ck-out 11:30 am. Business servs avail. Some refrigerators. Cr cds: A, C, D, DS, ER, JCB, MC, V.

[D] [🐾] [⊠] [🐾] [SC]

★★ **HOLIDAY INN.** *2125 N Sheridan Way (L5K 1A3), QEW Exit Erin Mills Pkwy. 905/855-2000; fax 905/855-1433. Email holinn.miss.qew@sympatico.ca.* 151 rms, 6 story, 80 suites. S, D, suites $140-$160; each addl $10; under 19 free. Crib free. TV; cable (premium), VCR avail. Heated pool; poolside serv. Coffee in rms. Restaurant 6:30 am-10 pm. Rm serv 7 am-midnight. Bar 11-1 am. Ck-out 1 pm. Meeting rms. Bellhops. Valet serv. Sundries. Airport transportation. Health club privileges. Wet bars; some in-rm whirlpools; refrigerators, microwaves avail. Cr cds: A, C, D, DS, ER, JCB, MC, V.

D ⌨ ⊠ 🔥 SC

★★ **HOLIDAY INN TORONTO WEST.** *100 Britannia Rd (L4Z 2G1). 905/890-5700; fax 905/568-0868. www.holiday-inn.com.* 132 air-cooled rms, 6 story. S, D $145; each addl $8; under 20 free. Crib free. Pet accepted, some restrictions. TV; cable (premium), VCR avail. Coffee in rms. Restaurant from 6:30 am. Bar. Ck-out noon. Meeting rms. Business servs avail. In-rm modem link. Valet serv. Free airport transportation. Exercise equipt; sauna. Whirlpool. Refrigerators avail. Cr cds: A, D, DS, ER, JCB, MC, V.

D ⚡ 🏋 ⊠ 🔥 SC

★ **HOWARD JOHNSON.** *2420 Surveyor Rd (L5N 4E6). 905/858-8600; fax 905/858-8574.* 117 rms, 2 story. June-Sep: S $69-$74; D $74-$84; each addl $5; under 18 free; package plans; lower rates rest of yr. Crib free. Pet accepted, some restrictions. TV; cable (premium). Complimentary continental bkfst, coffee in rms. Restaurant opp open 24 hrs. Ck-out 1 pm. Coin lndry. Meeting rms. Business servs avail. Downhill/x-country ski 15 mi. Game rm. Some refrigerators. Picnic tables. Cr cds: A, D, DS, ER, MC, V.

⚡ ▶ ⊠ 🔥 SC

★★ **QUALITY INN.** *50 Britannia Rd E (L4Z 2G2). 905/890-1200; fax 905/890-5183.* 108 rms, 2 story. S, D $78-$96; each addl $7; suites $123-$149; under 18 free; monthly rates. Crib free. TV; cable (premium). Restaurant 7 am-10 pm. Serv bar 11-1 am. Ck-out noon. Meeting rms. Business servs avail. Exercise equipt; sauna.

Refrigerators avail. Cr cds: A, C, D, DS, ER, MC, V.

D 🏋 ⊠ SC

★★★ **RADISSON.** *2501 Argentia Rd (L5N 4G8). 905/858-2424; fax 905/821-1592.* 207 rms, 8 story. S, D $155-$165; each addl $10; suites $185; under 18 free; wkend rates. Crib free. TV; cable (premium). Indoor pool; whirlpool. Coffee in rms. Restaurant. Bar 11-1 am. Ck-out noon. Coin lndry. Meeting rms. Business servs avail. In-rm modem link. Bellhops. Valet serv. Sundries. Gift shop. Free airport transportation. Exercise equipt; sauna. Refrigerators; bathrm phone in suites; microwaves avail. Picnic tables. Cr cds: A, D, DS, ER, JCB, MC, V.

D ⌨ 🏋 ⊠ 🔥 SC

★ **TRAVELODGE.** *5599 Ambler Dr (L4W 3Z1), SW of jct ON 401, Dixie Rd. 905/624-9500; fax 905/624-1382.* 225 rms, 6 story. S $59; D $68; under 18 free; suites $89.95. Crib free. Pet accepted. TV; cable. Indoor pool; whirlpool. Complimentary coffee in rms. Restaurant 7-1 am. Bar from noon. Ck-out 11 am. Guest lndry. Meeting rms. Business servs avail. Valet serv. Sundries. Cr cds: A, D, DS, ER, JCB, MC, V.

D ⚡ ⌨ ⊠ 🔥 SC

★ **TRAVELODGE TORONTO SW/CARRIAGE INN.** *1767 Dundas St E (L4X 1L5), off on 427. 905/238-3400; fax 905/238-9457; toll-free 800/578-7878.* 85 rms, 2 story. June-Sep: S $70; D $75; each addl $5; suites $125-$150; under 12 free; wkly rates; lower rates rest of yr. Crib $5. TV; cable (premium). Complimentary continental bkfst. Coffee in rms. Restaurant nearby. Ck-out 11 am. Meeting rms. Health club privileges. Many refrigerators. Cr cds: A, D, DS, ER, MC, V.

D ⊠ 🔥 SC

Hotels

★★ **DELTA MEADOWVALE RESORT.** *6750 Mississauga Rd (L5N 2L3), in Meadowvale Business Park. 905/821-1981; fax 905/542-4036. www.deltahotels.com.* 374 rms, 15 story. S, D $190-$205; each addl $15; suites $150-$300; under 18 free. Crib free. Pet accepted. TV; cable (premium), VCR avail. 2 pools, 1 indoor; whirlpool, poolside serv. Supervised children's activities; ages 2-14. Restaurant 6:30 am-10 pm. Rm serv 24 hrs. Bar 11-1 am. Ck-out 1 pm. Meeting rms. Business servs avail. Barber, beauty shop. Airport transportation. Indoor tennis, pro shop. Golf privileges. Exercise rm. Minibars; some fireplaces. Microwaves avail. Balconies. Cr cds: A, D, DS, JCB, MC, V.

⊡ 🐾 🐫 ⛱ 🏃 ⊠ 🔥 SC 🎿

★★★ **FOUR POINTS BY SHERA-TON.** *5444 Dixie Rd (L4W 2L2), ON 401, Dixie Rd S Exit. 905/624-1144; fax 905/624-9477; toll-free 800/737-3211. www.fourpoints.com/toronto airport.* 296 rms, 10 story. S, D $99-$209; each addl $15; suites $225-$395; under 18 free; package plans. Crib free. Pet accepted, some restrictions. TV; cable (premium), VCR avail. Heated pool. Supervised children's activities; ages 2-12. Complimentary coffee in rms. Restaurant 6:30 am-10 pm; Sat, Sun from 7 am. Bars 11:30-1 am. Ck-out 1 pm. Meeting rms. Business center. In-rm modem link. Gift shop. Beauty shop. Garage parking. Free airport transportation. Exercise equipt; sauna. Game rm. Refrigerators, minibars. Cr cds: A, C, D, DS, ER, JCB, MC, V.

⊡ 🐾 ⛱ 🏃 ⊠ 🔥 SC 🎿

★★★ **HILTON INTERNATIONAL.** *5875 Airport Rd (L4V 1N1), 1 mi W of jct ON 427, Dixon Rd, near Lester B. Pearson Intl Airport. 905/677-9900; fax 905/677-5073. Email salestoronto-apt@hilton.com; www.hilton.com.* 413 rms, 11 story. S, D $165-$185; each addl $20; suites $185-$225; family rates; wkend packages. Crib free. Pet accepted, some restrictions. TV. Heated pool; poolside serv. Coffee in rms. Restaurant 6 am-midnight. Bars 11-2 am; entertainment. Ck-out noon. Meeting rms. Business center. Barber. Garage parking $6. Free airport transportation. Exercise equipt; sauna. Minibars; many bathrm phones. Cr cds: A, D, DS, ER, JCB, MC, V.

⊡ 🐾 ⛱ 🏃 ✈ ⊠ 🔥 SC 🎿

★★ **NOVOTEL.** *3670 Hurontartio St (L5B 1P3), jct ON 10 and Burn-hamthorpe Rd. 905/896-1000; fax 905/896-2521; res 800/668-6835. Email missmail@aol.com; novojack@aol.com.* 325 air-cooled rms, 14 story. S, D $169-$189; each addl $15; suite $250; under 16 free; wkend rates. Crib free. Pet accepted. TV; cable (premium). Indoor pool. Restaurant 6 am-midnight. Bar 11-1 am. Ck-out 1 pm. Meeting rms. Business servs avail. In-rm modem link. Shopping arcade. Beauty shop. Covered parking. Free airport transportation. Exercise equipt. Health club privileges. Minibars; some bathrm phones. Shopping center opp. Cr cds: A, C, D, DS, ER, JCB, MC, V.

⊡ 🐾 ⛱ 🏃 ⊠ 🔥 SC

★★★ **STAGE WEST HOTEL.** *5400 Dixie Rd (O4W 4T4). 905/238-0159; fax 905/238-9820; toll-free 800/668-9887. Email reservations@stagewest. com.* 224 suites, 16 story. Suites $175; family, wkly rates; package plans. Crib free. TV; cable (premium), VCR avail. Indoor pool; whirlpool, lifeguard, water slide. Supervised children's activities; ages 1-12. Restaurant 6:30 am-midnight. Bar 11-1 am. Ck-out noon. Meeting rms. Business center. In-rm modem link. Concierge serv. Shopping arcade. Barber, beauty shop. Valet parking $5/day. Free airport transportation. Downhill/x-country ski 20 mi. Exercise equipt. Microwaves avail. Complex incl Stage West Dinner Theatre. Cr cds: A, D, ER, MC, V.

⊡ 🎿 ⛱ 🏃 ✈ ⊠ 🔥 SC 🎿

B&B/Small Inn

★★★ **GLENERIN.** *1695 The College-way (L5L 3S7), off Mississauga Rd. 905/828-6103; fax 905/828-6103; res 800/267-0525. Email wersdl@connect. reach.net.* 39 rms, 2½ story, 13 suites. S $115; D $165; each addl $10; suites $195-$375; under 18 free; wkly rates; wkend packages. Crib free. TV; cable (premium), VCR avail. Complimentary bkfst. Dining rm 7 am-11 pm. Ck-out 11 am, ck-in 4 pm. Meeting rms. Business servs avail. Downhill/x-country ski 10 mi. Health club privileges. Some fireplaces. English-style manor house (1927); antique and modern furnishings. Rms vary in size and style. Cr cds: A, D, ER, MC, V.

⊡ 🎿 ⊠ 🔥 SC

Restaurants

★★★ **CHERRINGTON'S.** *7355 Torbram Rd (L4T 3W3). 905/672-0605.* Specializes in fresh fish, steak, pasta. Hrs: 11 am-11 pm; Sat from 4 pm. Closed Sun; Easter, Dec 25. Res accepted. Bar. Lunch $9.95-$14.95; dinner $15.95-$31.95. Child's menu. Entertainment: Fri, Sat. Parking. Elegant dining rm divided by bar. Cr cds: A, D, ER, MC, V.

D ⊐

★★ **CHERRY HILL HOUSE.** *680 Silvercreek Blvd (L5A 3Z1), in Silvercreek Mall. 905/275-9300.* Specializes in rack of lamb, pasta with lobster. Hrs: 11:30 am-10:30 pm; Sat from 5:30 pm; Sun 5:30-9 pm. Closed hols. Res accepted. Bar. Lunch a la carte entrees: $8.75-$13.25; dinner $13.50-$19.75. Converted house (ca 1850) is designated historic site. Cr cds: A, D, ER, MC, V.

D ⊐

★ **DECKER-TEN.** *1170 Burnhamthorpe Rd W (L5C 4E6). 905/276-7419.* Specializes in sashimi, beef teriyaki. Sushi bar. Hrs: 11:45 am-2:15 pm, 5:30-10 pm; Sat from 5:30 pm; Sun 5-9:30 pm. Closed Jan 1, July 1, Dec 24, 25. Res accepted. Bar. Lunch a la carte entrees: $7-$15; dinner a la carte entrees: $9-$20. Complete meals: $14-$28. Child's menu. Japanese art. Cr cds: A, C, MC, V.

⊐

★★ **LA CASTILE.** *2179 Dundas St E (L4X 1M3). 905/625-1137.* Specializes in shrimp cocktail, prime rib, barbecued ribs. Hrs: 11:30 am-midnight; Mon, Tues to 11 pm. Closed Sun; Dec 25. Res accepted. Bar. Lunch $9.95-$18.95; dinner $16.95-$36.95. Entertainment: pianist Wed-Sat. Parking. 16th-century castle decor; cathedral ceiling, tapestries, original oil painting. Cr cds: A, D, ER, MC, V.

D ⊐

★★★ **MOLINARO.** *50 Burnhamthorpe Rd W (L5B 3C2). 905/566-1330.* Specializes in pasta. Hrs: 11:30 am-11:30 pm. Closed Sun; hols. Res accepted; required Fri, Sat (dinner). Bar. Wine list. Lunch a la carte entrees: $10.95-

$14.95; dinner a la carte entrees: $12.95-$25.95. Entertainment: Thurs-Sat. Large windows; city views. Cr cds: A, D, MC, V.

D ⊐

★★ **MUSKY SUPPER HOUSE.** *261 Lakeshore Rd E (L5H 1G8). 905/271-9727. Email musky@istar.ca.* Specializes in hickory-smoked pork with sour cherries. Hrs: 5:30-11 pm. Closed Sun, Mon; some hols. Res accepted. Bar. Dinner a la carte entrees: $15-$24. Original art and carvings. Cr cds: A, DS, MC, V.

D

★★★ **OLD BARBER HOUSE.** *5155 Mississauga Rd (L5M 2L9). 905/858-7570.* Specializes in veal, pasta, lamb. Own pastries. Hrs: 11 am-11 pm; Sat from 5 pm. Closed Sun; Jan 1, Dec 25. Res accepted. Bar. Lunch a la carte entrees: $9.95-$13.95; dinner a la carte entrees: $11.95-$34.95. Parking. Victorian house (1862). Cr cds: A, MC, V.

⊐

★★ **OUTRIGGER STEAK AND SEAFOOD.** *2539 Dixie Rd (L4Y 2A1). 905/275-7000.* Specializes in steak, seafood. Salad bar. Own baking. Hrs: 4-10:30 pm. Closed Dec 25. Res accepted. Bar. Dinner a la carte entrees: $10.95-$36.99. Child's menu. Cr cds: A, C, D, DS, MC, V.

D ⊐

★★ **SNUG HARBOUR.** *14 Stavebank Rd S (L5G 2T1). 905/274-5000.* Specializes in fresh seafood, pasta. Hrs: 11:30 am-10:30 pm. Closed Jan 1, Dec 24-26. Res accepted. Bar. Lunch $6.95-$18.50; dinner $6.95-$18.50. Child's menu. Entertainment: jazz Fri, Sat. On Lake Ontario. Cr cds: A, MC, V.

D ⊐

Morrisburg

See also Cornwall

Pop 2,308 **Elev** 250 ft (76 m)
Area code 613

Information Chamber of Commerce, PO Box 288, K0C 1X0; 613/543-3443

Rising waters of the St. Lawrence Seaway forced the removal of Morrisburg and many other towns to higher ground. This was one of the earliest settled parts of Canada, and homes, churches, and buildings of historic note were moved and reconstructed on the Crysler Farm located in Upper Canada Village, itself a historic spot.

What to See and Do

Crysler Farm Battlefield Park. Scene of a decisive battle of the War of 1812, where 800 British and Canadians defeated 4,000 American troops. Also here are Crysler Park Marina, Upper Canada Golf Course, Crysler Beach (fee), Battle of Crysler's Farm Visitor Centre and Memorial Mound, Pioneer Memorial, Loyalist Memorial, Air Strip, and Queen Elizabeth Gardens. Varying fees. 7 mi (11 km) E on ON 2. Nearby is

Upper Canada Village. Authentic re-creation of rural 1860s riverfront village. Demonstrations by staff in period costumes. Historic bldgs incl operating woolen mill, sawmill, gristmill; Willard's Hotel; blacksmith, tinsmith, dressmaker, shoemaker, and cabinetmaker shops; tavern, churches, school, bakery, working farms, canal. May be seen on foot, by carryall, or *bateau*. (Mid-May-mid-Oct, daily; closed hols) Phone 613/543-3704. ¢¢¢

Fort Wellington National Historic Site. Original British fort first built in 1813, rebuilt in 1838 after Canadian Rebellions of 1837-38. Restored blockhouse, officers' quarters, latrine; guides in period costume depict fort life ca 1846. Underground stone tunnel designed to defend the fort's flank. Large military pageant with mock battles (3rd wkend July). (Mid-May-Sep, daily; rest of yr, by appt) 33 mi (53 km) SW via Hwy 401, in Prescott. Phone 613/925-2896. **FREE**

Prehistoric World. Life-size reproductions of prehistoric animals along a ¾-mi (1-km) nature trail. More than 40 exhibits completed, incl Brontosaurus and Tyrannosaurus Rex; others in various stages of construction. (Late May-Labour Day, daily) 5

mi (7 km) E via Hwy 401, Exit 758. Phone 613/543-2503. ¢¢

Motel/Motor Lodge

★ **BUDGET INN.** *Hwy 2 & 31 (K0C 1X0). 613/543-2932; fax 613/543-3316.* 31 rms, 1-2 story. S $39-$49; D $49-$69; wkend rates. Pet accepted. TV; cable. Heated pool. Restaurant 11:30 am-2 pm, 5-9:30 pm. Bar noon-1 am. Ck-out 11 am. Cr cds: A, MC, V.
⊗ ⊵ ⊠ ⊠ SC

Niagara Falls

(E-5) *See Niagara-on-the-Lake, St. Catharines*

Pop 70,960 **Elev** 589 ft (180 m)
Area code 905
Web www.tourismniagara.com/nfcvcb

Information Visitor & Convention Bureau, 5433 Victoria Ave, L2G 3L1; 905/356-6061 or 800/563-2557

The Canadian side of Niagara Falls offers viewpoints different from, and in many ways superior to, those on the American side. Center of a beautiful 35-mile (60-kilometer) stretch of parks and home of a tremendous range of man-made attractions, this area is popular all year with tourists from all over the world.

What to See and Do

Boat ride. *Maid of the Mist* leaves from foot of Clifton Hill on Niagara River Pkwy near Rainbow Bridge. Phone 716/284-4233 (NY) or 905/358-5781 (Canada). ¢¢¢

Canada One Factory Outlets. Outlet Centre sells many nationally recognized brands of merchandise. 7500 Lundy's Ln. Phone 416/323-3977.

Great Gorge Adventure. Niagara River at its narrowest point. Elevator and 240-ft (73-m) tunnel takes visitors to the boardwalk at edge of whirlpool rapids. (Apr-Oct, daily) 2 mi (3 km) N at 4330 River Rd. Contact PO Box 150, L2E 6T2. Phone 905/374-1221. ¢¢

Horseshoe Falls, Niagara Falls

Guinness World of Records Museum. Based on the popular book of records; hundreds of original exhibits, artifacts; laser video galleries; re-creations of many of the world's greatest accomplishments. (Daily) 4943 Clifton Hill. Phone 905/356-2299. ¢¢¢

Historic Fort Erie. Site of some of the fiercest fighting of the War of 1812; restored to period. Guided tours by interpreters dressed in uniform of the Glengarry Light Infantry. (Mid-Apr-late-Oct) 21 mi (34 km) S via QEW, at 250 Lake Shore Rd in Fort Erie. Phone 905/871-0540. ¢¢¢

Journey Behind the Falls. Elevator descends to point about 25 ft (8 m) above river, offering excellent view of Falls from below and behind; waterproof garments are supplied. (Daily; closed Dec 25) 1 mi S of Rainbow Bridge on Niagara Pkwy in Queen Victoria Park. Phone 905/354-1551. ¢¢ Also in park is

> **Greenhouse.** Tropical and native plants; animated fountain, garden shop. (Daily) Phone 905/354-1721. **FREE**

Louis Tussaud's Waxworks. Life-size, historically costumed wax figures of the past and present; Chamber of Horrors. (Daily; closed Dec 25) 4915 Clifton Hill. Phone 905/374-6601 or 905/374-4534. ¢¢

Lundy's Lane Historical Museum. (1874) On the site of the Battle of Lundy's Lane (1814). Interprets early settlement and tourism of Niagara Falls; 1812 war militaria; Victorian parlor, early kitchen, toys, dolls, photographs; galleries and exhibits. (May-Nov, daily; rest of yr, Mon-Fri; closed Jan 1, Dec 25) 5810 Ferry St. Phone 905/358-5082. ¢

Marineland. Performing killer whales, dolphins, sea lions; wildlife displays with deer, bears, buffalo, and elk; thrill rides, incl one of the world's largest steel roller coasters; restaurants, picnic areas. Park (Mar-mid-Dec, daily); rides (mid-May-early Oct). 7657 Portage Rd. Phone 905/356-8250. ¢¢¢¢

Niagara Falls Museum. One of North America's oldest museums, founded in 1827. Twenty-six galleries of rare, worldwide artifacts, incl "Niagara's Original Daredevil Hall of Fame"; Egyptian mummy collection; dinosaur exhibit. (Summer, daily; winter, schedule varies) 5651 River Rd. Phone 905/356-2151 (Canada) or 716/285-4898 (US). ¢¢

Niagara Parks Botanical Gardens. Nearly 100 acres of horticultural exhibits. Nature shop. (Daily) Niagara Pkwy N. Phone 905/356-8554. **FREE**. On grounds is the

> **Niagara Parks Butterfly Conservatory.** Approx 2,000 butterflies make

their home in this 11,000-sq-ft (1,022-sq-m), climate-controlled conservatory filled with exotic greenery and flowing water. Nearly 50 species of butterflies can be viewed from a 600-ft (180-m) network of walking paths. Outdoor butterfly garden (seasonal). Gift shop. (Daily) Phone 905/358-0025. ¢¢¢

Niagara Spanish Aero Car. The 1,800-ft (549-m) cables support a car that crosses the whirlpool and rapids of the Niagara River. Five-min trip each way. (Mid-Apr-mid-Oct, daily) 3½ mi (5 km) N on Niagara Parkway. Phone 905/354-5711. ¢¢¢

Observation towers.

IMAX Theatre and Daredevil Adventure. Six-story-high movie screen shows *Niagara: Miracles, Myths, and Magic,* a film highlighting the Falls. Daredevil Adventure has displays, exhibits, and some of the actual barrels used to traverse the Falls. (Daily; closed Dec 25) 6170 Buchanan Ave. Phone 905/374-IMAX (recording) or 905/358-3611. ¢¢¢

⭐ **Minolta Tower Centre.** This awesome 325-ft (99.06-m) tower offers a magnificent 360° view of the Falls and surrounding areas. Eight levels at top; specially designed glass for ideal photography; Minolta exhibit floor; "Waltzing Waters" water and light spectacle (free; seasonal); gift shops; incline railway to Falls (fee; free parking); "Top of the Rainbow" dining rms overlooking Falls (res suggested). (Daily; closed Dec 24, 25) 6732 Oakes Dr. Phone 905/356-1501. ¢¢¢

Skylon Tower. Stands 775 ft (236 m) above base of Falls. Three-level dome contains an indoor/outdoor observation deck and revolving and stationary dining rms served by 3 external, glass-enclosed "Yellow Bug" elevators. Specialty shops at base of tower. (Daily) 5200 Robinson St. Phone 905/356-2651. ¢¢¢ Adj is

Annual Event

Winter Festival of Lights. Queen Victoria Park. Phone 800/563-2557. Late Nov-late Jan.

Motels/Motor Lodges

★★ **BEST WESTERN CAIRN CROFT.** *6400 Lundy's Ln (ON 20) (L3G 1T6), 1¼ mi W of Falls. 905/ 356-1161; fax 905/356-8664. Email bestwestern@niagara.net; www.niagara. net/cairncroft.* 165 rms, 5 story. Late June-Aug: S, D $99.50-$149.50; each addl $10; suites $150-$199; under 18 free; lower rates rest of yr. Crib free. TV. Playground. Indoor pool. Restaurant 7 am-2 pm, 5-8 pm. Bar 4 pm-1 am; entertainment Tues-Sat. Ck-out 11 am. Meeting rms. Business servs avail. Bellhops. Valet serv. X-country ski 3 mi. Health club privileges. Enclosed courtyard. Cr cds: A, C, D, DS, ER, MC, V.
🐾 🏊 ⛷ 🐾 SC

★★ **BEST WESTERN FALLSVIEW.** *5551 Murray St (L2G 2J4), 1 blk to Falls. 905/356-0551; fax 905/356-7773. www.bestwestern.com.* 244 rms, 4-6 story. June-Sep: S, D $79-$169; each addl $10; lower rates rest of yr. Crib $5. Pet accepted. TV; cable. Indoor pool; whirlpool. Sauna. Restaurant 6 am-10 pm. Bar 11-1 am. Ck-out 11 am. Coin lndry. Meeting rms. Business servs avail. Bellhops. Gift shop. Sundries. Game rm. Some in-rm whirlpools. Cr cds: A, C, D, DS, ER, JCB, MC, V.
D 🐾 🏊 ⛷ 🐾 SC

★★ **CARRIAGE HOUSE.** *8004 Lundy's Ln (ON 20) (L2H 1H1), ½ mi W of QEW. 905/356-7799; fax 905/ 358-6431; toll-free 800/267-9887.* 120 rms, 2 story. July-Aug: S, D $65-$105; each addl $10; suites $100-$150; family rates; higher rates special events; lower rates rest of yr. Crib free. TV. 2 pools, 1 indoor; whirlpool. Restaurant 7 am-noon. Ck-out 11 am. Business servs avail. Sundries. X-country ski 4 mi. Some in-rm whirlpools. Some balconies. Cr cds: A, C, D, DS, ER, MC, V.
D 🐾 🏊 ⛷ 🐾 SC

★ **CASCADE INN.** *5305 Murray St (L2G 2J3), 1 blk W of Falls. 905/354-2796; fax 905/354-2797. Email niagara@cascade.on.ca; www.cascade. on.ca.* 65 rms, 3-6 story. Mid-May-Labour Day: D $98-$129; lower rates rest of yr. Crib free. TV. Pool. Restaurant 7-11 am. Ck-out 11 am. Gift shop. X-country ski 2 mi. Near Sky-lon Tower. Cr cds: A, DS, MC, V.

🏊 ≋ ⛷ 🐾 SC

★ **CAVALIER.** *5100 Centre St (L2G 3P2), 3 blks W of Falls.* 905/358-3288; fax 905/358-3289. 39 rms, 2 story. July-Aug: S, D $66-$94; under 5 free; lower rates rest of yr. Crib free. TV; cable (premium). Heated pool. Restaurant opp from 7 am. Ck-out 11 am. French Provincial decor. Cr cds: A, JCB, MC, V.

≋ ⛷ 🐾 SC

★ **CRYSTAL MOTEL.** *4249 River Rd (Niagara River Pkwy) (L2E 3E7), 1 blk N of Whirlpool Rapids Bridge.* 905/354-0460; fax 905/374-4972. 38 rms, 2 story. Mid-June-mid-Sep: S, D $68-$95; each addl $8; lower rates rest of yr. Crib $4. TV; cable (premium). Heated pool. Restaurant nearby. Ck-out 11 am. Refrigerators; some in-rm whirlpools. Some balconies. Cr cds: A, DS, MC, V.

≋ ⛷ 🐾 SC

★ **DAYS INN FALLSVIEW DISTRICT.** *6408 Stanley Ave (L2G 3Y5), 2 blks W of Falls.* 905/356-5877; fax 905/356-9452. 102 rms, 3 story, 4 suites. June-Sep: S, D $89-$165; each addl $10; suites $150-$180; under 13 free; lower rates rest of yr. Crib $10. TV. Indoor pool. Restaurant 7 am-midnight; hrs vary rest of yr. Bar from noon. Ck-out 11 am. X-country ski 5 mi. Sauna. Balconies. Picnic tables. Cr cds: A, D, ER, JCB, MC, V.

🏊 ≋ 🐾 SC

★ **ECONO LODGE.** *5781 Victoria Ave (L2G 3L6), at Lundy's Ln.* 905/356-2034; fax 905/374-2866. 57 rms, 2 story. Late June-Sep: S, D $89.95-$156.95; each addl $10; suites $156.95-$199.95; under 18 free; lower rates rest of yr. Crib free. TV; cable. Indoor pool; whirlpool. Restaurant adj open 24 hrs. Ck-out 11 am. X-country ski 2 mi. Cr cds: A, D, DS, MC, V.

🏊 ≋ ⛷ 🐾 SC

★ **ECONO LODGE.** *7514 Lundy's Ln (ON 20) (L2H 1G8), 2¾ mi W of Falls at QEW.* 905/354-1849. 45 rms. Late June-mid-Sep: S, D $45-$115; each addl $5; higher rates hol wkends; lower rates rest of yr. Crib free. TV. Heated pool. Restaurant nearby. Ck-

out 11 am. X-country ski 3 mi. Picnic tables. On landscaped grounds; back from hwy. Cr cds: A, D, DS, MC, V.

🏊 ⛷ ≋ ⛷ 🐾 SC

★★ **FLAMINGO MOTOR INN.** *7701 Lundy's Ln (L2H 1H3), 1½ mi W of Falls.* 905/356-4646; fax 905/356-9373; toll-free 800/738-7701. 95 rms, 2 story. Mid-June-Labour Day: S, D $72-$104; each addl $10; whirlpool rm $104-$200; lower rates rest of yr. Crib free. Pet accepted, some restrictions. TV; cable. Heated pool. Restaurant adj 7 am-10 pm. Ck-out 11 am. Gift shop. Picnic tables. Cr cds: A, C, D, DS, MC, V.

🐾 ≋ ⛷ 🐾 SC

★★ **HAMPTON INN AT THE FALLS.** *5591 Victoria Ave (L2Z 3L4).* 905/357-1626; fax 905/357-5869. 127 units, 3-6 story. Mid-June-Labour Day: S, D $89-$189; suites $139-$269; under 18 free; lower rates rest of yr. Crib free. TV; cable (premium). Indoor pool; whirlpool. Sauna. Complimentary continental bkfst, coffee in rms. Bar 4 pm-1 am (in season). Ck-out 11 am. Meeting rms. Business servs avail. In-rm modem link. Sundries. Game rm. Balconies. Cr cds: A, D, DS, ER, MC, V.

D ≋ ⛷ 🐾 SC

★★ **HOLIDAY INN BY THE FALLS.** *5339 Murray St (L2G 2J3), 2 blks W of Falls.* 905/356-1333; fax 905/356-7128. Email res@holidayinn.com; www.holidayinn.com. 122 rms, 6 story. Mid-June-mid-Sep: S, D $95-$195; each addl $10; bridal suite $175-$225; lower rates rest of yr. Crib $5. Pet accepted. TV. 2 pools, 1 indoor; whirlpool. Restaurant 7 am-10 pm; winter from 8 am. Bar noon-2 am. Ck-out noon. Sundries. Sauna. Some in-rm whirlpools. Balconies. Cr cds: A, C, D, DS, ER, JCB, MC, V.

D 🐾 ≋ ⛷ 🐾 SC

★★ **HONEYMOON CITY.** *4943 Clifton Hill (L2G 3N5).* 905/357-4330; fax 905/357-0423. www.niagara.com/falls/. 77 rms, 2 story. Mid-June-early Sep: S, D $48-$169; suites, kits. $129-$239; under 12 free; wkend, hol rates; lower rates rest of yr. Crib free. Pet accepted, some restrictions. TV; cable, VCR avail (movies). Heated pool. Restaurant 7 am-11 pm. Ck-out

11 am. Business servs avail. Shopping arcade. X-country ski 2 mi. Some balconies. Cr cds: A, MC, V.

⬛ ⬛ ⬛ ⬛ SC

★ **HOWARD JOHNSON BY THE FALLS.** *5905 Victoria Ave (L2G 3L8). 905/357-4040; fax 905/357-6202.* 199 rms, 6-7 story. S, D $59-$299; each addl $10; suites $69-$349; under 18 free. Crib free. TV; cable, VCR avail. Indoor/outdoor pool; whirlpool. Restaurant open 24 hrs. Ck-out noon. Meeting rms. Business servs avail. Gift shop. X-country ski 2 mi. Sauna. Game rm. Some in-rm whirlpools. Some balconies. Cr cds: A, C, D, DS, ER, JCB, MC, V.

⬛ ⬛ ⬛ ⬛ ⬛ SC

★★ **IMPERIAL HOTEL AND SUITES.** *5851 Victoria St (L2G 3L6). 905/356-2648; fax 905/356-4068.* 104 suites, 10 story. July-Aug: S, D $104-$179; each addl $15; under 16 free; lower rates rest of yr. Crib $10. TV. Indoor pool; whirlpool. Restaurant adj 7 am-10 pm. Bar 11-2 am. Ck-out noon. Coin lndry. Meeting rms. Business servs avail. Gift shop. X-country ski 2 mi. Game rm. Refrigerators; microwaves avail. Cr cds: A, D, DS, ER, MC, V.

⬛ ⬛ ⬛ ⬛ ⬛ SC

★★★ **MICHAEL'S INN.** *5599 River Rd (L2E 3H3), N of Rainbow Bridge. 905/354-2727; fax 905/374-7706. Email michaels@michaelsinn.com; www.michaelsinn.com.* 130 rms, 4 story. May-Oct: S, D $59-$228; suites $125-$375; lower rates rest of yr. Crib $5. TV; cable (premium). Indoor pool; wading pool, whirlpool, lifeguard in season. Restaurant 7 am-11:30 pm. Bar. Ck-out 11 am. Meeting rms. Business servs avail. Bellhops. Valet serv. Sauna. Some refrigerators. Overlooks the Falls. Cr cds: A, C, D, ER, JCB, MC, V.

⬛ ⬛ ⬛ ⬛ SC

★★ **OLD STONE INN.** *5425 Robinson St (L2G 7L6). 905/357-1234; fax 905/357-9299. Email atiene@oldstone. on.ca.* 114 rms, 3 story. May-Oct: S, D $125-$225; each addl $10; suites $195-$349; under 12 free; wkend rates; higher rates hols; lower rates rest of yr. Crib free. TV; cable. 2 pools, 1 indoor; whirlpool, poolside serv. Restaurant (see also THE MILLERY). Bar 11-2 am. Ck-out 11

am. Meeting rms. Business servs avail. Bellhops. Gift shop. Valet serv. X-country ski 2 mi. Main bldg former flour mill built 1904. Cr cds: A, D, DS, ER, JCB, MC, V.

⬛ ⬛ ⬛ ⬛ ⬛

★ **PILGRIM MOTOR INN.** *4955 Clifton Hill (L2G 3N5). 905/374-7777; fax 905/354-8086.* 40 rms, 3 story. Mid-June-mid-Sep: S, D $58-$149.50; each addl $10; higher rates: hols, wkends; lower rates rest of yr. Crib free. TV; cable. Ck-out noon. Balconies. Sun deck. Cr cds: A, MC, V.

⬛ ⬛ ⬛ SC

★★ **RAMADA-CORAL INN RESORT.** *7429 Lundy's Ln (ON 20) (L2H 1G9), 2 mi W of Falls. 905/356-6116; fax 905/356-7204. Email ramada.niagara@sympatico.ca; www.tourismniagara.com/ramcoral.* 130 units, 2-4 story. Mid-June-early Sep: S, D $89-$139; each addl $10; suites, studio rms $129-$169; under 18 free; package plans; higher rates: Sat in season, hols, special events; lower rates rest of yr. Crib free. TV. 2 heated pools, 1 indoor; whirlpool. Restaurant 7 am-10 pm. Ck-out 11 am. Meeting rms. Business center. Valet serv. Gift shop. Exercise equipt; sauna. Health club privileges. Playground. Game rm. Refrigerators, in-rm whirlpools; fireplace in suites. Cr cds: A, C, D, DS, ER, JCB, MC, V.

⬛ ⬛ ⬛ ⬛ SC ⬛ ⬛

★ **SURFSIDE INN.** *3665 Macklem St (L2Q 6C8). 905/295-4354; fax 905/295-4374; toll-free 800/263-0713. Email surfside@niagarafalls.net; www.niagarafalls.net/motel.* 31 rms. Mid-Apr-mid-Nov: D $55-$125; each addl $6; suites $99-$185; lower rates rest of yr. Crib free. TV. Pool. Coffee in rms. Restaurant nearby. Ck-out 11 am. Refrigerators; microwaves avail. Some whirlpools in suites. Bicycle trail. Cr cds: A, C, D, DS, ER, JCB, MC, V.

⬛ ⬛ ⬛ ⬛ SC

★ **TRAVELODGE BONAVENTURE.** *7737 Lundy's Ln (L2H 1H3). 905/374-7171; fax 905/374-1151.* 118 rms, 3 story, 16 suites. Mid-June-Sep: S, D $59.50-$159; each addl $8; whirlpool rm $139-$179; under 17 free; 2-day min wkends in season; lower rates rest of yr. Crib free. TV; cable (premium). 2 pools, 1 indoor.

Complimentary coffee in lobby. Restaurant opp 7-1 am. Ck-out 11 am. X-country ski 4 mi. Cr cds: A, D, DS, ER, MC, V.

D ⊠ ⛱ ⛷ 🔥 SC

★ **TRAVELODGE NEAR THE FALLS.** *5234 Ferry St (L2G 1R5). 905/374-7771; fax 905/374-7771.* 81 rms, 4 story, 22 suites. July-Aug: S, D $99-$149; each addl $10; suites $129-$199; family, wkly rates; higher rates hol wknds, lower rates rest of yr. Crib free. TV; cable (premium). Indoor pool; whirlpool. Sauna. Complimentary coffee in lobby. Restaurant 7 am-3 pm. Ck-out 11 am. X-country ski 2 mi. Whirlpool in suites. Cr cds: A, D, MC, V.

D ⊠ ⛱ ⛷ 🔥 SC

★ **VILLAGE INN.** *5685 Falls Ave (L2E 6W7), off QEW spur at Rainbow Bridge, in Maple Leaf Village Complex. 905/374-4444; fax 905/374-0800. www.falls.net/skyline.* 206 rms, 2 story. Late June-early Sep: S, D $119.99; lower rates rest of yr. Crib free. TV; cable. Playground. Complimentary continental bkfst. Restaurant 6:30-11 am. Business servs avail. Health club privileges. Microwaves avail. Cr cds: A, C, D, DS, ER, JCB, MC, V.

⛷ 🔥 SC

Hotels

★ **DAYS INN NEAR THE FALLS.** *5943 Victoria Ave (L2G 3L8). 905/374-3333; fax 905/374-0669.* 117 rms, 7 story. S, D $99-$199; each addl $10; under 18 free. Crib free. TV; cable. Indoor pool; whirlpool. Restaurant adj open 24 hrs. No rm serv. Ck-out noon. No bellhops. Gift shop. X-country ski 2 mi. Sauna. Game rm. Cr cds: A, D, DS, ER, MC, V.

⊠ ⛱ ⛷ 🔥 SC

★ **DAYS INN OVERLOOKING THE FALLS.** *6361 Buchanan Ave (L2G 3V9). 905/357-7377; fax 905/374-6707. www.daysinn.com/daysinn.html.* 193 rms, 15 story. Late June-late Sep: S, D $99-$499; each addl $10; under 17 free; lower rates rest of yr. Crib free. TV. Indoor pool; whirlpool. Complimentary coffee in rms. Restaurant adj open 24 hrs. No rm serv. Bar. Ck-out 11 am. Meeting rms. Business servs avail. No bellhops. Gift

shop. X-country ski 2 mi. Sauna. Game rm. Cr cds: A, D, DS, ER, MC, V.

⊠ ⛱ ⛷ 🔥 SC

★★★ **FOUR POINTS SHERATON BY THE FALLS.** *6045 Stanley Ave (L2G 3Y3). 905/374-4142; fax 905/358-3430.* 112 rms, 8 story. Late June-mid-Sep: S, D $129-$269; each addl $10; under 14 free; wkends (2-day min); higher rates hol wkends; lower rates rest of yr. Crib free. TV; cable. Indoor pool; whirlpool, poolside serv. Restaurant 7 am-2 pm, 5-10 pm. Bar from 5 pm. Ck-out 11 am. Meeting rms. Business center. Gift shop. X-country ski 2 mi. Cr cds: A, D, DS, ER, JCB, MC, V.

D ⊠ ⛱ ⛷ 🔥 🚶 SC

★★ **OAKES INN.** *6546 Buchanan Ave (L2G 3W2), 2 blks S of Falls. 905/356-4514; fax 905/356-3651.* 167 units, 12 story. Mid-June-mid-Sep: S, D $89-$309; each addl $5; suites $209-$349; family units; lower rates rest of yr. Crib $10. TV; cable. 2 heated pools, 1 indoor; whirlpool. Restaurants 7 am-midnight; off-season 8 am-9 pm. Bar noon-1 am. Ck-out 11 am. Meeting rms. Business servs avail. Gift shop. X-country ski 2 mi. Exercise equipt; sauna. Some in-rm whirlpools. Some rms with view of Falls. Enclosed observation deck. Cr cds: A, C, D, DS, ER, JCB, MC, V.

⛱ ⛱ 🚴 ⛷ 🔥 SC

★★ **QUALITY HOTEL.** *5257 Ferry St (L2G 1R6). 905/356-2842; fax 905/356-6629; toll-free 800/263-6917. www.hotelchoice.com.* 80 rms, 8 story. Mid-June-mid-Sep: S, D $89.99-$249.99; each addl $10-$50; lower rates rest of yr. Crib free. TV; cable. Indoor pool; whirlpool. Restaurant 7 am-noon. No rm serv. Ck-out noon. Meeting rms. Business servs avail. No bellhops. Gift shop. X-country ski 2 mi. Sauna. Cr cds: A, C, D, DS, ER, JCB, MC, V.

⛱ ⛱ ⛷ 🔥 SC

★★ **RAMADA SUITES NIAGARA.** *7389 Lundy's Ln (L2H 2W9). 905/356-6119; fax 905/356-7204. www.ramada.com.* 73 suites, 7 story. Mid-June-early Sep: S, D $109-$159; each addl $10; under 18 free; suites $129-$169; family rates; higher rates: hol wknds, Sat in season; lower rates rest of yr. Crib free. TV. Indoor pool;

whirlpool. Restaurant 7 am-11 pm. No rm serv. Bar 11:30 am-midnight. Ck-out 11 am. Meeting rms. Business center. In-rm modem link. Exercise equipt; sauna. Refrigerators; whirlpool in suites. Cr cds: A, C, D, DS, ER, JCB, MC, V.

D ⇆ 🕇 🖳 🔥 SC 🕇

★★★ **RENAISSANCE FALLSVIEW.** 6455 Buchanan Ave (L2G 3Z9). 905/ 357-5200; fax 905/357-3422. Email renfalls@niagara.com; www.niagara. com/nf-renaissance. 262 rms, 19 story. Mid-June-Sep: S, D $185-$309; each addl $20; under 18 free; lower rates rest of yr. Crib free. TV; cable. Indoor pool. Restaurants 7 am-11 pm. Bar 11-1 am. Ck-out 11 am. Meeting rms. Business servs avail. Exercise equipt; sauna. Cr cds: A, D, DS, ER, JCB, MC, V.

D ⇆ 🕇 🖳 🔥 SC

★★ **SKYLINE BROCK.** 5685 Falls Ave (L2E 6W7), off QEW spur at Rainbow Bridge, in Maple Leaf Village Complex. 905/374-4445; fax 905/357-4804. www.falls.net/skyline. 233 rms, 12 story. June-Sep: S, D $129-$369; each addl $10; suites $249-$429; under 18 free; lower rates rest of yr. Crib free. TV; cable. Parking $4-$6 (in season). Restaurant 7 am-10 pm. Bar in season 11-1 am. Ck-out 11 am. Meeting rms. Business servs avail. Health club privileges. Most rms overlook Falls. Cr cds: A, C, D, DS, ER, JCB, MC, V.

🖳 🔥 SC

★★ **SKYLINE FOXHEAD.** 5875 Falls Ave (L2E 6W7), in Maple Leaf Village Complex. 905/374-4444; fax 905/351-0157; res 800/263-7135. www.falls.net/skyline. 399 rms, 14 story. June-Sep: S, D $119-$269; each addl $10; under 18 free; higher rates hol wkends; lower rates rest of yr. Crib free. Valet parking $12/day in season. TV; cable (premium). Pool. Restaurant 6:30 am-10 pm. Bar from 11 am. Ck-out 11 am. Meeting rms. Business center. Concierge serv. Shopping arcade. X-country ski 2 mi. Exercise equipt. Some balconies overlooking Falls. Cr cds: A, C, D, DS, ER, JCB, MC, V.

D ⇆ 🕇 🖳 🔥 SC 🕇

Restaurants

★★ **CAPRI.** 5438 Ferry St (L2G 1S1). 905/354-7519. Specializes in seafood, steak, pasta. Hrs: 11 am-11 pm. Closed Dec 24-26. Res accepted. Bar. Lunch a la carte entrees: $5.75-$12.50; dinner a la carte entrees: $8.95-$34.95. Child's menu. Parking. Family-owned. Cr cds: A, C, D, ER, MC, V.

D 🖳

★ **FOUR BROTHERS.** 5383 Ferry St (L2G 1R6). 905/358-6951. Specializes in steak, seafood, gourmet pasta dishes. Hrs: 11 am-10:30 pm. Closed Dec 24, 25. Res accepted. Bar. Lunch a la carte entrees: $1.95-$10.95; dinner a la carte entrees: $7.95-$19.95. Child's menu. Parking. Old World decor. Family-owned. Cr cds: A, C, D, DS, ER, MC, V.

D 🖳

★★ **THE MILLERY.** 5425 Robinson St. 905/357-1234. www.oldstoneinn.on. ca. Specializes in prime rib, rack of lamb. Hrs: 7 am-10 pm; early-bird dinner 4:30-6 pm. Res accepted (dinner). Bar. Bkfst $1.95-$8.95; lunch $4.95-$9.95; dinner $15.50-$40. Child's menu. In historic mill. Cr cds: A, D, DS, MC, V.

D 🖳

★★★ **QUEENSTON HEIGHTS.** 14184 Niagara Pkwy (L2E 6T2), 6 mi N of Falls. 905/262-4274. Specializes in prime rib, lamb, steak. Hrs: noon-3 pm, 5-9 pm; Sat noon-9 pm; high tea 3-5 pm; mid-June-Labour Day to 9:30 pm; Sun brunch 11 am-3 pm. Res accepted. Bar. Lunch a la carte entrees: $9.25-$11.95; dinner a la carte entrees: $15.95-$24.95. Sun brunch $17.95. Child's menu. Parking. Enclosed balcony dining overlooks river, orchards. War of 1812 battle site. Cr cds: A, D, MC, V.

D 🖳

★★ **VICTORIA PARK.** Niagara Pkwy, in Queen Victoria Park. 905/356-2217. Specializes in prime rib. Menu changes seasonally. Hrs: 11 am-9 pm; late June-Aug to 10 pm; early-bird dinner 4-6:30 pm. Closed mid-Oct-Apr. Res accepted. Bar. Lunch $8.29-$12.49; dinner $16.99-$21.99. Child's menu. Parking. Victorian decor. Cr cds: A, C, D, ER, MC, V.

D

Niagara-on-the-Lake

(D-5) *See also Niagara Falls, St. Catharines*

Settled 1776 **Pop** 12,186 **Elev** 262 ft (80 m) **Area code** 905
Web www.niagara-on-the-lake.com
Information Chamber of Commerce, 153 King St, PO Box 1043, L0S 1J0; 905/468-4263

Often called the loveliest in Ontario, this picturesque town has a long and distinguished history which parallels the growth of the province. Originally the Neutral village of Onghiara, it attracted Loyalist settlers after the American Revolution, many of whom were members of the feared Butler's Rangers. Pioneers followed from many European countries, and after a succession of names including Newark, the town finally received its present name. In 1792 it became the first capital of Upper Canada and remained so until 1796. Governor John Graves Simcoe, considering the proximity to the United States in case of war, moved the seat of government to York, near Toronto. The town played a significant role in the War of 1812, was occupied, and eventually burned along with Fort George in 1813.

Once a busy shipping, shipbuilding, and active commercial center, the beautiful old homes lining the tree-shaded streets testify to the area's prosperity. The town's attractions now include theater, historic sites, beautiful gardens, and Queen Street, with its shops, hotels, and restaurants. Delightful in any season, this is one of the best-preserved and prettiest remnants of the Georgian era.

What to See and Do

Brock's Monument. Massive, 185-ft (56-m) memorial to Sir Isaac Brock, who was felled by a sharpshooter while leading his troops against American forces at the Battle of Queenston Heights in Oct 1812. Narrow, winding staircase leads to tiny observation deck inside monument. Other memorial plaques in park; walking tour of important points on the Queenston Heights Battlefield begins at Brock Monument; brochure avail here. Brock and his aide-de-camp, Lieutenant-Colonel Macdonell, are buried here. (Mid-May-Labour Day, daily) 7 mi (11 km) S in Queenston Heights Park. Phone 905/468-4257. **FREE**

Court House. (1847) Built on site of original government house, 3-story bldg is now the home of Court House Theatre. First home of the Shaw Festival (see SEASONAL EVENT). Queen St. Opp is

Clock Tower. (1921) Erected in memory of those who died in world wars. Set in center of road surrounded by floral displays.

Fort George National Historic Site. (1797) Once the principal British post on the frontier, this fort saw much action during the War of 1812. Eleven restored, refurnished bldgs and massive ramparts. (Mid-May-Oct, daily; rest of yr, by appt; living history mid-May-Labour Day) Guided tours by appt. On Niagara Pkwy. Phone 905/468-6614. ¢¢

Laura Secord Homestead. Restored home of Canadian heroine is furnished with early Upper Canada furniture. After overhearing the plans of Americans billetted in her home, Laura Secord made an exhausting and difficult 19 mi (30 km) walk to warn British troops, which resulted in a victory over the Americans at Beaverdams in 1813. (Victoria Day-Labour Day, daily) Partition St, 5 mi (8 km) S in Queenston. Phone 905/371-0254 or 877/642-7275. Tours ¢

McFarland House. (1800) Georgian brick home used as hospital in War of 1812; furnished in the Loyalist tradition, 1835-45. (July-Labour Day, daily; mid-May-June and Labour Day-Sep, wkends only) McFarland Point Park, Niagara Pkwy, 1 mi (1.6 km) S. Phone 905/356-2241. ¢

Niagara Apothecary. (ca 1820) Restoration of pharmacy which operated on the premises from 1866-1964. Has large golden mortar and pestle over door; original walnut and butternut fixtures, apothecary glass, and interesting remedies of the past.

(May-Labour Day, daily) Queen & King Sts. Phone 905/468-3845. **FREE**

Niagara Historical Society Museum. Opened in 1907, the earliest museum bldg in Ontario. Items from the time of the United Empire Loyalists, War of 1812, early Upper Canada, and the Victorian era. (Mar-Dec, daily; rest of yr, wkends or by appt; closed hols) Contact the Niagara Historical Society, PO Box 208, L0S 1J0. 43 Castlereagh St. Phone 905/468-3912. ¢¢

St. Mark's Anglican Church. (1805, 1843) Original church damaged by fire after being used as a hospital and barracks during the War of 1812. Rebuilt in 1822 and enlarged in 1843. Unusual 3-layer stained-glass window. Churchyard dates from earliest British settlement. (July-Aug, daily; rest of yr, by appt) 41 Byron St, opp Simcoe Park. Phone 905/468-3123.

St. Vincent de Paul Roman Catholic Church. (1835) First Roman Catholic parish in Upper Canada. Excellent example of Gothic Revival architecture; enlarged in 1965; older part largely preserved. Picton & Wellington Sts.

Annual Event

The Days of Wine and Roses. Phone 905/468-4263. Wkends in Feb.

Seasonal Event

Shaw Festival. Shaw Festival Theatre, specializing in works of George Bernard Shaw and his contemporaries, presents 10 plays each yr in repertory. Housed in 3 theaters, incl Court House Theatre. Staged by internationally acclaimed ensemble company. Also lunchtime theater featuring one-act plays by Shaw. Queen's Parade & Wellington St. Contact PO Box 774, L0S 1J0; 800/724-2934 (US) or 800/267-4759 (Canada). Mid-Apr-Oct.

Motel/Motor Lodge

★★★ **WHITE OAKS CONFERENCE RESORT AND SPA.** *253 Taylor Rd (L0F 1J0), 10 mi NW on QEW, Glendale Ave Exit.* 905/688-2550; fax 905/688-2220. Email hotel@whiteoaks. on.ca; www.whiteoaks.on.ca. 150 rms, 3 story. S $115-$169; D $125-$189;

each addl $10; suites $189-$279; under 13 free; wkend rates. TV; cable, VCR avail. Indoor pool; poolside serv. Playground. Supervised children's activities; to age 10. Complimentary coffee in rms. Restaurant 7 am-11 pm. Bar 11-1 am. Ck-out noon. Meeting rms. Business center. In-rm modem link. Concierge serv. Valet serv. Indoor, outdoor tennis, pro. Putting green. Exercise rm. Spa. Rec rm. Bathrm phones. Private patios, balconies. Cr cds: A, D, ER, MC, V.

🄳 🖾 🌊 🏃 🖾 🌊 SC 🏃

Hotel

★★★ **PRINCE OF WALES.** *6 Picton St (L0S 1J0).* 905/468-3246; fax 905/468-5521; toll-free 888/669-5566. www.princeofwaleshotel.on.ca. 101 rms. May-Oct: S, D $129-$225; each addl $20; suites $275; wkend rates (winter); lower rates rest of yr. Crib free. TV; cable (premium). Indoor pool; whirlpool. Restaurant 11 am-midnight. Bar 11:30-1 am. Ck-out 11 am. Meeting rms. Business servs avail. In-rm modem link. Exercise equipt; sauna. Health club privileges. Sun deck. Victorian bldg (1864). Cr cds: A, D, DS, ER, MC, V.

🄳 🌊 🏃 🏃 🖾 🌊 SC

B&Bs/Small Inns

★★★ **GATE HOUSE HOTEL.** *142 Queen St (L0S 1J0).* 905/468-3263; fax 905/468-7400. 10 rms, 2 story. June-Sep: S, D $160-$180; each addl $10; under 12 free; lower rates Mar-May, Oct-Dec. Closed rest of yr. Crib free. TV; cable (premium). Complimentary continental bkfst. Dining rm noon-2:30 pm, 5-10 pm. Bar 11:30-2 am. Ck-out 11 am. X-country ski 2 mi. Minibars. Modern decor. Cr cds: A, D, ER, JCB, MC, V.

🄳 🌊 🖾 🌊

★★ **KIELY HOUSE HERITAGE INN.** *209 Queen St (L0S 1J0).* 905/468-4588; fax 905/468-2194. 11 rms, 2 story, 4 suites. No A/C. Mid-Apr-Oct: S $75; D $119; suites $145-$175; under 12 free; lower rates rest of yr. Crib free. Complimentary bkfst buffet. Restaurant 11:30 am-9 pm. Ck-out 11 am, ck-in 1 pm. Lighted tennis privileges, pro. X-country ski 1 mi. Balconies. Built 1832 as private summer residence; several screened porches. Cr cds: A, MC, V.

★★ **MOFFAT INN.** *60 Picton St (L0S 1J0), QEW via ON 55.* 905/468-4116; *fax 905/468-4747.* 22 rms, 2 story. May-Oct: S, D $79-$125; each addl $10; lower rates rest of yr. TV. Complimentary coffee in rms. Dining rm 8 am-midnight. Bar. Ck-out 11 am, ck-in 2 pm. Business servs avail. In-rm modem link. Some private patios. Historic inn (1835); individually decorated rms, many with brass bed; some with fireplace. Totally nonsmoking. Cr cds: A, MC, V.

★★★ **PILLAR AND POST.** *48 John St (L0S 1J0), at King St.* 905/468-2123; *fax 905/468-3551; res 800/ 361-6788; toll-free 888/669-5566. www.pillarandpost.com.* 123 rms. S, D $170; each addl $20; suites $225-$375; under 12 free; winter packages. TV; cable (premium). Heated pool; whirlpool. Restaurant (see also THE CARRIAGES). Bar 11-1 am. Ck-out 11 am, ck-in 3 pm. Meeting rm. Business center. In-rm modem link. Bellhops. Gift shop. Bicycle rentals. Exercise rm; sauna. Spa. Minibars; some fireplaces. Turn-of-the-century fruit canning factory. Cr cds: A, D, DS, ER, MC, V.

★★★ **QUEEN'S LANDING.** *155 Byron St (L0S 1J0), at Melville.* 905/ 468-2195; *fax 905/468-2227; toll-free 888/669-5566. www.queenslanding. com.* 142 rms, 3 story. S, D $195-$255; each addl $20; suites $350-$450; under 18 free; some lower rates off-season. Crib free. TV; cable (premium), VCR avail. Indoor pool; whirlpool. Dining rm 7 am-10 pm. Rm serv to midnight. Bar 11-1 am. Ck-out 11 am, ck-in 3 pm. Meeting rms. Business servs avail. In-rm modem link. Bellhops. Valet serv. Concierge serv. Tennis privileges. 18-hole golf privileges. X-country ski 6 mi. Exercise equipt; sauna. Health club privileges. Minibars. Antique furnishings; distinctive appointments. Many in-rm whirlpools, fireplaces. Located at mouth of Niagara River, opp historic Fort Niagara. Bicycle rentals. Cr cds: A, D, DS, ER, MC, V.

Restaurants

★★ **BUTTERY THEATRE.** *19 Queen St (L0S 1J0).* 905/468-2564. Specializes in spareribs, roast leg of lamb, lobster Newburg. Hrs: 11 am-9:30 pm. Closed Dec 25. Res accepted. Bar. Lunch a la carte entrees: $7.50-$15.50; dinner a la carte entrees: $15-$23. Child's menu. Entertainment: medieval feast Fri, Sat. Family-owned. Cr cds: A, D, DS, MC, V.

★★★ **THE CARRIAGES.** *48 John St.* 905/468-2123. *www.vintageinn. com.* Specializes in rack of lamb. Hrs: Open 24 hrs. Res required. Bar. Wine list. Bkfst $1.95-$7.25. Buffet: $11; lunch $9-$14.95; dinner $15.95-$26.95. Child's menu. Entertainment. Intimate dining. Cr cds: A, D, DS, MC, V.

★★★ **ESCABECHE.** *6 Picton St.* 905/468-3246. *www.vintageinn.com.* French menu. Specializes in rack of lamb, fresh salmon. Own pastries. Hrs: 7 am-10 pm; Sun 11:30 am-2 pm. Res accepted. Bar. Bkfst a la carte entrees: $5.50-$12.95; lunch a la carte entrees: $11.50-$14.95; dinner a la carte entrees: $17.50-$29.95. Sun brunch $21.95. Child's menu. Entertainment. Greenhouse dining. Victorian decor. Built 1864. Cr cds: A, C, D, DS, MC, V.

★ **FANS COURT.** *135 Queen St (L0S 1J0).* 905/468-4511. Hrs: noon-3 pm, 5-9 pm. Closed Mon. Res accepted. Bar. Lunch a la carte entrees: $5-$7.50; dinner a la carte entrees: $9-$15.80. Entertainment. Large display of antique Chinese vases, jade, and figurines. Cr cds: A, MC, V.

Ottawa (B-7)

Founded 1827 **Pop** 295,163
Elev 374 ft (114 m) **Area code** 613
Web www.tourottawa.org
Information Tourism & Convention Authority, 130 Albert St, Suite 1800, K1P 5G4; 613/237-5150 or 800/363-4465

The capital city of Canada, Ottawa is situated at the confluence of the Ottawa, Gatineau, and Rideau rivers. A camp established by Champlain in 1615 served as headquarters for explorations from Québec to Lake Huron. For nearly two centuries, fur traders and missionaries used the Ottawa River—their only transportation route—for travel to the interior.

The first European settlement in the area was Hull, Québec, founded across the Ottawa River in 1800. In 1823 the Earl of Dalhousie secured ground for the crown on what is now Parliament Hill. Shortly after, two settlements bordered this: Upper Town and Lower Town.

The area was named Bytown in 1827 after Colonel John By, an engineer in charge of construction of the Rideau Canal, which bisects the city and connects the Ottawa River to Lake Ontario. In 1854 Bytown was renamed Ottawa. About this time four cities were rivals for capital of the United Provinces of Upper and Lower Canada: Montréal, Québec City, Kingston, and Toronto. Queen Victoria, in anticipation of confederation, unexpectedly selected Ottawa as capital in 1857, because the city was a meeting point of French and English cultures. Ten years later confederation took place and Ottawa became capital of Canada.

Today Ottawa is an important cultural center with few heavy industries. With its parks full of flowers and its universities, museums, and diplomatic embassies, Ottawa is one of Canada's most beautiful cities.

What to See and Do

By Ward Market. Traditional farmers market; bldg houses boutiques and art galleries; outdoor cafes. Exterior market (daily); interior market (Apr-Dec, daily; rest of yr, Tues-Sun). Bounded by Dalhousie & Sussex Dr, George & Clarence Sts. Phone 613/562-3325. **FREE**

Bytown Museum. Artifacts, documents, and pictures relating to Colonel By, Bytown, and the history and social life of the region. Tours (by appt). (Early May-mid-Oct, daily; rest of yr, Mon-Fri or by appt) Commissariat Bldg, 50 Canal Ln, beside the Ottawa Locks, Rideau Canal. Phone 613/234-4570. ¢¢

⭐ **Canadian Museum of Civilization.** This vast facility employs state-of-the-art exhibition technology to illustrate Canada's history and heritage over 1,000 yrs of settlement. Permanent attractions incl **The Children's Museum**, offering a variety of hands-on displays, workshops, and activities; **CINEPLUS**, the world's first convertible IMAX/Omnimax theater; **History Hall**, a setting for many life-size reconstructions of various bldgs and environments in Canada's past; and **The Grand Hall**, an expansive space housing 6 Pacific Coast indigenous houses as well as demonstrations, native ceremonies, and participatory activities. Large galleries with changing exhibits; theater. Tours. (May-mid-Oct, daily; rest of yr, Tues-Sun; closed Jan 1, Dec 25) Free admission to museum Sun mornings. 100 Laurier St, Hull, PQ. Phone 819/776-7000. Museum ¢¢; CINEPLUS ¢¢¢-¢¢¢¢

Canadian Museum of Contemporary Photography. Showcases the work of Canada's preeminent photographers. (Daily) 1 Rideau Canal. Phone 613/990-8527.

Canadian Parliament Buildings. Neo-Gothic architecture dominates this part of the city. House of Commons and Senate meet here; visitors may request tickets (free) to both chambers when Parliament is in session. Forty-five-min guided tour incl House of Commons, Senate Chamber, Parliamentary Library. (Daily; closed Jan 1, July 1, Dec 25) (See SEASONAL EVENTS) Also here are the **Centennial Flame**, lit in 1967 as a symbol of Canada's 100th birthday, and **Memorial Chapel**, dedicated to Canadian servicemen who lost their lives in the Boer War, WWI, WWII, and the Korean War. **Observation**

Canadian Parliament, Ottawa

Deck atop the Peace Tower. Wellington St on Parliament Hill. Phone 613/996-0896. **FREE**

Canadian Ski Museum. History of skiing; collection of old skis and ski equipment from Canada and around the world. (Daily; closed hols) 1960 Scott St. Phone 613/722-3584. ¢

Canadian War Museum. Exhibits tracing Canada's military history incl arms, aircraft, military vehicles, uniforms, and action displays. (May-mid-Oct, daily; rest of yr, Tues-Sun; closed Dec 25) 330 Sussex Dr. Phone 819/776-8600. ¢¢

Central Experimental Farm. Approx 1,200 acres (486 hectares) of field crops, ornamental gardens, arboretum; showcase herds of beef and dairy cattle, sheep, swine, horses. Tropical greenhouse (daily). Agricultural museum (daily; closed Dec 25). Clydesdale horse-drawn wagon or sleigh rides. Picnicking. (May-mid-Oct) Grounds (daily). Some fees. Prince of Wales Drive. Phone 613/991-3044.

City Hall. Situated on Green Island, on the Rideau River. View of city and surrounding area from 8th floor. Guided tours (Mon-Fri, by appt; closed hols). Opp are the Rideau Falls. 111 Sussex Dr. Phone 613/244-5464. **FREE**

Currency Museum. Artifacts, maps, and exhibits tell the story of money and its use throughout the world. (Tues-Sun) 245 Sparks St. Phone 613/782-8914. **FREE**

Laurier House. Former residence of 2 prime ministers: Sir Wilfrid Laurier and W. L. Mackenzie King. Re-created study of Prime Minister Lester B. Pearson. Books, furnishings, and memorabilia. (Tues-Sun; closed hols) 335 Laurier Ave E. Phone 613/992-8142. ¢¢

Museum of Canadian Scouting. Depicts the history of Canadian Scouting; exhibits on the life of Lord R. S. S. Baden-Powell, founder of the Boy Scouts; pertinent documents, photographs, and artifacts. (Mon-Fri; closed hols) 1345 Base Line Rd, 8 mi (13 km) SW. Phone 613/224-5131. **FREE**

National Archives of Canada. Collections of all types of material relating to Canadian history. Changing exhibits. (Daily) Opp is **Garden of the Provinces.** Flags representing all Canadian provinces and territories; fountain illuminated at night. (May-Nov) 395 Wellington St. Phone 613/995-5138. **FREE**

National Arts Centre. Center for performing arts; houses a concert hall and 2 theaters for music, dance, variety, and drama; home of the National Arts Centre Orchestra; more than 800 performances each yr; canal-side cafe. Landscaped terraces with panoramic view of Ottawa. Guided tours (free). 53 Elgin St at Confederation Sq. Phone 613/996-5051 or 613/755-1111 (Ticketmaster).

⭐ **National Gallery of Canada.** Permanent exhibits incl European paintings from 14th century-present; Canadian art from 17th century-present; contemporary and decorative arts, prints, drawings, photos, and Inuit art; video, and film. Reconstructed 19th-century Rideau convent chapel with Neo-Gothic fan-vaulted ceiling, only known example of its kind in North America. Changing exhibits (fee), gallery talks, films; restaurants, bookstore. Guided tours (daily). (Daily; closed hols) 380 Sussex Dr, at St. Patrick St. Phone 613/990-1985. **FREE**

National Museum of Science and Technology. More than 400 exhibits with many do-it-yourself experiments; Canada's role in science and technology shown through displays on Canada in space, transportation, agriculture, computers, communications, physics, and astronomy. Unusual open restoration bay allows viewing of various stages of artifact repair and refurbishment. Cafeteria. (May-Labour Day, daily; rest of yr, Tues-Sun; closed Dec 25) 1867 St. Laurent Blvd. Phone 613/991-3044. ¢¢¢ The museum also maintains

National Aviation Museum. More than 100 historic aircraft, 49 on display in a "Walkway of Time." Displays demonstrate the development of aircraft in peace and war, emphasizing Canadian aviation. (Daily) Rockcliffe Airport, NE end of city. Phone 613/993-2010 or 800/463-2038. ¢¢

Nepean Point. Lovely view of the area; Astrolabe Theatre, a 700-seat amphitheater, is the scene of musical, variety, and dramatic shows in summer. Just W of Sussex Dr & St. Patrick. Phone 613/239-5000. **FREE**

Professional sports.

NHL (Ottawa Senators). Corel Center. 1000 Palladium Dr, in Kanata. Phone 613/755-1166.

Recreational facilities. For information on canoes, rowboats, docking and launching, swimming at outdoor beaches and pools, phone 613/239-5000. Gatineau Park, across the Ottawa River in Québec, offers swimming, fishing; bicycling, cross-country skiing, picnicking, and camping. There are more than 87 mi (140 km) of recreational trails and approx 50 golf courses in the area. Boats may be rented on the Rideau Canal at Dow's Lake, Queen Elizabeth Driveway & Preston St. Contact the National Capital Commission, 90 Wellington St, opp Parliament Hill, phone 613/239-5000. Fishing licenses (required in Québec for nonresidents) may be obtained at the Québec Dept of Tourism, Fish & Game, 13 rue Buteau, J8Z 1V4 in Hull, PQ (wkdays, closed hols); 613/771-4840.

★ **Rideau Canal.** Constructed under the direction of Lieutenant-Colonel John By of the Royal Engineers between 1826-32 as a safe supply route to Upper Canada. The purpose was to bypass the St. Lawrence River

in case of an American attack. There are 24 lock stations where visitors can picnic, watch boats pass through the hand-operated locks, and see wooden lock gates, cut stone walls, and many historic structures. In summer there are interpretive programs and exhibits at various locations. Areas of special interest incl Kingston Mills Locks, Jones Falls Locks (off ON 15), Smith Falls Museum (off ON 15), Merrickville Locks (on ON 43), and Ottawa Locks. Boating is popular (mid-May-mid-Oct, daily) and ice-skating is avail (mid-Dec-late Feb, daily). Runs 125 mi (202 km) between Kingston and Ottawa. Phone 613/283-5170. **FREE**

Royal Canadian Mint. Production of coins; collection of coins and medals. Guided tours and film; detailed process of minting coins and printing bank notes is shown. (Daily; tours by appt) 320 Sussex Dr. Phone 613/991-6554. ¢

Sightseeing tours.

Double-Decker bus tours. Capital Trolley Tours. Buses seen in service in Britain visit various highlights of the city. (Apr-mid-Nov, daily) Phone 613/749-3666. ¢¢¢¢

Gray Line bus tours. (May-Oct, daily) Phone 613/725-1441.

Ottawa Riverboat Company. Two-hr cruises on Ottawa River. Boats depart from Hull and Ottawa docks (daily). Also evening dinner/dance cruises (Wed-Fri). Phone 613/562-4888. ¢¢-¢¢¢¢

Paul's Boat Lines, Ltd. Rideau Canal sightseeing cruises depart from Conference Centre (mid-May-mid-Oct, daily). Ottawa River sightseeing cruises depart from foot of Rideau Canal Locks (mid-May-mid-Oct, daily). Phone 613/225-6781. ¢¢¢

Victoria Memorial Museum Building. Castle like structure houses museum that interrelates man and his natural environment. Houses the **Canadian Museum of Nature.** Natural history exhibits from dinosaurs to present day plants and animals. Outstanding collection of minerals and gems. (Daily; closed Dec 25) Metcalfe & McLeod Sts. Phone 613/566-4700. ¢¢

Annual Events

Winterlude. Extravaganza devoted to outdoor concerts, fireworks, skating contests, dances, music, ice sculptures. Phone 613/239-5000. Three wkends Feb.

Canadian Tulip Festival. Part of a 2-wk celebration, culminated by the blooming of more than 3 million tulips presented to Ottawa by Queen Juliana of the Netherlands after she sought refuge here during WWII. Tours of flower beds; craft market and demonstrations, kite flying, boat parade. Phone 613/567-5757. May.

Canada Day. Celebration of Canada's birthday with many varied events throughout the city, incl canoe and sailing regattas, concerts, music and dance, art and craft demonstrations, children's entertainment, fireworks. Phone 613/239-5000. July 1.

Ottawa International Jazz Festival. Phone 613/594-3580. Ten days July.

Seasonal Events

Sound & Light Show on Parliament Hill. Phone 613/239-5000. Mid-May-Labour Day.

Changing the Guard. Parliament Hill. Phone 613/239-5000. Late June-late Aug.

Motel/Motor Lodge

★★ **RAMADA INN.** *480 Metcalfe St (K1F 3N6), ON 417 Exit Metcalfe St. 613/237-5500; fax 613/237-6705.* 157 rms, 9 story. S, D $79; each addl $10; suites $110; under 18 free; wkend rates. Crib free. TV; cable. Indoor pool. Complimentary coffee in rms. Restaurant 7 am-2 pm, 5-10 pm; Sun to 2 pm. Ck-out noon. Meeting rms. Business servs avail. In-rm modem link. Valet serv. Downhill/x-country ski 10 mi. Cr cds: A, D, DS, ER, MC, V.

⊠ ◺ ◹ ◳ SC

Hotels

★★★ **ALBERT AT BAY.** *435 Albert St (K1R 7X4). 613/238-8858; fax 613/238-1433; toll-free 800/267-6644. Email info@absuites.com; www.albertat bay.com.* 195 kit. suites, 12 story. S, D $124-$144; under 16 free; wkend, monthly rates. Crib free. Garage $8.50. TV; cable. Restaurant 6:30 am-midnight; Sat, Sun from 11 am. Ck-out noon. Coin lndry. Meeting rms. Business servs avail. In-rm modem link. Downhill ski 8 mi; x-country ski 5 mi. Exercise equipt; sauna. Whirlpool. Microwaves. Balconies. Renovated apartment bldg. Rooftop garden with picnic tables, lawn chairs. Cr cds: A, C, D, DS, ER, JCB, MC, V.

D ◺ ◹ ◳ ◵ SC

★★ **BEST WESTERN VICTORIA PARK SUITES.** *377 O'Connor St (K2P 2M2). 613/567-7275; fax 613/567-1161. Email steph@vpsuites.com; www. vpsuites.com.* 100 kit. units, 8 story. May-Oct: S, D $100-$145; wkend rates; lower rates rest of yr. Crib free. Garage parking $7. TV; cable. Complimentary continental bkfst. Restaurant nearby. Ck-out noon. Coin lndry. Meeting rms. Business servs avail. Exercise equipt. Microwaves. Cr cds: A, D, DS, ER, MC, V.

◹ ◳ ◵ SC

★★★★ **CHATEAU LAURIER.** *1 Rideau St (K1N 8S7), opp Rideau Canal from Parliament Hill. 613/241-1414; fax 613/562-7030.* This French castle-like landmark has stood since 1912 and welcomes guests with expanses of orange tulips in summer and snow-tipped turrets in winter. A popular home for many visiting politicians, the hotel is convenient to most capital city destinations. There are also several well-respected restaurants on site, including Wilfrid's, with its views of Parliament Hill and the canal. 426 rms, 8 story. S, D $149-$339; each addl $20; suites $339-$1,800; business suites avail. Under 18 free. Crib free. Garage parking (fee). TV; cable (premium), VCR avail. Indoor pool. Supervised children's activities (summer). Complimentary coffee in rms. Restaurant 6:30 am-10 pm; dining rm (Mid-May-Labor Day) 11:30 am-10 pm. Rm serv 24 hrs. Bar 11:30-1 am. Ck-out noon. Convention facilities. Business center. In-rm modem link. Concierge serv. Shopping arcade. Downhill/x-country ski 12 mi. Exercise rm; sauna. Massage. Rec rm. Minibars. Luxury level. Cr cds: A, C, D, DS, ER, JCB, MC, V.

D ◺ ◹ ◳ ◵ ◹

★★★ **CROWNE PLAZA OTTAWA.**
*101 Lyon St (K1R 5T9). 613/237-3600;
fax 613/237-2351.* 411 rms, 26 story. S,
D $89-$155; each addl $12; suites
$150-$450; under 18 free; package
plans. Crib free. Garage (fee). TV;
cable. Indoor pool. Restaurant 6:30
am-10 pm. Bar 11-1 am. Ck-out 1 pm.
Meeting rms. Business center.
Concierge serv. Gift shop. Downhill/x-
country ski 12 mi. Exercise rm; sauna.
Cr cds: A, D, DS, ER, MC, V.

D ⊠ ⌨ 🛠 ⛷ 🐾 SC 🏃

★★ **DELTA HOTEL.** *361 Queen St
(K1R 7F9), off Lyon St. 613/238-6000;
fax 613/238-2290. Email jwilliams@
deltahotels.com; www.deltahotels.com.*
328 units, 18 story. May-June, Sep-
Oct: S, D $155-$175; each addl $15;
suites $180-$200; under 18 free;
wkend rates; special summer rates;
lower rates rest of yr. Crib free. Pet
accepted. Garage $11.50. TV; cable.
Indoor pool; whirlpool. Restaurant
6:30 am-10 pm. Rm serv 6 am-11
pm. Bars 11-2 am. Ck-out noon.
Meeting rms. Business center. In-rm
modem link. Barber, beauty shop.
Downhill/x-country ski 12 mi. Exercise rm; saunas. Minibars. Some balconies. Luxury level. Cr cds: A, D,
ER, JCB, MC, V.

D 🐾 ⊠ ⌨ 🛠 ⛷ 🐾 SC 🏃

★★★ **LE CHATEAU MONTE-
BELLO.** *392 rue Notre Dame, 40 mi E
on Hwy 148. 819/423-6341; fax
819/423-5283; toll-free 800/441-1414.
Email yeserve@icm.cphotels.ca; www.
fairmont.com.* 210 rms, 3 story. Mid-
May-mid-Oct, MAP: S $186.50; D
$238; each addl $71.50; under 4 free;
lower rates rest of yr. Crib free. Pet
accepted. TV; cable. 2 pools, 1 indoor;
whirlpool, lifeguard. Playground.
Supervised children's activities (mid-
June-early Sep); ages 3-12. Dining rm.
Rm serv 7 am-11 pm. Bar 11-1 am;
entertainment Fri-Sat. Ck-out noon,
ck-in 3 pm. Meeting rms. Business
center. In-rm modem link. Bellhops.
Valet serv. Gift shop. Sports dir.
Indoor and outdoor tennis. 18-hole
golf, greens fee (incl cart) $62, pro,
putting green. X-country ski on site
(rentals). Sleighing. Curling. Bicycles.
Lawn games. Soc dir. Rec rm. Game
rm. Squash courts. Exercise rm; sauna,
steam rm. Massage. Fishing, hunting
guides. Minibars. Marina. On 65,000
acres. Cr cds: A, DS, MC, V.

🎣 ⊠ 🛠 🏌 ⌨ 🛠 🏃 🔥

★★ **LORD ELGIN.** *100 Elgin St (K1P
5K8), at Laurier Ave. 613/235-3333;
fax 613/235-3223; toll-free 800/267-
4298. www.interconti.com.* 311 rms, 11
story. S $109-$135; D $115-$141;
each addl $5; suites $180-$200;
under 18 free; wkend rates. Crib free.
Pet accepted, some restrictions.
Garage; valet, in/out $11.50. TV;
cable. Coffee in rms. Restaurant 7
am-11 pm. Bar 11:30-1 am. Ck-out 1
pm. Meeting rms. Business servs
avail. In-rm modem link. Gift shop.
Downhill/x-country ski 12 mi. Exercise equipt. Originally opened 1941;
completely renovated. Cr cds: A, C,
D, ER, JCB, MC, V.

D 🐾 ⊠ 🛠 ⛷ 🐾 SC

★★★ **RADISSON OTTAWA CEN-
TRE.** *100 Kent St (K1P 5R7). 613/238-
1122; fax 613/783-4229.* 478 rms, 26
story. S, D $125-$155; each addl $10;
suites $300-$400; under 19 free;
wkend rates. Crib free. Pet accepted.
Garage (fee). TV; cable (premium).
Indoor pool; whirlpool. Restaurant
6:30 am-11 pm; revolving rooftop
dining rm 11:30 am-2:30 pm, 6-11
pm; Sat from 6 pm. Bar 11-1 am. Ck-
out 1 pm. Meeting rms. Business servs
avail. In-rm modem link. Downhill
ski 15 mi. Exercise rm; sauna. Minibars. Many balconies. Adj underground shopping mall. Luxury level.
Cr cds: A, C, D, DS, ER, JCB, MC, V.

D 🐾 ⊠ ⌨ 🛠 ⛷ 🐾 SC

★★★ **SHERATON.** *150 Albert St
(K1P 5G2). 613/238-1500; fax 613/
235-2723; toll-free 800/489-8333.* 236
rms, 18 story. S $200; D $215; each
addl $20; suites $280-$450; family
rates; package plans. Crib free. Garage
(fee). Pet accepted. TV; cable. Indoor
pool; poolside serv. Coffee in rms.
Restaurant 6:30 am-11 pm. Ck-out
noon. Meeting rms. Business center.
In-rm modem link. Gift shop. Down-
hill/x-country ski 12 mi. Exercise
equipt; sauna. Minibars. Luxury level.
Cr cds: A, D, DS, ER, JCB, MC, V.

D 🐾 ⊠ ⌨ 🛠 ⛷ 🐾 SC 🏃

★★★ **THE WESTIN OTTAWA.**
*11 Colonel By Dr (K1N 9H4), connects
with Ottawa Congress Center, Rideau
Center. 613/560-7000; fax 613/569-
2013.* 484 rms, 24 story. Mid-Apr-
June, mid-Sep-mid-Nov: S, D
$190-$211; each addl $20; suites
$265-$700; under 18 free; wkend
rates; lower rates rest of yr. Crib

free. Pet accepted, some restrictions. TV; cable. Indoor pool; whirlpool. Restaurants 6:30 am-11 pm. Rm serv 24 hrs. Bar 11:30-2 am. Ck-out 1 pm. Convention facilities. Business center. Concierge serv. Shopping arcade adj. Barber, beauty shop. Valet parking. Downhill/x-country ski 12 mi. Exercise rm; sauna. Massage. Minibars; some bathrm phones. Opp Rideau Canal; near Parliament Hill. Cr cds: A, C, D, DS, ER, JCB, MC, V.

D ⚑ ✈ ⌢ 🖈 🏂 🔥 SC 🚶

B&Bs/Small Inns

★★★ **GASTHAUS SWITZERLAND INN.** *89 Daly Ave (K1N 6E6). 613/237-0335; fax 613/594-3327. Email switzinn@magi.com; www.gasthaus switzerlandinn.com.* 22 rms, 3 story. May-Oct: S, D $78-$128; each addl $20; suites $188; lower rates rest of yr. Children over 12 yrs only. TV; cable. Complimentary full bkfst. Restaurant nearby. Ck-out 11 am, ck-in 3 pm. In-rm modem link. Some in-rm whirlpools, fireplaces. Picnic tables. In restored 1872 house. Totally nonsmoking. Cr cds: A, D, ER, MC, V.

🏂 🔥

★ **VOYAGEUR'S GUEST HOUSE.** *95 Arlington Ave (K1R 5S4). 613/238-6445; fax 613/236-5551. www. bbcanada.com/897.html.* 6 rms, 3 share bath, 2 story. No rm phones. S $34; D $44; each addl $10; higher rates Canada Day. TV; cable (premium). Complimentary full bkfst. Restaurant nearby. Ck-out 11 am, ck-in 11 am. Downhill ski 20 mi; x-country ski 3 mi. Totally nonsmoking. Cr cds: D, ER, MC, V.

⛟ 🏂 🔥

Restaurants

★★★ **AUX CHANTIGNOLES.** *392 rue Notre Dame. 819/423-6341. www. chateaumontebello.com.* Specializes in seafood, veal, game. Own baking. Hrs: open 24 hrs. Res accepted. Wine list. Bkfst buffet: $14.25; lunch complete meals: $19.50; dinner a la carte entrees: $24.50-$29.50. Sun brunch

$28.50. Child's menu. Parking. Rustic decor; fireplace. Cr cds: A, MC, V.

D 🔥

★★ **CHEZ BUNTHA.** *64 Queen St (K1P 5C6), off Elgin St. 613/234-0064.* Specializes in lamb with fine herbs, sirloin flambe, seafood. Hrs: 11 am-2 pm, 5-8 pm; Fri to 11 pm; Sat 5-11 pm. Closed Sun. Res accepted. Wine list. Lunch a la carte entrees: $7.50-$12. Buffet: $8.50; dinner a la carte entrees: $12.95-$19.95. Child's menu. Entertainment: Fri, Sat. Formal, contemporary decor. Cr cds: A, ER, MC, V.

🔥

★★★ **DOMUS CAFI.** *87 Murray St (K2A 0E7). 613/241-6007.* Canadian regional cuisine menu. Specializes in panseared Québec foie gras, New foundland sea scallops. Hrs: Mon-Sat 11:30 am-2:30 pm, 6-9 pm, Sun 11 am-2:30 pm. Closed Canada Day, Christmas. Res. Wine list. Lunch $6-$15; dinner $17-$35. Brunch $6-$15. Entertainment. Cr cds: A, D, DS, ER, MC, V.

D 🔥

★★ **LA GONDOLA.** *188 Bank St (K2P 1W8). 613/235-3733. www. ottawaguide.com.* Specializes in veal, pasta. Hrs: 11 am-11 pm; Sat from 10 am; Sun 10 am-10 pm. Closed Dec 25. Res accepted. Bar. Lunch a la carte entrees: $5.95-$12.95; dinner a la carte entrees: $8.95-$22. Sat, Sun brunch, $3.25-$7. Child's menu. Cr cds: A, D, ER, MC, V.

D 🔥

★ **LAS PALMAS.** *111 Parent Ave (K1N 7B3). 613/241-3738.* Specializes in fajitas, enchiladas. Hrs: 11 am-11 pm. Bar. Lunch a la carte entrees: $6-$15.95; dinner a la carte entrees: $6-$15.95. Mexican village setting. Cr cds: A, D, DS, ER, MC, V.

D 🔥

★★ **LE CAFE.** *53 Elgin St (K1P 5W1), National Arts Centre, Confederation Sq. 613/594-5127.* Own pastries. Hrs: noon-11 pm; Sun to 8 pm. Closed Jan 1, Dec 24, 25; also Sun Sep-May. Res accepted. Bar. Lunch a la carte entrees: $7.95-$13.95; dinner a la carte entrees: $12.95-$22.95.

Child's menu. Parking. Cr cds: A, D, ER, MC, V.

D

★★ **MARBLE WORKS STEAK-HOUSE.** *14 Waller St (K1N 9C4).* *613/241-6764.* Specializes in steak. Hrs: 11:30 am-2 pm, 5-10 pm; Sat, Sun from 5 pm. Closed Dec 25. Res accepted. Bar. Lunch a la carte entrees: $8-$16; dinner a la carte entrees: $12-$24. Child's menu. Entertainment: Sat. Parking. In renovated 1866 bldg. Cr cds: A, D, MC, V.

★★ **THE MILL.** *555 Ottawa River Pkwy (K1P 5R4), Wellington Ave and Portage Bridge. 613/237-1311.* Specializes in prime rib, fish, chicken. Hrs: 11:30 am-2:30 pm, 4:30-10 pm. Closed July 1. Bar. Lunch a la carte entrees: $5.95-$9.95; dinner a la carte entrees: $9.95-$17.95. Sun brunch $4.95-$9.95. Child's menu. Parking. Former mill (1850); mill structure visible through glass wall. Cr cds: A, D, MC, V.

D

★★ **SITAR.** *417A Rideau St (K1N 5Y6). 613/789-7979.* Specializes in tandoori-prepared dishes, vegetarian dishes. Own breads. Hrs: 11:45 am-2 pm, 5-10:30 pm. Closed Jan 1, Dec 25. Lunch complete meals: $7.95; dinner complete meals: $14.95-$18.75. Cr cds: A, D, ER, MC, V.

D

Quetico Provincial Park

See also Fort Frances, Thunder Bay

Web www.ontarioparks.com
Information Superintendent, Ministry of Natural Resources, 108 Saturn Ave, Atikokan P0T 1C0; 807/597-2735

Quetico is a wilderness park and as such is composed largely of rugged landscape. There are no roads in the park, but its vast network of connecting waterways allows for some of the best canoeing in North America. More than 900 miles (1,450 kilometers) of canoe routes are within Quetico's 1,832-square-mile (4,622-square-kilometer) area. Canoeing (no motor-powered craft allowed), fishing, and swimming are primary activities in the park. Appropriate fishing licenses are required. Interior fee/person/night ¢¢¢¢

Car camping is permitted at 107 sites in two areas of the Dawson Trail Campgrounds. Permits can be obtained at Park Ranger Stations. Payments may be made in Canadian or US currency (no personal checks). For reservations phone 807/597-2737 (Canadian residents) or 807/597-2735 (nonresidents). Camping ¢¢¢¢-¢¢¢¢

Picnic facilities, trails, and a large assortment of pictographs may be enjoyed. In winter the vacationer can ice fish and cross-country ski, although there are no maintained facilities. Park (Victoria Day wkend-Thanksgiving wkend, daily). Day-use fee/vehicle ¢¢¢

Rideau Canal, Ottawa

Sarnia

(E-2) *See also London*

Founded 1856 **Pop** 50,892 **Elev** 610 ft (186 m) **Area code** 519

Information Convention and Visitors Bureau of Sarnia-Lambton, 224 N Vidal St, N7T 5Y3; 519/336-3232 or 800/265-0316

Sarnia was originally known as "The Rapids" and was renamed Port Sarnia in 1836. The town grew because of timber stands in the area, the discovery of oil, and the arrival of the Great Western Railway in 1858. Today it is Canada's most important petrochemical center.

Sarnia is located in the center of one of Canada's most popular recreation areas. Lake Huron offers beaches from Canatara Park to nearby Lambton County; the St. Clair River flows south of Sarnia into Lake St. Clair. Facilities for water sports and boating are excellent. The city and surrounding area have many golf courses, campsites, and trailer parks. Easy access to the United States is provided by the International Blue Water Bridge (toll) spanning the St. Clair River between Sarnia and Port Huron, Michigan (see Border Crossing Regulations in MAKING THE MOST OF YOUR TRIP).

What to See and Do

Canatara Park. Information center housed in reconstructed 19th-century log cabin (Victoria Day wkend-Labour Day wkend, Mon-Fri afternoons; rest of yr, wkends). Facilities for swimming, beach, and bathhouse; picnicking, barbecuing, refreshments, lookout tower, fitness trail, natural area, toboggan hill, playground equipt, and ball diamond. (Daily) At Cathcart Blvd, off N Christina St. Phone 800/265-0316. **FREE** Also in the park are

  Children's Animal Farm. Farm bldgs; animals, poultry, and waterfowl. (Daily) **FREE**

  Log Cabin. Two-floor cabin with natural wooden peg flooring, 2 fireplaces; interpretive programs featured in summer. Adj are carriage shed with farm implement artifacts from 1850, and a smokehouse. (Open for special events) **FREE**

The Gardens. Wide variety of plant life. The park also offers facilities for swimming (fee); tennis, lawn bowling, horseshoes, baseball, and soccer. Germain Park, East St. Phone 519/332-0330.

Lambton Heritage Museum. Features more than 400 Currier & Ives prints, Canada's largest collection of antique pressed-glass water pitchers; 2 farm machinery barns; slaughterhouse, chapel, and main exhibit center with a chronological natural and human history of Lambton County. (Mar-Oct, daily; rest of yr, Mon-Fri; closed Dec 25-Jan 1) Picnicking. 45 mi (72 km) NE via ON 21, Grand Bend, opp Pinery Provincial Park. Phone 519/243-2600. ¢¢

Moore Museum. Country store, early switchboard, late-1800s church organ in main bldg; Victorian cottage; log cabin; farm implements; 1-rm schoolhouse; 1890 lighthouse. (Mar-June, Wed-Sun; July and Aug, daily; Sep-mid Dec, Mon-Fri) 12 mi (19 km) S in Mooretown, 94 Moore Line, 2 blks E of St. Clair Pkwy (County Rd 33). Phone 519/867-2020. ¢

Oil Museum of Canada. On site of first commercialized oil well in North America; historic items and data regarding the discovery. Six acres (2½ hectares) of landscaped grounds w/blacksmith shop, pioneer home, and post office; railroad station, working oil field using 1860 methods; picnic pavilion. Guided tours. (May-Oct, daily; rest of yr, Mon-Fri) 30 mi SE in Oil Springs on Kelly Rd. Phone 519/834-2840. ¢¢

Sombra Township Museum. Pioneer home with displays of household goods, clothes, books and deeds, marine artifacts, indigenous and military items, music boxes, photographic equipment, and farming tools. (June-Sep, afternoons; May, wkends; also by appt) 3470 St. Clair Pkwy, S in Sombra. Phone 519/892-3982. ¢

Annual Event

Sarnia Highland Games. Centennial Park. Caber and hammer tossing, stone throwing, haggis-hurling; clan village, bands, dancers. Phone 519/336-5054. Mid-Aug.

Seasonal Events

Sarnia Waterfront Festival. Centennial Park. More than 80 events incl singers, dancers; children's shows. Phone 800/265-0316. Late Apr-Labour Day wkend.

Celebration of Lights. Seven-wk festive season featuring 60,000 lights in waterfront park. Residential, commercial displays. Phone 800/265-0316. Late Nov-Dec.

Motels/Motor Lodges

★★ **COMFORT INN.** *815 Mara St (N7V 1X5), on 402 Exit Front St. 519/383-6767; fax 519/383-8710; toll-free 800/228-5150.* 100 rms, 3 story. S $55-$75; D $65-$85; each addl $5; family rates. Crib free. TV; cable. Complimentary continental bkfst. Restaurant adj 6:30 am-midnight. Ck-out noon. Meeting rms. Business center. In-rm modem link. Exercise equipt. Refrigerators avail. Cr cds: A, D, DS, ER, MC, V.

[D] [icons]

★★★ **DRAWBRIDGE INN.** *283 N Christina St (N7T 5V4). 519/337-7571; fax 519/332-8181; toll-free 800/663-0376.* 97 rms, 3 story. S, D $82; each addl $9; suites $115-$135; under 12 free; wkend rates. Crib free. Pet accepted. TV; cable. Indoor pool. Sauna. Restaurant 7 am-2 pm, 5-9 pm; Fri-Sun 8 am-2 pm, 5-9 pm. Bar noon-11 pm. Ck-out noon. Meeting rms. Business center. In-rm modem link. Bellhops. Valet serv. Health club privileges. Cr cds: A, D, DS, ER, MC, V.

[icons]

★★ **HARBOURFRONT INN.** *505 Harbour Rd (N7T 5R8), ½ mi SW of Bluewater Bridge. 519/337-5434; fax 519/332-5882; toll-free 800/787-5010.* 105 rms, 2 story. S $51-$58; D $59-$67; each addl $4; under 16 free. Crib free. Pet accepted, some restrictions. TV; cable, VCR avail. Restaurant adj 11-1 am. Ck-out 11 am. Valet serv. Picnic tables. On river. Cr cds: A, D, ER, JCB, MC, V.

[D] [icons]

★★ **HOLIDAY INN.** *1498 Venetian Blvd (N7T 7W6). 519/336-4130; fax 519/332-3326. Email hi-sarnia@bristol hotels.com; www.hi-online.com.* 151 rms, 2 story. S, D $69-$89; suites $180-$240; under 19 free; wkend rates. Crib free. Pet accepted. TV; cable (premium). 2 pools, 1 indoor; whirlpool. Playground. Restaurant 6:30 am-10:30 pm. Bar 11-1 am. Ck-out 1 pm. Meeting rms. Bellhops. Valet serv. Golf privileges, greens fee $10, putting green. Exercise equipt; sauna. Lawn games. Balconies. Cr cds: A, C, D, DS, ER, JCB, MC, V.

[D] [icons]

[gas pump icon]

Sault Ste. Marie

Pop 83,300 (est) **Elev** 580 ft (177 m) **Area code** 705 **Web** www.sault-canada.com

Information Chamber of Commerce, 334 Bay St, P6A 1X1; 705/949-7152

Founded and built on steel, Sault Ste. Marie is separated from its sister city in Michigan by the St. Mary's River. Lake and ocean freighters traverse the river, which links Lake Huron and Lake Superior—locally known as "the Soo."

What to See and Do

Agawa Canyon Train Excursion. A scenic day trip by Algoma Central Railway through a wilderness of hills and fjord like ravines. Two-hr stopover at the canyon. Dining car on train. (June-mid-Oct, daily; Jan-Mar, wkends only) Advance ticket orders avail by phone. Phone 705/946-7300 or 800/242-9287. ¢¢¢¢

Boat cruises. Two-hr boat cruises from Norgoma dock, next to Holiday Inn on MV *Chief Shingwauk* and MV *Bon Soo* through American locks; also 3-hr dinner cruises. (June-mid-Oct) Contact Lock Tours Canada, PO Box 424, P6A 5M1. Phone 705/253-9850. ¢¢¢

Sault Ste. Marie Museum. Local and national exhibits in a structure originally built as a post office. Skylight Gallery traces history of the region dating back 9,000 yrs; incl prehistoric artifacts, displays of early industries, re-creation of 1912 Queen St house interiors. Durham Gallery displays traveling exhibits from the Royal Ontario Museum and locally curated displays. Discovery Gallery for children features hands-on exhibits. (Daily; closed hols) 690 Queen St E. Phone 705/759-7278. **Donation**

Annual Events

Ontario Winter Carnival Bon Soo. Features more than 100 events: fireworks, fiddle contest, winter sports, polar bear swim, winter playground sculptured from snow. Last wkend Jan-1st wkend Feb.

Algoma Fall Festival. Visual and performing arts presentations by Canadian and international artists. Late Sep-late Oct.

Motels/Motor Lodges

★ ★ ★ **ALGOMA'S WATER TOWER INN.** *360 Great Northern Rd (P6A 5N3). 705/949-8111; fax 705/949-1912. Email awtinn@age.net; www.watertowerinn.com.* 180 rms, 5 story. S, D $79-$99; each addl $7; suites $130-$290; under 18 free; ski plans. Crib free. Pet accepted. TV; cable (premium), VCR avail. Heated pool; whirlpool. Restaurant 7 am-11 pm. Rm serv 7-11 am, 5-10 pm. Bar noon-1 am. Ck-out noon. Meeting rms. Valet serv. Airport transportation. Sundries. X-country ski 5 mi. Exercise equipt. Some refrigerators, microwaves; whirlpool in suites. Cr cds: A, C, D, DS, ER, JCB, MC, V.

D ⬤ ⬤ ⬤ ⬤ ⬤ ⬤ SC

★ ★ **BAY FRONT QUALITY INN.** *180 Bay St (P6A 6S2). 705/945-9264; fax 705/945-9766.* 109 rms, 7 story. Sep-mid-Oct: S $102-$165; D $112-$165; each addl $10; family rates; ski, package plans; lower rates rest of yr. Crib free. TV; cable (premium), VCR avail. Indoor pool; whirlpool. Coffee in rms. Restaurant 7 am-midnight. Bar from 11:30 am. Ck-out 1 pm. Meeting rms. Bellhops. Valet serv. Downhill/x-country ski 8 mi. Exercise equipt; sauna. Some refrigerators. Cr cds: A, C, D, DS, ER, JCB, MC, V.

D ⬤ ⬤ ⬤ ⬤ ⬤ ⬤ SC

★ ★ **HOLIDAY INN.** *208 St. Mary's River Dr (P6A 5V4). 705/949-0611; fax 705/945-6972; res 888/713-3482.*

Email yamca.071@sympatico.ca. 195 rms, 9 story. June-mid-Oct: S, D $92-$139; each addl $10; suites $175-$275; under 12 free; lower rates rest of yr. Crib free. Pet accepted. TV; cable (premium). Indoor pool; whirlpool. Restaurant 6:30 am-10 pm. Bar 11-1 am. Ck-out 4 pm. Meeting rms. In-rm modem link. Bellhops. Valet serv. Sundries. Gift shop. Airport transportation. Exercise equipt; sauna. Game rm. Refrigerator in some suites. Cr cds: A, C, D, DS, ER, JCB, MC, V.

D ⬤ ⬤ ⬤ ⬤ ⬤ ⬤ SC

★ ★ **RAMADA INN AND CONVENTION CENTRE.** *229 Great Northern Rd; Hwy 17 N (P6V 4Z2). 705/942-2500; fax 705/942-2570; res 800/563-7262.* 211 units, 2-7 story. S $86-$109; D $96-$122; each addl $10; suites $150-$275; under 18 free; package plans. Crib free. Pet accepted. TV; cable, VCR avail. 2 pools, 1 indoor; whirlpool. Restaurant 7 am-11 pm. Bar to midnight. Ck-out noon. Meeting rms. Business servs avail. Bellhops. Valet serv (Mon-Fri). Sundries. Downhill ski 20 mi; x-country ski 3 mi. Exercise equipt. Miniature golf; water slide. Bowling. Game rms. Some refrigerators. Cr cds: A, C, D, DS, ER, JCB, MC, V.

D ⬤ ⬤ ⬤ ⬤ ⬤ ⬤ SC

Restaurants

★ **GIOVANNI'S.** *516 Great Northern Rd (P6B 4Z9). 705/942-3050.* Specializes in family-style dinners. Hrs: 11:30 am-11 pm. Closed Jan 1, Labor Day, Dec 25. Res accepted. Bar. Lunch $5-$8; dinner $7-$15. Child's menu. Cr cds: A, MC, V.

D ⬤

★ ★ **NEW MARCONI.** *480 Albert St W (P6A 1C3). 705/759-8250.* Specializes in barbecued ribs, steak, seafood. Own pasta. Hrs: 11:30 am-11 pm. Closed Sun; Jan 1, Dec 25. Res accepted. Lunch $4.25-$8.50; dinner $8-$50. Complete meals: $16.95. Family-owned. Cr cds: A, D, ER, MC, V.

D ⬤

St. Catharines

(D-5) *See also Hamilton, Niagara-on-the-Lake, Niagara Falls*

Pop 124,018 **Elev** 321 ft (98 m)
Area code 905
Web www.st.catharines.com
Information Tourism Marketing Coordinator, City Hall, 50 Church St, PO Box 3012, L2R 7C2; 905/688-5601, ext 1999

St. Catharines, "The Garden City of Canada," is located in the heart of the wine country and the Niagara fruit belt, which produces half of the province's entire output of fresh fruit. Originally a Loyalist settlement, it was also a depot of the Underground Railway. Located on the Welland Ship Canal, and the site of the first canal, St. Catharines was also the home of the first electric streetcar system in North America.

What to See and Do

Brock University. (1964) 6,000 students. A 540-acre (219-hectare) campus encompasses some of the finest woods and countryside in the Niagara region. Named in honor of General Sir Isaac Brock, commander of the British forces at the Battle of Queenston Heights in 1812. Tours (Mon-Fri, by appt). Glenridge Ave/Merrittville Hwy, at St. David's Rd. Phone 905/688-5550, ext 3245.

The Farmers Market. Large variety of fruit and vegetables from fruit belt farms of the surrounding area. (Tues, Thurs, and Sat) Church & James Sts, behind City Hall. Phone 905/688-5601, ext 1999.

Happy Rolph Bird Sanctuary and Children's Farm. Feeding station for native fowl and farm animals; 3 ponds; nature trail, picnicking, playground. (Victoria Day-Thanksgiving, daily; ponds all yr) Queen Elizabeth Way, Lake St Exit N to Lakeshore Rd E, cross ship canal, then N on Read Rd. Phone 905/937-7210. **FREE**

Morningstar Mill. Waterpowered, fine old mill containing rollers and millstones for grinding flour and feed. Picnic area. (Victoria Day wkend-Thanksgiving wkend, daily; rest of yr, Sat, Sun) De Cew Rd, at De Cew Falls. Phone 905/937-7210. **FREE**

Old Port Dalhousie. An 18th-century harborfront village, once the northern terminus of the first 3 Welland Ship Canals; now part of a larger recreation area with hand-crafted wooden carousel, restaurants, and shops. Ontario St, N of QEW to Lakeport Rd. Phone 905/935-7555.

Prudhomme's Wet 'n Wild Water Park. Park features wave pool, water and tube slides; rides, arcades. Roller rink, miniature golf, playground, beach; picnicking, snack bar, restaurant (June-Labour Day). 8 mi (13 km) W off Queen Elizabeth Way, Victoria Ave Exit 57, near Vineland. Phone 905/562-7304 or 905/562-7121. Day pass ¢¢¢¢

Rodman Hall Arts Centre. Art exhibitions, films, concerts, children's theater. (Tues-Sun; closed hols) 109 St. Paul Crescent. Phone 905/684-2925. **FREE**

Welland Canal Viewing Complex at Lock III. Unique view of lock operations from an elevated platform. Ships from over 50 countries can be seen as they pass through the canal. Arrival times are posted. Large information center; picnicking, restaurant. Via Queen Elizabeth Way Exit at Glendale Ave to Canal Rd then N. Phone 905/688-5601, ext 1999. Also here is

    St. Catharines Museum. Illustrates development, construction, and significance of Welland Canal; working scale model lock; displays on history of St. Catharines. Exhibitions on loan from major museums. (Daily; closed Jan 1, Dec 25-26) 1932 Government Rd. Phone 905/984-8880. ¢¢

Annual Events

Salmon Derby. Open season on Lake Ontario for coho and chinook salmon; rainbow, brown, and lake trout. Prizes for all categories. Phone 905/935-6700. Mid-Apr-mid-May.

Folk Arts Festival. Folk Art Multicultural Centre, 85 Church St. Open houses at ethnic clubs, concerts, ethnic dancing, and singing. Art and craft exhibits; big parade. Phone 905/685-6589. Two wks late May.

Can-Am Soapbox Derby. Jaycee Park, QEW N, Exit Ontario St. More than 100 competitors from US and Canada. June.

Niagara Grape and Wine Festival. Wine and cheese parties, athletic events, grape stomping, arts and crafts, ethnic concerts, and parade with bands and floats to honor ripening of the grapes. Grand Parade last Sat of festival. Phone 905/688-2570. Ten days late Sep.

Seasonal Events

Niagara Symphony Association. 73 Ontario St, Unit 104. (Sep-May) Professional symphony orchestra; amateur chorus; summer music camp. Phone 905/687-4993.

Royal Canadian Henley Regatta. Henley Rowing Course. Champion rowers from all parts of the world. Second in size only to the famous English regatta. Several nation- and continent-wide regattas take place on this world-famous course. Phone 905/935-9771. Apr-Oct.

Motels/Motor Lodges

★★ **HIGHWAYMAN MOTOR INN.** *420 Ontario St (L2R 5M1).* 905/688-1646; *fax 905/688-1646. www.ont.net/ highwayman/owerche.* 50 rms, 2 story. Mid-May-Sep: S $51.95; D $99.95; each addl $5; under 12 free; lower rates rest of yr. Crib $5. TV; cable (premium). Heated pool. Restaurant 7 am-2 pm. Ck-out noon. Meeting rms. Business servs avail. In-rm modem link. Valet serv. Sundries. Cr cds: A, C, D, DS, ER, MC, V.
⚏ ⬆ ♿ SC

★★ **HOLIDAY INN.** *2 N Service Rd (L2N 4G9), at QEW Lake St Exit.* 905/934-8000; *fax 905/934-9117. Email holiday@niagra.com; www. niagra.com/holidayinn_stc.* 140 rms, 2 story. July-Sep: S $105-$135; D $115-$145; each addl $10; under 18 free; lower rates rest of yr. Crib free. Pet accepted. TV; cable (premium) VCR avail (movies). Indoor/outdoor pool; lifeguard. Playground. Complimentary coffee in rms. Restaurant 6:30 am-9 pm. Bar 11-1 am.

Ck-out noon. Meeting rms. Business servs avail. In-rm modem link. Bellhops. Valet serv. Gift shop. Exercise rm; sauna. Balconies. Cr cds: A, C, D, DS, ER, JCB, MC, V.
⚏ ⬆ ♿ ⬆ ⬆ ♿ SC

★ **HOWARD JOHNSON.** *89 Meadowvale Dr (L2N 3Z8), off QEW Lake St N Exit.* 905/934-5400; *fax 905/646-8700.* 96 rms, 5 story. S $69-$149; D $79-$159; each addl $10; under 18 free. Crib free. Pet accepted. TV. Indoor pool. Coffee in rms. Restaurant open 24 hrs. Bar 11-2 am. Ck-out noon. Coin lndry. Meeting rm. Business servs avail. In-rm modem link. X-country ski 10 mi. Exercise equipt; sauna. Microwaves avail. Cr cds: A, D, DS, ER, MC, V.
⚏ ⬆ ♿ ⬆ ⬆ ♿ SC

★★★ **NIAGARA SUITES.** *3530 Schmon Pkwy (L2V 4Y6).* 905/984-8484; *fax 905/984-6691. www. embassy-suites.com.* 128 kit. suites, 4 story. S, D $94-$200; each addl $10; under 18 free. Crib free. Pet accepted. TV; cable, VCR avail. Indoor pool. Complimentary full bkfst. Coffee in rms. Restaurant 11 am-11 pm. Bar. Ck-out noon. Guest lndry. Meeting rms. Business center. In-rm modem link. Valet serv. Sundries. Exercise equipt; sauna. Lawn games. Microwaves. Cr cds: A, D, DS, ER, MC, V.
⚏ ⬆ ♿ ⬆ ⬆ ♿ SC ⬆

★★ **RAMADA PARKWAY INN.** *327 Ontario St (L2R 5L3), QEW Exit 47 S.* 905/688-2324; *fax 905/684-6432.* 125 rms, 5 story. Late June-Labor Day: S $89.99; D $149.99; each addl $10; under 18 free; wkend plan off-season; lower rates rest of yr. Crib free. TV; cable. Indoor pool; whirlpool. Sauna. Coffee in rms. Restaurant 6:30 am-11 pm. Bar 11-2 am. Ck-out 11 am. Meeting rms. Business servs avail. Health club privileges. Bowling alley. Refrigerators; some in-rm whirlpools. Plaza adj. Cr cds: A, C, D, DS, ER, MC, V.
⚏ ♿ ⬆ ♿ SC

St. Lawrence Islands National Park

See also Gananoque, Kingston

Information Superintendent, 2 County Rd 5, RR 3, Mallorytown, ON, K0E 1R0; 613/923-5261

Established in 1904, this park lies on a 50 mile (80 kilometer) stretch of the St. Lawrence River between Kingston and Brockville. It consists of 21 island areas and a mainland headquarters at Mallorytown Landing. The park offers boat launching facilities, beaches, natural and historic interpretive programs, island camping, picnicking, hiking, and boating. A visitor reception center and the remains of an 1817 British gunboat are at Mallorytown Landing (mid-May-mid-Oct, daily; rest of yr, by appt).

The islands can be accessed by water taxi or by boat rentals at numerous marinas along both the Canadian and American sides.

Stratford

(D-3) *See also Brantford, Kitchener-Waterloo*

Pop 27,500 (est) **Elev** 119 ft (36 m)
Area code 519
Information Tourism Stratford, 88 Wellington St, N5A 2L2; 519/271-5140 or 800/561-SWAN

The names Stratford and Avon River can conjure up only one name in most travelers' minds—Shakespeare. And that is exactly what you will find in this lovely city. World-renowned, this festival of fine theater takes place here every year.

What to See and Do

The Gallery/Stratford. Public gallery in parkland setting; historical and contemporary works. Guided tours on request. (Daily) 54 Romeo St N. Phone 519/271-5271. Admission (June-mid-Nov) ¢¢ Adj is

Shakespearean Gardens. Fragrant herbs, shrubs, and flowering plants common to William Shakespeare's time. Huron St. Phone 519/271-5140. **FREE**

Confederation Park. Features rock hill, waterfall, fountain, Japanese garden, and commemorative court.

Annual Event

Kinsmen Antique Show. Stratford Arena. Late July-Aug.

Seasonal Event

Stratford Festival. Contemporary, classical, and Shakespearean dramas and modern musicals. Performances at Festival, Avon, and Tom Patterson theaters. Contact Box Office, Stratford Festival, PO Box 520, N5A 6V2; 519/273-1600, 416/363-4471 (Toronto) or 800/567-1600. May-Nov, matinees and eves.

Motels/Motor Lodges

★★★ **FESTIVAL INN.** *1144 Ontario St (N5A 6W1). 519/273-1150; fax 519/273-2111.* 183 rms, 1-2 story. May-mid-Nov: S $74-$135; D $80-$139; each addl $10; suites $150; under 12 free; lower rates rest of yr. Crib free. TV; cable (premium), VCR avail. Indoor pool; whirlpool; poolside serv. Restaurant 7 am-9 pm; Sat from 7:30 am; Sun 7:30 am-9 pm. Bar 11:30-1 am. Ck-out 11 am. Meeting rms. Business servs avail. Exercise equipt; sauna. Lawn games. Many refrigerators. Cr cds: A, D, DS, ER, JCB, MC, V.

D 🛏 🖎 🖎 🖎 **SC**

★ **MAJER'S.** *2970 Ontario St E (M5A 6S5), 1¼ mi E (ON 7/8). 519/271-2010; fax 519/273-7951.* 31 rms. May-Oct: S $57-$65; D $70-$75; each addl $10; lower rates rest of yr. Crib free. TV; cable (premium). Heated pool. Playground. Complimentary coffee in lobby. Restaurant adj 11 am-11 pm. Ck-out 10:30 am. Refrigerators. Picnic tables. Cr cds: A, MC, V.

🛏 🖎 🖎

★★ **STRATFORD SUBURBAN.** *2808 Ontario St E (N5A 6S5), 2½ mi E (ON 7/8). 519/271-9650; fax 519/271-0193.* 25 rms. S $58-$67; D $68-$79; each addl $10. TV; cable. Heated pool. Restaurant nearby. Ck-out 11 am. Tennis. Refrigerators. Cr cds: MC, V.

★★ **VICTORIAN INN.** *10 Romeo St N (N5A 5M7).* 519/271-4650; fax 519/271-2030; toll-free 800/741-2135. Email *victorian-inn@orc.ca; www. victorian-inn.on.ca.* 115 rms, 4 story. Mid-May-mid-Nov: S, D $79-$139; each addl $10; under 12 free; lower rates rest of yr. Crib $10. TV; cable (premium), VCR avail. Heated pool; poolside serv. Complimentary coffee in rms. Dining rm 7 am-11 am, 5-9 pm. Ck-out noon. Meeting rms. Business servs avail. In-rm modem link. Valet serv. Sundries. Exercise equipt. Game rm. Balconies. On Lake Victoria. Cr cds: A, D, DS, ER, JCB, MC, V.

B&B/Small Inn

★★★ **QUEEN'S INN.** *161 Ontario St (N5A 3H3).* 519/271-1400; fax 519/271-7373; res 800/461-6450. Email *queens@stratford.webgate.net.* 32 rms, 3 story, 7 suites. May-Oct: S $75-$110; D $85-$120; each addl $25; suites $130-$200; kit. units $190-$200; under 12 free; ski plans; lower rates rest of yr. Crib free. Pet accepted, some restrictions. TV; cable, VCR avail (movies). Restaurant 7 am-10 pm. Ck-out 11 am, ck-in 2 pm. Business servs avail. Bellhops. Valet serv. Concierge serv. Downhill ski 20 mi; x-country ski 10 mi. Exercise equipt. Microwaves avail. Built 1850. Cr cds: A, D, ER, MC, V.

Restaurants

★★★ **THE CHURCH RESTAURANT AND THE BELFRY.** *70 Brunswick St (N5A 6V6), at Waterloo St.* 519/273-3424. *www.church restaurant.com.* Specializes in salmon monette, filet mignon, loin of lamb. Own baking. Hrs: 11:30-1 am; Sun 11:30 am-8 pm. Closed Mon; Jan 1, Dec 25. Res accepted. Wine cellar. Lunch a la carte entrees: $9.50-$16.25; dinner a la carte entrees: $26.50-$33.50. Complete meals: $49.50-$58.50. Child's menu. Parking. In 1870 Gothic church. Cr cds: A, D, DS, MC, V.

★ **GENE'S.** *81 Ontario St (N5A 3H1).* 519/271-9678. Specializes in Cantonese, Szechwan dishes. Own pies. Hrs: 11 am-midnight. Closed Dec 25, 26. Res accepted. Bar. Lunch a la carte entrees: $6-$7.50; dinner a la carte entrees: $8.25-$16.95. Child's menu. Entertainment. Asian decor. Family-owned. Cr cds: A, C, D, DS, ER, MC, V.

★★ **HOUSE OF GENE.** *108 Downie St (N5A 1X1).* 519/271-3080. Specializes in Cantonese, Szechwan dishes. Hrs: 11:30 am-8 pm; Sun from noon. Closed Dec 25, 26. Res accepted. Bar. Lunch a la carte entrees: $6.25-$7.95. Buffet: $6.95; dinner a la carte entrees: $6.25-$16.75. Buffet: $8.95. Child's menu. Entertainment. Modern Asian decor. Cr cds: A, D, MC, V.

★★ **KEYSTONE ALLEY CAFE.** *34 Brunswick St (N5A 3L8).* 519/271-5645. Specializes in pasta, fresh fish. Hrs: 11:30 am-3 pm, 5-9 pm; Mon to 3 pm. Closed Sun; most major hols. Res accepted. Bar. Lunch a la carte entrees: $7.95-$9.95; dinner $15.95-$24.95. Child's menu. Entertainment. Open kitchen. Cr cds: A, D, MC, V.

★ **MADELYN'S DINER.** *377 Huron St (N5A 5T6).* 519/273-5296. Specializes in English fish and chips, homemade pies. Hrs: 7 am-8 pm; Sun 8 am-1:30 pm. Closed Mon; Dec 25. Res accepted. Bar. Bkfst $2.50-$7.95; lunch $2.75-$7.25; dinner $6.95-$10.95. Entertainment. Parking. Cr cds: A, MC, V.

★★ **OLD PRUNE.** *151 Albert St (N5A 3K5).* 519/271-5052. *www.cyg. net/~oldprune.* Eclectic menu. Specializes in seafood, lamb. Hrs: 11:30 am-1:30 pm, 5-8 pm. Res accepted. Bar. Lunch a la carte entrees: $8.50-$14.95; dinner complete meals: $53.50. Child's menu. Parking. Restored Edwardian residence;

enclosed garden terrace. Cr cds: A, MC, V.

★ ★ ★ **RUNDLE'S.** *9 Cobourg St (N5A 3E4). 519/271-6442.* Specializes in regional wine country cuisine. Hrs: 5-8:30 pm; Sun to 7 pm. Closed Mon; hols. Res accepted. Bar. Dinner a la carte entrees: $11.50-$17.95. Child's menu. Entertainment. Intimate atmosphere. Cr cds: D, DS, MC, V.

Thunder Bay (G-6)

Pop 112,486 **Elev** 616 ft (188 m)
Area code 807
Web http://tourism.city.thunder-bay.on.ca
Information Tourism Thunder Bay, 500 Donald St E, P7E 5V3; 800/667-8386 or 807/983-2041

Thunder Bay was formed with the joining of the twin cities of Fort William and Port Arthur. Located on Lake Superior, it is a major grain shipping port. The history of Thunder Bay is tied very closely to the fur trade in North America. In the early 19th century, the North West Company had acquired most of the fur trade. Fort William became the inland headquarters for the company, and today much of the activity and spirit of those days can be relived at the fort.

Thunder Bay offers the vacationer outdoor recreation including skiing, parks, and historical attractions and serves as a starting point for a drive around Lake Superior.

What to See and Do

Amethyst Centre. Full lapidary shop and gem cutting operation; retail, gift, and jewelry shop. Tours. (Mon-Sat; closed hols) 400 E Victoria Ave. Phone 807/622-6908. **FREE**

Amethyst Mine Panorama. Open-pit quarry adj to Elbow Lake. The quarrying operation, geological faults, Canadian Pre-Cambrian shield, and sample gem pockets are readily visible. Gem picking; tours. (Mid-May-

mid-Oct, daily) 35 mi (56 km) NE, 5 mi (8 km) off Hwy 11/17 on E Loon Rd. Phone 807/622-6908. ¢

Centennial Conservatory. Wide variety of plant life incl banana plants, palm trees, cacti. (Daily; closed hols) Balmoral & Dease Sts. Phone 807/622-7036. **FREE**

Centennial Park. Summer features incl a reconstructed 1910 logging camp; logging camp museum. Playground. Cross-country skiing, sleigh rides (by appt; fee) in winter. (Daily) Near Boulevard Lake, at Centennial Park Rd. Phone 807/683-6511. **FREE**

⭐ **International Friendship Gardens.** Park is composed of individual gardens designed and constructed by various ethnic groups incl Slovakian, Polish, German, Italian, Finnish, Danish, Ukranian, Hungarian, and Chinese. (Daily) 2000 Victoria Ave. Phone 807/625-3166. **FREE**

Kakabeka Falls Provincial Park. Spectacular waterfall on the historic Kaministiquia River, formerly a voyageur route from Montréal to the West. The 128-ft (39-km) high falls may be seen from highway stop. Waterflow is best in spring and on wkends—flow is reduced during the wk. Sand beach in the park; hiking and interpretive trails, camping (day-use, electrical hookups; fee), playground, visitor service center. 20 mi (32 km) W via ON 11/17. Phone 807/475-1535 (Oct-Apr) or 807/473-9231 (May-Sep). Per vehicle ¢¢¢

Old Fort William. Authentic reconstruction of the original Fort William as it was from 1803-21. Visitors experience the adventure of the Nor'westers convergence for the Rendezvous (re-creation staged 10 days mid-July). Costumed staff populate 42 bldgs on the site, featuring tradesmen's shops, farm, apothecary, fur stores, warehouses, Great Hall, voyageur encampment, indigenous encampment; historic restaurant. Gift shop. Walking tours (exc winter). (May-Oct, daily) 1 King Rd, off Hwy 61S. Phone 807/577-8461. ¢¢¢

Quetico Provincial Park. (see) 27 mi W on ON 11/17.

Thunder Bay Art Gallery. Changing exhibitions from major national and international museums; regional art; contemporary native art. Tours, films, lectures, concerts. Gift shop. (Tues-Sun; closed hols) On Confederation College Campus; use Harbour Expy from Hwy 11/17. Phone 807/577-6427. **FREE**

Motels/Motor Lodges

★ ★ **BEST WESTERN CROSS-ROADS.** *655 W Arthur St (P7E 5R6), jct ON 11/17 and ON 61, near Thunder Bay Airport. 807/577-4241; fax 807/ 475-7059.* 60 rms, 2 story. May-Oct: S $73; D $78; under 12 free; lower rates rest of yr. Crib free. Pet accepted. TV; cable. Complimentary coffee. Restaurant opp 7 am-midnight. Ck-out 11 am. Business servs avail. In-rm modem link. Valet serv. Free airport transportation. Some refrigerators. Cr cds: A, C, D, DS, ER, MC, V.

🐾 ✈ 🖬 🔥 SC

★ ★ **COMFORT INN.** *660 W Arthur St (P7E 5R8), near Thunder Bay Airport. 807/475-3155; fax 807/475-3816.* 80 rms, 2 story. S $70-$85; D $75-$93; each addl $8; under 19 free. Crib free. Pet accepted. TV; cable. Complimentary coffee in lobby. Restaurant adj 7 am-11 pm. Ck-out 11 am. Business servs avail. In-rm modem link. Cr cds: A, D, DS, ER, MC, V.

D 🐾 🖬 🔥 SC

★ ★ **LANDMARK INN.** *1010 Dawson Rd (P7B 5J4), jct ON 11/17 and 102, County Fair Plz. 807/767-1681; fax 807/767-1439. www.landmark.thunder bay.on.ca.* 106 rms, 4 story. S $80; D $86; each addl $8; under 12 free. Crib free. Pet accepted; $50. TV; cable. Indoor pool; whirlpool, water slide, poolside serv. Sauna. Complimentary continental bkfst., coffee in rms. Restaurant 7-1 am. Bar 11-1 am. Ck-out 11 am. Meeting rms. Business servs avail. In-rm modem link. Valet serv. Sundries. Free airport transportation. Downhill ski 20 mi. Cr cds: A, D, DS, ER, MC, V.

D 🐾 ✇ 🖬 🔥 SC

★ ★ **PRINCE ARTHUR.** *17 N Cumberland (P7A 4K8). 807/345-5411; fax 807/345-8565. Email pahotel@tbaytel. net; www.princearthur.on.ca.* 121 rms, 6 story. S $59-$77; D $67-$85; each addl $8; suites $115-$145; under 16 free. Crib free. Pet accepted. TV; cable. Indoor pool; wading pool, whirlpool. Saunas. Coffee in rms. Restaurant 6:30 am-10 pm. Bar 11-1

am. Ck-out noon. Meeting rms. Business servs avail. In-rm modem link. Valet serv. Sundries. Free airport transportation. Health club privileges. Some refrigerators; microwaves avail. Downhill ski 10 mi. Overlooks harbor. Shopping mall opp. Cr cds: A, C, D, ER, MC, V.

D 🐾 ⚓ ✇ 🖬 🔥 SC

★ **TRAVELODGE.** *450 Memorial Ave (P7B 3Y7), adj Auditorium. 807/345-2343; fax 807/345-3246. www.jwg. com/ventureinns/.* 93 rms, 3 story. S $75; D $85; each addl $10; under 20 free. Crib free. Pet accepted. TV; cable. Indoor pool. Sauna. Complimentary continental bkfst. Restaurant adj 11-1 am. Ck-out 1 pm. Meeting rms. Business servs avail. In-rm modem link. Sun deck. Downhill ski 15 mi. Cr cds: A, C, D, DS, ER, MC, V.

🐾 ✇ 🖬 🔥 SC

★ **TRAVELODGE AIRLANE HOTEL.** *698 W Arthur St (P7E 5R8), jct ON 11/17 and on 61, near Thunder Bay Airport. 807/577-1181; fax 807/475-4852. Email inquire@travelodge-airlane. com; www.travelodge.com.* 160 rms, 2-3 story. S $79-$105; D $85-$110; each addl $5; wkend rates. Crib free. Pet accepted. TV; cable (premium), VCR avail. Indoor pool; whirlpool. Restaurants 7 am-11 pm. Bar 4 pm-1 am, closed Sun; entertainment. Ck-out 11 am. Meeting rms. Business center. In-rm modem link. Bellhops. Valet serv. Sundries. Free airport transportation. Exercise equipt; sauna. Minibars. Cr cds: A, C, D, ER, MC, V.

D 🐾 ✇ 🏋 ✈ 🖬 SC 🚶

★ ★ ★ **VALHALLA INN.** *1 Valhalla Inn Rd (P7E 6J1), jct ON 11/17 and ON 61, near Thunder Bay Airport. 807/577-1121; fax 807/475-4723; res 800/964-1121. Email valbay@baynet. net; www.valhallainn.com.* 267 rms, 5 story. S $175-$190; D $185-$200; each addl $10; suites $295-$305; under 18 free; ski, wkend rates. Crib free. Pet accepted; $10. TV. Indoor pool; whirlpool. Complimentary coffee in rms. Restaurant 6:30 am-11:30 pm. Bar 4:30 pm-2 am. Ck-out 1 pm. Meeting rms. Business servs avail. In-rm modem link. Bellhops. Valet serv. Sundries. Free airport transportation. Downhill ski 3 mi; x-country ski 4 mi. Exercise equipt; sauna. Bicycle rentals. Game rm. Some bathrm phones, minibars; microwaves avail. Luxury level. Cr cds: A, C, D, DS, ER, MC, V.

★ ★ ★ **VICTORIA INN.** *555 W Arthur St (P7E 5R5), near airport. 807/577-8481; fax 807/475-8961; res 800/387-3331. Email vicinn@tbaytel. net; www.tbaytel.net/vicinn.* 182 rms, 3 story. S $76.95-$155; D $86.95-$155; each addl $10; suites $179-$229; under 16 free. Crib free. Pet accepted; $5. Indoor pool; wading pool, whirlpool, poolside serv, lifeguard. TV; cable. Complimentary coffee in rms. Restaurant 7 am-11 pm. Bar 11:30-1 am. Ck-out noon. Meeting rms. Business servs avail. In-rm modem link. Valet serv. Sundries. Coin lndry. Free airport transportation. Downhill ski 8 mi; x-country ski 5 mi. Exercise equipt; sauna. Health club privileges. Some refrigerators. Cr cds: A, C, D, DS, ER, MC, V.

Restaurant

★ ★ **THE KEG.** *735 Hewitson Ave (P7B 6B5), Balmoral at Harbour Expy. 807/623-1960.* Specializes in steak, seafood. Salad bar. Own cheesecake. Hrs: 4 pm-1 am; Fri, Sat to 2 am. Closed Dec 24, 25. Bar. Dinner $15.99-$32.99. Child's menu. Pub atmosphere. Cr cds: A, D, MC, V.

Toronto

(D-4) *See also Hamilton, Mississauga*

Founded 1793 **Pop** 3,400,000 (metro)
Elev 569 ft (173 m) **Area code** 416
Web www.torontotourism.com

Information Tourism Toronto, Queens Quay Terminal at Harbourfront, 207 Queens Quay W, M5J 1A7; 416/203-2500 or 800/363-1990

Toronto is one of Canada's leading industrial, commercial, and cultural centers. From its location on the shores of Lake Ontario, it has performed essential communications and transportation services throughout Canadian history. Its name derives from the native word for meeting place, as the area was called by the Hurons who led the first European, Etienne Brule, to the spot. In the mid-1800s the Grand Trunk and Great Western Railroad and the Northern Railway connected Toronto with the upper St. Lawrence; Portland, Maine; and Chicago, Illinois.

After French fur traders from Québec established Fort Rouille in 1749, Toronto became a base for further Canadian settlement. Its population of Scottish, English, and US emigrants was subject to frequent armed attacks, especially during the War of 1812 and immediately thereafter. From within the United States, the attackers aimed at annexation; from within Canada, they aimed at emancipation from England. One result of these unsuccessful threats was the protective confederation of Lower Canada, which later separated again as the province of Québec, and Upper Canada, which still later became the province of Ontario with Toronto as its capital.

Toronto today is a cosmopolitan city with many intriguing features. Once predominantly British, the population is now exceedingly multi-cultural—the United Nations deemed Toronto the world's most ethnically diverse city in 1989. A major theater center with many professional playhouses, including the Royal Alexandra Theatre, Toronto is also a major banking center, with several architecturally significant banks. Good shopping can be found throughout the city, but Torontonians are most proud of their "Underground City," a series of subterranean malls linking more than 300 shops and restaurants in the downtown area. For professional sports fans, Toronto offers the Maple Leafs (hockey), the Blue Jays (baseball), the Raptors (basketball), and the Argonauts (football). A visit to the Harbourfront, a boat tour to the islands, or enjoying an evening on the town should round out your stay in Toronto.

What to See and Do

Art Gallery of Ontario. Changing exhibits of paintings, drawings, sculpture, and graphics from the

14th-20th centuries incl Henry Moore Collection; permanent Canadian Collection and Contemporary Galleries; films, lectures, concerts. (Tues-Sun; winter Wed-Sun; closed Jan 1, Dec 25) Free admission Wed eves. 317 Dundas St W. Phone 416/979-6648. ¢¢ Behind gallery is

The Grange. A Georgian house (ca 1817) restored and furnished in early Victorian style (1835-40). (Same hrs as Art Gallery) **Free** with admission to Art Gallery.

Black Creek Pioneer Village. More than 30 bldgs restored to re-create life in a rural Canadian village of mid-19th-century; incl general store, printing office, town hall, church, firehouse, blacksmith shop; special events wkends. Visitor reception centre has exhibit gallery, theater, restaurant. (Early Mar-Dec, variable schedule; closed Dec 25) 1000 Murray Ross Pkwy. Jane St & Steeles Ave, 2 mi (3 km) N on Hwy 400, E on Steeles, then ½ mi (1 km) to Jane St. Phone 416/736-1733. ¢¢

Casa Loma. A medieval-style castle built by Sir Henry Pellatt between 1911-14. Furnished rms, secret passages, underground tunnel, and stables. Restored gardens (May-Oct). Gift shop, cafe. (Daily; closed Jan 1, Dec 25) One Austin Ter, 1½ mi (2 km) NW of downtown. Phone 416/923-1171. ¢¢ Adj is

Spadina. (ca 1865) Home of financier James Austin and his descendants; Victorian and Edwardian furnishings and fine art; restored gardens. (Tues-Sun afternoons; closed hols) 285 Spadina Rd. Phone 416/392-6910. ¢

City Hall. (1965) Distinctive modern design features twin towers that appear to support round, elevated council chambers. Exhibits, concerts in Nathan Phillips Sq in front of bldg. Self-guided tours; guided tours (summer). (Mon-Fri) 100 Queen St W. Phone 416/392-7341. **FREE**

City parks. Listed below are some of Toronto's many parks. Contact the Dept of Parks & Recreation. Phone 416/392-1111.

Allan Gardens. Indoor/outdoor botanical displays, wading pool, picnicking, concerts. (Daily) W side of Sherbourne St to Jarvis St

between Carlton St & Gerrard St E. Phone 416/392-7288. **FREE**

Edwards Gardens. Civic garden center; rock gardens, pools, pond, rustic bridges. (Daily) NE of downtown, at Leslie Ave E & Lawrence St. Phone 416/392-8186. **FREE**

Grange Park. Wading pool, playground. Natural ice rink (winter, weather permitting). (Daily) Dundas & Beverley Sts, located behind the Art Gallery of Ontario. **FREE**

High Park. The largest park in the city (399 acres or 161 hectares). Swimming, wading pool; tennis, playgrounds, picnicking, hiking, floral display and rock falls in Hillside Gardens, animal paddocks. Shakespeare performances at Dream Site outdoor theater. Restaurant, concessions; trackless tour train. Ice-skating. Also here is Colborne Lodge at S end of park. (Daily) Between Bloor St W & The Queensway at Parkside Dr, near lakeshore. **FREE**

Queen's Park. Ontario Parliament Bldgs are located in this park. (Daily) Queen's Park Crescent. **FREE**

Riverdale Park. Summer: tennis, swimming, wading pools; playgrounds, picnicking, band concerts. Winter: skating; 19th-century farm. (Daily) W side of Broadview Ave, between Danforth Ave & Gerrard St E.

Toronto Island Park. Accessible by ferry (fee; phone 416/392-8193) from foot of Bay St. Historic lighthouse, other bldgs. Fishing, boating, swimming; bicycling, children's farmyard, scenic tram ride (free), amusement area (fee), mall with fountains and gardens, fine views of city and lake. (May-Oct, daily) S across Inner Harbour. Phone 416/392-8186. **FREE**

✪ **CN Tower.** World's tallest freestanding structure (1,815 ft/553 m). Three observation decks (daily), revolving restaurant (see 360 REVOLVING RESTAURANT), and nightclub. Also various activities incl SkyQuest Theatre, Maple Leaf Cinema, and 4 motion simulator rides (fees). 301 Front St W, just W of University Ave. Phone 416/360-8500 (information) or 416/362-5411 (dining res). ¢¢¢¢

Colborne Lodge. (1837) Built by John G. Howard, architect and surveyor; restored to 1870 style; art gallery houses changing exhibits; artifacts of 1830s; artist's studio. (Tues-Sun; closed Good Fri, Dec 25-26) Colborne Lodge Dr & The Queensway in High Park. Phone 416/392-6916. ¢¢

Exhibition Place. Designed to accommodate the Canadian National Exhibition (see ANNUAL EVENTS), this 350-acre (141-hectare) park has events yr-round. (Aug-Sep, daily) S off Gardener Expy, on Lakeshore Blvd. Phone 416/393-6000.

George R. Gardiner Museum of Ceramic Art. One of the world's finest collections of Italian majolica, English Delftware, and 18th-century continental porcelain. (Daily; closed Jan 1, Dec 25) 111 Queen's Park, opp Royal Ontario Museum. Phone 416/586-8080. **Donation**

Gibson House. Home of land surveyor and local politician David Gibson; restored and furnished to 1850s style. Costumed interpreters conduct demonstrations. Tours. (Tues-Sun; closed hols) 5172 Yonge St (ON 11), in North York. Phone 416/395-7432. ¢¢

Harbourfront Centre. This 10-acre waterfront community is alive with theater, dance, films, art shows, music, crafts, and children's programs. Most events free. (Daily) 235 Queens Quay W at foot of York St. Phone 416/973-3000.

Historic Fort York. Restored War of 1812 fort and battle site. Costumed staff provide military demonstrations; 8 original bldgs house period environments and exhibits. Tours. (Daily; closed hols) Garrison Rd, SE near jct Bathurst & Fleet Sts by Strachan Ave. Phone 416/392-6907. ¢¢

Hummingbird Centre for the Performing Arts. Stage presentations of Broadway musicals, dramas, and concerts by international artists. Home of the Canadian Opera Company and National Ballet of Canada. Pre-performance dining; gift shop. 1 Front St E at Yonge St. Phone 416/393-7469 or 416/872-2262 (tickets).

Huronia Historical Parks. Two living history sites animated by costumed interpreters. (Daily) 63 mi (101 km) N via Hwy 400, then 34 mi (55 km) N to Midland on Hwy 93. Phone 705/526-7838. ¢¢¢ Consists of

Discovery Harbour. Marine heritage center and reconstructed 19th-century British Naval dockyard. Established in 1817, site incl 19th-century military base. Now rebuilt, the site features 8 furnished bldgs and orientation center. Replica of 49-ft (15-m) British naval schooner HMS *Bee;* also HMS *Tecumseth* and *Perseverance.* Costumed interpreters bring base to life, ca 1830. Sail training and excursions (daily). Audiovisual display; free parking, docking, picnic facilities. Theater; gift shop, restaurant. (Victoria Day-Labour Day, Mon-Fri; after Labour Day-Sep, daily) Church St, Penetanguishene. ¢¢¢

Ste. Marie among the Hurons. (1639-49) Reconstruction of 17th-century Jesuit mission that was Ontario's first European community. Twenty-two furnished bldgs incl native dwellings, workshops, barn, church, cookhouse, hospital. Candlelight tours, canoe excursions. Cafe features period-inspired meals and snacks. Orientation center, interpretive museum. Free parking and picnic facilities. (Victoria Day wkend-Oct, daily) E of Midland on Hwy 12. ¢¢¢ World-famous Martyrs' Shrine (site of Papal visit) is located across the highway. Other area highlights incl pioneer museum, replica indigenous village, Wye Marsh Wildlife Centre.

Kortright Centre for Conservation. Environmental center with trails, beehouse, maple syrup shack, wildlife pond, and plantings. Naturalist-guided hikes (daily). Cross-country skiing (no rentals); picnic area, cafe; indoor exhibits and theater. (Daily; closed Dec 24 and 25) 9550 Pine Valley Dr, Woodbridge; 12 mi (19.3 km) NW via Hwy 400, Major MacKenzie Dr Exit, then 2 mi (3 km) W, then S on Pine Valley Dr. Phone 905/832-2289. ¢¢

Mackenzie House. Restored 19th-century home of William Lyon Mackenzie, first mayor of Toronto; furnishings and artifacts of the 1850s; 1840s print shop. Group tours (by appt). (Tues-Sat, afternoons; closed hols) 82 Bond St. Phone 416/392-6915. ¢¢

The Market Gallery. Exhibition center for Toronto Archives; displays on city's historical, social, and cultural heritage; art, photographs, maps, documents, and artifacts. (Wed-Sat, also Sun afternoons; closed hols) 95 Front St E. Phone 416/392-7604. **FREE**

McMichael Canadian Art Collection. Works by Canada's most famous artists—the Group of Seven, Tom Thomson, Emily Carr, David Milne, Clarence Gagnon, and others. Also Inuit (Eskimo) and contemporary indigenous art and sculpture. Restaurant; book, gift shop. Constructed from hand-hewn timbers and native stone, the gallery stands in 100 acres (40 hectares) on the crest of Humber Valley; nature trail. (June-early Nov, daily; rest of yr, Tues-Sun; closed Dec 25) N via ON 400 or 427, 10365 Islington Ave in Kleinburg. Phone 905/893-1121. ¢¢¢

⚃ Metro Toronto Zoo. Approx 710 acres (287 hectares) of native and exotic plants and animals in 6 geographic regions: Indo-Malaya, Africa, North and South America, Eurasia, and Australia. The North American Domain can be seen on a 3-mi (5-km) A/C vehicle ride. The Zoomobile takes visitors on ½-hr drive through Eurasian, South American, and African areas. Parking fee. (Daily; closed Dec 25) 10 mi (16 km) E of Don Valley Pkwy on Hwy 401, then N on Meadowvale Rd, in Scarborough. Phone 416/393-4636. ¢¢¢

Ontario Parliament Buildings. Guided tours of the Legislature Bldg and walking tour of grounds. Gardens; art collection; historic displays. (Victoria Day-Labour Day, daily; rest of yr, Mon-Fri; closed hols) Queen's Park. Phone 416/325-7500. **FREE**

Ontario Place. A 96-acre (39-hectare) cultural, recreational, and entertainment complex on 3 man-made islands in Lake Ontario. Incl outdoor amphitheater for concerts, 2 pavilions with multimedia presentations, Cinesphere theater with IMAX films (yr-round; fee); children's village. Three villages of snack bars, restaurants, and pubs; miniature golf; lagoons, canals, 2 marinas, 370-ft (113-m) water slide, showboat, pedal and bumper boats; Wilderness Adventure Ride. (Mid-May-early Sep; daily) Parking fee. 955 Lakeshore Blvd W. Phone 416/314-9900 (recording) or 416/314-9811. ¢¢¢¢

Ontario Science Centre. Hundreds of hands-on exhibits in the fields of space, technology, communications, food, chemistry, and earth science. Demonstrations on electricity, papermaking, metal casting, lasers, cryogenics. OmniMax theater (fee). Special exhibitions. (Daily; closed Dec 25) 770 Don Mills Rd, at Eglinton Ave E, 6 mi (10 km) NE via Don Valley Pkwy, in Don Mills. Phone 416/696-3127 (recording). Per person ¢¢¢; Parking ¢¢

Paramount Canada's Wonderland. More than 140 attractions in 8 themed areas offer 11 live stage shows and 50 rides, incl Vortex and Top Gun (suspended roller coasters). Splash Works, a 10-acre area offers 15 water-related rides and attractions (mid-June-Labour Day, weather permitting; free with Pay-One-Price admission). Special events, fireworks displays, top-name entertainment. (May and Sep, wkends; June-Aug, daily) 9580 Jane St, 18 mi (29 km) N on Hwy 400. Phone 905/832-7000. Pay-One-Price Passport ¢¢¢¢

The Pier: Toronto's Waterfront Museum. Original 1930s pier bldg on Toronto's celebrated waterfront incl 2 floors of hands-on interactive displays, rare historical artificacts, recreations of marine history stories, art gallery, boat-building center, narrated walking excursions, children's programs. (Mar-Oct, Daily) Central Harbourfront at 245 Queen's Quay W. Phone 416/597-0965. ¢¢

Professional sports.

American League baseball (Toronto Blue Jays). SkyDome. 1 Blue Jays Way. Phone 416/341-1000.

NBA (Toronto Raptors). SkyDome. 1 Blue Jays Way. Phone 416/214-2255.

NHL (Toronto Maple Leafs). Air Canada Centre. 40 Bay St. Phone 416/815-5700.

Royal Ontario Museum. (ROM) Extensive permanent displays of fine and decorative art, archaeology, and earth and life sciences. The collection incl Chinese temple wall paintings; 12 dinosaur skeletons; the Ming

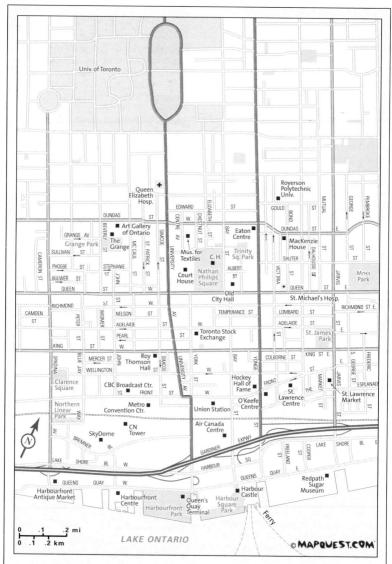

Univ. of Toronto

Queen Elizabeth Hosp.

Royerson Polytechnic Univ.

Art Gallery of Ontario
The Grange
Grange Park

Mus. for Textiles

Eaton Centre

MacKenzie House

Trinity Sq. Park

Court House

Nathan Phillips Square

Old City Hall

St. Michael's Hosp.

Toronto Stock Exchange

St. James Park

Roy Thomson Hall

Hockey Hall of Fame

CBC Broadcast Ctr.

St. Lawrence Centre

St. Lawrence Market

O'Keefe Centre

Metro Convention Ctr.

Clarence Square

Northern Linear Park

Union Station

Air Canada Centre

SkyDome

CN Tower

Redpath Sugar Museum

Harbourfront Antique Market

Harbourfront Centre

Harbourfront Park

Queen's Quay Terminal

Harbour Square Park

Harbour Castle

Ferry

0   .1   .2 mi
0   .1   .2 km

LAKE ONTARIO

©MAPQUEST.COM

This is one of a number of "Discovery Walks" offered by Metropolitan Toronto. It follows ravine footpaths and a beach boardwalk and offers views of the Lake Ontario shoreline, Toronto's charming "Beaches" neighborhood, gardens, and wooded ravine parklands. Other points of interest include an Art Deco water treatment plant.

Tomb Gallery; the hands-on Discovery Gallery; Greek, Etruscan, Chinese, European, and Egypt and Nubia galleries; special programs. (Daily; closed Jan 1, Dec 25) 100 Queen's Park. Phone 416/586-5549 or 416/586-8000 (recording). ¢¢¢¢

Sightseeing tours.

Gray Line bus tours. Contact 184 Front St E, Suite 601, M5A 4N3. Phone 416/594-3310.

Toronto Tours Ltd. Four different boat tours of Toronto Harbour. Phone 416/869-1372. ¢¢¢¢

SkyDome. State-of-the-art sports stadium with a fully retractable roof; contains a hotel and restaurants. Guided tours (1 hr) begin with 15-min film *The Inside Story* and incl visits to a skybox, media center, locker rm, and playing field (all subject to availability). Tour (daily, schedule permitting). 1 Blue Jays Way, adj CN Tower. Phone 416/341-2770. ¢¢¢

St. Lawrence Centre for the Arts. Performing arts complex features theater, music, dance, films, and other public events. 27 Front St E. Phone 416/367-8243 (box office).

Todmorden Mills Heritage Museum & Arts Centre. Restored historic houses; Parshall Terry House (1797) and William Helliwell House (1820). Also museum; restored 1899 train station. Picnicking. (May-Sep, Tues-Sun; Oct-Dec, Mon-Fri) 67 Pottery Rd, 2¼ mi (4 km) N, off Don Valley Pkwy in East York on Pottery Rd. between Broadview and Bayview Aves. Phone 416/396-2819. Museum **FREE**; Tours ¢¢

Toronto Stock Exchange. Stock Market Place visitor center has multimedia displays, interactive games, and archival exhibits to aid visitors in understanding the market. The Exchange Tower, 2 First Canadian Pl (King & York Sts). Phone 416/947-4676. **FREE**

Toronto Symphony. Classical, pops, and children's programs; Great Performers series. Wheelchair seating, audio enhancement for hearing-impaired. Roy Thomson Hall, 60 Simcoe St. Phone 416/593-4828.

University of Toronto. (1827) 55,000 students. Largest univ in Canada. Guided walking tours of magnificent Gothic bldgs begin at Hart House and incl account of campus ghost (June-Aug, Mon-Fri; free). Downtown, W of Queen's Park. Phone 416/978-5000 (tours).

Woodbine Racetrack. Thoroughbred racing (late Apr-Oct, Wed-Sun afternoons; Queen's Plate race in mid-July). 15 mi (24 km) N via Hwy 427 in Etobicoke. Phone 416/675-RACE. ¢¢

Young People's Theatre. Professional productions for the entire family. (Sep-May, daily; Aug, wkends only) 165 Front St E. Phone 416/862-2222.

Annual Events

International Caravan. Fifty pavilions scattered throughout the city present ethnic food, dancing, crafts. Phone 416/977-0466. Third wk June.

Chin International Picnic. At Paramount Canada's Wonderland. Contests, sports, picnicking. Phone 416/531-9991. First wkend July.

Outdoor Art Show. Nathan Phillips Sq. Phone 416/408-2754. Mid-July.

Caribana. Caribbean music, grand parade, floating nightclubs, dancing, costumes, food at various locations throughout city. Phone 416/465-4884. Late July-early Aug.

Canadian National Exhibition. Exhibition Place on the lakefront. This gala celebration originated in 1879 as the Toronto Industrial Exhibition for the encouragement of agriculture, industry, and the arts, although agricultural events dominated the show. Today sports, industry, labor, and the arts are of equal importance to CNE. The "Ex," as it is locally known, is so inclusive of the nation's activities that it is a condensed Canada. A special 350-acre (141-hectare) park has been built to accommodate the exhibition. Hundreds of events incl animal shows, parades, exhibits, a midway, water and air shows. Virtually every kind of sporting event is represented, from frisbee-throwing to the National Horse Show. Phone 416/393-6000. Mid-Aug-Labour Day.

Toronto International Film Festival. Celebration of world cinema in downtown theaters; Canadian and foreign films, international movie makers, and stars. Phone 416/967-7371. Early Sep.

Canadian International. Woodbine Racetrack. World-class thoroughbreds compete in one of Canada's most important races. Mid-late Oct.

Royal Agricultural Winter Fair. Coliseum Bldg, Exhibition Place. World's largest indoor agricultural fair exhibits the finest livestock. Food shows; Royal Horse Show features intl competitions in several categories. Phone 416/263-3400. Early Nov.

Additional Visitor Information

For further information contact Tourism Toronto, Queens Quay Terminal at Harbourfront, 207 Queens Quay W, M5J 1A7; 416/203-2500 or 800/363-1990 (US and Canada). Toronto's public transportation system is extensive and incl buses, subways, streetcars, and trolley buses; for maps phone 416/393-4636.

City Neighborhoods

Many of the restaurants, unrating dining establishments, and some lodgings listed under Toronto incl neighborhoods as well as exact street addresses. Geographic descriptions of these areas are given.

Cabbagetown. N of Gerrard St, E of Parliament St, S of Rosedale Valley Rd, and W of the Don River.

Downtown. N of Inner Harbour, E of Spadina Ave, S of Bloor St, and W of Sherbourne St. **N of Downtown:** N of Bloor St. **E of Downtown:** E of Sherbourne St. **W of Downtown:** W of Spadina Ave.

Harbourfront. N of Inner Harbour, E of Bathurst St, S of Gardiner Expy, and W of Yonge St.

Yorkville. N of Bloor St, E of Ave Rd, S of Davenport Rd, and W of Yonge St.

Motels/Motor Lodges

★★ **HOLIDAY INN EXPRESS.** 50 Estates Dr (M1H 2Z1), jct ON 48 and 401. 416/439-9666; fax 416/439-4295. 138 rms, 2-3 story. No elvtrs. S $59; D $79; each addl $10; under 19 free; wkend rates. Crib free. TV; cable (premium). Complimentary continental bkfst. Restaurant adj 11:30-1 am, Sat, Sun from 4:30 pm. Ck-out 11 am. Meeting rms. Business servs avail. Health club privileges. Cr cds: A, C, D, DS, ER, JCB, MC, V.
🄳 ⊠ 🔥 SC

★ **HOWARD JOHNSON EAST.** 940 Progress Ave (M1G 3T5). 416/439-6200; fax 416/439-5689. Email inquiry@hojotoronto.com. 186 rms, 6 story. S $109; D $119; each addl $10; under 18 free; wkend rates; package plan. Crib free. Pet accepted. TV; cable (premium). Heated pool; whirlpool. Restaurant 6:30 am-2 pm, 5-10 pm. Bar 4:30 pm-1 am. Ck-out noon. Coin lndry. Meeting rms. Business servs avail. Valet serv. Sundries. Gift shop. Exercise equipt; sauna. Health club privileges. Microwaves avail. Cr cds: A, C, D, DS, ER, JCB, MC, V.
🄳 ⊠ ⊠ 🕂 ⊠ 🔥 SC

★ **HOWARD JOHNSON INN.** 89 Avenue Rd (M5R 2G3), Downtown. 416/964-1220; fax 416/964-8692. Email venture.cro@sympatico.ca; www.ventureinn.com. 71 rms, 8 story. S $124; D $134; each addl $10; under 19 free; wkend rates off-season. Crib free. Pet accepted, some restrictions. Parking $6.50/day. TV; cable (premium), VCR avail. Complimentary continental bkfst. Ck-out 1 pm. Meeting rms. Business servs avail. Health club privileges. Cr cds: A, D, DS, ER, MC, V.
⊠ ⊠ 🔥 SC

★★ **RAMADA HOTEL TORONTO AIRPORT.** 2 Holiday Dr (M9C 2Z7), near Lester B. Pearson Intl Airport. 416/621-2121; fax 416/621-9840. 179 rms, 2-6 story. June-Aug: S, D $150-$160; each addl $10; suites $250-$350; under 18 free; wkly, wkend rates; lower rates rest of yr. Crib free. Pet accepted. TV; cable (premium). Indoor/outdoor pool; whirlpool. Complimentary coffee in rms. Restaurant 6 am-11 pm. Bar 11:30-1 am. Ck-out noon. Business servs avail. In-rm modem link. Bellhops. Valet serv. Free airport transportation. Exercise equipt; sauna. Some minibars; microwaves avail. Cr cds: A, C, D, DS, ER, JCB, MC, V.
🄳 ⊠ ⊠ 🕂 ✈ ⊠ 🔥 SC

★ **SEA HORSE INN.** 2095 Lakeshore Blvd W (ON 2) (M8V 1A1), jct QEW, W of Downtown. 416/255-4433; fax 416/251-5121. Email seahorse@simpatico.ca; www.toronto.com/seahorse inn. 74 rms, 1-3 story. S $57-$72; D $57-$89; each addl $5; suites $85-$170; under 18 free. TV; cable (premium). Pool; whirlpool. Playground. Complimentary continental bkfst.

Ck-out 11 am. Meeting rms. Sauna. Refrigerators. Picnic tables, grills. On Lake Ontario. Cr cds: A, C, D, DS, ER, MC, V.

★ **TRAVELODGE EAST.** *20 Milner Business Ct (M1B 3C6). 416/299-9500; fax 416/299-6172. www.travelodge. com.* 156 rms, 6 story. S, D $71-$81; each addl $6; suites $85-$105; under 17 free. Pet accepted. TV; cable (premium). Indoor pool; whirlpool. Complimentary coffee in rms. Restaurant 11-2 am. Rm serv noon-11 pm. Ck-out 11 am. Meeting rms. Business servs avail. Sundries. Health club privileges. Microwaves avail. Cr cds: A, D, DS, ER, MC, V.

★ **TRAVELODGE NORTH.** *50 Norfinch Dr (M3N 1X1), N ON 400 to Finch Ave, then E to Norfinch Dr. 416/663-9500; fax 416/663-8480. www. travelodge.com.* 184 rms, 6 story. S $89; D $97; each addl $8; under 17 free. Crib free. Pet accepted, some restrictions. TV; cable (premium). Indoor pool; whirlpool. Coffee in rms. Restaurant 7-1 am. Bar. Ck-out 11 am. Meeting rms. Business servs avail. Sundries. Cr cds: A, D, DS, ER, MC, V.

★★★ **VALHALLA INN.** *1 Valhalla Inn Rd (M9B 1S9), W of Downtown. 416/239-2391; fax 416/239-8764. Email valhalla@globalserve.net; www. valhalla-inn.com.* 240 rms, 2-12 story. S $160; D $170; each addl $10; suites $150-$275; under 18 free; wkend rates. Crib free. Pet accepted. TV; cable (premium). Heated pool. Coffee in rms. Restaurant 6 am-11 pm; dining rm noon-2:30 pm, 6-10 pm. Bars 11-2 am; entertainment. Ck-out 1 pm. Meeting rms. Business center. In-rm modem link. Bellhops. Valet serv. Sundries. Free airport transportation. Health club privileges. Some bathrm phones. Private patios, balconies. Grills. Cr cds: A, C, D, DS, ER, MC, V.

Hotels

★★ **BEST WESTERN PRIMROSE.** *111 Carlton St (M5B 2G3), at Jarvis St, Downtown. 416/977-8000; fax 416/ 977-6323. www.bestwestern.com.* 338 rms, 23 story. S, D $149; each addl $10; suites $275; under 16 free. Crib free. Garage $12.50. TV; cable. Pool. Complimentary coffee in rms. Restaurant 6:30 am-10 pm. Bar 11-1 am. Ck-out 11 am. Meeting rms. Business center. Exercise equipt; sauna. Cr cds: A, C, D, DS, ER, JCB, MC, V.

★★ **BEST WESTERN TORONTO AIRPORT-CARLTON PLACE.** *33 Carlson Ct (M9W 6H5), near Lester B. Pearson Intl Airport, W of Downtown. 416/675-1234; fax 416/675-3436.* 524 rms, 12 story. S $160-175; D $175-$190; each addl $15; suites $250-$350; under 18 free; wkend, mid-wk rates. Crib free. Parking in/out $5/day. TV; cable (premium). Indoor pool; whirlpool. Complimentary coffee in rms. Restaurant 6:30-1 am. Rm serv 24 hrs. Bar 11-1 am. Ck-out 1 pm. Meeting rms. Business center. Gift shop. Airport transportation. Exercise equipt; sauna. Health club privileges. Minibars. Cr cds: A, D, DS, ER, JCB, MC, V.

★ **BOND PLACE.** *65 Dundas St E (N5B 2G8), E of Downtown. 416/362-6061; fax 416/360-6406.* 286 rms, 18 story, 51 suites. May-Oct: S, D $89-$109; each addl $15; suites $104-$134; under 15 free; lower rates rest of yr. Crib free. Parking, in/out $11. TV; cable (premium), VCR avail. Restaurant 7 am-11 pm. Rm serv 11 am-10 pm. Bar 5 pm-1 am. Ck-out 11 am. Meeting rms. Business servs avail. Cr cds: A, C, D, DS, ER, MC, V.

★★ **COMFORT HOTEL DOWNTOWN.** *15 Charles St E (M4Y 1S1), Downtown. 416/924-1222; fax 416/927-1369.* 108 rms, 10 story. S $109; D $119; each addl $10; suites $129-$139; under 18 free; wkend rates. Crib $10. Parking $9. TV; cable (premium), VCR avail. Restaurant noon-10 pm. Piano bar. Ck-out 11 am. Meeting rms. Business servs avail. Health club privileges. Refrigerators; microwaves avail. Cr cds: A, C, D, DS, ER, MC, V.

★★★ **CROWNE PLAZA TORONTO CENTRE.** *225 Front St*

W (M5V 2X3), Downtown. 416/597-1400; fax 416/597-8128. www.crowneplaza.com. 587 rms, 25 story. S, D $239-$279; each addl $20; suites $375-$600; under 12 free; wkend rates. Crib free. TV; cable (premium), VCR avail. Indoor pool; wading pool, whirlpool, poolside serv. Coffee in rms. Restaurant 6-2 am. Fine dining (see also ACCOLADE) open lunch and dinner 6-11 pm. Bar 11:30-2 am; Nightly entertainment. Ck-out noon. Ck-in 3 pm. Meeting rms. Business center. In-rm modem link. Concierge serv. Valet parking. Exercise rm; sauna. Massage. Minibars; microwaves avail. Upscale and luxurious decor. Cr cds: A, C, D, DS, ER, JCB, MC, V.

D ⇌ 🏌 ⛵ 🔥 SC 🚶

★ **DAYS INN DOWNTOWN.** *30 Carlton St (M5B 2E9), adj to Maple Leaf Gardens, between Yonge and Church Sts, Downtown. 416/977-6655; fax 416/977-0502; toll-free 800/329-7466. www.daysinn.com/daysinn.html.* 536 rms, 23 story. S, D $119-$135; each addl $15; under 16 free. Crib free. Pet accepted, some restrictions. Covered parking $15/day. TV; cable. Indoor pool. Restaurant 7 am-10 pm. Bar 11:30-2 am. Ck-out 11 am. Coin lndry. Meeting rms. Business servs avail. Sundries. Barber, beauty shop. Sauna. Some refrigerators. Sun deck. Cr cds: A, D, DS, ER, JCB, MC, V.

🐾 ⇌ ⛵ 🔥 SC

★★ **DELTA CHELSEA INN.** *33 Gerrard St W (M5G 1Z4), between Bay and Yonge Sts, Downtown. 416/595-1975; fax 416/585-4362. Email reservations@deltachelsea.com; www.deltahotels.com.* 1,590 rms, 26 story. S $245-$275; D $265-$295; each addl $15; suites, kit. units $255-$375; under 18 free; wkend rates. Crib free. Pet accepted, some restrictions. Valet parking $22 in/out. TV; cable, VCR avail. 2 heated pools; whirlpool. Supervised children's activities; ages 2-13. Restaurant 6:30-1 am. Rm serv 24 hrs. Bar 11-1 am; entertainment. Ck-out 11 am. Convention facilities. Business center. Gift shop. Exercise equipt; sauna. Health club privileges. Game rm. Refrigerator in some suites. Microwaves avail. Many balconies. Cr cds: A, C, D, DS, ER, JCB, MC, V.

D 🐾 ⇌ 🏌 ⛵ 🔥 SC 🚶

★★ **DELTA TORONTO AIRPORT.** *801 Dixon Rd (N9W 1J5), near Lester B. Pearson Intl Airport. 416/675-6100; fax 416/675-4022. Email delta@nbnet.nb.ca; www.deltahotels.com.* 251 rms, 8 story. S, D $115-$165; each addl $15; suites $170-$220; under 18 free; package plans. Crib free. Pet accepted, some restrictions. TV; cable (premium). Indoor pool. Supervised children's activities (June-Aug). Restaurant 6 am-11 pm. Rm serv 24 hrs. Bar 11:30-2 am. Ck-out 1 pm. Convention facilities. Business center. Bellhops. Valet serv. Gift shops. Exercise equipt; sauna. Health club privileges. Minibars; microwaves avail. Cr cds: A, C, D, DS, ER, JCB, MC, V.

D 🐾 ⇌ 🏌 ⛵ 🔥 SC 🚶

★★★ **EMBASSY SUITES.** *8500 Warden Ave (L6G 1A5). 905/470-8500; fax 905/477-8611.* 332 suites, 10 story. S, D $160-$180; each addl $20; wkend rates; under 18 free. Crib free. Valet parking $3. TV; cable (premium). Indoor pool; whirlpool. Complimentary full bkfst, coffee in rms. Restaurant 6:30 am-midnight. Bar 11-2 am. Ck-out noon. Convention facilities. Business center. Shopping arcade. Barber, beauty shop. Exercise rm; sauna, steam rm. Game rm. Minibars; microwaves avail. Extensive grounds; elaborate landscaping. Elegant atmosphere. Cr cds: A, C, D, ER, MC, V.

D ⇌ 🏌 ⛵ 🔥 SC 🚶

★★★★ **FOUR SEASONS HOTEL TORONTO.** *21 Avenue Rd (M5R 2G1), Downtown. 416/964-0411; fax 416/964-2301. www.fourseasons.com.* Visitors will enjoy all the expected luxuries at this 230-room, 150-suite hotel located in the heart of fashionable Yorkville, near the Royal Ontario Museum and Queen's Park. Business travelers can even reserve a complimentary limousine ride to the nearby financial district during weekday mornings. Several culinary experiences are avail, including tasting the flavors of Provence at the renowned Truffles restaurant. 380 rms, 32 story. S $325-$485; D $365-$525; each addl $30; suites $755; under 18 free; wkend rates. Crib free. Pet accepted. Self-park $22/day, valet $24/day. TV; cable (premium), VCR avail (movies). Indoor/outdoor pool; whirlpool, poolside serv. Restaurants

6:30 am-11 pm, Sat, Sun from 7 am. Rm serv 24 hrs. Bar 11:30-2 am; entertainment Thurs-Sat only. Ck-out noon, ck-in 3 pm. Convention facilities. Business center. In-rm modem link/fax capabilities. Concierge serv. Exercise rm; sauna. Massage. Bathrm phones, minibars; microwaves avail. Some balconies. Cr cds: A, D, DS, JCB, MC, V.

★★★ **HILTON.** 145 Richmond St W (M5H 2L2), at University Ave, Downtown. 416/869-3456; fax 416/869-1478. www.hilton.com. 601 rms, 32 story. Apr-Nov: S, D $239-$259; each addl $20; suites $249-$1,600; family rates; package plans; lower rates rest of yr. Crib free. Garage $17.50. TV; cable (premium). Indoor/outdoor pool; whirlpool, poolside serv in summer. Restaurant 6:30 am-11 pm. Rm serv 24 hrs. Bar 11:30-2 am. Ck-out noon. Convention facilities. Business center. Exercise equipt; sauna. Massage. Minibars. Luxury level. Cr cds: A, C, D, DS, ER, JCB, MC, V.

★★ **HOLIDAY INN.** 970 Dixon Rd (M9W 1J9), near Lester B. Pearson Intl Airport. 416/675-7611; fax 416/675-9162. www.hype.com/holiday_inn/airport/home.htm. 445 rms, 12 story. S, D $160-$175; suites $230-$430; wkend rates. Crib free. Pet accepted. TV; cable (premium). 2 heated pools, 1 indoor; whirlpool. Playground. Coffee in rms. Restaurant 6 am-11 pm. Rm serv to 1 am. Bar 11-2 am; Sun noon-11 pm. Ck-out 1 pm. Meeting rms. Business center. Concierge serv. Barber, beauty shop. Free airport transportation. Exercise equipt; sauna. Rec rm. Minibars. Cr cds: A, C, D, DS, ER, JCB, MC, V.

★★ **HOLIDAY INN.** 370 King St W (M5V 1J9), Downtown. 416/599-4000; fax 416/599-7394. Email info@hiok. com; www.hiok.com. 425 rms, 20 story. S, D $189; each addl $15; suites $269; family rates; package plans. Crib free. Garage $16. TV; cable, VCR avail. Heated rooftop pool; poolside serv, lifeguard. Complimentary coffee in rms. Restaurant 6:30-2 am. Bar from 11 am. Ck-out noon. Convention facilities. Business

center. Concierge serv. Gift shop. Exercise equipt; sauna. Massage. Wet bars. Cr cds: A, C, D, DS, ER, JCB, MC, V.

★★ **HOLIDAY INN.** 600 Dixon Rd (M9W 1J1). 416/240-7511; fax 416/240-7519. 186 rms, 2-5 story. S, D $89-$150; each addl $10; suites $129-$155; under 18 free. Crib free. Pet accepted, some restrictions. TV; cable. Heated pool; wading pool, poolside serv. Coffee in rms. Restaurant open 24 hrs. Ck-out 1 pm. Meeting rms. Business servs avail. Airport transportation. Exercise equipt. Cr cds: A, C, D, DS, ER, JCB, MC, V.

Huron Indian Village

★★ **HOLIDAY INN - DON VALLEY.** 1100 Eglinton Ave E (M3C 1H8), N of Downtown. 416/446-3700; fax 416/446-3701; res 800/465-4329. 298 rms, 14 story. S, D $115-$155; each addl $10; suites $175-$325; family, wkend, wkly rates. Crib free. Pet accepted, some restrictions. TV; cable (premium), VCR avail (movies). Complimentary coffee in lobby. Restaurant 6:30 am-11 pm. Bar 6 pm-2 am; entertainment Thurs-Sat. Ck-out noon. Convention facilities. Business center. In-rm modem link. Concierge serv. Shopping arcade. Barber, beauty shop. Free valet parking. Airport, railroad station transportation. Indoor tennis, pro. X-country ski ¼ mi. Exercise equipt; sauna. Indoor/outdoor pool; whirlpool, poolside serv, lifeguard. Playground. Supervised children's activities (June-Sep); ages 5-12. Game rm. Lawn games. Bathrm phones, refrigerators. Many balconies. Cr cds: A, C, D, DS, ER, JCB, MC, V.

★★ HOLIDAY INN YORKDALE.
3450 Dufferin St (M6A 2V1), 1 blk S of ON 401 Dufferin St Exit, N of Downtown. 416/789-5161; fax 416/785-6845. 365 rms, 12 story. S $149.95; D $164.95; each addl $15; suites $350; under 12 free; wkend rates. Crib free. TV; cable (premium). Heated pool; whirlpool. Supervised children's activities. Complimentary coffee in rms. Restaurant 6 am-11 pm. Bar 11-1 am. Ck-out noon. Meeting rms. Business center. Exercise equipt; sauna. Rec rm. Minibars. Some balconies. Cr cds: A, C, D, DS, ER, JCB, MC, V.

★★★★ HOTEL INTER-CONTINENTAL TORONTO. *220 Bloor St W (M5S 1T8), Downtown. 416/960-5200; fax 416/960-8269. www.interconti.com.* Located in the fashionable Yorkville district, this property has 208 rooms and suites appropriate for business and leisure guests. The wood paneling, brass accents, fresh flowers, and Art Deco-type style of the lobby create a refreshing decor that flows into the brightly colored rooms. 208 rms, 8 story. S, D $365-$405; suites $450-$2,000. Crib free. Valet parking $24. TV; cable (premium), VCR avail in business rms and suites (movies). Indoor pool. Restaurants 7 am-11 pm. Rm serv 24 hrs. Bar noon-1 am. Ck-out 1 pm. Meeting rms. Business center. In-rm modem link. Concierge serv. Gift shop. Exercise equipt; sauna. Massage. Bathrm phones, minibars. Patios. Cr cds: A, C, D, ER, JCB, MC, V.

★★★ HOTEL TORONTO - EAST.
2035 Kennedy Rd (M1T 3G2). 416/299-1500; fax 416/299-8959. Email net@hte.cphotels.ca; www.cphotels.ca. 368 rms, 14 story. S, D $219; each

addl $15; suites $365-$620; under 18 free; wkend rates. Crib free. Pet accepted. TV; cable. Indoor pool; wading pool; whirlpool. Free supervised children's activities (wkends, school hols); ages 3-15. Restaurants 6:30-2 am. Rm serv 24 hrs. Bar 11-2 am. Ck-out noon. Convention facilities. Business servs avail. In-rm modem link. Concierge serv. Gift shop. Barber, beauty shop. Covered valet parking. Putting green. Exercise rm; sauna. Game rm. Luxury level. Cr cds: A, D, DS, ER, JCB, MC, V.

★ HOWARD JOHNSON PLAZA.
2737 Keele St (M3M 2E9), N ON 401, Exit Keele St, then 1 blk N. 416/636-4656; fax 416/633-5637. www.hojo.com. 367 rms, most A/C, 10 story, 27 suites. S, D $129-$179; each addl $10; suites $175-$375; family rates; package plans. Crib free. Pet accepted. TV; cable (premium), VCR avail. Indoor pool. Supervised children's activities (June-Sep); ages 4-12. Complimentary coffee in rms. Restaurant 6:30 am-11 pm; Sun to 10 pm. Bar 11-1 am. Ck-out noon. Meeting rms. Business servs avail. Free garage parking. Downhill/x-country ski 10 mi. Exercise equipt; sauna. Game rm. Rec rm. Some minibars; microwaves avail. Cr cds: A, C, D, DS, ER, JCB, MC, V.

★ INN ON THE PARK. *1100 Eglinton Ave E (M3C 1H8), at Leslie St, N of Downtown. 416/444-2561; fax 416/446-3308.* 270 rms, 23 story. S, D $175-$235; each addl $20; suites $250-$800; under 18 free; wkend rates. Compllimentary parking. Crib free. TV; cable (premium), VCR avail (movies). 2 heated pools, 1 indoor; whirlpool, lifeguards (in season). Free supervised children's activities (June-Sep); ages 5-12. Restaurants 6:30 am-midnight. Bar 11:30-1 am; vocalist Fri-Sat. Ck-out noon. Meeting rms. Business center. In-rm modem link. Concierge serv. Barber, beauty shop. X-country ski opp hotel. Exercise equipt; sauna. Rec rm. Courtyard/playground games. Iron/board. Bathrm phones. Business rm. Some minibars. Some private patios, balconies. Cr cds: A, C, D, DS, ER, JCB, MC, V.

★★★ INTERNATIONAL PLAZA.
655 Dixon Rd (M9W 1J4), near Lester B. Pearson Intl Airport, W of Downtown. 416/244-1711; fax 416/244-8031. Email sales@internationalplaza. com; www.internationalplaza.com. 415 rms, 12 story. S, D $170; each addl $10; suites $350-$500; under 18 free; wkend rates. Crib free. Pet accepted. Valet parking $6. TV; cable (premium). Indoor pool; wading pool, poolside serv, lifeguard. Supervised children's activities; ages 3-12. Restaurant 6:30 am-11 pm. Rm serv 24 hrs. Bar 11-2 am. Ck-out noon. Convention facilities. Business center. Concierge serv. Gift shop. Beauty, barber shop. Exercise equipt; sauna. Massages. Game rm. Refrigerators. Minibars in suites. Cr cds: A, D, DS, ER, MC, V.

★★★★ LE ROYAL MERIDIEN KING EDWARD.
37 King St E (M5C 1E9), Downtown. 416/863-9700; fax 416/367-5515. Built in 1903 during the time of Edward VII, this stately hotel has a luxurious lobby of rich fabrics, marble pillars, and soaring ceilings. Both business and leisure guests will find the business-district location convenient with theaters, restaurants, and shops nearby. From martinis in the plush lounge to bedtime mints on pillows, this is classy service the old-fashioned way. 294 rms, 9 and 16 story. S $205-$360; D $230-$385; suites $435-$510; under 12 free; wkend rates. Covered parking, valet $24. TV; cable (premium), VCR avail. Restaurants 6:30 am-2:30 pm, 5-11 pm (see also CHIARO'S). Rm serv 24 hrs. Bars 11:30-1 am. Ck-out noon. Convention facilities. Business center. In-rm modem link. Concierge serv. Shopping arcade. Beauty shop. Exercise equipt; sauna. Whirlpools. Massage. Health club privileges. Bathrm phones, minibars; microwaves avail. Cr cds: A, C, D, ER, JCB, MC, V.

★★★ MARRIOTT AIRPORT.
901 Dixon Rd (M9W 1J5), near Lester B. Pearson Intl Airport. 416/674-9400; fax 416/674-8292. 424 rms, 9 story. S, D $240; suites $300-$1,200; under 18 free; wkend rates. Crib free. TV; cable (premium). Indoor pool; whirlpool. Restaurants 6 am-11 pm. Bar noon-2 am. Ck-out noon. Convention facilities. Business center. Gift shop. Covered parking. Free airport transportation. Exercise equipt; sauna. Luxury level. Cr cds: A, C, D, ER, JCB, MC, V.

★★★ MARRIOTT EATON CENTRE.
525 Bay St (N5G 2L2), Downtown. 416/597-9200; fax 416/597-9211; res 888/440-9300. www.marriott.com/marriott/yyzec. 459 rms, 18 story. May-Oct: S, D $350; suites $600-$1,800; family rates; package plans; higher rates special events; lower rates rest of yr. Crib free. Garage parking $14, valet $18. TV; cable (premium), VCR avail. Indoor pool; whirlpool, poolside serv. Restaurant 6:30 am-10 pm. Rm serv 24 hrs. Bar 11-1 am. Ck-out noon. Convention facilities. Business center. Concierge serv. Shopping arcade. Drug store. Barber, beauty shop. Exercise equipt; sauna. Cr cds: A, D, DS, ER, JCB, MC, V.

★★★★ THE METROPOLITAN HOTEL.
108 Chestnut St (M5G 1R3), adj to City Hall Downtown. 416/977-5000; fax 416/599-3317; res 800/668-6600. Email reservations@ metropolitan.com; www.metropolitan. com. A good value for the quality of accommodations and services offered, this hotel's guestrooms are fairly intimate but the comfortable beds covered in fine linens and feather duvets more than compensate. Add to this a friendly, enthusiastic staff and two restaurants that stand up to the competition, Lai Wah Heen and Hemispheres, and guests are guaranteed to have a great experience. 425 rms, 26 story. S, D $240-$380; each addl $30; suites $490-$1,800; wkend rates. Crib free. Parking, in/out $19-$24 Pet accepted, some restrictions. TV; cable (premium), VCR avail (free movies). Indoor pool; whirlpool. Restaurant 6:30 am-11:30 pm. Bar 11-1 am. Ck-out noon. Meeting rms. Business center. In-rm modem link. Concierge serv. Gift shop. Exercise equipt; sauna. Bathrm phones, minibars. Eaton Centre 2 blks. Cr cds: A, D, DS, ER, JCB, MC, V.

★★ **NOVOTEL AIRPORT.** *135 Carlingview Dr (M9W 5E7), near Lester B. Pearson Intl Airport. 416/798-9800; fax 416/798-3257. Email tairmail@aol. com.* 192 rms, 7 story. S $165; D $175; suites $175; family, wkly, wkend rates. Crib free. Pet accepted. TV; cable (premium). Indoor pool; whirlpool. Restaurant 6 am-11 pm. Bar 11-1 am. Ck-out 1 pm. Meeting rms. Business center. In-rm modem link. Gift shop. Garage parking. Free airport transportation. Downhill/x-country ski 20 mi. Exercise equipt; sauna. Minibars. Cr cds: A, D, DS, ER, JCB, MC, V.

⊡ ⚓ ⛴ ⚒ 🧍 ✈ ⛵ 🔥 SC 🎿

★★★ **NOVOTEL TORONTO CENTRE.** *45 The Esplanade (M5E 1W2), Downtown. 416/367-8900; fax 416/360-8285. www.novotel-northamerica. com/welcome.* 262 rms, 9 story. S, D $205; each addl $20; suites $215; under 16 free; wkend rates. Crib free. Pet accepted. Garage, in/out $13.50. TV; cable (premium). Indoor pool; whirlpool. Restaurant 6 am-midnight. Bar 11-2 am. Ck-out 1 pm. Meeting rms. Business servs avail. Exercise equipt; sauna. Minibars. Cr cds: A, D, DS, ER, JCB, MC, V.

⊡ ⚓ ⚒ 🧍 ⛵ 🔥 SC

★★★★ **PARK HYATT, TORONTO.** *4 Avenue Rd (M5R 2E8), downtown. 416/925-1234; fax 416/924-4933; res 800/233-1234; toll-free 800/977-1497. www.hyatt.com.* After a recent $60 million dollar renovation, this hotel offers elegance and glamour in the heart of fashionable Yorkville. All 346 spacious guestrooms have opulent bathrooms and the public spaces are filled with relaxing dark wood, gold tones, and rich, cream-colored couches. Visitors will enjoyed getting pampered with warm and gracious service on either a business trip or a romantic getaway. 300 rms, 18 story, 46 suites. May-Sep: S, D $499; suites $559; each addl $40; under 17 free; lower rates rest of yr. Crib avail. Pet accepted. Valet parking avail. TV; cable, VCR avail. Complimentary newspaper. Restaurant 6 am-11 pm. 24-hr rm serv. Bar. Ck-out noon, ck-in 3 pm. Conference center, meeting rms. Business center. Bellhops. Concierge serv. Dry cleaning. Gift shop. Salon/barber avail. Free airport transportation. Exercise equipt;

sauna, steam rm. Golf, 18 holes. Cr cds: A, D, DS, JCB, MC, V.

⊡ ⚓ 🍴 🧍 ⛵ 🔥 SC 🎿

★★ **QUALITY HOTEL.** *111 Lombard St (M5C 2T9), Downtown. 416/367-5555; fax 416/367-3470.* 196 rms, 16 story. S $139; D $149; each addl $10; under 18 free. Crib free. Pet accepted. Garage $11.75/day. TV; cable. Ck-out 11 am. Business servs avail. Exercise equipt. Health club privileges. Cr cds: A, D, DS, ER, JCB, MC, V.

⊡ ⚓ 🧍 ⛵ 🔥 SC

★★ **QUALITY HOTEL.** *280 Bloor St W (M5S 1V8), Downtown. 416/968-0010; fax 416/968-7765.* 210 rms, 14 story. Mid-Mar-Oct: S $120-$145; D $130-$155; under 18 free; wkend rates; higher rates special events; lower rates rest of yr. Crib free. Pet accepted, some restrictions. Garage in/out $11.50. TV; cable. Restaurant 7 am-11 pm. Ck-out 11 am. Meeting rms. Business servs avail. No bellhops. Health club privileges. Cr cds: A, D, DS, JCB, MC, V.

⊡ ⚓ ⛵ 🔥 SC

★★ **QUALITY INN AIRPORT EAST.** *2180 Islington Ave (N9P 3P1), near/ Lester B. Pearson Intl Airport, W of Downtown. 416/240-9090; fax 416/240-9944. Email quality@ica.net; www.qualityinn.com.* 198 rms, 12 story. S, D $89-$139; each addl $10; under 18 free; package plans; higher rates special events. Crib free. Pet accepted. TV; cable (premium). Restaurant 6 am-midnight. Bar from 11 am. Ck-out 11 am. Meeting rms. In-rm modem link. Microwaves avail. Near airport. Cr cds: A, D, DS, ER, JCB, MC, V.

⊡ ⚓ ✈ ⛵ 🔥 SC

★★ **QUALITY SUITES.** *262 Carlingview Dr (M9W 5G1), near Lester B. Pearson Intl Airport, W of Downtown. 416/674-8442; fax 416/674-3088. www.hotelchoice.com.* 254 suites, 12 story. S, D $120-$145; each addl $5; under 18 free; wkend, hol rates. Crib free. Pet accepted. TV; cable (premium). Complimentary coffee in rms. Restaurant 6:30-1 am. Bar. Ck-out 11 am. Meeting rms. Business servs avail. No bellhops. Gift shop. Downhill/x-country ski 15 mi. Exercise equipt. Health club privileges.

Minibars; microwaves avail. Cr cds: A, D, DS, ER, JCB, MC, V.

⊡ ⬛ ⬛ ⬛ ⬛ ⬛ **SC**

★★★ **RADISSON.** *50 E Valhalla Dr (L3R 0A3), N ON 404, jct ON 7. 905/ 477-2010; fax 905/477-2026.* 204 rms, 15 story, 26 suites. S, D $220; each addl $15; suites $250; under 19 free; wkly, wkend rates; golf plans; higher rates Dec 31. Crib free. Indoor pool; whirlpool. Complimentary continental bkfst, coffee in rms. Restaurant 6:30 am-11 pm. Bar 11-2 am. Ck-out noon. Meeting rms. Business servs avail. Gift shop. Tennis privileges. 18-hole golf privileges. Downhill/x-country ski 12 mi. Exercise equipt; sauna. Rec rm. Minibars; microwaves avail. Picnic tables. Cr cds: A, C, D, DS, ER, JCB, MC, V.

⊡ ⬛ ⬛ ⬛ ⬛ ⬛ ⬛ **SC**

★★★ **RADISSON PLAZA - HOTEL ADMIRAL.** *249 Queens Quay W (M5J 2N5), Downtown. 416/203-3333; fax 416/203-3100.* 157 air-cooled rms, 8 story, 17 suites. Early-May-mid-Nov: S, D $265-$295; each addl $20; suites from $495; family, wkend rates. Crib free. Parking $15/day. TV; cable (premium). Heated pool; whirlpool, poolside serv. Complimentary coffee in rms. Restaurant 7 am-11 pm. Rm serv 24 hrs. Bar 11:30-1 am. Ck-out noon. Meeting rms. Business servs avail. Concierge serv. Gift shop. Health club privileges. Bathrm phones, minibars. On waterfront; nautical theme throughout. View of Harbour. Cr cds: A, C, D, DS, ER, JCB, MC, V.

⊡ ⬛ ⬛ ⬛ **SC**

★★★ **RADISSON SUITE TORONTO AIRPORT.** *640 Dixon Rd (N9W 1J1), near Lester B. Pearson Intl Airport, W of Downtown. 416/242-7400; fax 416/242-9888. www. radisson.com.* 215 suites, 14 story. S, D $204-$216; under 18 free. Crib free. Pet accepted, some restrictions. TV; cable, VCR avail. Complimentary continental bkfst. Restaurant 6:30 am-11 pm. Bar 11-1 am. Ck-out noon. Meeting rms. Business center. In-rm modem link. Concierge serv. Gift shop. Free valet parking. Exercise equipt. Minibars, microwaves avail. Cr cds: A, C, D, DS, ER, JCB, MC, V.

⊡ ⬛ ⬛ ⬛ ⬛ **SC** ⬛

★★ **RAMADA DON VALLEY.** *185 Yorkland Blvd (M2J 4R2), jct ON 401, Don Valley Pkwy, N of Downtown. 416/493-9000; fax 416/493-5729. www.ramada.com/ramada.html.* 285 rms, 10 story. S, D $105-$165; each addl $15; suites $175-$300; under 18 free; wkend rates. Crib free. TV; cable (premium). Indoor pool. Coffee in rms. Restaurant 6:30 am-10:30 pm; Sat from 7 am. Bar 11-2 am; Sun to 11 pm. Ck-out noon. Meeting rms. Business center. In-rm modem link. Exercise equipt; sauna. Health club privileges. Game rm. Rec rm. Some in-rm whirlpools. Luxury level. Cr cds: A, C, D, DS, ER, JCB, MC, V.

⊡ ⬛ ⬛ ⬛ ⬛ **SC** ⬛

★★ **RAMADA INN AND SUITES.** *300 Jarvis St (M5B 2C5), Downtown. 416/977-4823; fax 416/977-4830. Email clarion@net.com.ca; www. hotelchoice.com.* 102 rms, 10 story, 44 suites. S $155; D $170; each addl $15; suites $185-$265; under 18 free. Crib free. Garage parking $15. TV; cable (premium). Indoor pool; whirlpool. Complimentary coffee in rms. Restaurant 7 am-2 pm, 5-9 pm. Bar from 11 am. Ck-out 11 am. Meeting rms. Business servs avail. Concierge serv. Downhill/x-country ski 10 mi. Exercise equipt; sauna. Rec rm. Refrigerators. Cr cds: A, C, D, DS, ER, JCB, MC, V.

⬛ ⬛ ⬛ ⬛ ⬛ **SC**

★★★ **REGAL CONSTELLATION.** *900 Dixon Rd (M9W 1J7), near Lester B. Pearson Intl Airport, W of Downtown. 416/675-1500; fax 416/675-1737. www.regal-hotels.com.* 710 rms, 8-16 story. S, D $95-$165; each addl $15; suites from $275; under 18 free; wkend package plan. Crib free. Pet accepted, some restrictions. Valet parking $9.25/day. TV; cable (premium), VCR avail. 2 heated pools, 1 indoor/outdoor; whirlpool, poolside serv in season. Restaurant 6:30 am-11 pm; dining rm 11 am-2 pm, 5:30-10 pm. Rm serv 24 hrs. Bar 11-1 am; entertainment Thurs-Sat. Ck-out noon. Concierge serv. Convention facilities. Business center. Gift shop. Beauty shop. Airport transportation. Exercise equipt; sauna. Some balconies. Cr cds: A, C, D, DS, ER, MC, V.

⊡ ⬛ ⬛ ⬛ ⬛ ⬛ ⬛ **SC** ⬛

★★★ **ROYAL YORK.** *100 Front St W (M5J 1E3), opp Union Station, Downtown.* 416/368-2511; fax 416/368-2884. *Email reserve@ryh.cphotels.ca; www.cphotels.ca.* 1,365 rms, 22 story. S, D $189-$289; each addl $20; suites $295-$1,750; under 18 free; package plans. Crib free. Pet accepted. Garage (fee). TV; cable. Pool; wading pool, whirlpool. Restaurant 6:30 am-10:30 pm. Rm serv 24 hrs. Bars noon-2 am; entertainment. Ck-out noon. Convention facilities. Business center. Concierge serv. Shopping arcade. Barber, beauty shop. Exercise rm; sauna. Massage. Health club privileges. Minibars; refrigerators, microwaves avail. Luxury level. Cr cds: A, D, DS, ER, JCB, MC, V.

D 🐾 ⇌ 🏋 ✕ 🔥 SC 🚶

★★★ **SHERATON CENTRE.** *123 Queen St W (M5H 2M9), opp City Hall, Downtown.* 416/361-1000; fax 416/947-4854. *www.sheratonctr.toronto.on.ca.* 1,382 rms, 43 story. Late June-Dec: S $275; D $285; each addl $20; suites $450-$850; under 18 free; wkend rates; lower rates rest of yr. Covered parking, valet $22/day. TV; cable (premium), VCR avail. Indoor/outdoor pool; whirlpool, poolside serv (summer); lifeguard. Supervised children's activities (daily July-mid-Sep; wkends rest of yr). Complimentary coffee in rms. Restaurant 6 am-11 pm. Rm serv 24 hrs. Bars. Ck-out noon. Convention facilities. Business center. Concierge serv. Shopping arcade. Barber, beauty shop. Exercise equipt; sauna. Massage. Rec rm. Minibars; microwaves avail. Private patios, balconies. Waterfall in lobby; pond with live ducks. Cr cds: A, C, D, ER, JCB, MC, V.

D ⇌ 🏋 ✕ 🔥 SC 🚶

★★★ **SHERATON GATEWAY.** *at Lester B. Pearson Intl Airport, W of Downtown.* 905/672-7000; fax 905/672-7100. *www.sheraton.com.* 474 rms, 8 story. S, D $190-$240; each addl $15; suites $420-$800; under 18 free; wkly, wkend rates. Crib free. Pet accepted. Garage parking $9.50; valet $18. TV; cable (premium), VCR avail. Indoor pool; whirlpool. Restaurant 6 am-11 pm. Rm serv 24 hrs. Bar 11-1 am. Ck-out noon. Convention facilities. Business center. Concierge serv. Shopping arcade. Barber, beauty shop. Free airport transportation. Exercise equipt; sauna. Massage.

Minibars. Modern facility connected by climate-controlled walkway to Terminal 3. Cr cds: A, C, D, DS, ER, JCB, MC, V.

D 🐾 ⇌ 🏋 ✈ 🔥 SC 🚶

★★★ **SKYDOME.** *1 Blue Jays Way (M5V 1J4), adj CN Tower, Downtown.* 416/341-7100; fax 416/341-5091. *www.cphotels.ca.* 346 rms, 11 story, 26 suites. May-Oct: S, D $169-$179; each addl $30; suites from $299-$559; under 18 free; wkend rates; package plans; lower rates rest of yr. Crib avail. Pet accepted. Garage parking $16; valet $22. TV; cable, VCR avail. Indoor pool. Complimentary coffee in rms. Supervised children's activities (June-Sep). Restaurant 7-1 am. Rm serv 24 hrs. Bar. Ck-out noon. Convention facilities. Business center. Concierge serv. Gift shop. Health club privileges. Massage. Minibars. Modern facility within SkyDome complex; lobby and some rms overlook playing field. Cr cds: A, C, D, DS, ER, JCB, MC, V.

D 🐾 ⇌ 🔥 SC 🚶

★★★ **SUTTON PLACE.** *955 Bay St (M5S 2A2), Downtown.* 416/924-9221; fax 416/324-5617; res 800/268-3790. *Email res@tor.suttonplace.com; www.travelweb.com/sutton.html.* 292 rms, 33 story, 62 suites. S, D $320; each addl $20; suites $390-$1,500; under 18 free; wkend rates. Crib free. Garage parking $18, valet $21. TV; cable (premium), VCR avail (movies). Indoor pool; poolside serv. Restaurant (see also ACCENTS). Rm serv 24 hrs. Bar 11-1:30 am; entertainment Thurs-Sat. Ck-out noon. Convention facilities. Business center. Concierge serv.. Gift shop. Barber, beauty shop. Exercise equipt; sauna. Health club privileges. Massage. Minibars. Cr cds: A, C, D, ER, JCB, MC, V.

D ⇌ 🏋 ✕ 🔥 SC 🚶

★★ **TOWN INN.** *620 Church St (M4Y 2G2), Downtown.* 416/964-3311; fax 416/924-9466. *Email mitch@town inn.com; www.towninn.com/.* 200 kit. units (1-2 bedrm), 26 story. June-Dec: S $95-$125; D $110-$135; each addl $15; under 12 free; monthly rates; lower rates rest of yr. Crib free. Pet accepted. Garage $14. TV; cable (premium). Heated pool. Complimentary continental bkfst. Restaurant 7-10 am. Ck-out 11 am. Meeting rms. Business servs avail. Tennis. Exercise equipt. Health club privileges; saunas. Refrigerators, microwaves. Balconies. Cr cds: A, C, D, ER, MC, V.

[icons]

★ **TRAVELODGE.** *55 Hallcrown Pl (M2J 4R1), ON 401 Exit 376, then N on Victoria Park Ave, off Consumer Rd. 416/493-7000; fax 416/493-6577. www.travelodge.com.* 228 rms, 9 story. S, D $98-$103; each addl $10; suites $225; under 17 free; wknd rates. Crib free. TV; cable (premium). Indoor pool; whirlpool. Complimentary coffee in rms. Restaurant 7 am-10 pm. Bar. Ck-out noon. Meeting rms. Business servs avail. Sauna. Cr cds: A, C, D, DS, ER, JCB, MC, V.

[icons]

★ **TRAVELODGE - AIRPORT.** *925 Dixon Rd (M9W 1J8), near Lester B. Pearson Intl Airport, W of Downtown. 416/674-2222; fax 416/674-5757. www.ventureinn.com.* 283 rms, 17 story. S $120; D $140; each addl $10; suites $140-$275; under 18 free; wkend rates. Crib free. Pet accepted. TV, cable (premium). Indoor pool; whirlpool. Complimentary continental bkfst. Restaurant 11-2 am. Bar. Ck-out 1 pm. Convention facilities. Business servs avail. In-rm modem link. Airport transportation. Sauna. Health club privileges. Gift shop. Cr cds: A, D, DS, ER, MC, V.

[icons]

★★★ **WESTIN PRINCE.** *900 York Mills Rd (M3B 3H2), N on Don Valley Pkwy, W on York Mills Rd. 416/444-2511; fax 416/444-9597. Email toprince@idirect.com; www.princehotels. co.jp.* 381 rms, 22 story. S $210-$245; D $230-$265; each addl $20; suites $340-$1,800; under 18 free; wknd rates. Crib free. TV; cable (premium), VCR avail (movies). Pool; whirlpool, poolside serv. Playground. Restaurant 6:30 am-10 pm. Rm serv 24 hrs. Bar 11:30-2 am; entertainment Mon-Sat. Ck-out 1 pm. Convention facilities. Business center. In-rm modem link. Concierge serv. Shopping arcade. Barber, beauty shop. Tennis. 18-hole golf privileges. Exercise equipt; sauna. Health club privileges. Game rm. Refrigerators. Balconies. Cr cds: A, C, D, DS, ER, JCB, MC, V.

[icons]

★★★★ **WINDSOR ARMS HOTEL.** *18 Ste. Thomas St, Downtown, QVW E to Gardner Expy, left on Bloor St to St. Thomas St. 416/971-9666.* This hotel's century-old building, located in the uptown Yorkville shopping district, houses 28 luxurious suites. Public spaces are modern with a warm, countrylike aura while rooms are urban sleek with a gray-toned color scheme. Guests can dine at the socially respected Courtyard Cafe, have tea by day and caviar by night in The Tea Room, or a drink at Club 22. 7 rms, 21 suites. S, D $295-$495. Cribs. TV. Pool. Valet. Ck-out noon. Business center. Spa. Exercise rm. Dining. Cr cds: A, DS, MC, V.

[icons]

★★ **WYNDHAM BRISTOL PLACE.** *950 Dixon Rd (M9W 5N4), near Lester B. Pearson Intl Airport, W of Downtown. 416/675-9444; fax 416/675-4426. Email bristol@interlog.com; www. wyndham.com.* 287 rms, 15 story. S, D $214-$350; each addl $10; suites from $625; under 18 free; wknd rates; package plans. Crib free. TV; cable (premium); pay per view movies. Indoor/outdoor pool; poolside serv. Coffee in rooms. Restaurant 6:30 am-10 pm (see also ZACHARY'S). Rm serv 24 hrs. Bars 11-2 am; entertainment Mon-Fri. Ck-out 1 pm. Convention facilities. Business center. In-rm modem link. Concierge serv. Valet parking. Free airport transportation. Exercise equipt; sauna. Minibars; bathrm phone, whirlpool in some suites. Some private patios. Cr cds: A, C, D, DS, ER, JCB, MC, V.

[icons]

B&Bs/Small Inns

★★ **GUILD INN.** *201 Guildwood Pkwy (M1E 1T6). 416/261-3331; fax 416/261-5675.* 96 rms, 3-6 story. Apr-Dec: S, D $79; each addl $10; suites $140; under 18 free; AP, MAP avail; wkly rates; lower rates rest of yr. Crib free. TV; cable (premium). Pool. Restaurant (see also GUILD INN). Ck-out noon, ck-in 3 pm. Business servs avail. Tennis. Balconies. Opened in 1923 as art community. On 90 acres overlooking Lake Ontario. Log cabin (1805) on grounds. Cr cds: A, C, D, DS, ER, MC, V.

[icons]

★★★ **MILLCROFT.** *55 John St (L0N 1A0), ON 10 to ON 24, W to ON 136, then N to John St.* *519/941-8111; fax 519/941-9192; res 800/383-3976. Email millcroft@millcroft.com; www. millcroft.com.* 52 rms, 2 story, 20 chalets. S, D $185-$275. Crib free. Heated pool; whirlpool, poolside serv. Complimentary continental bkfst. Restaurant (see also MILLCROFT INN). Bar. Ck-out noon, ck-in 4 pm. Guest lndry. Meeting rm. Business servs avail. Valet serv. Tennis. Golf privileges. X-country ski on site. Exercise equipt; sauna. Volleyball. Game rm. Some private patios. 100 acres on Credit River. Former knitting mill (1881). Cr cds: A, D, ER, MC, V.

Restaurants

★★★ **360.** *301 Front St. W (M5V 2T6), in CN Tower, Downtown. 416/ 362-5411. www.cntower.ca.* Specializes in fresh rack of lamb, prime rib, corn-fed free-range chicken. Own baking. Hrs: 11 am-1:45 pm, 5-9:45 pm; Fri, Sat 5-10:15 pm. Res accepted. Bar. Wine cellar. Lunch a la carte entrees: $19-$38; dinner a la carte entrees: $19-$38. Sun brunch from $35. Revolving restaurant; view of harbor and city. Cr cds: A, C, D, DS, ER, MC, V.

★★★ **ACCENTS.** *955 Bay St, Downtown. 416/324-5633.* Specializes in market-fresh cuisine. Hrs: 6:30 am-10:30 pm. Res accepted. Bar. Wine cellar. Bkfst a la carte entrees: $2.95-$10.50; lunch a la carte entrees: $11.50-$14.50; dinner a la carte entrees: $22-$36. Entertainment: pianist Thurs-Sat. Parking. Continental atmosphere. Cr cds: A, D, ER, MC, V.

★★★ **ACCOLADE.** *225 Front St. W. 416/597-1400. www.crowneplaza.com.* Eclectic menu. Specializes in rack of lamb. Own baking. Hrs: 11:45 am-2 pm, 5:45-10 pm; Sat from 5:45 pm. Closed Sun. Res accepted. Bar. Wine list. Lunch $11.95-$21.95; dinner $26-$32. Complete meals: $34.95. Valet parking. Cr cds: A, D, DS, MC, V.

★★ **ARKADIA HOUSE.** *2007 Eglinton Ave E (M1L 2M9), approx 10 mi E ON 2. 416/752-5685.* Specializes in roast lamb, souvlaki. Hrs: 11:30 am-3 pm, 4 pm-midnight. Closed Dec 24. Res accepted. Bar. Wine list. Lunch a la carte entrees: $6.95-$12.95; dinner a la carte entrees: $10.95-$19.95. Child's menu. Entertainment. Parking. Garden cafe atmosphere. Cr cds: A, C, D, ER, MC, V.

Toronto Skyline

★ **ARLEQUIN.** *134 Avenue Rd (M5R 2H6), N of Downtown. 416/928-9521.* Hrs: 9 am-10 pm. Closed Sun; hols. Res accepted. Bar. Lunch a la carte entrees: $7.95-$12.95; dinner a la carte entrees: $12.95-$18.95. Complete meals: Mon-Wed $18.95; Thurs-Sat $22.95. Small bistro with harlequin motif. Cr cds: A, C, D, DS, ER, MC, V.

D ⊐

★★★ **AUBERGE DU POMMIER.** *4150 Yonge St (M2P 2C6). 416/222-2220. www.oliverbonacini.com.* Hrs: 11:30 am-2:30 pm, 5-10 pm; Sat from 5 pm. Closed Sun; hols. Res required. Bar. Child's menu. Entertainment. Cr cds: A, D, MC, V.

★★★ **AVALON.** *270 Adelaide St W (M5H 1X6), Downtown. 416/979-9918. Email avalonrestaurant@msn.com.* Chinese menu. Specializes in wood-roasted chicken, yellowfin tuna steak, grilled dry-aged rib steak. Hrs: 5:30-10 pm; Fri, Sat to 11 pm; Thurs noon-2:30 pm, 5:30-10 pm. Closed Sun; hols. Res accepted. Bar. Wine list. Lunch a la carte entrees: $13-$22; dinner $20-$30. Artwork by local artists. Cr cds: A, D, ER, MC, V.

★★★ **BANGKOK GARDEN.** *18 Elm St (M5G 1G7), Downtown. 416/977-6748. www.elmwoodcomplex.com.* Specializes in soup, curry dishes, seafood. Hrs: 11:30 am-2:30 pm, 5-10 pm; Sat from 5 pm. Res accepted. Bar. Lunch a la carte entrees: $8.95-$10.95. Buffet: (Mon, Fri) $9.95; dinner a la carte entrees: $14.95-$19.25. Complete meals: $25.95-$39.95. Child's menu. Thai decor; indoor garden. Cr cds: A, D, ER, MC, V.

D ⊐

★★ **BAROOTES.** *220 King St W (M5H 1K4), Downtown. 416/979-7717.* Specializes in fresh stir-fry, Thai satay combination, grilled marinated lamb tenderloin. Hrs: 11:30 am-2 pm, 5-11 pm; Sat from 5 pm. Closed Sun; Jan 1, Dec 25. Res accepted. Bar. Lunch a la carte entrees: $8.95-$12.95; dinner a la carte entrees: $11.50-$24.95. Traditional dining rm. Cr cds: A, D, MC, V.

D ⊐

★★★ **BIAGIO.** *155 King St E (M5C 1G9). 416/366-4040.* Specializes in risotto, veal. Hrs: noon-2:30 pm, 5:30-10 pm; Sat 5:30-10:30 pm. Closed Sun. Lunch $15-$33; dinner $15-$33. Cr cds: D, MC, V.

D ⊐

★★ **BISTRO 990.** *990 Bay St (M5S 2A5), Downtown. 416/921-9990.* Specializes in lamb, fresh fish. Hrs: noon-2:30 pm, 5:30-11 pm. Closed Sun. Res accepted. Bar. Lunch a la carte entrees: $13.50-$29. Prix fixe: $19.90; dinner a la carte entrees: $14-$32. Prix fixe: $19.90. French bistro decor. Cr cds: A, C, D, DS, MC, V.

D ⊐

★★★ **BOBA.** *90 Avenue Rd (M5R 2H2), in Yorkville. 416/961-2622.* Specializes in vegetarian dishes, desserts. Hrs: 5:30-10 pm. Closed Sun; Jan 1, Dec 25, 26. Res required. Bar. Dinner a la carte entrees: $19.50-$29.95. Patio dining. Intimate dining rm; bistro atmosphere. Cr cds: A, C, D, DS, ER, MC, V.

D

★★ **BUMPKINS.** *21 Gloucester St (M4Y 1L8), between Church and Yonge Sts, Downtown. 416/922-8655. www.wheremags.com.* Specializes in shrimp Bumpkins. Hrs: 11 am-11 pm. Lunch a la carte entrees: $3.95-$8.50; dinner a la carte entrees: $8.75-$20.95. Child's menu. Cr cds: A, D, ER, MC, V.

D ⊐

★★★ **CARMAN'S CLUB.** *26 Alexander St (M8V 2K8), Downtown. 416/924-8558. www.toronto.com/carmans.* Specializes in rack of lamb, Dover sole. Own pastries. Hrs: 5-11 pm. Closed Sun; Good Fri, Dec 25. Res accepted. Wine cellar. Dinner complete meals: $31.95-$35.95. Child's menu. Entertainment. In pre-1900 house; fireplaces. Family-owned. Cr cds: A, MC, V.

D ⊐

★★★★ **CENTRO GRILL & WINE BAR.** *2472 Yonge St (M4P 2H5), N of Downtown. 416/483-2211. www.centrorestaurant.com.* A lot of tastes are rolled into one destination at this contemporary European restaurant with a downstairs sushi and oyster bar. The wood floors, red, high-backed chairs, white tablecloths, and silver-accented decor create a colorful, New-Age-style dining rm, and the worldly menu is never a bore with novelties like caribou chop with juniper berry oil, Alsatian spatzle, and Arctic cloudberry sauce. Specializes in rack of lamb in honey-mustard crust a la Provencal with rosemary and garlic jus. Own baking. Hrs: 5-11 pm. Closed Sun. Res accepted. Bar. Dinner a la carte entrees: $25.95-$39.95. Entertainment: pianist Mon-Wed; 4-piece band Thurs-Sat. Valet parking. Cr cds: A, D, ER, MC, V.

D ➘

★★★★ **CHIADO.** *864 College St (M6H 1A3), W of Downtown. 416/538-1910.* Guests will feel like they've dined at a small, authentic bistretto after experiencing this restaurant's warm decor, friendly service, and Mediterranean-influenced Portuguese menu. Named after Lisbon's oldest neighborhood, this restaurant is housed in a charming three-story home that is both beautifully sophisticated and comfortably Old World. The seasonal menu offers perfectly grilled fish and more and the all-Portuguese wine list is stellar. Specializes in Portuguese classical cuisine. Hrs: noon-3 pm, 5-11 pm; Sun from 5 pm. Closed Dec 24-26. Res accepted. Wine cellar. Lunch a la carte entrees: $14-$25; dinner a la carte entrees: $17.75-$30. Child's menu. Cr cds: A, C, D, DS, ER, MC, V.

➘

★★★ **CHIARO'S.** *37 King St E, Downtown. 416/863-9700. www.top restaurants.com/toronto/chiaros.htm.* Specializes in rack of lamb, Dover sole. Hrs: 6-11 pm. Closed Sun. Res accepted. Bar. Wine cellar. Dinner $24-$43. Child's menu. Valet parking. Cr cds: A, D, ER, MC, V.

D ➘

★★★ **DAVID DUNCAN HOUSE.** *125 Moatfield Dr, 1 mi S of ON 401, Leslie St Exit. 416/391-1424.* Specializes in steak, seafood, rack of lamb. Hrs: 11:30 am-3 pm, 5-11 pm; Sat, Sun from 5 pm. Res accepted. Bar. Wine list. Lunch $9.95-$14.95; dinner $17.95-$41.95. Entertainment. Valet parking. Jacket. In restored Gothic Revival house (1865); elaborate gingerbread and millwork, antiques, stained-glass skylight. Cr cds: A, D, MC, V.

D ➘

★★★ **THE DOCTOR'S HOUSE.** *21 Nashville Rd (L0J 1C0), 20 mi N ON 27/427 to Kleinburg, right ON Nashville Rd to top of hill. 905/893-1615. www.toronto.com/thedoctors house.* Hrs: 11 am-10 pm. Closed Mon. Res accepted; required Sun brunch. Bar. Lunch $13-$16.50; dinner $16-$36.50. Sun brunch $29.50. Child's menu. Entertainment: pianist Fri, Sat. Parking. Early Canadian atmosphere; antique cabinets with artifacts. Cr cds: A, MC, V.

D

★★ **DYNASTY CHINESE.** *131 Bloor St W (M5S 1R1). 416/923-3323. www. torontolife.com.* Cantonese menu. Specializes in Peking duck, dim sum. Hrs: 11 am-11 pm; Sat, Sun from 10 am. Res accepted. Wine, beer. Lunch, dinner $10.95-$22.95. Entertainment. Cr cds: A, JCB, MC, V.

D ➘

★★★ **ED'S WAREHOUSE.** *270 King St W (M5V 1H8), Downtown. 416/593-6676.* Specializes in roast beef, steak. Own baking. Hrs: 5-9 pm. Closed Sun, Mon; Dec 24, 25. Wine list. Dinner a la carte entrees: $10.95-$20.95. Unusual theatrical decor; many French antiques and statues, Tiffany lamps. Family-owned. Cr cds: A, D, DS, MC, V.

D

★★★ **ELLAS.** *702 Pape Ave (M4K 3S7), E of Downtown. 416/463-0334. Email eria@ellas.com; www.ellas.com.* Kosher menu. Specializes in lamb, shish kebab, seafood. Own pastries. Hrs: 11 am-midnight; Sat to 1 am. Closed Dec 25. Res accepted. Bar. Lunch $7.95-$9.95; dinner $9.95-$24.95. Entertainment. Ancient Athenian decor; sculptures. Family-owned. Cr cds: A, C, D, DS, MC, V.

D SC ➘

★★★★ **THE FIFTH.** *225 Richmond St W. 416/979-3000. www.easyand thefifth.com.* This unique, highly coherent concept combines elegant cuisine and a candlelit atmosphere of rich sensory and social delights. It's a hidden gem, through the Easy nightclub and up a freight elevator to the fifth floor, which offers a limited prix fixe, classic-French menu with state-of-the-art execution. Service is knowledgeable, friendly, and professional.

Classical French menu. Hrs: 6-10 pm. Closed Sun-Wed. Res required. Beer, Wine, extensive wine list. Dinner price fix $75. Entertainment: pianist, trio. Cr cds: A, D, ER, MC, V.

★★ **GRANO.** *2035 Yonge St (M4S 2A2), N of Downtown.* 416/440-1986. Specializes in pasta. Hrs: 10 am-10:30 pm; Sat to 11 pm. Closed Sun; major hols. Res accepted. Bar. Lunch $7.95-$13.95; dinner $8.95-$15.95. Italian street cafe ambience. Cr cds: A, D, DS, MC, V.

★★ **GRAZIE.** *2373 Yonge St (M4P 2C8), N of Downtown.* 416/488-0822. *www.grazie.net.* Specializes in pizza, pasta. Hrs: noon-midnight. Closed hols. Res accepted. Bar. Lunch, dinner a la carte entrees: $7.50-$14. Child's menu. Bistro atmosphere. Cr cds: A, MC, V.

★★★ **GUILD INN.** *201 Guildwood Pkwy.* 416/261-3331. Specializes in rack of lamb, prime rib. Salad bar. Own baking. Hrs: open 24 hrs. Res accepted. Bar. Wine list. Bkfst $2.75-$8.50; lunch $6.50-$15.95; dinner $15.90-$29.50. Sun brunch $17.95. Child's menu. Garden setting in former artist colony. Cr cds: A, MC, V.

★ **HAPPY SEVEN.** *358 Spadina Ave (M5T 2G4), W of Downtown.* 416/971-9820. Hrs: 11-5 am. Res accepted. Bar. Wine, beer. Lunch $7.95-$8.95. A la carte entrees: $4.75-$6.50; dinner $7.95-$8.95. A la carte entrees: $7.95-$14.99. Street parking. Fish, crab, lobster tanks. Cr cds: MC, V.

★★★ **HARVEST CAFE.** *1100 Eglinton Ave E (M3C 1H8).* 416/444-2561. Own baking. Hrs: 7 am-11 pm; Sat to midnight. Res accepted. Wine list. Bkfst a la carte entrees: $3.95-$11.95; lunch a la carte entrees: $8.50-$18.95; dinner a la carte entrees: $8.50-$18.95. Child's menu. Valet parking. Cr cds: A, D, DS, MC, V.

★★★★ **HEMISPHERES.** *110 Chestnut St* 416/599-8000. *www.*

metropolitan.com. Located in the Metropolitan Hotel, chef Neal Noble turns out innovative, fusion cuisine such as his lobster Bolognese, tagliatelle pasta tossed with lobster meat, tomatoes, tarragon, lemon grass, and cream. The modern, stylish dining room has an open kitchen and service is attentive, caring, and well-paced. Guests can splurge for the chef's table and its action-packed, eight-course tasting experience. Asian cuisine with a contemporary Mediterranean-influenced menu. Hrs: Mon-Sat 6:30 am-10:30 pm. Closed Sun. Res accepted. Beer, wine, extensive wine list. Lunch $10.50-$23; dinner $12-$48. Child's menu. Cr cds: A, C, D, MC, V.

★★ **IL POSTO.** *148 Yorkville Ave (M5R 1C2), in Yorkville.* 416/968-0469. Specializes in liver and veal chops, pasta with lobster, carpaccio. Hrs: 11:30 am-3 pm, 5:30-11 pm. Closed Sun; hols. Res accepted. Lunch a la carte entrees: $12-$18.50; dinner a la carte entrees: $14-$33. Cr cds: A, D, DS, MC, V.

★★ **JACQUES BISTRO DUPARC.** *126-A Cumberland St (M5R 1A6).* 416/961-1893. *www.toronto.com/E/V/toron/0012/80/63.* Specializes in sweet bread, rack of lamb. Hrs: 11:30 am-3 pm, 5-10:30 pm. Closed Sun. Res required. Wine, beer. Lunch $10.95-$18.50; dinner $10.95-$26.95. Entertainment. Cr cds: A, C, D, DS, ER, MC, V.

★★★ **JAMIE KENNEDY AT THE ROME.** *100 Queen's Park, 4th Fl (M5S 2C6), at Museum subway stop.* 416/586-5577. Hrs: 11:30 am-3 pm. Res required. Dinner $6-$16. Cr cds: MC, V.

★★★ **JOSO'S.** *202 Davenport Rd (M5R 1J2), in Yorkville.* 416/925-1903. Specializes in Italian dishes, seafood. Hrs: 11:30 am-2:30 pm, 5:30-11 pm; Sat from 5:30 pm. Closed Sun; hols. Res accepted. Wine cellar. Lunch a la carte entrees: $7-$19; dinner a la carte entrees: $14-$27. Child's menu. Cr cds: A, D, MC, V.

★★ **KALLY'S.** *430 Nugget Ave (M1S 4A4), N of Downtown. 416/293-9292. Email kallys@aidal.com.* Specializes in steak, ribs. Salad bar. Hrs: 11:30 am-10 pm; Sat from 4 pm; Sun 4-9 pm. Closed hols; also 1st Mon in Aug. Lunch a la carte entrees: $4.45-$14.95; dinner a la carte entrees: $8.45-$14.95. Child's menu. Parking. Pyramid-shaped skylights. Cr cds: A, D, DS, ER, MC, V.
D SC ⊟

★★★ **LA FENICE.** *319 King St W (M5V 1J5), Downtown. 416/585-2377.* Specializes in fresh seafood, pasta. Hrs: noon-2:30 pm, 5:30-10:30 pm; Sat from 5:30 pm. Closed Sun; major hols. Res accepted. Bar. Wine list. Lunch a la carte entrees: $10.50-$24; dinner a la carte entrees: $16.50-$26. Sleek Milanese-style trattoria. Near theater district. Cr cds: A, D, DS, MC, V.
⊟

★★★★ **LAI WAH HEEN.** *108 Chestnut St. 416/977-9899.* The name of this Metropolitan Hotel dining room means "beautiful meeting place" and that it is with swirling, recessed lighting overhead and a silky, yellow and black color scheme. Nouvelle Cantonese offerings include coffee-smoked mango fish with citrus mayonnaise and tropical fruit. Whether visiting for dinner or dim sum (including over 40 offerings), the Pacific Rim flavors are authentic and exciting. Hrs: 11 am-3 pm, 5:30-11 pm. Res accepted. Wine cellar. Lunch a la carte entrees: $16-$20. Complete meals: $16-$32; dinner a la carte entrees: $16-$48. Complete meals: $32-$42. Cr cds: A, C, D, DS, ER, MC, V.
D

★★ **LE PAPILLION.** *16 Church St (M5E 1M1), Downtown. 416/363-0838. www.toronto.com/lepapillion.* Specializes in crêpes Bretonne, French onion soup. Hrs: noon-2:30 pm, 5-10 pm; Thurs to 11 pm; Fri to midnight; Sat 11 am-midnight; Sun 11 am-10 pm. Closed Mon. Res accepted. Bar. Lunch, dinner $7.75-$18.95. Sun brunch $18. Child's menu. French country kitchen decor. Braille menu. Cr cds: A, D, DS, ER, MC, V.
D ⊟

★ **LE PARADIS.** *166 Bedford Rd (M5R 2K9), Downtown. 416/921-0995. www.leparadis.com.* Specializes in steak frites, moules a la mariniere, cassoulet. Menu changes daily. Hrs: noon-3 pm, 6-11 pm; Sat from 6 pm; Sun, Mon 5:30-10 pm. Closed Jan 1, Dec 24, 25. Res required Fri, Sat (dinner). Bar. Lunch a la carte entrees: $3.95-$14.95; dinner $8.50-$14.95. Street parking. Cr cds: A, D, MC, V.
⊟

★ **MARCHE BCE PLACE.** *42 Yonge St (M5E 1T1). 416/366-8986.* Specializes in caesar salad, crêpes, waffles. Hrs: 7:30-2 am; Fri, Sat to 4 am. Res accepted. Wine list. Lunch $10-$15; dinner $15-$20. Child's menu. Entertainment: Latin band, clowns; Tues, Wed, Sun. Cr cds: A, C, D, DS, ER, MC, V.
D ⊟

★★ **MATIGNON.** *51 Ste. Nicholas St (M4Y 1W6), Downtown. 416/921-9226. www.starcitysearch.com.* Specializes in rack of lamb, duck breast, la darne de saumon aux capres. Hrs: 11:30 am-2:30 pm, 5-10 pm; Fri, Sat 5-11 pm. Closed Sun. Res accepted. Bar. Lunch a la carte entrees: $8.25-$15.95; dinner a la carte entrees: $13.50-$17.95. French atmosphere. Cr cds: A, MC, V.
⊟

★★ **MERCER STREET GRILL.** *36 Mercer St (M5V 1H3). 416/599-3399. www.mercerstreetgrill.com.* Specializes in lentil-crusted sea bass with jasmine rice papaya mint sambal and light green curry sauce, hand-rolled Belgian chocolate sushi. Hrs: 5-10 pm; Fri, Sat to 11 pm. Res accepted. Wine list. Dinner $24-$29.95. Entertainment. exotic Japanese garden. Cr cds: A, D, MC, V.
D ⊟

★★★ **MILLCROFT INN.** *55 John St. 519/941-8111. Email millcroft@millcroft.com; www.millcroft.com.* Specializes in game meat. Hrs: 7:30 am-9 pm; Sun brunch noon-2:30 pm. Res accepted. Bar. Bkfst a la carte entrees: $6.95-$9.95; lunch a la carte entrees: $16.25-$18.50; dinner a la carte entrees: $23.50-$32. Sun brunch $27.95. Entertainment. Valet parking. Restored knitting mill (1881) on the Credit River. Cr cds: A, D, DS, ER, MC, V.

D

★ **MILLER'S COUNTRY FARE.** *5140 Dundas St W (M9A 1C2). 416/234-5050.* Specializes in ribs, chicken, beef stew. Hrs: 10 am-10 pm; Sat, Sun from 9 am; Sat, Sat, Sun brunch to 2:30 pm. Closed Dec 25. Bar. Lunch, dinner $6.25-$13.95. Sun brunch, $3.95-$10.95. Child's menu. Entertainment. Parking. Country decor. Cr cds: A, D, ER, MC, V.

D

★★ **MISTURA.** *265 Davenport Rd (M5R 1J9), in Yorkville. 416/515-0009. Email mistura@attcanada.ca.* Specializes in beet risotto, veal chops, turkey breast. Hrs: 5:30-10 pm; Fri, Sat to 11 pm. Closed Sun; hols; also Victoria Day. Res accepted. Dinner a la carte entrees: $18.50-$21.75. Parking. Cr cds: A, C, D, DS, ER, MC, V.

D

★★ **MOVENPICK OF SWITZER-LAND.** *165 York St (M5H 3R8), Downtown. 416/366-5234. www.movenpick canada.com.* Specializes in Swiss dishes. Salad bar. Hrs: 7:30 am-midnight; Sat from 9 am; Sun 9 am-midnight. Res accepted. Bar. Bkfst $2.50-$13.80; lunch $6.50-$18.50; dinner $9.25-$22.50. Buffet: (Mon-Sat) $16.80-$28.50. Sun brunch $27.80. Child's menu. Parking. European decor. Cr cds: A, D, DS, MC, V.

D

★★★★ **NORTH 44 DEGREES.** *2537 Yonge St (M4P 2H9), N of Downtown. 416/487-4897. www.toronto.com.* Chef Mark McEwan offers world-inspired, continental cuisine in this chic, modern dining room. Although there are hints of exclusivity in the air, service is humble and the room's wood floors, soft lighting, and frosted-glass, "compass" centerpiece create a sexy, comfortable environment. Creative presentations include squab "two ways", a roasted breast with preserved lemon, sea salt, and honey and a foie-gras-stuffed leg. Specializes in mixed appetizer platters, angel hair pasta, rack of lamb. Hrs: 5-11 pm. Closed Sun; hols. Res accepted. Bar. Dinner a la carte entrees: $14.95-$39.95. Entertainment: Wed-Sat. Valet parking. Cr cds: A, D, MC, V.

D

★★ **OLD MILL.** *21 Old Mill Rd (M8X 1G5), W of Downtown. 416/236-2641. Email isto@oldmilltoronto. com; www.oldmilltoronto.com.* Specializes in roast beef, prime rib. Own baking. Hrs: noon-11 pm; Sat 6 pm-1 am; Sun 10:30 am-10:30 pm. Closed Dec 24. Res accepted. Bar. Lunch a la carte entrees: $10.95-$16.95. Buffet: (Mon-Fri) $19.95; dinner $25.95-$34. Sun brunch $23.95. Child's menu. Entertainment: Parking. Jacket. Old English castle motif. Cr cds: A, C, DS, ER, MC, V.

D

★ **OLD SPAGHETTI FACTORY.** *54 The Esplanade (M5E 1A6), Downtown. 416/864-9761.* Specializes in fettucine with seafood, chicken parmigiana. Hrs: 11:30 am-11 pm; Fri, Sat to midnight. Closed Dec 24. Bar. Lunch $5.99-$9.49; dinner $7.99-$14.50. Child's menu. Bright decor; carousel effect. Family-owned. Cr cds: A, C, D, DS, ER, MC, V.

D

★★★ **OPUS.** *37 Prince Arthur Ave (M5R 1B2), in Yorkville. 416/921-3105. www.opusrestaurant.com.* Own baking. Hrs: 5:30-11:30 pm. Bar. Extensive wine list. Dinner $24-$32. Cr cds: A, D, ER, MC, V.

★★★ **ORO.** *45 Elm St (M5G 1H1). 416/597-0155. www.ororestaurant.com.* Specializes in sea bass, rack of lamb. Hrs: Mon-Fri noon-2 pm, 5-10 pm, Sat 5:30-10 pm. Closed Sun, hols. Res accepted. Beer, wine. Lunch $14-$27; dinner $16-$36. Entertainment. Street. Smart casual. Cr cds: A, D, ER, MC, V.

D

★★★★ **PANGAEA.** *1221 Bay St (M5R 3P5), in Yorkville. 416/920-2323.* This modern eatery's industrial facade doesn't do its interior space justice. Once guests enter, they'll relish the softer, calming effects of the dining room's vaulted ceiling and exotic floral arrangements. Chef Martin Kouprie creates sophisticated continental cuisine utilizing the wealth of each season's harvest. Tired Bloor

Street shoppers will find this a great place to break for lunch or tea. Specializes in calamari, wild mushroom risotto, rack of lamb. Hrs: 11:30 am-11:30 pm. Closed Sun; hols. Res accepted. Bar. Wine list. Lunch a la carte entrees: $12-$19; dinner a la carte entrees: $18-$29. Street parking. Cr cds: A, D, MC, V.

[D] [≥]

★★★ **PASTIS.** *1158 Yonge St (M4W 2L9). 416/928-2212.* Hrs: 5:30-11 pm. Closed Sun, Mon. Res accepted. Dinner $18-$35. Cr cds: D, MC, V.

[D] [≥]

★★ **PIER 4 STOREHOUSE.** *245 Queen's Quay W (M5J 2K9), Harbourfront. 416/203-1440. Email sales@pier. 4rest.com.* Specializes in pepper steak Peru, red snapper. Hrs: 11:30 am-11 pm. Closed Jan 1, Dec 25. Res accepted. Bar. Lunch $9.50-$14.95; dinner $16.50-$35.95. Child's menu. Located at water end of a quay on Toronto Bay. Cr cds: A, D, DS, MC, V.

[D] [≥]

★★ **PREGO.** *15474 Yonge St (L4G 1P2), approx 30 mi (48 km) N of Downtown. 905/727-5100.* Specializes in baked rack of lamb, pasta. Hrs: 11:30 am-10 pm; Sun 5-9 pm. Closed Mon; Jan 1, Good Fri, Dec 25, 26. Res accepted. Bar. Lunch a la carte entrees: $7.50-$11.95; dinner a la carte entrees: $9.50-$23.50. Entertainment. Parking. Casual atmosphere. Cr cds: A, ER, MC, V.

[D] [≥]

★★★ **PRONTO.** *692 Mnt Pleasant Rd (M4S 2N3), N of Downtown. 416/486-1111.* Hrs: 5-10:30 pm; Fri, Sat to 11 pm. Closed Jan 1, Dec 24, 25. Res accepted. Bar. Dinner a la carte entrees: $12.95-$27.95. Valet parking. Elegant modern decor; local artwork. Cr cds: A, D, DS, MC, V.

[≥]

★★★ **PROVENCE.** *12 Amelia St (M4X 1A1), in Cabbagetown. 416/924-9901. Email elie@provencerestaurant. com.* Specializes in rack of lamb, duck confit, steak. Hrs: noon-2 pm, 6-10 pm. Closed Dec 25. Res accepted. Bar. Lunch $9.95-$32; dinner $9.95-$32. Sat, Sun brunch, $12.95. French country cottage decor; original artwork. Cr cds: A, ER, MC, V.

[D] [≥]

★★ **QUARTIER.** *2112 Yonge St (M4S 2A5), N of Downtown. 416/545-0505.* Specializes in fresh fish, lamb. Hrs: 11:30 am-2:30 pm, 5:30-10 pm; Sat 5:30-11 pm. Closed hols. Res required Sat (dinner). Bar. Lunch a la carte entrees: $7.50-$12; dinner a la carte entrees: $13-$19. Street parking. Cr cds: A, C, D, DS, ER, MC, V.

[D]

★ **RIVOLI CAFE.** *332 Queen St W (M5V 2A2), Downtown. 416/596-1908. www.home.1star.cia/~rivoli.* Specializes in Sri Malay Bombay, Laotian spring rolls. Hrs: 11:30-2 am. Bar. Lunch a la carte entrees: $6.50-$8.75; dinner a la carte entrees: $8.75-$14.95. Cr cds: A, MC, V.

[D] [≥]

★★ **RODNEY'S OYSTER HOUSE.** *209 Adelaide St E (M5A 1M8). 416/363-8105. Email rodneys@interlog.com; www.tasteoflife.com.* Specializes in oysters, mollusks. Hrs: 11:30-1 am. Closed Sun. Res required. Wine, beer. Lunch, dinner $6.50-$30. Entertainment. Cr cds: A, C, D, DS, ER, MC, V.

[≥]

★ **THE ROSEDALE DINER.** *1164 Yonge St (M4W 2L9), in Yorkville. 416/923-3122. Email dubi@zeygezunt.com; www.zeygezunt.com.* Specializes in herb-crusted rack of lamb, fresh saffron spaghettini, slow-roasted chicken Dijonaise. Hrs: 11 am-midnight. Closed Easter, Dec 25. Res accepted. Bar. Lunch a la carte entrees: $9.50-$15; dinner a la carte entrees: $10-$28. Sat, Sun brunch, $6.95-$15. Child's menu. Street parking. 1940s decor and music. Cr cds: A, D, DS, MC, V.

[≥]

★★★ **ROSEWATER SUPPER CLUB.** *19 Toronto St (M5C 2R1), E of Downtown. 416/214-5888. Email rosewater@idirect.com.* Hrs: 11:30 am-2:30 pm, 5:30-10:30 pm; Thurs-Sun 5:30-11:30 pm. Closed Sun; hols; also July 1, Dec 26. Res accepted. Bar. Wine cellar. Lunch a la carte entrees: $9.95-$15.95; dinner $19-$32. Entertainment: pianist. Early 20th-century atmosphere; elaborate Victorian crown moldings and cathedral-style windows. Cr cds: A, D, DS, MC, V.

[D]

★★ **SARKIS.** *67 Richmond St E (M5C 1N9). 416/214-1337.* Hrs: 5:30-10:30 pm; Fri, Sat to 11:30 pm. Closed Sun hols. Res accepted. Wine list. Dinner $15-$25. Entertainment. Cr cds: A, D, ER, MC, V.

D

★★ **SASSAFRAZ.** *100 Cumberland St (M5R 1A6). 416/964-2222. www. toronto.com/sassafraz.* French menu. Specializes in signature salmon, black Angus strip sirloin. Hrs: 11:30-2 am. Res accepted. Wine, beer. Lunch $11-$20; dinner $25-$35. Cr cds: A, ER, MC, V.

D ⫞

★★★★ **SCARAMOUCHE.** *1 Benvenuto Pl (M4V 2L1), N of Downtown. 416/961-8011. www.toronto.com.* This restaurant and pasta bar has been attracting well-to-do regulars to its Benvenuto-building location for years. What draws them? It could be the sparkling view of the Toronto skyline, one of the city's best wine lists, the superb French-influenced cuisine, or simply the comfortable chairs. Most likely, it's all of these things combined with a gentle atmosphere and divine creme brulee. Specializes in grilled Atlantic salmon, roasted rack of lamb. Pasta bar. Own baking. Hrs: 5:30-10:30 pm. Closed Sun; hols. Res accepted. Bar. Dinner a la carte entrees: $22.75-$36.75. Free valet parking. Cr cds: A, D, DS, MC, V.

D ⫞

★★ **SENATOR.** *253 Victoria St (M5B 1T8), Downtown. 416/364-7517. www. toronto.com/senator.* Specializes in steak, seafood. Hrs: 5-11:30 pm. Closed Mon; hols. Res accepted. Bar. Dinner a la carte entrees: $20.95-$36.95. Parking. 1920s decor; in heart of theatre district. Cr cds: A, D, MC, V.

D ⫞

★★★ **SENSES.** *15 Bloor St W (M4W 1A3), W of Yonge St. 416/935-0400. www.senses.ca.* Hrs: 11:30 am-2:30 pm, 5:30-10 pm; Sun to 2:30 pm. Res accepted. Valet parking. Cr cds: D, MC, V.

★★★ **SPLENDIDO.** *88 Harbord St (M5S 1G5), Downtown. 416/929-7788.* Specializes in roast rack of veal, roast jumbo tiger shrimp. Hrs: 5-11 pm.

Closed Sun. Res accepted. Bar. Dinner $16.95-$35.95. Valet parking. Fashionable trattoria with inviting atmosphere. Cr cds: A, ER, MC, V.

D ⫞

★ **SPRING ROLL ON YONGE.** *693 Yonge St (M4Y 2B3). 416/972-7655.* Specializes in seafood. Hrs: Mon-Thurs 11 am-11 pm, Fri, Sat to midnight, Sun noon-11 pm. Res accepted. Wine, beer. Lunch $6.95-$8.95; dinner $6.95-$13.95. Entertainment. Cr cds: MC, V.

D ⫞

★ **SUSHI BISTRO.** *204 Queen St W (M5V 1Z2), Downtown. 416/971-5315.* Specializes in shrimp and mushrooms, sushi rolls, sashimi. Hrs: noon-10 pm; Fri, Sat to 11:30 pm. Closed Sun; hols. Res accepted. Bar. Lunch a la carte entrees: $7.25-$11; dinner a la carte entrees: $8.50-$18. Child's menu. Traditional Japanese food in modern setting. Cr cds: A, D, DS, MC, V.

D

★ **TAKE SUSHI.** *22 Front St W (M5J 1N7), Downtown. 416/862-1891.* Specializes in lobster sushi. Hrs: 11:45 am-2:30 pm, 5:30-10 pm. Closed hols. Res accepted. Lunch a la carte entrees: $11-$29. Complete meals: $9.50-$45; dinner a la carte entrees: $11-$29. Complete meals: $22-$30. Parking. Cr cds: A, D, MC, V.

D SC ⫞

★ **THAI FLAVOUR.** *1554 Avenue Rd (M5M 3X5), N of Downtown. 416/782-3288.* Specializes in cashew nut chicken, pad Thai, basil shrimp. Hrs: 11 am-11 pm; Sun 5-10 pm. Closed Jan 1, Dec 25. Res accepted. Lunch, dinner a la carte entrees: $7.45-$9.50. Cr cds: A, D, MC, V.

⫞

★★ **TIGER LILY'S NOODLE HOUSE.** *257 Queen St W (M5V 1Z4), Downtown. 416/977-5499.* Specializes in home-style egg roll. Hrs: 11:30 am-9 pm; Wed to 10 pm; Thurs-Sat to 11 pm; Sun from noon. Closed hols. Lunch a la carte entrees: $7.95-$12.95; dinner a la carte entrees: $7.95-$12.95. Cr cds: A, MC, V.

D

★★ **TOMMY COOKS.** *1911 Eglinton Ave E (M1L 2L6). 416/759-4448.* Specializes in steak, seafood. Salad bar. Hrs: 9-2 am. Res accepted. Bar. Lunch $7.95-$12.95; dinner $14.95-$29.95. Sun brunch $12.95. Child's menu. Entertainment. Parking. Mediterranean decor. Cr cds: A, D, ER, MC, V. **D** ⊟

★★ **TRAPPER'S.** *3479 Yonge St (M4N 2N3), N of Downtown. 416/482-6211. www.toronto.com/trappers.* Specializes in fresh fish, steak, pasta. Hrs: 11 am-2:30 pm, 5-10 pm; Sat, Sun from 5 pm. Closed Dec 25. Res accepted. Bar. Lunch a la carte entrees: $8.50-$11.50; dinner a la carte entrees: $13.95-$25.95. Child's menu. Entertainment. Casual dining. Cr cds: A, D, DS, MC, V. **D** ⊟

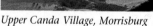
Upper Canda Village, Morrisburg

★★★★ **TRUFFLES.** *21 Avenue Rd, at Bloor St. 416/964-0411. www.fourseasons.com.* Housed in the Four Seasons Hotel, this dining room has received nationwide rave reviews. After walking past the entrance's boar sculptures, an elegant, well-spaced room awaits complete with vaulted ceilings and French garden murals. The menu, blending flavors of Provence with local ingredients, presents twists on the traditional, including a seafood and pearl pasta paella in a tomato-fennel broth. Specializes in pan-seared fillet of beef, foie gras, spaghettini with Perigord black gold. Hrs: 6-11 pm. Closed Sun. Res required. Bar. Dinner a la carte entrees: $28-$40. Prix fixe: 5-course $62, 3-course $49.

Valet parking. Cr cds: A, D, DS, MC, V. **D**

★★ **VANIPHA LANNA.** *471 Eglinton Ave W (M5N 1A7), N of Downtown. 416/484-0895.* Specializes in northern Thai dishes. Hrs: noon-10:30 pm; Tues, Thurs from 5 pm; Fri, Sat to 11:30 pm. Closed Sun; hols. Res accepted Fri, Sat. Lunch a la carte entrees: $6.25-$9.95; dinner a la carte entrees: $8.25-$12.50. Thai decor. Cr cds: A, MC, V. **D**

★★ **VILLA BORGHESE.** *2995 Bloor St W (M8X 1C1). 416/239-1286.* Specializes in fresh fish, veal, pepper steak. Own pasta. Hrs: 11 am-11 pm; Sat, Sun from 4 pm. Closed Mon; Easter, Dec 25. Res accepted. Bar. Lunch $8-$15; dinner $11.95-$23.95. Entertainment. Italian villa decor. Cr cds: A, D, DS, ER, MC, V. **D** ⊟

★★ **XANGO.** *106 John St (M5V 2E1), Downtown. 416/593-4407. Email xangorestaurant@wiznet.ca.* Specializes in raw fish marinated in lime juice. Hrs: 5 pm-midnight; Thurs, Fri from noon. Closed Sun; Dec 24-26. Res accepted. Bar. Lunch a la carte entrees: $19-$28; dinner a la carte entrees: $19-$28. Converted house with veranda. Cr cds: A, MC, V. ⊟

★ **YAMASE.** *317 King St W (M5V 1J5), Downtown. 416/598-1562.* Specializes in sushi, teriyaki, tempura dishes. Hrs: noon-2:30 pm, 5:30-11 pm; Sat from 5 pm; Sun 5-10 pm. Closed Sun; Jan 1. Res accepted. Bar. Lunch a la carte entrees: $5.50-$14.50; dinner a la carte entrees: $7.50-$24.50. Complete meals: $15-$50. Intimate atmosphere. Japanese decor, artwork. Cr cds: A, D, MC, V. **D** ⊟

★★★ **ZACHARY'S.** *950 Dixon Rd. 416/675-9444. Email bristol@interlog.*

com. Specializes in rack of lamb. Own baking. Hrs: noon-2 pm, 6-10 pm; Sat from 6 pm; Sun brunch 11 am-2 pm. Res accepted. Bar. Wine list. Lunch a la carte entrees: $12.50-$16.95. Complete meals: $19.75; dinner a la carte entrees: $22.50-$31.95. Complete meals: $29.50. Sun brunch $23.95. Valet parking. Modern decor with Chinese prints. Cr cds: A, D, DS, MC, V.

D SC ➡

Unrated Dining Spots

PATACHOU. *1095 Yonge St (M4W 2L7), in Yorkville. 416/927-1105.* Eclectic menu. Specializes in cafe au lait, croque Monsieur, pastries. Own baking. Hrs: 8:30 am-7 pm. Closed Sun; hols. Bkfst $5-$10; lunch, dinner $5-$10. Entertainment. Cr cds: V.

D

SHOPSY'S DELICATESSEN. *33 Yonge St (M5E 1G4), Downtown. 416/365-3333.* Hrs: 7 am-11 pm; Thurs, Fri to midnight; Sat 8 am-midnight; Sun 8 am-10 pm. Bar. Bkfst a la carte entrees: $2.10-$6.75; lunch a la carte entrees: $3.95-$8.95; dinner a la carte entrees: $3.75-$11.75. Cr cds: A, D, V.

D

UNITED BAKERS DAIRY RESTAU-RANT. *506 Lawrence Ave W (M6A 1A1), in Lawrence Plz, N of Downtown. 416/789-0519.* Specializes in cheese blintzes, soups, gefilte fish. Hrs: 7 am-8:30 pm; Fri to 8 pm; Sun from 8:30 am. Bkfst a la carte entrees: $5-$10; lunch a la carte entrees: $5-$10; dinner a la carte entrees: $7-$12. Parking. Bakery on premises. Family-owned. Cr cds: MC, V.

Windsor (E-2)

Pop 192,083 **Elev** 622 ft (190 m)
Area code 519
Web www.city.windsor.on.ca/cvb

Information Convention & Visitors Bureau of Windsor, Essex County and Pelee Island, 333 Riverside Dr W, City Centre Mall, Suite 103, N9A 5K4; 519/255-6530 or 800/265-3633

Windsor is located at the tip of a peninsula and is linked to Detroit, Michigan by the Ambassador Bridge and the Detroit-Windsor Tunnel. Because of its proximity to the United States, it is often referred to as the Ambassador City. Windsor is also known as the City of Roses for its many beautiful parks. The Sunken Gardens and Rose Gardens in Jackson Park boast more than 500 varieties of roses. Coventry Garden & Peace Fountain has the only fountain floating in international waters. Whatever the nickname, for many people traveling from the United States, Canada begins here.

Windsor is a cosmopolitan city, designated a bilingual-bicultural area because of the French influence so much in evidence. Windsor also has a symphony orchestra, theaters, a light opera company, art galleries, nightlife, and all the amenities of a large city. Within its boundaries are 900 acres (364 hectares) of parks giving the city the charm of a rural environment. With easy access to lakes Erie and St. Clair and such pleasure troves as Pelee Island, it is also the major city in Canada's "Sun Parlor," Essex County. Mild climate and beautiful beaches make Windsor an excellent place to visit all year.

What to See and Do

Art Gallery of Windsor. Collections consist of Canadian art, incl Inuit prints and carvings, with emphasis on Canadian artists from the late 18th century-present. Children's gallery; gift shop. (Tues-Sun; closed hols) 3100 Howard Ave. Phone 519/969-4494. **FREE**

Casino Windsor. The casino overlooks the Detroit skyline and is easily accessible from a number of hotels. (Daily) Riverside Dr in City Centre. Phone 519/258-7878 or 800/991-7777.

Colasanti Farms, Ltd. Over 25 greenhouses with acres of exotic plants; large collection of cacti; farm animals, parrots and tropical birds; crafts; mini-putt; restaurant. (Daily; closed Jan 1, Dec 25) 28 mi (45 km) SE, on Hwy 3 near Ruthven. Phone 519/326-3287. **FREE**

✪ **Coventry Gardens and Peace Fountain.** Riverfront park and floral gardens with 75-ft-high (23-m) floating fountain; a myriad of 3-D water displays with spectacular night illumination (May-Sep, daily). (Daily) Riverside Dr E & Pillette Rd. Phone 519/253-2300. **FREE**

Fort Malden National Historic Park. Ten-acre (4-hectare) park with remains of fortification, original 1838 barracks, and 1851 pensioner's cottage; visitor and interpretation centers with exhibits. (Daily) Contact PO Box 38, 100 Laird Ave, N9V 2Z2. 100 Laird Ave, 18 mi (29 km) S via City Rd 20, in Amherstburg. Phone 519/736-5416. ¢¢

Heritage Village. Historical artifacts and structures on 54 acres (22 hectares). Log cabins (1826 and 1835), railway station (1854), house (1869), church (1885), schoolhouse (1907), barber shop (ca 1920), general store (1847); transportation museum. Special events. Picnic facilities. 20 mi (32 km) SE via ON 3, then 5 mi (8 km) S of Essex on County Rd 23. Phone 519/776-6909. ¢¢

Jack Miner Bird Sanctuary. Canadian geese and other migratory waterfowl; ponds; picnicking; museum. Canadian geese "air shows" during peak season (Mar and late Oct-Nov; daily). (Mon-Sat) 27 mi (44 km) SE via ON 3 & 29S, 2 mi (3 km) N of Kingsville. Phone 519/733-4034. **FREE**

John Freeman Walls Historic Site & Underground Railroad Museum. John Freeman Walls, a fugitive slave from North Carolina, built this log cabin in 1846. It subsequently served as a terminal of the Underground Railroad and the first meeting place of the Puce Baptist Church. It has remained in the possession of Walls's descendants. (May-Oct, by appt only) At Puce in Maidstone Township; Hwy 401 E from Windsor to Puce Rd Exit N. Phone 519/258-6253.

North American Black Historical Museum. Chronicles achievements of black North Americans, many of whom fled the US for freedom in Canada. Permanent exhibits on Underground Railroad; artifacts, archives, genealogical library. (Apr-Nov, Wed-Fri, also Sat and Sun afternoons) 18 mi (29 km) S on City Rd 20, Exit Richmond St E, at 227 King

St in Amherstburg. Phone 519/736-5433. ¢¢

Park House Museum. Solid log, clapboard-sided house (ca 1795), considered to be oldest house in area. Built in Detroit, moved here in 1799. Restored and furnished as in the 1850s. Demonstrations of tinsmithing; pieces for sale. (June-Aug, daily; rest of yr, Tues-Fri and Sun) 219 Dalhousie St, 18 mi (29 km) S via City Rd 20, on the King's Naval Yard, near Fort Malden in Amherstburg. Phone 519/736-2511. ¢

Point Pelee National Park. The park is a 6-sq-mi (16-sq-km) tip of the Point Pelee peninsula. Combination dry land and marshland, the park also has a deciduous forest and is situated on 2 major bird migration flyways. More than 350 species have been sighted in the park. A boardwalk winds through the 2,500 acres (1,011 hectares) of marshland. Fishing, swimming, canoeing; picnicking, trails, and interpretive center, biking (rentals), transit ride (free). (Daily) Contact Chief of Visitor Services, RR 1, Leamington, N8H 3V4. 30 mi (48 km) SE via ON 3, near Leamington. Phone 519/322-2365 or 519/322-2371(migration line). Entrance fee ¢¢-¢¢¢

University of Windsor. 16,000 students. On campus is Essex Hall Theatre, featuring 7 productions/season (Sep-Mar, fee). 401 Sunset Ave. Phone 519/253-3000 or 519/253-4565 (box office).

Willistead Manor. (1906) Restored English Tudor mansion built for Edward Chandler Walker, son of famous distiller Hiram Walker, on 15 acres (6 hectares) of wooded parkland; elegant interiors with hand-carved woodwork; furnished in turn-of-the-century style. (July-Aug, Sun and Wed; Sep-June, 1st and 3rd Sun of each month) 1899 Niagara St, at Kildare Rd. Phone 519/253-2365. ¢¢

Windsor's Community Museum. Exhibits and collections interpret the history of Windsor and southwestern Ontario. Located in the historic Francois Baby House. (Tues-Sat; closed hols) 254 Pitt St W. Phone 519/253-1812. **FREE**

Wreck Exploration Tours. Exploration of a 130-yr-old wreck site. Shoreline cruise; artifact orientation. (May-Oct, res required) 303 Conces-

sion 5, Leamington, ON N8H 3V5.
Phone 313/510-2592 or 888/229-7325.

Annual Events

International Freedom Festival. Two-wk joint celebration by Detroit and Windsor with many events, culminating in fireworks display over the river. Phone 519/252-7264. Late June-1st wk July.

Leamington Tomato Festival. Leamington. Phone 519/326-2878. Mid-Aug.

Motels/Motor Lodges

★★ **BEST WESTERN CONTINENTAL INN.** 3345 Huron Church Rd (N9E 4H5). 519/966-5541; fax 519/972-3384. 71 rms, 2 story. S $66-$76; D $70-$80; each addl $6-$10; under 12 free. TV; cable (premium), VCR avail. Heated pool. Restaurant 7 am-10 pm. Ck-out 11 am. Meeting rms. Cr cds: A, D, DS, MC, V.

★★ **BEST WESTERN WHEELS INN.** 615 Richmond St (N7M 1R2), NE ON 2, at Keil Dr. 519/351-1100; fax 519/436-5541. www.wheelsinn.com. 350 rms, 2-10 story. S, D $102.88-$154.88; each addl $5; suites $188.88-$208.88; under 18 free; lower rates mid-wk. Crib free. TV; cable. 2 pools, 1 indoor/outdoor; whirlpools, water slides. Restaurant 7-1 am. Rm serv 7-11 am, 5 pm-midnight. Bar noon-1 am; entertainment Mon-Sat. Ck-out 11:30 am. Convention facilities. Business center. Gift shop. Miniature golf. Exercise rm; sauna, steam rm. Bowling. Game rm. Rec rm. Some balconies. Resort atmosphere; more than 7 acres of indoor facilities. Atrium. Cr cds: A, C, D, DS, ER, JCB, MC, V.

★★ **COMFORT INN.** 1100 Richmond St (N7M 5J5), E ON 401 to Exit 81. 519/352-5500; fax 519/352-2520. 81 rms, 2 story. May-Sep: S $57-$95; D $65-$105; each addl $4; under 19 free; wkend rates; lower rates rest of yr. Crib free. Pet accepted. TV; cable. Complimentary coffee in lobby. Restaurant adj 9 am-10 pm. Ck-out

11 am. Cr cds: A, C, D, DS, ER, JCB, MC, V.

★★ **MARQUIS PLAZA.** 2530 Ouellette Ave (N8X 1L7). 519/966-1860; fax 519/966-6619. 97 rms, 2 story. S $48-$150; D $60; each addl $5; suites $90-$150. Crib $5. Pet accepted, some restrictions; $10. TV; cable (premium), VCR avail. Ck-out noon. Meeting rms. Cr cds: A, D, ER, MC, V.

★★★ **ROYAL MARQUIS.** 590 Grand Marais E (M8X 3H4), near Intl Airport. 519/966-1900; fax 519/966-4689. 99 rms, 5 story, 14 suites. S $70; D $80; each addl $5; suites $90-$175; under 12 free; wkend rates; higher rates prom. Crib $5. Pet accepted, some restrictions; $10. TV; cable (premium), VCR avail. Indoor pool; whirlpool. Supervised children's activities; ages 5-10. Restaurant 6:30 am-10 pm. Bar; entertainment Thurs-Sun. Ck-out noon. Meeting rms. Valet serv. Concierge serv. Barber, beauty shop. X-country ski 5 mi. Exercise equipt; sauna. Luxurious furnishings, atmosphere. Cr cds: A, D, ER, MC, V.

Hotel

★★★ **RADISSON.** 333 Riverside Dr W. 519/977-9777; fax 519/977-1411; toll-free 800/267-9777. 207 rms, 19 story. S, D $95; under 12 free. Crib free. Pet accepted, some restrictions. Garage avail. TV; cable (premium). Indoor pool; whirlpool. Complimentary full bkfst. Restaurant nearby. Ck-out noon. Meeting rms. In-rm modem link. Exercise equipt; saunas. Minibars. Cr cds: A, D, DS, ER, MC, V.

Restaurants

★★ **CHATHAM STREET GRILL.** 149 Chatham St W (N9A 5M7). 519/256-2555. Specializes in fresh seafood, certified Angus beef. Hrs: 11:30 am-11 pm; Fri to midnight; Sat noon-midnight; Sun 5-9 pm. Closed hols; Good Fri. Res accepted. Bar.

Lunch $5.95-$10; dinner $14.95-$24.95. Cr cds: A, C, D, ER, MC, V.
⊟

★★ **COOK SHOP.** *683 Ouellette Ave (N9A 4J4). 519/254-3377.* Specializes in pasta, steak, rack of lamb. Hrs: 5-10 pm; Fri, Sat to midnight. Closed Mon; Dec 24, 25; also Aug. Res required. Dinner $7.65-$16.85. Parking. Cr cds: A, MC, V.

★★ **PASTA SHOP.** *683 Ouellette Ave (N9A 4J4). 519/254-1300.* Specializes in steak Diane, veal scallopini. Hrs: 5-10 pm; Fri, Sat to midnight. Closed Mon; Dec 24, 25; Aug. Res required. Dinner $11.50-$16.85. Parking. Open kitchen. Intimate dining. Cr cds: A, MC, V.

★★ **TOP HAT SUPPER CLUB.** *73 University Ave E (N9A 2Y6). 519/253-4644.* Specializes in steak, seafood, babyback ribs. Hrs: 11 am-midnight; Fri, Sat to 2 am. Res accepted. Bar. Lunch $4-$10; dinner $6.50-$25. Child's menu. Entertainment: Fri, Sat. Parking. Fireplace. Family-owned. Cr cds: A, D, DS, MC, V.
[D] ⊟

★★ **TUNNEL BAR-B-Q.** *58 Park St E (N9A 3A7), at Tunnel Exit. 519/258-3663. www.tunnel-b-q.com.* Specializes in barbecued ribs, chicken, steak. Hrs: 8-2 am. Closed Dec 25. Wine, beer. Bkfst $3.25-$5.95; lunch $4.25-$7.95; dinner $7.45-$18.95. Child's menu. Old English decor. Family-owned. Cr cds: D, MC, V.
[D] ⊟

★★ **YE OLDE STEAK HOUSE.** *46 Chatham St W (N9A 5M6). 519/256-0222.* Specializes in soup, char-broiled steak, fresh seafood. Hrs: 11:30 am-10 pm; Sat 4-11 pm: Sun 4-9 pm. Closed Jan 1, Good Fri, Dec 25. Res accepted. Bar. Lunch $3.75-$12; dinner $11-$24. Child's menu. Old English decor. Family-owned. Cr cds: A, D, MC, V.
[D] ⊟

PROVINCE OF PRINCE EDWARD ISLAND

Prince Edward Island is located in the Gulf of St. Lawrence on Canada's east coast, off the shores of Nova Scotia and New Brunswick. Although it is the smallest province, it is known as the "Birthplace of Canada" because Charlottetown hosted the Charlottetown Conference in 1864. This laid the foundation for the Confederation in 1867.

Pop 122,506 **Land area** 2,186 sq mi (5,662 sq km) **Capital** Charlottetown **Web** www.peiplay.com

Information Tourism PEI, PO Box 940, Charlottetown, C1A 7M5; 902/368-4444 or 888/734-7529

The island is 40 miles (64 kilometers) wide at its broadest point, narrowing to only four miles (six kilometers) wide near Summerside, and 140 miles (224 kilometers) long. Famous for its red soil, warm waters, fine white beaches, and deep-cut coves, it can be reached by air, ferry, and the Confederation Bridge, an eight-mile (12.9-kilometer) link between Borden-Carleton, PE and Cape Jourimain, New Brunswick.

Prince Edward Island is divided into six daytour regions. The North by Northwest daytour region encompasses the northwestern parts of the province from North Cape to Cedar Dunes Provincial Park. It is an area of unspoiled beauty with secluded beaches, picturesque fishing and farming communities, and quaint churches. (Visitor Information Centre on Rte 2 in Portage.)

The Ship to Shore daytour region covers the southwest. It introduces the visitor to the history of shipbuilding and fox farming, and the Malpeque oysters. Also here is the city of Summerside, located on the Bedeque Bay, which is gaining a reputation for hosting international sporting events. (Visitor Information Centre on Rte 1A, east of downtown.)

The Anne's Land daytour region features the central north shore of the province. It is home to many sites related to *Anne of Green Gables*, the children's story written by Lucy Maud Montgomery. The stunning white sand beaches of Prince Edward Island National Park (see) are also here. (Visitor Information Centre at jct Rtes 6 & 13 in Cavendish and on Rte 15 at Brackley Beach.)

The Charlotte's Shore daytour encompasses the south central region of Prince Edward Island. It is here that the visitor is introduced to Charlottetown, the provincial capital and birthplace of the Canadian Confederation. The scenic red cliffs and warm waters of the south shore beaches are also inviting. (Visitor Information Centre on Water St in Charlottetown and at Gateway Village in Borden-Carleton.)

The Bays & Dunes daytour region covers the northeastern corner of the province. It offers the island's best coastline views, with miles of uncrowded white sand beaches and spectacular dunes bordering the scenic countryside. (Visitor Information Centre on Rte 2 in Souris.)

The Hills & Harbours daytour details the southeastern region. It is home to some of the most pleasing vistas and peaceful fishing villages in the province. (Visitor Information Centre at jct Rte 3 & 4 in Pooles Corner at the Wood Islands Ferry Terminal.)

Safety belts are mandatory for all persons anywhere in vehicle. Children under 40 pounds in weight must be in an approved safety seat anywhere in vehicle. Children 20-39 pounds may face forward in seat; however, children under 20 pounds must face backward in seat. For further information phone 902/368-5200.

Tuna fishery

Cavendish (C-5)

See also Charlottetown

Pop 93 **Elev** 75 ft (23 m)
Area code 902
Web www.peiplay.com
Information Tourism PEI, PO Box 940; Charlottetown C1A 7M5; 800/463-4734

Located near the western end of Prince Edward Island National Park (see), Cavendish encompasses more than 15 miles (24 kilometers) of beach area. World famous as the setting for *Anne of Green Gables,* the area also boasts excellent recreational facilities.

What to See and Do

Birthplace of Lucy Maud Montgomery. A replica of the "Blue Chest", the writer's personal scrapbooks, containing copies of her many stories and poems, and her wedding dress and veil are stored here. (May-Thanksgiving, daily) Jct Hwy 6, 20 in New London. Phone 902/436-7329 or 902/886-2099. ¢ Nearby is

> **Lucy Maud Montgomery's Cavendish Home.** Site where Montgomery was raised by her grandparents from 1876-1911. Bookstore and museum houses the original desk, scales, and crown stamp used in post office. (June-Sep, daily) ¢

The Great Island Science & Adventure Park. Science centre; space shuttle replica; dinosaur museum; planetarium. (Mid-June-Labor Day, daily) 2.5 mi (4 km) W of Cavendish on Rte 6 at Stanley Bridge. Phone 902/886-2252. ¢¢¢

Green Gables. Famous as the setting for Lucy Maud Montgomery's *Anne of Green Gables*. Surroundings portray the Victorian setting described in the novel. Tours avail off-season (fee). (May-Oct, daily) Prince Edward Island National Park, on Hwy 6. Phone 902/672-6350 (Bilingual Guide Service). ¢¢

Prince Edward Island National Park. (see).

Rainbow Valley Family Fun Park. Approx 40 acres of woodland, lakes, and landscaped areas; children's farm with petting areas; playground, swan boats, flumes, water slides; entertainment, picnicking, cafe. Monorail ride. (June-Labour Day, daily) On Hwy 6 near Green Gables. Phone 902/963-2221. ¢¢

⭐ **Woodleigh Replicas & Gardens.** Extensive outdoor display of large-scale models of famous castles and bldgs of legendary, historic, and literary interest. Incl are the Tower of London, Dunvegan Castle, and Anne Hathaway Cottage. Several models are large enough to enter and are furnished. Flower, shrub garden; children's playground; food service. (Early June-mid-Oct, daily) 14 mi (23 km) SW via Hwy 6, right on Hwy 20, left on Hwy 234 to Burlington. Phone 902/836-3401. ¢¢

Motels/Motor Lodges

★★ **CAVENDISH.** *Rte 6 (C0A 1M0), jct PE 6, 13.* 902/963-2244; *fax* 902/963-2244; *res* 800/565-2243. 38 rms, some A/C, 2 story, 3 kit. units, 8 kit. cottages. May-late Sep: S $72-$78; D $78-$88; each addl $3-$6; kit. units $88; cottages (1-4 persons) $81-$105. Closed rest of yr. TV; cable. Heated pool. Complimentary continental bkfst (June-Sep). Restaurant adj 8 am-10 pm. Ck-out 10 am. Picnic tables, grills. Cr cds: A, MC, V.
🏊 🔥

★★ **SILVERWOOD MOTEL.** *Green Gables Post Office (C0A 1M0), 1 mi W of jct PE 6, 13.* 902/963-2439; *fax* 902/963-2439; *toll-free* 800/565-4753. 50 rms, 35 A/C, 1-2 story, 23 kits. Mid-May-mid-Oct: S, D $82; each addl $8; kit. units $90-$120. Closed rest of yr. TV. Heated pool. Playground. Restaurant adj 7:30 am-9 pm. Ck-out 10 am. Meeting rms. Picnic tables, grills. Cr cds: A, MC, V.
🏊 🛏 🐾

Restaurants

★★ **IDLE OARS.** *N Rustico (C0A 1X0), 3 mi E on PE 6.* 902/963-2534. Specializes in steak, seafood. Hrs: 8 am-10:30 pm. Bkfst, lunch $4.95-

$12.95. Dinner $5.95-$18.95. Entertainment. Cr cds: A, C, D, ER, MC, V.
D ⬛

★★ **NEW GLASGOW LOBSTER SUPPER.** *Rte 258 New Glasgow (C0A 1N0), 5 mi S off PE 13.* 902/964-2870. Seafood menu. Hrs: 4-8:30 pm. Closed Nov-May. Complete meals: $15.95-$26.95. Entertainment. Cr cds: A, C, D, ER, MC, V.
D SC ⬛

Charlottetown

(D-5) *See also Cavendish*

Pop 15,282 **Elev** 25 ft (8 m)
Area code 902
Web www.peiplay.com
Information Tourism PEI, PO Box 940, C1A 7M5; 902/368-4444 or 888/734-7529

Named for Queen Charlotte, King George III's wife, Charlottetown was chosen in 1765 as the capital of Colonial St. John's Island, as it was then known. The name was changed to Prince Edward Island in 1799. The first settlement in the area was at Port la Joye across the harbour and was ruled by the French until ceded to Great Britain after the fall of Louisbourg. Known as the birthplace of Canada because the conference that led to confederation was held here in 1864, the city has many convention facilities, cultural and educational institutions, and attractions located within easy reach. Encircled by a scenic natural harbour, boating, yachting, swimming, golf, other sports, and a variety of seafood are all popular and readily available. Charlottetown is a main feature of the Charlotte's Shore daytour region; a Visitor Information Centre is here.

Prince Edward Island may be reached from the mainland at Caribou, NS, by car ferry to Wood Islands, PE, 38 mi (61 km) southeast of Charlottetown. Contact Northumberland Ferries, PO Box 634, Charlottetown, PE, C1A 7L3; 902/566-3838 or 888/249-7245. (Daily, May-mid-Dec; 1¼-hr crossing; fee) The island can also be reached from Cape Jourimain, New Brunswick, via the Confederation Bridge, an eight-mile bridge that leads to Borden-Carleton, PE (toll).

What to See and Do

Basin Head Fisheries Museum. Depicts history of fishing in the province. Fishing equipment, scale models showing methods; old photographs, fish charts, and other marine articles. Film and slide projections. (Mid-June-late Sep, daily) 58 mi (93 km) E via Rte 2 to Souris, then Rte 16 to Kingsboro. Phone 902/357-2966 or 902/368-6600. ¢¢

Beaconsfield. (1877) Mansard-style house built for shipbuilder is architecturally intact; guided tours. Headquarters of Prince Edward Island Museum & Heritage Foundation; bookstore. Regular and annual events. (Mid-June-Labor Day, daily; after Labor Day, Sun and Tues-Fri afternoons) 2 Kent St. Phone 902/368-6600. Museum ¢¢

Confederation Centre of the Arts. (1964) Canada's National Memorial to the Fathers of Confederation; opened by Queen Elizabeth II to honor the centennial of the 1864 Confederation Conference. Contains provincial library, Confederation Centre Museum and Art Gallery, theatres, and the Robert Harris Collection of portraiture. Courtyard restaurant, gift shop. Home of the Charlottetown Festival (see SEASONAL EVENT). Gallery and museum (Tues-Sat, also Sun afternoons). Centre (daily; closed hols). 145 Richmond St. Phone 902/628-1864, 800/565-0278, or 902/566-1267 (tickets). ¢

Fort Amherst/Port La Joye National Historic Park. Only earthworks of the former French fort Port la Joye (built 1720) are still visible. Captured by British in 1758, abandoned in 1768. Cafe, boutique. Interpretive center. (Mid-June-Labor Day, daily) Near Rocky Point, on Hwy 19 across the harbour mouth. Phone 902/672-6350.

Green Park Shipbuilding Museum. Former estate of James Yeo, Jr, whose family members were leading shipbuilders of the 19th century. House (1865) restored to reflect life during the prosperous shipbuilding era. Photos of famous ships and artifacts in interpretive center; audiovisual presentation in museum

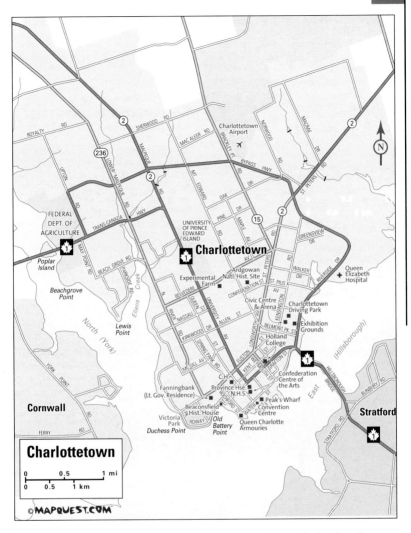

Charlottetown

theater. Lecture series and concerts. Annual events. Camping, swimming at Malpeque Bay. (Mid-June-Labour Day, daily) 63 mi (101 km) NW via Hwy 2 to Hwy 132 just past Richmond, right to jct with Hwy 12, left to Port Hill. Phone 902/831-7947 or 902/368-6600 (off-season). ¢¢

Orwell Corner Historic Village.
Reconstructed rural crossroads community of late 19th century. Combined store, post office, and farmhouse; school, church, cemetery, and barns. Farming activities as they were practiced 100 yrs ago. Annual events. Ceilidhs (Wed eves). (Late June-early Sep, daily; mid-May-late

June, Mon-Fri; early Sep-late Oct, Tues-Sun) 18 mi (29 km) E via Trans Canada Hwy. Phone 902/651-2013 or 902/368-6600 (off-season). ¢¢

Prince Edward Island National Park. (see).

Province House. (1847) Birthplace of the Canadian nation and a national historic site. Confederation rm where delegates met in 1864 to discuss confederation. National memorial, seat of Provincial Legislature. Tours. (June-early Oct, daily; rest of yr, Mon-Fri; closed hols) Richmond St. Phone 902/566-7626.

Sightseeing tour.
Abegweit Tours. Charlottetown tours

on authentic London double-decker buses; also N and S shore tours. Bilingual guide service avail. Contact 157 Nassau St, C1A 2X3. Phone 902/894-9966. ¢¢¢-¢¢¢¢¢

St. Dunstan's Cathedral Basilica. Largest church on the island. Gothic cathedral with distinctive triple towers contains beautiful stained-glass windows and an impressive altar 37 ft (11 m) high made of many types of marble and crowned with a beautiful rose window. Audio loop for hearing impaired. Restoration in progress. (Daily) 45 Great George St. Phone 902/894-3486.

Annual Event

Festival of Lights. Charlottetown Waterfront. Buskers, children's concerts, Waterfront Magic, children's midway. Fireworks display over Charlottetown Harbour on July 1 (Canada Day). Late June-early July.

Seasonal Event

Charlottetown Festival. Confederation Centre of the Arts. Original Canadian musicals, incl *Anne of Green Gables* and other productions; special gallery presentations and theater. Box office 902/566-1267; information 902/628-1864. Late June-late Sep.

Motels/Motor Lodges

★★★ **BEST WESTERN CHARLOTTETOWN.** *(C1A 1L5). 902/892-2461; toll-free 800/528-1234. Email maclauchlans@pei.sympatico.ca; www.bestwestern.com.* 143 rms, 2-3 story, 26 kits. June-mid-Oct: S $139-$149; D $149-$159; each addl $10; studio rms $149-$159; suites $169-$209; kit. units $149-$159; under 18 free; lower rates rest of yr. Pet accepted, some restrictions. TV; cable. Indoor pool; whirlpool. Complimentary coffee in rms. Restaurants 7 am-9 pm; Sun from 8 am. Ck-out noon. Meeting rms. Valet serv. Exercise equipt; sauna. Sundries. Microwaves avail. Cr cds: A, C, D, DS, ER, JCB, MC, V.
D 🐾 ➾ 🏋 ⊠ 🔥 SC

★★ **ISLANDER MOTOR LODGE.** *146-148 Pownal St (C1A 7N4). 902/892-1217; fax 902/566-1623; toll-free 800/268-6261.* 49 rms, 2 story, 3 kits. Mid-May-mid-Oct: S, D $86-$96; each addl $8; suites, kit. units $96-$120; under 12 free; lower rates rest of yr. Crib $7. Pet accepted. TV; cable. Restaurant 7 am-8 pm. Ck-out 11 am. Meeting rms. Sundries. Microwaves avail. Cr cds: A, ER, MC, V.
D 🐾 🔥

★★ **QUALITY INN ON THE HILL.** *150 Euston St (C1A 1W5). 902/894-8572; fax 902/368-3556.* 48 rms, 5 story. Late June-mid-Oct: S $116; D $127; each addl $9; studio rms $137-$142; suites $152-$174; under 16 free; lower rates rest of yr. Pet accepted. TV; cable. Coffee in rms. Restaurant 7 am-8 pm. Bar 11-1 am. Ck-out noon. Meeting rms. Bellhops. Health club privileges. Sundries. Cr cds: A, C, D, DS, ER, MC, V.
🐾 ⊠ 🔥

★★ **SUNNY KING.** *Trans-Can Hwy 1 (C0A 1H0), on 902/566-2209; fax 902/566-4209.* 39 rms, 1-2 story, 30 kits. No A/C. Late June-early Sep: S $54-$64; D $60-$70; each addl $8; suites, kit. units $68-$92; under 16 free; lower rates rest of yr. Crib $6. Pet accepted. TV; cable. Heated pool. Playground. Free supervised children's activities (May-mid-Nov). Restaurant adj 8 am-11 pm. Ck-out 11 am. Coin lndry. Business servs avail. Valet serv. Many microwaves. Picnic tables, grills. Cr cds: A, C, D, DS, ER, MC, V.
D 🐾 ➾ ⊠ 🔥 🐾 SC

★★★ **THRIFT LODGE.** *Trans-Can Hwy (C1A 7K7), 2 mi W. 902/892-2481; fax 902/368-3247; toll-free 800/565-7633. Email rodds@rodd-hotels.ca; www.rodd-hotels.ca/.* 62 rms, 2 story, 31 suites. Mid-June-Sep: S, D $85-$94; suites $99-$115; under 16 free; lower rates rest of yr. Crib free. Pet accepted. TV; cable. Heated pool. Restaurant 7-10 am, 5-9 pm. Bar 11-1 am; closed Sun. Ck-out 11 am. Health club privileges. Refrigerators, microwaves avail. Cr cds: A, C, D, DS, ER, JCB, MC, V.
🐾 ➾ ⊠ 🔥 SC

★★★ **TRAVELODGE HOTEL.** *Hwy 1 & Hwy 2 (C1A 8C2) 902/894-8566; fax 902/892-8488; res 800/578-7878; toll-free 800/565-7633.* 132 rms, 1-3 story, 6 kits. June-Oct: S $87; D $99; each addl $10; suites $125-$175; under 16 free; lower rates rest of yr. Crib free. TV; cable. Indoor pool.

Charlottetown

Restaurant 7 am-10 pm. Bar 4:30 pm-1 am; closed Sun. Ck-out noon. Meeting rms. Bellhops. Sundries. Exercise equipt; sauna. Balconies. Indoor courtyard adj to pool area. Cr cds: A, C, D, ER, MC, V.

Hotels

★★ **THE CHARLOTTETOWN.** *75 Kent St (C1A 7K4), at Pownal St. 902/894-7371; fax 902/368-2178; toll-free 800/565-7633. Email rodds@rodd-hotels.ca; www.rodd-hotels.ca/.* 115 rms, 5 story. June-mid-Oct: S, D $135-$215; each addl $10; under 16 free; lower rates rest of yr. Crib free. Pet accepted. TV; cable. Indoor pool; whirlpool. Restaurant 7 am-2 pm, 5-10 pm. Bar 4 pm-1 am; closed Sun. Ck-out 11 am. Meeting rms. Exercise equipt; sauna. Cr cds: A, D, DS, ER, JCB, MC, V.

★★★ **THE PRINCE EDWARD.** *18 Queen St (C1A 8B9). 902/566-2222; fax 902/566-1745; toll-free 800/441-1414. Email vdowne@peh.cphotels.ca; www.peisland.com/prince/edward.htm.* 211 rms, 10 story. May-mid-Oct: S $139-$229; D $159-$249; each addl $20; suites $299-$799; lower rates rest of yr. Crib avail. Pet accepted. TV; cable. Indoor pool; wading pool, whirlpool. Restaurants 6:30 am-11 pm. Bar; entertainment. Ck-out noon. Meeting rms. Business center. Exercise rm; sauna. Massage. On waterfront in Olde Charlottetown. Cr cds: A, D, DS, MC, V.

Prince Edward Island National Park

See also Cavendish, Charlottetown

Information Field Unit Superintendant, Department of Canadian Heritage/Parks Canada, 2 Palmer's Lane, Charlottetown, PEI, C1A 5V6; 902/566-7050 or 902/672-6350

Prince Edward Island National Park, 25 square miles (40 square kilometers), is one of eastern Canada's most popular vacation destinations.

Warm salt waters and sandy beaches abound. There are several supervised beach areas for swimmers and miles of secluded shoreline to explore. In addition to golf, tennis, bicycling, and picnicking, the park offers an interpretation program highlighting the natural and cultural features and stories of the area; campfires; beach walk; and more. Green Gables and its association with Lucy Maud Montgomery's *Anne of Green Gables* is a major attraction, with daily walks offered around the house and grounds (see CAVENDISH). Camping is also available (maximum stay 21 nights, reservations accepted). Dalvay-by-the-Sea offers hotel accommodations in a unique setting. Many private cabins, hotels, and campgrounds are available bordering the park.

Prince Edward Island may be reached by a car ferry. For further information, contact Marine Atlantic Reservation Bureau, PO Box 250, North Sydney, NS, B2A 3M3; 800/341-7981 (US). Another ferry crosses in 1¼ hours at Caribou, NS to Wood Islands, PEI (see CHARLOTTE-TOWN, PEI).

PROVINCE OF QUÉBEC

The Québéçois, whose ancestors came from France more than 400 years ago, made their stronghold in the St. Lawrence River valley. These ancestors also gave this province its decidedly French character.

The geography of Québec is largely determined by the St. Lawrence River, the Laurentian mountains, lakes that are really inland seas, and streams that swell into broad rivers.

These magnificent natural settings provide the tourist with year-round vacation wonders. The Laurentians, only an hour's drive from Montréal, have some of the finest skiing, outdoor recreation, and restaurants in North America.

Pop 6,438,403 **Land area** 643,987 sq mi (1,667,926 sq km)
Capital Québec
Web www.tourisme.gouv.qc.ca

Information Tourisme/Québec, CP 979, Montréal H3C 2W3; 514/873-2015 or 800/363-7777

Combine the natural beauty of the area, the cosmopolitan yet historic ambience of Montréal and Québec City, and a tour of the unspoiled Gaspé Peninsula, and you will have a vacation destination nonpareil.

When dining in Québec, travelers should be aware that there is a 15.2% federal and provincial tax on food and alcohol added to all restaurant checks.

In addition to national holidays, Québec observes St. Jean Baptiste Day (June 24).

Safety belts are mandatory for all persons anywhere in vehicle. Children under 5 years or under 40 pounds in weight must be in an approved safety seat. Radar detectors are strictly forbidden. For further information phone 800/361-7620.

Drummondville

(D-6) *See also Montréal, Sherbrooke*

Pop 27,347 **Elev** 350 ft (107 m)
Area code 819
Information Bureau du Tourisme et des Congrès, 1350 Michaud St, J2C 2Z5; 819/477-5529

Known as the "Center of Québec," this industrial and commercial center is advantageously located on the St. Francois River where the Trans-Canada and Trans-Québec highways intersect.

What to See and Do

Le Village Québécois d'Antan. Historical village (1810-1910) typical of the area. (June-Labour Day) N via Hwy 20, exit 181 on rue Montplaisir. Phone 819/478-1441. ¢¢¢

Manoir et Domaine Trent. Period home (1836) restored by artisans; restaurant. Camping (late June-Aug). Parc des Voltigeurs. Phone 819/472-3662. **FREE**

Annual Event

World Folklore Festival. One of the major folklore events in North America. International singers, dancers, and musicians participate at 4 different sites. Phone 819/472-1184. Ten days July.

Motel/Motor Lodge

★★ **HOTEL UNIVERSEL.** *915 Hains St (J2C 3A1). 819/478-4971; fax 819/477-6604; toll-free 800/668-3521. Email aub-uni@9bit.qc.ca.* 115 rms, 4 story. S $75.95; D $85.95; each addl $10; suites $120-$150; under 15 free. Crib free. Pet accepted. TV; cable. Indoor pool; poolside serv. Restaurant 7 am-10 pm. Bar 11-3 am; entertainment Wed-Sat. Ck-out noon. Meeting rms. Business servs avail. Cr cds: A, C, D, DS, ER, MC, V.

Restaurant

★★ **RESTAURANT DU BOIS-JOLI.** *505 St. Joseph Blvd W (J2E 1K8).* 819/472-4366. Specializes in roti de boeuf au jus. Hrs: 11 am-10 pm; Sun brunch to 2 pm. Res accepted. Lunch a la carte entrees: $5.75-$15.50. Complete meals: $5.50-$9.75; dinner a la carte entrees: $5.75-$15.50. Complete meals: $9.95-$15.50. Sun brunch $9.25. Child's menu. Cr cds: A, C, D, MC, V.

Gaspé Peninsula

Web www.tourisme.gouv.qc.ca
Information Tourism Québec, CP 979, Montréal H3C 2W3; 514/873-2015 or 800/363-7777

Jutting out into the Gulf of St. Laurent, the Gaspé Peninsula is a region of varying landforms including mountains, plateaus, beaches, and cliffs. It is blessed with abundant and rare wildlife and some unique flora, including 12-foot-high (4-meter), centuries-old fir trees. Landscapes are incredibly beautiful. The rivers, teeming with trout, flow to meet the salmon coming from the sea. Called "Gespeg" (meaning "land's end") by the aborigines, the area was settled primarily by Basque, Breton, and Norman fishermen, whose charming villages may be seen clinging to the shore beneath the gigantic cliffs. The French influence is strong; English is spoken in few villages.

With the exception of suggested side trips, the entire Gaspé Peninsula Auto Tour follows Highway 132, making it very easy to follow. Until this highway was developed, access to most of the peninsula was only by boat, accounting for much of its unspoiled character.

Auto Tour

RIVIÈRE-DU-LOUP

Rivière-du-Loup is an educational, administrative, and commercial center offering remarkable panoramas by virtue of its location on a rocky spur overlooking the majestic St. Lawrence River. In the center of town is a 98-ft (30-m) waterfall, which for many years provided the town with electrical power. Excursions to the islands of the St. Lawrence River (or *Fleuve St.-Laurent*), whale-watching trips, the Musée du Bas-St.-Laurent, and the public beach and marina at the "Pointe" of Rivière-du-Loup constitute points of particular interest in this region.

For further information contact Association Touristique du Bas St.-Laurent, 148 rue Froser, Rivière-du-Loup G5R 1C8; 418/867-3015 or 800/563-5268.

Hunting and freshwater and deep sea fishing are popular activities. Whale-watching tours are conducted by Croisières Navimex; phone 418/867-3361. A ferry may be taken across the St. Lawrence River to St.-Siméon from mid-Apr-early Jan. For schedule, fees phone 418/862-9545 or 514/849-4466. Travel 25 miles (40 km) to

TROIS-PISTOLES

Named for three old French coins, supposedly the price of a silver cup that fell into the river here, this well-known resort is an important port for tourist fishing. Found here are an imposing church built between 1882-87, and the **Musée St.-Laurent**, at 552 rue Notre Dame O, displaying antique cars, farm equipment, and various antiques (mid-June-mid-Sep; fee). For further information phone 418/851-2345.

Three islands off the coast are bird sanctuaries. **Île-aup-Basques**, the largest, shows restored furnaces used long ago by the Basque fishermen to extract oil from whales. Île-aup-Basques and the two smaller islands, the Îles Rasades, shelter blue herons, gulls, eider ducks, cormorants, and many other birds. Naturalists, bird-watchers, and photographers are allowed to visit Île-aup-Basques with permission of the warden, in groups of five or more (mid-June-mid-Oct; fee). Phone 418/851-1202. Whales and seals also visit off this coast each summer and autumn. ¢¢¢¢ Continue driving along the coast 38 miles (61 km) to

RIMOUSKI

Established in 1696, one-quarter of this center of the Lower St. Lawrence region was destroyed by fire in 1950, yet no traces of the damage remain today. Its large and important harbor is open all year. The beach at Ste.-Luce and Lepage Park with its monument to Lepage, the first settler, are places to see, as is the covered bridge at Mont-Lebel on the Rivière Neigette.

The **Musée Régional de Rimouski**, 35 rue Germain O, is located in the third Catholic church of Rimouski (1824); it houses a National Arts Center with major national, local, and regional events and expositions; arts, crafts. Phone 418/724-2272.

Inland via Road 232 and a local road, you may take a small side excursion to Réserve Faunique de Rimouski, approximately 30 miles (48 km) to the south. Here you will find 284 square miles (735 sq km) of beautiful area with camping, picnicking, nature interpretation, hunting, fishing, and boating; phone 418/779-2212 or 800/665-6527. Return via the same routes to Hwy 132 and follow it 19 mi (31 km) to

STE.-FLAVIE

This farming and resort village is indeed the Gateway to Gaspé and the Atlantic provinces. From Ste.-Flavie, along Highway 132, around to the town of Percé, is some of the most incredibly beautiful scenery to be found anywhere. Enjoying this remarkable landscape, follow the highway 208 miles (335 km) around to the very tip of the Gaspé to Forillon National Park.

A few interesting sights on your way include **Jardins de Métis** at Grand-Métis, a few miles east of Ste.-Flavie. The 40-acre (16-hectare) Reford Estate comprising Jardins de Métis is a British-style garden. There are alpine shrubs, perennial and annual plants, some exotic species, and many native plants. A section of wild and aquatic plants has been started and a waterfall-fed stream meanders through the garden, spanned by small bridges. Expanses of green lawn accented by coniferous and deciduous trees complete the lovely setting, surrounding the

Gaspé Peninsula

Reford Villa, a distinctive 37-room mansion now housing a museum, restaurant, and craft shop. The gardens are unique in North America because more than 800 species and 100,000 plants have been successfully cultivated in this northern climate. Visits to mansion museum (fee), natural harbor and picnic grounds. (1st wkend June-Sep, daily) Phone 418/775-2221. ¢¢

Along Highway 132, about 32 mi (51 km), you pass through the town of Matane, where you may see a salmon migration channel right in the middle of town, or stop at the lighthouses and tourist information office in Musée du Vieux Phare (Old Lighthouse) at 968 du Phare O (June-Labour Day, daily). At St.-Anne-des-Monts, 57 miles (91 km) farther, you reach the first access route, Road 299, to **Parc de la Gaspésie** (Gaspesian Park), a vast area noted for its rugged terrain, mountain excursions, panoramic mountain rides, and summit climbs; also fishing, canoeing, hiking, cross-country skiing; phone 418/763-3301. Returning to Hwy 132 and traveling 70 miles (112 km), you will come to the town of Grande-Vallée. Watch for the many bread ovens along the highway. The final 38-mile (61-km) drive brings you to your intended destination.

PARC NATIONAL FORILLON

This 95-square-mile (245-sq-km) park was established in 1970 to protect a special region of highly varied plant and animal life and geological formations. Escarpments rising over 500 feet (15 m) on the eastern shore and the Monts Notre-Dame, an eastern arm of the Appalachians rising to 1,700 feet (518 m), along with a rugged coastline, give the park a most varied topography. The area embraces the Lower St. Lawrence forest region and the Boreal Forest, with abundant and varied wildlife and vegetation. Unique plant ecosystems are found in the arctic Alpine flora of Cap Bon-Ami and the pioneer (sand dune) plants at Penouille.

Forillon National Park was developed to reflect both the unique coastal environment and the rich human history of the Gaspé region. Headquarters are at Gaspé, 122 de. Gaspé Blvd, phone 418/368-5505. Camping is available at Cap-Bon-Ami, Des Rosiers, and Petit-Gaspé. Visitors may enjoy nature walks, hiking trails, cross-country ski trails, snowshoeing, cycling, and picnic areas. Cruising and deep sea fishing expeditions (fee) also leave from here; whales and seals can be seen from the tip of the Forillon Peninsula.

Returning to the highway and rounding the tip of the peninsula for 42 miles (68 km), you will come to the deep seaport and large sheltered bay of

GASPÉ

Three salmon rivers (the Dartmouth, York, and St.-Jean) empty into the bay at Gaspé, site of **Piscicole de Gaspé**, a 100-year-old fish hatchery (the oldest in Canada) that raises and releases more than a million salmon and trout fry into the rivers of eastern Canada every year (mid-June-mid-Sep, daily). For fishing information contact Société de Gestion des rivières du Grand Gaspé, Inc, CP 826, Gaspé, G0C 1R0; 418/368-2324.

A religious, educational, and administrative center, Gaspé has a college and **Cathédrale de Gaspé**, a remarkable wooden cathedral, the only one in North America. It contains some very beautiful stained glass windows. In front of the cathedral is a granite cross erected during celebrations for the 400th anniversary of the discovery of Canada and commemorating the cross planted here by Jacques Cartier on his first voyage in 1534.

The **Musée de la Gaspésie**, located on Jacques Cartiers's Point on Highway 132, offers a panoramic view of the bay and Forillon Park. The museum presents a chronological history dating from the Gaspé. Exhibits feature traditional occupations and contemporary culture of the area. (Late June-Sep, daily; limited hrs rest of yr) Contact CP 680, G0C 1R0; 418/368-1534. ¢

Side trips available from Gaspé are by air to the picturesque and peaceful Magdalen Islands, 157 miles (253 km) to the east via Inter-Canadien. 40-min flight (Mon-Fri). For reservations phone Inter-Canadien (514/847-2211 or 800/363-7530). Deep sea fishing excursions at Forillon National Park are offered from late June to Labour Day. Gaspé is another of the entrances to Parc de la Gaspésie (Gaspesian Park) to the west, leading to Lake Madeleine.

Just before arriving at Percé, 47 miles (76 km) away, you pass through the village of Coin-du-Banc, where you may find agates on the cliff-hugging beach, view fossilized tree trunks, and see a beautiful waterfall set in sedimentary rock.

PERCÉ

One of the most astonishingly beautiful and interestingly situated towns is Percé, with its colossal rock formation, Rocher Percé (Percé Rock). The village takes the form of a semicircle surrounded left to right by Cap Blanc, 1,143-foot (375-m) Mont Sainte-Anne, 1,116-foot (340-m) Mont Blanc, Pic de l'Aurore (Peak of Dawn), Trois-Soeurs (Three Sisters), and Cap Barré and opening onto two bays, separated by two capes and Percé Rock. Jacques Cartier anchored his three ships behind this famed rock in July 1534.

Percé Rock, 288 feet (88 m) high, 1,421 feet (433 m) long and weighing approximately 400 million tons (406 million metric tons), is formed of siliceous limestone of the Devonian period, which means it contains many fossils. It resembles a large ship at anchor and is pierced by a large arch near one end, 18 feet (6 m) high, which gives the rock and town their names. Formerly joined to shore and providing shelter for a large cod fleet, the rock can now be reached at low tide across a gravel bar. Be sure to inquire about the tide schedule. Phone 418/782-2240.

Craft shops, painters' galleries, and fine food abound in this area, and deep sea fishing excursions leave from the harbor. A trail behind Mont Ste.-Anne leads to an area of great crevasses; lookout points are good from Pic de l'Aurore, and Côte Surprise and the southeast side of Mont Ste.-Anne.

Excursion boats leave daily (mid-May-early Oct) for trips around Percé Rock, landing at Bonaventure Island; phone 418/782-2974. **L'Île-Bonaventure Park** comprises the entire island, 2 miles (3.5 km) offshore. Rocky ledges and cliffs 250 feet (76 m) high give sanctuary to thousands of sea birds. The major inhabitants are kittiwakes, razor-billed auks, black guillemots, a few Arctic puffins, and especially gannets, with the largest and most accessible of the 22 known colonies in the world here. The island has rich and diverse vegetation. Climbs may be made to the cliff and four guided nature trails are available from mid-June-mid-Oct. Phone Gaspé, 418/782-2240; Percé (summer only), 418/782-2721.

Returning to the highway and traveling southwest and then west 161 mi (258 km) to Restigouche, more than a few points of interest may be noted on the way.

At **Cap-d'Espoir**, approximately 10 miles (16 km), and Anse-aux-Gascons, 33 miles (53 km) farther, agates may be found on the beautiful beaches. Striking red cliffs at Shigawake may be viewed about 18 miles (29 km) farther on. At Bonaventure, reached by proceeding 22 miles (38 km) and rounding the cape, are a church of granite built in 1960 and noteworthy Musée Acadien du Québec, on the highway.

Continuing along Highway 132 for another 78 miles (126 km), you will come to the deep seaport and large sheltered bay of

RESTIGOUCHE

A reservation and site of an ancient Recollet mission (1620) served by the Capuchin Fathers, Restigouche Reserve is today the location of a Ste.-Anne Shrine and museum in the monastery of the Capuchin Fathers. The church of Ste.-Anne is the 12th built on the site, the previous 11 having burned.

Pointe-à-la-Croix is a work site of the **Historic National Park Batsille-de-la-Ristigouche.** Archaeologists are reclaiming the 18th-century French supply ship *Machault*, scuttled during a battle in 1760. It has been underwater in front of the mission. Some cargo and structural elements have been excavated and are exhibited. Phone 418/788-5676. ¢¢

Turning northwest from Restigouche, the highway enters the Matapédia River Valley, which is tightly ensconced between mountains. The river flows in a deep hollow with steep embankments which separate the mass of the Chic-Chocs Mountains from the highland zone to the southwest. The most striking section of the valley begins at Causapscal, the earlier section of the road having followed the former Kempt military road, itself developed from an old indigenous track. Causapscal is noted for its covered bridges across the Matapédia River and its excellent salmon fishing. The Domaine Matamajaw, situated along the river, is the only historic Atlantic salmon sportfishing site in Québec; exhibitions are presented at the interpretation center, phone 418/756-5999.

Twenty-three miles (37 kilometers) beyond Causapscal you pass through the town of Val-Brillant (called "Queen of the Valley") with its Gothic church, one of the most beautiful religious structures in the region. Having traveled 94 miles (151 km) from Restigouche, you return again to Ste.-Flavie.

Granby

(E-6) *See also Montréal, Sherbrooke*

Pop 38,069 **Elev** 270 ft (82 m)
Area code 450
Web www.tourisme.granby.qc.ca
Information Tourism Granby, 650 Principale St, J2G 8L4; 450/372-7273 or 800/567-7273

Begun as a mission in 1824, with the first settlers arriving in 1813, Granby was named for an English nobleman, the Marquis of Granby. Only 45 miles (71 kilometers) east of Montréal, the town is a favorite excursion spot for Montréalers, with 18 beautiful parks containing a collection of old European fountains and its devotion to good food. Located on the north bank of the Yamaska River, Granby manufactures rubber products, candy, electrical products, and cement. Because of the abundance of maple groves, sugaring-off parties are a popular activity.

What to See and Do

Granby Zoological Garden. More than 1,000 animals of 225 species from every continent; education and African pavillions, amusement park. (May-Sep, daily) 525 rue Bourget. Phone 450/372-9113. ¢¢¢

Nature Interpretation Centre of Lake Boivin. Guided walking tours through woodland and marsh; concentrations of waterfowl and nature exhibits. (Daily) 700 rue Drummond. Phone 450/375-3861. **FREE**

Yamaska Provincial Park. Newly developed park with swimming, fishing, boating (rentals); paths, hiking, cross-country skiing (fee), picnicking, snack bar. Parking (fee). 3 mi (5 km) E. Phone 450/372-3204.

Annual Event

Granby International. Antique car show. Phone 450/777-1330. Last wkend July.

Resort

★★ **AUBERGE BROMONT.** *95 Rue Montmorency (G2H 2G1), Hwy 139 to*

CAN 10E, Exit 78 and follow tourist signs. 450/534-1199; fax 450/534-1700; toll-free 888/276-6668. 50 rms, 3 story. No elvtr. S, D $98-$118; MAP avail; family rates; ski, golf plans. Crib free. TV; cable (premium). Pool; poolside serv, lifeguard. Dining rm (public by res) 7 am-3 pm, 6-10 pm. Bar 11-3 am. Ck-out noon, ck-in 4 pm. Business servs avail. Concierge serv. Lighted tennis, pro. 18-hole golf, greens fee $26-$33. Downhill ski 1 mi; x-country ski on site (rentals). Exercise equipt. Some minibars. Cr cds: C, D, ER, MC, V.

Hull

(see Ottawa, Ontario)

The Laurentians (D-6 - E-4)

Information Laurentian Tourism Association, 14142 rue de la Chapelle, RR #1, St. Jérôme, PQ, J7Z 5T4; 450/436-8532 or 800/561-6673

The Laurentian region, just 45 miles from Montréal, is a rich tourist destination. Surrounded by forests, lakes, rivers, and the Laurentian Mountains, this area provides ample settings for open-air activities year-round. Water sports abound in summer, including canoeing, kayaking, swimming, rafting, scuba diving, and excellent fishing. Hunting, golfing, horseback riding, and mountain climbing are also popular in warmer months, as is bicycling along the 125-mile P'tit train du Nord trail. Brilliant fall colors lead into a winter ideal for snow lovers. The Laurentian region boasts a huge number of downhill ski centers, 600 miles of cross-country trails, and thousands of miles of snowmobiling trails. The territory of the Laurentian tourist zone is formed on the south by the Outaouais River, des Deux-Montagnes Lake, and the Milles-Iles River. On the east, its limits stretch from the limit of Terrebonne to Entrelacs. It is bounded on the north by Ste.-Anne du Lac and Baskatong Reservoir and on the west by the towns of Des Ruisseaux, Notre-Dame de Pontmain, and Notre Dame du Laus. Places listed are Mont Tremblant Provincial Park, St. Jérôme, and St.-Jovite.

Montréal (E-5)

Settled 1642 **Pop** 1,005,000
Elev 117 ft (36 m) **Area code** 514
Web www.tourisme.gouv.qc.ca

Information Tourisme-Québec, CP 979, H3C 2W3; 514/873-2015 or 800/363-7777

Blessed by its location on an island at the junction of the St. Lawrence and Ottawa rivers, Montréal has served for more than three centuries as a gigantic trading post; its harbor can accommodate more than 100 ocean-going vessels. While it is a commercial, financial, and industrial center, Montréal is also an internationally recognized patron of the fine arts, hosting several acclaimed festivals attended by enthusiasts worldwide.

A stockaded indigenous settlement called Hochelaga when it was discovered in 1535 by Jacques Cartier, the area contained a trading post by the early 1600s; but it was not settled as a missionary outpost until 1642 when the Frenchman Paul de Chomedey, Sieur de Maisonneuve, and a group of settlers, priests, and nuns founded Ville-Morie. This later grew as an important fur trading center and from here men such as Jolliet, Marquette, Duluth, and Father Hennepin set out on their western expeditions. Montréal remained under French rule until 1763 when Canada was surrendered as a possession to the British under the Treaty of Paris. For seven months during the American Revolution, Montréal was occupied by Americans, but it was later regained by the British.

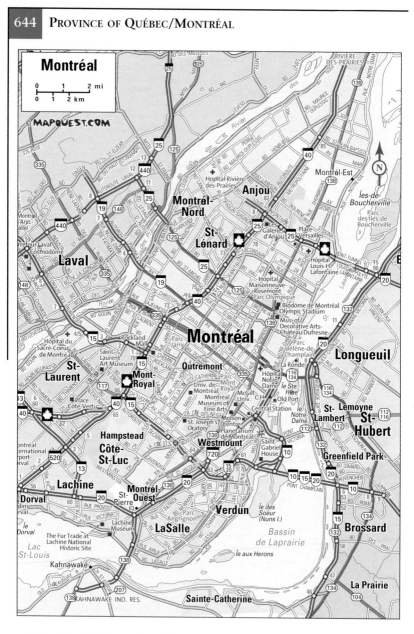

Today Montréal is an elegantly sophisticated city. Two-thirds of its people are French-speaking, and its French population is the largest outside of Europe. It is made up of two parts: the Old City, in the same area as the original Ville-Morie, which is a maze of narrow streets, restored buildings, and old houses, best seen on foot; and the modern Montréal, with its many skyscrapers, museums, theaters, nearly 7,600 restaurants, and glittering nightlife.

There is an underground Montréal also, with miles of shops, galleries, restaurants, and access to one of the most unique subway systems in the world. Each station has been decorated by a different architect in a different style, and visitors have called it "the largest underground art gallery in the world." Mont-Royal rises from the center of the island-city to a height of 764 feet (233 meters), affording a panoramic view. Calèches (horse-drawn carriages) provide tourists with a charming means of viewing the city and are, with the exception of bicycles, the only vehicles permitted in some areas of Mount Royal Park. Adjacent to the park is the Westmount area, a section of meandering roads and charming older homes of the early 1900s with delightful English-style gardens.

In 1967, Montréal hosted Expo '67, celebrating Canada's centennial. The summer Olympic games were held here in 1976.

What to See and Do

Angrignon Park. 262 acres (106 hectares) with more than 21,600 trees; lagoons, river; playground, picnicking, bicycling, ice-skating, cross-country skiing. Park (daily). 3400 des Trinitaires Blvd. Phone 514/872-3816. Zoo ¢¢

Byzantine Museum. On Gallery for icons and other works by Romanian-born artist Rosette Mociornitza, produced in the unique style of the Byzantine period using old wood, traditional techniques, materials from Europe. Works may be purchased. (Daily, by appt) 6780 Biarritz Ave, Brossard. Phone 450/656-0188. **FREE**

Casino Montréal. The Casino de Montréal offers guests a variety of games, with 112 gaming tables as well as 2,700 slot machines. (Open 24 hrs) 1 Ave du Casino, housed in Expo 67's famous French Pavilion. Phone 514/392-2746 or 800/665-2274.

Dorchester Square. In the center of Montréal, this park is a popular meeting place. Also here is Mary Queen of the World Cathedral, a ⅓-scale replica of St. Peter's in Rome. Also information centre of Montréal and Tourisme Québec. René-Lévesque Blvd O between Peel & Metcalfe Sts. **FREE**

Fort Lennox. 45 mi (72.4 km) SE.

iSci Centre. Interactive science exhibits, IMAX, IMAX 3D, and the first immersion theater (interactive video game on giant screen) in Canada. Also boutiques, restaurants. (Daily) 2 de la Commune Street. Phone 514/496-4724 or 877/496-4724. ¢¢¢¢

La Fontaine Park. Illuminated fountain, playground, monuments; 2

lakes, paddleboats; cycling trail. (Mid-May-Oct, daily) Winter activities incl ice-skating, cross-country skiing; hockey rink. Sherbrooke St & Papineau St. Phone 514/872-2644. **FREE**

Maison St.-Gabriel. Built in late 17th century as a farm; also served as school for Marguerite Bourgeoys, founder of the Sisters of the Congrégatun de Notre-Dame, who looked after young French girls who were to marry the early colonists. Period furnishings; altar built in 1700s; items of French-Canadian heritage incl woodcuts from ancient churches and chapels. (Mid-Apr-mid-Dec, Tues-Sun) 2146 Dublin Pl. Phone 514/935-8136. ¢¢

McGill University. (1821) 31,000 students. The 80-acre main campus is set between the lower slopes of Mt Royal and the downtown commercial district. Guided tours by appt (free). Welcome Centre at 805 Sherbrooke St O. Phone 514/398-4455.

⚔ **Montréal Botanical Garden.** Within 180 acres (73 hectares) grow more than 26,000 species and varieties of plants; 30 specialized sections incl rose, perennial plant, heath gardens, flowery brook, bonsai, carnivorous plants, and arboretum; one of the world's largest orchid collections; seasonal flower shows. The bonsai and penjing collections are two of the most diversified in North America. Chinese and Japanese gardens; restaurant, tea rm. Parking (fee). (Daily) 4101 Sherbrooke St E. Phone 514/872-1400. ¢¢ Also here (and incl in admission) is

Insectarium de Montreal. Collection of more than 350,000 insects in a bldg designed to resemble a stylized insect. Interactive and participatory concept takes visitors through aviaries and living displays in 6 geographically themed areas. Hands-on exhibits; Outside Gardens; butterfly aviary (summer); traveling exhibits; children's amusement center. (Daily)

The Montréal Museum of Fine Arts. (Musée des beaux-arts de Montréal) Canada's oldest art museum (founded 1860) has a wide variety of displays, ranging from Egyptian statues to 20th-century abstracts. Cana-

dian section features old Québec furniture, silver, and paintings. (Tues-
Sun; closed Jan 1, Dec 25) 1379-80
Sherbrooke St O. Phone 514/285-
2000. ¢¢¢¢-¢¢¢¢¢

Montréal Planetarium. Astronomy
shows: projectors create all features
of the night sky; special effects.
(Tues-Sun) Phone 514/872-4530. ¢¢

Mount Royal Park. On #430 acres
(174 hectares) in center of city; lake,
picnicking, bicycling, calèche tours,
winter sports (skating, downhill/cross-
country skiing); observation point at
chalet lookout. Permanent exhibits
at Chalet de la Montagne, a nature-
appreciation center (daily). Côte des
Neiges & Remembrance Rds. Phone
514/843-8240. **FREE**

Museum of Decorative Arts. Historic
mansion Chateau Dufresne (1918),
partially restored and refurnished,
now houses international exhibitions
of glass, textiles, and ceramic art;
changing exhibits. (Wed-Sun; closed
Jan 1, Dec 25) 2200 rue Crescent.
Phone 514/284-1252. ¢¢

⭐ **Old (Vieux) Montréal.** The city of
Montréal evolved from the small settlement of Ville-Marie founded by de
Maisonneuve in 1642. The largest
concentration of 19th-century bldgs
in North America is found here; several original dwellings remain, while
many other locations are marked by
bronze plaques throughout the area.
The expansion of this settlement led
to what is now known as Old Montréal. The area roughly forms a 100-
acre (40-hectare) quadrangle which
corresponds approx to the area
enclosed within the original fortifications. Bounded by McGill, Berri,
Notre-Dame Sts and the St. Lawrence
River. Some major points of interest
are

   Place d'Armes. A square of great
   historical importance and center of
   Old Montréal. The founders of
   Ville-Marie encountered the Iroquois here in 1644 and rebuffed
   them. In the square's center is a
   statue of de Maisonneuve, first
   governor of Montréal, and at one
   end is the St. Sulpice seminary
   (1685) with an old wooden clock
   (1710), oldest bldg in Montréal. St.
   Sulpice & Notre-Dame Sts. At 119
   St. Jacques St is the **Bank of Montréal.** This magnificent bldg contains a museum with collection of

currency, mechanical savings
banks, photographs, reproduction
of old-fashioned teller's cage.
(Mon-Fri; closed hols) Some of the
most important financial houses of
the city are grouped around the
square. Phone 514/877-6810.
FREE Across the square is

Notre-Dame Basilica. (1824) In
1672, a church described as "one
of the most beautiful churches in
North America" was erected on
the present Notre-Dame St. When
this became inadequate for the
growing parish, a new church
designed by New Yorker James
O'Donnell was built. It was completed in 1829 and 2 towers and
interior decorations were added
later. *Le Gros Bourdon,* a bell cast
in 1847 and weighing 24,780 lbs,
is in Perseverance Tower; there is a
10-bell chime in Temperance
Tower. Built of Montréal limestone, the basilica is Neo-Gothic
in design with a beautiful main
altar, pulpit, and numerous statues, paintings, and stained-glass
windows. (Daily; concerts in summer) 110 Notre-Dame St O. **FREE**

Notre-Dame Basilica Museum.
Works of religious and historical
art; old furniture, statues; local
folklore paintings. (*Closed for renovation; opening in 2001*) 424 St.
Sulpice St. Phone 514/842-2925. ¢

St.-Paul St. Oldest street in Montréal. The mansions of Ville-Marie
once stood here but they have been
replaced by commercial houses and
office bldgs. Here is **Notre-Dame-
de-Bonsecours Church** (1773).
Founded in 1657 and rebuilt 115
yrs later, this is one of the oldest
churches still standing in the city;
tower has view of the river and city;
museum (fee) has objects pertaining to early settlers. Miniature ships
suspended from vault in church are
votive offerings from sailors who
worshiped here.

Château Ramezay. (1705) Historical museum, once the home of the
governors of Montréal, the West
Indies Co of France, and the
Governors-General of British North
America. Furniture, paintings, costumes, porcelain, manuscripts, art
objects of the 17th-19th centuries.
(Tues-Sun) 280 Notre-Dame E, in

front of City Hall. Phone 514/861-3708. ¢¢¢

Place Jacques-Cartier. Named for the discoverer of Canada, this was once a busy marketplace. Oldest monument in the city, the Nelson Column (1809) is in the square's upper section. Notre-Dame St.

Olympic Park. Stadium was site of 1976 Summer Olympic Games and is now home of Montréal Expos baseball team and les Alouettes de Montréal football team; observatory of world's tallest inclined tower. Cafeteria, souvenir shop. Tours (daily). 4141 Pierre de Coubertin St. Phone 514/252-8687. Tours (with tower) ¢¢ Adj stadium is

Biodôme de Montréal. Former Olympic Velodrome has been transformed into an environmental museum that combines elements of botanical garden, aquarium, zoo, and nature center. Four ecosystems—Laurentian Forest, Tropical Forest, Polar World, and St.-Laurent Marine—sustain thousands of plants and small animals. Incl 500-m Nature Path with text panels and maps, interpreters; and discovery rm "Naturalia." (Daily; closed Jan 1, Dec 25) 4777 Pierre de Coubertin St. Phone 514/868-3000. ¢¢

Parc Safari. Features 750 animals, rides, and shows; children's theater and play area, swimming beach; drive-through wild animal reserve; picnicking, restaurants, boutiques. (Mid-May-mid-Sep, daily) 33 mi (56 km) S on Hwy 15 to exit 6, then follow zoo signs. Phone 800/465-8724. ¢¢¢¢

Parc des Îles. Two islands in the middle of the St. Lawrence River; access via Jacques-Cartier Bridge or Metro subway. Île Ste.-Hélène (St. Helen's Island) was the main anchor site for Expo '67; now a 342-acre (138-hectare) multipurpose park with 3 swimming pools; picnicking, cross-country skiing, snowshoeing. Île Notre-Dame (Notre Dame Island), to the south, was partly built up from the river bed and was an important activity site for Expo '67. Here is Gilles-Villeneuve Formula One race track (see ANNUAL EVENTS); also beach, paddle boats, windsurfing, and sailing. Some fees.

(Daily) Phone 514/872-6093. Located here are

The Old Fort. (1820-24). Oldest remaining fortification of Montréal, only the arsenal, powder magazine, and barracks bldg still stand. Two military companies dating from the 18th century, La Compagnie Franche de la Marine and the 78th Fraser Highlanders, perform colorful military drills and parades (late June-Aug, Wed-Sun). ¢¢ In the fort's arsenal is

David M. Stewart Museum. Artifacts trace Canadian history from the 15th century through maps, firearms, kitchen utensils, engravings, navigational and scientific instruments. (Wed-Mon; closed Jan 1, Dec 25) Phone 514/861-6701. ¢¢¢

Floral Park. Site of Les Floralies Internationales 1980; now permanent, it displays collection of worldwide flowers and plants. Walking trails; pedal boats, canoeing; picnic area, snack bar, and restaurant. Some fees. (Third wk June-mid-Sep, daily) Île Notre-Dame. **FREE**

Théâtre des Lilas. Open-air theater with a variety of shows, including music and dance. Île Notre-Dame.

La Ronde. A 135-acre amusement park with 35 rides, incl 132-ft (40-m) high wooden roller coaster; arcades, entertainment on a floating stage; waterskiing; live cartoon characters, children's village; circus, boutiques, and restaurants. (June-Labour Day, daily; May, wkends; closed 4 days late Aug) Île Ste.-Hélène. Phone 514/872-4537 or 800/797-4537. ¢¢¢¢

Place des Arts. This 4-theater complex is the heart of Montréal's artistic life. L'Opéra de Montréal, the Montréal Symphony Orchestra, les Grands Ballets Canadiens, and La Compagnie Jean-Duceppe theatrical troupe have their permanent home here. Other entertainment incl chamber music, recitals, jazz, folk singers, variety shows, music hall, theater, musicals, and modern and classical dance. Corner of Ste.-Catherine and Jeonne-Mance. Phone 514/790-2787 (recording) or 514/842-2112 (tickets).

☒ **Pointe-à-Callière, the Montréal Museum of Archaeology and History.** Deals with the founding and development of the City of Montréal. Built in 1992 over the actual site of the founding of Montréal, the main museum bldg, the **Éperon**, actually rests on pillars built around ruins dating from the town's first cemetery and its earliest fortifications, which are now in its basement. Two balconies overlook this archaeological site and a 16-min multimedia show is presented using the actual remnants as a backdrop. From here visitors continue underground, amid still more remnants, to the **Archaeological Crypt**, a structure that allows access to many more artifacts and remains; architectural models beneath a transparent floor illustrate 5 different periods in the history of Place Royale. The **Old Customs House (Ancienne-Douane)** houses thematic exhibits on Montréal in the 19th-20th centuries. Permanent and changing exhibits. Cafe; gift shop. (Tues-Sun; extended hrs summer) 350 Place Royale, corner of Place Youville in Old Montréal. Phone 514/872-9150. ¢¢¢

Professional sports.

National League baseball (Montréal Expos). Olympic Stadium. 4549 Pierre de Coubertin St. Phone 514/790-1245.

NHL (Montréal Canadiens). Molson Center. 1260 La Gaucheti`ere O. Phone 514/932-2582.

Rafting Montréal. Rafting and hydrojet trips on the Lachine Rapids of the St. Lawrence River. (May-Sep, daily; res required) Phone 514/767-2230 or 800/324-7238. ¢¢¢¢

Sightseeing tours.

Calèche tours. Horse-drawn carriages depart from Place d'Armes, Mount Royal Park, or Old Port of Montréal. ¢¢¢

Gray Line bus tours. Contact 1140 Wellington St, H3C 1V8. Phone 514/934-1222.

Montréal Harbour Cruises. Various guided cruises and dinner excursions (1-4 hrs); bar service. Res advised. (May-mid-Oct, daily) Contact Croisières Vieure-Port de Montréal, Quai de l'Horlage, C.P. 1085, Succ. Place d'Armes, H2Y 3J6. Depart from Quai de L'Horloge in Old Montréal, at the foot of Berri St and from Quai Jacque Cartier. Phone 514/842-9300 or 800/667-3131. ¢¢¢¢

St. Joseph's Oratory. Chapel (1904), crypt church (1916); museum. Main church is a famous shrine attracting more than 2 million pilgrims yearly; basilica founded 1924; built in Italian Renaissance style; dome towers over city. 56-bell carillon made in France is outstanding. (Daily) 3800 Queen Mary Rd, on N slope of Mt Royal. Phone 514/733-8211. **FREE**

Université de Montréal. (1920) 58,000 students. On N slope of Mt Royal. 2900 boul Édouord-Montpetit. Phone 514/343-6111.

Annual Events

Canadian Grand Prix. Parc des Îles. Formula One racing at Gilles-Villeneuve track, Îles Notre-Dame. Phone 514/350-0000. Early June.

Antiques Bonaventure. East Exhibition Hall, Place Bonaventure. Exhibits of private and public collections for sale; more than 100 dealers participate. Phone 514/397-2222. Mid-June.

Fête Nationale. St.-Jean-Baptiste, patron saint of the French Canadians, is honored with 3 days of festivities surrounding provincial holiday. Celebration incl street festivals, bonfire, fireworks, musical events. June 24.

Montréal Jazz Festival. Downtown. More than 1,200 musicians and a million music lovers from around the world gather to celebrate jazz. Ten-day fest incl more than 500 indoor and outdoor concerts. Phone 514/871-1881 or 888/515-0515. Late June-early July.

Just for Laughs. International comedy festival. Phone 514/845-2322. Mid-July.

World Film Festival. Contact 1432 Bleury St; 514/848-3883. Late Aug-early Sep.

Additional Visitor Information

Québec Tourism, PO Box 979, Montréal, H3C 2W3; phone 800/363-7777 or in person at Infotouriste, 1001 rue du Square-Dorchester (between Peel & Metcalfe Sts); also office at Old Montréal, Place Jacques-

Cartier, 174 Notre-Dame St E; all have helpful information for tourists. The Consulate General of the United States is located on 1155 rue St.-Alexandre, at Placé Felip-Martin, at the corner of René Levesque Blvd; phone 514/398-9695. Public transportation is provided by the Societé de Transport de la Communauté Urbaine de Montréal (STCUM), phone 514/288-6287.

Motels/Motor Lodges

★★ **AUBERGES WANDLYN.** *7200 Sherbrooke St E (H1N 1E7).* 514/256-1613; fax 514/256-5150. 123 rms, 2 story. June-Oct: S $63-$89.50; D $63-$99.50; each addl $10; suites $99.50-$129.50; under 18 free; lower rates rest of yr. TV; cable. Heated pool; poolside serv; lifeguard. Restaurant 7 am-2 pm. Bar 4 pm-midnight. Ck-out noon. Meeting rms. Business servs avail. Balconies. Cr cds: A, C, D, DS, ER, MC, V.

★ **COCONUT.** *7531 rue Notre Dame (G9B 1L7).* 819/377-3221; fax 819/377-1344; toll-free 800/838-3221. 39 rms. Mid-June-Sep: S $42-$65; D $42-$70; each addl $5; suites $118; under 18 free; lower rates rest of yr. TV; cable (premium). Ck-out noon. Meeting rms. Refrigerator avail. Cr cds: A, C, D, ER, MC, V.

★★★ **HOSTELLERIE LES TROIS TILLEULS.** *290 Richelieu St (G0L 2E0), 26 mi SE on Hwy 20E, Exit 112, then 5 mi N on Hwy 223.* 514/856-7787; fax 514/584-3146. Email host.3tilleuls@ sympatico.ca; saveurs.essympatico.ca/ encroy/quebec/tilleuls.htm. 24 rms, 3 story. S $92-$125; D $110-$145; each addl $20; suites $225-$390. Crib free. TV; cable (premium), VCR. Heated pool. Restaurant (see also LES TROIS TILLEULS). Bar 11-2 am. Ck-out noon. Meeting rms. Business center. In-rm modem link. Lighted tennis. X-country ski 10 mi. Hunting trips. Private marina. Boat tours. Some in-rm whirlpools. Balconies. Golf nearby. In 1880 farmhouse. On Richelieu River. Cr cds: A, C, D, ER, MC, V.

★★★ **HOSTELLERIE RIVE GAUCHE.** *1810 Richelieu Blvd (J3G 4S4), Hwy 20 E Exit 112, jct Hwy 223.* 450/467-4477; fax 450/467-0525. 22 rms, 3 story. S $92-$110; D $125-$145; each addl $20; suites $225-$235. Crib free. TV; cable (premium). Pool. Restaurant 7:30 am-10:30 pm. Bar 11 am-midnight. Ck-out noon. Meeting rms. Business servs avail. Lighted tennis. X-country ski 8 mi. Balconies. View of Richelieu River and Mont Ste.-Hilaire. Cr cds: A, D, ER, MC, V.

★ **HOTEL LE SAINTE-ANDRE.** *1285 rue Ste.-Andre (H2L 3T1).* 514/849-7070; fax 514/849-8167; toll-free 800/265-7071. 61 rms, 4 story. May-Oct: S $64.50; D $69.50; each addl $5; lower rates rest of yr. TV; cable. Parking free. Complimentary continental bkfst. Restaurants nearby. Ck-out noon. Business servs avail. Cr cds: A, C, D, DS, ER, MC, V.

★★ **QUALITY HOTEL DORVAL.** *7700 Cote de Liesse (H4T 1E7), near Dorval Intl Airport.* 514/731-7821; fax 514/731-1538; toll-free 800/361-2643. Email qualityyul@aol.com, www. qualityinn.com. 159 rms, 4 story, 47 kit suites. S, D $145-$170; kit suites $185-$395. each addl $10; wkend rates. Parking. Crib free. Small pet accepted. TV; cable (premium), In-rm movies. Outdoor heated pool; 2 whirlpools. Restaurant 6:30 am-2 pm, 6-11 pm. Bar 5 pm-1 am. Ck-out noon. Coin lndry. Meeting rms. Business servs avail. Concierge serv. Valet serv. Free airport transportation. Exercise equipt; sauna. Health club privileges. Massage. Minibars. Cr cds: A, C, D, DS, ER, JCB, MC, V.

★★ **QUALITY INN AND SUITES.** *6680 Taschereau Blvd (J4W 1M8), E on Hwy 10, Exit 8E.* 450/671-7213; fax 450/671-7041; res 800/267-3837. 91 rms, 3 story, 9 suites. May-Oct: S, D $75-$85; each addl $10; suites $165; under 18 free; lower rates rest of yr. TV. Pool. Complimentary continental bkfst. Restaurant 11:30 am-10:30 pm. Bar. Ck-out noon. Meeting rms.

Business servs avail. Health club privileges. Cr cds: A, ER, MC, V.

Hotels

★★ **CHATEAU ROYAL HOTEL SUITES.** *1420 Crescent St (H3G 2B7), Downtown. 514/848-0999; fax 514/ 848-1891; toll-free 800/363-0335. Email reservations@chateauroyal.com; www.chateauroyal.com.* 112 kit. suites, 21 story. May-Oct S, D $112-$214; each addl $20; under 14 free; wkend rates. Special seasonal rates avail. Crib free. Indoor garage. Valet parking. TV; cable (premium); Spectravision movies. Complimentary coffee/tea in rms. Restaurant 7-1 am. Rm serv to 11 pm. Ck-out noon. Ck-in 3 pm. Meeting rms. Business servs avail. Coin lndry. Some microwaves. Balconies. Walking distance to Museum of Fine Arts, Molson Centre, Casino, Plaza des Arts. Cr cds: A, C, D, DS, ER, MC, V.

★★★ **CHATEAU VAUDREUIL.** *21700 Trans-Canada Hwy (J7V 8P3), Exit 36. 450/455-0955; fax 450/455-6617.* 117 rms, 6 story, 103 suites. May-Dec: S, D $125-$165; each addl $20; suites $135-$400; under 16 free; wkend rates; higher rates special events; lower rates rest of yr. Crib free. TV; cable, VCR (movies). Indoor pool; whirlpool. Complimentary coffee in rms. Restaurant 6:30 am-11 pm. Bar 11-2 am; entertainment Tues-Sun. Ck-out noon. Meeting rms. Business servs avail. In-rm modem link. Concierge serv. Tennis. Downhill/x-country ski 15 mi. Exercise equipt; sauna. Minibars. Some balconies. On lake. Cr cds: A, D, DS, ER, MC, V.

★★★ **CHATEAU VERSAILLES.** *1659 Sherbrooke St W (H3H 1E3), At Ste.-Mathieu. 514/933-3611; fax 514/933-6867; toll-free 800/361-3664.* 176 rms, 3-14 story. S, D $107-$190; each addl $15; suites $325-$350; under 16 free. Crib free. Heated garage; valet $12.50. TV; cable. Coffee in rms. Restaurant (see also CHAMPS ELYSEES). Meeting rms. In-rm modem link. Some minibars. Comprised of 4 renovated Victorian

houses and a 14-story tower. Cr cds: A, D, DS, ER, MC, V.

★ **DAYS INN MIDTOWN.** *1005 Guy St (H3H 2K4), at René Levesque Blvd W. 514/938-4611; fax 514/938-8718; toll-free 800/567-0880. www.daysinn. qc.ca.* 205 rms, 7 story. May-Oct: S $129; D $139; each addl $10; suites $200-$350; under 12 free; wkend rates; lower rates rest of yr. Crib free. Parking (fee). TV; cable. Heated pool; lifeguard. Restaurant 7 am-10 pm; closed Nov-Apr. Ck-out noon. Meeting rms. Business servs avail. Gift shop. Cr cds: A, D, DS, ER, MC, V.

★★ **DELTA.** *1620 Notre Dame St (G9A 6E5). 819/376-1991; fax 819/372-5975. www.deltahotels.com.* 159 rms, 12 story. S, D $72-$150; each addl $15; suites $150-$300; under 18 free; higher rates Formula Grand Prix (Aug). Crib free. Pet accepted. TV; cable. Indoor pool; whirlpool. Coffee in rms. Restaurant 7 am-9:30 pm. Bar 4 pm-midnight. Ck-out noon. Meeting rms. Business servs avail. In-rm modem link. Gift shop. Free garage parking. Downhill ski 15 mi; x-country ski 5 mi. Exercise equipt; sauna. Massage. Minibars; some bathrm phones. Cr cds: A, D, DS, ER, JCB, MC, V.

★★ **DELTA MONTREAL.** *475 President Kennedy Ave (H3A 1J4). 514/286-1986; fax 514/284-4342; toll-free 877/ 286-1986. www.deltamontreal.com.* 446 rms, 7 suites, 23 story. S, D $205-$220; each addl $20; suites $450-$950; under 12 free; wkend packages. Crib free. Pet accepted, some restrictions, fee. Covered parking $12/day. TV; cable (premium), Sony Playstation. Complimentary coffee, tea in rms. Heated pools indoor/outdoor, whirlpool. Supervised children's activities; ages 4-12. Restaurant 7 am-9:30 pm. Rm serv 5 am-midnight. Bar 11:00-midnight. Ck-out noon. Ck-in 3 pm. Meeting rms. Business center. In-rm modem link. Fax machines in suites. Concierge serv. Barber, beauty shop. Fitness center, exercise rm, sauna, spa. Massage. Minibars. Balconies. Suites, meeting rooms, bars, rooms renovated in 1999. Located in the heart of downtown Montréal, near Cultural Arts

Center, Place des Arts. Cr cds: A, C, D, DS, ER, JCB, MC, V.

⬛ 🦮 ≈ 🛋 ⤢ 🔥 🚶

★★★★ **HILTON MONTREAL BONAVENTURE.** *1 Place Bonaventure (H5A 1E4). 514/878-2332; fax 514/878-3881; res 800/HILTONS. Email info@hiltonmontreal.com; www. hiltonmontreal.com.* Penthouse life is glorious inside this 393-room hotel perched on top of the Place Bonaventure Exhibition Hall. There are acres of rooftop gardens to explore and a year-round outdoor pool. The central city location is perfect for sightseeing in Old Montreal, gambling at the casino, or shopping the underground boutiques. 393 rms, 2 story. S, D $190-$340 Can; under 18 free. Crib free. Pet accepted, some restrictions (call). TV, cable, radio. Two restaurants. Bar. Heated pool. Exercise rm. Concierge serv; valet. Business center. Suites provide bathrobe, kit, wet bar, fax. Ck-out noon, ck-in 3 pm. Cr cds: A, C, D, DS, ER, MC, V.

≈ 🚶 🔥

★★ **HOLIDAY INN SELECT CENTRE VILLE.** *99 Viger Ave W (H2Z 1E9). 514/878-9888; fax 514/878-6341.* 235 rms, 8 story. May-Oct: S $160-$185; D $170-$195; each addl $10; suites $399-$499; family, wkly, wkend rates; lower rates rest of yr. Crib free. Garage fee in/out. TV; cable. Indoor pool; whirlpool. Coffee in rms. Restaurant 6:30 am-11 pm. Bar 11-1 am. Ck-out noon. Meeting rms. Business center. In-rm modem link. Gift shop. Barber, beauty shop. Exercise equipt; saunas, steam rm. Massage. Some balconies. Pagoda-topped bldg in Chinatown area. Cr cds: A, C, D, DS, ER, JCB, MC, V.

⬛ ≈ 🛋 ⤢ 🔥 **SC** 🚶

★★ **HOTEL AUBERGE UNIVERSEL MONTREAL.** *5000 Sherbrooke St E (H1V 1A1). 514/253-3365; fax 514/253-9958.* 231 rms, 7 story. S $97; D $107; each addl $12; suites $175-$225; under 16 free. TV; cable (premium), VCR avail. 2 pools, 1 indoor; whirlpool. Sauna. Restaurant 7 am-11 pm. Bar; entertainment Tues-Sat. Ck-out noon. Meeting rms. Business servs avail. Gift shop. Valet serv. Free covered parking. Refrigerator in suites. Microwaves avail. Across from Olympic Stadium, Biôdome,

botanical gardens. Cr cds: A, C, D, ER, MC, V.

≈ ⤢ 🔥 **SC**

★★★ **HOTEL DU PARC.** *3625 Parc Ave (H2X 3P8). 514/288-6666; fax 514/288-2469; res 800/363-0735. Email rooms@duparc.com.* 459 rms, 16 story. May-Oct: S, D $99-$139; each addl $15; suites $160-$350; under 18 free; wkend rates; lower rates rest of yr. Crib free. Pet accepted, some restrictions. Garage (fee). TV; cable, VCR avail. Complimentary coffee in rms. Restaurant 6:30 am-10:30 pm. Bar from noon. Ck-out noon. Meeting rms. Business center. Shopping arcade. Barber, beauty shop. Exercise rm. Health club privileges. Luxury level. Cr cds: A, C, D, DS, ER, JCB, MC, V.

⬛ 🦮 🛋 ⤢ 🔥 **SC** 🚶

★★ **HOTEL GOUVERNEUR TROIS-RIVIÉRES.** *975 rue Hart (G9A 4S3). 819/379-4550; fax 819/379-3941; res 888/910-1111. www.gouverneur.com.* 127 rms, 1 suite, 5 story. S, D $52; each addl $10; suite $150; under 18 free; wkend rates. Crib free. TV; cable (premium). Outdoor pool. Complimentary continental bkfst. Ck-out 1 pm. Business servs avail. In-rm modem link. Some minibars. Located downtown; walking distance to St. Lawrence River, Trois-Riviéres old district. Cr cds: A, D, DS, ER, MC, V.

⬛ ≈ ≈ 🛋 🚶 ⤢ 🔥

★★★ **HOTEL INTER-CONTINENTAL MONTREAL.** *360 rue Ste.-Antoine W (H2Y 3X4), at the World Trade Centre. 514/987-9900; fax 514/847-8550; toll-free 800/361-3600.* 357 rms, 23 suites, on 10th-26th floors of 26-story bldg. May-mid-Oct: S, D $235-$325; each addl $25; suites $360-$2,200; under 17 free; family, wkend rates; lower rates rest of yr. Crib free. Pet accepted, some restrictions. Valet parking $19/day. TV; cable (premium),VCR avail, Nintendo. Indoor heated pool. Restaurant 6:30 am-11:30 pm. Rm serv 24 hrs. Bar 11:30-1 am; Mon-Fri entertainment. Ck-out 1 pm. Ck-in 3 pm. Club Inter-Continental floors, complimentary continental bkfst, private lounge, afternoon refreshments. Meeting rms. Convention facilities. Business center. In-rm modem link. Concierge serv. Barber, beauty shop.

Exercise rm. Massage. Bathrm phones, minibars. Connected to shop and boutiques, metro system. Near Old Montréal. Next to Convention Center. Cr cds: A, DS, MC, V.

★ HOTEL LA RESIDENCE DU VOYAGEUR.
847 Sherbrooke E (H2O 1K6). 514/527-9515; fax 514/526-1070. Email twng@ican.net; www.hotel residencevoyager.com. 28 units, 4 story. June-mid-Sep: S $50-$90; D $65-$105; each addl $5; under 12 free; wkly rates winter; lower rates rest of yr. TV; cable. Complimentary continental bkfst. Restaurants nearby. Ck-out noon. Business servs avail. Free parking. Airport transportation. Refrigerators, microwaves avail. Cr cds: A, DS, MC, V.

★★★★ HOTEL LE GERMAIN.
2050 Mansfield (H3A 1Y9). 514/849-2050; fax 514/849-1437; toll-free 877/333-2050. www.hotelboutique. com. 100 rms, 16 story, 2 suites. July-Aug: S $230; D $250; lower rates rest of yr. Crib avail. Pet accepted, some restrictions, fee. Valet parking avail. TV; cable (DSS), VCR avail, CD avail. Complimentary full bkfst, newspaper, toll-free calls. Restaurant nearby. Bar. Ck-out noon, ck-in 3 pm. Meeting rms. Business servs avail. Bellhops. Concierge serv. Dry cleaning, coin lndry. Gift shop. Exercise privileges. Tennis. Downhill skiing. Bike rentals. Picnic facilities. Cr cds: A, D, ER, MC, V.

★★ HOTEL WYNDHAM MONTREAL.
1255 Jeanne Mance (H5B 1E5), opp Place Des Arts, Downtown. 514/285-1450; fax 514/285-1243; res 800/-WYNDHAM; toll-free 800/361-8234. Email info@wyndham.mtl.com; www.wyndham.com. 575 rms, 12 story, 28 suites. May-Oct: S, D $189; suites $340; lower rates rest of yr. Crib avail. Pet accepted, some restrictions. Valet parking avail. Indoor pool, lifeguard, whirlpool. TV; cable (premium). Complimentary coffee in rms, newspaper. Restaurant 6:30 am-2 pm. Bar. Ck-out noon, ck-in 3 pm. Conference center, meeting rms. Business center. Bellhops. Concierge serv. Dry cleaning, coin lndry. Gift shop. Salon/barber avail. Exercise equipt, sauna, steam rm. Golf. Tennis. Video games. Cr cds: A, C, D, DS, ER, JCB, MC, V.

★★★ LE CENTRE SHERATON.
1201 René Levesque W (H3B 2L7). 514/878-2000; fax 514/878-3958; res 800/325-3535. www.sheraton.com/ Lecentre. 825 rms, 37 story, 42 suites. S, D $210; each addl $25; suites $375-$1,800; under 17 free; wkend packages. Crib free. Valet parking $20/day. TV; cable (premium), VCR (suites), tendo. Indoor heated pool; whirlpool, lifeguard. Complimentary coffee in rms. Restaurant 6:30 am-2 pm, 5:30 pm-midnight. 2 Bar 11:30-2 am. Ck-out noon. Ck-in 3 pm. Meeting rms. Convention facilities. Business center. In-rm modem link. Fax machines, exec level. Some bathrm phones, two-line phones. Shopping arcade. Barber, beauty shop. Fitness center. Massage. Minibars avail. Across from the Molson Center. In the heart of downtown Montréal; minutes from Old Montréal. Cr cds: A, D, DS, ER, JCB, MC, V.

★★ LE NOUVEL HOTEL.
1740 René Levesque Blvd W (H3H 1R3). 514/931-8841; fax 514/931-3233; toll-free 800/363-6063. www.lenouveauhotel. com. 126 rms, 32 studios, 8 story. S, D $130-$150; each addl $10; studio $150-$170; under 12 free. Crib free. Indoor parking $9.50. TV; cable (premium). Pool; whirlpool. Restaurant 7 am-11 pm. Bar. Ck-out noon. Meeting rms. Business servs avail. In-rm modem link. Valet serv. Gift shop. Beauty shop. Game rm. Microwaves avail. Near Molson Centre. Cr cds: A, D, DS, ER, MC, V.

★★★★ LOEWS HOTEL VOGUE.
1425 rue de la Montagne (H3G 1Z3). 514/285-5555; fax 514/849-8903; res 800/465-6654. Email loewsvogue@ loewshotels.com. Located in the center of the city's golden square mile, this 126-room, 16-suite property has an intimate feel for such a central city location. Exclusive shops, museums, bars, and restaurants are within walking distance for those interested in exploring the city while the needs of business travelers are also taken into account: personal fax machines, three boardroom and six executive boardroom suites. 126 rms, 9 story,

16 suites. Mid-May-mid-Oct: S, D $195-$315; each addl $20; suites $425-$1,275; under 18 free; wkend rates; lower rates rest of yr. Crib free. Pet accepted. Garage; valet parking $15. TV; cable, VCR (movies). Restaurant 7 am-11 pm. Rm serv 24 hrs. Bar 3 pm-1 am. Ck-out 1 pm, ck-in 3 pm. Meeting rms. Business servs avail. In-rm modem link. Concierge serv. Gift shop. Exercise equipt. Massage. Health club privileges. Bathrm phones, TV. Some mircowaves. In-rm whirlpools, minibars. Cr cds: A, C, D, ER, JCB, MC, V.

★ **MARRIOTT CHATEAU CHAMPLAIN.** *1 Place du Canada (H3B 4C9). 514/878-9000; fax 514/878-6761; toll-free 800/200-5909. Email info@chateauchamplain.com; www.marriotthotels.com/yulcc.* 592 rms, 36 story, 19 suites. Apr-Oct: S, D $200; suites $600; each addl $30; under 12 free; lower rates rest of yr. Crib avail, fee. Valet parking avail. Indoor pool, whirlpool. TV; cable (premium), VCR avail. Complimentary coffee in rms, newspaper, toll-free calls. Restaurant 7 am-10 pm. Bar. Ck-out noon, ck-in 3 pm. Conference center, meeting rms. Business center. Bellhops. Concierge serv. Dry cleaning. Gift shop. Salon/barber avail. Exercise equipt, steam rm. Golf. Cr cds: A, C, D, DS, ER, JCB, MC, V.

★ ★ ★ **NOVOTEL MONTREAL CENTRE.** *1180 rue de la Montagne (H3G 1Z1). 514/861-6000; fax 514/861-0992; res 800/668-6835. Email novomtl@aol.com; www.novotel.com.* 226 rms, 9 story, 1 suite. May-Oct: S, D $150; suites $1,500; each addl $15; under 2 free; lower rates rest of yr. Crib avail. Pet accepted, some restrictions, fee. Parking garage. TV; cable. Restaurant 6:30 am-11 pm. Bar. Ck-out 1 pm, ck-in 3 pm. Meeting rms. Business center. Concierge serv. Dry cleaning. Exercise equipt, sauna, whirlpool. Supervised children's activities. Cr cds: A, C, D, DS, ER, JCB, MC, V.

★ ★ ★ **OMNI MONT-ROYAL.** *1050 Sherbrooke St W (H2A 2R6), at Peel St, Downtown. 514/284-1110; fax 514/845-3025; toll-free 800/842-6664.*

Email omni.montreal@omnihotels.com; www.omnihotels.com. 271 rms, 29 suites, 31 story. May-Oct: S, D deluxe $295-$425; each addl $30; suites $500-$1,750; under 18 free; wkend rates; lower rates rest of yr. Crib free. Pet accepted, some restrictions. Valet parking $20/day. TV; cable (premium), VCR avail. Outdoor heated pool; whirlpool, poolside serv, lifeguard (summer only). Restaurants (see also ZEN). Rm serv 24 hrs. Bar noon-midnight. Ck-out 1 pm. Ck-in 3 pm. Meeting rms. Business center. In-rm modem link. Fax machine avail. Concierge serv.. Shopping boutiques. Barber, beauty shop. Fully-equipped fitness center, sauna, steam rm. Massage. Bathrm phones, minibars. Located at the foot of Mt Royal, near all attractions and shopping. Cr cds: A, C, D, DS, MC, V.

★ ★ ★ **QUEEN ELIZABETH.** *900 René Levesque Blvd W (H3B 4A5). 514/861-3511; fax 514/954-2256; toll-free 800/441-1414. www.ephotels.ca.* 1,020 rms, 21 story. S, D $120-$220; each addl $30; suites $225-$1,850; under 18 free; wkend rates. Crib free. Garage $14. TV; cable (premium). Indoor pool; whirlpool. Coffee in rms. Restaurant (see also THE BEAVER CLUB). Rm serv 24 hrs. Bars from 11 am. Ck-out noon. Convention facilities. Business center. In-rm modem link. Shopping arcade. Beauty shop. Exercise rm. Massage. Minibars. Underground passage to Place Ville Marie. Luxury level. Cr cds: A, C, D, DS, ER, JCB, MC, V.

★ ★ ★ **RITZ-CARLTON.** *1228 Sherbrooke St W (H3G 1H6), at Drummond, Downtown. 514/842-4212; fax 514/842-3383; res 800/241-3333; toll-free 800/363-0366. Email ritz@citenet. net; www.ritzcarlton.com.* 229 rms, 9 story, 45 suites. May-Oct: S, D $425; suites $525; each addl $35; lower rates rest of yr. Crib avail. Pet accepted, some restrictions, fee. Valet parking avail. TV; cable (premium). Complimentary newspaper. Restaurant. Rm serv 24hrs. Bar. Meeting rms. Business center. Bellhops. Concierge serv. Dry cleaning. Gift shop. Salon/barber avail. Exercise privileges. Golf, 18 holes. Tennis, 10 courts. Bike rentals. Supervised children's activities. Hiking trail. Picnic facilities. Video games. Cr cds: A, D, DS, ER, MC, V.

★★★ SHERATON FOUR POINTS HOTEL & SUITES, MONTREAL CENTRE-VILLE. *475 Sherbrooke St W (H3A 2L9). 514/842-3961; fax 514/844-0945; res 800/325-3535; toll-free 800/842-3961. www.fourpoints.com.* 108 rms, 20 story, 87 suites. May-July, Sep-Oct: S, D $149; suites $179; each addl $15; under 17 free; lower rates rest of yr. Crib avail. Pet accepted. Valet parking avail. TV; cable (premium). Complimentary coffee in rms, newspaper. Restaurant 6:30 am-10:30 pm. Bar. Ck-out noon, ck-in 3 pm. Meeting rms. Business center. Bellhops. Concierge serv.. Dry cleaning. Exercise equipt, sauna. Golf, 18 holes. Tennis, 13 courts. Downhill skiing. Video games. Cr cds: A, C, D, ER, JCB, MC, V.

Changing of the guards, Old Québec City

B&Bs/Small Inns

★★★ AUBERGE DE LA FOUN-TAINE. *1301 rue Rachel E (H2J 2K1). 514/597-0166; fax 514/597-0496.* 21 rms, 3 story, 3 suites. May-Nov: S $139-$163; D $154-$178; each addl $15; suites $221-$233; under 12 free. TV; cable, VCR avail. Complimentary bkfst buffet. Ck-out noon, ck-in 3 pm. Meeting rm. Business servs avail. In-rm modem link. Sun deck. Some in-rm whirlpools. Some balconies. Former residence; quiet setting in urban location; opp La Fontaine Parc. Cr cds: A, MC, V.

★★★ AUBERGE HANDFIELD. *555 Chemin Du Prince (J0L 2E0), 28 mi SE on Hwy 20, Exit 112; 6 mi N on Hwy 223. 450/584-2226; fax 450/584-3650.* 53 rms, 2 story. S $70; D $80-$195; each addl $10; under 4 free; theatre, winter package plans. Crib free. TV; cable (premium). Outdoor pool; whirlpool, poolside serv. Restaurant (see also AUBERGE HANDFIELD). Bar 11 am-midnight. Ck-out noon, ck-in 3 pm. Meeting rms. Business servs avail. Golf privileges. Tennis privileges. Downhill/x-country ski 15 mi. Exercise rm; sauna. Bathrm phones. Theater boat (late June-early Sep). Marina. Sugar cabin (late Feb-late Apr). Built in 1880. Cr cds: A, C, D, DS, ER, MC, V.

★★★ AUBERGE HATLEY. *325 Virgin St, CP330 (J0B 2C0), off Autoroute 10 Exit 121. 819/842-2451; fax 819/842-2907; toll-free 800/336-2451. Email hatley@realschateaux.fr; www.northhatley.com.* 25 rms, 3 story, 5 suites. MAP: D $245-$390; each addl $90; wkly, wkend rates; ski plans. Heated pool. Complimentary full bkfst. Dining rm 8-10 am, 6 pm-closing. Ck-out noon, ck-in 4 pm. Business servs avail. Downhill ski 1 mi; x-country ski on site. Many fireplaces; some in-rm whirlpools, balconies. Lake opp; swimming, boats avail for guest use. 1903 Victorian-style mansion. Cr cds: A, ER, MC, V.

★ LE BRETON. *1609 rue St.-Hubert (H2L 3Z1). 514/524-7273; fax 514/527-7016.* 13 rms, 11 with private bath, 3 story. S $35-$55; D $45-$70; each addl $8. TV; cable. Complimentary continental bkfst. Restaurant nearby. Ck-out noon, ck-in 2 pm. Some rm phones. Business servs avail. Self-parking. Cr cds: MC, V.

★ MANOIR AMBROSE. *3422 Stanley St (H3A 1R8). 514/288-6922; fax*

514/288-5757. Email webmaster@
manoirambrose.com. 22 rms, 15 with
bath, 8 A/C, 3 story. May-Oct: S, D
$50-$85; each addl $10; under 12
free; winter wkly rates; lower rates
rest of yr. Crib free. Parking $5/day.
TV; cable. Complimentary continental bkfst. Breakfast rm. Ck-out noon,
ck-in 2:30 pm. Business servs avail.
Near Peel metro station. Victorian
mansion built 1883; large windows,
high ceilings. Cr cds: MC, V.
🔾 🐾

Conference Center

★★ HOTEL CHERIBOURG. 2603
Chemin du Parc (J1X 8C8), Hwy 10,
Exit 118, then 2 mi N on Hwy 141.
819/843-3308; fax 819/843-2639;
toll-free 800/567-6132. Email info@
cheribourg.com; www.cheribourg.com.
100 rms, 3 story, 3 suites. May-Oct:
S, D $84; suites $150; lower rates rest
of yr. Crib avail. Parking lot.
Indoor/outdoor pools, lifeguard,
whirlpool. TV; cable (premium), VCR
avail. Complimentary coffee in rms.
Restaurant 7:30 am-9:30 pm. Bar. Ck-
out noon, ck-in 4:30 pm. Meeting
rms. Business center. Dry cleaning.
Exercise equipt, sauna. Golf, 18
holes. Tennis, 4 courts. Downhill skiing. Bike rentals. Supervised children's activities. Hiking trail. Picnic
facilities. Video games. Cr cds: A, C,
D, DS, ER, MC, V.
D 🔾 🔾 🔾 🔾 🔾 🔾 🔾 🔾 🔾 🔾

Restaurants

★★ AU PETIT EXTRA. 1690 rue
Ontario E (H2L 1S7). 514/527-5552.
www.infoAubegite.com. Specializes in
hot goat cheese, fish soup, homemade paté. Hrs: 11:30 am-10 pm; Fri,
Sat to 10:30 pm. Res required. Wine,
beer. Lunch $10.25-$13.50; dinner
$14.50-$22. Entertainment. Cr cds:
A, C, D, MC, V.
D 🔾

★★ AUBERGE HANDFIELD. 555
Chemin du Prince. 450/584-2226.
www.aubergehandfield.com. Specializes
in lapin saute, petit cochon de lait,
rago and circut de pattes. Hrs: 8 am-9
pm. Res accepted. Bar. Bkfst a la carte
entrees: $14-$25; lunch, dinner a la
carte entrees: $14-$25. Sun brunch

$19.50. Child's menu. Entertain-
ment. Parking. In 1880 bldg. Indoor
terrace with view of Richelieu River.
Family-owned. Cr cds: A, C, D, DS,
ER, MC, V.
🔾

★★★ THE BEAVER CLUB. 900
René Levesque Blvd W. 514/861-3511.
Specializes in steak Charles, calf's
sweetbread scallopine, duckling foie
gras with a gyromitre mushroom
sauce. Hrs: 6-10:30 pm. Closed Sun,
Mon. Res accepted. Bar. Wine cellar.
Dinner a la carte entrees: $27-$32.
Complete meals: (Sat) $30-$39.
Child's menu. Entertainment: social
dancing with live music Sat. Valet
parking. Jacket. Cr cds: A, D, DS, ER,
MC, V.
D SC 🔾

★★★ BISTRO A CHAMPLAIN. 75
Chemin Masson. 450/228-4988. Email
champlain@cedarnet.net; www.bistro
champlain.qc.ca. Eclectic menu. Hrs:
6-9:30 pm. Closed Mon. Extensive
wine cellar. Dinner $24-$36. Entertainment. Parking. Elegant restaurant
is an 1864 old general store; located
across from Lake Masson. Cr cds: A,
C, D, ER, MC, V.
D 🔾

★★★ CAFE DE PARIS. 1228 Sherbrooke St W. 514/842-4212. Email
ritz@sitenet.net; www.ritzcarlton.com.
Specializes in feuillete de saumon,
scallops. Own pastries. Hrs: 6:30 am-
11 pm; Sat, Sun brunch noon-2:30
pm. Res accepted; required for
brunch. Bar. Wine list. Bkfst a la carte
entrees: $11.95-$21.95; lunch a la
carte entrees: $11.95-$21.95; dinner a
la carte entrees: $25-$40. Sun brunch
$28.95, $42.50. Child's menu. Entertainment: Tues-Sat. Valet parking. Cr
cds: A, C, D, DS, ER, MC, V.
D 🔾

★ CAFE STE. ALEXANDRE. 518
Duluth St E (H2L 1A7). 514/849-4251.
Specializes in pikilia, shish kebab.
Salad bar. Hrs: 11 am-10 pm; Fri, Sat
to 11 pm. Res accepted. Lunch a la
carte entrees: $7.95-$15.95; dinner a la
carte entrees: $7.95-$15.95. Complete
meals: $15.95-$17.95. Child's menu.
Entertainment. Cr cds: A, MC, V.
D 🔾

★★★ **CAFI FERREIRA.** *1446 rue Peel (H3A 1S8). 514/848-0988. www. ferrieracafe.com.* Mediterranean and Portuguese menu. Hrs: Mon-Fri 11 am-11 pm, Sat 5 pm-11 pm. Closed Sun. Res required. Beer, wine, extensive wine list. Lunch $15-$40; dinner $20-$40. Jacket. Cr cds: A, D, DS, ER, MC, V.

D ⟡ ⊐

★★★ **CHAMPS ELYSEES.** *1800 Sherbrooke W. 514/939-1212.* Specializes in braised salmon, rib steak with fresh onions, crepes Suzette. Hrs: 7-10:30 am, noon-2:30 pm, 6-10:30 pm. Res accepted. Bar. Wine cellar. Bkfst complete meals: $7.25-$9.75; lunch complete meals: $13.95-$35; dinner complete meals: $19.50-$26.50. Entertainment: jazz trio Fri, Sat. Valet parking. Elegant French bistro. Cr cds: A, D, MC, V.

D ⊐

★★ **CHEZ DELMO.** *211-215 Rue Notre Dame W (H2Y 1T4). 514/849-4061.* Specializes in poached salmon, filet of halibut. Hrs: 11:30 am-10 pm. Closed Sun. Res accepted. Wine, beer. Lunch $11.75-$42.75; dinner $15.75-$43.75. Entertainment. Cr cds: A, D, ER, MC, V.

⊐

★★★★ **CHEZ LA MERE MICHEL.** *1209 Guy St (H3H 2K5). 514/934-0473.* In a city with volumes of competition, this fine French restaurant has succeeded in its downtown, historic-home location since 1965. Guests will feel like they've stepped into a painting, from the quaint flower-lined walkway to the small, slightly cluttered rooms filled with eclectic collectibles. The menu is classic and well prepared, including a fantastic strawberry Napoleon for dessert. Specializes in pintade au vinaigre de framboises, almond soufflé. Own pastries. Hrs: 11:30 am-2:15 pm, 5:30-10:30 pm; Mon from 5:30 pm. Closed Sun. Res required. Wine cellar. Lunch table d'hote: $14.50-$17.50; dinner a la carte entrees: $22-$30. Entertainment. Cr cds: A, ER, MC, V.

D ⊐

★★ **GLOBE.** *3455 St. Laurent (H2X 2V2). 514/284-3823. www.restaurant-globe.com.* Menu changes seasonally. Hrs: 6-11 pm; Thurs-Sat to midnight.

Res required. Wine, beer. Dinner $22-$35. Entertainment. Cr cds: A, MC, V.

D ⊐

★★ **IL CORTILE.** *1442 Sherbrooke W (H3G 1K3). 514/843-8230.* Hrs: 11 am-2:30 pm, 6-9:30 pm. Res required. Lunch $15-$20; dinner $17-$29. Entertainment. Italian cuisine. Cr cds: MC, V.

⊐

★★★ **JONGLEUX CAFI.** *3434 St. Denis (H2X 3L3). 514/841-8080.* Modern with classic twist menu. Specializes in menu changes monthly. Hrs: Mon-Sat noon-2 pm, 6-10:30 pm. Closed Sun. Res recommended. Beer, wine. Lunch $18-$22; dinner $18-$26. Lot, street. Smart casual. Chef/owned: Nicolas Jonleux. Cr cds: A, C, D, ER, MC, V.

★★★ **KATSURA MONTREAL.** *2170 rue de la Montagne (H3G 1Z7). 514/849-1172.* Specializes in sushi, steak, teriyaki. Sushi bar. Hrs: 11:30 am-2:30 pm, 5:30-10 pm; Fri, Sat 5:30-11 pm; Sun 5:30-9:30 pm. Closed hols. Res preferred. Wine list. Lunch a la carte entrees: $8.10-$14.50; dinner a la carte entrees: $11-$27. Complete meals: $27-$37. Entertainment. Cr cds: A, D, ER, MC, V.

D ⊐

★★★★ **L'EAU A LA BOUCHE.** *3003 Blvd Ste.-Adele. 450/227-1416. Email eaubouche@sympatico.ca.* This hotel restaurant is tucked away just north of Montreal in what's called "cottage country" where charming Alpine houses dot the landscape. The name, meaning "mouth watering," is an apt description of chef Anne Desjardin's exquisite menu highlighting local ingredients. Lovely details of the original builder, a German cabinet-maker, are evident in the French-Canadian chalet's detailed paneling and wall carvings. Specializes in French and original cuisine. Menu changes weekly. Hrs: 6:30 pm-midnight. Closed hols. Bar. Dinner prix fixe: 5-course $55, 7-course $65, 9-course $75. Entertainment. Cr cds: C, D, DS, ER, MC, V.

D

★★★ **L'EXPRESS.** *3927 Ste.-Denis (H2W 2M4). 514/845-5333.* Specializes in steak Tartare, fresh salmon, chicken liver mousse with pistachio. Hrs: 8-3 am; Sat from 10 am; Sun 10-2 am. Closed Dec 25. Res accepted. Bar. Bkfst a la carte entrees: $2.45-$3.45; lunch, dinner a la carte entrees: $9.95-$16.50. Entertainment. Cr cds: A, C, D, DS, ER, MC, V.

D ⬛

★★ **L'ORCHIDEE DE CHINE.** *2017 rue Peel.* 514/287-1878. Szechwan menu. Specializes in orange beef. Hrs: noon-2:30 pm, 5:30-10:30 pm; Fri, Sat 5:30-11:30 pm. Closed Sun. Res accepted. Wine, beer. Lunch $11-$16; dinner $20-$30. Entertainment. Cr cds: A, DS, ER, MC, V.

⬛ ⬛

★ **LA CAVERNE GREQUE.** *105 Prince Arthur E (H2X 1B6).* 514/844-5114. Specializes in seafood, steak, chicken. Hrs: 11 am-midnight; Fri, Sat to 1 am. Res accepted. Lunch complete meals: $5-$10; dinner a la carte entrees: $8.95-$19.95. Child's menu. Entertainment. Cr cds: A, ER, MC, V.

⬛

★★★ **LA CHRONIQUE.** *99 rue Laurier W (H2T 2N6).* 514/271-3095. Specializes in menu changes daily. Hrs: Tues-Sat 11:30 am-2:30 pm, Tue-Sat 6-10 pm. Closed Sun, Mon. Res required. Beer, wine. Lunch $16-$24; dinner $22-$26. Street. Smart casual. Chef/owned: Mark Dacenk. Cr cds: A, D, ER, MC, V.

D

★★★ **LA CLEF DES CHAMPS.** *875 Chemin Pierre Peladeau (J3B 1Z3).* 450/229-2875. Specializes in venison, foie gras. Hrs: 4-10 pm; winter hrs vary. Closed 2 wks in April. Res required. Wine list. Dinner $22-$34. Child's menu. Cr cds: A, D, MC, V.

★★ **LA GAUDRIOLE.** *825 Laurier E.* 514/276-1580. *Email emve@total.net; www.total.net/~emve.* French menu. Hrs: 11:30 am-2 pm, 5:30-9:30 pm; Sat 5:30-10:30 pm. Res accepted. Wine, beer. Lunch $9-$14; dinner $26-$29. Entertainment. Cr cds: A, D, ER, MC, V.

D ⬛

★ **LA LOUISIANE.** *5850 rue Sherbrooke W (H4A 1X5).* 514/369-3073. Specializes in jambalaya, prime rib, shrimp magnolia. Hrs: 5:30-10:30

pm; Thurs, Fri 11:30 am-10:30 pm. Closed Mon. Wine, beer. Lunch $6.50-$13; dinner $9-$19. Entertainment. Cr cds: A, D, MC, V.

D ⬛

★★★ **LALOUX.** *250 Ave Des Pins (H2W 1P3).* 514/287-9127. Specializes in shrimps and scallops duo with orange and tarragon sauce, grilled lamb tenderloin with mango chutney and liquorice sauce. Hrs: Mon-Fri 11:30 am-3 pm, Sun-Wed 5:30 pm-10:30 pm, Thurs-Sat 5:30 pm-11:30 pm. Closed Confederation Day. Res accepted. Wine list. Lunch $9.95-$15.95; dinner $19.95-$29. Entertainment: jazz music. Street. Casual. Cr cds: A, D, MC, V.

D ⬛

★★★★ **LA MAREE.** *404 Place Jacques Cartier (H2Y 3B2), in Old Montréal.* 514/861-8126. Situated in Old Montréal, this romantic dining room offers classic French cuisine in an ornate, Louis XIII atmosphere. The historic 1808 building is just the place to enjoy old-fashioned, formal service and a great bottle of wine from the cellar. Specializes in homard brunetiere, chateaubriand grille. Own pastries, sherbets. Hrs: noon-3 pm, 5:30-11 pm; Sat, Sun from 5:30 pm. Closed Jan 1, Dec 25. Res required. Wine cellar. Lunch complete meals: $14.50-$17.50; dinner a la carte entrees: $24-$33. Entertainment. Cr cds: A, D, DS, ER, MC, V.

⬛

★★★ **LA RAPIERE.** *1155 rue Metcalfe (H3B 2V6).* 514/871-8920. Specializes in foie gras de canard, le confit de canard au vinaigre de framboise, le cassoulet a la Toulousaine. Hrs: 11 am-3 pm, 5-10 pm; Sat from 5 pm. Closed Sun; hols; mid-July-mid-Aug. Res accepted. Bar. Wine list. Lunch a la carte entrees: $17.75-$26.50; dinner a la carte entrees: $24.25-$27.75. Entertainment. Jacket. French decor. Cr cds: A, D, ER, MC, V.

D ⬛

★★ **LE CAFE FLEURI.** *1255 Jeanne Mance.* 514/285-1450. *www.hotel desjardins.com.* Specializes in marinated Canadian salmon, casserole of scallops, puffed pastry shell stuffed with wild mushrooms. Salad bar.

Own pastries. Hrs: 6:30 am-2 pm. Res accepted. Bkfst a la carte entrees: $9.75-$12.75. Buffet: $14.75; lunch a la carte entrees: $13.75-$16.75. Buffet: $16.95. Child's menu. Entertainment. Parking. Cr cds: A, DS, ER, MC, V.

D ⌐

★★★ **LE CHRYSANTHEME.** *1208 Crescent (H3G 2A9). 514/397-1408.* Specializes in jumbo shrimp, beef. Hrs: 12:30-2:30 pm, 5:30-10:30 pm. Closed Mon; Jan 1, Dec 24, 25. Res accepted. Bar. Lunch a la carte entrees: $10.80-$14. Complete meals: $10-$13; dinner $12-$20. Entertainment. Chinese decor, artifacts. Cr cds: A, C, D, DS, ER, MC, V.

D ⌐

★ **LE JARDIN DE PANOS.** *521 Duluth St E (H2L 1A8). 514/521-4206.* German menu. Specializes in calmars frites, cotelettes d'agneau, brochette de poulet. Hrs: 11 am-11 pm. Res accepted. Lunch complete meals: $7-$15; dinner a la carte entrees: $9-$19. Entertainment. Mediterranean decor. Cr cds: A, MC, V.

D ⌐

★ **LE KEG/BRANDY'S.** *25 St. Paul E (H2Y 1G2). 514/871-9093.* Specializes in steak, chicken, seafood. Hrs: 11 am-10:30 pm. Closed Dec 25. Res accepted. Bar. Lunch a la carte entrees: $4.29-$14.99; dinner $13.99-$26.99. Child's menu. Entertainment. Cr cds: A, D, DS, ER, MC, V.

D ⌐

★★★ **LE LUTETIA.** *1430 rue de la Montagne (H3G 1Z5). 514/288-5656. www.hotellelamontagen.com.* Specializes in steak tartar, rack of lamb. Hrs: 11:30-1 am, Mon, Tues to 11 pm. Res accepted. Wine list. Lunch $3.50-$19 a la carte; dinner $5-$24.50. Entertainment. Cr cds: A, D, ER, MC, V.

⌐ ⌐

★★ **LE MAISTRE.** *5700 Monkland (H4A 1E6). 514/481-2109.* Specializes in rack of lamb with thyme and honey sauce, duck confit with cremone mustard. Hrs: 5:30-9:30 pm; Thur, Fri from 11:30 am. Closed Sun, Mon. Res accepted. Wine, beer. Lunch $10.50-$16; dinner $24-$31. Entertainment. Cr cds: A, D, ER, MC, V.

★★★ **LE MAS DES OLIVIERS.** *1216 rue Bishop (H3X 2R2). 514/861-*

6733. Specializes in rack of lamb, blue tuna. Hrs: 10:30 am-11 pm, Sat 6-11 pm, Sun 6-10:30pm. Res required. Wine list. Lunch $12-$22; dinner $21-$37. Lot. Casual. Cozy southern French house. Cr cds: A, D, ER, MC, V.

⌐

★★★ **LE MITOYEN.** *652 Place Publique Ste.-Dorothee Laval (H7X 1G1). 450/689-2977. Email lemitoyen@ yahoo.ca.* Specializes in medaillons de caribou aux framboises, magrets de canard. Own pastries, baking. Hrs: 6 pm-midnight. Closed Mon. Res accepted. Wine list. Dinner a la carte entrees: $20.50-$28.50. Complete meals: $29.50-$58. Child's menu. Entertainment. Parking. Renovated 1870 house. Fireplace. Cr cds: A, C, D, DS, ER, MC, V.

D ⌐

★★ **LE MUSCADIN.** *100 St. Paul W (H1P 2Z3). 514/842-0588.* Specializes in rack of lamb, rack of veal, seafood. Hrs: 11:30 am-2:30 pm, 6-10 pm. Closed Sun; most major hols. Res accepted. Wine list. Lunch $19-$23; dinner $23-$34. Entertainment. Cr cds: A, D, DS, MC, V.

⌐

★★ **LE PARCHEMIN.** *1333 rue University (H3A 2A4). 514/844-1619.* Specializes in beef Wellington, chateaubriand, Dover sole. Hrs: 11 am-3 pm, 5 pm-midnight. Closed Sun. Res accepted. Wine, beer. Lunch $10-$26; dinner $14-$26. Entertainment. Cr cds: A, C, D, ER, JCB, MC, V.

D ⌐

★★ **LE PARIS.** *1812 Ste.-Catherine W (H3H 1M1). 514/937-4898.* Specializes in fish, liver, steak. Hrs: noon-3 pm, 5:30-10:30 pm; Fri, Sat 5:30-11 pm; Sun from 5:30 pm. Closed Sun; Dec 25. Res accepted. Lunch a la carte entrees: $13-$20; dinner a la carte entrees: $13-$20. Entertainment. Parisian atmosphere. Cr cds: A, D, MC, V.

⌐

★★★ **LE PASSE-PARTOUT.** *3857 Boul Decarie (H4A 3J6). 514/487-7750.* Specializes in smoked salmon, red snapper a la Provencal. Own baking. Hrs: 11:30 am-2 pm, 6:30-9:30 pm; Tues, Wed to 2 pm. Closed Sun, Mon, hols. Res accepted. Lunch complete meals: $18.50; dinner complete meals: $40-$50. Entertainment. Classic French decor. Cr cds: A, D, DS, MC, V.

[D] [⊐]

★ ★ ★ **LE PIEMONTAIS.** *1145-A Rue de Bullion. 514/861-8122.* Closed Sun. Res accepted. Wine list. Lunch $15-$20; dinner $22-$33. lots. casual. Cr cds: A, C, D, DS, ER, MC, V.

[D] [🐾] [⊐]

★ ★ ★ ★ **LE PIMENT ROUGE.** *1170 Peel (H3B 4P2). 514/866-7816.* Proprietor Hazel Mah, who also owns Sherlock's and Boston's Ma Soba Pan Asian Noodles, has overseen this landmark for 20 years. The dining room is in the renovated Windsor Hotel annex (a building now used for office space) and serves some of the city's best Chinese cuisine. The space is quiet and elegant, the service refined and attentive. Specializes in general tao chicken. Hrs: 11:30 am-11 pm; Fri to midnight; Sat noon-midnight; Sun noon-11 pm. Res reqiured. Wine, beer. Lunch $16.95-$21.95; dinner $4.95-$19.95. Entertainment. Cr cds: A, D, ER, JCB, MC, V.

[D] [⊐]

★ ★ ★ ★ **LES CAPRICES DE NICO-LAS.** *2072 rue Drummond (H3G 1W9). 514/282-9790. www.lescaprices.com.* The intimate candlelight and romantic indoor/outdoor garden combine to make this restaurant a true, special-occasion destination. Given the classic, very formal service, it is a pleasant surprise to find the French dishes on the menu refreshingly updated with light, vibrant flavors and seasonal market produce. A wine list of 500 labels only adds to the excitement. Specializes in modern French cuisine. Hrs: 6-10 pm. Res required. Bar. Dinner $27-$40. Entertainment. Cr cds: A, D, MC, V.

[⊐]

★ ★ **LES CONTENENTS.** *360 rue St.- Antoine W (H2Y 3X4). 514/847-8729. www.montreal.interconti.com.* Menu changes wkly. Hrs: 6:30 am-2:30 pm, 5-10:30 pm. Res accepted. Wine, beer. Lunch, dinner $12.95-$31.75. Child's menu. Entertain-

ment: pianist. Cr cds: A, D, DS, ER, MC, V.

[D] [⊐]

★ ★ ★ **LES HALLES.** *1450 Crescent St (H3G 2B6). 514/844-2328. www.restaurantleshalles.com.* Specializes in grapefruit Marie Louise, mariner soup tureen, caribou (seasonal). Own pastries. Hrs: 11:45 am-2:30 pm, 6-10:30 pm; Sat from 6 pm. Closed Sun, Mon. Res accepted. Bar. Extensive wine cellar. Lunch complete meals: $13.50-$25; dinner a la carte entrees: $22.95-$33.50, Table d'hote: $47. Entertainment. Jacket. Warm French bistro atmosphere; mural. Family-owned. Cr cds: A, C, D, DS, ER, MC, V.

[D] [⊐]

★ ★ ★ **LES REMPARTS.** *93 rue de la Commune E. 514/392-1649. www.lesremparts.restaurant.ca.* Menu changes seasonally. Hrs: Sun-Sat 7-10 am, Mon-Fri 11:30 am-3 pm, Sun-Sat 6-10:30 pm. Res required. Beer, wine. Lunch $13-$16; dinner $29.95-$36.95. Cr cds: A, D, DS, MC, V.

[D] [⊐]

★ **LE STE.-AMABLE.** *410 Place Jacques Cartier (X2Y 3B2). 514/866-3471.* Hrs: 11 am-2 pm, 5-10 pm; summer hrs vary. Bar. Lunch $12-$16; dinner $16-$35. Entertainment: Fri, Sat. Cr cds: C, MC, V.

[⊐]

★ ★ ★ **LES TROIS TILLEULS.** *290 Richelieu St. 514/856-7787. Email host.3tilleuls@sympatico.ca; www.saveurs.sympatico.ca/enc-roy/quebec/tilleuls.h.* Specializes in ris de veau Trois Tilleuls, cuisse de canard confite et son aiguillette. Own baking. Hrs: 7:30 am-10 pm. Res accepted. Bar. Wine cellar. Bkfst complete meals: $18.50-$22; lunch complete meals: $18.50-$22; dinner a la carte entrees: $32.50-$44.50. Child's menu. Entertainment. Parking. In 1880 farmhouse with garden, terrace; view of river. Cr cds: A, ER, MC, V.

[D] [⊐]

★ ★ ★ ★ **MEDITERRANEO GRILL & WINE BAR.** *3500 Boul St.-Laurent. 514/844-0027.* Chef Claude Pelletier's Mediterranean cuisine is fresh, innovative in taste, and appealingly presented. The dining room atmosphere, including an impressive 63-foot-long bar, makes guests feel like they've stepped into the Mediterranean's warm sun, even in the cold Montréal winters. Service is friendly and professional and despite the trendiness, the overall experience is genuinely first-rate. Californian with French influence menu. Hrs: Mon-Sun 6 pm-11 pm. Res accepted. Wine list. Dinner $35-$65. Child's menu. Lot. Casual. Cr cds: A, D, ER, MC, V. D ⬛

★★ **MIKADO.** *368 rue Laurier W. 514/279-4809.* Specializes in teriyaki plate, sushi. Hrs: 11:30 am-11 pm; Sun 5:30-10 pm. Res accepted. Wine, beer. Lunch $9-$14; dinner $12.50-$24. Entertainment. Cr cds: A, ER, MC, V. ⬛

★★★★ **NUANCES.** *1 Ave de Casino (H3C 4W7), in Casino de Montréal. 514/392-2708. www.casinos quebec. com.* Ten minutes from downtown, the Casino de Montréal may seem an unlikely place for this elegant restaurant. But this space rivals the most stunning dining rooms in all of Montréal and has a view to match. Although the interesting menu is not quite as mesmerizing as the room or service, which is warm, gracious, and unhurried, it is still fine and ambitious. Specializes in French cuisine. Hrs: 5:30 pm-midnight. Res required. Bar. Dinner a la carte entrees: $28-$40. Prix fixe: 5-course $62, 3-course $49. Entertainment. Valet parking. Cr cds: A, D, ER, MC, V. D ⬛

★★ **PRIMADONNA.** *3479 Boul St.-Laurent (H2X 2T6). 514/282-6644.* Italian menu. Hrs: 11:30 am-3 pm, 5:30-11 pm; Sat, Sun 5:30 pm-1 am. Res required. Extensive wine list. Lunch $20-$30; dinner $30-$40. Entertainment: musician. Cr cds: A, D, ER, MC, V. ⬛

★★ **QUELLI DELLA NOTTE.** *6834 Boul St.-Laurent (H2S 3C7). 514/271-3929. www.quelli.com.* Specializes in sushi. Menu changes seasonally. Hrs: noon-3 pm, 5:30-11 pm; Fri 5:30 pm-midnight; Sat 5:30 pm-1 am. Res accepted. Wine, beer. Lunch $15-$22;

dinner $13-$29. Entertainment. Cr cds: A, C, D, DS, JCB, MC, V. ⬛

★★ **RESTAURANT CHEZ LEVEQUE.** *1030 rue Laurier W (H2V 2K8). 514/279-7355.* French menu. Specializes in sea scallops over potato mousseline, torchon foie gras. Hrs: 8 am-midnight; Sat, Sun from 10 am. Res accepted. Wine, beer. Lunch $10-$32.50; dinner $15-$32.50. Entertainment. Chef owned. Cr cds: A, D, DS, MC, V. D

★★ **RESTAURANT LE LATINI.** *1130 rue Jeanne Mance (H2Z 1L7). 514/861-3166.* Hrs: 11:30 am-3 pm, 5:30-11:45 pm; Sat 5-11:45 pm; Sun 4-10 pm. Wine list. Lunch $14-$28; dinner $24-$38. Entertainment. Cr cds: A, DS, MC, V. ⬛

★★ **RESTAURANT SHO-DAN.** *2020 Metcalfe (H3A 1X8). 514/987-9987. Email sushi@sho-dan.com; www. sushi@sho-dan.com.* Specializes in tempura, sushi, teriyaki. Hrs: 11:30 am-2:30 pm, 5-10:30 pm; Fri, Sat to 11 pm. Closed Sun. Res accepted. Wine, beer. Lunch $10.95-$14.95; dinner $10.95-$21.75. Entertainment. Cr cds: A, D, ER, MC, V. D ⬛

★★★ **RISTORANTE BICE.** *1504 rue Sherbrooke W. 514/937-6009.* Hrs: noon-3 pm, 6-11 pm; Sat, Sun from 6 pm. Res accepted. Wine list. Lunch $20-$26; dinner $50-$75. Cr cds: A, C, D, ER, MC, V. ⬛

★★★ **RISTORANTE DA VINCI.** *1180 Bishop (H3G 2E3). 514/874-2001. Email davinci@aei.ca; www. davinci.qc.ca/.* Specializes in osso bucco, meats, pasta. Hrs: Mon-Fri noon-midnight, Sat 5pm-midnight. Closed Sun. Res accepted. Wine, beer. Lunch $15-$20; dinner $20-$35. Cr cds: A, C, D, DS, ER, MC, V. ⬛

★ **SAWATDEE.** *457 rue Ste.-Pierre (H2Y 2M8). 514/849-8854.* Specializes in som tum, chicken/shrimp with peanut sauce. Hrs: 11:30 am-3 pm, 5-10:30 pm. Res accepted. Bar. Lunch a la carte entrees: $8.95-$15.95. Complete meals: $18.50-$24.50. Buffet: $8.95; dinner a la carte entrees:

$8.95-$15.95. Complete meals: $18.50-$24.50. Buffet: $8.95. Child's menu. Entertainment. Thai decor; art. Cr cds: A, D, DS, MC, V.

SC ⌐

★★★ **SOCIETE CAFI.** *1425 Rue de La Montagne. 514/285-5555.* Specializes in lobster. Hrs: Mon-Sun 7 am-10 pm. Res accepted. Wine list. Lunch $18-$28; dinner $22-$39. Brunch $25. Child's menu. Garage. Casual. Cr cds: A, D, ER, MC.

D ⌐

★★ **SOTO RESTAURANT.** *3527 rue Ste. Laurent (H2X 2T6). 514/842-1150.* Japanese menu. Specializes in Omakase sushi, Maguro Yaki. Hrs: noon-2:30 pm, 6-10:30 pm; Sat, Sun from 6 pm. Res accepted. Wine. Lunch $10-$30; dinner $20-$35. Entertainment. Cr cds: A, DS, MC, V.

⌐

★★ **SOUVENIRS D'INDOCHINE.** *243 Mont-Royal W. 514/848-0336.* Hrs: 11:30 am-2:30 pm, 5:30-10:30 pm. Res accepted. Wine, beer. Lunch $6.50-$10; dinner $20-$30. Entertainment. Cr cds: MC, V.

D 🐾 ⌐

★★ **SZECHUAN.** *400 Notre Dame St W (H2Y 1V3). 514/844-4456.* Specializes in Szechuan, Hunan dishes. Hrs: 11:30 am-2:30 pm, 5:30-10:30 pm; Sat 5:30-11 pm. Closed Sun; Jan 1, Dec 24, 25. Res accepted. Lunch $10.95-$15.95; dinner $15-$25. Entertainment. Cr cds: A, ER, MC, V.

D ⌐

★★ **TOKYO SUKIYAKI.** *7355 Mountain Sights Ave (H4P 2A7). 514/737-7245.* Specializes in shabu shabu, sushi, sukiyaki. Hrs: 5:30-11 pm. Closed Mon; Jan 1, Dec 25. Res accepted. Wine, beer. Dinner complete meals: $27. Entertainment. Parking. Japanese decor; traditional Japanese seating. Family-owned. Cr cds: A, D, DS, MC, V.

★★★★ **TOQUE!.** *3842 rue Ste.-Denis (H2W 2M2). 514/499-2084. Email toque@viveotron.ca.* It would not be a stretch to call this restaurant the best in Canada; it's certainly Montréal's finest. The food is always the star and the kitchen, under the direction of chef Normand Laprise, is not afraid to take chances; how many

others would dare to serve duck magret roasted with liquorice and caramelized kumquats? The service is also without equal. Specializes in roasted back of salmon, Atlantic halibut, roasted haunch of Boileau venison. Hrs: 5:30-10:30 pm. Closed Sun. Res required. Dinner $19-$42. Entertainment. Cr cds: A, DS, MC, V.

D ⌐

★★★ **TREEHOUSE.** *4120 St. Catherine St W (H3Z 1P4). 514/932-5654. Email info@kaizen-sushi-bar. com; www.kaizen-sushi-bar.com.* Specializes in new style sashimi, cobe cow steak. Hrs: 5:30-10:30 pm; Thurs-Sat to midnight. Closed Mon; Jan 1, Dec 25. Ews accepted. Wine list. Dinner $45-$50. Entertainment: jazz Sun, Tues, Wed. Tatami rms. Cr cds: A, MC, V.

D ⌐

★★ **ZEN.** *1050 Sherbrooke St W. 514/499-0801.* Specializes in Szechuan duck, General Tso's chicken, sesame orange beef. Hrs: 11 am-2:30 pm, 5:30-11 pm. Closed Dec 25. Res required. Lunch a la carte entrees: $10.50-$20. Complete meals: $12-$25; dinner a la carte entrees: $10.50-$20. Complete meals: $27. Entertainment. Cr cds: A, C, D, DS, ER, MC, V.

D ⌐

Unrated Dining Spots

AU TOURNANT DE LA RIVIERE. *5070 Salaberry (J3L 3P9). 450/658-7372. Email tournantriviere@qc-air.com.* French menu. Hrs: 11 am-2 pm, 6:30-9 pm; Sun brunch 11 am-2 pm. Lunch, dinner $28-$45. Entertainment. Cr cds: D, ER, MC, V.

D

BEN'S DELICATESSEN. *990 de Maisonneuve Blvd (H3A 1M5), W at Metcalfe. 514/844-1001.* Specializes in pastrami, smoked meat, corned beef. Hrs: 7:30-2 am; Thurs to 3 am; Fri, Sat to 4 am. Bkfst $3.60-$9.95; lunch, dinner $3.60-$9.95. Entertainment. Family-owned. Cr cds: MC, V.

D

BIDDLE'S JAZZ AND RIBS. *2060 Aylmer (H3A 2E3). 514/842-8656.* Specializes in chicken, ribs, steak. Hrs: 11-1 am; Sat 5 pm-2 am; Sun from 6 pm. Res accepted. Bar. Lunch a la carte entrees: $6.25-$11.95; dinner a la carte entrees: $7.95-$17.95. Entertainment: jazz. Cr cds: A, C, D, ER, MC, V.

LA SAUVAGINE. *1592 Rte 329 (J8C 2Z8). 819/326-7673. Email sauvagine@polyinter.com.* Hrs: 6:30-8:30 pm; hrs vary off-season. Closed Mon, Tues. Res accepted. Dinner $36. Entertainment. Cr cds: MC, V.

D

PIZZA MELLA. *107 Prince Arthur E (H2X 1B6). 514/849-4680.* Indian menu. Specializes in 30 types of pizza. Hrs: 11 am-11:30 pm. Closed Dec 25. Lunch $7.95-$10.95; dinner $7.95-$10.95. Entertainment. Open kitchen; 3 wood-burning brick ovens. Cr cds: A, C, D, DS, ER, MC, V.

D

RESTAURANT DAOU. *519 Faillon E (H2R 1L6). 514/276-8310.* Lebanese menu. Hrs: 11:30 am-10 pm; Sun to 9 pm. Closed Mon. Res required. Extensive wine list. Lunch, dinner $8-$22. Entertainment. Cr cds: A, D, DS, ER, MC, V.

D SC

Mont Tremblant Provincial Park

(Approx 15 mi or 24 km N of St.-Jovite on PQ 327)

In 1894 the provincial government of Québec established this 482-square-mile (1,248-square-kilometer) wilderness reserve as a park. A vast territory gifted with abundant wildlife and a large variety of plants, it is filled with 300 lakes, three rivers, three major hydrographical basins, innumerable streams, waterfalls, and mountains reaching as high as 3,120 feet (960 meters). Today it is a leisure haven for thousands of people interested in fishing, hiking, canoeing, biking, swimming, sailing, snowmobiling, snowshoeing, and cross-country and downhill skiing. Many come just to see the spectacular foliage in fall. Entrances are at St. Donat, on Hwy

125, St.-Faustin on Hwy 117 North, or St.-Côme on Hwy 343. Canoes and boats for rent. Reception areas, picnicking. Some facilities for the disabled; inquire for details.

Camping is available from mid-May to early October; some trailer hookups available (fee). Winter activities may be enjoyed mid-November-mid-March. Phone 819/688-2281 or 819/688-6176.

Hotels

★★ **BEST WESTERN HOTEL.** *131 Laurier St (J8X 3W3), on N side of Alexandria Bridge (to Ottawa). 819/770-8550; fax 819/770-9705; res 800/265-8550.* 144 rms, 9 story. Mid-May-mid-Oct: S, D $86-$125; each addl $10; kit. units $100-$125; under 18 free; lower rates rest of yr. Crib $10. TV; cable. Indoor pool; lifeguard. Restaurant 7 am-2 pm, 5-10 pm; wkend hrs vary. Bar 11-3 am; entertainment. Ck-out noon. Meeting rms. Business servs avail. Many refrigerators. Some balconies. Opp Museum of Civilization. Cr cds: A, C, D, DS, ER, MC, V.

⊠ ⊠ ⊠ SC

★★★ **PINOTEAU VILLAGE.** *126 Pinoteau St (J0T 1Z0), 8 mi N of St. Jovite on Hwy 327. 819/425-2795; fax 819/425-9177.* 50 condos, 2 story. No A/C. Mid-June-mid-Sep and Nov-mid-Apr: 1-bedrm $125-$160; 2-bedrm $180-$210; 3-bedrm $260-$280; under 12 free; ski plans; lower rates rest of yr. TV; cable (premium). Heated pool. No rm serv. Ck-out noon. Tennis. Golf privileges. Downhill ski ¼ mi; x-country ski adj. Exercise equipt. Microwaves. Private patios. On lake, private beach; boat rentals. Ski shop; rentals. Cr cds: A, MC, V.

⊠ ⊠ ⊠ ⊠ ⊠ ⊠

Resorts

★★★ **CLUB TREMBLANT.** *121 Cuttle St (J1T 1Z0), 9 mi N of St.-Jovite on Hwy 327. 819/425-2731; fax 819/425-5617; toll-free 800/567-8341. Email club@tremblant; www.clubtremblant.com.* 100 condos. No A/C. MAP, mid-July-mid-Aug: suites $250; wkly rates; ski plan; under 6 free; lower rates rest of yr. TV; cable. 2 pools, 1 indoor; whirlpool. Playground. Free supervised children's activities (July-Aug). Dining rm 7:30-9:30 am, 6-8:30 pm; wkends to 9 pm. Bar 4 pm-1 am. Ck-out noon, ck-in 4:30 pm. Meeting rms. Business servs avail. In-rm modem link. Tennis, pro. Canoes, rowboats, sailboats, kayaks. Downhill ski ¼mi; x-country ski adj. Ski shop; equipt rental. Rec dir. Rec rm. Exercise rm; sauna. Massage. Fireplaces. On Lake Tremblant; beach club. Cr cds: A, D, ER, JCB, MC, V.

★ ★ ★ GRAY ROCKS RESORT AND CONVENTION CENTER. *525 Chemin Principal (J0T 1Z0), on Hwy 327, 4 mi N of Hwy 117. 819/425-2771; fax 819/425-3474; res 800/567-6767. Email info@grayrocks.com; www.grayrocks.com.* 213 rms. Jan-Feb, Jun-Jul: Pet accepted, fee. Parking lot. Indoor pool, whirlpool. TV; cable. Complimentary full bkfst, coffee in rms, toll-free calls. Restaurant. Bar. Ck-out 11 am, ck-in 4 pm. Meeting rms. Business center. Bellhops. Concierge serv. Gift shop. Exercise rm, sauna, steam rm. Golf. Tennis, 22 courts. Downhill skiing. Beach access. Bike rentals. Supervised children's activities. Hiking trail. Picnic facilities. Cr cds: A, D, DS, ER, MC, V.

Restaurants

★ AUBERGE SAUVIGNON. *2723 Chemin Principal (J0T 120). 818/425-5466. www.aubergesauvignon.qbc.net.* French menu. Specializes in gradlax salmon, warm French goat cheese. Hrs: 6-11 pm. Res required. Wine list. Dinner $6.95-$8.95. Entertainment. Built in 1939 and in operation since 1957. Cr cds: A, D, DS, ER, JCB, MC, V.

★ ★ AUX TRUFFES. *3035 Chemin Principale (J0T 2H0). 819/681-4544.* Specializes in caribou, fish with truffle sauce, beef. Hrs: 6-10 pm. Res accepted. Wine, beer. Dinner $28-$36. Entertainment. Cr cds: A, D, ER, MC, V.

★ ★ ★ ★ CAFE HENRY BURGER. *69 rue Laurier (J8X 3V7). 819/777-5646.* This establishment has been delighting the region's most refined palates since 1922 with state-of-the-art classical French cuisine. Chef/owner Robert Bourassa presides over the elegant, warm dining room that occupies the first floor of a free-standing cafe in front of the Canadian Museum of Civilization. Guests will cherish the excellent preparations of the freshest ingredients, professional service, and excellent wine list. Specializes in smoked salmon, venison, duck. Hrs: noon-3:30 pm, 6-10 pm. Res accepted. Extensive wine list. Lunch $3-$18; dinner $4-$44. Child's menu. Entertainment. Cr cds: A, D, DS, ER, JCB, MC, V.

★ ★ LA FOURCHETTE FOLLE. *2713 Chemin Principal (J0T 1Z0). 819/425-7666.* Specializes in pan-roasted salmon, duck, grain-fed chicken, risotto. Hrs: 6-10 pm; hrs vary per season. Res accepted. Wine, beer. Dinner $15-$25. Child's menu. Entertainment. Name of restaurant means "Crazy Fork." Mountain terrace view. Cr cds: A, D, ER, MC, V.

★ LE GASCON. *Village Center (J0T 1Z0). 819/681-4606. Email legascon@ qc.airaraira.com; www.tremblant.com.* Specializes in pasta, seafood, steak. Hrs: 11 am-midnight. Res accepted. Wine, beer. Lunch $7-$15; dinner $10-$30. Child's menu. Entertainment: vocalist. Cr cds: A, D, ER, MC, V.

★ LE SHACK. *3035 Principal (J0T 1Z0). 819/681-4700. Email leshack@ leshack.com; www.tremblant.com.* Menu changes seasonally. Hrs: 7-10 pm. Res required. Wine, beer. Lunch, dinner $8.95-$26.95. Child's menu. Entertainment. Cr cds: A, D, ER, MC, V.

★ MEXICALI ROSA'S. *Place St. Bernard (G0T 1Z0). 819/681-2439.* Mexican menu. Specializes in fajitas, quesadillas, chimichangas. Hrs: 11 am-10 pm; Fri, Sat to 11 pm. Res accepted. Wine, beer. Lunch $7-$30;

dinner $7-30. Child's menu. Entertainment. Cr cds: A, D, ER, MC, V.

[D] [≡]

★ **PIZZATERIA.** *Village Center (G0T 1Z0). 819/681-4522.* Specializes in pizza. Hrs: 11 am-11 pm. Wine, beer. Lunch, dinner $6.75-$10.95. Child's menu. Entertainment. Cr cds: A, D, DS, MC, V.

[D] [≡]

Québec City

Founded 1608 **Pop** 166,474
Elev 239 ft (73 m) **Area code** 418
Web www.quebecregion.com
Information Greater Québec Area Tourism & Convention Bureau, 399 rue St.-Joseph E, G1K 8E2; 418/522-3511

The city of Québec, one of the most beautiful in the Western Hemisphere, is 150 miles (240 kilometers) northeast of Montréal. Nestled on an historic rampart, Québec is antique, medieval, and lofty, a place of mellowed stone buildings and weathered cannon, horse-drawn calèches, ancient trees, and narrow, steeply angled streets. Here and there the 20th century has intruded, but Québec has preserved the ambience of the past.

Québec is a split-level city. Above is the sheer cliff and rock citadel that once made Québec the Gibraltar of the north. The Upper Town, built high on the cliff and surrounded by fortresslike walls, has one of the city's best-known landmarks, Le Château Frontenac, a hotel towering so high it is visible from ten miles (16 kilometers) away. The Lower Town is the region surrounding Cape Diamond and spreading up the valley of the St. Charles River, a tributary of the St. Lawrence. The two sections are divided by the Funicular, which affords magnificent views of the harbor, river, and hills beyond.

In soul and spirit Québec is French; the population is nine-tenths French. Although French is the official language, English is understood in many places. The city streets are perfect for a casual stroll and many of the things you'll want to see are convenient to one another. Winters here are quite brisk.

The first known visitor to what is now Québec was Jacques Cartier, who spent the winter of 1535 at what was then the local village of Stadacone. Undoubtedly, Cartier recognized the strategic significance of this site, but a European colony was not established until 1608 when Samuel de Champlain, a French nobleman acting in the name of the King of France, established Kebec (native for "the narrowing of the waters"). The French began to put down roots in 1617 when Louis Hebert, the first agricultural pioneer, arrived with his family. The first settlement was wiped out in 1629 by British seafarers, but was later ceded back to France. For more than a century, Québec thrived despite constant harassment and siege from both the English and the Iroquois.

The decisive date in Québec history—and in the history of the British colonies to the south—was September 13, 1759. After an heroic ascent up the towering cliffs, General James Wolfe led his British troops to the Plains of Abraham (named after an early settler) and engaged the forces of the brilliant French General, Louis Joseph, Marquis de Montcalm. In 15 minutes the battle was over; both generals were among the fatalities and French dreams of an empire in America were shattered. (The last siege of Québec took place in 1775, when American troops under the command of Benedict Arnold attacked and were repelled.)

From its earliest days, Québec has been a center for military, administrative, religious, educational, and medical activities. Today the provincial capital, it still is a center for these endeavors and also for industry.

What to See and Do

Artillery Park National Historic Site. A 4-acre (2-hectare) site built by the French to defend the opening of the St. Charles River. By the end of the 17th century it was known as a strategic site, and military engineers began to build fortifications here. Until 1871 the park housed French and British soldiers, eventually

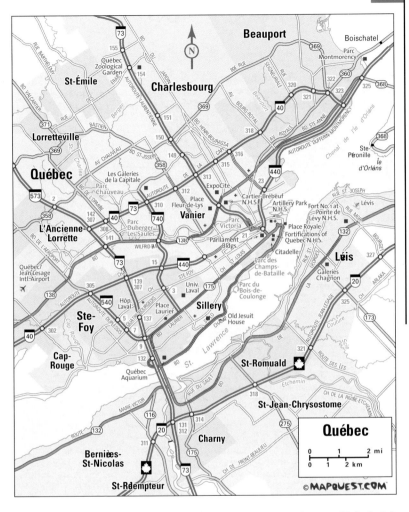

becoming a large industrial complex. Dauphine Redoubt (1712-48), gun carriage shed (1813-15), officers' quarters (1818), and arsenal foundry (1903) have been restored. Interpretation center. (Daily; closed Jan 1, Easter, Dec 25) St. Jean & D'Auteuil Sts. Phone 418/648-4205. Admission (June 24-Labour Day) ¢¢

Basilica of Ste.-Anne-de-Beaupré. (1923) Noted as the oldest pilgrimage in North America. First chapel was built on this site in 1658; the present basilica, built of white Canadian granite, is a Romanesque masterpiece. Capitals tell story of Jesus' life in 88 scenes; vaults decorated with mosaics; unusual technique used for 240 stained-glass windows outlined in concrete. Fourteen life-size Stations of

the Cross and *Scala Santa* (Holy Stairs) on hillside. (Daily) 22 mi (35 km) NE on Hwy 138. Phone 418/827-3781.

Cartier-Brébeuf National Historic Site. Commemorates Jacques Cartier, first European known to have wintered in mainland Canada (1535-36), and Jean de Brébeuf, a martyred Jesuit priest. The *Grande Hermine,* a full-size replica of Cartier's 16th-century flagship, is in dry dock; the hold and between deck can be viewed. Interpretation center with videotaped material. Guided tours by res. Indigenous habitation on site is open to visitors. (Feb-Nov, daily; Dec-Jan by appt) 175 de l'Espinay St. Phone 418/648-4038. **FREE**

Explore. High-tech sound and visual art are used to illustrate the founding of Québec and the beginnings of New France during the Golden Age of Exploration, when Columbus, Cartier, Champlain, and others began to venture into the Americas. (Daily; closed Dec 1-26) 63 rue Dalhousie. Phone 418/692-1759. ¢¢

Grand Théâtre. Ultramodern theater has giant mural by sculptor Jordi Bonet in lobby; home of the Québec Symphony Orchestra and Opera; theatrical performances, concerts. 269 Blvd René Levesque. Phone 418/643-4975.

Île d'Orléans. This 23-mi-long (37-km) island was visited by Champlain in 1608 and colonized in 1648. Old stone farmhouses and churches of the 18th century remain. Farms grow an abundance of fruits and vegetables, especially strawberries, for which the island is famous. Across bridge, in St. Lawrence River.

Jacques-Cartier Park. Beautiful views in boreal forest valley. Fishing, rafting, canoeing; mountain climbing, wilderness camping, cross-country skiing, hiking, mountain biking, picnicking, magnificent nature trail; nature interpretation. (Late May-mid-Oct, mid-Dec-mid-Apr) 25 mi (40.2 km) N via Hwy 175. Phone 418/848-3169. **FREE**

⭐ **La Citadelle.** Forming the eastern flank of the fortifications of Québec, La Citadelle was begun in 1820 and work continued on it until 1850. Vestiges of the French regime, such as the Cap Diamant Redoubt (1693) and a powder magazine (1750), can still be seen. Panoramic views; 50-min guided tours. Changing of the guard (mid-June-Labour Day, daily); Beating the Retreat, re-creation of a 16th-century ceremony (late June-Labour Day, Tues, Thurs, Sat, and Sun; fee). On Cap Diamant. Phone 418/694-2815. ¢¢¢ In La Citadelle is

Museum of the Royal 22e Régiment. Located in 2 bldgs. Powder magazine (ca 1750), flanked on both sides by massive buttresses, contains replicas of old uniforms of French regiments, war trophies, 17th-20th-century weapons; diorama of historic battles under the French; old military prison contains insignias, rifle, and bayonet collections, last cell left intact. (Mid-Mar-Oct, daily) Changing of

the guard (mid-June-Labour Day, daily at 10 am). ¢¢

Laurentides Wildlife Reserve. Camping, canoeing, fishing; cottages, lodges, picnicking, small and big game hunting, cross-country and backcountry skiing, snowshoeing. (Late May-Labour Day, mid-Dec-mid-Apr) Some fees. 35 mi (48 km) N via Hwy 175. Phone 418/528-6868 or 418/848-2422 (in season). **FREE**

Mont-Ste.-Anne Park. Gondola travels to summit of mountain (2,625 ft or 800 m), affording beautiful view of St. Lawrence River (late June-early Sep, daily). Skiing (Nov-May), 12 lifts, 50 trails; 85% snowmaking; cross-country, full service. Two 18-hole golf courses; bicycle trail; 166 campsites (Phone 418/826-2323). The migration of 250,000 snow geese occurs in spring and fall at nearby wildlife reserve Cap Tourmente. Park (daily; closed May). Some fees. 23 mi (37 km) NE via ON 138, then N 3 mi (5 km) on Hwy 360. Phone 418/827-4561 or 800/463-1568 (lodging information).

Montmorency Park. Montmorency Falls; Wolfe's Redoubt, historic house (June-early Sep, by appt), artifacts. Picnicking. (May-Oct) 10 mi (16 km) E via Hwy 138. Phone 418/663-2877.

Musée du Fort. Narrated historical re-creation of the 6 sieges of Québec between 1629-1775; sound and light show. (Daily; closed Dec 1-26) Place d'Armes, corner of Ste.-Anne & du Fort Sts. Phone 418/692-2175. ¢¢¢

Museum of Civilization (Musée de la Civilisation). At entrance is *La Débâcle,* a massive sculpture representing ice breaking up in spring. Separate exhibition halls present 4 permanent and several changing exhibitions dealing with history of Québec and the French Canadian culture as well as cultures of other civilizations from around the world. All narrative panels and signs are in French; bilingual guides on duty in most exhibit areas and English guide books are avail (fee). Guided tours (1 hr; fee). (Late June-Labour Day, daily; rest of yr, Tues-Sun; closed Dec 25) 85 rue Dalhousie, near Place-Royale. Phone 418/643-2158. ¢¢¢

National Assembly of Québec. Guided tours (30 min) of century-old Parliament Bldg. Dufferin Ave. Phone 418/643-7239. **FREE**

National Battlefields Park. Two hundred fifty acres (101 hectares) along edge of bluff overlooking St. Lawrence River from Citadel to Gilmour Hill. Also called the Plains of Abraham, park was site of 1759 battle between the armies of Wolfe and Montcalm and 1760 battle of Ste.-Foy between the armies of Murray and Lévis. Visitor reception and interpretation center presents history of the Plains of Abraham from the New France period to the present. Bus tour of the park. Entrances along Grand-Allée. Phone 418/648-4071. ¢ In the park are two Martello towers, part of the fortifications, a sunken garden, many statues, and the

Jeanne d'Arc Garden. Floral jewel created in 1938 by landscape architect Louis Perron. Combines the French Classical style with British-style flower beds. More than 150 species of annuals, bulbs, and perennials. Phone 418/649-6159.

Musée du Québec. Collection of ancient, modern, and contemporary Québec paintings, sculpture, photography, drawings, decorative arts; changing exhibits. (Daily; closed Jan 1, Dec 25) Parc des Champs-de-Bataille. Phone 418/643-2150. ¢¢¢

Old Port of Québec Interpretation Centre. Located in an ancient cement works and integrated into harbor installations of Louise Basin. Permanent exhibit shows importance of city as a gateway to America in the mid-19th century; timber trade and shipbuilding displays; films, exhibits; guides. (Early May-early Sep, daily; rest of yr, Tues-Sun) 100 St.-André St. Phone 418/648-3300. Admission (June 24-Labour Day) ¢¢

Place-Royale. Encompasses earliest vestiges of French civilization in North America; ongoing restoration of 17th-19th-century bldgs, which make this the greatest concentration of such structures in North America. Notre-Dame-des-Victoires Church (1688), exhibit, and several houses are open to the public; information center at 215 rue du Marché Finlay, G1K 8R5. One-hr guided tours by appt. Lower Town along St. Lawrence Riverfront. Phone 418/643-6631.

Québec Aquarium. Extensive collection of tropical, fresh, and saltwater fish, marine mammals, and reptiles; overlooks St. Lawrence River. Seal feeding (morning and afternoon); films (mid-May-Aug; daily). Cafeteria, picnicking. (Daily) 1675 des Hôtels Ave in Ste.-Foy. Phone 418/659-5266. ¢¢

★ **Québec City Walls and Gates.** Encompassing Old Québec. Eighteenth-century fortifications encircle the only fortified city in North America; incl Governor's Promenade and provides scenic views of The Citadel, St. Lawrence River, and Lévis. (Daily exc Governor's Promenade) **FREE**

Québec Zoo. More than 270 species of native and exotic animals and birds in a setting of forests, fields, and streams; children's zoo, sea lion shows; gift shops; restaurant, picnicking. (Daily; closed Dec 25) 9300 Faune St, in Charlesbourg, 7 mi (11.3 km) NW on Hwy 73 175. Phone 418/622-0312. ¢¢

Sightseeing tours.

Baillairgé Cultural tours. Group tours lasting between 3 days and 1 wk. Specialized tours in art, cuisine, and education. (Late June-mid-Oct, daily) Phone 418/692-5737. ¢¢¢

Calèches. Horse-drawn carriages leave Esplanade parking lot on d'Auteuil St, next to Tourist Bureau.

Gray Line bus tours. Contact 1576 Ave des Hôtels G1W 3Z5. Phone 418/523-9722.

Harbour Cruises. M/V *Louis Jolliet* offers daytime, evening dance, and dinner cruises on the St. Lawrence River. Bar service, entertainment. (May-Oct) Contact Croisières AML, 124 rue St-Pierre G1K 4A7. Chouinard Pier, opp Place Royale. Phone 418/692-1159 or 800/563-4643. ¢¢¢¢

St. Andrew's Presbyterian Church. (1810) Serving the oldest English-speaking congregation of Scottish origin in Canada. Church interior is distinguished by a long front wall with a high center pulpit. Original petition to King George III asking for a "small plot of waste ground" on which to build a "Scotch" church; spiral stairway leading to century-old organ. Stained-glass windows, historic plaques. Guide service. (July-

Aug, Mon-Fri) Ste.-Anne & Cook Sts. Phone 418/656-0625. **FREE**

St.-Jean-Port-Joli. Tradition of wood sculpture began in this town about 1936, initiated by the famed Bourgault family. Other craftsmen came and made this a premier handicraft center; sculptures, enamels, mosaics in copper and wood, fabrics, paintings. Golf club (May-Sep); tennis courts, mountain bike trails, marina. Guided tour. Approx 60 mi (96.6 km) NE on Hwy 132 halfway to the Gaspé Peninsula (see). Phone 418/598-3084. Also here are

> **Church.** (1779) Designed and decorated by famous woodcarvers. Renowned for the beauty of its lines and interior decor; has not been altered since built. Sculpted wood vault, tabernacle, and reredos all by different artisans. **FREE**

> **Musée des Anciens Canadiens.** Wood sculptures by St.-Jean artisans. Original carvings by Bourgault brothers. (Mid-May-Oct, daily) Phone 418/598-3392. ¢¢

Université Laval. (1663) 35,900 students. Oldest French university on the continent, Laval evolved from Québec Seminary, which was founded in 1663 by Québec's first bishop, Msgr. de Laval. In 1950 the university moved from "Le Quartier Latin" in old Québec to a 470-acre (190-hectare) site in suburban Ste.-Foy, where it developed into the present, modern campus. Guided tours by appt. Sir Wilfrid Laurier Blvd & Du Vallon Route, in Ste.-Foy. Phone 418/656-3333.

Annual Events

Carnaval Québec Kellogg's. Internationally acclaimed French Canadian festival celebrated throughout the city. Main attraction is the Snow Palace, a 2-story structure built of blocks of ice, open to visitors. Other highlights incl snow and ice sculptures, parades, canoe race on the St. Lawrence, fireworks, many special events. Contact Carnaval de Québec, Inc, 290 rue Joly, G1L 1N8; 418/626-3716. Late Jan-mid Feb.

du Maurier Québec Summer Festival. Outdoor festival held at 15 locations throughout Old Québec. International event of the performing arts; more than 400 shows, most free. Contact 160 rue St.-Paul, CP 24,

Succ B, G1K 7A1; 418/692-4540. Eleven days beginning 1st Thurs July.

International Fireworks Competition. Montmorency Falls Park. Musical fireworks competition attracts master fireworks handlers from around the world. Phone 418/523-3389. Late July-early Aug.

New France Celebration. Family-oriented historical event that re-creates life of the colonists in New France and fills the streets with theatrical events, song and dance, and children's entertainment. Phone 418/694-3311. Early Aug.

Expo Québec. Exhibition Park. Agricultural, commercial, and industrial fair; shows, games. Phone 418/691-7110. Late Aug.

Additional Visitor Information

Information centers are located at Tourism Québec, 12 Ste.-Anne St, phone 800/363-7777 (US and Canada) (Mon-Fri); and at the Greater Québec Area Tourism & Convention Bureau, 835 Ave Wilfrid-Laurier, G1R 2L3; 418/649-2608 (daily). The US Consulate is located at 2 Terrasse Dufferin, phone 418/692-2095. Public transportation is operated throughout the city by the Québec Urban Community Transportation Commission.

Motels/Motor Lodges

★★ **BEST WESTERN L'ARTISTO-CRATE.** *3100 Chemin Ste.-Louis, Hwy 20 Exit Chemin Ste.-Louis. 418/653-2841; fax 418/653-8525.* 100 rms, 2 story. July-Aug: S, D $89-$119; each addl $5; under 18 free; wkend rates; lower rates rest of yr. Crib free. TV; cable, VCR avail. Pool; poolside serv, lifeguard. Restaurant 7 am-10 pm. Bar noon-10 pm. Ck-out noon. Meeting rms. Business servs avail. In-rm modem link. Valet serv. Health club privileges. Some refrigerators. Cr cds: A, C, D, DS, ER, MC, V.

D ⊷ ⇶ ▨ SC

★★ **CHALETS MONTMORENCY.** *1768 Ave Royale (G0A 3R0), E on Hwy 138, E on Hwy 360. 418/826-2600; fax 418/826-1123; toll-free 800/463-2612. www.holidayjunction.com.* 35 rms, 3 story, 25 kit. suites. S $48-$51; D $64-$68; suites $79-$390; ski, golf plans. Crib $5. TV; cable, VCR avail.

2 pools, 1 indoor; whirlpool. Sauna. Restaurant adj 8 am-11 pm. Ck-out noon. Business servs avail. Coin lndry. 18-hole golf course. Downhill/x-country ski 1 mi. Rec rm. Microwaves. Balconies. Picnic tables. Cr cds: MC, V.

Upper Town, Québec City

★ **DAYS INN.**
2250 Ste.-Anne Blvd (Hwy 138) (G1J 1Y2). 418/661-7701; fax 418/661-5221; toll-free 800/463-5568. Email voyageur@mediom.qc.ca. 62 rms, 2 story. Mid-June-mid-Sep: S $70; D $75; each addl $10; suites $130; under 12 free; wkly rates off-season; lower rates rest of yr. Crib free. TV; cable (premium). 2 pools, 1 indoor; poolside serv. Sauna. Coffee in rms. Restaurant 7-10 am; Sat, Sun to 11 am. Ck-out noon. Meeting rms. Business servs avail. Free parking. Some refrigerators. Balconies. Cr cds: A, D, ER, JCB, MC, V.

★★ **HOTEL CHATEAU LAURIER.**
1220 Georges 5th W (G1R 5B8). 418/522-8108; fax 418/524-8768; toll-free 800/463-4453. www.old-quebec.com/laurier. 57 rms, 4 story. May-Oct: S $79-$99; D $89-$109; each addl $10; under 12 free; lower rates rest of yr. Crib free. Pet accepted, some restrictions. TV; cable, VCR avail. Restaurant 7:30 am-3:30 pm. Bar 11-3 am. Ck-out noon. Business servs avail. Cr cds: A, D, DS, ER, MC, V.

★ **MOTEL SPRING.** *8520 Ste.-Anne (G0A 1N0), N on Hwy 138. 418/824-4953; fax 418/824-4117; toll-free 888/824-4953.* July-Aug: S, D $45; lower rates rest of yr. TV; cable. Restaurant 7 am-9 pm. Ck-out 11 am, ck-in 1 pm. Golf. Cr cds: MC, V.

★ **ONCLE SAM.** *7025 W Hamel Blvd (G2G 1V6), 5½ mi W on Hwy 138, jct Hwy 540. 418/872-1488; fax 418/871-5519; toll-free 800/414-1488.* 44 rms, 1-2 story. Mid-June-mid-Sep: S, D $59-$79; each addl $10; under 14 free; lower rates rest of yr. Pet accepted. TV; cable, VCR avail. Heated pool. Playground. Ck-out noon. Coin lndry. Business servs avail. X-country ski 5 mi. Picnic table. Cr cds: A, C, D, ER, MC, V.

★★ **SELECTOTEL ROND-POINT.**
53 Kennedy Blvd (J6W 6C7), jct Rive-Sud Blvd (Hwy 132) and Hwy 173; 1 mi N of Autoroute Jean Lesage (Hwy 20), Exit 325N. 418/833-4920; fax 418/833-0634. 124 rms, 2 story. July-mid-Sep: S $95—$105; D $119-$129; each addl $5; suites $150; each addl $10; lower rates rest of yr. Crib $5. TV; cable. Indoor heated pool. Restaurant 7 am-2 pm, 4:30-9:30 pm. Ck-out noon. Ck-in 2 pm. Coin lndry. Meeting rms. Business servs avail. Barber. Downhill/x-country ski 30 mi. Massage. 18- and 9-hole golf nearby. Miniature golf. Some refrigerators. Some balconies. Ferry 5 min to Old Québec. Cr cds: A, C, D, DS, ER, MC, V.

Hotels

★ **CHATEAU BELLVUE.** *16 rue Laporte (G1R 4M9). 418/692-2573; fax 418/692-4876; toll-free 800/463-5256. Email lmorin@loews.com.,www.loews hotels.com.* 58 rms, 3 story. May-Oct: S, D $129-$149; each addl $10; winter packages; under 12 free; lower rates rest of yr. Parking. A/C. Crib free. TV; cable. Complimentary continental bkfst (Mid-Oct-Apr). Restaurants nearby. No rm serv. Ck-out noon. Ck-in 2 pm. In-rm modem link. Business servs avail. View of St Lawrence River. Cr cds: A, D, DS, ER, JCB, MC, V.

★★★ **CHATEAU BONNE ENTENTE.** *3400 Chemin Ste.-Foy (G1X 1S6), 6 mi W on CAN 73, Duplessis Exit, then Chemin Ste.-Foy Exit W.* 418/653-5221; fax 418/653-3098; toll-free 800/463-4390. www.chateau bonneentente.com. 109 rms, 3 story. May-Oct: S $168-$188; D $174-$194; each addl $15; suites $298-$314; under 17 free; wkend rates; lower rates rest of yr. Crib free. TV; cable, VCR avail. Heated pool; poolside serv, lifeguard. Playground. Free supervised children's activities; ages 6 month and up. Complimentary coffee in lobby. Restaurant 6:30-11 am, noon-2 pm, 5-10 pm; Sat, Sun from 7 am (see also LE PAILLEUR). High tea service 2-4 pm. Bar 11-2 am. Ck-out 1 pm. Meeting rms. Business center. In-rm modem link. Valet serv. Sundries. Free airport, bus depot, Rail Road station transportation. Tennis. X-country ski 5 mi. Exercise equipt. Massage. Rec rm. Lawn games. Whirlpool in suites. Picnic table. Stocked pond. Cr cds: A, DS, ER, MC, V.

★★ **CLARENDON.** *57 rue Ste. Anne (G1R 3X4).* 418/692-2480; fax 418/692-4652; res 888/554-6001. Email m.tanguay@hotelclarendon; www.hotel clarendon.com. 151 rms, 7 story. June-mid-Oct: S, D $99-$119; each addl $20; suites $189-$199; under 12 free; lower rates rest of yr. Crib free. Parking $6. TV; cable. Restaurant 7-10:30 am, noon-2 pm, 6-10 pm. Bar 11-3 am; entertainment. Ck-out noon. Meeting rms. Business servs avail. Historic hotel (1870), the oldest in Québec. Cr cds: A, MC, V.

★★★ **GOUVERNEUR HOTEL STE.-FOY.** *3030 Laurier Blvd (G1V 2M5), 5 mi SW on Hwy 73, ½ mi E of Laurier Blvd Exit.* 418/651-3030; fax 418/651-6797; toll-free 888/910-1111. 317 rms, 4 story, 3 suites. May-Sep: S $165; D $180; each addl $15; under 18 free; lower rates rest of yr. Crib avail. Parking lot. Pool, lifeguard. TV; cable (premium), VCR avail. Complimentary coffee in rms, newspaper. Restaurant. Bar. Conference center, meeting rms. Business center. Bellhops. Dry cleaning. Gift shop. Exercise privileges. Golf. Downhill skiing. Video games. Cr cds: A, D, DS, ER, JCB, MC, V.

★★★ **HILTON.** *1100 Blvd René Levesque E (G1K 7M9).* 418/647-2411; fax 418/647-3737; res 800/447-2411. 571 rms, 23 story. Mid-May-mid-Oct: S $138-$187; D $160-$209; each addl $22; suites $355-$835; wkend rates. Crib free. Pet accepted, some restrictions. Parking $16. TV; cable. Pool; poolside serv, lifeguard. Coffee in rms. Restaurant 7 am-midnight. Bars 11 am-midnight. Ck-out noon. Meeting rms. Business center. Barber, beauty shop. Downhill ski 11 mi; x-country ski nearby. Exercise rm; sauna. Massage. Québec Convention Center opp. Luxury level. Cr cds: A, C, D, DS, ER, JCB, MC, V.

★★ **HOTEL CLASSIQUE.** *2815 Blvd Laurier (G1Z 4H3), 1 mi E of Hwy 73, Blvd Laurier Exit.* 418/658-2793; fax 418/658-6816; res 888/463-0083. 237 rms, 32 A/C, 12 story, 102 suites, 60 kit. units (no equipt). May-Sep: S $80-$110; D $110-$140; each addl $10; suites, kit. units $110-$180; under 12 free; wkly rates; lower rates rest of yr. Crib $10. TV; cable. 2 pools, 1 indoor; lifeguard. Restaurant open 24 hrs. Bar 11-3 am. Ck-out noon. Coin lndry. Meeting rms. Business servs avail. In-rm modem link. Free indoor parking. Gift shop. Health club privileges. Balconies. Cr cds: A, C, D, ER, MC, V.

★★★ **HOTEL GERMAIN-DES-PRES.** *1200 Ave Germain-Des-Pres (G1V 3M7), 3 mi W on Blvd Laurier.* 418/658-1224; fax 418/658-8846. 126 rms, 8 story. June-mid-Oct: S $130; D $140; each addl $15; wkend rates; lower rates rest of yr. Crib free. TV; cable, VCR avail. Coffee in rms. Restaurant 7-10 am, 5-11 pm (see also BISTANGO). Bar 5-11 pm. Ck-out noon. Business servs avail. In-rm modem link. Some free covered parking. Free airport, railroad station, bus depot transportation. Health club privileges. Bathrm phones, minibars. Cactus garden in lobby. Cr cds: A, C, D, ER, MC, V.

★★ HOTEL PLAZA QUEBEC.

3031 Blvd Laurier (G1Z 2M2), 6 mi W. 418/658-2727; fax 418/658-6587; toll-free 800/567-5276. 231 rms, 7 story. May-Oct: S $105-$125; D $120-$140; each addl $10-$15; suites $150-$250; family, wkend rates; lower rates rest of yr. Crib free. Free garage parking. TV; cable. Indoor pool; lifeguard, whirlpool. Saunas. Restaurant 6 am-11 pm. Bar. Ck-out noon. Meeting rms. Business center. Gift shop. Refrigerator in suites. Some balconies. Indoor garden. Cr cds: A, D, DS, ER, MC, V.

★★ HOTEL UNIVERSEL. *2300 Chemin Ste.-Foy (G1V 1S5), 3 mi NE of Pierre-Laporte Bridge via Quatre Bourgeois Exit from Hwy 73. 418/653-5250; fax 418/653-4486; res 800/463-4495. Email infi@hoteluniversel.qc.ca; www.hoteluniversel.qc.ca.* 127 rms, 3 story, 47 kits. S, D, suites $79; each addl $5; under 14 free. Crib free. TV; cable. Indoor pool. Sauna. Playground. Restaurant noon-11 pm. Bar 5 pm-1 am. Ck-out noon. Meeting rms. Business servs avail. Bellhops. X-country ski 3 mi. Some refrigerators. Balconies. Cr cds: A, DS, MC, V.

★★★ LE CHATEAU FRONTENAC.

1 rue Des Carrieres (G1R 4P5). 418/692-3861; fax 418/692-1751; res 800/441-1414. www.cphotels.ca. 613 rms, 18 story. May-Oct: S, D $189-$359; each addl $25; suites $399-$1,000; under 18 free; lower rates rest of yr. Crib free. Garage parking $15.45. TV; cable, VCR avail. Indoor pool; whirlpool, wading pool, poolside serv. Restaurant 7 am-midnight (see also LE CHAMPLAIN). Bar 11-2 am; entertainment. Ck-out noon. Meeting rms. Business center. In-rm modem link. Shopping arcade. Ice skating. Downhill ski 11 mi; x-country ski 3 mi. Exercise rm. Minibars. Landmark chateau-style hotel (1893); site of historic conferences during WWII. Cr cds: A, C, D, DS, ER, JCB, MC, V.

★★★★ LOEWS LE CONCORDE.

1225 Place Montcalm (G1R 4W6), on Grande Allée. 418/647-2222; fax 418/647-4710; toll-free 800/463-5256. www.loewshotels.com. See a vision of Paris out your window from this 404-room hotel on Quebec City's "Champs-Elysees". Just 15 minutes from the airport, the tower has views of the St. Lawrence River, the city lights, and the historic Plains of Abraham. A visit is not complete without a peek, and hopefully a meal, at L'Astral, the revolving, rooftop restaurant. 404 rms, 26 story. May-Oct: S, D $99-$215; each addl $20; suites $180-$750; wkend, ski plans; lower rates rest of yr. Crib free. Pet accepted. Garage $14; valet parking $18. TV; cable. Heated pool; whirlpool, poolside serv, lifeguard. Restaurant 6:45 am-midnight (see also L'ASTRAL). Bars 11-3 am. Ck-out 1 pm. Meeting rms. Business center. In-rm modem link. Concierge serv. Downhill ski 11 mi; x-country ski on site. Tennis privileges. Exercise rm; sauna. Health club privileges. Refrigerators, minibars; fireplace in 2 bilevel suites. Luxury level. Cr cds: A, C, D, DS, ER, JCB, MC, V.

★★ QUEBEC INN. *7175 W Hamel Blvd (G2G 1B6), 6½ mi W on Hwy 138. 418/872-9831; fax 418/872-1336; res 800/567-5276. Email quebecinn@jaro. qc.ca; www.jaro.com.* 135 rms, 2 story. June-mid-Oct: S $76.95-$86.95; D $86.95-$96.95; each addl $10; family rates; package plans; lower rates rest of yr. TV; cable. Indoor pool; whirlpool, poolside serv. Restaurant 6:30 am-11 pm. Bar 11-3 am; entertainment Wed-Sun. Ck-out noon. Meeting rms. Business servs avail. In-rm modem link. Beauty, barber shop. X-country ski 5 mi. Exercise rm; sauna. Massage. Balconies. Indoor garden. Cr cds: A, D, ER, MC, V.

★★★ RADISSON HOTEL GOUVERNEUR QUEBEC. *690 Blvd René-Levesque E (G1R 5A8), in Place Haute-Ville. 418/647-1717; fax 418/647-2146; res 800/333-3333; toll-free 888/884-7777. Email bhollingworth@ chipreit.com; www.radisson.com.* 371 rms, 12 story, 6 suites. May-Oct: S, D $245; suites $675; each addl $20; under 17 free; lower rates rest of yr. Crib avail, fee. Pet accepted, some restrictions, fee. Valet parking avail. Pool, lifeguard, whirlpool. TV; cable (premium). Complimentary coffee in rms, newspaper. Restaurant 7 am-10 pm. Bar. Ck-out noon, ck-in 3 pm. Conference center, meeting rms. Busi-

ness center. Bellhops. Dry cleaning. Gift shop. Salon/barber avail. Exercise rm, sauna. Golf. Downhill skiing. Cr cds: A, C, D, DS, ER, MC, V.

Oldest street in Québec City

Resort

★★★ MANOIR DU LAC DELAGE.
40 Ave Du Lac (G0A 4P0), 13 mi N via Hwy 175 to Hwy 371, then W to Lac Delage and follow signs. 418/848-2551; fax 418/848-1352; toll-free 800/463-8841. www.lacdelage.com. 105 rms, 54 A/C, 1-3 story. MAP: S $119-$145; D $164-$190; each addl $60; EP avail. Crib free. TV; cable. 2 pools; 1 indoor, poolside serv. Playground. Dining rm 7-10 am, noon-2 pm, 6-9 pm. Bar 11-1 am; pianist. Ck-out noon, ck-in 3 pm. Meeting rms. Business servs avail. Lighted tennis. Marina; canoes, paddleboats, sailboats, windsurfing. Downhill ski 2 mi; x-country ski on site. Snowshoe activities, sledding, skating. Bicycles. Lawn games. Exercise equipt; sauna. Massage. Some minibars. Balconies. On lake. Summer theater performances. Cr cds: A, D, MC, V.

B&Bs/Small Inns

★ AU CHATEAU FLEUR DE LYS.
15 Ste.-Genevieve Ave (G1R 4A8), 1 blk N of Citadel. 418/694-1884; fax 418/694-1666; toll-free 877/691-1884. 18 rms, 3 story. May-Oct: S, D $75-$120; each addl $10. Under 6 free, 12 yrs $6. Crib free. Parking $8/day. TV; cable. Restaurants nearby. Ck-out noon, ck-in 1 pm. Business servs

avail. Refrigerators. Located in Old Québec in an 1873 greystone house. Panoramic view of gardens. Cr cds: A, DS, MC, V.

★★ AU MANOIR STE.-GENEVIEVE.
13 Ste.-Genevieve Ave (G1R 4A7), 1 blk N of Citadel. 418/694-1666; fax 418/694-1666; toll-free 877/694-1666. 9 rms, 3 story, 3 kit. suites. No rm phones. May-Oct: S $87; D, kit. units $100; each addl $10; under 12 free; lower rates rest of yr. Crib free. Parking $6. TV; cable. Continental bkfst. Ck-out noon, ck-in 1 pm. Business servs avail. Greystone house (1895) with terrace on upper level. Cr cds: A, MC, V.

Restaurants

★ AU CAFE SUISSE.
32 Ste.-Anne St (G1R 3X3), in front of Chateau Frontenac. 418/694-1320. Email reservations@cafesuisse.qc.ca. Specializes in fondues, seafood, steak. Hrs: 8 am-11 pm; summer to midnight. Res accepted. Bar. Bkfst a la carte entrees: $3.95-$9.95; lunch a la carte entrees: $7.95-$24.95; dinner a la carte entrees: $7.95-$24.95. Complete meals: $19.95-$24.95. Entertainment: pianist Sat. Parking. Turn-of-the-century greystone house. Cr cds: A, MC, V.

★★ AUX ANCIENS CANADIENS.
34 rue Ste.-Louis (G1R 4P3). 418/692-1627. www.auxancienscanadiens.qc.ca. Specializes in country-style meat pie, small game. Own pastries. Hrs: noon-9:30 pm. Res accepted. Bar. Wine list. Lunch a la carte entrees: $20-$29.; dinner a la carte entrees: $20-$29. Table d'hote: $24.50-$35. Entertainment. In bldg reputedly used as headquarters by General Montcalm; antiques. Family-owned. Cr cds: A, ER, MC, V.

★★ **BACO RESTAURANT AND WINE BAR.** *200 Beachwood Ave (K1L 8A9). 613/747-0272. Email baccus@ skybiz.com.* Specializes in fresh fish, Canadian lamb. Hrs: 5-9 pm. Closed Sun, Mon. Res accepted. Wine list. Dinner $17-$32. Entertainment. Cr cds: A, C, D, DS, ER, JCB, MC, V.
D ⊣

★★ **BISTANGO.** *1200 Ave Germain des Pres, 3 mi W at Blvd Laurier. 418/658-8780.* Specializes in light French and California-style cuisine. Hrs: 7 am-11 pm; Sat from 5:30 pm. Res accepted. Bar. Lunch a la carte entrees: $9.95-$11.95; dinner complete meals: $22-$25. Child's menu. Entertainment. Valet parking. French bistro decor. Cr cds: A, D, MC, V.
D ⊣

★ **CAFE DE PARIS.** *66 rue Ste.-Louis (G1R 3Z3). 418/694-9626.* Specializes in seafood, veal. Hrs: 11 am-11 pm. Res accepted. Lunch a la carte entrees: $9.95-$14.95; dinner a la carte entrees: $19.95-$29.95. Child's menu. Entertainment. Free valet parking. Built in 1827. Rustic decor; many original oil paintings. Cr cds: A, D, ER, MC, V.
⊣

★★★ **L'ASTRAL.** *1225 place Montcalm. 418/647-2222.* Specializes in rack of lamb, filet of veal, duckling with maple syrup. Salad bar. Own pastries. Hrs: 8 am-9 pm. Res required. Bar. Wine cellar. Lunch a la carte entrees: $9.50-$16.50. Buffet: $16.50; dinner a la carte entrees: $19.50-$35.50. Buffet: $38.95. Sun brunch $23.75. Child's menu. Entertainment: pianist. Valet parking. Revolving rooftop restaurant. Cr cds: A, D, MC, V.
D ⊣

★ **L'OMELETTE.** *64 rue Ste.-Louis (G1R 3Z3). 418/694-9626.* Specializes in omelets, seafood, beef. Hrs: 7 am-11 pm. Closed Nov-Mar. Res accepted. Bkfst a la carte entrees: $3.50-$5.25; lunch a la carte entrees: $3-$6.95; dinner a la carte entrees: $5-$13.75. Entertainment. Valet parking. Cr cds: A, D, ER, MC, V.
⊣

★★★ **LA MAISON SERGE BRUYERE.** *1200 rue Ste.-Jean (G1R 1S8). 418/694-0618.* Specializes in caribou (seasonal), grilled salmon. Own pastries. Hrs: 6-10 pm. Res accepted. Wine list. Dinner prix fixe: $8.95-$100. Entertainment. Valet parking. Fireplaces, original oil paintings; view of Ste. John's gate and City Hall. Family-owned. Cr cds: A, D, ER, MC, V.
D ⊣

★★ **LA RIPAILLE.** *9 rue de Buade (G1R 3Z9). 418/692-2450.* Specializes in seafood, rack of lamb, veal tenderloin. Own pastries. Hrs: 9 am-11 pm; early-bird dinner 5-7 pm. Res accepted. Lunch a la carte entrees: $10-$15. Complete meals: $8.95-$13.50; dinner a la carte entrees: $17-$20.95. Complete meals: $25.95. Child's menu. Entertainment. Valet parking. In 1835 bldg. Cr cds: A, D, DS, ER, MC, V.
SC ⊣

★★★★ **LAURIE RAPHAEL.** *117 Dalhousis (G1K 9C8), in the Old Port next to the Civilization Museum. 418/ 692-4555. www.resto-laurie-raphael. com/anglais.html.* Owner/chef Daniel Vezina and Suzanne Gagnon preside over this cheerful, Old-Port-district eatery with red-checked, upholstered chairs, red walls and sparkling windows. The menu is adventurous, "market cuisine" changing every two weeks to incorporate local ingredients and worldly spices. Try dishes such as Moroccan-style roast lamb with maple syrup and confit of leeks with one of the nearly 40 by-the-glass wines. Specializes in Asian, French dishes. Hrs: 9 am-9 pm; Sat, Sun 5 pm-midnight. Res required. Bkfst $19-$32; lunch, dinner $19-$32. Child's menu. Entertainment. Cr cds: C, D, DS, ER, MC, V.
D ⊣

★★ **LE BONAPARTE.** *680 E Grande-Allee (G1R 2K5). 418/647-4747.* Specializes in rack of lamb, steak, seafood. Own pastries. Hrs: noon-4 pm, 5:30-10:30 pm; hrs vary Nov-Mar. Res accepted. Bar. Lunch complete meals: $7.95-$14.95; dinner complete meals: $22.95-$28.95. A la carte entrees: $10.95-$28.95. Child's menu. Entertainment: French murder mystery Fri dinner. In 1823 bldg. Cr cds: A, MC, V.

D 🍴

★★★ **LE CHAMPLAIN.** *1 rue Des Carrieres. 418/692-3861. www. cphotels.ca.* Specializes in Quebec smoked salmon, rack of lamb. Own pastries. Hrs: 6:30-9 pm. Res accepted. Extensive wine list. Dinner a la carte entrees: $27-$66. Table d'hote $55-$59. Entertainment: harpist Fri, Sat. Valet parking. Jacket. Classic French atmosphere. Cr cds: A, C, D, DS, ER, MC, V.

D 🍴

★★★ **LE CONTINENTAL.** *26 rue Ste.-Louis (G1R 3Y9), 1 blk W of Place D'Armes. 418/694-9995. www.le continental.com.* Specializes in steak tartare, curried shrimp, orange duck-ing flambe. Own pastries. Hrs: noon-11 pm. Closed Dec 24, 25. Res accepted. Wine cellar. Lunch com-plete meals: $9.75-$16.95; dinner a la carte entrees: $19-$31. Complete meals: $29-$35. Entertainment. Valet parking. Tableside cooking. Near Chateau Frontenac. Family-owned. Cr cds: A, C, D, DS, ER, MC, V.

D

★ **LE MANOIR DU SPAGHETTI.** *3077 Chemin Ste.-Louis (G1W 1R6). 418/659-5628. Email manoir@ videotron.net.* Specializes in pasta, veal. Hrs: 11 am-10 pm; Thurs to 10:30 pm; Fri, Sat to 11 pm. Res accepted. Lunch a la carte entrees: $5.50-$16.99. Complete meals: $5.49-$9.99; dinner a la carte entrees: $5.50-$16.99. Complete meals: $13-$24. Child's menu. Enter-tainment. Parking. Cafe bar. Cr cds: A, D, MC, V.

D 🍴

★★★ **LE PAILLEUR.** *3400 Chemin Ste.-Foy. 418/653-5221. www.chateau donneentent.ca.* Specializes in grilled meats, seafood. Hrs: 6 am-9:30 pm; Sun brunch 10 am-2 pm. Res accepted. Bar. Wine list. Bkfst a la carte entrees: $4.95-$9.95. Buffet: $9.95; lunch buffet: $12.95; dinner complete meals: $22-$33.95. Child's menu. Entertainment: pianist Fri-Sun. Parking. Traditional and original Québec cooking, using local prod-ucts. Cr cds: A, C, D, DS, ER, MC, V.

D 🍴

★★★ **LE ST.-AMOUR.** *48 Ste.-Ursule (G1R 4E2). 418/694-0667. www.saint-amour.com.* Specializes in foie gras, rack of lamb, royale chocolate. Hrs: 11:30 am-2:30 pm, 6-11 pm; Sat-Mon from 6 pm. Closed Dec 24. Res accepted. Wine cellar. Lunch a la carte entrees: $19.50-$28.50; dinner a la carte entrees: $19.50-$28.50. Child's menu. Entertainment. Valet parking. Family-owned since 1978. Cr cds: A, C, D, DS, ER, MC, V.

🍴

★★ **LE VENDOME.** *36 Cote de la Montagne (G1K 4E2). 418/692-0557.* Specializes in steaks, seafood, veal. Hrs: 11:30 am-2 pm, 5:30-11 pm. Closed Dec 24. Res accepted. Bar. Lunch a la carte entrees: $7.50-$12.50; dinner a la carte entrees: $14.50-$23. Child's menu. Entertain-ment. Valet parking. Parisian decor; murals. Family-owned since 1951. Cr cds: A, C, D, DS, ER, MC, V.

🍴

★★ **RESTAURANT AU PARMESAN.** *38 rue Ste.-Louis (G1R 3Z1). 418/692-0341.* Italian menu. Specializes in seafood, veal. Own pasta, pastries. Hrs: noon-midnight. Closed Dec 24, 25. Res accepted. Bar. Wine cellar. Lunch a la carte entrees: $9.95-$31. Complete meals: $9.50-$13.50; din-ner a la carte entrees: $9.95-$31. Complete meals: $17.75-$26.95. Child's menu. Entertainment: accor-dionist. Valet parking. 4,000 liqueur bottles displayed; many oil paintings. Chestnuts roasted in fireplaces in winter. Cr cds: A, D, DS, ER, MC, V.

🍴

St.Jérôme

(E-5) *See also Montréal, St.-Jovite*

Pop 25,123 **Elev** 362 ft (110 m)
Area code 450
Web www.laurentides.com

Information Laurentian Tourism Association, 14142, rue de Lachapelle, RR 1, J7Z 5T4; 450/436-8532 or 800/561-6673

Founded in 1834 on the Rivière du Nord is the "Gateway to the Lauren-tians," St. Jérôme. In this resort area, amid the magnificent setting of mountains, forests, lakes and rivers, summer sports and recreation are unlimited, fall colors spectacular, and winter sports and festivals delightful. Outfitters are available to help plan a wilderness vacation, but visitors may also choose from over 200 accommodations of every price and type.

Under the fierce leadership (1868-91) of Curé Labelle, a huge man and a near legendary figure, this area began to grow. Curé Labelle hoped to open the whole country, north and to the Pacific, which was nearly empty at that time. Making over 60 canoe and foot trips of exploration, he selected sites for new parishes and founded more than 20. By pen and pulpit he sought to stop the flow of labor to the United States, and in 1876, due to his inexhaustible efforts, the railroad came to St. Jérôme, bringing new prosperity. Curé Labelle became the Minister of Agriculture and Colonization in 1888. A bronze monument honoring him is in the park opposite the cathedral.

What to See and Do

Centre d'exposition du Vieux Palais. Exhibition centre of visual arts. 185 rue du Palais, Hwy 15 N, Exit 43. Phone 514/432-7171.

St.-Jovite (D-4)

Pop 3,841 **Elev** 790 ft (241 m)
Area code 819
Web www.laurentides.com
Information Laurentian Tourism Association, 14142, rue de La Chapelle, RR 1, Saint-Jérôme, PQ, J7Z 5T4; 450/436-8532

Nestled in the valley of the du Diable River and situated close to Mont Tremblant Provincial Park (see), this major all-year tourist area is one of the oldest in the Laurentians. Hunting, fishing, snowmobiling, and skiing are among the many available activities. Three public beaches around Lac des Sables in Ste.-Agathe make this a water sports paradise; international dogsled races on ice in nearby Ste.-Agathe-des-Monts add to the excite-

ment. French summer theater, mountain climbing on Monts Condor and Césaire, antique shops, and a Santa Claus Village are other options in Val-David, to the southeast.

What to See and Do

Antiques, arts, and crafts. Interesting artisan's shops and galleries: **Le Coq Rouge**, an antique shop (phone 819/425-3205); **Alain Plourde**, Artisan (phone 819/425-7873).

Restaurant

★ **ANTIPASTO.** *855 rue Ouimet (J0T 2H0). 819/425-7580.* Specializes in pasta. Hrs: 11 am-11 pm. Wine list. Lunch, dinner $10-$29. Child's menu. Entertainment. Cr cds: A, MC, V.

Sherbrooke

(E-6) See also Granby

Pop 85,000 **Elev** 600 ft (183 m)
Area code 819
Web www.sders.com/tourism
Information Office of Tourism, 3010 King W St, J1H 5G1; 819/821-1919 or 800/561-8331

Nestled in a land of natural beauty at the confluence of the Magog and St.-François rivers, Sherbrooke is a bilingual and bicultural community. Originally settled in 1791 by the French, an influx of Loyalist settlers and English colonists brought English influence to the city, which remains today despite the 95 percent French population. More than 150 types of industries, including pulp and paper, textile, and heavy machinery manufacturing, are carried on in this major railroad center. The principal city of Québec's Eastern Townships, Sherbrooke is the center of one of Canada's fastest developing winter sports areas. There are many beautiful open areas, such as the Howard Estate with its lovely pond and grounds and the Lake of Nations.

What to See and Do

Basilica of St. Michel. Center of archbishopric.

Beauvoir Sanctuary. Setting of natural splendor on a hill. Church built in 1920. Statue of the Sacred Heart here since 1916, making it a regional pilgrimage site. Gospel scenes in outdoor mountain setting. (May-Oct, daily; Nov-Apr, Sun) Summer: picnic tables, restaurant, gift shop. 4 mi (6 km) N, Exit 146 off Hwy 10. On the east bank of the St.-François River. Phone 819/569-2535. **FREE**

Louis S. St. Laurent National Historic Site. Birthplace of Prime Minister Louis S. St. Laurent (1882-1973); landscaped grounds; general store and adj warehouse with sound and light show. (May-mid-Oct, daily) S on Hwy 147, at 6 Main St in Compton. Phone 819/835-5448. **FREE**

Mena'Sen Place. Site of large illuminated cross. Many legends surround island and its original lone pine, destroyed in a storm in 1913 and replaced by the cross in 1934.

⭐ **Mount Orford.** 2,800 ft (864 m) high with range stretching across the border into Vermont. Recreational park with swimming; campground, golf course, hiking, picnicking, lake, and wildlife. Downhill and cross-country skiing in winter. Some fees. 22 mi (35 km) SW near Hwy 10, Exit 118. Phone 819/843-6233, 800/462-5349 (PQ), or 819/462-9855 (campground res). Here are

Orford Arts Centre. World renowned hall is one of the finest auditoriums anywhere. Pavilion with teaching and practice studios, 500-seat concert hall. Performances given by noted artists during Orford Summer Festival. Visual arts program. (May-Sep) Phone 819/843-3981 or 800/567-6155 (seasonal).

Ski Mont Orford. Outstanding area and some of the best facilities in Québec. Thirty-nine runs, 8 lifts; patrol, school, rentals; day care, cafeteria, restaurant, bar. Longest run 2½ mi (4 km). (Nov-Apr, daily) 20 acres (8.09 hectares) of glade, 25 mi (40.2 km) of cross-country skiing. 18-hole golf (fee; rentals). Scenic chairlift (July-mid-Aug, daily; rest of summer, wkends only). 22 mi (36 km) SW. Phone 819/843-6548. ¢¢¢¢

Musée du Séminaire de Sherbrooke. More than 90,000 objects of natural history. (Tues-Sun afternoons) 195 rue Marquette. Phone 819/564-3200. ¢¢ Fee incl

Léon Marcotte Exhibition Centre. Presents traveling exhibitions from other museums and assembles others from the Seminary Museum. (Tues-Sun afternoons) 222 rue Frontenac. Phone 819/564-3200. ¢¢

Uplands Museum and Cultural Centre. This neo-Georgian home built in 1862 is located on 4 acres of beautifully wooded grounds. Changing exhibits interpret heritage of Lennoxville-Ascot and eastern townships. Museum contains period furniture. Red Barn, on grounds, is home to children's theater. Afternoon tea served all yr (res required in winter). (Tues-Sun; extended summer hrs) 50 Park St; S via Rte 143, W on Church to Park St in Lennoxville. Phone 819/564-0409.

Hotel

★★★ **HOTEL GOUVERNEUR SHERBROOKE.** *3131 King St W (J1L 1C8), ¼ mi E of jct Hwy 55. 819/565-0464; fax 819/565-5505; res 888/910-1111. www.gouverneur.com.* 124 rms, 4 story, 1 suite. May-Oct: S, D $79; suites $140; each addl $10; under 12 free; lower rates rest of yr. Crib avail. Pet accepted. Parking lot. Pool. TV; cable (premium). Complimentary coffee in rms. Restaurant 8 am-10 pm. Bar. Ck-out 1 pm, ck-in 3 pm. Meeting rms. Business servs avail. Dry cleaning. Exercise privileges. Golf, 18 holes. Video games. Cr cds: A, MC, V.

🄳 ➤ 🄺 🏊 🏃 🛝 🖼 🔥

Trois-Rivières

(D-6)

Pop 50,466 **Elev** 120 ft (37 m)
Area code 819
Information Tourism Information
Bureau, 1457 Notre Dame St, G9A
4X4; 819/375-1122

Considered the second-oldest French
city in North America, Trois-Rivières
was founded in 1634. Many 17th-
and 18th-century buildings remain,
and the Old Town area is a favorite
haunt for visitors. The St. Maurice
River splits into three channels here
as it joins the St. Lawrence, giving
the name to this major commercial
and industrial center and important
inland seaport. Paper milling and
shipment of cereals are some of the
more important industries. Trois-
Rivières is a cathedral and university
(Université du Québec) center as well.

What to See and Do

The Cathedral. (1854) Built in
Gothic Westminster style; contains
huge stained-glass windows, brilliantly designed by Nincheri, considered finest of their kind in North
America. Renovated in 1967. 362 rue
Bonaventure.

De Tonnancour Manor. (1723) Oldest
house in city; housed soldiers in
1812; in 1852 became the bishop's
home. Displays of painting, pottery,
sculpture, engravings, serigraphy,
and jewelry. (Tues-Sun) 864 rue des
Ursulines, Place Pierre-Boucher.
Phone 819/374-2355. **FREE**

**Les Forges du St.-Maurice National
Historic Site.** Remains of the first
ironworks industry in Canada (1729-
1883). Blast furnace and Ironmaster's
House interpretation centers; models,
audiovisual displays. Guided tours.
(Mid-May-Labour Day, daily; Labour
Day-late Oct, Wed-Sun) 8 mi (13 km)
N at 10000 boul des Forges. Phone
819/378-5116. ¢¢

Notre Dame-du-Cap. Small stone
church (1714) and large octagonal
basilica renowned for its stained-

glass windows. Important pilgrimage
site. (May-Oct, daily) Across the river,
at 626 rue Notre Dame in Cap-de-la-
Madeleine. Phone 819/374-2441.
FREE

Old Port. Magnificent view of the St.
Lawrence River. Built over part of the
old fortifications. Pulp and paper
interpretation center; riverside park;
monument to La Vérendrye, discoverer of the Rockies (1743). Off rue
Ste.-François-Xavier, overlooking
river. Phone 819/372-4633. Interpretation center ¢

Sightseeing tour. M/S *Jacques-Cartier*.
Around Trois-Rivières Harbour and
on the St. Lawrence River. Four-
hundred-passenger ship. Orchestra
on wkend evening cruises. Contact
1515 rue du Fleuve, CP 64, G9A 5E3.
(Mid-May-mid-Sep) Wharf on des
Forges St. Phone 819/375-3000. ¢¢¢

St. James Anglican Church. (1699)
Rebuilt in 1754; used at various
times as a storehouse and court; rectory used as prison, hospital, and
sheriff's office. In 1823 it became an
Anglican church and is now shared
with the United Church; carved
woodwork added in 1917; cemetery
dates from 1808. Still used for
church services. 811 rue des Ursulines. Phone 819/374-6010.

Ursuline Convent. (1700) Norman-
style architecture; bldg has been
enlarged and restored many times.
Historic chapel; museum and art collection. (May-Aug, Tues-Sun; Oct-
Apr, Wed-Sun) 734 rue des Ursulines.
Phone 819/375-7922. ¢

Annual Event

**Trois-Rivières International Vocal
Arts Festival.** Downtown. A celebration of song. Religious, lyrical, popular, ethnic, traditional singing. Phone
819/372-4635. Late June-early July.

ATTRACTION LIST

Attraction names are listed in alphabetical order followed by a symbol identifying their classification and then city. The symbols for classification are: [A] for Annual Events, [S] for Seasonal Events, and [W] for What to See and Do.

1000 Islands Camping Resort [W] *Gananoque, ON*
1000 Islands Skydeck [W] *Gananoque, ON*
1627 Pilgrim Village [W] *Plymouth, MA*
1800 House [W] *Nantucket Island, MA*
Abbe Museum, The [W] *Bar Harbor, ME*
Abbot Hall [W] *Marblehead, MA*
Abigail Adams House [W] *Braintree, MA*
Academy of Performing Arts [W] *Orleans (Cape Cod), MA*
Acadia National Park [W] *Bar Harbor, ME*
Acadia National Park [W] *Cranberry Isles, ME*
Acadia National Park [W] *Northeast Harbor, ME*
Acadia National Park [W] *Southwest Harbor, ME*
Acadian Memorial Church [W] *Grand Pre, NS*
Accursed Tombstone [W] *Bucksport, ME*
Acres of the Golden Pheasant [W] *Truro, NS*
Adams National Historic Site, The [W] *Quincy, MA*
Adams National Historic Sites Visitor Center [W] *Quincy, MA*
Addison Gallery of American Art [W] *Andover and North Andover, MA*
African Lion Safari [W] *Hamilton, ON*
Agawa Canyon Train Excursion [W] *Sault Ste. Marie, ON*
Agnes Etherington Art Centre [W] *Kingston, ON*
Aldrich Museum of Contemporary Art [W] *Ridgefield, CT*
Ale Trail [A] *Kitchener-Waterloo, ON*
Alexander Graham Bell National Historic Park [W] *Baddeck, NS*
Algoma Fall Festival [A] *Sault Ste. Marie, ON*
Algonquin Golf Courses [W] *St. Andrews, NB*
Allan Gardens [W] *Toronto, ON*
Allis-Bushnell House and Museum [W] *Madison, CT*

Altrusa Annual Antique Show and Sale [A] *Meredith, NH*
Amasa Day House [W] *East Haddam, CT*
American Antiquarian Society [W] *Worcester, MA*
American Clock and Watch Museum [W] *Bristol, CT*
American Eagle [W] *Rockland, ME*
American Independence Museum [W] *Exeter, NH*
American League baseball (Boston Red Sox) [W] *Boston, MA*
American League baseball (Toronto Blue Jays) [W] *Toronto, ON*
American Stage Festival [S] *Nashua, NH*
American Textile History Museum [W] *Lowell, MA*
America's Stonehenge [W] *Salem, NH*
Amesbury Sports Park [W] *Amesbury, MA*
Amethyst Centre [W] *Thunder Bay, ON*
Amethyst Mine Panorama [W] *Thunder Bay, ON*
Amherst College [W] *Amherst, MA*
Amherst History Museum [W] *Amherst, MA*
Amistad Memorial [W] *New Haven, CT*
Amos Blanchard House [W] *Andover and North Andover, MA*
Andrés Wines [W] *Hamilton, ON*
Androscoggin Historical Society Library and Museum [W] *Auburn, ME*
Angelique [W] *Camden, ME*
Angrignon Park [W] *Montreal, QE*
Anheuser-Busch, Inc [W] *Nashua, NH*
Antique Auto Museum [W] *Edmundston, NB*
Antique Dealers Outdoor Show and Sale [A] *Westport, CT*
Antiques, arts, and crafts [W] *St.-Jovite, QE*
Antique Show [A] *Boothbay Harbor, ME*
Antiques Bonaventure [A] *Montreal, QE*
Appledore [W] *Camden, ME*

Apple Harvest Festival [A] *Meriden, CT*
Apple Squeeze Festival [A] *Lenox, MA*
Aptucxet Trading Post [W] *Bourne (Cape Cod), MA*
Aquaboggan Water Park [W] *Saco, ME*
Arcade, The [W] *Providence, RI*
Arcadia Nature Center and Wildlife Sanctuary, Massachusetts Audubon Society [W] *Northampton, MA*
Architectural Walking Tour [W] *Kennebunkport, ME*
Arethusa Falls [W] *Bretton Woods, NH*
Aroostook Farm--Maine Agricultural Experiment Station [W] *Presque Isle, ME*
Aroostook Historical and Art Museum [W] *Houlton, ME*
Aroostook State Park [W] *Presque Isle, ME*
Around the Bay Road Race [A] *Hamilton, ON*
Arrowhead [W] *Pittsfield, MA*
Art Exhibit [A] *Bar Harbor, ME*
Art Gallery of Hamilton [W] *Hamilton, ON*
Art Gallery of Nova Scotia [W] *Halifax, NS*
Art Gallery of Ontario [W] *Toronto, ON*
Art Gallery of Windsor [W] *Windsor, ON*
Artillery Company of Newport Military Museum [W] *Newport, RI*
Artillery Park National Historic Site [W] *Quebec City, QE*
Arts and Crafts Show [A] *Old Saybrook, CT*
Arts in the Park Performance Series [S] *Pawtucket, RI*
Ashumet Holly & Wildlife Sanctuary [W] *Falmouth (Cape Cod), MA*
Astors' Beechwood [W] *Newport, RI*
Atlantic Crew Classic Rowing Regatta [A] *Fredericton, NB*
Atlantic Jazz Festival [A] *Halifax, NS*
Atlantic Seal Cruises [W] *Freeport, ME*
Attitash Bear Peak Ski Resort [W] *Bartlett, NH*
Audubon Center in Greenwich [W] *Greenwich, CT*
August Meeting of the Narragansett Indian Tribe [A] *Charlestown, RI*
Auto road [W] *Mount Washington, NH*
Autumnal Feasting [A] *Plymouth, MA*
Autumn Celebration [A] *Auburn, ME*
Awesome August Festival [A] *Cornwall, ON*

Babcock-Smith House [W] *Westerly, RI*
Back Bay area [W] *Boston, MA*
Bailey Island Cribstone Bridge [W] *Bailey Island, ME*
Baillairgé Cultural tours [W] *Quebec City, QE*
Baker Memorial Library [W] *Hanover, NH*
Balch House [W] *Beverly, MA*
Ballard Institute and Museum of Puppetry [W] *Storrs, CT*
Balloons Over Bristol [A] *Bristol, CT*
Balmy Days Cruises [W] *Boothbay Harbor, ME*
Balsams/Wilderness Ski Area [W] *Dixville Notch, NH*
Band concerts [S] *Bangor, ME*
Band concerts [S] *Beverly, MA*
Band Concerts [S] *Chatham (Cape Cod), MA*
Band concerts [S] *Hampton Beach, NH*
Bangor Fair [A] *Bangor, ME*
Bangor Historical Museum [W] *Bangor, ME*
Barbour's General Store [W] *St. John, NB*
Bar Harbor Historical Society Museum [W] *Bar Harbor, ME*
Bar Harbor Whale Watch Co [W] *Bar Harbor, ME*
Barn Playhouse [S] *New London, NH*
Barnstable County Fair [A] *Falmouth (Cape Cod), MA*
Barnum Festival [S] *Bridgeport, CT*
Barnum Museum, The [W] *Bridgeport, CT*
Barracks Museum [W] *Eastport, ME*
Barrett House "Forest Hall" [W] *Jaffrey, NH*
Barrett's Tours [W] *Nantucket Island, MA*
Bartlett Museum [W] *Amesbury, MA*
Baseball [S] *New Britain, CT*
Basilica of Sainte-Anne-de-Beaupré [W] *Quebec City, QE*
Basilica of St. Michel [W] *Sherbrooke, QE*
Basin, The [W] *Franconia Notch State Park, NH*
Basin Head Fisheries Museum [W] *Charlottetown, PE*
Basketball Hall of Fame [W] *Springfield, MA*
Baskin Robbins Putt 'n Play [W] *Gananoque, ON*
Bates College [W] *Lewiston, ME*
Battlefield House and Monument [W] *Hamilton, ON*
Battle Green [W] *Lexington, MA*
Battleship Cove [W] *Fall River, MA*

Baxter State Park [W] *Greenville, ME*

Baxter State Park [W] *Millinocket, ME*

Bay Chamber Concerts [S] *Camden, ME*

Bay State Cruise Company [W] *Boston, MA*

Bay View Cruises [W] *Portland, ME*

Beaconsfield [W] *Charlottetown, PE*

Beardsley Zoological Gardens [W] *Bridgeport, CT*

Beartown State Forest [W] *Great Barrington, MA*

"Beauport," the Sleeper-McCann House [W] *Gloucester, MA*

Beauvoir Sanctuary [W] *Sherbrooke, QE*

Beaverbrook Art Gallery [W] *Fredericton, NB*

Beaver Brook Falls [W] *Colebrook, NH*

Beaverbrook Playhouse , The [W] *Fredericton, NB*

Belcourt Castle [W] *Newport, RI*

Belfast Bay Festival [A] *Belfast, ME*

Bellevue House National Historic Site [W] *Kingston, ON*

Bell Homestead [W] *Brantford, ON*

Bell's Laboratory [W] *Boston, MA*

Ben Veldhuis Limited [W] *Hamilton, ON*

Berkshire Botanical Garden [W] *Stockbridge and West Stockbridge, MA*

Berkshire Craft Fair [A] *Great Barrington, MA*

Berkshire Museum [W] *Pittsfield, MA*

Berkshire Theatre Festival [S] *Stockbridge and West Stockbridge, MA*

Bingeman Park [W] *Kitchener-Waterloo, ON*

Biodôme de Montréal [W] *Montreal, QE*

Birthplace of Lucy Maud Montgomery [W] *Cavendish, PE*

Black Creek Pioneer Village [W] *Toronto, ON*

Black Cultural Centre [W] *Dartmouth, NS*

Black Heritage Trail [W] *Boston, MA*

Black Mountain [W] *Jackson, NH*

Blacksmith House, The [W] *Cambridge, MA*

Blackstone River Valley National Heritage Corridor [W] *Worcester, MA*

Blaine House [W] *Augusta, ME*

Blessing of the Fleet [A] *New Bedford, MA*

Blithewold Mansion and Gardens [W] *Bristol, RI*

Blithewold Mansion and Gardens [S] *Bristol, RI*

Blockhouse Historic Site [W] *St. Andrews, NB*

Block Island Ferry [W] *Narragansett, RI*

Block Island/Montauk, Long Island [W] *Block Island, RI*

Block Island/New London, CT [W] *Block Island, RI*

Block Island/Point Judith [W] *Block Island, RI*

Block Island/Providence/Newport [W] *Block Island, RI*

Bluegrass Festival [A] *Brunswick, ME*

Blue Grass Festival [A] *Norwich, CT*

Blue Hill Fair [A] *Blue Hill, ME*

Blue Hills Trailside Museum [W] *Boston, MA*

Bluenose II [W] *Halifax, NS*

Boat cruises [W] *Sault Ste. Marie, ON*

Boat ride [W] *Niagara Falls, ON*

Boat trips [W] *Portland, ME*

Boat trips. Hyannis-Nantucket Day Round Trip [W] *Nantucket Island, MA*

Boothbay Railway Village [W] *Boothbay Harbor, ME*

Boothbay Region Historical Society Museum [W] *Boothbay Harbor, ME*

Boothe Memorial Park [W] *Stratford, CT*

Boott Cotton Mills Museum [W] *Lowell, MA*

Boston African American National Historic Site [W] *Boston, MA*

Boston Common [W] *Boston, MA*

Boston Harbor Islands National Park Area [W] *Boston, MA*

Boston Marathon [A] *Boston, MA*

Boston Massacre Monument [W] *Boston, MA*

Boston Public Library [W] *Boston, MA*

Boston Tea Party Ship and Museum [W] *Boston, MA*

Boston Tours from Suburban Hotels [W] *Boston, MA*

Boston University [W] *Boston, MA*

Bourne Scenic Park [W] *Bourne (Cape Cod), MA*

Bousquet [W] *Pittsfield, MA*

Bowdoin College [W] *Brunswick, ME*

Bowdoin Summer Music Festival and School [S] *Brunswick, ME*

Bradley House Museum [W] *Woods Hole (Cape Cod), MA*

Brandeis University [W] *Waltham, MA*

Brant County Museum [W] *Brantford, ON*

Brass Mill Center [W] *Waterbury, CT*

Breakers, The [W] *Newport, RI*

Bretton Woods Ski Area [W] *Bretton Woods, NH*

Brick Market [W] *Newport, RI*

Brick Store Museum [W] *Kennebunk, ME*

Brimfield [W] *Springfield, MA*

Brock's Monument [W] *Niagara-on-the-Lake, ON*

Brockton Fair [A] *Brockton, MA*

Brockton Historical Society Museums [W] *Brockton, MA*

Brock University [W] *St. Catharines, ON*

Brockville Museum [W] *Brockville, ON*

Brodie Mountain [W] *Pittsfield, MA*

Brooks Free Library [W] *Harwich (Cape Cod), MA*

Brown & Hopkins Country Store [W] *Glocester, RI*

Brown University [W] *Providence, RI*

Bruce Museum [W] *Greenwich, CT*

Brush Hill Tours [W] *Boston, MA*

Buckman Tavern [W] *Lexington, MA*

Bullet Hill Schoolhouse [W] *Southbury, CT*

Bunker Hill Day [A] *Boston, MA*

Bunker Hill Monument [W] *Boston, MA*

Burial Hill [W] *Plymouth, MA*

Burlingame State Park [W] *Charlestown, RI*

Burlington Trout Hatchery [W] *Bristol, CT*

Burnham Tavern Museum [W] *Machias, ME*

Bush-Holley House [W] *Greenwich, CT*

Bushnell Park [W] *Hartford, CT*

Busker Carnival Festival [A] *Kitchener-Waterloo, ON*

Butler-McCook Homestead [W] *Hartford, CT*

Butterfly Zoo, The [W] *Portsmouth, RI*

Butternut Basin [W] *Great Barrington, MA*

Buttolph-Williams House [W] *Wethersfield, CT*

Buttonwood Park and Zoo [W] *New Bedford, MA*

Bytown Museum [W] *Ottawa , ON*

By Ward Market [W] *Ottawa , ON*

Byzantine Museum [W] *Montreal, QE*

Cabot House [W] *Beverly, MA*

Cadillac Shopping Outlet [W] *Warwick, RI*

Caléches [W] *Quebec City, QE*

Caléche tours [W] *Montreal, QE*

Calvin Coolidge Memorial Room [W] *Northampton, MA*

Camden Hills State Park [W] *Camden, ME*

Camden Opera House [S] *Camden, ME*

Camelot Cruises, Inc [W] *East Haddam, CT*

Campbell Falls [W] *Norfolk, CT*

Camping [W] *Rangeley, ME*

Canada Day [A] *Ottawa , ON*

Canada Day Celebration [A] *Fredericton, NB*

Canada One Factory Outlets [W] *Niagara Falls, ON*

Canadian Empress [W] *Kingston, ON*

Canadian Football Hall of Fame and Museum [W] *Hamilton, ON*

Canadian Grand Prix [A] *Montreal, QE*

Canadian International [A] *Toronto, ON*

Canadian Museum of Civilization [W] *Ottawa, ON*

Canadian Museum of Contemporary Photography [W] *Ottawa, ON*

Canadian National Exhibition [A] *Toronto, ON*

Canadian Parliament Buildings [W] *Ottawa, ON*

Canadian Ski Museum [W] *Ottawa, ON*

Canadian Tulip Festival [A] *Ottawa, ON*

Canadian War Museum [W] *Ottawa, ON*

Can Am Crown Sled Dog Races [A] *Fort Kent, ME*

Can-Am Soapbox Derby [A] *St. Catharines, ON*

Canatara Park [W] *Sarnia, ON*

Candlewood Lake [W] *Danbury, CT*

Cannon Mountain Ski Area [W] *Franconia Notch State Park, NH*

Canobie Lake Park [W] *Salem, NH*

Canoeing [W] *Fort Kent, ME*

Canoe Meadows Wildlife Sanctuary [W] *Pittsfield, MA*

Canterbury Shaker Village [W] *Concord, NH*

Cape Ann Historical Museum [W] *Gloucester, MA*

Cape Breton Highlands National Park [W] *Baddeck, NS*

Cape Cod Art Association Gallery [W] *Barnstable (Cape Cod), MA*

Cape Cod Canal Cruises [W] *Buzzards Bay (Cape Cod), MA*

Cape Cod Melody Tent [S] *Hyannis (Cape Cod), MA*

Cape Cod Museum of Natural History [W] *Brewster (Cape Cod), MA*

Cape Forchu Lighthouse [W] *Yarmouth, NS*

Cape Island Express Lines [W] *Martha's Vineyard, MA*

Cape Island Express Lines [W] *New Bedford, MA*

Cape Playhouse [S] *Dennis (Cape Cod), MA*

Capitol Center for the Arts [W] *Concord, NH*

Cap'n Fish's Boat Trips and Deep Sea Fishing [W] *Boothbay Harbor, ME*

Caprilands Herb Farm [W] *Storrs, CT*

Captain Bangs Hallet House [W] *South Yarmouth (Cape Cod), MA*

Captain David Judson House [W] *Stratford, CT*

Captain's Cove Seaport [W] *Bridgeport, CT*

Cardinal Spellman Philatelic Museum [W] *Waltham, MA*

Caribana [A] *Toronto, ON*

Caribou Historical Center [W] *Caribou, ME*

Carlton Martello Tower National Historic Park [W] *St. John, NB*

Carnaval Québec Kellogg's [A] *Quebec City, QE*

Car/passenger boat trips [W] *Woods Hole (Cape Cod), MA*

Carrabassett Valley Ski Touring Center [W] *Kingfield, ME*

Carter's X-C Ski Center [W] *Bethel, ME*

Cartier-Brébeuf National Historic Site [W] *Quebec City, QE*

Casa Loma [W] *Toronto, ON*

Casco Bay Lines [W] *Chebeague Islands, ME*

Casco Bay Lines [W] *Portland, ME*

Casey Farm [W] *North Kingstown, RI*

Casimir Pulaski State Park [W] *Glocester, RI*

Casino Montréal [W] *Montreal, QE*

Casino Windsor [W] *Windsor, ON*

Castle Craig Tower [W] *Meriden, CT*

Catamount [W] *Great Barrington, MA*

Catharine B. Mitchell Museum [W] *Stratford, CT*

Cathedral, The [W] *Trois-Rivieres, QE*

Cathedral of St. John [W] *Providence, RI*

Cathedral of the Pines [W] *Jaffrey, NH*

Cat, The [W] *Yarmouth, NS*

CCInc Auto Tape Tours [W] *Newport, RI*

Celebration of Lights [S] *Sarnia, ON*

Centennial Conservatory [W] *Thunder Bay, ON*

Centennial Park [W] *Thunder Bay, ON*

Center Church and Ancient Burying Ground [W] *Hartford, CT*

Centerville Historical Society Museum [W] *Centerville (Cape Cod), MA*

Central Burying Ground [W] *Boston, MA*

Central Connecticut State University [W] *New Britain, CT*

Central Experimental Farm [W] *Ottawa , ON*

Centre d'exposition du Vieux Palais [W] *St. Jerome, QE*

Chamard Vinyards [W] *Clinton, CT*

Chamber Arts and Crafts Festival [A] *Fairfield, CT*

Chamber Music Hall [W] *Lenox, MA*

Changing the Guard [S] *Ottawa , ON*

Chapel of Our Lady of Sorrows [W] *Halifax, NS*

Chapman-Hall House [W] *Damariscotta, ME*

Charles Hayden Planetarium [W] *Boston, MA*

Charles Ives Center for the Arts [S] *Danbury, CT*

Charles River Regatta [A] *Boston, MA*

Charlottetown Festival [S] *Charlottetown, PE*

Charter fishing trips [W] *Groton, CT*

Charter fishing trips [W] *Norwalk, CT*

Château Ramezay [W] *Montreal, QE*

Chateau-sur-Mer [W] *Newport, RI*

Chatfield Hollow State Park [W] *Clinton, CT*

Chebeague Transportation [W] *Chebeague Islands, ME*

Chelsea Street Festival [A] *Norwich, CT*

Cheney Homestead [W] *Manchester, CT*

Cheshire Fair [A] *Keene, NH*

Chesterwood [W] *Stockbridge and West Stockbridge, MA*

Chestnut Street [W] *Salem, MA*

Children's Animal Farm [W] *Sarnia, ON*

Children's Chimes Bell Tower [W] *Stockbridge and West Stockbridge, MA*

Children's Museum of Boston [W] *Boston, MA*

Children's Museum [W] *Hamilton, ON*

Children's Museum [W] *Holyoke, MA*

Children's Museum [W] *New Bedford, MA*

Children's Museum of Maine [W] *Portland, ME*

Children's Museum of Portsmouth [W] *Portsmouth, NH*

Chin International Picnic [A] *Toronto, ON*

Christa McAuliffe Planetarium [W] *Concord, NH*

Christ Church [W] *Cambridge, MA*

Christian Science Publishing Society [W] *Boston, MA*

Christmas by the Sea [A] *Camden, ME*

Christmas Crafts Expo I & II [A] *Hartford, CT*

Christmas in Newport [A] *Newport, RI*

Christmas Stroll [A] *Nantucket Island, MA*

Christmas Torchlight Parade [A] *Old Saybrook, CT*

Chronicle of Salem [W] *Salem, MA*

Chrysanthemum Festival [A] *Bristol, CT*

Church [W] *Quebec City, QE*

City Hall [W] *Fredericton, NB*

City Hall [W] *Kingston, ON*

City Hall [W] *Ottawa , ON*

City Hall [W] *Toronto, ON*

City parks [W] *Toronto, ON*

Civilian Conservation Corps Museum [W] *Stafford Springs, CT*

Clam Festival [A] *Yarmouth, ME*

Clark House [W] *Wolfeboro, NH*

Clark's Trading Post [W] *Lincoln/North Woodstock Area, NH*

Cliff Walk [W] *Newport, RI*

Clock Tower [W] *Niagara-on-the-Lake, ON*

Clydesdale Hamlet [W] *Nashua, NH*

CN Tower [W] *Toronto, ON*

Cobscook Bay [W] *Machias, ME*

Cocheco Arts Festival [S] *Dover, NH*

Codman House [W] *Concord, MA*

Coffin House [W] *Newburyport, MA*

Coggeshall Farm Museum [W] *Bristol, RI*

Cog railway [W] *Mount Washington, NH*

Colasanti Farms, Ltd [W] *Windsor, ON*

Colborne Lodge [W] *Toronto, ON*

Colby College [W] *Waterville, ME*

Colchester County Museum [W] *Truro, NS*

Cole Land Transportation Museum [W] *Bangor, ME*

Coleman State Park [W] *Colebrook, NH*

Cole's Hill [W] *Plymouth, MA*

Collection of Musical Instruments [W] *New Haven, CT*

College Light Opera Co at Highfield Theatre [S] *Falmouth (Cape Cod), MA*

Colonel Ashley House [W] *Great Barrington, MA*

Colonial Pemaquid State Memorial [W] *Damariscotta, ME*

Colony Mill Marketplace [W] *Keene, NH*

Colt State Park [W] *Bristol, RI*

Colt State Park [S] *Bristol, RI*

Columbia Covered Bridge [W] *Colebrook, NH*

Computer Museum [W] *Boston, MA*

Concord Arts & Crafts [W] *Concord, NH*

Concord Free Public Library [W] *Concord, MA*

Concord Museum [W] *Concord, MA*

Confederation Centre of the Arts [W] *Charlottetown, PE*

Confederation Park [W] *Stratford, ON*

Confederation Tour Trolley [W] *Kingston, ON*

Congregational Christian Church [W] *Franklin, NH*

Connecticut Audubon Society Birdcraft Museum and Sanctuary [W] *Fairfield, CT*

Connecticut Audubon Society Fairfield Nature Center and Larsen Sanctuary [W] *Fairfield, CT*

Connecticut Audubon Society Holland Brook Nature Center [W] *Hartford, CT*

Connecticut Firemen's Historical Society Fire Museum [W] *Manchester, CT*

Connecticut Fire Museum [W] *Windsor Locks, CT*

Connecticut Historical Society [W] *Hartford, CT*

Connecticut Repertory Theatre [S] *Storrs, CT*

Connecticut River Cruise [W] *Hartford, CT*

Connecticut River Museum [W] *Essex, CT*

Connecticut State Museum of Natural History [W] *Storrs, CT*

Connecticut Storytelling Festival [A] *New London, CT*

Connecticut Trolley Museum [W] *Windsor, CT*

Conway Homestead-Cramer Museum [W] *Camden, ME*

Conway Scenic Railroad [W] *North Conway, NH*

Copley Square [W] *Boston, MA*

Copp's Hill Burying Ground [W] *Boston, MA*

Correctional Service of Canada Museum [W] *Kingston, ON*

Court House [W] *Niagara-on-the-Lake, ON*

Coventry Gardens and Peace Fountain [W] *Windsor, ON*

Covered bridge [W] *Cornwall Bridge, CT*

Covered bridges [W] *North Conway, NH*

Craft Centre [W] *Baddeck, NS*

Cranberry Cove Boating Co [W] *Southwest Harbor, ME*

Cranberry Harvest Festival [A] *Harwich (Cape Cod), MA*

Cranberry World [W] *Plymouth, MA*

Crane Beach [W] *Ipswich, MA*

Crane Museum [W] *Pittsfield, MA*

Crawford Notch State Park [W] *Bretton Woods, NH*

Crescent Beach [W] *Portland, ME*

Cross-country skiing [W] *Fort Kent, ME*

Crowninshield-Bentley House [W] *Salem, MA*

Crysler Farm Battlefield Park [W] *Morrisburg, ON*

Crystal Palace Amusement Park [W] *Moncton, NB*

Culinary Archives & Museum [W] *Providence, RI*

Culturama Festival [A] *Fort Frances, ON*

Currency Museum [W] *Ottawa, ON*

Currier Gallery of Art [W] *Manchester, NH*

Cushing House Museum [W] *Newburyport, MA*

Custom House [W] *Salem, MA*

Custom House Maritime Museum [W] *Newburyport, MA*

Daffodil Festival [A] *Meriden, CT*

Daffodil Festival [A] *Nantucket Island, MA*

Damon House [W] *Northampton, MA*

Danforth Museum of Art [W] *Framingham, MA*

Danvers Family Festival [A] *Danvers, MA*

Dartmouth College [W] *Hanover, NH*

Dartmouth Natal Day [A] *Dartmouth, NS*

Dartmouth Row [W] *Hanover, NH*

Dartmouth Skiway [W] *Hanover, NH*

David M. Stewart Museum [W] *Montreal, QE*

Days of Wine and Roses, The [A] *Niagara-on-the-Lake, ON*

Deacon John Grave House [W] *Madison, CT*

DeCordova Museum & Sculpture Park [W] *Concord, MA*

Dedham Historical Society [W] *Dedham, MA*

Deep River Ancient Muster [A] *Essex, CT*

Denison Homestead [W] *Mystic, CT*

Denison Pequotsepos Nature Center [W] *Mystic, CT*

Dennis Hill [W] *Norfolk, CT*

Derby House [W] *Salem, MA*

Derby Wharf [W] *Salem, MA*

Destination Plymouth Sprint Triathlon [A] *Plymouth, MA*

De Tonnancour Manor [W] *Trois-Rivieres, QE*

Dinosaur State Park. [W] *Wethersfield, CT*

Discovery Harbour [W] *Toronto, ON*

Discovery Museum [W] *Bridgeport, CT*

Dogwood Festival [A] *Fairfield, CT*

Dolly Copp Campground [W] *Gorham, NH*

Donald G. Trayser Memorial Museum [W] *Barnstable (Cape Cod), MA*

Doon Heritage Crossroads [W] *Kitchener-Waterloo, ON*

Dorchester Square [W] *Montreal, QE*

Double-decker Bus Tour of London [W] *London, ON*

Double-Decker bus tours. Capital Trolley Tours [W] *Ottawa, ON*

Double Decker Tours [W] *Halifax, NS*

Double Eagle II Launch Site Monument [W] *Presque Isle, ME*

Downeast Whitewater Rafting [W] *North Conway, NH*

Downtown Summertime Street Festival [A] *New Haven, CT*

Dozynki Polish Harvest Festival [A] *New Britain, CT*

Dragon Boat Festival [A] *London, ON*

Dr. Moses Mason House Museum [W] *Bethel, ME*

Drumlin Farm Education Center [W] *Concord, MA*

du Maurier Québec Summer Festival [A] *Quebec City, QE*

Dundurn Castle [W] *Hamilton, ON*

Durham Fair [A] *Middletown, CT*

Dyer Library and York Institute Museum [W] *Saco, ME*

Eagle Aviation [W] *East Haddam, CT*

Eagle Tours Inc [W] *Portland, ME*

Eastern National Morgan Horse Show [A] *Northampton, MA*

Eastern Slope Playhouse [S] *North Conway, NH*

Eastern States Exposition (The Big E) [A] *Springfield, MA*

Eastham Historical Society [W] *Eastham (Cape Cod), MA*

Eastham Windmill [W] *Eastham (Cape Cod), MA*

Easton's Beach [W] *Newport, RI*

East Rock Park [W] *New Haven, CT*

Echo Lake State Park [W] *North Conway, NH*

Edgartown [W] *Martha's Vineyard, MA*

Edith Wharton Restoration (The Mount) [W] *Lenox, MA*

Edmundston Golf Club [W] *Edmundston, NB*

Edward King House [W] *Newport, RI*

Edwards Gardens [W] *Toronto, ON*

Eldon House [W] *London, ON*

Eli Terry, Jr Waterwheel [W] *Bristol, CT*

Elizabeth Park [W] *Hartford, CT*

Elizabeth Perkins House [W] *York, ME*

Elms, The [W] *Newport, RI*

Emerson-Wilcox House [W] *York, ME*

Emily Dickinson Homestead [W] *Amherst, MA*

ESCAPE (Exciting, Scenic, Canadian/American Powerboat Excursion) [A] *Kenora, ON*

Esplanade Concerts [A] *Boston, MA*

Eugene O'Neill Theater Center [W] *New London, CT*

Exhibition Place [W] *Toronto, ON*

Expedition Whydah's Sea Lab and Learning Center [W] *Provincetown (Cape Cod), MA*

Explore [W] *Quebec City, QE*

Expo Québec [A] *Quebec City, QE*

Factory Outlet District [W] *Fall River, MA*

Factory outlet stores [W] *Freeport, ME*

Factory Outlet Stores [W] *Kittery, ME*

Factory outlet stores [W] *North Conway, NH*

Fairbanks House [W] *Dedham, MA*

Fairfield Historical Society [W] *Fairfield, CT*

Fall Festival [A] *Kent, CT*

Fall Foliage Festival [A] *Boothbay Harbor, ME*

Fall Foliage Festival [A] *North Adams, MA*

Fall Harvest Festival [A] *Newburyport, MA*

Fall River Heritage State Park [W] *Fall River, MA*

Fall River Historical Society [W] *Fall River, MA*

Falmouth Historical Society Museums. Julia Wood House [W] *Falmouth (Cape Cod), MA*

Faneuil Hall Marketplace [W] *Boston, MA*

Fanshawe Pioneer Village [W] *London, ON*

Farmers' Market, The [W] *St. Catharines, ON*

Farmers' Market [W] *Kitchener-Waterloo, ON*

Farmington Antiques Weekend [A] *Farmington, CT*

Farmington Valley Arts Center [W] *Avon, CT*

Farnsworth Art Museum and Wyeth Center [W] *Rockland, ME*

Farnsworth Homestead [W] *Rockland, ME*

Feast of the Blessed Sacrament [A] *New Bedford, MA*

Felix Neck Sanctuary [W] *Martha's Vineyard, MA*

Ferries [W] *New London, CT*

Ferry Beach State Park [W] *Saco, ME*

Ferry from Port Clyde [W] *Monhegan Island, ME*

Ferry service [W] *Block Island, RI*

Ferry service [W] *Cranberry Isles, ME*

Ferry Service [W] *Northeast Harbor, ME*

Ferry Service to Digby, NS [W] *St. John, NB*

Ferry Service to St. John, NB [W] *Digby, NS*

Ferry service to Yarmouth, Nova Scotia [W] *Bar Harbor, ME*

Ferry to Deer Island, New Brunswick [W] *Eastport, ME*

Ferry to Port Jefferson, Long Island [W] *Bridgeport, CT*

Ferry to Sheffield Island Lighthouse [W] *Norwalk, CT*

Festitalia [A] *Hamilton, ON*

Festival Acadien de Wedgeport [A] *Yarmouth, NS*

Festival by the Sea [A] *St. John, NB*

Festival de Joie [A] *Lewiston, ME*

Festival of Arts [A] *Stamford, CT*

Festival of Friends [A] *Hamilton, ON*

Festival of Lights [A] *Charlottetown, PE*

Festival of Lights [A] *North Kingstown, RI*

Festival Week [A] *Dennis (Cape Cod), MA*

Fête Nationale [A] *Montreal, QE*

Fife & Drum Muster and Colonial Fair [A] *Sudbury Center, MA*

Fine Arts Center and Gallery [W] *Amherst, MA*

Firefighters' Museum of Nova Scotia [W] *Yarmouth, NS*

First Baptist Meeting House [W] *Providence, RI*

First Church in Windsor, The [W] *Windsor, CT*

First Church of Christ, Congregational United Church of Christ [W] *Wethersfield, CT*

First Night Celebration [A] *Boston, MA*

First Night New Bedford [A] *New Bedford, MA*

First Presbyterian Church [W] *Stamford, CT*

First Unitarian Church [W] *Providence, RI*

Fisheries Museum of the Atlantic [W] *Peggy's Cove, NS*

Fishermen's Wharf [W] *Digby, NS*

Fishing [W] *Bar Harbor, ME*

Fishing [W] *Block Island, RI*

Fishing [W] *Boothbay Harbor, ME*

Fishing [W] *Eastport, ME*

Fishing [W] *Fort Kent, ME*

Fishing [W] *Hampton Beach, NH*

Fishing [W] *Jamestown, RI*

Fishing [W] *Narragansett, RI*

Fishing [W] *Rangeley, ME*

Fishing [W] *Truro and North Truro (Cape Cod), MA*

Fishing, boating on bay [W] *Searsport, ME*

Flamboro Downs [W] *Hamilton, ON*

Flanders Nature Center [W] *Woodbury, CT*

Floral Park [W] *Montreal, QE*

Florence Griswold Museum [W] *Old Lyme, CT*

Flume Cascade [W] *Bretton Woods, NH*

Flume Gorge and Park Information Center [W] *Franconia Notch State Park, NH*

Flying Horse Carousel [W] *Westerly, RI*

Fogg Art Museum [W] *Cambridge, MA*

Foire Brayonne [A] *Edmundston, NB*

Folger-Franklin Seat & Memorial Boulder [W] *Nantucket Island, MA*

Folk Arts Festival [A] *St. Catharines, ON*

Forest Park [W] *Springfield, MA*

Formal Gardens [W] *Lenox, MA*

Fort Adams State Park [W] *Newport, RI*

Fort Amherst/Port La Joye National Historic Park [W] *Charlottetown, PE*

Fort Anne National Historic Site [W] *Digby, NS*

Fort at No. 4 [W] *Newport, NH*

Fort Beausejour National Historic Site [W] *Moncton, NB*

Fort Constitution [W] *Portsmouth, NH*

Fort Foster Park [W] *Kittery, ME*

Fort Frances Museum [W] *Fort Frances, ON*

Fort Frederick & College Museum [W] *Kingston, ON*

Fort George National Historic Site [W] *Niagara-on-the-Lake, ON*

Fort Griswold Battlefield State Park [W] *Groton, CT*

Fort Hale Park and Restoration [W] *New Haven, CT*

Fort Henry [W] *Kingston, ON*

Fort Kent Block House [W] *Fort Kent, ME*

Fort Kent Historical Society Museum and Gardens [W] *Fort Kent, ME*

Fort Knox State Park [W] *Bucksport, ME*

Fort Lennox [W] *Montreal, QE*

Fort Malden National Historic Park [W] *Windsor, ON*

Fort McClary Memorial [W] *Kittery, ME*

Fort O'Brien Memorial [W] *Machias, ME*

Fort Phoenix Beach State Reservation [W] *New Bedford, MA*

Fort Point State Park [W] *Bucksport, ME*

Fort Popham Memorial [W] *Bath, ME*

Fort Saybrook Monument Park [W] *Old Saybrook, CT*

Fort Stark State Historic Site [W] *Portsmouth, NH*

Fort Wellington National Historic Site [W] *Morrisburg, ON*

Fort William Henry State Memorial [W] *Damariscotta, ME*

Foundation Headquarters [W] *Concord, NH*

Franconia Notch State Park [W] *Franconia, NH*

Franconia Notch State Park [W] *Lincoln/North Woodstock Area, NH*

Franklin County Fair [A] *Greenfield, MA*

Franklin Park Zoo [W] *Boston, MA*

Fred Benson Town Beach [W] *Block Island, RI*

Frederick Law Olmsted National Historic Site [W] *Boston, MA*

Fredericton [W] *Fredericton, NB*

Fredericton Exhibition [A] *Fredericton, NB*

Freedom Trail, The [W] *Boston, MA*

French Cable Station Museum [W] *Orleans (Cape Cod), MA*

Friends Meeting House [W] *Newport, RI*

Frost Park [W] *Yarmouth, NS*

Frost Place [W] *Franconia, NH*

Fruitlands Museums [W] *Concord, MA*

Fuller Gardens [W] *Hampton Beach, NH*

Fuller Museum of Art [W] *Brockton, MA*

Fun in the Sun Festival [A] *Fort Frances, ON*

Funtown USA [W] *Saco, ME*

Gaelic College, The [W] *Baddeck, NS*
Gail's Tours [W] *Nantucket Island, MA*
Gallery/Stratford, The [W] *Stratford, ON*
Gananoque Boat Line [W] *Gananoque, ON*
Gananoque Historical Museum [W] *Gananoque, ON*
Garden Club Open House Day [A] *Camden, ME*
Garden in the Woods [W] *Framingham, MA*
Gardens, The [W] *Sarnia, ON*
Gardner-Pingree House [W] *Salem, MA*
Garlicfest [A] *Fairfield, CT*
Gaspee Days [A] *Warwick, RI*
General Sylvanus Thayer Birthplace [W] *Braintree, MA*
General William Hart House [W] *Old Saybrook, CT*
George Marshall Store [W] *York, ME*
George R. Gardiner Museum of Ceramic Art [W] *Toronto, ON*
George Washington State Campground [W] *Glocester, RI*
Giant Staircase [W] *Bailey Island, ME*
Giant Waterslide [W] *Gananoque, ON*
Gibbs Avenue Museum [W] *Bridgton, ME*
Gibson House [W] *Toronto, ON*
Gibson House Museum [W] *Boston, MA*
Gilbert Stuart Birthplace [W] *North Kingstown, RI*
Gillette Castle State Park [W] *East Haddam, CT*
Gilman Garrison House [W] *Exeter, NH*
Glebe House and Gertrude Jekyll Garden [W] *Woodbury, CT*
Glendi Greek Celebration [A] *Springfield, MA*
Glen Ellis Falls Scenic Area [W] *Pinkham Notch, NH*
Glenhyrst Art Gallery of Brant [W] *Brantford, ON*
Glen Magna Farms [W] *Danvers, MA*
Glockenspiel [W] *Kitchener-Waterloo, ON*
Gloucester Fisherman [W] *Gloucester, MA*
Goddard Memorial State Park [W] *East Greenwich, RI*
Goodspeed Opera House [W] *East Haddam, CT*
Gore Place [W] *Waltham, MA*
Governor John Langdon House [W] *Portsmouth, NH*
Governor Stephen Hopkins House [W] *Providence, RI*

Grafton Notch State Park [W] *Bethel, ME*
Granary Burying Ground [W] *Boston, MA*
Granby International [A] *Granby, QE*
Granby Zoological Garden [W] *Granby, QE*
Grand Army of the Republic Museum [W] *Lynn, MA*
Grand Falls [W] *Edmundston, NB*
Grand Pré National Historic Site [W] *Grand Pre, NS*
Grand Prix at Lime Rock [A] *Lakeville, CT*
Grand Theatre [W] *Kingston, ON*
Grand Theatre [W] *London, ON*
Grand Théâtre [W] *Quebec City, QE*
Grange, The [W] *Toronto, ON*
Grange Park [W] *Toronto, ON*
Granville [W] *Springfield, MA*
Gray's Store (1788) [W] *Little Compton, RI*
Gray Line bus tours [W] *Halifax, NS*
Gray Line bus tours [W] *Montreal, QE*
Gray Line bus tours [W] *Ottawa, ON*
Gray Line bus tours [W] *Quebec City, QE*
Gray Line bus tours [W] *Toronto, ON*
Great Balloon Rodeo [A] *Brockville, ON*
Great Glen Trails [W] *Mount Washington, NH*
Great Gorge Adventure [W] *Niagara Falls, ON*
Great Hall of the Clans, The [W] *Baddeck, NS*
Great Island Science & Adventure Park, The [W] *Cavendish, PE*
Great Meadows National Wildlife Refuge [W] *Concord, MA*
Great Meadows National Wildlife Refuge [W] *Sudbury Center, MA*
Great Rotary Fishing Derby [A] *Meredith, NH*
Great Whatever Family Festival Week [A] *Augusta, ME*
Green, The [W] *New Haven, CT*
Green Animals [W] *Portsmouth, RI*
Greenfield State Park [W] *Peterborough, NH*
Green Gables [W] *Cavendish, PE*
Greenhouse [W] *Niagara Falls, ON*
Green Park Shipbuilding Museum [W] *Charlottetown, PE*
Green River Music and Balloon Festival [A] *Greenfield, MA*
Gristmill [W] *Chatham (Cape Cod), MA*
Gristmill [W] *Sudbury Center, MA*
Gropius House [W] *Concord, MA*

Grove Street Cemetery [W] *New Haven, CT*

Guided walking tours. Boston by Foot [W] *Boston, MA*

Guild of Boston Artists [W] *Boston, MA*

Guinness World of Records Museum [W] *Niagara Falls, ON*

Gunstock Recreation Area [W] *Laconia, NH*

Guy Lombardo Music Centre [W] *London, ON*

Hadley Farm Museum [W] *Amherst, MA*

Hadwen House [W] *Nantucket Island, MA*

Haffenreffer Museum of Anthropology [W] *Bristol, RI*

Haight Vineyard and Winery [W] *Litchfield, CT*

Hale House [W] *Beverly, MA*

Halifax Citadel National Historic Park [W] *Halifax, NS*

Hall of Fame Tip-off Classic [A] *Springfield, MA*

Hamilton's Farmers' Market [W] *Hamilton, ON*

Hamilton House [W] *Kittery, ME*

Hamilton International Air Show [A] *Hamilton, ON*

Hamilton Military Museum [W] *Hamilton, ON*

Hamilton Mum Show [A] *Hamilton, ON*

Hamilton Place [W] *Hamilton, ON*

Hammersmith Farm [W] *Newport, RI*

Hammonasset Beach State Park [W] *Madison, CT*

Hammond Castle Museum [W] *Gloucester, MA*

Hampton Beach State Park [W] *Hampton Beach, NH*

Hampton Playhouse [S] *Hampton Beach, NH*

Hancock Barracks [W] *Houlton, ME*

Hancock-Clarke House [W] *Lexington, MA*

Hancock Shaker Village [W] *Pittsfield, MA*

Happy Rolph Bird Sanctuary and Children's Farm [W] *St. Catharines, ON*

Harbor Day [A] *Norwich, CT*

Harborfest [A] *Boston, MA*

Harborfest [A] *Nantucket Island, MA*

Harbor Lights Festival [A] *Boothbay Harbor, ME*

Harbour Cruises [W] *Quebec City, QE*

Harbourfront Centre [W] *Toronto, ON*

Harbour Hopper Tours [W] *Halifax, NS*

Harlow Old Fort House [W] *Plymouth, MA*

Harness racing [S] *Scarborough, ME*

Harriet Beecher Stowe House [W] *Hartford, CT*

Harrison Gray Otis House [W] *Boston, MA*

Harrison House [W] *Branford, CT*

Hartford on Tour [W] *Hartford, CT*

Hart Nautical Galleries [W] *Cambridge, MA*

Harvard Museum Natural History [W] *Cambridge, MA*

Harvard University [W] *Cambridge, MA*

Harvest Fair [A] *Bristol, RI*

Harvest Fest [A] *York, ME*

Harvest Festival [A] *Stockbridge and West Stockbridge, MA*

Harvest Jazz and Blues Festival [A] *Fredericton, NB*

Harwich Historical Society [W] *Harwich (Cape Cod), MA*

Harwich Junior Theatre [S] *Harwich (Cape Cod), MA*

Hatstack Mountain [W] *Norfolk, CT*

Haunted Happenings [A] *Salem, MA*

Haverhill Historical Society [W] *Haverhill, MA*

Hawthorne Cottage [W] *Lenox, MA*

H.C. Barnes Memorial Nature Center [W] *Bristol, CT*

Hedge House [W] *Plymouth, MA*

Helme House [W] *Kingston, RI*

Henry Phipps & Sarah Juliette Ross Memorial Museum, The [W] *St. Andrews, NB*

Henry Whitfield State Museum [W] *Guilford, CT*

Heritage Days [A] *Auburn, ME*

Heritage Days Celebration [A] *Salem, MA*

Heritage-New Hampshire [W] *Jackson, NH*

Heritage Plantation [W] *Sandwich (Cape Cod), MA*

Heritage, The [W] *Rockland, ME*

Heritage Trails Sightseeing [W] *Hartford, CT*

Heritage Village [W] *Windsor, ON*

Her Majesty's Royal Chapel of the Mohawks [W] *Brantford, ON*

Herreshoff Marine Museum [W] *Bristol, RI*

Higgins Armory Museum [W] *Worcester, MA*

Highland Games [A] *Antigonish, NS*

Highland Games [A] *Halifax, NS*

High Park [W] *Toronto, ON*

Hiking trails [W] *Mount Washington, NH*

Hill-Stead Museum [W] *Farmington, CT*

Historical Museum [W] *Norfolk, CT*

Historical Museum of Gunn Memorial Library [W] *New Preston, CT*

Historical Society Museum [W] *Wellfleet (Cape Cod), MA*

Historic Deerfield, Inc [W] *Deerfield, MA*

Historic Fort Erie [W] *Niagara Falls, ON*

Historic Fort York [W] *Toronto, ON*

Historic Mansions and Houses [W] *Newport, RI*

Historic Northampton Museum houses [W] *Northampton, MA*

Historic Norwichtown Days [A] *Norwich, CT*

Historic Pontiac Mills [W] *Warwick, RI*

Historic Properties (Privateers Wharf) [W] *Halifax, NS*

Historic Ship *Nautilus* & Submarine Force Museum [W] *Groton, CT*

Historic South Norwalk (SoNo) [W] *Norwalk, CT*

History House [W] *Skowhegan, ME*

Hitchcock Museum [W] *Riverton, CT*

Hobbamock's (Wampanoag) Homesite [W] *Plymouth, MA*

Hobo Railroad [W] *Lincoln/North Woodstock Area, NH*

Holley House [W] *Lakeville, CT*

Holt House [W] *Blue Hill, ME*

Holyoke Heritage State Park [W] *Holyoke, MA*

Home County Folk Festival [A] *London, ON*

Hood Museum and Hopkins Center for the Arts [W] *Hanover, NH*

Hope Street [W] *Bristol, RI*

Horatio Colony House Museum [W] *Keene, NH*

Hot Air Balloon Festival [A] *Kingston, RI*

Houlton Fair [A] *Houlton, ME*

Houlton Potato Feast Days [A] *Houlton, ME*

Housatonic Meadows State Park [W] *Cornwall Bridge, CT*

House of Seven Gables [W] *Salem, MA*

Houses of Harvard-Radcliffe, The [W] *Cambridge, MA*

House Tours of Historic Lenox [A] *Lenox, MA*

Howland House [W] *Plymouth, MA*

Hoxie House and Dexter Gristmill [W] *Sandwich (Cape Cod), MA*

Hudson Museum [W] *Orono, ME*

Hummingbird Centre for the Performing Arts [W] *Toronto, ON*

Hungerford Outdoor Education Center [W] *New Britain, CT*

Hunter House [W] *Newport, RI*

Huntsman Marine Science Center/Aquarium-Museum [W] *St. Andrews, NB*

Hurlburt-Dunham House [W] *Wethersfield, CT*

Huronia Historical Parks [W] *Toronto, ON*

Hyannis-Martha's Vineyard Day Round Trip [W] *Martha's Vineyard, MA*

Hyannis-Nantucket or Martha's Vineyard Day Round Trip [W] *Hyannis (Cape Cod), MA*

Hyannis Whale Watcher Cruises [W] *Barnstable (Cape Cod), MA*

Hyland House [W] *Guilford, CT*

Île d'Orléans [W] *Quebec City, QE*

IMAX Theatre and Daredevil Adventure [W] *Niagara Falls, ON*

Indian Day [A] *Springfield, MA*

Indian Festival [A] *Eastport, ME*

Indian Leap [W] *Norwich, CT*

Indian Motocycle Museum [W] *Springfield, MA*

Industrial tour. Abitibi Consolidated [W] *Fort Frances, ON*

Industrial tour. Pairpoint Crystal Co [W] *Bourne (Cape Cod), MA*

Information Center [W] *Cambridge, MA*

Insectarium de Montreal [W] *Montreal, QE*

InSight Tours [W] *Portsmouth, NH*

Institute for American Indian Studies, The [W] *New Preston, CT*

Institute of Contemporary Art [W] *Boston, MA*

International Buskerfest [A] *Halifax, NS*

International Caravan [A] *Toronto, ON*

International Festival of Arts and Ideas [A] *New Haven, CT*

International Festival Week [A] *Calais, ME*

International Fireworks Competition [A] *Quebec City, QE*

International Freedom Festival [A] *Windsor, ON*

International Friendship Gardens [W] *Thunder Bay, ON*

International Ice Hockey Federation Museum [W] *Kingston, ON*

International In-water Boat Show [A] *Norwalk, CT*

International Snowmobilers Festival [A] *Edmundston, NB*

International Tennis Hall of Fame & Museum [W] *Newport, RI*

International Tulip Festival [A] *Truro, NS*

International Villages Festival [A] *Brantford, ON*

Inverarden Regency Cottage Museum [W] *Cornwall, ON*

Iroquois Village [W] *London, ON*

Irving Nature Park [W] *St. John, NB*

Isaac Royall House [W] *Boston, MA*

Isaak Walton Killam Library [W] *Yarmouth, NS*

Isabella Stewart Gardner Museum [W] *Boston, MA*

iSci Centre [W] *Montreal, QE*

Island Queen [W] *Falmouth (Cape Cod), MA*

Island Queen [W] *Kingston, ON*

Island Queen [W] *Martha's Vineyard, MA*

Isle au Haut [W] *Deer Isle, ME*

Isle au Haut Ferry Service [W] *Deer Isle, ME*

Islesford Historical Museum [W] *Cranberry Isles, ME*

Issac Evans [W] *Rockland, ME*

It's a Grand Summer [S] *Kingston, ON*

Jack Miner Bird Sanctuary [W] *Windsor, ON*

Jackson Homestead [W] *Newton, MA*

Jackson Laboratory, The [W] *Bar Harbor, ME*

Jackson Ski Touring Foundation [W] *Jackson, NH*

Jacob's Pillow Dance Festival [S] *Lee, MA*

Jacques-Cartier Park [W] *Quebec City, QE*

Jamestown Museum [W] *Jamestown, RI*

J. & E. Riggin [W] *Rockland, ME*

Jazz Festival [A] *Edmundston, NB*

Jeanne d'Arc Garden [W] *Quebec City, QE*

Jed Prouty Tavern [W] *Bucksport, ME*

Jefferds Tavern and Schoolhouse [W] *York, ME*

Jeremiah Lee Mansion [W] *Marblehead, MA*

Jericho House and Historical Center [W] *Dennis (Cape Cod), MA*

Jethro Coffin House [W] *Nantucket Island, MA*

Jiminy Peak [W] *Pittsfield, MA*

John Adams and John Quincy Adams Birthplaces [W] *Quincy, MA*

John Black Mansion [W] *Ellsworth, ME*

John Brown House [W] *Providence, RI*

John Carter Brown Library [W] *Providence, RI*

John F. Kennedy Hyannis Museum [W] *Hyannis (Cape Cod), MA*

John F. Kennedy Memorial [W] *Hyannis (Cape Cod), MA*

John F. Kennedy National Historic Site [W] *Boston, MA*

John F. Kennedy School of Government [W] *Cambridge, MA*

John Freeman Walls Historic Site & Underground Railroad Museum [W] *Windsor, ON*

John Greenleaf Whittier Birthplace [W] *Haverhill, MA*

John Greenleaf Whittier Home [W] *Amesbury, MA*

John Hancock Observatory [W] *Boston, MA*

John Hancock Warehouse [W] *York, ME*

John Hay Library [W] *Providence, RI*

John Heard House [W] *Ipswich, MA*

John Paul Jones House [W] *Portsmouth, NH*

John Paul Jones State Memorial [W] *Kittery, ME*

John Ward House [W] *Salem, MA*

John Whipple House, The [W] *Ipswich, MA*

Jones Library [W] *Amherst, MA*

Jones Museum of Glass and Ceramics, The [W] *Sebago Lake, ME*

Joseph Allen Skinner Museum [W] *South Hadley, MA*

Joseph Schneider Haus [W] *Kitchener-Waterloo, ON*

Joshua Hempsted House [W] *New London, CT*

Joshua L. Chamberlain Museum [W] *Brunswick, ME*

Josiah Dennis Manse [W] *Dennis (Cape Cod), MA*

Josiah Quincy House [W] *Quincy, MA*

Journey Behind the Falls [W] *Niagara Falls, ON*

Just for Laughs [A] *Montreal, QE*

JVC Jazz Festival [A] *Newport, RI*

Kakabeka Falls Provincial Park [W] *Thunder Bay, ON*

Keeler Tavern [W] *Ridgefield, CT*

Kelmscott Farm [W] *Camden, ME*

Kenduskeag Stream Canoe Race [A] *Bangor, ME*

Kenora Agricultural Fair [A] *Kenora, ON*

Kenora International Bass Fishing Tournament [A] *Kenora, ON*

Kent Falls State Park [W] *Kent, CT*

Kentish Guards Armory [W] *East Greenwich, RI*

Keppoch Mountain Ski Area [W] *Antigonish, NS*

Kettletown [W] *Southbury, CT*

Kidspace [W] *North Adams, MA*

Kimball Wildlife Refuge [W] *Charlestown, RI*

King Hooper Mansion [W] *Marblehead, MA*

King Park and Beach [W] *Newport, RI*

King Pine Ski Area [W] *Center Ossipee, NH*

King's Chapel [W] *Boston, MA*

Kingscote [W] *Newport, RI*

Kings Landing Historical Settlement [W] *Fredericton, NB*

Kingston Library [W] *Kingston, RI*

Kinsmen Antique Show [A] *Stratford, ON*

Kitchener-Waterloo Art Gallery [W] *Kitchener-Waterloo, ON*

Kitchener-Waterloo Multicultural Festival [A] *Kitchener-Waterloo, ON*

Kittery Historical and Naval Museum [W] *Kittery, ME*

Kortright Centre for Conservation [W] *Toronto, ON*

Koussevitzky Music Shed [W] *Lenox, MA*

La Citadelle [W] *Quebec City, QE*

Lafayette Campground [W] *Franconia Notch State Park, NH*

La Festa [A] *North Adams, MA*

La Fontaine Park [W] *Montreal, QE*

Lake Compounce Theme Park [W] *Bristol, CT*

Lake cruises. Lake Navigation, Ltd [W] *Kenora, ON*

Lake of the Woods Museum [W] *Kenora, ON*

Lakes Region Factory Stores [W] *Franklin, NH*

Lakes Region Fine Arts and Crafts Festival [A] *Meredith, NH*

Lake St. George State Park [W] *Belfast, ME*

Lake Waramaug State Park [W] *New Preston, CT*

Lake Winnipesaukee cruises [W] *Wolfeboro, NH*

Lambton Heritage Museum [W] *Sarnia, ON*

Lamoine State Park [W] *Ellsworth, ME*

Lancaster Fair [A] *Jefferson, NH*

La Ronde [W] *Montreal, QE*

Laughing Brook Education Center and Wildlife Sanctuary [W] *Springfield, MA*

Laura Secord Homestead [W] *Niagara-on-the-Lake, ON*

Laurel Creek Conservation Area [W] *Kitchener-Waterloo, ON*

Laurentides Wildlife Reserve [W] *Quebec City, QE*

Laurier House [W] *Ottawa , ON*

Lawrence Heritage State Park [W] *Lawrence, MA*

League of New Hampshire Craftsmen [W] *Hanover, NH*

League of New Hampshire Craftsmen [W] *North Conway, NH*

League of New Hampshire Craftsmen's Fair [A] *Sunapee, NH*

League of New Hampshire Craftsmen/Exeter [W] *Exeter, NH*

League of New Hampshire Craftsmen—Meredith/Laconia Arts and Crafts [W] *Meredith, NH*

League of New Hampshire Craftsmen—Sandwich Home Industries [W] *Holderness, NH*

Leamington Tomato Festival [A] *Windsor, ON*

Leffingwell Inn [W] *Norwich, CT*

"Le Grand David and his own Spectacular Magic Company." [W] *Beverly, MA*

Léon Marcotte Exhibition Centre [W] *Sherbrooke, QE*

Les Forges du St.-Maurice National Historic Site [W] *Trois-Rivieres, QE*

Les Jardins de la République Provincial Park [W] *Edmundston, NB*

Le Village Québécois d'Antan [W] *Drummondville, QE*

Levitt Pavilion for the Performing Arts [S] *Westport, CT*

Lewiston-Auburn Garden Tour [A] *Lewiston, ME*

Lexington Historical Society [W] *Lexington, MA*

Libby Memorial Pool and Recreation Area [W] *Gorham, NH*

Library [W] *Providence, RI*

Library Gallery [W] *Salem, MA*

Lighthouse [W] *Westerly, RI*

Lighthouse Point [W] *New Haven, CT*

Lilac Time Festival [A] *Franconia, NH*

Lily Bay State Park [W] *Greenville, ME*

Lincoln County Museum and Old Jail [W] *Wiscasset, ME*

Lincoln Woods State Park [W] *Providence, RI*

List Visual Arts Center at MIT [W] *Cambridge, MA*

Litchfield Historical Society Museum [W] *Litchfield, CT*

Littleton Historical Museum [W] *Littleton, NH*

Little White Schoolhouse Museum [W] *Truro, NS*

Lobsterfest [A] *Mystic, CT*

Lobster Hatchery [W] *Bar Harbor, ME*

Lock Museum of America [W] *Bristol, CT*

Lockwood-Mathews Mansion Museum [W] *Norwalk, CT*

Log Cabin [W] *Sarnia, ON*

Logging Museum Field Days [A] *Rangeley, ME*

London Air Show & Balloon Festival, The [A] *London, ON*

London Fringe Theatre Festival [A] *London, ON*

London Museum of Archaeology [W] *London, ON*

London Regional Art and Historical Museums [W] *London, ON*

London Regional Children's Museum [W] *London, ON*

Longfellow National Historic Site [W] *Cambridge, MA*

Longfellow's Wayside Inn [W] *Sudbury Center, MA*

Long Sault Parkway [W] *Cornwall, ON*

Long Wharf Theatre [S] *New Haven, CT*

Look Park [W] *Northampton, MA*

Lost River Gorge [W] *Lincoln/North Woodstock Area, NH*

Louisburg Square [W] *Boston, MA*

Louis S. St.-Laurent National Historic Site [W] *Sherbrooke, QE*

Louis Tussaud's Waxworks [W] *Niagara Falls, ON*

Lowell Folk Festival [A] *Lowell, MA*

Lowell Heritage State Park [W] *Lowell, MA*

Lowell National Historical Park [W] *Lowell, MA*

Loyalist Days' Heritage Celebration [A] *St. John, NB*

Loyalist House [W] *St. John, NB*

Lucy Maud Montgomery's Cavendish Home [W] *Cavendish, PE*

Lundy's Lane Historical Museum [W] *Niagara Falls, ON*

Lutz Children's Museum [W] *Manchester, CT*

Lyman Allyn Art Museum [W] *New London, CT*

Lyman Estate "The Vale" [W] *Waltham, MA*

Lynn Heritage State Park [W] *Lynn, MA*

Lynn Historical Society Museum/Library [W] *Lynn, MA*

Lynn Woods Reservation [W] *Lynn, MA*

Macedonia Brook State Park [W] *Kent, CT*

Mackenzie House [W] *Toronto, ON*

MacLachlan Woodworking Museum [W] *Kingston, ON*

Mactaquac [W] *Fredericton, NB*

Mactaquac Fish Hatchery [W] *Fredericton, NB*

Mactaquac Generating Station [W] *Fredericton, NB*

Mactaquac Provincial Park [W] *Fredericton, NB*

Magnetic Hill Zoo [W] *Moncton, NB*

Maine Aquarium [W] *Saco, ME*

Maine Art Gallery [W] *Wiscasset, ME*

Maine History Gallery [W] *Portland, ME*

Maine Lobster Festival [A] *Rockland, ME*

Maine Maritime Museum and Shipyard [W] *Bath, ME*

Maine State Ferry Service [W] *Camden, ME*

Maine State Ferry Service [W] *Southwest Harbor, ME*

Maine State Ferry Service [W] *Rockland, ME*

Maine State Museum [W] *Augusta, ME*

Maine State Music Theater [S] *Brunswick, ME*

Maine State Parade [A] *Lewiston, ME*

Maine Windjammer Cruises [W] *Camden, ME*

Main Gate Area [W] *Lenox, MA*

Main House [W] *Lenox, MA*

Main Stage Auditorium [W] *Salem, MA*

Main Street [W] *Nantucket Island, MA*

Main Street, USA [A] *New Britain, CT*

Main Street, Wickford Village [W] *North Kingstown, RI*

Maison Saint-Gabriel [W] *Montreal, QE*

Manchester Historic Association [W] *Manchester, NH*

Manoir et Domaine Trent [W] *Drummondville, QE*

Map and Globe Museum [W] *Wellesley, MA*

Maple Days [A] *Auburn, ME*

Maple sugaring [S] *Amherst, MA*

Maple sugaring [S] *Northampton, MA*

Marble House [W] *Newport, RI*

Marginal Way [W] *Ogunquit, ME*

Marineland [W] *Niagara Falls, ON*

Marine Museum [W] *Fall River, MA*

Marine Museum of the Great Lakes at Kingston [W] *Kingston, ON*

Maritime Aquarium at Norwalk [W] *Norwalk, CT*

Maritime Museum of the Atlantic [W] *Halifax, NS*

Market Gallery, The [W] *Toronto, ON*

Market Square [W] *Portsmouth, NH*

Market Square Days [A] *Portsmouth, NH*

Market Square Historic District [W] *Houlton, ME*

Mark Twain Days [A] *Hartford, CT*

Mark Twain House [W] *Hartford, CT*

Marrett House and Garden [W] *Sebago Lake, ME*

Martha A. Parsons House [W] *Enfield, CT*

Martha Mary Chapel [W] *Sudbury Center, MA*

Mary Baker Eddy Historical Home [W] *Lynn, MA*

Mary Baker Eddy Historic House [W] *Plymouth, NH*

Massachusetts Hall [W] *Cambridge, MA*

Massachusetts Institute of Technology [W] *Cambridge, MA*

Massacoh Plantation-Simsbury Historic Center [W] *Simsbury, CT*

MASS MoCA [W] *North Adams, MA*

Mast Landing Sanctuary [W] *Freeport, ME*

Mattatuck Museum [W] *Waterbury, CT*

Mayflower II [E] [W] *Plymouth, MA*

Mayflower Society House Museum [W] *Plymouth, MA*

McFarland House [W] *Niagara-on-the-Lake, ON*

McGill University [W] *Montreal, QE*

McMichael Canadian Art Collection [W] *Toronto, ON*

Mead Art Museum [W] *Amherst, MA*

Meduxnekeag River Canoe Race [A] *Houlton, ME*

Memorial Hall Museum [W] *Deerfield, MA*

Mena'Sen Place [W] *Sherbrooke, QE*

Merwin House "Tranquility" [W] *Stockbridge and West Stockbridge, MA*

Metro Toronto Zoo [W] *Toronto, ON*

Mid-winter New England Surfing Championship [A] *Narragansett, RI*

Milford Historical Society Wharf Lane Complex [W] *Milford, CT*

Milford Jai-Alai [W] *Milford, CT*

Military Communications and Electronics Museum [W] *Kingston, ON*

Miller Museum of Geology and Mineralogy [W] *Kingston, ON*

Miller State Park [W] *Peterborough, NH*

Mill Hill Historic Park [W] *Norwalk, CT*

Mineral Springs [W] *Stafford Springs, CT*

Minolta Tower Centre [W] *Niagara Falls, ON*

Minute Man National Historical Park [W] *Concord, MA*

Misquamicut State Beach [W] *Westerly, RI*

Mission House [W] *Stockbridge and West Stockbridge, MA*

MIT Museum [W] *Cambridge, MA*

Moffatt-Ladd House [W] *Portsmouth, NH*

Mohawk Mountain Ski Area [W] *Cornwall Bridge, CT*

Mohawk Trail State Forest [W] *North Adams, MA*

Mohegan Park and Memorial Rose Garden [W] *Norwich, CT*

Monadnock State Park [W] *Jaffrey, NH*

Monhegan Lighthouse [W] *Monhegan Island, ME*

Monomoy National Wildlife Refuge [W] *Chatham (Cape Cod), MA*

Monomoy Theatre [S] *Chatham (Cape Cod), MA*

Monte Cristo Cottage [W] *New London, CT*

Montmorency Park [W] *Quebec City, QE*

Montréal Botanical Garden [W] *Montreal, QE*

Montréal Harbour Cruises [W] *Montreal, QE*

Montréal Jazz Festival [A] *Montreal, QE*

Montréal Museum of Fine Arts, The [W] *Montreal, QE*

Montréal Planetarium [W] *Montreal, QE*

Mont-Ste.-Anne Park [W] *Quebec City, QE*

Monument to Paul Bunyan [W] *Bangor, ME*

Moore Museum [W] *Sarnia, ON*

Moose Brook State Park [W] *Gorham, NH*

Moosehead Lake [W] *Rockwood, ME*

Moosehead Marine Museum [W] *Greenville, ME*

Moosehorn National Wildlife Refuge [W] *Calais, ME*

Moose Mainea [A] *Greenville, ME*

Moose Tours [W] *Gorham, NH*

Morningstar Mill [W] *St. Catharines, ON*

Mother Church, The First Church of Christ, Scientist, The [W] *Boston, MA*

Mount Blue State Park [W] *Rumford, ME*

Mount David [W] *Lewiston, ME*

Mount Desert Oceanarium [W] *Southwest Harbor, ME*

Mount Greylock State Reservation [W] *North Adams, MA*

Mount Holyoke College [W] *South Hadley, MA*

Mount Holyoke College Art Museum [W] *South Hadley, MA*

Mount Jefferson Ski Area [W] *Lincoln, ME*

Mount Orford [W] *Sherbrooke, QE*

Mount Royal Park [W] *Montreal, QE*

Mount Southington Ski Area [W] *Meriden, CT*

Mount Sunapee State Park [W] *Sunapee, NH*

Mount Tom Ski Area and Summer-Side [W] *Holyoke, MA*

Mount Washington [W] *Gorham, NH*

Mount Washington [W] *Twin Mountain, NH*

Mount Washington Summit Museum [W] *Mount Washington, NH*

Mount Washington Valley Equine Classic [A] *North Conway, NH*

M/S *Mount Washington* [W] *Laconia, NH*

M/S *Scotia Prince* [W] *Portland, ME*

MS *Scotia Prince* [W] *Yarmouth, NS*

Mud Bowl [A] *North Conway, NH*

Multicultural Festival [A] *Halifax, NS*

Municipal Group [W] *Springfield, MA*

Munroe Tavern [W] *Lexington, MA*

Murney Tower Museum [W] *Kingston, ON*

Murphy's on the Water [W] *Halifax, NS*

Musée des Anciens Canadiens [W] *Quebec City, QE*

Musée du Fort [W] *Quebec City, QE*

Musée du Québec, [W] *Quebec City, QE*

Musée du Séminaire de Sherbrooke [W] *Sherbrooke, QE*

Museum & Archive of Games [W] *Kitchener-Waterloo, ON*

Museum at Portland Headlight, The [W] *Portland, ME*

Museum at the John Fitzgerald Kennedy Library [W] *Boston, MA*

Museum of American Political Life [W] *Hartford, CT*

Museum of Art [W] *Brunswick, ME*

Museum of Canadian Scouting [W] *Ottawa , ON*

Museum of Civilization (Musée de la Civilisation) [W] *Quebec City, QE*

Museum of Decorative Arts [W] *Montreal, QE*

Museum of Fine Arts [W] *Boston, MA*

Museum of Nantucket History (Macy Warehouse) [W] *Nantucket Island, MA*

Museum of Natural History [W] *Providence, RI*

Museum of New Hampshire History [W] *Concord, NH*

Museum of Our National Heritage [W] *Lexington, MA*

Museum of Primitive Art and Culture [W] *Kingston, RI*

Museum of Rhode Island History at Aldrich House [W] *Providence, RI*

Museum of Science [W] *Boston, MA*

Museum of Steam and Technology [W] *Hamilton, ON*

Museum of the Royal 22e Régiment [W] *Quebec City, QE*

Museum of Vintage Fashions [W] *Houlton, ME*

Musical Wonder House-Music Museum [W] *Wiscasset, ME*

Music Mountain Summer Music Festival [S] *Lakeville, CT*

Music on the Mall [S] *Brunswick, ME*

M/V *Kearsarge* Restaurant Ship [W] *Sunapee, NH*

M/V *Mount Sunapee II* Excursion Boat [W] *Sunapee, NH*

Myles Standish State Forest [W] *Plymouth, MA*

Myrtleville House Museum [W] *Brantford, ON*

Mystic Marinelife Aquarium [W] *Mystic, CT*

Mystic Seaport [W] *Mystic, CT*

Nantucket Maria Mitchell Association [W] *Nantucket Island, MA*

Narbonne House [W] *Salem, MA*

Nathan Hale Homestead [W] *Storrs, CT*

Nathan Hale Schoolhouse [W] *East Haddam, CT*

Nathaniel Bowditch [W] *Rockland, ME*

Nathaniel Hempsted House [W] *New London, CT*

National Archives of Canada [W] *Ottawa , ON*

National Arts Centre [W] *Ottawa, ON*

National Assembly of Québec [W] *Quebec City, QE*

National Aviation Museum [W] *Ottawa , ON*

National Battlefields Park [W] *Quebec City, QE*

National Exhibit Centre [W] *Yarmouth, NS*

National Gallery of Canada [W] *Ottawa , ON*

National League baseball (Montréal Expos) [W] *Montreal, QE*

National Monument to the Forefathers [W] *Plymouth, MA*

National Museum of Science and Technology [W] *Ottawa , ON*

National Yiddish Book Center [W] *Amherst, MA*

Native American Burial Grounds [W] *Norwich, CT*

Natural Bridge State Park [W] *North Adams, MA*

Natural formations. Mohegan Bluffs [W] *Block Island, RI*

Natural History Museum [W] *Bar Harbor, ME*

Nature Interpretation Centre of Lake Boivin [W] *Granby, QE*

Naumkeag [W] *Stockbridge and West Stockbridge, MA*

Nauset Beach [W] *Orleans (Cape Cod), MA*

NBA (Boston Celtics) [W] *Boston, MA*

NBA (Toronto Raptors) [W] *Toronto, ON*

NB Highland Games [A] *Fredericton, NB*

Nepean Point [W] *Ottawa , ON*

Neptune Theatre [W] *Halifax, NS*

New Bedford-Cuttyhunk Ferry [W] *New Bedford, MA*

New Bedford Whaling Museum [W] *New Bedford, MA*

New Britain Museum of American Art [W] *New Britain, CT*

New Britain Youth Museum [W] *New Britain, CT*

New Brunswick Botanical Garden [W] *Edmundston, NB*

New Brunswick Legislative Assembly [W] *Fredericton, NB*

New Brunswick Museum [W] *St. John, NB*

New Brunswick Summer Chamber Music Festival [A] *Fredericton, NB*

New Canaan Historical Society [W] *New Canaan, CT*

New Canaan Nature Center [W] *New Canaan, CT*

New Denmark Memorial Museum [W] *Edmundston, NB*

New England Airlines [W] *Block Island, RI*

New England Air Museum [W] *Windsor Locks, CT*

New England Aquarium [W] *Boston, MA*

New England Carousel Museum [W] *Bristol, CT*

New England Fire and History Museum [W] *Brewster (Cape Cod), MA*

New England Marionette Opera [W] *Peterborough, NH*

New England Music Camp [S] *Waterville, ME*

New England Quilt Museum [W] *Lowell, MA*

New England Science Center [W] *Worcester, MA*

New England Ski Museum [W] *Franconia, NH*

New England Thanksgiving [A] *Sturbridge, MA*

New France Celebration [A] *Quebec City, QE*

New Hampshire Highland Games [A] *Lincoln/North Woodstock Area, NH*

New Hampshire Music Festival [S] *Laconia, NH*

New Haven Colony Historical Society Museum [W] *New Haven, CT*

New Haven Symphony Orchestra [S] *New Haven, CT*

New London-Block Island, RI [W] *New London, CT*

New London-Fishers Island, NY [W] *New London, CT*

New London-Orient Point, NY [W] *New London, CT*

Newport Art Museum and Art Association [W] *Newport, RI*

Newport Historical Society Museum [W] *Newport, RI*

Newport Irish Heritage Month [A] *Newport, RI*

Newport Jai Alai [W] *Newport, RI*

Newport Music Festival [A] *Newport, RI*

Newport Navigation [W] *Newport, RI*

New Year's Eve Portland [A] *Portland, ME*

NFL (New England Patriots) [W] *Foxboro, MA*

NHL (Boston Bruins) [W] *Boston, MA*

NHL (Montréal Canadiens) [W] *Montreal, QE*

NHL (Ottawa Senators) [W] *Ottawa , ON*

NHL (Toronto Maple Leafs) [W] *Toronto, ON*

Niagara Apothecary [W] *Niagara-on-the-Lake, ON*

Niagara Falls Museum [W] *Niagara Falls, ON*

Niagara Grape and Wine Festival [A] *St. Catharines, ON*

Niagara Historical Society Museum [W] *Niagara-on-the-Lake, ON*

Niagara Parks Botanical Gardens [W] *Niagara Falls, ON*

Niagara Parks Butterfly Conservatory [W] *Niagara Falls, ON*

Niagara Spanish Aero Car [W] *Niagara Falls, ON*

Niagara Symphony Association [S] *St. Catharines, ON*

Nichols House Museum [W] *Boston, MA*

Nickels-Sortwell House [W] *Wiscasset, ME*

Nickerson State Park [W] *Brewster (Cape Cod), MA*

Night Heron Nature Cruises [W] *Kingston, RI*

Noah Webster Foundation and Historical Society [W] *Hartford, CT*

Noden Causeway [W] *Fort Frances, ON*

Noden-Reed House and Barn [W] *Windsor Locks, CT*

Norfolk Chamber Music Festival [S] *Norfolk, CT*

Norlands Living History Center [W] *Auburn, ME*

Norman Rockwell Museum [W] *Stockbridge and West Stockbridge, MA*

North American Black Historical Museum [W] *Windsor, ON*

North Burial Ground [W] *Providence, RI*

Northeast Historic Film [W] *Bucksport, ME*

Northern Maine Fair [A] *Presque Isle, ME*

Northern Outdoors, Inc [W] *Rockwood, ME*

Northfield Mountain Recreation and Environmental Center [W] *Greenfield, MA*

North Light [W] *Block Island, RI*

North Shore Music Theatre [S] *Beverly, MA*

Notre-Dame Basilica [W] *Montreal, QE*

Notre-Dame Basilica Museum [W] *Montreal, QE*

Notre-Dame-de-Bonsecours Church [W] *Montreal, QE*

Notre Dame-du-Cap [W] *Trois-Rivieres, QE*

Nott House, The [W] *Kennebunkport, ME*

Nova Scotia Air Show [A] *Halifax, NS*

Nova Scotia Museum of Natural History [W] *Halifax, NS*

Nylander Museum [W] *Caribou, ME*

Oak Bluffs [W] *Martha's Vineyard, MA*

Oak Grove Nature Center [W] *Manchester, CT*

Oceanarium-Bar Harbor [W] *Bar Harbor, ME*

Ocean Beach Park [W] *New London, CT*

Oceanographic cruise [W] *Groton, CT*

Octoberfest Parade and Craft Fair [A] *Pawtucket, RI*

October Mountain State Forest [W] *Lee, MA*

Odell Park [W] *Fredericton, NB*

Officers' Square [W] *Fredericton, NB*

Ogden House [W] *Fairfield, CT*

Ogunquit Museum of American Art [W] *Ogunquit, ME*

Ogunquit Playhouse [S] *Ogunquit, ME*

Oil Museum of Canada [W] *Sarnia, ON*

Oktoberfest [A] *Kitchener-Waterloo, ON*

Olad and Northwind [W] *Camden, ME*

Old (Vieux) Montréal [W] *Montreal, QE*

Old Atwood House [W] *Chatham (Cape Cod), MA*

Old Burying Ground, The [W] *Norwich, CT*

Old Campus, The [W] *New Haven, CT*

Old Castle [W] *Rockport, MA*

Old City Market [W] *St. John, NB*

Old Colony and Newport Railroad [W] *Newport, RI*

Olde Mistick Village [W] *Mystic, CT*

Olde Port Mariner Fleet, Inc [W] *Portland, ME*

Old Fire Hose Cart House [W] *Nantucket Island, MA*

Old Firehouse Museum [W] *South Hadley, MA*

Old Fort, The [W] *Montreal, QE*

Old Fort Halifax [W] *Waterville, ME*

Old Fort Western [W] *Augusta, ME*

Old Fort William [W] *Thunder Bay, ON*

Old Gaol [W] *York, ME*

Old Gaol [W] *Nantucket Island, MA*

Old Government House [W] *Fredericton, NB*

Old Homestead, The [A] *Keene, NH*

Old Ipswich Days [A] *Ipswich, MA*

Old Kent County Court House [W] *East Greenwich, RI*

Old Ledge School [W] *Yarmouth, ME*

Old Lighthouse Museum [W] *Stonington, CT*

Old Man of the Mountains [W] *Franconia Notch State Park, NH*

Old Manse, The [W] *Concord, MA*

Old Narragansett Church [W] *North Kingstown, RI*

Old New Gate Prison [W] *Windsor Locks, CT*

Old North Church [W] *Boston, MA*

Old Officers' Quarters [W] *Fredericton, NB*

Old Port [W] *Trois-Rivieres, QE*

Old Port Dalhousie [W] *St. Catharines, ON*

Old Port Exchange [W] *Portland, ME*

Old Port Festival [A] *Portland, ME*

Oldport Marine Harbor Tours [W] *Newport, RI*

Old Port of Québec Interpretation Centre [W] *Quebec City, QE*

Old South Meeting House [W] *Boston, MA*

Old Sow Whirlpool [W] *Eastport, ME*

Old State House [W] *Boston, MA*

Old State House [W] *Hartford, CT*

Old State House [W] *Providence, RI*

Old Stone Mill [W] *Newport, RI*

Old Sturbridge Village [W] *Sturbridge, MA*

Old Town Hall (Purple Heart Museum) [W] *Enfield, CT*

Old Whaling Church [W] *Martha's Vineyard, MA*

Old Windmill [W] *Jamestown, RI*

Old Windmill [W] *Nantucket Island, MA*

Old York Historical Society [W] *York, ME*

Olin Arts Center [W] *Lewiston, ME*

Oliver Ellsworth Homestead [W] *Windsor, CT*

Olympic Park [W] *Montreal, QE*

Ontario Parliament Buildings [W] *Toronto, ON*

Ontario Place [W] *Toronto, ON*

Ontario Science Centre [W] *Toronto, ON*

Ontario Winter Carnival Bon Soo [A] *Sault Ste. Marie, ON*

Ontario Workers Art & Heritage Centre [W] *Hamilton, ON*

Open House Tour [A] *Litchfield, CT*

Orchard House and School of Philosophy [W] *Concord, MA*

Orford Arts Centre [W] *Sherbrooke, QE*

Orwell Corner Historic Village [W] *Charlottetown, PE*

Osterville Historical Society Museum [W] *Centerville (Cape Cod), MA*

Otis Ridge [W] *Great Barrington, MA*

Ottawa International Jazz Festival [A] *Ottawa , ON*

Ottawa Riverboat Company [W] *Ottawa , ON*

Outdoor Art Show [A] *Toronto, ON*

Outdoor summer concerts [S] *Portland, ME*

Owls Head Transportation Museum [W] *Rockland, ME*

Oyster Festival [A] *Milford, CT*

Oyster Festival [A] *Norwalk, CT*

Palace Playland [W] *Old Orchard Beach, ME*

Palace Theatre [W] *Manchester, NH*

Panorama Ethnic Festival [A] *London, ON*

Paper House, The [W] *Rockport, MA*

Paramount Canada's Wonderland [W] *Toronto, ON*

Parc des Îles [W] *Montreal, QE*

Parc Safari [W] *Montreal, QE*

Pardee-Morris House [W] *New Haven, CT*

Parker River National Wildlife Refuge [W] *Newburyport, MA*

Park House Museum [W] *Windsor, ON*

Park Street Church [W] *Boston, MA*

Parson Fisher House [W] *Blue Hill, ME*

Parsons House [W] *Northampton, MA*

Passamaquoddy Indian Reservation [W] *Eastport, ME*

Pat's Peak Ski Area [W] *Concord, NH*

Patrick J Mogan Cultural Center [W] *Lowell, MA*

Patriots Day Celebration [A] *Boston, MA*

Patriots' Day Parade [A] *Concord, MA*

Paul's Boat Lines, Ltd [W] *Ottawa , ON*

Paul Revere House [W] *Boston, MA*

Pawtucket Red Sox [S] *Pawtucket, RI*

Peabody Museum and Essex Institute [W] *Salem, MA*

Peabody Museum of Natural History [W] *New Haven, CT*

Peary-MacMillan Arctic Museum [W] *Brunswick, ME*

Peirce-Nichols House [W] *Salem, MA*

Pejepscot Historical Society Museum [W] *Brunswick, ME*

Pemaquid Point Lighthouse Park [W] *Damariscotta, ME*

Pennesseewasee Lake [W] *Norway, ME*

Penobscot Marine Museum [W] *Searsport, ME*

Peterborough Historical Society [W] *Peterborough, NH*

Phillips Academy [W] *Andover and North Andover, MA*

Phillips Exeter Academy [W] *Exeter, NH*

Pickering Wharf [W] *Salem, MA*

Picnicking [W] *Boothbay Harbor, ME*

Pier, The [W] *Old Orchard Beach, ME*
Pier: Toronto's Waterfront Museum, The [W] *Toronto, ON*
Pier 21 [W] *Halifax, NS*
Pierce Manse [W] *Concord, NH*
Pilgrim Hall Museum [W] *Plymouth, MA*
Pilgrim Heights Area [W] *Truro and North Truro (Cape Cod), MA*
Pilgrim Monument and Museum [W] *Provincetown (Cape Cod), MA*
Pilgrim's Progress [A] *Plymouth, MA*
Pilot Pen International Tennis Tournament [A] *New Haven, CT*
Pines Golf Course [W] *Digby, NS*
Pinkham Notch [W] *Mount Washington, NH*
Pioneer Memorial Tower [W] *Kitchener-Waterloo, ON*
Pioneer Village: Salem In 1630 [W] *Salem, MA*
Pither's Point Park [W] *Fort Frances, ON*
Pittsburgh Sheepdog Trials [A] *Kingston, ON*
Place d'Armes [W] *Montreal, QE*
Place des Arts [W] *Montreal, QE*
Place Jacques-Cartier [W] *Montreal, QE*
Place-Royale [W] *Quebec City, QE*
Plainfield Greyhound Park [W] *Plainfield, CT*
Pleasant Valley Wildlife Sanctuary [W] *Lenox, MA*
Plimoth Plantation [W] *Plymouth, MA*
Plymouth Colony Winery [W] *Plymouth, MA*
Plymouth Harbor Cruises [W] *Plymouth, MA*
Plymouth National Wax Museum [W] *Plymouth, MA*
Plymouth Rock [W] *Plymouth, MA*
Plymouth State College [W] *Plymouth, NH*
Pointe-à-Calliére, the Montréal Museum of Archaeology and History [W] *Montreal, QE*
Point Judith [W] *Narragansett, RI*
Point Pelee National Park [W] *Windsor, ON*
Point Pleasant Park [W] *Halifax, NS*
Point Prim Lighthouse [W] *Digby, NS*
Poker Run [A] *Brockville, ON*
Polar Caves Park [W] *Plymouth, NH*
Popham Beach [W] *Bath, ME*
Popham Colony [W] *Bath, ME*
Porter Thermometer Museum [W] *Buzzards Bay (Cape Cod), MA*
Portland Museum of Art [W] *Portland, ME*

Portland Observatory [W] *Portland, ME*
Port Royal National Historic Site [W] *Digby, NS*
Portsmouth Harbor Cruises [W] *Portsmouth, NH*
Portsmouth Historic Homes [W] *Portsmouth, NH*
Portsmouth Jazz Festival [A] *Portsmouth, NH*
Portuguese Festival [A] *Provincetown (Cape Cod), MA*
Portuguese Princess [E] Whale Watch [W] *Provincetown (Cape Cod), MA*
Powder House Day [A] *New Haven, CT*
Powder Ridge Ski Area [W] *Middletown, CT*
Pownalborough Court House [W] *Wiscasset, ME*
Pratt Museum of Geology [W] *Amherst, MA*
Prehistoric World [W] *Morrisburg, ON*
Prescott Farm and Windmill [W] *Portsmouth, RI*
Prince Edward Island National Park [W] *Cavendish, PE*
Prince Edward Island National Park [W] *Charlottetown, PE*
Prince of Wales Tower National Historic Park [W] *Halifax, NS*
Providence Athenaeum Library [W] *Providence, RI*
Providence Children's Museum [W] *Providence, RI*
Providence Preservation Society [W] *Providence, RI*
Province House [W] *Charlottetown, PE*
Province House [W] *Halifax, NS*
Provincetown Art Association & Museum [W] *Provincetown (Cape Cod), MA*
Provincetown Ferry [W] *Plymouth, MA*
Provincetown Museum [W] *Provincetown (Cape Cod), MA*
Prudence Crandall House [W] *Plainfield, CT*
Prudence Island [W] *Bristol, RI*
Prudhomme's Wet 'n Wild Water Park [W] *St. Catharines, ON*
Public Archives of Nova Scotia [W] *Halifax, NS*
Public Garden [W] *Boston, MA*
Public Gardens [W] *Halifax, NS*
Public Gardens Band Concerts [S] *Halifax, NS*
Public wharves [W] *Yarmouth, NS*
Pump House Steam Museum [W] *Kingston, ON*

Putnam Cottage/Knapp Tavern [W] *Greenwich, CT*

Québec Aquarium [W] *Quebec City, QE*

Québec City Walls and Gates [W] *Quebec City, QE*

Québec Zoo [W] *Quebec City, QE*

Quaker Whaler's House [W] *Dartmouth, NS*

Quassy Amusement Park [W] *Waterbury, CT*

Queen of Winnipesaukee [W] *Laconia, NH*

Queen's Park [W] *Toronto, ON*

Queen's University [W] *Kingston, ON*

Quetico Provincial Park [W] *Thunder Bay, ON*

Quilt Show [A] *Bridgton, ME*

Quincy Bay Race Week [A] *Quincy, MA*

Quincy Historical Society [W] *Quincy, MA*

Quincy Homestead [W] *Quincy, MA*

Quinebaug Valley Trout Hatchery [W] *Plainfield, CT*

Rachel Carson National Wildlife Refuge [W] *Wells, ME*

Rackliffe Pottery [W] *Blue Hill, ME*

Radcliffe College [W] *Cambridge, MA*

Rafting Montréal [W] *Montreal, QE*

Ragged Mountain [W] *New London, NH*

Railroad Museum [W] *Chatham (Cape Cod), MA*

Rainbow Valley Family Fun Park [W] *Cavendish, PE*

Raisin River Canoe Races [A] *Cornwall, ON*

Ralph Waldo Emerson House [W] *Concord, MA*

Rangeley Lake State Park [W] *Rangeley, ME*

Raymond E. Baldwin Museum of Connecticut History [W] *Hartford, CT*

Rebecca Nurse Homestead [W] *Danvers, MA*

Reconstructed 18th-Century Barn [W] *Braintree, MA*

Recreation [W] *Provincetown (Cape Cod), MA*

Recreational facilities [W] *Ottawa , ON*

Recreation. Swimming [W] *Martha's Vineyard, MA*

Recreation. The Weirs [W] *Laconia, NH*

Redington Museum [W] *Waterville, ME*

Red River Beach [W] *Harwich (Cape Cod), MA*

Redstone School [W] *Sudbury Center, MA*

Redwood Library and Athenaeum [W] *Newport, RI*

Reenactment of March of Sudbury Minutemen to Concord on Apr 19, 1775 [A] *Sudbury Center, MA*

Reenactment of the Battle of Lexington and Concord [A] *Lexington, MA*

Reid [W] *Bath, ME*

Research Library [W] *Portland, ME*

Rhode Island School of Design [W] *Providence, RI*

Rhode Island State House [W] *Providence, RI*

Richard Sparrow House [W] *Plymouth, MA*

Rideau Canal [W] *Ottawa, ON*

RISD Museum [W] *Providence, RI*

Riverboat Cruises. Big Creek Boat Farm [W] *Brantford, ON*

Riverdale Park [W] *Toronto, ON*

Riverfest [A] *Brantford, ON*

Riverfest [A] *Brockville, ON*

Riverfest [A] *Hartford, CT*

Riverfest [A] *Manchester, NH*

Riverside Park [W] *Springfield, MA*

Riverton Fair [A] *Riverton, CT*

Roaring Brook Nature Center [W] *Avon, CT*

Robert Frost Farm [W] *Salem, NH*

Robert S. Peabody Foundation for Archaeology [W] *Andover and North Andover, MA*

Rockefeller Library [W] *Providence, RI*

Rockingham Park [W] *Salem, NH*

Rockport Art Association [W] *Rockport, MA*

Rockport Chamber Music Festival [A] *Rockport, MA*

"The Rocks" Provincial Park [W] *Moncton, NB*

Rockwood Park [W] *St. John, NB*

Rocky Neck State Park [W] *Old Lyme, CT*

Rodman Hall Arts Centre [W] *St. Catharines, ON*

Roger Williams National Memorial [W] *Providence, RI*

Roger Williams Park [W] *Providence, RI*

Roosevelt Campobello International Park [W] *Lubec, ME*

Ropes Mansion and Garden [W] *Salem, MA*

Roque Bluffs [W] *Machias, ME*

Rose-Arts Festival [A] *Norwich, CT*

Rosecliff [W] *Newport, RI*

Roseland Cottage [W] *Putnam, CT*

Rosie O'Grady's Balloon of Peace Monument [W] *Caribou, ME*

Rotch-Jones-Duff House and Garden Museum [W] *New Bedford, MA*

Round Hill Scottish Games [A] *Norwalk, CT*

Rowantrees Pottery [W] *Blue Hill, ME*

Royal Agricultural Winter Fair [A] *Toronto, ON*

Royal Botanical Gardens [W] *Hamilton, ON*

Royal Canadian Big Band Music Festival [A] *London, ON*

Royal Canadian Henley Regatta [S] *St. Catharines, ON*

Royal Canadian Mint [W] *Ottawa, ON*

Royal Canadian Regiment Museum, The [W] *London, ON*

Royal Military College of Canada [W] *Kingston, ON*

Royal Ontario Museum [W] *Toronto, ON*

Ruggles House [W] *Machias, ME*

Rundlet-May House [W] *Portsmouth, NH*

Rushing River Provincial Park [W] *Kenora, ON*

Saddleback Ski and Summer Lake Preserve [W] *Rangeley, ME*

Sail Festival [A] *New London, CT*

Sailing [W] *Wellfleet (Cape Cod), MA*

Sailing races [S] *Marblehead, MA*

Saint-Gaudens National Historic Site [W] *Hanover, NH*

Sakonnet Point [W] *Little Compton, RI*

Sakonnet Vineyards [W] *Little Compton, RI*

Salem Maritime National Historic Site [W] *Salem, MA*

Salem State College [W] *Salem, MA*

Salem Witch Museum [W] *Salem, MA*

Salisbury Cannon Museum [W] *Lakeville, CT*

Salisbury Mansion [W] *Worcester, MA*

Salmon Derby [A] *St. Catharines, ON*

Salmon Festival [A] *Eastport, ME*

Samuel C. Moore Station [W] *Littleton, NH*

Samuel Whitehorne House [W] *Newport, RI*

Sand Castle Contest [A] *Nantucket Island, MA*

Sanderson Centre for the Performing Arts [W] *Brantford, ON*

Sandwich Glass Museum [W] *Sandwich (Cape Cod), MA*

Sandy Bay Historical Society & Museums [W] *Rockport, MA*

Santarella "Tyringham's Gingerbread House" [W] *Lee, MA*

Santa's Village [W] *Jefferson, NH*

Saquatucket Municipal Marina [W] *Harwich (Cape Cod), MA*

Sarah Orne Jewett House [W] *Kittery, ME*

Sargent House Museum [W] *Gloucester, MA*

Sarnia Highland Games [A] *Sarnia, ON*

Sarnia Waterfront Festival [S] *Sarnia, ON*

Saugus Iron Works National Historic Site [W] *Saugus, MA*

Sault Ste. Marie Museum [W] *Sault Ste. Marie, ON*

Savoy Mountain State Forest [W] *North Adams, MA*

Sayward-Wheeler House [W] *York, ME*

Scale House [W] *Salem, MA*

Scallop Days [A] *Digby, NS*

Scarborough Marsh Nature Center [W] *Scarborough, ME*

School House [W] *Kennebunkport, ME*

Schooner *Lewis R. French* [W] *Camden, ME*

Schooner *Mary Day* [W] *Camden, ME*

Schooner *Roseway* [W] *Camden, ME*

Schooner *Surprise* [W] *Camden, ME*

Schooner *Timberwind* [W] *Camden, ME*

Schooner Days and North Atlantic Blues Festival [A] *Rockland, ME*

Schooner Festival [A] *Gloucester, MA*

Science Center of Connecticut [W] *Hartford, CT*

Science Center of Eastern Connecticut [W] *New London, CT*

Science Center of New Hampshire [W] *Holderness, NH*

Science Enrichment Encounters Museum [W] *Manchester, NH*

Scott-Fanton Museum [W] *Danbury, CT*

Scusset Beach [W] *Sandwich (Cape Cod), MA*

Seafest [A] *Yarmouth, NS*

Seafood Festival [A] *Charlestown, RI*

Seamen's Bethel [W] *New Bedford, MA*

Seashore Trolley Museum [W] *Kennebunkport, ME*

Sebago Lake State Park [W] *Sebago Lake, ME*

Seiji Ozawa Concert Hall [W] *Lenox, MA*

Seventh Day Baptist Meeting House [W] *Newport, RI*

Shaker Museum [W] *Poland Spring, ME*

Shakespeare & Co [S] *Lenox, MA*

Shakespearean Gardens [W] *Stratford, ON*

Sharon Arts Center [W] *Peterborough, NH*

Sharon Audubon Center [W] *Cornwall Bridge, CT*

Shaw Festival [S] *Niagara-on-the-Lake, ON*

Shawme-Crowell State Forest [W] *Sandwich (Cape Cod), MA*

Shawnee Peak at Pleasant Mountain Ski Area [W] *Bridgton, ME*

Shaw Perkins Mansion [W] *New London, CT*

Shearwater Aviation Museum [W] *Dartmouth, NS*

Shepherd House [W] *Northampton, MA*

Sherbrooke Village [W] *Antigonish, NS*

Shopping [W] *Boston, MA*

Shore Line Trolley Museum [W] *New Haven, CT*

Shore Village Museum [W] *Rockland, ME*

Shrine of Our Lady of Grace [W] *Colebrook, NH*

Shubert Performing Arts Center [W] *New Haven, CT*

Sidewalk Art Show [A] *Portland, ME*

Sightseeing cruises on Penobscot Bay [W] *Camden, ME*

Sightseeing tour. Abegweit Tours [W] *Charlottetown, PE*

Sightseeing tour. M/S *Jacques-Cartier* [W] *Trois-Rivieres, QE*

Sightseeing tours and boat cruises [W] *Rockport, MA*

Silver Cascade [W] *Bretton Woods, NH*

Silver Lake State Park [W] *Nashua, NH*

Silvermine Guild Arts Center [W] *New Canaan, CT*

Simsbury Farms [W] *Simsbury, CT*

Site of the Boston Massacre [W] *Boston, MA*

Site of the first US free public school [W] *Boston, MA*

Six Gun City [W] *Jefferson, NH*

Six Nations Native Fall Fair [A] *Brantford, ON*

Six Nations Native Pageant [A] *Brantford, ON*

Ska Nah Doht Iroquois Village [W] *London, ON*

Skiing. Camden Snow Bowl [W] *Camden, ME*

Skiing. Lonesome Pine Trails [W] *Fort Kent, ME*

Skiing. Loon Mountain Recreation Area [W] *Lincoln/North Woodstock Area, NH*

Skiing. Lost Valley Ski Area [W] *Auburn, ME*

Skiing. Moosehead Resort on Big Squaw Mountain [W] *Greenville, ME*

Skiing. Mount Cranmore [W] *North Conway, NH*

Ski Mont Orford [W] *Sherbrooke, QE*

Ski Sundown [W] *Avon, CT*

Skolfield-Whittier House [W] *Brunswick, ME*

Skowhegan Log Days [A] *Skowhegan, ME*

Skowhegan State Fair [A] *Skowhegan, ME*

SkyDome [W] *Toronto, ON*

Skylon Tower [W] *Niagara Falls, ON*

Slater Memorial Museum and Converse Art Gallery [W] *Norwich, CT*

Slater Memorial Park [W] *Pawtucket, RI*

Slater Mill National Historic Site [A] *Pawtucket, RI*

Sled Dog Race [A] *Rangeley, ME*

Sleepy Hollow Cemetery [W] *Concord, MA*

Sloane-Stanley Museum and Kent Furnace [W] *Kent, CT*

Smith's Castle [W] *North Kingstown, RI*

Smith College [W] *Northampton, MA*

Snowhill at Eastman Ski Area [W] *Sunapee, NH*

Solomon Goffe House [W] *Meriden, CT*

Solomon Rockwell House [W] *Riverton, CT*

Sombra Township Museum [W] *Sarnia, ON*

SoNo Arts Celebration [A] *Norwalk, CT*

Sound & Light Show on Parliament Hill [S] *Ottawa , ON*

South County Museum [W] *Narragansett, RI*

Southford Falls [W] *Southbury, CT*

South Mountain Concerts [S] *Pittsfield, MA*

South Shore Christmas Festival [A] *Quincy, MA*

Southworth Planetarium [W] *Portland, ME*

Spadina [W] *Toronto, ON*

Splashdown Amphibious Tours [W] *Plymouth, MA*

Spooner House [W] *Plymouth, MA*

Sports car racing [S] *Lakeville, CT*

Spring Arts & Flower Festival [A] *Newburyport, MA*

Spring Festival of Historic Houses [A] *Providence, RI*

Springfield Armory National Historic Site [W] *Springfield, MA*

Springfield Library and Museums [W] *Springfield, MA*

Springtime in Paradise [A] *Northampton, MA*

Spudland Open Amateur Golf Tournament [A] *Presque Isle, ME*

Squam Lake Tours [W] *Holderness, NH*

Squantz Pond State Park [W] *Danbury, CT*

Stafford Motor Speedway [S] *Stafford Springs, CT*

St. Andrew's Presbyterian Church [W] *Quebec City, QE*

Stanley-Whitman House [W] *Farmington, CT*

St. Anne's Church and Shrine [W] *Fall River, MA*

Stanton House [W] *Clinton, CT*

Stanwood Sanctuary (Birdsacre) and Homestead Museum [W] *Ellsworth, ME*

Star Island and Isles of Shoals [W] *Portsmouth, NH*

State Capitol [W] *Hartford, CT*

State House [W] *Augusta, ME*

State House [W] *Concord, NH*

State House [W] *Boston, MA*

Statue of Benjamin Franklin [W] *Boston, MA*

Statue of Tom Thumb [W] *Bridgeport, CT*

St. Basile Chapel Museum [W] *Edmundston, NB*

St. Catharines Museum [W] *St. Catharines, ON*

St. Croix Island International Historic Site [W] *Calais, ME*

St. Dunstan's Cathedral Basilica [W] *Charlottetown, PE*

Ste.-Marie among the Hurons [W] *Toronto, ON*

Stephen Phillips Memorial Trust House [W] *Salem, MA*

Stephen Taber [W] *Rockland, ME*

Sterling and Francine Clark Art Institute [W] *Williamstown, MA*

Sterling Memorial and Beinecke Rare Book and Manuscript Libraries [W] *New Haven, CT*

Stevens-Coolidge Place [W] *Andover and North Andover, MA*

St. George's Round Church [W] *Halifax, NS*

St. James Anglican Church [W] *Trois-Rivieres, QE*

St.-Jean-Port-Joli [W] *Quebec City, QE*

St. Joseph's Oratory [W] *Montreal, QE*

St. Lawrence Centre for the Arts [W] *Toronto, ON*

St. Lawrence Islands National Park [W] *Gananoque, ON*

St. Mark's Anglican Church [W] *Niagara-on-the-Lake, ON*

St. Ninian's Cathedral [W] *Antigonish, NS*

Stockbridge Main Street at Christmas [A] *Stockbridge and West Stockbridge, MA*

Stone Consolidated [W] *Kenora, ON*

Stoney Brook Mill [W] *Brewster (Cape Cod), MA*

Storrowton Village [W] *Springfield, MA*

Storybook Gardens [W] *London, ON*

Story Land [W] *Jackson, NH*

St. Patrick's Church [W] *Damariscotta, ME*

St. Patrick's Day Parade [A] *Pawtucket, RI*

St. Paul's-on-the-Green [W] *Norwalk, CT*

St.-Paul St [W] *Montreal, QE*

St. Peter's Fiesta [A] *Gloucester, MA*

Stratford Festival [S] *Stratford, ON*

Strawbery Banke Museum [W] *Portsmouth, NH*

Striped Bass and Bluefish Derby [S] *Martha's Vineyard, MA*

Sturgis Library [W] *Barnstable (Cape Cod), MA*

St. Vincent de Paul Roman Catholic Church [W] *Niagara-on-the-Lake, ON*

Sugarloaf/USA Ski Area [W] *Kingfield, ME*

Summer [W] *Laconia, NH*

Summer [W] *Sunapee, NH*

Summerfest [S] *Quincy, MA*

Sunbeam Fleet Nature Cruises [W] *New London, CT*

Sunday River Ski Resort [W] *Bethel, ME*

Sunfest [A] *London, ON*

Supersports Family Fun Park [W] *Plymouth, MA*

Surf Coaster [W] *Laconia, NH*

Swift-Daley House [W] *Eastham (Cape Cod), MA*

Swimming [W] *Center Ossipee, NH*

Swimming [W] *Damariscotta, ME*

Swimming [W] *Dartmouth, NS*

Swimming [W] *Kennebunkport, ME*

Swimming [W] *Plymouth, MA*

Swimming [W] *South Yarmouth (Cape Cod), MA*

Swimming [W] *Wellfleet (Cape Cod), MA*

Swimming [W] *Narragansett, RI*

Swimming, boating [W] *Rangeley, ME*

Swimming. Craigville Beach [W] *Hyannis (Cape Cod), MA*

Swimming, fishing [W] *Charlestown, RI*

Swimming. Head of the Meadow [W] *Truro and North Truro (Cape Cod), MA*

Swimming, picnicking, camping, boating, fishing [W] *Bethel, ME*

Sydney L. Wright Museum [W] *Jamestown, RI*

Symphony Hall [W] *Boston, MA*

Table Rock [W] *Dixville Notch, NH*

Talcott Arboretum [W] *South Hadley, MA*

Talcott Mountain State Park [W] *Hartford, CT*

Tanglewood [W] *Lenox, MA*

Tanglewood Music Festival [S] *Lenox, MA*

Tantaquidgeon Indian Museum [W] *Norwich, CT*

Tapping Reeve House [W] *Litchfield, CT*

Taste O' Danbury [A] *Danbury, CT*

Taste of Hartford [A] *Hartford, CT*

Taste of Springfield [A] *Springfield, MA*

Tate House [W] *Portland, ME*

Taylor-Barry House [W] *Kennebunk, ME*

Thanksgiving Week [A] *Plymouth, MA*

Theatre-by-the-Sea [S] *Charlestown, RI*

Théâtre des Lilas [W] *Montreal, QE*

Thimble Islands Cruise [W] *Branford, CT*

Thomas Griswold House Museum [W] *Guilford, CT*

Thomas Point Beach [W] *Brunswick, ME*

Thousand Island Cruises [W] *Brockville, ON*

Three-County Fair [A] *Northampton, MA*

Thunder Bay Art Gallery [W] *Thunder Bay, ON*

Tidal bore [W] *Moncton, NB*

Tidal bore [W] *Truro, NS*

Todmorden Mills Heritage Museum & Arts Centre [W] *Toronto, ON*

Topsham Fair [A] *Brunswick, ME*

Topsmead State Forest [W] *Litchfield, CT*

Toronto International Film Festival [A] *Toronto, ON*

Toronto Island Park [W] *Toronto, ON*

Toronto Stock Exchange [W] *Toronto, ON*

Toronto Symphony [W] *Toronto, ON*

Toronto Tours Ltd [W] *Toronto, ON*

Touro Synagogue National Historic Site [W] *Newport, RI*

Towers, The [W] *Narragansett, RI*

Town Clock [W] *Halifax, NS*

Town of Lunenburg [W] *Peggy's Cove, NS*

Town Wharf (MacMillan Wharf) [W] *Provincetown (Cape Cod), MA*

Trinity Church [W] *Boston, MA*

Trinity Church [W] *Digby, NS*

Trinity Church [W] *Newport, RI*

"Trinity Royal" Heritage Preservation Area [W] *St. John, NB*

Trips from Boothbay Harbor [W] *Monhegan Island, ME*

Trois-Rivieres International Vocal Arts Festival [A] *Trois-Rivieres, QE*

Trolley Museum [W] *Windsor Locks, CT*

Truro Historical Society Museum [W] *Truro and North Truro (Cape Cod), MA*

Tuck Memorial Museum [W] *Hampton Beach, NH*

Two-Cent Footbridge [W] *Waterville, ME*

Two Lights [W] *Portland, ME*

United Counties Museum [W] *Cornwall, ON*

United First Parish Church [W] *Quincy, MA*

Université de Montréal [W] *Montreal, QE*

Université Laval [W] *Quebec City, QE*

University Hall [W] *Cambridge, MA*

University Hall [W] *Providence, RI*

University of Connecticut [W] *Storrs, CT*

University of Connecticut-Bartlett Arboretum [W] *Stamford, CT*

University of Hartford [W] *Hartford, CT*

University of Maine at Presque Isle [W] *Presque Isle, ME*

University of Maine-Orono [W] *Orono, ME*

University of MA-Lowell [W] *Lowell, MA*

University of Massachusetts [W] *Amherst, MA*

University of New Brunswick [W] *Fredericton, NB*

University of Toronto [W] *Toronto, ON*

University of Windsor [W] *Windsor, ON*

Uplands Museum and Cultural Centre [W] *Sherbrooke, QE*

Upper Canada Village [W] *Cornwall, ON*

Upper Canada Village [W] *Morrisburg, ON*

Ursuline Convent [W] *Trois-Rivieres, QE*

US Coast Guard Academy [W] *New London, CT*

USS *Constitution* [W] *Boston, MA*

Valley Railroad [W] *Essex, CT*

Varnum House Museum [W] *East Greenwich, RI*

Varnum Memorial Armory and Military Museum [W] *East Greenwich, RI*

Victoria Mansion [W] *Portland, ME*

Victoria Memorial Museum Building [W] *Ottawa , ON*

Victoria Park [W] *Truro, NS*

Victory Chimes [W] *Rockland, ME*

Viking Boat Tour [W] *Newport, RI*

Viking Bus Tour [W] *Newport, RI*

Vincent House [W] *Martha's Vineyard, MA*

Visitor Center [W] *Plymouth, MA*

Visitor Information [W] *Salem, MA*

Wadsworth Atheneum [W] *Hartford, CT*

Wadsworth Falls State Park [W] *Middletown, CT*

Wadsworth-Longfellow House [W] *Portland, ME*

Walden Pond State Reservation [W] *Concord, MA*

Walking tour [W] *Boston, MA*

Walking Tour of Historic Apponaug Village [W] *Warwick, RI*

Wanton-Lyman-Hazard House [W] *Newport, RI*

Warner House [W] *Portsmouth, NH*

Warwick Heritage Festival [A] *Warwick, RI*

Warwick Mall [W] *Warwick, RI*

Watch Hill [W] *Westerly, RI*

WaterFire [A] *Providence, RI*

Waterfront Festival [A] *Gloucester, MA*

Waterloo County Quilt Festival [A] *Kitchener-Waterloo, ON*

Waterloo Park [W] *Kitchener-Waterloo, ON*

Waterloo-St. Jacobs Railway [W] *Kitchener-Waterloo, ON*

Waterville Valley Ski Area [W] *Waterville Valley, NH*

Watson Farm [W] *Jamestown, RI*

Wayside, The [W] *Concord, MA*

Webb-Deane-Stevens Museum [W] *Wethersfield, CT*

Webster Cottage [W] *Hanover, NH*

Welland Canal Viewing Complex at Lock III [W] *St. Catharines, ON*

Wellesley Apple Butter & Cheese Festival [A] *Kitchener-Waterloo, ON*

Wellesley College [W] *Wellesley, MA*

Wellfleet Bay Wildlife Sanctuary [W] *Wellfleet (Cape Cod), MA*

Wells Auto Museum [W] *Wells, ME*

Wells Natural Estuarine Research Reserve [W] *Wells, ME*

Wendell Gilley Museum [W] *Southwest Harbor, ME*

Wenham Museum [W] *Beverly, MA*

Wentworth-Gardner House [W] *Portsmouth, NH*

Wentworth State Park [W] *Wolfeboro, NH*

Western Fair [A] *London, ON*

Western Gateway Heritage State Park [W] *North Adams, MA*

Western Nova Scotia Exhibition [A] *Yarmouth, NS*

West India Goods Store [W] *Salem, MA*

West Parish Meetinghouse [W] *Barnstable (Cape Cod), MA*

Westport Country Playhouse [S] *Westport, CT*

Westport Handcrafts Fair [A] *Westport, CT*

West Rock Nature Center [W] *New Haven, CT*

Wethersfield Museum [W] *Wethersfield, CT*

Whale's Tale Water Park [W] *Lincoln/North Woodstock Area, NH*

Whale Watching [S] *Gloucester, MA*

Whale watching [W] *Plymouth, MA*

Whale Watching [W] *Provincetown (Cape Cod), MA*

Whale-watching trips [W] *Eastport, ME*

Whaling Museum [W] *Nantucket Island, MA*

Whistler House Museum of Art [W] *Lowell, MA*

Whitehall Museum House [W] *Newport, RI*

Whitehern [W] *Hamilton, ON*

White Horse Tavern [W] *Newport, RI*

White Lake State Park [W] *Center Ossipee, NH*

White Memorial Foundation, Inc [W] *Litchfield, CT*

White Mountain National Forest [W] *Bartlett, NH*

White Mountain National Forest [W] *Bethel, ME*

White Mountain National Forest [W] *Franconia, NH*

White Mountain National Forest [W] *Jackson, NH*

White Mountain National Forest [W] *Lincoln/North Woodstock Area, NH*

White Mountain National Forest [W] *Mount Washington, NH*

White Mountain National Forest [W] *North Conway, NH*

White Mountain National Forest [W] *Twin Mountain, NH*
"Whites of Their Eyes" [W] *Boston, MA*
Whitney Museum of American Art at Champion [W] *Stamford, CT*
Wickford Art Festival [A] *North Kingstown, RI*
Wickham Park [W] *Manchester, CT*
Widener Library [W] *Cambridge, MA*
Wilbor House [W] *Little Compton, RI*
Wild Blueberry Festival [A] *Machias, ME*
Wildcat Ski & Recreation Area [W] *Pinkham Notch, NH*
Wilderness Expeditions [W] *Bingham, ME*
Wilderness Expeditions, Inc [W] *Rockwood, ME*
Wilhelm Reich Museum [W] *Rangeley, ME*
William Benton Museum of Art [W] *Storrs, CT*
Williams College [W] *Williamstown, MA*
Williams College Museum of Art [W] *Williamstown, MA*
Williamstown Fair [A] *Cornwall, ON*
Willistead Manor [W] *Windsor, ON*
Wilmot Park [W] *Fredericton, NB*
Wilson Museum [W] *Bucksport, ME*
Windjammer Days [A] *Boothbay Harbor, ME*
Windjammers [W] *Camden, ME*
Windjammers [W] *Rockland, ME*
Windjammer Weekend [A] *Camden, ME*
Windsor Historical Society [W] *Windsor, CT*
Windsor's Community Museum [W] *Windsor, ON*
Winfisky Art Gallery [W] *Salem, MA*
Winnipesaukee Railroad [W] *Laconia, NH*
Winnipesaukee Scenic Railroad [W] *Meredith, NH*
Winslow Crocker House [W] *South Yarmouth (Cape Cod), MA*
Winslow Memorial Park [W] *Freeport, ME*
Winter [W] *Laconia, NH*
Winter [W] *Sunapee, NH*
Winter Carnival [A] *Caribou, ME*
Winter Carnival [A] *Kennebunk, ME*
Winterfest [A] *Halifax, NS*
Winter Festival of Lights [A] *Niagara Falls, ON*
Winterlude [A] *Ottawa , ON*
Wistariahurst Museum [W] *Holyoke, MA*

Witchcraft Victims' Memorial [W] *Danvers, MA*
Witch Dungeon Museum [W] *Salem, MA*
Witch House [W] *Salem, MA*
Women's National Rowing Regatta [A] *New Preston, CT*
Women's Regatta [A] *South Hadley, MA*
Woodbine Racetrack [W] *Toronto, ON*
Wooden Boat School [W] *Blue Hill, ME*
Woodland Cultural Centre [W] *Brantford, ON*
Woodleigh Replicas & Gardens [W] *Cavendish, PE*
Woodman Institute [W] *Dover, NH*
Woods-Gerry Gallery [W] *Providence, RI*
Woods Hole, Martha's Vineyard, and Nantucket Steamship Authority [W] *Martha's Vineyard, MA*
Woodside National Historic Site [W] *Kitchener-Waterloo, ON*
Worcester Art Museum [W] *Worcester, MA*
Worcester Common Outlets [W] *Worcester, MA*
Worcester Music Festival of the Worcester County Music Assn [S] *Worcester, MA*
Worldfest/Festimonde [A] *Cornwall, ON*
World Film Festival [A] *Montreal, QE*
World Folklore Festival [A] *Drummondville, QE*
World's Largest Pancake Breakfast [A] *Springfield, MA*
WPA Murals [W] *Norwalk, CT*
Wreck Exploration Tours [W] *Windsor, ON*
Wright Museum [W] *Wolfeboro, NH*
Wriston Quadrangle [W] *Providence, RI*
Wyman Tavern [W] *Keene, NH*
Yale Art Gallery [W] *New Haven, CT*
Yale Bowl [W] *New Haven, CT*
Yale Center for British Art [W] *New Haven, CT*
Yale Repertory Theater [S] *New Haven, CT*
Yale University [W] *New Haven, CT*
Yamaska Provincial Park [W] *Granby, QE*
Yankee Homecoming [A] *Newburyport, MA*
Yarmouth Arts Regional Centre [W] *Yarmouth, NS*
Yarmouth County Museum [W] *Yarmouth, NS*

Yarmouth Cup Races [A] *Yarmouth, NS*

Yarmouth Historical Society Museum [W] *Yarmouth, ME*

Ye Antientiest Burial Ground [W] *New London, CT*

Ye Olde Towne Mill [W] *New London, CT*

Yesteryears Doll and Miniature Museum [W] *Sandwich (Cape Cod), MA*

York Redoubt National Historic Site [W] *Halifax, NS*

York-Sunbury Historical Society Museum [W] *Fredericton, NB*

Young People's Theatre [W] *Toronto, ON*

Zoo [W] *Providence, RI*

LODGING LIST

Establishment names are listed in alphabetical order followed by a symbol identifying their classification and then city and state. The symbols for classification are: [AS] for All Suites, [BB] for B&Bs/Small Inns, [CAS] for Casinos, [CC] for Cottage Colonies, [CON] for Villas/Condos, [CONF] for Conference Centers, [EX] for Extended Stays, [HOT] for Hotels, [MOT] for Motels/Motor Lodges, [RAN] for Guest Ranches, and [RST] for Resorts.

181 MAIN STREET BED & BREAKFAST [BB] *Freeport, ME*
1661 INN & GUEST HOUSE, THE [BB] *Block Island, RI*
1785 INN & RESTAURANT [BB] *North Conway, NH*
1811 HOUSE [BB] *Manchester and Manchester Center, VT*
1824 HOUSE INN BED AND BREAKFAST [BB] *Waitsfield, VT*
1830 ADMIRAL'S QUARTERS INN [BB] *Boothbay Harbor, ME*
1896 HOUSE [MOT] *Williamstown, MA*
ABOVE TIDE INN [BB] *Ogunquit, ME*
ACADIA CABINS [CC] *Southwest Harbor, ME*
ACADIA INN [HOT] *Bar Harbor, ME*
A CAMBRIDGE HOUSE BED AND BREAKFAST INN [BB] *Cambridge, MA*
ACWORTH INN [BB] *Barnstable (Cape Cod), MA*
ADAIR COUNTRY INN [BB] *Littleton, NH*
ADAMS MOTEL AND RESTAURANT, THE [CC] *Brandon, VT*
ADAM'S TERRACE GARDENS INN [BB] *Centerville (Cape Cod), MA*
ADDISON CHOATE INN [BB] *Rockport, MA*
ADMIRAL DIGBY INN [MOT] *Digby, NS*
ADMIRAL INN [MOT] *Hamilton, ON*
ADMIRAL PEARY HOUSE [BB] *Center Lovell, ME*
ADMIRALTY INN [MOT] *Falmouth (Cape Cod), MA*
AIME'S MOTEL INC [MOT] *St. Johnsbury, VT*
AIRPORT HOTEL HALIFAX [HOT] *Halifax, NS*
ALBERT AT BAY [HOT] *Ottawa , ON*
ALDEN COUNTRY INN [BB] *Hanover, NH*
ALGOMA'S WATER TOWER INN [MOT] *Sault Ste. Marie, ON*
ALGONQUIN, THE [RST] *St. Andrews, NB*

ALLEN HOUSE VICTORIAN INN [BB] *Amherst, MA*
ALL SEASON MOTOR INN [MOT] *South Yarmouth (Cape Cod), MA*
AMERICANA HOLIDAY MOTEL [MOT] *South Yarmouth (Cape Cod), MA*
ANCHORAGE BY THE SEA [RST] *Ogunquit, ME*
ANCHORAGE MOTOR INN [RST] *York, ME*
ANCHOR WATCH BED & BREAKFAST [BB] *Boothbay Harbor, ME*
ANDOVER INN [BB] *Andover and North Andover, MA*
ANDRIE ROSE INN [BB] *Ludlow, VT*
APPLEBUTTER INN [BB] *Woodstock, VT*
APPLEGATE [BB] *Lee, MA*
APPLE TREE INN [BB] *Lenox, MA*
APPLEWOOD FARMS INN [BB] *Mystic, CT*
ARABIAN HORSE INN, THE [BB] *Sudbury Center, MA*
ARBOR INN, THE [BB] *Martha's Vineyard, MA*
ARLINGTON INN [BB] *Arlington, VT*
ARLINGTONS WEST MOUNTAIN INN [BB] *Arlington, VT*
ARUNDEL MEADOWS INN [BB] *Kennebunk, ME*
ASHLEY INN [BB] *Martha's Vineyard, MA*
ASHLEY MANOR [BB] *Barnstable (Cape Cod), MA*
ASHWORTH BY THE SEA [HOT] *Hampton Beach, NH*
ASPEN MOTEL [MOT] *Manchester and Manchester Center, VT*
ASTICOU INN [BB] *Northeast Harbor, ME*
ATLANTIC BIRCHES INN [BB] *Old Orchard Beach, ME*
ATLANTIC EYRIE LODGE [MOT] *Bar Harbor, ME*
ATLANTIC MOTOR INN [MOT] *Wells, ME*
ATLANTIS MOTOR INN [MOT] *Gloucester, MA*

ATRIUM [MOT] *Millinocket, ME*
ATRIUM TRAVELODGE [MOT]
  Brunswick, ME
ATTITASH MOUNTAIN VILLAGE
  [RST] *Bartlett, NH*
AUBERGE BROMONT [RST] *Granby,
  QE*
AUBERGE DE LA FOUNTAINE [BB]
  Montreal, QE
AUBERGE GISELE'S INN [MOT]
  Baddeck, NS
AUBERGE HANDFIELD [BB] *Montreal,
  QE*
AUBERGE HATLEY [BB] *Montreal, QE*
AUBERGES WANDLYN [MOT]
  Montreal, QE
AU CHATEAU FLEUR DE LYS [BB]
  Quebec City, QE
AUGUSTUS SNOW HOUSE [BB]
  Harwich (Cape Cod), MA
AU MANOIR STE.-GENEVIEVE [BB]
  Quebec City, QE
AUSTINS INN TOWN HOTEL [HOT]
  Kennebunkport, ME
AUTUMN INN [MOT] *Northampton,
  MA*
AVON OLD FARMS HOTEL [HOT]
  Avon, CT
BAGLEY HOUSE, THE [BB] *Freeport,
  ME*
BAILEY ISLAND MOTEL [BB] *Bailey
  Island, ME*
BALSAMS, THE [RST] *Dixville Notch,
  NH*
BAR HARBOR HOTEL - BLUENOSE
  INN [MOT] *Bar Harbor, ME*
BAR HARBOR INN [HOT] *Bar Harbor,
  ME*
BAR HARBOR MOTEL [MOT] *Bar
  Harbor, ME*
BAR HARBOR QUALITY INN [MOT]
  Bar Harbor, ME
BAR HARBOR REGENCY [RST] *Bar
  Harbor, ME*
BARNSTEAD INN [BB] *Manchester and
  Manchester Center, VT*
BARRINGTON COURT [MOT] *Great
  Barrington, MA*
BARROWS HOUSE INN [BB] *Dorset,
  VT*
BARTON'S MOTEL [MOT] *Laconia,
  NH*
BASIN HARBOR CLUB [RST]
  Vergennes, VT
BASS RIVER MOTEL [MOT] *South
  Yarmouth (Cape Cod), MA*
BATTENKILL INN [BB] *Arlington, VT*
BAY BEACH BED & BREAKFAST [BB]
  Sandwich (Cape Cod), MA
BAY FRONT QUALITY INN [MOT]
  Sault Ste. Marie, ON
BAY MOTOR INN [MOT] *Buzzards
  Bay (Cape Cod), MA*
BAYVIEW, THE [HOT] *Bar Harbor, ME*
BAY VIEW INN & COTTAGES [CC]
  Wiscasset, ME

BAY VOYAGE, THE [BB] *Jamestown, RI*
BEACH HOUSE, THE [BB] *Kennebunk,
  ME*
BEACH HOUSE, THE [BB] *Martha's
  Vineyard, MA*
BEACH HOUSE AT FALMOUTH
  HEIGHTS [BB] *Falmouth (Cape
  Cod), MA*
BEACHMERE INN, THE [MOT]
  Ogunquit, ME
BEACH N TOWNE MOTEL [MOT]
  South Yarmouth (Cape Cod), MA
BEACH PLUM INN [BB] *Martha's
  Vineyard, MA*
BEACON RESORT [MOT]
  *Lincoln/North Woodstock Area,
  NH*
BEAUSEJOUR [HOT] *Moncton, NB*
BEDFORD VILLAGE INN [BB]
  Manchester, NH
BEE AND THISTLE INN [BB] *Old
  Lyme, CT*
BEECHWOOD HOTEL [HOT]
  Worcester, MA
BEECHWOOD INN [BB] *Barnstable
  (Cape Cod), MA*
BELFAST BAY MEADOWS INN [BB]
  Belfast, ME
BELFAST HARBOR INN [MOT] *Belfast,
  ME*
BELFRY INN & BISTRO, THE [BB]
  Sandwich (Cape Cod), MA
BELKNAP MOTEL [MOT] *Laconia, NH*
BELMONT MOTEL [MOT] *Skowhegan,
  ME*
BENNINGTON MOTOR INN [MOT]
  Bennington, VT
BERKSHIRE HILLS MOTEL [MOT]
  Williamstown, MA
BERNERHOF INN & PRINCE PLACE
  RESTAURANT [BB] *Jackson, NH*
BEST INN BANGOR [MOT] *Bangor,
  ME*
BEST WESTERN [HOT] *Boston, MA*
BEST WESTERN [MOT] *Brockton, MA*
BEST WESTERN [MOT] *Bucksport, ME*
BEST WESTERN [HOT] *Burlington, VT*
BEST WESTERN [MOT] *Cambridge,
  MA*
BEST WESTERN [MOT] *Camden, ME*
BEST WESTERN [HOT] *Concord, MA*
BEST WESTERN [HOT] *Haverhill, MA*
BEST WESTERN [MOT] *Kingston, ON*
BEST WESTERN [MOT] *London, ON*
BEST WESTERN AT THE JUNCTION
  [HOT] *White River Junction, VT*
BEST WESTERN BASS ROCKS OCEAN
  INN [MOT] *Gloucester, MA*
BEST WESTERN BERKSHIRE INN
  [HOT] *Danbury, CT*
BEST WESTERN BLACK BEAR INN
  [MOT] *Orono, ME*
BEST WESTERN BLACK SWAN INN
  [MOT] *Lee, MA*

BEST WESTERN BLUE ROCK MOTOR INN [MOT] *South Yarmouth (Cape Cod), MA*

BEST WESTERN BRANT PARK INN [MOT] *Brantford, ON*

BEST WESTERN CAIRN CROFT [MOT] *Niagara Falls, ON*

BEST WESTERN CHARLOTTETOWN [MOT] *Charlottetown, PE*

BEST WESTERN CHATEAU MOTOR INN [RST] *Provincetown (Cape Cod), MA*

BEST WESTERN CHELMSFORD INN [HOT] *Lowell, MA*

BEST WESTERN CONTINENTAL INN [MOT] *Windsor, ON*

BEST WESTERN CROSSROADS [MOT] *Thunder Bay, ON*

BEST WESTERN FALLSVIEW [MOT] *Niagara Falls, ON*

BEST WESTERN FALMOUTH MARINA TRADEWINDS [MOT] *Falmouth (Cape Cod), MA*

BEST WESTERN GLENGARRY [HOT] *Truro, NS*

BEST WESTERN HERITAGE MOTOR INN [MOT] *Millinocket, ME*

BEST WESTERN HOTEL [HOT] *Mont Tremblant Provincial Park, QE*

BEST WESTERN INN [MOT] *Bar Harbor, ME*

BEST WESTERN INN & SUITES [EX] *Rutland, VT*

BEST WESTERN INN AND CONFERENCE CENTER [MOT] *Portsmouth, NH*

BEST WESTERN LAKESIDE INN [HOT] *Kenora, ON*

BEST WESTERN L'ARTISTOCRATE [MOT] *Quebec City, QE*

BEST WESTERN MAINSTAY INN [HOT] *Newport, RI*

BEST WESTERN MERMAID [MOT] *Yarmouth, NS*

BEST WESTERN MERRY MANOR INN [MOT] *Portland, ME*

BEST WESTERN NEW ENGLANDER MOTOR INN [MOT] *Bennington, VT*

BEST WESTERN NORTHAMPTON [MOT] *Northampton, MA*

BEST WESTERN PARKWAY INN [MOT] *Cornwall, ON*

BEST WESTERN PRIMROSE [HOT] *Toronto, ON*

BEST WESTERN PROVINCIAL [MOT] *Gananoque, ON*

BEST WESTERN ROYAL PLAZA HOTEL & TRADE CENTER [HOT] *Sudbury Center, MA*

BEST WESTERN SENATOR INN [MOT] *Augusta, ME*

BEST WESTERN SOVEREIGN [HOT] *Keene, NH*

BEST WESTERN SOVEREIGN HOTEL [MOT] *Mystic, CT*

BEST WESTERN STONY HILL INN [RST] *Danbury, CT*

BEST WESTERN TIDES BEACHFRONT [RST] *Provincetown (Cape Cod), MA*

BEST WESTERN TLC HOTEL [HOT] *Waltham, MA*

BEST WESTERN TORONTO AIRPORT-CARLTON PLACE [HOT] *Toronto, ON*

BEST WESTERN VICTORIA PARK SUITES [HOT] *Ottawa , ON*

BEST WESTERN WATERVILLE [HOT] *Waterville, ME*

BEST WESTERN WHEELS INN [MOT] *Windsor, ON*

BEST WESTERN WHITE HOUSE INN [MOT] *Bangor, ME*

BEST WESTERN WHITE HOUSE [MOT] *Brockville, ON*

BETHEL INN AND COUNTRY CLUB [RST] *Bethel, ME*

BETSY'S BED AND BREAKFAST [BB] *Montpelier, VT*

BINGHAM MOTOR INN & SPORTS COMPLEX [MOT] *Bingham, ME*

BIRCHES & CATERING, THE [CC] *Rockwood, ME*

BIRCH KNOLL [MOT] *Laconia, NH*

BIRCHWOOD INN [BB] *Lenox, MA*

BISHOPSGATE INN [BB] *East Haddam, CT*

BLACK BEAR LODGE [HOT] *Waterville Valley, NH*

BLACK FRIAR INN [BB] *Bar Harbor, ME*

BLACK HORSE INN [MOT] *Camden, ME*

BLACK LOCUST INN [BB] *Waterbury, VT*

BLACK POINT INN [RST] *Portland, ME*

BLANTYRE [HOT] *Lenox, MA*

BLOMIDON [BB] *Grand Pre, NS*

BLUEBERRY HILL INN [BB] *Brandon, VT*

BLUEBIRD MOTEL [MOT] *Machias, ME*

BLUE DOLPHIN INN [MOT] *Eastham (Cape Cod), MA*

BLUE GENTIAN LODGE [BB] *Londonderry, VT*

BLUE HARBOR HOUSE, A VILLAGE INN [BB] *Camden, ME*

BLUE HILL INN [BB] *Blue Hill, ME*

BLUE IRIS MOTOR INN [MOT] *Rumford, ME*

BLUE MOON MOTEL [MOT] *St. Andrews, NB*

BLUENOSE INN AND SUITES [MOT] *Halifax, NS*

BLUE SEA MOTOR INN [MOT] *Provincetown (Cape Cod), MA*

BLUE SPRUCE MOTEL [MOT]
Middlebury, VT
BLUE SPRUCE MOTEL &
TOWNHOUSES [MOT]
Plymouth, MA
BLUE WATER ON THE OCEAN
[MOT] South Yarmouth (Cape
Cod), MA
B MAE'S RESORT INN & SUITES
[MOT] Laconia, NH
BONACCORD HOUSE B&B [BB]
Moncton, NB
BOND PLACE [HOT] Toronto, ON
BOSTON HARBOR HOTEL [HOT]
Boston, MA
BOSTON MARRIOTT [HOT]
Burlington, MA
BOSTON MARRIOTT LONG WHARF
[HOT] Boston, MA
BOSTON PARK PLAZA HOTEL, THE
[HOT] Boston, MA
BOULDERS INN [BB] New Preston, CT
BRADFORD GARDENS INN [BB]
Provincetown (Cape Cod), MA
BRADFORD HOUSE MOTEL [MOT]
Provincetown (Cape Cod), MA
BRADLEY INN, THE [BB]
Damariscotta, ME
BRAESIDE MOTEL [MOT] Woodstock,
VT
BRAMBLE INN [BB] Brewster (Cape
Cod), MA
BRANDON INN, THE [BB] Brandon,
VT
BRANDT HOUSE [HOT] Greenfield,
MA
BRANNON-BUNKER INN [BB]
Damariscotta, ME
BRASS LANTERN INN [BB] Stowe, VT
BRASS LANTERN INN BED &
BREAKFAST [BB] Searsport, ME
BREAKERS MOTEL [MOT] Dennis
(Cape Cod), MA
BREAKWATER INN AND
RESTAURANT [BB]
Kennebunkport, ME
BREEZEWAY RESORT L [RST] Westerly,
RI
BRETTON ARMS COUNTRY INN,
THE [BB] Bretton Woods, NH
BREWSTER FARMHOUSE INN [BB]
Brewster (Cape Cod), MA
BREWSTER HOUSE BED &
BREAKFAST [BB] Freeport, ME
BREWSTER INN [BB] Newport, ME
BRIARBROOK MOTOR INN [MOT]
Ogunquit, ME
BRIAR LEA INN & RESTAURANT [BB]
Bethel, ME
BRIARWOOD MOTOR INN [MOT]
Lincoln, ME
BRICK TOWER MOTOR INN [MOT]
Concord, NH
BRIDGES FAMILY RESORT AND
TENNIS CLUB [MOT] Warren,
VT

BRINELY VICTORIAN INN [BB]
Newport, RI
BRITTANY INN MOTEL, THE [MOT]
Manchester and Manchester
Center, VT
BROOK FARM INN [BB] Lenox, MA
BROWN'S WHARF MOTEL
RESTAURANT & MARINA
[RST] Boothbay Harbor, ME
BUCCANEER COUNTRY LODGE
[MOT] Stowe, VT
BUCKSPORT MOTOR INN [MOT]
Bucksport, ME
BUDGET HOST MOTEL [MOT]
Hyannis (Cape Cod), MA
BUDGET INN [MOT] Morrisburg, ON
BUDGET TRAVELER MOTOR LODGE
[MOT] Presque Isle, ME
BUFFLEHEAD COVE [BB]
Kennebunkport, ME
BURKHAVEN AT SUNAPEE [MOT]
Sunapee, NH
BURNSIDE [MOT] Dartmouth, NS
BUTTERNUT INN AND COUNTRY
GUEST HOUSE [BB] Stowe, VT
BUTTONWOOD INN [BB] North
Conway, NH
BY THE SEA GUESTS [BB] Dennis
(Cape Cod), MA
CADILLAC MOTEL [MOT] St. Albans,
VT
CADILLAC MOTOR INN [MOT] Bar
Harbor, ME
CAMBRIDGE CENTER MARRIOTT
[HOT] Cambridge, MA
CAMBRIDGE SUITES HOTEL
HALIFAX [AS] Halifax, NS
CAMDEN WINDWARD HOUSE [BB]
Camden, ME
CANDLELIGHT INN AND
RESTAURANT [BB] Lenox, MA
CANDLELIGHT MOTEL [MOT]
Arlington, VT
CANDLELITE INN [BB] Sunapee, NH
CANTERBURY COTTAGE [BB] Bar
Harbor, ME
CANTERBURY HOUSE BED AND
BREAKFAST [BB] Woodstock, VT
CAPE ARUNDEL INN [MOT]
Kennebunkport, ME
CAPE COD CLADDAGH INN [BB]
Harwich (Cape Cod), MA
CAPITOL PLAZA HOTEL AND
CONFERENCE CENTER [HOT]
Montpelier, VT
CAP'N FISH'S MOTE & MARINA
[MOT] Boothbay Harbor, ME
CAPRI MOTEL [MOT] Yarmouth, NS
CAPTAIN BOUNTY MOTOR INN
[MOT] Rockport, MA
CAPTAIN DANIEL STONE INN [BB]
Brunswick, ME
CAPATAIN DEXTER HOUSE [BB]
Martha's Vineyard, MA

CAPTAIN DEXTER HOUSE OF VINEYARD HAVEN, THE [BB] *Martha's Vineyard, MA*

CAPTAIN EZRA NYE HOUSE BED & BREAKFAST [BB] *Sandwich (Cape Cod), MA*

CAPTAIN FAIRFIELD INN [BB] *Kennebunkport, ME*

CAPTAIN FARRIS HOUSE BED & BREAKFAST [BB] *South Yarmouth (Cape Cod), MA*

CAPTAIN FREEMAN INN [BB] *Brewster (Cape Cod), MA*

CAPTAIN GOSNOLD VILLAGE [MOT] *Hyannis (Cape Cod), MA*

CAPTAIN JEFFERDS INN, THE [BB] *Kennebunkport, ME*

CAPTAIN JONATHAN MOTEL [MOT] *South Yarmouth (Cape Cod), MA*

CAPTAIN LINDSEY HOUSE INN [BB] *Rockland, ME*

CAPTAIN LORD MANSION, THE [BB] *Kennebunkport, ME*

CAPTAIN NICKERSON INN [BB] *Dennis (Cape Cod), MA*

CAPT. TOM LAWRENCE HOUSE [BB] *Falmouth (Cape Cod), MA*

CAPTAIN'S HOUSE INN [BB] *Chatham (Cape Cod), MA*

CAPTAIN'S LODGE MOTEL [MOT] *Gloucester, MA*

CAPTAIN'S QUARTERS MOTEL AND CONFERENCE CENTER [MOT] *Eastham (Cape Cod), MA*

CARIBOU INN & CONVENTION CENTER [MOT] *Caribou, ME*

CARLISLE HOUSE INN [BB] *Nantucket Island, MA*

CAROLINA MOTEL [MOT] *Old Orchard Beach, ME*

CARRIAGE HOUSE, THE [BB] *Nantucket Island, MA*

CARRIAGE HOUSE [MOT] *Niagara Falls, ON*

CASCADE INN [MOT] *Niagara Falls, ON*

CASCADES LODGE [HOT] *Killington, VT*

CASCO BAY INN [MOT] *Freeport, ME*

CASTELMAINE [BB] *Bar Harbor, ME*

CASTINE INN [BB] *Bucksport, ME*

CATAMOUNT MOTEL [MOT] *Bennington, VT*

CAVALIER [MOT] *Niagara Falls, ON*

CAVALIER MOTOR LODGE [MOT] *South Yarmouth (Cape Cod), MA*

CAVENDISH [MOT] *Cavendish, PE*

CEDAR CREST MOTEL [MOT] *Camden, ME*

CENTENNIAL INN [AS] *Farmington, CT*

CENTERBOARD GUEST HOUSE [BB] *Nantucket Island, MA*

CENTER OF NH HOLIDAY INN [HOT] *Manchester, NH*

CENTERVILLE CORNERS MOTOR LODGE [MOT] *Centerville (Cape Cod), MA*

CENTRAL INN AND CONFERENCE CENTER [MOT] *New Britain, CT*

CENTRE STREET INN [BB] *Nantucket Island, MA*

CHALET [MOT] *Lewiston, ME*

CHALET MOOSEHEAD LAKEFRONT MOTEL [MOT] *Greenville, ME*

CHALETS MONTMORENCY [MOT] *Quebec City, QE*

CHAMBERY INN [BB] *Lee, MA*

CHARLES, THE [HOT] *Cambridge, MA*

CHARLES STREET INN [HOT] *Boston, MA*

CHARLESTON HOUSE [BB] *Woodstock, VT*

CHARLOTTE INN [BB] *Martha's Vineyard, MA*

CHARLOTTETOWN, THE [HOT] *Charlottetown, PE*

CHATEAU BELLVUE [HOT] *Quebec City, QE*

CHATEAU BONNE ENTENTE [HOT] *Quebec City, QE*

CHATEAU LAURIER [HOT] *Ottawa, ON*

CHATEAU ROYAL HOTEL SUITES [HOT] *Montreal, QE*

CHATEAU VAUDREUIL [HOT] *Montreal, QE*

CHATEAU VERSAILLES [HOT] *Montreal, QE*

CHATHAM BARS INN [RST] *Chatham (Cape Cod), MA*

CHATHAM HIGHLANDER [MOT] *Chatham (Cape Cod), MA*

CHATHAM MOTEL, THE [MOT] *Chatham (Cape Cod), MA*

CHATHAM TIDES WATERFRONT MOT [MOT] *Chatham (Cape Cod), MA*

CHATHAM TOWN HOUSE INN [BB] *Chatham (Cape Cod), MA*

CHESTERFIELD INN [BB] *Keene, NH*

CHIEFTAN MOTOR INN [MOT] *Hanover, NH*

CHIMNEY CREST MANOR [BB] *Bristol, CT*

CHRISTMAS FARM INN [BB] *Jackson, NH*

CITADEL [HOT] *Halifax, NS*

CLARENDON [HOT] *Quebec City, QE*

CLARION CARRIAGE HOUSE INN [MOT] *Sudbury Center, MA*

CLARION HOTEL AND CONFERENCE CENTER [HOT] *Burlington, VT*

CLARION INN [MOT] *Groton, CT*

CLARION INN [MOT] *Kitchener-Waterloo, ON*

CLARION SUITES INN [AS] *Manchester, CT*

CLARK CURRIER INN [BB]
Newburyport, MA
CLASSIC [MOT] Saco, ME
CLEARWATER LODGES [CC]
Wolfeboro, NH
CLEFTSTONE MANOR [BB] Bar
Harbor, ME
CLIFFSIDE INN [EX] Newport, RI
CLINTON MOTEL [MOT] Clinton, CT
CLUB TREMBLANT [RST] Mont
Tremblant Provincial Park, QE
COACH HOUSE INN [BB] Salem, MA
COACHMAN INN [BB] Kittery, ME
COACHMAN MOTOR LODGE [RST]
Harwich (Cape Cod), MA
COASTAL INN KINGFISHER [MOT]
Digby, NS
COASTLINE INN [MOT] Freeport, ME
COBBLESTONE INN [BB] Nantucket
Island, MA
COCONUT [MOT] Montreal, QE
COD COVE INN [MOT] Wiscasset,
ME
COLBY HILL INN [BB] Concord, NH
COLD SPRING MOTEL & GUEST
SUITES [MOT] Plymouth, MA
COLONADE INN [MOT] Lyndonville,
VT
COLONEL EBENEZER CRAFTS INN
[BB] Sturbridge, MA
COLONIAL HOUSE, THE [BB]
Weston, VT
COLONIAL HOUSE INN &
RESTAURANT [BB] South
Yarmouth (Cape Cod), MA
COLONIAL INN [BB] Concord, MA
COLONIAL INN [MOT] Moncton, NB
COLONIAL INN [MOT] St. John, NB
COLONIAL INN OF MARTHA'S
VINEYARD [BB] Martha's
Vineyard, MA
COLONIAL TRAVELODGE [MOT]
Ellsworth, ME
COLONIAL VILLAGE RESORT [MOT]
Dennis (Cape Cod), MA
COLONIAL VILLAGE RESORT [RST]
Ogunquit, ME
COLONNADE HOTEL, THE [HOT]
Boston, MA
COLONY, THE [HOT] New Haven, CT
COLONY HOTEL [RST]
Kennebunkport, ME
COMBES FAMILY INN [BB] Ludlow,
VT
COMFORT HOTEL DOWNTOWN
[HOT] Toronto, ON
COMFORT INN [MOT] Augusta, ME
COMFORT INN [MOT] Bangor, ME
COMFORT INN [MOT] Brunswick, ME
COMFORT INN [MOT] Burlington, VT
COMFORT INN [HOT] Concord, NH
COMFORT INN [MOT] Kenora, ON
COMFORT INN [MOT] Kitchener-
Waterloo, ON
COMFORT INN [HOT] Manchester,
NH

COMFORT INN [MOT] Middletown,
CT
COMFORT INN [HOT] Mystic, CT
COMFORT INN [MOT] Nashua, NH
COMFORT INN, THE [HOT] New
Bedford, MA
COMFORT INN [MOT] Pawtucket, RI
COMFORT INN [MOT] Portland, ME
COMFORT INN [MOT] Sarnia, ON
COMFORT INN [MOT] Thunder Bay,
ON
COMFORT INN [HOT] Warwick, RI
COMFORT INN [HOT] White River
Junction, VT
COMFORT INN [MOT] Windsor, ON
COMFORT INN & SUITES [HOT] St.
Albans, VT
COMFORT INN & SUITES [HOT]
Sturbridge, MA
COMFORT INN & SUITES [MOT]
Waterville, ME
COMFORT INN AT THE PARWICK
CENTRE [HOT] Springfield, MA
COMFORT INN @ MAPLEWOOD
LTD [MOT] Montpelier, VT
COMFORT INN-CAPE
COD/HYANNIS [HOT] Hyannis
(Cape Cod), MA
COMFORT INN PORTSMOUTH
[HOT] Portsmouth, NH
COMFORT INN TROLLEY SQUARE
[HOT] Rutland, VT
COMFORT SUITES [AS] Haverhill, MA
COMMODORES INN [RST] Stowe, VT
CONNECTICUT MOTOR LODGE
[MOT] Manchester, CT
COOK'S ISLAND VIEW MOTEL
[MOT] Bailey Island, ME
COPLEY INN [HOT] Boston, MA
COPLEY SQUARE [HOT] Boston, MA
COPPER BEECH INN, THE [BB] Essex,
CT
CORNER HOUSE INN [BB] Nantucket
Island, MA
CORNWALL INN AND RESTAURANT
[BB] Cornwall Bridge, CT
CORSAIR OCEANFRONT MOTEL
[MOT] Dennis (Cape Cod), MA
CORTINA INN AND RESORT [RST]
Killington, VT
COUNTRY ACRES MOTEL [MOT]
Sandwich (Cape Cod), MA
COUNTRY CLUB INN [MOT]
Rangeley, ME
COUNTRY GARDEN INN & MOTEL
[MOT] Ipswich, MA
COUNTRY INN [BB] Harwich (Cape
Cod), MA
COUNTRY LAKE LODGE [MOT]
Hyannis (Cape Cod), MA
COURTYARD BY MARRIOTT [MOT]
Burlington, MA
COURTYARD BY MARRIOTT [MOT]
Danvers, MA
COURTYARD BY MARRIOTT [HOT]
Newport, RI

COURTYARD BY MARRIOTT [MOT] *Windsor, CT*
COURTYARD BY MARRIOTT - FOXBOROUGH [HOT] *Foxboro, MA*
COVE, THE [MOT] *Orleans (Cape Cod), MA*
CRAIGNAIR INN [BB] *Rockland, ME*
CRANBERRY COTTAGES [CC] *Eastham (Cape Cod), MA*
CRANBERRY INN [BB] *Chatham (Cape Cod), MA*
CRANMORE INN [BB] *North Conway, NH*
CRANMORE MOUNTAIN LODGE [BB] *North Conway, NH*
CRANWELL RESORT AND GOLF CLUB [HOT] *Lenox, MA*
CROMWELL HARBOR MOTEL [MOT] *Bar Harbor, ME*
CROW'S NEST MOTEL [MOT] *Truro and North Truro (Cape Cod), MA*
CROWNE PLAZA [HOT] *Hartford, CT*
CROWNE PLAZA [HOT] *Pittsfield, MA*
CROWNE PLAZA AT THE CROSSING [HOT] *Warwick, RI*
CROWNE PLAZA HOTEL [HOT] *Nashua, NH*
CROWNE PLAZA HOTEL BOSTON - NATICK [HOT] *Natick, MA*
CROWNE PLAZA OTTAWA [HOT] *Ottawa , ON*
CROWNE PLAZA TORONTO CENTRE [HOT] *Toronto, ON*
CROWNE PLAZA WORCESTER [HOT] *Worcester, MA*
CROWN PARK INN [MOT] *Caribou, ME*
CRYSTAL MOTEL [MOT] *Niagara Falls, ON*
CURTIS HOUSE [BB] *Woodbury, CT*
DAGGETT HOUSE [BB] *Martha's Vineyard, MA*
DANA PLACE INN [BB] *Jackson, NH*
DAN'L WEBSTER INN [BB] *Sandwich (Cape Cod), MA*
DARBY FIELD COUNTRY INN & RESTAURANT [BB] *North Conway, NH*
DARK HARBOR HOUSE [BB] *Camden, ME*
DAUPHINEE INN [BB] *Halifax, NS*
DAYS [HOT] *Providence, RI*
DAYS HOTEL TORONTO AIRPORT [MOT] *Mississauga, ON*
DAYS INN [MOT] *Bangor, ME*
DAYS INN [MOT] *Branford, CT*
DAYS INN [MOT] *Brantford, ON*
DAYS INN [MOT] *Brockville, ON*
DAYS INN [HOT] *Burlington, VT*
DAYS INN [MOT] *Concord, NH*
DAYS INN [MOT] *Dover, NH*
DAYS INN [MOT] *Gananoque, ON*
DAYS INN [MOT] *Hamilton, ON*
DAYS INN [MOT] *Kittery, ME*

DAYS INN [MOT] *Mississauga, ON*
DAYS INN [HOT] *Mystic, CT*
DAYS INN [MOT] *Quebec City, QE*
DAYS INN [MOT] *Shelburne, VT*
DAYS INN [MOT] *Springfield, MA*
DAYS INN [MOT] *Worcester, MA*
DAYS INN BOSTON/SALEM [MOT] *Danvers, MA*
DAYS INN BRAINTREE-BOSTON [MOT] *Braintree, MA*
DAYS INN DOWNTOWN [HOT] *Toronto, ON*
DAYS INN FALLSVIEW DISTRICT [MOT] *Niagara Falls, ON*
DAYS INN MIDTOWN [HOT] *Montreal, QE*
DAYS INN NEAR THE FALLS [HOT] *Niagara Falls, ON*
DAYS INN OF BARRE [MOT] *Barre, VT*
DAYS INN OVERLOOKING THE FALLS [HOT] *Niagara Falls, ON*
DEERFIELD INN [BB] *Deerfield, MA*
DELTA [HOT] *Montreal, QE*
DELTA BARRINGTON [MOT] *Halifax, NS*
DELTA BRUNSWICK [HOT] *St. John, NB*
DELTA CHELSEA INN [HOT] *Toronto, ON*
DELTA HALIFAX [HOT] *Halifax, NS*
DELTA HOTEL [HOT] *Ottawa , ON*
DELTA LONDON ARMOURIES [HOT] *London, ON*
DELTA MEADOWVALE RESORT [HOT] *Mississauga, ON*
DELTA MONTREAL [HOT] *Montreal, QE*
DELTA TORONTO AIRPORT [HOT] *Toronto, ON*
DEVONFIELD INN [BB] *Lee, MA*
DEXTERS INN & TENNIS CLUB [BB] *Sunapee, NH*
DIAMOND DISTRICT BREAKFAST INN [BB] *Lynn, MA*
DOCKSIDE GUEST QUARTERS [BB] *York, ME*
DOCKSIDE INN [BB] *Martha's Vineyard, MA*
DOLPHIN OF CHATHAM INN AND MOTEL [MOT] *Chatham (Cape Cod), MA*
DORSET INN [BB] *Dorset, VT*
DOSTAL'S RESORT LODGE [MOT] *Londonderry, VT*
DOUBLETREE [HOT] *Lowell, MA*
DOUBLETREE CLUB HOTEL - NORWALK [HOT] *Norwalk, CT*
DOUBLETREE GUEST SUITES BOSTON/WALTHAM [AS] *Waltham, MA*
DOUBLETREE HOTEL [MOT] *Windsor Locks, CT*
DOUBLETREE SUITES [HOT] *Boston, MA*

DOWD'S COUNTRY INN [BB]
Hanover, NH
DOWN EASTER INN [BB]
Damariscotta, ME
DRAWBRIDGE INN [MOT] Sarnia, ON
DREAMWOOD PINES MOTEL [MOT]
Bar Harbor, ME
DRUMMER BOY MOTOR INN [MOT]
Lincoln/North Woodstock Area,
NH
DUNBAR HOUSE [BB] Sandwich (Cape
Cod), MA
DUNSCROFT BY THE SEA [BB]
Harwich (Cape Cod), MA
D.W.'S OCEANSIDE INN [BB]
Hampton Beach, NH
EAGLE HOUSE MOTEL [MOT]
Rockport, MA
EAGLE MOUNTAIN HOUSE [RST]
Jackson, NH
EAGLE WING GUEST MOTEL [MOT]
Eastham (Cape Cod), MA
EARL OF SANDWICH MOTEL [MOT]
Sandwich (Cape Cod), MA
EASTERN SLOPE INN RESORT [MOT]
North Conway, NH
EASTGATE MOTOR INN [MOT]
Littleton, NH
EASTHAM OCEAN VIEW MOTEL
[MOT] Eastham (Cape Cod), MA
EAST HARBOUR MOTEL &
COTTAGES [RST] Truro and
North Truro (Cape Cod), MA
EASTLAND [MOT] Lubec, ME
EASTLAND PARK HOTEL [HOT]
Portland, ME
EASTMAN INN [BB] North Conway,
NH
EASTVIEW [MOT] Saco, ME
ECHO LAKE INN [BB] Ludlow, VT
ECONO LODGE [MOT] Bangor, ME
ECONO LODGE [MOT] Brunswick,
ME
ECONO LODGE [MOT] Hamilton, ON
ECONO LODGE [MOT] Kingston, ON
ECONO LODGE [MOT] Manchester,
NH
ECONO LODGE [MOT] Moncton, NB
ECONO LODGE [MOT] Niagara Falls,
ON
ECONO LODGE [MOT] Sturbridge,
MA
ECONO LODGE AND SUITES [MOT]
Shelburne, VT
ECONO LODGE KENNEBUNK [MOT]
Kennebunk, ME
ECONO LODGE SPRING'S INN
[MOT] Pittsfield, MA
EDENBROOK MOTEL [MOT] Bar
Harbor, ME
EDGARTOWN INN, THE [BB]
Martha's Vineyard, MA
EDGEWATER, THE [MOT] Old
Orchard Beach, ME
EDGEWATER BEACH RESORT [RST]
Dennis (Cape Cod), MA

EDGEWATER COTTAGES AND
MOTEL [MOT] Bar Harbor, ME
EDSON HILL MANOR [BB] Stowe, VT
EDWARDS HARBORSIDE INN [BB]
York, ME
EGREMONT INN, THE [BB] Great
Barrington, MA
ELIOT HOTEL, THE [AS] Boston, MA
ELLIS RIVER HOUSE [HOT] Jackson,
NH
ELLSWORTH MOTEL [MOT]
Ellsworth, ME
ELM ARCH INN [BB] Falmouth (Cape
Cod), MA
ELMS BED & BREAKFAST [BB]
Camden, ME
ELMS INN, THE [BB] Ridgefield, CT
ELORA MILL [BB] Kitchener-Waterloo,
ON
EMBASSY SUITES [AS] Portland, ME
EMBASSY SUITES [HOT] Toronto, ON
EMERSON GUEST HOUSE [BB]
Vergennes, VT
EMERSON INN BY THE SEA [BB]
Rockport, MA
EMERY'S COTTAGES ON THE SHORE
[CC] Bar Harbor, ME
ENGLISH MEADOWS INN [BB]
Kennebunkport, ME
EQUINOX, THE [RST] Manchester and
Manchester Center, VT
ESSEX STREET INN [BB] Newburyport,
MA
EVEN'TIDE MOTEL & COTTAGES
[MOT] Wellfleet (Cape Cod), MA
EVERGREEN MOTEL [MOT] Jefferson,
NH
EYRIE MOTEL [MOT] Manchester and
Manchester Center, VT
FAIRBANKS INN [BB] Provincetown
(Cape Cod), MA
FAIRBANKS MOTOR INN [MOT] St.
Johnsbury, VT
FAIRFIELD INN [MOT] Bangor, ME
FAIRFIELD INN [MOT] Nashua, NH
FAIRFIELD INN [HOT] Scarborough,
ME
FAIRFIELD INN [MOT] Warwick, RI
FAIRFIELD INN AND RESTAURANT
[MOT] Fairfield, CT
FAIRHAVEN INN [BB] Bath, ME
FAIRMONT COPLEY PLAZA, THE
[HOT] Boston, MA
FAIRWAY MOTEL [MOT] New London,
NH
FAMOUTH RAMADA ON THE
SQUARE, THE [HOT] Falmouth
(Cape Cod), MA
FARMBROOK MOTEL [MOT]
Plymouth, VT
FARMINGTON INN OF GREATER
HARTFORD [EX] Farmington,
CT
FEDERAL HOUSE INN [BB] Lee, MA
FERRY POINT HOUSE [BB] Laconia,
NH

FESTIVAL INN [MOT] *Stratford, ON*
FIFE 'N DRUM [MOT] *Bennington, VT*
FIFE N DRUM RESTAURANT & INN [BB] *Kent, CT*
FIRST CANADA INN [MOT] *Kingston, ON*
FISHERMAN'S WHARF INN [HOT] *Boothbay Harbor, ME*
FIVE GABLES INN [BB] *Boothbay Harbor, ME*
FLAGSHIP MOTEL [MOT] *Old Orchard Beach, ME*
FLAGSHIP MOTOR INN [MOT] *Boothbay Harbor, ME*
FLAGSHIP MOTOR INN [MOT] *South Yarmouth (Cape Cod), MA*
FLAMINGO MOTOR INN [MOT] *Niagara Falls, ON*
FOLLANSBEE INN [BB] *New London, NH*
FORSET, A COUNTRY INN, THE [BB] *North Conway, NH*
FOUNDER'S BROOK MOTEL & SUITES [MOT] *Portsmouth, RI*
FOUR ACRES MOTEL [MOT] *Williamstown, MA*
FOUR CHIMNEYS INN [BB] *Bennington, VT*
FOUR CHIMNEYS INN [BB] *Dennis (Cape Cod), MA*
FOUR CHIMNEYS INN [BB] *Nantucket Island, MA*
FOUR COLUMNS INN [BB] *Newfane, VT*
FOUR PILLARS [BB] *Woodstock, VT*
FOUR POINTS BY SHERATON [HOT] *Bangor, ME*
FOUR POINTS BY SHERATON [HOT] *Mississauga, ON*
FOUR POINTS HOTEL [HOT] *Manchester, NH*
FOUR POINTS HOTEL BY SHERATON [MOT] *Norwalk, CT*
FOUR POINTS HOTEL LEOMINSTER [HOT] *Leominster, MA*
FOUR POINTS SHERATON BY THE FALLS [HOT] *Niagara Falls, ON*
FOUR SEASONS HOTEL BOSTON [HOT] *Boston, MA*
FOUR SEASONS HOTEL TORONTO [HOT] *Toronto, ON*
FOUR SEASONS MOTOR INN [MOT] *Twin Mountain, NH*
FOURWINDS COUNTRY MOTEL [MOT] *Manchester and Manchester Center, VT*
FOXGLOVE INN [BB] *Franconia, NH*
FOX RIDGE, THE [RST] *North Conway, NH*
FOXWOODS RESORT AND CASINO LEDYARD [HOT] *Mystic, CT*
FRANCIS MALBONE HOUSE [BB] *Newport, RI*
FRANCONIA INN [BB] *Franconia, NH*

FREDERICTON INN [MOT] *Fredericton, NB*
FREEPORT INN [HOT] *Freeport, ME*
FRESH START [BB] *Halifax, NS*
FRIENDSHIP MOTOR INN [MOT] *Old Orchard Beach, ME*
FROG'S LEAP INN [BB] *Londonderry, VT*
GABLES INN, THE [BB] *Lenox, MA*
GALEN C. MOSES HOUSE [BB] *Bath, ME*
GALE RIVER [MOT] *Franconia, NH*
GANANOQUE INN [MOT] *Gananoque, ON*
GARDEN GABLES INN [BB] *Lenox, MA*
GARLANDS, THE [MOT] *Dennis (Cape Cod), MA*
GARRISON INN [HOT] *Newburyport, MA*
GARRISON SUITES [RST] *Wells, ME*
GASTHAUS SWITZERLAND INN [BB] *Ottawa , ON*
GATE HOUSE HOTEL [BB] *Niagara-on-the-Lake, ON*
GATEWAY INN [MOT] *Kitchener-Waterloo, ON*
GATEWAYS INN [BB] *Lenox, MA*
GEORGE FULLER HOUSE [BB] *Gloucester, MA*
GLEN COVE MOTEL [MOT] *Rockland, ME*
GLENERIN [BB] *Mississauga, ON*
GLENMOOR BY THE SEA [MOT] *Camden, ME*
GLYNN HOUSE INN [BB] *Holderness, NH*
GOLDEN ANCHOR INN [MOT] *Bar Harbor, ME*
GOLDEN EAGLE RESORT [RST] *Stowe, VT*
GOLDEN GABLES INN [MOT] *North Conway, NH*
GOLDEN LION RIVERSIDE INN [MOT] *Warren, VT*
GOLDEN STAGE INN [BB] *Ludlow, VT*
GOODWIN HOTEL [HOT] *Hartford, CT*
GOODWIN'S MOTOR INN [MOT] *Norway, ME*
GOOSE COVE LODGE [RST] *Deer Isle, ME*
GORGES GRANT HOTEL [HOT] *Ogunquit, ME*
GORHAM MOTOR INN [MOT] *Gorham, NH*
GOUVERNEUR HOTEL SAINTE-FOY [HOT] *Quebec City, QE*
GOVERNOR'S INN, THE [BB] *Ludlow, VT*
GOVERNOR BRADFORD ON THE HARBOUR [MOT] *Plymouth, MA*
GOVERNORS ROCK [MOT] *Bennington, VT*

GRAFTON INN [BB] *Falmouth (Cape Cod), MA*
GRAND BEACH INN [MOT] *Old Orchard Beach, ME*
GRAND HOTEL, THE [HOT] *Ogunquit, ME*
GRAND SUMMIT [RST] *Bethel, ME*
GRAND SUMMIT HOTEL [RST] *Kingfield, ME*
GRAND VIEW [MOT] *Halifax, NS*
GRAYCOTE INN [BB] *Bar Harbor, ME*
GRAY ROCKS RESORT AND CONVENTION CENTER [RST] *Mont Tremblant Provincial Park, QE*
GREEN ACRES [MOT] *Kingston, ON*
GREENFIELD BED & BREAKFAST INN [BB] *Peterborough, NH*
GREEN GRANITE INN & CONFERENCE CENTER [BB] *North Conway, NH*
GREENHOUSE INN, THE [BB] *Newport, RI*
GREEN MOUNTAIN INN [RST] *Stowe, VT*
GREENSBORO INN [MOT] *Grand Pre, NS*
GREEN TRAILS INN [BB] *Barre, VT*
GREENVILLE INN [BB] *Greenville, ME*
GREEN WAY CLAYMORE INN AND CONFERENCE CENTER [MOT] *Antigonish, NS*
GREENWOOD [HOT] *Greenville, ME*
GREENWOOD HOUSE [BB] *Martha's Vineyard, MA*
GREY BONNET INN [MOT] *Killington, VT*
GREY FOX INN & RESORT [RST] *Stowe, VT*
GREYLIN HOUSE [BB] *Brewster (Cape Cod), MA*
GREYSTONE MOTEL [MOT] *Middlebury, VT*
GRISWOLD INN [BB] *Essex, CT*
GRUNBERG HAUS BED AND BREAKFAST [BB] *Waterbury, VT*
GUILD INN [BB] *Toronto, ON*
GULL MOTEL [MOT] *Belfast, ME*
GULL MOTEL INN & COTTAGES, THE [MOT] *Old Orchard Beach, ME*
GULL WING SUITES [MOT] *South Yarmouth (Cape Cod), MA*
HADDON HALL [BB] *Halifax, NS*
HAMMETT HOUSE INN [BB] *Newport, RI*
HAMPSHIRE INN [AS] *Hampton Beach, NH*
HAMPTON BEACH REGAL INN [MOT] *Hampton Beach, NH*
HAMPTON FALLS INN [HOT] *Hampton Beach, NH*
HAMPTON INN [MOT] *Brattleboro, VT*
HAMPTON INN [HOT] *Burlington, MA*

HAMPTON INN [HOT] *Burlington, VT*
HAMPTON INN [HOT] *Concord, NH*
HAMPTON INN [HOT] *Lawrence, MA*
HAMPTON INN [MOT] *Meriden, CT*
HAMPTON INN [HOT] *Milford, CT*
HAMPTON INN [MOT] *Natick, MA*
HAMPTON INN [HOT] *Portland, ME*
HAMPTON INN [MOT] *Springfield, MA*
HAMPTON INN [MOT] *Worcester, MA*
HAMPTON INN AT THE FALLS [MOT] *Niagara Falls, ON*
HAMPTON INN WESTPORT [MOT] *Fall River, MA*
HANCOCK INN [BB] *Peterborough, NH*
HANDKERCHIEF SHOALS MOTEL [MOT] *Harwich (Cape Cod), MA*
HANOVER HOUSE, THE [BB] *Martha's Vineyard, MA*
HANOVER INN [MOT] *Hanover, NH*
HARBOR HOUSE HOTEL [MOT] *Nantucket Island, MA*
HARBOR HOUSE INN [BB] *Greenwich, CT*
HARBOR LIGHT INN [BB] *Marblehead, MA*
HARBORSIDE HYATT CONFERENCE CENTER AND HOTEL [HOT] *Boston, MA*
HARBORSIDE INN [HOT] *Boston, MA*
HARBOR VIEW HOTEL OF MARTHA'S VINEYARD [HOT] *Martha's Vineyard, MA*
HARBOR VIEW VILLAGE [MOT] *Truro and North Truro (Cape Cod), MA*
HARBOURFRONT INN [MOT] *Sarnia, ON*
HARBOUR TOWNE INN ON WATERFRONT [BB] *Boothbay Harbor, ME*
HARRASEEKET INN [BB] *Freeport, ME*
HARRISON HOUSE [BB] *Lenox, MA*
HARTFORD FARMINGTON MARRIOTT [HOT] *Farmington, CT*
HARTNESS HOUSE [HOT] *Springfield, VT*
HARTWELL HOUSE [BB] *Ogunquit, ME*
HARVARD SQUARE HOTEL [MOT] *Cambridge, MA*
HATFIELD BED & BREAKFAST [BB] *Bar Harbor, ME*
HAWK INN AND MOUNTAIN RESORT [RST] *Plymouth, VT*
HAWTHORNE, THE [MOT] *Chatham (Cape Cod), MA*
HAWTHORNE HOTEL [HOT] *Salem, MA*
HAWTHORNE INN [BB] *Concord, MA*
HAWTHORN INN [BB] *Camden, ME*
HEARTHSIDE BED & BREAKFAST [BB] *Bar Harbor, ME*

HEATHER HOTEL AND
    CONVENTION CENTRE [HOT]
    Antigonish, NS
HERBERT HOTEL, THE [HOT]
    Kingfield, ME
HERITAGE HOUSE HOTEL [MOT]
    Hyannis (Cape Cod), MA
HERITAGE INN [MOT] *Blue Hill, ME*
HERITAGE MOTOR INN [MOT] *Old
    Saybrook, CT*
HERMITAGE INN [BB] *Wilmington,
    VT*
HESLIN'S MOTEL DINIG ROOM
    [MOT] *Calais, ME*
HICHBORN INN [BB] *Searsport, ME*
HIGGINS HOLIDAY HOTEL [MOT]
    Bar Harbor, ME
HIGH BREWSTER [BB] *Brewster (Cape
    Cod), MA*
HIGHLANDER MOTEL [MOT]
    Jeffersonville, VT
HIGHLAND LAKE INN [BB] *Franklin,
    NH*
HIGH SEAS [MOT] *Bar Harbor, ME*
HIGHWAYMAN MOTOR INN [MOT]
    St. Catharines, ON
HIGHWAY MOTOR INN [MOT]
    Providence, RI
HILL FARM INN [BB] *Arlington, VT*
HILLSIDE ACRES CABINS & MOTEL
    [CC] *Boothbay Harbor, ME*
HILLTOP INN [BB] *Franconia, NH*
HILTON [HOT] *Hartford, CT*
HILTON [HOT] *Mystic, CT*
HILTON [HOT] *Quebec City, QE*
HILTON [HOT] *Toronto, ON*
HILTON AT DEDHAM PLACE [HOT]
    Dedham, MA
HILTON BACK BAY [HOT] *Boston, MA*
HILTON DANBURY AND TOWERS
    [HOT] *Danbury, CT*
HILTON HOTEL LONDON [HOT]
    London, ON
HILTON INTERNATIONAL [HOT]
    Mississauga, ON
HILTON LOGAN AIRPORT [HOT]
    Boston, MA
HILTON MONTREAL
    BONAVENTURE [HOT]
    Montreal, QE
HILTON SAINT JOHN [HOT] *St. John,
    NB*
HILTON SOUTHBURY HOTEL [HOT]
    Southbury, CT
HISTORIC MERRELL INN [BB] *Lee,
    MA*
HO-HUM MOTEL [MOT] *Burlington,
    VT*
HOB KNOB INN [BB] *Martha's
    Vineyard, MA*
HOB KNOB INN [MOT] *Stowe, VT*
HOCHELAGA [BB] *Kingston, ON*
HOLDEN INN, THE [BB] *Wellfleet
    (Cape Cod), MA*

HOLIDAY HOUSE INN & MOTEL
    [MOT] *Scarborough, ME*
HOLIDAY INN [MOT] *Andover and
    North Andover, MA*
HOLIDAY INN [HOT] *Bangor, ME*
HOLIDAY INN [HOT] *Bangor, ME*
HOLIDAY INN [HOT] *Bridgeport, CT*
HOLIDAY INN [MOT] *Burlington, VT*
HOLIDAY INN [HOT] *Cambridge, MA*
HOLIDAY INN [HOT] *Danbury, CT*
HOLIDAY INN [MOT] *Ellsworth, ME*
HOLIDAY INN [MOT] *Foxboro, MA*
HOLIDAY INN [HOT] *Hartford, CT*
HOLIDAY INN [MOT] *Holyoke, MA*
HOLIDAY INN [MOT] *Kingston, RI*
HOLIDAY INN [MOT] *Kitchener-
    Waterloo, ON*
HOLIDAY INN [MOT] *Middletown, CT*
HOLIDAY INN [MOT] *Mississauga,
    ON*
HOLIDAY INN [HOT] *Nashua, NH*
HOLIDAY INN [MOT] *Portland, ME*
HOLIDAY INN [MOT] *Portsmouth, NH*
HOLIDAY INN [HOT] *Salem, NH*
HOLIDAY INN [MOT] *Sarnia, ON*
HOLIDAY INN [MOT] *Sault Ste. Marie,
    ON*
HOLIDAY INN [HOT] *Springfield, MA*
HOLIDAY INN [MOT] *St. Catharines,
    ON*
HOLIDAY INN [HOT] *Toronto, ON*
HOLIDAY INN [HOT] *Toronto, ON*
HOLIDAY INN [HOT] *Toronto, ON*
HOLIDAY INN [MOT] *Waterville, ME*
HOLIDAY INN & SPA WATERBURY
    [HOT] *Waterbury, VT*
HOLIDAY INN - DON VALLEY [HOT]
    Toronto, ON
HOLIDAY INN AT YALE UNIVERSITY
    [HOT] *New Haven, CT*
HOLIDAY INN BATH [MOT] *Bath, ME*
HOLIDAY INN BOSTON-DEDHAM
    [MOT] *Dedham, MA*
HOLIDAY INN BOSTON METRO
    SOUTH [HOT] *Brockton, MA*
HOLIDAY INN BOXBOROUGH
    WOODS [MOT] *Concord, MA*
HOLIDAY INN BY THE BAY [MOT]
    Portland, ME
HOLIDAY INN BY THE FALLS [MOT]
    Niagara Falls, ON
HOLIDAY INN EXPRESS [HOT]
    Braintree, MA
HOLIDAY INN EXPRESS [MOT]
    Lexington, MA
HOLIDAY INN EXPRESS [MOT]
    London, ON
HOLIDAY INN EXPRESS [MOT]
    Meriden, CT
HOLIDAY INN EXPRESS [MOT]
    Springfield, VT
HOLIDAY INN EXPRESS [MOT]
    Toronto, ON
HOLIDAY INN EXPRESS HOTEL &
    SUITES [AS] *Burlington, VT*

HOLIDAY INN HARBOURVIEW [HOT] *Dartmouth, NS*

HOLIDAY INN NEWTON-BOSTON [HOT] *Newton, MA*

HOLIDAY INN RANDOLPH [MOT] *Braintree, MA*

HOLIDAY INN RUTLAND-KILLINGTON [HOT] *Rutland, VT*

HOLIDAY INN SELECT [HOT] *Stamford, CT*

HOLIDAY INN SELECT BOSTON [HOT] *Boston, MA*

HOLIDAY INN SELECT CENTRE VILLE [HOT] *Montreal, QE*

HOLIDAY INN SELECT HALIFAX CENTRE [MOT] *Halifax, NS*

HOLIDAY INN TORONTO WEST [MOT] *Mississauga, ON*

HOLIDAY INN YORKDALE [HOT] *Toronto, ON*

HOLIDAY MOTEL [MOT] *St. Johnsbury, VT*

HOLLOW INN AND HOTEL [MOT] *Barre, VT*

HOME PORT INN [BB] *Lubec, ME*

HOMESTEAD INN, THE [BB] *Danbury, CT*

HOMESTEAD INN [HOT] *Greenwich, CT*

HOMESTEAD INN BED AND BREAKFAST [BB] *York, ME*

HOMESTEAD MOTEL [MOT] *Ellsworth, ME*

HOME SUITES INN [MOT] *Waltham, MA*

HOMEWOOD SUITES BY HILTON [MOT] *Windsor Locks, CT*

HONEYMOON CITY [MOT] *Niagara Falls, ON*

HONEYSPOT LODGE [MOT] *Stratford, CT*

HONEYSUCKLE HILL B&B [BB] *Barnstable (Cape Cod), MA*

HONEYWOOD COUNTRY LODGE [MOT] *Stowe, VT*

HOPKINS INN [BB] *New Preston, CT*

HORIZON [AS] *Old Orchard Beach, ME*

HORIZON INN [HOT] *Wilmington, VT*

HORSE & HOUND INN, THE [BB] *Franconia, NH*

HOSTELLERIE LES TROIS TILLEULS [MOT] *Montreal, QE*

HOSTELLERIE RIVE GAUCHE [MOT] *Montreal, QE*

HOTEL AUBERGE UNIVERSEL MONTREAL [HOT] *Montreal, QE*

HOTEL CHATEAU LAURIER [MOT] *Quebec City, QE*

HOTEL CHERIBOURG [MOT] *Montreal, QE*

HOTEL CLASSIQUE [HOT] *Quebec City, QE*

HOTEL COURTENAY BAY [MOT] *St. John, NB*

HOTEL DU PARC [HOT] *Montreal, QE*

HOTEL GERMAIN-DES-PRES [HOT] *Quebec City, QE*

HOTEL GOUVERNEUR SHERBROOKE [HOT] *Sherbrooke, QE*

HOTELGOUVERNEURTROIS-RIVIERES [HOT] *Montreal, QE*

HOTEL INTER-CONTINENTAL MONTREAL [HOT] *Montreal, QE*

HOTEL INTER-CONTINENTAL TORONTO [HOT] *Toronto, ON*

HOTEL LA RESIDENCE DU VOYAGEUR [HOT] *Montreal, QE*

HOTEL LE GERMAIN [HOT] *Montreal, QE*

HOTEL LE SAINTE-ANDRE [MOT] *Montreal, QE*

HOTEL NORTHAMPTON [HOT] *Northampton, MA*

HOTEL PLAZA QUEBEC [HOT] *Quebec City, QE*

HOTEL TORONTO - EAST [HOT] *Toronto, ON*

HOTEL UNIVERSEL [MOT] *Drummondville, QE*

HOTEL UNIVERSEL [HOT] *Quebec City, QE*

HOTEL VIKING, THE [HOT] *Newport, RI*

HOTEL WYNDHAM MONTREAL [HOT] *Montreal, QE*

HOUSE ON THE HILL BED & BREAKFAST [BB] *Waterbury, CT*

HOWARD HOUSE LODGE [BB] *Boothbay Harbor, ME*

HOWARD JOHNSON [MOT] *Fredericton, NB*

HOWARD JOHNSON [HOT] *Hamilton, ON*

HOWARD JOHNSON [MOT] *Hyannis (Cape Cod), MA*

HOWARD JOHNSON [MOT] *Kingston, ON*

HOWARD JOHNSON [MOT] *Mississauga, ON*

HOWARD JOHNSON [MOT] *St. Catharines, ON*

HOWARD JOHNSON BY THE FALLS [MOT] *Niagara Falls, ON*

HOWARD JOHNSON EAST [MOT] *Toronto, ON*

HOWARD JOHNSON EXPRESS INN [MOT] *Lenox, MA*

HOWARD JOHNSON HOTEL [MOT] *Burlington, VT*

HOWARD JOHNSON HOTEL [HOT] *Cambridge, MA*

HOWARD JOHNSON HOTEL [HOT] *Portland, ME*

HOWARD JOHNSON HOTEL [HOT] *St. John, NB*

HOWARD JOHNSON INN [MOT]
    Amherst, MA
HOWARD JOHNSON INN [MOT]
    Rutland, VT
HOWARD JOHNSON INN [MOT]
    Toronto, ON
HOWARD JOHNSON INN NEWPORT
    [HOT] Newport, RI
HOWARD JOHNSON LODGE [MOT]
    Greenfield, MA
HOWARD JOHNSON PLAZA [HOT]
    Toronto, ON
HUGGING BEAR INN [BB] Springfield,
    VT
HUNTERS GREEN MOTEL [MOT]
    South Yarmouth (Cape Cod), MA
HUNTSMAN MOTOR LODGE [MOT]
    Dennis (Cape Cod), MA
HYANNIS DAYS INN [MOT] Hyannis
    (Cape Cod), MA
HYATT REGENCY [HOT] Cambridge,
    MA
HYATT REGENCY GREENWICH
    [HOT] Greenwich, CT
HYATT REGENCY NEWPORT [MOT]
    Newport, RI
IDLEWYLD [BB] London, ON
IMPERIAL HOTEL AND SUITES
    [MOT] Niagara Falls, ON
INDIAN HEAD RESORT [RST]
    Lincoln/North Woodstock Area,
    NH
INDIAN HILL [MOT] Greenville, ME
INN AT BAY LEDGE [BB] Bar Harbor,
    ME
INN AT BAY POINT, THE [BB]
    Meredith, NH
INN AT BLUSH HILL [BB] Waterbury,
    VT
INN AT CASTLE HILL, THE [BB]
    Newport, RI
INN AT CHRISTIAN SHORE, THE [BB]
    Portsmouth, NH
INN AT DUCK CREEKE [BB] Wellfleet
    (Cape Cod), MA
INN AT ESSEX [HOT] Burlington, VT
INN AT ETHAN ALLEN, THE [HOT]
    Danbury, CT
INN AT FOREST HILLS [BB] Franconia,
    NH
INN AT HARBOR HEAD, THE [BB]
    Kennebunkport, ME
INN AT HARVARD, THE [MOT]
    Cambridge, MA
INN AT IRON MASTERS [MOT]
    Lakeville, CT
INN AT LEWIS BAY [BB] South
    Yarmouth (Cape Cod), MA
INN AT LONG LAKE, THE [BB]
    Bridgton, ME
INN AT LONGSHORE, THE [BB]
    Westport, CT
INN AT MANCHESTER [BB]
    Manchester and Manchester
    Center, VT

INN AT MILL FALLS, THE [BB]
    Meredith, NH
INN AT MONTPELIER [BB] Montpelier,
    VT
INN AT MYSTIC [MOT] Mystic, CT
INN AT NATIONAL HALL, THE
    [HOT] Westport, CT
INN AT NORTHAMPTON, THE [HOT]
    Northampton, MA
INN AT OCEAN'S EDGE [HOT]
    Camden, ME
INN AT PLEASANT LAKE [BB] New
    London, NH
INN AT QUAIL RUN, THE [BB] West
    Dover, VT
INN AT RUTLAND BED AND
    BREAKFAST [BB] Rutland, VT
INN AT SAW MILL FARM, THE [BB]
    West Dover, VT
INN AT ST. JOHN [BB] Portland, ME
INN AT STOCKBRIDGE, THE [BB]
    Stockbridge and West Stockbridge,
    MA
INN AT SUNRISE POINT [BB]
    Camden, ME
INN AT THE EGG [BB] Brewster (Cape
    Cod), MA
INN AT THE MOUNTAIN [MOT]
    Stowe, VT
INN AT THE ROSTAY [MOT] Bethel,
    ME
INN AT THE ROUND BARN, THE [BB]
    Waitsfield, VT
INN AT THORN HILL [BB] Jackson,
    NH
INN AT WEATHERSFIELD, THE [BB]
    Springfield, VT
INN AT WEST VIEW FARM [BB]
    Dorset, VT
INN AT WOODCHUCK HILL FARM
    [BB] Grafton, VT
INN AT WOODSTOCK HILL [BB]
    Putnam, CT
INN BY THE SEA [RST] Portland, ME
INN OF EXETER [BB] Exeter, NH
INN OF HAMPTON [HOT] Hampton
    Beach, NH
INN OF THE SIX MOUNTAINS [RST]
    Killington, VT
INN ON CARLETON [BB] Portland,
    ME
INN ON COVE HILL, THE [BB]
    Rockport, MA
INN ON GOLDEN POND [BB]
    Holderness, NH
INN ON LONG WHARF [MOT]
    Newport, RI
INN ON THE COMMON, THE [BB]
    Montpelier, VT
INN ON THE HARBOR [MOT]
    Newport, RI
INN ON THE LAKE [HOT] Halifax, NS
INN ON THE PARK [HOT] Toronto,
    ON

INN ON THE SOUND [BB] *Falmouth (Cape Cod), MA*
INNSBRUCK INN [MOT] *Stowe, VT*
INTERLAKEN INN [RST] *Lakeville, CT*
INTERNATIONAL INN [HOT] *Hyannis (Cape Cod), MA*
INTERNATIONAL MOTEL [MOT] *Calais, ME*
INTERNATIONAL PLAZA [HOT] *Toronto, ON*
INVERARY RESORT [RST] *Baddeck, NS*
IRON HORSE INN [MOT] *Simsbury, CT*
IRON KETTLE [MOT] *Bennington, VT*
ISAIAH CLARK HOUSE [BB] *Brewster (Cape Cod), MA*
ISAIAH HALL BED AND BREAKFAST INN [BB] *Dennis (Cape Cod), MA*
ISAIAH JONES HOMESTEAD [BB] *Sandwich (Cape Cod), MA*
ISAIAH TUBBS RESORT [RST] *Kingston, ON*
ISLANDER MOTOR LODGE [MOT] *Charlottetown, PE*
ISLAND INN [RST] *Martha's Vineyard, MA*
ISLAND VIEW MOTEL [MOT] *Old Orchard Beach, ME*
IVEYS MOTOR LODGE [MOT] *Houlton, ME*
IVY LODGE [BB] *Newport, RI*
JACK DANIELS MOTOR INN [MOT] *Peterborough, NH*
JACK O'LANTERN RESORT [RST] *Lincoln/North Woodstock Area, NH*
JARED COFFIN HOUSE [BB] *Nantucket Island, MA*
JEFFERSON INN [BB] *Jefferson, NH*
JIMINY PEAK MOUNTAIN RESORT [RST] *Pittsfield, MA*
JOHN CARVER INN [BB] *Plymouth, MA*
JOHNSON AND WALES INN [HOT] *Seekonk, MA*
JUNGE'S MOTEL [MOT] *North Conway, NH*
JUNIPER HILL INN [MOT] *Ogunquit, ME*
JUNPIER HILL INN [BB] *Windsor, VT*
KADEE'S GRAY ELEPHANT [BB] *Orleans (Cape Cod), MA*
KALMAR VILLAGE [CC] *Truro and North Truro (Cape Cod), MA*
KANCAMABUS MOTOR LODGE [MOT] *Lincoln/North Woodstock Area, NH*
KEDDY'S HALIFAX [MOT] *Halifax, NS*
KEDRON VALLEY INN [BB] *Woodstock, VT*
KELLEY HOUSE [HOT] *Martha's Vineyard, MA*
KELTIC LODGE [RST] *Cape Breton Highlands National Park, NS*
KEMBLE INN [BB] *Lenox, MA*

KENDALL TAVERN B&B [BB] *Freeport, ME*
KENNEBUNK INN, THE [BB] *Kennebunk, ME*
KENNEBUNKPORT INN [HOT] *Kennebunkport, ME*
KENNISTON HILL INN [BB] *Boothbay Harbor, ME*
KIELY HOUSE HERITAGE INN [BB] *Niagara-on-the-Lake, ON*
KILLINGTON PICO MOTOR INN [MOT] *Killington, VT*
KIMBALL TERRACE INN [MOT] *Northeast Harbor, ME*
KINEO VIEW MOTOR LODGE [MOT] *Greenville, ME*
KING EDWARD [HOT] *Toronto, ON*
KING PHILIP INN [MOT] *Bristol, RI*
KINGSBRAE ARMS [HOT] *St. Andrews, NB*
KINGS INN [MOT] *Putnam, CT*
KINGSLEIGH INN 1904 [BB] *Southwest Harbor, ME*
KINGSTON EAST [MOT] *Kingston, ON*
KNIGHTS INN [MOT] *Waterbury, CT*
KNOTTY PINE [MOT] *Bennington, VT*
LAFAYETTES OCEANFRONT RESORT [MOT] *Wells, ME*
LAGUE INN [MOT] *Montpelier, VT*
LAKELAWN MOTEL [MOT] *Yarmouth, NS*
LAKE MOREY INN [RST] *Fairlee, VT*
LAKE MOTEL [MOT] *Wolfeboro, NH*
LAKESHORE INN BED & BREAKFAST, THE [BB] *Rockland, ME*
LAKEVIEW INN & MOTOR LODGE [MOT] *Wolfeboro, NH*
LAMAISON CAPPELLARI AT MOSTLY HALL [BB] *Falmouth (Cape Cod), MA*
LAMB'S EAR INN BED AND BREAKFAST [BB] *Southwest Harbor, ME*
LAMBERT'S COVE COUNTRY INN [BB] *Martha's Vineyard, MA*
LAMIE'S INN & TAVERN [BB] *Hampton Beach, NH*
LAMPLIGHTER MOTOR INN [MOT] *New London, NH*
LANDMARK INN [MOT] *Thunder Bay, ON*
LANGDON HALL [HOT] *Kitchener-Waterloo, ON*
LANTERN HOUSE MOTEL [MOT] *Great Barrington, MA*
LANTERN MOTOR INN [MOT] *Jefferson, NH*
LA PLACE RENDEZ-VOUS [MOT] *Fort Frances, ON*
LARCHWOOD INN [BB] *Kingston, RI*
LAREAU FARM COUNTRY INN [BB] *Waitsfield, VT*
LA REINE MOTEL [MOT] *Yarmouth, NS*
LATCHIS HOTEL [HOT] *Brattleboro, VT*

LAWNMEER INN [MOT] *Boothbay Harbor, ME*
LE BRETON [BB] *Montreal, QE*
LE CENTRE SHERATON [HOT] *Montreal, QE*
LE CHATEAU FRONTENAC [HOT] *Quebec City, QE*
LE CHATEAU MONTEBELLO [RST] *Montreal, QE*
LE MERIDIEN BOSTON [HOT] *Boston, MA*
LE NOUVEL HOTEL [HOT] *Montreal, QE*
LENOX [HOT] *Boston, MA*
LENOX MOTEL [MOT] *Lenox, MA*
LEWIS BAY LODGE [MOT] *South Yarmouth (Cape Cod), MA*
LIBERTY HILL INN [BB] *South Yarmouth (Cape Cod), MA*
LIFTLINE LODGE [MOT] *Stratton Mountain, VT*
LIGHTHOUSE INN [RST] *Dennis (Cape Cod), MA*
LIGHTHOUSE MOTOR INN [MOT] *Scarborough, ME*
LILAC INN [BB] *Brandon, VT*
LINCOLN INN AT THE COVERED BRIDGE, THE [BB] *Woodstock, VT*
LINDEN TREE INN [BB] *Rockport, MA*
LINNELL MOTEL & RESTINN CONFERENCE CENTER [MOT] *Rumford, ME*
LITCHFIELD INN [BB] *Litchfield, CT*
LOCH LYME LODGE [RST] *Hanover, NH*
LODGE AT CAMDEN HILLS, THE [BB] *Camden, ME*
LODGE AT JACKSON VILLAGE [MOT] *Jackson, NH*
LODGE AT MOOSEHEAD LAKE, THE [BB] *Greenville, ME*
LOEWS HOTEL VOGUE [HOT] *Montreal, QE*
LOEWS LE CONCORDE [HOT] *Quebec City, QE*
LOG CABIN ISLAND INN [BB] *Bailey Island, ME*
LONDONDERRY INN [BB] *Londonderry, VT*
LONGFELLOWS WAYSIDE INN [BB] *Sudbury Center, MA*
LORD BEAVERBROOK HOTEL [HOT] *Fredericton, NB*
LORD ELGIN [HOT] *Ottawa , ON*
LORD HAMPSHIRE MOTEL & COTTAGES [RST] *Laconia, NH*
LORD JEFFREY INN [BB] *Amherst, MA*
LORD NELSON [HOT] *Halifax, NS*
LOVETTS INN [BB] *Franconia, NH*
LOVLEY'S MOTEL [MOT] *Newport, ME*
LUCERNE INN, THE [BB] *Bangor, ME*
MABBETT HOUSE, THE [BB] *Plymouth, MA*

MADISON [MOT] *Gorham, NH*
MADISON BEACH HOTEL [BB] *Madison, CT*
MADISON RESORT INN [MOT] *Rumford, ME*
MAINELAND MOTEL [MOT] *Machias, ME*
MAINE STAY BED & BREAKFAST [BB] *Camden, ME*
MAINE STAY INN & COTTAGES [BB] *Kennebunkport, ME*
MAINE STREET MOTEL [MOT] *Bar Harbor, ME*
MAISON SUISSE INN [BB] *Northeast Harbor, ME*
MAJER'S [MOT] *Stratford, ON*
MANCHESTER HIGHLANDS INN [BB] *Manchester and Manchester Center, VT*
MANCHESTER VIEW [MOT] *Manchester and Manchester Center, VT*
MANCHESTER VILLAGE MOTOR INN [MOT] *Manchester, CT*
MANNSVIEW INN [BB] *Jeffersonville, VT*
MANOIR AMBROSE [BB] *Montreal, QE*
MANOIR DU LAC DELAGE [RST] *Quebec City, QE*
MANOR HOUSE INN [BB] *Bar Harbor, ME*
MANOR INN, THE [MOT] *Gloucester, MA*
MANOR INN, THE [BB] *Yarmouth, NS*
MANOR ON GOLDEN POND [BB] *Holderness, NH*
MAPLE LEAF INN [BB] *Woodstock, VT*
MAPLES INN [BB] *Bar Harbor, ME*
MAPLEWOOD INN [BB] *Rutland, VT*
MARBLEHEAD INN [BB] *Marblehead, MA*
MARIA ATWOOD INN [BB] *Franklin, NH*
MARINER MOTEL [MOT] *Falmouth (Cape Cod), MA*
MARINER MOTOR LODGE [MOT] *South Yarmouth (Cape Cod), MA*
MARITIME INN ANTIGONISH [MOT] *Antigonish, NS*
MARLBOROUGH [BB] *Woods Hole (Cape Cod), MA*
MARQUIS PLAZA [MOT] *Windsor, ON*
MARRIOTT [HOT] *Nashua, NH*
MARRIOTT [HOT] *Newton, MA*
MARRIOTT [MOT] *Portland, ME*
MARRIOTT [HOT] *Springfield, MA*
MARRIOTT-EATON CENTRE [HOT] *Toronto, ON*
MARRIOTT AIRPORT [HOT] *Toronto, ON*
MARRIOTT CHATEAU CHAMPLAIN [HOT] *Montreal, QE*
MARRIOTT COPLEY PLACE [HOT] *Burlington, MA*

MARRIOTT COURTYARD [MOT]
Lowell, MA
MARRIOTT EATON CENTRE [HOT]
Toronto, ON
MARRIOTT HOTEL [MOT] Providence,
RI
MARRIOTT TRUMBULL HOTEL
[HOT] Bridgeport, CT
MARTHA'S PLACE B&B [BB] Martha's
Vineyard, MA
MARTIN HOUSE INN [BB] Nantucket
Island, MA
MASTHEAD RESORT, THE [RST]
Provincetown (Cape Cod), MA
MATTERHORN MOTOR LODGE
[MOT] Meredith, NH
MAYFLOWER INN, THE [BB]
Washington, CT
MEADOWMERE [MOT] Ogunquit, ME
MEADOWS LAKESIDE LODGING
[MOT] Meredith, NH
MELVILLE HOUSE [BB] Newport, RI
MERRILL [BB] Kingston, ON
MERRILL FARM RESORT [BB] North
Conway, NH
METROPOLITAN HOTEL [HOT]
Toronto, ON
MICHAEL'S INN [MOT] Niagara Falls,
ON
MIDDLEBURY INN [HOT] Middlebury,
VT
MIDWAY MOTEL & COTTAGES
[MOT] Eastham (Cape Cod), MA
MIGIS LODGE [RST] Sebago Lake, ME
MILES RIVER COUNTRY INN B&B
[BB] Ipswich, MA
MILESTONE, THE [MOT] Ogunquit,
ME
MILFORD MOTEL ON THE RIVER
[MOT] Orono, ME
MILLBROOK [MOT] Scarborough, ME
MILLCROFT [BB] Toronto, ON
MILL HOUSE INN [MOT]
Lincoln/North Woodstock Area,
NH
MILL STREET INN [BB] Newport, RI
MIRA MONTE INN & SUITES [BB] Bar
Harbor, ME
MOFFAT INN [BB] Niagara-on-the-
Lake, ON
MOFFETT HOUSE B & B [BB]
Brandon, VT
MONUMENT MOUNTAIN MOTEL
[MOT] Great Barrington, MA
MOORINGS INN, THE [BB] Southwest
Harbor, ME
MOOSEHEAD MOTEL [MOT]
Rockwood, ME
MOOSE MOUNTAIN LODGE [BB]
Hanover, NH
MORGAN HOUSE [BB] Lee, MA
MORRILL PLACE [BB] Newburyport,
MA
MOSES NICKERSON HOUSE INN
[BB] Chatham (Cape Cod), MA
MOTEL 6 [MOT] Augusta, ME

MOTEL EAST, THE [MOT] Eastport,
ME
MOTEL PEG LEG [MOT] Rockport, MA
MOTEL SPRING [MOT] Quebec City,
QE
MOUNTAIN CLUB ON LOON [RST]
Lincoln/North Woodstock Area,
NH
MOUNTAIN GAP RESORT [RST]
Digby, NS
MOUNTAIN RESORT AT STOWE,
THE [MOT] Stowe, VT
MOUNTAIN TOP INN [RST] Rutland,
VT
MOUNTAIN VIEW INN [BB] Norfolk,
CT
MOUNT BATTEL HOTEL [MOT]
Camden, ME
MOUNT COOLIDGE MOTEL [MOT]
Lincoln/North Woodstock Area,
NH
MOUNT WASHINGTON HOTEL
[RST] Bretton Woods, NH
MULBURN [BB] Littleton, NH
NANTUCKET INN [RST] Nantucket
Island, MA
NAUSET KNOLL MOTOR LODGE
[MOT] Orleans (Cape Cod), MA
NAUTILUS MOTOR INN [RST] Woods
Hole (Cape Cod), MA
NAVIGATOR MOTOR INN [MOT]
Rockland, ME
NEPTUNE MOTEL [MOT] Old Orchard
Beach, ME
NER BEACH MOTEL [MOT] Wells, ME
NESTLENOOK FARM RESORT [BB]
Jackson, NH
NEWBURG INN [MOT] Kitchener-
Waterloo, ON
NEWBURY GUEST HOUSE [BB]
Boston, MA
NEWCASTLE INN [BB] Damariscotta,
ME
NEW ENGLAND CENTER HOTEL
[MOT] Dover, NH
NEW LONDON INN [BB] New
London, NH
NEWPORT CITY MOTEL [MOT]
Newport, VT
NEWPORT HARBOR HOTEL &
MARINA [HOT] Newport, RI
NEWPORT MARRIOTT HOTEL [HOT]
Newport, RI
NEWPORT MOTEL [MOT] Newport,
NH
NEWPORT RAMADA INN &
CONFERENCE CENTER [HOT]
Newport, RI
NEW SEABURY RESORT AND
CONFERENCE CENTER [HOT]
Falmouth (Cape Cod), MA
NIAGARA SUITES [MOT] St.
Catharines, ON
NIANTIC INN [MOT] New London, CT
NONANTUM RESORT [RST]
Kennebunkport, ME

NORDIC HILLS LODGE [RST] *Wilmington, VT*
NORSEMAN INN [MOT] *Bethel, ME*
NORSEMAN MOTOR INN [MOT] *Ogunquit, ME*
NORTH CONWAY GRAND HOTEL [HOT] *North Conway, NH*
NORTH CONWAY MOUNTAIN INN [HOT] *North Conway, NH*
NORTHERN COMFORT MOTEL [MOT] *Colebrook, NH*
NORTHERN LIGHTS [MOT] *Presque Isle, ME*
NORTHERN ZERMATT INN & MOTEL [BB] *Twin Mountain, NH*
NORTHFIELD INN [BB] *Montpelier, VT*
NORTH HERO HOUSE INN [BB] *North Hero, VT*
NORTH SHIRE MOTEL [MOT] *Manchester and Manchester Center, VT*
NORUMBEGA INN [BB] *Camden, ME*
NOTCHLAND INN [BB] *Bretton Woods, NH*
NOVOTEL [HOT] *Mississauga, ON*
NOVOTEL AIRPORT [HOT] *Toronto, ON*
NOVOTEL MONTREAL CENTRE [HOT] *Montreal, QE*
NOVOTEL TORONTO CENTRE [HOT] *Toronto, ON*
OAKES INN [HOT] *Niagara Falls, ON*
OAK HOUSE, THE [BB] *Martha's Vineyard, MA*
OAK ISLAND RESORT AND MARINA [RST] *Halifax, NS*
OCEAN EDGE RESORT AND GOLF CLUB [RST] *Brewster (Cape Cod), MA*
OCEAN GATE INN [MOT] *Boothbay Harbor, ME*
OCEAN MIST MOTOR LODGE [MOT] *South Yarmouth (Cape Cod), MA*
OCEAN POINT INN [BB] *Boothbay Harbor, ME*
OCEAN VIEW INN AND RESORT [RST] *Gloucester, MA*
OLD COLONY MOTEL [MOT] *Sandwich (Cape Cod), MA*
OLD COURT BED & BREAKFAST [BB] *Providence, RI*
OLD CUTTER INN, THE [BB] *Lyndonville, VT*
OLDE ORCHARD INN [BB] *Meredith, NH*
OLDE TAVERN MOTEL AND INN [MOT] *Orleans (Cape Cod), MA*
OLD FORT INN [BB] *Kennebunkport, ME*
OLD HARBOR INN [BB] *Chatham (Cape Cod), MA*
OLD LYME INN [BB] *Old Lyme, CT*

OLD MYSTIC INN, THE [BB] *Mystic, CT*
OLD NEWFANE INN [BB] *Newfane, VT*
OLD ORCHARD INN [RST] *Grand Pre, NS*
OLD SEA PINES INN [BB] *Brewster (Cape Cod), MA*
OLD STONE INN [MOT] *Niagara Falls, ON*
OLD STURBRIDGE VILLAGE LODGES [MOT] *Sturbridge, MA*
OLD TAVERN AT GRAFTON [BB] *Grafton, VT*
OLYMPIA MOTOR LODGE [MOT] *Manchester and Manchester Center, VT*
OMNI MONT-ROYAL [HOT] *Montreal, QE*
OMNI PARKER HOUSE [HOT] *Boston, MA*
ONCLE SAM [MOT] *Quebec City, QE*
ORCHARDS HOTEL, THE [HOT] *Williamstown, MA*
OTTAUQUECHEE MOTEL [MOT] *Woodstock, VT*
OUTERMOST INN [BB] *Martha's Vineyard, MA*
OVERLOOK INN OF CAPE COD [BB] *Eastham (Cape Cod), MA*
OWEN HOUSE [BB] *Lubec, ME*
OXFORD HOUSE INN [BB] *Center Lovell, ME*
OYSTER SHELL MOTEL [MOT] *Damariscotta, ME*
PALLISER MOTEL [MOT] *Truro, NS*
PALMER HOUSE [RST] *Manchester and Manchester Center, VT*
PALMER HOUSE INN, THE [BB] *Falmouth (Cape Cod), MA*
PALMER INN [BB] *Mystic, CT*
PAMOLA MOTOR LODGE [MOT] *Millinocket, ME*
PANSY PATCH [RST] *St. Andrews, NB*
PAQUETTE'S MOTOR INN [MOT] *Twin Mountain, NH*
PARK ENTRANCE MOTEL [MOT] *Bar Harbor, ME*
PARKER HOUSE INN [BB] *Woodstock, VT*
PARK HYATT, Toronto[HOT] *Toronto, ON*
PARK PLACE RAMADA PLAZA [HOT] *Dartmouth, NS*
PARKVIEW INN [MOT] *Salem, NH*
PARSONAGE INN, THE [BB] *Orleans (Cape Cod), MA*
PEGLEG RESTAURANT AND INN [BB] *Rockport, MA*
PENNY HOUSE INN [BB] *Eastham (Cape Cod), MA*
PENTAGOET INN [BB] *Bucksport, ME*
PEQUOT HOTEL [BB] *Martha's Vineyard, MA*

PHILBROOK FARM INN [BB] *Gorham, NH*

PICKET FENCE [MOT] *St. Andrews, NB*

PILGRAM INN [MOT] *Lee, MA*

PILGRIM HOUSE [BB] *Newport, RI*

PILGRIM MOTOR INN [MOT] *Niagara Falls, ON*

PILGRIM SANDS [MOT] *Plymouth, MA*

PILGRIMS INN [BB] *Deer Isle, ME*

PILLAR AND POST [BB] *Niagara-on-the-Lake, ON*

PINE HAVEN MOTEL [MOT] *Portsmouth, NH*

PINE HILL INN, THE [BB] *Ogunquit, ME*

PINE LODGE, THE [CC] *Westerly, RI*

PINES MOTEL [MOT] *Boothbay Harbor, ME*

PINES RESORT, THE [RST] *Digby, NS*

PINE VIEW LODGE [MOT] *Wolfeboro, NH*

PINK BLOSSOMS FAMILY RESORT [RST] *Ogunquit, ME*

PINOTEAU VILLAGE [HOT] *Mont Tremblant Provincial Park, QE*

PLAINFIED YANKEE MOTOR INN [MOT] *Plainfield, CT*

PLAINFIELD MOTEL [MOT] *Plainfield, CT*

PLEASANT BAY VILLAGE RESORT [RST] *Chatham (Cape Cod), MA*

POINT WAY INN [BB] *Martha's Vineyard, MA*

POMEGRANATE INN [BB] *Portland, ME*

POND RIDGE MOTEL [MOT] *Woodstock, VT*

PORT FORTUNE INN [BB] *Chatham (Cape Cod), MA*

PORTLAND REGENCY HOTEL [HOT] *Portland, ME*

PORT MOTOR INN [MOT] *Portsmouth, NH*

POWDER HOUND INN [MOT] *Warren, VT*

PRINCE ARTHUR [MOT] *Thunder Bay, ON*

PRINCE EDWARD, THE [HOT] *Charlottetown, PE*

PRINCE GEORGE [HOT] *Halifax, NS*

PRINCE OF WALES [HOT] *Niagara-on-the-Lake, ON*

PROFILE DELUXE MOTEL [MOT] *Twin Mountain, NH*

PROVIDENCE BILTMORE, THE [HOT] *Providence, RI*

PROVINCETOWN INN [RST] *Provincetown (Cape Cod), MA*

PUBLICK HOUSE HISTORIC INN [MOT] *Sturbridge, MA*

PURITY SPRING RESORT [RST] *North Conway, NH*

QUALITY HOTEL [HOT] *Niagara Falls, ON*

QUALITY HOTEL [HOT] *Toronto, ON*

QUALITY HOTEL [HOT] *Toronto, ON*

QUALITY HOTEL DORVAL [MOT] *Montreal, QE*

QUALITY INN [MOT] *Danvers, MA*

QUALITY INN [MOT] *Groton, CT*

QUALITY INN [MOT] *Mississauga, ON*

QUALITY INN [MOT] *New Bedford, MA*

QUALITY INN AIRPORT EAST [HOT] *Toronto, ON*

QUALITY INN AND CONFERENCE CENTER [MOT] *Vernon, CT*

QUALITY INN AND SUITES [HOT] *Brattleboro, VT*

QUALITY INN AND SUITES [MOT] *Montreal, QE*

QUALITY INN FALL [HOT] *Fall River, MA*

QUALITY INN ON THE HILL [MOT] *Charlottetown, PE*

QUALITY INN PHENIX [BB] *Bangor, ME*

QUALITY SUITES [HOT] *Toronto, ON*

QUEBEC INN [HOT] *Quebec City, QE*

QUECHEE INN AT MARSHLAND FARM [BB] *Woodstock, VT*

QUEEN'S INN [BB] *Stratford, ON*

QUEEN'S LANDING [BB] *Niagara-on-the-Lake, ON*

QUEEN ANNE INN [BB] *Chatham (Cape Cod), MA*

QUEEN ANNE INN [BB] *New London, CT*

QUEEN ELIZABETH [HOT] *Montreal, QE*

QUISISANA LODGE [RST] *Center Lovell, ME*

RABBIT HILL INN [BB] *St. Johnsbury, VT*

RACE BROOK LODGE [BB] *Great Barrington, MA*

RADDISON [HOT] *Windsor, ON*

RADISSON [HOT] *Boston, MA*

RADISSON [HOT] *Burlington, VT*

RADISSON [MOT] *Mississauga, ON*

RADISSON [MOT] *New London, CT*

RADISSON [HOT] *Toronto, ON*

RADISSON AIRPORT HOTEL [MOT] *Warwick, RI*

RADISSON HOTEL [MOT] *Lowell, MA*

RADISSON HOTEL AND CONFERENCE CENTER [HOT] *Middletown, CT*

RADISSON HOTEL GOUVERNEUR QUEBEC [HOT] *Quebec City, QE*

RADISSON HOTEL SPRINGFIELD [HOT] *Enfield, CT*

RADISSON INN [MOT] *Sudbury Center, MA*

RADISSON OTTAWA CENTRE [HOT] *Ottawa , ON*

RADISSON PLAZA - HOTEL ADMIRAL [HOT] *Toronto, ON*

RADISSON SUITE TORONTO AIRPORT [HOT] *Toronto, ON*

RAGAMONT INN [BB] *Lakeville, CT*
RAMADA [HOT] *Hamilton, ON*
RAMADA-CORAL INN RESORT
    [MOT] *Niagara Falls, ON*
RAMADA AIRPORT HOTEL [MOT]
    Boston, MA
RAMADA DON VALLEY [HOT]
    Toronto, ON
RAMADA HOTEL [MOT] *Andover and
    North Andover, MA*
RAMADA HOTEL TORONTO
    AIRPORT [MOT] *Toronto, ON*
RAMADA INN [MOT] *Bedford, MA*
RAMADA INN [MOT] *Brantford, ON*
RAMADA INN [MOT] *Danbury, CT*
RAMADA INN [MOT] *London, ON*
RAMADA INN [HOT] *New London, CT*
RAMADA INN [HOT] *Norwich, CT*
RAMADA INN [MOT] *Ottawa , ON*
RAMADA INN [MOT] *Seekonk, MA*
RAMADA INN [MOT] *Wethersfield, CT*
RAMADA INN-WHITE RIVER JCT
    [MOT] *White River Junction, VT*
RAMADA INN AND CONVENTION
    CENTRE [MOT] *Sault Ste.
    Marie, ON*
RAMADA INN AND SUITES [HOT]
    Toronto, ON
RAMADA INN CAPITOL HILL [HOT]
    Hartford, CT
RAMADA INN CONFERENCE
    CENTER [MOT] *Lewiston, ME*
RAMADA INN REGENCY [MOT]
    Hyannis (Cape Cod), MA
RAMADA INN STRATFORD [HOT]
    Stratford, CT
RAMADA LIMITED [MOT] *Rutland,
    VT*
RAMADA PARKWAY INN [MOT] *St.
    Catharines, ON*
RAMADA PLAZA INN [HOT] *Meriden,
    CT*
RAMADA SUITES NIAGARA [HOT]
    Niagara Falls, ON
RANDALL'S ORDINARY [BB]
    Stonington, CT
RANGELEY INN [RST] *Rangeley, ME*
RED APPLE INN [MOT] *Jackson, NH*
RED BROOK INN [BB] *Mystic, CT*
RED CLOVER INN [BB] *Killington, VT*
REDCLYFFE SHORE MOTOR INN
    [MOT] *Calais, ME*
RED COACH INN [MOT] *Franconia,
    NH*
RED CRICKET INN [BB] *West Dover,
    VT*
RED DOORS MOTEL [MOT]
    *Lincoln/North Woodstock Area,
    NH*
RED HILL INN [BB] *Meredith, NH*
RED HORSE INN [MOT] *Falmouth
    (Cape Cod), MA*
RED JACKET BEACH MOTOR INN
    [MOT] *South Yarmouth (Cape
    Cod), MA*

RED JACKET MOUNTAIN VIEW [RST]
    North Conway, NH
RED LION INN [BB] *Stockbridge and
    West Stockbridge, MA*
RED ROOF INN [MOT] *Enfield, CT*
RED ROOF INN [MOT] *Nashua, NH*
RED ROOF INN [MOT] *New London,
    CT*
REGAL BOSTONIAN [HOT] *Boston,
    MA*
REGAL CONSTELLATION [HOT]
    Toronto, ON
RELUCTANT PANTHER INN AND
    RESTAURANT [BB] *Manchester
    and Manchester Center, VT*
RENAISSANCE [HOT] *Bedford, MA*
RENAISSANCE CHARLOTTE SUITES
    HOTEL [AS] *Charlotte, NC*
RENAISSANCE FALLSVIEW [HOT]
    Niagara Falls, ON
RESIDENCE INN [MOT] *Burlington,
    VT*
RESIDENCE INN [EX] *New Haven, CT*
RESIDENCE INN [MOT] *Windsor, CT*
RESIDENCE INN BY MARRIOTT
    [MOT] *Danvers, MA*
RESIDENCE INN BY MARRIOTT
    [MOT] *Nashua, NH*
RESIDENCE INN BY MARRIOTT
    [MOT] *Warwick, RI*
RHUMB LINE MOTOR LODGE
    [MOT] *Kennebunkport, ME*
RIDGEWAY INN, THE [BB] *Bar
    Harbor, ME*
RIDGEWOOD MOTEL AND
    COTTAGES [MOT] *Orleans
    (Cape Cod), MA*
RITZ-CARLTON [HOT] *Montreal, QE*
RITZ-CARLTON, BOSTON COMMON
    [HOT] *Boston, MA*
RITZ-CARLTON, BOSTON, THE
    [HOT] *Boston, MA*
RIVERSIDE [MOT] *Ogunquit, ME*
RIVER VIEW [MOT] *Bethel, ME*
RIVIERA BEACH RESORT [RST] *South
    Yarmouth (Cape Cod), MA*
ROAD COLONY HARBOUR INN
    [MOT] *Yarmouth, NS*
ROBERTS HOUSE INN [BB] *Nantucket
    Island, MA*
ROCKWELL HOUSE INN [BB] *Bristol,
    RI*
ROCKY SHORES INN & COTTAGES
    [BB] *Rockport, MA*
RODD GRAND YARMOUTH [HOT]
    Yarmouth, NS
RODD PARK HOUSE INN [MOT]
    Moncton, NB
ROGER SHERMAN INN [BB] *New
    Canaan, CT*
ROOKWOOD INN [BB] *Lenox, MA*
ROSEMOUNT INN [BB] *Kingston, ON*
ROYAL ANCHOR RESORT [MOT] *Old
    Orchard Beach, ME*
ROYAL BROCK [HOT] *Brockville, ON*

ROYAL MARQUIS [MOT] *Windsor, ON*

ROYAL PLAZA HOTEL [MOT] *Newport, RI*

ROYAL SONESTA [HOT] *Cambridge, MA*

ROYALTY INN [MOT] *Gorham, NH*

ROYAL YORK [HOT] *Toronto, ON*

RUDDY TURNSTONE [BB] *Brewster (Cape Cod), MA*

RUTHCLIFFE LODGE & RESORT [BB] *North Hero, VT*

SALEM INN [BB] *Salem, MA*

SAMOSET RESORT [RST] *Rockland, ME*

SAND PIPER BEACHFRONT MOTEL [HOT] *Old Orchard Beach, ME*

SANDPIPER MOTOR INN [MOT] *Old Saybrook, CT*

SANDWICH LODGE & RESORT [MOT] *Sandwich (Cape Cod), MA*

SANDY BAY MOTOR INN [MOT] *Rockport, MA*

SANDY NECK MOTEL [MOT] *Sandwich (Cape Cod), MA*

SAYBROOK POINT INN AND SPA [MOT] *Old Saybrook, CT*

SCANDINAVIA INN AND CHALETS [BB] *Stowe, VT*

SCHOONERS INN [HOT] *Kennebunkport, ME*

SCOTTISH INN [MOT] *Houlton, ME*

SEA BREEZE INN [BB] *Hyannis (Cape Cod), MA*

SEA CHAMBERS MOTOR LODGE [MOT] *Ogunquit, ME*

SEA CLIFF HOUSE & MOTEL [MOT] *Old Orchard Beach, ME*

SEACREST MANOR [BB] *Rockport, MA*

SEA CREST RESORT AND CONFERENCE CENTER [RST] *Falmouth (Cape Cod), MA*

SEADAR INN [RST] *Harwich (Cape Cod), MA*

SEAFARER INN [BB] *Rockport, MA*

SEAFARER OF CHATHAM [MOT] *Chatham (Cape Cod), MA*

SEAGATE [MOT] *Boothbay Harbor, ME*

SEAGULL INN [BB] *Marblehead, MA*

SEA GULL MOTEL [MOT] *Truro and North Truro (Cape Cod), MA*

SEAGULL MOTOR INN [MOT] *Wells, ME*

SEA HEATHER INN [BB] *Harwich (Cape Cod), MA*

SEA HORSE INN [MOT] *Toronto, ON*

SEA LORD RESORT MOTEL [MOT] *Dennis (Cape Cod), MA*

SEA MIST RESORT MOTEL [MOT] *Wells, MA*

SEAPORT [HOT] *Boston, MA*

SEA SHELL [MOT] *Dennis (Cape Cod), MA*

SEASHORE PARK MOTOR INN [MOT] *Orleans (Cape Cod), MA*

SEASIDE BEACH RESORT [MOT] *St. Andrews, NB*

SEASIDE HOUSE & COTTAGES [HOT] *Kennebunkport, ME*

SEASONS MOTOR INN [MOT] *Dartmouth, NS*

SEASONS MOTOR INN [MOT] *Halifax, NS*

SEAVIEW CAMPGROUND [CC] *Eastport, ME*

SEA VIEW MOTEL [MOT] *Ogunquit, ME*

SEAWARD INN & COTTAGES [BB] *Rockport, MA*

SELECTOTEL ROND-POINT [MOT] *Quebec City, QE*

SERENITY MOTEL [CC] *Bennington, VT*

SESUIT HARBOR [MOT] *Dennis (Cape Cod), MA*

SEVEN OAKES [MOT] *Kingston, ON*

SEVEN SEA STREET INN [BB] *Nantucket Island, MA*

SHADY NOOK INN & MOTEL [MOT] *Sandwich (Cape Cod), MA*

SHAKER INN AT THE GREAT STONE DWELLING, THE [BB] *Enfield, CT*

SHARON MOTOR LODGE [MOT] *Lakeville, CT*

SHAWMUT INN [MOT] *Kennebunkport, ME*

SHELBURNE FARMS [BB] *Shelburne, VT*

SHELTER HARBOR INN [BB] *Westerly, RI*

SHERATON [HOT] *Hamilton, ON*

SHERATON [HOT] *Kitchener-Waterloo, ON*

SHERATON [HOT] *Ottawa , ON*

SHERATON [MOT] *Portsmouth, NH*

SHERATON [HOT] *Warwick, RI*

SHERATON BOSTON HOTEL [HOT] *Boston, MA*

SHERATON BRADLEY [HOT] *Windsor Locks, CT*

SHERATON BRAINTREE HOTEL [MOT] *Braintree, MA*

SHERATON CENTRE [HOT] *Toronto, ON*

SHERATON COLONIAL HOTEL AND GOLF CLUB [HOT] *Lynnfield, MA*

SHERATON COMMANDER HOTEL [HOT] *Cambridge, MA*

SHERATON FERNCROFT RESORT [HOT] *Danvers, MA*

SHERATON FOUR POINTS HOTEL [MOT] *Eastham (Cape Cod), MA*

SHERATON FOUR POINTS HOTEL [HOT] *Hyannis (Cape Cod), MA*

SHERATON FOUR POINTS HOTEL & SUITES, MONTREAL CENTRE-VILLE [HOT] *Montreal, QE*

SHERATON FRAMINGHAM HOTEL [HOT] *Framingham, MA*

SHERATON FREDERICTON [HOT]
Fredericton, NB
SHERATON GATEWAY [HOT] Toronto,
ON
SHERATON HALIFAX HOTEL [HOT]
Halifax, NS
SHERATON HARTFORD HOTEL
[HOT] Hartford, CT
SHERATON HOTEL [HOT] Newton,
MA
SHERATON HOTEL [HOT] Springfield,
MA
SHERATON HOTEL AND
CONFERENCE CENTER [HOT]
Burlington, VT
SHERATON HYANNIS RESORT [RST]
Hyannis (Cape Cod), MA
SHERATON INN [HOT] Plymouth, MA
SHERATON LEXINGTON INN [HOT]
Lexington, MA
SHERATON NASHUA HOTEL [HOT]
Nashua, NH
SHERATON NEWTON HOTEL [HOT]
Newton, MA
SHERATON SOUTH PORTLAND
HOTEL [HOT] Portland, ME
SHERATON STANFORD HOTEL
[HOT] Stamford, CT
SHERATON WATERBURY [HOT]
Waterbury, CT
SHERBORN INN [HOT] Natick, MA
SHERBURNE-KILLINGTON MOTEL
[MOT] Killington, VT
SHERBURNE INN [BB] Nantucket
Island, MA
SHIP'S BELL INN & MOTEL [MOT]
Provincetown (Cape Cod), MA
SHIPS INN [BB] Nantucket Island, MA
SHIPS KNEES INN [BB] Orleans (Cape
Cod), MA
SHIRE INN [BB] Barre, VT
SHIRE MOTEL, THE [MOT]
Woodstock, VT
SHIRETOWN INN [BB] Martha's
Vineyard, MA
SHIRETOWN MOTOR INN [MOT]
Houlton, ME
SHORE ACRES INN [MOT] North
Hero, VT
SILAS GRIFFITH INN [BB] Manchester
and Manchester Center, VT
SILVER DART LODGE [MOT] Baddeck,
NS
SILVER MAPLE LODGE + COTTAGES
[BB] Fairlee, VT
SILVERMINE TAVERN, THE [BB]
Norwalk, CT
SILVER STREET INN [BB] Dover, NH
SILVERWOOD MOTEL [MOT]
Cavendish, PE
SIMMONS HOMESTEAD INN [BB]
Hyannis (Cape Cod), MA
SIMSBURY 1820 HOUSE [BB]
Simsbury, CT
SIMSBURY INN [HOT] Simsbury, CT

SINCLAIR INN BED & BREAKFAST
[BB] Jeffersonville, VT
SISE INN [HOT] Portsmouth, NH
SKAKET BEACH MOTEL [MOT]
Orleans (Cape Cod), MA
SKYDOME [HOT] Toronto, ON
SKYLARK MOTEL [MOT] Old Orchard
Beach, ME
SKYLINE BROCK [HOT] Niagara Falls,
ON
SKYLINE FOXHEAD [HOT] Niagara
Falls, ON
SKYVIEW MOTEL [MOT] Vergennes,
VT
SLEEPY HOLLOW MOTOR INN
[MOT] Woods Hole (Cape Cod),
MA
SLEEPY PILGRIM MOTEL [MOT]
Plymouth, MA
SLUMBER INN-NEW MINAS [MOT]
Grand Pre, NS
SMUGGLER'S COVE MOTOR INN
[MOT] Boothbay Harbor, ME
SMUGGLER'S NOTCH INN AND
RESTAURANT [BB]
Jeffersonville, VT
SMUGGLER'S NOTCH RESORT [RST]
Jeffersonville, VT
SNOWDON MOTEL [MOT]
Londonderry, VT
SNOW HILL LODGE [MOT] Camden,
ME
SNOW VILLAGE INN [BB] North
Conway, NH
SNOWY OWL INN [RST] Waterville
Valley, NH
SOMERSET HOUSE [BB] Provincetown
(Cape Cod), MA
SOUDINGS SEASIDE RESORT [MOT]
Dennis (Cape Cod), MA
SOUTHFLEET MOTOR INN [MOT]
Wellfleet (Cape Cod), MA
SOUTH SHIRE INN [BB] Bennington,
VT
SPA AT NORWICH INN, THE [RST]
Norwich, CT
SPARHAWK RESORT MOTEL [MOT]
Ogunquit, ME
SPOUTER WHALE MOTOR INN
[MOT] Dennis (Cape Cod), MA
SPRAY CLIFF ON THE OCEAN [BB]
Marblehead, MA
SPRING HILL MOTOR LODGE [MOT]
Sandwich (Cape Cod), MA
SPRING HOUSE [HOT] Block Island,
RI
SPRUCE POINT INN [RST] Boothbay
Harbor, ME
SQUIRE TARBOX INN [BB] Wiscasset,
ME
ST. MORITZ TERRACE RESORT [RST]
Laconia, NH
STAGE NECK INN [RST] York, ME
STAGE RUN MOTEL [MOT] Ogunquit,
ME

STAGE WEST HOTEL [HOT]
Mississauga, ON
STAMFORD MARRIOTT HOTEL
[HOT] Stamford, CT
STAMFORD MOTEL [MOT]
Manchester and Manchester
Center, VT
STAMFORD SUITES [EX] Stamford, CT
STANTON HOUSE INN [BB]
Greenwich, CT
STARDUST [MOT] Halifax, NS
STARDUST [MOT] Halifax, NS
STARDUST [MOT] Houlton, ME
STARLIGHT MOTOR INN [MOT] New
London, CT
STATE HOUSE INN [BB] Providence, RI
STERLING RIDGE INN & CABINS
[CC] Jeffersonville, VT
STONCREST FARM BED AND
BREAKFAST [BB] White River
Junction, VT
STONE HEARTH INN [BB] Springfield,
VT
STONEHEDGE INN [RST] Lowell, MA
STONEHENGE INN [BB] Ridgefield,
CT
STONE HOUSES MOTEL & REST
[MOT] Truro, NS
STONYBROOK MOTEL & LODGE
[MOT] Franconia, NH
STORYBOOK RESORT INN [RST]
Jackson, NH
STOWEFLAKE MOUNTAIN RESORT
& SPA [RST] Stowe, VT
STOWEHOF INN [BB] Stowe, VT
STOWE INN AT LITTLE RIVER [BB]
Stowe, VT
STOWE MOTEL [MOT] Stowe, VT
STRATFORD HOUSE INN [BB] Bar
Harbor, ME
STRATFORD SUBURBAN [MOT]
Stratford, ON
STRATTON MOUNTAIN INN AND
VILLAGE LODGE [RST] Stratton
Mountain, VT
STRONG HOUSE INN [BB] Vergennes,
VT
ST STEPHEN INN [MOT] St. Andrews,
NB
STURBRIDGE COACH MOTOR
LODGE [MOT] Sturbridge, MA
STURBRIDGE HOST HOTEL &
CONFERENCE CENTER [MOT]
Sturbridge, MA
SUBURBAN PINES [MOT] Sebago
Lake, ME
SUGARBUSH INN [BB] Warren, VT
SUGARBUSH VILLAGE CONDOS
[RST] Warren, VT
SUGAR HILL INN [BB] Franconia, NH
SUGARTREE COUNTRY INN [BB]
Warren, VT
SUMMER WHITE HOUSE, THE [BB]
Lenox, MA
SUMMIT LODGE [HOT] Killington,
VT

SUN AND SKI MOTOR INN [MOT]
Stowe, VT
SUNNY KING [MOT] Charlottetown,
PE
SUNRISE MOTEL [MOT] Saco, ME
SUNSET HILL HOUSE — A GRAND
INN [BB] Franconia, NH
SUNSET MOTOR INN [MOT] Stowe,
VT
SUPER 8 [MOT] Brattleboro, VT
SUPER 8 [MOT] Danvers, MA
SUPER 8 [MOT] Franklin, NH
SUPER 8 [HOT] Kitchener-Waterloo,
ON
SUPER 8 [MOT] Lewiston, ME
SUPER 8 [MOT] Newport, VT
SUPER 8 [MOT] Stamford, CT
SUPER 8 [MOT] Wells, ME
SUPER 8-AIRPORT [MOT] Manchester,
NH
SUPER 8 MOTEL [MOT] Brunswick,
ME
SURF MOTEL [HOT] Block Island, RI
SURFSIDE INN [MOT] Niagara Falls,
ON
SUSSE CHALET HOTEL [HOT] Boston,
MA
SUSSE CHALET HOTEL [HOT]
Plymouth, NH
SUSSE CHALET INN [MOT] Andover
and North Andover, MA
SUSSE CHALET INN [MOT] Augusta,
ME
SUSSE CHALET INN [MOT]
Manchester, NH
SUSSE CHALET INN [MOT]
Newburyport, MA
SUSSE CHALET INN [MOT] Newton,
MA
SUSSE CHALET INN [MOT]
Portsmouth, NH
SUSSE CHALET INN [MOT] Salem,
NH
SUSSE CHALET LODGE [MOT]
Portland, ME
SUSSE CHALET MOTOR LODGE
[MOT] Waltham, MA
SUTTON PLACE [HOT] Toronto, ON
SWIFT HOUSE INN [BB] Middlebury,
VT
SWISS CHALETS VILLAGE INN
[MOT] North Conway, NH
SWISS INN & RESTAURANT [BB]
Londonderry, VT
SWISSOTEL BOSTON [HOT] Boston,
MA
T-BIRD MOTOR INN [MOT]
Shelburne, VT
TAGE INN-ANDOVER [HOT] Andover
and North Andover, MA
TAGGART HOUSE, THE [BB]
Stockbridge and West Stockbridge,
MA
TARA MANOR INN [BB] St. Andrews,
NB

TATTINGSTONE INN [BB] *Grand Pre, NS*
TELEGRAPH HOUSE [MOT] *Baddeck, NS*
TERRACE BY THE SEA, THE [RST] *Ogunquit, ME*
THATCHER BROOK INN [BB] *Waterbury, VT*
THAYER'S INN [BB] *Littleton, NH*
THOMAS MOTT HOMESTEAD B&B [BB] *North Hero, VT*
THORNCROFT INN [BB] *Martha's Vineyard, MA*
THORNEWOOD INN & RESTAURANT [BB] *Great Barrington, MA*
THORNHEDGE INN [BB] *Bar Harbor, ME*
THREE BEARS AT THE FOUNTAIN [BB] *Stowe, VT*
THREE CHIMNEYS [BB] *New Haven, CT*
THREE CHIMNEYS INN [BB] *Dover, NH*
THREE SEASONS MOTOR LODGE [MOT] *Dennis (Cape Cod), MA*
THRIFT LODGE [MOT] *Charlottetown, PE*
TIDES INN BY THE SEA [BB] *Kennebunkport, ME*
TIDEWATER MOTOR LODGE [MOT] *South Yarmouth (Cape Cod), MA*
TODD HOUSE [BB] *Eastport, ME*
TOLLAND INN [BB] *Vernon, CT*
TOLLGATE HILL INN & REST [BB] *Litchfield, CT*
TOLL ROAD MOTOR INN [MOT] *Manchester and Manchester Center, VT*
TOPNOTCH AT STOWE [RST] *Stowe, VT*
TOPSIDE MOTEL [MOT] *Boothbay Harbor, ME*
TOWER SUITES MOTEL [AS] *Guilford, CT*
TOWN & COUNTRY MOTOR INN [MOT] *Gorham, NH*
TOWN AND COUNTRY RESORT [MOT] *Stowe, VT*
TOWN CRIER MOTEL [RST] *Eastham (Cape Cod), MA*
TOWNE LYNE MOTEL [MOT] *Ogunquit, ME*
TOWNE MOTEL, THE [MOT] *Skowhegan, ME*
TOWN INN [HOT] *Toronto, ON*
TRADE WINDS INN [MOT] *Centerville (Cape Cod), MA*
TRAIL'S END - A COUNTRY INN [BB] *Wilmington, VT*
TRAPP FAMILY LODGE [RST] *Stowe, VT*
TRAVELODGE [MOT] *Bedford, MA*
TRAVELODGE [MOT] *Kenora, ON*
TRAVELODGE [MOT] *Mississauga, ON*

TRAVELODGE [MOT] *Natick, MA*
TRAVELODGE [MOT] *Pittsfield, MA*
TRAVELODGE [MOT] *Thunder Bay, ON*
TRAVELODGE [HOT] *Toronto, ON*
TRAVELODGE - AIRPORT [HOT] *Toronto, ON*
TRAVELODGE AIRPLANE HOTEL [MOT] *Thunder Bay, ON*
TRAVELODGE BONAVENTURE [MOT] *Niagara Falls, ON*
TRAVELODGE EAST [MOT] *Toronto, ON*
TRAVELODGE HOTEL [HOT] *Augusta, ME*
TRAVELODGE HOTEL [MOT] *Charlottetown, PE*
TRAVELODGE HOTEL LA SALLE [MOT] *Kingston, ON*
TRAVELODGE NEAR THE FALLS [MOT] *Niagara Falls, ON*
TRAVELODGE NORTH [MOT] *Toronto, ON*
TRAVELODGE TORONTO SW/CARRIAGE INN [MOT] *Mississauga, ON*
TREMONT BOSTON, THE [HOT] *Boston, MA*
TRINITY HOUSE [BB] *Gananoque, ON*
TUCKER HILL INN & RESTAURANT [RST] *Waitsfield, VT*
TUCKERNUCK INN [BB] *Nantucket Island, MA*
TUCK INN B&B, THE [BB] *Rockport, MA*
TUGBOAT INN [HOT] *Boothbay Harbor, ME*
TULIP TREE INN [BB] *Rutland, VT*
TURK'S HEAD MOTOR INN [MOT] *Rockport, MA*
TURNPIKE MOTEL [MOT] *Kennebunk, ME*
TUSCANY INN [BB] *Martha's Vineyard, MA*
TWILITE MOTEL [MOT] *Ellsworth, ME*
TWIN FARMS [BB] *Woodstock, VT*
TWO TREES INN [MOT] *Mystic, CT*
TYLER PLACE FAMILY RESORT [RST] *Highgate Springs, VT*
UNIVERSITY MOTOR INN [MOT] *Orono, ME*
VALHALLA INN [MOT] *Thunder Bay, ON*
VALHALLA INN [MOT] *Toronto, ON*
VALLEY INN & TAVERN [RST] *Waterville Valley, NH*
VAL ROC MOTEL [MOT] *Killington, VT*
VENTURE INN [MOT] *Hamilton, ON*
VERMONTER MOTOR LODGE [MOT] *Bennington, VT*
VERMONT INN [BB] *Killington, VT*
VICTORIA'S HISTORIC INN [BB] *Grand Pre, NS*

VICTORIA INN [MOT] *Thunder Bay, ON*

VICTORIAN BY THE SEA, THE [BB] *Camden, ME*

VICTORIAN INN [MOT] *Stratford, ON*

VICTORIAN LADIES INN [BB] *Newport, RI*

VIKING MOTOR INN [MOT] *Brunswick, ME*

VIKING SHORES RESORT [MOT] *Eastham (Cape Cod), MA*

VILLA BED & BREAKFAST [BB] *Westerly, RI*

VILLAGE BY THE SEA [AS] *Wells, ME*

VILLAGE COUNTRY INN [BB] *Manchester and Manchester Center, VT*

VILLAGE COVE INN [MOT] *Kennebunkport, ME*

VILLAGE GREEN MOTEL & COTTAGES [MOT] *Wells, ME*

VILLAGE INN, THE [BB] *Lenox, MA*

VILLAGE INN [MOT] *Narragansett, RI*

VILLAGE INN [MOT] *Niagara Falls, ON*

VILLAGE INN [BB] *Sandwich (Cape Cod), MA*

VILLAGER MOTEL [MOT] *Bar Harbor, ME*

VISTA MOTEL [MOT] *Gloucester, MA*

VOYAGEUR [MOT] *Yarmouth, NS*

VOYAGEUR'S GUEST HOUSE [BB] *Ottawa , ON*

WACHUSETT VILLAGE INN [BB] *Leominster, MA*

WAITSFIELD INN, THE [BB] *Waitsfield, VT*

WAKE ROBIN INN [BB] *Lakeville, CT*

WALKER HOUSE [BB] *Lenox, MA*

WALPER TERRACE [HOT] *Kitchener-Waterloo, ON*

WANDLYN INN [MOT] *Fredericton, NB*

WANDLYN INN [MOT] *Grand Pre, NS*

WANDLYN INN HALIFAX [MOT] *Halifax, NS*

WATER'S EDGE MOTEL, THE [MOT] *Boothbay Harbor, ME*

WATER'S EDGE RESORT AND CONFERANCE CENTER [RST] *Old Saybrook, CT*

WATERCREST COTTAGES & MOTEL [CC] *Wells, ME*

WATERFORD INN [BB] *Norway, ME*

WATERLOO INN [MOT] *Kitchener-Waterloo, ON*

WATERMARK INN [AS] *Provincetown (Cape Cod), MA*

WATERSHIP INN [BB] *Provincetown (Cape Cod), MA*

WAUWINET, THE [BB] *Nantucket Island, MA*

WAVERLEY INN [BB] *Halifax, NS*

WAYBURY INN [BB] *Middlebury, VT*

WAYFARER INN AND CONVENTION CENTER [BB] *Manchester, NH*

WAYSIDE [BB] *Littleton, NH*

WEATHERVANE HOTEL [MOT] *Manchester and Manchester Center, VT*

WEDGEWOOD MOTEL [MOT] *Manchester and Manchester Center, VT*

WELLESLEY INN ON THE SQUARE [MOT] *Wellesley, MA*

WELLFLEET MOTEL & LODGE [MOT] *Wellfleet (Cape Cod), MA*

WELLS-MOODY MOTEL [MOT] *Wells, ME*

WENTWORTH RESORT HOTEL [BB] *Jackson, NH*

WEQUASSETT INN [RST] *Chatham (Cape Cod), MA*

WEST DENNIS MOTOR LODGE [MOT] *Dennis (Cape Cod), MA*

WEST DOVER INN [BB] *West Dover, VT*

WESTFORD REGENCY INN [HOT] *Lowell, MA*

WESTIN [HOT] *Providence, RI*

WESTIN [HOT] *Waltham, MA*

WESTIN COPLEY PLACE HOTEL [HOT] *Boston, MA*

WESTIN OTTAWA, THE [HOT] *Ottawa , ON*

WESTIN PRINCE [HOT] *Toronto, ON*

WESTIN STAMFORD, THE [HOT] *Stamford, CT*

WEST LANE INN [BB] *Ridgefield, CT*

WEST MAIN LODGE [MOT] *Newport, RI*

WESTON HOUSE BED & BREAKFAST [BB] *Eastport, ME*

WESTPORT INN [HOT] *Westport, CT*

WHALER'S INN [BB] *Mystic, CT*

WHARF COTTAGES [MOT] *Nantucket Island, MA*

WHEATLEIGH HOTEL [HOT] *Lenox, MA*

WHETSTONE INN [BB] *Marlboro, VT*

WHISTLER INN [BB] *Lenox, MA*

WHITE BARN INN, THE [BB] *Kennebunkport, ME*

WHITE CEDAR INN [BB] *Freeport, ME*

WHITE ELEPHANT RESORT [HOT] *Nantucket Island, MA*

WHITE GATES INN [MOT] *Rockland, ME*

WHITE GOOSE INN [BB] *Hanover, NH*

WHITEHALL INN INC [BB] *Camden, ME*

WHITE HORSE INN [BB] *Waitsfield, VT*

WHITE HOUSE OF WILMINGTON [BB] *Wilmington, VT*

WHITE MOUNTAIN HOTEL & RESORT [RST] *North Conway, NH*

WHITE OAKS CONFERENCE RESORT AND SPA [MOT] *Niagara-on-the-Lake, ON*

WHITE TRELLIS MOTEL [MOT] *North Conway, NH*
WHITE WIND INN [BB] *Provincetown (Cape Cod), MA*
WILBURTON INN [BB] *Manchester and Manchester Center, VT*
WILDER HOMESTEAD INN [BB] *Weston, VT*
WILDERNESS INN BED & BREAKFAST [BB] *Lincoln/North Woodstock Area, NH*
WILDFLOWER INN [BB] *Falmouth (Cape Cod), MA*
WILDFLOWER INN, THE [BB] *Lyndonville, VT*
WILLIAMS GRANT INN [BB] *Bristol, RI*
WILLIAMS INN [HOT] *Williamstown, MA*
WILLIAMSVILLE INN [BB] *Stockbridge and West Stockbridge, MA*
WILLOW BEND MOTEL [MOT] *Truro, NS*
WILLOW OF NEWPORT ROMANTIC INN, THE [BB] *Newport, RI*
WILSON INN [AS] *Burlington, VT*
WINDFLOWER INN [BB] *Great Barrington, MA*
WINDHAM HILL INN [BB] *Newfane, VT*
WINDING BROOK...A CLASSIC MOUNTAIN LODGE [BB] *Stowe, VT*
WINDJAMMER [MOT] *Peggy's Cove, NS*
WINDSOR ARMS HOTEL [HOT] *Toronto, ON*
WINDSOR HOUSE [BB] *Newburyport, MA*
WINGS HILL INN [BB] *Augusta, ME*
WINNAPAUG INN [RST] *Westerly, RI*
WINSLOW HOUSE [BB] *Woodstock, VT*
WISCASSET MOTOR LODGE [MOT] *Wiscasset, ME*
WOLFEBORO INN, THE [BB] *Wolfeboro, NH*
WONDERVIEW COTTAGES [MOT] *Belfast, ME*
WONDER VIEW INN [MOT] *Bar Harbor, ME*
WOODSTOCKER BED AND BREAKFAST [BB] *Woodstock, VT*
WOODSTOCK INN [BB] *Lincoln/North Woodstock Area, NH*
WOODSTOCK INN &RESORT [RST] *Woodstock, VT*
WOODWARD RESORT [RST] *Lincoln/North Woodstock Area, NH*
WORCHESTER INN AND SUITES [MOT] *Worcester, MA*
WYCHMERE VILLAGE [MOT] *Harwich (Cape Cod), MA*

WYNDHAM [MOT] *Andover and North Andover, MA*
WYNDHAM BOSTON [HOT] *Boston, MA*
WYNDHAM BRISTOL PLACE [HOT] *Toronto, ON*
WYNDHAM GARDEN HOTEL [HOT] *Waltham, MA*
XV BEACON [HOT] *Boston, MA*
YACHTSMAN LODGE & MARINA [MOT] *Kennebunkport, ME*
YANKEE CLIPPER INN [BB] *Rockport, MA*
YANKEE HOME COMFORT, THE [MOT] *Lenox, MA*
YANKEE PEDLAR INN [BB] *Holyoke, MA*
YARDARM MOTEL [MOT] *Searsport, ME*
YE OLDE ENGLAND INNE [BB] *Stowe, VT*
YORK COMMONS INN [MOT] *York, ME*
YORK HARBOR INN [BB] *York, ME*

RESTAURANT LIST

Establishment names are listed in alphabetical order followed by a symbol identifying their classification and then city and state. The symbols for classification are: [RES] for Restaurants and [URD] for Unrated Dining Spots.

1640 HART HOUSE [RES] *Ipswich, MA*
176 MAIN [RES] *Keene, NH*
1785 INN [RES] *North Conway, NH*
21 FEDERAL [RES] *Nantucket Island, MA*
360 [RES] *Toronto, ON*
A.J.'S [RES] *White River Junction, VT*
ABBICCI [RES] *South Yarmouth (Cape Cod), MA*
ACCENTS [RES] *Toronto, ON*
ACCOLADE [RES] *Toronto, ON*
ADESSO [RES] *Providence, RI*
ADRIAN'S [RES] *Truro and North Truro (Cape Cod), MA*
AESOP'S TABLES [RES] *Wellfleet (Cape Cod), MA*
ALDARIO'S [RES] *Milford, CT*
ALEIA'S [RES] *Old Saybrook, CT*
AL FORNO [RES] *Providence, RI*
ALFREDO, WEINSTEIN AND HO [RES] *Halifax, NS*
ALISSON'S [RES] *Kennebunkport, ME*
AMBROSIA ON HUNTINGTON [RES] *Boston, MA*
AMERICAN SEASONS [RES] *Nantucket Island, MA*
ANAGO [RES] *Boston, MA*
ANCASTER OLD MILL INN [RES] *Hamilton, ON*
ANDIAMO [RES] *Greenfield, MA*
ANDREW'S HARBORSIDE [RES] *Boothbay Harbor, ME*
ANTHONY'S PIER 4 [RES] *Boston, MA*
ANTIPASTO [RES] *St.-Jovite, QE*
APPLE TREE [RES] *Lenox, MA*
APRICOT'S [RES] *Farmington, CT*
AQUITAINE [RES] *Boston, MA*
ARKADIA HOUSE [RES] *Toronto, ON*
ARLEQUIN [RES] *Toronto, ON*
ARLINGTON INN [RES] *Arlington, VT*
ARMANDO'S [RES] *Ellsworth, ME*
ARROW'S [RES] *Ogunquit, ME*
ARUNDEL WHARF [RES] *Kennebunkport, ME*
ATLANTIC CAFE [RES] *Nantucket Island, MA*
AUBERGE DU POMMIER [RES] *Toronto, ON*
AUBERGE HANDFIELD [RES] *Montreal, QE*
AUBERGE SAUVIGNON [RES] *Mont Tremblant Provincial Park, QE*
AU CAFE SUISSE [RES] *Quebec City, QE*

AUJOURD'HUI [RES] *Boston, MA*
AUNT LUCY'S [RES] *Kingston, ON*
AU PETIT EXTRA [RES] *Montreal, QE*
AUSTRIAN INN [RES] *Yarmouth, NS*
AU TOURNANT DE LA RIVIERE [URD] *Montreal, QE*
AUX ANCIENS CANADIENS [RES] *Quebec City, QE*
AUX CHANTIGNOLES [RES] *Ottawa , ON*
AUX TRUFFES [RES] *Mont Tremblant Provincial Park, QE*
AVALON [RES] *Toronto, ON*
AVON OLD FARMS INN [RES] *Avon, CT*
BACK BAY GRILL [RES] *Portland, ME*
BACKSTREET LANDING [RES] *Damariscotta, ME*
BACO RESTAURANT AND WINE BAR [RES] *Quebec City, QE*
BANGKOK GARDEN [RES] *Toronto, ON*
BARBYANN'S [URD] *Hyannis (Cape Cod), MA*
BARJO [RES] *Norway, ME*
BARLEY NECK INN [RES] *Orleans (Cape Cod), MA*
BARNACLE BILLY'S [RES] *Ogunquit, ME*
BARNARD INN [RES] *Woodstock, VT*
BARNHOUSE TAVERN RESTAURANT [RES] *Sebago Lake, ME*
BARNSTABLE TAVERN AND GRILLE [RES] *Barnstable (Cape Cod), MA*
BAROOTES [RES] *Toronto, ON*
BARRELS [RES] *Kitchener-Waterloo, ON*
BARROWS HOUSE INN [RES] *Dorset, VT*
BARTLEY'S DOCKSIDE DINING [RES] *Kennebunkport, ME*
BASS [RES] *Warren, VT*
BAY TOWER [RES] *Boston, MA*
BEAL'S LOBSTER PIER [URD] *Southwest Harbor, ME*
BEAVER CLUB, THE [RES] *Montreal, QE*
BEDFORD VILLAGE INN [RES] *Manchester, NH*
BEE AND THISTLE INN [RES] *Old Lyme, CT*
BELLINI'S [RES] *North Conway, NH*
BELVEDERE ROOM, THE [RES] *Kennebunkport, ME*

BEN'S DELICATESSEN [URD]
Montreal, QE
BENJAMIN'S [RES] Kitchener-Waterloo,
ON
BENNINGTON STATION [RES]
Bennington, VT
BENTLEY'S [RES] Woodstock, VT
BEVERLY DEPOT [RES] Beverly, MA
BIAGIO [RES] Toronto, ON
BIBA [RES] Boston, MA
BIDDLE'S JAZZ AND RIBS [URD]
Montreal, QE
BIG G'S DELI [URD] Waterville, ME
BILLY'S ETC [RES] Ogunquit, ME
BISHOP'S [RES] Lawrence, MA
BISTANGO [RES] Quebec City, QE
BISTRO, THE [RES] Chatham (Cape
Cod), MA
BISTRO 990 [RES] Toronto, ON
BISTRO A CHAMPLAIN [RES]
Montreal, QE
BLACK HORSE TAVERN [RES]
Bridgton, ME
BLACK ROCK CASTLE [RES]
Bridgeport, CT
BLACKSMITH SHOP RESTAURANT
[RES] Truro and North Truro
(Cape Cod), MA
BLANTYRE [RES] Lenox, MA
BLUE GINGER [RES] Wellesley, MA
BLUE ROOM [RES] Cambridge, MA
BOARDING HOUSE [RES] Nantucket
Island, MA
BOBA [RES] Toronto, ON
BOBBY BYRNE'S PUB [RES] Sandwich
(Cape Cod), MA
BOB THE CHEF'S [RES] Boston, MA
BOMBAY CLUB [RES] Cambridge, MA
BOONE'S [RES] Portland, ME
BOULDERS [RES] New Preston, CT
BRACKETT'S OCEANIEW [RES]
Rockport, MA
BRAMBLE INN [RES] Brewster (Cape
Cod), MA
BRANNIGAN'S [RES] Meriden, CT
BRASSERIE JO [RES] Boston, MA
BRAVO BRAVO [RES] Mystic, CT
BREAKWATER INN [RES]
Kennebunkport, ME
BRIDGE RESTAURANT [RES] Sandwich
(Cape Cod), MA
BRISTOL LOUNGE [RES] Boston, MA
BROWN SUGAR CAFE [RES] Boston,
MA
BUMPKINS [RES] Toronto, ON
BUTTERFLY [RES] Hartford, CT
BUTTERY THEATRE [RES] Niagara-on-
the-Lake, ON
CAFE ALLEGRA [RES] Madison, CT
CAFE BUDAPEST [RES] Boston, MA
CAFE DE PARIS [RES] Montreal, QE
CAFE DE PARIS [RES] Quebec City, QE
CAFE EDWIGE [RES] Provincetown
(Cape Cod), MA
CAFE FLEURI [RES] Boston, MA

CAFE HENRY BURGER [RES] Mont
Tremblant Provincial Park, QE
CAFE LOUIS [RES] Boston, MA
CAFE LUCIA [RES] Lenox, MA
CAFE MARLIAVE [RES] Boston, MA
CAFE SHELBURNE [RES] Shelburne,
VT
CAFE STE. ALEXANDRE [RES]
Montreal, QE
CAFFE BELLA [RES] Braintree, MA
CAFFE VITTORIA [URD] Boston, MA
CAFI FERREIRA [RES] Montreal, QE
CAMERON'S [RES] Gloucester, MA
CANDLELIGHT [RES] Skowhegan, ME
CANFIELD HOUSE [RES] Newport, RI
CANNERY [RES] Yarmouth, ME
CAP'N TOBEY'S CHOWDER HOUSE
[RES] Nantucket Island, MA
CAPE NEDDICK INN [RES] York, ME
CAPITAL GRILLE, THE [RES] Boston,
MA
CAPRI [RES] Niagara Falls, ON
CAPTAIN LINNELL HOUSE [RES]
Orleans (Cape Cod), MA
CAPTAIN NICK'S SEAFOOD HOUSE
[RES] Bangor, ME
CAPTAIN SIMON'S GALLEY [RES]
Kittery, ME
CAPTAIN WILLIAM'S HOUSE [RES]
Dennis (Cape Cod), MA
CARBONE'S [RES] Hartford, CT
CARBUR'S [RES] Burlington, VT
CARMAN'S CLUB [RES] Toronto, ON
CAROL'S [RES] Lenox, MA
CAROLE PECK'S GOOD NEWS CAFE
[RES] Woodbury, CT
CARRIAGES, THE [RES] Niagara-on-
the-Lake, ON
CASA ROMERO [RES] Boston, MA
CASCADE INN [RES] Saco, ME
CASCADES LODGE [RES] Killington,
VT
CASSIS [RES] Andover and North
Andover, MA
CASTLE [RES] Worcester, MA
CASTLE STREET CAFE [RES] Great
Barrington, MA
CAVEY'S FRENCH RESTAURANT
[RES] Manchester, CT
CAVEY'S ITALIAN RESTAURANT
[RES] Manchester, CT
CENTRO GRILL & WINE BAR [RES]
Toronto, ON
CHAMPS ELYSEES [RES] Montreal, QE
CHANTICLEER [RES] Manchester and
Manchester Center, VT
CHANTICLEER [RES] Nantucket
Island, MA
CHARCOAL STEAK HOUSE [RES]
Kitchener-Waterloo, ON
CHARLEY'S [RES] Boston, MA
CHART HOUSE [RES] Simsbury, CT
CHASE HOUSE [RES] Salem, MA
CHATHAM SQUIRE [RES] Chatham
(Cape Cod), MA

CHATHAM STREET GRILL [RES] Windsor, ON

CHEF'S HARVEST [RES] Newburyport, MA

CHEF'S TABLE [RES] Montpelier, VT

CHERRINGTON'S [RES] Mississauga, ON

CHERRY HILL HOUSE [RES] Mississauga, ON

CHEZ BUNTHA [RES] Ottawa , ON

CHEZ DELMO [RES] Montreal, QE

CHEZ HENRI [RES] Cambridge, MA

CHEZ LA MERE MICHEL [RES] Montreal, QE

CHIADO [RES] Toronto, ON

CHIARO'S [RES] Toronto, ON

CHILE PEPPERS [RES] Waterville Valley, NH

CHILLINGSWORTH [RES] Brewster (Cape Cod), MA

CHINA BLOSSOM [RES] Andover and North Andover, MA

CHINA BY THE SEA [RES] Boothbay Harbor, ME

CHINA COURT [RES] Yarmouth, NS

CHRISTIAN'S [RES] Chatham (Cape Cod), MA

CHRISTIE'S OF NEWPORT [RES] Newport, RI

CHRISTINE'S [RES] Dennis (Cape Cod), MA

CHRISTMAS FARM INN [RES] Jackson, NH

CHRISTOS [RES] Brockton, MA

CHURCH RESTAURANT AND THE BELFRY, THE [RES] Stratford, ON

CHURCH STREET CAFE [RES] Lenox, MA

CIAO BELLA [RES] Boston, MA

CIAO CAFE AND WINE BAR [RES] Danbury, CT

CIOPPINO'S [RES] Nantucket Island, MA

CLAM SHELL [RES] Littleton, NH

CLAREMONT CAFE [RES] Boston, MA

CLIFF HOUSE [RES] Stowe, VT

CLIO [RES] Boston, MA

COACH HOUSE [RES] Martha's Vineyard, MA

COAST GUARD HOUSE [RES] Narragansett, RI

COBB'S MILL INN [RES] Westport, CT

COBBLESTONES [RES] Lowell, MA

COLBY HILL INN [RES] Concord, NH

COLONIAL INN [RES] Concord, MA

COMMON MAN [RES] Holderness, NH

COMMON MAN [RES] Lincoln/North Woodstock Area, NH

COMMON MAN, THE [RES] Warren, VT

CONNOLLY'S [RES] Westport, CT

CONSTANTINE'S [RES] New London, CT

COOK'S LOBSTER HOUSE [RES] Bailey Island, ME

COOK SHOP [RES] Windsor, ON

COONAMESSETT INN [RES] Falmouth (Cape Cod), MA

COPPER BEECH INN [RES] Essex, CT

CORK [RES] Camden, ME

CORK N' HEARTH [RES] Lee, MA

CORNER HOUSE INN [RES] Holderness, NH

CORSICAN [RES] Freeport, ME

COTTONWOOD CAFE [RES] Cambridge, MA

COUNTRY GOURMET [RES] Nashua, NH

COUNTRYMAN'S PLEASURE [RES] Rutland, VT

CRAB SHELL [RES] Stamford, CT

CREAMERY [RES] St. Johnsbury, VT

CREMALDI'S [URD] Cambridge, MA

CURTIS HOUSE [RES] Woodbury, CT

DAILY PLANET [RES] Burlington, VT

DAKOTA [RES] Avon, CT

DAKOTA [RES] Pittsfield, MA

DALI [RES] Cambridge, MA

DAN'L WEBSTER INN [RES] Sandwich (Cape Cod), MA

DANCING LOBSTER CAFE [RES] Provincetown (Cape Cod), MA

DANDELION INN [RES] Burlington, MA

DARBY'S [RES] Belfast, ME

DAVID'S [RES] Newburyport, MA

DAVID DUNCAN HOUSE [RES] Toronto, ON

DAVIDE [RES] Boston, MA

DAVIO'S [RES] Boston, MA

DECKER-TEN [RES] Mississauga, ON

DEERFIELD INN [RES] Deerfield, MA

DELANY HOUSE [RES] Holyoke, MA

DI MILLO'S FLOATING RESTAURANT [RES] Portland, ME

DINING ROOM, THE [RES] Boston, MA

DOCK AND DINE [RES] Old Saybrook, CT

DOCKSIDE [RES] York, ME

DOCKSIDER [RES] Northeast Harbor, ME

DOCTOR'S HOUSE, THE [RES] Toronto, ON

DOG TEAM TAVERN [RES] Middlebury, VT

DOME RESTAURANT [RES] Woods Hole (Cape Cod), MA

DOMUS CAFI [RES] Ottawa , ON

DONATELLO [RES] Saugus, MA

DORSET INN [RES] Dorset, VT

DOUBLE DRAGON INN [RES] Orleans (Cape Cod), MA

DRAGON LITE [RES] Hyannis (Cape Cod), MA

DUCK CREEK TAVERN ROOM [RES] Wellfleet (Cape Cod), MA

DURGIN PARK [RES] Boston, MA

DYNASTY CHINESE [RES] Toronto, ON

EAST COAST GRILL [URD]
    Cambridge, MA
EASTGATE [RES] *Littleton, NH*
EAST SIDE [RES] *New Britain, CT*
EASTSIDE GRILL [RES] *Northampton,
    MA*
EAST SIDE RESTAURANT AND PUB
    [RES] *Newport, VT*
EASY & THE FIFTH [RES] *Toronto, ON*
EBB TIDE [RES] *Boothbay Harbor, ME*
ED'S WAREHOUSE [RES] *Toronto, ON*
EGG & I [RES] *Hyannis (Cape Cod),
    MA*
ELLAS [RES] *Toronto, ON*
ELMS, THE [RES] *Ridgefield, CT*
ELORA MILL [RES] *Kitchener-Waterloo,
    ON*
ESCABECHE [RES] *Niagara-on-the-
    Lake, ON*
EXCHANGE, THE [RES] *Boston, MA*
F. PARKER REIDY'S [RES] *Portland, ME*
FABYAN'S STATION [RES] *Bretton
    Woods, NH*
FAMOUS BILL'S [RES] *Greenfield, MA*
FANS COURT [RES] *Niagara-on-the-
    Lake, ON*
FAZIO'S ITALIAN [RES] *York, ME*
FEDERALIST, THE [RES] *Boston, MA*
FELLINI KOOLINI'S [RES] *London, ON*
FIFE 'N DRUM [RES] *Kent, CT*
FIFTH, THE [RES] *Toronto, ON*
FILIPPO [RES] *Boston, MA*
FINN'S SEAFOOD [RES] *Block Island,
    RI*
FIRE AND ICE [RES] *Middlebury, VT*
FIREHOUSE ONE [RES] *Dover, NH*
FISHERMAN'S LANDING [URD] *Bar
    Harbor, ME*
FIVE FISHERMEN [RES] *Halifax, NS*
FLOOD TIDE [RES] *Mystic, CT*
FLYING BRIGE [RES] *Falmouth (Cape
    Cod), MA*
FORE STREET [RES] *Portland, ME*
FOUR BROTHERS [RES] *Niagara Falls,
    ON*
FOUR CHIMNEYS [RES] *Bennington,
    VT*
FOUR COLUMNS [RES] *Newfane, VT*
FRANCONIA INN, THE [RES]
    Franconia, NH
FREDDIE'S ROUTE 66 [RES] *Bar
    Harbor, ME*
FREESTONE'S CITY GRILL [RES] *New
    Bedford, MA*
FRIENDS AND COMPANY [RES]
    Madison, CT
FRONT STREET [RES] *Provincetown
    (Cape Cod), MA*
FUNDY [RES] *Digby, NS*
GALLERIA ITALIANO [RES] *Boston,
    MA*
GATEWAYS INN [RES] *Lenox, MA*
GATHERING, THE [RES] *Milford, CT*
GENE'S [RES] *Stratford, ON*
GINZA [RES] *Boston, MA*

GIOVANNI'S [RES] *Sault Ste. Marie,
    ON*
GIOVANNI'S [RES] *Stamford, CT*
GLENN'S GALLEY [RES] *Newburyport,
    MA*
GLOBE [RES] *Montreal, QE*
GLOUCESTER HOUSE RESTAURANT
    [RES] *Gloucester, MA*
GO FISH [RES] *Mystic, CT*
GOLDEN APPLE [RES] *Gananoque, ON*
GOLDEN SAILS CHINESE [RES]
    Falmouth (Cape Cod), MA
GORDI'S FISH & STEAK HOUSE [RES]
    *Lincoln/North Woodstock Area,
    NH*
GOVONI'S ITALIAN [RES]
    *Lincoln/North Woodstock Area,
    NH*
GRAND CHAU-CHOWS [RES] *Boston,
    MA*
GRANO [RES] *Toronto, ON*
GRAPE VINE [RES] *Salem, MA*
GRAZIE [RES] *Toronto, ON*
GREAT IMPASTA [RES] *Brunswick, ME*
GRENDEL'S DEN [RES] *Cambridge,
    MA*
GREY GULL [RES] *Wells, ME*
GRILL 23 [RES] *Boston, MA*
GRILL AT HOBBS BROOK [RES]
    Waltham, MA
GRISSINI [RES] *Kennebunk, ME*
GRIST MILL [RES] *Concord, NH*
GRISWOLD INN [RES] *Essex, CT*
GRITTY MCDUFF'S [RES] *Freeport, ME*
GROG, THE [RES] *Newburyport, MA*
GRUBSTAKE [RES] *Fortress of
    Louisbourg National Historic Site,
    NS*
GUILD INN [RES] *Toronto, ON*
GYPSY SWEETHEARTS [RES]
    Ogunquit, ME
HAMERSLEY'S BISTRO [RES] *Boston,
    MA*
HANCOCK INN [RES] *Peterborough,
    NH*
HANNAH JACK TAVERN [RES]
    Nashua, NH
HAPPY SEVEN [RES] *Toronto, ON*
HARBOR POINT [RES] *Barnstable
    (Cape Cod), MA*
HARBOR VIEW [RES] *Rockland, ME*
HARDCOVER, THE [RES] *Danvers, MA*
HART'S TURKEY FARM [RES]
    Meredith, NH
HARTNESS HOUSE INN [RES]
    Springfield, VT
HARVEST [RES] *Cambridge, MA*
HARVEST CAFE [RES] *Toronto, ON*
HAVILLAND'S GRILLE [URD] *Bedford,
    MA*
HAYLOFT [RES] *Wells, ME*
HEARTH, THE [RES] *Danbury, CT*
HEARTH AND KETTLE [RES]
    Plymouth, MA
HELM, THE [RES] *Camden, ME*

HELMAND [RES] *Cambridge, MA*
HEMENWAY'S SEAFOOD GRILL [RES] *Providence, RI*
HEMINGWAY'S [RES] *Killington, VT*
HEMISPHERES [RES] *Toronto, ON*
HENRIETTA'S TABLE [RES] *Cambridge, MA*
HERITAGE HOUSE [RES] *Skowhegan, ME*
HERM'S [RES] *Greenfield, MA*
HERMITAGE [RES] *Wilmington, VT*
HICKORY STICK FARM [RES] *Laconia, NH*
HIGH BREWSTER INN [RES] *Brewster (Cape Cod), MA*
HILLTOP HOUSE [RES] *Ellsworth, ME*
HILLTOP STEAK HOUSE [RES] *Saugus, MA*
HOFBRAUHAUS [RES] *Springfield, MA*
HOME PORT [RES] *Martha's Vineyard, MA*
HOME PORT INN [RES] *Lubec, ME*
HOPKINS INN [RES] *New Preston, CT*
HORIZON'S [RES] *Sandwich (Cape Cod), MA*
HORSE & HOUND [RES] *Franconia, NH*
HORSEFEATHERS [RES] *North Conway, NH*
HOTEL MANISSES DINING ROOM [RES] *Block Island, RI*
HOT TOMATOES [RES] *Hartford, CT*
HOUSE OF GENE [RES] *Stratford, ON*
HOWE'S COTTAGE [RES] *South Yarmouth (Cape Cod), MA*
HUNGRY I [RES] *Boston, MA*
HURRICANE [RES] *Ogunquit, ME*
ICARUS [RES] *Boston, MA*
ICE HOUSE [RES] *Burlington, VT*
IDLE OARS [RES] *Cavendish, PE*
IL CAPRICCIO [RES] *Waltham, MA*
IL CORTILE [RES] *Montreal, QE*
IL FALCO [RES] *Stamford, CT*
IL POSTO [RES] *Toronto, ON*
IMPUDENT OYSTER [RES] *Chatham (Cape Cod), MA*
INAHO-JAPANESE RESTAURANT [RES] *South Yarmouth (Cape Cod), MA*
INDOCHINE PAVILLION [RES] *New Haven, CT*
INN AT SAWMILL FARM, THE [RES] *West Dover, VT*
INN AT THORN HILL [RES] *Jackson, NH*
INN AT WESTVIEW FARM [RES] *Dorset, VT*
ISLAND CHOWDER HOUSE [RES] *Bar Harbor, ME*
ISLE DE FRANCE [RES] *Stowe, VT*
ITALIAN OASIS [RES] *Littleton, NH*
IVANHOE [RES] *Springfield, MA*
J. P. DANIELS [RES] *Mystic, CT*
JACOB MARLEY'S [RES] *Newburyport, MA*

JACQUES BISTRO DUPARC [RES] *Toronto, ON*
JADE PALACE [RES] *Caribou, ME*
JAE'S CAFE AND GRILL [RES] *Boston, MA*
JAMESON TAVERN [RES] *Freeport, ME*
JAMIE KENNEDY AT THE ROME [RES] *Toronto, ON*
JEAN-LOUIS [RES] *Greenwich, CT*
JESSE'S [RES] *Hanover, NH*
JIGGER JOHNSON'S [RES] *Plymouth, NH*
JIMMY'S HARBORSIDE [RES] *Boston, MA*
JODI'S COUNTRY CAFE [RES] *Great Barrington, MA*
JOHN ANDREW'S RESTAURANT [RES] *Great Barrington, MA*
JOHN MARTIN'S MANOR [RES] *Waterville, ME*
JOLLY BUTCHER'S [RES] *Brattleboro, VT*
JONATHAN'S [RES] *Blue Hill, ME*
JONATHAN'S [RES] *Ogunquit, ME*
JONGLEUX CAFI [RES] *Montreal, QE*
JORDAN POND HOUSE [RES] *Northeast Harbor, ME*
JOSO'S [RES] *Toronto, ON*
JULIEN [RES] *Boston, MA*
KALLY'S [RES] *Toronto, ON*
KASHMIR [RES] *Boston, MA*
KATSURA MONTREAL [RES] *Montreal, QE*
KEDRON VALLEY [RES] *Woodstock, VT*
KEG, THE [RES] *Thunder Bay, ON*
KENNEBUNK INN, THE [RES] *Kennebunk, ME*
KENSINGTON ROOM [RES] *Norwich, CT*
KERNWOOD [RES] *Lynnfield, MA*
KEYSTONE ALLEY CAFE [RES] *Stratford, ON*
KING'S ROOK [RES] *Marblehead, MA*
KRISTINA'S [RES] *Bath, ME*
L'ALOUETTE [RES] *Harwich (Cape Cod), MA*
L'ASTRAL [RES] *Quebec City, QE*
L'EAU A LA BOUCHE [RES] *Montreal, QE*
L'ESPALIER [RES] *Boston, MA*
L'EXPRESS [RES] *Montreal, QE*
L'OMELETTE [RES] *Quebec City, QE*
L'ORCHIDEE DE CHINE [RES] *Montreal, QE*
LA BONICHE [RES] *Lowell, MA*
LA BRETAGNE [RES] *Stamford, CT*
LA CASTILE [RES] *Mississauga, ON*
LA CAVERNE GREQUE [RES] *Montreal, QE*
LA CHRONIQUE [RES] *Montreal, QE*
LA CLEF DES CHAMPS [RES] *Montreal, QE*
LAFAYETTE HOUSE [RES] *Foxboro, MA*
LA FENICE [RES] *Toronto, ON*

LA FORGE CASINO [RES] *Newport, RI*
LA FOURCHETTE FOLLE [RES] *Mont Tremblant Provincial Park, QE*
LA GAUDRIOLE [RES] *Montreal, QE*
LA GONDOLA [RES] *Ottawa , ON*
LA GROCERIA [RES] *Cambridge, MA*
LA HACIENDA [RES] *Stamford, CT*
LAI WAH HEEN [RES] *Toronto, ON*
LALA ROKH [RES] *Boston, MA*
LA LOUISIANE [RES] *Montreal, QE*
LALOUX [RES] *Montreal, QE*
LA MAISON SERGE BRUYERE [RES] *Quebec City, QE*
LA MAREE [RES] *Montreal, QE*
LA MIRAGE [RES] *New Haven, CT*
LANGDON HALL [RES] *Kitchener-Waterloo, ON*
LA PETITE AUBERGE [RES] *Newport, RI*
LA PLACE RENDEZ-VOUS [RES] *Fort Frances, ON*
LA RAPIERE [RES] *Montreal, QE*
LARCHWOOD INN [RES] *Kingston, RI*
LA RIPAILLE [RES] *Quebec City, QE*
LA SAUVAGINE [URD] *Montreal, QE*
LAS PALMAS [RES] *Ottawa , ON*
LAURIE RAPHAEL [RES] *Quebec City, QE*
LE BISTRO [RES] *Newport, RI*
LE BONAPARTE [RES] *Quebec City, QE*
LE BON COIN [RES] *New Preston, CT*
LE CAFE [RES] *Ottawa , ON*
LE CAFE FLEURI [RES] *Montreal, QE*
LE CHAMPLAIN [RES] *Quebec City, QE*
LE CHRYSANTHEME [RES] *Montreal, QE*
LE CHRYSANTHEME [RES] *Montreal, QE*
LE CONTINENTAL [RES] *Quebec City, QE*
LEESIDE [RES] *Woods Hole (Cape Cod), MA*
LEGAL SEAFOODS [RES] *Danvers, MA*
LEGAL SEAFOODS [RES] *Newton, MA*
LEGAL SEAFOODS [RES] *Warwick, RI*
LE GARAGE [RES] *Wiscasset, ME*
LE GASCON [RES] *Mont Tremblant Provincial Park, QE*
LE GRENIER FRENCH RESTAURANT [RES] *Martha's Vineyard, MA*
LE JARDIN [RES] *Williamstown, MA*
LE JARDIN DE PANOS [RES] *Montreal, QE*
LE KEG/BRANDY'S [RES] *Montreal, QE*
LE LANGUEDOC [RES] *Nantucket Island, MA*
LE LUTETIA [RES] *Montreal, QE*
LE MAISTRE [RES] *Montreal, QE*
LE MANOIR DU SPAGHETTI [RES] *Quebec City, QE*
LE MAS DES OLIVIERS [RES] *Montreal, QE*
LE MITOYEN [RES] *Montreal, QE*
LE MUSCADIN [RES] *Montreal, QE*

LENOX 218 RESTAURANT [RES] *Lenox, MA*
LENOX HOUSE [RES] *Lenox, MA*
LE PAILLEUR [RES] *Quebec City, QE*
LE PAPILLION [RES] *Toronto, ON*
LE PARADIS [RES] *Toronto, ON*
LE PARCHEMIN [RES] *Montreal, QE*
LE PARIS [RES] *Montreal, QE*
LE PASSE-PARTOUT [RES] *Montreal, QE*
LE PIEMONTAIS [RES] *Montreal, QE*
LE PIMENT ROUGE [RES] *Montreal, QE*
LE SAINT-AMOUR [RES] *Quebec City, QE*
LES CAPRICES DE NICOLAS [RES] *Montreal, QE*
LES CONTENENTS [RES] *Montreal, QE*
LE SHACK [RES] *Mont Tremblant Provincial Park, QE*
LES HALLES [RES] *Montreal, QE*
LES REMPARTS [RES] *Montreal, QE*
LE STE.-AMABLE [RES] *Montreal, QE*
LES TROIS TILLEULS [RES] *Montreal, QE*
LES ZYGOMATES [RES] *Boston, MA*
LE VENDOME [RES] *Quebec City, QE*
LILAC INN [RES] *Brandon, VT*
LITCHFIELD'S [RES] *Wells, ME*
LOBSTER CLAW [RES] *Orleans (Cape Cod), MA*
LOBSTER COOKER [RES] *Freeport, ME*
LOBSTER POT [RES] *Bristol, RI*
LOBSTER POT [RES] *Montpelier, VT*
LOBSTER POT [RES] *Provincetown (Cape Cod), MA*
LOBSTER POUND [RES] *Camden, ME*
LOBSTER TREAT [RES] *Antigonish, NS*
LOCKE OBER [RES] *Boston, MA*
LOG CABIN DINER [RES] *Newport, ME*
LOG CABIN RESTAURANT AND LOUNGE [RES] *Clinton, CT*
LONGFELLOW'S [RES] *Kingfield, ME*
LONGFELLOW'S WAYSIDE INN [RES] *Sudbury Center, MA*
LORD'S HARBORSIDE [RES] *Wells, ME*
LOUIS' TISBURY CAFE [RES] *Martha's Vineyard, MA*
LOVETT'S INN BY LAFAYETTE BROOK [RES] *Franconia, NH*
LUCIA [RES] *Boston, MA*
LUMIERE [RES] *Newton, MA*
LYCEUM [RES] *Salem, MA*
MABEL'S LOBSTER CLAW [RES] *Kennebunkport, ME*
MADELYN'S DINER [RES] *Stratford, ON*
MAINE DINER [RES] *Wells, ME*
MAINE DINING ROOM, THE [RES] *Freeport, ME*
MAIN STREET GRILL AND BAR [RES] *Montpelier, VT*
MAISON ROBERT [RES] *Boston, MA*

MAME'S [RES] *Meredith, NH*
MAMMA MARIA [RES] *Boston, MA*
MANOR ON GOLDEN POND [RES]
    Holderness, NH
MAPLES [RES] *Dover, NH*
MARBLEHEAD LANDING [RES]
    Marblehead, MA
MARBLE WORKS STEAKHOUSE [RES]
    Ottawa , ON
MARCHE BCE PLACE [RES] *Toronto,
    ON*
MARCUCCIO'S [RES] *Boston, MA*
MARGARITA'S [RES] *Orono, ME*
MARIENBAD [RES] *London, ON*
MARINA [RES] *Brattleboro, VT*
MARK ANTHONY'S YE OLDE
    TAVERN [RES] *Manchester and
    Manchester Center, VT*
MARLA JANE'S [RES] *London, ON*
MARSHSIDE [RES] *Dennis (Cape Cod),
    MA*
MARTIN'S [URD] *Great Barrington,
    MA*
MATIGNON [RES] *Toronto, ON*
MATTAKEESE WHARF [RES]
    Barnstable (Cape Cod), MA
MAURICE RESTAURANT FRANCAIS
    [RES] *Norway, ME*
MAX DOWNTOWN [RES] *Hartford,
    CT*
MCGOVERN'S [RES] *Fall River, MA*
MEDITERRANEO GRILL & WINE BAR
    [RES] *Montreal, QE*
MEERA INDIAN CUISINE [RES]
    Stamford, CT
MERCER STREET GRILL [RES]
    Toronto, ON
MESON GALICIA [RES] *Norwalk, CT*
METRO [RES] *Portsmouth, NH*
METROPOLIS CAFE [RES] *Boston, MA*
MEXICALI ROSA'S [RES] *Mont
    Tremblant Provincial Park, QE*
MICHAEL'S [RES] *Stockbridge and West
    Stockbridge, MA*
MICHAEL'S-ON-THE-THAMES [RES]
    London, ON
MICHAEL'S HARBORSIDE [RES]
    Newburyport, MA
MIGUEL'S MEXICAN [RES] *Bar
    Harbor, ME*
MIKADO [RES] *Montreal, QE*
MILL, THE [RES] *Ottawa , ON*
MILLCROFT INN [RES] *Toronto, ON*
MILLER'S [RES] *Bangor, ME*
MILLER'S COUNTRY FARE [RES]
    Toronto, ON
MILLERY, THE [RES] *Niagara Falls, ON*
MILLSTONE [RES] *New London, NH*
MIRAMAR [RES] *Westport, CT*
MISTER UP'S [RES] *Middlebury, VT*
MISTRAL [RES] *Boston, MA*
MISTURA [RES] *Toronto, ON*
MODERN [RES] *Nashua, NH*
MOHEGAN CAFE [RES] *Block Island,
    RI*
MOLINARO [RES] *Mississauga, ON*

MOLLY'S [RES] *Hanover, NH*
MONTANO'S [RES] *Truro and North
    Truro (Cape Cod), MA*
MONTE CARLO [RES] *Springfield, MA*
MOORING, THE [RES] *Newport, RI*
MORTON'S OF CHICAGO [RES]
    Boston, MA
MOTHER'S [RES] *Bethel, ME*
MOVENPICK OF SWITZERLAND
    [RES] *Toronto, ON*
MR D'S [RES] *Franklin, NH*
MUSKY SUPPER HOUSE [RES]
    Mississauga, ON
MYSTIC PIZZA [RES] *Mystic, CT*
NAPI'S [RES] *Provincetown (Cape Cod),
    MA*
NATHANIEL PORTER INN [RES]
    Bristol, RI
NAUSET BEACH CLUB [RES] *Orleans
    (Cape Cod), MA*
NAVIGATOR [RES] *Martha's Vineyard,
    MA*
NEW GLASGOW LOBSTER SUPPER
    [RES] *Cavendish, PE*
NEWICK'S [RES] *Nashua, NH*
NEWICK'S FISHERMAN'S LANDING
    [RES] *Hampton Beach, NH*
NEWICK'S SEAFOOD [RES] *Dover, NH*
NEWICK'S SEAFOOD [RES] *Portland,
    ME*
NEW LONDON INN [RES] *New
    London, NH*
NEW MARCONI [RES] *Sault Ste.
    Marie, ON*
NIKKI'S [RES] *Ludlow, VT*
NISTICO'S RED BARN [RES] *Westport,
    CT*
NO. 9 PARK [RES] *Boston, MA*
NORTH 44 DEGREES [RES] *Toronto,
    ON*
NORTH HERO HOUSE [RES] *North
    Hero, VT*
NUANCES [RES] *Montreal, QE*
OAK ROOM, THE [RES] *Boston, MA*
OARWEED COVE [RES] *Ogunquit, ME*
OGUNQUIT LOBSTER POUND [RES]
    Ogunquit, ME
OLD BARBER HOUSE [RES]
    Mississauga, ON
OLD CUTTER INN [RES] *Lyndonville,
    VT*
OLDE HOUSE [RES] *Sebago Lake, ME*
OLDE SCHOOL RESTAURANT [RES]
    Brantford, ON
OLD GRIST MILL TAVERN [RES]
    Providence, RI
OLD JAILHOUSE TAVERN [RES]
    Orleans (Cape Cod), MA
OLD LYME INN [RES] *Old Lyme, CT*
OLD MANSE INN AND RESTAURANT
    [RES] *Brewster (Cape Cod), MA*
OLD MILL, THE [RES] *Great
    Barrington, MA*
OLD MILL [RES] *Toronto, ON*
OLD NEWFANE [RES] *Newfane, VT*
OLD PRUNE [RES] *Stratford, ON*

OLD SPAGHETTI FACTORY [RES] *Toronto, ON*
OLD STORROWTON TAVERN [RES] *Springfield, MA*
OLD TIMBERMILL PUB & RESTAURANT [RES] *Lincoln/North Woodstock Area, NH*
OLD VILLAGE INN [RES] *Ogunquit, ME*
OLIVER'S [RES] *Franklin, NH*
ONE-WAY FARE [RES] *Simsbury, CT*
OPUS [RES] *Toronto, ON*
ORCHARDS, THE [RES] *Williamstown, MA*
ORIGINAL GOURMET BRUNCH [RES] *Hyannis (Cape Cod), MA*
ORO [RES] *Toronto, ON*
OUTRIGGER STEAK AND SEAFOOD [RES] *Mississauga, ON*
PADDOCK [RES] *Hyannis (Cape Cod), MA*
PADDY'S PUB AND BREWERY [RES] *Grand Pre, NS*
PAINTED LADY [RES] *Great Barrington, MA*
PALM [RES] *Boston, MA*
PANDA HOUSE CHINESE RESTAURANT [RES] *Lenox, MA*
PANE E SALUTE [URD] *Woodstock, VT*
PANGAEA [RES] *Toronto, ON*
PAPARAZZI [RES] *Truro and North Truro (Cape Cod), MA*
PARKER'S [RES] *Boston, MA*
PARTRIDGE INN SEAFOOD RESTAURANT [RES] *Stowe, VT*
PASTA NOSTRA [RES] *Norwalk, CT*
PASTA SHOP [RES] *Windsor, ON*
PASTIS [RES] *Hartford, CT*
PASTIS [RES] *Toronto, ON*
PATACHOU [URD] *Toronto, ON*
PAULINE'S [RES] *Burlington, VT*
PEACH'S [URD] *North Conway, NH*
PEG LEG RESTAURANT [RES] *Rockport, MA*
PELLINO'S [RES] *Marblehead, MA*
PENGUINS SEA GRILL [RES] *Hyannis (Cape Cod), MA*
PEOPLE'S CHOICE [RES] *Rangeley, ME*
PEPPERCORN'S GRILL [RES] *Hartford, CT*
PERRY'S FISH HOUSE [RES] *Burlington, VT*
PETER OTT'S [RES] *Camden, ME*
PIER [RES] *Newport, RI*
PIER 4 STOREHOUSE [RES] *Toronto, ON*
PIER II [RES] *Portsmouth, NH*
PIGNOLI [RES] *Boston, MA*
PILLAR HOUSE [RES] *Newton, MA*
PILOTS GRILL [RES] *Bangor, ME*
PIZZA MELLA [URD] *Montreal, QE*
PIZZATERIA [RES] *Mont Tremblant Provincial Park, QE*

PLAZA III KANSAS CITY STEAK [RES] *Boston, MA*
POLLY'S PANCAKE PARLOR [RES] *Franconia, NH*
POOR RICHARD'S TAVERN [RES] *Ogunquit, ME*
POT AU FEU [RES] *Providence, RI*
POTTER PLACE INN [RES] *New London, NH*
PREGO [RES] *Toronto, ON*
PRIMADONNA [RES] *Montreal, QE*
PRIMO [RES] *Rockland, ME*
PRINCE AND THE PAUPER [RES] *Woodstock, VT*
PRINCE ARTHUR STEAK AND SEAFOOD HOUSE [RES] *Yarmouth, NS*
PRINCE PLACE [RES] *Jackson, NH*
PRONTO [RES] *Toronto, ON*
PROVENCE [RES] *Ogunquit, ME*
PROVENCE [RES] *Toronto, ON*
PUB, THE [RES] *Keene, NH*
PUBLICK HOUSE [RES] *Sturbridge, MA*
PUBLYK HOUSE [RES] *Bennington, VT*
PUCCI'S HARBORSIDE [RES] *Provincetown (Cape Cod), MA*
PURITAN BACKROOM [RES] *Manchester, NH*
PUTNEY INN, THE [RES] *Brattleboro, VT*
QUARTER DECK [RES] *Bar Harbor, ME*
QUARTIER [RES] *Toronto, ON*
QUECHEE INN AT MARSHLAND FARM [RES] *Woodstock, VT*
QUEENSTON HEIGHTS [RES] *Niagara Falls, ON*
QUELLI DELLA NOTTE [RES] *Montreal, QE*
RABBIT HILL [RES] *St. Johnsbury, VT*
RADIUS [RES] *Boston, MA*
RANGELEY INN [RES] *Rangeley, ME*
READING ROOM [RES] *Bar Harbor, ME*
REDBONES [RES] *Cambridge, MA*
RED INN RESTAURANT [RES] *Provincetown (Cape Cod), MA*
RED LION, THE [RES] *Stockbridge and West Stockbridge, MA*
RED PARKA PUB [RES] *Jackson, NH*
RED PHEASANT INN [RES] *Dennis (Cape Cod), MA*
RED RAVEN'S LIMP NOODLE [RES] *Salem, MA*
REGATTA OF COTUIT [RES] *Centerville (Cape Cod), MA*
REGATTA OF FALMOUTH BY THE SEA [RES] *Falmouth (Cape Cod), MA*
REIN'S NEW YORK-STYLE DELI [RES] *Vernon, CT*
RENO'S [RES] *Caribou, ME*
RESTAURANT AU PARMESAN [RES] *Quebec City, QE*
RESTAURANT BRICCO [URD] *Hartford, CT*

RESTAURANT CHEZ LEVEQUE [RES] *Montreal, QE*
RESTAURANT DAOU [URD] *Montreal, QE*
RESTAURANT DEN [RES] *Waitsfield, VT*
RESTAURANT DU BOIS-JOLI [RES] *Drummondville, QE*
RESTAURANT LE LATINI [RES] *Montreal, QE*
RESTAURANT SHO-DAN [RES] *Montreal, QE*
RESTAURANT THOMAS HENKELMANN [RES] *Greenwich, CT*
RHODE ISLAND QUAHOG COMPANY [RES] *Newport, RI*
RIALTO [RES] *Cambridge, MA*
RIBOLITA [RES] *Portland, ME*
RINEHART DINING PAVILLION [RES] *Bar Harbor, ME*
RISTORANTE BAROLO [RES] *Hyannis (Cape Cod), MA*
RISTORANTE BICE [RES] *Montreal, QE*
RISTORANTE DA VINCI [RES] *Montreal, QE*
RISTORANTE TOSCANO [RES] *Boston, MA*
RIVERWAY LOBSTER HOUSE [RES] *South Yarmouth (Cape Cod), MA*
RIVOLI CAFE [RES] *Toronto, ON*
ROADHOUSE CAFE [RES] *Hyannis (Cape Cod), MA*
ROCCO'S [RES] *Dartmouth, NS*
RODNEY'S OYSTER HOUSE [RES] *Toronto, ON*
ROM'S RESTAURANT [RES] *Sturbridge, MA*
ROMA, THE [RES] *Portland, ME*
ROPE WALK [RES] *Nantucket Island, MA*
ROSA FLAMINGOS [RES] *Littleton, NH*
ROSEDALE DINER, THE [RES] *Toronto, ON*
ROSEWATER SUPPER CLUB [RES] *Toronto, ON*
ROWES WHARF [RES] *Boston, MA*
ROYAL'S 121 HEARTHSIDE [RES] *Rutland, VT*
ROYAL PALACE [RES] *Dennis (Cape Cod), MA*
R PLACE [RES] *Waltham, MA*
RUBIN'S KOSHER DELICATESSEN [URD] *Boston, MA*
RUNDLE'S [RES] *Stratford, ON*
SACHEM COUNTRY HOUSE [RES] *Guilford, CT*
SAGE [RES] *Boston, MA*
SAGE AMERICAN BAR & GRILL [RES] *Essex, CT*
SAL'S PLACE [RES] *Provincetown (Cape Cod), MA*
SALTS [RES] *Boston, MA*
SALTY'S ON THE WATERFRONT [RES] *Halifax, NS*

SAM DIEGO'S [RES] *Hyannis (Cape Cod), MA*
SANDRINE'S [RES] *Cambridge, MA*
SARKIS [RES] *Toronto, ON*
SASSAFRAZ [RES] *Toronto, ON*
SAVOIR FAIRE [RES] *Martha's Vineyard, MA*
SAWATDEE [RES] *Montreal, QE*
SAYBROOK FISH HOUSE [RES] *Old Saybrook, CT*
SCANDIA [RES] *Newburyport, MA*
SCARAMOUCHE [RES] *Toronto, ON*
SCARGO CAFE [RES] *Dennis (Cape Cod), MA*
SCRIBNER'S [RES] *Milford, CT*
SEAFARE INN [RES] *Portsmouth, RI*
SEAMEN'S INNE [RES] *Mystic, CT*
SEASCAPES [RES] *Kennebunkport, ME*
SEASONS [RES] *Boston, MA*
SEAWALL DINING ROOM [RES] *Southwest Harbor, ME*
SEL DE LA TERRE [RES] *Boston, MA*
SENATOR [RES] *Toronto, ON*
SENSES [RES] *Toronto, ON*
SHAKESPEARE'S DINING LOUNGE [RES] *Hamilton, ON*
SHED, THE [RES] *Stowe, VT*
SHERBORN INN [RES] *Natick, MA*
SHOPSY'S DELICATESSEN [URD] *Toronto, ON*
SIENNA [RES] *Deerfield, MA*
SILKS [RES] *Lowell, MA*
SILVERMINE TAVERN [RES] *Norwalk, CT*
SIMON PEARCE [RES] *Woodstock, VT*
SIRLOIN CELLAR [RES] *Hamilton, ON*
SIRLOIN SALOON [RES] *Burlington, VT*
SIRLOIN SALOON [RES] *Manchester and Manchester Center, VT*
SIRLOIN SALOON [RES] *Rutland, VT*
SITAR [RES] *Ottawa , ON*
SKIPPER RESTAURANT [RES] *South Yarmouth (Cape Cod), MA*
SKYLINE [RES] *Marlboro, VT*
SNUG HARBOUR [RES] *Mississauga, ON*
SOCIETE CAFI [RES] *Montreal, QE*
SOTO RESTAURANT [RES] *Montreal, QE*
SOU'WESTER [RES] *Peggy's Cove, NS*
SOUVENIRS D'INDOCHINE [RES] *Montreal, QE*
SPENCER'S [RES] *Great Barrington, MA*
SPLENDIDO [RES] *Toronto, ON*
SPRING ROLL ON YOUNGE [RES] *Toronto, ON*
SQUARE RIGGER [RES] *Martha's Vineyard, MA*
ST. ANDREWS LIGHTHOUSE [RES] *St. Andrews, NB*
STARBUCKS [RES] *Hyannis (Cape Cod), MA*
STEAKHOUSE [RES] *Wells, ME*
STEAK LOFT [RES] *Mystic, CT*

STEAK PLACE AT TUCKER HILL, THE [RES] *Waitsfield, VT*
STEEP HILL GRILL [RES] *Ipswich, MA*
STEVE CENTERBROOK CAFE [RES] *Essex, CT*
STONE CROCK [RES] *Kitchener-Waterloo, ON*
STONEHENGE [RES] *Ridgefield, CT*
STONEWELL [RES] *Farmington, CT*
STREET & CO [RES] *Portland, ME*
STUDENT PRINCE & FORT [RES] *Springfield, MA*
SULLIVAN STATION RESTAURANT [RES] *Lee, MA*
SUSHI BISTRO [RES] *Toronto, ON*
SWAN RIVER [RES] *Dennis (Cape Cod), MA*
SWEETWATERS [RES] *Burlington, VT*
SWISS CASTLE INN [RES] *Kitchener-Waterloo, ON*
SWISSPOT [RES] *Stowe, VT*
SZECHUAN [RES] *Montreal, QE*
TAKE SUSHI [RES] *Toronto, ON*
TAPEO [RES] *Boston, MA*
TARTUFO [RES] *Southbury, CT*
TASTE OF MAINE [RES] *Bath, ME*
TATSUKICHI [RES] *Boston, MA*
TAVERN AT HARBOR SQUARE [RES] *Nantucket Island, MA*
TEN CENTER STREET [RES] *Newburyport, MA*
TERRAMIA [RES] *Boston, MA*
TERRA RISTORANTE ITALIANO [RES] *Greenwich, CT*
THAI FLAVOUR [RES] *Toronto, ON*
THATCHER BROOK [RES] *Waterbury, VT*
TIGER LILY'S NOODLE HOUSE [RES] *Toronto, ON*
TIO JUAN'S [RES] *Concord, NH*
TOKYO SUKIYAKI [RES] *Montreal, QE*
TOLLGATE HILL [RES] *Litchfield, CT*
TOMMY COOKS [RES] *Toronto, ON*
TOP HAT SUPPER CLUB [RES] *Windsor, ON*
TOP OF THE HUB [RES] *Boston, MA*
TOPPER'S [RES] *Nantucket Island, MA*
TOQUE! [RES] *Montreal, QE*
TORCH [RES] *Boston, MA*
TRAPPER'S [RES] *Toronto, ON*
TRATTORIA IL PANINO [RES] *Boston, MA*
TREEHOUSE [RES] *Montreal, QE*
TREE HOUSE [RES] *Plymouth, NH*
TRUANTS TAVERNE [RES] *Lincoln/North Woodstock Area, NH*
TRUC [RES] *Boston, MA*
TRUC ORIENT EXPRESS [RES] *Stockbridge and West Stockbridge, MA*
TRUFFLES [RES] *Toronto, ON*
TUCSON CAFE [RES] *Greenwich, CT*
TUNNEL BAR-B-Q [RES] *Windsor, ON*
TURNER FISHERIES [RES] *Boston, MA*

TUSCAN GRILL [RES] *Waltham, MA*
TWO STEPS DOWNTOWN GRILLE [RES] *Danbury, CT*
UNITED BAKERS DAIRY RESTAURANT [URD] *Toronto, ON*
UPSTAIRS AT THE PUDDING [RES] *Cambridge, MA*
VALLE'S STEAK HOUSE [RES] *Portland, ME*
VANIPHA LANNA [RES] *Toronto, ON*
VANRENSSELAER'S [RES] *Wellfleet (Cape Cod), MA*
VAULT [RES] *Boston, MA*
VERANDA AT THE YANKEE CLIPPER [RES] *Rockport, MA*
VERMONT INN [RES] *Killington, VT*
VICTORIA PARK [RES] *Niagara Falls, ON*
VICTORIA STATION [RES] *Salem, MA*
VILLA BORGHESE [RES] *Toronto, ON*
VILLAGE CAFE [RES] *Portland, ME*
VILLAGE RESTAURANT [RES] *Litchfield, CT*
VILLA TRAGARA [RES] *Waterbury, VT*
VILLA TROMBINO [RES] *Westerly, RI*
WALTER'S CAFE [RES] *Portland, ME*
WARREN'S LOBSTER HOUSE [RES] *Kittery, ME*
WARREN HOUSE RESTAURANT AND RUPERT'S BAR, THE [URD] *Warren, VT*
WATERFRONT [RES] *Camden, ME*
WATERLOT [RES] *Kitchener-Waterloo, ON*
WATER STREET GRILL [RES] *Williamstown, MA*
WAYBURY INN [RES] *Middlebury, VT*
WEATHERVANE [RES] *Waterville, ME*
WEST CREEK CAFE [RES] *Nantucket Island, MA*
WEST STREET GRILL [RES] *Litchfield, CT*
WHARF & WHARF PUB [RES] *Martha's Vineyard, MA*
WHEATLEIGH [RES] *Lenox, MA*
WHISKERS [RES] *Stowe, VT*
WHISTLING SWAN [RES] *Sturbridge, MA*
WHITE'S OF WESTPORT [RES] *Fall River, MA*
WHITE BARN RESTAURANT, THE [RES] *Kennebunkport, ME*
WHITEHALL DINING ROOM [RES] *Camden, ME*
WHITE HORSE TAVERN [RES] *Newport, RI*
WHITE HOUSE [RES] *Wilmington, VT*
WHITE RAINBOW [RES] *Gloucester, MA*
WHITE STAR TAVERN [RES] *Boston, MA*
WICKACHEE [RES] *Calais, ME*
WILD AMBER GRILL [RES] *Williamstown, MA*

WILDCAT TAVERN [RES] *Jackson, NH*
WILLIAMSVILLE INN [RES]
    Stockbridge and West Stockbridge,
    MA
WILLIAM TELL [RES] *Waterville*
    Valley, NH
WIMPY'S SEAFOOD CAFE AND
    MARKET [URD] *Centerville*
    (Cape Cod), MA
WINDOWS ON THE WATER [RES]
    Kennebunk, ME
WINDRIDGE INN [URD] *Jeffersonville,*
    VT
WINDSOR STATION [RES] *Windsor,*
    VT
WOODSTOCK INN [RES]
    Lincoln/North Woodstock Area,
    NH
WOODSTOCK INN [RES] *Woodstock,*
    VT
WYNDHURST RESTAURANT, THE
    [RES] *Lenox, MA*
XANGO [RES] *Toronto, ON*
YAMASE [RES] *Toronto, ON*
YANKEE PEDLAR [RES] *Holyoke, MA*
YARMOUTH HOUSE [RES] *South*
    Yarmouth (Cape Cod), MA
YE OLDE STEAK HOUSE [RES]
    Windsor, ON
YE OLDE UNION OYSTER HOUSE
    [RES] *Boston, MA*
YOKEN'S THAR SHE BLOWS [RES]
    Portsmouth, NH
YOKOHAMA [RES] *Gorham, NH*
YORK HARBOR INN [RES] *York, ME*
ZACHARY'S [RES] *Toronto, ON*
ZEN [RES] *Montreal, QE*
ZOLA'S GRILLE [RES] *Killington, VT*
ZUMA'S TEX-MEX CAFE [RES] *Boston,*
    MA

CITY INDEX

Mobil Travel Guides

Please check the guides you would like to order:

☐ 0-7853-4629-5
California
$16.95

☐ 0-7803-4630-9
Florida
$16.95

☐ 0-7853-4635-X
Great Lakes
Illinois, Indiana, Michigan
Ohio, Wisconsin
$16.95

☐ 0-7853-4636-8
Great Plaines
Iowa, Kansas, Minnesota,
Missouri, Nebraska, North
Dakota, Oklahoma, South
Dakota
$16.95

☐ 0-7853-4633-3
Mid-Atlantic
Delaware, Maryland,
Pennsylvania, Virginia,
Washington DC, West
Virginia
$16.95

☐ 0-7853-4631-7
**New England and Eastern
Canada**
Connecticut, Maine, Massachu-
setts, New Hampshire, Rhode
Island, Vermont, Canada
$16.95

☐ 0-7853-4632-5
New York/New Jersey
$16.95

☐ 0-7853-4638-4
Northwest
Idaho, Montana, Oregon, Wash-
ington, Wyoming, Canada
$16.95

☐ 0-7853-4634-1
Southeast
Alabama, Arkansas, Georgia, Ken-
tucky, Louisiana, Mississippi,
North Carolina, South Carolina,
Tennessee
$16.95

☐ 0-7853-4637-6
Southwest
Arizona, Colorado, Nevada, New
Mexico, Texas, Utah
$16.95

Please ship the books above to:

Name: _____

Address: _____

City: _____ State _____ Zip _____

Total Cost of Book(s)	$ _____	☐ Please charge my credit card.
Shipping & Handling	$ _____	☐ Discover ☐ Visa
(Please add $2.00 for first book $1.00 for each additional book)		☐ MasterCard ☐ American Express
Add 8.75% sales tax	$ _____	Card # _____
Total Amount	$ _____	Expiration _____
☐ My Check is enclosed.		Signature _____

Please mail this form to: **Mobil Travel Guides**
7373 N. Cicero Avenue
Lincolnwood, IL 60712

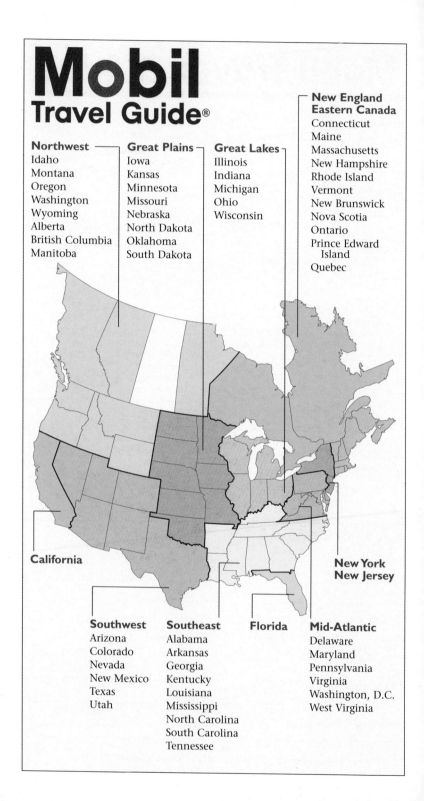

Mobil
Travel Guide®

New England Eastern Canada
Connecticut
Maine
Massachusetts
New Hampshire
Rhode Island
Vermont
New Brunswick
Nova Scotia
Ontario
Prince Edward
  Island
Quebec

Northwest
Idaho
Montana
Oregon
Washington
Wyoming
Alberta
British Columbia
Manitoba

Great Plains
Iowa
Kansas
Minnesota
Missouri
Nebraska
North Dakota
Oklahoma
South Dakota

Great Lakes
Illinois
Indiana
Michigan
Ohio
Wisconsin

California

New York New Jersey

Southwest
Arizona
Colorado
Nevada
New Mexico
Texas
Utah

Southeast
Alabama
Arkansas
Georgia
Kentucky
Louisiana
Mississippi
North Carolina
South Carolina
Tennessee

Florida

Mid-Atlantic
Delaware
Maryland
Pennsylvania
Virginia
Washington, D.C.
West Virginia

Add your opinion!

Help make the Guide even more useful. Tell us about your experiences with the hotels and restaurants listed in the Guide (or ones that should be added).

Find us on the Internet at www.exxonmobiltravel.com/feedback

Or copy the form below and mail to Mobil Travel Guide, 7373 N. Cicero Ave, Lincolnwood, IL 60712 or fax to 847/329-5877. All information will be kept confidential.

Your name _____   Were children with you on trip? ☐ Yes ☐ No

Street _____   Number of people in your party _____

City/State/Zip _____   Your occupation _____

Establishment name _____
☐ Hotel ☐ Resort ☐ Restaurant
☐ Motel ☐ Inn ☐ Other

Street_____ City_____ State _____

Do you agree with out description? ☐ Yes ☐ No. If not, give reason _____

Please give us your opinion of the following::   2001 Guide rating _____ ★

Decor	Cleanliness	Service	Food
☐ Excellent	☐ Spotless	☐ Excellent	☐ Excellent
☐ Good	☐ Clean	☐ Good	☐ Good
☐ Fair	☐ Unclean	☐ Fair	☐ Fair
☐ Poor	☐ Dirty	☐ Poor	☐ Poor

Check your suggested rating
☐ ★good, satisfactory
☐ ★★very good
☐ ★★★excellent
☐ ★★★★outstanding
☐ ★★★★★ one of best in country
☐ ✓unusually good value

Date of visit _____   First visit? ☐ Yes ☐ No

Comments x x x x x x x x x x x x x x x x x x x x x x x x x x x x x x x x x x x x x x x x x x x x x x x x

_____

Establishment name_____
☐ Hotel ☐ Resort ☐ Restaurant
☐ Motel ☐ Inn ☐ Other

Street_____ City_____ State _____

Do you agree with out description? ☐ Yes ☐ No. If not, give reason _____

Please give us your opinion of the following::   2001 Guide rating _____ ★

Decor	Cleanliness	Service	Food
☐ Excellent	☐ Spotless	☐ Excellent	☐ Excellent
☐ Good	☐ Clean	☐ Good	☐ Good
☐ Fair	☐ Unclean	☐ Fair	☐ Fair
☐ Poor	☐ Dirty	☐ Poor	☐ Poor

Check your suggested rating
☐ ★good, satisfactory
☐ ★★very good
☐ ★★★excellent
☐ ★★★★outstanding
☐ ★★★★★ one of best in country
☐ ✓unusually good value

Date of visit _____   First visit? ☐ Yes ☐ No

Comments x x x x x x x x x x x x x x x x x x x x x x x x x x x x x x x x x x x x x x x x x x x x x x x x

_____

Notes